AN INDEX
TO BOOK REVIEWS
IN THE HUMANITIES

VOLUME 16

1975

PHILLIP THOMSON

WILLIAMSTON, MICHIGAN

STANDARD BOOK NUMBER: 0-911504-16-8

INTERNATIONAL STANDARD SERIAL NUMBER:
US ISSN 0073-5892

LIBRARY OF CONGRESS CATALOG CARD NUMBER:
62-21757

PRINTED IN THE U.S.A.

THIS VOLUME OF THE INDEX CONTAINS DATA COLLECTED UP TO 31 DECEMBER 1975.

THIS IS AN INDEX TO BOOK REVIEWS IN HUMANITIES PERIODICALS. BEGINNING WITH VOLUME 12 OF THIS INDEX (DATED 1971), THE FORMER POLICY OF SELECTIVELY INDEXING REVIEWS OF BOOKS IN CERTAIN SUBJECT CATEGORIES ONLY WAS DROPPED IN FAVOR OF A POLICY OF INDEXING ALL REVIEWS IN THE PERIODICALS INDEXED, WITH THE ONE EXCEPTION OF CHILDREN'S BOOKS--THE REVIEWS OF WHICH WILL NOT BE INDEXED.

THE FORM OF THE ENTRIES USED IS AS FOLLOWS:

> AUTHOR. TITLE.
> REVIEWER. IDENTIFYING LEGEND.

THE AUTHOR'S NAME USED IS THE NAME THAT APPEARS ON THE TITLE-PAGE OF THE BOOK BEING REVIEWED, AS WELL AS WE ARE ABLE TO DETERMINE, EVEN THOUGH THIS NAME IS KNOWN TO BE A PSEUDONYM. THE TITLE ONLY IS SHOWN; SUBTITLES ARE INCLUDED ONLY WHERE THEY ARE NECESSARY TO IDENTIFY A BOOK IN A SERIES. THE IDENTIFYING LEGEND CONSISTS OF THE PERIODICAL, EACH OF WHICH HAS A CODE NUMBER, AND THE DATE AND PAGE NUMBER OF THE PERIODICAL WHERE THE REVIEW IS TO BE FOUND. PMLA ABBREVIATIONS ARE ALSO SHOWN (WHEN A PERIODICAL HAS SUCH AN ABBREVIATION, BUT SUCH ABBREVIATIONS ARE LIMITED TO FOUR LETTERS) IMMEDIATELY FOLLOWING THE CODE NUMBER OF THE PERIODICAL. TO LEARN THE NAME OF THE PERIODICAL IN WHICH THE REVIEW APPEARS, IT IS NECESSARY TO REFER THE CODE NUMBER TO THE NUMERICALLY-ARRANGED LIST OF PERIODICALS BEGINNING ON PAGE III. THIS LIST ALSO SHOWS THE VOLUME AND NUMBER OF THE PERIODICALS INDEXED.

REVIEWS ARE INDEXED AS THEY APPEAR AND NO ATTEMPT IS MADE TO HOLD THE TITLE UNTIL ALL THE REVIEWS ARE PUBLISHED. FOR THIS REASON IT IS NECESSARY TO REFER TO PREVIOUS AND SUBSEQUENT VOLUMES OF THIS INDEX TO BE SURE THAT THE COMPLETE ROSTER OF REVIEWS OF ANY TITLE IS SEEN. AS AN AID TO THE USER, AN ASTERISK (*) HAS BEEN ADDED IMMEDIATELY FOLLOWING ANY TITLE THAT WAS ALSO INDEXED IN VOLUME 15 (1974) OF THIS INDEX.

AUTHORS WITH HYPHENATED SURNAMES ARE INDEXED UNDER THE NAME BEFORE THE HYPHEN, AND THE NAME FOLLOWING THE HYPHEN IS NOT CROSS-INDEXED. AUTHORS WITH MORE THAN ONE SURNAME, BUT WHERE THE NAMES ARE NOT HYPHENATED, ARE INDEXED UNDER THE FIRST OF THE NAMES AND THE LAST NAME IS CROSS-INDEXED. WHEN ALPHABETIZING SURNAMES CONTAINING UMLAUTS, THE UMLAUTS ARE IGNORED. EDITORS ARE ALWAYS SHOWN IN THE AUTHOR-TITLE ENTRY, AND THEY ARE CROSS-INDEXED (EXCEPT WHERE THE EDITOR'S SURNAME IS THE SAME AS THAT OF THE AUTHOR). TRANSLATORS ARE SHOWN ONLY WHEN THEY ARE NECESSARY TO IDENTIFY THE BOOK BEING REVIEWED (AS IN THE CLASSICS), AND THEY ARE NOT CROSS-INDEXED UNLESS THE BOOK BEING REVIEWED HAS NO AUTHOR OR EDITOR. CERTAIN REFERENCE WORKS AND ANONYMOUS WORKS THAT ARE KNOWN PRIMARILY BY THEIR TITLE ARE INDEXED UNDER THAT TITLE AND THEIR EDITORS ARE CROSS-INDEXED.

A LIST OF ABBREVIATIONS USED IS SHOWN ON PAGE II.

ABBREVIATIONS

```
ANON  ................. ANONYMOUS
APR   ................. APRIL
AUG   ................. AUGUST
BK    ................. BOOK
COMP(S) .............. COMPILER(S)
CONT. ................ CONTINUED
DEC   ................. DECEMBER
ED(S) ................ EDITOR(S) [OR] EDITION(S)
FASC  ................. FASCICULE
FEB   ................. FEBRUARY
JAN   ................. JANUARY
JUL   ................. JULY
JUN   ................. JUNE
MAR   ................. MARCH
NO. (OR #) ........... NUMBER
NOV   ................. NOVEMBER
OCT   ................. OCTOBER
PREV  ................. PREVIOUS VOLUME OF THIS INDEX
PT    ................. PART
REV   ................. REVISED
SEP   ................. SEPTEMBER
SER   ................. SERIES
SUPP  ................. SUPPLEMENT
TRANS ................ TRANSLATOR(S)
VOL   ................. VOLUME
* (ASTERISK) ......... THIS TITLE WAS ALSO SHOWN IN THE VOLUME
                       OF THIS INDEX IMMEDIATELY PRECEDING
                       THIS ONE
```

THE PERIODICALS IN WHICH THE REVIEWS APPEAR ARE IDENTIFIED IN
THIS INDEX BY A NUMBER. TO SUPPLEMENT THIS NUMBER, AND TO PROMOTE
READY IDENTIFICATION, PMLA ABBREVIATIONS ARE ALSO GIVEN FOLLOWING
THIS NUMBER. EVERY ATTEMPT WILL BE MADE TO INDEX THOSE ISSUES
SHOWN HERE AS "MISSING" IN A LATER VOLUME OF THIS INDEX.
THE FOLLOWING IS A LISTING OF THE PERIODICALS INDEXED IN VOLUME
16:

71(ALS) - AUSTRALIAN LITERARY STUDIES. HOBART, TASMANIA. TWICE
YEARLY.
MAY75 & OCT75 (VOL 7 #1&2)
72 - ARCHIV FÜR DAS STUDIUM DER NEUEREN SPRACHEN UND LITERATUREN.
BRAUNSCHWEIG, GERMANY. SIX YEARLY.
BAND 211 COMPLETE
73 - ART MAGAZINE. TORONTO. QUARTERLY.
FALL73 THRU SUMMER74 (VOL 5 COMPLETE)
75 - BABEL. GERLINGEN, GERMANY. QUARTERLY.
1/1973 THRU 4/1973 (VOL 19 COMPLETE)
78(BC) - BOOK COLLECTOR. LONDON. QUARTERLY.
SPRING73 THRU WINTER73 (VOL 22 COMPLETE)
84 - THE BRITISH JOURNAL FOR THE PHILOSOPHY OF SCIENCE. CAMBRIDGE,
ENGLAND. QUARTERLY.
MAR73 THRU DEC73 (VOL 24 COMPLETE)
85 - STUDIES IN BROWNING & HIS CIRCLE (EX-THE BROWNING NEWS-
LETTER). WACO, TEXAS. TWICE YEARLY.
SPRING73 (VOL 1 #1)
86(BHS) - BULLETIN OF HISPANIC STUDIES. LIVERPOOL. QUARTERLY.
JAN73 THRU OCT73 (VOL 50 COMPLETE)
89(BJA) - THE BRITISH JOURNAL OF AESTHETICS. LONDON. QUARTERLY.
WINTER73 THRU AUTUMN73 (VOL 13 COMPLETE)
90 - BURLINGTON MAGAZINE. LONDON. MONTHLY.
JAN73 THRU DEC73 (VOL 115 COMPLETE)
96 - ARTSCANADA. OTTAWA.
FEB/MAR73 THRU DEC73/JAN74 (VOL 30 COMPLETE)
98 - CRITIQUE. PARIS. MONTHLY.
JAN73 THRU DEC73 (VOL 29 COMPLETE)
99 - CANADIAN FORUM. TORONTO. MONTHLY.
JAN75 THRU DEC75/JAN76 (VOL 54 #647-649, VOL 55
#650-657) [VOL BEGINS WITH APR/MAY75 ISSUE]
102(CANL) - CANADIAN LITERATURE. VANCOUVER, B.C. QUARTERLY.
WINTER73 THRU AUTUMN74 (#55-62)
104 - CANADIAN-AMERICAN SLAVIC STUDIES/REVUE CANADIENNE-AMERICAINE
D'ÉTUDES SLAVES. PITTSBURGH, PA. QUARTERLY.
SPRING73 THRU WINTER74 (VOLS 7 & 8 COMPLETE)
109 - THE CARLETON MISCELLANY. NORTHFIELD, MINN. TWICE YEARLY.
FALL/WINTER73/74 & SPRING/SUMMER74 (VOL 14 COM-
PLETE)
111 - CAMBRIDGE REVIEW. CAMBRIDGE, ENGLAND. SIX YEARLY.
26OCT73 THRU 30MAY74 (VOL 95 #2216-2221)
113 - CENTRUM. MINNEAPOLIS, MINN. TWICE YEARLY.
SPRING73 THRU FALL74 (VOLS 1 & 2 COMPLETE)
114(CHIR) - CHICAGO REVIEW. QUARTERLY.
VOLUME 25 COMPLETE
121(CJ) - CLASSICAL JOURNAL. TALLAHASSEE, FLORIDA. QUARTERLY.
OCT/NOV72 THRU FEB/MAR73 & OCT/NOV73 THRU
APR/MAY74 (VOL 68 #1-3, VOL 69 COMPLETE)
[APR/MAY73 ISSUE IS MISSING]
122 - CLASSICAL PHILOLOGY. CHICAGO. QUARTERLY.
JAN73 THRU OCT74 (VOLS 68 & 69 COMPLETE)
123 - CLASSICAL REVIEW. LONDON. TWICE YEARLY.
MAR74 & NOV74 (VOL 24 COMPLETE)
124 - CLASSICAL WORLD. UNIVERSITY PARK, PA. MONTHLY.
SEP72 THRU APR/MAY74 (VOLS 66 & 67 COMPLETE)
125 - CLIO. KENOSHA, WISC. THREE YEARLY.
OCT73 THRU JUN74 (VOL 3 COMPLETE)
127 - ART JOURNAL. NEW YORK. QUARTERLY.
FALL73 THRU SUMMER74 (VOL 33 COMPLETE)
128(CE) - COLLEGE ENGLISH. CHAMPAIGN, ILLINOIS. MONTHLY.
OCT73 THRU MAY74 (VOL 35 COMPLETE)
131(CL) - COMPARATIVE LITERATURE. EUGENE, OREGON. QUARTERLY.
WINTER73 THRU FALL74 (VOLS 25 & 26 COMPLETE)
133 - COLLOQUIA GERMANICA. BERN, SWITZERLAND. THREE YEARLY.
1973/1 THRU 1973/3
134(CP) - CONCERNING POETRY. BELLINGHAM, WASH. TWICE YEARLY.
SPRING73 & FALL73 (VOL 6 COMPLETE)
135 - CONNOISSEUR. LONDON & NEW YORK. MONTHLY.
JAN73 THRU DEC73 (VOLS 182, 183 & 184 COMPLETE)
136 - CONRADIANA. ABILENE, TEXAS. THREE YEARLY.
VOLUME 5 COMPLETE
139 - CRAFT HORIZONS. NEW YORK. BI-MONTHLY.
FEB73 THRU DEC73 (VOL 33 COMPLETE)

140(CR) - THE CRITICAL REVIEW. MELBOURNE, AUSTRALIA. ANNUAL.
            #15 THRU #17
141 - CRITICISM. DETROIT. QUARTERLY.
            WINTER72 THRU FALL74 (VOLS 14, 15 & 16 COMPLETE)
145(CRIT) - CRITIQUE. ATLANTA, GEORGIA. THREE YEARLY.
            VOLUME 15 COMPLETE
148 - CRITICAL QUARTERLY. MANCHESTER, ENGLAND.
            SPRING72 THRU WINTER73 (VOLS 14 & 15 COMPLETE)
149 - COMPARATIVE LITERATURE STUDIES. URBANA, ILL. QUARTERLY.
            MAR74 THRU DEC74 (VOL 11 COMPLETE)
150(DR) - DALHOUSIE REVIEW. HALIFAX, N.S., CANADA. QUARTERLY.
            SPRING73 THRU WINTER73/74 (VOL 53 COMPLETE)
151 - DANCE MAGAZINE. NEW YORK. MONTHLY.
            FEB70 & JAN73 THRU DEC73 (VOL 44 #2, VOL 47 COM-
            PLETE)
154 - DIALOGUE. MONTREAL. QUARTERLY.
            MAR73 THRU DEC73 (VOL 12 COMPLETE)
155 - THE DICKENSIAN. LONDON. THREE YEARLY.
            JAN73 THRU SEP73 (VOL 69 COMPLETE)
157 - DRAMA/THE QUARTERLY THEATRE REVIEW. LONDON.
            SPRING73 THRU WINTER 73 (#108-111)
159(DM) - DUBLIN MAGAZINE. DUBLIN. QUARTERLY.
            AUTUMN72 & WINTER/SPRING73 THRU AUTUMN/WINTER73/74
            (VOL 9 #4, VOL 10 #1-3)
160 - DRAMA & THEATRE. FREDONIA, N.Y. THREE YEARLY.
            FALL72 THRU SPRING73 (VOL 11 COMPLETE)
165 - EARLY AMERICAN LITERATURE. AMHERST, MASS. THREE YEARLY.
            WINTER75 THRU FALL75 (VOL 9 #3, VOL 10 #1&2)
172(EDDA) - EDDA. OSLO. SIX YEARLY.
            1973/1 THRU 1973/6 (VOL 73 COMPLETE)
173(ECS) - EIGHTEENTH-CENTURY STUDIES. DAVIS, CALIF. QUARTERLY.
            FALL73 THRU SUMMER74 (VOL 7 COMPLETE)
175 - ENGLISH. LONDON. THREE YEARLY.
            SPRING72 THRU AUTUMN73 (VOLS 21 & 22 COMPLETE)
177(ELT) - ENGLISH LITERATURE IN TRANSITION. TEMPE, ARIZ. QUARTERLY.
            VOLUME 16 COMPLETE
179(ES) - ENGLISH STUDIES. AMSTERDAM. BI-MONTHLY.
            FEB72 THRU DEC73 (VOLS 53 & 54 COMPLETE)
180(ESA) - ENGLISH STUDIES IN AFRICA. JOHANNESBURG. TWICE YEARLY.
            MAR73 THRU SEP74 (VOLS 16 & 17 COMPLETE)
181 - EPOCH. ITHACA, N.Y. THREE YEARLY.
            AUTUMN73 THRU SPRING74 (VOL 23 COMPLETE)
182 - ERASMUS. WIESBADEN, GERMANY. MONTHLY.
            VOLUME 26 COMPLETE
184(EIC) - ESSAYS IN CRITICISM. OXFORD, ENGLAND. QUARTERLY.
            JAN72 THRU OCT73 (VOLS 22 & 23 COMPLETE)
185 - ETHICS. CHICAGO. QUARTERLY.
            OCT73 THRU JUL74 (VOL 84 COMPLETE)
186(ETC.) - ETC. SAN FRANCISCO. QUARTERLY.
            MAR73 THRU DEC73 (VOL 30 COMPLETE)
187 - ETHNOMUSICOLOGY. ANN ARBOR, MICH. THREE YEARLY.
            JAN75 THRU SEP75 (VOL 19 COMPLETE)
188(ECR) - L'ESPRIT CRÉATEUR. LAWRENCE, KANSAS. QUARTERLY.
            SPRING73 THRU WINTER73 (VOL 13 COMPLETE)
189(EA) - ETUDES ANGLAISES. PARIS. QUARTERLY.
            JAN-MAR73 THRU OCT-DEC73 (VOL 26 COMPLETE)
190 - EUPHORION. HEIDELBERG. QUARTERLY.
            BAND 67 COMPLETE
191(ELN) - ENGLISH LANGUAGE NOTES. BOULDER, COLORADO. QUARTERLY.
            SEP73 THRU JUN74 (VOL 11 COMPLETE)
196 - FABULA. BERLIN. THREE YEARLY.
            BAND 14 COMPLETE
198 - THE FIDDLEHEAD. FREDERICTON, N.B., CANADA. QUARTERLY.
            WINTER75 THRU FALL75 (#104-107)
200 - FILMS IN REVIEW. NEW YORK. MONTHLY.
            JAN73 THRU DEC73 (VOL 24 COMPLETE)
202(FMOD) - FILOLOGÍA MODERNA. MADRID. THREE YEARLY.
            NOV72/FEB73 & JUN73 (VOL 13 COMPLETE)
203 - FOLKLORE. LONDON. QUARTERLY.
            SPRING73 THRU WINTER73 (VOL 84 COMPLETE)
204(FDL) - FORUM DER LETTEREN. LEIDEN. QUARTERLY.
            MAR73 THRU DEC73 (VOL 14 COMPLETE)

205(FMLS) - FORUM FOR MODERN LANGUAGE STUDIES. ST. ANDREWS, SCOT-
           LAND. QUARTERLY.
                 JAN73 THRU OCT73 (VOL 9 COMPLETE)
206 - FOUNDATIONS OF LANGUAGE. DORDRECHT, THE NETHERLANDS. SIX
      YEARLY.
                 MAY73 THRU NOV73 (VOL 10 COMPLETE)
207(FR) - FRENCH REVIEW. BALTIMORE. SIX YEARLY.
                 OCT72 THRU MAY73 (VOL 46 COMPLETE)
208(FS) - FRENCH STUDIES. OXFORD, ENGLAND. QUARTERLY.
                 JAN74 THRU OCT74 (VOL 28 COMPLETE)
209(FM) - LE FRANÇAIS MODERNE. PARIS. QUARTERLY.
                 JAN73 THRU OCT73 (VOL 41 COMPLETE)
214 - GAMBIT. LONDON.
                 VOLUME 6 COMPLETE
215(GL) - GENERAL LINGUISTICS. UNIVERSITY PARK, PA. QUARTERLY.
                 VOLUME 13 COMPLETE
219(GAR) - GEORGIA REVIEW. ATHENS, GA. QUARTERLY.
                 SPRING73 THRU WINTER73 (VOL 27 COMPLETE)
220(GL&L) - GERMAN LIFE & LETTERS. OXFORD, ENGLAND. QUARTERLY.
                 OCT73 THRU JUL74 (VOL 27 COMPLETE)
221(GQ) - GERMAN QUARTERLY. PHILADELPHIA.
                 JAN73 THRU NOV73 (VOL 46 COMPLETE)
222(GR) - GERMANIC REVIEW. NEW YORK. QUARTERLY.
                 JAN73 THRU NOV73 (VOL 48 COMPLETE)
223 - GENRE. CHICAGO. QUARTERLY.
                 MAR73 THRU DEC73 (VOL 6 COMPLETE)
224(GRM) - GERMANISCH-ROMANISCHE MONATSSCHRIFT. HEIDELBERG.
           QUARTERLY.
                 BAND 23 COMPLETE
228(GSLI) - GIORNALE STORICO DELLA LETTERATURA ITALIANA. TORINO.
            QUARTERLY.
                 VOLUME 150 COMPLETE
231 - HARPER'S MAGAZINE. NEW YORK. MONTHLY.
                 JAN75 THRU DEC75 (VOLS 250 & 251 COMPLETE)
238 - HISPANIA. QUARTERLY.
                 MAR73 THRU DEC73 (VOL 56 COMPLETE)
240(HR) - HISPANIC REVIEW. PHILADELPHIA. QUARTERLY.
                 WINTER73 THRU AUTUMN73 (VOL 41 COMPLETE)
241 - HISPANÓFILA. CHAPEL HILL, N.C. THREE YEARLY.
                 JAN73 THRU SEP73 (#47-49)
244(HJAS) - HARVARD JOURNAL OF ASIATIC STUDIES. CAMBRIDGE, MASS.
            ANNUAL.
                 VOLUME 33 COMPLETE
249(HUDR) - HUDSON REVIEW. NEW YORK. QUARTERLY.
                 SPRING74 THRU WINTER74/75 (VOL 27 COMPLETE)
255(HAB) - HUMANITIES ASSOCIATION BULLETIN. FREDERICTON, N.B.,
           CANADA. QUARTERLY.
                 WINTER73 THRU FALL73 (VOL 24 COMPLETE)
258 - INTERNATIONAL PHILOSOPHICAL QUARTERLY. NEW YORK & HEVERLEE-
      LEUVEN, BELGIUM.
                 MAR73 THRU DEC73 (VOL 13 COMPLETE)
260(IF) - INDOGERMANISCHE FORSCHUNGEN. BERLIN.
                 BAND 77 HEFT2/3 & BAND 78
262 - INQUIRY. OSLO. QUARTERLY.
                 SPRING73 THRU WINTER73 (VOL 16 COMPLETE)
263 - INTER-AMERICAN REVIEW OF BIBLIOGRAPHY. WASHINGTON, D.C.
      QUARTERLY.
                 JAN-MAR74 THRU OCT-DEC74 (VOL 24 COMPLETE)
268 - THE INTERNATIONAL FICTION REVIEW. FREDERICTON, N.B., CANADA.
      TWICE YEARLY.
                 JAN75 & JUL75 (VOL 2 COMPLETE)
269(IJAL) - INTERNATIONAL JOURNAL OF AMERICAN LINGUISTICS. BALTI-
            MORE. QUARTERLY.
                 JAN73 THRU OCT73 (VOL 39 COMPLETE)
270 - INTERNATIONAL P.E.N. LONDON. QUARTERLY.
                 VOLUME 23 COMPLETE
273(IC) - ISLAMIC CULTURE. HYDERABAD-DECCAN, INDIA. QUARTERLY.
                 JAN73 THRU OCT73 (VOL 47 COMPLETE)
275(IQ) - ITALIAN QUARTERLY. RIVERSIDE, CALIFORNIA.
                 SUMMER73 THRU SPRING74 (VOL 17 COMPLETE)
276 - ITALICA. NEW YORK. QUARTERLY.
                 SPRING73 THRU WINTER73 (VOL 50 COMPLETE)

279 - INTERNATIONAL JOURNAL OF SLAVIC LINGUISTICS & POETICS.
    'S-GRAVENHAGE, THE NETHERLANDS. ANNUAL.
        VOLUME 16 COMPLETE
285(JAPQ) - JAPAN QUARTERLY. TOKYO.
        JAN-MAR73 THRU OCT-DEC74 (VOLS 20 & 21 COMPLETE)
287 - JEWISH FRONTIER. NEW YORK. MONTHLY.
        JAN73 THRU DEC73 (VOL 40 COMPLETE)
290(JAAC) - JOURNAL OF AESTHETICS & ART CRITICISM. BALTIMORE.
    QUARTERLY.
        FALL73 THRU SUMMER74 (VOL 32 COMPLETE)
292(JAF) - JOURNAL OF AMERICAN FOLKLORE. QUARTERLY.
        JAN-MAR73 THRU OCT-DEC73 (VOL 86 COMPLETE)
293(JAST) - JOURNAL OF ASIAN STUDIES. ANN ARBOR, MICH. QUARTERLY.
        NOV72 THRU AUG73 (VOL 32 COMPLETE)
295 - JOURNAL OF MODERN LITERATURE. PHILADELPHIA. FIVE YEARLY.
        FEB74 THRU JUL74 (VOL 3 #3-5)
296 - JOURNAL OF CANADIAN FICTION. MONTREAL. QUARTERLY.
        VOL 3 #4 THRU VOL 4 #3
297(JL) - JOURNAL OF LINGUISTICS. READING, ENGLAND. TWICE YEARLY.
        FEB73 & SEP73 (VOL 9 COMPLETE)
301(JEGP) - JOURNAL OF ENGLISH & GERMANIC PHILOLOGY. URBANA, ILL.
    QUARTERLY.
        JAN74 THRU OCT74 (VOL 73 COMPLETE)
302 - JOURNAL OF ORIENTAL STUDIES. HONG KONG. TWICE YEARLY.
        JAN73 & JUL73 (VOL 11 COMPLETE)
303 - JOURNAL OF HELLENIC STUDIES. LONDON. ANNUAL.
        VOLUME 93
307 - JOURNAL OF LITERARY SEMANTICS. THE HAGUE, NETHERLANDS.
        #1 THRU #3
308 - JOURNAL OF MUSIC THEORY. NEW HAVEN, CONN. TWICE YEARLY.
        SPRING73 & FALL73 (VOL 17 COMPLETE)
311(JP) - JOURNAL OF PHILOSOPHY. NEW YORK. BI-WEEKLY.
        16JAN75 THRU 18DEC75 (VOL 72 COMPLETE)
313 - JOURNAL OF ROMAN STUDIES. LONDON. ANNUAL.
        VOLUME 63
315(JAL) - JOURNAL OF AFRICAN LANGUAGES. LONDON. THREE YEARLY.
        VOLUME 11 COMPLETE
316 - JOURNAL OF SYMBOLIC LOGIC. PROVIDENCE, R.I. QUARTERLY.
        MAR73 THRU DEC73 (VOL 38 COMPLETE)
317 - JOURNAL OF THE AMERICAN MUSICOLOGICAL SOCIETY. RICHMOND, VA.
    THREE YEARLY.
        SPRING73 & FALL73 (VOL 26 #1&3) [SUMMER73 ISSUE
          IS MISSING]
318(JAOS) - JOURNAL OF THE AMERICAN ORIENTAL SOCIETY. BALTIMORE.
    QUARTERLY.
        JAN-MAR73 THRU OCT-DEC73 (VOL 93 COMPLETE)
319 - JOURNAL OF THE HISTORY OF PHILOSOPHY. ST. LOUIS, MO.
    QUARTERLY.
        JAN75 THRU OCT75 (VOL 13 COMPLETE)
320(CJL) - CANADIAN JOURNAL OF LINGUISTICS. TORONTO. TWICE YEARLY.
        SPRING74 & FALL74 (VOL 19 COMPLETE)
321 - THE JOURNAL OF VALUE INQUIRY. THE HAGUE. QUARTERLY.
        SPRING73 THRU WINTER73 (VOL 7 COMPLETE)
322(JHI) - JOURNAL OF THE HISTORY OF IDEAS. NEW YORK. QUARTERLY.
        JAN-MAR73 THRU OCT-DEC73 (VOL 34 COMPLETE)
325 - JOURNAL OF THE SOCIETY OF ARCHIVISTS. LONDON. TWICE YEARLY.
        APR73 & OCT73 (VOL 4 #7&8)
329(JJQ) - JAMES JOYCE QUARTERLY. TULSA, OKLAHOMA.
        FALL74/WINTER75 THRU SUMMER75 (VOL 12 COMPLETE)
342 - KANT-STUDIEN. BONN. QUARTERLY.
        BAND 64 COMPLETE
343 - KRATYLOS. WIESBADEN. TWICE YEARLY.
        BAND 16 & 17 COMPLETE
349 - LANGUAGE & STYLE. CARBONDALE, ILL. QUARTERLY.
        WINTER73 THRU FALL73 (VOL 6 COMPLETE)
350 - LANGUAGE. BALTIMORE. QUARTERLY.
        MAR74 THRU DEC74 (VOL 50 COMPLETE)
351(LL) - LANGUAGE LEARNING. ANN ARBOR, MICH. TWICE YEARLY.
        JUN74 & DEC74 (VOL 24 COMPLETE)
352(LE&W) - LITERATURE EAST & WEST. AUSTIN, TEXAS. QUARTERLY.
        VOL 16 #3 & VOL 16 #4
353 - LINGUISTICS. THE HAGUE, NETHERLANDS. 24 ISSUES YEARLY.
        1JAN73 THRU 15DEC73 (#95-118)

354 - THE LIBRARY. LONDON. QUARTERLY.
            MAR73 THRU DEC73 (VOL 28 COMPLETE)
361 - LINGUA. AMSTERDAM. MONTHLY.
            VOL 31 #1 THRU DEC73 (VOLS 31 & 32 COMPLETE)
362 - THE LISTENER. LONDON. WEEKLY.
            2JAN75 THRU 25DEC75/1JAN76 (VOLS 93 & 94 COMPLETE)
364 - LONDON MAGAZINE. LONDON. BI-MONTHLY.
            APR-MAY74 THRU FEB-MAR75 (VOL 14 COMPLETE)
376 - THE MALAHAT REVIEW. VICTORIA, B.C., CANADA. QUARTERLY.
            JAN73 THRU OCT73 (#25-28)
377 - MANUSCRIPTA. ST. LOUIS, MO. THREE YEARLY.
            MAR74 THRU NOV74 (VOL 18 COMPLETE)
381 - MEANJIN QUARTERLY. PARKVILLE, VICTORIA, AUSTRALIA.
            MAR73 THRU DEC73 (VOL 32 COMPLETE)
382(MAE) - MEDIUM AEVUM. OXFORD, ENGLAND. THREE YEARLY.
            1974/1 THRU 1974/3 (VOL 43 COMPLETE)
385(MQR) - MICHIGAN QUARTERLY REVIEW. ANN ARBOR.
            WINTER75 THRU FALL75 (VOL 14 COMPLETE)
390 - MIDSTREAM. NEW YORK. MONTHLY.
            JAN73 THRU DEC73 (VOL 19 COMPLETE)
391(JFI) - JOURNAL OF THE FOLKLORE INSTITUTE. BLOOMINGTON, IND.
            THREE YEARLY.
            JUN/AUG73 & DEC73 (VOL 10 COMPLETE) [NO REVIEWS
            INDEXED]
393(MIND) - MIND. LONDON. QUARTERLY.
            JAN73 THRU OCT73 (VOL 82 COMPLETE)
396(MODA) - MODERN AGE. CHICAGO. QUARTERLY.
            WINTER74 THRU FALL74 (VOL 18 COMPLETE)
397(MD) - MODERN DRAMA. TORONTO. QUARTERLY.
            JUN73 THRU DEC73 (VOL 16 COMPLETE)
398 - MODERN POETRY STUDIES. BUFFALO, N.Y. THREE YEARLY.
            SPRING75 THRU WINTER75 (VOL 6 COMPLETE)
399(MLJ) - MODERN LANGUAGE JOURNAL. BOULDER, COLORADO. EIGHT
            YEARLY.
            JAN-FEB73 THRU DEC74 (VOLS 57 & 58 COMPLETE)
400(MLN) - MODERN LANGUAGE NOTES. BALTIMORE. SIX YEARLY.
            JAN73 THRU DEC73 (VOL 88 COMPLETE)
401(MLQ) - MODERN LANGUAGE QUARTERLY. SEATTLE, WASH.
            MAR74 THRU DEC74 (VOL 35 COMPLETE)
402(MLR) - MODERN LANGUAGE REVIEW. LONDON. QUARTERLY.
            JAN74 THRU OCT74 (VOL 69 COMPLETE)
405(MP) - MODERN PHILOLOGY. CHICAGO. QUARTERLY.
            AUG73 THRU MAY74 (VOL 71 COMPLETE)
406 - MONATSHEFTE. MADISON, WISC. QUARTERLY.
            SPRING74 THRU WINTER74 (VOL 66 COMPLETE)
410(M&L) - MUSIC & LETTERS. LONDON. QUARTERLY.
            JAN74 THRU OCT74 (VOL 55 COMPLETE)
412 - MUSIC REVIEW. CAMBRIDGE, ENGLAND. QUARTERLY.
            FEB73 THRU AUG-NOV73 (VOL 34 COMPLETE)
414(MQ) - MUSICAL QUARTERLY. NEW YORK.
            JAN73 THRU OCT73 (VOL 59 COMPLETE)
415 - MUSICAL TIMES. LONDON. MONTHLY.
            JAN74 THRU DEC74 (VOL 115 COMPLETE)
418(MR) - THE MASSACHUSETTS REVIEW. AMHERST, MASS. QUARTERLY.
            WINTER-SPRING74 THRU AUTUMN74 (VOL 15 COMPLETE)
            [NO REVIEWS INDEXED]
424 - NAMES. POTSDAM, N.Y. QUARTERLY.
            MAR73 THRU DEC73 (VOL 21 COMPLETE)
430(NS) - DIE NEUEREN SPRACHEN. FRANKFURT AM MAIN. MONTHLY.
            JAN73 THRU SEP73 (VOL 72 #1-9)
432(NEQ) - NEW ENGLAND QUARTERLY. BRUNSWICK, MAINE.
            MAR73 THRU DEC74 (VOLS 46 & 47 COMPLETE)
433 - NEOPHILOLOGUS. GRONINGEN, THE NETHERLANDS. QUARTERLY.
            JAN73 THRU OCT73 (VOL 57 COMPLETE)
439(NM) - NEUPHILOLOGISCHE MITTEILUNGEN. HELSINKI. QUARTERLY.
            1973/1 THRU 1973/4 (VOL 74 COMPLETE)
441 - THE NEW YORK TIMES. DAILY.
            1JAN75 THRU 31DEC75 [SUNDAY DATES FOR THIS PERIODICAL
            REFER TO THE NEW YORK TIMES BOOK REVIEW SECTION]
442(NY) - THE NEW YORKER. WEEKLY.
            6JAN75 THRU 29DEC75 (VOL 50 #46-52, VOL 51 #1-45)
            [VOLUME 51 BEGINS WITH THE 24FEB75 ISSUE]
445(NCF) - NINETEENTH-CENTURY FICTION. BERKELEY, CALIF. QUARTERLY.
            JUN73 THRU MAR74 (VOL 28 COMPLETE)

```
446 - NINETEENTH-CENTURY FRENCH STUDIES.  FREDONIA, N.Y.  QUARTERLY.
          FALL-WINTER73/74 & SPRING-SUMMER74 (VOL 2 COMPLETE)
447(N&Q) - NOTES & QUERIES.  LONDON.  MONTHLY.
          JAN73 THRU DEC73 (VOL 20 COMPLETE)
448 - NORTHWEST REVIEW.  EUGENE, OREGON.  THREE YEARLY.
          VOL 13 #1 & VOL 13 #2
453 - THE NEW YORK REVIEW OF BOOKS.  BI-WEEKLY.
          23JAN75 THRU 11DEC75 (VOL 21 #21/22 & VOL 22 #1-20)
          [VOL 22 BEGINS WITH THE 6FEB75 ISSUE]
454 - NOVEL.  PROVIDENCE, R.I.  THREE YEARLY.
          FALL73 THRU SPRING74 (VOL 7 COMPLETE)
462(OL) - ORBIS LITTERARUM.  COPENHAGEN.  QUARTERLY.
          VOL 28 #1, 2 & 4 [VOL 28 #3 ISSUE IS MISSING]
463 - ORIENTAL ART.  RICHMOND, SURREY, ENGLAND.  QUARTERLY.
          SPRING73 THRU WINTER73 (VOL 19 COMPLETE)
470 - PAN PIPES.  DES MOINES, IOWA.  QUARTERLY.
          NOV72 THRU MAY74 (VOLS 65 & 66 COMPLETE)
473(PR) - PARTISAN REVIEW.  NEW YORK.  QUARTERLY.
          1/1974 THRU 4/1974 (VOL 41 COMPLETE)
477 - PERSONALIST.  LOS ANGELES.  QUARTERLY.
          WINTER73 THRU AUTUMN73 (VOL 54 COMPLETE) [NO RE-
          VIEWS INDEXED]
478 - THE PHILOSOPHICAL JOURNAL.  EDINBURGH.  TWICE YEARLY.
          JAN73 & JUL73 (VOL 10 COMPLETE)
479(PHQ) - PHILOSOPHICAL QUARTERLY.  ST. ANDREWS, SCOTLAND.
          JAN73 THRU OCT73 (VOL 23 COMPLETE)
480(P&R) - PHILOSOPHY & RHETORIC.  UNIVERSITY PARK, PA.  QUARTERLY.
          WINTER73 THRU FALL73 (VOL 6 COMPLETE)
481(PQ) - PHILOLOGICAL QUARTERLY.  IOWA CITY, IOWA.
          JAN73 THRU OCT73 (VOL 52 COMPLETE)
482(PHR) - PHILOSOPHICAL REVIEW.  ITHACA, N.Y.  QUARTERLY.
          JAN73 THRU OCT74 (VOLS 82 & 83 COMPLETE)
483 - PHILOSOPHY.  LONDON.  QUARTERLY.
          JAN73 THRU OCT73 (VOL 48 COMPLETE)
484(PPR) - PHILOSOPHY & PHENOMENOLOGICAL RESEARCH.  BUFFALO, N.Y.
          QUARTERLY.
          SEP73 THRU JUN74 (VOL 34 COMPLETE)
485(PE&W) - PHILOSOPHY EAST & WEST.  HONOLULU.  QUARTERLY.
          JAN-APR73 THRU OCT73 (VOL 23 COMPLETE)
486 - PHILOSOPHY OF SCIENCE.  EAST LANSING, MICH.  QUARTERLY.
          MAR73 THRU DEC73 (VOL 40 COMPLETE)
487 - PHOENIX.  TORONTO.  QUARTERLY.
          SPRING73 THRU WINTER73 (VOL 27 COMPLETE)
488 - PHILOSOPHY OF THE SOCIAL SCIENCES.  TORONTO.  QUARTERLY.
          MAR73 THRU DEC73 (VOL 3 COMPLETE)
491 - POETRY.  CHICAGO.  MONTHLY.
          OCT74 THRU SEP75 (VOLS 125 & 126 COMPLETE)
492 - POETICS.  THE HAGUE, NETHERLANDS.
          #5 THRU 7 & #9 [#8 IS MISSING]
497(POLR) - POLISH REVIEW.  NEW YORK.  QUARTERLY.
          VOLUME 18 COMPLETE
502(PRS) - PRAIRIE SCHOONER.  LINCOLN, NEBRASKA.  QUARTERLY.
          SPRING73 THRU WINTER73/74 (VOL 47 COMPLETE)
503 - THE PRIVATE LIBRARY.  PINNER, MIDDLESEX, ENGLAND.  QUARTERLY.
          AUTUMN73 THRU WINTER73 (VOL 5 #3&4, VOL 6 COMPLETE)
505 - PROGRESSIVE ARCHITECTURE.  NEW YORK.  MONTHLY.
          JAN73 THRU DEC73 (VOL 54 COMPLETE)
513 - PERSPECTIVES OF NEW MUSIC.  PRINCETON.  TWICE YEARLY.
          FALL-WINTER72 THRU FALL-WINTER73/SPRING-SUMMER74
          (VOLS 11 & 12 COMPLETE)
517(PBSA) - PAPERS OF THE BIBLIOGRAPHICAL SOCIETY OF AMERICA.
          NEW HAVEN, CONN.  QUARTERLY.
          JAN-MAR74 THRU OCT-DEC74 (VOL 68 COMPLETE)
518 - PHILOSOPHICAL BOOKS.  LEICESTER, ENGLAND.  THREE YEARLY.
          JAN74 THRU OCT74 (VOL 15 COMPLETE)
529(QQ) - QUEEN'S QUARTERLY.  KINGSTON, ONT., CANADA.
          SPRING73 THRU WINTER73 (VOL 80 COMPLETE)
535(RHL) - REVUE D'HISTOIRE LITTÉRAIRE DE LA FRANCE.  PARIS.
          SIX YEARLY.
          JAN-FEB73 THRU NOV-DEC73 (VOL 73 COMPLETE)
536 - RATIO.  OXFORD, ENGLAND.  TWICE YEARLY.
          JUN73 & DEC73 (VOL 15 COMPLETE)
541(RES) - REVIEW OF ENGLISH STUDIES.  LONDON.  QUARTERLY.
          FEB73 THRU NOV73 (VOL 24 COMPLETE)
```

542 - REVUE PHILOSOPHIQUE DE LA FRANCE ET DE L'ÉTRANGER. PARIS.
    QUARTERLY.
        JAN-MAR73 THRU OCT-DEC73 (VOL 163 COMPLETE)
543 - REVIEW OF METAPHYSICS. NEW HAVEN, CONN. QUARTERLY.
        SEP72 THRU JUN73 (VOL 26 COMPLETE)
544 - REVIEW OF NATIONAL LITERATURES. JAMAICA, N.Y. TWICE YEARLY.
        SPRING74 & FALL74 (VOL 5 COMPLETE)
545(RPH) - ROMANCE PHILOLOGY. BERKELEY, CALIF. QUARTERLY.
        AUG73 THRU MAY74 (VOL 27 COMPLETE)
546(RR) - ROMANIC REVIEW. NEW YORK. QUARTERLY.
        JAN73 THRU NOV74 (VOLS 64 & 65 COMPLETE)
548(RCSF) - RIVISTA CRITICA DI STORIA DELLA FILOSOFIA. FIRENZE,
    ITALY. QUARTERLY.
        JAN-MAR73 THRU OCT-DEC73 (VOL 28 COMPLETE)
549(RLC) - REVUE DE LITTÉRATURE COMPARÉE. PARIS. QUARTERLY.
        JAN-MAR73 THRU OCT-DEC73 (VOL 47 COMPLETE)
550(RUSR) - RUSSIAN REVIEW. HANOVER, N.H. QUARTERLY.
        JAN73 THRU OCT73 (VOL 32 COMPLETE)
551(RENQ) - RENAISSANCE QUARTERLY. NEW YORK.
        SPRING73 THRU WINTER73 (VOL 26 COMPLETE)
555 - REVUE DE PHILOLOGIE. PARIS. TWICE YEARLY.
        VOLUME 47 COMPLETE
556(RLV) - REVUE DES LANGUES VIVANTES/TIJDSCHRIFT VOOR LEVENDE TALEN.
    BRUXELLES. SIX YEARLY.
        1973/1 THRU 1973/6 (VOL 39 COMPLETE)
557(RSH) - REVUE DES SCIENCES HUMAINES. LILLE, FRANCE. QUARTERLY.
        JAN-MAR73 THRU OCT-DEC73 (#149 THRU #152)
563(SS) - SCANDINAVIAN STUDIES. QUARTERLY.
        WINTER74 THRU FALL74 (VOL 46 COMPLETE)
564 - SEMINAR. TORONTO. THREE YEARLY.
        MAR73 THRU OCT73 (VOL 9 COMPLETE)
565 - STAND. NEWCASTLE UPON TYNE, ENGLAND. QUARTERLY.
        VOLUME 14 COMPLETE
566 - THE SCRIBLERIAN. PHILADELPHIA. TWICE YEARLY.
        AUTUMN73 & SPRING74 (VOL 6 COMPLETE)
568(SCN) - SEVENTEENTH-CENTURY NEWS. NEW YORK. QUARTERLY.
        SPRING-SUMMER74 THRU WINTER74 (VOL 32 COMPLETE)
569(SR) - SEWANEE REVIEW. SEWANEE, TENN. QUARTERLY.
        WINTER74 THRU FALL74 (VOL 82 COMPLETE)
570(SQ) - SHAKESPEARE QUARTERLY. NEW YORK.
        WINTER73 THRU AUTUMN73 (VOL 24 COMPLETE)
571 - THE SHAVIAN. LONDON.
        SUMMER73 (VOL 4 #7)
572 - SHAW REVIEW. UNIVERSITY PARK, PA. THREE YEARLY.
        JAN73 THRU SEP73 (VOL 16 COMPLETE)
573(SSF) - STUDIES IN SHORT FICTION. NEWBERRY, S.C. QUARTERLY.
        WINTER73 THRU FALL73 (VOL 10 COMPLETE)
574(SEEJ) - SLAVIC & EAST EUROPEAN JOURNAL. QUARTERLY.
        SPRING72 THRU WINTER73 (VOLS 16 & 17 COMPLETE)
575(SEER) - SLAVONIC & EAST EUROPEAN REVIEW. LONDON. QUARTERLY.
        JAN74 THRU OCT74 (VOL 52 COMPLETE)
576 - JOURNAL OF THE SOCIETY OF ARCHITECTURAL HISTORIANS. PHILA-
    DELPHIA. QUARTERLY.
        MAR73 THRU DEC73 (VOL 32 COMPLETE)
577(SHR) - SOUTHERN HUMANITIES REVIEW. AUBURN, ALA. QUARTERLY.
        WINTER73 THRU FALL73 (VOL 7 COMPLETE)
578 - SOUTHERN LITERARY JOURNAL. CHAPEL HILL, N.C. TWICE YEARLY.
        SPRING75 & FALL75 (VOL 7 #2 & VOL 8 #1)
579(SAQ) - SOUTH ATLANTIC QUARTERLY. DURHAM, N.C.
        WINTER74 THRU AUTUMN74 (VOL 73 COMPLETE)
581 - SOUTHERLY. SYDNEY, AUSTRALIA. QUARTERLY.
        MAR74 THRU DEC74 (VOL 34 COMPLETE)
582(SFQ) - SOUTHERN FOLKLORE QUARTERLY. GAINESVILLE, FLA.
        MAR73 THRU DEC73 (VOL 37 COMPLETE)
583 - SOUTHERN SPEECH COMMUNICATION JOURNAL. WINSTON-SALEM, N.C.
    QUARTERLY.
        FALL73 THRU SUMMER74 (VOL 39 COMPLETE)
584(SWR) - SOUTHWEST REVIEW. DALLAS, TEXAS. QUARTERLY.
        WINTER74 THRU AUTUMN74 (VOL 59 COMPLETE)
588 - STUDIES IN SCOTTISH LITERATURE. COLUMBIA, S.C. QUARTERLY.
        JUL-OCT73 THRU APR74 (VOL 11 COMPLETE)
589 - SPECULUM. CAMBRIDGE, MASS. QUARTERLY.
        JAN74 THRU OCT74 (VOL 49 COMPLETE)

590 - SPIRIT. SOUTH ORANGE, N.J. TWICE YEARLY.
               SPRING/SUMMER74 & FALL/WINTER74/75 (VOL 41 COM-
               PLETE) [NO REVIEWS INDEXED]
591(SIR) - STUDIES IN ROMANTICISM. BOSTON. QUARTERLY.
               WINTER74 THRU FALL74 (VOL 13 COMPLETE)
592 - STUDIO INTERNATIONAL. LIVERPOOL. MONTHLY.
               JAN73 THRU DEC73 (VOLS 185 & 186 COMPLETE)
593 - SYMPOSIUM. SYRACUSE, N.Y. QUARTERLY.
               SPRING74 THRU WINTER74 (VOL 28 COMPLETE)
594 - STUDIES IN THE NOVEL. DENTON, TEX. QUARTERLY.
               SPRING73 THRU WINTER73 (VOL 5 COMPLETE)
595(SCS) - SCOTTISH STUDIES. EDINBURGH. ANNUAL.
               VOLUME 18 COMPLETE
597(SN) - STUDIA NEOPHILOLOGICA. UPPSALA, SWEDEN. TWICE YEARLY.
               VOLUME 45 COMPLETE
598(SOR) - THE SOUTHERN REVIEW. BATON ROUGE, LA. QUARTERLY.
               WINTER75 THRU AUTUMN75 (VOL 11 COMPLETE)
599 - STYLE. FAYETTEVILLE, ARK. THREE YEARLY.
               WINTER73 THRU FALL73 (VOL 7 COMPLETE)
606(TAMR) - TAMARACK REVIEW. TORONTO. QUARTERLY.
               1STQTR74 THRU MAR75 (#62 THRU #65)
607 - TEMPO. LONDON. QUARTERLY.
               #104 THRU SEP73 (#104 THRU #106)
608 - TESOL QUARTERLY. HONOLULU.
               MAR74 THRU DEC74 (VOL 8 COMPLETE)
613 - THOUGHT. BRONX, N.Y. QUARTERLY.
               SPRING73 THRU WINTER73 (VOL 48 COMPLETE)
617(TLS) - TIMES LITERARY SUPPLEMENT. LONDON. WEEKLY.
               3JAN75 THRU 26DEC75 (#3800 THRU #3850)
627(UTQ) - UNIVERSITY OF TORONTO QUARTERLY.
               FALL73 THRU SUMMER74 (VOL 43 COMPLETE) [SUMMER
               ISSUES OF THIS PERIODICAL ARE NOT INDEXED]
628 - UNIVERSITY OF WINDSOR REVIEW. WINDSOR, ONT. TWICE YEARLY.
               FALL73 & SPRING74 (VOL 9 COMPLETE)
636(VP) - VICTORIAN POETRY. MORGANTOWN, W. VA. QUARTERLY.
               SPRING73 THRU WINTER73 (VOL 11 COMPLETE)
637(VS) - VICTORIAN STUDIES. BLOOMINGTON, IND. QUARTERLY.
               SEP73 THRU JUN74 (VOL 17 COMPLETE)
639(VQR) - VIRGINIA QUARTERLY REVIEW. CHARLOTTESVILLE, VA.
               WINTER74 THRU AUTUMN74 (VOL 50 COMPLETE)
646(WWR) - WALT WHITMAN REVIEW. DETROIT. QUARTERLY.
               MAR73 THRU SEP73 (VOL 19 #1-3)
648 - WEST COAST REVIEW. BURNABY, B.C., CANADA. QUARTERLY.
               JUN73 & OCT73 (VOL 8 #1&2)
649(WAL) - WESTERN AMERICAN LITERATURE. FORT COLLINS, COLORADO.
               QUARTERLY.
               SPRING&SUMMER73 THRU WINTER74 (VOL 8 COMPLETE)
650(WF) - WESTERN FOLKLORE. BERKELEY, CALIF. QUARTERLY.
               JAN73 THRU OCT73 (VOL 32 COMPLETE)
651(WHR) - WESTERN HUMANITIES REVIEW. SALT LAKE CITY. QUARTERLY.
               WINTER74 THRU AUTUMN74 (VOL 28 COMPLETE)
654(WB) - WEIMARER BEITRÄGE. BERLIN. MONTHLY.
               1/1973 THRU 12/1973 (VOL 19 COMPLETE)
656(WMQ) - WILLIAM & MARY QUARTERLY. WILLIAMSBURG, VA.
               JAN74 THRU OCT74 (VOL 31 COMPLETE)
657(WW) - WIRKENDES WORT. DUSSELDORF. SIX YEARLY.
               JAN-FEB73 THRU NOV-DEC73 (VOL 23 COMPLETE)
659 - CONTEMPORARY LITERATURE. MADISON, WISC. QUARTERLY.
               WINTER75 THRU AUTUMN75 (VOL 16 COMPLETE)
660(WORD) - WORD. NEW YORK. THREE YEARLY.
               DEC70 (VOL 26 #3)
661 - WORKS. NEW YORK.
               WINTER72/73 THRU SPRING74 (VOL 3 #3/4 THRU VOL 4
               #3)
676(YR) - YALE REVIEW. NEW HAVEN, CONN. QUARTERLY.
               AUTUMN73 THRU SUMMER74 (VOL 63 COMPLETE)
677 - THE YEARBOOK OF ENGLISH STUDIES. LONDON. ANNUAL.
               VOLUME 4 COMPLETE
680(ZDP) - ZEITSCHRIFT FÜR DEUTSCHE PHILOLOGIE. BERLIN. QUARTERLY.
               BAND 92 COMPLETE [BAND 91 HEFT 4 IS MISSING]
682(ZPSK) - ZEITSCHRIFT FÜR PHONETIK, SPRACHWISSENSCHAFT UND KOMMUNI-
               KATIONSFORSCHUNG. BERLIN. SIX YEARLY.
               BAND 26 COMPLETE

683 - ZEITSCHRIFT FÜR KUNSTGESCHICHTE. MÜNCHEN. FIVE YEARLY.
BAND 36 COMPLETE

EACH YEAR WE ARE UNABLE (FOR ONE REASON OR ANOTHER) TO INDEX
THE REVIEWS APPEARING IN ALL OF THE PERIODICALS SCANNED. THE
FOLLOWING IS A LIST OF THE PERIODICALS WHOSE REVIEWS WERE NOT
INCLUDED IN THIS VOLUME OF THE INDEX. EVERY ATTEMPT WILL BE
MADE TO INDEX THESE REVIEWS IN THE NEXT VOLUME OF THE INDEX:

42(AR) - ANTIOCH REVIEW. YELLOW SPRINGS, OHIO. QUARTERLY.
47(ARL) - ARCHIVUM LINGUISTICUM. GLASGOW. ANNUAL.
48 - ARCHIVO ESPAÑOL DE ARTE. MADRID. QUARTERLY.
58 - ARTS MAGAZINE. NEW YORK. MONTHLY.
62 - ARTFORUM. NEW YORK. MONTHLY.
70(ANQ) - AMERICAN NOTES & QUERIES. NEW HAVEN, CONN. MONTHLY.
97(CQ) - THE CAMBRIDGE QUARTERLY. CAMBRIDGE, ENGLAND.
192(EP) - LES ÉTUDES PHILOSOPHIQUES. PARIS. QUARTERLY.
312 - JOURNAL OF PHONETICS. LONDON. QUARTERLY.
341 - KONSTHISTORISK TIDSKRIFT. STOCKHOLM.
355 - LANGUAGE IN SOCIETY. LONDON. TWICE YEARLY.
368 - LANDFALL. CHRISTCHURCH, N.Z. QUARTERLY.
395(MFS) - MODERN FICTION STUDIES. WEST LAFAYETTE, IND. QUARTERLY.
490 - POETICA. MÜNCHEN. QUARTERLY.
586(SORA) - SOUTHERN REVIEW. ADELAIDE, SOUTH AUSTRALIA. THREE
          YEARLY.
587(SAF) - STUDIES IN AMERICAN FICTION. BOSTON. TWICE YEARLY.
596(SL) - STUDIA LINGUISTICA. LUND, SWEDEN. TWICE YEARLY.
618 - TRANSITION. ACCRA, GHANA. SIX YEARLY.
684(ZDA) - ZEITSCHRIFT FÜR DEUTSCHES ALTERTUM UND DEUTSCHE LIT-
          ERATUR [ANZEIGER SECTION]. WIESBADEN, GERMANY. QUAR-
          TERLY.
685 - ZEITSCHRIFT FÜR DIALEKTOLOGIE UND LINGUISTIK. WIESBADEN,
      GERMANY. THREE YEARLY.

ACKERMAN, J.S. PALLADIO.
P. SCHNEIDER, 98:APR73-318
ACKERSON, D. WEATHERING.
M. GROSSMAN, 448:VOL13#2-90
ACKOFF, R.L. & F.E. EMERY. ON PUR-
POSEFUL SYSTEMS.
W. SCHÄFER, 182:VOL26#3/4-65
ACLAND, J.H. MEDIEVAL STRUCTURE.
R. BRANNER, 589:APR74-308
R. MARK, 576:DEC73-334
K. MORAND, 255:FALL73-304
"ACTA LINGUISTICA ACADEMIAE SCIEN-
TIARUM HUNGARICAE." (VOLS 19 & 20)
B. CARSTENSEN, 430(NS):JAN73-49
"ACTES DU COLLOQUE INTERNATIONAL DU
CENTRE NATIONAL DE LA RECHERCHE
SCIENTIFIQUE, 9 AU 13 JUIN 1969."
M. LASSÈGUE, 542:JAN-MAR73-27
G.J.P. O'DALY, 123:NOV74-228
"ACTES DU XIIE CONGRÈS INTERNATIONAL
D'HISTOIRE DES SCIENCE."
A. VIRIEUX-REYMOND, 542:JUL-SEP73-
345
"ACTES DU PREMIER CONGRÈS INTERNA-
TIONAL DES ÉTUDES BALKANIQUES ET
SUD-EST EUROPÉENNES." (VOL 6)
H. GALTON, 353:10CT73-115
ACTON, H. MEMOIRS OF AN AESTHETE,
1939-1969.
295:FEB74-362
ACTON, H. NANCY MITFORD.
R. BLYTHE, 362:25SEP75-405
A. FORBES, 617(TLS):12SEP75-1020
ACTON, H.B. THE MORALS OF MARKETS.
D.A.L. THOMAS, 479(PHQ):APR73-186
ADACHI, B. THE LIVING TREASURES OF
JAPAN.* (D. BIRDSALL, ED)
S. SITWELL, 39:DEC73-516
ADAIR, V. & L. EIGHTEENTH-CENTURY
PASTEL PORTRAITS.
M. WYNNE, 39:JUL73-71
ADAM DE LA HALLE. THE CHANSONS.*
(J.H. MARSHALL, ED)
N. WILKINS, 402(MLR):JAN74-170
ADAM, A. - SEE DE MALHERBE, F.
ADAM, A. - SEE RIMBAUD, A.
ADAM, F. - SEE GLÖCKNER, E.
ADAM, H., ED. SOUTH AFRICA.
S. PATTERSON, 69:APR73-177
ADAMEC, L.W., ED. BADAKHSHAN, HIS-
TORICAL & POLITICAL GAZETTEER OF
AFGHANISTAN. (VOL 1)
L. DUPREE, 293(JAST):MAY73-547
ADAMI, G. - SEE PUCCINI, G.
ADAMIETZ, J. UNTERSUCHUNGEN ZU
JUVENAL.
F. LASSERRE, 182:VOL26#3/4-119
ADAMS, A. FAMILIES & SURVIVORS.
A. BROYARD, 441:30JAN75-39
A. GOTTLIEB, 441:16MAR75-28
442(NY):10FEB75-115
ADAMS, A. & J. THE BOOK OF ABIGAIL
& JOHN. (L.H. BUTTERFIELD, M.
FRIEDLAENDER & M-J. KLINE, EDS)
P.U. BONOMI, 441:16NOV75-2
442(NY):10NOV75-193
ADAMS, C.C. BOONTLING.
R.A. DWYER, 35(AS):WINTER69-293
D.L. HAYES, 650(WF):JAN73-65
ADAMS, E. FRANCIS DANBY.*
639(VQR):SPRING74-LXII

ADAMS, H. THE EDUCATION OF HENRY
ADAMS.* (E. & J.N. SAMUELS, EDS)
J.C. LEVENSON, 27(AL):JAN75-590
P. SHAW, 432(NEQ):DEC74-603
"JOHN ADAMS, A BIOGRAPHY IN HIS OWN
WORDS."* (J.B. PEABODY, ED)
P.H. SMITH, 432(NEQ):MAR74-163
ADAMS, L., COMP. NORMAN MAILER.
617(TLS):30MAY75-601
ADAMS, N.S. & A.W. MC COY, EDS.
LAOS.
M. LEIFER, 293(JAST):NOV72-121
ADAMS, P., ED. LANGUAGE IN THINK-
ING.
J. MORTON, 399(MLJ):SEP-OCT74-278
ADAMS, R. SHARDIK.*
P. ADAMS, 61:JUN75-94
K. GRAHAM, 362:2JAN75-30
C. LEHMANN-HAUPT, 441:29APR75-37
A. LURIE, 453:12JUN75-34
P. ZWEIG, 441:4MAY75-1
442(NY):5MAY75-142
ADAMS, R. WATERSHIP DOWN.*
E.J. DEVEREUX, 99:MAR75-39
639(VQR):SUMMER74-LXXXII
ADAMS, R.F. COME AN' GET IT.
H.W. MARSHALL, 650(WF):JUL73-215
ADAMS, R.F. THE COWMAN SAYS IT
SALTY.
J.H. BRUNVAND, 292(JAF):APR-JUN73-
197
ADAMS, R.M. THE ROMAN STAMP.
F. KERMODE, 617(TLS):10JAN75-27
ADAMS, R.P. FAULKNER.
G. VAN CROMPHOUT, 179(ES):DEC72-
572
ADAMS, S. THE BOY INSIDE.
A. CLUYSENAAR, 565:VOL14#4-75
ADAMSON, D. - SEE SENCOURT, R.
ADAMSON, D. & P.B. DEWAR. THE
HOUSE OF NELL GWYN.
617(TLS):14FEB75-177
ADAMSON, J.H. & H.F. FOLLAND. SIR
HARRY VANE.*
H.M. JONES, 385(MQR):SPRING75-236
D.B. RUTMAN, 432(NEQ):MAR74-158
P.C. STURGES, 651(WHR):SUMMER74-
279
J.W. WILLIAMSON, 141:FALL74-345
ADAMUS, M. PHONEMTHEORIE UND DAS
DEUTSCHE PHONEMINVENTAR.
G. LINDNER, 682(ZPSK):BAND26HEFT
3/4-408
ADBURGHAM, A. LIBERTY'S.
G. HAVENHAND, 362:13NOV75-658
ADCOCK, F. THE SCENIC ROUTE.
R. GARFITT, 364:DEC74/JAN75-103
ADCOCK, F. & D.J. MOSLEY. DIPLOMACY
IN ANCIENT GREECE.
P. CARTLEDGE, 617(TLS):14NOV75-
1348
ADDISON, J. & R. STEELE. CRITICAL
ESSAYS FROM THE SPECTATOR BY JOSEPH
ADDISON WITH FOUR ESSAYS BY RICHARD
STEELE. (D.F. BOND, ED)
R. LONSDALE, 447(N&Q):MAY73-197
ADDISON, J. & R. STEELE. SELECTED
ESSAYS FROM "THE TATLER," "THE
SPECTATOR," & "THE GUARDIAN." (D.
MC DONALD, ED)
566:AUTUMN73-37
ADDISON, P. THE ROAD TO 1945.
M. BENTLEY, 362:30OCT75-570
K.O. MORGAN, 617(TLS):17OCT75-1222

ADELMAN, C. NO LOAVES, NO PARABLES.
442(NY):10FEB75-116
ADELMAN, I. & C.T. MORRIS. ECONOMIC
GROWTH & SOCIAL EQUITY IN DEVELOP-
ING COUNTRIES.
H. MYINT, 617(TLS):18APR75-432
ADELMAN, J. THE COMMON LIAR.
S.J. GREENBLATT, 676(YR):SPRING74-
447
C. HOY, 569(SR):SPRING74-363
R.P. WHEELER, 301(JEGP):OCT74-545
639(VQR):SUMMER74-LXXVII
ADELSON, R. MARK SYKES.
J. GRIGG, 362:8MAY75-620
G. WHEELER, 617(TLS):22AUG75-936
ADHÉMAR, J. & F. CACHIN. DEGAS.
J. CANADAY, 441:28MAR75-31
R. PICKVANCE, 617(TLS):21MAR75-317
J. RUSSELL, 441:3AUG75-7
ADHVARIN, D. - SEE UNDER DHARMARĀJA
ADHVARIN
ADJAN, S.I. DEFINING RELATIONS &
ALGORITHMIC PROBLEMS FOR GROUPS &
SEMIGROUPS.
A. YASUHARA, 316:JUN73-338
ADKINS, A.W.H. FROM THE MANY TO THE
ONE.*
C.T. MURPHY, 24:SPRING74-67
A. NEHAMAS, 482(PHR):JUL73-395
ADKINS, A.W.H. MORAL VALUES & POL-
ITICAL BEHAVIOR IN ANCIENT GREECE.
H.A. DEANE, 639(VQR):WINTER74-127
ADKINS, E. THE DEVIL'S LIMELIGHT.
D.M. DAY, 157:WINTER73-89
ADLARD, J. THE SPORTS OF CRUELTY.
K.M. BRIGGS, 203:SPRING73-80
I.H. CHAYES, 591(SIR):SPRING74-155
T.R. HENN, 402(MLR):APR74-379
ADLARD, M. MULTIFACE.
T.A. SHIPPEY, 617(TLS):5DEC75-1438
ADLEMAN, B. DOWN HOME. (S. HALL,
ED)
O. STROUD, 577(SHR):FALL73-454
ADLER, A. HOLZBENGEL MIT HERZENS-
BILDUNG.
H. HINTERHÄUSER, 72:BAND211HEFT
1/3-245
ADLER, F. SISTERS IN CRIME.
L. FRANKS, 441:6JUL75-7
ADMUSSEN, R.L. LES PETITES REVUES
LITTÉRAIRES, 1914-1939.*
R. DE SMEDT, 535(RHL):JUL-AUG73-
724
S.S. WEINER, 546(RR):NOV73-314
ADNÈS, A. ADENÈS, DERNIER GRAND
TROUVÈRE.
K.V. SINCLAIR, 589:APR74-311
ADORNO, T.W. NEGATIVE DIALECTICS.*
R. GEUSS, 311(JP):27MAR75-167
ADORNO, T.W. PHILOSOPHY OF MODERN
MUSIC.
R. MIDDLETON, 410(M&L):APR74-219
F.E. SPARSHOTT, 415:APR74-303
ADORNO, T.W. & E. KRENEK. BRIEF-
WECHSEL. (W. ROGGE, ED)
F.E. SPARSHOTT, 617(TLS):7NOV75-
1336
ADRIAANSZ, W. THE KUMIUTA & DANMONO
TRADITION OF JAPANESE KOTO MUSIC.
W.P. MALM, 414(MQ):OCT73-649
B. WADE, 187:JAN75-137

AEBISCHER, P. PRÉHISTOIRE ET PROTO-
HISTOIRE DU "ROLAND" D'OXFORD.
D.J.A. ROSS, 382(MAE):1974/2-159
K.V. SINCLAIR, 67:MAY74-107
AEBISCHER, P. TEXTES NORROIS ET
LITTÉRATURE FRANÇAISE DU MOYEN AGE.
(VOL 2)
D.J.A. ROSS, 382(MAE):1974/2-159
H.F. WILLIAMS, 207(FR):APR73-1003
AERS, D. PIERS PLOWMAN & CHRISTIAN
ALLEGORY.
J. BURROW, 617(TLS):21NOV75-1380
AESCHYLUS. THE PERSIANS. (A.J.
PODLECKI, TRANS)
D. PARKER, 5:SPRING73-205
AESCHYLUS. SEVEN AGAINST THEBES.*
(H. BACON & A. HECHT, TRANS)
G.E. DIMOCK, JR., 676(YR):SUMMER
74-573
B.M.W. KNOX, 453:27NOV75-27
AESCHYLUS. SUPPLIANTS. (J. LEMBKE,
TRANS) PROMETHEUS BOUND. (J.
SCULLY & C.J. HERINGTON, TRANS)
B.M.W. KNOX, 453:27NOV75-27
"AESTHETICS I." [TULANE STUDIES IN
PHILOSOPHY]
P.N., 543:MAR73-548
AFFRON, C. A STAGE FOR POETS.*
W.D. HOWARTH, 402(MLR):OCT74-880
J. MALL, 400(MLN):MAY73-917
AGAR, H. THE DARKEST YEAR.
W. BARBER, 150(DR):WINTER73/74-780
AGASSI, J. FARADAY AS A NATURAL
PHILOSOPHER.
J.L. SYNGE, 488:DEC73-351
J.O. WISDOM, 488:DEC73-354
AGBODEKA, F. AFRICAN POLITICS &
BRITISH POLICY IN THE GOLD COAST.
A.F. ROBERTSON, 69:APR73-173
AGEE, P. INSIDE THE COMPANY.
G. GARCÍA MÁRQUEZ, 453:7AUG75-32
R.R. LINGEMAN, 441:31JUL75-25
W. PINCUS, 441:3AUG75-2
AGESTHIALINGOM, S. & S.V. SHANMUGAM.
THE LANGUAGE OF TAMIL INSCRIPTIONS,
1250-1350 A.D.
K.V. ZVELEBIL, 318(JAOS):APR-JUN
73-246
AGGELER, W.F. BAUDELAIRE JUDGED BY
SPANISH CRITICS 1857-1957.*
W.T. BANDY, 535(RHL):JAN-FEB73-147
F.S. HECK, 188(ECR):FALL73-265
AGIRRE, J. OPERACIÓN OGRO.
R. EDER, 441:25OCT75-27
P. PRESTON, 617(TLS):4JUL75-740
AGNELLI, S. VESTIVAMO ALLA MARINARA.
A. FORBES, 617(TLS):19DEC75-1510
AGNELLI, S. WE ALWAYS WORE SAILOR
SUITS.
J. DASH, 441:12OCT75-6
AGRIPPA D'AUBIGNÉ - SEE UNDER D'AUB-
IGNÉ, A.
AGUILERA, R. INTENCIÓN Y SILENCIO
EN EL QUIJOTE.
E.H. FRIEDMAN, 400(MLN):MAR73-448
AGUINAGA, C.B. - SEE UNDER BLANCO
AGUINAGA, C.
AGULHON, M. LA RÉPUBLIQUE AU VIL-
LAGE.
R.E. SANDSTROM, 207(FR):DEC72-455
AGYEYA - SEE UNDER VATSYAYAN, S.H.
AHLBERG, G. FIGHTING ON LAND & SEA
IN GREEK GEOMETRIC ART.*
K. DE VRIES, 124:SEP-OCT73-37

AHLSTROM, S.E. A RELIGIOUS HISTORY
OF THE AMERICAN PEOPLE.*
   F.X. CURRAN, 613:WINTER73-548
AHMAD, I., ED. CASTE & SOCIAL
STRATIFICATION AMONG THE MUSLIMS.
   B. TYABJI, 273(IC):JUL73-283
AHMAD, N. ECONOMIC RESOURCES OF THE
UNION OF BURMA.
   R.E. HUKE, 293(JAST):AUG73-743
AHMAD, Z. SINO-TIBETAN RELATIONS
IN THE SEVENTEENTH CENTURY.
   T.V. WYLIE, 318(JAOS):JUL-SEP73-
   409
AHMED, U. & B. DAURA. AN INTRODUC-
TION TO CLASSICAL HAUSA & THE
MAJOR DIALECTS.
   C. GOUFFÉ, 69:JAN73-86
AHNLUND, K. OMKRING LYKKE-PER.
   B.G. MADSEN, 563(SS):WINTER74-76
AHRENS, C. INSTRUMENTALE MUSIKSTILE
AN DER OSTTÜRKISCHEN SCHWARZMEER-
KÜSTE.
   S. BLUM, 187:JAN75-141
AI. CRUELTY.*
   G. FRENCH, 181:SPRING74-338
   J.N. MORRIS, 249(HUDR):SPRING74-
   107
   M.G. PERLOFF, 659:WINTER75-84
AI. POEMS.
   G. BURNS, 584(SWR):WINTER74-103
AIKEN, J. VOICES IN AN EMPTY HOUSE.
   J. MELLORS, 362:13MAR75-349
   617(TLS):11JUL75-784
AINSZTEIN, R. JEWISH RESISTANCE IN
NAZI-OCCUPIED EASTERN EUROPE.
   L. DAWIDOWICZ, 617(TLS):20JUN75-
   694
AIRD, C. SLIGHT MOURNING.
   T.J. BINYON, 617(TLS):26DEC75-1544
   M. LASKI, 362:25DEC75&1JAN76-893
AITCHISON, J. SPHERES.
   A. MACLEAN, 617(TLS):1AUG75-866
AITKEN, A.J., R.W. BAILEY & N.
HAMILTON-SMITH, EDS. THE COMPUTER
& LITERARY STUDIES.
   D.A. WELLS, 402(MLR):JUL74-597
AITKEN, A.J., A. MC INTOSH & H.
PÁLSSON, EDS. EDINBURGH STUDIES
IN ENGLISH & SCOTS.*
   R.D., 179(ES):FEB72-88
   D. MINDT, 38:BAND91HEFT2-246
AJAYI, J.F.A. & M. CROWDER, EDS.
HISTORY OF WEST AFRICA. (VOL 1)
   R. SMITH, 69:OCT73-370
AJAYI, J.F.A. & R.S. SMITH. YORUBA
WARFARE IN THE 19TH CENTURY. (2ND
ED)
   W. GUTTERIDGE, 69:JAN73-87
AJIBOLA, J.O. ORIN YORUBA/YORUBA
SONGS.
   D.B. WELCH, 187:SEP75-495
AKINARI, U. TALES OF MOONLIGHT &
RAIN.* (K. HAMADA, TRANS)
   D.H., 502(PRS):FALL73-278
   L.M. ZOLBROD, 293(JAST):NOV72-156
   L.M. ZOLBROD, 352(LE&W):VOL16#3-
   1080
AKINARI, U. UGETSU MONOGATARI.
(L.M. ZOLBROD, ED & TRANS)
   A. THWAITE, 617(TLS):11APR75-388
"ÄKSPERIMENTAL'NAJA FONETIKA."
   G·F. MEIER, 682(ZPSK):BAND26HEFT
   3/4-411
ALAIN. THE GODS.
   M. TURNELL, 617(TLS):5SEP75-1004

ALAND, K., ED. QUELLEN ZUR GESCHICH-
TE DES PAPSTTUMS UND DES RÖMISCHEN
KATHOLIZISMUS. (REIHE 2, VOL 1)
   G. MAY, 182:VOL26#9-268
ALARCOS LLORACH, E. ESTUDIOS DE
GRAMÁTICA FUNCIONAL DEL ESPAÑOL.*
   R.G. KEIGHTLEY, 86(BHS):JAN73-73
ALATORRE, M.F. - SEE UNDER FRENK
ALATORRE, M.
ALATORRE, M.F. & Y. JIMÉNEZ DE BÁEZ
- SEE UNDER FRENK ALATORRE, M. &
Y. JIMÉNEZ DE BÁEZ
ALAVI, B. & M. LORENZ. LEHRBUCH DER
PERSISCHEN SPRACHE.
   D.L.F. NILSEN, 353:15JAN73-123
ALAYA, F.M. WILLIAM SHARP - "FIONA
MACLEOD" 1855-1905.*
   A. DEDIO, 179(ES):APR73-186
ALAZRAKI, J. JORGE LUIS BORGES.
(W.Y. TINDALL, ED)
   J.R. AYORA, 399(MLJ):JAN-FEB73-69
ALBA, V. THE LATIN AMERICANS.
   P. FLYNN, 86(BHS):JAN73-107
ALBERT, M. THE SECOND STORY MAN.
   T. LASK, 441:30NOV75-61
ALBERT, M.H. THE GARGOYLE CONSPIR-
ACY.
   N. CALLENDAR, 441:10AUG75-10
ALBERTI, L.B. THE ALBERTIS OF FLOR-
ENCE. (G.A. GUARINO, ED & TRANS)
   F.S. MIRRI, 399(MLJ):SEP-OCT73-303
ALBERTI, L.B. ON PAINTING & ON
SCULPTURE. (C. GRAYSON, ED &
TRANS)
   C.H. CLOUGH, 39:MAY73-533
   J.R. SPENCER, 54:DEC73-627
ALBERTI, L.B. OPERE VOLGARI. (VOL
3) (C. GRAYSON, ED)
   C. FAHY, 402(MLR):OCT74-887
ALBORG, J.L. HISTORIA DE LA LITERA-
TURA ESPAÑOLA. (VOL 1) (2ND ED)
   A.D. DEYERMOND, 86(BHS):JUL73-281
ALBORG, J.L. HISTORIA DE LA LITERA-
TURA ESPAÑOLA. (VOL 3)
   K. KISH, 481(PQ):JUL73-423
ALBRECHT, E. BESTIMMT DIE SPRACHE
UNSER WELTBILD?
   K. KRÜGER, 682(ZPSK):BAND26HEFT6-
   719
ALBRECHT, F. DEUTSCHE SCHRIFTSTEL-
LER IN DER ENTSCHEIDUNG.*
   J·H. REID, 182:VOL26#3/4-103
ALBRECHT, G. & G. DAHLKE, EDS. IN-
TERNATIONALE BIBLIOGRAPHIE ZUR
GESCHICHTE DER DEUTSCHEN LITERATUR
VON DEN ANFÄNGEN BIS ZUR GEGENWART.
(PT 2, VOL 1)
   R.M., 191(ELN):SEP73(SUPP)-104
VON ALBRECHT, M. MEISTER RÖMISCHER
PROSA VON CATO BIS APULEIUS.*
   P-Y. CHANUT, 555:VOL47FASC2-356
   W.L. WATSON, 124:MAY73-494
   M. WINTERBOTTOM, 123:NOV74-219
ALBRIGHT, D. THE MYTH AGAINST
MYTH.*
   F.S. COLWELL, 529(QQ):WINTER73-645
   I. FLETCHER, 617(TLS):2MAY75-490
   R.N. PARISIOUS, 159(DM):WINTER/
   SPRING73-125
   H. PESCHMANN, 175:SUMMER73-83
ALCAIDE, V.N. - SEE UNDER NIETO
ALCAIDE, V.
ALCALÁ, H.R. - SEE UNDER RODRÍGUEZ
ALCALÁ, H.

ALCHOURRÓN, C.E. & E. BULYGIN. NOR-
MATIVE SYSTEMS.*
M.J. CRESSWELL, 316:JUN73-326
D.G. LONDEY, 479(PHQ):JUL73-280
ALCOCK, L. ARTHUR'S BRITAIN.
J.D.A. OGILVY, 191(ELN):SEP73-57
ALCORTA, G. LA PAREJA DE NÚÑEZ.
J. WALKER, 238:MAY73-508
ALCOTT, L.M. BEHIND A MASK (M.
STERN, ED)
J. O'REILLY, 441:1 JUN75-4
442(NY):30 JUN75-98
ALCOVER, M. LA PENSÉE PHILOSOPHIQUE
ET SCIENTIFIQUE DE CYRANO DE BER-
GERAC.*
A.M. BEICHMAN, 546(RR):MAR74-128
M. LAUGAA, 535(RHL):JUL-AUG73-681
ALDCROFT, D.H. BRITISH TRANSPORT
SINCE 1914.
T.C. BARKER, 617(TLS):4JUL75-737
ALDEN, J.R. ROBERT DINWIDDIE.
R.M. GEPHART, 656(WMQ):OCT74-690
639(VQR):SPRING74-XL
ALDERSON, W.L. & A.C. HENDERSON.
CHAUCER & AUGUSTAN SCHOLARSHIP.*
T.A. BIRRELL, 433:OCT73-426
ALDISS, B., ED. EVIL EARTHS.
J. HAMILTON-PATERSON, 617(TLS):
5DEC75-1438
ALDISS, B., ED. THE GOLLANCZ/SUNDAY
TIMES BEST SF STORIES.
S. CLARK, 617(TLS):5DEC75-1438
ALDISS, B., COMP. SCIENCE FICTION
ART.
G. JONAS, 441:14DEC75-29
ALDISS, B.W. BILLION YEAR SPREE.
J. COTTON, 503:WINTER73-196
ALDISS, B.W., ED. SPACE OPERA.
J. HAMILTON-PATERSON, 617(TLS):
7MAR75-260
ALDISS, B.W. & H. HARRISON, EDS.
HELL'S CARTOGRAPHERS.
J. BLISH, 617(TLS):23MAY75-554
ALDRIDGE, A.O., ED. THE IBERO-
AMERICAN ENLIGHTENMENT.
D-H. PAGEAUX, 549(RLC):OCT-DEC73-
637
ALDRIDGE, J. MOCKERY IN ARMS.
N. CALLENDAR, 441:9MAR75-22
ALDRIDGE, J. THE UNTOUCHABLE JULI.
P.D. JAMES, 617(TLS):10OCT75-1217
ALDRIDGE, J.W. THE DEVIL IN THE
FIRE.
R. FOSTER, 109:FALL/WINTER73/74-
111
ALEGRÍA, F., ED. LA PRENSA (LATIN
AMERICAN PRESS READER).
L. PEARSON, 399(MLJ):NOV74-353
ALEIXANDRE, V. DIÁLOGOS DEL CONOCI-
MIENTO.
A. TERRY, 617(TLS):23MAY75-559
ALEWYN, R. PROBLEME UND GESTALTEN.
617(TLS):14FEB75-160
ALEXANDER, A., ED. STORIES OF
SICILY.
I. QUIGLY, 617(TLS):31 JAN75-102
ALEXANDER, A. GIOVANNI VERGA.
O. RAGUSA, 276:AUTUMN73-466
A. WILKIN, 402(MLR):JAN74-192
ALEXANDER, H.G. THE LANGUAGE &
LOGIC OF PHILOSOPHY.
B.G.H., 543:JUN73-744

ALEXANDER, J. RUSSIAN AIRCRAFT
SINCE 1940.
E. COLSTON-SHEPHERD, 617(TLS):
12DEC75-1493
ALEXANDER, J. YUGOSLAVIA: BEFORE
THE ROMAN CONQUEST. (G. DANIEL, ED)
M. GIMBUTAS, 574(SEEJ):WINTER72-
514
R.R. HOLLOWAY, 124:NOV72-187
ALEXANDER, J.J.G. NORMAN ILLUMINA-
TION AT MONT ST. MICHEL, 966-1100.
J. BACKHOUSE, 90:MAR73-169
E.G. CARLSON, 56:SPRING-SUMMER73-
100
ALEXANDER, J.J.G. & A.C. DE LA MARE.
THE ITALIAN MANUSCRIPTS IN THE LIB-
RARY OF MAJOR J.R. ABBEY.
J. BACKHOUSE, 90:MAR73-168
ALEXANDER, L.G. NEW CONCEPT ENG-
LISH. (VOL 5)
K. OLTMANN, 430(NS):JUL73-384
ALEXANDER, L.G. QUESTION & ANSWER.
K. OLTMANN, 430(NS):JUL73-383
ALEXANDER, L.G. & J. TADMAN. TAR-
GET 1.
K. OLTMANN, 430(NS):JUL73-384
ALEXANDER, M., ED & TRANS. THE EAR-
LIEST ENGLISH POEMS.
J. VERDONCK, 179(ES):FEB73-97
ALEXANDER, M. - SEE "BEOWULF, A
VERSE TRANSLATION"
ALEXANDER, M.V. CHARLES I'S LORD
TREASURER.
K. SHARPE, 617(TLS):26SEP75-1082
ALEXANDER, R.J. LATIN AMERICAN POL-
ITICAL PARTIES.
H. KANTOR, 263:JUL-SEP74-315
ALEXANDER, R.L. THE ARCHITECTURE OF
MAXIMILIAN GODEFROY.
S. BAYLEY, 617(TLS):26DEC75-1547
ALEXANDER, S. WOMEN'S LEGAL RIGHTS.
S. HARRIMAN, 441:4MAY75-14
ALEXANDRIAN, S. LE SURRÉALISME ET
LE RÊVE.
M. BOWIE, 617(TLS):19SEP75-1039
ALEXANDROU, A. TO KIVOTIO.
A. ARGYRIOU, 617(TLS):14NOV75-1368
ALEXIS, P. & É. ZOLA. "NATURALISME
PAS MORT." (B.H. BAKKER, ED)
C.A. BURNS, 402(MLR):JUL74-649
S. VIA, 557(RSH):JAN-MAR73-176
P. WALKER, 207(FR):FEB73-621
ALFASSIO GRIMALDI, U. & G. BOZZETTI.
DIECI GIUGNO 1940.
S. WOOLF, 617(TLS):11 JUL75-783
ALFIERI, V. THE PRINCE & LETTERS.
(B. CORRIGAN, ED)
A. WILKIN, 402(MLR):JUL74-665
ALFÖLDI-ROSENBAUM, E. ANAMUR NEK-
ROPOLÜ.
P. CARRINGTON, 313:VOL63-292
ALFÖLDY, G. NORICUM.
J.M.C. TOYNBEE, 617(TLS):10 JAN75-
40
ALFORD, D.V. BUMBLEBEES.
G.E.J. NIXON, 617(TLS):30CT75-1122
ALHAZRED, A. AL AZIF (THE NECRO-
NOMICON).
J.B. POST, 503:AUTUMN73-149
ALI, M., WITH R. DURHAM. THE GREAT-
EST.
C. LEHMANN-HAUPT, 441:5NOV75-35
I. REED, 441:30NOV75-6
G. WILLS, 453:30OCT75-3

ALI-BAB. ENCYCLOPEDIA OF PRACTICAL
GASTRONOMY.*
M.F.K. FISHER, 442(NY):10NOV75-187
ALIGHIERI, D. - SEE UNDER DANTE
ALIGHIERI
ALINEI, M., ED. SPOGLI ELETTRONICI
DELL'ITALIANO DELLE ORIGINI E DEL
DUECENTO.* (VOL 2, PTS 2-10)
G.C. LEPSCHY, 353:15DEC73-125
ALLAN, M. T.S. ELIOT'S IMPERSONAL
THEORY OF POETRY.
A. AUSTIN, 27(AL):NOV74-407
G. HOUGH, 617(TLS):1AUG75-866
R. KIRK, 569(SR):FALL74-698
ALLAND, G., W. WASKIW & T. HISS.
KNOW-HOW.
A. RUDER, 441:29JUN75-22
ALLBEURY, T. OMEGA-MINUS.
N. CALLENDAR, 441:15JUN75-24
ALLBEURY, T. PALOMINO BLONDE.
617(TLS):21FEB75-184
ALLBEURY, T. THE SPECIAL COLLEC-
TION.
T.J. BINYON, 617(TLS):26DEC75-1544
M. LASKI, 362:25DEC75&1JAN76-893
ALLDRIDGE, J. - SEE BÖLL, H.
ALLDRITT, K. THE VISUAL IMAGINATION
OF D.H. LAWRENCE.*
K. WIDMER, 295:APR74-1044
ALLEE, A. ANDALUSIA.
N. GLENDINNING, 617(TLS):21FEB75-
202
ALLEMAN, G.S. & OTHERS - SEE "ENG-
LISH LITERATURE 1660-1800"
ALLEMAND, A. UNITÉ ET STRUCTURE DE
L'UNIVERS BALZACIEN.
M.G. WORTHINGTON, 545(RPH):NOV73-
228
ALLEMANN, F.R. MACHT UND OHNMACHT
DER GUERRILLA.
W. LAQUEUR, 617(TLS):1AUG75-862
ALLEN, C., ED. PLAIN TALES FROM THE
RAJ.
J. GRIGG, 362:20NOV75-676
ALLEN, D. - SEE O'HARA, F.
ALLEN, D. & W. TALLMAN, EDS. THE
POETICS OF THE NEW AMERICAN POETRY.
J.M. BRINNIN, 441:2MAR75-4
ALLEN, D.C. MYSTERIOUSLY MEANT.*
M.A. DI CESARE, 551(RENQ):AUTUMN
73-342
M-S. RØSTVIG, 179(ES):DEC73-615
ALLEN, E.D. & R.M. VALLETTE. MODERN
LANGUAGE CLASSROOM TECHNIQUES.
S.I. ARELLANO, 238:SEP73-745
J-P. BERWALD, 399(MLJ):APR73-218
ALLEN, G.W. CARL SANDBURG.
R. ASSELINEAU, 189(EA):APR-JUN73-
248
ALLEN, H.B. & R.N. CAMPBELL, EDS.
TEACHING ENGLISH AS A SECOND LAN-
GUAGE.
J.W. NEY, 608:JUN74-193
ALLEN, H.B. & G.N. UNDERWOOD, EDS.
READINGS IN AMERICAN DIALECTOLOGY.
J. APPLEBY, 35(AS):SPRING-SUMMER
71-158
ALLEN, J.W.T. TENDI.
L. HARRIES, 315(JAL):VOL11PT1-98
ALLEN, M. WHERE HAVE YOU GONE, JOE
DI MAGGIO?
J. DURSO, 441:1JUN75-34
E. WEEKS, 61:JUN75-92

ALLEN, P.M. & A. SEGAL. THE TRAV-
ELER'S AFRICA.
J. POVEY, 2:SPRING74-86
ALLEN, R. IMPERIALISM & NATIONALISM
IN THE FERTILE CRESCENT.
J.B. KELLY, 617(TLS):12DEC75-1485
ALLEN, R. THE SOCIAL PASSION.
H.V. NELLES, 529(QQ):AUTUMN73-459
ALLEN, R.C. THE SYMBOLIC WORLD OF
FEDERICO GARCÍA LORCA.*
J.M. AGUIRRE, 402(MLR):JAN74-209
V.F. DE BECK-AGULAR, 149:DEC74-344
D.K. LOUGHRAN, 400(MLN):MAR73-487
ALLEN, R.E. PLATO'S "EUTHYPHRO" &
THE EARLIER THEORY OF FORMS.*
J.J. MULHERN, 321:SPRING73-71
ALLEN, R.E. & D.J. FURLEY, EDS.
STUDIES IN PRESOCRATIC PHILOSOPHY.
(VOL 2)
E. HUSSEY, 617(TLS):16MAY75-535
ALLEN, R.F. FIRE & IRON.*
R. KELLOGG, 131(CL):SUMMER73-280
ALLEN, R.L. ENGLISH GRAMMARS & ENG-
LISH GRAMMAR.
M. RENSKY, 399(MLJ):DEC73-439
ALLÉN, S. NUSVENSK FREKVENSORDBOOK
BASERAD PÅ TIDNINGSTEXT. (VOLS
1&2) TIOTUSEN I TOPP.
H. BLUME, 260(IF):BAND78-326
ALLEN, V.F. & S. FORMAN. ENGLISH
AS A SECOND LANGUAGE.
H.C. WOODBRIDGE, 399(MLJ):NOV74-
371
ALLEN, W. WITHOUT FEATHERS.
R.R. LINGEMAN, 441:9JUL75-41
M. RICHLER, 441:1JUN75-4
ALLEN, W. - SEE BOIS, J.
ALLENTUCK, M.E. - SEE GRAHAM, J.
ALLEVI, F. FORTUNA ED EREDITÀ DEL
PARINI.*
P.Z., 228(GSLI):VOL150FASC470/471-
474
ALLINGHAM, M. FLOWERS FOR THE JUDGE.
N. CALLENDAR, 441:29JUN75-30
ALLISON, A.F. THOMAS DEKKER, C.
1572-1632.*
E.D. PENDRY, 677:VOL4-281
ALLISON, A.F. THOMAS LODGE, 1558-
1625.
C.W. WHITWORTH, 402(MLR):APR74-371
354:JUN73-173
ALLISON, H.E., ED. THE KANT-EBER-
HARD CONTROVERSY.*
W. SCHWARZ, 484(PPR):JUN74-606
ALLISON, L. ENVIRONMENTAL PLANNING.
J. BAILEY, 617(TLS):4JUL75-742
ALLODI, M. CANADIAN WATERCOLOURS &
DRAWINGS IN THE ROYAL ONTARIO MUS-
EUM.
M. BELL, 99:JUL75-40
ALLWORTH, E. NATIONALITIES OF THE
SOVIET EAST.*
M.M. SHORISH, 574(SEEJ):WINTER72-
515
D. SINOR, 318(JAOS):JUL-SEP73-405
ALLWORTH, E., ED. SOVIET NATIONAL-
ITY PROBLEMS.
R. PIPES, 550(RUSR):JAN73-82
ALMANSI, G. THE WRITER AS LIAR.
P. SHAW, 617(TLS):31OCT75-1302
DE ALMAS, F.A. THE FOUR INTERPOLAT-
ED STORIES IN THE ROMAN "COMIQUE."
R. GODENNE, 535(RHL):JAN-FEB73-125

ALONSO, D. OBRAS COMPLETAS. (VOL 1)
R.J. PENNY, 402(MLR):JAN74-194
E.L. RIVERS, 400(MLN):MAR73-508
ALONSO, D. PLURALITÀ E CORRELAZIONE
IN POESIA.
A.L. LEPSCHY, 402(MLR):JUL74-655
400(MLN):MAR73-507
ALONSO DE HERRERA, G. OBRA DE AGRI-
CULTURA. (J.U. MARTÍNEZ CARRERAS,
ED)
M. ROBINSON, 86(BHS):JAN73-79
ALONSO DE LOS RÍOS, C. CONVERSA-
CIONES CON MIGUEL DELIBES.
D.R. MC KAY, 400(MLN):MAR73-496
ALONSO MONTERO, X. ROSALÍA DE
CASTRO.
270:VOL23#3-67
DE ALOYSIO, F. DA DEWEY A JAMES.
E. NAMER, 542:APR-JUN73-218
ALPATOV, M.A. TREASURES OF RUSSIAN
ART IN THE XI-XVITH CENTURIES
(PAINTINGS).
M. CHAMOT, 39:DEC73-514
ALPERS, E.A. IVORY & SLAVES IN EAST
CENTRAL AFRICA.
T.O. RANGER, 617(TLS):17OCT75-1240
ALPHONSO-KARKALA, J.B., ED. AN
ANTHOLOGY OF INDIAN LITERATURE.
U. ARYA, 318(JAOS):JUL-SEP73-388
AL ROY, G.C. THE KISSINGER EXPERI-
ENCE.
G. WILLS, 453:12JUN75-7
ALSDORF, L. - SEE TRENCKNER, V.
ALSOP, S.M. TO MARIETTA FROM PARIS.
L. LYON, 441:14SEP75-37
ALTABÉ, D.F. TEMAS Y DIÁLOGOS.
D.H. DARST, 238:SEP73-753
T.J. PEAVLER, 238:MAR73-198
F.M. WALTMAN, 238:MAR73-198
ALTAMIRANO, I.M. LA NAVIDAD EN LAS
MONTAÑAS. (H.L. JOHNSON, ED)
J. AYORA, 399(MLJ):SEP-OCT74-293
ALTENHOFER, N. HARZREISE IN DIE
ZEIT.
J.L.S., 191(ELN):SEP73(SUPP)-129
ALTENHOFER, N. - SEE VON HOFMANNS-
THAL, H. & A. WILDGANS
ALTENMÜLLER, R. DIE SCHIEDSRICHTER-
LICHE ENTSCHEIDUNG KARTELLRECHT-
LICHER STREITIGKEITEN.
A.F. SCHNITZLER, 182:VOL26#13/14-
472
ALTER, R. PARTIAL MAGIC.
R. KIELY, 441:16NOV75-61
"ALTERNATIVE LONDON."
R. NORTH, 362:24APR75-542
ALTHAN, J.E.J. THE LOGIC OF PLURAL-
ITY.
R. BLANCHÉ, 542:JUL-SEP73-347
ALTHAUS, H. ÄSTHETIK, ÖKONOMIE UND
GESELLSCHAFT.*
H-U. KÜHL, 654(WB):1/1973-181
ALTHAUS, H.P., H. HENNE & H.E. WIE-
GAND, EDS. LEXIKON DER GERMANIS-
TISCHEN LINGUISTIK.
B.A. LEWIS, 399(MLJ):NOV74-362
ALTHUSSER, L. ELÉMENTS D'AUTOCRIT-
IQUE. PHILOSOPHIE ET PHILOSOPHIE
SPONTANÉE DES SAVANTS.
F. JAMESON, 617(TLS):22AUG75-942
"ALTKLEINASIATISCHE SPRACHEN."
V. ŠEVOROŠKIN, 353:1JUL73-46

ALTMAN, H.B., ED. INDIVIDUALIZING
THE FOREIGN LANGUAGE CLASSROOM.
T.B. FRYER, 399(MLJ):MAR74-129
ALTMANN, A. MOSES MENDELSSOHN.*
J. COLLINS, 377:NOV74-181
L. WIESELTIER, 617(TLS):21NOV75-
1392
639(VQR):WINTER74-XXVIII
ALVAR, M. ESTUDIOS Y ENSAYOS DE
LITERATURA CONTEMPORÁNEA.
D.L. SHAW, 86(BHS):JUL73-300
ALVAR, M. EL ROMANCERO.*
C. SMITH, 402(MLR):JAN74-197
ALVAR, M. VARIEDAD Y UNIDAD DEL
ESPAÑOL.
H.T. STURCKEN, 238:MAY73-499
ALVAREZ, A. SAMUEL BECKETT.
L. GRAVER, 473(PR):4/1974-622
ALVAREZ, A. HERS.*
P. ADAMS, 61:APR75-100
A. BROYARD, 441:19MAR75-47
P. DELANY, 441:30MAR75-5
D. DURRANT, 364:FEB/MAR75-136
442(NY):31MAR75-98
ALVERSON, C. GOODEY'S LAST STAND.
N. CALLENDAR, 441:14DEC75-30
ALVES PEREIRA, T. PELIGRO.
D.J. NOËL, 268:JUL75-189
ALVIN, J. MUSIC THERAPY. (REV)
A. STORR, 617(TLS):20JUN75-702
ALWALL, E. THE RELIGIOUS TREND IN
SECULAR SCOTTISH SCHOOLBOOKS 1850-
1861 & 1873-1882 WITH A SURVEY OF
THE DEBATE ON EDUCATION IN SCOTLAND
IN THE MIDDLE & LATE 19TH CENTURY.
A. LAW, 588:JUL-OCT73-117
AMABILE, G. BLOOD TIES.
D. BAILEY, 529(QQ):SPRING73-99
S. DRAGLAND, 102(CANL):AUTUMN74-
118
AMADO, J. TEREZA BATISTA.
T. LASK, 441:21SEP75-38
AMADO, J. WERKSTATT DER WUNDER.
A. DESSAU, 654(WB):7/1973-160
AMAN, R. BAYRISCH-ÖSTERREICHISCHES
SCHIMPFWÖRTERBUCH.
T.L. KELLER, 399(MLJ):SEP-OCT74-
284
AMAURY, F. LE PETIT PARISIEN 1876-
1944.
D. JOHNSON, 617(TLS):10OCT75-1180
AMBACHER, M. LA MATIÈRE DANS LES
SCIENCES ET EN PHILOSOPHIE.
G. LANE, 154:DEC73-711
AMBASZ, E., ED. ITALY: THE NEW
DOMESTIC LANDSCAPE.
P. OWEN, 89(BJA):SPRING73-199
T. DEL RENZIO, 592:JUL-AUG73-51
AMBLER, E. RUSSIAN JOURNALISM &
POLITICS 1861-1881.*
H.J. ELLISON, 550(RUSR):APR73-198
M. ZIRIN, 574(SEEJ):SUMMER73-231
ST. AMBROSE. S. AMBROSII "DE BONO
MORTIS." (W.T. WIESNER, ED & TRANS)
D. BREARLEY, 124:FEB73-302
M. TESTARD, 555:VOL47FASC2-363
P.G. WALSH, 123:MAR74-142
ST. AMBROSE. SEVEN EXEGETICAL
WORKS. (M.P. MC HUGH, TRANS)
H. MUSURILLO, 613:WINTER73-542
AMBROSE, A. & M. LAZEROWITZ, EDS.
LUDWIG WITTGENSTEIN: PHILOSOPHY &
LANGUAGE.*
M. PROUDFOOT, 479(PHQ):JUL73-263

AMBROSI, L.A.M. - SEE UNDER MUSSO
AMBROSI, L.A.
AMBROZ, O. REALIGNMENT OF WORLD
POWER.
  H. HANAK, 575(SEER):JUL74-475
  R.L. WALKER, 550(RUSR):APR73-189
AMBROZE, A. RACINE POÈTE DU SACRI-
FICE.
  R.W. TOBIN, 207(FR):FEB73-607
AMELN, K., ED. LOCHAMER-LIEDERBUCH
UND DAS FUNDAMENTUM ORGANISANDI VON
CONRAD PAUMANN.
  J.A. WESTRUP, 410(M&L):JAN74-109
"AMERICAN BOOK-PRICES CURRENT 1970."
  (VOL 76)
  P.H. MUIR, 78(BC):WINTER73-540
"THE AMERICAN COURTHOUSE."
  A. GREENBERG, 45:JUN73-51
"AMERICA'S BIRTHDAY."*
  H. MITGANG, 441:4JAN75-21
AMES, D.W. & A.V. KING. GLOSSARY OF
HAUSA MUSIC & ITS SOCIAL CONTEXTS.
  A.H.M. KIRK-GREENE, 315(JAL):VOL11
  PT3-92
AMES, H.B. THE CITY BELOW THE HILL.
  W.P. WARD, 529(QQ):SPRING73-114
AMIN, S., ED. MODERN MIGRATIONS IN
WESTERN AFRICA.
  L. MAIR, 617(TLS):25APR75-462
AMIRANASHVILI, S. GEORGIAN METAL-
WORK FROM ANTIQUITY TO THE 18TH
CENTURY.
  J. BECKWITH, 39:APR73-436
AMIS, K. ENDING UP.*
  M. HODGART, 453:20MAR75-32
  R. SALE, 249(HUDR):WINTER74/75-624
AMIS, K. GIRL, 20.*
  J.C. FIELD, 556(RLV):1973/1-93
AMIS, K. RUDYARD KIPLING & HIS
WORLD.
  D.A.N. JONES, 362:25DEC75&1JAN76-
  890
AMIS, K. WHAT BECAME OF JANE
AUSTEN? & OTHER QUESTIONS.
  295:FEB74-465
AMIS, M. DEAD BABIES.
  M. MASON, 617(TLS):17OCT75-1225
  J. MELLORS, 362:30OCT75-582
AMMON, H. THE GENET MISSION.
  L.S. KAPLAN, 656(WMQ):APR74-336
  639(VQR):SPRING74-XLIV
AMMON, U. PROBLEME DER SOZIOLIN-
GUISTIK.
  M. CLYNE, 67:NOV74-241
AMMONS, A.R. COLLECTED POEMS: 1951-
1971.*
  J. DITSKY, 577(SHR):FALL73-457
  P. ZWEIG, 473(PR):4/1974-608
AMMONS, A.R. DIVERSIFICATIONS.
  D. IGNATOW, 441:30NOV75-54
AMMONS, A.R. SPHERE.*
  D. DAVIE, 453:6MAR75-10
AMMONS, A.R. TAPE FOR THE TURN OF
THE YEAR.*
  W. HARMON, 578:SPRING75-3
AMOR Y VÁZQUEZ, J. - SEE LOBO LASSO
DE LA VEGA, G.
ANAHAREO. DEVIL IN DEERSKINS.
  J. POLK, 102(CANL):SPRING73-110
ANAN'ICH, B.V. ROSSIIA I MEZHDUNAR-
ODNYI KAPITAL, 1897-1914.
  J.E. TUVE, 104:SUMMER73-266
ANAYA, R.A. BLESS ME, ULTIMA.*
  A.D. TREJO, 50(ARQ):SPRING73-95

ANCESCHI, L. LE POETICHE DEL NOVE-
CENTO IN ITALIA.
  M.E. BROWN, 290(JAAC):SPRING74-439
  F.J. JONES, 402(MLR):JUL74-666
ANCET, J. LUIS CERNUDA.
  P. BACARISSE, 205(FMLS):JUL73-301
"THE ANCIENT EMPIRES & THE ECONOMY."
  E. WILL, 555:VOL47FASC2-324
ANDELSON, R.V. IMPUTED RIGHTS.*
  H.F., 543:DEC72-349
ANDERSCH, A. WINTERSPELT.
  D.S. LOW, 617(TLS):22AUG75-950
ANDERSEN, J.K. & L. EMEREK. HANS
KIRKS FORFATTERSKAB.
  T. ALSVIK, 172(EDDA):1973/3-184
ANDERSEN, K.E. INTRODUCTION TO COM-
MUNICATION THEORY & PRACTICE.
  T.R. KING, 583:FALL73-100
ANDERSEN, T. MALEVICH. VLADIMIR
TATLIN. MODERNE RUSSISK KUNST
1910-1930.
  A.C. BIRNHOLZ, 56:SPRING-SUMMER73-
  109
ANDERSON, B.L. & P.L. COTTRELL, EDS.
MONEY & BANKING IN ENGLAND.
  J. REDWOOD, 617(TLS):17JAN75-54
ANDERSON, B.R.O. JAVA IN TIME OF
REVOLUTION.
  B. DAHM, 293(JAST):MAY73-567
ANDERSON, C.L. POE IN NORTHLIGHT.*
  N. INGWERSEN, 301(JEGP):APR74-273
  P. MICHEL, 556(RLV):1973/5-476
  G.B. TENNYSON, 445(NCF):SEP73-245
ANDERSON, C.R. - SEE THOREAU, H.D.
ANDERSON, D. JAMES KERR POLLOCK.
  K.J. PIKE, 14:JUL73-411
ANDERSON, F. ALFONSO SASTRE.*
  A.M. PASQUARIELLO, 238:MAR73-178
ANDERSON, F., ED. MARK TWAIN: THE
CRITICAL HERITAGE.
  A. EASSON, 447(N&Q):JUL73-273
ANDERSON, F. & E.M. BRANCH - SEE
TWAIN, M.
ANDERSON, H. & L.J. BLAKE. JOHN
SHAW NEILSON.
  V. VALLIS, 381:JUN73-225
ANDERSON, J. THE ABOLITION OF DEATH.
  N. CALLENDAR, 441:17AUG75-26
ANDERSON, J. THE AFFAIR OF THE
BLOOD STAINED EGG COSY.
  T.J. BINYON, 617(TLS):26DEC75-1544
ANDERSON, J. THE COMMANDANT.
  R. BUCKLER, 362:1MAY75-590
ANDERSON, J. IN SEPIA.
  J. MARTIN, 491:MAY75-103
  V. YOUNG, 249(HUDR):WINTER74/75-
  597
ANDERSON, J. & E. HANNA. THE DOUBLE-
DAY COOKBOOK.
  R.A. SOKOLOV, 441:7DEC75-78
ANDERSON, J.F. PAUL TILLICH.
  H.F., 543:DEC72-350
ANDERSON, J.K. MILITARY THEORY &
PRACTICE IN THE AGE OF XENOPHON.
  R.J. BUCK, 121(CJ):DEC72/JAN73-187
ANDERSON, J.M. THE GRAMMAR OF CASE.
  R.W. LANGACKER, 297(JL):SEP73-319
  G. SAMPSON, 307:#1-116
ANDERSON, J.R.L. THE NINE-SPOKED
WHEEL.
  617(TLS):11JUL75-784

ANDERSON, M. & OTHERS. CROWELL'S HANDBOOK OF CONTEMPORARY DRAMA.
  C.A. CARPENTER, 397(MD):DEC73-396
  295:FEB74-355
ANDERSON, P. PASSAGES FROM ANTIQUITY TO FEUDALISM. LINEAGES OF THE ABSOLUTIST STATE.
  J. DUNN, 362:17JUL75-91
  D. HAY, 617(TLS):25APR75-452
  K. THOMAS, 453:17APR75-26
ANDERSON, Q. THE IMPERIAL SELF.
  295:FEB74-387
ANDERSON, R. THE PURPLE HEART THROBS.*
  R. GADNEY, 364:APR/MAY74-139
ANDERSON, R.G. FACES, FORMS, FILMS.
  M.R. PITTS, 200:JUN-JUL73-369
ANDERSON, R.L. JOSEPH SMITH'S NEW ENGLAND HERITAGE.
  M.S. HILL, 432(NEQ):MAR73-155
ANDERSON, S. SONG OF THE EARTH SPIRIT. (D.R. BROWER, ED)
  639(VQR):SPRING74-LXII
ANDERSON, S. & G. STEIN. SHERWOOD ANDERSON/GERTRUDE STEIN: CORRESPONDENCE & PERSONAL ESSAYS.* (R.L. WHITE, ED)
  D.D. ANDERSON, 219(GAR):FALL73-424
ANDERSON, W. THE WILD MAN FROM SUGAR CREEK.
  617(TLS):13JUN75-656
ANDERSON, W. - SEE THEOPHRASTUS
ANDERSON, W.E.K. - SEE SCOTT, W.
ANDERSON, W.S. THE ART OF THE "AENEID."
  K. QUINN, 121(CJ):DEC73/JAN74-175
ANDERSON IMBERT, E. LA FLECHA EN EL AIRE. LOS DOMINGOS DEL PROFESOR.
  A. RODRÍGUEZ-SEDA, 572:SEP73-136
ANDERSSON-SCHMITT, M. MANUSCRIPTA MEDIAEVALIA UPSALIENSIA.*
  P. MC GURK, 123:MAR74-146
ANDRADE, J.C. - SEE UNDER CARRERA ANDRADE, J.
ANDRÉ, J. - SEE PLINY
ANDRÉ, R. L'AMOUR ET LA VIE D'UNE FEMME.
  J.P. GOLLUB, 207(FR):OCT72-200
ANDREACH, R.J. THE SLAIN & RESURRECTED GOD.
  R.A. CASSELL, 136:VOL5#1-52
ANDREAE, J.V. THEOPHILUS. (R. VAN DÜLMEN, ED)
  W. BIESTERFELD, 182:VOL26#17/18-577
ANDREIS, J. MUSIC IN CROATIA.
  N. O'LOUGHLIN, 415:OCT74-848
ANDRESEN, C., ED. DIE GNOSIS. (VOL 2)
  G.W. MAC RAE, 124:SEP72-54
ANDRESEN, C. - SEE ST. AUGUSTINE
ANDRESKI, S. THE SOCIAL SCIENCES AS SORCERY.
  I.C. JARVIE, 84:JUN73-193
ANDREWS, B. & R. BARANIK, EDS. THE ATTICA BOOK.
  B. SCHWARTZ, 59(ASOC):FALL-WINTER 74-479
ANDREWS, K.R. THE LAST VOYAGE OF DRAKE & HAWKINS.
  J.H. PARRY, 551(RENQ):AUTUMN73-323
ANDREWS, L. A DICTIONARY OF THE HAWAIIAN LANGUAGE.
  J.H. WARD, 399(MLJ):NOV74-352

ANDREWS, P. & M. THE TURCOMAN OF IRAN.
  M. LEVEY, 39:AUG73-151
ANDREWS, T. THE STORY OF HAROLD.*
  W. FEAVER, 617(TLS):30MAY75-585
ANDREWS, W. AMERICAN GOTHIC.
  J. RUSSELL, 441:7DEC75-24
ANDREWS, W. ARCHITECTURE IN MICHIGAN.
  M.B. LAPPING, 576:OCT73-262
ANDREWS, W. ARCHITECTURE IN NEW ENGLAND.
  B.F. TOLLES, JR., 432(NEQ):SEP73-487
ANDRIEUX, A. & J. LIGNON. LE MILITANT SYNDICALISTE D'AUJOURD'HUI.
  W. SCHÄFER, 182:VOL26#10-334
ANGEL, H. THE WORLD OF AN ESTUARY.
  617(TLS):28FEB75-232
ANGEL, J.L. LERNA. (VOL 2)
  C. NYLANDER, 124:MAR73-372
ANGELI, G. "L'ENEAS" E I PRIMI ROMANZI VOLGARI.
  J.M. FERRANTE, 545(RPH):NOV73-267
ANGER, K. HOLLYWOOD BABYLON.
  P. ANDREWS, 441:31AUG75-9
  R.R. LINGEMAN, 441:30JUN75-27
  J. SEELYE, 231:JUN75-84
ANGIOLIERI, C. THE SONNETS OF A HANDSOME & WELL-MANNERED ROGUE.
  G.P. ORWEN, 276:AUTUMN73-445
MARQUESS OF ANGLESEY - SEE HODGE, E.C.
ANGLIN, J.M. THE GROWTH OF WORD MEANING.*
  J. DEESE, 215(GL):VOL13#1-47
ANGOFF, C., ED. WILLIAM CARLOS WILLIAMS.
  L.W. WAGNER, 659:SUMMER75-378
ANGOLD, M. A BYZANTINE GOVERNMENT IN EXILE.
  A. BRYER, 617(TLS):5SEP75-1005
ANGRESS, R.K. THE EARLY GERMAN EPIGRAM.
  P.M. DALY, 564:MAR73-78
  G.F. MERKEL, 221(GQ):MAY73-452
  W.F. SCHERER, 406:FALL74-294
  P.N. SKRINE, 402(MLR):JAN74-224
ANGULO IÑIGUEZ, D. & A.E. PÉREZ SÁNCHEZ. HISTORIA DE LA PINTURA ESPAÑOLA. (VOL 2)
  E. YOUNG, 617(TLS):23MAY75-558
ANGYAL, D. EMLÉKEZESEK.
  M.D. BIRNBAUM, 574(SEEJ):SUMMER72-272
"ANNALES DE LA SOCIÉTÉ JEAN-JACQUES ROUSSEAU." (VOL 37)
  R. GRIMSLEY, 208(FS):OCT74-466
ANOBILE, R.J., ED. A FINE MESS.
  R. SCHICKEL, 441:7DEC75-88
ANSARI, K.H. JOHN WEBSTER.*
  S.G. PUTT, 175:SPRING72-26
ANSCOMBE, G.E.M. & G.H. VON WRIGHT - SEE WITTGENSTEIN, L.
ANSHEN, R.N. THE REALITY OF THE DEVIL.
  W.G., 543:MAR73-523
ANSLEY, C. THE HERESY OF WU HAN.*
  LI YU-NING, 318(JAOS):APR-JUN73-212
ANSTEY, F. VICE VERSA.
  A. RENDLE, 157:SUMMER73-79

9

ANSTEY, R. THE ATLANTIC SLAVE TRADE & BRITISH ABOLITION 1760-1810.
D.B. DAVIS, 617(TLS):24OCT75-1263

ANSTRUTHER, I. THE SCANDAL OF THE ANDOVER WORKHOUSE.
D. ROBERTS, 637(VS):DEC73-237

ANTAL, E. & J. HARTHAN - SEE KLING-ENDER, F.

ANTHONY, J.R. FRENCH BAROQUE MUSIC FROM BEAUJOYEULX TO RAMEAU.*
P. HOWARD, 415:MAR74-219
J. RUSHTON, 410(M&L):JUL74-348

ANTON, J.P. - SEE PAPANOUTSOS, E.P.

ANTRIM, H.T. T.S. ELIOT'S CONCEPT OF LANGUAGE.
J.M. LUCCIONI, 189(EA):JAN-MAR73-113

ANUŠKIN, A. TAJNY STAROPEČATNOJ KNIGI.
D. TSCHIŽEWSKIJ, 72:BAND211HEFT 1/3-248

ANZAI HITOSHI, SHIRAISHI KAZUKO & TANIKAWA SHUNTARŌ. THREE CONTEM-PORARY JAPANESE POETS.* (G. WILSON & ATSUMI IKUKO, TRANS) [SHOWN IN PREV UNDER TITLE]
D. MORAES, 285(JAPQ):APR-JUN73-230

ANZELEWSKY, F. ALBRECHT DÜRER, DAS MALERISCHE WERK.
J.K. ROWLANDS, 683:BAND36HEFT2/3-209

ANZENBACHER, A. DIE INTENTIONALITÄT BEI THOMAS VON AQUIN UND EDMUND HUSSERL.
S. DECLOUX, 182:VOL26#1/2-11

AOKI, M.Y., ED & TRANS. IZUMO FUDOKI.*
F.G. BOCK, 318(JAOS):OCT-DEC73-628

APEL, W. THE HISTORY OF KEYBOARD MUSIC TO 1700.* (REV & TRANS BY H. TISCHLER)
H.M. BROWN, 415:JAN74-38

APOLLINAIRE, G. ALCOOLS. (A.E. PILKINGTON, ED)
S.I. LOCKERBIE, 208(FS):OCT74-483

APOLLINAIRE, G. APOLLINAIRE ON ART.* (L.C. BREUNIG, ED)
A. ABEL, 399(MLJ):JAN-FEB74-63
J. GOLDING, 90:SEP73-616
W.T. STARR, 207(FR):MAR73-839

APOLLINAIRE, G. L'ENCHANTEUR POUR-RISSANT [SUIVI DE] LES MAMELLES DE TIRÉSIAS [ET] COULEUR DU TEMPS.
M. PIERSSENS, 207(FR):FEB73-650

APOLLINAIRE, G. SELECTED WRITINGS OF GUILLAUME APOLLINAIRE. (R. SHATTUCK, ED)
A.H. GREET, 399(MLJ):DEC73-444

APOLLINAIRE, G. & A. BILLY. LA BRÉHATINE. (C. TOURNADRE, ED)
H. BÉHAR, 535(RHL):NOV-DEC73-1105
M. DAVIES, 208(FS):OCT74-483

APOLLINAIRE, G. & P. GUILLAUME. SCULPTURES NEGRES [TOGETHER WITH] BELLIER, A. & OTHERS. SCULPTURES D'AFRIQUE, D'AMERIQUE, D'OCEANIE.
D.J. CROWLEY, 2:AUTUMN73-84

APONTE, B.B. ALFONSO REYES & SPAIN.*
H.L. JOHNSON, 238:DEC73-1126
W.D. RAAT, 37:AUG-SEP73-57
H.M. RASI, 399(MLJ):JAN-FEB74-75

APPADORAI, A. INDIAN POLITICAL THINKING IN THE TWENTIETH CENTURY FROM NAOROJI TO NEHRU.
D. DALTON, 293(JAST):MAY73-525

APPEL, A., JR. NABOKOV'S DARK CINE-MA.
A. DE JONGE, 617(TLS):16MAY75-526

APPELHANS, P. UNTERSUCHUNGEN ZUR SPÄTMITTELALTERLICHEN MARIENDICH-TUNG.
F.V. SPECHTLER, 680(ZDP):BAND92 HEFT3-461

APPLETON, J. THE EXPERIENCE OF LANDSCAPE.
G. JELLICOE, 617(TLS):20JUN75-703

"APPROCHES: ESSAI SUR LA POÉSIE MOD-ERNE DE LANGUE FRANÇAISE."
W. ALBERT, 207(FR):MAR73-847

APTEKAR, J. ICONS OF JUSTICE.*
C.B. LOWER, 599:SPRING73-217

APTER, M.J. THE COMPUTER SIMULATION OF BEHAVIOR.*
J.F., 543:SEP72-149

APTHEKER, H. - SEE DU BOIS, W.E.B.

AQUILECCHIA, G., S.N. CRISTEA & S. RALPHS, EDS. COLLECTED ESSAYS ON ITALIAN LANGUAGE & LITERATURE PRE-SENTED TO KATHLEEN SPEIGHT.*
N.J. PERELLA, 399(MLJ):DEC73-437

AQUILINA, J., COMP. A COMPARATIVE DICTIONARY OF MALTESE PROVERBS.
L. HARRIES, 292(JAF):JUL-SEP73-310

ARA, G. & OTHERS. QUÉ ES LA ARGEN-TINA.
J.M. FLINT, 86(BHS):APR73-197

ARAGON, L. HENRI MATISSE.
A. FORGE, 592:MAR73-138

ARAGONE TERNI, E. - SEE DE VEGA, L.

ARAMÓN I SERRA, R., ED. ESTUDIS DE LINGÜÍSTICA I DE FILOLOGIA CATA-LANES DEDICATS A LA MEMÒRIA DE POMPEU FABRA EN EL CENTENARI DE LA SEVA NAIXENÇA.
J. GULSOY, 545(RPH):FEB74-399

ARANDA, F. LUIS BUÑUEL.
E. RHODE, 617(TLS):24OCT75-1257

ARANGUREN, J.L. LA CRUZ DE LA MON-ARQUÍA ESPAÑOLA ACTUAL.
P. PRESTON, 617(TLS):4JUL75-740

ARATUS. ARATOS, "PHAINOMENA." (M. ERREN, ED & TRANS)
M.A.T. NATUNEWICZ, 124:MAY73-471

ARAYA, G. CLAVES FILOLÓGICAS PARA LA COMPRENSIÓN DE ORTEGA.
J.W. DÍAZ, 238:MAY73-503

ARBASINO, A. LA BELLA DI LODI.
B. MERRY, 270:VOL23#3-63

ARBASINO, A. SPECCHIO DELLE MIE BRAME.
F. DONINI, 617(TLS):2MAY75-492

ARBASINO, A. & OTHERS. LE INTERVIS-TE IMPOSSIBILI.
G. ALMANSI, 617(TLS):31OCT75-1305

ARBMAN, E. ECSTASY OR RELIGIOUS TRANCE. (VOLS 2&3)
J. BRUNO, 98:MAY73-417

ARCHER, M. COMPANY DRAWINGS IN THE INDIA OFFICE LIBRARY.*
G. EYRE, 39:FEB73-197
I. STUEBE, 90:DEC73-814

ARCHER, M.S., ED. STUDENTS, UNIVER-SITY & SOCIETY.
M. FELD, 255(HAB):WINTER73-46

ARCHER, W.G. THE HILL OF FLUTES.
N.C. CHAUDHURI, 617(TLS):3!JAN75-
118
ARCHER, W.G. A SURVEY & HISTORY OF
PAHARI MINIATURE PAINTING.
R.C. CRAVEN, JR., 60:JUL-AUG74-68
ARCHIMEDES. ARCHIMÈDE. (VOLS 2&3)
(C. MUGLER, ED & TRANS)
I. BULMER-THOMAS, 123:NOV74-200
P. LOUIS, 555:VOL47FASC1-137
ARCHIMEDES. ARCHIMÈDE, "'COMMEN-
TAIRES' D'EUTOCIUS ET FRAGMENTS."
(VOL 4) (C. MUGLER, ED & TRANS)
P. LOUIS, 555:VOL47FASC2-322
"ARCHITECTURE OF THE GOLLINS MELVIN
WARD PARTNERSHIP."
617(TLS):28MAR75-330
"THE ARCHITECTURE OF YORKE ROSEN-
BERG & MARDALL: 1944-1972."
M. MANSER, 46:JUL73-64
ARDALAN, N. & L. BAKHTIAR. THE
SENSE OF UNITY.
639(VQR):SUMMER74-CX
ARDENER, E., ED. SOCIAL ANTHROPOLO-
GY & LANGUAGE.*
R.B. LE PAGE, 297(JL):FEB73-140
ARDIES, T. KOSYGIN IS COMING.*
J. PARR, 296:VOL3#4-101
ARDOIN, J. & G. FITZGERALD. CAL-
LAS.*
J. ROCKWELL, 441:19JAN75-32
ARE, G. ECONOMIA E POLITICA NELL'-
ITALIA LIBERALE (1890-1915).
S.J. WOOLF, 617(TLS):31OCT75-1306
ARELLANES, A.S., ED. BOOKPLATES.
B.N. LEE, 503:AUTUMN72-167
P.H. MUIR, 78(BC):SPRING73-100
ARENAS, J.F. - SEE UNDER FERNANDEZ
ARENAS, J.
ARENDT, D. DER "POETISCHE NIHILIS-
MUS" IN DER ROMANTIK.
D.G. LITTLE, 402(MLR):OCT74-920
ARETHAS. ARETHAE ARCHIEPISCOPI
CAESARIENSIS "SCRIPTA MINORA."
(VOL 2) (L.G. WESTERINCK, ED)
H. MUSURILLO, 124:MAY73-480
ARGÜELLES, J.A. CHARLES HENRY & THE
FORMATION OF A PSYCHOPHYSICAL AES-
THETIC.*
M.H. BORNSTEIN, 127:SPRING74-276
DE ARGUIJO, J. OBRA POÉTICA. (S.B.
VRANICH, ED)
E. BERGMANN, 400(MLN):MAR73-451
ARGYLE, B. AN INTRODUCTION TO THE
AUSTRALIAN NOVEL 1830-1930.
L.T. HERGENHAN, 67:MAY74-105
H.P. HESELTINE, 541(RES):AUG73-378
J. JONES, 594:FALL73-402
W.H. NEW, 102(CANL):WINTER74-87
M. WILDING, 677:VOL4-322
ARIAS-LARRETA, A. LITERATURA COL-
ONIAL.
J.L. WALKER, 238:MAR73-179
DEGLI ARIENTI, G.S. - SEE UNDER
SABADINO DEGLI ARIENTI, G.
ARIÈS, P. WESTERN ATTITUDES TOWARD
DEATH.*
C. RICKS, 617(TLS):18JUL75-790
ARIOSTO, L. LUDOVICO ARIOSTO'S
"ORLANDO FURIOSO." (J. HARINGTON,
TRANS; R. MC NULTY, ED)
E.T. FALASCHI, 402(MLR):APR74-429
R.B. GOTTFRIED, 551(RENQ):WINTER
73-520   [CONTINUED]

[CONTINUING]
J. ROBERTSON, 541(RES):AUG73-327
E. SACCONE, 400(MLN):JAN73-149
ARIOSTO, L. THE COMEDIES OF ARIOS-
TO. (E.M. BEAME & L.G. SBROCCHI,
EDS & TRANS)
C.P. BRAND, 617(TLS):31OCT75-1304
ARIOSTO, L. ORLANDO FURIOSO. (PT
1) (B. REYNOLDS, TRANS)
D.S. CARNE-ROSS, 617(TLS):31OCT75-
1303
ARIOSTO, L. ORLANDO FURIOSO.* (G.
WALDMAN, TRANS)
J. BUXTON, 617(TLS):10JAN75-39
ARISTAENETUS. ARISTAENETI EPISTUL-
ARUM LIBRI II. (O. MAZAL, ED)
F.H. SANDBACH, 303:VOL93-236
ARISTOTLE. ARISTOTE, "POLITIQUE."
(VOL 2, PT 1, BKS 3&4) (J. AUBON-
NET, ED & TRANS)
J. BARNES, 123:NOV74-292
P. LOUIS, 555:VOL47FASC2-336
T. TRACY, 124:APR73-428
ARISTOTLE. ARISTOTLE'S "DE PARTIBUS
ANIMALIUM I" & "DE GENERATIONE ANI-
MALIUM I." (D.M. BALME, ED & TRANS)
J.D.G. EVANS, 483:OCT73-404
M.D. ROHR, 482(PHR):OCT74-548
ARISTOTLE. ARISTOTLE'S PHYSICS,
BOOKS I & II. (W. CHARLTON, ED &
TRANS)
C.J.F. WILLIAMS, 393(MIND):OCT73-
617
ARISTOTLE. LETTRE D'ARISTOTE À
ALEXANDRE SUR LA POLITIQUE ENVERS
LES CITÉS. (J. BIELAWSKI & M.
PLEZIA, EDS & TRANS)
P. LOUIS, 555:VOL47FASC1-138
C. MONTAGU & O. MURRAY, 303:VOL93-
226
ARISTOTLE. METAPHYSICS.* (BOOKS
GAMMA, DELTA, EPSILON) (C. KIRWAN,
ED & TRANS)
W. CHARLTON, 393(MIND):JUL73-452
P. LOUIS, 555:VOL47FASC1-138
C.C.W. TAYLOR, 479(PHQ):APR73-162
ARIZA, F. & OTHERS. ZARABANDA.
D.R. MC KAY, 399(MLJ):APR73-213
ARLEN, M.J. PASSAGE TO ARARAT.
C. LEHMANN-HAUPT, 441:7AUG75-29
P. THEROUX, 441:17AUG75-3
ARLOTT, J., ED. THE OXFORD COMPANION
TO SPORTS & GAMES.
I. HAMILTON, 617(TLS):4JUL75-724
G. SCOTT, 362:24JUL75-126
ARMANI, G. GLI SCRITTI SU CARLO
CATTANEO.
E.B., 228(GSLI):VOL150FASC470/471-
477
DE ARMAS, F.A. THE FOUR INTERPOLAT-
ED STORIES IN THE "ROMAN COMIQUE."
C.G.S. WILLIAMS, 399(MLJ):JAN-FEB
73-51
ARMBRISTER, T. ACT OF VENGEANCE.
B.A. FRANKLIN, 441:9NOV75-28
ARMENTANO, D.T. THE MYTHS OF ANTI-
TRUST.
T.W. ROGERS, 396(MODA):WINTER74-
103
ARMES, R. FILM & REALITY.*
D. FREDERICKSEN, 290(JAAC):WINTER
74-241
ARMES, R. PATTERNS OF REALISM.
B.L., 275(IQ):SUMMER73-120

ARMFELT, N. SMUDGE.
  C. PETERS, 617(TLS):23MAY75-577
ARMISTEAD, S.G. & J.H. SILVERMAN.
  THE JUDEO-SPANISH BALLAD CHAPBOOKS
  OF YACOB ABRAHAM YONÁ.
  M.E. BARRICK, 292(JAF):JUL-SEP73-
  304
  D. EISENBERG, 400(MLN):MAR73-407
  I. LERNER, 149:DEC74-337
ARMISTEAD, S.G. & J.H. SILVERMAN,
  WITH B. ŠLJIVIĆ-SIMŠIC, EDS. JUDEO-
  SPANISH BALLADS FROM BOSNIA.*
  M.E. BARRICK, 292(JAF):JUL-SEP73-
  304
  P. BÉNICHOU, 240(HR):SPRING73-443
  C. BLAYLOCK, 574(SEEJ):FALL72-363
  A.D. DEYERMOND, 86(BHS):JUL73-286
  J. LIHANI, 582(SFQ):JUN73-131
ARMITAGE, R. & W. MEIDEN. BEGINNING
  SPANISH. (3RD ED)
  D.R. MC KAY, 399(MLJ):JAN-FEB73-71
ARMOUR, L. LOGIC & REALITY.
  P.G.W.S., 543:DEC72-351
  P. SMALE, 154:MAR73-174
ARMS, S. IMMACULATE DECEPTION.
  A. RICH, 453:20CT75-25
  J. WILSON, 441:22JUN75-7
"THE ARMS TRADE WITH THE THIRD
  WORLD." (REV)
  E. ROTHSCHILD, 453:20CT75-7
ARMSTRONG, A. BERLINERS.
  639(VQR):SUMMER74-CI
ARMSTRONG, D.M. BELIEF, TRUTH &
  KNOWLEDGE.
  F.I. DRETSKE, 311(JP):4DEC75-793
  S.J. NOREN, 484(PPR):MAR74-446
ARMSTRONG, E.A. THE LIFE & LORE OF
  THE BIRD.
  R. CARAS, 441:7DEC75-92
ARMSTRONG, F.H. & OTHERS, EDS. AS-
  PECTS OF NINETEENTH-CENTURY ONTARIO.
  K.M. MC LAUGHLIN, 99:MAR75-37
ARMSTRONG, I., ED. ROBERT BROWNING.
  M. ROBERTS, 617(TLS):16MAY75-543
ARMSTRONG, I., ED. VICTORIAN SCRU-
  TINIES.*
  R.G. COX, 148:SUMMER73-189
  S.M. SMITH, 89(BJA):WINTER73-96
  P. TURNER, 541(RES):MAY73-229
ARMSTRONG, W. - SEE GODKIN, E.L.
ARMSTRONG, W.A., ED. SHAKESPEARE'S
  HISTORIES.
  J.C. MAXWELL, 447(N&Q):APR73-152
ARMYTAGE, W.H.G. FOUR HUNDRED YEARS
  OF ENGLISH EDUCATION. (2ND ED)
  P.A. SLACK, 447(N&Q):AUG73-316
ARNASON, H.H. HISTORY OF MODERN ART.
  B. HAYES, 54:DEC73-645
ARNASON, H.H. THE SCULPTURES OF
  HOUDON.
  J. RUSSELL, 441:7DEC75-20
  D. THOMAS, 362:25DEC75&1JAN76-892
ARNASON, J.P. VON MARCUSE ZU MARX.
  S. DECLOUX, 182:VOL26#15/16-521
ARNDT, K.J.R. - SEE SEALSFIELD, C.
ARNHEIM, M.T.W. THE SENATORIAL
  ARISTOCRACY IN THE LATER ROMAN EM-
  PIRE.
  T.D. BARNES, 487:AUTUMN73-305
  A. CHASTAGNOL, 555:VOL47FASC2-373
  W. LIEBESCHUETZ, 313:VOL63-258
  S.I. OOST, 124:MAR73-364
ARNHEIM, R. VISUAL THINKING.*
  M. BORNSTEIN, 486:MAR73-141

ARNOLD, A. NEFARIO.
  M. CAMBER, 617(TLS):31JAN75-101
ARNOLD, D. DIE POLYKLETNACHFOLGE.
  R.V. NICHOLLS, 303:VOL93-266
ARNOLD, D. & N. FORTUNE, EDS. THE
  BEETHOVEN READER.
  M. PETERSON, 470:NOV72-46
ARNOLD, G. KENYATTA & THE POLITICS
  OF KENYA.
  M. TWADDLE, 617(TLS):3JAN75-8
ARNOLD, H.L., ED. BERTOLT BRECHT
  I/II.
  R. GRIMM, 406:FALL74-322
ARNOLD, H.L., ED. LITERATURBETRIEB
  IN DEUTSCHLAND.
  H.J. BERNHARD, 654(WB):1/1973-174
ARNOLD, K. JOHANNES TRITHEMIUS
  (1462-1516).*
  L.W. SPITZ, 551(RENQ):WINTER73-471
ARNOLD, M. THE COMPLETE PROSE
  WORKS. (VOL 8) (R.H. SUPER, ED)
  P. TURNER, 541(RES):AUG73-385
ARNOLD, M. THE COMPLETE PROSE
  WORKS. (VOL 10) (R.H. SUPER, ED)
  J. HOLLOWAY, 617(TLS):8AUG75-897
ARNOTT, P.D. THE ROMANS & THEIR
  WORLD.
  J.E. REXINE, 121(CJ):DEC73/JAN74-
  167
ARNTZEN, H. LITERATUR IM ZEITALTER
  DER INFORMATION.
  U. KARTHAUS, 680(ZDP):BAND92HEFT4-
  634
ARON, J-P. THE ART OF EATING IN
  FRANCE.
  M. PRINGLE, 362:25DEC75&1JAN76-891
  J. WEIGHTMAN, 617(TLS):19DEC75-
  1504
ARON, J-P. LE MANAGEUR DU XIXE
  SIÈCLE.
  M. REBERIOUX, 98:NOV73-1031
ARON, R. HISTOIRE DE L'EPURATION.
  (PT 3)
  R. GRIFFITHS, 617(TLS):29AUG75-965
ARON, R. HISTORY & THE DIALECTIC
  OF VIOLENCE.
  K. MINOGUE, 617(TLS):7NOV75-1318
ARON, R. THE IMPERIAL REPUBLIC.*
  (FRENCH TITLE: RÉPUBLIQUE IMPÉRI-
  ALE.)
  H. BERKELEY, 362:15MAY75-651
  R. CUFF, 99:APR/MAY75-47
  D.C. WATT, 617(TLS):240CT75-1268
ARONOWITZ, S. FALSE PROMISES.
  N. MILLS, 676(YR):SUMMER74-566
ARONSON, A. PSYCHE & SYMBOL IN
  SHAKESPEARE.
  M. MC CANLES, 141:SPRING74-172
ARP, J. ARP ON ARP. (M. JEAN, ED)
  A. ABEL, 399(MLJ):JAN-FEB74-63
ARPINO, G. DOMINGO IL FAVOLOSO.
  617(TLS):310CT75-1310
ARRIAN. THE CAMPAIGNS OF ALEXANDER.
  (A. DE SÉLINCOURT, TRANS)
  E.N. BORZA, 124:MAR73-368
  P.A. STADTER, 399(MLJ):SEP-OCT73-
  279
ARRIGHI, M. THE HATCHET MAN.
  P. ADAMS, 61:SEP75-85
  M. LEVIN, 441:31AUG75-13
ARRIVÉ, M. LES LANGAGES DE JARRY.
  C. BOUCHÉ, 209(FM):JUL73-303

12

ARROM, J.J. HISPANOAMÉRICA.*
  N. GARCÍA, 238:DEC73-1143
  J.K. KNOWLES, 238:DEC73-1143
  M. MARIS, 238:SEP73-756
  M.A. SALGADO, 238:MAR73-195
ARROYO, C.M. - SEE UNDER MORÓN AR-
  ROYO, C.
ARSLAN, E. GOTHIC ARCHITECTURE IN
  VENICE.
  J. BECKWITH, 46:JAN73-79
"THE ART OF BEATRIX POTTER." (NEW
  ED)
  V. POWELL, 39:JUL73-72
"ART TREASURES OF THE VATICAN."
  J. RUSSELL, 441:7DEC75-24
ARTAUD, A. COLLECTED WORKS.* (VOL
  4) OEUVRES COMPLÈTES. (VOLS 10-13)
  J.G. WEIGHTMAN, 617(TLS):8AUG75-
  888
ARTÉMOVA, V.A., ED. ISSLEDOVANIJA
  JAZYKA I RECI.
  G.F. MEIER, 682(ZPSK):BAND26HEFT
  3/4-425
ARTHOS, J. SHAKESPEARE: THE EARLY
  WRITINGS.
  R.A. FOAKES, 175:AUTUMN72-107
ARTHUR, E. & D. WITNEY. THE BARN.
  C.P., 505:APR73-146
  J. WARKENTIN, 96:FEB/MAR73-85
  G. WOODCOCK, 102(CANL):SPRING73-97
"THE ARTIST CRAFTSMAN IN AUSTRALIA."
  R.S., 139:OCT73-64
ARVAY, H. ELEVEN BULLETS FOR
  MOHAMMED.
  N. CALLENDAR, 441:23FEB75-40
ARVAY, H. OPERATION KUWAIT.
  N. CALLENDAR, 441:30MAR75-24
ARVON, H. MARXIST ESTHETICS.*
  (FRENCH TITLE: L'ESTHÉTIQUE MARX-
  ISTE.)
  A. BERLEANT, 484(PPR):MAR74-452
  W.H. TRUITT, 290(JAAC):SPRING74-
  431
"AS I CROSSED A BRIDGE OF DREAMS."*
  (I. MORRIS, TRANS)
  P. BEER, 617(TLS):21FEB75-186
  D.J. ENRIGHT, 362:20FEB75-252
  L.M. ZOLBROD, 352(LE&W):VOL16#3-
  1080
ASCHENBRENNER, K. THE CONCEPT OF
  VALUE.*
  M. OPPENHEIMER, JR., 186(ETC.):
  MAR73-102
ASCHER, A. PAVEL AXELROD & THE DE-
  VELOPMENT OF MENSHEVISM.
  D. LA BELLE, 104:WINTER73-555
  A. WILDMAN, 550(RUSR):OCT73-431
ASCHERI, M. UN MAESTRO DEL "MOS
  ITALICUS."
  W. ULLMANN, 551(RENQ):WINTER73-481
ASCOLI, D. A VILLAGE IN CHELSEA.
  617(TLS):31JAN75-121
ASCOLI, G. LA GRANDE-BRETAGNE DE-
  VANT L'OPINION FRANÇAISE DEPUIS LA
  GUERRE DE CENT ANS JUSQU'À LA FIN
  DU XVIe SIÈCLE.
  M. HUGHES, 535(RHL):NOV-DEC73-1053
ASHBEE, P. ANCIENT SCILLY.
  C. THOMAS, 617(TLS):18APR75-434
ASHBERY, J. SELF-PORTRAIT IN A CON-
  VEX MIRROR.
  P. AUSTER, 231:NOV75-106
  J.M. BRINNIN, 441:10AUG75-7
                          [CONTINUED]

[CONTINUING]
  I. EHRENPREIS, 453:16OCT75-3
  D. KALSTONE, 617(TLS):25JUL75-834
ASHDOWN, D.M., ED. OVER THE TEACUPS.
  R.C. TOBIAS, 637(VS):DEC73-209
ASHE, A., WITH F. DEFORD. ARTHUR
  ASHE.
  J. DURSO, 441:1JUN75-32
  R. SMITH, 441:7DEC75-34
ASHE, G. CAMELOT & THE VISION OF
  ALBION.
  205(FMLS):OCT73-407
ASHER, J.A. - SEE VON EMS, R.
ASHER, R.E., ED. PROCEEDINGS OF THE
  SECOND INTERNATIONAL CONFERENCE
  SEMINAR OF TAMIL STUDIES. (VOL 1)
  G.L. HART 3D, 293(JAST):MAY73-541
ASHER, R.E. & R. RADHAKRISHNAN. A
  TAMIL PROSE READER.
  K.V. ZVELEBIL, 318(JAOS):JAN-MAR
  73-118
ASHLEY, F. JAMES DICKEY.
  354:SEP73-264
ASHLEY, R. COCAINE.
  N.E. ZINBERG, 453:30OCT75-32
ASHMARIN, N.I. THESAURUS LINGUAE
  TSCHUVASCHORUM.
  G. HAZAI, 682(ZPSK):BAND26HEFT6-
  718
ASHMOLE, B. THE ARCHITECT & SCULP-
  TOR IN ANCIENT GREECE.
  M. ROSENTHAL, 135:MAR73-216
ASHMOLE, B. ARCHITECT & SCULPTOR IN
  CLASSICAL GREECE.
  R.M. COOK, 123:NOV74-309
  J.M. COOK, 303:VOL93-264
  R. HIGGINS, 39:SEP73-240
  C. VERMEULE, 90:NOV73-747
ASHTON, D. THE LIFE & TIMES OF THE
  NEW YORK SCHOOL.*
  G.S. WHITTET, 135:APR73-291
ASHTON, D. - SEE PICASSO, P.
ASHTON, T.L. - SEE LORD BYRON
ASHTOR, E. LES MÉTAUX PRECIEUX ET
  LA BALANCE DES PAYEMENTS DU PROCHE-
  ORIENT À LA BASSE ÉPOQUE.
  J.L. BACHARACH, 589:JAN74-91
  H.L. MISBACH, 318(JAOS):OCT-DEC
  73-573
ASIMOV, I. BEFORE THE GOLDEN AGE.
  J. HAMILTON-PATERSON, 617(TLS):
  7MAR75-260
ASIMOV, I. PLEASE EXPLAIN.
  617(TLS):11APR75-397
ASKWITH, B. THE LYTTELTONS.
  G. BATTISCOMBE, 617(TLS):31OCT75-
  1301
ASKWITH, B. TWO VICTORIAN FAMILIES.
  M. ROSE, 637(VS):MAR74-319
ASLANAPA, O. TURKISH ART & ARCHI-
  TECTURE.*
  S. LLOYD, 90:MAR73-181
ASPATURIAN, V.V., ED. PROCESS &
  POWER IN SOVIET FOREIGN POLICY.
  E.B. MORRELL, 104:WINTER73-559
ASPETSBERGER, F. WELTEINHEIT UND
  EPISCHE GESTALTUNG.
  C. HAMLIN, 301(JEGP):APR74-292
ASPLER, T. ONE OF MY MARIONETTES.
  G. WOODCOCK, 102(CANL):SPRING74-96
ASPREY, R.B. WAR IN THE SHADOWS.
  W. LAQUEUR, 617(TLS):1AUG75-862

13

ASSARSSON-RIZZI, K. "FRIAR BACON &
FRIAR BUNGAY."
N. SANDERS, 402(MLR):APR74-370
ASSELINEAU, R. EDGAR ALLAN POE.
L. BONNEROT, 189(EA):OCT-DEC73-494
ASSÉNOV, D. NUITS TORRIDES EN
ARCADIE.
270:VOL23#1-15
ASSION, P. ALTDEUTSCHE FACHLITERA-
TUR.
E.A. PHILIPPSON, 301(JEGP):JUL74-
390
DE ASSIS, J.M.M. - SEE UNDER MACHADO
DE ASSIS, J.M.
ASTON, M. & T. ROWLEY. LANDSCAPE
ARCHAEOLOGY.
C. TAYLOR, 617(TLS):14MAR75-282
ASTRO, R. & J.J. BENSON, EDS. HEM-
INGWAY IN OUR TIME.
S. MOORE, 385(MQR):FALL75-466
ASTURIAS, M.A. MEN OF MAIZE.
P. ADAMS, 61:SEP75-85
V. PERERA, 441:30NOV75-60
ATANASIJEVIC, K. THE METAPHYSICAL &
GEOMETRICAL DOCTRINE OF BRUNO.
M. CAPEK, 484(PPR):JUN74-611
ATHENAGORAS. LEGATIO [&] DE RESUR-
RECTIONE. (W.R. SCHOEDEL, ED &
TRANS)
J.N. BIRDSALL, 123:NOV74-295
ATHERTON, J.S. THE BOOKS AT THE
WAKE. (REV)
J. VAN VOORHIS, 329(JJQ):SPRING75-
340
ATHERTON, S. WELCOME TO THE MARI-
TIMES.
G.S. MC CAUGHEY, 99:APR/MAY75-63
ATKINS, G.P. & L.C. WILSON. THE
UNITED STATES & THE TRUJILLO REGIME.
W.F. BARBER, 150(DR):SPRING73-179
ATKINS, M.E. BY THE NORTH DOOR.
N. CALLENDAR, 441:20APR75-27
ATKINS, S. - SEE HEINE, H.
ATKINSON, D. ORTHODOX CONSENSUS &
RADICAL ALTERNATIVE.
M. FELD, 255(HAB):WINTER73-46
ATKINSON, D.M. & A.H. CLARKE, EDS.
HISPANIC STUDIES IN HONOUR OF
JOSEPH MANSON.
N.G. ROUND, 402(MLR):JUL74-668
ATKINSON, F. DICTIONARY OF PSEUDO-
NYMS & PEN-NAMES.
617(TLS):30CT75-1138
ATKINSON, G. & A.C. KELLER. PRELUDE
TO THE ENLIGHTENMENT.*
A.S. CRISAFULLI, 188(ECR):FALL73-
263
L.G. CROCKER, 546(RR):MAY74-230
ATSALOS, B. LA TERMINOLOGIE DU
LIVRE-MANUSCRIT À L'ÉPOQUE BYZAN-
TINE. (PT 1)
R. CLAVAUD, 555:VOL47FASC2-345
N.G. WILSON, 123:MAR74-145
AL-ATTAS, S.M.N. THE MYSTICISM OF
ḤAMZAH FANṢŪRĪ.
J.A. BELLAMY, 318(JAOS):JUL-SEP73-
368
ATTENBOROUGH, J. A LIVING MEMORY.
W. HALEY, 617(TLS):240CT75-1265
ATWOOD, M. THE EDIBLE WOMAN.
L. BURTON & D. MORLEY, 99:SEP75-57
ATWOOD, M. POWER POLITICS.*
H. ZINNES, 109:SPRING/SUMMER74-122

ATWOOD, M. SURFACING.*
L. BURTON & D. MORLEY, 99:SEP75-57
E. GLOVER, 565:VOL14#4-69
P. GROSSKURTH, 102(CANL):WINTER73-
108
J. HARCOURT, 529(QQ):SUMMER73-278
C. MC LAY, 296:VOL4#1-82
ATWOOD, M. SURVIVAL.*
G. GEDDES, 376:APR73-233
M. ROSS, 150(DR):SPRING73-159
ATWOOD, M. YOU ARE HAPPY.*
T. LASK, 441:2AUG75-19
L. SANDLER, 606(TAMR):NOV74-89
H. VENDLER, 441:6APR75-4
AUBERT, R. - SEE GUITTARD DE FLORI-
BAN, C.
AUBIN, F., ED. ÉTUDES SONG IN MEM-
ORIAM ETIENNE BALAZS. (SER 1, PTS
1&2)
B.E. MC KNIGHT, 318(JAOS):OCT-DEC
73-638
A.F. WRIGHT, 293(JAST):NOV72-138
AUBIN, J. & G. BUCHON. MARE LUSO-
INDICUM.
R. CALLAHAN, 318(JAOS):APR-JUN73-
250
AUBINEAU, M., ED. HOMÉLIES PASCALES.
C.W. MACLEOD, 123:NOV74-295
AUBONNET, J. - SEE ARISTOTLE
AUBRETON, R., ED & TRANS. ANTHOLOGIE
GRECQUE. (PT 1, VOL 10)
Z. PAVLOVSKIS, 124:SEP-OCT73-49
AUCHINCLOSS, L., ED. FABLES OF WIT
& ELEGANCE.
F. RICHIE, 573(SSF):SPRING73-218
AUCHINCLOSS, L. A WRITER'S CAPI-
TAL.* THE PARTNERS.
J.W. TUTTLETON, 569(SR):SUMMER74-
XLVIII
AUDEN, W.H. A CERTAIN WORLD.
H. PESCHMANN, 175:SPRING72-30
AUDEN, W.H. CITY WITHOUT WALLS &
OTHER POEMS. A NEW YEAR GREETING.
E. CALLAN, 295:APR74-1055
AUDEN, W.H. EPISTLE TO A GODSON.*
E. CALLAN, 295:APR74-1055
H. MURPHY, 159(DM):WINTER/SPRING
73-120
AUDEN, W.H. FOREWORDS & AFTERWORDS.*
(E. MENDELSON, ED)
G. WOODCOCK, 569(SR):FALL74-685
AUDEN, W.H. POEMS 1928.
P. DAVISON, 354:DEC73-361
AUDEN, W.H. THANK YOU, FOG.*
J. ATLAS, 491:JUN75-175
H. MOSS, 441:12JAN75-1
AUDEN, W.H. - SEE DRYDEN, J.
VON AUE, H. - SEE UNDER HARTMANN
VON AUE
AUERBACH, E. & C.K. ADAMS, COMPS.
PAINTINGS & SCULPTURE AT HATFIELD
HOUSE.*
G. REYNOLDS, 39:FEB73-196
AUGEROT, J.E. & F.D. POPESCU. MOD-
ERN ROMANIAN.
J.E. ALGEO, 399(MLJ):NOV73-369
"UN AUGURIO A RAFFAELE MATTIOLI."
400(MLN):JAN73-161
ST. AUGUSTINE. AUGUSTINUS PHILOSO-
PHISCHE FRÜHDIALOGE. (C. ANDRESEN,
ED)
D. WIESEN, 124:MAY73-495

ST. AUGUSTINE. THE CITY OF GOD
AGAINST THE PAGANS. (VOL 7, BKS
21&22) (W.M. GREEN, TRANS)
  J. ANDRÉ, 555:VOL47FASC1-174
ST. AUGUSTINE [AURELIUS AUGUSTINUS].
DIE ORDNUNG. NUTZEN DES GLAUBENS
[&] DIE ZWEI SEELEN. DREI BÜCHER
ÜBER DEN GLAUBEN. GEIST UND BUCH-
STABE. 83 VERSCHIEDENE FRAGEN.
(C.J. PERL, ED OF ALL)
  H. RONDET, 182:VOL26#21/22-774
AULD, D.A.L., ED. ECONOMIC THINK-
ING & POLLUTION PROBLEMS.
  P.A. LARKIN, 529(QQ):SUMMER73-286
AULT, D. VISIONARY PHYSICS.
  G.S. ROUSSEAU, 617(TLS):20JUN75-
  701
AULT, W.O. OPEN-FIELD FARMING IN
MEDIEVAL ENGLAND.
  E. SEARLE, 589:APR74-314
AURENHAMMER, H. J.B. FISCHER VON
ERLACH.*
  639(VQR):AUTUMN74-CXXX
AURENHAMMER, H. & G. DAS BELVEDERE
IN WIEN.
  R. WAGNER-RIEGER, 683:BAND36HEFT1-
  83
AUSONIUS. OPERE DI DECIMO MAGNO
AUSONIO. (A. PASTORINO, ED)
  P.G. WALSH, 123:MAR74-141
AUSTEN, J. SENSE & SENSIBILITY.*
(C. LAMONT, ED) PRIDE & PREJU-
DICE.* (F.W. BRADBROOK, ED) MANS-
FIELD PARK.* (J. LUCAS, ED)
  T.A. SHIPPEY, 402(MLR):JAN74-156
AUSTEN, J. & ANOTHER LADY. SANDITON.
  G. ANNAN, 362:24JUL75-125
  P. BEER, 617(TLS):25JUL75-821
  V.S. PRITCHETT, 453:17JUL75-26
  442(NY):14APR75-127
AUSTIN, A.E. ELIZABETH BOWEN.
  J. GINDIN, 141:WINTER73-81
  A.A.A. JOHNSON, 573(SSF):FALL73-
  432
AUSTIN, B. SOULCATCHER.
  M. LEVIN, 441:26OCT75-56
AUSTIN, J.L. HOW TO DO THINGS WITH
WORDS. (2ND ED) (M. SBISÀ & J.O.
URMSON, EDS)
  617(TLS):19SEP75-1067
AUSTIN, M. ACUPUNCTURE THERAPY.
  617(TLS):21MAR75-295
AUSTIN, M. & P. VIDAL-NAQUET. ÉCON-
OMIE ET SOCIÉTÉS EN GRÈCE ANCIENNE
(PÉRIODES ARCHAÏQUE ET CLASSIQUE).
  J.A.O. LARSEN, 122:OCT73-299
AUSTIN, R.G. - SEE VERGIL
"AUSTRALIAN NATIONAL BIBLIOGRAPHY
1974."
  C.D. NEEDHAM, 617(TLS):30MAY75-605
AUTY, R., J.L.I. FENNELL & I.P.
FOOTE, EDS. OXFORD SLAVONIC PAPERS.
(NEW SER, VOL 5)
  A.G.F. VAN HOLK, 402(MLR):OCT74-
  945
AUTY, R., J.L.I. FENNELL & I.P.
FOOTE, EDS. OXFORD SLAVONIC PAPERS.
(NEW SER, VOL 6)
  G. STONE, 402(MLR):OCT74-948
AUTY, R., J.L.I. FENNELL & I.P.
FOOTE, EDS. OXFORD SLAVONIC PAP-
ERS. (NEW SER, VOL 7)
  I. DE MADARIAGA, 617(TLS):4JUL75-
  716

AUZAS, P-M. - SEE MÉRIMÉE, P.
AVAKUMOVIC, I. THE COMMUNIST PARTY
IN CANADA.
  G. WOODCOCK, 617(TLS):10OCT75-1188
AVALLE, D.S. MODELLI SEMIOLOGICI
NELLA COMMEDIA DI DANTE.
  D. ROBEY, 617(TLS):31OCT75-1304
AVALLE-ARCE, J.B. EL CRONISTA PEDRO
DE ESCAVIAS.
  R.B. TATE, 402(MLR):OCT74-901
AVALLE-ARCE, J.B. TEMAS HISPÁNICOS
MEDIEVALES.
  617(TLS):23MAY75-576
AVALLE-ARCE, J.B. - SEE DE CERVANTES
SAAVEDRA, M.
AVALLE-ARCE, J.B. - SEE VALERA, J.
AVANESOV, R.I. MODERN RUSSIAN
STRESS.
  G.F. MEIER, 682(ZPSK):BAND26HEFT
  1/2-171
AVANESOV, R.I. RUSSKOE LITERATURNOE
PROIZNOŠENIE. (5TH ED)
  W.J. DANIELS, 574(SEEJ):FALL73-355
AVARY, M.L. DIXIE AFTER THE WAR.
  S.W. WIGGINS, 9(ALAR):APR73-145
AVEDON, R. - SEE LARTIGUE, J.H.
AVERCH, H.A., F.H. DENTON & J.E.
KOEHLER. THE MATRIX OF POLICY IN
THE PHILIPPINES.* A CRISIS OF AM-
BIGUITY.
  B.J. KERKVLIET, 293(JAST):MAY73-
  489
AVI-YONAH, M. & OTHERS - SEE JONES,
A.H.M.
AVINERI, S. HEGEL'S THEORY OF THE
MODERN STATE.
  M.J.D., 543:JUN73-745
  P. FUSS, 319:APR73-235
  W.L. MC BRIDE, 390:NOV73-74
  A. QUINTON, 453:29MAY75-34 [& CONT
  IN] 453:12JUN75-39
AVINERI, S. THE SOCIAL & POLITICAL
THOUGHT OF KARL MARX.
  A.W. WOOD, 543:SEP72-118
AVINOV, M. PILGRIMAGE THROUGH HELL.
  M.S. SHATZ, 104:SUMMER73-250
"EL AVISO DE ESCARMENTADOS DEL AÑO
QUE ACABA Y ESCARMIENTO DE AVISADOS
PARA EL QUE EMPIEZA DE 1935." (J.
BERGAMÍN, ED)
  A. TERRY, 617(TLS):9MAY75-519
AVRICH, P., ED. THE ANARCHISTS IN
THE RUSSIAN REVOLUTION.
  G. BOSHYK, 575(SEER):OCT74-636
AVRICH, P. RUSSIAN REBELS, 1600-
1800.*
  J.L. WIECZYNSKI, 550(RUSR):JUL73-
  316
AXELBANK, A. BLACK STAR OVER JAPAN.
  A.D. COOX, 293(JAST):AUG73-709
  MUSHAKŌJI KINHIDE, 285(JAPQ):JAN-
  MAR74-95
AXELOS, K. POUR UNE ÉTHIQUE PROBLÉ-
MATIQUE.
  M. ADAM, 542:OCT-DEC73-480
  C. PANACCIO, 154:SEP73-563
AXELSON, S. CULTURE CONFRONTATION
IN THE LOWER CONGO.
  J. VANSINA, 69:JAN73-85
AXLER, B. METHODS & MANNERS OF
COOKING.
  M.F.K. FISHER, 442(NY):10NOV75-176
AYALA, F. EL LAZARILLO REEXAMINADO.
  C.A. LONGHURST, 86(BHS):OCT73-392

15

AYALA, F.J. & T. DOBZHANSKY, EDS.
STUDIES IN THE PHILOSOPHY OF BIOL-
OGY.
  M. CHANCE, 617(TLS):6JUN75-631
DE AYALA, R.P. - SEE UNDER PÉREZ DE
AYALA, R.
AYER, A.J. THE CENTRAL QUESTIONS OF
PHILOSOPHY.*
  M. LEBOWITZ, 598(SOR):AUTUMN75-949
  J. RACHELS, 441:5JAN75-17
AYER, A.J. METAPHYSICS & COMMON
SENSE.
  M. FOX, 255(HAB):WINTER73-43
AYER, A.J. PROBABILITY & EVIDENCE.*
  P. HORWICH, 482(PHR):OCT73-547
  W. KNEALE, 393(MIND):JAN73-144
  J.L., 543:MAR73-523
  D.H. MELLOR, 479(PHQ):JUL73-272
AYER, A.J. RUSSELL.
  J.L., 543:MAR73-524
  H. LAYCOCK, 529(QQ):AUTUMN73-485
AYERS, H.B. & T.H. NAYLOR, EDS. YOU
CAN'T EAT MAGNOLIAS.
  W.D. LEWIS, 9(ALAR):APR73-147
AYERS, J. THE BAUR COLLECTION,
GENEVA: CHINESE CERAMICS. (VOL 3)
  M. MEDLEY, 463:AUTUMN73-318
  B. NEAVE-HILL, 135:APR73-292
AYERS, J. THE BAUR COLLECTION,
GENEVA: CHINESE CERAMICS. (VOL 4)
  M. TREGEAR, 617(TLS):2MAY75-493
AYERS, R.H. & W.T. BLACKSTONE, EDS.
RELIGIOUS LANGUAGE & KNOWLEDGE.
  R.B., 543:JUN73-746
AYERS, W. CHANG CHIH-TUNG & EDUCA-
TIONAL REFORM IN CHINA.*
  D. PONG, 318(JAOS):APR-JUN73-218
AYLING, A. A FURTHER COLLECTION OF
CHINESE LYRICS & OTHER POEMS.
  D. HAWKES, 318(JAOS):OCT-DEC73-635
AYLMER, G.E., ED. THE INTERREGNUM.
  T. HAYES, 568(SCN):SPRING-SUMMER
  74-21
AYRE, L. THE GILBERT & SULLIVAN
COMPANION.
  C. KLEINHANS, 637(VS):SEP73-117
AYRTON, E. THE COOKERY OF ENGLAND.
  S. PAKENHAM, 617(TLS):20JUN75-703
AZAÑA, M. OBRAS COMPLETAS. (J.
MARICHAL, ED)
  H. THOMAS, 617(TLS):21FEB75-195
AZIMOV, P.A. & OTHERS, EDS. PROB-
LEMY DVUJAZYČIJA I MNOGOJAZYČIJA.
  H. JACHNOW, 343:BAND17HEFT2-141
AZIZ, K.K., ED. THE ALL INDIA MUS-
LIM CONFERENCE 1928-1935.
  M. MINES, 293(JAST):AUG73-715
AZIZ, M. - SEE JAMES, H.
AL-AZM, S.J. THE ORIGIN OF KANT'S
ARGUMENTS IN THE ANTINOMIES.*
  J.D. GLENN, JR., 482(PHR):JUL74-
  416

BÂ, S.W. THE CONCEPT OF NEGRITUDE
IN THE POETRY OF LÉOPOLD SÉDAR
SENGHOR.
  G. MOORE, 617(TLS):1AUG75-880
  639(VQR):SUMMER74-LXXX
BABCOCK, R.H. GOMPERS IN CANADA.
  I. ABELLA, 99:APR/MAY75-27

BABCOCK, S.S. THE SYNTAX OF SPANISH
REFLEXIVE VERBS.*
  M. ROLDÁN, 238:SEP73-749
BABIĆ, G. LES CHAPELLES ANNEXES DES
ÉGLISES BYZANTINES.
  S. ČURČIĆ, 54:SEP73-448
BABLET, D. & J. JACQUOT, EDS.
L'EXPRESSIONNISME DANS LE THÉÂTRE
EUROPÉEN.
  R. FURNESS, 402(MLR):JAN74-230
BABUT, D. PLUTARQUE ET LE STOÏ-
CISME.
  P. DE LACY, 122:JUL73-227
BACH, R. JONATHAN LIVINGSTON SEA-
GULL.*
  B. MERRY, 364:AUG/SEP74-80
BACHELARD, G. LE DROIT DE RÊVER.
  J-L. BACKÈS, 98:MAR73-237
BACHELARD, G. EPISTÉMOLOGIE. (D.
LECOURT, ED)
  R. BLANCHÉ, 542:JUL-SEP73-348
BACHELARD, G. L'ENGAGEMENT RATION-
ALISTE.
  R. BLANCHÉ, 542:JUL-SEP73-348
  M-A. SINACEUR, 98:JAN73-53
BACHELARD, G. ON POETIC IMAGINATION
& REVERIE. (C. GAUDIN, ED & TRANS)
  E.K. KAPLAN, 207(FR):APR73-1030
"BACHELARD: COLLOQUE DE CÉRISY."
  J. CULLER, 617(TLS):28FEB75-230
VON BACHERACH, T. & K. GUTZKOW.
UNVERÖFFENTLICHTE BRIEFE (1842-
1849). (W. VORDTRIEDE, ED)
  G.K. FRIESEN, 400(MLN):OCT73-1055
BACHRACH, B.S. MEROVINGIAN MILITARY
ORGANIZATION, 481-751.
  R. BRILL, 124:FEB74-229
  C. GAIER, 589:JUL74-549
BACKHOUSE, J. JOHN SCOTTOWE'S
ALPHABET BOOKS.
  N. BARKER, 617(TLS):4JUL75-735
BÄCKMAN, S. THIS SINGULAR TALE.*
  R. QUINTANA, 405(MP):AUG73-59
BACKSTROM, P.N. CHRISTIAN SOCIALISM
& CO-OPERATION IN VICTORIAN ENG-
LAND.
  N. MASTERMAN, 617(TLS):3JAN75-17
BACKWELL, H.F., ED. THE OCCUPATION
OF HAUSALAND: 1900-1904.
  A.H.M. KIRK-GREENE, 69:OCT73-356
BACON, F. THE HISTORY OF THE REIGN
OF KING HENRY THE SEVENTH. (F.J.
LEVY, ED)
  R.W. KENNY, 551(RENQ):SUMMER73-219
BACQUE, J. A MAN OF TALENT.*
  D. BROWN, 376:JAN73-164
  L. MC DONALD, 102(CANL):AUTUMN74-
  112
BADER, J. CRYSTAL LAND.*
  J. VISWANATHAN, 648:OCT73-58
BADIAN, E. PUBLICANS & SINNERS.*
  P.A. BRUNT, 313:VOL63-250
  T.P. WISEMAN, 487:SUMMER73-189
BADIR, M.G. VOLTAIRE ET L'ISLAM.
  H. MASON, 617(TLS):30MAY75-594
BAEHR, R. EINFÜHRUNG IN DIE FRANZÖ-
SISCHE VERSLEHRE.
  H. RHEINFELDER, 430(NS):MAR73-178
BAEHR, R., ED. ENEAS.
  W.G. VAN EMDEN, 208(FS):JAN74-51
BAELEN, J. LA VIE DE FLORA TRISTAN.
  S. DEBOUT, 98:JAN73-81

BAER, G., ED. ASIAN & AFRICAN
STUDIES. (VOL 7)
  S.A. AKBARABADI, 273(IC):OCT73-362
BAGCHI, A.K. PRIVATE INVESTMENT IN
INDIA, 1900-1939.
  J. ADAMS, 293(JAST):FEB73-343
BAGDANAVIČIUS, V. CULTURAL WELL-
SPRINGS OF FOLKTALES.
  E. ANDERSON, 650(WF):JUL73-213
BAGEHOT, W. THE COLLECTED WORKS OF
WALTER BAGEHOT.* (VOLS 5-8) (N.
ST. JOHN-STEVAS, ED)
  E. BOYLE, 362:23JAN75-122
BAGG, R. THE SCRAWNY SONNETS &
OTHER NARRATIVES.
  J.R. CARPENTER, 491:DEC74-166
  M.G. PERLOFF, 659:WINTER75-84
  639(VQR):WINTER74-XIV
BAGLEY, J.J. LANCASHIRE DIARISTS.
  R. FULFORD, 617(TLS):5DEC75-1436
BAGLIANI, A.P. CARDINALI DI CURIA
E "FAMILIAE" CARDINALIZIE DAL 1227
AL 1254.
  W.M. BOWSKY, 589:JUL74-551
BAGLIONI, G. L'IDEOLOGIA DELLA
BORGHESIA INDUSTRIALE NELL'ITALIA
LIBERALE.
  S.J. WOOLF, 617(TLS):31OCT75-1306
BAGNALL, N., ED. PARENT POWER.
  617(TLS):28FEB75-232
BAGRIANA, E. CONTRAPUNKTI.
  N. DONTCHEV, 270:VOL23#2-33
BAGUELEY, D. FÉCONDITE D'EMILE
ZOLA.*
  R.J. NIESS, 399(MLJ):NOV74-359
BAGWELL, P.S. INDUSTRIAL RELATIONS.
  P. HOLLIS, 617(TLS):28MAR75-340
BAHM, A.J. THE HEART OF CONFUCIUS.
  D. LANCASHIRE, 302:JAN73-162
BAHNER, W., ED. BEITRÄGE ZUR FRANZ-
ÖSISCHEN AUFKLÄRUNG UND ZUR SPAN-
ISCHEN LITERATUR.
  H.T. MASON, 208(FS):OCT74-462
BAHR, E. DIE IRONIE IM SPÄTWERK
GOETHES "...DIESE SEHR ERNSTEN
SCHERZE..."*
  G.W. FIELD, 564:JUN73-161
  N.H. SMITH, 182:VOL26#3/4-101
  I.H. SOLBRIG, 406:SPRING74-77
BAHR, E. & R.G. KUNZER. GEORG LU-
KÁCS.*
  S.G. NICHOLS, JR., 131(CL):SPRING
  74-184
BAHR, E-J. HELP, PLEASE.
  N. CALLENDAR, 441:20APR75-28
BAÏCHE, A. - SEE DU BARTAS, G.S.
BAILEY, A.G. CULTURE & NATIONALITY.
  J. FINGARD, 150(DR):SUMMER73-358
  G.A. RAWLYK, 529(QQ):AUTUMN73-463
BAILEY, A.G. THANKS FOR A DROWNED
ISLAND.*
  F. COGSWELL, 102(CANL):SUMMER74-
  119
  A.J.M. SMITH, 150(DR):WINTER73/74-
  752
BAILEY, C. GUIDE TO FAMOUS LONDON
GRAVES.
  E.S. TURNER, 362:5JUN75-738
  617(TLS):20JUN75-696
BAILEY, D. IF YOU HUM ME A FEW BARS
I MIGHT REMEMBER THE TUNE.*
  F. SUTHERLAND, 102(CANL):AUTUMN74-
  109

BAILEY, D. IN THE BELLY OF THE
WHALE.
  M. BAXTER, 99:DEC75/JAN76-48
  S. OVERBURY, 198:WINTER75-124
  D. WILSON, 617(TLS):15AUG75-912
BAILEY, D.R.S. - SEE UNDER SHACKLE-
TON BAILEY, D.R.
BAILEY, F.L., WITH J. GREENYA. FOR
THE DEFENSE.
  T. LASK, 441:5JUL75-15
BAILEY, H. POLLY PUT THE KETTLE ON.
  G. EWART, 617(TLS):15AUG75-913
BAILEY, H.W. SAD-DHARMA-PUNDARIKA-
SŪTRA.
  M.J. DRESDEN, 318(JAOS):OCT-DEC73-
  599
BAILEY, P. DUEY'S TALE.
  M. LEVIN, 441:16MAR75-30
BAILEY, T.A. & P.B. RYAN. THE LUSI-
TANIA DISASTER.
  P.G. FREDERICKS, 441:12OCT75-46
BAILLET, T.S. DIE FRAUEN IM WERK
EICHENDORFFS.
  J.F.F., 191(ELN):SEP73(SUPP)-120
BAILY, L. GILBERT & SULLIVAN.*
(BRITISH TITLE: GILBERT & SULLIVAN
& THEIR WORLD.)
  639(VQR):AUTUMN74-CXXX
BAILYN, B. THE ORDEAL OF THOMAS
HUTCHINSON.*
  J. CATANZARITI, 432(NEQ):SEP74-459
  R. MIDDLEKAUFF, 639(VQR):SUMMER74-
  463
  J.H. PLUMB, 617(TLS):13JUN75-640
BAIN, I. - SEE BEWICK, T.
BAINBRIDGE, B. THE BOTTLE FACTORY
OUTING.*
  P. ADAMS, 61:JUN75-95
  A. BROYARD, 441:26MAY75-13
  G. DAVENPORT, 441:8JUN75-6
BAINBRIDGE, B. SWEET WILLIAM.
  S. CLAPP, 617(TLS):30CT75-1125
  J. MELLORS, 362:90CT75-485
BAINTON, R.H. BEHOLD THE CHRIST.
  P. HEBBLETHWAITE, 617(TLS):3JAN75-
  20
BAIRD, E. CLASSIC CANADIAN COOKING.
  J.M. COLE, 99:DEC75/JAN76-37
BAIRD, J.D., ED. EDITING TEXTS OF
THE ROMANTIC PERIOD.
  P. DAVISON, 354:DEC73-358
  J.D. JUMP, 677:VOL4-305
BAIRD, K.E. - SEE CHUKS-ORJI, O.
BAIRD, R.D. & A. BLOOM. RELIGION &
MAN.
  H.B. EARHART, 485(PE&W):OCT73-556
BAIROCH, P. THE ECONOMIC DEVELOP-
MENT OF THE THIRD WORLD SINCE 1900.
  B. WARREN, 617(TLS):12DEC75-1496
BAKER, C. HEMINGWAY. (4TH ED)
  K. MC SWEENEY, 529(QQ):AUTUMN73-
  499
BAKER, H.A., JR. LONG BLACK SONG.*
  M. FABRE, 189(EA):OCT-DEC73-490
  H.S. JARRETT, 27(AL):NOV74-395
BAKER, H.A., JR. TWENTIETH CENTURY
INTERPRETATIONS OF "NATIVE SON."
  M. FABRE, 189(EA):OCT-DEC73-491
BAKER, I. - SEE UNDER L.M.
BAKER, J. THIRD BACK TO NATURE
ALMANAC.
  J. CANADAY, 441:13APR75-16
BAKER, K.M. CONDORCET.
  F.E. MANUEL, 617(TLS):28NOV75-1402

BAKER, L.   JOHN MARSHALL.*
  617(TLS):13JUN75-680
BAKER, W.E.   JACQUES PRÉVERT.
  D.H. MORRIS 4TH, 577(SHR):WINTER
  73-103
BAKISH, D.   RICHARD WRIGHT.
  M. FABRE, 189(EA):OCT-DEC73-491
BAKKER, B.H. - SEE ALEXIS, P. & É.
ZOLA
BALAKIAN, A.   ANDRÉ BRETON.*
  K.R. ASPLEY, 402(MLR):JAN74-186
  R. CARDINAL, 208(FS):APR74-229
  M.A. CAWS, 207(FR):DEC72-422
  E. SELLIN, 295:FEB74-550
  E. SELLIN, 546(RR):NOV73-316
BALAKIAN, A.   SURREALISM.*   (REV)
  A. POWELL, 39:MAR73-316
BALANDIER, G.   ANTHROPO-LOGIQUES.
  L. MAIR, 617(TLS):14FEB75-172
BALANDIER, G.   GURVITCH.
  S. LUKES, 617(TLS):12SEP75-1019
BALAYÉ, S.   LES CARNETS DE VOYAGE
DE MADAME DE STAËL.
  M.J. COX, 402(MLR):JUL74-643
  P. DEGUISE, 535(RHL):NOV-DEC73-
  1087
  M. GUTWIRTH, 207(FR):MAY73-1226
  M. LEHTONEN, 439(NM):1973/1-179
  J.F. MARSHALL, 399(MLJ):MAR74-142
BALD, R.C.   JOHN DONNE.*   (W. MIL-
GATE, ED)
  T.A. BIRRELL, 179(ES):FEB73-71
  R. ELLRODT, 189(EA):OCT-DEC73-468
BALD, W-D., B. CARSTENSEN & M. HEL-
LINGER.   DIE BEHANDLUNG GRAMMAT-
ISCHER PROBLEME IN LEHRWERKEN FÜR
DEN ENGLISCHUNTERRICHT.
  K. OLTMANN, 430(NS):JUL73-381
BALDERSTON, M. & D. SYRETT, EDS.
THE LOST WAR.
  P-L. ADAMS, 61:NOV75-124
BALDERSTONE, G.   WHERE THE WORDS ARE
UNSPOKEN.
  E. LANCZOS, 648:OCT73-61
BALDINGER, K., WITH J-D. GENDRON &
G. STRAKA.   DICTIONNAIRE ÉTYMOLO-
GIQUE DE L'ANCIEN FRANÇAIS.   (FASC
G1)
  B. FOSTER, 208(FS):OCT74-500
BALDUCCI, G.   ITALIA MODERNA.
  A. MOLLICA, 399(MLJ):NOV74-367
  J. NARDIELLO, 399(MLJ):SEP-OCT74-
  295
BALDWIN, J.   SONNY'S BLUES.   (G.
KIRBY, ED)
  K. OLTMANN, 430(NS):JUL73-391
BALDWIN, J.W. & R.A. GOLDTHWAITE,
EDS.   UNIVERSITIES IN POLITICS.*
  J.K. MC CONICA, 529(QQ):AUTUMN73-
  474
BALIBAR, R. & D. LAPORTE.   LE FRAN-
ÇAIS NATIONAL.
  S. ULLMAN, 617(TLS):24JAN75-89
BALIBAR, R., WITH G. MERLIN & G.
TRET.   LES FRANÇAIS FICTIFS.
  S. ULLMAN, 617(TLS):24JAN75-89
BALIGAND, R.A.   LES POÈMES DE RAY-
MOND QUENEAU.
  J-M. KLINKENBERG, 209(FM):JUL73-
  313
BALJIEU, J.   THEO VAN DOESBURG.
  S. BANN, 617(TLS):11JUL75-754
BALKA, M.   LA NUIT.
  A. CAPRIO, 207(FR):DEC72-429

BALL, G. - SEE GINSBERG, A.
BALL, P.M.   THE SCIENCE OF ASPECTS.*
  G. THOMAS, 175:SPRING72-27
  R. TRICKETT, 447(N&Q):AUG73-307
"BALLAD OF THE HIDDEN DRAGON (LIU
CHIH-YÜAN CHU-KUNG-TIAO)."   (M.
DOLEŽELOVÁ-VELINGEROVÁ & J.I.
CRUMP, TRANS)
  A.R. DAVIS, 302:JAN73-164
  C.J. WIVELL, 293(JAST):NOV72-137
BALLANCHE, P-S.   LA VISION D'HÉBAL.
  (A.J.L. BUSST, ED)
  A.J. STEELE, 402(MLR):OCT74-879
BALLAND, A. & OTHERS.   BOLSENA.
  (VOL 2)
  H. PLOMMER, 123:MAR74-114
BALLANTYNE, S.   NORMA JEAN THE TER-
MITE QUEEN.
  M. LEVIN, 441:22JUN75-10
BALLARD, E.G.   PHILOSOPHY AT THE
CROSSROADS.
  O.T., 543:SEP72-150
BALLARD, J.G.   HIGH RISE.
  N. HEPBURN, 362:11DEC75-806
  J. SUTHERLAND, 617(TLS):5DEC75-
  1438
BALLEM, J.   THE DEVIL'S LIGHTER.
  J. PARR, 296:VOL3#4-101
BALLINGER, R.E. - SEE USIGLI, R.
BALME, D.M. - SEE ARISTOTLE
BAL'MONT, K.D.   STIXOTVORENIJA.
  R.L. PATTERSON, 574(SEEJ):SPRING72-
  103
BALOGUN, O.   SHANGO, SUIVI DE LE
ROI-ELÉPHANT.
  G. & M. LEVILAIN & H. & N. FUYET,
  207(FR):FEB73-653
VON BALTHASAR, H.U.   ENGAGEMENT WITH
GOD.   ELUCIDATIONS.
  P. HEBBLETHWAITE, 617(TLS):25APR
  75-464
DE BALZAC, H.   LE DOIGT DE DIEU.
  (G. JACQUES, ED)
  P. LAUBRIET, 535(RHL):SEP-OCT73-
  911
DE BALZAC, H.   LE SECRET DES RUGGI-
ERI.   (W.L. CRAIN, ED)
  N. CAZAURAN, 535(RHL):SEP-OCT73-
  912
DE BALZAC, H.   SPLENDEURS ET MISÈRES
DES COURTISANES.   (J. GAUTREAU, ED)
  205(FMLS):APR73-211
BAMBOROUGH, J.B.   BEN JONSON.
  R. SOUTHALL, 184(EIC):JAN72-83
BAMBROUGH, R., ED.   WISDOM.*
  H.O. MOUNCE, 518:OCT74-1
BAMFIELD, V.   ON THE STRENGTH.
  D. CANNAN, 617(TLS):18APR75-429
BANASIEWICZ, C.Z., T. BIELECKI & L.
SZYMAŃSKI.   WARSAW AFLAME.
  A. IWAŃSKA, 497(POLR):VOL18#3-103
BANATHY, B.H. & D.L. LANGE.   A DE-
SIGN FOR FOREIGN LANGUAGE CURRICU-
LUM.
  D.E. BARTLEY, 399(MLJ):MAR74-149
BANCE, A.F. - SEE ROTH, J.
BANCHINI, F.   LE THÉÂTRE DE MONTHER-
LANT.
  A. BLANC, 535(RHL):NOV-DEC73-1116
BANDINELLI, R.B. - SEE UNDER BIANCHI
BANDINELLI, R.
BANDLE, O.   DIE GLIEDERUNG DES NORD-
GERMANISCHEN.
  H-J. GRAF, 72:BAND211HEFT1/3-95

BANDYOPADHYAYA, J. THE MAKING OF
INDIA'S FOREIGN POLICY.
S.P. COHEN, 293(JAST):NOV72-191
BANG, J. SYNSPUNKTER PÅ FOLKEVISEN.
W.E. RICHMOND, 563(SS):SPRING74-
196
"BANGLA DESH DOCUMENTS: MINISTRY OF
EXTERNAL AFFAIRS."
B.M. MORRISON, 293(JAST):AUG73-716
BANGS, C. ARMINIUS.
J. HITCHCOCK, 613:SPRING73-154
BANHAM, R. AGE OF THE MASTERS.
W. FEAVER, 362:26JUN75-852
R.C. TWOMBLY, 441:16NOV75-64
BANK, J.A. TACTUS, TEMPO & NOTATION
IN MENSURAL MUSIC FROM THE 13TH TO
THE 17TH CENTURY.
H.M. BROWN, 415:OCT74-847
BANKO, D. VERY DRY WITH A TWIST.
N. CALLENDAR, 441:21SEP75-41
BANKS, R. FAMILY LIFE.
M. LEVIN, 441:20APR75-30
BANKS, R. SEARCHING FOR SURVIVORS.
T. LE CLAIR, 441:18MAY75-6
BANN, S. EXPERIMENTAL PAINTING.
G. RICKEY, 54:DEC73-648
BANN, S. & J.E. BOWLT, EDS. RUS-
SIAN FORMALISM.
A. SHUKMAN, 402(MLR):JUL74-713
G. STEINER, 111:23NOV73-52
BANOV, A. PAINTS & COATINGS HAND-
BOOK.
45:MAY73-91
BANTA, M. HENRY JAMES & THE OCCULT.*
H. KERR, 445(NCF):JUN73-101
D.K. KIRBY, 432(NEQ):JUN73-331
G. MONTEIRO, 401(MLQ):SEP74-326
T. ROGERS, 175:AUTUMN73-119
BANTI, L. THE ETRUSCAN CITIES &
THEIR CULTURE.
639(VQR):AUTUMN74-CLVI
BANTON, M. & J. HARWOOD. THE RACE
CONCEPT.
M. RICHARDS, 617(TLS):7NOV75-1341
BANULS, A. HEINRICH MANN.*
H.R. WARDER, 222(GR):JAN73-76
BANY, J. MON EAU BLEUE.
M. SAKHAROFF, 207(FR):MAY73-1237
BANZAI, M. A PILGRIMAGE TO THE 88
TEMPLES IN SHIKOKU ISLAND.
R. STORRY, 285(JAPQ):JUL-SEP74-302
BAO RUO-WANG [J. PASQUALINI] & R.
CHELMINSKI. PRISONER OF MAO.
W.J.F. JENNER, 617(TLS):19DEC75-
1522
BAQUÉ, F. LE NOUVEAU ROMAN.
205(FMLS):APR73-211
BAR-ADON, A. & W.F. LEOPOLD, EDS.
CHILD LANGUAGE.*
B.T. TERVOORT, 361:OCT73-271
BAR-HILLEL, Y. ASPECTS OF LANGUAGE.
J.L. MACKIE, 84:JUN73-190
G. SAMPSON, 307:#2-101
BAR-HILLEL, Y., ED. PRAGMATICS OF
NATURAL LANGUAGES.
J.L., 543:JUN73-747
BAR-LEWAW M., I., ED. LA REVISTA
"TIMÓN" Y JOSÉ VASCONCELOS.
P.G. EARLE, 240(HR):SUMMER73-583
BAR-ZOHAR, M. THE SPY WHO DIED
TWICE.
T.J. BINYON, 617(TLS):26DEC75-1544
N. CALLENDAR, 441:22JUN75-18

BARASCH, F.K. THE GROTESQUE.*
G.D. JOSIPOVICI, 541(RES):FEB73-
110
BARATTA, E.A. SURREALISTISCHE ZÜGE
IM WERKE JEAN PAULS.
M.H., 191(ELN):SEP73(SUPP)-146
BARATTA, G. L'IDEALISMO FENOMENO-
LOGICO DI EDMUND HUSSERL.
A.M., 543:SEP72-151
BARATTO, M. REALTÀ E STILE NEL
DECAMERON.
N.L.F., 275(IQ):FALL-WINTER73(VOL
17#66)-60
M. POZZI, 228(GSLI):VOL150FASC
470/471-449
BARBEAU, A.T. THE INTELLECTUAL
DESIGN OF JOHN DRYDEN'S HEROIC
PLAYS.*
L. POTTER, 179(ES):AUG73-391
BARBER, C.L. SHAKESPEARE'S FESTIVE
COMEDY.
G. SALGADO, 402(MLR):APR74-374
BARBER, D. UNMARRIED FATHERS.
C.H. ROLPH, 617(TLS):22AUG75-940
BARBER, E.A. THE CERAMIC COLLECTORS'
GLOSSARY.
C. OMAN, 39:FEB73-202
BARBER, I. THE PINK ELEPHANT.
J. WILLIAMS, 186(ETC.):SEP73-327
BARBER, J.D. THE PRESIDENTIAL CHAR-
ACTER.
T.E. VADNEY, 529(QQ):SPRING73-111
BARBER, W.J. BRITISH ECONOMIC
THOUGHT & INDIA 1600-1858.
D. WINCH, 617(TLS):1AUG75-871
BARBERI SQUAROTTI, G. GLI INFERI E
IL LABERINTO DA PASCOLI A MONTALE.
617(TLS):31OCT75-1310
BARBERI SQUAROTTI, G. L'ARTIFICIO
DELL'ETERNITÀ.
M. MARTI, 228(GSLI):VOL150FASC470/
471-411
L. PEIRONE, 275(IQ):FALL-WINTER73
(VOL17#66)-55
BARBEY D'AUREVILLY, J. OMNIA. (A.
HIRSCHI & J. PETIT, EDS)
H. HOFER, 535(RHL):NOV-DEC73-1105
BARBIER, C.P., ED. DOCUMENTS STÉ-
PHANE MALLARMÉ.* (VOL 3)
C. CHADWICK, 402(MLR):JUL74-648
BARBIER, C.P., ED. DOCUMENTS STÉ-
PHANE MALLARMÉ. (VOL 4)
D.H. MC KEEN, 399(MLJ):DEC74-422
BARBIERI, F. CORPUS PALLADIANUM.
(VOL 2: LA BASILICA PALLADIANA.)
C.K. LEWIS, 127:WINTER73/74-176
M.N. ROSENFELD, 576:DEC73-335
F.J.B. WATSON, 39:MAY73-531
BARBIERI, F. ILLUMINISTI E NEOCLAS-
SICI A VICENZA.
J.S. ACKERMAN, 576:MAR73-73
BARBOUR, D. WHITE.*
D. BAILEY, 529(QQ):SPRING73-99
BARBUDO, A.S. - SEE UNDER SÁNCHEZ
BARBUDO, A.
DE LA BARCA, P.C. - SEE UNDER CAL-
DERÓN DE LA BARCA, P.
BARDON, H. PROPOSITIONS SUR CAT-
ULLE.*
R.E. GRIMM, 24:SUMMER74-171
BAREA, A. THE FORGING OF A REBEL.
G. BRENAN, 453:6MAR75-3

19

BAREISS, D. DIE VIERPERSONENKON-
STELLATION IM ROMAN.
 P. GOETSCH, 179(ES):FEB73-76
BARFIELD, L. NORTHERN ITALY BEFORE
ROME.
 D. RIDGWAY, 313:VOL63-282
 S.P. VINSON, 124:MAR73-365
BARFIELD, O. WHAT COLERIDGE
THOUGHT.*
 J.R. BARTH, 191(ELN):SEP73-61
 B. LUPINI, 175:AUTUMN72-111
 R.K. MEINERS, 141:SPRING73-174
 W.J.B. OWEN, 541(RES):MAY73-222
BARI NADVI, M.A. MAZHAB AUR SCIENCE.
 M. ABIDI, 273(IC):OCT73-367
BARILLI, R. LA LINEA SVEVO-PIRAN-
DELLO.
 N.L.F., 275(IQ):FALL-WINTER73(VOL
 17#66)-71
BARING-GOULD, S. & G. HITCHCOCK.
FOLK-SONGS OF THE WEST COUNTRY.
 F. HOWES, 415:JUN74-480
BARISH, J.A., ED. JONSON: "VOLPONE."
 G.K. HUNTER, 148:WINTER73-374
BARKAS, J. THE VEGETABLE PASSION.
 G. ANNAN, 617(TLS):30MAY75-595
BARKER, A.J. THE VAINGLORIOUS WAR,
1854-56.
 B.D. GOOCH, 637(VS):DEC73-217
BARKER, A.L. A SOURCE OF EMBARRASS-
MENT.*
 J. MELLORS, 364:JUN/JUL74-135
BARKER, C.M. & M.H. FOX. CLASSIFIED
FILES.
 L.J. HACKMAN, 14:APR73-237
BARKER, G. IN MEMORY OF DAVID
ARCHER.
 A. STEVENSON, 362:30OCT75-571
BARKER, M. GLADSTONE & RADICALISM.
 K.O. MORGAN, 617(TLS):22AUG75-941
BARKER, M.A-A-R., H.J. HAMDANI &
K.M.S. DIHLAVI. AN URDU NEWSPAPER
WORD COUNT.
 R.N. SRIVASTAVA, 353:1JUL73-64
BARKER, M.A-A-R. & A.K. MENGAL. A
COURSE IN BALUCHI.*
 W.A. COATES, 353:1JUL73-97
BARKER, M.A-A-R., S. RAHMAN & H.J.
HAMDANI. AN URDU NEWSPAPER READER.
KEY TO AN URDU NEWSPAPER READER.
 C.J. DASWANI, 353:1JUL73-58
BARKER, N. STANLEY MORISON.
 J. DREYFUS, 78(BC):SUMMER73-254
BARKER, N. - SEE MORISON, S.
BARKER, R. LOVE FORTY.
 M. LEVIN, 441:15JUN75-27
BARKER, R. ONE MAN'S JUNGLE.
 R. LEWIN, 362:11SEP75-349
 C. SYKES, 617(TLS):26SEP75-1076
BARKER, T., ED. THE LONG MARCH OF
EVERYMAN.
 T. ZELDIN, 362:19JUN75-819
BARKER, T.C. & M. ROBBINS. A HIS-
TORY OF LONDON TRANSPORT. (VOL 2)
 A. BRIGGS, 362:2JAN75-28
 J. NAUGHTON, 617(TLS):4JUL75-726
BARKUN, M. DISASTER & THE MILLEN-
NIUM.*
 639(VQR):AUTUMN74-CLII
BARLOUGH, J.E., ED. MINOR BRITISH
POETRY, 1680-1800.
 C. JOHNSON, 568(SCN):FALL74-49

BARLOW, E. FREDERICK LAW OLMSTED'S
NEW YORK.*
 I.R. STEWART, 576:DEC73-348
BARLOW, F. & OTHERS. LEOFRIC OF
EXETER.
 T.A. SHIPPEY, 677:VOL4-244
BARLOW, S.A. THE IMAGERY OF EURIP-
IDES.
 C.R. BEYE, 121(CJ):FEB/MAR74-255
 D. GARRISON, 124:OCT72-109
 G. RONNET, 555:VOL47FASC1-132
 E.W. WHITTLE, 123:MAR74-21
BARMANN, L.F. BARON FRIEDRICH VON
HÜGEL & THE MODERNIST CRISIS IN
ENGLAND.
 A. LOUIS-DAVID, 189(EA):APR-JUN73-
 242
 A. LOUIS-DAVID, 377:MAR74-53
 M. ROSE, 637(VS):MAR74-319
BARMEYER, E., ED. SCIENCE FICTION.
 W. BIESTERFELD, 182:VOL26#9-289
BARNABY, F. & R. HUISKEN. ARMS UN-
CONTROLLED.
 E. ROTHSCHILD, 453:2OCT75-7
BARNARD, C. & S. STANDER. THE UN-
WANTED.
 M. LEVIN, 441:16NOV75-76
BARNARD, D.S., JR. - SEE GOODMAN, N.
BARNARD, H. ADVANCED ENGLISH VOCAB-
ULARY. (WORKBOOK 1)
 D.L.F. NILSEN, 399(MLJ):NOV73-367
 C.K. WICKLOW, 351(LL):JUN74-167
BARNARD, J., ED. POPE: THE CRITICAL
HERITAGE.
 P. ROGERS, 566:AUTUMN73-32
BARNARD, J. VICTORIAN CERAMIC TILES.
 G.A. GODDEN, 135:FEB73-138
BARNARD, T.C. CROMWELLIAN IRELAND.
 J.C. BECKETT, 617(TLS):11JUL75-758
BARNDS, W.J. INDIA, PAKISTAN, & THE
GREAT POWERS.
 N.D. PALMER, 293(JAST):FEB73-358
BARNER, W. BAROCK-RHETORIK.*
 R. TAROT, 221(GQ):JAN73-103
BARNES, B. PARTHENOPHIL & PARTHENO-
PHE.* (V.A. DOYNO, ED)
 H. MORRIS, 551(RENQ):AUTUMN73-360
 M. RUDICK, 405(MP):NOV73-188
BARNES, B. SCIENTIFIC KNOWLEDGE &
SOCIOLOGICAL THEORY.
 J.R. RAVETZ, 617(TLS):6JUN75-631
BARNES, J. THE ONTOLOGICAL ARGU-
MENT.*
 M. PATERSON, 154:DEC73-733
 G. SLATER, 479(PHQ):JUL73-283
BARNES, J., M. SCHOFIELD & R. SORAB-
JI, EDS. ARTICLES ON ARISTOTLE.
(VOL 1)
 G.R. LLOYD, 617(TLS):12DEC75-1482
BARNES, J.J. AUTHORS, PUBLISHERS &
POLITICIANS.
 C.H. HOLMAN, 617(TLS):13JUN75-678
BARNES, K.C. A VAST BUNDLE OF
OPPORTUNITIES.
 J. WILSON, 617(TLS):24OCT75-1273
BARNES, T.D. TERTULLIAN.
 W.H.C. FREND, 123:MAR74-72
 D.E. GROH, 124:FEB74-227
 R.D. SIDER, 24:FALL74-302
BARNET, R.J. & R.E. MÜLLER. GLOBAL
REACH.
 N. FAITH, 617(TLS):19DEC75-1523
 P. GROSE, 441:4APR75-31
 [CONTINUED]

BARNET, R.J. & R.E. MÜLLER. GLOBAL
REACH. [CONTINUING]
  R.L. HEILBRONER, 453:20MAR75-6
  A. ROTSTEIN, 99:APR/MAY75-42
  A. SAMPSON, 441:26JAN75-2
BARNETT, A.D. UNCERTAIN PASSAGE.
  A. AUSTIN, 441:17MAY75-25
BARNETT, D. THE PERFORMANCE OF
MUSIC.
  V. WATTS, 255(HAB):WINTER73-54
BARNETT, F.J. & OTHERS, EDS. HIS-
TORY & STRUCTURE OF FRENCH.*
  J.R. ALLEN, 207(FR):MAY73-1273
  L. CHALON, 209(FM):APR73-200
BARNEY, W.L. THE SECESSIONIST IM-
PULSE.
  639(VQR):AUTUMN74-CXLIII
BARNICOAT, J. CONCISE HISTORY OF
POSTERS.
  R. LEVIN, 73:FALL73-43
BARNOUW, D. ENTZÜCKTE ANSCHAUUNG.
  H.B. JÜRSCHICK, 406:SUMMER74-196
BARNOUW, E. TUBE OF PLENTY.
  J. LEONARD, 441:30NOV75-6
BARNSLEY, J.H. THE SOCIAL REALITY
OF ETHICS.
  D. EMMET, 479(PHQ):OCT73-376
BARNSTONE, W., ED. SPANISH POETRY
FROM ITS BEGINNINGS THROUGH THE
NINETEENTH CENTURY.
  F. PIERCE, 86(BHS):APR73-166
BARNSTONE, W., WITH KO CHING-PO -
SEE MAO TSE-TUNG
BAROJA, J.C. - SEE UNDER CARO
BAROJA, J.
BARON, F. - SEE HOEST, S.
BARON, M. LETTERS FOR THE NEW ENG-
LAND DEAD.*
  R. DICKINSON-BROWN, 598(SOR):
  AUTUMN75-953
  R. LATTIMORE, 249(HUDR):AUTUMN74-
  463
  R.B. SHAW, 491:SEP75-352
BARON, S.W. & OTHERS. ECONOMIC HIS-
TORY OF THE JEWS. (N. GROSS, ED)
  H. SCHWARTZ, 441:10DEC75-51
BARON, W. SICKERT.
  C. HARRISON, 592:NOV73-203
  R. PICKVANCE, 39:DEC73-519
  P. SKIPWITH, 135:SEP73-67
BAROOSHIAN, V.D. RUSSIAN CUBO-
FUTURISM 1910-1930.
  J.E. BOWLT, 617(TLS):16MAY75-540
BARR, A.H., JR. CUBISM & ABSTRACT
ART. PICASSO. MATISSE.
  C. GREEN, 617(TLS):21FEB75-186
BARR, A.P. VICTORIAN STAGE PULPI-
TEER.
  639(VQR):SUMMER74-CIV
BARR, D. SPACE RELATIONS.
  G. JONAS, 441:4MAY75-51
BARRACLOUGH, G. - SEE GRAUS, F. &
OTHERS
BARRATT, G. THE REBEL ON THE BRIDGE.
  L. SCHAPIRO, 617(TLS):26DEC75-1539
BARRATT, G.R.V. IVAN KOZLOV.
  R.M. DAVISON, 402(MLR):OCT74-950
  A. GLASSE, 574(SEEJ):FALL73-332
  J.D. GOODLIFFE, 104:FALL73-423
BARRATT, G.R.V., ED. VOICES IN
EXILE.
  L. SCHAPIRO, 617(TLS):26DEC75-1539

BARRELL, J. THE IDEA OF LANDSCAPE &
THE SENSE OF PLACE 1730-1840.*
  M.R. BROWNELL, 481(PQ):JUL73-425
  D.V.E., 191(ELN):SEP73(SUPP)-42
  B. LUPINI, 175:AUTUMN72-111
  J.E. RAPF, 591(SIR):WINTER74-79
  J. WAINWRIGHT, 565:VOL14#3-42
  J.R. WATSON, 148:SUMMER73-188
  J.R. WATSON, 148:AUTUMN73-283
BARRELL, J. & J. BULL, EDS. THE
PENGUIN BOOK OF ENGLISH PASTORAL
VERSE.
  S. HEANEY, 617(TLS):11JUL75-750
BARRENO, M.I., M.T. HORTA & M. VELHO
DA COSTA. THE THREE MARIAS. (BRIT-
ISH TITLE: NEW PORTUGUESE LETTERS.)
  N. ASCHERSON, 453:20MAR75-11
  A. DE FIGUEIREDO, 362:20CT75-451
  J. KRAMER, 441:2FEB75-1
  H.M. MACEDO, 617(TLS):12DEC75-1484
  442(NY):24FEB75-142
BARRERA VIDAL, A. PARFAIT SIMPLE ET
PARFAIT COMPOSÉ EN CASTILLAN MOD-
ERNE.
  H. MEIER, 72:BAND211HEFT3/6-463
BARRÈRE, J-B. L'IDÉE DE GOÛT DE
PASCAL À VALÉRY.*
  H. GODIN, 208(FS):JUL74-359
BARRETT, D. EARLY COLA ARCHITECTURE
& SCULPTURE.
  J.C. HARLE, 617(TLS):24JAN75-92
BARRETT, E.B. & B.R. HAYDON. INVIS-
IBLE FRIENDS. (W.B. POPE, ED)
  R.W. GLADISH, 85:SPRING73-47
BARRETT-AYRES, R. JOSEPH HAYDN &
THE STRING QUARTET.
  M. DONAT, 617(TLS):25JUL75-854
BARROLL, J.L. - SEE SHAKESPEARE, W.
BARRÓN, C.G. - SEE UNDER GARCÍA BAR-
RÓN, C.
BARRON, F. ARTISTS IN THE MAKING.
  E.L. KAMARCK, 59(ASOC):SUMMER-FALL
  74-320
BARROW, L.L. NEGATION IN BAROJA.
  G. FLYNN, 238:SEP73-734
BARROW, L.L. & R.M. HAMMOND. MAC-
ARIO.
  J.S. BAILEY, 399(MLJ):APR74-215
BARRUTIA, R. LANGUAGE LEARNING &
MACHINE TEACHING.
  W.J. CAMERON & C.P. RICHARDSON,
  238:MAY73-521
BARRY, B. THE LIBERAL THEORY OF
JUSTICE.*
  M.T. DALGARNO, 518:MAY74-18
BARRY, E. ROBERT FROST.
  R. FOSTER, 432(NEQ):SEP74-469
BARRY, E. - SEE FROST, R.
BARRY, G. THE HISTORY OF THE ORKNEY
ISLANDS.
  J.A. SMITH, 617(TLS):22AUG75-937
BARRY, J.B. THE MICHAELMAS GIRLS.
  S. KENNEDY, 617(TLS):11JUL75-784
BARRY, J.G. DRAMATIC STRUCTURE.*
  S.F.R., 131(CL):WINTER73-79
BARRY, M. DETROIT MASSACRE.
  N. CALLENDAR, 441:25MAY75-16
BARRY, P. STATES OF GRACE. (B.
GILL, ED)
  F. WYNDHAM, 617(TLS):19DEC75-1507
BARSAM, R.M. NONFICTION FILM.
  J. REEVE, 255:FALL73-343
BARSON, A.T. A WAY OF SEEING.*
  J.R. PARISH, 200:FEB73-115

DU BARTAS, G.S. OEUVRES: LA JUDIT.*
(A. BAÏCHE, ED)
  A.E. CREORE, 207(FR):DEC72-398
BARTELINK, G.J.M., L.J. ENGELS &
A.A.R. BASTIAENSEN. GRAECITAS ET
LATINITAS CHRISTIANORUM PRIMAEVA.
(SUPP 3)
  R.E. DENGLER, 124:SEP-OCT73-44
  C.W. MACLEOD, 123:MAR74-143
BARTFELD, F. SAINTE-BEUVE ET ALFRED
DE VIGNY.
  E.M. PHILLIPS, 208(FS):JAN74-89
BARTH, J.R., ED. RELIGIOUS PERSPEC-
TIVES IN FAULKNER'S FICTION.*
  J. GOLD, 255:FALL73-335
BARTHELL, E.E., JR. GODS & GOD-
DESSES OF ANCIENT GREECE.
  K. ALDRICH, 124:FEB73-315
  F.E. BRENK, 122:JAN74-66
BARTHELME, D. THE DEAD FATHER.
  T.R. EDWARDS, 453:11DEC75-54
  C. LEHMANN-HAUPT, 441:3NOV75-33
  R. SHATTUCK, 441:9NOV75-1
  R. TODD, 61:DEC75-112
  442(NY):24NOV75-194
BARTHELME, D. SADNESS.*
  J. KLINKOWITZ, 114(CHIR):VOL25#1-
  172
BARTHES, R. BARTHES PAR LUI-MÊME.
  A. LAVERS, 617(TLS):1AUG75-878
BARTHES, R. MYTHOLOGIES.* (A.
LAVERS, ED & TRANS)
  A.A. BERGER, 186(ETC.):JUN73-216
  E.J. SHARPE, 148:WINTER73-382
  295:FEB74-466
BARTHES, R. THE PLEASURE OF THE
TEXT. (FRENCH TITLE: LE PLAISIR
DU TEXTE.)
  P. BROOKS, 441:14SEP75-38
  J.A. MOREAU, 98:JUL73-583
  D. NEWTON-DE MOLINA, 402(MLR):
  APR74-362
  J. UPDIKE, 442(NY):24NOV75-189
BARTHES, R. S/Z.*
  P. BROOKS, 441:14SEP75-38
  A. LAVERS, 617(TLS):1AUG75-878
  D. MAY, 362:20MAR75-379
  A.R. PUGH, 268:JUL75-173
  J. UPDIKE, 442(NY):24NOV75-189
BÄRTHLEIN, K. DIE TRANSZENDENTAL-
IENLEHRE DER ALTEN ONTOLOGIE.
(PT 1)
  P. SELIGMAN, 154:SEP73-527
  G. TONELLI, 319:OCT75-517
BARTHOLOMEUSZ, D. MACBETH & THE
PLAYERS.
  J.G. BARRY, 570(SQ):SPRING73-239
  A.C. SPRAGUE, 179(ES):APR72-158
BARTLETT, R.A. THE NEW COUNTRY.*
  P.A.M. TAYLOR, 617(TLS):4JUL75-725
BARTLEY, D.E. SOVIET APPROACHES TO
BILINGUAL EDUCATION. (R.C. LUGTON,
ED)
  P.A. DAVIS, 574(SEEJ):SUMMER72-250
BARTLEY, R.H. & S.L. WAGNER. LATIN
AMERICA IN BASIC HISTORICAL COLLEC-
TIONS.
  W.R. LUX, 14:APR73-247
BARTLEY, W.W. 3D. WITTGENSTEIN.*
  R.L. GOODSTEIN, 483:OCT73-403
BARTRAM, G. A JOB ABROAD.
  A. BROYARD, 441:11MAR75-39
  N. CALLENDAR, 441:15JUN75-24

BARTSOS, I.A. ATHENAIKAI KLEROU-
CHIAI.
  M.B. WALLACE, 487:AUTUMN73-310
BARZUN, J. CLIO & THE DOCTORS.*
  E. KEDOURIE, 617(TLS):7MAR75-238
BARZUN, J. THE USE & ABUSE OF ART.*
  J. FISHER, 290(JAAC):WINTER74-239
BASCH, F. RELATIVE CREATURES.*
  P. MC CALLUM, 99:NOV75-39
BASCOM, W. AFRICAN ART IN CULTURAL
PERSPECTIVE.
  G.N. PRESTON, 2:SUMMER74-89
BASILIKOS, B. TO IMEROLOGIO TOU Z.
  617(TLS):14NOV75-1368
"BASIS." (VOL 1) (R. GRIMM & J.
HERMAND, EDS)
  H. LEHNERT, 221(GQ):SEP73-163
  S.P. SCHER, 406:SUMMER74-203
"BASIS." (VOLS 2&3) (R. GRIMM & J.
HERMAND, EDS)
  S.P. SCHER, 406:SUMMER74-203
BASKIN, W., ED. CLASSICS IN CHINESE
PHILOSOPHY.
  W.G., 543:MAR73-525
BASS, E. I'M NOT YOUR LAUGHING
DAUGHTER.
  H. CARRUTH, 249(HUDR):SUMMER74-311
  M. MADIGAN, 385(MQR):SPRING75-220
BASS, T.J. THE GODWHALE.
  T.A. SHIPPEY, 617(TLS):23MAY75-554
BASSAN, F. & S. CHEVALLEY. ALEXAN-
DRE DUMAS PÈRE ET LA COMÉDIE-
FRANÇAISE.
  M. LEHTONEN, 439(NM):1973/3-544
BASSANI, G. BEHIND THE DOOR.* THE
GARDEN OF THE FINZI-CONTINIS.
  S.G. ESKIN, 390:JUN-JUL73-71
BASSANI, G. THE SMELL OF HAY.
  H. MITGANG, 441:19OCT75-39
BASSETT, J. WILLIAM FAULKNER.
  N. POLK, 255:FALL73-338
BASSETT, J., ED. WILLIAM FAULKNER:
THE CRITICAL HERITAGE.
  H. BEAVER, 617(TLS):12DEC75-1479
BASSI, E. CORPUS PALLADIANUM.
(VOL 6: IL CONVENTO DELLA CARITÀ.)
  M.N. ROSENFELD, 576:DEC73-335
BASTIANELLI, E.B. LA FRANCIA IN
AZORÍN.
  S. BACARISSE, 86(BHS):OCT73-407
BASTID, M. ASPECTS DE LA REFORME
DE L'ENSEIGNEMENT EN CHINE AU
DEBUT DU XXE SIÈCLE.
  V.D. MEDLIN, 293(JAST):NOV72-145
BASTID, M., M.C. BERGÈRE & J. CHES-
NEAUX. HISTOIRE DE LA CHINE. (VOL
2)
  E. LAFFEY, 293(JAST):FEB73-318
BASTIDE, G. ESSAI D'ÉTHIQUE FONDA-
MENTALE.*
  M. LASSÈGUE, 542:OCT-DEC73-481
BASTIDE, R. AS RELIGIÕES AFRICANAS
NO BRASIL.
  J.P. RENSHAW, 263:JUL-SEP74-293
BASTIN, T., ED. QUANTUM THEORY &
BEYOND.*
  J. BUB, 84:MAR73-78
BASTOS, A.R. - SEE UNDER ROA BASTOS,
A.
BATAILLE, M. LE CHAT SAUVAGE.
  N.L. GOODRICH, 207(FR):DEC72-430
BATCHELOR, J. BREATHLESS HUSH.
  S. CLAPP, 617(TLS):3JAN75-5

BATCHELOR, J. MERVYN PEAKE.
H. BROGAN, 617(TLS):4APR75-354
BATCHELOR, R.E. UNAMUNO NOVELIST.
J. LÓPEZ-MORILLAS, 402(MLR):JUL74-
682
BATE, S. CHRISTMAS SPIRIT.
D.M. DAY, 157:AUTUMN73-86
BATE, S. RUMOUR.
D.M. DAY, 157:WINTER73-89
BATE, W.J. & A.B. STRAUSS - SEE
JOHNSON, S.
BATES, A.J. SEEDS BENEATH THE SNOW.
P. ADAMS, 61:FEB75-122
BATES, D.V. A CITIZEN'S GUIDE TO
AIR POLLUTION.
P.A. LARKIN, 529(QQ):SUMMER73-286
BATES, G.E. ARCHAEOLOGICAL EXPLOR-
ATION OF SARDIS: BYZANTINE COINS.
J.F. HEALY, 123:NOV74-312
J. SCARBOROUGH, 121(CJ):FEB/MAR74-
273
BATES, R. NORTHROP FRYE.
C. THOMAS, 102(CANL):SPRING73-103
BATESON, F.W. THE SCHOLAR-CRITIC.*
H. SERVOTTE, 179(ES):JUN73-305
R. SKELTON, 376:JAN73-162
BATESON, M.C. STRUCTURAL CONTINUITY
IN POETRY.*
W.O. HENDRICKS, 297(JL):FEB73-148
BATLEY, E.M. A PREFACE TO "THE
MAGIC FLUTE."
R. CRAFT, 453:27NOV75-16
BATLLE, C.M. DIE "ADHORTATIONES
SANCTORUM PATRUM" ("VERBA SENIOR-
UM") IM LATEINISCHEN MITTELALTER.
A. KEMMER, 182:VOL26#7/8-201
BATLLORI, M. CATALUNYA A L'ÉPOCA
MODERNA.
R.B. TATE, 86(BHS):JUL73-315
BATTENHOUSE, R.W. SHAKESPEAREAN
TRAGEDY.*
R.E. LYNCH, 125:JUN74-378
H. OPPEL, 430(NS):AUG73-451
BATTESTIN, M.C. THE PROVIDENCE OF
WIT.
P. FUSSELL, 617(TLS):7FEB75-134
BATTISCOMBE, G. SHAFTESBURY.*
J. CLIVE, 231:DEC75-96
442(NY):7APR75-138
"BATTLE OF STYLES."
617(TLS):19SEP75-1048
BATTS, M.S. GOTTFRIED VON STRASS-
BURG.*
H. BEKKER, 221(GQ):MAR73-250
R.G. KUNZER, 406:SUMMER74-188
O. SAYCE, 220(GL&L):OCT73-77
BATTS, M.S. - SEE "DAS NIBELUNGEN-
LIED"
BAUCHHENSS-THÜRIEDL, C. DER MYTHOS
VON TELEPHOS IN DER ANTIKEN BILD-
KUNST.
G.B. WAYWELL, 123:NOV74-310
BAUDELAIRE, C. ECRITS SUR L'ART.
(Y. FLORENNE, ED)
P. GUERRE, 98:JAN73-67
BAUDELAIRE, C. SALON DE 1846. (D.
KELLEY, ED)
A. BROOKNER, 617(TLS):7MAR75-248
BAUDLER, G. "IM WORTE SEHEN."
E.F. RITTER, 481(PQ):JUL73-520

BAUDOUIN DE COURTENAY, J. A BAU-
DOUIN DE COURTENAY ANTHOLOGY. (E.
STANKIEWICZ, ED & TRANS)
G.M. ERAMIAN, 104:FALL73-416
R.A. ROTHSTEIN, 574(SEEJ):WINTER
72-495
BAUDRILLARD, J. LA SOCIÉTÉ DE CON-
SOMMATION.
B.A. LENSKI, 207(FR):OCT72-194
BAUER, G. CLAUSTRUM ANIMAE. (VOL 1)
R. RUDOLF, 182:VOL26#10-326
BAUER, G. STUDIEN ZUM SYSTEM UND
GEBRAUCH DER "TEMPORA" IN DER
SPRACHE CHAUCERS UND GOWERS.*
K.C. PHILLIPPS, 179(ES):OCT72-456
BAUER, MRS. G., ED. TRADITIONAL
INDIAN RECIPES.
J.M. COLE, 99:DEC75/JAN76-37
BAUER, G.H. SARTRE & THE ARTIST.*
T.R.F., 543:SEP72-152
BAUER, J. KAFKA & PRAGUE.*
295:FEB74-688
BAUER, P.T. DISSENT ON DEVELOPMENT.
P.C. ROBERTS, 396(MODA):FALL74-430
BAUER, W. ALL CHANGE; PARTY FOR
SIX; MAGIC AFTERNOON.
A. RENDLE, 157:WINTER73-87
BAUER, W.A. & O.E. DEUTSCH, EDS.
MOZART: BRIEFE UND AUFZEICHNUNGEN.
A.H. KING, 182:VOL26#20-745
BAUGHMAN, J.P. THE MALLORYS OF
MYSTIC.
E.S. DODGE, 432(NEQ):MAR73-138
BAUM, D.J. THE BANKS OF CANADA IN
THE COMMONWEALTH CARIBBEAN.
G.K. HELLEINER, 99:APR/MAY75-20
BAUM, D.J. THE FINAL PLATEAU.
K. BRYDEN, 99:FEB75-35
BAUM, D.L. TRADITIONALISM IN THE
WORKS OF FRANCISCO DE QUEVEDO Y
VILLEGAS.
F.A. DE ARMAS, 241:MAY73-69
M. DURÁN, 399(MLJ):MAR73-143
H. ETTINGHAUSEN, 86(BHS):JAN73-86
A.E. WILTROUT, 238:MAY73-500
BAUMAN, R. & J. SHERZER, EDS. EX-
PLORATIONS IN THE ETHNOGRAPHY OF
SPEAKING.
R.B. LE PAGE, 617(TLS):23MAY75-568
BAUMGART, W. DER FRIEDE VON PARIS
1856.*
E. ANDERSON, 550(RUSR):OCT73-449
BAUSANI, A. THE PERSIANS.
R.A. HADLEY, 124:MAR73-377
BAUTIER, R-H. & M. GILLES - SEE
DE SENS, O.
BAWDEN, N. GEORGE BENEATH A PAPER
MOON.*
M. LEVIN, 441:9FEB75-12
442(NY):24FEB75-140
BAXANDALL, L., ED. RADICAL PERSPEC-
TIVES IN THE ARTS.*
R.J. LONGHURST, 89(BJA):AUTUMN73-
417
BAXANDALL, M. GIOTTO & THE ORATORS.*
M.P. GILMORE, 54:MAR73-148
W. KEMP, 52:BAND8HEFT1-92
A.R. TURNER, 551(RENQ):AUTUMN73-
335
BAXANDALL, M. PAINTING & EXPERIENCE
IN FIFTEENTH-CENTURY ITALY.*
B. GOLDMAN, 141:WINTER74-88
C. GOULD, 39:DEC73-521
[CONTINUED]

23

BAXANDALL, M. PAINTING & EXPERIENCE
IN FIFTEENTH-CENTURY ITALY.* [CON-
TINUING]
  G. HERMERÉN, 290(JAAC):FALL73-130
  676(YR):WINTER74-XXII
BAXTER, T.W. & E.E. BURKE. GUIDE TO
THE HISTORICAL MANUSCRIPTS IN THE
NATIONAL ARCHIVES OF RHODESIA.*
  E.D. ANTHONY, 14:JAN73-78
BAYES, R.H. THE CASKETMAKER.*
  A.A. JOHNSON, 134(CP):SPRING73-91
BAYET, J. CROYANCES ET RITES DANS
LA ROME ANTIQUE.*
  J. ANDRÉ, 555:VOL47FASC1-180
  J. POLLARD, 313:VOL63-271
BAYLEN, J.O. & A. CONWAY - SEE REID,
D.A.
BAYLEY, J. PUSHKIN.*
  H. GIFFORD, 184(EIC):JUL72-313
BAYLEY, P. EDMUND SPENSER.*
  R.A. FOAKES, 175:AUTUMN72-107
BAYLIS, T.A. THE TECHNICAL INTELLI-
GENTSIA & THE EAST GERMAN ELITE.
  L. HOLMES, 617(TLS):24OCT75-1266
BAZIN, H. JOUR [SUIVI DE] A LA
POURSUITE D'IRIS.
  W. ALBERT, 207(FR):APR73-1039
BAZIN, N.T. VIRGINIA WOOLF & THE
ANDROGYNOUS VISION.*
  L.D. BLOOM, 454:SPRING74-255
  A. FLEISHMAN, 594:WINTER73-559
  J. GUIGUET, 189(EA):JUL-SEP73-338
BAZYLOW, L. DZIEJE ROSJI, 1801-
1917.
  W. SUKIENNICKI, 550(RUSR):JUL73-
  329
BAZYLOW, L. HISTORIA ROSJI.
  L. HACZYŃSKI, 104:SPRING74-156
BAZYLOW, L. OSTATNIE LATA ROSJI
CARSKIEJ.*
  M.K. DZIEWANOWSKI, 550(RUSR):OCT
  73-450
BAZYLOW, L. SPOŁECZEŃSTWO ROSYJSKIE
W PIERWSZEJ POŁOWIE XIX WIEKU.
  M. SZEFTEL, 575(SEER):OCT74-632
BEACH, V.W. CHARLES X OF FRANCE.
  L.C. JENNINGS, 207(FR):MAY73-1270
BEALE, T.W. AN ORIENTAL BIOGRAPHI-
CAL DICTIONARY. (REV BY H.G.
KEENE)
  293(JAST):NOV72-226
BEALS, R.L. THE PEASANT MARKETING
SYSTEM OF OAXACA, MEXICO.
  L. WHITEHEAD, 617(TLS):12DEC75-
  1497
BEAME, E.M. & L.G. SBROCCHI - SEE
ARIOSTO, L.
BEAN, G.E. TURKEY BEYOND THE MAEAN-
DER.
  R.H. DYSON, JR., 124:SEP72-56
BEARD, J. AMERICAN COOKERY.
  S. CAMPBELL, 617(TLS):20JUN75-703
BEARD, P., ED. LONGING FOR DARK-
NESS.
  N. ASCHERSON, 453:18SEP75-13
  E. BREDSDORFF, 617(TLS):15AUG75-
  912
  E. WEEKS, 61:JUL75-80
BEARDSLEY, M.C. THE POSSIBILITY OF
CRITICISM.*
  K.W. BRITTON, 447(N&Q):FEB73-78
  W.J. CLINE, 399(MLJ):NOV74-371
  W. MARTIN, 131(CL):WINTER73-81

BEARDSLEY, T.S., JR. HISPANO-CLASS-
ICAL TRANSLATIONS PRINTED BETWEEN
1482 & 1699.
  E.M. WILSON, 240(HR):WINTER73-98
BEARDSMORE, R.W. ART & MORALITY.*
  M.R. HAIGHT, 479(PHQ):APR73-187
BEASLEY, J.C. A CHECK LIST OF PROSE
FICTION PUBLISHED IN ENGLAND 1740-
1749.
  P.J. KORSHIN, 481(PQ):JUL73-324
BEASLEY, W.G. THE MEIJI RESTORATION.
  R. STORRY, 285(JAPQ):OCT-DEC73-457
BEATON, C. & G. BUCKLAND. THE MAGIC
IMAGE.
  H. KRAMER, 441:7DEC75-5
BEAUJOUR, E.K. THE INVISIBLE LAND.*
  P.M. AUSTIN, 104:FALL73-431
BEAULIEU, M. SYLVIE STONE.
  R. HATHORN, 296:VOL3#4-92
BEAUMONT, E.M., J.M. COCKING & J.
CRUICKSHANK, EDS. ORDER & ADVEN-
TURE IN POST-ROMANTIC POETRY.
  L. WELCH, 399(MLJ):SEP-OCT74-277
BEAUNE, J-C. LA TECHNOLOGIE.
  P. GERMAIN, 154:JUN73-383
BEAURLINE, L.A. - SEE SUCKLING, J.
BEAZLEY, J.D. PARALIPOMENA.*
  J. FREL, 124:APR-MAY74-398
BEBBINGTON, G. LONDON STREET NAMES.
  E.C. SMITH, 424:JUN73-118
BEBEY, F. AFRICAN MUSIC.
  J. BLACKING, 617(TLS):15AUG75-917
  G. GIDDINS, 441:14SEP75-16
BECATTI, G. SCAVI DI OSTIA, EDIFI-
CIO CON "OPUS SECTILE" FUORI PORTA
MAXIMA.
  H. STERN, 54:JUN73-285
BECCARI, A. LE RIME DI MAESTRO AN-
TONIO DA FERRARA (ANTONIO BECCARI).
(L. BELLUCCI, ED)
  D.D., 275(IQ):SUMMER73-105
  M.M., 228(GSLI):VOL150FASC470/471-
  471
BECCO, H.J. BIBLIOGRAFÍA DE BIBLIO-
GRAFÍAS LITERARIAS ARGENTINAS.
  L.S. THOMPSON, 263:APR-JUN74-167
BECH, G. BEITRÄGE ZUR GENETISCHEN
IDG. VERBALMORPHOLOGIE.
  F. BADER, 555:VOL47FASC1-113
BECHER, U. WILLIAM'S EX-CASINO.
  P. PROCHNIK, 617(TLS):3OCT75-1152
BECHERT, H. - SEE GEIGER, W.
BECHERT, H. & M. BIDOLI, COMPS.
SINGHALESISCHE HANDSCHRIFTEN.
(PT 1)
  J. FILLIOZAT, 182:VOL26#13/14-451
BECHERT, J. & OTHERS. EINFÜHRUNG IN
DIE GENERATIVE TRANSFORMATIONSGRAM-
MATIK.*
  H.W. FELTKAMP, 361:SEP73-135
  G.F. MEIER, 682(ZPSK):BAND26HEFT
  1/2-172
BECK, E.T. KAFKA & THE YIDDISH
THEATRE.*
  M. SACHAROFF, 295:FEB74-689
BECK, H. FOLKLORE & THE SEA.
  639(VQR):SUMMER74-CVI
BECK, H.G. GESCHICHTE DER BYZANTIN-
ISCHEN VOLKSLITERATUR.
  D.M. NICOL, 123:NOV74-223
BECK, J.H. - SEE DI JACOPO, M.
BECK, R.T. THE CUTTING EDGE.
  C. WELLS, 617(TLS):14MAR75-283

24

BECKER, A. "TÊTE D'OR" (1889) ET
"LA VILLE" (1890-1891).*
  W.H. MATHESON, 207(FR):FEB73-626
BECKER, B. & M. VALKHOFF - SEE CAS-
TELLION, S.
BECKER, C.L. "WHAT IS THE GOOD OF
HISTORY?" (M. KAMMEN, ED)
  B. CLAYTON, 579(SAQ):AUTUMN74-572
  A. EZERGAILIS, 676(YR):WINTER74-
  296
  R.H. ROBINSON, 432(NEQ):DEC74-610
  639(VQR):WINTER74-XXIV
BECKER, E. ESCAPE FROM EVIL.
  A. BROYARD, 441:7OCT75-39
  R.J. LIFTON, 441:14DEC75-3
BECKER, H. DIE RESPONSORIEN DES
KARTÄUSERBREVIERS.
  R. RUDOLF, 182:VOL26#11/12-397
BECKER, J. AFTER GENEVA.
  S. CLAPP, 617(TLS):1AUG75-865
  J. MELLORS, 362:18SEP75-386
BECKER, L.F. LOUIS ARAGON.
  Y. GINDINE, 546(RR):MAR74-145
  A.H. GREET, 207(FR):APR73-1025
BECKER, P. DAS MONASTISCHE REFORM-
PROGRAMM DES JOHANNES RODE, ABTES
VON ST. MATTHIAS IN TRIER.
  H. RÜTHING, 182:VOL26#17/18-578
BECKER, S. THE CHINESE BANDIT.
  T. BUCKLEY, 441:21DEC75-18
  C. LEHMANN-HAUPT, 441:13NOV75-45
BECKERMAN, B. DYNAMICS OF DRAMA.
  P. GOETSCH, 430(NS):FEB73-117
BECKERMAN, W. TWO CHEERS FOR THE
AFFLUENT SOCIETY.
  E. ROTHSCHILD, 453:26JUN75-31
BECKETT, J.C. CONFRONTATIONS.
  C. FITZ GIBBON, 159(DM):SUMMER73-
  101
BECKETT, L. WALLACE STEVENS.*
  R. GARFITT, 364:OCT/NOV74-138
BECKETT, R.B. - SEE CONSTABLE, J.
BECKETT, S. FIRST LOVE.* (FRENCH
TITLE: PREMIER AMOUR.)
  H. MURPHY, 159(DM):AUTUMN/WINTER
  73/74-118
BECKETT, S. THE LOST ONES.
  L. GRAVER, 473(PR):4/1974-622
BECKETT, S. MERCIER & CAMIER.*
  P. ADAMS, 61:MAY75-104
  D. BAIR, 441:9MAR75-19
  J. UPDIKE, 442(NY):1SEP75-62
BECKFORD, W. DREAMS, WAKING
THOUGHTS & INCIDENTS.* (R.J.
GEMMETT, ED)
  A. PARREAUX, 189(EA):APR-JUN73-232
BECKFORD, W. THE HISTORY OF THE
CALIPH VATHEK INCLUDING THE EPI-
SODES OF VATHEK. (L. CARTER, ED)
  T.J. MAYNARD, 648:OCT73-61
BECKFORD, W. VATHEK.
  D.W. FRESE, 481(PQ):JUL73-461
BECKMAN, G.M. & O. GENJI. THE JAP-
ANESE COMMUNIST PARTY, 1922-1945.
  B.H. HAZARD, 318(JAOS):JUL-SEP73-
  406
BECKSON, K., ED. OSCAR WILDE: THE
CRITICAL HERITAGE.*
  J.J. MC AULEY, 376:OCT73-145
BECKWITH, C.E., ED. TWENTIETH CEN-
TURY INTERPRETATIONS OF "A TALE OF
TWO CITIES."
  G. WOODCOCK, 155:JAN73-53

BECKWITH, J. IVORY CARVINGS IN
EARLY MEDIEVAL ENGLAND.
  G. ZARNECKI, 39:JUN73-623
BEDBROOK, G.S. KEYBOARD MUSIC FROM
THE MIDDLE AGES TO THE BEGINNINGS
OF THE BAROQUE.
  P. WILLIAMS, 415:FEB74-135
BEDELL, G.C. KIERKEGAARD & FAULK-
NER.
  L.B. CEBIK, 219(GAR):SUMMER73-286
  R. GRIMSLEY, 149:DEC74-353
BEDFORD, S. ALDOUS HUXLEY.* (VOL 2)
  G. EWART, 364:DEC74/JAN75-134
BEDFORD, S. ALDOUS HUXLEY.* (1-VOL
ED)
  W. ABRAHAMS, 61:JAN75-84
  R.S. BAKER, 659:AUTUMN75-492
  R. CRAFT, 453:23JAN75-9
  J. RICHARDSON, 231:APR75-105
  G. STEINER, 442(NY):17FEB75-103
BEDIENT, C. ARCHITECTS OF THE
SELF.*
  R. BEARDS, 295:FEB74-445
  M.S. HELFAND, 454:FALL73-88
BEDIENT, C. EIGHT CONTEMPORARY
POETS.*
  J. NAREMORE, 659:SUMMER75-381
BEDINGER, M. INDIAN SILVER.
  F.J. DOCKSTADER, 139:DEC73-15
BEEKES, R.S.P. THE DEVELOPMENT OF
THE PROTO-INDO-EUROPEAN LARYNGEALS
IN GREEK.*
  F.O. LINDEMAN, 260(IF):BAND77HEFT
  2/3-307
BEEMAN, R.R. PATRICK HENRY.
  G.F. SCHEER, 441:6APR75-3
BEER, G. MEREDITH.*
  B.F. FISHER 4TH, 594:SUMMER73-258
  M. HARRIS, 72:BAND211HEFT1/3-128
  R. NOLL-WIEMANN, 430(NS):SEP73-510
BEER, J., ED. COLERIDGE'S VARIETY.
  G. HOUGH, 617(TLS):11JUL75-756
BEER, P. AN INTRODUCTION TO THE
METAPHYSICAL POETS.*
  D.C. JUDKINS, 568(SCN):WINTER74-74
  H. SERGEANT, 175:SPRING73-28
BEER, P. READER, I MARRIED HIM.*
  C-G. HEILBRUN, 441:11MAY75-40
BEERBOHM, M. ZULEIKA DOBSON.
  A. BELL, 617(TLS):29AUG75-962
BEERBOHM, M. & W. ROTHENSTEIN. MAX
& WILL. (M.M. LAGO & K. BECKSON,
EDS)
  A. BELL, 617(TLS):29AUG75-962
BEESTON, A.F.L. THE ARABIC LANGUAGE
TODAY.* WRITTEN ARABIC.
  C-G. KILLEAN, 350:MAR74-186
BEEVOR, A. THE VIOLENT BRINK.
  R. FOSTER, 617(TLS):31OCT75-1285
BÉGUE, C. "LA CHANSON DU MAL-AIMÉ"
D'APOLLINAIRE.
  C. TOURNADRE, 535(RHL):SEP-OCT73-
  923
BEHLMER, R. - SEE SELZNICK, D.O.
BEHLMER, R. & T. THOMAS. HOLLYWOOD'S
HOLLYWOOD.
  R. SCHICKEL, 441:7DEC75-88
BEHN, W. - SEE GOLDZIHER, I.
BEHNSTEDT, P. VIENS-TU? EST-CE QUE
TU VIENS? TU VIENS?
  A. GRIEVE, 72:BAND211HEFT3/6-444
BEHREND, D. ATTISCHE PACHTURKUNDEN.
  R.S. STROUD, 24:SPRING74-84
BEHRMAN, S.N. DUVEEN.*
  T. LASK, 55:NOV72-17

BEIER, U., ED. WORDS OF PARADISE.
  V. YOUNG, 249(HUDR):WINTER74/75-
  597
BEIERWALTES, W. PLATONISMUS UND
  IDEALISMUS.
  H. FUHRMANS, 182:VOL26#1/2-12
BEIK, P.H., ED. THE FRENCH REVOLU-
  TION.
  N. HAMPSON, 208(FS):APR74-203
BEINHOFF, H. & K-H. FÄRBER, EDS.
  CHANTONS GAIEMENT.
  H. PULS, 430(NS):MAR73-174
BEISECKER, T.D. & D.W. PARSON, EDS.
  THE PROCESS OF SOCIAL INFLUENCE.
  J.L. JELLICORSE, 583:WINTER73-202
"BEITRÄGE ZUR OBERDEUTSCHEN DIALEK-
  TOLOGIE."
  G.F. MEIER, 682(ZPSK):BAND26HEFT
  3/4-413
BEITTEL, K.R. ALTERNATIVES FOR ART
  EDUCATION RESEARCH.
  D.W. ECKER, 290(JAAC):SPRING74-436
BEJA, M. EPIPHANY IN THE MODERN
  NOVEL.*
  D. HAYMAN, 141:FALL72-401
  S. SPENCER, 659:SPRING75-249
  F.L. WALZI, 295:FEB74-388
  E. WEBB, 648:JUN73-61
BEJA, M., ED. JAMES JOYCE, "DUBLIN-
  ERS" & "A PORTRAIT OF THE ARTIST
  AS A YOUNG MAN."
  J. VAN VOORHIS, 329(JJQ):SPRING75-
  339
BEK, A. NOVOE NAZNACHENIE.
  D. POSPIELOVSKY, 550(RUSR):JAN73-
  96
BEKKER, H. THE NIBELUNGENLIED.*
  W.H. JACKSON, 402(MLR):OCT74-912
  G.F. JONES, 400(MLN):APR73-620
BEKKERS, J.A.F. - SEE MORRIS, J.
BELDEN, R. THE LIMIT.*
  E. FEINSTEIN, 364:OCT/NOV74-134
BELCHER, J. & D. WEST. PATTY/TANIA.
  F. CARNEY, 453:26JUN75-8
BELFER, N. DESIGNING IN BATIK & TIE
  DYE.
  M. CLAYDEN, 139:FEB73-8
BELGARDT, R. ROMANTISCHE POESIE.
  D. HARTH, 224(GRM):BAND23HEFT4-486
  G. RODGER, 220(GL&L):JAN74-153
BÉLIČ, J. NÁSTIN ČESKÉ DIALEKTOLO-
  GIE.
  H. RÖSEL, 182:VOL26#17/18-596
BELINKOV, N. & OTHERS, EDS. NOVY
  KOLOKOL.
  M. FRIEDBERG, 550(RUSR):OCT73-452
BELITT, B. - SEE NERUDA, P.
BELL, A., ED. AN ANGLO-NORMAN BRUT
  (ROYAL 13 A.XXI).
  J. FRAPPIER, 545(RPH):AUG73-121
BELL, C. & H. NEWBY, EDS. THE
  SOCIOLOGY OF COMMUNITY.
  A. CURLE, 617(TLS):21FEB75-203
BELL, D. THE COMING OF POST-INDUS-
  TRIAL SOCIETY.*
  L.A. COSER, 473(PR):1/1974-128
BELL, D. A TIME TO BE BORN.
  M.G. MICHAELSON, 441:2FEB75-7
BELL, M. PAINTERS IN A NEW LAND.
  J. MORRIS, 73:SPRING74-40
BELL, M. RESIDUE OF SONG.
  R. HOWARD, 491:SEP75-346

BELL, M.D. HAWTHORNE & THE HISTORI-
  CAL ROMANCE OF NEW ENGLAND.*
  H-J. LANG, 38:BAND91HEFT4-548
  J. NORMAND, 189(EA):JAN-MAR73-118
BELL, P.M.H. A CERTAIN EVENTUALITY.
  D. JOHNSON, 617(TLS):14MAR75-280
BELL, Q. VIRGINIA WOOLF.* (VOL 1)
  A. FLEISHMAN, 594:WINTER73-559
  J. GUIGUET, 189(EA):JUL-SEP73-331
BELL, Q. VIRGINIA WOOLF.* (VOL 2)
  A. FLEISHMAN, 594:WINTER73-559
  J. GUIGUET, 189(EA):JUL-SEP73-331
  K. MC SWEENEY, 529(QQ):SUMMER73-
  324
BELL, Q. VIRGINIA WOOLF.* (VOLS
  1&2 BOUND IN ONE VOL)
  L.D. BLOOM, 454:SPRING74-255
  A. FLEISHMAN, 594:WINTER73-559
BELL, S.F. CHARLES NODIER.
  R.T. DENOMMÉ, 207(FR):APR73-1013
  S. RAPHAEL, 402(MLR):APR74-416
  P.J. WHYTE, 208(FS):JAN74-87
"BELL'S INTRODUCTION TO THE QUR'ÂN."
  (REV BY W.M. WATT)
  G. KROTKOFF, 318(JAOS):JUL-SEP73-
  363
DE BELLAIGUE, G. FURNITURE, CLOCKS
  & GILT BRONZES.
  P.K. THORNTON, 617(TLS):11APR75-
  407
BELLAK, L. THE BEST YEARS OF YOUR
  LIFE.
  R.M. HENIG, 441:14SEP75-12
BELLAMY, J.A. - SEE IBN ABĪ D-DUNYĀ
BELLAMY, J.D. THE NEW FICTION.
  L. ZIFF, 617(TLS):13JUN75-674
BELLAMY, J.D., ED. SUPERFICTION, OR
  THE AMERICAN STORY TRANSFORMED.
  A. BROYARD, 441:5SEP75-33
BELLARD, A. GONE FOR A SOLDIER.
  (D.H. DONALD, ED)
  442(NY):17NOV75-194
BELLEN, H. STUDIEN ZUR SKLAVEN-
  FLUCHT IM RÖMISCHEN KAISERREICH.*
  S.M. TREGGIARI, 124:NOV72-181
BELLENGER, C. & OTHERS, EDS. HIS-
  TOIRE GÉNÉRALE DE LA PRESSE FRAN-
  ÇAISE. (VOLS 1-4)
  D. JOHNSON, 617(TLS):100CT75-1180
BELLERBY, F. THE FIRST-KNOWN.
  A. STEVENSON, 362:30OCT75-571
BELLET, R. - SEE VALLÈS, J.
BELLIDO, A.G. - SEE UNDER GARCÍA Y
  BELLIDO, A.
BELLIER, A. & OTHERS - SEE UNDER
  APOLLINAIRE, G. & P. GUILLAUME
BELLMANN, G. SLAVOTEUTONICA.
  J.W. MARCHAND, 574(SEEJ):FALL72-
  361
BELLOW, S. HUMBOLDT'S GIFT.
  A. BROYARD, 441:14AUG75-35
  R. GILMAN, 441:17AUG75-1
  D. LODGE, 617(TLS):100CT75-1173
  R. MAYNE, 362:90CT75-484
  C. NEWMAN, 231:0CT75-82
  R. SHATTUCK, 453:18SEP75-21
  R. TODD, 61:SEP75-83
  J. UPDIKE, 442(NY):15SEP75-122
BELLOW, S. MR. SAMMLER'S PLANET.
  F.M. KUNA, 179(ES):DEC72-531
BELLUCCI, L. - SEE BECCARI, A.
BELOTTI, E.G. LITTLE GIRLS.
  M. PRINGLE, 362:13NOV75-658

BELOTTI, G. F. CHOPIN L'UOMO.
G. ABRAHAM, 617(TLS):9MAY75-506
BELSHAW, C.S. TOWERS BESIEGED.
R. STORR, 99:DEC75/JAN76-62
BELY, A. KOTIK LETAEV.*
M.L. GIES, 574(SEEJ):FALL72-347
BELY, A. [A. BIELY] THE SILVER
DOVE.*
H. MUCHNIC, 453:17APR75-35
BEN-AMI, A. SOCIAL CHANGE IN A
HOSTILE ENVIRONMENT.
J. PRAWER, 589:JAN74-93
BEN-CHORIN, S. HEAR, O ISRAEL.
B. FREIDENREICH, 287:JUL-AUG73-29
BEN-DASAN, I. THE JAPANESE & THE
JEWS.
S.M. LYMAN, 390:JUN-JUL73-75
BENAMOU, M. POUR UNE NOUVELLE PÉDA-
GOGIE DU TEXTE LITTÉRAIRE.
D. BRODIN, 207(FR):FEB73-679
J. CANTERA, 202(FMOD):NOV72/FEB73-
174
M. GUINEY, 399(MLJ):JAN-FEB74-62
BENAMOU, M. WALLACE STEVENS & THE
SYMBOLIST IMAGINATION.*
I. EHRENPREIS, 402(MLR):JAN74-159
BENAMOU, M. & J. CARDUNER. LE
MOULIN À PAROLES.
M.M. CELLER, 207(FR):DEC72-462
BENBOW, R.M., E.M. BLISTEIN & F.S.
HOOK - SEE PEELE, G.
BENCHLEY, P. JAWS.*
P.M. SPACKS, 249(HUDR):SUMMER74-
293
BENDER, B.W. SPOKEN MARSHALLESE.*
A.S. KAYE, 353:15AUG73-122
BENDER, J.B. SPENSER & LITERARY
PICTORIALISM.*
R.F. HILL, 402(MLR):JUL74-618
BENDER, R. A CRACK IN THE REAR-VIEW
MIRROR.
J.P. EBERHARD, 505:SEP73-154
BENDINER, E. A TIME FOR ANGELS.
A. WHITMAN, 441:1SEP75-13
BENDIXSON, T. INSTEAD OF CARS.
E. WILSON, 617(TLS):17JAN75-54
BENÉ, C. ÉRASME ET SAINT AUGUSTIN.*
I.D. MC FARLANE, 208(FS):APR74-183
BENE, E., ED. LES LUMIÈRES EN HON-
GRIE, EN EUROPE CENTRALE ET EN
EUROPE ORIENTALE.*
E. WANGERMANN, 575(SEER):JAN74-155
BENECKE, G. SOCIETY & POLITICS IN
GERMANY 1500-1750.
F.L. CARSTEN, 617(TLS):7FEB75-133
BENEDICT, P.K. SINO-TIBETAN.
P. DENWOOD, 302:JUL73-261
KUN CHANG, 293(JAST):FEB73-335
BENEDIKT, M. MOLE NOTES.
W.G. REGIER, 502(PRS):SPRING73-86
BENEDIKT, M., ED. THE POETRY OF
SURREALISM.
D. DONOGHUE, 441:11MAY75-46
BENEDIKTSSON, H., ED. THE NORDIC
LANGUAGES & MODERN LINGUISTICS.*
U. GROENKE, 343:BAND16HEFT2-140
BENEDIKZ, B.S., ED. ON THE NOVEL.*
H. SERGEANT, 175:SPRING72-29
BENELLO, C.G. & D. ROUSSOPOULOS,
EDS. THE CASE FOR PARTICIPATORY
DEMOCRACY.
C.E.S. FRANKS, 529(QQ):WINTER73-
663

BENEVENTO, A. STUDI SU PIETRO
JAHIER.
J.R. DASHWOOD, 402(MLR):OCT74-890
BENEVOLO, L. ROMA DA IERI A DOMANI.
S. KOSTOF, 576:OCT73-239
BENGTSON, H. INTRODUCTION TO AN-
CIENT HISTORY.*
J-C. DUMONT, 555:VOL47FASC1-179
BENGTSON, H. DIE OLYMPISCHE SPIELE
IN DER ANTIKE.
J.M. BALCER, 124:MAY73-485
BÉNICHOU, P. MAN & ETHICS.
R.J. NELSON, 399(MLJ):JAN-FEB74-63
BÉNICHOU, P. NERVAL ET LA CHANSON
FOLKLORIQUE.
M. SORIANO, 400(MLN):MAY73-890
BENIMELI, J.A.F. - SEE UNDER FERRER
BENIMELI, J.A.
BENÍTEZ, R. BÉCQUER TRADICIONALIS-
TA.*
191(ELN):SEP73(SUPP)-175
BENJAMIN, R. NOTION DE PERSONNE ET
PERSONNALISME CHRÉTIEN.
M. ADAM, 542:OCT-DEC73-483
BENJAMIN, W. CHARLES BAUDELAIRE.
S. DEANE, 111:23NOV73-56
BENJAMIN, W. UNDERSTANDING BRECHT.
S. GOOCH, 214:VOL6#23-53
BENKŐ, L. & S. IMRE, EDS. THE HUN-
GARIAN LANGUAGE.
J.T. JENSEN, 574(SEEJ):SPRING73-
111
BENN, G. GOTTFRIED BENN: SELECTED
POEMS.* (F.W. WODTKE, ED)
J.P.J. MAASSEN, 433:JAN73-104
BENN, M. PRIVATE PRACTICE.
M. LEVIN, 441:2MAR75-18
BENNASSAR, B. L'HOMME ESPAGNOL.
M. FRAGA IRIBARNE, 617(TLS):29AUG
75-966
BENNETT, D. IRISH GEORGIAN SILVER.
J. STUART, 135:AUG73-317
BENNETT, D. VICKY.
R.C. TOBIAS, 637(VS):DEC73-212
BENNETT, G.N. THE REALISM OF WIL-
LIAM DEAN HOWELLS, 1889-1920.*
G.C. CARRINGTON, JR., 445(NCF):
DEC73-354
E. CARTER, 219(GAR):WINTER73-591
J.W. CROWLEY, 432(NEQ):SEP73-481
D.J. NORDLOH, 594:SUMMER73-256
BENNETT, H.S. ENGLISH BOOKS & READ-
ERS 1603-1640.*
G. BULLOUGH, 179(ES):AUG72-358
BENNETT, J. LOCKE, BERKELEY, HUME.*
J. BARNES, 479(PHQ):JAN73-73
E.J. FURLONG, 447(N&Q):JAN73-32
C.E. MARKS, 482(PHR):JAN74-126
BENNETT, J.A.W. - SEE LANGLAND, W.
BENNETT, M. CROSS-COUNTRY SKIING.
J. SAVERCOOL, 441:23MAR75-37
BENNETT, P.J. CONFERENCE UNDER THE
TAMARIND TREE.
D.K. WYATT, 293(JAST):FEB73-378
BENNETT, W.A. APPLIED LINGUISTICS
& LANGUAGE LEARNING.
M.H.A. BLANC & P. MEARA, 617(TLS):
23MAY75-568
BENNING, H.A. DIE VORGESCHICHTE VON
NEUENGLISCH "DUTY."
G. KRISTENSSON, 353:1MAR73-118

BENOIT, J. ENJOYING THE ART OF CAN-
ADIAN COOKING. THE CANADIANA COOK-
BOOK.
J.M. COLE, 99:DEC75/JAN76-37
BENOT, J.M.C. - SEE UNDER CAPOTE
BENOT, J.M.
BENSIMON, P. & R. MARTIN. LORD
BYRON: LE CAPTIF DE CHILLON; LE
CHEVALIER HAROLD (CHANT III).
J.D. BONE, 447(N&Q):AUG73-308
BENSON, M., WITH B. ŠLJIVIĆ-ŠIMŠIĆ.
SERBOCROATIAN-ENGLISH DICTIONARY.
K.E. NAYLOR, 574(SEEJ):FALL72-370
BENTLEY, G.E. THE PROFESSION OF
DRAMATIST IN SHAKESPEARE'S TIME,
1590-1642.*
R.A. FOAKES, 175:AUTUMN72-107
S. SCHOENBAUM, 405(MP):FEB74-326
F.B. WILLIAMS, JR., 570(SQ):AUTUMN
73-474
BENTLEY, G.E., JR. BLAKE RECORDS.
H.B. DE GROOT, 179(ES):AUG73-398
BENTLEY, J. THE THRESHER DISASTER.
T. BUCKLEY, 441:26JAN75-18
BENTON, J. OKLAHOMA TENOR.
B. CARR, 415:OCT74-849
BENTON, K. CRAIG & THE TUNISIAN
TANGLE.
N. CALLENDAR, 441:11MAY75-26
BENTON, T. & C., EDS. FORM & FUNC-
TION.
C. AMERY, 617(TLS):30OCT75-1153
BENVENISTI, M. THE CRUSADERS IN THE
HOLY LAND.
M.S. CHERTOFF, 287:FEB73-28
BENZING, B. DIE GESCHICHTE UND DAS
HERRSCHAFTSSYSTEM DER DAGOMBA.
R. SCHOTT, 69:OCT73-375
"BEOWULF." (L.D. PEARSON, TRANS;
R.L. COLLINS, ED)
G. BOURQUIN, 189(EA):APR-JUN73-221
"BEOWULF, A VERSE TRANSLATION."*
(M. ALEXANDER, TRANS)
G.S. FRASER, 473(PR):2/1974-289
BERADT, C. - SEE LUXEMBURG, R.
BÉRARD, C. L'HÉRÔON A LA PORTE DE
L'OUEST.
D.G. MITTEN, 182:VOL26#1/2-42
BERARDINELLI, A. & F. CORDELLI, EDS.
IL PUBBLICO DELLA POESIA ANTOLOGIA.
F. FORTINI, 617(TLS):31OCT75-1308
BERCÉ, Y-M. HISTOIRE DES CROQUANTS.
D. PARKER, 617(TLS):1AUG75-877
DE BERCEO, G. MARTIRIO DE SAN LOR-
ENZO. (P. TESAURO, ED)
B. DUTTON, 86(BHS):OCT73-389
DE BERCEO, G. LOS MILAGROS DE
NUESTRA SEÑORA. (B. DUTTON, ED)
R.P. KINKADE, 589:JAN74-108
C. SMITH, 382(MAE):1974/1-90
BERCHEM, T. STUDIEN ZUM FUNKTIONS-
WANDEL BEI AUXILIARIEN UND SEMI-
AUXILIARIEN IN DEN ROMANISCHEN
SPRACHEN.
A-J. HENRICHSEN, 72:BAND211HEFT3/6-
446
BERCOVITCH, S., ED. THE AMERICAN
PURITAN IMAGINATION.
M. MC GIFFERT, 165:WINTER75-328
BERCOVITCH, S. HOROLOGICALS TO
CHRONOMETRICALS.*
W.S. GREAVES, 551(RENQ):SPRING73-
99

BEREND, I.T. & G. RÁNKI. HUNGARY.
C.A. MACARTNEY, 575(SEER):OCT74-
636
BERENDSOHN, W.A. PHANTASIE UND
WIRKLICHKEIT IN DEN "MÄRCHEN UND
GESCHICHTEN" HANS CHRISTIAN ANDER-
SENS.
N.H. SMITH, 182:VOL26#3/4-106
BERENSOHN, P. FINDING ONE'S WAY
WITH CLAY.
R. CHARLIP, 139:JUN73-9
BERESFORD-HOWE, C. THE BOOK OF
EVE.*
L. BURTON & D. MORLEY, 99:SEP75-57
A. THOMAS, 102(CANL):SUMMER74-79
VAN DEN BERG, B. FONIEK VAN HET
NEDERLANDS.
D.T. BRINK, 361:OCT73-266
BERG, S. THE DAUGHTERS.*
J.D. MC CLATCHY, 134(CP):SPRING73-
77
B. MATHIEU, 584(SWR):SPRING74-209
BERGAMÍN, J. LA IMPORTANCIA DEL
DEMONIO.
A. TERRY, 617(TLS):9MAY75-519
BERGAMÍN, J. - SEE "EL AVISO DE ES-
CARMENTADOS DEL AÑO QUE ACABA Y ES-
CARMIENTO DE AVISADOS PARA EL QUE
EMPIEZA DE 1935"
BERGE, C. FROM A SOFT ANGLE.
P. CALLAHAN, 134(CP):SPRING73-81
BERGER, A.A. POP CULTURE.
J.S. KEEL, 186(ETC.):MAR73-101
BERGER, B. & H. RUPP, EDS. DEUT-
SCHES LITERATUR-LEXIKON. (3RD ED)
(VOL 2)
J.G. KUNSTMANN, 221(GQ):JAN73-129
BERGER, E.L. LABOUR, RACE & COLON-
IAL RULE.
J. LEWIN, 617(TLS):3JAN75-8
BERGER, J. G.*
E. GLOVER, 565:VOL14#2-36
K. MC SWEENEY, 529(QQ):SUMMER73-
320
J. MILLS, 648:JUN73-57
BERGER, J. & J. MOHR, WITH S. BLOM-
BERG. A SEVENTH MAN.
J. NAUGHTON, 362:12JUN75-788
BERGER, P. THE LAST LAUGH.
R. LASSON, 441:6APR75-6
C. LEHMANN-HAUPT, 441:15APR75-39
BERGER, P. & T. LUCKMANN. THE
SOCIAL CONSTRUCTION OF REALITY.
J.O. WISDOM, 488:SEP73-257
BERGER, R. IMPEACHMENT.
C.T. CULLEN, 432(NEQ):DEC73-631
BERGER, R., ED. SCIENTIFIC METHODS
IN MEDIEVAL ARCHAEOLOGY.*
D.W. LAGING, 54:MAR73-142
BERGER, R.W. ANTOINE LE PAUTRE.*
A. BRAHAM, 54:DEC73-642
BERGER, T. REGIMENT OF WOMEN.*
E.R. WIDMER, 59(ASOC):SPRING-SUM-
MER74-153
BERGER, T. SNEAKY PEOPLE.
A. BROYARD, 441:14APR75-29
D.K. MANO, 441:20APR75-4
R. TODD, 61:SEP75-84
442(NY):9JUN75-126
BERGER, W.R. DIE MYTHOLOGISCHEN
MOTIVE IN THOMAS MANNS ROMAN "JOS-
EPH UND SEINE BRÜDER."
S. MANNESMANN, 224(GRM):BAND23
HEFT2-244
D.F. NELSON, 221(GQ):NOV73-642

BERGERON, B. PRAIRIE STATE BLUES.
J. NORDYKE, 114(CHIR):VOL25#3-37
BERGERON, D.M. ENGLISH CIVIC PAG-
EANTRY, 1558-1642.*
G.R. HIBBARD, 447(N&Q):DEC73-472
S.G. PUTT, 175:SPRING72-26
G. WICKHAM, 541(RES):MAY73-205
M.L. WILLIAMSON, 570(SQ):AUTUMN73-
476
BERGHAHN, K.L. - SEE SCHILLER, F.
BERGIN, T.G. DANTE'S "DIVINE COM-
EDY."
J.A. TURSI, 399(MLJ):JAN-FEB74-81
BERGIN, T.G. A DIVERSITY OF DANTE.
P. CHERCHI, 405(MP):AUG73-70
BERGIN, T.G. - SEE PETRARCH
BERGIN, T.G. - SEE WILKINS, E.H.
BERGLUND, B. & C.E. BOLSBY. THE
EDIBLE WILD.
J.M. COLE, 99:DEC75/JAN76-37
BERGMAN, A. THE BIG KISS-OFF OF
1944.*
R. DAVIES, 617(TLS):7MAR75-241
BERGMAN, A. HOLLYWOOD & LE VINE.
N. CALLENDAR, 441:7SEP75-39
R.R. LINGEMAN, 441:4SEP75-39
BERGMAN, A. WE'RE IN THE MONEY.
J. MELLEN, 295:FEB74-511
BERGMAN, I. SCENES FROM A MARRI-
AGE.*
L. SAGE, 617(TLS):28FEB75-226
BERGMAN, R. TROUT.
H. HENKIN, 441:29JUN75-20
BERGMANN, A. GRABBE-BIBLIOGRAPHIE.
H. THOMKE, 182:VOL26#20-740
BERGMANN, R. VERZEICHNIS DER ALT-
HOCHDEUTSCHEN UND ALTSÄCHSISCHEN
GLOSSENHANDSCHRIFTEN.
H. VON GADOW, 182:VOL26#5/6-129
BERGONZI, B. T·S. ELIOT.*
M. DODSWORTH, 184(EIC):JUL73-310
R. ELLIS, 148:WINTER72-381
H. PESCHMANN, 175:SPRING73-35
A. RIDLER, 541(RES):AUG73-386
295:FEB74-584
BERGONZI, B. THE SITUATION OF THE
NOVEL.
H. SERGEANT, 175:SPRING72-29
P. WOLFE, 141:SPRING72-197
295:FEB74-485
BERGONZI, B. THE TURN OF A CEN-
TURY.*
D.E.S. MAXWELL, 402(MLR):JAN74-158
BERGOUNIOUX, A., J. LEMARTINEL & G.
ZONANA - SEE DE VEGA, L.
BERGQUIST, M. SVERIGE OCH EEC.
J.B. BOARD, 563(SS):FALL74-429
BERGSON, L. DIE RELATIVITÄT DER
WERTE IM FRÜHWERK DES EURIPIDES.
O. TAPLIN, 123:MAR74-127
BERGSTEIN, E. ADVANCING PAUL NEW-
MAN.*
T. EDWARDS, 473(PR):3/1974-469
P.M. SPACKS, 249(HUDR):SUMMER74-
283
BERGSTEN, C.F. TOWARD A NEW INTER-
NATIONAL ECONOMIC ORDER.
G. BARRACLOUGH, 453:7AUG75-23
BERGSTEN, G. THOMAS MANN'S "DOCTOR
FAUSTUS."
R. CRAFT, 453:7AUG75-18.
BERGSTEN, S. JAGET OCH VÄRLDEN.
C.L. ANDERSON, 563(SS):WINTER74-82

BERGUA, E.J. - SEE UNDER JARNÉS BER-
GUA, E.
VAN DEN BERK, C.A., ED. DER "SERB-
ISCHE" ALEXANDERROMAN. (VOL 1)
D.F. ROBINSON, 574(SEEJ):WINTER72-
491
VAN DEN BERK, C.A. - SEE IVŠIĆ, S.
BERKELEY, E. & D.S. JOHN BECKLEY.
R.R. BEEMAN, 656(WMQ):JUL74-519
BERKELEY, E. & D.S. DR. JOHN MIT-
CHELL.
639(VQR):AUTUMN74-CXXXIV
BERKIN, C. JONATHAN SEWALL.
B. WOOD, 617(TLS):24OCT75-1261
BERKOVITS, I. ILLUMINATED MANU-
SCRIPTS IN HUNGARY.
J. BACKHOUSE, 90:MAR73-169
BERLIN, B. TZELTAL NUMERAL CLASSI-
FIERS.
K.C. KELLER, 353:15MAY73-116
BERLIN, I. FATHERS & CHILDREN.*
A. WALKER, 402(MLR):APR74-477
BERLIN, I. SLAVES WITHOUT MASTERS.
H. MITGANG, 441:25JAN75-25
W.L. ROSE, 453:18SEP75-46
P.H. WOOD, 441:9FEB75-3
BERLIOZ, H. OEUVRES LITTÉRAIRES:
CORRESPONDANCE GÉNÉRALE. (VOL 1)
(P. CITRON, ED)
D.K. HOLOMAN, 317:SPRING73-167
BERMAN, J.J. & M.H. HALPERIN, EDS.
THE ABUSES OF THE INTELLIGENCE
AGENCIES.
G. WILLS, 453:13NOV75-20
BERMAN, L. THE THOUGHT & THEMES OF
THE MARQUIS DE SADE.
E. BAGNALL, 402(MLR):OCT74-876
BERMAN, M. THE POLITICS OF AUTHEN-
TICITY.*
N. HAMPSON, 208(FS):APR74-199
BERMAN, R.J. BROWNING'S DUKE.*
J.C. MAXWELL, 447(N&Q):JUL73-269
BERMANT, C. THE COUSINHOOD.
H. MACCOBY, 390:JAN73-78
BERNADETE, S. HERODOTEAN INQUIRIES.
J.K. ANDERSON, 121(CJ):DEC73/JAN
74-165
BERNAND, A. & E. LES INSCRIPTIONS
GRECQUES ET LATINES DE PHILAE.
J. DESANGES, 182:VOL26#7/8-231
BERNARD, J. GRANDEUR ET TENTATIONS
DE LA MÉDECINE...
J-C. POLACK, 98:JUL73-659
BERNARD, J-P. LES ROUGES.
E.J. TALBOT, 207(FR):FEB73-645
BERNARD, Y. PSYCHO-SOCIOLOGIE DU
GOÛT EN MATIÈRE DE PEINTURE.
H. JÖRG, 182:VOL26#19-647
DE BERNARDI FERRERO, D. TEATRI
CLASSICI IN ASIA MINORE.* (VOLS
2&3)
R. STILLWELL, 54:MAR73-139
BERNARDO, G.A., COMP. A CRITICAL &
ANNOTATED BIBLIOGRAPHY OF PHILIP-
PINE, INDONESIAN & OTHER MALAYAN
FOLKLORE. (F. DEMETRIO Y RADAZA,
ED)
D.V. HART, 293(JAST):MAY73-573
BERNAS, J.G. A HISTORICAL & JURIDI-
CAL STUDY OF THE PHILIPPINE BILL OF
RIGHTS.
M.D. ZAMORA, 293(JAST):AUG73-757

BERNASCONI, J.R. THE COLLECTORS'
GLOSSARY OF ANTIQUES & FINE ARTS.
G. WILLS, 39:SEP73-240
BERNAYS, A. GROWING UP RICH.
M. LEVIN, 441:5OCT75-48
BERND, C.A. - SEE STORM, T. & P.
HEYSE
BERNEKER, E. & M. VASMER. RUSSISCHE
GRAMMATIK.* (7TH ED REV BY M.
BRÄUER-POSPELOVA)
K. STRUNK, 343:BAND17HEFT1-106
BERNETTI, G. SAGGI E STUDI SUGLI
SCRITTI DI ENEA SILVIO PICCOLOMINI
PAPA PIO II (1405-1464).*
R.C., 228(GSLI):VOL150FASC469-152
BERNHARD, R. THE ULLMAN CODE.
N. CALLENDAR, 441:9MAR75-24
BERNHARDT, R. IMPERIUM UND ELEU-
THARIA.
B.L. FORTE, 124:MAR74-302
BERNIKOW, L., ED. THE WORLD SPLIT
OPEN.
W.H. PRITCHARD, 441:18MAY75-36
BERNINGER, H. & J-A. CARTIER. JEAN
POUGNY (IWAN PUNI) 1892-1956.*
(VOL 1)
J.E. BOWLT, 592:NOV73-213
BERNSTEIN, B. THURBER.
C. LEHMANN-HAUPT, 441:3APR75-41
J.D. O'HARA, 441:23MAR75-6
J. MILLER, 617(TLS):31OCT75-1284
V.S. PRITCHETT, 442(NY):23JUN75-
104
J. RUSSELL, 617(TLS):13JUN75-646
D. THOMAS, 362:20OCT75-452
E. WEEKS, 61:APR75-97
M. WOOD, 453:15MAY75-13
BERNSTEIN, H. DOM PEDRO II.
D. CARNEIRO, 263:OCT-DEC74-461
BERNSTEIN, R.J. PRAXIS & ACTION.*
R.D. DEARIN, 480(P&R):SUMMER73-192
J.E. HANSEN, 484(PPR):SEP73-129
A.W.J. HARPER, 154:SEP73-560
M.J. SCOTT-TAGGART, 479(PHQ):JUL
73-277
J.W. YOLTON, 488:MAR73-81
BERNSTEIN, T.M. BERNSTEIN'S REVERSE
DICTIONARY.
J. LEONARD, 441:25OCT75-27
BERNSTORFF, D. & OTHERS. WAHLKAMPF
IN INDIEN.
T.P. THORNTON, 293(JAST):FEB73-364
BERNUS, S. HENRI BARTH CHEZ LES
TOUAREGS DE L'AÏR.
A.H.M. KIRK-GREENE, 69:APR73-178
BEROFSKY, B. DETERMINISM.
P. VAN INWAGEN, 482(PHR):JUL73-399
S. WATERLOW, 479(PHQ):JUL73-276
BÉROUL. LE ROMAN DE "TRISTAN ET
YSEUT." (D. GROJNOWSKI, ED & TRANS)
A. PETIT, 557(RSH):JAN-MAR73-163
DE BERRÊDO CARNEIRO, P.E. & P. AR-
NAUD - SEE COMTE, A.
BERRIGAN, D. JESUS CHRIST.
J.W.H., 502(PRS):FALL73-280
BERRIGAN, D. SELECTED & NEW POEMS.
D. BROMWICH, 491:JAN75-229
F. MORAMARCO, 651(WHR):WINTER74-93
P. RAMSEY, 569(SR):SPRING74-401
BERRY, C. VOICE & THE ACTOR.
C. BARKER, 157:WINTER73-86
BERRY, D. CENTRAL IDEAS IN SOCIOL-
OGY.
P. ABRAMS, 617(TLS):30MAY75-593

BERRY, D.C. SAIGON CEMETERY.*
J.B. MAYS, 219(GAR):SUMMER73-282
BERRY, F. THOUGHTS ON POETIC TIME.
P.N. LOCKHART, 124:MAR73-353
BERRY, J. THE MADINA PROJECT, GHANA.
315(JAL):VOL11PT2-106
BERRY, J. & N.A. KOTEI. AN INTRO-
DUCTORY COURSE IN GÃ.
P.F.A. KOTEY, 315(JAL):VOL11PT2-94
BERRY, J.W. & G.J.S. WILDE, EDS.
SOCIAL PSYCHOLOGY: THE CANADIAN
CONTEXT.
C. MILLER, 255(HAB):SUMMER73-210
BERRY, M. MULK RAJ ANAND.*
M.E. DERRETT, 293(JAST):NOV72-189
BERRY, R. THE ART OF JOHN WEBSTER.*
C.A. ASP, 568(SCN):SPRING-SUMMER
74-13
R.W. DENT, 405(MP):MAY74-427
I-S. EWBANK, 541(RES):NOV73-486
R.A. FOAKES, 175:AUTUMN72-107
F. LAGARDE, 189(EA):OCT-DEC73-476
G.A.E. PARFITT, 89(BJA):WINTER73-
95
K.T. VON ROSADOR, 72:BAND211HEFT
1/3-120
BERRY, R. SHAKESPEARE'S COMEDIES.*
A. GILMAN, 191(ELN):DEC73-131
M. GRIVELET, 189(EA):OCT-DEC73-466
BERRY, S.S. COCOA, CUSTOM & SOCIO-
ECONOMIC CHANGE IN RURAL WESTERN
NIGERIA.
L. MAIR, 617(TLS):17OCT75-1230
BERRY, T.E. A.K. TOLSTOY.
J. PADRO, 574(SEEJ):FALL72-346
BERRY, W. THE COUNTRY OF MARRIAGE.*
J.K. ROBINSON, 598(SOR):SUMMER75-
668
BERRY, W. THE MEMORY OF OLD JACK.*
P.M. SPACKS, 249(HUDR):SUMMER74-
288
J. YARDLEY, 569(SR):SUMMER74-537
639(VQR):AUTUMN74-CXX
BERRYMAN, J. DELUSIONS, ETC.*
H. SERGEANT, 175:AUTUMN73-121
BERRYMAN, J. LOVE & FAME.*
G. LINDOP, 148:WINTER72-379
H. SERGEANT, 175:SUMMER72-75
BERRYMAN, J. RECOVERY.*
W. HEYEN, 598(SOR):SUMMER75-721
BERSANI, J., ED. LES CRITIQUES DE
NOTRE TEMPS ET PROUST.*
J. ONIMUS, 557(RSH):OCT-DEC73-664
BERSANI, J. & OTHERS. LA LITTÉRA-
TURE EN FRANCE DEPUIS 1945.*
A. ABEL, 399(MLJ):SEP-OCT73-286
BERSANI, L. BALZAC TO BECKETT.*
J. CRUICKSHANK, 208(FS):JAN74-111
E. KERN, 295:FEB74-417
L. LE SAGE, 546(RR):JAN74-66
BERST, C.A. BERNARD SHAW & THE ART
OF DRAMA.
S. WEINTRAUB, 401(MLQ):SEP74-328
BERTAGAEV, T.A. MORFOLOGIČESKAJA
STRUKTURA SLOVA V MONGOL'SKIX JAZY-
KAX.
N. POPPE, 353:15MAR73-115
BERTAUD, J-P. LES ORIGINES DE LA
RÉVOLUTION FRANÇAISE.
N. HAMPSON, 208(FS):JUL74-335
BERTEAUT, S. PIAF.
A.D. CAPRIO, 207(FR):DEC72-456

BERTHOFF, A.E. THE RESOLVED SOUL.*
W. VON KOPPENFELS, 38:BAND91HEFT4-
532
M-S. RØSTVIG, 179(ES):JUN73-287
BERTHOFF, W. FICTIONS & EVENTS.*
295:FEB74-466
DE BERTIER DE SAUVIGNY, G. METTER-
NICH ET LA FRANCE APRÈS LE CONGRÈS
DE VIENNE. (VOL 2)
F. BASSAN, 535(RHL):JAN-FEB73-141
BERTIN, C. JE T'APPELLERAI AMÉR-
IQUE.
N.L. GOODRICH, 207(FR):APR73-1040
BERTINI, F. - SEE PLAUTUS
BERTOLINO, J. EMPLOYED.
N. LAVERS, 134(CP):SPRING73-87
BERTON, P. KLONDIKE.
102(CANL):SUMMER74-124
BERTON, P. THE LAST SPIKE, 1881-
1885.*
D. SWAINSON, 529(QQ):SPRING73-143
BERTON, P. & J. CANADIAN FOOD
GUIDE.
J.M. COLE, 99:DEC75/JAN76-37
BERTONASCO, M.F. CRASHAW & THE
BAROQUE.*
A.R. CIRILLO, 405(MP):MAY74-430
G.W. WILLIAMS, 551(RENQ):SPRING73-
86
BERTOTTI SCAMOZZI, O. LE FABBRICHE
E I DISEGNI DI ANDREA PALLADIO.
P. SCHNEIDER, 98:APR73-318
BERTRAND, G. L'ILLUSTRATION DE LA
POÉSIE A L'ÉPOQUE DU CUBISME.
J.A. ARGUELLES, 290(JAAC):SPRING
74-441
BESCH, W. SPRACHLANDSCHAFTEN UND
SPRACHAUSGLEICH IM 15. JAHRHUN-
DERT.*
I.T. PIIRAINEN, 439(NM):1973/1-169
BESOMI, O. RICERCHE INTORNO ALLA
"LIRA" DI G.B. MARINO.
A.N. MANCINI, 400(MLN):JAN73-125
BESSÈDE, R. LA CRISE DE LA CON-
SCIENCE CATHOLIQUE DANS LA LITTÉRA-
TURE ET LA PENSÉE FRANÇAISES A LA
FIN DU XIXE SIÈCLE.
M. TURNELL, 617(TLS):3OCT75-1150
BESSINGER, J.B., JR., ED. A CONCOR-
DANCE TO "BEOWULF."
G. BOURQUIN, 189(EA):APR-JUN73-221
BESSO, M. ROMA E IL PAPA NEI PRO-
VERBI E NEI MODI DI DIRE.
W. KÖNIG, 683:BAND36HEFT2/3-213
BEST, O.F. PETER WEISS.*
I. HILTON, 402(MLR):JUL74-710
BEST, T.W. MACROPEDIUS.
L. GILLET, 556(RLV):1973/6-572
BESTER, A. THE COMPUTER CONNECTION.
G. JONAS, 441:20JUL75-10
BESTER, A. EXTRO.
T.A. SHIPPEY, 617(TLS):5DEC75-1438
BESTERMAN, T., ED. STUDIES ON VOL-
TAIRE & THE EIGHTEENTH CENTURY.*
(VOL 76)
M.H. WADDICOR, 208(FS):JAN74-73
BESTERMAN, T., ED. STUDIES ON VOL-
TAIRE & THE EIGHTEENTH CENTURY.*
(VOL 79)
M.H. WADDICOR, 208(FS):JAN74-75

BESTERMAN, T., ED. STUDIES ON VOL-
TAIRE & THE EIGHTEENTH CENTURY.
(VOL 81)
N. SUCKLING, 208(FS):JAN74-76
J. VERCRUYSSE, 535(RHL):JAN-FEB73-
135
BESTERMAN, T., ED. STUDIES ON VOL-
TAIRE & THE EIGHTEENTH CENTURY.
(VOL 86)
H. DURANTON, 535(RHL):NOV-DEC73-
1078
BESTERMAN, T., ED. STUDIES ON VOL-
TAIRE & THE EIGHTEENTH CENTURY.
(VOLS 87-90)
D.C. POTTS, 402(MLR):OCT74-870
BESTERMAN, T., ED. STUDIES ON VOL-
TAIRE & THE EIGHTEENTH CENTURY.
(VOL 97)
J. UNDANK, 400(MLN):MAY73-867
BESTERMAN, T., ED. STUDIES ON VOL-
TAIRE & THE EIGHTEENTH CENTURY.
(VOLS 124 & 127)
H. MASON, 617(TLS):30MAY75-594
BESTERMAN, T., ED. STUDIES ON VOL-
TAIRE & THE EIGHTEENTH CENTURY.
(VOLS 129 & 132)
H.T. MASON, 617(TLS):12SEP75-1032
BESTERMAN, T. VOLTAIRE ON THE ARTS.
J. SEZNEC, 208(FS):OCT74-458
BESTERMAN, T. - SEE DE VOLTAIRE,
F.M.A.
BÉSUS, R. FRANCE DERNIÈRE.
S.R. ALFONSI, 207(FR):MAR73-848
BETH, E.W. ASPECTS OF MODERN LOGIC.*
R. BLANCHÉ, 542:JUL-SEP73-349
BETHELL, N. THE LAST SECRET.
K. FITZLYON, 364:FEB/MAR75-123
442(NY):10FEB75-115
BETHLEN, I. BETHLEN ISTVÁN TIKOS
IRATAI. (M. SZINAI & L. SZÜCS,
EDS)
T.L. SAKMYSTER, 104:SPRING74-161
BETJEMAN, J. A NIP IN THE AIR.*
J. PRESS, 617(TLS):10JAN75-38
BETJEMAN, J. A PICTORIAL HISTORY OF
ENGLISH ARCHITECTURE.*
T. LASK, 55:NOV72-16
BETTARINI, R. JACOPONE E IL LAUDAR-
IO URBINATE.
L. BANFI, 228(GSLI):VOL150FASC470/
471-393
"BETTER HOMES & GARDENS HERITAGE
COOKBOOK."
R.A. SOKOLOV, 441:7DEC75-78
BETTETINI, G. THE LANGUAGE & THE
TECHNIQUE OF THE FILM.
B.L., 275(IQ):SPRING74-116
A. SESONSKE, 290(JAAC):WINTER74-
240
BETTI, F. STORIA CRITICA DELLE LET-
TERE VIRGILIANE.
B.L., 275(IQ):SUMMER73-111
BETTINI, S. & OTHERS. VENEZIA E
BIZANZIO.
P. BROWN & S. MAC CORMACK, 453:
20FEB75-19
BETTS, D. BEASTS OF THE SOUTHERN
WILD & OTHER STORIES.
W. PEDEN, 569(SR):FALL74-712
639(VQR):SPRING74-LVI
BETTS, G.G. & W.D. ASHWORTH. INDEX
TO UPPSALA EDITION OF COLUMELLA.
J. ANDRÉ, 555:VOL47FASC2-351

BETZ, A. ÄSTHETIK UND POLITIK.*
R. RESCHKE, 654(WB):9/1973-186
BEUGNOT, B. L'ENTRETIEN AU XVIIE
SIÈCLE.
H.T. BARNWELL, 208(FS):JAN74-65
BEVINGTON, D., ED. THE MACRO PLAYS.
E.T. DONALDSON, 617(TLS):16MAY75-
542
BEVINGTON, D. TUDOR DRAMA & POLI-
TICS.
W.G. ZEEVELD, 570(SQ):WINTER73-96
BEWICK, T. A MEMOIR. (I. BAIN, ED)
A. BELL, 617(TLS):3OCT75-1123
BEYEN, R. MICHEL DE GHELDERODE OU
LA HANTISE DU MASQUE.*
J. BLANCART, 557(RSH):JAN-MAR73-
177
H. HELLMAN, 207(FR):APR73-1022
R. LORRIS, 405(MP):AUG73-107
M. VOISIN, 549(RLC):JAN-MAR73-167
BEYER, A. PICKING WINNERS.
C. LEHMANN-HAUPT, 441:18MAR75-41
E. PERLMUTTER, 441:18MAY75-14
BEYER, J. & F. KOPPE, EDS. GRUND-
RISS DER ROMANISCHEN LITERATUREN
DES MITTELALTERS. (VOL 6, PT 2)
W. ROTHWELL, 208(FS):APR74-177
BEYER, S. THE CULT OF TĀRĀ.*
639(VQR):AUTUMN74-CLIII
BEYLSMIT, J.J. & OTHERS, COMPS.
BIBLIOGRAPHIE LINGUISTIQUE DE L'AN-
NÉE 1967 ET COMPLÉMENT DES ANNÉES
PRÉCÉDENTES/LINGUISTIC BIBLIOGRAPHY
FOR THE YEAR 1967 & SUPPLEMENT FOR
THE PREVIOUS YEARS.
E.F.K. KOERNER, 353:15APR73-94
BHARADWAJ, K. PRODUCTION CONDITIONS
IN INDIAN AGRICULTURE.
M. DESAI, 617(TLS):31JAN75-119
BHASA. AVIMARAKA (LOVE'S ENCHANTED
WORLD). (J.L. MASSON & D.D. KOSAM-
BI, TRANS) THREE PLAYS OF BHASA.
(A. & B.G. RAO, TRANS)
B.S. MILLER, 293(JAST):MAY73-538
BHASKAR, R. A REALIST THEORY OF
SCIENCE.
S. KÖRNER, 617(TLS):11APR75-397
BHASKARARAO, P. PRACTICAL PHONET-
ICS. (PT 1)
G.F. MEIER, 682(ZPSK):BAND26HEFT
3/4-414
BHATIA, K. INDIRA.*
N. SAHGAL, 364(DEC74/JAN75-116
BHATIA, K. THE ORDEAL OF NATION-
HOOD.
I. TINKER, 293(JAST):NOV72-181
BHATTACHARYA, K. L'ÂTMAN-BRAHMAN
DANS LE BOUDDHISME ANCIEN.
R.E. EMMERICK, 182:VOL26#20-713
BHATTACHARYA, T. THE CULT OF BRAH-
MĀ. (2ND ED)
D. SRINIVASAN, 318(JAOS):JAN-MAR
73-118
BHAVEN, B.K. CHHAVI.
M.W. MEISTER, 463:AUTUMN73-318
BIANCHI BANDINELLI, R. ROME: THE
LATE EMPIRE.* ROME: THE CENTER OF
POWER.
R. BRILLIANT, 54:JUN73-282
BIANCHINI, F. LE THÉÂTRE DE MON-
THERLANT.
J. VIER, 557(RSH):JAN-MAR73-179

BIANCO, G. LA FONTE GRECA DELLE
METAMORFOSI DI APULEIO.
P.G. WALSH, 123:NOV74-215
BIARD, J.D. LE STYLE DES FABLES DE
LA FONTAINE.
J. MARMIER, 535(RHL):JUL-AUG73-686
DA BIBBIENA, B.D. CALANDRIA. (G.
PADOAN, ED)
R. ALONGE, 228(GSLI):VOL150FASC
470/471-451
"BIBLIOGRAPHIE INTERNATIONALE DE
L'HUMANISME ET DE LA RENAISSANCE."
(VOL 6)
C.H. CLOUGH, 402(MLR):JUL74-662
"BIBLIOTHECA AMERICANA: CATALOGUE OF
THE JOHN CARTER BROWN LIBRARY IN
BROWN UNIVERSITY; SHORT-TITLE LIST
OF ADDITIONS, BOOKS PRINTED 1471-
1700."* "BIBLIOTHECA AMERICANA:
CATALOGUE OF THE JOHN CARTER BROWN
LIBRARY IN BROWN UNIVERSITY; BOOKS
PRINTED 1675-1700."*
M.A. MC CORISON, 432(NEQ):DEC74-
631
"BIBLIOTHECA SOCIETATIS TEUTONICAE
SAECULI XVI-XVIII: KATALOG DER
BÜCHERSAMMLUNG DER DEUTSCHEN GE-
SELLSCHAFT IN LEIPZIG."
L. FORSTER, 220(GL&L):APR74-259
BIČANIČ, R. ECONOMIC POLICY IN
SOCIALIST YUGOSLAVIA.*
A. OCKER, 182:VOL26#10-336
"BICENTENAIRE DE CHATEAUBRIAND."
J. GAULMIER, 535(RHL):JAN-FEB73-
141
J.B. SANDERS, 207(FR):DEC72-408
BICHARD, J.D. & D. MC CLINTOCK.
WILD FLOWERS OF THE CHANNEL ISLANDS.
617(TLS):17OCT75-1245
BICHSEL, P. AND REALLY FRAU BLUM
WOULD VERY MUCH LIKE TO MEET THE
MILKMAN.
D.P. DENEAU, 573(SSF):FALL73-436
BICKEL, A.M. THE MORALITY OF CON-
SENT.
C.M. CURTIS, 61:DEC75-114
A.M. DERSHOWITZ, 441:21SEP75-1
BICKERTON, D. DYNAMICS OF A CREOLE
SYSTEM.
R.B. LE PAGE, 617(TLS):19SEP75-
1067
BICKHAM, J.M. A BOAT NAMED DEATH.
M. LEVIN, 441:31AUG75-13
BIDDLE, A.W. & P.A. ESCHHOLZ, EDS.
THE LITERATURE OF VERMONT.
R.C. BARRET, 432(NEQ):JUN74-315
BIDDLE, S. BOLINGBROKE & HARLEY.
G. HOLMES, 617(TLS):21NOV75-1391
442(NY):13JAN75-94
BIDEAU, P-A. D'UN MUR À L'AUTRE.
R. SUTHERLAND, 102(CANL):WINTER73-
114
BIDWELL, C.E. OUTLINE OF POLISH
MORPHOLOGY.
G.M. ERAMIAN & R.K. WILSON, 104:
FALL73-417
BIDWELL, C.E. THE STRUCTURE OF
RUSSIAN IN OUTLINE.
S.S. BIRKENMAYER, 215(GL):VOL13#1-
67
V. ŠEVOROŠKIN, 353:15FEB73-94
BIEBUYCK, D. LEGA CULTURE.
R.A. BRAVMANN, 2:SPRING74-82

BIEBUYCK, D.P., ED. TRADITION &
CREATIVITY IN TRIBAL ART.*
  V.L. GROTTANELLI, 69:APR73-169
BIEHL, W. - SEE EURIPIDES
BIELAWSKI, J. & M. PLEZIA - SEE
ARISTOTLE
BIELER, A., O. HAAC & P. LÉON. PER-
SPECTIVES DE FRANCE. (REV)
  G.R. DANNER, 207(FR):FEB73-686
BIELER, L. - SEE LOWE, E.A.
BIELFELDT, H.H. RUSSISCH-DEUTSCHES
WÖRTERBUCH.
  K. GINGOLD, 75:2/1973-98
BIELY, A. - SEE UNDER BELY, A.
BIEN, P. NIKOS KAZANTZAKIS.
  M.P. LEVITT, 295:FEB74-691
BIEN, P. KAZANTZAKIS & THE LINGUIS-
TIC REVOLUTION IN GREEK LITERATURE.
  A. HORTON, 149:SEP74-259
  M.P. LEVITT, 295:FEB74-691
  P. MACKRIDGE, 402(MLR):JAN74-239
  G. NIKETAS, 219(GAR):FALL73-452
BIEN, P., J. RASSIAS & C. BIEN.
DEMOTIC GREEK.* (3RD ED)
  J.E. REXINE, 399(MLJ):DEC73-430
BIENEK, H. THE CELL.*
  L.T. LEMON, 502(PRS):SUMMER73-183
BIENEN, H. KENYA.
  M. TWADDLE, 617(TLS):3JAN75-8
BIENERT, W.A. - SEE DIONYSIUS VON
ALEXANDRIEN
BIENIARZÓWNA, J. MIESZCZAŃSTWO KRA-
KOWSKIE XVII W.
  P. BUSHKOVITCH, 497(POLR):VOL18#3-
  86
BIERI, P. ZEIT UND ZEITERFAHRUNG.
  S.L. HART, 484(PPR):MAR74-453
BIERLAIRE, F. LA FAMILIA D'ERASME.
  A.J. GAIL, 657(WW):JAN/FEB73-69
BIERLEY, P.E. JOHN PHILIP SOUSA.
  B. CARR, 415:MAR74-221
BIERSTEDT, R. POWER & PROGRESS.
  D. MAC RAE, 617(TLS):14FEB75-162
BIEZAIS, H. DIE HIMMLISCHE GÖTTER-
FAMILIE DER ALTEN LETTEN.
  E. ETTLINGER, 203:SPRING73-82
BIGGS, P., P. CHICKEN & R. LEESON.
LA FRANCE.
  R. MERKER, 399(MLJ):DEC73-443
BIGSBY, C.W.E. DADA & SURREALISM.*
  I.B. WHYTE, 111:3MAY74-128
  A. YOUNG, 148:SPRING73-90
BIJLEVELD, M. BIRDS OF PREY IN
EUROPE.
  P. BURTON, 617(TLS):7MAR75-258
BILL, E.G.W. A CATALOG OF MANU-
SCRIPTS IN LAMBETH PALACE LIBRARY,
MSS. 1222-1860.
  R.E. WALTON, 14:JUL73-409
BILLINGTON, M. THE MODERN ACTOR.
  J. HAMMOND, 214:VOL6#23-56
BILLINGTON, R. A PAINTED DEVIL.
  A. BARNES, 617(TLS):19SEP75-1041
  K. POLLITT, 441:28DEC75-18
BILLINGTON, R.A. FREDERICK JACKSON
TURNER.*
  T. COLBOURN, 432(NEQ):JUN74-302
  C. EARLE, 656(WMQ):JAN74-146
BILODEAU, F. BALZAC ET LE JEU DES
MOTS.*
  G. DELATTRE, 207(FR):MAR73-832
  H. GODIN, 208(FS):JAN74-90
  W. WALLING, 188(ECR):FALL73-267
  205(FMLS):APR73-211

BINDER, G. AENEAS UND AUGUSTUS.*
  G.K. GALINSKY, 24:SPRING74-77
  K.W. GRANSDEN, 123:MAR74-50
BINDING, G. & OTHERS. RHEINISCHE
AUSGRABUNGEN.
  M.R. COLTON, 313:VOL63-286
BINFIELD, C. GEORGE WILLIAMS & THE
Y.M.C.A.
  N.F. POPE, JR., 637(VS):JUN74-441
BINGHAM, C. THE STEWART KINGDOM OF
SCOTLAND 1371-1603.
  B.P. LENMAN, 617(TLS):10JAN75-33
BINGHAM, M. SHERIDAN.*
  C.J. RAWSON, 175:AUTUMN72-110
BINH, D.T. A TAGMEMIC COMPARISON OF
THE STRUCTURE OF ENGLISH & VIETNAM-
ESE SENTENCES.
  D. THOMAS, 361:VOL31#1-77
BINKLEY, L.J. CONFLICT OF IDEALS.
  W.E.M., 543:SEP72-153
BINKLEY, R., R. BRONAUGH & A. MAR-
RAS, EDS. AGENT, ACTION, & REASON.
  R. TRIGG, 479(PHQ):JAN73-87
  A.R. WHITE, 393(MIND):JAN73-149
  J.W. YOLTON, 488:MAR73-81
BINSWANGER, L. BEING-IN-THE-WORLD.
  P. LOMAS, 617(TLS):18JUL75-797
"BIOGRAPH BULLETINS 1908-1912."
(ANNOTATIONS BY G.W. BITZER)
  C.P.R., 200:OCT73-497
BIRBARI, E. DRESS IN ITALIAN PAINT-
ING 1460-1500.
  Q. BELL, 617(TLS):5SEP75-999
BIRCH, C., ED. ANTHOLOGY OF CHINESE
LITERATURE. (VOL 2)
  H.H. FRANKEL, 293(JAST):MAY73-510
BIRCHER, M., ED. DIE FRUCHTBRIN-
GENDE GESELLSCHAFT.
  G. REBING, 680(ZDP):BAND92HEFT2-
  283
BIRCHER, M. JOHANN WILHELM VON
STUBENBERG (1619-1663) UND SEIN
FREUNDESKREIS.*
  K.G. KNIGHT, 220(GL&L):OCT73-85
BIRCHER, M. & K.S. GUTHKE - SEE FÜS-
SLI, J.H.
BIRCHER, M. & H. STRAUMANN. SHAKE-
SPEARE UND DIE DEUTSCHE SCHWEIZ BIS
ZUM BEGINN DES 19. JAHRHUNDERTS.
  P.M. DALY, 564:JUN73-156
  K.S. GUTHKE, 133:1973/1-85
  H. OPPEL, 430(NS):AUG73-448
BIRD, G. PHILOSOPHICAL TASKS.
  J.D. CARNEY, 484(PPR):DEC73-287
  M.A. SLOTE, 482(PHR):OCT74-553
BIRD, R. - SEE MOORE, G.
BIRDSALL, D. - SEE ADACHI, B.
BIRKENMAYER, S.S., COMP. SUPPLEMENT
TO AN ACCENTED DICTIONARY OF PLACE
NAMES IN THE SOVIET UNION.
  M. BENSON, 574(SEEJ):SUMMER72-261
BIRKENMAYER, S.S. & J.R. KRZYŻANOW-
SKI, EDS. A MODERN POLISH READER.
  M.Z. BROOKS, 574(SEEJ):SPRING72-
  119
BIRKOS, A.S. & L.A. TAMBS, EDS.
ACADEMIC WRITER'S GUIDE TO PERIOD-
ICALS. (VOL 2)
  G.D. WIGGINS, 574(SEEJ):SPRING73-
  113
BIRKS, T. - SEE MEYER, F.S.
BIRLEY, A. SEPTIMIUS SEVERUS.
  W.R. CHALMERS, 123:NOV74-278
  R. MAC MULLEN, 124:NOV74-181
  S.I. OOST, 122:JAN74-67

BIRMINGHAM, S. THE LATE JOHN MAR-
QUAND.
T.K. MEIER, 454:FALL73-83
BIRNEY, A.L. SATIRIC CATHARSIS IN
SHAKESPEARE.*
C. HOY, 569(SR):SPRING74-363
B. MC ELROY, 301(JEGP):APR74-244
BIRNEY, E. THE COLLECTED POEMS OF
EARLE BIRNEY.
D.G. JONES, 99:DEC75/JAN76-51
BIRNEY, E. RAG & BONESHOP.
H. SERGEANT, 175:SUMMER72-75
BIRNEY, E. WHAT'S SO BIG ABOUT
GREEN?*
G. BOWERING, 102(CANL):SUMMER74-95
P. STEVENS, 628:SPRING74-103
BIRX, H.J. PIERRE TEILHARD DE CHAR-
DIN'S PHILOSOPHY OF EVOLUTION.*
F. CRONIN, 154:SEP73-559
BISCHOFF, H. SETZUNG UND TRANSPOS-
ITION DES -MENTE- ADVERBS ALS AUS-
DRUCK DER ART UND WEISE IM FRANZO-
SISCHEN UND ITALIENISCHEN MIT
BESONDERER BERÜCKSICHTIGUNG DER
TRANSPOSITION IN ADJEKTIVEN.*
L. WOLF, 209(FM):APR73-195
BISHOP, E. & E. BRASIL, EDS. AN
ANTHOLOGY OF TWENTIETH CENTURY
BRAZILIAN POETRY.
R. SAYERS, 399(MLJ):APR73-232
BISHOP, M., ED. A ROMANTIC STORY-
BOOK.
205(FMLS):APR73-215
BISHOP, T.A.M. ENGLISH CAROLINE
MINISCULE.*
N. BARKER, 78(BC):SPRING73-95
K.W. HUMPHREYS, 354:SEP73-252
BISSAINTHE, M. DICTIONNAIRE DE BIB-
LIOGRAPHIE HAITIENNE. (1ST SUPP)
W. GOLDWATER, 517(PBSA):JUL-SEP74-
344
BISSELL, C. HALFWAY UP PARNASSUS.
H.I. MACDONALD, 99:JUL75-18
A. WERNICK, 99:JUL75-19
BISSELL, R. NEW LIGHT ON 1776 & ALL
THAT.
M. KITMAN, 441:28DEC75-8
BISSETT, B. DRIFTING INTO WAR.
S. SCOBIE, 102(CANL):SPRING73-89
BISSETT, B. MEDICINE MY MOUTHS ON
FIRE.
D. BARBOUR, 198:SPRING75-121
BISSETT, B. NOBODY OWNS TH EARTH.*
D. WYNAND, 376:APR73-238
BISSETT, B. POMES FOR YOSHI.
S. SCOBIE, 102(CANL):SPRING74-120
BISWAS, R.K. ARTHUR HUGH CLOUGH.*
K. ALLOTT, 677:VOL4-329
P.M. BALL, 637(VS):SEP73-105
K. MC SWEENEY, 529(QQ):WINTER73-
669
G. THOMAS, 175:SPRING73-32
M. THORPE, 179(ES):DEC73-602
BITTKER, B.I. THE CASE FOR BLACK
REPARATIONS.
N. MILLS, 676(YR):AUTUMN73-146
J.W. NICKEL, 185:JAN74-180
BITTLE, D. TOUCH.
D. BESSAI, 99:JUL75-36
BITZER, G.W. BILLY BITZER.
J. SPEARS, 200:AUG-SEP73-432
BITZER, G.W. - SEE "BIOGRAPH BULLE-
TINS 1908-1912"

BITZER, H. GOETHE ÜBER DEN DILET-
TANTISMUS.
R. NOVAK, 400(MLN):OCT73-1068
BITZER, L.F. & E. BLACK, EDS. THE
PROSPECT OF RHETORIC.*
W.R. WINTEROWD, 480(P&R):WINTER73-
47
BIVINS, J., JR. THE MORAVIAN POT-
TERS IN NORTH CAROLINA.*
T. ROSE, 139:FEB73-8
BIVON, R. ELEMENT ORDER.*
B. COMRIE, 297(JL):FEB73-157
G.F. HOLLIDAY, 574(SEEJ):SUMMER72-
255
M.K. LAUNER, 104:WINTER73-542
BIVONA, L. ISCRIZIONI LATINE LAPI-
DARIE DEL MUSEO DI PALERMO.
J.F. GILLIAM, 24:FALL74-312
BIZARDEL, Y. THE FIRST EXPATRIATES.
A. WHITMAN, 441:12JUL75-23
BIZOS, M. - SEE XENOPHON
BJERRUM, A. LINGUISTIC PAPERS.
A.S.C. ROSS, 447(N&Q):JUN73-222
269(IJAL):OCT73-273
BJÖRKEGREN, H. ALEKSANDR SOLZHEN-
ITSYN.*
A.P. OBOLENSKY, 399(MLJ):MAR74-145
BJØRNEBOE, J. HERTUG HANS.
E. HASLUND, 270:VOL23#3-66
E. HASLUND, 270:VOL23#4-93
BJØRNEBOE, J. MOMENT OF FREEDOM.
P. ADAMS, 61:JUL75-83
BJØRNVIG, T. PAGTEN.
E. BREDSDORFF, 617(TLS):24OCT75-
1269
BJORVAND, E., ED. A CONCORDANCE TO
SPENSER'S "FOWRE HYMNES."
E.F. HENLEY, 568(SCN):WINTER74-73
BLACK, C.L., JR. CAPITAL PUNISH-
MENT.*
M.E. GALE, 441:5JAN75-1
BLACK, G. A BIG WIND FOR SUMMER.
M. LASKI, 362:20NOV75-684
BLACK, G. THE GOLDEN COCKATRICE.*
N. CALLENDAR, 441:8JUN75-10
BLACK, H., JR. MY FATHER.
L.L. KING, 441:28SEP75-22
BLACK, L. ARAFAT IS NEXT!
N. CALLENDAR, 441:22JUN75-16
BLACK, M. MARGINS OF PRECISION.*
L.A., 543:JUN73-748
BLACK, M. OLD NEW YORK IN EARLY
PHOTOGRAPHS.
639(VQR):SUMMER74-CX
BLACK, M., J. HOCHBERG & E.M. GOM-
BRICH. ART, PERCEPTION, & REALITY.
W.A.F., 543:MAR73-525
BLACK-MICHAUD, J. ORDERED FORCE.
L. MAIR, 617(TLS):21NOV75-1394
BLACKBURN, S. REASON & PREDICTION.
D.C. STOVE, 63:MAY74-72
BLACKER, H. JUST LIKE IT WAS.
E.S. TURNER, 362:13FEB75-219
BLACKFORD, P.W. - SEE MILTON, J.
BLACKING, J. HOW MUSICAL IS MAN?
L. DURAN, 415:MAR74-218
M. HERNDON, 187:JAN75-143
BLACKMAN, D. OPERANT CONDITIONING.
O.L. ZANGWILL, 617(TLS):28MAR75-
343
BLACKMORE, H.L. HUNTING WEAPONS.
N. HALL, 135:MAY73-62
BLACKMORE, J.T. ERNST MACH.
F. SEAMAN, 319:APR75-273

BLACKWELL, J.E. & M. JANOWITZ, EDS.
BLACK SOCIOLOGISTS.
D. MAC RAE, 617(TLS):14FEB75-162
BLACKWOOD, C. FOR ALL THAT I FOUND
THERE.*
D. DURRANT, 364:OCT/NOV74-131
BLAFFER, S.C. THE BLACK-MAN OF
ZINACANTAN.
P.M. GARDNER, 292(JAF):OCT-DEC73-
403
BLAIR, C., JR. SILENT VICTORY.
R. TRUMBULL, 441:9JUN75-29
BLAIR, H. & M. GREENE - SEE NEKRAS-
SOV, V.
BLAIR, H. & M. GREENE - SEE ZOSH-
CHENKO, M.
BLAIR, R. THE GRAVE (1743).
566:SPRING74-99
BLAIR, W. - SEE TWAIN, M.
BLAIS, J. PRÉSENCE D'ALAIN GRAND-
BOIS. DE L'ORDRE ET DE L'AVENTURE.
C. MAY, 617(TLS):10OCT75-1188
BLAIS, M-C. ST. LAWRENCE BLUES.*
G. DAVIES, 198:WINTER75-128
A. DUCHÊNE, 617(TLS):14MAR75-269
442(NY):24MAR75-115
BLAIS, M-C. THE WOLF.
G. DAVIES, 198:WINTER75-128
BLAISE, C. A NORTH AMERICAN EDUCA-
TION.*
R.M. BROWN, 102(CANL):AUTUMN73-114
BLAISE, C. TRIBAL JUSTICE.*
S. ESCHE, 606(TAMR):NOV74-85
BLAKE, H. THE ISLAND SELF. (R.
KENT, ED)
D. BROMWICH, 491:MAR75-352
BLAKE, N.F. - SEE CAXTON, W.
BLAKE, R.L.V.F. - SEE UNDER FFRENCH
BLAKE, R.L.V.
BLAKE, W. THE BOOK OF THEL.* (N.
BOGEN, ED)
D.D. AULT, 405(MP):NOV73-218
M.F. SCHULZ, 173(ECS):FALL73-120
BLAKE, W. THE NOTEBOOK OF WILLIAM
BLAKE.* (D.V. ERDMAN, WITH D.K.
MOORE, EDS)
D.R. FAULKNER, 676(YR):SUMMER74-
590
639(VQR):SPRING74-LXII
BLAKE, W. THE POEMS OF WILLIAM
BLAKE. (W.H. STEVENSON, ED)
J.B. BEER, 447(N&Q):AUG73-305
"WILLIAM BLAKE'S WATERCOLOURS, ILL-
USTRATING THE POEMS OF THOMAS
GRAY."* [VARIANT TITLE SHOWN IN
PREV]
I.H. CHAYES, 591(SIR):SPRING74-155
K. GARLICK, 39:JUL73-71
BLAKEMORE, H. & C.T. SMITH, EDS.
LATIN AMERICA.
D.A. PRESTON, 86(BHS):JUL73-317
BLAMIRES, D. DAVID JONES.*
J.P. GEMMILL, 295:FEB74-674
N. JACOBS, 447(N&Q):OCT73-399
BLAMIRES, H. MILTON'S CREATION.*
G. BULLOUGH, 175:SPRING72-24
R. LEJOSNE, 189(EA):JAN-MAR73-98
B. RUDDICK, 148:SPRING72-90
W. WEISS, 430(NS):JUN73-346
BLANCHÉ, R. L'ÉPISTÉMOLOGIE.
J-M. GABAUDE, 542:JUL-SEP73-349
BLANCHÉ, R. LA LOGIQUE ET SON HIS-
TOIRE D'ARISTOTE À RUSSELL.
H. BARREAU, 542:JUL-SEP73-349

BLANCHET, A. - SEE BLONDEL, H.B-M.
BLANCK, J., COMP. BIBLIOGRAPHY OF
AMERICAN LITERATURE.* (VOL 6)
J.D. HART, 27(AL):NOV74-417
BLANCO, R.L. WELLINGTON'S SURGEON
GENERAL.
A. BRETT-JAMES, 617(TLS):4APR75-
355
BLANCO AGUINAGA, C. JUVENTUD DEL
98.
E.I. FOX, 400(MLN):MAR73-478
BLANCO GONZÁLEZ, B. - SEE HURTADO DE
MENDOZA, D.
BLANCO WHITE, J.M. ANTOLOGÍA DE
OBRAS EN ESPAÑOL. (V. LLORENS, ED)
191(ELN):SEP73(SUPP)-176
BLANCPAIN, M. & J-P. COUCHOUD. LA
CIVILISATION FRANÇAISE.
O. ANDREWS, JR., 399(MLJ):DEC73-
426
BLAND, J. DEATH IN WAITING.
N. CALLENDAR, 441:19OCT75-47
BLAND, J. ODD & UNUSUAL ENGLAND.
617(TLS):7MAR75-261
BLANK, W. DIE DEUTSCHE MINNEALLE-
GORIE.*
P.F. GANZ, 382(MAE):1974/2-206
BLANKERT, A. JOHANNES VERMEER VAN
DELFT, 1632-1675.
A. NOACH, 617(TLS):28NOV75-1413
BLANKOFF, J. LA SOCIÉTÉ RUSSE DE LA
SECONDE MOITIÉ DU XIXE SIÈCLE.
I.P. FOOTE, 402(MLR):OCT74-951
BLANNING, T.C.W. REFORM & REVOLU-
TION IN MAINZ 1743-1803.
S. SCHAMA, 617(TLS):28MAR75-333
BLASER, R. - SEE SPICER, J.
BLASHFIELD, J. APARTMENT GARDENER.
J. CANADAY, 441:13APR75-16
BLASI, A.O. GÜIRALDES Y LARBAUD.
P.R. BEARDSELL, 86(BHS):APR73-196
BLASSINGAME, J.W. THE SLAVE COM-
MUNITY.*
R.F. DURDEN, 579(SAQ):SPRING74-273
BLASUCCI, L. STUDI SU DANTE E ARI-
OSTO.
B.L., 275(IQ):SUMMER73-106
BLATTMANN, E. "HENRI QUATRE SALVA-
TOR."
R.N. LINN, 406:FALL74-315
U. WEISSTEIN, 301(JEGP):JUL74-419
BLAU, J.L. MODERN VARIETIES OF
JUDAISM.
P.B., 502(PRS):SPRING73-92
BLAUG, M. THE CAMBRIDGE REVOLUTION.
R. SOLOW, 617(TLS):14MAR75-277
BLAUKOPF, K. GUSTAV MAHLER.
R-S. CLARK, 249(HUDR):AUTUMN74-412
BLAZER, J.S. LEND A HAND.
N. CALLENDAR, 441:19OCT75-47
BLEAKLEY, D. FAULKNER.
G. Ó TUATHAIGH, 617(TLS):10JAN75-
30
BLEASDALE, A. SCULLY.
S. CLAPP, 617(TLS):21MAR75-293
BLECUA, J.M. - SEE GUILLÉN, J.
BLECUA, J.M. - SEE DE QUEVEDO, F.
BLEICHER, T. HOMER IN DER DEUTSCHEN
LITERATUR (1450-1740).
E. BERNSTEIN, 131(CL):SPRING73-185
H. ERBSE, 52:BAND8HEFT3-322
BLEICKEN, J. STAATLICHE ORDNUNG UND
FREIHEIT IN DER RÖMISCHEN REPUBLIK.
T.J. LUCE, 487:WINTER73-417

BLEILER, E.F. - SEE LE FANU, J.S.
BLEZNICK, D.W. QUEVEDO.
  D.L. BAUM, 238:SEP73-733
  H. SIEBER, 400(MLN):MAR73-454
BLEZNICK, D.W., ED. VARIACIONES
INTERPRETATIVAS EN TORNO A LA
NUEVA NARRATIVA HISPANOAMERICANA.
  R.M. REEVE, 238:DEC73-1121
BLICKER, S. SHMUCKS.*
  D. BROWN, 376:OCT73-140
  T.E. TAUSKY, 102(CANL):WINTER74-
  119
BLICKLE, P. LANDSCHAFTEN IM ALTEN
REICH.
  F.L. CARSTEN, 617(TLS):7FEB75-133
BLIER, B. MAKING IT.
  J. LANDRY, 617(TLS):7NOV75-1338
BLISH, J. THE QUINCUNX OF TIME.
  T.A. SHIPPEY, 617(TLS):23MAY75-554
BLISS, M., ED. SOCIAL PLANNING FOR
CANADA.
  K. MC NAUGHT, 99:NOV75-38
BLISS, W.R. SIDE GLIMPSES FROM THE
COLONIAL MEETING-HOUSE.
  D.P. WHARTON, 568(SCN):WINTER74-90
BLISSETT, W., J. PATRICK & R.W. VAN
FOSSEN, EDS. A CELEBRATION OF BEN
JONSON.*
  J.K. GARDINER, 568(SCN):WINTER74-
  75
BLIT, L. THE ORIGINS OF POLISH
SOCIALISM.
  L. BUSHKOFF, 104:SPRING74-151
BLOCH, E. EXPERIMENTUM MUNDI.
  G. STEINER, 617(TLS):30CT75-1128
BLOCH, P.A. SCHILLER UND DIE FRAN-
ZÖSISCHE KLASSISCHE TRAGÖDIE.
  K.L. BERGHAHN, 406:WINTER74-401
BLOCH, P.A., ED. DIE SCHRIFTSTELLER
UND SEIN VERHÄLTNIS ZUR SPRACHE,
DARGESTELLT AM PROBLEM DER TEMPUS-
WAHL.
  H. GELHAUS, 182:VOL26#10-341
  G. RAUSCHER, 406:SUMMER74-197
BLOCH, R. AMERICAN GOTHIC.*
  N. CALLENDAR, 441:30MAR75-24
BLOCH, R. & OTHERS - SEE PIGANIOL,
A.
BLOCH, V. REMBRANDT TODAY.
  K.R., 90:JAN73-47
BLOCH-MICHEL, J. DANIEL ET NOÉMI.
  N.L. GOODRICH, 207(FR):OCT72-201
BLOCK, H.M. NATURALISTIC TRIPTYCH.*
  R. DUMONT, 549(RLC):JAN-MAR73-165
BLODGETT, E.D. TAKE AWAY THE NAMES.
  R.A. SWANSON, 398:AUTUMN75-184
BLOK, A. SELECTED POEMS. (A. PY-
MAN, ED)
  J.D. ELLSWORTH, 575(SEER):JAN74-
  153
BLOK, A. THE TWELVE & OTHER POEMS.
  H. GIFFORD, 447(N&Q):JUN73-238
BLOM-COOPER, L. PROGRESS IN PENAL
REFORM.
  R. HOOD, 617(TLS):26SEP75-1099
BLONDEL, H.B-M. CORRESPONDANCE.
(A. BLANCHET, ED)
  P. MOREAU, 535(RHL):JUL-AUG73-636
BLONDEL, M. LE LIEN SUBSTANTIEL ET
LA SUBSTANCE COMPOSÉE D'APRÈS LEIB-
NIZ.*
  M. RENAULT, 154:JUN73-392
  J.M. SOMERVILLE, 258:DEC73-588

BLONDET, O. & A. TUDISCO - SEE VILLA-
VERDE, C.
BLOODWORTH, D. THE CLIENTS OF
OMEGA.
  M. LASKI, 362:5JUN75-748
  617(TLS):18APR75-416
BLOOM, A. - SEE KOJÈVE, A.
BLOOM, E.A. & L.D. JOSEPH ADDISON'S
SOCIABLE ANIMAL.*
  F. RAU, 405(MP):MAY74-440
  W.A. SPECK, 447(N&Q):JUN73-223
  C. TRACY, 529(QQ):SUMMER73-296
BLOOM, E.A. & L.D. - SEE BURNEY, F.
BLOOM, H. THE ANXIETY OF INFLUENCE.*
  M.E. BROWN, 659:SPRING75-241
  K. MC SWEENEY, 591(SIR):WINTER74-
  84
  P. DE MAN, 131(CL):SUMMER74-269
  D. NEWTON-DE MOLINA, 111:30MAY74-
  169
  A.H. ROSENFELD, 598(SOR):SPRING75-
  444
  R. SCHOLES, 301(JEGP):APR74-266
  P. SCHWABER, 128(CE):OCT73-86
BLOOM, H. KABBALAH & CRITICISM.
  R. TOWERS, 441:21DEC75-15
BLOOM, H. A MAP OF MISREADING.
  E.W. SAID, 441:13APR75-23
  M. WOOD, 453:17APR75-15
BLOOM, H. THE RINGERS IN THE TOW-
ER.*
  A.H. ROSENFELD, 598(SOR):SPRING75-
  444
BLOOM, H. YEATS.*
  J.R. MULRYNE, 402(MLR):JUL74-629
  A.H. ROSENFELD, 598(SOR):SPRING75-
  444
BLOOM, L. LANGUAGE DEVELOPMENT.
  E.P. HAMP, 269(IJAL):JUL73-199
BLOOMFIELD, B.C. & E. MENDELSON.
W.H. AUDEN.* (2ND ED)
  E. CALLAN, 295:APR74-1055
  J. COTTON, 503:SUMMER73-100
  P. DAVISON, 354:DEC73-361
  G. WOODCOCK, 569(SR):FALL74-685
BLOOMFIELD, H.H. & OTHERS. TM.
  A. BROYARD, 441:17MAR75-27
  L.C. LEWIN, 441:13APR75-6
BLOOMFIELD, L. A LEONARD BLOOMFIELD
ANTHOLOGY. (C.F. HOCKETT, ED)
  Z.S. HARRIS, 269(IJAL):OCT73-252
  G.C. LEPSCHY, 353:15JUL73-120
BLOOMFIELD, L. LE LANGAGE.
  A. BOUDREAU, 343:BAND16HEFT2-210
BLOOMFIELD, M.W. ESSAYS & EXPLORA-
TIONS.*
  H. BERGNER, 38:BAND91HEFT1-111
  J.R. SIMON, 189(EA):OCT-DEC73-456
BLOOMFIELD, M.W., ED. IN SEARCH OF
LITERARY THEORY.*
  M.C. BEARDSLEY, 113:SPRING73-77
  F. BERRY, 541(RES):NOV73-530
  J.V. HAGOPIAN, 128(CE):OCT73-72
  D. NEWTON-DE MOLINA, 89(BJA):
  AUTUMN73-413
BLOOMGARDEN, H.S. THE GUN.
  W.J. HELMER, 441:6JUL75-10
BLOTNER, J. FAULKNER.*
  R.P. ADAMS, 27(AL):NOV74-392
  C. BAKER, 639(VQR):SUMMER74-438
  H. BEAVER, 617(TLS):30MAY75-600
  R.M. LUDWIG, 385(MQR):SPRING75-232
  L.P. SIMPSON, 578:FALL75-126
  F.C. WATKINS, 569(SR):SUMMER74-518

36

BLOW, S. RHETORIC IN THE PLAYS OF
THOMAS DEKKER.*
    T. HAWKES, 677:VOL4-282
BLOY, L. OEUVRES DE LÉON BLOY.
(VOL 15) (J. PETIT, ED)
    R. HEPPENSTALL, 617(TLS):30CT75-
    1147
BLUCK, R.S. PLATO'S SOPHIST. (G.C.
NEAL, ED)
    M.F. BURNYEAT, 617(TLS):18APR75-
    435
BLUEFARB, S. THE ESCAPE MOTIF IN
THE AMERICAN NOVEL.*
    G.B. TENNYSON, 445(NCF):SEP73-247
    295:FEB74-389
BLUEM, A.W. & J.E. SQUIRE, EDS.
THE MOVIE BUSINESS.
    R. CAMPION, 200:MAY73-302
BLUESTEIN, G. THE VOICE OF THE
FOLK.
    J.T. FLANAGAN, 292(JAF):APR-JUN73-
    186
    J.W. HEALY, 502(PRS):FALL73-272
    W.T. LHAMON, JR., 651(WHR):SPRING
    74-180
BLUM, A. THEORIZING.
    R. ENFIELD, 617(TLS):24JAN75-88
BLUM, C. DIDEROT.
    F. BROWN, 31(ASCH):SUMMER75-504
    P. FRANCE, 617(TLS):17JAN75-47
BLUM, O. DANCE IN GHANA.
    B.L. HAMPTON, 187:SEP75-481
BLUMBERG, G. A KILLER IN MY MIND.
    N. CALLENDAR, 441:31AUG75-12
BLUME, B. & R.H. PEARCE - SEE BURCK-
HARDT, S.
BLUME, J. FOREVER.
    M. LEVIN, 441:28DEC75-20
BLUNT, A. NEAPOLITAN BAROQUE &
ROCOCO ARCHITECTURE.
    A. BRAHAM, 617(TLS):7NOV75-1322
BLUNT, A. - SEE UNDER SCHILLING, E.
BLUNT, W. THE DREAM KING.
    M. PETERSON, 470:MAY74-24
BLUNT, W. "ENGLAND'S MICHELANGELO."
    D.A.N. JONES, 362:17JUL75-90
    D. PIPER, 617(TLS):4JUL75-715
BLUNT, W. ON WINGS OF SONG.*
    E. SAMS, 415:0CT74-849
BLUSKE, M.K. & E.K. WALTHER. DAS
ERSTE JAHR. (REV)
    L. KRESSLEY, 221(GQ):JAN73-136
BLY, R. SLEEPERS JOINING HANDS.*
    P. RAMSEY, 569(SR):SPRING74-402
BLY, R. THE TEETH MOTHER NAKED AT
LAST. THE MORNING GLORY.
    K. SKINNER, 134(CP):FALL73-89
BLY, R. - SEE IGNATOW, D.
BLY, R. - SEE MARTINSON, H., G.
EKELÖF & T. TRANSTRÖMER
BLY, R. - SEE NERUDA, P. & C. VALLE-
JO
BLYTH, H. CARO.*
    E.E.B., 191(ELN):SEP73(SUPP)-37
BLYTH, H. MADELEINE SMITH.
    R. DAVIES, 617(TLS):26SEP75-1097
BLYTH, M. COUSIN SUZANNE.
    M. LEVIN, 441:9NOV75-54
BLYTHE, P. THE MAN WHO WAS UNCLE.
    D. HUNT, 617(TLS):8AUG75-890
BLYTHE, R., ED. ALDEBURGH ANTHOL-
OGY.*
    G. GRIGSON, 607:SEP73-38

BOA, E. & J.H. REID. CRITICAL
STRATEGIES.
    G.W. FIELD, 529(QQ):SUMMER73-291
    I. TIESLER, 406:WINTER74-436
BOALCH, D.H. MAKERS OF THE HARPSI-
CHORD & CLAVICHORD 1440-1840.*
(2ND ED)
    P. WILLIAMS, 415:DEC74-1049
BOARDMAN, G.R. GRAHAM GREENE.
    R.M. DAVIS, 594:WINTER73-530
    H.D. SPEAR, 295:FEB74-625
BOAS, F.S. - SEE FLETCHER, G. & P.
BOASE, A.M. THE FORTUNES OF MON-
TAIGNE.*
    I.D. MC FARLANE, 208(FS):APR74-189
BOASE, T.S.R. DEATH IN THE MIDDLE
AGES.*
    B.A. DOEBLER, 124:SEP-OCT73-53
BOBBIO, N. UNA FILOSOFIA MILITANTE.
    W.T.S., 191(ELN):SEP73(SUPP)-165
BOBERG, I.M. MOTIF-INDEX OF EARLY
ICELANDIC LITERATURE.
    R. GRAMBO, 196:BAND14HEFT1/2-156
BOBRI, V. & C. MILLER. TWO GUITARS.
    E.F. STANTON, 582(SFQ):MAR73-75
BOBROWSKI, J. & H. BIENEK. SELECTED
POEMS.
    R. SIEBURTH, 565:VOL14#4-32
BOCCACCIO, G. DECAMERON. (C.S.
SINGLETON, ED)
    C. GRAYSON, 617(TLS):10JAN75-39
BOCHENSKI, J.M. & OTHERS, EDS.
GUIDE TO MARXIST PHILOSOPHY.
    M.A.W., 543:JUN73-749
BOCK, H. SAVE!
    M. RICHLER, 441:5JAN75-6
BOCK, S. - SEE SEGHERS, A.
BÖCKENFÖRDE, E-W., ED. MODERNE
DEUTSCHE VERFASSUNGSGESCHICHTE
(1815-1918).
    W. RÜFNER, 182:VOL26#13/14-505
BÖCKMANN, P. SCHILLERS "DON KAR-
LOS."
    J.L. SAMMONS, 301(JEGP):OCT74-596
BODE, C., ED. MIDCENTURY AMERICA.
    H. SCHWARTZ, 432(NEQ):JUN73-308
    G.B. TENNYSON, 445(NCF):SEP73-247
BODROGLIGETI, A., ED. A FOURTEENTH
CENTURY TURKIC TRANSLATION OF
SA'DI'S GULISTAN.
    J.M. KELLY, 318(JAOS):APR-JUN73-
    238
BODTKE, R. TRAGEDY & THE JACOBEAN
TEMPER.
    J. FELTES, 568(SCN):SPRING-SUMMER
    74-12
BOECK, O. HEINES NACHWIRKUNG UND
HEINE-PARALLELEN IN DER FRANZÖ-
SISCHEN DICHTUNG.
    L.R. FURST, 220(GL&L):APR74-267
    C.R. OWEN, 400(MLN):OCT73-1054
    J.L.S., 191(ELN):SEP73(SUPP)-130
BOEHRINGER, R. EWIGER AUGENBLICK.
    I. JONES, 172(EDDA):1973/2-125
BOER, C. VARMINT Q.
    P.D. MORROW, 649(WAL):FALL73-153
BOER, C. & G.F. BUTTERICK - SEE
OLSON, C.
BOEREN, P.C. JOCUNDUS, BIOGRAPHE
DE SAINT SERVAIS.
    G. CONSTABLE, 589:APR74-316
BOERNER, P. TAGEBUCH.*
    W. EMMERICH, 221(GQ):JAN73-114

37

BOESCH, B., ED. GERMAN LITERATURE.*
M. WINKLER, 399(MLJ):NOV73-380
BOESIGER, W., ED. LE CORBUSIER.
505:APR73-146
BOETHIUS. BOETHII DACI OPERA. (VOL
5, PT 1) (G. SAJÖ, ED)
A. ZIMMERMANN, 53(AGP):BAND55HEFT
2-243
BOETHIUS. THE THEOLOGICAL TRACTATES
(H.F. STEWART, E.K. RAND & S.J.
TESTER, TRANS) [TOGETHER WITH] THE
CONSOLATION OF PHILOSOPHY. (S.J.
TESTER, TRANS)
J. ANDRÉ, 555:VOL47FASC2-362
BOFFEY, P. THE BRAIN BANK OF AMER-
ICA.
S.J. GOULD, 441:4MAY75-8
BOGARD, T. CONTOUR IN TIME.*
T.P. ADLER, 160:SPRING73-192
D.V. FALK, 295:FEB74-738
H.F. FOLLAND, 651(WHR):SUMMER74-
270
J.P. LOVERING, 613:WINTER73-540
B.J. MANDEL, 579(SAQ):SUMMER74-410
T.E. PORTER, 191(ELN):JUN74-316
BOGATYREV, P. THE FUNCTIONS OF
FOLK COSTUME IN MORAVIAN SLOVAKIA.
K.L. COTHRAN, 292(JAF):JAN-MAR73-
78
BOGDAN, R., ED. ANDREESCU. (VOL 1)
Z. BARBU, 89(BJA):SUMMER73-306
BOGDANOR, V. - SEE DISRAELI, B.
BOGDANOVICH, P. PICTURE SHOWS.
G. MILLAR, 362:28AUG75-284
D. WILSON, 617(TLS):24OCT75-1257
BOGEL, E. & E. BLÜHM. DIE DEUTSCHEN
ZEITUNGEN DES 17. JAHRHUNDERTS.
P. RIES, 402(MLR):APR74-455
BOGEN, J. WITTGENSTEIN'S PHILOSOPHY
OF LANGUAGE.*
J.E. LLEWELYN, 262:WINTER73-431
R.A. SHINER, 154:DEC73-683
BOGEN, N. - SEE BLAKE, W.
BOGER, L.A. THE DICTIONARY OF WORLD
POTTERY & PORCELAIN.
G. WILLS, 39:SEP73-240
BOGUSLAWSKI, A. & S. KAROLAK. GRAM-
ATYKA ROSYJSKA W UJĘCIU FUNKCJONAL-
NYM.
A.M. SCHENKER, 574(SEEJ):WINTER72-
501
BOHLEN, C.E. WITNESS TO HISTORY
1929-1969.
W.F. BARBER, 50(ARQ):WINTER73-373
BÖHME, G. STIMM-, SPRACH- UND
HÖRSTÖRUNGEN.
I. KOSSEL, 682(ZPSK):BAND26HEFT
3/4-401
BÖHME, H. DEUTSCHLANDS WEG ZUR
GROSSMACHT.
G.G. WINDELL, 182:VOL26#10-370
BÖHME, R. PELOPIDEN UND POETEN.
M. GRIFFITH, 123:NOV74-213
BOHROD, A. A DECADE OF STILL LIFE.
M.S. YOUNG, 39:APR73-442
BOIARDO, M.M. ORLANDO INNAMORATO.
(S. FERRARI, ED; REV BY G. NEN-
CIONI)
A. DI BENEDETTO, 228(GSLI):VOL150
FASC469-118
BOIARDO, M.M. ORLANDO INNAMORATO.
(L. GARBATO, ED)
400(MLN):JAN73-164

BOILEAU, N. L'ART POÉTIQUE.* (A.
BUCK, ED)
B. BRAY, 535(RHL):JAN-FEB73-127
BOIME, A. THE ACADEMY & FRENCH
PAINTING IN THE NINETEENTH CEN-
TURY.*
F.A. TRAPP, 56:WINTER73-416
BOINE, G. & G. PREZZOLINI. CARTEG-
GIO I. (M. MARCHIONE & S.E. SCAL-
IA, EDS)
R.S. DOMBROSKI, 275(IQ):SPRING74-
92
BOIS, J. TRANSLATING FOR KING
JAMES. (W. ALLEN, ED & TRANS)
M. VAN BEEK, 179(ES):JUN72-256
DE BOISDEFFRE, P. VIE D'ANDRÉ GIDE.
(VOL 1)
M. PHILIP, 207(FR):FEB73-622
BOITANI, P. PROSATORI NEGRI AMERI-
CANI DEL NOVECENTO.
J. WOODRESS, 27(AL):JAN75-586
BOL, H. LA BASSE DE VIOLE DU TEMPS
DE MARIN MARAIS ET D'ANTOINE FOR-
QUERAY.
N. DOLMETSCH, 410(M&L):OCT74-489
BOLAND, E. THE WAR HORSE.
J. FULLER, 617(TLS):7NOV75-1327
BOLDREWOOD, R. THE MINER'S RIGHT.
H.W. RHODES, 67:NOV74-233
BOLDRINI, M. SCIENTIFIC TRUTH &
STATISTICAL METHOD.
R. BLANCHÉ, 542:JUL-SEP73-352
BOLELLI, T. LINGUISTICA GENERALE,
STRUTTURALISMO, LINGUISTICA STORICA.
G.C. LEPSCHY, 353:1DEC73-115
BOLES, J.B., ED. AMERICA.
639(VQR):SPRING74-XLVI
BOLES, J.B. A GUIDE TO THE MICRO-
FILM EDITION OF THE WILLIAM WIRT
PAPERS.
D.A. YANCHISIN, 14:OCT73-567
BOLES, P.D. THE LIMNER.
M. LEVIN, 441:4MAY75-52
442(NY):17MAR75-126
BOLGAR, R.R., ED. CLASSICAL INFLU-
ENCES ON EUROPEAN CULTURE A.D. 500-
1500.*
F.P. PICKERING, 220(GL&L):APR74-
256
LORD BOLINGBROKE. HISTORICAL WRIT-
INGS.* (I. KRAMNICK, ED)
R.W. GREAVES, 481(PQ):JUL73-468
BOLINGER, D. ASPECTS OF LANGUAGE.
R. QUIRK, 617(TLS):19DEC75-1509
BOLINGER, D. THE PHRASAL VERB IN
ENGLISH.*
B. FRASER, 350:SEP74-568
F.R. PALMER, 349:SUMMER73-230
BOLITHO, H. TREASURES AMONG MEN.
R. STORRY, 617(TLS):21MAR75-319
BÖLL, H. CHILDREN ARE CIVILIANS
TOO. AND WHERE WERE YOU, ADAM?
THE TRAIN WAS ON TIME. NEUE POLI-
TISCHE UND LITERARISCHE SCHRIFTEN.
P. PROCHNIK, 617(TLS):31JAN75-120
BÖLL, H. GROUP PORTRAIT WITH LADY.*
(GERMAN TITLE: GRUPPENBILD MIT
DAME.)
L.T.L., 502(PRS):FALL73-279
BÖLL, H. IM TAL DER DONNERNDEN
HUFE. (J. ALLDRIDGE, ED)
P. PROCHNIK, 220(GL&L):JUL74-339

BÖLL, H. THE LOST HONOR OF KATHAR-
INA BLUM.* (GERMAN TITLE: DIE VER-
LORENE EHRE DER KATHARINA BLUM.)
D.J. ENRIGHT, 362:30OCT75-578
C. LEHMANN-HAUPT, 441:21MAY75-43
M. WOOD, 441:27APR75-1
442(NY):19MAY75-119
BOLLACK, J. EMPÉDOCLE.* (VOLS 1-4)
A.A. LONG, 53(AGP):BAND55HEFT1-76
BOLLACK, J., M. BOLLACK & H. WIS-
MANN. LA LETTRE D'ÉPICURE.*
O-R. BLOCH, 542:OCT-DEC73-453
A.A. LONG, 123:MAR74-46
BOLLACK, J. & H. WISMANN. HÉRACLITE
OU LA SÉPARATION.
C. MUGLER, 555:VOL47FASC2-329
BOLSTER, R. STENDHAL, BALZAC ET LE
FÉMINISME ROMANTIQUE.*
G.R. BESSER, 207(FR):FEB73-614
H.J. HUNT, 208(FS):JAN74-91
R. LELIÈVRE, 557(RSH):JAN-MAR73-
170
BOLZANO, B. THEORY OF SCIENCE. (R.
GEORGE, ED & TRANS)
J. BERG, 488:SEP73-267
J. CORCORAN, 484(PPR):DEC73-282
J.J. KOCKELMANS, 486:MAR73-136
BOMANS, G. DICKENS, WAAR ZIJN UW
SPOKEN?
M.S., 155:SEP73-183
BONACHEA, R.E. & N.P. VALDÉS - SEE
CASTRO, F.
BONADEO, A. CORRUPTION, CONFLICT, &
POWER IN THE WORKS & TIMES OF NIC-
COLÒ MACHIAVELLI.
B.L., 275(IQ):SPRING74-105
BONANNO, M.G. STUDI SU CRATETE
COMICO.
N.G. WILSON, 123:NOV74-289
BONAPARTE, N. NAPOLEON WROTE FIC-
TION. (C. FRAYLING, ED & TRANS)
F.G. HEALEY, 208(FS):OCT74-474
BONARD, O. LA PEINTURE DANS LA CRÉ-
ATION BALZACIENNE.
J-L. BOURGET, 546(RR):NOV73-286
BONATH, G. UNTERSUCHUNGEN ZUR ÜBER-
LIEFERUNG DES PARZIVAL WOLFRAMS VON
ESCHENBACH.* (VOL 1)
G.R. DIMLER, 221(GQ):MAR73-270
D. STELLMACHER, 439(NM):1973/1-174
BONATTI, W. THE GREAT DAYS.
N. MORIN, 617(TLS):28MAR75-344
BOND, D.F. - SEE ADDISON, J. & R.
STEELE
BOND, R.P. THE TATLER.*
A.R. HUMPHREYS, 541(RES):MAY73-217
BONE, P.J. THE GUITAR & THE MANDO-
LIN.
I. HARWOOD, 415:JUN74-479
BONE, Q. HENRIETTA MARIA.*
A.J. LOOMIE, 613:WINTER73-547
BONELLI, M.L.R. & W.R. SHEA, EDS.
REASON, EXPERIMENT, & MYSTICISM IN
THE SCIENTIFIC REVOLUTION.
P. HEIMANN, 617(TLS):20JUN75-701
BONFANTE, G. & P. FERRERO. SCHOLA
NOVA, NOVA RATIO.
G. SERBAT, 555:VOL47FASC2-347
BONGARD-LEVIN, G.M. & G.F. IL'IN.
DREVNIJA INDIJA.
L. STERNBACH, 318(JAOS):JUL-SEP73-
378
BONHAM, B. WILLA CATHER.
J.H. RANDALL 3D, 295:FEB74-558

BONHEIM, H. & OTHERS. THE ENGLISH
NOVEL BEFORE RICHARDSON.*
L. BORINSKI, 38:BAND91HEFT2-259
BONI, D. LES PAYS AKYÉ (CÔTE
D'IVOIRE).
D.J. SIDDLE, 69:APR73-174
BONINO, J.M. - SEE UNDER MIGUEZ BON-
INO, J.
BÓNIS, F. BÉLA BARTÓK.
P. GRIFFITHS, 415:APR74-306
J.A. WESTRUP, 410(M&L):APR74-245
BONJOUR, E. DIE SCHWEIZ UND EUROPA.
H.S. OFFLER, 182:VOL26#21/22-813
BONNEROT, J. - SEE SAINTE-BEUVE,
C-A.
BONNEROT, J. & A. - SEE SAINTE-
BEUVE, C-A.
BONNEROT, L. L'OEUVRE DE WALTER DE
LA MARE.
P-S. MACAULAY, 179(ES):JUN72-266
BONNEROT, L., ED. "ULYSSES" CIN-
QUANTE ANS APRÈS.
G. ECKLEY, 659:AUTUMN75-504
N. HALPER, 329(JJQ):SPRING75-330
BONNET, H. MARCEL PROUST DE 1907 À
1914. (2ND ED)
J. ONIMUS, 557(RSH):OCT-DEC73-663
C. QUÉMAR-HOF, 535(RHL):NOV-DEC73-
1106
BONNEY, R. KEDAH 1771-1821.
C.S. GRAY, 293(JAST):MAY73-557
BONNIE, R.J. & C.H. WHITEBREAD 2D.
THE MARIHUANA CONVICTION.
639(VQR):AUTUMN74-CL
DE BONO, E., ED. EUREKA!*
M.W. THRING, 617(TLS):3JAN75-7
BONOMI, P.U. A FACTIOUS PEOPLE.*
J.A. SCHUTZ, 173(ECS):FALL73-109
BONSAL, P.W. CUBA, CASTRO, & THE
UNITED STATES.*
W.F. BARBER, 150(DR):SPRING73-179
BONSET, I.K. NIEUWE WOORDBEELDIN-
GEN. (K. SCHIPPERS, ED)
C. LEVENSON, 617(TLS):28NOV75-1427
BONTADINI, G. - SEE KANT, I.
BONTINCK, F., ED & TRANS. DIAIRE
CONGOLAIS DE FRA LUCA DA CALTANI-
SETTA (1690-1701).
D. BIRMINGHAM, 69:JAN73-80
BONURA, G. INVITO ALLA LETTURA DI
ITALO CALVINO.
R. ADAMS, 275(IQ):FALL-WINTER73
(VOL17#66)-72
400(MLN):JAN73-171
BONVESIN DE LA RIVA. DE MAGNALIBUS
MEDIOLANI/LE MERAVIGLIE DI MILANO.
617(TLS):31OCT75-1295
BONWETSCH, B. KRIEGSALLIANZ UND
WIRTSCHAFTSINTERESSEN.
M. MC CAULEY, 575(SEER):APR74-302
BONYTHON, K. MODERN AUSTRALIAN
PAINTING 1960-70.
L. KLEPAC, 39:FEB73-203
BONZON, A. LA NOUVELLE CRITIQUE ET
RACINE.
O. DE MOURGUES, 535(RHL):SEP-OCT
73-893
"THE BOOK OF KELLS."*
P. BROWN & S. MAC CORMACK, 453:
20FEB75-19
442(NY):24FEB75-144
BOOKCHIN, M. POST-SCARCITY ANAR-
CHISM.*
H. LOMAS, 364:AUG/SEP74-130

BOON, J.A. FROM SYMBOLISM TO STRUC-
TURALISM.
  R. MACKSEY, 400(MLN):DEC73-1338
BOON, J-P. MONTAIGNE, GENTILHOMME
ET ESSAYISTE.*
  F.S. BROWN, 188(ECR):SPRING73-87
  R.C. LA CHARITÉ, 207(FR):DEC72-401
  I.D. MC FARLANE, 208(FS):APR74-189
  205(FMLS):APR73-211
BOORSTIN, D.J. THE AMERICANS: THE
DEMOCRATIC EXPERIENCE.*
  R.A. RUTLAND, 639(VQR):WINTER74-
  109
BOORSTIN, D.J. DEMOCRACY & ITS DIS-
CONTENTS.*
  R. NISBET, 639(VQR):AUTUMN74-606
BOOTH, M. CORONIS.
  R. GARFITT, 364:AUG/SEP74-111
BOOTH, M.R., ED. ENGLISH PLAYS OF
THE NINETEENTH CENTURY.* (VOLS
3&4)
  P. DAVISON, 402(MLR):APR74-385
  A. RENDLE, 157:AUTUMN73-81
BOOTH, W.C. A RHETORIC OF IRONY.*
  W. EMPSON, 453:12JUN75-37
BOOTON, K. THE TOY.
  N. CALLENDAR, 441:23NOV75-52
BORASTON, I., H. CLEGG & M. RIMMER.
WORKPLACE & UNION.
  R.J. BEISHON, 617(TLS):18APR75-431
BORCHARDT, F.L. GERMAN ANTIQUITY IN
RENAISSANCE MYTH.*
  F.H. BÄUML, 405(MP):MAY74-415
  G.R. DIMLER, 613:WINTER73-546
  R.T. LLEWELLYN, 551(RENQ):SUMMER
  73-204
BORCHMEYER, D. TRAGÖDIE UND ÖFFENT-
LICHKEIT - SCHILLERS DRAMATURGIE.
  K.L. BERGHAHN, 406:WINTER74-401
  N.H. SMITH, 182:VOL26#13/14-487
"BORDAS-ENCYCLOPÉDIE." (VOL 12B:
LINGUISTIQUE)
  J. ANDRÉ, 555:VOL47FASC2-348
BOREL, J. MÉDECINE ET PSYCHIATRIE
BALZACIENNES.*
  C.F. COATES, 207(FR):DEC72-412
  H.J. HUNT, 208(FS):JAN74-92
BOREL, J. LE RETOUR.
  A. MARISSEL, 207(FR):FEB73-654
BOREL, J. - SEE VERLAINE, P.
BOREN, C.E. & OTHERS. ESSAYS ON THE
GILDED AGE.
  K.O. MORGAN, 617(TLS):14FEB75-154
BORETZ, B. & E.T. CONE, EDS. PER-
SPECTIVES ON SCHOENBERG & STRAV-
INSKY. (REV)
  M. PETERSON, 470:MAY73-15
BORG, A. ARCHITECTURAL SCULPTURE IN
ROMANESQUE PROVENCE.*
  A. REINLE, 182:VOL26#21/22-808
BORGER, R. & F. CIOFFI, EDS. EX-
PLANATION IN THE BEHAVIOURAL SCI-
ENCES.*
  J. WATLING, 262:SPRING73-101
  W.B. WEIMER, 215(GL):VOL13#2-133
BORGES, J.L. BORGES: SUS MEJORES
PÁGINAS. (M. ENGUÍDANOS, ED)
  H.D. OBERHELMAN, 238:MAY73-536
BORGES, J.L. DOCTOR BRODIE'S RE-
PORT.*
  T.E. LYON, 399(MLJ):NOV73-373
BORGES, J.L. IN PRAISE OF DARKNESS.*
PRÓLOGOS.
  J. STURROCK, 617(TLS):15AUG75-925

BORGES, J.L. EL LIBRO DE ARENA.
OBRAS COMPLETAS.
  J. STURROCK, 617(TLS):14NOV75-1349
BORGES, J.L., WITH E.Z. DE TORRES.
AN INTRODUCTION TO AMERICAN LITERA-
TURE. (L.C. KEATING & R.O. EVANS,
EDS & TRANS)
  A. BORINSKY, 400(MLN):MAR73-498
  295:FEB74-466
BORGHINI, V. SCRITTI INEDITI O RARI
SULLA LINGUA. (J.R. WOODHOUSE, ED)
  D.D., 275(IQ):SUMMER73-109
  V. LUCCHESI, 402(MLR):JAN74-190
BORGMEIER, R. SHAKESPEARES SONETT
"WHEN FORTY WINTERS..." UND DIE
DEUTSCHEN ÜBERSETZER.*
  S.L. GILMAN, 52:BAND8HEFT2-201
  H. OPPEL, 430(NS):AUG73-449
  H. WEINSTOCK, 179(ES):APR73-174
BORIE, J. ZOLA ET LES MYTHES OU DE
LA NAUSÉE AU SALUT.*
  N. SCHOR, 546(RR):NOV73-311
BORIS, C. LES TIGRES DE PAPIER.
  M. PALMER, 617(TLS):10OCT75-1203
BORKOWSKI, L. - SEE ŁUKASIEWICZ, J.
BORKOWSKI, P. THE GREAT RUSSIAN-
ENGLISH DICTIONARY OF IDIOMS & SET
EXPRESSIONS.
  R. SUSSEX, 67:MAY74-137
BORMANN, E.G. & N.C. EFFECTIVE
SMALL GROUP COMMUNICATION.
  J.C. MELE, 583:FALL73-98
BORMANN, K. PARMENIDES.*
  J.P. HERSHBELL, 124:OCT72-111
BORN, H. THE RARE WIT & THE RUDE
GROOM.*
  H. WEINSTOCK, 179(ES):DEC73-589
BORN, W. THE CONCISE ATLAS OF WINE.
  617(TLS):31OCT75-1313
BORNE, W.C., ED. TOWARD STUDENT-
CENTERED FOREIGN-LANGUAGE PROGRAMS.
  L.K. MEYER, 399(MLJ):NOV74-376
BORNEMANN, E. DIE UMWELT DES KINDES
IM SPIEGEL SEINER "VERBOTENEN" LIE-
DER, REIME, VERSE UND RÄTSEL.
  A. BOSTOCK, 617(TLS):25APR75-465
BORRAS, F.M. & R.F. CHRISTIAN. RUS-
SIAN SYNTAX.* (2ND ED)
  R.E. BEARD, 399(MLJ):DEC73-442
  R.A. ROTHSTEIN, 574(SEEJ):SUMMER
  72-251
BORRELL, C. & B. CASHINELLA. CRIME
IN BRITAIN TODAY.
  C.H. ROLPH, 617(TLS):26SEP75-1105
BORRELLO, A. H.G. WELLS.
  W.J. SCHEICK, 177(ELT):VOL16#4-307
BORROFF, E. MUSIC IN EUROPE & THE
UNITED STATES.
  P. DENNISON, 410(M&L):JUL74-352
BÖRSCH-SUPAN, H. CASPAR DAVID
FRIEDRICH.*
  P. CONRAD, 617(TLS):15AUG75-911
BORSI, F. L'ARCHITETTURA DELL'
UNITÀ D'ITALIA.
  S. KOSTOF, 576:OCT73-239
BORST, A. DER TURMBAU ZU BABEL.
  L. WEISGERBER, 680(ZDP):BAND92HEFT
  1-116
BORTOLI, G. THE DEATH OF STALIN.
  N. BETHELL, 441:25MAY75-4
BOS, C.A. INTERPRETATIE, VADERSCHAP
EN DATERING VAN DE ALCIBIADES
MAIOR.
  L.G. WESTERINK, 24:SPRING74-72

40

BOS, G.F. CATEGORIES & BORDER-LINE
CATEGORIES.
  O. REICHMANN, 680(ZDP):BAND92HEFT
  1-149
BOSCH, R. LA NOVELA ESPAÑOLA DEL
SIGLO XX. (VOL 1)
  J.W. KRONIK, 238:DEC73-1120
BOSCH, R. LA NOVELA ESPAÑOLA DEL
SIGLO XX. (VOL 2)
  L. HICKEY, 86(BHS):OCT73-411
  J.W. KRONIK, 238:DEC73-1120
BOSCO, H. LE RÉCIF.
  S. MAX, 207(FR):DEC72-431
BOSCO, M. LOT'S WIFE.
  G. DAVIES, 198:FALL75-137
BOSE, A.C. INDIAN REVOLUTIONARIES
ABROAD, 1905-1922.
  E.C. BROWN, 293(JAST):MAY73-522
BOSE, B.M., S.N. SEN & B.V. SUBBARA-
YAPPA, EDS. A CONCISE HISTORY OF
SCIENCE IN INDIA.
  S. PRAKASH, 273(IC):JAN73-80
BÖSING, L. GRIECHEN UND RÖMER IM
AUGUSTUSBRIEF DES HORAZ.
  O.A.W. DILKE, 313:VOL63-307
  J. PERRET, 555:VOL47FASC1-161
  N. RUDD, 123:NOV74-296
BOSL, K. DIE GESCHICHTE DER REPRÄ-
SENTATION IN BAYERN.
  F.L. CARSTEN, 617(TLS):7FEB75-133
BOSL, K. DIE GRUNDLAGEN DER MODERN-
EN GESELLSCHAFT IM MITTELALTER.
  D. NICHOLAS, 589:OCT74-708
BOSLEY, K., ED & TRANS. THE WAR
WIFE.
  T. EAGLETON, 565:VOL14#1-65
BOSMAJIAN, H.A., ED. DISSENT.
  C. LOGUE, 583:SPRING74-301
"BOSO'S LIFE OF ALEXANDER III."
(G.M. ELLIS, TRANS)
  M. CHENEY, 382(MAE):1974/3-313
BOSQUET, A. NOTES POUR UN AMOUR.
  G. BRÉE, 207(FR):APR73-1040
BOSS, V. NEWTON & RUSSIA.*
  J.T. ALEXANDER, 481(PQ):JUL73-378
BOSSANO, L. LOS PROBLEMAS DE LA
SOCIOLOGÍA. (5TH ED)
  A. CARRIÓN, 263:JAN-MAR74-78
VAN DEN BOSSCHE, E. - SEE GROOTEN,
J. & G.J. STEENBERGEN
BOSSCHER, P.M. ZEEGESCHIEDENIS VAN
DE LAGE LANDEN.
  C.R. BOXER, 617(TLS):28NOV75-1423
BOSTON, R. - SEE URQUHART, T.
"BOSTON PRINTS & PRINTMAKERS, 1670-
1775."
  A. FERN, 127:SPRING74-274
  C.C. SELLERS, 432(NEQ):DEC73-657
BOSWELL, J. BOSWELL'S BOOK OF BAD
VERSE. (J. WERNER, ED)
  D.J. ENRIGHT, 362:22MAY75-685
  K. WALKER, 617(TLS):4JUL75-734
BOTHA, R.P. METHODOLOGICAL ASPECTS
OF TRANSFORMATIONAL GENERATIVE
PHONOLOGY.
  G. BROWN, 297(JL):FEB73-162
BOTHE, D. DIREKTE UND INDIREKTE
TRANSKRIPTION.
  K. RYDLAND, 597(SN):VOL45#2-443
  J. VACHEK, 682(ZPSK):BAND26HEFT
  1/2-217
BÖTTCHER, I. - SEE HARSDÖRFFER, G.P.

BÖTTGER, F. HERMANN HESSE.
  T. ZIOLKOWSKI, 617(TLS):26SEP75-
  1108
BÖTTGER, P. DIE ALTE PINAKOTHEK IN
MÜNCHEN.
  N. PEVSNER, 54:DEC73-643
BOTTRALL, R. POEMS 1955-1973.
  P. BEER, 617(TLS):4JUL75-718
BOTZ, G. DIE EINGLIEDERUNG ÖSTER-
REICHS IN DAS DEUTSCHE REICH.
  F.L. CARSTEN, 575(SEER):JAN74-155
BOUAZIS, C., ED. ESSAIS DE LA
THÉORIE DU TEXTE.
  J. CULLER, 307:#2-114
BOUCÉ, P-G. LES ROMANS DE SMOLLETT.*
  H. AUFFRET, 549(RLC):JUL-SEP73-478
  D.F. BOND, 405(MP):NOV73-213
  B. GASSMAN, 72:BAND211HEFT3/6-438
BOUCHER, J.G. & R.L. PARIS. CON-
TRASTES.
  W. STAAKS, 207(FR):MAR73-878
DU BOUCHERON, G.B. - SEE UNDER BRA-
MOND DU BOUCHERON, G.
BOUDOT, M. LOGIQUE INDUCTIVE ET
PROBABILITÉ.
  R. BLANCHÉ, 542:JUL-SEP73-353
BOUILLON, J-P. - SEE ZOLA, É.
BOULANGER, A. & S. FERY. COURS
D'INITIATION AU RUSSE SCIENTIFIQUE.
  G.M. ERAMIAN, 104:WINTER74-586
BOULANGER, D. LES PRINCES DU QUAR-
TIER BAS.
  B. WRIGHT, 617(TLS):31JAN75-120
DU BOULAY, J. PORTRAIT OF A GREEK
MOUNTAIN VILLAGE.
  P. LEVI, 617(TLS):28MAR75-341
BOULLE, P. QUIA ABSURDUM.
  S.G. STARY, 207(FR):FEB73-655
BOULLE, P. THE VIRTUES OF HELL.
  N. CALLENDAR, 441:5JAN75-24
BOULTER, C.G. CORPUS VASORUM ANTI-
QUORUM: THE CLEVELAND MUSEUM OF ART.
(FASC 1)
  R.M. COOK, 123:MAR74-158
  B.A. SPARKES, 303:VOL93-267
BOULTON, D. THE MAKING OF TANIA
HEARST.
  K. MINOGUE, 617(TLS):7NOV75-1318
BOULTON, J.T., ED. JOHNSON: THE
CRITICAL HERITAGE.*
  D. FAIRER, 447(N&Q):JUN73-227
BOULTON, J.T. & R.S. SMITH, EDS.
RENAISSANCE & MODERN STUDIES. (VOL
14)
  C.J. RAWSON, 447(N&Q):JAN73-38
BOULVERT, G. ESCLAVES ET AFFRANCHIS
IMPÉRIAUX SOUS LE HAUT EMPIRE RO-
MAIN, RÔLE POLITIQUE ET ADMINISTRA-
TIF.
  J-C. DUMONT, 555:VOL47FASC1-186
BOUMA, L. THE SEMANTICS OF THE
MODAL AUXILIARIES IN CONTEMPORARY
GERMAN.
  R.L. KYES, 399(MLJ):DEC74-429
BOUQUET, H. THE PAPERS OF HENRY
BOUQUET.* (VOL 1) (S.K. STEVENS,
D.H. KENT & A.L. LEONARD, EDS)
  W.E.A. BERNHARD, 14:JAN73-69
BOUR, J-A. & W.L. HENDRICKSON.
QUINZE LEÇONS DE FRANÇAIS.
  A. CAPRIO, 207(FR):OCT72-240
BOURAOUI, H.A. CRÉACULTURE 1. CRÉ-
ACULTURE 2.
  W. WRAGE, 207(FR):FEB73-674

BOURAOUI, H.A. PAROLE ET ACTION.
W. WRAGE, 207(FR):FEB73-676
BOURGEADE, P. LES IMMORTELLES.
C. ST. LÉON, 207(FR):OCT72-202
BOURGEOIS, B. - SEE HEGEL, G.W.F.
BOURGOINT, J. LE RETOUR DE L'ENFANT
TERRIBLE. (J. HUGO & J. MOUTON,
EDS)
R. SPEAIGHT, 617(TLS):18JUL75-808
DU BOURGUET, P. EARLY CHRISTIAN ART.
P. HETHERINGTON, 90:NOV73-748
DU BOURGUET, P. MUSÉE NATIONAL DU
LOUVRE: CATALOGUE DES ÉTOFFES
COPTES. (VOL 1)
J. BECKWITH, 90:AUG73-547
BOURNE, G. & M. COHEN. THE GENTLE
GIANTS.
S. HEMPSTONE, 441:19OCT75-18
BOURNEUF, R. & R. OUELLET. L'UNIVERS
DU ROMAN.
A. FAIRLIE, 208(FS):OCT74-490
BOUTON, C.P., LES MÉCANISMES D'AC-
QUISITION DU FRANÇAIS, LANGUE
ÉTRANGÈRE CHEZ L'ADULTE.*
F. ABEL, 430(NS):AUG73-452
A. VALDMAN, 399(MLJ):SEP-OCT73-277
BOUVIER, J. & L. ONE SPECIAL SUM-
MER.
E. WEEKS, 61:JAN75-89
BOUVIER-CAVORET, J. LA MÉMOIRE VER-
TICALE.
S. MAX, 207(FR):DEC72-432
BOUYSSY, M.T. & OTHERS. LIVRE ET
SOCIÉTÉ DANS LA FRANCE DU XVIIIE
SIÈCLE. (VOL 2)
M. DUCHET, 535(RHL):JUL-AUG73-691
BOWBEER, R. & G. SCHERI - SEE SASTRE,
A.
BOWDEN, G.H. BRITISH GASTRONOMY.
N. SHRAPNEL, 617(TLS):12SEP75-1026
BOWDITCH, N.D. GEORGE DE FOREST
BRUSH.
T.B. BRUMBAUGH, 127:FALL73-76
BOWEN, A. THE JOURNALS OF ASHLEY
BOWEN (1728-1813) OF MARBLEHEAD.
(P.C.F. SMITH, ED)
G.A. BILLIAS, 432(NEQ):MAR74-140
BOWEN, B.C. THE AGE OF BLUFF.*
G.J. BRAULT, 207(FR):OCT72-146
BOWEN, C.D. THE MOST DANGEROUS MAN
IN AMERICA.*
G.F. SCHEER, 441:6APR75-3
BOWEN, E. PICTURES & CONVERSATIONS.
W. ABRAHAMS, 61:MAR75-133
G. ANNAN, 362:30OCT75-580
E. WELTY, 441:5JAN75-4
F. WYNDHAM, 617(TLS):24OCT75-1254
442(NY):20JAN75-99
BOWEN, J. A HISTORY OF WESTERN
EDUCATION. (VOL 2)
H. KEARNEY, 617(TLS):25APR75-452
BOWEN, J.D. & R.P. STOCKWELL. PAT-
TERNS OF SPANISH PRONUNCIATION.
G.S. GIAUQUE, 399(MLJ):NOV73-377
BOWEN, P., M. HAYDEN & F. RIESS.
SCREEN TEST.
G. MILLAR, 362:28AUG75-284
BOWEN, Z. MUSICAL ALLUSIONS IN THE
WORKS OF JAMES JOYCE.
R. BOYLE, 329(JJQ):SUMMER75-454
G. ECKLEY, 659:AUTUMN75-504
E. SAMS, 617(TLS):11APR75-395

BOWERING, G. FLYCATCHER & OTHER
STORIES.
M. BAXTER, 99:DEC75/JAN76-48
BOWERING, G. GEORGE, VANCOUVER.
M. DOYLE, 102(CANL):AUTUMN73-108
BOWERS, E. LIVING TOGETHER.
D. BROMWICH, 491:JAN75-229
R. LATTIMORE, 249(HUDR):AUTUMN74-
461
P. RAMSEY, 569(SR):SPRING74-399
L. STALL, 598(SOR):SUMMER75-662
BOWERS, F. THE NEW SCRIABIN.*
P. DICKINSON, 415:DEC74-1048
BOWERS, F., ED. STUDIES IN BIBLIO-
GRAPHY. (VOL 27)
G.T. TANSELLE, 617(TLS):8AUG75-904
BOWERS, F. - SEE CRANE, S.
BOWERS, F. - SEE MARLOWE, C.
BOWERS, J. THE COLONY.*
295:FEB74-362
BOWERS, J.Z. WESTERN MEDICINE IN A
CHINESE PALACE.
M.B. BULLOCK, 293(JAST):AUG73-689
BOWERSOCK, G.W. - SEE PHILOSTRATUS
BOWES, P. CONSCIOUSNESS & FREEDOM.
Y.N. CHOPRA, 393(MIND):JUL73-465
BOWICK, D.M. TAPESTRY OF DEATH.
N. CALLENDAR, 441:23NOV75-52
BOWIE, M. HENRI MICHAUX.*
C.A. HACKETT, 208(FS):APR74-231
639(VQR):AUTUMN74-CXXVII
BOWIE, N.E. TOWARDS A NEW THEORY OF
DISTRIBUTIVE JUSTICE.
N.L. NATHAN, 393(MIND):APR73-315
BOWIE, T. & D. THIMME. THE CARREY
DRAWINGS OF THE PARTHENON SCULP-
TURES.*
B. ASHMOLE, 90:NOV73-747
BOWKER, A. - SEE LEACOCK, S.
BOWLE, J. THE IMPERIAL ACHIEVEMENT.
J. MORRIS, 441:13JUL75-25
BOWLE, J. NAPOLEON.
J.E. HOWARD, 617(TLS):21FEB75-193
BOWLES, P. WITHOUT STOPPING.*
295:FEB74-363
BOWMAN, A. THE TOWN COUNCILS OF
ROMAN EGYPT.
J.A.S. EVANS, 487:WINTER73-419
BOWMAN, A.H. THE STRUGGLE FOR
NEUTRALITY.
639(VQR):AUTUMN74-CXXXIX
BOWMAN, D. LIFE INTO AUTOBIOGRAPHY.
D.G. LITTLE, 402(MLR):APR74-457
H. REISS, 133:1973/2-189
BOWN, W., ED. TWO CENTURIES OF
AFRICAN ENGLISH.
E. WRIGHT, 315(JAL):VOL11PT3-100
BOWNESS, A. COURBET'S "ATELIER DU
PEINTRE."
C.R. BRIGHTON, 89(BJA):SPRING73-
201
BOWRA, C.M. PERICLEAN ATHENS.*
M.E. WHITE, 487:AUTUMN73-309
BOWRING, J. THE KINGDOM & PEOPLE OF
SIAM.
C.M. WILSON, 293(JAST):MAY73-561
BOWSKILL, D. ACTING & STAGECRAFT
MADE SIMPLE.
R. STACEY, 157:SUMMER73-77
BOWSKILL, D. SEAVENTURES. GILGA-
MESH.
G. TYLER, 157:AUTUMN73-75

BOXER, A. NO ADDRESS.
D. BARBOUR, 529(QQ):SPRING73-141
S. MAYNE, 102(CANL):SPRING73-119
BOXER, C.R. THE ANGLO-DUTCH WARS OF
THE 17TH CENTURY 1652-1674.
G. PARKER, 617(TLS):28NOV75-1411
BOXER, C.R. MARY & MISOGYNY.
J. LYNCH, 617(TLS):30CT75-1129
BOYANCE, P. ÉTUDES SUR LA RELIGION
ROMAINE.
J-C. RICHARD, 555:VOL47FASC2-369
BOYCE, C. CATCHWORLD.
S. CLARK, 617(TLS):5DEC75-1438
BOYCE, D.G. ENGLISHMEN & IRISH
TROUBLES.
L.P. CURTIS, JR., 676(YR):AUTUMN
73-137
BOYCE, M. & I. GERSHEVITCH, EDS.
W.B. HENNING MEMORIAL VOLUME.
W. HINZ, 260(IF):BAND77HEFT2/3-290
D. WEBER, 260(IF):BAND77HEFT2/3-
296
BOYD, A. THE COMPANION GUIDE TO
MADRID & CENTRAL SPAIN.
N. GLENDINNING, 617(TLS):21FEB75-
202
BOYD, A.F. ASPECTS OF THE RUSSIAN
NOVEL.
N. MORAVCEVICH, 149:DEC74-354
BOYD, D. ROLLING THUNDER.
M.G. MICHAELSON, 441:2FEB75-7
BOYD, M. NUNS IN JEOPARDY.
M. LEVIN, 441:27APR75-34
BOYD, S. AMERICAN MADE.
A. NELSON, 441:29JUN75-15
BOYDE, P. DANTE'S STYLE IN HIS
LYRIC POETRY.*
P.M. BROWN, 205(FMLS):OCT73-403
A. FREEDMAN, 402(MLR):JUL74-657
G. MAZZOTTA, 546(RR):JAN74-71
A.L. PELLEGRINI, 589:JAN74-94
BOYDSTON, J.A. - SEE DEWEY, J.
BOYENS, A. KIRCHENKAMPF UND OKUMENE
1939-45.
J.S. CONWAY, 617(TLS):15AUG75-923
BOYER, F. LE MONDE DES ARTS EN
ITALIE ET LA FRANCE DE LA RÉVOLU-
TION ET DE L'EMPIRE.*
H-F. IMBERT, 535(RHL):JUL-AUG73-
708
BOYER, P. NON LIEU.
B.L. KNAPP, 207(FR):FEB73-657
BOYER, P. & S. NISSENBAUM. SALEM
POSSESSED.*
R. BRIGGS, 617(TLS):3JAN75-13
N. SALISBURY, 432(NEQ):SEP74-472
639(VQR):AUTUMN74-CXXXVIII
BOYLAN, J. HORIZONS.
G. TYLER, 157:AUTUMN73-75
BOYLAN, J., ED. THE WORLD & THE
20'S.*
S. DONALDSON, 569(SR):SUMMER74-527
BOYLE, C.M. - SEE MARSHALL, D.C.
BOYLE, H.J. THE GREAT CANADIAN
NOVEL.
L. MC DONALD, 102(CANL):AUTUMN74-
112
BOYLE, J.H. CHINA & JAPAN AT WAR,
1937-1945.
J.R. SHIRLEY, 293(JAST):FEB73-320
BOYLE, K. THE UNDERGROUND WOMAN.
J.D. O'HARA, 441:2FEB75-4
442(NY):20JAN75-97

BOYLE, L.E. A SURVEY OF THE VATICAN
ARCHIVES & OF ITS MEDIEVAL HOLDINGS.
R.H. ROUSE, 589:OCT74-711
BOYSEN, G. SUBJONCTIF ET HIÉRARCHIE.
H. NORDAHL, 1(ALH):VOL15#1-119
W. ROTHE, 343:BAND16HEFT2-185
BOZZOLI, A. MANZONIANA.*
A. PALLOTTA, 276:WINTER73-586
BRABAZON, J. ALBERT SCHWEITZER.
M.E. MARTY, 441:20JUL75-6
BRACEWELL, R.N. THE GALACTIC CLUB.
P. ADAMS, 61:MAY75-104
DE BRACH, P. LES AMOURS D'AYMÉE.*
(J. DAWKINS, ED)
F. JOUKOVSKY, 545(RPH):FEB74-436
I.D. MC FARLANE, 208(FS):APR74-193
A. SAUNDERS, 402(MLR):JAN74-173
M.S. WHITNEY, 207(FR):FEB73-603
BRACHER, F. - SEE ETHEREGE, G.
BRACHER, K.D. THE GERMAN DILEMMA.
J. JOLL, 617(TLS):8AUG75-892
BRACHIN, P. & OTHERS, EDS. DUTCH
STUDIES. (VOL 1)
M. RIGELSFORD, 617(TLS):28NOV75-
1425
BRACKEN, J.A. FREIHEIT UND KAUSALI-
TÄT BEI SCHELLING.
J.G. HART, 258:SEP73-454
BRACKMAN, A.C. THE DREAM OF TROY.
G. BIBBY, 441:2MAR75-10
BRACKMAN, A.C. THE LAST EMPEROR.
J. SPENCE, 441:14SEP75-34
"BRACTON ON THE LAWS & CUSTOMS OF
ENGLAND." (VOLS 1&2) (S.E. THORNE,
TRANS)
B. NICHOLAS, 382(MAE):1974/1-97
BRADBROOK, F.W. - SEE AUSTEN, J.
BRADBROOK, M. MALCOLM LOWRY, HIS
ART & EARLY LIFE.
S. GRACE, 296:VOL4#3-169
BRADBROOK, M.C. LITERATURE IN AC-
TION.
K.J. ATCHITY, 149:SEP74-263
W.H. NEW, 102(CANL):WINTER74-87
BRADBURY, M. THE HISTORY MAN.
H. SPURLING, 617(TLS):7NOV75-1325
J. VAIZEY, 362:4DEC75-760
BRADBURY, M., E. MOTTRAM & J. FRANCO,
EDS. THE PENGUIN COMPANION TO
AMERICAN LITERATURE.
K. CONGDON, 37:MAR73-38
BRADBURY, M. & D. PALMER, EDS. THE
AMERICAN NOVEL & THE NINETEEN
TWENTIES.*
T. ROGERS, 175:SUMMER73-81
295:FEB74-467
BRADBURY, M. & D. PALMER, EDS. META-
PHYSICAL POETRY.
L. POTTER, 179(ES):DEC73-591
BRADBURY, M. & D.J. PALMER, EDS.
SHAKESPEARIAN COMEDY.*
R.A. FOAKES, 175:SUMMER73-72
P. SWINDEN, 148:WINTER73-375
BRADBURY, M. & D. PALMER, EDS. VIC-
TORIAN POETRY.
P.J. MC CARTHY, 301(JEGP):OCT74-
558
H. SERGEANT, 175:SUMMER73-78
BRADBURY, R. WHEN ELEPHANTS LAST IN
THE DOORYARD BLOOMED.
A. MACLEAN, 617(TLS):23MAY75-552
BRADEN, W., ED. REPRESENTATIVE AMER-
ICAN SPEECHES: 1971-72.
W.S. TOWNS, 583:FALL73-94

BRAUDEL, F. THE MEDITERRANEAN & THE
MEDITERRANEAN WORLD IN THE AGE OF
PHILIP II.* (VOL 2)
 R.M. ANDREWS, 441:18MAY75-1
 H. MITGANG, 441:31MAY75-25
 639(VQR):SUMMER74-XCVII
BRAUDY, L. NARRATIVE FORM IN HIS-
TORY & FICTION.*
 I. SIMON, 179(ES):AUG73-395
BRAUDY, S. BETWEEN MARRIAGE &
DIVORCE.
 A. NELSON, 441:9NOV75-24
BRAUER, G.C., JR. JUDAEA WEEPING.
 L.H. FELDMAN, 121(CJ):FEB/MAR74-
 263
BRÄUER-POSPELOVA, M. - SEE BERNEKER,
E. & M. VASMER
BRAULT, G.J. EARLY BLAZON.
 C. BULLOCK-DAVIES, 382(MAE):
 1974/3-314
 D. EVANS, 447(N&Q):FEB73-61
 D.J.A. ROSS, 208(FS):OCT74-436
 M.A. STONES, 589:APR74-319
BRAULT, G.J. EIGHT THIRTEENTH-CEN-
TURY ROLLS OF ARMS IN FRENCH &
ANGLO-NORMAN BLAZON.
 R. EDWARDS, 651(WHR):SUMMER74-286
BRAULT, J. & B. LACROIX - SEE GAR-
NEAU, H.S-D.
BRAUN, H-J. L. FEUERBACHS LEHRE VOM
MENSCHEN.
 C. CESA, 548(RCSF):JUL-SEP73-352
BRAUN, L. DIE CANTICA DES PLAUTUS.*
 R.J. TARRANT, 122:APR74-140
BRAUN, T.E.D. UN ENNEMI DE VOL-
TAIRE.
 M. WACHS, 481(PQ):JUL73-562
BRAUN, V. DAS UNGEZWUNGENE LEBEN
KASTS.
 S. SCHLENSTEDT, 654(WB):3/1973-136
BRAUNSTEIN, J. MUSICA AETERNA.
 A. JACOBS, 415:JAN74-41
BRAUTIGAN, R. THE HAWKLINE MON-
STER.*
 V. CUNNINGHAM, 617(TLS):11APR75-
 389
 R. SALE, 249(HUDR):WINTER74/75-624
BRAUTIGAN, R. WILLARD & HIS BOWLING
TROPHIES.
 M. ROGERS, 441:14SEP75-4
 442(NY):10NOV75-189
BRAVERMAN, H. LABOR & MONOPOLY CAP-
ITAL.
 R.L. HEILBRONER, 453:23JAN75-6
BRAVMANN, R.A. OPEN FRONTIERS.
 P.J. IMPERATO, 2:AUTUMN73-82
BRAVO, A.P. & OTHERS. LA ESCUELA
INTERMEDIA EN DEBATE.
 J.R. LUNA, 37:APR73-39
DEL BRAVO, C. SCULTURA SENESE DEL
QUATTROCENTO.
 J.T. PAOLETTI, 56:SPRING-SUMMER73-
 102
DE BRAY, R.G.A. GUIDE TO THE SLAV-
ONIC LANGUAGES. (2ND ED)
 T.M.S. PRIESTLY, 104:FALL73-389
BRAY, T. BANTOCK.
 C. PALMER, 415:FEB74-133
BRAYBROOKE, N. - SEE ACKERLEY, J.R.
BRAZELL, J. SHELLEY & THE CONCEPT
OF HUMANITY.
 P.H. BUTTER, 402(MLR):JUL74-624

BRAZILL, W.J. THE YOUNG HEGELIANS.
 M. FOX, 529(QQ):SUMMER73-289
 A. QUINTON, 453:12JUN75-39
BREBNER, J.A. THE DEMON WITHIN.*
 H. COOMBES, 598(SOR):AUTUMN75-779
BRECH, U. - SEE KOBS, J.
BRECHER, E.M. & OTHERS. LICIT &
ILLICIT DRUGS.
 M. SEGAL, 150(DR):WINTER73/74-769
BRECHER, I. & S.A. ABBAS. FOREIGN
AID & INDUSTRIAL DEVELOPMENT IN
PAKISTAN.*
 J.J. STERN, 293(JAST):MAY73-545
BRÉCHON, R. LE SURRÉALISME.*
 R. CARDINAL, 208(FS):APR74-229
BRECHT, B. ARBEITSJOURNAL 1938-
1955. (W. HECHT, ED)
 M. KANE, 270:VOL23#3-61
BRECHT, B. KALENDERGESCHICHTEN.
(K.A. DICKSON, ED)
 205(FMLS):APR73-211
BRECHT, B. TAGEBÜCHER 1920-1922.
(H. RAMTHUN, ED)
 J. WILLETT, 617(TLS):3OCT75-1145
BRECKENRIDGE, J.D. LIKENESS.
 F.M. WASSERMANN, 121(CJ):OCT/NOV73-
 84
BREDE, W. - SEE HORKHEIMER, M.
BREDIUS, A. & H. GERSON. REMBRANDT
PAINTINGS.
 E. LARSEN, 127:WINTER73/74-172
BREDNICH, R.W., ED. JAHRBUCH FÜR
VOLKSLIEDFORSCHUNG. (VOL 15)
 W. MÜLLER-BLATTAU, 680(ZDP):BAND
 92HEFT3-471
VON BREDOW, W. VOM ANTAGONISMUS ZUR
KONVERGENZ?
 M. ROCK, 182:VOL26#9-277
BREDSDORFF, E. HANS CHRISTIAN AN-
DERSEN.
 A. WHITMAN, 441:31DEC75-19
BREDSDORFF, E. DEN STORE NORDISKE
KRIG OM SEKSUALMORALEN.
 P. VINTEN-JOHANSEN, 563(SS):FALL74-
 443
BREDVOLD, L.I. & OTHERS, EDS.
EIGHTEENTH-CENTURY POETRY & PROSE.
(3RD ED)
 566:AUTUMN73-35
BRÉE, G. CAMUS & SARTRE.*
 R. CHAMPIGNY, 295:FEB74-447
 A. VAN DEN HOVEN, 628:FALL73-113
BRÉE, G. WOMEN WRITERS IN FRANCE.
 S. RUDIKOFF, 249(HUDR):SUMMER74-
 273
BRÉE, G. & G. MARKOW-TOTEVY, EDS.
CONTES ET NOUVELLES.* (REV)
 W. STAAKS, 207(FR):FEB73-685
BREED, P.F. & F.M. SNIDERMAN, EDS.
DRAMATIC CRITICISM INDEX.
 L-L. MARKER, 397(MD):JUN73-110
BREESKIN, A.D. MARY CASSATT.
 R. PICKVANCE, 90:NOV73-745
BREICHA, O. GEORG EISLER.
 P. VERGO, 90:AUG73-550
BREINES, S. & W.J. DEAN. THE PEDES-
TRIAN REVOLUTION.
 C. TUNNARD, 441:2MAR75-6
BREITENSTEIN, T. HÉSIODE ET ARCH-
ILOQUE.*
 D.A. CAMPBELL, 123:MAR74-125

BREKLE, H.E. GENERATIVE SATZSEMAN-
TIK UND TRANSFORMATIONELLE SYNTAX
IM SYSTEM DER ENGLISCHEN NOMINAL-
KOMPOSITION.*
  U. OOMEN, 260(IF):BAND77HEFT2/3-
  353
BREKLE, H.E. SEMANTIK.
  G.F. MEIER, 682(ZPSK):BAND26HEFT
  1/2-184
BREMAN, P., ED. YOU BETTER BELIEVE
IT.
  C.W.E. BIGSBY, 617(TLS):28MAR75-
  342
BREMEN, W. DIE ALTEN GLASGEMÄLDE
UND HOHLGLÄSER DER SMLG. BREMEN IN
KREFELD.
  U-D. KORN, 182:VOL26#21/22-810
BRENAN, G. ST. JOHN OF THE CROSS.
  E.L. RIVERS, 402(MLR):OCT74-902
BRENAN, G. PERSONAL RECORD: 1920-
1972.*
  A. BROYARD, 441:28APR75-27
  I. EHRENPREIS, 453:17APR75-9
  P. STANSKY, 441:1JUN75-7
  442(NY):28APR75-139
BREND, R.M. A TAGMEMIC ANALYSIS OF
MEXICAN SPANISH CLAUSES.*
  J.R. CRADDOCK, 353:15NOV73-127
BRENDON, P. HURRELL FROUDE & THE
OXFORD MOVEMENT.
  J.W. BURROW, 617(TLS):14MAR75-274
  S. MINOGUE, 362:13FEB75-220
BRENDON, P. HAWKER OF MORWENSTOW.
  P. BEER, 362:17JUL75-93
  E.F.W. TOMLIN, 617(TLS):1AUG75-864
BRENGUES, J. CHARLES DUCLOS (1704-
1772) OU L'OBSESSION DE LA VERTU.*
  R. NIKLAUS, 535(RHL):JUL-AUG73-705
BRENGUES, J. - SEE DUCLOS, C.
BRENNAN, A. THE CARBON COPY.*
  R.A. HUNT, 296(VOL4#3-176
  G. WOODCOCK, 102(CANL):SPRING74-96
BRENNAN, A. THE CRAZY HOUSE.
  A. DONALDSON, 198:SUMMER75-115
BRENNAN, C.J. POEMS (1913).*
  H.W. RHODES, 67:NOV74-233
BRENNAN, N. THE POLITICS OF CATHO-
LICS.
  M. LYONS, 381:MAR73-106
BRENNI, V.J., COMP. WILLIAM DEAN
HOWELLS.
  D.J. NORDLOH, 27(AL):MAY74-229
  T. WORTHAM, 445(NCF):MAR74-497
BRENT, M. MOONRAKER'S BRIDE.
  E.M. EWING, 441:11MAY75-10
BRENT, P. THE VIKING SAGA.
  C.L. MEE, JR., 441:7DEC75-46
BRENT, R.L. INVITATION TO A STRANG-
LING.
  N. CALLENDAR, 441:31AUG75-12
BRENTANO, C. DIE CHRONIKA DES FAHR-
ENDEN SCHÜLERS.
  J.F.F., 191(ELN):SEP73(SUPP)-115
BRENTANO, F. THE FOUNDATION & CON-
STRUCTION OF ETHICS. (E.H. SCHNEE-
WIND, ED & TRANS)
  483:APR73-198
BRENTANO, R. ROME BEFORE AVIGNON.
  W. ULLMANN, 617(TLS):31JAN75-117
BRENTNALL, M. OLD CUSTOMS & CERE-
MONIES OF LONDON.
  617(TLS):8AUG75-906

BRÈS, Y. LA PSYCHOLOGIE DE PLATON.
  M. BUCCELLATO, 548(RCSF):OCT-DEC
  73-457
BRESLIN, J. HOW THE GOOD GUYS
FINALLY WON.
  C. LEHMANN-HAUPT, 441:19MAY75-27
  M.F. NOLAN, 441:11MAY75-2
  R. TODD, 61:JUL75-73
BRESLOW, M.A. A MIRROR OF ENGLAND.
  W.L. SACHSE, 551(RENQ):SPRING73-67
BRETON, A. SURREALISM & PAINTING.*
  A. POWELL, 39:MAR73-316
BRETT, R.L., ED. S.T. COLERIDGE.*
  D.V.E., 191(ELN):SEP73(SUPP)-43
  G. THOMAS, 175:SPRING72-27
BRETT, S. CAST, IN ORDER OF DISAP-
PEARANCE.
  P.D. JAMES, 617(TLS):26SEP75-1079
  M. LASKI, 362:25DEC75&1JAN76-893
BRETTSCHNEIDER, W. DIE MODERNE
DEUTSCHE PARABEL.
  C.P. MAGILL, 402(MLR):APR74-472
BRETTSCHNEIDER, W. ZWISCHEN LITER-
ARISCHER AUTONOMIE UND STAATS-
DIENST.*
  P. HUTCHINSON, 220(GL&L):JUL74-335
  D. JOST, 182:VOL26#15/16-546
  G. SCHULZ, 67:MAY74-126
  J.J. WHITE, 402(MLR):OCT74-943
BREUER, R. & R. SCHÖWERLING, EDS.
ALTENGLISCHE LYRIK.
  E.G. STANLEY, 38:BAND91HEFT4-514
BREUNIG, L.C. - SEE APOLLINAIRE, G.
BREUNINGER, M. FUNKTION UND WERTUNG
DES ROMANS IM FRÜHVIKTORIANISCHEN
ROMAN.
  G. KRIEGER, 430(NS):MAY73-289
BREWER, D., ED. GEOFFREY CHAUCER.
  617(TLS):14FEB75-177
BREWER, D.S. CHAUCER. (3RD ED)
  R.M. WILSON, 402(MLR):JUL74-616
BREWSTER, E. IN SEARCH OF EROS.
  G.S. MC CAUGHEY, 99:APR/MAY75-63
  A. RAVEL, 198:SPRING75-116
BREWSTER, E. THE SISTERS.
  M. BAXTER, 99:DEC75/JAN76-48
  F. GIBB, 617(TLS):10OCT75-1217
  M. LUND, 198:SPRING75-134
BREWSTER, E. SUNRISE NORTH.
  S. SOLECKI, 529(QQ):SUMMER73-311
BRICHAUT, C.D. LA FRANCE AU COURS
DES AGES.
  L.C. KEATING, 399(MLJ):NOV74-358
BRICHLER-LABAEYE, C. LES VOYELLES
FRANÇAISES.
  M. MONNOT, 207(FR):MAR73-888
BRIDBURY, A.R. HISTORIANS & THE
OPEN SOCIETY.
  R.H.C., 125:OCT73-95
BRIDEL, C. AUX SEUILS DE L'ESPÉR-
ANCE.
  T.H.L. PARKER, 182:VOL26#1/2-14
BRIDGEMAN, H. & E. DRURY, EDS. THE
BRITISH ECCENTRIC.
  A. BOYLE, 362:13NOV75-657
BRIDGEMAN, H. & E. DRURY, EDS. THE
ENCYCLOPEDIA OF VICTORIANA.
  R. REIF, 441:29DEC75-29
BRIDGES, K. A CALENDAR OF THE EGAN
FAMILY COLLECTION.
  A.L. NOLEN, 14:JAN73-76
BRIDGES-ADAMS, W. A BRIDGES-ADAMS
LETTER BOOK. (R. SPEAIGHT, ED)
  J. HAMILTON, 157:SPRING73-80

BRIDGMAN, R. GERTRUDE STEIN IN
PIECES.*
  S.B. PURDY, 295:FEB74-787
BRIDGWATER, P. NIETZSCHE IN ANGLO-
SAXONY.
  R.A. NICHOLLS, 131(CL):SUMMER74-
  284
BRIDLE, P., ED. DOCUMENTS ON RELA-
TIONS BETWEEN CANADA & NEWFOUNDLAND.
(VOL 1)
  P. NEARY, 99:APR/MAY75-37
BRIEGER, P., M. MEISS & C. SINGLE-
TON. ILLUMINATED MANUSCRIPTS OF
THE "DIVINE COMEDY."*
  J. BACKHOUSE, 90:MAR73-169
DE BRIEL, H. - SEE "LE ROMAN DE MER-
LIN L'ENCHANTEUR"
BRIELS, J.G.C.A. ZUIDNEDERLANDSE
BOEKDRUKKERS EN BOEKVERKOPERS IN DE
REPUBLIEK DER VERENIGDE NEDERLANDEN
OMSTREEKS 1570-1630.
  A.C. DUKE, 617(TLS):28NOV75-1408
BRIGGS, A., ED. ESSAYS IN THE HIS-
TORY OF PUBLISHING.*
  R.G. LANDON, 99:DEC75/JAN76-64
BRIGGS, A. - SEE MORRIS, W.
BRIGGS, D. IN PLACE OF PRISON.
  S. MC CONVILLE, 617(TLS):26SEP75-
  1105
BRIGGS, K.M. THE FOLKLORE OF THE
COTSWOLDS.
  R. HAYNES, 617(TLS):4JUL75-742
BRIGGS, S. KEEP SMILING THROUGH.
  F. DILLON, 362:4SEP75-316
BRILL, R.H., ED. SCIENCE & ARCHAE-
OLOGY.
  M. FARNSWORTH, 124:OCT72-115
BRILLAT-SAVARIN, A. PHYSIOLOGIE DU
GOÛT.
  J. WEIGHTMAN, 617(TLS):19DEC75-
  1504
BRIMO, A. LES MÉTHODES DES SCIENCES
SOCIALES.
  D. MERLLIÉ, 542:JAN-MAR73-53
BRINDLE, R.S. THE NEW MUSIC.
  617(TLS):12SEP75-1030
BRINEY, R.E. & E. WOOD, EDS. SF
BIBLIOGRAPHIES.
  J.B. POST, 503:SPRING73-48
BRINGMANN, K. UNTERSUCHUNGEN ZUM
SPÄTEN CICERO.
  M. RUCH, 555:VOL47FASC1-103
BRINK, A.P. LOOKING ON DARKNESS.*
  442(NY):25AUG75-86
BRINK, C.O. HORACE ON POETRY.*
(VOL 2)
  W.R. JOHNSON, 121(CJ):FEB/MAR74-
  275
  Z. PAVLOVSKIS, 122:JUL74-233
  G.W. WILLIAMS, 123:MAR74-52
BRINKER, K. DAS PASSIV IM HEUTIGEN
DEUTSCH.
  B.J. KOEKKOEK, 221(GQ):MAR73-240
BRINKMANN, R., WITH W. WIETHÖLTER -
SEE "THEODOR FONTANE"
BRINKMANN, R.D. WESTWÄRTS 1 & 2.
  M. HAMBURGER, 617(TLS):6JUN75-623
BRINKWORTH, E.R.C. SHAKESPEARE &
THE BAWDY COURT OF STRATFORD.
  M. ECCLES, 402(MLR):APR74-373
BRION-GUERRY, L., ED. L'ANNÉE
1913.* (VOLS 1&2)
  R. MICHA, 98:FEB73-99

BRIOSI, S. DA CROCE AGLI STRUTTUR-
ALISTI.
  E.G. CASERTA, 545(RPH):AUG73-113
BRISMAN, L. MILTON'S POETRY OF
CHOICE & ITS ROMANTIC HEIRS.
  R.W. FRENCH, 568(SCN):FALL74-52
  J.A. WITTREICH, JR., 301(JEGP):
  JUL74-435
DE BRISSAC, E. UN LONG MOIS DE SEP-
TEMBRE.
  J.M. SCHNEIDER, 207(FR):DEC72-433
BRISSENDEN, C., ED. WEST COAST
PLAYS.
  E. MULLALY, 198:SUMMER75-38
BRISSENDEN, R.F., ED. STUDIES IN
THE EIGHTEENTH CENTURY II.
  A.C. KEYS, 67:NOV74-227
  566:SPRING74-94
"THE BRITANNICA REVIEW OF FOREIGN
LANGUAGE EDUCATION." (VOL 1)
  E.C. CONDON, 207(FR):APR73-1075
BRITTEN, A. THE MIGNONETTE.
  A. RENDLE, 157:SUMMER73-79
BRITTEN, B. CHILDREN'S CRUSADE.
  J. WARRACK, 415:FEB74-132
"BENJAMIN BRITTEN: A COMPLETE CATA-
LOGUE OF HIS PUBLISHED WORKS."
  P. EVANS, 415:JUL74-570
BRITTON, J. LANGUAGE & LEARNING.
  R.C. LUGTON, 399(MLJ):SEP-OCT74-
  279
BROAD, C.D. BROAD'S CRITICAL ESSAYS
IN MORAL PHILOSOPHY. (D. CHENEY,
ED)
  A.R.C. DUNCAN, 154:JUN73-341
BROAD, C.D. LEIBNIZ. (C. LEWY, ED)
  G.H.R. PARKINSON, 617(TLS):15AUG
  75-914
BROADFOOT, B. SIX WAR YEARS 1939-
1945.*
  R. WEAVER, 606(TAMR):MAR75-101
BROADIE, F. AN APPROACH TO DES-
CARTES' "MEDITATIONS."*
  D.R.P., 543:DEC72-351
BROADIE, F. THE DRY CONSPIRACY.
  A. BARNES, 617(TLS):4JUL75-732
BROCCIA, G. LEXEIS.
  R. SCHMITT, 343:BAND16HEFT1-91
BROCH, H. & D. BRODY. HERMANN BROCH
- DANIEL BRODY: BRIEFWECHSEL 1930-
1951.* (B. HACK & M. KLEISS, EDS)
  G. BRUDE-FIRNAU, 224(GRM):BAND23
  HEFT2-250
  J. STRELKA, 133:1973/2-190
BROCHIER, J-J. - SEE NIZAN, P.
BROCK, E. INVISIBILITY IS THE ART
OF SURVIVAL.*
  R.J. SMITH, 598(SOR):SPRING75-464
BROCK, E. THE PORTRAITS & THE
POSES.*
  D. BROMWICH, 491:JAN75-229
  H. CARRUTH, 249(HUDR):SUMMER74-311
BROCK, M. THE GREAT REFORM ACT.
  J. CLIVE, 453:23JAN75-29
BROCK, P. PACIFISM IN EUROPE TO
1914.*
  J.M. STAYER, 529(QQ):AUTUMN73-475
BROCK, S. THE SYRIAC VERSION OF THE
PSEUDO-NONNOS MYTHOLOGICAL SCHOLIA.
  B.M. METZGER, 124:SEP72-53

"THE BROCK BIBLIOGRAPHY OF PUBLISHED
CANADIAN STAGE PLAYS IN ENGLISH
1900-1972."
L.T.C., 102(CANL):SUMMER73-128
J. NOONAN, 529(QQ):AUTUMN73-466
BROCKETT, O.G. PERSPECTIVES ON CON-
TEMPORARY THEATRE.
F. HODGE, 583:SPRING74-297
BROCKMAN, J. & E. ROSENFELD. REAL
TIME.
E. KORN, 617(TLS):28MAR75-342
R. NORTH, 362:24APR75-542
BRODERICK, A. - SEE HAURIOU, M., G.
RENARD & J.T. DELOS
BRODERICK, J. AN APOLOGY FOR ROSES.
T. HARAN, 159(DM):WINTER/SPRING73-
122
BRODERICK, W.J. CAMILO TORRES.
E. HEGEMAN, 441:9MAR75-6
BRODIE, F.M. THOMAS JEFFERSON.*
P.F. BOLLER, JR., 584(SWR):SUMMER
74-321
M-J. KLINE, 432(NEQ):DEC74-623
R.E. SPILLER, 27(AL):JAN75-580
639(VQR):AUTUMN74-CXXXV
BRODINE, V. & M. SELDEN. OPEN SEC-
RET.
J.H. FINCHER, 293(JAST):AUG73-702
BRODORICK, A.H., ED. ANIMALS IN
ARCHAEOLOGY.
H.A. FRANKFORT, 54:MAR73-136
BRODSKIJ, I. OSTANOVKA V PUSTYNE.
E. BRISTOL, 574(SEEJ):SPRING72-107
BRODSKY, I. SYDNEY'S PHANTOM BOOK-
SHOPS.
G.A.W., 581:MAR74-102
BRODSKY, J. SELECTED POEMS.*
V. ERLICH, 473(PR):4/1974-617
R. GARFITT, 364:JUN/JUL74-104
R. LATTIMORE, 249(HUDR):AUTUMN74-
473
639(VQR):SUMMER74-LXXXV
BRODWIN, L.L. ELIZABETHAN LOVE
TRAGEDY 1587-1625.
R.A. FOAKES, 175:SUMMER72-67
A. HOLADAY, 551(RENQ):SUMMER73-228
E.M. YEARLING, 541(RES):MAY73-203
BRODY, A. COMING TO.
M. LEVIN, 441:23MAR75-33
BRODY, A. THE ENGLISH MUMMERS &
THEIR PLAYS.*
N. PEACOCK, 203:SUMMER73-167
R.M. WILSON, 175:SPRING72-23
BRODY, E.C. THE DEMETRIUS LEGEND &
ITS LITERARY TREATMENT IN THE AGE
OF THE BAROQUE.*
J.V. HANEY, 574(SEEJ):WINTER73-454
I.K. LILLY, 104(WINTER74-587
E. KOSTKA, 549(RLC):OCT-DEC73-628
L. TURKEVICH, 550(RUSR):JUL73-329
BRODY, S.N. THE DISEASE OF THE
SOUL.
639(VQR):SUMMER74-LXXX
BROER, L.R. HEMINGWAY'S SPANISH
TRAGEDY.
S. MOORE, 385(MQR):FALL75-466
B. OLDSEY, 27(AL):JAN75-597
639(VQR):SUMMER74-LXXIII
BROGAN, H., ED. THE AMERICAN CIVIL
WAR.
617(TLS):13JUN75-680
BROKHIN, Y. HUSTLING ON GORKY
STREET.
S. JACOBY, 441:19OCT75-42

BROMBERG, R. CANALETTO'S ETCHINGS.
J.B. SHAW, 617(TLS):21MAR75-299
BROMBERT, V. FLAUBERT PAR LUI-
MÊME.*
B.F. BART, 207(FR):DEC72-417
F.P. BOWMAN, 546(RR):NOV73-309
C. GOTHOT-MERSCH, 535(RHL):JAN-
FEB73-148
M. TILLETT, 208(FS):APR74-221
BROME, V. THE DAY OF DESTRUCTION.
J. MELLORS, 362:23JAN75-126
BROMELL, H. THE SLIGHTEST DISTANCE.
A. GOTTLIEB, 441:5JAN75-16
BROMFIELD, J.G. DE LORENZINO DE
MÉDICIS À LORENZACCIO.
R. TROUSSON, 549(RLC):OCT-DEC73-
641
BROMHEAD, P. BRITAIN'S DEVELOPING
CONSTITUTION.
617(TLS):31JAN75-121
BROMHEAD, P. LIFE IN MODERN BRIT-
AIN. (3RD ED)
E. QUENON-PAQUES, 556(RLV):1973/3-
282
BROMIGE, D. THREADS.*
S. DRAGLAND, 102(CANL):AUTUMN74-
188
BRONEER, O. ISTHMIA. (VOL 1)
J.M. COOK, 123:MAR74-122
A.T. HODGE, 487:SPRING73-93
N. NABERS, 124:NOV72-185
BRONK, W. THE NEW WORLD.
R. ELMAN, 441:9MAR75-12
BRONSEN, D. JOSEPH ROTH.
E. TUCKER, 617(TLS):11APR75-406
BRONSON, B.H. THE TRADITIONAL TUNES
OF THE CHILD BALLADS.* (VOL 4)
C.M. SIMPSON, JR., 317:SPRING73-
159
BRONTË, C. FIVE NOVELETTES.* (W.
GÉRIN, ED)
N. SHERRY, 402(MLR):JUL74-626
BRONZWAER, W.J.M. TENSE IN THE
NOVEL.*
R. COPPITERS, 179(ES):APR73-195
R. FOWLER, 307:#1-119
BROOK, R.J. BERKELEY'S PHILOSOPHY
OF SCIENCE.
L.A. MIRARCHI, 319:OCT75-530
BROOKE, C. THE MONASTIC WORLD, 1000-
1300.*
G. WILLS, 231:JUL75-85
BROOKE, C., WITH G. KEIR. LONDON
800-1216.
A. JOHNSON, 362:24APR75-543
H.R. LOYN, 617(TLS):9MAY75-504
BROOKE, J. KING GEORGE III.*
R.W. GREAVES, 481(PQ):JUL73-338
J.J. HECHT, 432(NEQ):MAR74-161
BROOKE, J. & M. SORENSEN - SEE
GLADSTONE, W.E.
BROOKE, R. THE LETTERS OF RUPERT
BROOKE. (G. KEYNES, ED)
A.S. MONOD, 189(EA):JAN-MAR73-72
BROOKE-ROSE, C. THRU.
W. FEAVER, 362:14AUG75-221
M. MASON, 617(TLS):11JUL75-753
BROOKE-ROSE, C. A ZBC OF EZRA
POUND.*
B. ALPERT, 295:FEB74-751
D. BARBOUR, 529(QQ):AUTUMN73-450
A.P. HINCHLIFFE, 148:SUMMER72-189
H. SERGEANT, 175:SUMMER72-75

BROOKES, G.H. THE RHETORICAL FORM
OF CARLYLE'S "SARTOR RESARTUS."*
 M. BAUMGARTEN, 125:OCT73-98
 S. MONOD, 189(EA):JUL-SEP73-374
 E. SHARPLES, 141:SPRING74-180
 E.M. VIDA, 255(HAB):SUMMER73-227
 E.M. VIDA, 637(VS):DEC73-225
BROOKES, H.F. & C.E. FRAENKEL - SEE
GRASS, G.
BROOKHOUSE, C., ED. "SIR AMADACE"
& "THE AVOWING OF ARTHUR."*
 F.C. DE VRIES, 179(ES):FEB72-64
BROOKNER, A. GREUZE.*
 D. MANNINGS, 89(BJA):SPRING73-205
 M. ROSENTHAL, 135:MAY73-63
BROOKS, A.R. JAMES BOSWELL.
 R. FOLKENFLIK, 481(PQ):JUL73-469
BROOKS, C. A SHAPING JOY.*
 R. BUFFINGTON, 219(GAR):WINTER73-
 586
 H. PESCHMANN, 175:SPRING72-30
 295:FEB74-467
BROOKS, C. & R.P. WARREN. MODERN
RHETORIC. (3RD ED)
 R.J. REDDICK, 113:SPRING73-61
BROOKS, C.E. THE TROUT & THE STREAM.
 H. HENKIN, 441:29JUN75-16
BROOKS, D. RACE & LABOUR IN LONDON
TRANSPORT.
 D. COLLARD, 617(TLS):4JUL75-727
BROOKS, D.H. GONE AWAY.
 M. LEVIN, 441:18MAY75-50
BROOKS, J.R. THOMAS HARDY.*
 C.J.P. BEATTY, 447(N&Q):JUL73-276
 D. KRAMER, 445(NCF):DEC73-347
 B. SANKEY, 301(JEGP):JUL74-452
BROOKS, M.Z. NASAL VOWELS IN CON-
TEMPORARY STANDARD POLISH.
 G.F. MEIER, 682(ZPSK):BAND26HEFT
 3/4-459
BROOKS, R.A. A CRITICAL BIBLIOGRA-
PHY OF FRENCH LITERATURE. (VOL 4)
 D.A. BONNEVILLE, 207(FR):OCT72-156
BROPHY, R.J. ROBINSON JEFFERS.
 L.C. POWELL, 584(SWR):SPRING74-196
 H.H. WAGGONER, 27(AL):NOV74-409
BROSSARD, N. FRENCH KISS.
 A. POKORNY, 296:VOL4#3-183
BROTHERS, J. OX.
 M. LEVIN, 441:29JUN75-28
BROUGH, J. THE PRINCE & THE LILY.
 J. O'REILLY, 441:23FEB75-30
 S. SECKER, 617(TLS):26SEP75-1085
BROUGH, J. PRINCESS ALICE.
 M.S. KENNEDY, 441:13APR75-26
BROUWER, J.W., J.L. SIESLING & J.
VIS. ANTHON VAN RAPPARD.
 R. PICKVANCE, 617(TLS):11JUL75-754
BROWER, D.R. - SEE ANDERSON, S.
BROWER, R., H. VENDLER & J. HOLLAN-
DER, EDS. I.A. RICHARDS.*
 R.G. COX, 569(SR):FALL74-705
 R. FULLER, 364:AUG/SEP74-127
 D.J. GORDON, 676(YR):SPRING74-424
 P. HUGHES, 113:FALL74-90
 G.W. RUOFF, 651(WHR):SUMMER74-284
BROWER, R.A., ED. FORMS OF LYRIC.*
 C. RAINE, 447(N&Q):MAR73-119
BROWER, R.A. HERO & SAINT.*
 J. BRITTON, 613:SPRING73-121
 G. BULLOUGH, 551(RENQ):SPRING73-81
 R.A. FOAKES, 175:SUMMER72-67
 R. FRASER, 141:WINTER73-70
                  [CONTINUED]

[CONTINUING]
 J.C. MAXWELL, 447(N&Q):APR73-152
 M. MUELLER, 72:BAND21HEFT3/6-431
BROWER, R.A. ALEXANDER POPE.
 I. SIMON, 179(ES):JUN72-258
BROWER, R.A., ED. TWENTIETH-CENTURY
LITERATURE IN RETROSPECT.
 S. GILL, 447(N&Q):SEP73-360
 V.M. HAMM, 613:SPRING73-136
 W.W. ROBSON, 541(RES):FEB73-105
 295:FEB74-467
BROWN, A.C. BODYGUARD OF LIES.
 T. MORGAN, 441:9NOV75-3
 442(NY):29DEC75-56
BROWN, A.E. BOSWELLIAN STUDIES.
 I.S. LUSTIG, 481(PQ):JUL73-469
BROWN, C. MANDELSTAM.*
 J. BAINES, 402(MLR):OCT74-954
 J. BAINES, 575(SEER):JUL74-441
 G. DAVENPORT, 249(HUDR):SUMMER74-
 299
 G.J. JANECEK, 399(MLJ):APR74-219
 M.G. LEVINE, 473(PR):3/1974-462
 G. STRUVE, 574(SEEJ):WINTER73-461
 639(VQR):WINTER74-XXII
BROWN, C. NEGATIVE IN BLUE.
 N. CALLENDAR, 441:23FEB75-40
BROWN, C. A SHADOW ON SUMMER.*
 A. BROYARD, 441:3FEB75-23
BROWN, C.H. WILLIAM CULLEN BRYANT.*
 S.J. HASELTON, 613:SPRING73-127
BROWN, D. MIKHAIL GLINKA.
 A. FITZLYON, 364:APR/MAY74-128
 E. GARDEN, 410(M&L):JUL74-341
 G. NORRIS, 415:JUN74-476
BROWN, D. WILBYE.
 P. BRETT, 415:DEC74-1046
BROWN, D. - SEE PAUL, A.
BROWN, F.A. GOTTHOLD EPHRAIM LES-
SING.
 J. GLENN, 564:MAR73-80
 L.P. WESSELL, JR., 399(MLJ):SEP-
 OCT73-296
BROWN, G. MY STRUGGLE.
 E. KORN, 617(TLS):24JAN75-73
BROWN, G.E. GEORGE BERNARD SHAW.*
 F.P.W. MC DOWELL, 295:FEB74-772
BROWN, G.G. A LITERARY HISTORY OF
SPAIN: THE TWENTIETH CENTURY.*
 J.R. CORTINA, 399(MLJ):JAN-FEB74-
 75
 C. DE COSTER, 149:DEC74-358
BROWN, G.M. GREENVOE.*
 E. GLOVER, 565:VOL14#2-36
BROWN, G.M. HAWKFALL.* THE TWO
FIDDLERS.
 J. MELLORS, 362:9JAN75-61
BROWN, I. A CHARM OF NAMES.
 L.R.N. ASHLEY, 424:SEP73-196
BROWN, I. SHAKESPEARE & THE ACTORS.
 J.A. ROBERTS, 570(SQ):SUMMER73-335
BROWN, J. SLAVE LIFE IN GEORGIA.
 J.E. TALMADGE, 219(GAR):SPRING73-
 143
BROWN, J. ZURBARÁN.
 F. HASKELL, 453:2OCT75-14
BROWN, J.M. GANDHI'S RISE TO POWER.
 G. MINAULT, 293(JAST):AUG73-721
 L. STERNBACH, 318(JAOS):OCT-DEC73-
 612
BROWN, J.M. THE ORDEAL OF A PLAY-
WRIGHT.* (N. COUSINS, ED)
 J.M. WARE, 295:FEB74-778

BROWN, J.R., ED. SHAKESPEARE: "AN-
TONY & CLEOPATRA."
   M.T. JONES-DAVIES, 189(EA):JUL-SEP
   73-360
"THE JOHN CARTER BROWN LIBRARY,
BROWN UNIVERSITY: ANNUAL REPORTS
1901-1966."
   R.B. DRAKE, 517(PBSA):APR-JUN74-
   191
   E. WOLF 2D, 432(NEQ):DEC73-649
BROWN, K. ADVENTURES WITH D.W.
GRIFFITH. (K. BROWNLOW, ED)
   J. SPEARS, 200:DEC73-619
BROWN, L.R., WITH E.P. ECKHOLM. BY
BREAD ALONE.*
   G. BARRACLOUGH, 453:23JAN75-20
BROWN, L.W. BITS OF IVORY.*
   M.A. BURGAN, 301(JEGP):JAN74-127
   G.M. HARVEY, 150(DR):WINTER73/74-
   788
   S.M. TAVE, 445(NCF):DEC73-364
BROWN, M. THE POLITICS OF IRISH
LITERATURE FROM THOMAS DAVIS TO
W.B. YEATS.*
   J. FRAYNE, 301(JEGP):JAN74-141
   J.J. MC AULEY, 376:OCT73-143
   N.H. MACKENZIE, 529(QQ):AUTUMN73-
   481
   H. SERGEANT, 175:AUTUMN72-114
BROWN, M.E. WALLACE STEVENS.*
   J. HARDIE, 295:FEB74-791
BROWN, M.P. THE AUTHENTIC WRITINGS
OF IGNATIUS.
   J. DANIÉLOU, 182:VOL26#10-329
BROWN, P. RELIGION & SOCIETY IN THE
AGE OF SAINT AUGUSTINE.
   W.H.C. FREND, 123:NOV74-283
BROWN, P.L. STAR & PLANET SPOTTING.
   617(TLS):7FEB75-149
BROWN, R. A FIRST LANGUAGE: THE
EARLY STAGES.*
   C.Y. DULL, 351(LL):JUN74-135
   D.L.F. NILSEN, 399(MLJ):SEP-OCT74-
   268
BROWN, R., ED. KNOWLEDGE, EDUCATION,
& CULTURE CHANGE.
   T. POOT, 182:VOL26#15/16-534
BROWN, R. & R.J. HERRNSTEIN. PSY-
CHOLOGY.
   N.S. SUTHERLAND, 617(TLS):19SEP75-
   1064
BROWN, R.A. THE PRESIDENCY OF JOHN
ADAMS.
   M.M. MINTZ, 441:30NOV75-51
BROWN, R.D. REVOLUTIONARY POLITICS
IN MASSACHUSETTS.*
   R. MIDDLETON, 173(ECS):SPRING74-
   368
BROWN, R.H. I AM OF IRELAND.
   R. EDER, 441:13APR75-28
BROWN, S. NEW FORCES IN WORLD POLI-
TICS.
   G. BARRACLOUGH, 453:7AUG75-23
BROWN, S., WITH G. GÁL - SEE OCKHAM,
WILLIAM OF
BROWN, T. LOUIS MAC NEICE.
   R. PADEL, 617(TLS):28MAR75-327
BROWN, T. & A. REID, EDS. TIME WAS
AWAY.
   R. PADEL, 617(TLS):28MAR75-327
BROWN, T.H. & K. SANDBERG. CONVER-
SATIONAL ENGLISH.
   F. GOMES DE MATOS, 399(MLJ):JAN-
   FEB73-75

BROWN, T.J., ED. THE DURHAM RITUAL.*
   G. STORMS, 179(ES):AUG72-351
BROWN, W. ON THE COAST.*
   A. CLUYSENAAR, 565:VOL14#3-70
BROWN, W.H., JR. A SYNTAX OF KING
ALFRED'S "PASTORAL CARE."*
   D.L. SHORES, 179(ES):APR73-163
BROWNE, H. YOU CAN PROFIT FROM A
MONETARY CRISIS.*
   B.G. MALKIEL, 441:26JAN75-19
BROWNE, M.L. THE AROUSERS.
   M. LEVIN, 441:12JAN75-18
BROWNE, R.B., ED. FOLKSONGS & THEIR
MAKERS.
   N.V. ROSENBERG, 292(JAF):JAN-MAR
   73-69
BROWNE, R.B. MELVILLE'S DRIVE TO
HUMANISM.
   K. WIDMER, 594:SPRING73-117
BROWNING, E.B. LETTERS TO MRS.
DAVID OGILVY 1849-1861. (P.N. HEY-
DON & P. KELLEY, EDS)
   A. HAYTER, 617(TLS):25JUL75-837
BROWNING, F. & OTHERS. PRISON LIFE.
   N. WARDEN, 109:FALL/WINTER73/74-98
BROWNING, R. BROWNING: POETICAL
WORKS 1833-1864. (I. JACK, ED)
BROWNING: MEN & WOMEN 1855. (P.
TURNER, ED)
   J.C. MAXWELL, 447(N&Q):JUL73-269
BROWNING, R. BYZANTIUM & BULGARIA.
   D. OBOLENSKY, 617(TLS):2MAY75-477
BROWNING, R. THE COMPLETE WORKS OF
ROBERT BROWNING.* (VOLS 1&2) (R.A.
KING, JR., GENERAL ED)
   J. PETTIGREW, 184(EIC):OCT72-436
BROWNING, R. THE DUKE OF NEWCASTLE.
   P. LANGFORD, 617(TLS):18JUL75-794
BROWNING, R. JUSTINIAN & THEODORA.*
   W.R. CHALMERS, 123:NOV74-281
BROWNING, R.M. GERMAN BAROQUE
POETRY, 1618-1723.*
   F.R. LEHMEYER, 399(MLJ):DEC73-434
BROWNJOHN, A. WARRIOR'S CAREER.*
   A. CLUYSENAAR, 565:VOL14#2-62
BROWNLOW, K. - SEE BROWN, K.
BROWNMILLER, S. AGAINST OUR WILL.
   M.E. GALE, 441:12OCT75-1
   A. HELLER, 61:NOV75-118
   D. JOHNSON, 453:11DEC75-36
   C. LEHMANN-HAUPT, 441:16OCT75-43
   442(NY):3NOV75-171
BROWNRIGG, R. THE TWELVE APOSTLES.
   P. HEBBLETHWAITE, 617(TLS):3JAN75-
   20
BROYARD, A. AROUSED BY BOOKS.
   B. DE MOTT, 61:FEB75-111
BROZEK, J. & D.I. SLOBIN, EDS.
PSYCHOLOGY IN THE USSR.
   J. KOLAJA & L.M. SIZER, 104:WINTER
   74-610
BROZOVIĆ, D. STANDARDNI JEZIK.
   R. DUNATOV, 574(SEEJ):SUMMER72-264
BRUCCOLI, M.J. APPARATUS FOR F.
SCOTT FITZGERALD'S "THE GREAT GATS-
BY" ("UNDER THE RED, WHITE & BLUE").
   D.S. SMITH, 617(TLS):5SEP75-1002
BRUCCOLI, M.J., ED. THE CHIEF GLORY
OF EVERY PEOPLE.
   W.B. DILLINGHAM, 569(SR):SPRING74-
   XXXV
   T. WORTHAM, 445(NCF):MAR74-497

BRUCCOLI, M.J.   F. SCOTT FITZGERALD:
A DESCRIPTIVE BIBLIOGRAPHY.
   295:FEB74-600
BRUCCOLI, M.J.   THE O'HARA CONCERN.
   J. ATLAS, 441:26OCT75-6
   A. BROYARD, 441:4NOV75-39
   R. TODD, 61:NOV75-116
   442(NY):20OCT75-170
BRUCCOLI, M.J. - SEE HEMINGWAY, E.
BRUCCOLI, M.J., WITH J.M. ATKINSON
   - SEE FITZGERALD, F.S. & H. OBER
BRUCCOLI, M.J. & J.R. BRYER, EDS.
F. SCOTT FITZGERALD IN HIS OWN
TIME.
   295:FEB74-600
BRUCCOLI, M.J. & C.E.F. CLARK, JR.,
COMPS.   HEMINGWAY AT AUCTION, 1930-
1973.
   27(AL):NOV74-425
BRUCE, C.   THE CHANNEL SHORE.
   S.L. DUREN, 296:VOL4#3-153
BRUCE, D.   SUN PICTURES.*
   639(VQR):AUTUMN74-CLVIII
BRUCE, G., M. LINDSAY & E. MORGAN,
EDS.   SCOTTISH POETRY 6.
   A. CLUYSENAAR, 565:VOL14#2-62
BRUCE, J.   BREATHING SPACE.
   J. DOAN, 606(TAMR):OCT74-76
   R. WILLMOT, 296:VOL4#1-181
BRUCE, N.   PORTUGAL.
   C.R. BOXER, 617(TLS):11APR75-392
BRUCE-MITFORD, R.   ASPECTS OF ANGLO-
SAXON ARCHAEOLOGY.*
   P. ADAMS, 61:FEB75-122
BRUCH, J-L. - SEE KANT, I.
BRÜCKNER, H-D.   HELDENGESTALTUNG IM
PROSAWERK CONRAD FERDINAND MEYERS.
   G. FOLKERS, 221(GQ):NOV73-639
BRÜCKNER, P. & OTHERS.   DAS UNVER-
MÖGEN DER REALITÄT.
   P. LABANYI, 617(TLS):25JUL75-855
BRUDE-FIRNAU, G.   MATERIALEN ZU HER-
MANN BROCHS "DIE SCHLAFWANDLER."
   P.M. LÜTZELER, 680(ZDP):BAND92
   HEFT4-624
BRUDNER, N.Y.   PAINTING WITH A
NEEDLE.
   P. GREENBERG, 139:FEB73-8
BRUDNOY, D., ED.   THE CONSERVATIVE
ALTERNATIVE.
   H.B. GOW, 396(MODA):WINTER74-93
BRUEGEL, J.W.   CZECHOSLOVAKIA BEFORE
MUNICH.
   F.L. CARSTEN, 575(SEER):APR74-319
BRUFORD, W.H.   CHEKHOV & HIS RUSSIA.
   K.D. KRAMER, 574(SEEJ):SPRING72-
   102
BRUFORD, W.H.   THE GERMAN TRADITION
OF SELF-CULTIVATION.
   T.J. REED, 617(TLS):25APR75-458
BRÜGEL, J.W., ED.   STALIN UND HIT-
LER.*
   H. HANAK, 575(SEER):OCT74-621
BRÜGGEMANN, D.   DIE SÄCHSISCHE KOMÖ-
DIE.
   M.G. FLAHERTY, 221(GQ):JAN73-116
BRUIJN, J.R.   DE ADMIRALITEIT VAN
AMSTERDAM IN RUSTIGE JAREN, 1713-
1751.
   C.R. BOXER, 617(TLS):28NOV75-1423
BRUIJN, J.R. & OTHERS.   VIER EEUWEN
VAREN.
   C.R. BOXER, 617(TLS):28NOV75-1423

DE BRUIN, M.P.   AAN DE REDE, ZEELAND
AAN DE WATERKANT.
   C.R. BOXER, 617(TLS):28NOV75-1423
BRUMFITT, J.H.   THE FRENCH ENLIGHT-
ENMENT.
   V. GOUREVITCH, 481(PQ):JUL73-379
BRUMM, U.   PURITANISMUS UND LITERA-
TUR IN AMERIKA.
   C. RIVERS, 165:SPRING75-93
BRUNEAU, J. - SEE FLAUBERT, G.
BRUNEAU, T.C.   THE POLITICAL TRANS-
FORMATION OF THE BRAZILIAN CATHOLIC
CHURCH.
   E. DE KADT, 617(TLS):14FEB75-163
BRUNEL, P.   CLAUDEL ET SHAKESPEARE.
   J. PETIT, 535(RHL):SEP-OCT73-926
BRUNEL, P., ED.   LA MORT DE GODOT.
   E.C. JACQUART, 207(FR):OCT72-168
BRUNEL, P.   LE MYTHE D'ELECTRE.*
   S. MAX, 207(FR):MAR73-846
BRUNEL, P. - SEE BUCHER, B. & OTHERS
BRUNEL, P. & OTHERS.   HISTOIRE DE LA
LITTÉRATURE FRANÇAISE.
   K.R. DUTTON, 67:NOV74-234
BRUNÈS, T.   THE SECRETS OF ANCIENT
GEOMETRY - & ITS USE.
   C. KREN, 124:DEC73-JAN74-182
BRÜNING, D.   CLÉMENT MAROTS BEAR-
BEITUNG DES ROSENROMANS (1526).
   E.T. DUBOIS, 182:VOL26#21/22-796
BRÜNING, E., ED.   AMERIKANISCHE PRO-
TESTDRAMEN.
   U. BEITZ, 654(WB):7/1973-153
BRÜNING, H.   BRIEFE 1946-1960.   (C.
NIX, ED)
   K. VON KLEMPERER, 617(TLS):4JUL75-
   723
BRUNIUS, T.   MUTUAL AID IN THE ARTS.
   S. BAYLEY, 89(BJA):SPRING73-195
   L.R. FURST, 131(CL):SUMMER73-267
   W.H. TRUITT, 290(JAAC):SPRING74-
   444
BRUNNER, B.   SIX DAYS TO SUNDAY.
   M. LEVIN, 441:19OCT75-45
BRUNNER, F. & OTHERS.   VOM WESEN DER
SPRACHE.
   C.M. KIEFFER, 343:BAND16HEFT2-129
BRUNNER, J.   THE SHOCKWAVE RIDER.
   G. JONAS, 441:20JUL75-10
BRUNNER, J.   THE WRONG END OF TIME.
   T.A. SHIPPEY, 617(TLS):8AUG75-903
BRUNNER, R.J.   JOHANN ANDREAS SCHMEL-
LER - SPRACHWISSENSCHAFTLER UND
PHILOLOGE.
   P. WIESINGER, 343:BAND16HEFT1-76
BRUNNSÅKER, S.   THE TYRANT-SLAYERS
OF KRITIOS & NESIOTES.*
   G.B. WAYWELL, 123:NOV74-312
   B.S. RIDGWAY, 124:FEB74-240
BRUNOT, F.   LA PENSÉE ET LA LANGUE.
   J. STÉFANINI, 209(FM):OCT73-419
BRUNS, G.   KÜCHENWESEN UND MAHL-
ZEITEN.
   P. CHANTRAINE, 555:VOL47FASC2-317
BRUNS, G.L.   MODERN POETRY & THE
IDEA OF LANGUAGE.
   M.D. UROFF, 301(JEGP):OCT74-572
BRUNS, T.   KANT ET L'EUROPE.
   C. ZORGBIBE, 98:JAN73-95
BRUNSDEN, D. & J.C. DOORNKAMP, EDS.
THE UNQUIET LANDSCAPE.
   K. DUNHAM, 617(TLS):3JAN75-7

51

BUCKLEY, W.F., JR. EXECUTION EVE.
A. BROYARD, 441:11SEP75-45
S.R. WEISMAN, 441:28SEP75-3
BUCKLEY, W.F., JR. FOUR REFORMS.*
C.P. IVES, 396(MODA):SUMMER74-312
BUCKLEY, W.F., JR. UNITED NATIONS
JOURNAL.*
P. WHITEHEAD, 362:3JUL75-28
BUCKMASTER, H. WAIT UNTIL EVENING.*
P.M. SPACKS, 249(HUDR):SUMMER74-
283
BUDAGOV, R.A. JAZYK, ISTORIJA I
SOVREMENNOST'.
J. VEYRENC, 353:1AUG73-120
BUDDE, L. ANTIKE MOSAIKEN IN KILI-
KIEN.
E. KITZINGER, 54:MAR73-140
BUDDEN, J. THE OPERAS OF VERDI.*
(VOL 1)
R. CRAFT, 453:20MAR75-3
A. PORTER, 415:FEB74-130
BUDGEN, F. JAMES JOYCE & THE MAKING
OF "ULYSSES."
P. RECONDO, 202(FMOD):JUN73-410
BUECHNER, F. LOVE FEAST.*
R. SALE, 249(HUDR):WINTER74/75-628
N. SHRAPNEL, 617(TLS):23MAY75-577
BUEL, R., JR. SECURING THE REVOLU-
TION.*
M.B. NORTON, 432(NEQ):JUN73-319
J.A. SCHUTZ, 481(PQ):JUL73-339
C. WILSON, 396(MODA):WINTER74-94
BUELL, F. W.H. AUDEN AS A SOCIAL
POET.*
B. DUFFEY, 27(AL):MAR74-121
C. DUNCAN, 150(DR):AUTUMN73-564
M. KIRKHAM, 529(QQ):WINTER73-646
J. REPLOGLE, 301(JEGP):APR74-268
G. WOODCOCK, 569(SR):FALL74-685
BUELL, J. THE SHREWSDALE EXIT.
D. BROWN, 376:OCT73-140
H. ROSENGARTEN, 102(CANL):AUTUMN
73-92
BUELL, L. LITERARY TRANSCENDENTAL-
ISM.
C.H. FOSTER, 27(AL):NOV74-399
F. MURPHY, 432(NEQ):JUN74-304
639(VQR):WINTER74-XX
BUERKLE, J.V. & D. BARKER. BOURBON
STREET BLACK.*
639(VQR):WINTER74-XXX
BUERO VALLEJO, A. EL SUEÑO DE LA
RAZÓN.* (J. DOWLING, ED)
K. SCHWARTZ, 399(MLJ):JAN-FEB73-72
BUFFER, J. SKULL.
N. CALLENDAR, 441:29JUN75-30
BUFFIÈRE, F., ED & TRANS. ANTHOLO-
GIE GRECQUE.* (PT 1, VOL 12)
G. LUCK, 24:SPRING74-71
BUGAULT, B.G. LA NOTION DE "PRAJÑA"
OU DE SAPIENCE SELON LES PERSPEC-
TIVES DU "MADĀYĀNA."
A. WAYMAN, 318(JAOS):JAN-MAR73-110
BUGLIOSI, V., WITH C. GENTRY. HEL-
TER SKELTER.* (BRITISH TITLE: THE
MANSON MURDERS.)
C. RYCROFT, 617(TLS):18APR75-418
BUGNICOURT, J. DISPARITÉS RÉGION-
ALES ET AMÉNAGEMENT DU TERRITOIRE
EN AFRIQUE.
R.C. O'BRIEN, 69:OCT73-376
BÜHLER, C.F. EARLY BOOKS & MANU-
SCRIPTS.
K.W. HUMPHREYS, 402(MLR):JUL74-617

BÜHLER, C.F. - SEE DE PISAN, C.
BÜHLER, H. & OTHERS. LINGUISTIK I.*
R. BARTSCH, 133:1973/1-88
U. SCHEUERMANN, 260(IF):BAND77HEFT
2/3-348
BÜHLER, K. AMERICAN SILVER 1655-
1825 IN THE MUSEUM OF FINE ARTS,
BOSTON.
C. OMAN, 39:DEC73-521
BÜHLER, K.C. & G. HOOD. AMERICAN
SILVER, GARVAN & OTHER COLLECTIONS
IN THE YALE UNIVERSITY ART GALLERY.
C. OMAN, 39:AUG73-153
BUIJTENHUIJS, R. MAU MAU.
M. TWADDLE, 617(TLS):3JAN75-8
BUIJTENHUIJS, R. LE MOUVEMENT "MAU-
MAU."
B. BERNARDI, 69:OCT73-374
BUIST, M.G. AT SPES NON FRACTA.
D. ORMROD, 617(TLS):28NOV75-1422
VAN BUITENEN, J.A.B., ED & TRANS.
THE MAHĀBHĀRATA.* (VOL 1)
639(VQR):AUTUMN74-CLIII
DE BUJANDA, J.M. ÉRASME DE ROTTER-
DAM.
A. HYMA, 551(RENQ):WINTER73-463
BUJNOCH, J., ED & TRANS. ZWISCHEN
ROM UND BYZANZ. (2ND ED)
N.W. INGHAM, 574(SEEJ):WINTER72-
512
BULATKIN, E.W. STRUCTURAL ARITHME-
TIC METAPHOR IN THE OXFORD "ROLAND."
A.K. HIEATT, 382(MAE):1974/1-37
G.F. JONES, 589:JAN74-98
A. KNAPTON, 545(RPH):FEB74-428
BULGAKOV, M. A COUNTRY DOCTOR'S
NOTEBOOK.
E. MORGAN, 617(TLS):30MAY75-584
BULGAKOV, M. DIABOLIAD & OTHER
STORIES.* (E. & C.R. PROFFER, EDS)
E. STENBOCK-FERMOR, 574(SEEJ):WIN-
TER72-483
BULGAKOV, M. THE EARLY PLAYS OF
MIKHAIL BULGAKOV.* (E. PROFFER, ED)
C.H. BEDFORD, 397(MD):JUN73-106
E. STENBOCK-FERMOR, 574(SEEJ):WIN-
TER72-483
BULGAKOV, M. SELECTED WORKS. (A.
PYMAN, ED)
R.D.B. THOMSON, 575(SEER):JUL74-
471
205(FMLS):APR73-211
BULK, W. DAS PROBLEM DES IDEALEN
AN-SICH-SEINS BEI NICOLAI HARTMANN.
S. DECLOUX, 182:VOL26#5/6-133
BULL, J. BIRDS OF NEW YORK STATE.*
442(NY):9JUN75-128
BULL, W.E. & OTHERS. SPANISH FOR
COMMUNICATION. (LEVEL 1)
T.W. KELLY, 238:MAY73-526
T. TERRELL, 399(MLJ):NOV74-364
BULL, W.E. & OTHERS. SPANISH FOR
COMMUNICATION. (LEVEL 2)
T. TERRELL, 238:MAY73-527
BULL, W.E., L.A. BRISCO & E.E. LAMA-
DRID. COMMUNICATING IN SPANISH.
T. TERRELL, 399(MLJ):NOV74-364
BULLARD, E.J. MARY CASSATT, OILS &
PASTELS.*
A.D. BREESKIN, 127:SPRING74-280
BULLEN, R. PALMERSTON, GUIZOT &
THE COLLAPSE OF THE ENTENTE COR-
DIALE.
C. LUCAS, 617(TLS):21FEB75-193

BULLER, F. & H. FALKUS. FRESHWATER
FISHING.
  S. VAUGHAN, 617(TLS):30MAY75-608
BULLER, H. DAYS OF RAGE.*
  B. SPROXTON, 296:VOL4#1-203
BULLOCK, A., ED. THE TWENTIETH
CENTURY.
  295:FEB74-364
BULLOUGH, G., ED. NARRATIVE & DRA-
MATIC SOURCES OF SHAKESPEARE.*
(VOL 7)
  J.B. FORT, 189(EA):JUL-SEP73-362
  K. MUIR, 402(MLR):JAN74-148
BULLOUGH, G., ED. NARRATIVE & DRA-
MATIC SOURCES OF SHAKESPEARE. (VOL
8)
  J. CAREY, 362:20MAR75-376
BULMER, K., ED. NEW WRITINGS IN
SF - 25.
  617(TLS):23MAY75-555
BULMER, K., ED. NEW WRITINGS IN
SF - 26.
  J. HAMILTON-PATERSON, 617(TLS):
  5DEC75-1438
BULWER-LYTTON, E.G. PELHAM, OR THE
ADVENTURES OF A GENTLEMAN. (J.J.
MC GANN, ED)
  G.P. LANDOW, 454:SPRING74-269
BUMPUS, J. THINGS IN PLACE.
  T. LASK, 441:30NOV75-61
BUNCHE, R.J. THE POLITICAL STATUS
OF THE NEGRO IN THE AGE OF FDR.
(D.W. GRANTHAM, ED)
  R. GAVINS, 579(SAQ):AUTUMN74-564
BUNGE, H. FRAGEN SIE MEHR ÜBER
BRECHT.
  C.L. HART-NIBBRIG, 657(WW):MAY/JUN
  73-215
BUNGE, M. PHILOSOPHY OF PHYSICS.
  W.K. BURTON, 478:JUL73-124
BUNGE, M., ED. PROBLEMS IN THE
FOUNDATIONS OF PHYSICS.
  R.S. METZGER, 486:SEP73-464
BUNGERT, H., ED. DIE AMERIKANISCHE
SHORT STORY.
  H. OPPEL, 38:BAND91HEFT3-412
BUNGERT, H. FORMEN DER EINSAMKEIT
IM ZEITGENÖSSISCHEN AMERIKANISCHEN
ROMAN.
  L. TRUCHLAR, 430(NS):JAN73-51
BUNKER, G.E. THE PEACE CONSPIRACY.*
  J.R. SHIRLEY, 293(JAST):FEB73-320
BURCH, F.F. TRISTAN CORBIÈRE.*
  L. FORESTIER, 535(RHL):JUL-AUG73-
  721
BURCHFIELD, J.D. LORD KELVIN.
  K. DUNHAM, 617(TLS):24OCT75-1272
BURCHFIELD, R.W. - SEE "A SUPPLEMENT
TO THE OXFORD ENGLISH DICTIONARY"
BURCKHARDT, C.J. RICHELIEU & HIS
AGE.* (VOL 3)
  J. LOUGH, 208(FS):JUL74-318
BURCKHARDT, S. THE DRAMA OF LAN-
GUAGE. (B. BLUME & R.H. PEARCE,
EDS)
  B.K. BENNETT, 221(GQ):SEP73-135
  J. GEAREY, 405(MP):NOV73-221
BURD, V.A., ED. THE RUSKIN FAMILY
LETTERS.
  A.D. CULLER, 676(YR):WINTER74-287
  G.P. LANDOW, 301(JEGP):JAN74-135
BURD, V.A. - SEE RUSKIN, J.

BURDEN, V. GOING PLACES IN THE
THAMES VALLEY.
  617(TLS):8AUG75-906
VON BÜREN, E. ZUR BEDEUTUNG DER
PSYCHOLOGIE IM WERK ROBERT MUSILS.*
  J.J. WHITE, 220(GL&L):JUL74-331
BURFORD, A. CRAFTSMEN IN GREEK &
ROMAN SOCIETY.
  M. REINHOLD, 124:MAR74-300
  C. ROEBUCK, 487:SUMMER73-187
BURGER, H. ZEIT UND EWIGKEIT.
  D.H. GREEN, 402(MLR):JUL74-691
  M. KAEMPFERT, 680(ZDP):BAND92HEFT
  2-278
BURGER, H.O., ED. ANNALEN DER
DEUTSCHEN LITERATUR. (2ND ED)
  J.C. BRUCE, 221(GQ):SEP73-160
  I.F., 191(ELN):SEP73(SUPP)-106
BURGER, H.O. RENAISSANCE, HUMANIS-
MUS, REFORMATION.*
  S. JAFFE, 405(MP):FEB74-304
BURGER, H.O. & K. VON SEE, EDS.
FESTSCHRIFT GOTTFRIED WEBER.
  R.G. FINCH, 220(GL&L):OCT73-72
BÜRGER, P. DER FRANZÖSISCHE SUR-
REALISMUS.
  H. RÜCK, 430(NS):SEP73-505
  N. SCHWAB-BAKMAN, 535(RHL):JAN-FEB
  73-154
BÜRGER, P. DIE FRÜHEN KOMÖDIEN
PIERRE CORNEILLES UND DAS FRANZÖ-
SISCHE THEATER UM 1630.
  P.J. YARROW, 208(FS):JUL74-321
BÜRGER, P. THEORIE DER AVANTGARDE.
  P. LABANYI, 617(TLS):25JUL75-855
BURGESS, A. THE CLOCKWORK TESTA-
MENT, OR ENDERBY'S END.*
  P. ADAMS, 61:FEB75-122
  A. BROYARD, 441:1FEB75-25
  T.R. EDWARDS, 453:20FEB75-34
  J.D. O'HARA, 441:2FEB75-4
  442(NY):10MAR75-118
BURGESS, A. JOYSPRICK.*
  G. ECKLEY, 659:AUTUMN75-504
BURGESS, A. MF.*
  J.C. FIELD, 556(RLV):1973/1-91
BURGESS, A. NAPOLEON SYMPHONY.*
  J.L. HALIO, 598(SOR):AUTUMN75-942
  R. SALE, 249(HUDR):WINTER74/75-624
  P. VANSITTART, 364:FEB/MAR75-130
BURGESS, A. OEDIPUS THE KING.
  A. RENDLE, 157:AUTUMN73-81
BURGESS, G.S. CONTRIBUTION À
L'ÉTUDE DU VOCABULAIRE PRÉ-COUR-
TOIS.*
  S.G. NICHOLS, JR., 207(FR):OCT72-
  143
BURGHARDT, L.H., ED. DIALECTOLOGY.
  R.K. O'CAIN, 35(AS):FALL-WINTER71-
  246
BURGIN, V. WORK & COMMENTARY.
  W. FEAVER, 364:JUN/JUL74-129
BURGOS, J., ED. CIRCÉ.
  L. DAVIS, 208(FS):OCT74-504
BURIAN, J. & A. HARTMANN. PRAGUE
CASTLE.
  S. SMITH, 441:7DEC75-95
BURICH, N.J. ALEXANDER THE GREAT.*
  E.N. BORZA, 122:APR73-138
BURKE, E. THE CORRESPONDENCE OF
EDMUND BURKE.* (VOL 9) (R.B.
MC DOWELL & J.A. WOODS, EDS)
  J.T. BOULTON, 447(N&Q):JAN73-36

BURKE, J. ENGLISH VILLAGES.
617(TLS):7NOV75-1339
BURKE, J. ROGUE'S PROGRESS.
G. WEALES, 441:19JAN75-20
BURKE, J.F. DEATH TRICK.
N. CALLENDAR, 441:2NOV75-51
BURKE, K. LANGUAGE AS SYMBOLIC
ACTION.
J.M. FERRANTE, 545(RPH):NOV73-214
BURKE, K. THE RHETORIC OF RELIGION.
F.P. DINNEEN, 215(GL):VOL13#3-176
BURKE, P. CULTURE & SOCIETY IN
RENAISSANCE ITALY, 1420-1540.
R. HATFIELD, 54:DEC73-630
H. HIBBARD, 551(RENQ):WINTER73-491
BURKE, P. VENICE & AMSTERDAM.
S. SCHAMA, 617(TLS):17JAN75-52
BURKERT, W. HOMO NECANS.*
E.B. HOLTSMARK, 124:MAR74-294
BURKHART, K.W. WOMEN IN PRISON.
S. TOTH, 109:SPRING/SUMMER74-127
BURKHART, T. KITE FOLIO.
C. HART, 617(TLS):7FEB75-136
BURKHOLZ, H. MULLIGAN'S SEED.
N. CALLENDAR, 441:30NOV75-63
BURKILL, T.A. THE EVOLUTION OF
CHRISTIAN THOUGHT.*
W.D., 543:SEP72-154
BURKMAN, K.H. THE DRAMATIC WORLD OF
HAROLD PINTER.
S.H. GALE, 295:FEB74-746
BURLAND, B. SURPRISE.
M. LEVIN, 441:12JAN75-16
BURLEIGH, A.H., ED. EDUCATION IN A
FREE SOCIETY.
J.M. LALLEY, 396(MODA):SPRING74-
197
BURLEY, W.J. WYCLIFFE & THE PEA-
GREEN BOAT.
P.D. JAMES, 617(TLS):26DEC75-1544
BURMEISTER, K.H. ACHILLES PIRMIN
GASSER.
V.A. TUMINS, 551(RENQ):SUMMER73-
206
BURNAM, T. THE DICTIONARY OF MIS-
INFORMATION.
C. LEHMANN-HAUPT, 441:25DEC75-19
BURNE, G.S. JULIAN GREEN.
L.C. KEATING, 149:SEP74-260
BURNETT, A.P. CATASTROPHE SURVIVED.*
H.C. BALDRY, 123:MAR74-23
C. GARTON, 24:WINTER74-398
J.R. WILSON, 487:SUMMER73-204
BURNEY, C. MEMOIRS OF DOCTOR BUR-
NEY. (MADAME D'ARBLAY, ED)
B.H. DAVIS, 173(ECS):FALL73-106
BURNEY, C. & D.M. LANG. THE PEOPLES
OF THE HILLS, ANCIENT ARARAT & CAU-
CASUS.
K.S. RUBINSON, 318(JAOS):OCT-DEC73-
578
BURNEY, F. CAMILLA, OR A PICTURE OF
YOUTH. (E.A. & L.D. BLOOM, EDS)
B.H. DAVIS, 173(ECS):FALL73-107
BURNEY, F. THE JOURNALS & LETTERS
OF FANNY BURNEY (MADAME D'ARBLAY).*
(VOL 1 ED BY J. HEMLOW, WITH C.D.
CECIL & A. DOUGLAS; VOL 2 ED BY J.
HEMLOW & A. DOUGLAS)
R.L. BRETT, 541(RES):MAY73-219
B.H. DAVIS, 173(ECS):FALL73-106
R. HALSBAND, 481(PQ):JUL73-475
C.J. HORNE, 67:MAY74-85

BURNHAM, B. THE ART CRISIS.
D. THOMAS, 362:12JUN75-790
BURNHAM, H.B. & D.K. "KEEP ME WARM
ONE NIGHT."
M. SONDAY, 139:DEC73-15
102(CANL):SUMMER73-125
BURNIM, K.A. DAVID GARRICK, DIREC-
TOR.
I. BROWN, 157:AUTUMN73-72
BURNS, A. & J. GIBBS - SEE DE CER-
VANTES SAAVEDRA, M.
BURNS, E. THEATRICALITY.
639(VQR):SUMMER74-CVI
BURNS, E. - SEE TOKLAS, A.B.
BURNS, E.B. A HISTORY OF BRAZIL.
J.C. KINNEAR, 86(BHS):APR73-198
BURNS, J. A SINGLE FLOWER.
A. CLUYSENAAR, 565:VOL14#2-62
BURNS, N.T. CHRISTIAN MORTALISM
FROM TYNDALE TO MILTON.
J.R. MC ADAMS, 568(SCN):SPRING-
SUMMER74-4
BURNS, R.I. ISLAM UNDER THE CRU-
SADERS.
P. LINEHAN, 617(TLS):17JAN75-52
639(VQR):AUTUMN74-CXLVII
BURNS, S. HOME, INC.
B. KUTTNER, 441:21SEP75-20
BURNSHAW, S. IN THE TERRIFIED
RADIANCE.
639(VQR):WINTER74-XIV
BURR, J.R. & M. GOLDINGER, EDS.
PHILOSOPHY & CONTEMPORARY ISSUES.
W.G., 543:DEC72-352
BURRELL, B. COMBAT WEAPONS.
617(TLS):7FEB75-149
BURROUGHS, W.S. EXTERMINATOR!*
P. STEVICK, 473(PR):2/1974-302
BURROUGHS, W.S. THE LAST WORDS OF
DUTCH SCHULTZ.
A. FRIEDMAN, 441:22JUN75-4
BURROW, J.A. RICARDIAN POETRY.*
G.C. BRITTON, 447(N&Q):JAN73-29
A.B. FRIEDMAN, 191(ELN):DEC73-126
J.B. FRIEDMAN, 301(JEGP):APR74-241
V.M. LAGORIO, 377:MAR74-50
M.C. SEYMOUR, 179(ES):JUN73-274
T.A. STROUD, 405(MP):AUG73-71
BURROW, T. THE SANSKRIT LANGUAGE.
(3RD ED)
R. SCHMITT, 343:BAND17HEFT2-202
BURROW, T. & S. BHATTACHARYA. THE
PENGO LANGUAGE.*
K. DE VREESE, 318(JAOS):OCT-DEC73-
594
BURSILL-HALL, G.L. SPECULATIVE
GRAMMARS OF THE MIDDLE AGES.*
M.W. BLOOMFIELD, 589:JAN74-102
D.L., 543:DEC72-352
BURSILL-HALL, G.L. - SEE THOMAS OF
ERFURT
BURT, C. ESP & PSYCHOLOGY. (A.
GREGORY, ED)
C.W.K. MUNDLE, 617(TLS):29AUG75-
976
BURT, M.K. & C. KIPARSKY. THE
GOOFICON.
R. NASH, 608:MAR74-85
G.R. TUCKER, 608:JUN74-191
BURTON, T.G. & A.N. MANNINGS, EDS.
THE EAST TENNESSEE STATE UNIVERSITY
COLLECTION OF FOLKLORE: FOLKSONGS
II.
A. JABBOUR, 650(WF):JAN73-63

BURY, J.B. & R. MEIGGS. A HISTORY
OF GREECE. (4TH ED)
617(TLS):2MAY75-476
BUSA, R. SANCTI THOMAE AQUINATIS
OPERUM OMNIUM INDICES ET CONCOR-
DANTIAE.
H.E. BREKLE, 343:BAND17HEFT2-210
BUSCH, F. HAWKES.*
B. TISDALE, 109:FALL/WINTER73/74-
104
BUSCHOR, E. DAS HELLENISTISCHE
BILDNIS. (2ND ED) (H. WALTER, ED)
D.G. RICE, 124:MAY73-486
BUSETTE, C. OBRA DRAMÁTICA DE
GARCÍA LORCA.
C. COBB, 238:MAY73-502
J.M. RILEY, 86(BHS):OCT73-410
BUSH, D. MATTHEW ARNOLD.*
G. THOMAS, 175:SUMMER72-72
J. TURNER, 541(RES):FEB73-115
BUSH, D. JANE AUSTEN.
W. HALEY, 31(ASCH):AUTUMN75-684
V.S. PRITCHETT, 453:17JUL75-26
BUSH, D. - SEE MILTON, J.
BUSH, D., J.E. SHAW & A.B. GIAMATTI,
EDS. A VARIORUM COMMENTARY ON THE
POEMS OF JOHN MILTON.* (VOL 1)
R. LEJOSNE, 189(EA):JAN-MAR73-99
BUSH, E.W. GALLIPOLI.
A. BRETT-JAMES, 617(TLS):22AUG75-
936
BUSH, M.H. DORIS CAESAR.
M-S. YOUNG, 39:APR73-441
BUSH, V.G. CONSTRUCTION MANAGEMENT.
B. PERKINS, 45:DEC73-43
BUSHRUI, S.B., ED. A CENTENARY
TRIBUTE TO JOHN MILLINGTON SYNGE,
1871-1909.
R. HOGAN, 295:APR74-1031
BUSIRI VICI, A. I PONIATOWSKI E
ROMA.
P. CANNON-BROOKES, 39:JUN73-624
F. HASKELL, 90:AUG73-548
BUSSAGLI, M. ORIENTAL ARCHITECTURE.
J. RUSSELL, 441:7DEC75-3
BUSSMANN, H., ED. EILHART VON
OBERG: TRISTRANT.
C. SOETEMAN, 433:JAN73-103
BUSST, A.J.L. - SEE BALLANCHE, P-S.
BUTCHER, F. MANY LIVES - ONE LOVE.
295:FEB74-364
BUTCHER, J. COPY-EDITING.
W. HALEY, 617(TLS):16MAY75-537
BUTLER, A.J.P. & B.H. SKITT. IN
SERVICE TRAINING.
M. CAIN, 617(TLS):26SEP75-1102
BUTLER, B.C. SEARCHINGS. (V. RICE,
ED)
P. HEBBLETHWAITE, 617(TLS):18JUL
75-812
BUTLER, C. NUMBER SYMBOLISM.*
M-S. RØSTVIG, 179(ES):FEB72-67
BUTLER, C. & A. FOWLER. TOPICS IN
CRITICISM.
H. JECHOVA', 549(RLC):OCT-DEC73-
626
BUTLER, D. & A. SLOMAN. BRITISH
POLITICAL FACTS. (4TH ED)
617(TLS):15AUG75-920
BÜTLER, H-P. DIE GEISTIGE WELT DES
JÜNGEREN PLINIUS.
W.C. MC DERMOTT, 124:OCT72-106
BUTLER, J. THE GARBAGEMAN.
D. BAILEY, 529(QQ):SPRING73-99

BUTLER, M. MARIA EDGEWORTH.*
D.V.E., 191(ELN):SEP73(SUPP)-48
S. MONOD, 189(EA):APR-JUN73-227
J. NEWCOMER, 445(NCF):JUN73-98
G. THOMAS, 175:SUMMER73-80
J.M.S. TOMPKINS, 541(RES):NOV73-
499
BUTLER, R.N. WHY SURVIVE?
R.M. HENIG, 441:14SEP75-12
BUTLER, S. HUDIBRAS, PARTS I & II,
& SELECTED OTHER WRITINGS. (J.
WILDERS & H. DE QUEHEN, EDS)
P.A. TROUT, 566:SPRING74-98
"SAMUEL BUTLER 1612-1680: CHARAC-
TERS." (C.W. DAVES, ED)
L. POTTER, 179(ES):DEC72-561
P. ROBERTS, 447(N&Q):MAY73-196
BUTOR, M. MATIÈRE DE RÊVES.
G. CRAIG, 617(TLS):18JUL75-791
BUTOW, R.J.C. THE JOHN DOE ASSOCI-
ATES.
R. STORRY, 617(TLS):13JUN75-655
BUTT, J., ED. ROBERT OWEN.
J.F.C. HARRISON, 637(VS):DEC73-227
BUTTER, P.H. - SEE MUIR, E.
BUTTERFIELD, L.H. & M. FRIEDLAENDER,
EDS. THE ADAMS PAPERS. (SER 2,
VOLS 3&4)
C.W. AKERS, 432(NEQ):DEC73-627
J. HUTSON, 656(WMQ):APR74-326
639(VQR):WINTER74-XXIV
BUTTERFIELD, L.H., M. FRIEDLAENDER
& M-J. KLINE - SEE ADAMS, A. & J.
BUTTERFIELD, S. BLACK AUTOBIOGRAPHY
IN AMERICA.
J. WHITE, 617(TLS):18JUL75-810
BUTTERWORTH, M. THE MAN IN THE
SOPWITH CAMEL.
N. CALLENDAR, 441:15JUN75-24
BUTTINGER, J. A DRAGON DEFIANT.
S. PARKER, 293(JAST):AUG73-754
BUTTMANN, G. THE SHADOW OF THE
TELESCOPE.
J. NORTH, 617(TLS):14MAR75-283
BÜTTNER, L. VON BENN ZU ENZENSBER-
GER.
J. GLENN, 133:1973/3-282
BUXBAUM, M.H. BENJAMIN FRANKLIN &
THE ZEALOUS PRESBYTERIANS.
J.A.L. LEMAY, 165:FALL75-222
BUXTON, J. THE POETRY OF LORD
BYRON.
F. MC COMBIE, 447(N&Q):MAR73-119
BUZÁS, L. & F. JUNGINGER. BAVARIA
LATINA.
R. SCHMITT, 343:BAND16HEFT1-100
BUZZI, G. INVITO ALL LETTURA DI
GIUSEPPE TOMASI DI LAMPEDUSA.
R. ADAMS, 275(IQ):FALL-WINTER73
(VOL17#66)-72
BYCK, R. - SEE FREUD, S.
BYNUM, T.W. - SEE FREGE, G.
BYRD, E. I'LL GET BY.
A. BARNES, 617(TLS):29AUG75-961
BYRD, M. VISITS TO BEDLAM.
M. HODGART, 617(TLS):28MAR75-328
BYRNE, R. & I. NEI. BOTH SIDES OF
THE CHESSBOARD.
617(TLS):7NOV75-1342
BYRNES, R.F. - SEE EPSTEIN, F.T.
LORD BYRON. BYRON'S HEBREW MELO-
DIES.* (T.L. ASHTON, ED)
E.E.B., 191(ELN):SEP73(SUPP)-36
A.H. ELLIOTT, 541(RES):AUG73-353
G. THOMAS, 175:AUTUMN72-113

56

LORD BYRON. BYRON'S LETTERS & JOUR-
NALS.* (VOLS 1&2) (L.A. MARCHAND,
ED)
  R.H. FOGLE, 569(SR):SPRING74-383
  C. ROSEN, 453:15MAY75-15
LORD BYRON. BYRON'S LETTERS & JOUR-
NALS.* (VOL 3) (L.A. MARCHAND, ED)
  C. ROSEN, 453:15MAY75-15
  442(NY):13JAN75-93
LORD BYRON. BYRON'S LETTERS & JOUR-
NALS. (VOL 4) (L.A. MARCHAND, ED)
  P. CONRAD, 617(TLS):29AUG75-962
  R. MITCHISON, 362:23OCT75-548
LORD BYRON. FROM CAMBRIDGE TO MISS-
OLONGHI. (T.G. STEFFAN, ED)
  E.E.B., 191(ELN):SEP73(SUPP)-39
"LORD BYRON: WERNER, A TRAGEDY."*
[ACTING VERSION BY W.C. MACREADY]
  J.D. BONE, 447(N&Q):FEB73-73
BYRON, B. LOYALTY IN THE SPIRITUAL-
ITY OF ST. THOMAS MORE.
  L. MILES, 677:VOL4-252

"CSP DIRECTORY OF SUPPLIERS OF SPAN-
ISH MATERIALS."
  C.W. STANSFIELD, 399(MLJ):JAN-FEB
  74-77
CABALLERO CALDERÓN, E. ANCHA ES
CASTILLA. (L.C. PÉREZ & L.F. LY-
DAY, EDS)
  M.M. DÍAZ, 399(MLJ):JAN-FEB73-70
CABANIS, J. SAINT-SIMON L'ADMIRABLE.
  J. RAYMOND, 617(TLS):20JUN75-691
CABLE, M. THE LITTLE DARLINGS.
  442(NY):28JUL75-80
CABLE, T. THE METER & MELODY OF
BEOWULF.
  T. SHIPPEY, 617(TLS):29AUG75-974
CABRERA, R.M. JULIÁN DEL CASAL.*
  I.A. SCHULMAN, 240(HR):SUMMER73-
  577
DE CADALSO, J. DEFENSA DE LA
NACIÓN ESPAÑOLA CONTRA LA "CARTA
PERSIANA LXXVIII" DE MONTESQUIEU
(TEXTO INÉDITO). (G. MERCADIER, ED)
  J. DOWLING, 240(HR):AUTUMN73-704
CADBURY, H.J. JOHN WOOLMAN IN ENG-
LAND 1772.
  W.A. SPECK, 447(N&Q):NOV73-439
CADELL, E. THE FLEDGLING.
  N. CALLENDAR, 441:16MAR75-32
CADÈRE, V-G. L'ECONOMIE PLANIFIÉE
ET LA FAMILLE EN DROIT SOCIALISTE
ROUMAIN.
  M. ROCK, 182:VOL26#19-653
CADY, E.H. THE LIGHT OF COMMON
DAY.*
  J.J. MC ALEER, 594:SPRING73-140
CADY, E.H. - SEE HOWELLS, W.D.
CAEIRO, O. LA OBRA NARRATIVA DE
REINHOLD SCHNEIDER.
  E. SAGARRA, 220(GL&L):JAN74-169
CAESARIUS OF ARLES. CÉSAIRE D'AR-
LES, "SERMONS AU PEUPLE." (VOL 1)
(M-J. DELAGE, ED)
  J. ANDRÉ, 555:VOL47FASC1-177
CAFFREY, K. THE MAYFLOWER.
  D. QUINN, 617(TLS):1AUG75-876
"CAHIER PAUL CLAUDEL 9."
  H.A. WATERS, 207(FR):FEB73-624

"CAHIERS BARBEY D'AUREVILLY, NO. 5."
  J-H. BORNECQUE, 535(RHL):JAN-FEB
  73-149
CAHILL, J. SCHOLAR PAINTERS OF
JAPAN: THE NANGA SCHOOL.*
  C. MAC SHERRY, 293(JAST):NOV72-154
CAHM, E. POLITICS & SOCIETY IN CON-
TEMPORARY FRANCE (1789-1971).*
  R.D. ANDERSON, 402(MLR):OCT74-886
CAHN, S.M., ED. THE PHILOSOPHICAL
FOUNDATIONS OF EDUCATION.
  J.T.K., 543:MAR73-528
CAHN, W. THE ROMANESQUE WOODEN
DOORS OF AUVERGNE.
  C.M. KAUFFMANN, 617(TLS):10OCT75-
  1196
CAILLAT, C. LES EXPIATIONS DANS LE
RITUEL ANCIEN DES RELIGIEUX JAINA.
  G. LANCZKOWSKI, 343:BAND16HEFT1-90
CAILLOIS, R. APPROCHES DE L'IMAGI-
NAIRE.
  J. STURROCK, 617(TLS):14FEB75-173
CAIN, J.M. RAINBOW'S END.
  442(NY):15SEP75-131
CAINE, L. WIDOW.*
  A. NELSON, 441:6JUL75-4
CAIRNCROSS, A. & OTHERS. ECONOMIC
POLICY FOR THE EUROPEAN COMMUNITY.
  A. SHONFIELD, 617(TLS):18APR75-431
CAIRNS, D. GUIDE FOR TRANSLATING
HUSSERL.
  P. DUBOIS, 182:VOL26#10-321
CAIRNS, D. RESPONSES.*
  D. WULSTAN, 410(M&L):JAN74-109
CAIRNS, F. GENERIC COMPOSITION IN
GREEK & ROMAN POETRY.
  K. QUINN, 487:WINTER73-403
CAIRNS, H., ED. THE LIMITS OF ART.
(VOL 3)
  N. SUCKLING, 208(FS):APR74-246
CAIS, J. & P. ENOCH. HABET USHMA.
(PT 1)
  W. CHOMSKY, 399(MLJ):MAR74-144
CALAME, A. ANNE DE LA ROCHE GUIL-
HEN, ROMANCIÈRE HUGUENOTE, 1644-
1707.
  D.L. RUBIN, 207(FR):APR73-1009
CALDER, N. TECHNOPOLIS.
  C. MITCHAM, 258:JUN73-277
CALDER, N. THE WEATHER MACHINE.*
  P. ADAMS, 61:MAY75-103
  C. LEHMANN-HAUPT, 441:17APR75-43
CALDER, R., WITH M.A. SCREECH - SEE
RABELAIS, F.
CALDER, R.L. W. SOMERSET MAUGHAM &
THE QUEST FOR FREEDOM.
  R. BOWEN, 50(ARQ):WINTER73-363
CALDERÓN, E.C. - SEE UNDER CABALLERO
CALDERÓN, E.
CALDERÓN DE LA BARCA, P. EN LA VIDA
TODO ES VERDAD Y TODO MENTIRA.*
(D.W. CRUICKSHANK, ED)
  C.F. SMITH, 238:DEC73-1118
CALDERÓN DE LA BARCA, P. LA HIJA
DEL AIRE.* (G. EDWARDS, ED)
  P.N. DUNN, 240(HR):SUMMER73-567
CALDWELL, G. GRISTMILL.
  A. BARNES, 617(TLS):29AUG75-961
CALDWELL, H. MACHADO DE ASSIS.*
  F.P. ELLISON, 240(HR):SPRING73-463
CALHOON, R.M. THE LOYALISTS IN
REVOLUTIONARY AMERICA, 1760-1781.*
  D.V.J. BELL, 656(WMQ):JUL74-495
  R.D. BROWN, 432(NEQ):JUN74-344

CALHOUN, D. THE INTELLIGENCE OF A
PEOPLE.
R.D. BROWN, 656(WMQ):JUL74-496
R.A. LEWIS, 639(VQR):WINTER74-112
CALIFANO, J.A., JR. A PRESIDENTIAL
NATION.
R. MANNING, 61:NOV75-118
M.F. NOLAN, 441:28SEP75-4
CALISHER, H. THE COLLECTED STORIES
OF HORTENSE CALISHER.
A. BROYARD, 441:13OCT75-27
D. GRUMBACH, 441:19OCT75-3
CALLAGHAN, C.A. LAKE MIWOK DICTION-
ARY.
H. BERMAN, 269(IJAL):OCT73-260
CALLAGHAN, M. AN AUTUMN PENITENT.
G.W., 102(CANL):WINTER74-127
CALLAGHAN, M. A FINE & PRIVATE
PLACE.
F.W. WATT, 99:AUG75-35
CALLAHAN, R. THE EAST INDIA COMPANY
& ARMY REFORM, 1783-1798.
S.P. COHEN, 293(JAST):AUG73-713
M.N. PEARSON, 318(JAOS):OCT-DEC73-
621
CALLAN, R.J. MIGUEL ÁNGEL ASTURIAS.*
G. MARTIN, 240(HR):SUMMER73-586
G.A. DE LOS REYES, 577(SHR):WINTER
73-106
M.A. SALGADO, 241:MAY73-77
M.E. VENIER, 400(MLN):MAR73-502
CALLOW, P. BARE WIRES.
A. CLUYSENAAR, 565:VOL14#2-62
CALLOW, P. SON & LOVER.
M. GREEN, 441:21SEP75-7
J. MOYNAHAN, 617(TLS):5SEP75-990
CALLU, J.P. - SEE SYMMACHUS
CALVERT, B. THE ROLE OF THE PUPIL.
617(TLS):310CT75-1313
CALVET, L-J. ROLAND BARTHES.
A. LAVERS, 617(TLS):1AUG75-878
CALVET, M. THE ELABORATION OF BASIC
WOLOF.
315(JAL):VOL11PT2-105
CALVIN, J. THREE FRENCH TREATISES.*
(F.M. HIGMAN, ED)
R.D. LINDER, 551(RENQ):SUMMER73-
191
CALVINO, I. INVISIBLE CITIES.*
(ITALIAN TITLE: LE CITTÀ INVISI-
BILI.)
P. BAILEY, 617(TLS):21FEB75-185
E. TENNANT, 362:20FEB75-253
J. UPDIKE, 442(NY):24FEB75-137
CALVINO, I. THE WATCHER & OTHER
STORIES.*
P. COURTINES, 573(SSF):WINTER73-
117
CALVO, L.N. - SEE UNDER NOVÁS CALVO,
L.
CAMARA, J.M., JR. THE PORTUGUESE
LANGUAGE.
L. LOCKETT, 238:SEP73-752
N.P. SACKS, 399(MLJ):SEP-OCT74-296
CAMBITOGLOU, A. & OTHERS. ZAGORA.
(VOL 1)
J. BOARDMAN, 123:MAR74-158
CAMBON, G. EUGENIO MONTALE.
E. SACCONE, 400(MLN):JAN73-158
"CAMBRIDGE LATIN COURSE." (UNITS
1&2)
W.C. STEPHENS, 124:NOV72-176

CAMERON, A. AGATHIAS.*
M.T.W. ARNHEIM, 313:VOL63-298
G. DOWNEY, 121(CJ):DEC72/JAN73-188
CAMERON, A. CLAUDIAN.*
J. MARTIN, 24:SPRING74-82
CAMERON, D. CONVERSATIONS WITH
CANADIAN NOVELISTS.
A. MAC KINNON, 150(DR):AUTUMN73-
546
CAMERON, H.D. STUDIES ON THE SEVEN
AGAINST THEBES OF AESCHYLUS.
E.W. WHITTLE, 123:MAR74-18
CAMERON, J. AN INDIAN SUMMER.*
E.R. LIPSON, 441:13JUL75-24
442(NY):3MAR75-99
CAMERON, K. - SEE DE CHANTELOUVE, F.
CAMERON, L. THE CLOSING CIRCLE.
N. CALLENDAR, 441:26JAN75-23
CAMERON, R. THE GOLDEN RIVIERA.
D. LEITCH, 617(TLS):31OCT75-1281
CAMERON, W.J., ED. POEMS ON AFFAIRS
OF STATE.* (VOL 5)
A. POYET, 189(EA):APR-JUN73-226
C.J. RAWSON, 677:VOL4-293
CAMILLERI, C. JEUNESSE, FAMILLE ET
DÉVELOPPEMENT.
E. DAMMANN, 182:VOL26#19-659
CAMOIN, F. BENBOW & PARADISE.
M. LEVIN, 441:28SEP75-37
DE CAMP, L.S. LOVECRAFT.
P. ADAMS, 61:MAR75-146
G. JONAS, 441:29JUN75-27
C. LEHMANN-HAUPT, 441:29JAN75-33
CAMPBELL, A., ED. ANGLO-SAXON CHAR-
TERS I.
D.E. GREENWAY, 382(MAE):1974/3-309
CAMPBELL, G.F. CHINA TEA CLIPPERS.
B. GREENHILL, 617(TLS):21FEB75-202
CAMPBELL, J. THE MYTHIC IMAGE.
J. GARDNER, 441:28DEC75-15
W. SARGEANT, 442(NY):21JUL75-86
CAMPBELL, J. & P. SHERRARD. MODERN
GREECE.
R.C. CLARK, 544:FALL74-137
CAMPBELL, J.I. THE LANGUAGE OF
RELIGION.
H.A.D., 543:DEC72-354
CAMPBELL, J.W., ED. ANALOG 7.
617(TLS):5DEC75-1439
CAMPBELL, M. DOLMETSCH.
D. ARNOLD, 362:3JUL75-29
H.M. BROWN, 617(TLS):7NOV75-1334
CAMPBELL, P.N. RHETORIC-RITUAL.
D. STEWART, 480(P&R):WINTER73-66
CAMPBELL, R.N. NOUN SUBSTITUTES IN
MODERN THAI.*
D.W. DELLINGER, 353:15MAR73-103
CAMPBELL, R.N. & M. BRACY. LETTERS
FROM ROGER.
W.R. SLAGER, 399(MLJ):APR73-230
CAMPBELL, T.D. ADAM SMITH'S SCIENCE
OF MORALS.*
P.S. ÁRDAL, 482(PHR):OCT73-542
CAMPBELL, T.M. & G.C. HERRING - SEE
STETTINIUS, E.R., JR.
CAMPI, E. - SEE MÜNTZER, T.
CAMPION, T. THE WORKS OF THOMAS
CAMPION: COMPLETE SONGS, MASQUES, &
TREATISES WITH A SELECTION OF THE
LATIN VERSE. (W.R. DAVIS, ED)
J.J. YOCH, JR., 568(SCN):SPRING-
SUMMER74-10

CAMPOREALE, S.I. LORENZO VALLA,
UMANESIMO E TEOLOGIA.
C.H. CLOUGH, 402(MLR):JUL74-662
CAMPRA, A. ANDRÉ CAMPRA: LES FÊTES
VÉNITIENNES, OPERA-BALLET (1710).
(M. LÜTOLF, ED)
M. CYR, 414(MQ):OCT73-639
CANADAY, J. THE LIVES OF THE PAINT-
ERS.
J.K. NELSON, 290(JAAC):FALL73-134
"CANADIAN ARTISTS IN EXHIBITION
1972-73."
J. ZEMENS, 73:SUMMER74-38
"THE CANADIAN OXFORD DESK ATLAS OF
THE WORLD." (3RD ED)
102(CANL):SUMMER73-126
CANAN, J.W. THE SUPERWARRIORS.
J.W. FINNEY, 441:10AUG75-5
CANART, P. & V. PERI. SUSSIDI BIB-
LIOGRAFICI PER I MANOSCRITTI GRECI
DELLA BIBLIOTECA VATICANA.
N.G. WILSON, 123:MAR74-146
CANAWAY, W.H. THE GLORY OF THE
SEAS.
M. LEVIN, 441:16MAR75-30
CANBY, V. LIVING QUARTERS.
R.R. LINGEMAN, 441:16APR75-41
W. SCHOTT, 441:13APR75-4
CANCIAN, F.M. WHAT ARE NORMS?
P. RIVIÈRE, 617(TLS):21NOV75-1394
CANE, M. THE FIRST FIREFLY.
639(VQR):SUMMER74-LXXXV
CANETTI, E. KAFKA'S OTHER TRIAL.*
I. PARRY, 617(TLS):28FEB75-231
442(NY):6JAN75-83
CANETTI, E. DER OHRENZEUGE.
I. PARRY, 617(TLS):10JAN75-38
CANFIELD, C. THE INCREDIBLE PIER-
PONT MORGAN.*
E. WEEKS, 61:JAN75-88
CANFORA, L. DEMOSTENE: "DISCORSO
ALL'ASSEMBLEA PER AMBASCERIE IN
ASIA E IN GRECIA (TERZA FILIP-
PICA)."
D.M. MAC DOWELL, 123:MAR74-41
CANFORA, L. TUCIDIDE CONTINUATO.*
S.I. OOST, 122:JUL73-234
CANGUILHEM, G., ED. INTRODUCTION À
L'HISTOIRE DES SCIENCES. (VOL 1)
R. BLANCHÉ, 542:JUL-SEP73-354
CANGUILHEM, G. & OTHERS. INTRODUC-
TION À L'HISTOIRE DES SCIENCES.
(VOL 2)
R. BLANCHÉ, 542:JUL-SEP73-354
CANNING, V. FIRECREST.
N. CALLENDAR, 441:26JAN75-24
CANNING, V. THE KINGSFORD MARK.
M. LASKI, 362:20NOV75-684
CANNING, V. THE LIMBO LINE.
N. CALLENDAR, 441:31AUG75-12
CANNING, V. THE MASK OF MEMORY.*
N. CALLENDAR, 441:22JUN75-18
CANNON, J. THE FOX-NORTH COALITION.
H.L. SNYDER, 481(PQ):JUL73-340
CANO, J.L. LA POESÍA DE LA GENERA-
CIÓN DEL 27.
A. SÁNCHEZ-BARBUDO, 240(HR):WIN-
TER73-109
CANO-BALLESTA, J., ED. MAESTROS DEL
CUENTO ESPAÑOL MODERNO.
F.H. NUESSEL, JR., 399(MLJ):NOV74-
366

CANOSSA, L. SECRETOS Y SORPRESAS
DEL IDIOMA.
D.L. GOLD, 75:4/1973-192
CANOVA, G.M. LA MINIATURA VENETA
DEL RINASCIMENTO, 1450-1500.
J. BACKHOUSE, 90:MAR73-168
CANTELLI, G. DISEGNI DI FRANCESCO
FURINI E DEL SUO AMBIENTE.
E. YOUNG, 39:JUL73-66
CANTELLI, G. VICO E BAYLE.
E. GIANTURCO, 276:WINTER73-598
CANTEMIR, D. DESCRIPTIO MOLDAVIAE.
E. TAPPE, 575(SEER):OCT74-631
CANTER, D. & T. LEE, EDS. PSYCHOL-
OGY & THE BUILT ENVIRONMENT.
617(TLS):5SEP75-999
CANTILLO, G. - SEE HEGEL, G.W.F.
CANTIN, A. - SEE DAMIEN, P.
ČAPEK, K. APOCRYPHAL STORIES.
I. HAJEK, 617(TLS):6JUN75-629
ČAPEK, M. BERGSON & MODERN PHYS-
ICS.*
J.A. MC GILVRAY, 482(PHR):APR74-
274
D.R.P., 543:DEC72-355
CAPELL, A. A SURVEY OF NEW GUINEA
LANGUAGES.
A.M. STEVENS, 353:15AUG73-125
CAPELLANUS, A. DE AMORE DEUTSCH.*
(J. HARTLIEB, TRANS; A. KARNEIN,
ED)
S.L. WAILES, 221(GQ):MAY73-484
CAPIZZI, A. SOCRATE E I PERSONAGGI
FILOSOFI DI PLATONE.*
P. LOUIS, 555:VOL47FASC2-334
CAPLAN, A.P. PRIESTS & COBBLERS.
J.F. FISHER, 293(JAST):AUG73-723
CAPLAN, F. & T. THE POWER OF PLAY.
O. JENKINS, 109:FALL/WINTER73/74-
137
CAPLAN, H. OF ELOQUENCE.* (A.
KING & H. NORTH, EDS)
M. MC CALL, 24:SUMMER74-183
CAPOTE BENOT, J.M. EL PERÍODO
SEVILLANO DE LUIS CERNUDA.
P. BACARISSE, 205(FMLS):JUL73-301
D.R. HARRIS, 86(BHS):JUL73-306
CAPP, B.S. THE FIFTH MONARCHY MEN.*
G.D. HAMILTON, 125:JUN74-390
CAPRONI, G. IL MURO DELLA TERRA.
F. FORTINI, 617(TLS):31OCT75-1308
DE CAPUA, A.G. GERMAN BAROQUE
POETRY.
R.M. BROWNING, 301(JEGP):JUL74-399
F.R. LEHMEYER, 399(MLJ):SEP-OCT74-
287
DE CAPUA, A.G. & E.A. METZGER - SEE
"BENJAMIN NEUKIRCHS ANTHOLOGIE"
CAPUT, J-P. LA LANGUE FRANCAISE,
HISTOIRE D'UNE INSTITUTION. (VOL 1)
J. ANDRÉ, 555:VOL47FASC1-149
G. PRICE, 208(FS):OCT74-496
CARACCIOLO-TREJO, E., ED. THE PEN-
GUIN BOOK OF LATIN AMERICAN VERSE.
T.O. BENTE, 37:MAR73-38
M.E. CAROSSINO, 399(MLJ):SEP-OCT73-
300
CARAS, R. SOCKEYE.
C. LEHMANN-HAUPT, 441:27NOV75-31
CARASSUS, E. BARRÈS ET SA FORTUNE
LITTÉRAIRE.*
M. DAVANTURE, 535(RHL):JUL-AUG73-
723

CARASSUS, E. LE MYTHE DU DANDY.
  C. AFFRON, 207(FR):DEC72-413
  J.S.P., 191(ELN):SEP73(SUPP)-69
CARAWAN, G. & C., COMPS. VOICES
FROM THE MOUNTAINS.
  S. SANBORN, 441:27APR75-2
CARBALLIDO, E. MEDUSA. (J. GAUCHER-
SHULTZ & A. MORALES, EDS)
  E.M. DIAL, 238:SEP73-751
  M.S. PEDEN, 399(MLJ):NOV73-374
CARBONNIER, J. FLEXIBLE DROIT. (2ND
ED) SOCIOLOGIE JURIDIQUE.
  N. HERPIN, 542:JAN-MAR73-97
CARDEN, P. THE ART OF ISAAC BABEL.*
  T.L. AMAN, 550(RUSR):APR73-212
  M. FRIEDBERG, 390:APR73-74
  M.H. SHOTTON, 402(MLR):JAN74-237
  D. WHITE, 399(MLJ):MAR74-146
CARDEW, C. STOCKHAUSEN SERVES IM-
PERIALISM.
  R. MACONIE, 617(TLS):9MAY75-506
CARDINAL, R. OUTSIDER ART.
  M. YAFFE, 592:MAR73-141
CARDONA, G. STUDIES IN INDIAN GRAM-
MARIANS. (VOL 1)
  H. BERGER, 353:1JUL73-38
CARDONA, G., H.M. HOENIGSWALD & A.
SENN, EDS. INDO-EUROPEAN & INDO-
EUROPEANS.*
  C.E. REED, 399(MLJ):JAN-FEB73-52
  R. ROCHER, 318(JAOS):OCT-DEC73-615
  R. SCHMITT, 343:BAND16HEFT2-148
CARDOZO, N. HELMET OF THE WIND.*
  M. PERLBERG, 491:JUN75-172
CARDWELL, M. - SEE DICKENS, C.
CARDWELL, R.A. BLASCO IBAÑEZ: "LA
BARRACA."
  E. RODGERS, 402(MLR):JUL74-683
CARETTI, L. MANZONI.
  V.A.S., 275(IQ):FALL-WINTER73(VOL
  17#66)-68
CARETTI, L. MANZONI E LA CRITICA.
(3RD ED)
  B.L., 275(IQ):SUMMER73-113
CAREW, D. A FRAGMENT OF FRIENDSHIP.
  D. PRYCE-JONES, 617(TLS):25APR75-
  444
CAREY, C. LES PROVERBES ÉROTIQUES
RUSSES.
  J.L. RICE, 574(SEEJ):FALL73-343
CAREY, G.G. MARYLAND FOLK LEGENDS
& FOLK SONGS.
  J.A. BURRISON, 292(JAF):APR-JUN73-
  189
DE CARLE, D. WATCH & CLOCK ENCYCLO-
PEDIA.
  617(TLS):30MAY75-609
CARLISLE, C.J. SHAKESPEARE FROM THE
GREENROOM.
  D.S. SMITH, 570(SQ):SPRING73-240
CARLISLE, E.F. THE UNCERTAIN SELF.*
  S.A. BLACK, 646(WWR):JUN73-73
CARLSON, M. THE GERMAN STAGE IN
THE NINETEENTH CENTURY.
  W.E. YATES, 402(MLR):OCT74-926
CARLSON, R.J., ED. THE FRONTIERS OF
SCIENCE & MEDICINE.
  W.A.R. THOMSON, 617(TLS):29AUG75-
  973
CARLSSON, A. & V. MICHELS - SEE
HESSE, H. & T. MANN
CARLTON, C. THE COURT OF ORPHANS.
  R.B. PUGH, 617(TLS):4APR75-379

CARLTON, C.R. A DESCRIPTIVE SYNTAX
OF THE OLD ENGLISH CHARTERS.*
  E.A. EBBINGHAUS, 215(GL):VOL13#1-
  53
  D.L. SHORES, 179(ES):APR73-163
  A. SZWEDEK, 353:1MAR73-115
CARLTON, D. & C. SCHAERF, EDS. THE
DYNAMICS OF THE ARMS RACE.
  E. LUTTWAK, 617(TLS):15AUG75-923
CARLUT, C. LA CORRESPONDANCE DE
FLAUBERT.
  J. BRUNEAU, 546(RR):JAN74-68
CARMICHAEL, J. TROTSKY.
  A. GAMBLE, 362:13MAR75-348
  B. KNEI-PAZ, 617(TLS):4APR75-356
CARNAP, R. & R.C. JEFFREY, EDS.
STUDIES IN INDUCTIVE LOGIC & PROBA-
BILITY.* (VOL 1)
  R.G. SWINBURNE, 393(MIND):OCT63-
  624
CARNEGY, P. FAUST AS MUSICIAN.
  R. ANDERSON, 415:NOV74-948
  M. BEDDOW, 111:26OCT73-26
  R. CRAFT, 453:7AUG75-18
  R. MIDDLETON, 410(M&L):APR74-219
CARNEIRO, P.E.D.B. & P. ARNAUD - SEE
UNDER DE BERRÊDO CARNEIRO, P.E. &
P. ARNAUD
CARNER, M. - SEE PUCCINI, G.
CARNES, R.J. HORSEBACK GOVERNMENT.
  W. GARD, 584(SWR):SUMMER74-V
CARNEY, T.F. THE ECONOMIES OF AN-
TIQUITY.
  W.R. CONNOR, 5:VOL1#4-731
CARNOCHAN, W.B. LEMUEL GULLIVER'S
MIRROR FOR MAN.*
  P. DIXON, 447(N&Q):JAN73-35
CARNOIS, B. LA COHÉRENCE DE LA DOC-
TRINE KANTIENNE DE LA LIBERTÉ.
  O. REBOUL, 154:DEC73-746
CARO, R.A. THE POWER BROKER.*
  R. BANHAM, 617(TLS):17JAN75-57
  M. BLISS, 99:APR/MAY75-48
  C.R. HATCH, 231:JAN75-86
  G. KATEB, 31(ASCH):SPRING75-306
CARO BAROJA, J. LOS BAROJA (MEMOR-
IAS FAMILIARES).
  O.P. FERRER, 399(MLJ):JAN-FEB74-76
CARO BAROJA, J. TEATRO POPULAR Y
MAGIA.
  J.E. VAREY, 617(TLS):23MAY75-575
CAROTHERS, R.L. FREEDOM & OTHER
TIMES.
  K. SKINNER, 134(CP):FALL73-89
CARPENTER, A., ED. IRISH WRITINGS
FROM THE AGE OF SWIFT. (VOL 1)
  566:AUTUMN73-38
CARPENTER, D. THE TRUE LIFE STORY
OF JODY MC KEEGAN.
  T. LE CLAIR, 441:9FEB75-6
CARPENTER, K.E., ED. BRITISH LABOUR
STRUGGLES.
  K.O. MORGAN, 617(TLS):9MAY75-514
CARPENTIER, A. CONCIERTO BARROCO.
  617(TLS):22AUG75-950
CARPENTIER, A. EL RECURSO DEL
MÉTODO.
  J. STURROCK, 617(TLS):14MAR75-284
CARPENTIER, H. & J. BROF, EDS.
DOORS & MIRRORS.
  T.O. BENTE, 37:JUN-JUL73-39
CARPOZI, G., JR. THE JOHN WAYNE
STORY.
  R. CAMPION, 200:JAN73-48

CARR, E.B. DA KINE TALK.
  R.A. HALL, JR., 350:SEP74-604
CARR, E.H. & R.W. DAVIES. A HISTORY
  OF SOVIET RUSSIA: FOUNDATIONS OF A
  PLANNED ECONOMY, 1926-1929.* (VOL
  1)
  G. GROSSMAN, 550(RUSR):APR73-195
CARR, G. THE ANGRY BRIGADE.
  J.P. MACKINTOSH, 362:17JUL75-92
  K. MINOGUE, 617(TLS):7NOV75-1318
CARR, J., ED. KITE-FLYING & OTHER
  IRRATIONAL ACTS.*
  W.T. LHAMON, JR., 651(WHR):WINTER
  74-77
  E. LYONS, 584(SWR):SPRING74-205
CARR, J.L. HOW STEEPLE SINDERBY
  WANDERERS WON THE FA CUP.
  F. PIKE, 617(TLS):2MAY75-492
CARR, P. THE LION TRIUMPHANT.
  E.M. EWING, 441:11MAY75-10
CARR, T., ED. THE BEST SCIENCE FIC-
  TION OF THE YEAR 4.
  J. HAMILTON-PATERSON, 617(TLS):
  5DEC75-1438
CARR, T., ED. FELLOWSHIP OF THE
  STARS.
  G. JONAS, 441:12JAN75-32
CARR, V.S. THE LONELY HUNTER.
  R.R. LINGEMAN, 441:21AUG75-39
  R. PHILLIPS, 441:24AUG75-7
  442(NY):28JUL75-80
CARRASQUER, F., ED & TRANS. ANTOLO-
  GÍA DE LA POESÍA NEERLANDESA MOD-
  ERNA.
  J. CANTERA, 202(FMOD):JUN73-407
CARRASQUER, F. "IMÁN" Y LA NOVELA
  HISTÓRICA DE SENDER.*
  G. CONNELL, 86(BHS):JUL73-310
  J.W. KRONIK, 400(MLN):MAR73-491
  J. RIVAS, 238:MAY73-504
LE CARRÉ, J. TINKER, TAILOR, SOL-
  DIER, SPY.*
  R. GADNEY, 364:OCT/NOV74-73
  R. SALE, 249(HUDR):WINTER74/75-624
CARRERA ANDRADE, J. REFLECTIONS ON
  SPANISH-AMERICAN POETRY.
  S. BACIU, 263:JUL-SEP74-304
CARRERA ANDRADE, J. EL VOLCÁN Y EL
  COLIBRÍ.
  A. CARRIÓN, 263:APR-JUN74-175
CARRERAS, J.U.M. - SEE UNDER MARTÍN-
  EZ CARRERAS, J.U.
CARRIÈRE, C. NÉGOCIANTS MARSEILLAIS
  AU XVIIIE SIÈCLE.
  W. SCOTT, 617(TLS):5SEP75-1001
CARRIGHAR, S. THE TWILIGHT SEAS.
  C. LEHMANN-HAUPT, 441:25APR75-39
CARRILLO, S. DEMAIN L'ESPAGNE.
  HACIA EL POST-FRANQUISMO.
  P. PRESTON, 617(TLS):4JUL75-740
CARRITHERS, G.H., JR. DONNE AT
  SERMONS.
  W.J. ONG, 401(MLQ):MAR74-66
CARROLL, C.F. THE TIMBER ECONOMY
  OF PURITAN NEW ENGLAND.
  J.R. DANIELL, 656(WMQ):OCT74-686
CARROLL, J. LIVING AT THE MOVIES.
  G. MALANGA, 491:DEC74-162
CARROLL, J.T. IRELAND IN THE WAR
  YEARS, 1939-1945.
  R. O'RORKE, 362:13FEB75-220
CARROLL, K.L. JOHN PERROT.
  C. HILL, 447(N&Q):MAY73-196

CARROLL, L. ALICE'S ADVENTURES IN
  WONDERLAND & THROUGH THE LOOKING-
  GLASS. (R.L. GREEN, ED)
  S.H. GOODACRE, 447(N&Q):JUL73-279
CARROLL, L. SYLVIE ET BRUNO. (F.
  DELEUZE, TRANS)
  H. TOUBEAU, 98:FEB73-131
CARROLL, R. A DISAPPEARANCE.
  N. CALLENDAR, 441:17AUG75-26
CARROLL, V., ED. ADOPTION IN EAST-
  ERN OCEANIA.
  R. MC KINLEY, 293(JAST):AUG73-734
CARRUBA, O. DAS PALAISCHE.*
  A. KAMMENHUBER, 343:BAND16HEFT1-54
  G. KELLERMAN & V. ŠEVOROŠKIN, 353:
  1JUL73-115
CARRUBA, O. DIE SATZEINLEITENDEN
  PARTIKELN IN DEN INDOGERMANISCHEN
  SPRACHEN ANATOLIENS.
  H.A. HOFFNER, JR., 318(JAOS):OCT-
  DEC73-520
  E. NEU, 260(IF):BAND77HEFT2/3-284
CARRUTH, H. THE BLOOMINGDALE PAPERS.
  H. VENDLER, 441:6APR75-4
CARRUTH, H. FROM SNOW & ROCK, FROM
  CHAOS.*
  P. RAMSEY, 569(SR):SPRING74-396
DES CARS, G. UNE CERTAINE DAME.
  D. O'CONNELL, 207(FR):DEC72-438
CARSON, M.E. PABLO NERUDA.
  T.A. PÉREZ, 238:DEC73-1124
CARSWELL, J. FROM REVOLUTION TO
  REVOLUTION.
  639(VQR):SUMMER74-XCVI
CARSWELL, J. KÜTAHYA TILES & POT-
  TERY FROM THE ARMENIAN CATHEDRAL OF
  ST. JAMES, JERUSALEM.
  A. BORG, 135:SEP73-69
  G. REITLINGER, 463:SUMMER73-202
CARTEANU, A., L. LEVITCHI & V. STEF-
  ANESCU-DRĂGĂNESTI. A COURSE IN
  MODERN RUMANIAN. AN ADVANCED
  COURSE IN MODERN RUMANIAN. (BOTH
  2ND ED)
  J.E. ALGEO, 399(MLJ):NOV73-368
CARTER, A.C. NEUTRALITY OR COMMIT-
  MENT.
  S. SCHAMA, 617(TLS):25JUL75-829
CARTER, A.E. VERLAINE.*
  D.F. MC CORMICK, 399(MLJ):NOV73-
  365
CARTER, A.T. ELITE POLITICS IN
  RURAL INDIA.
  D. POCOCK, 617(TLS):31JAN75-118
CARTER, D. GHOST WRITER.
  N. CALLENDAR, 441:17AUG75-26
CARTER, F. GONE TO TEXAS.
  M. LEVIN, 441:29JUN75-29
  617(TLS):14NOV75-1349
CARTER, H. A HISTORY OF THE OXFORD
  UNIVERSITY PRESS. (VOL 1)
  H. TREVOR-ROPER, 362:7AUG75-186
CARTER, J. ABC FOR BOOK COLLECTORS.
  (5TH ED)
  354:MAR73-79
CARTER, J.D. THE WARREN COURT &
  THE CONSTITUTION.
  T.W. ROGERS, 396(MODA):SPRING74-
  208
CARTER, L. - SEE BECKFORD, W.
CARTER, N. THE BLACK DEATH.
  N. CALLENDAR, 441:30MAR75-24

CASTILLO-PUCHE, J.L. EL CÍNGULO.
C.A. SULLIVAN, 238:MAY73-505
CASTLE, D. BEGINNER'S GUIDE TO
AMATEUR ACTING.
R. STACEY, 157:SUMMER73-77
CASTONGUAY, C. MEANING & EXISTENCE
IN MATHEMATICS.
Y. GAUTHIER, 154:DEC73-725
CASTRÉN, M.A. NORDISCHE REISEN UND
FORSCHUNGEN.
L. SCHIEFER, 343:BAND17HEFT1-108
CASTRÉN, P. & H. LILIUS. GRAFFITI
DEL PALATINO.* (VOL 2) (V. VÄÄNÄ-
NEN, ED)
A. ERNOUT, 555:VOL47FASC1-189
CASTRO, F. REVOLUTIONARY STRUGGLE
1947-1958. (R.E. BONACHEA & N.P.
VALDÉS, EDS & TRANS)
W.F. BARBER, 529(QQ):SPRING73-119
CATACH, N. L'ORTHOGRAPHE FRANÇAISE
À L'ÉPOQUE DE LA RENAISSANCE.
A. FOULET, 545(RPH):FEB74-441
CATACH, N., J. GOLFAND & R. DENUX.
ORTHOGRAPHE ET LEXICOGRAPHIE.*
(VOL 1)
M. GLATIGNY, 557(RSH):APR-JUN73-
312
P. RICKARD, 208(FS):OCT74-498
CATALÁN, D. POR CAMPOS DEL ROMAN-
CERO.*
E. ROGERS, 240(HR):SPRING73-441
CATALÁN, D. & M. SOLEDAD DE ANDRÉS,
EDS. CRÓNICA DE 1344 QUE ORDENÓ EL
CONDE DE BARCELOS DON PEDRO ALFON-
SO.
D.W. LOMAX, 86(BHS):JUL73-285
"CATALOG OF THE SOPHIA SMITH COLLEC-
TION."
A.L. NOLEN, 14:JAN73-76
"CATALOGUE OF AMERICAN PORTRAITS IN
THE NEW YORK HISTORICAL SOCIETY."
J. RUSSELL, 617(TLS):21MAR75-303
"CATALOGUE OF BOOKS FROM THE LIBRARY
OF LEONARD & VIRGINIA WOOLF."
A. BELL, 617(TLS):25JUL75-822
CATE, C. GEORGE SAND.
E. ABEEL, 441:24AUG75-6
P. ADAMS, 61:SEP75-85
C. CAMPOS, 617(TLS):21NOV75-1376
V.S. PRITCHETT, 442(NY):27OCT75-
162
A. WHITMAN, 441:15OCT75-35
TEN CATE, P.H.J.H. - SEE UNDER HOU-
WINK TEN CATE, P.H.J.
CATHER, W. UNCLE VALENTINE & OTHER
STORIES.
639(VQR):WINTER74-X
CATLIN, G. GEORGE CATLIN: LETTERS &
NOTES ON THE NORTH AMERICAN INDIAN.
(M.M. MOONEY, ED)
P-L. ADAMS, 61:NOV75-127
CATO. M. PORCIUS CATO: "DAS ERSTE
BUCH DER ORIGINES." (W.A. SCHRÖ-
DER, ED)
R.M. OGILVIE, 123:MAR74-64
CATON, H. THE ORIGIN OF SUBJECTIV-
ITY.*
H.M. CURTLER, 396(MODA):SPRING74-
213
R.A. WATSON, 319:APR75-251
CATTAFI, B. LA DISCESA AL TRONO
1972-1973.
K. BOSLEY, 617(TLS):31OCT75-1308
CATTAFI, B. L'ARIA SECCA DEL FUOCO.
270:VOL23#4-85

CATTELL, R.B. A NEW MORALITY FOR
SCIENCE.
N. WEYL, 396(MODA):FALL74-438
CATULLUS. C. VALERII CATULLI CAR-
MINA. (G.P. GOOLD, ED)
O. SKUTSCH, 122:APR74-126
CATULLUS. THE POEMS.* (K. QUINN,
ED)
M.C.J. PUTNAM, 121(CJ):DEC73/JAN
74-184
CATULLUS. THE POEMS OF CATULLUS.
(H. GREGORY, TRANS)
W.C. SCOTT, 124:APR-MAY74-406
CATULLUS. THE POEMS OF CATULLUS.*
(J. MICHIE, TRANS)
R.B. LLOYD, 399(MLJ):SEP-OCT73-279
CAU, J. LES ENTRAILLES DU TAUREAU.
E.J. TALBOT, 207(FR):APR73-1042
CAUGHEY, J.W. BERNARDO DE GALVEZ IN
LOUISIANA 1776-1783.
R.R. REA, 9(ALAR):JUL73-232
CAULFIELD, J. THE TINY PERFECT
MAYOR.
A. POWELL, 99:APR/MAY75-29
CAUSLEY, C. COLLECTED POEMS.
J. FULLER, 617(TLS):26SEP75-1080
CAUTE, D. CUBA, YES?
J. BIERMAN, 362:6MAR75-317
CAUVIN, P. BLIND LOVE.
M. LEVIN, 441:11MAY75-22
DELLA CAVA, R. MIRACLE AT JOASEIRO.
P.J. SCHOENBACH, 399(MLJ):JAN-FEB
73-62
CAVAFY, C.P. COLLECTED POEMS. (G.
SAVIDIS, ED)
J. MERRILL, 453:17JUL75-12
I. SCOTT-KILVERT, 617(TLS):14NOV
75-1357
CAVAFY, C.P. PASSIONS & ANCIENT
DAYS.
T. EAGLETON, 565:VOL14#2-74
CAVAGNA, G.G. LO DICA IN ITALIANO.
T. DE LAURETIS, 399(MLJ):DEC73-429
CAVALIERO, G. THE ANCIENT PEOPLE.
J. MARTIN, 491:MAY75-103
CAVALIERO, G. JOHN COWPER POWYS:
NOVELIST.*
H. COOMBES, 598(SOR):AUTUMN75-779
K. HOPKINS, 111:MAR74-105
W.J. KEITH, 301(JEGP):OCT74-567
CAVALLIUS, G. VELAZQUEZ' LAS HIL-
ANDERAS.
D. MANNINGS, 89(BJA):SUMMER73-307
CAVALLO, G. ROTOLI DI EXULTET DELL'
ITALIA MERIDIONALE.
J. BROWN, 617(TLS):31OCT75-1312
CAVE, R. THE PRIVATE PRESS.*
D. CHAMBERS, 503:AUTUMN72-168
CAVE, T., ED. RONSARD THE POET.
H.W. LAWTON, 208(FS):JUL74-316
CAVE, T.C. & M. JEANNERET, EDS.
MÉTAMORPHOSES SPIRITUELLES.
D.L. RUBIN, 188(ECR):FALL73-262
CAVELL, S. MUST WE MEAN WHAT WE
SAY?
M. MOTHERSILL, 311(JP):30JAN75-27
CAVELL, S. THE SENSES OF "WALDEN."
W. HARDING, 191(ELN):SEP73-70
M. MOTHERSILL, 011(JP):30JAN75-27
CAVELL, S. THE WORLD VIEWED.*
M. MOTHERSILL, 311(JP):30JAN75-27
G.M. WILSON, 482(PHR):APR74-240

CAVENDISH, J.M. A HANDBOOK OF COPY-RIGHT IN BRITISH PUBLISHING PRAC-TICE.
R.G. LANDON, 99:DEC75/JAN76-64
CAVENDISH, R., ED. ENCYCLOPEDIA OF THE UNEXPLAINED.*
639(VQR):AUTUMN74-CLIV
CAVENDISH, R. THE POWERS OF EVIL.
H. COX, 441:19OCT75-8
CAVITCH, D. D.H. LAWRENCE & THE NEW WORLD.*
P.S. MACAULAY, 179(ES):OCT72-473
CAWLEY, R.R. HENRY PEACHAM.*
H. SMITH, 405(MP):NOV73-208
CAWS, M.A. ANDRÉ BRETON.*
M. BERTRAND, 188(ECR):SUMMER73-166
L.S. ROUDIEZ, 546(RR):MAR74-142
E. SELLIN, 295:FEB74-550
CAWS, M.A. THE INNER THEATRE OF RECENT FRENCH POETRY.
L.C. BREUNIG, 546(RR):MAR74-144
CAWS, M.A. THE POETRY OF DADA & SURREALISM.*
M. BERTRAND, 188(ECR):SUMMER73-166
R. CARDINAL, 447(N&Q):SEP73-358
R.R. HUBERT, 207(FR):OCT72-165
CAXTON, W. SELECTIONS FROM WILLIAM CAXTON. (N.F. BLAKE, ED)
W. SAUER, 72:BAND211HEFT3/6-429
J.L. WILSON, 382(MAE):1974/3-304
CAYLEY, M. - SEE "RICHARD CRASHAW"
CAZACU, B. & OTHERS. A COURSE IN CONTEMPORARY ROMANIAN.
J.E. ALGEO, 399(MLJ):NOV73-368
CAZAMIAN, L. THE SOCIAL NOVEL IN ENGLAND 1830-1850.*
J.D. JUMP, 148:SUMMER73-192
S. MONOD, 155:SEP73-184
S.M. SMITH, 677:VOL4-321
G.B. TENNYSON, 445(NCF):DEC73-367
CAZDEN, R.E. GERMAN EXILE LITERA-TURE IN AMERICA 1933-1950.*
J. STRELKA, 399(MLJ):MAR73-149
CAZENEUVE, J., A. AKOUN & F. BALLE. GUIDE DE L'ÉTUDIANT EN SOCIOLOGIE.
D. MERLLIÉ, 542:JAN-MAR73-53
NA CEAPAICH, S. - SEE UNDER SÌLIS NA CEAPAICH
CÉARD, J. - SEE PARÉ, A.
CÈBE, J-P. - SEE VARRO
CECCHI, E. & N. SAPEGNO, EDS. STOR-IA DELLA LETTERATURA ITALIANA. (VOL 5)
A.N. MANCINI, 400(MLN):JAN73-125
DE CECCO, M. MONEY & EMPIRE.
J. REDWOOD, 617(TLS):30OCT75-1160
CECIL, D. THE CECILS OF HATFIELD HOUSE.
S.W. JACKMAN, 432(NEQ):JUN74-340
676(YR):WINTER74-XXXI
CECIL, D. LIBRARY LOOKING-GLASS.
LORD LAMBTON, 617(TLS):26DEC75-1532
CECIL, D. VISIONARY & DREAMER.*
M. PRAZ, 179(ES):AUG72-367
CECIL, H. JUST WITHIN THE LAW.
J. FOSTER, 617(TLS):26SEP75-1096
CECIL, M. HEROINES IN LOVE.
P. BEER, 617(TLS):17JAN75-48
CECIL, R. LIFE IN EDWARDIAN ENG-LAND.
F. DEBEER, 189(EA):APR-JUN73-234

CECIL, R. THE MYTH OF THE MASTER RACE.
R.F. HOPWOOD, 529(QQ):SUMMER73-290
CELA, C.J. DICCIONARIO SECRETO. (VOL 2)
H. SCHNEIDER, 72:BAND211HEFT1/3-201
C. SMITH, 86(BHS):JUL73-279
CELAN, P. SELECTED POEMS.
R. SIEBURTH, 565:VOL14#4-32
CELATI, G. LE AVVENTURE DI GUIZZAR-DI.
B. MERRY, 270:VOL23#4-87
ČELEBONOVIĆ, A. THE HEYDAY OF SALON PAINTING.
F. HASKELL, 617(TLS):21MAR75-297
ČELEBONOVIĆ, A. SOME CALL IT KITSCH.*
P. ADAMS, 61:JAN75-90
CELLIER, L. BAUDELAIRE ET HUGO.
D. KELLEY, 208(FS):JUL74-342
CELLIER, L. L'ÉPOPÉE HUMANITAIRE ET LES GRANDS MYTHES ROMANTIQUES.
J. DECOTTIGNIES, 557(RSH):JAN-MAR73-159
CELLIER, L. DE "SYLVIE" À "AURÉLIA."
W. BEAUCHAMP, 546(RR):MAY73-221
M. BOWIE, 208(FS):JUL74-339
"CENSUS OF INDIA, 1961." (VOL 1, PT 2-C[2])
J.P. HUGHES, 660(WORD):DEC70-430
CENTENO Y RILOVA, A. & D. SUTHERLAND. THE BLUE CLOWN, DIALOGUES.*
H.B. NORLAND, 502(PRS):SPRING73-83
CERMINARA, G. INSIGHTS FOR THE AGE OF AQUARIUS.
M.W. BUCKALEW, 186(ETC.):SEP73-321
CERNOVODEANU, P. ENGLAND'S TRADE POLICY IN THE LEVANT & HER EXCHANGE OF GOODS WITH THE ROMANIAN COUN-TRIES UNDER THE LATER STUARTS (1660-1714).
M.S. ANDERSON, 575(SEER):JAN74-140
CERNUDA, L. PERFIL DER AIRE CON OTRAS OBRAS OLVIDADAS E INÉDITAS, DOCUMENTOS Y EPISTOLARIO. (D. HARRIS, ED)
P. BACARISSE, 205(FMLS):JUL73-301
DE CERTEAU, M., D. JULIA & J. REVEL. UNE POLITIQUE DE LA LANGUE.
S. ULLMANN, 617(TLS):1AUG75-878
CERULLI, E. NUOVE RICERCHE SUL LIBRO DELLA SCALA E LA CONOSCENZA DELL'ISLAM IN OCCIDENTE.
F. GABRIELI, 228(GSLI):VOL150FASC470/471-443
DE CERVANTES SAAVEDRA, M. EL CASI-MIENTO ENGAÑOSO Y COLOQUIO DE LOS PERROS. LE MARIAGE TROMPEUR ET COLLOQUE DES CHIENS. (M. COLHO, ED & TRANS)
J.B. AVALLE-ARCE, 240(HR):SUMMER73-561
DE CERVANTES SAAVEDRA, M. DOS NOV-ELAS EJEMPLARES.* (A. BURNS & J. GIBBS, EDS) TWO CERVANTES SHORT NOVELS. (F. PIERCE, ED)
P.N. DUNN, 86(BHS):JUL73-293
DE CERVANTES SAAVEDRA, M. EXEMPLARY STORIES. (C.A. JONES, TRANS)
E.L. RIVERS, 400(MLN):MAR73-428
DE CERVANTES SAAVEDRA, M. OCHO ENTREMESES. (J.B. AVALLE-ARCE, ED)
M.C. ANDRADE, 399(MLJ):MAR73-154

DE CERVANTES SAAVEDRA, M. LOS TRAB-
AJOS DE PERSILES Y SIGISMUNDA.*
(J.B. AVALLE-ARCE, ED)
F.A. DE ARMAS, 241:JAN73-79
CEVESE, R. VILLE DELLA PROVINCIA
DI VICENZA.
J.S. ACKERMAN, 576:MAR73-73
CHABOD, F. OPERE. (VOL 1 THRU VOL
3, PT 2)
S. KINSER, 551(RENQ):WINTER73-501
CHACE, W.M. THE POLITICAL IDENTI-
TIES OF EZRA POUND & T.S. ELIOT.*
B. CRICK, 617(TLS):30MAY75-586
R. KIRK, 569(SR):FALL74-698
F. MORAMARCO, 651(WHR):AUTUMN74-
401
639(VQR):SUMMER74-LXXIII
CHADWICK, C. SYMBOLISM.*
M. BOWIE, 208(FS):JAN74-100
W.M. FROHOCK, 399(MLJ):SEP-OCT73-
283
CHADWICK, J. LE DÉCHIFFREMENT DU
LINÉAIRE B.
C. DOBIAS-LALOU, 555:VOL47FASC1-
119
CHAFE, W.L. MEANING & THE STRUCTURE
OF LANGUAGE.*
O. AKHMANOVA, 353:1MAY73-105
R. HARRIS, 297(JL):FEB73-115
G. KRESS, 307:#1-107
"CHAGALL'S POSTERS."
J.R. MELLOW, 441:7DEC75-82
CHAI, C. & W., EDS & TRANS. A TREAS-
URY OF CHINESE LITERATURE.
V. YOUNG, 249(HUDR):AUTUMN74-421
CHAI, W. THE NEW POLITICS OF COM-
MUNIST CHINA.
D. LOVELACE, 293(JAST):FEB73-323
CHAILLEY, J. "THE MAGIC FLUTE,"
MASONIC OPERA.
R. CRAFT, 453:27NOV75-16
CHAITIN, G.D. THE UNHAPPY FEW.*
L.B. PRICE, 207(FR):MAY73-1227
CHAKRAVARTI, P.C. THE EVOLUTION OF
INDIA'S NORTHERN BORDERS.
R.L. DIAL, 293(JAST):FEB73-361
CHALIDZE, V. TO DEFEND THESE RIGHTS.
M. GLENNY, 617(TLS):5SEP75-987
J. RUBENSTEIN, 441:12JAN75-4
CHALKLIN, C.W. THE PROVINCIAL TOWNS
OF GEORGIAN ENGLAND.
F.M.L. THOMPSON, 617(TLS):24JAN75-
72
CHAMBERLAIN, M. FENWOMEN.
J. MAPPLEBECK, 362:25SEP75-412
CHAMBERLIN, E.R. THE FALL OF THE
HOUSE OF BORGIA.
M. MALLETT, 617(TLS):24JAN75-91
CHAMBERS, D.S., ED. PATRONS & ART-
ISTS IN THE ITALIAN RENAISSANCE.*
R. HATFIELD, 54:DEC73-630
CHAMBERS, F.M. PROPER NAMES IN THE
LYRICS OF THE TROUBADOURS.*
P. CHERCHI, 405(MP):FEB74-325
N. ILIESCU, 589:JAN74-105
CHAMBERS, G. THE BONNYCLABBER.*
N. LAVERS, 454:FALL73-77
CHAMBERS, R. LA COMÉDIE AU CHÂT-
EAU.*
J. FOX, 208(FS):OCT74-502
CHAMBERS, R. AN EXPERIMENTAL PARA-
DISE.
A.R. CHISHOLM, 67:NOV74-238

CHAMBERS, R. L'ANGE ET L'AUTOMATE.*
GÉRARD DE NERVAL ET LA POÉTIQUE DU
VOYAGE.
M. JEANNERET, 98:NOV73-977
VON CHAMISSO, A. SÄMTLICHE WERKE.
S.S. PRAWER, 617(TLS):19DEC75-1521
CHAMPAGNE, M. FACING LIFE ALONE.
A. NELSON, 441:6JUL75-4
CHAMPIGNY, R. LA MISSION; LA DE-
MEURE; LA ROUE.
H.A. BOURAOUI, 207(FR):APR73-1043
CHAMPIGNY, R. ONTOLOGIE DU NARRA-
TIF.
G. BRÉE, 399(MLJ):MAR74-142
CHAMPION, L.S. THE EVOLUTION OF
SHAKESPEARE'S COMEDY.*
M. MINCOFF, 179(ES):APR73-171
J.M. WASSON, 570(SQ):WINTER73-101
CHAN, H-L. THE HISTORIOGRAPHY OF
THE CHIN DYNASTY.*
J-S. TAO, 318(JAOS):APR-JUN73-211
CHAN HENG CHEE. SINGAPORE, THE POL-
ITICS OF SURVIVAL: 1965-1967.
G.D. NESS, 293(JAST):AUG73-749
CHANAN, G. & L. GILCHRIST. WHAT
SCHOOL IS FOR.
S. CURTIS, 617(TLS):21FEB75-203
CHAND, G. POPULATION IN PERSPEC-
TIVE.
S. CHANDRASEKHAR, 293(JAST):AUG73-
724
CHANDAMAN, C.D. THE ENGLISH PUBLIC
REVENUE 1660-1688.
J.R. JONES, 617(TLS):4JUL75-737
CHANDLER, D. THE GANGSTERS.
617(TLS):18JUL75-793
CHANDLER, D. MARLBOROUGH AS MILI-
TARY COMMANDER.*
T. ROPP, 579(SAQ):AUTUMN74-571
CHANDLER, D. NAPOLEON.
J.E. HOWARD, 617(TLS):21FEB75-193
CHANDLER, D.L. BROTHERS IN BLOOD.
S. RAAB, 441:19APR75-29
CHANDLER, R. TRAVELS IN ASIA MINOR.
(ED & ABRIDGED BY E. CLAY)
J. BECKWITH, 39:SEP73-238
CHANDOLA, A. A SYSTEMATIC TRANSLA-
TION OF HINDI-URDU INTO ENGLISH
(THE DEVANAGARI VERSION).
V. MILTNER, 353:1JUL73-62
CHANDOS, J., ED. IN GOD'S NAME.
J.W. BLENCH, 677:VOL4-256
CHANG, G.C.C. THE BUDDHIST TEACHING
OF TOTALITY.
F.H. COOK, 485(PE&W):JUL73-397
K.K. INADA, 484(PPR):SEP73-116
A. WAYMAN, 293(JAST):NOV72-130
CHANG, H.C. CHINESE LITERATURE.*
V. YOUNG, 249(HUDR):AUTUMN74-421
CHANG, K-C. THE ARCHAEOLOGY OF
ANCIENT CHINA. (REV)
E. VON ERDBERG-CONSTEN, 318(JAOS):
APR-JUN73-208
CHANG, R.T. HISTORIANS & MEIJI
STATESMEN.
M.V. LAMBERTI, 318(JAOS):JUL-SEP
73-413
CHANLETT, E.T. ENVIRONMENTAL PRO-
TECTION.
505:JUN73-162

CHANNON, R. ON THE PLACE OF THE
PROGRESSIVE PALATALIZATION OF VEL-
ARS IN THE RELATIVE CHRONOLOGY OF
SLAVIC.
  L. NEWMAN, 574(SEEJ):SUMMER73-252
"LA CHANSON DE ROLAND." (G.F. JONES
& A. DEMAITRE, EDS)
  W.G. VAN EMDEN, 208(FS):APR74-180
DE CHANTELOUVE, F. LA TRAGÉDIE DE
FEU GASPARD DE COLIGNY. (K. CAM-
ERON, ED)
  E.S. GINSBERG, 207(FR):OCT72-148
  K.M. HALL, 402(MLR):APR74-401
  C.N. SMITH, 208(FS):JAN74-64
CHAO, K. AGRICULTURAL PRODUCTION
IN COMMUNIST CHINA, 1949-1965.*
  E. AXILROD, 302:JAN73-169
  N-R. CHEN, 318(JAOS):APR-JUN73-222
CHAO, T. - SEE UNDER TS'AO CHAO
CHAPLIN, C. MY LIFE IN PICTURES.
  R. SCHICKEL, 441:7DEC75-90
CHAPLIN, P. & S. KUPFER. CRY, WOLF.
  D.A.N. JONES, 362:5JUN75-743
CHAPMAN, A.H. IT'S ALL ARRANGED.
  M.G. MICHAELSON, 441:2FEB75-6
CHAPMAN, C.B. DARTMOUTH MEDICAL
SCHOOL.
  P.D. WHITE, 432(NEQ):JUN73-306
CHAPMAN, G. A KIND OF SURVIVOR.
  W. HALEY, 617(TLS):25JUL75-833
  R. LEWIN, 362:5JUN75-742
CHAPMAN, J.S. BYRON & THE HONOUR-
ABLE AUGUSTA LEIGH.
  442(NY):13OCT75-179
CHAPMAN, K. HOVEDLINJER I TARJEI
VESAAS' DIKTNING.
  E. POULENARD, 189(EA):JAN-MARS73-
  120
CHAPMAN, R. UNIDENTIFIED FLYING
OBJECTS.
  J. BLISH, 617(TLS):17JAN75-50
CHAPPEL, A.H. SAGA AF VIKTOR OK
BLAVUS.
  M.E. KALINKE, 563(SS):SPRING74-182
CHAPPELL, F. THE WORLD BETWEEN THE
EYES.
  K.S. BYER, 219(GAR):SPRING73-110
CHAPPELOW, A. SHAW - THE "CHUCKER-
OUT."*
  A.E. KALSON, 160:FALL72-71
  R.S. NELSON, 50(ARQ):AUTUMN73-283
  A. RODRÍGUEZ-SEDA, 149:DEC74-359
  295:FEB74-776
CHAPPLE, J.A.V. DOCUMENTARY & IMAG-
INATIVE LITERATURE, 1880-1920.*
  295:FEB74-364
CHAR, R. LE NU PERDU.
  R. NUGENT, 207(FR):MAR73-849
CHAR, R. LA NUIT TALISMANIQUE.
  P-A. JOURDAN, 98:APR73-366
CHARBONNEAU, R. ÉTUDE SUR LES VOY-
ELLES NASALES DU FRANÇAIS CANAD-
IEN.*
  N.A. POULIN, 399(MLJ):DEC74-424
CHARBONNEAUX, J., R. MARTIN & F.
VILLARD. CLASSICAL GREEK ART, 480-
330 B.C.
  R. HIGGINS, 39:SEP73-240
CHARD, L.F., 2D. DISSENTING REPUB-
LICAN.
  B.C.H., 191(ELN):SEP73(SUPP)-62
DE CHARDIN, P.T. - SEE UNDER TEIL-
HARD DE CHARDIN, P.

CHARIG, A. & B. HORSFIELD. BEFORE
THE ARK.
  P. GOODWIN, 362:15MAY75-654
CHARITY, A.C. EVENTS & THEIR AFTER-
LIFE.*
  L.J. FRIEDMAN, 545(RPH):NOV73-235
CHARLES D'ORLÉANS. CHOIX DE
POÉSIES. (J. FOX, ED)
  C. CLARK, 382(MAE):1974/2-201
CHARLES, B.H. POTTERY & PORCELAIN.
  617(TLS):17JAN75-65
CHARLES-ROUX, E. CHANEL.
  P-L. ADAMS, 61:DEC75-119
  R. BILLINGTON, 441:2NOV75-24
  F. GRAY, 453:11DEC75-44
CHARLES-ROUX, E. L'IRRÉGULIÈRE.
  N. ROBERTS, 617(TLS):3JAN75-9
CHARLESWORTH, M.J. PHILOSOPHY OF
RELIGION.
  K. WARD, 479(PHQ):APR73-188
CHARLTON, D.G., J. GAUDON & A.R.
PUGH, EDS. BALZAC & THE NINETEENTH
CENTURY.*
  D.R. HAGGIS, 208(FS):APR74-213
CHARLTON, W. - SEE ARISTOTLE
CHARNEY, A. DOBRYD.
  G. WOODCOCK, 102(CANL):WINTER74-95
CHARNEY, H. LE SCEPTICISME DE
VALÉRY.
  J. BUCHER, 207(FR):MAR73-840
CHARNEY, M. STYLE IN "HAMLET."*
  M.T. JONES-DAVIES, 189(EA):JUL-SEP
  73-360
CHARRON, G. DU LANGAGE.
  G. LANE, 154:JUN73-390
CHARTERS, A. KEROUAC.*
  H. LOMAS, 364:DEC74/JAN75-80
CHARTERS, S. SOME POEMS/POETS.
  295:FEB74-501
CHARTERS, S. & A. WYATT - SEE EIG-
NER, L.
CHARTIER, A. THE POETICAL WORKS OF
ALAIN CHARTIER. (J.C. LAIDLAW, ED)
  N. MANN, 617(TLS):18APR75-436
CHARYN, J. BLUE EYES.
  T. LE CLAIR, 441:9FEB75-6
  C. LEHMANN-HAUPT, 441:23JAN75-37
DE CHASCA, E. EL ARTE JUGLARESCO EN
EL "CANTAR DE MÍO CID."
  J. JOSET, 556(RLV):1973/3-279
CHASE, H. MORE THAN LAND.
  M. LEVIN, 441:16NOV75-77
CHASE, J.W. AFRO-AMERICAN ART &
CRAFT.
  E.L.R. MEYEROWITZ, 39:JUN73-625
  M.A. TWINING, 292(JAF):JUL-SEP73-
  308
CHASIN, H. CASTING STONES.
  T. LASK, 441:2AUG75-19
CHASTAGNOL, A. RECHERCHES SUR
L'HISTOIRE AUGUSTE.*
  H.W. BENARIO, 24:SPRING74-91
CHASTAIN, K. THE DEVELOPMENT OF
MODERN LANGUAGE SKILLS.*
  J-P. BERWALD, 399(MLJ):JAN-FEB73-
  45
  J.W. BROWN, 238:SEP73-743
  G.G. PFISTER, 221(GQ):JAN73-142
CHASTAIN, T. PANDORA'S BOX.
  617(TLS):11JUL75-784

CHATAGNIER, L.J. & G. TAGGART, EDS.
LABORATOIRES DE LANGUES: ORIENTA-
TIONS NOUVELLES/LANGUAGE LABORATORY
LEARNING: NEW DIRECTIONS.*
  R.W. NEWMAN, 207(FR):APR73-1076
CHATFIELD, M. A GALLERY OF BERK-
SHIRE CHURCHES.
  617(TLS):21MAR75-320
CHATHAM, J.R. & E. RUIZ-FORNELLS,
WITH S.M. SCALES. DISSERTATIONS IN
HISPANIC LANGUAGES & LITERATURES.
  D. EISENBERG, 241:JAN73-89
CHÂTILLON, P. LA MORT ROUSSE.
  R. HATHORN, 296:VOL4#3-186
CHATMAN, S., ED. APPROACHES TO
POETICS.
  J. CULLER, 676(YR):SPRING74-439
CHATMAN, S. THE LATER STYLE OF
HENRY JAMES.*
  D. LODGE, 454:WINTER74-187
  C. MAVES, 599:SPRING73-241
CHATMAN, S., ED. LITERARY STYLE.*
  J. CULLER, 297(JL):SEP73-356
  269(IJAL):OCT73-273
CHATTERJEE, B. JOHN KEATS.*
  A. RODWAY, 541(RES):NOV73-504
  G. THOMAS, 175:AUTUMN72-113
CHATTERJI, S.K. THE ORIGIN & DEVEL-
OPMENT OF THE BENGALI LANGUAGE.
  V. MILTNER, 353:1JUL73-96
CHATTERTON, T. THE COMPLETE WORKS
OF THOMAS CHATTERTON. (D.S. TAY-
LOR, WITH B.B. HOOVER, EDS)
  H. OPPEL, 430(NS):SEP73-501
  C. PRICE, 447(N&Q):NOV73-435
  I.N. ROTHMAN, 131(CL):WINTER73-84
  F.W. SCHULZE, 72:BAND211HEFT1/3-
  122
"THOMAS CHATTERTON." (G. LINDOP,
ED)
  J.D. JUMP, 148:SUMMER72-187
CHATTERTON, W. VARDIS FISHER.
  M. BUCCO, 649(WAL):FALL73-159
CHATTOPADHYAY, G. COMMUNISM & BEN-
GAL'S FREEDOM MOVEMENT. (VOL 1)
  M.F. FRANDA, 293(JAST):FEB73-363
CHATTOPADHYAYA, H.P. INDIANS IN
AFRICA.
  L. STERNBACH, 318(JAOS):APR-JUN73-
  253
CHATURVEDI, B. & M. SYKES. CHARLES
FREER ANDREWS.
  J.H. BROOMFIELD, 293(JAST):FEB73-
  351
CHAUDHURI, N.C. CLIVE OF INDIA.
  J. GRIGG, 362:20NOV75-676
CHAUDHURI, N.C. SCHOLAR EXTRAORDI-
NARY.*
  H. LLOYD-JONES, 453:20MAR75-19
CHAUDHURY, P.C.R. - SEE UNDER ROY
CHAUDHURY, P.C.
DE CHAULIAC, G. THE "CYRURGIE" OF
GUY DE CHAULIAC.* (VOL 1) (M.S.
OGDEN, ED)
  E.R. HARVEY, 447(N&Q):JUN73-237
  B. WALLNER, 179(ES):FEB73-62
CHAURAND, J. FOU: DIXIÈME CONTE DE
LA "VIE DES PÈRES."*
  J. MONFRIN, 209(FM):JAN73-73
  W. ROTHWELL, 208(FS):JUL74-309
  C. STOREY, 382(MAE):1974/1-66
CHAURAND, J. HISTOIRE DE LA LANGUE
FRANÇAISE.
  N.L. CORBETT, 545(RPH):MAY74-536

CHAUSSERIE-LAPRÉE, J-P. L'EXPRES-
SION NARRATIVE CHEZ LES HISTORIENS
LATINS.*
  M.P. CUNNINGHAM, 122:APR73-135
CHAVARDÈS, M. LA REPARATION.
  C. FRANÇOIS, 207(FR):DEC72-434
CHAVARRIA, G.L., ED. TRADITIONAL
INDIA.
  Z.Y. ALI KHAN, 273(IC):OCT73-366
CHEE, C.H. - SEE UNDER CHAN HENG
CHEE
CHEEVER, J. THE WORLD OF APPLES.*
  L.T. LEMON, 502(PRS):FALL73-270
  W. PEDEN, 569(SR):FALL74-712
CHEGODAYEV, A.D. JOHN CONSTABLE.
[IN RUSSIAN]
  M. CHAMOT, 39:DEC73-514
CHEKHOV, A. LETTERS OF ANTON CHEK-
HOV.* (S. KARLINSKY, ED)
  L.W. BAILEY, 157:WINTER73-83
  M. MUDRICK, 249(HUDR):SPRING74-33
CHEKHOV, A. LETTERS OF ANTON CHEK-
HOV.* (A. YARMOLINSKY, ED)
  M. MUDRICK, 249(HUDR):SPRING74-33
CHEKHOV, A. THE OXFORD CHEKHOV.*
(VOL 5) (R. HINGLEY, ED & TRANS)
  X. GASIOROWSKA, 574(SEEJ):SPRING
  72-101
CHEKHOV, A. THE OXFORD CHEKHOV.*
(VOL 6) (R. HINGLEY, ED & TRANS)
  K.D. KRAMER, 574(SEEJ):SPRING73-77
CHELHOD, J. LA STRUCTURE DU SACRÉ
CHEZ LES ARABES.
  C. SCHUWER, 542:JAN-MAR73-103
CHEN CHUNG-HO & TAN YEOK SEONG,
COMPS. HSIN-CHIA-P'O HUA-WEN PEI-
MING CHI-LU.
  CHUANG SHEN, 302:JAN73-166
CHEN, J. NEW EARTH.
  J. CH'EN, 293(JAST):AUG73-693
CH'EN, J. YUAN SHIH-K'AI. (2ND ED)
  R.A. KAPP, 293(JAST):NOV72-146
CH'EN, J. & M. BULLOCK - SEE "POEMS
OF SOLITUDE"
CHEN LI-FU. THE CONFUCIAN WAY.
  R.H. YANG, 396(MODA):WINTER74-100
CHENEY, A. MILLAY IN GREENWICH
VILLAGE.
  L. BERNIKOW, 441:16NOV75-22
CHENEY, C.R. NOTARIES PUBLIC IN
ENGLAND IN THE THIRTEENTH & FOUR-
TEENTH CENTURIES.*
  R. BRENTANO, 589:OCT74-713
CHENEY, D. - SEE BROAD, C.D.
CHENEY, T.E., ED. LORE OF FAITH &
FOLLY.
  K. CUNNINGHAM, 292(JAF):APR-JUN73-
  195
  H.H. LEE, 650(WF):APR73-143
CHENG, C-H. ANALYSE FORMELLE DE
L'OEUVRE POÉTIQUE D'UN AUTEUR DES
TANG, ZHANG RUO-XU.
  F.A. WESTBROOK, 318(JAOS):OCT-DEC
  73-632
CHENG, C-Y. TAI CHEN'S INQUIRY INTO
GOODNESS.
  D.E. MUNGELLO, 293(JAST):NOV72-142
CHENU, R., ED. L'IMAGINATION CRÉA-
TRICE.
  V.A. LA CHARITÉ, 207(FR):APR73-
  1035

CHERMAYEFF, I. OBSERVATIONS ON
AMERICAN ARCHITECTURE.
44:OCT73-18
505:JUN73-162
CHERMAYEFF, I. & OTHERS. THE DESIGN
NECESSITY.
M. & S. SOUTHWORTH, 505:JUN73-160
CHERNAIK, J. THE LYRICS OF SHEL-
LEY.*
K. ALLOTT, 447(N&Q):AUG73-311
P.H. BUTTER, 677:VOL4-316
S.C., 191(ELN):SEP73(SUPP)-57
A.T. ORZA, 141:SUMMER73-285
H. SERGEANT, 175:SUMMER73-78
T. WEBB, 541(RES):NOV73-502
CHESNEAUX, J., ED. POPULAR MOVE-
MENTS & SECRET SOCIETIES IN CHINA,
1840-1950.
J. POLACHEK, 293(JAST):MAY73-483
CHESNEAUX, J. SECRET SOCIETIES IN
CHINA.
J. POLACHEK, 293(JAST):MAY73-483
CHESNEAUX, J. & M. BASTID. HISTOIRE
DE LA CHINE. (VOL 1)
E. LAFFEY, 293(JAST):FEB73-318
CHESSEX, J. CARABAS.
Y. VELAN, 207(FR):DEC72-435
CHESSEX, J. A FATHER'S LOVE.
M. ENGEL, 441:24AUG75-16
442(NY):11AUG75-86
CHESTER, L. & S. BARBA, EDS. RISING
TIDES.*
R.E. SEBENTHALL, 59(ASOC):SPRING-
SUMMER74-165
CHESTERTON, G.K. G.F. WATTS.
D.A.N. JONES, 362:17JUL75-90
D. PIPER, 617(TLS):4JUL75-715
CHESTERTON, G.K. THE WISDOM OF
FATHER BROWN. THE INNOCENCE OF
FATHER BROWN. THE INCREDULITY OF
FATHER BROWN. THE SECRET OF FATHER
BROWN.
N. CALLENDAR, 441:28SEP75-38
CHEVALIER, J-C. & OTHERS. GRAMMAIRE
LAROUSSE DU FRANÇAIS CONTEMPORAINE.
H-W. KLEIN, 430(NS):JAN73-56
CHEVALIER, L. HISTOIRE ANACHRONIQUE
DES FRANÇAIS.
R. COBB, 617(TLS):7FEB75-126
CHEVALIER, L. LABORING CLASSES &
DANGEROUS CLASSES IN PARIS DURING
THE FIRST HALF OF THE NINETEENTH
CENTURY.
R. DARNTON, 453:2OCT75-17
CHEW, A.F. THE WHITE DEATH.
P.K. HAMALAINEN, 563(SS):SUMMER74-
290
CHEYNE, G.J.G. JOAQUÍN COSTA, EL
GRAN DESCONOZIDO. A BIBLIOGRAPHI-
CAL STUDY OF THE WRITINGS OF JOA-
QUÍN COSTA (1846-1911).
V.G. KIERNAN, 402(MLR):JUL74-685
CHI, R.S.Y. BUDDHIST FORMAL LOGIC.
D.D. DAYE, 485(PE&W):OCT73-525
CHIAPPELLI, F. - SEE MACHIAVELLI, N.
CHIARI, J. T.S. ELIOT.
H. PESCHMANN, 175:SPRING73-35
CHIARI, J. TWENTIETH CENTURY FRENCH
THOUGHT.
C. SMITH, 617(TLS):10OCT75-1216
CHIARINI, M. I DISEGNI ITALIANI DI
PAESAGGIO.
G. MASSON, 46:JUL73-64

DEL CHIARO, M.A. ETRUSCAN RED-FIG-
URED VASE-PAINTING AT CAERE.
617(TLS):17OCT75-1245
CHIBNALL, M. - SEE ORDERIC VITALIS
CHICAGO, J. THROUGH THE FLOWER.
C. LEHMANN-HAUPT, 441:10MAR75-27
"CHICANO BIBLIOGRAPHY."
A.D. TREJO, 50(ARQ):WINTER73-372
CHICHESTER, J. ALL THE LOVELY
PEOPLE.
R. USBORNE, 617(TLS):12SEP75-1013
CHICK, H., M. HUME & M. MACFARLANE.
WAR ON DISEASE.
M. ROSE, 637(VS):MAR74-319
CH'IEN CHUN-JUI. EDUCATIONAL THEORY
IN THE PEOPLE'S REPUBLIC OF CHINA.
(J.N. HAWKINS, ED & TRANS)
T.H.E. CHEN, 318(JAOS):APR-JUN73-
219
CH'IEN, T. - SEE UNDER T'AO CH'IEN
CHIH-T'UI, Y. - SEE UNDER YEN CHIH-
T'UI
CHIH-YÜAN, W. - SEE UNDER WANG CHIH-
YÜAN
CHIHARA, C.S. ONTOLOGY & THE VIC-
IOUS CIRCLE PRINCIPLE.
M. STEINER, 311(JP):10APR75-184
CHILCOTE, R.H. EMERGING NATIONALISM
IN PORTUGUESE AFRICA.
J.A. CASADA, 14:APR73-247
CHILCOTT, T. A PUBLISHER & HIS
CIRCLE.*
R.W. KING, 541(RES):MAY73-225
B. SAVAGE, 503:AUTUMN72-169
G. THOMAS, 175:SUMMER72-72
CHILD, H. & D. COLLES. CHRISTIAN
SYMBOLS, ANCIENT & MODERN.*
J. BECKWITH, 39:APR73-436
CHILD, I.L. ITALIAN OR AMERICAN?
E.S. FALBO, 275(IQ):SPRING74-67
CHILD, J. FROM JULIA CHILD'S KIT-
CHEN.
R.A. SOKOLOV, 441:7DEC75-6
CHILTON, C.W. - SEE DIOGENES
CHIN, F. & OTHERS, EDS. AIIIEEEEE!
R. COLES, 442(NY):2JUN75-107
CHIN-HSIUNG, H. - SEE UNDER HSÜ
CHIN-HSIUNG
"CHINESE RHYME-PROSE."* (B. WATSON,
TRANS)
C-I. TU, 293(JAST):NOV72-135
CHINWEIZU. THE WEST & THE REST OF
US.
P. ADAMS, 61:APR75-100
CHISHOLM, A.R. - SEE NEILSON, S.
CHITTY, S. THE BEAST & THE MONK.
J.W. BURROW, 617(TLS):24JAN75-70
D.A.N. JONES, 362:23JAN75-125
J. MORRIS, 441:9NOV75-30
CHIU, H. THE PEOPLE'S REPUBLIC OF
CHINA & THE LAW OF TREATIES.
G.P. JAN, 293(JAST):NOV72-148
CHIU, T.N. THE PORT OF HONG KONG.
J. GOTTMANN, 617(TLS):17JAN75-58
CHMIELEWSKI, I. DIE BEDEUTUNG DER
GÖTTLICHEN KOMÖDIE FÜR DIE LYRIK
T.S. ELIOTS.
A. HELLER, 430(NS):APR73-233
CHOCHEYRAS, J. LE THÉÂTRE RELIGIEUX
EN SAVOIE AU XVIE SIÈCLE (AVEC DES
FRAGMENTS INÉDITS).
J.L. ALLAIRE, 207(FR):DEC72-397
Y. GIRAUD, 535(RHL):NOV-DEC73-1059
C.N. SMITH, 208(FS):JUL74-314

CHODOROW, S. CHRISTIAN POLITICAL
THEORY & CHURCH POLITICS IN THE
MID-TWELFTH CENTURY.
J.A. BRUNDAGE, 377:NOV74-176
L. ORSY, 613:SUMMER73-317
CHODOS, R. & R. MURPHY, EDS. LET US
PREY.
C. ARMSTRONG, 99:APR/MAY75-39
CHOKSEY, R.D. MOUNTSTUART ELPHIN-
STONE.
A.J. GREENBERGER, 293(JAST):MAY73-
521
CHOLAKIAN, P.F. & R.C., EDS & TRANS.
THE EARLY FRENCH NOVELLA.
B.C. BOWEN, 551(RENQ):WINTER73-512
H.P. CLIVE, 207(FR):APR73-1004
P.W. ROGERS, 529(QQ):SUMMER73-299
CHOLAKIAN, R.C. THE WILLIAM P.
SHEPARD COLLECTION OF PROVENÇALIA.*
S.C. ASTON, 208(FS):APR74-182
CHOMSKY, C. THE ACQUISITION OF SYN-
TAX IN CHILDREN FROM 5 TO 10.*
R.J. DI PIETRO, 399(MLJ):NOV73-371
CHOMSKY, N. CARTESIAN LINGUISTICS.*
(GERMAN TITLE: CARTESIANISCHE LIN-
GUISTIK.)
W. BUMANN, 343:BAND16HEFT2-122
CHOMSKY, N. PEACE IN THE MIDDLE
EAST?*
B. AVISHAI, 453:23JAN75-34
J.B. KELLY, 617(TLS):12DEC75-1485
CHOMSKY, N. PROBLEMS OF KNOWLEDGE &
FREEDOM.*
A. FLEW, 483:APR73-194
CHOMSKY, N. & M. HALLE. THE SOUND
PATTERN OF ENGLISH.*
K.C. HILL & L. NESSLY, 353:15JUN73-
57
CHOPIN, K. THE COMPLETE WORKS OF
KATE CHOPIN. (P. SEYERSTED, ED)
M. FRAZEE, 189(EA):JAN-MAR73-119
C. KOCHUYT, 179(ES):APR73-184
CHOPRA, P., ED. THE CHALLENGE OF
BANGLA DESH.
B.M. MORRISON, 293(JAST):AUG73-716
CHOUDHARY, S. PEASANTS' & WORKERS'
MOVEMENT IN INDIA 1905-1929.
B.B. KLING, 293(JAST):MAY73-523
CHOUDHURY, G.W. THE LAST DAYS OF
UNITED PAKISTAN.
H. TINKER, 617(TLS):31OCT75-1288
CHRÉTIEN DE TROYES. ROMANS DE LA
TABLE RONDE. (J-P. FOUCHER, ED &
TRANS)
W.W. KIBLER, 207(FR):OCT72-245
CHRIMES, S.B., C.D. ROSS & R.A.
GRIFFITHS, EDS. FIFTEENTH-CENTURY
ENGLAND, 1399-1509.
W.H. DUNHAM, JR., 589:OCT74-715
CHRIST, K. VON GIBBON ZU ROSTOVT-
ZEFF.
M. HAMMOND, 124:DEC73-JAN74-180
CHRIST-JANER, A. GEORGE CALEB BING-
HAM.
J. RUSSELL, 441:7DEC75-24
CHRISTES, J. DER FRÜHE LUCILIUS.
W.S. ANDERSON, 121(CJ):FEB/MAR74-
247
W.C. WEST 3D, 124:NOV72-175
CHRISTGAU, R. ANY OLD WAY YOU
CHOOSE IT.
M. PETERSON, 470:MAY74-24

CHRISTIAN, J. FIVE GATES TO ARMA-
GEDDON.
N. CALLENDAR, 441:28DEC75-20
CHRISTIE, A. CURTAIN.
P-L. ADAMS, 61:NOV75-126
M. LASKI, 362:20NOV75-684
J. SYMONS, 441:12OCT75-3
F. WYNDHAM, 617(TLS):26SEP75-1078
442(NY):10NOV75-194
CHRISTIE, N., ED. SCANDINAVIAN
STUDIES IN CRIMINOLOGY. (VOL 3)
D. ORRICK, 563(SS):FALL74-433
CHRISTIN, P. & P. LEFEBVRE. COM-
PRENDRE LA FRANCE.*
J. GREENLEE, 207(FR):DEC72-460
CHRISTOFANI, M., ED. NUOVE LETTURE
DI MONUMENTI ETRUSCHI DOPO IL RES-
TAURO.
E.M. BOGGESS, 124:DEC73-JAN74-184
CHRISTOFF, P.K. AN INTRODUCTION TO
NINETEENTH-CENTURY RUSSIAN SLAVO-
PHILISM. (VOL 2)
J.D. MORISON, 575(SEER):JAN74-143
N.V. RIASANOVSKY, 550(RUSR):OCT73-
434
CHRISTOPHER, M. MEDIUMS, MYSTICS &
THE OCCULT.
P. GROSE, 441:23AUG75-19
CHROMAN, E. THE POTTER'S PRIMER.
B. GUTCHEON, 441:7DEC75-74
CHROMATIUS. CHROMACE D'AQUILÉE,
"SERMONS."* (VOL 2) (J. LEMARIÉ,
ED; H. TARDIF, TRANS)
J. DOIGNON, 555:VOL47FASC2-364
CHUBIN, S. & S. ZABIH. THE FOREIGN
RELATIONS OF IRAN.
R.M. BURRELL, 617(TLS):12DEC75-
1484
NÍ CHUILLEANÁIN, E. ACTS & MONU-
MENTS.
F. HARVEY, 159(DM):WINTER/SPRING
73-115
CHUKS-ORJI, O. NAMES FROM AFRICA.
(K.E. BAIRD, ED)
E.C. SMITH, 424:MAR73-56
CHUN-JUI, C. - SEE UNDER CH'IEN
CHUN-JUI
CHUNG, K.C. KOREA, THE THIRD RE-
PUBLIC.
S.S. CHO, 293(JAST):NOV72-165
CHUNG-GI, K. - SEE UNDER KWEI CHUNG-
GI
CHUNG-HO, C. & TAN YEOK SEONG - SEE
CHEN CHUNG-HO & TAN YEOK SEONG
CHURCHILL, A. THE LITERARY DECADE.
295:FEB74-365
CHURCHMAN, C.W. FILOSOFIA E SCIENZA
DEI SISTEMI.
A. TANZI, 548(RCSF):OCT-DEC73-472
CHURGIN, B. - SEE SAMMARTINI, G.B.
CIARDI, J. THE LITTLE THAT IS ALL.
J. PARISI, 491:JUL75-219
CIBBER, C. COLLEY CIBBER: THREE
SENTIMENTAL COMEDIES. (M. SULLI-
VAN, ED)
B.R.S. FONE, 566:SPRING74-92
DE CIBOULE, R. ÉDITION CRITIQUE DU
SERMON "QUI MANDUCAT ME" DE ROBERT
DE CIBOULE (1403-1458).* (N. MAR-
ZAC, ED)
M.D. LEGGE, 402(MLR):JAN74-169
C.C. WILLARD, 545(RPH):AUG73-137
CIBULKA, H. DORNBURGER BLÄTTER.
K-D. HÄHNEL, 654(WB):4/1973-162

69

CICCONE, S.D. - SEE UNDER DE STEFAN-
IS CICCONE, S.
CICERO. CICÉRON, "LAELIUS DE AMI-
CITIA."* (R. COMBÈS, ED & TRANS)
H.G. EDINGER, 124:OCT72-106
CICERO. M. TULLI CICERONIS, PRO P.
QUINCTIO ORATIO. (T.E. KINSEY, ED)
J. BRISCOE, 313:VOL63-305
D.R. SHACKLETON BAILEY, 24:SUMMER
74-174
CILVETI, A.L. EL SIGNIFICADO DE LA
VIDA ES SUEÑO.
A.K.G. PATERSON, 86(BHS):OCT73-402
CIORAN, E.M. THE NEW GODS.
D. BROMWICH, 441:19JAN75-24
J. UPDIKE, 442(NY):12MAY75-138
CIORAN, S.D. THE APOCALYPTIC SYM-
BOLISM OF ANDREJ BELYJ.
B. THOMSON, 617(TLS):16MAY75-540
CIORANESCU, A. VASILE ALECSANDRI.
D.J. DELETANT, 402(MLR):JUL74-719
CIORANESCU, A. L'AVENIR DU PASSÉ.
P. MERIVALE, 131(CL):SUMMER73-271
CIRLOT, J-E. PICASSO.*
R. KAUFMANN, 90:AUG73-545
CITRON, P. - SEE BERLIOZ, H.
"THE CITY." [PROVIDENCE PRESERVATION
SOCIETY]
J. HNEDAK, 576:OCT73-261
CIULICH, L.B. & P. BAROCCHI, EDS.
I RICORDI DI MICHELANGELO.*
P. JOANNIDES, 90:MAY73-332
CIVIL, M. - SEE UNDER LAMBERT, W.G.
& A.R. MILLARD
CIXOUS, H. THE EXILE OF JAMES
JOYCE.* (FRENCH TITLE: L'EXIL DE
JAMES JOYCE OU L'ART DU REMPLACE-
MENT.)
A. BELL, 159(DM):SUMMER73-106
S. BRIVIC, 295:FEB74-678
R.A. DAY, 569(SR):WINTER74-130
J. LEWIS, 255(HAB):SUMMER73-231
CIXOUS, H. UN VRAI JARDIN.
J. FLETCHER, 207(FR):MAR73-851
CIZEK, E. L'ÉPOQUE DE NÉRON ET SES
CONTROVERSES IDÉOLOGIQUES.
K.R. BRADLEY, 24:SUMMER74-200
ČIŽEVSKIJ, D. COMPARATIVE HISTORY
OF SLAVIC LITERATURES.* (S.A. ZEN-
KOVSKY, ED)
R. AUTY, 447(N&Q):AUG73-317
W.B. EDGERTON, 574(SEEJ):SPRING72-
84
R. EKMANIS, 125:OCT73-79
G.S.N. LUCKYJ, 104:FALL73-422
W.T. ZYLA, 399(MLJ):JAN-FEB73-64
CLAIBORNE, C. KITCHEN PRIMER.
M.F.K. FISHER, 442(NY):10NOV75-177
CLAIR, J. ART EN FRANCE.
R. MICHA, 98:OCT73-926
CLAIR, R. L'ETRANGE OUVRAGE DES
CIEUX.
B.L. KNAPP, 207(FR):FEB73-658
CLANCHY, M.T., ED. CIVIL PLEAS OF
THE WILTSHIRE EYRE, 1249.*
P.D.A. HARVEY, 325:OCT73-668
CLAPHAM, S. THE GREENHOUSE BOOK.
617(TLS):7FEB75-149
CLARE, J. BIRDS NEST POEMS. (A.
TIBBLE, ED)
J. WAINWRIGHT, 565:VOL14#3-42
CLAREMON, N. BORDERLAND.
M. LEVIN, 441:29JUN75-28

CLARESON, T. SCIENCE FICTION CRITI-
CISM.
J.B. POST, 503:SPRING73-48
CLARESON, T.D., ED. SF: THE OTHER
SIDE OF REALISM.*
R. PECK, 295:FEB74-486
DI CLARI, R. LA CONQUISTA DI COS-
TANTINOPOLI (1198-1216). (A.M.
NADA PATRONE, ED & TRANS)
D.E. QUELLER, 589:OCT74-719
CLARK, E. DR. HEART.*
P. SOURIAN, 441:12JAN75-7
CLARK, E. ROME & A VILLA.
A. BROYARD, 441:25MAR75-37
P. SOURIAN, 441:12JAN75-7
CLARK, F.M. OBJECTIVE METHODS FOR
TESTING AUTHENTICITY & THE STUDY OF
TEN DOUBTFUL COMEDIAS ATTRIBUTED TO
LOPE DE VEGA.
L.C. PÉREZ, 238:SEP73-731
CLARK, J.L.D. FOREIGN LANGUAGE
TESTING.
L.T. HORNER, 221(GQ):NOV73-658
C. STANSFIELD, 238:SEP73-746
CLARK, J.R. & A. MOTTO, EDS. SATIRE.
566:SPRING74-99
CLARK, K. ANOTHER PART OF THE
WOOD.*
C. LEHMANN-HAUPT, 441:7APR75-29
J. RUSSELL, 441:30MAR75-17
G. STEINER, 442(NY):28JUL75-76
E. WEEKS, 61:MAY75-98
R. WOLLHEIM, 453:1MAY75-29
CLARK, K. THE GOTHIC REVIVAL.
P.F. NORTON, 576:MAR73-75
CLARK, K. THE ROMANTIC REBELLION.*
639(VQR):SUMMER74-CX
CLARK, K.B. THE PATHOS OF POWER.*
R. NISBET, 639(VQR):AUTUMN74-606
CLARK, L. THE BROAD ATLANTIC.
T. EAGLETON, 617(TLS):28FEB75-214
CLARK, L. - SEE YOUNG, A.
CLARK, M. LOGIC & SYSTEM.*
R.J.G., 543:MAR73-528
CLARK, M. PERPLEXITY & KNOWLEDGE.
V.M. COOKE, 258:JUN73-303
K.R.M., 543:MAR73-530
CLARK, P. & P. STACK, EDS. CRISIS
& ORDER IN ENGLISH TOWNS 1500-1700.
R.J.W. SWALES, 255(HAB):SPRING73-
125
CLARK, R. - SEE DUMAS [FILS], A.
CLARK, R.W. THE LIFE OF BERTRAND
RUSSELL.
R. DINNAGE, 617(TLS):31OCT75-1282
M. WARNOCK, 362:30OCT75-569
CLARK, S.R.L. ARISTOTLE'S MAN.
M. SCHOFIELD, 617(TLS):12DEC75-
1482
CLARK, T.J. THE ABSOLUTE BOURGEOIS.
R. SHATTUCK, 676(YR):SPRING74-429
J. TAGG, 592:JUL-AUG73-53
CLARK, T.J. IMAGE OF THE PEOPLE.
M. ROSENTHAL, 135:OCT73-144
R. SHATTUCK, 676(YR):SPRING74-429
J. TAGG, 592:JUL-AUG73-53
CLARK, T.W., ED. THE NOVEL IN INDIA.
R.O. SWAN, 293(JAST):MAY73-539
CLARK-KENNEDY, A.E. ATTACK THE
COLOUR!
617(TLS):22AUG75-936
CLARKE, A. A BIBLIOGRAPHICAL DIC-
TIONARY.*
N.G. WILSON, 447(N&Q):DEC73-478

CLARKE, A. THE BIGGER LIGHT.
  M. LEVIN, 441:16FEB75-12
  442(NY):24FEB75-140
CLARKE, A. STORM OF FORTUNE.
  D. BESSAI, 102(CANL):SUMMER74-106
CLARKE, A.C. IMPERIAL EARTH.
  T.A. SHIPPEY, 617(TLS):5DEC75-1438
CLARKE, A.C. RENDEZVOUS WITH RAMA.
  639(VQR):WINTER74-VIII
CLARKE, B.L. LANGUAGE & NATURAL
THEOLOGY.
  E. ALBRECHT, 682(ZPSK):BAND26HEFT
  3/4-389
CLARKE, G. SNOW ON THE MOUNTAIN.
  P.E. LEWIS, 565:VOL14#4-52
CLARKE, J.F. & J.W. LEONARD, COMPS.
THE GENERAL STRIKE, 1926.
  W.B. STEPHENS, 325:APR73-621
CLARKE, K.M. & OTHERS. À LA FRAN-
ÇAISE.
  J.W. ZDENEK, 399(MLJ):DEC74-420
CLARKE, K.W. UNCLE BUD LONG.
  569(SR):WINTER74-XIV
CLARKE, M.L. HIGHER EDUCATION IN
THE ANCIENT WORLD.*
  E. BERRY, 124:OCT72-120
  S.F. BONNER, 313:VOL63-268
  G. KENNEDY, 121(CJ):APR/MAY74-374
  O. MURRAY, 123:NOV74-225
CLARKE, R. & G. HINDLEY. THE CHAL-
LENGE OF THE PRIMITIVES.
  A. BROYARD, 441:29OCT75-35
CLARKE, R.A. SOVIET ECONOMIC FACTS
1917-1970.
  A.H. SMITH, 575(SEER):JUL74-475
CLARKE, T. & J.J. TIGUE, JR. DIRTY
MONEY.
  P.E. ERDMAN, 441:6JUL75-6
  442(NY):8SEP75-126
CLAUDE, D. GESCHICHTE DES ERZBIS-
TUMS MAGDEBURG BIS IN DAS 12. JAHR-
HUNDERT. (VOL 1)
  B.H. HILL, JR., 589:APR74-321
CLAUDEL, P. RICHARD WAGNER. (M.
MALICET, ED)
  L. GUICHARD, 535(RHL):JUL-AUG73-
  728
CLAUDIA, S. CLOCK & BELL.
  N. CALLENDAR, 441:9FEB75-16
CLAUS, H. SCHAAMTE.
  A. DIXON, 270:VOL23#2-35
CLAUS, H. DE SPAANSE HOER.
  P. SMYTH, 131(CL):SPRING73-184
CLAUSSEN, E.N. & K.R. WALLACE - SEE
LAWSON, J.
CLAVEL, B. LE SEIGNEUR DU FLEUVE.
  R. LORRIS, 207(FR):APR73-1045
CLAVEL, M. & P. LÉVÊQUE. VILLES ET
STRUCTURES URBAINES DANS L'OCCI-
DENT ROMAIN.
  O. MURRAY, 313:VOL63-312
CLAVELIN, M. THE NATURAL PHILOSOPHY
OF GALILEO.
  I.B. COHEN, 617(TLS):2MAY75-479
CLAVELL, J. SHŌGUN.
  D.J. ENRIGHT, 453:18SEP75-44
  C. LEHMANN-HAUPT, 441:10JUL75-33
  W. SCHOTT, 441:22JUN75-5
  442(NY):28JUL75-80
CLAY, E. - SEE CHANDLER, R.
CLAY, L.D. THE PAPERS OF GENERAL
LUCIUS D. CLAY. (J.E. SMITH, ED)
  J. GIMBEL, 441:23FEB75-20
  M. HOWARD, 617(TLS):29AUG75-969

CLAYRE, A. WORK & PLAY.*
  F. KERMODE, 453:27NOV75-35
CLAYTON, A.J. ETAPES D'UN ITINÉR-
AIRE SPIRITUEL.
  G.H. BAUER, 207(FR):FEB73-634
CLAYTON, D., C. CORTIS & [?] WEISE.
TALKING OF BRITAIN.
  T.L. WULLEN, 430(NS):FEB73-119
CLAYTON, S. FRIENDS & ROMANS.
  N. HEPBURN, 362:11DEC75-806
  M. JOHNSON, 617(TLS):7NOV75-1338
CLAYTON, T. - SEE SUCKLING, J.
CLEARE, J. MOUNTAINS.
  N. MORIN, 617(TLS):19DEC75-1511
  C.S. WREN, 441:17AUG75-6
CLEARY, J. THE SAFE HOUSE.
  M. LEVIN, 441:27JUL75-11
CLEAVES, F.W. - SEE MOSTAERT, A.
CLEBSCH, W.A. AMERICAN RELIGIOUS
THOUGHT.*
  639(VQR):SUMMER74-CII
CLEMEN, W. SHAKESPEARE'S DRAMATIC
ART.*
  R.A. FOAKES, 175:AUTUMN72-107
  B. HARRIS, 541(RES):NOV73-481
  A. LEGGATT, 529(QQ):SPRING73-134
  P. SWINDEN, 148:WINTER73-375
CLEMENT, R.C. THE LIVING WORLD OF
AUDUBON.
  617(TLS):21NOV75-1397
CLEMENT, W. THE CANADIAN CORPORATE
ELITE.
  P. RESNICK, 99:OCT75-32
CLEMENTELLI, E. INVITO ALLA LET-
TURA DI NATALIA GINZBURG.
  400(MLN):JAN73-171
CLEMMENSEN, T. MØBLER OF N.H. JAR-
DIN, C.F. HARSDORFF & J.C. LILLIE,
OG EKSEMPLER PÅ DERES INTERIØR
DEKORATION.
  P. THORNTON, 39:OCT73-314
CLEMOES, P., ED. ANGLO-SAXON ENG-
LAND, I.
  C. CLARK, 179(ES):AUG73-378
  E.G. STANLEY, 72:BAND211HEFT3/6-
  418
  R.M. WILSON, 402(MLR):APR74-367
CLEUGH, J. THE MEDICI.
  A. WHITMAN, 441:22MAR75-29
CLEVER, G. COUNT DOWN.
  D. BESSAI, 99:JUL75-36
CLEVER, G. - SEE SCOTT, D.C.
CLIFFORD, G. THE TRANSFORMATIONS OF
ALLEGORY.
  G. HOUGH, 617(TLS):11APR75-391
CLIFFORD, J.L., ED. TWENTIETH CEN-
TURY INTERPRETATIONS OF BOSWELL'S
"LIFE OF JOHNSON."
  R. LONSDALE, 447(N&Q):JUN73-228
CLIFFORD, J.L. & D.J. GREENE, EDS.
SAMUEL JOHNSON.
  J.D. FLEEMAN, 447(N&Q):JUN73-230
CLIFFORD, R.J. THE COSMIC MOUNTAIN
IN CANAAN & THE OLD TESTAMENT.
  P.C. CRAIGIE, 255:FALL73-300
CLIFFORD, W. AN INTRODUCTION TO
AFRICAN CRIMINOLOGY.
  J. LEWIN, 617(TLS):26SEP75-1101
CLIFTON, L. AN ORDINARY WOMAN.
  H. VENDLER, 441:6APR75-4
CLINCH, N.G. THE KENNEDY NEUROSIS.
  P. MERKLEY, 529(QQ):AUTUMN73-492
CLINE, C.L. - SEE MEREDITH, G.

CLINE, C.T., JR. DAMON.
  M. LEVIN, 441:13APR75-31
CLINTON, I.W. THE DIVAN OF MANUCHI-
HRI DAMGHANI.
  Q.S. KALIMULLAH HUSSAINI, 273(IC):
  OCT73-364
CLIVE, G. THE BROKEN ICON.
  L. PEDROTTI, 574(SEEJ):SUMMER73-
  222
CLIVE, J. MACAULAY.
  W.H. NELSON, 639(VQR):WINTER74-157
  J.M. ROBSON, 637(VS):MAR74-327
CLOEREN, H-J. & S.J. SCHMIDT, EDS.
PHILOSOPHIE ALS SPRACHKRITIK IM 19.
JAHRHUNDERT.* (VOLS 1&2)
  E. ALBRECHT, 682(ZPSK):BAND26HEFT
  1/2-142
CLOETE, S. A VICTORIAN SON.
  R.C. TOBIAS, 637(VS):DEC73-214
CLOGAN, P.M., ED. MEDIEVALIA ET
HUMANISTICA.* (NEW SER. NO. 3)
  R. DAHOOD, 50(ARQ):WINTER73-374
CLOSSON, E. HISTORY OF THE PIANO.
(REV BY R. GOLDING)
  F. DAWES, 415:AUG74-659
CLOUDSLEY-THOMPSON, J.L. TERRESTRI-
AL ENVIRONMENTS.
  K. MELLANBY, 617(TLS):29AUG75-973
CLOUGH, A.H. THE POEMS OF ARTHUR
HUGH CLOUGH. (2ND ED) (F.L. MUL-
HAUSER, ED)
  J. HOLLOWAY, 617(TLS):10JAN75-37
CLOWSE, C.D. ECONOMIC BEGINNINGS
IN COLONIAL SOUTH CAROLINA, 1670-
1730.
  R.A. BECKER, 656(WMQ):JUL74-512
CLOYD, E.L. JAMES BURNETT LORD MON-
BODDO.
  A. PARREAUX, 189(EA):JAN-MAR73-104
  C.N. STOCKTON, 481(PQ):JUL73-381
CLUBB, O.E. CHINA & RUSSIA.*
  H. HANAK, 575(SEER):JUL74-464
  D.W. TREADGOLD, 318(JAOS):JUL-SEP
  73-408
CLUBB, O.E. TWENTIETH CENTURY
CHINA. (2ND ED)
  R.C., 293(JAST):MAY73-573
CLUBB, O.E. THE WITNESS & I.
  D. CAUTE, 617(TLS):13JUN75-657
  J. THOMSON, 441:23FEB75-1
  442(NY):24MAR75-116
CLURMAN, H. ALL PEOPLE ARE FAMOUS.*
  B. GILL, 442(NY):25AUG75-85
CLUTTERBUCK, R. LIVING WITH TERROR-
ISM.
  K. MINOGUE, 617(TLS):7NOV75-1318
CLUVER, A.D.D. MERKMALSGRAMMATIK
DER DEUTSCHEN SPRACHE. (VOL 1)
  C.V.J. RUSS, 402(MLR):OCT74-906
  G. STARKE, 682(ZPSK):BAND26HEFT6-
  730
COADY, M.M. THE MAN FROM MARGAREE.
(A.F. LAIDLAW, ED)
  G.F.G. STANLEY, 529(QQ):AUTUMN73-
  463
COATES, D. THE LABOUR PARTY & THE
STRUGGLE FOR SOCIALISM.
  J.P. MACKINTOSH, 362:6MAR75-315
COATS, A.M. THE BOOK OF FLOWERS.*
  R. MC EWEN, 592:NOV73-213
COATS, A.M. THE TREASURY OF FLOWERS.
  S. SMITH, 441:7DEC75-95
COBB, C.W. ANTONIO MACHADO.
  D.L. SHAW, 402(MLR):APR74-443

COBB, R. PARIS & ITS PROVINCES,
1792-1802.
  T. ZELDIN, 362:8MAY75-618
COBB, R. REACTIONS TO THE FRENCH
REVOLUTION.
  A.L. MOOTE, 173(ECS):WINTER73/74-
  238
COBBAN, A.B. THE MEDIEVAL UNIVER-
SITIES.
  H. KEARNEY, 617(TLS):25APR75-452
COBURN, K. - SEE COLERIDGE, S.T.
COCHRANE, E. FLORENCE IN THE FOR-
GOTTEN CENTURIES, 1527-1800.*
  G. MARTIN, 676(YR):SPRING74-421
COCHRANE, I. JESUS ON A STICK.
  V. GLENDINNING, 617(TLS):20JUN75-
  689
  J. MELLORS, 362:19JUN75-821
COCKBURN, A. IDLE PASSION.
  C. LEHMANN-HAUPT, 441:15JAN75-41
  M. WATKINS, 441:16MAR75-10
  442(NY):17FEB75-107
COCKBURN, H. CIRCUIT JOURNEYS.
  N. PHILLIPSON, 617(TLS):9MAY75-517
COCKBURN, R. & R. GIBBS, EDS. NINE-
TY SEASONS.
  T. INKSTER, 606(TAMR):OCT74-76
COCKE, R. PIER FRANCESCO MOLA.
  E. WATERHOUSE, 90:MAR73-187
COCKERHAM, H. - SEE GAUTIER, T.
COCKSHUT, A.O.J. TRUTH TO LIFE.*
  P. GROSSKURTH, 99:JAN75-49
  J. KAPLAN, 31(ASCH):AUTUMN75-673
COCLICO, A.P. MUSICAL COMPENDIUM
(COMPENDIUM MUSICES).
  R. BRAY, 410(M&L):JUL74-344
CODINO, F. EINFÜHRUNG IN HOMER.
  C. DOBIAS-LALOU, 555:VOL47FASC1-
  121
CODRESCU, A. THE HISTORY OF THE
GROWTH OF HEAVEN.
  J.R. CARPENTER, 491:DEC74-166
CODY, J. AFTER GREAT PAIN.*
  S.A. BLACK, 141:SPRING72-199
  D.E. STANFORD, 295:FEB74-576
CODY, J.P. YOUR DAUGHTER WILL DIE!
  N. CALLENDAR, 441:27JUL75-17
CODY, M.L. COMPETITION & THE STRUC-
TURE OF BIRD COMMUNITIES.
  J.C. COULSON, 617(TLS):31JAN75-106
COE, R.N. IONESCO.
  G. CRADDOCK, 207(FR):APR73-1027
COEDÈS, G. CATALOGUE DES MANUSCRITS
EN PĀLI, LAOTIEN ET SIAMOIS PROVE-
NANT DE LA THAILANDE.
  O. VON HINÜBER, 182:VOL26#5/6-131
COELHO, J-F. TERRA E FAMÍLIA NA
POESIA DE CARLOS DRUMMOND DE AN-
DRADE.
  R. SAYERS, 399(MLJ):APR74-218
COELHO, V.H. SIKKIM & BHUTAN.
  L.E. ROSE, 293(JAST):NOV72-196
COFFEY, B. THE WALL OF MASKS.
  N. CALLENDAR, 441:8JUN75-12
COFFEY, T.M. THE LONG THIRST.
  T. BUCKLEY, 441:19OCT75-22
  453:16OCT75-41
COFFIN, T.P. THE OLD BALL GAME.
  R.A. REUSS, 650(WF):APR73-145
COFFIN, T.P. UNCERTAIN GLORY.
  L.C. KEATING, 582(SFQ):MAR73-76
COFIÑO LÓPEZ, M. LA ÚLTIMA MUJER Y
EL PRÓXIMO COMBATE.
  K. SCHWARTZ, 238:MAR73-182

COGGAN, D. CONVICTIONS.
P. HEBBLETHWAITE, 617(TLS):5DEC75-
1465
COGSWELL, F. THE CHAINS OF LILLIPUT.
R. GUSTAFSON, 102(CANL):WINTER73-
105
COHANE, J.P. THE KEY.
I.J. GELB, 318(JAOS):JUL-SEP73-396
COHEN, A.A. SONIA DELAUNAY.
J.R. MELLOW, 441:7DEC75-2
COHEN, A.A. IN THE DAYS OF SIMON
STERN.*
A.H. ROSENFELD, 390:AUG-SEP73-72
COHEN, A.B. POOR PEARL, POOR GIRL.
J. BYRD, 584(SWR):SPRING74-201
COHEN, C. CIVIL DISOBEDIENCE.
C.D. JOHNSON, 321:FALL73-233
COHEN, C. DEMOCRACY.
H.A. BEDAU, 482(PHR):APR73-249
W.G., 543:DEC72-355
COHEN, E.H. EBENEZER COOKE.
R.D. ARNER, 578:FALL75-153
COHEN, I.B. INTRODUCTION TO NEW-
TON'S "PRINCIPIA."*
P.J. WALLIS, 354:MAR73-70
COHEN, J. JOURNEY TO THE TRENCHES.
C. BEDIENT, 441:14SEP75-27
K. MILLER, 453:16OCT75-27
W.W. ROBSON, 617(TLS):29AUG75-958
D. THOMAS, 362:22MAY75-685
442(NY):10NOV75-194
COHEN, J. STRUCTURE DU LANGAGE
POÉTIQUE.
M. CHASTAING, 542:JAN-MAR73-112
COHEN, J.A. & H. CHIU. PEOPLE'S
CHINA & INTERNATIONAL LAW.
P. ALLOTT, 617(TLS):25APR75-448
639(VQR):SUMMER74-CI
COHEN, J.M. JOURNEYS DOWN THE
AMAZON.
R.A. HUMPHREYS, 617(TLS):4JUL75-
733
COHEN, L. THE ENERGY OF SLAVES.*
J.H., 502(PRS):SUMMER73-185
C. LEVENSON, 529(QQ):AUTUMN73-469
S. SCOBIE, 255(HAB):SUMMER73-240
T. WAYMAN, 102(CANL):SPRING74-89
COHEN, M. COLUMBUS & THE FAT LADY.
D. EVANIER, 102(CANL):AUTUMN74-110
P. MORLEY, 529(QQ):AUTUMN73-468
COHEN, M. THE DISINHERITED.*
A. FRANK, 606(TAMR):OCT74-78
A. MITCHELL, 102(CANL):AUTUMN74-86
H. PORTER, 296:VOL4#1-187
E. THOMPSON, 99:MAR75-39
COHEN, M. LANGUAGE.
S. POTTER, 617(TLS):16MAY75-531
COHEN, M., ED. THE STORY SO FAR #2.
B. LEVER, 296:VOL4#1-190
COHEN, M. TOO BAD GALAHAD.
D. EVANIER, 102(CANL):AUTUMN74-110
COHEN, M. WOODEN HUNTERS.
J. MILLS, 198:FALL75-133
COHEN, M.A. URBAN POLICY & POLITI-
CAL CONFLICT IN AFRICA.
K. LITTLE, 617(TLS):17OCT75-1242
COHEN, N.W. NOT FREE TO DESIST.
J. REINHARZ, 390:JAN73-74
COHEN, P.S. MODERN SOCIAL THEORY.
J.O. WISDOM, 488:SEP73-257
COHEN, R.S. - SEE SCHAFF, A.

COHEN, R.S. & M.W. WARTOFSKY, EDS.
BOSTON STUDIES IN THE PHILOSOPHY
OF SCIENCE. (VOL 5)
J.C. GRAVES, 84:JUN73-183
COHEN, R.S. & M.W. WARTOFSKY, EDS.
BOSTON STUDIES IN THE PHILOSOPHY OF
SCIENCE. (VOL 10)
P.M. WILLIAMS, 84:DEC73-411
COHEN, S.B. SAUL BELLOW'S ENIGMATIC
LAUGHTER.
S. PINSKER, 659:SUMMER75-386
COHEN, S.J. DORIS HUMPHREY.
M. SCOTT, 151:JUN73-83
COHN, B.S. INDIA.
J.H. BROOMFIELD, 293(JAST):AUG73-
712
COHN, N. EUROPE'S INNER DEMONS.
J. DEMOS, 441:10AUG75-15
E. JANEWAY, 61:AUG75-80
F. KERMODE, 362:20MAR75-367
J. LEE, 617(TLS):7MAR75-247
G. STEINER, 442(NY):8SEP75-118
A. WHITMAN, 441:3MAY75-31
COHN, N. KING DEATH.
M. LEVIN, 441:19OCT75-46
COHN, R. BACK TO BECKETT.
639(VQR):SUMMER74-LXXIII
COHN, R. DIALOGUE IN AMERICAN DRAMA.
J. COAKLEY, 295:FEB74-506
COHN, R.G. THE POETRY OF RIMBAUD.*
639(VQR):AUTUMN74-CXXVII
COINDREAU, M.E. THE TIME OF WILLIAM
FAULKNER. (G.M. REEVES, ED & TRANS)
M. FABRE, 131(CL):SPRING73-189
295:FEB74-487
COINTET, J-P. LA FRANCE LIBRE.
D. JOHNSON, 617(TLS):14MAR75-280
COKER, W. MUSIC & MEANING.*
F. HANSEN, 308:SPRING73-172
J. RAHN, 513:FALL-WINTER72-255
COLBERT, R. BRIEF FRENCH REFERENCE
GRAMMAR.
R.W. BOYKIN, 207(FR):DEC72-466
J.C. EVANS, 399(MLJ):JAN-FEB74-64
COLBURN, C.W. STRATEGIES FOR EDUCA-
TIONAL DEBATE.
A.N. SHELBY, 583:WINTER73-198
COLBY, V. THE SINGULAR ANOMALY.*
R. LAWRENCE, 175:SPRING72-32
COLBY, V. YESTERDAY'S WOMAN.
M. MASON, 617(TLS):16MAY75-542
S. RUDIKOFF, 249(HUDR):WINTER
74/75-615
COLDSTREAM, J.N. & G.L. HUXLEY, EDS.
KYTHERA.
W.R. BIERS, 124:APR-MAY74-407
COLDSTREAM, N. GREEK GEOMETRIC POT-
TERY.
D.G. MITTEN, 54:JUN73-280
COLE, H. SOUNDS & SIGNS.*
J.A. WESTRUP, 410(M&L):APR74-238
COLE, H.C. A QUEST OF INQUIRIE.
V.K. WHITAKER, 301(JEGP):JAN74-116
COLE, J.P. THE PROBLEMATIC SELF IN
KIERKEGAARD & FREUD.*
G.L. STENGREN, 319:JAN75-117
COLE, P. MODERN & TRADITIONAL
ELITES IN THE POLITICS OF LAGOS.
M. PEIL, 617(TLS):17OCT75-1241
COLE, S. LEAKEY'S LUCK.
K. KYLE, 362:7AUG75-188
J. PFEIFFER, 441:16NOV75-7
D. ROE, 617(TLS):21NOV75-1396

COLECCHIA, F. PAISAJES Y PERSONAJES
LATINOAMERICANOS.
E. ECHEVARRÍA, 399(MLJ):MAR73-152
COLEMAN, A., ED. CINCO MAESTROS.
J.W. DÍAZ, 238:MAY73-533
E.R. SKINNER, 238:MAR73-196
L.H. STRATTON, 238:MAY73-532
COLEMAN, D.G. RABELAIS.*
A.M. BOASE, 402(MLR):OCT74-866
M. TETEL, 551(RENQ):AUTUMN73-349
COLEMAN, F.X.J. THE AESTHETIC
THOUGHT OF THE FRENCH ENLIGHTEN-
MENT.*
P.N., 543:MAR73-531
COLEMAN, V. THE MEDICINE MEN.
G.M. CARSTAIRS, 617(TLS):25JUL75-
831
COLEMAN, V. OLD FRIEND'S GHOSTS.
M. DOYLE, 102(CANL):AUTUMN73-108
COLEMAN, V. PARKING LOTS. AMERICA.
D. BARBOUR, 102(CANL):WINTER74-117
COLEMAN, V. STRANGER.
S. SOLECKI, 99:JAN75-46
COLERIDGE, S.T. COLERIDGE ON
SHAKESPEARE.* (R.A. FOAKES, ED)
J.K. WALTON, 447(N&Q):APR73-156
COLERIDGE, S.T. COLLECTED LETTERS
OF SAMUEL TAYLOR COLERIDGE.* (VOLS
5&6) (E.L. GRIGGS, ED)
K. COBURN, 677:VOL4-310
COLERIDGE, S.T. THE COLLECTED WORKS
OF SAMUEL TAYLOR COLERIDGE: THE
FRIEND.* (B.E. ROOKE, ED)
G.N.G. ORSINI, 131(CL):WINTER73-76
COLERIDGE, S.T. THE COLLECTED WORKS
OF SAMUEL TAYLOR COLERIDGE: LAY
SERMONS. (R.J. WHITE, ED)
I.H.C., 191(ELN):SEP73(SUPP)-47
G. CARNALL, 402(MLR):JAN74-154
W.J.B. OWEN, 541(RES):AUG73-344
COLERIDGE, S.T. THE COLLECTED WORKS
OF SAMUEL TAYLOR COLERIDGE: LEC-
TURES 1795 ON POLITICS & RELIGION.*
(L. PATTON & P. MANN, EDS)
L.W. DEEN, 405(MP):NOV73-222
COLERIDGE, S.T. THE NOTEBOOKS OF
SAMUEL TAYLOR COLERIDGE.* (VOL 3)
(K. COBURN, ED)
639(VQR):AUTUMN74-CXXIV
COLES, E. THE CLIMBER.
D.M. DAY, 157:SUMMER73-80
COLES, R. THE MIND'S FATE.
A. STORR, 441:28SEP75-8
COLES, R. WILLIAM CARLOS WILLIAMS.
H. LEIBOWITZ, 441:5OCT75-1
H. VENDLER, 453:13NOV75-17
442(NY):4AUG75-92
COLETTE. DUO [&] LE TOUTOUNIER.
442(NY):25AUG75-86
COLETTE. LOOKING BACKWARDS.
A. BROYARD, 441:7JUN75-25
B. WRIGHT, 617(TLS):4JUL75-741
442(NY):18AUG75-83
COLEY, W.B. - SEE FIELDING, H.
COLHO, M. - SEE DE CERVANTES SAAVED-
RA, M.
COLIE, R.L. "MY ECCHOING SONG."*
L. POTTER, 179(ES):AUG72-360
COLIE, R.L. THE RESOURCES OF KIND.*
(B.K. LEWALSKI, ED)
W. NELSON, 131(CL):FALL74-378
639(VQR):SUMMER74-LXXVII

COLLANGE, J-F. L'ÉPÎTRE DE ST.
PAUL AUX PHILIPPIENS.
F.F. BRUCE, 182:VOL26#23/24-841
COLLARD, C. SUPPLEMENT TO THE ALLEN
& ITALIE CONCORDANCE TO EURIPIDES.
N.G. WILSON, 123:MAR74-128
COLLET, P. MODERN FRENCH.
A. CAPRIO, 399(MLJ):NOV74-356
COLLETT, E. THE CHATELAINE COOK-
BOOK.
J.M. COLE, 99:DEC75/JAN76-37
COLLETTI, L. FROM ROUSSEAU TO LENIN.
D-H. RUBEN, 479(PHQ):OCT73-377
COLLETTI, L. - SEE MARX, K.
COLLEY, C.C., COMP. DOCUMENTS OF
SOUTHWESTERN HISTORY.*
H.P. BEERS, 14:APR73-245
COLLI, G. & M. MONTINARI - SEE
NIETZSCHE, F.W.
COLLIER, B. HOPE & FEAR IN WASHING-
TON.
A. COCKBURN, 453:11DEC75-28
J. FALLOWS, 441:2NOV75-5
M. JANEWAY, 61:NOV75-122
COLLIER, C. ROGER SHERMAN'S CONNEC-
TICUT.*
R. MIDDLETON, 173(ECS):SPRING74-
368
COLLIER, G., P. TOMLINSON & J. WIL-
SON, EDS. VALUES & MORAL DEVELOP-
MENT IN HIGHER EDUCATION.
M. WARNOCK, 617(TLS):18APR75-435
COLLIER, J. THE JOHN COLLIER READ-
ER.
E. KORN, 617(TLS):26DEC75-1533
COLLIN, F. MAURICE BLANCHOT ET LA
QUESTION DE L'ÉCRITURE.*
N. OXENHANDLER, 546(RR):MAR74-148
COLLIN, R. & R. THE NEW ORLEANS
COOKBOOK.
R.A. SOKOLOV, 441:7DEC75-78
COLLINET, J-P. LE MONDE LITTÉRAIRE
DE LA FONTAINE.
B. BEUGNOT, 535(RHL):JUL-AUG73-682
J-H. PERIVIER, 207(FR):MAY73-1220
COLLINS, D., ED. THE ORIGINS OF
EUROPE.
S. PIGGOTT, 617(TLS):18APR75-434
COLLINS, D.M. THE MENDING MAN.
A. MAC KINNON, 529(QQ):WINTER73-
649
COLLINS, F., JR. THE PRODUCTION OF
MEDIEVAL CHURCH MUSIC-DRAMA.*
B. RAW, 447(N&Q):NOV73-437
COLLINS, J. DESCARTES' PHILOSOPHY
OF NATURE.
R.A. WATSON, 319:OCT75-525
COLLINS, J. INTERPRETING MODERN
PHILOSOPHY.*
A. FLEW, 479(PHQ):JUL73-265
D. GADD, 154:MAR73-178
B-A. NACHBAHR, 613:AUTUMN73-438
H. VEATCH, 258:SEP73-446
COLLINS, L. & D. LAPIERRE. FREEDOM
AT MIDNIGHT.
J. CAMERON, 441:26OCT75-2
J. LELYVELD, 441:8NOV75-25
N. MAXWELL, 453:11DEC75-15
COLLINS, M. BLACK POETS IN FRENCH.
J. DECOCK, 207(FR):MAY73-1263
COLLINS, M. BLUE DEATH.
N. CALLENDAR, 441:20APR75-27

COLLINS, M.F. & T.M. PHAROAH. TRANS-
PORT ORGANISATION IN A GREAT CITY.
  J. NAUGHTON, 617(TLS):4JUL75-726
COLLINS, P. - SEE DICKENS, C.
COLLINS, R.G., ED. FROM AN ANCIENT
TO A MODERN THEATRE.
  R. ROBERTSON, 255:FALL73-318
  V. VALLIS, 89(BJA):SPRING73-207
COLLINS, R.G., ED. THE NOVEL & ITS
CHANGING FORM.
  J.E.J., 191(ELN):SEP73(SUPP)-12
COLLINS, R.L - SEE "BEOWULF"
COLLINS, W. TALES OF HORROR & THE
SUPERNATURAL. (H. VAN THAL, ED)
  J.M. PURCELL, 573(SSF):FALL73-435
"COLLINS DICTIONARY OF PEOPLE &
PLACES."
  617(TLS):30MAY75-606
COLLINSON, F. THE BAGPIPE.
  A. BAINES, 617(TLS):25JUL75-854
COLLINSON, H. COUNTRY MONUMENTS.
  617(TLS):7MAR75-261
COLLIOT, R. ADENET LE ROI, "BERTE
AUS GRANS PIÉS;" ÉTUDE LITTÉRAIRE
GÉNÉRALE.
  A. FOULET, 545(RPH):MAY74-539
COLLIS, D.R.F. POUR UNE SÉMIOLOGIE
DE L'ESQUIMAU.
  T. ULVING, 269(IJAL):JUL73-194
COLLIS, J.S. THE CARLYLES.
  E.M. VIDA, 637(VS):DEC73-225
COLLISON, R. THE STORY OF STREET
LITERATURE.
  G.B. TENNYSON, 445(NCF):DEC73-371
COLLISON, R.L. ABSTRACTS & AB-
STRACTING SERVICES.
  D. HARRISON, 14:JAN73-73
COLLODI, C. PINOCCHIO.
  E. SACCONE, 400(MLN):JAN73-154
COLLOMS, B. CHARLES KINGSLEY.
  J.W. BURROW, 617(TLS):24JAN75-70
  D.A.N. JONES, 362:23JAN75-125
COLLUTHUS. COLLOUTHOS: "L'ENLÈVE-
MENT D'HÉLÈNE." (P. ORSINI, ED &
TRANS)
  C.R. BEYE, 124:SEP-OCT73-46
  F.M. COMBELLACK, 122:OCT74-298
  G. GIANGRANDE, 123:MAR74-129
  F. WILLIAMS, 303:VOL93-239
COLMAN, J.B. A VERY PRIVATE PERSON.
  N. SHRAPNEL, 617(TLS):19DEC75-1506
COLODNY, R.G., ED. PARADIGMS & PARA-
DOXES.
  H. POST, 84:SEP73-277
COLOMBO, C. CULTURA E TRADIZIONE
NELL'"ADONE" DI G.B. MARINO.
  A.N. MANCINI, 400(MLN):JAN73-125
COLOMBO, J.R., ED. COLOMBO'S CANAD-
IAN QUOTATIONS.
  J.M. BLISS, 99:JUN75-44
  J. MOSS, 296:VOL4#1-200
COLOMBO, J.R. TRANSLATIONS FROM THE
ENGLISH. THE SAD TRUTHS.
  P. O'FLAHERTY, 99:JUL75-38
COLQUHOUN, K. ST. PETERSBURG RAIN-
BOW.
  N. HEPBURN, 362:5JUN75-746
  S. KENNEDY, 617(TLS):2MAY75-492
COLQUHOUN, N., ED. NEW ZEALAND
FOLKSONGS.
  R. MACONIE, 203:WINTER73-345
COLSON, E. TRADITION & CONTRACT.
  L. MAIR, 617(TLS):8AUG75-887

COLVILLE, D. VICTORIAN POETRY &
THE ROMANTIC RELIGION.
  U.C. KNOEPFLMACHER, 636(VP):SPRING
  73-77
COLVIN, C. - SEE EDGEWORTH, M.
COLWIN, L. DANGEROUS FRENCH MIS-
TRESS & OTHER STORIES.
  A. BARNES, 617(TLS):5SEP75-998
  J. MELLORS, 362:18SEP75-386
COLWIN, L. PASSION & AFFECT.*
  W. PEDEN, 569(SR):FALL74-712
COMBE, T.G.S. & P. RICKARD, EDS.
THE FRENCH LANGUAGE.
  L. CHALON, 209(FM):JAN73-87
  A. URECHIA, 353:15OCT73-121
COMBÈS, J. L'IDÉE CRITIQUE CHEZ
KANT.
  J. KOPPER, 342:BAND64HEFT1-130
COMBÈS, M. FONDEMENTS DES MATHÉMA-
TIQUES.*
  R. BLANCHÉ, 542:JUL-SEP73-355
COMBÈS, R. - SEE CICERO
DE COMBRAY, R. VENICE, FRAIL BAR-
RIER.
  A. BROYARD, 441:23SEP75-41
COMEAUX, M.L. ATCHAFALAYA SWAMP
LIFE.
  J.H. PETERSON, JR., 582(SFQ):MAR
  73-77
COMER, J.P. & A.F. POUSSAINT. BLACK
CHILD CARE.
  J. HASKINS, 441:15JUN75-28
COMFORT, A. COME OUT TO PLAY.
  A. BROYARD, 441:30APR75-41
COMFORT, A. MORE JOY.
  B. DE MOTT, 61:APR75-88
COMINI, A. GUSTAV KLIMT.
  P-L. ADAMS, 61:NOV75-126
  C.E. SCHORSKE, 453:11DEC75-39
COMINI, A. EGON SCHIELE'S PORTRAITS.
  J. CANADAY, 441:8FEB75-23
  C.E. SCHORSKE, 453:11DEC75-39
COMMAGER, H.S., ED. BRITAIN THROUGH
AMERICAN EYES.*
  H.G. BAETZHOLD, 27(AL):JAN75-581
COMPTON-BURNETT, I. THE LAST & THE
FIRST.*
  J.C. FIELD, 556(RLV):1973/1-86
COMSTOCK, M. & C. VERMEULE. GREEK,
ETRUSCAN & ROMAN BRONZES IN THE
MUSEUM OF FINE ARTS, BOSTON.
  A.B. COOPER, 124:DEC73-JAN74-186
COMTE, A. COURS DE PHILOSOPHIE
POSITIVE. (VOL 1 ED BY M. SERRES,
F. DAGOGNET & A. SINACEUR; VOL 2 ED
BY J-P. ENTHOVEN)
  A. GIDDENS, 617(TLS):14NOV75-1359
COMTE, A. ÉCRITS DE JEUNESSE, 1816-
1828 [SUIVIS DU] MÉMOIRE SUR LA
COSMOGONIE DE LAPLACE, 1835. (P.E.
DE BERRÊDO CARNEIRO & P. ARNAUD,
EDS)
  O. CECCONI, 535(RHL):SEP-OCT73-917
CONACHER, J.B. THE PEELITES & THE
PARTY SYSTEM, 1846-52.
  D.C. MOORE, 637(VS):SEP73-118
CONARROE, J. WILLIAM CARLOS WIL-
LIAMS' "PATERSON."*
  S. FERGUSON, 219(GAR):SUMMER73-291
CANCALON, E.D. TECHNIQUES ET PER-
SONNAGES DANS LES RÉCITS D'ANDRÉ
GIDE.*
  V. ROSSI, 207(FR):APR73-1017

CONCHA, J. NERUDA 1904-1936.
R. PRING-MILL, 617(TLS):19SEP75-
1068
"CONCISE CAMBRIDGE ITALIAN DICTION-
ARY."
617(TLS):30MAY75-589
CONDEMINE, O. - SEE CRÉMAZIE, O.
CONDIT, C.W. CHICAGO, 1910-1929.
639(VQR):WINTER74-XXX
CONDIT, C.W. CHICAGO, 1930-1970.
639(VQR):AUTUMN74-CLVI
CONDON, R. MONEY IS LOVE.
M. LEVIN, 441:25MAY75-12
442(NY):25AUG75-87
CONDRY, W. WOODLANDS.
617(TLS):10JAN75-41
CONE, E.T. THE COMPOSER'S VOICE.
A. WALKER, 617(TLS):7MAR75-259
CONELLAN, C. WHY DOES EVIL EXIST?
F.R. BARRY, 617(TLS):6JUN75-628
CONEY, M. HELLO SUMMER, GOODBYE.
J. HAMILTON-PATERSON, 617(TLS):
8AUG75-903
CONFINO, M., ED. DAUGHTER OF A
REVOLUTIONARY.*
W. HALEY, 31(ASCH):SPRING75-332
H.M. PACHTER, 231:AUG75-83
L. SCHAPIRO, 617(TLS):3JAN75-2
CONGREVE, W. THE COMPLETE PLAYS OF
WILLIAM CONGREVE. (H. DAVIS, ED)
D.R.M. WILKINSON, 179(ES):AUG72-
363
CONGREVE, W. THE OLD BATCHELOUR
1693.
P.E. PARNELL, 568(SCN):FALL74-59
CONKLIN, H.C. FOLK CLASSIFICATION.
J.H. BRUNVAND, 292(JAF):JUL-SEP73-
314
CONLON, D.J., ED. LI ROMANS DE
WITASSE LE MOINE.
L. THORPE, 382(MAE):1974/1-63
CONLON, K. A TWISTED SKEIN.
S. CLAPP, 617(TLS):7FEB75-129
J. MELLORS, 362:13MAR75-349
CONLON, P.M. PRÉLUDE AU SIÈCLE DES
LUMIÈRES EN FRANCE.* (VOL 1)
R.A. BROOKS, 546(RR):JAN73-72
CONN, S. THE BURNING.
A. RENDLE, 157:SUMMER73-79
CONNELL, D. THE VISION IN GOD.*
P. DI VONA, 548(RCSF):APR-JUN73-
238
CONNELLY, P. & R. PERLMAN. THE
POLITICS OF SCARCITY.
E.J. MISHAN, 617(TLS):7FEB75-142
CONNOLLY, C. THE EVENING COLONNADE.
N. ANNAN, 453:12JUN75-10
A. BROYARD, 441:24JAN75-35
442(NY):27JAN75-103
CONNOR, T. THE MEMOIRS OF UNCLE
HARRY.*
R. GARFITT, 364:DEC74/JAN75-104
CONNOR, W.D. DEVIANCE IN SOVIET
SOCIETY.*
D.J. KOENIG, 104:WINTER73-560
CONOLLY, M. FOR IRELAND.
D.M. DAY, 157:SUMMER73-80
CONOLLY, V. SIBERIA TODAY & TOMOR-
ROW.
G.E. WHEELER, 617(TLS):23MAY75-562
CONOMIS, N.C. - SEE LYCURGUS
CONQUEST, R. - SEE YAKIR, P.

CONRAD, P. THE VICTORIAN TREASURE-
HOUSE.
R. MANDER, 39:OCT73-318
CONRADY, K.O. LITERATUR UND GER-
MANISTIK ALS HERAUSFORDERUNG.
R.H. THOMAS, 617(TLS):11APR75-408
CONRON, B., ED. MORLEY CALLAGHAN.
J. ORANGE, 296:VOL4#3-149
CONROY, H. & T.S. MIYAKAWA, EDS.
EAST ACROSS THE PACIFIC.
R.J. SMITH, 293(JAST):AUG73-707
CONROY, W.T. DIDEROT'S "ESSAI SUR
SÉNÈQUE."
H.T. MASON, 617(TLS):12SEP75-1032
"THE CONSERVATION OF CITIES."
R. WORSKETT, 617(TLS):5SEP75-988
CONSIDINE, B. THE REMARKABLE LIFE
OF DR. ARMAND HAMMER.
R.C. ALBERTS, 441:13JUL75-3
CONSOLI, D. DALL'ARCADIA ALL'ILLU-
MINISMO.
V.S., 275(IQ):SUMMER73-112
J.T.S. WHEELOCK, 481(PQ):JUL73-427
CONSTABLE, J. JOHN CONSTABLE'S COR-
RESPONDENCE. (VOL 6) (R.B. BECKETT,
ED)
G. REYNOLDS, 39:AUG73-151
"JOHN CONSTABLE'S SKETCH-BOOKS OF
1813 & 1814 REPRODUCED IN FACSIM-
ILE."
P. CONRAD, 617(TLS):15AUG75-911
CONSTANT, B. DEUX CHAPITRES INÉDITS
DE "L'ESPRIT DES RELIGIONS" (1803-
1804). (P. THOMPSON, ED)
O. POZZO DI BORGO, 535(RHL):SEP-
OCT73-903
CONSTANT, B. RECUEIL D'ARTICLES:
"LE MERCURE," "LA MINERVE" ET "LA
RENOMMÉE." (É. HARPAZ, ED)
N. KING, 208(FS):JAN74-83
CONSTANTIN, M.M. ROSIE.
M. LEVIN, 441:5JAN75-21
CONSTANTINE, K.C. THE BLANK PAGE.
N. CALLENDAR, 441:12JAN75-18
CONSTANTINE, K.C. A FIX LIKE THIS.
M. LEVIN, 441:28DEC75-20
CONSTANTINE, M. & J.L. LARSEN. BE-
YOND CRAFT.
B. KESTER, 139:OCT73-18
L. TURNER, 73:SUMMER74-39
CONTAMINE, P. GUERRE, ÉTAT ET
SOCIÉTÉ A LA FIN DU MOYEN ÂGE.
T.N. BISSON, 589:JUL74-552
CONTE, G. LA METAFORA BAROCCA.
D. CONRIERI, 228(GSLI):VOL150FASC
472-616
"CONTES MODERNES." (3RD ED)
R.D. COTTRELL, 399(MLJ):JAN-FEB74-
66
CONTI, G. MUSEO NATIONALE DI FIR-
ENZE, PALAZZO DEL BARGELLO.
J.V.G. MALLET, 39:JUL73-67
CONTINI, G. ALTRI ESERCIZI (1942-
1971).
E. BONORA, 228(GSLI):VOL150FASC
472-635
CONTINI, G. & V. SANTOLI - SEE DE
LOLLIS, C.
CONWAY, L. MOMENT OF TRUTH.
M. LEVIN, 441:16NOV75-77
COOK, A. THE ARMIES OF THE STREETS.*
639(VQR):SUMMER74-XCIII

COOK, A. ENACTMENT: GREEK TRAGEDY.
J.S. MARGON, 124:OCT72-108
H. PARRY, 487:SPRING73-77
COOK, A. THE ROOT OF THE THING.
A.A. ANDERSON, 182:VOL26#7/8-203
COOK, A. & E. DOLIN, EDS. AN
ANTHOLOGY OF GREEK TRAGEDY.
T.C. BARRY, 124:MAR73-355
COOK, C., ED. SOURCES IN BRITISH
POLITICAL HISTORY 1900-1951. (VOL
1)
617(TLS):30MAY75-609
COOK, C.C. A DESCRIPTION OF THE
NEW YORK CENTRAL PARK.
I.R. STEWART, 576:DEC73-348
COOK, E. BROWNING'S LYRICS.
M. ROBERTS, 617(TLS):16MAY75-543
COOK, G.M., ED. ERNEST BUCKLER.
E. WATERSTON, 255(HAB):SPRING73-
150
COOK, H.E. SHAKER MUSIC.
F. HOWES, 410(M&L):JUL74-343
COOK, J. DIRECTORS' THEATRE.
J. BOWEN, 364:FEB/MAR75-139
COOK, J.M. IN DEFENSE OF HOMO
SAPIENS.
P. ADAMS, 61:MAR75-144
COOK, J.W. & H. KLOTZ. CONVERSA-
TIONS WITH ARCHITECTS.
676(YR):WINTER74-VI
COOK, K. BLOODHOUSE.*
N. CALLENDAR, 441:2MAR75-17
COOK, R.F., ED. LE BATARD DE BOUIL-
LON.
L. THORPE, 382(MAE):1974/2-178
COOK, R.L. ROBERT FROST.
P. BEER, 617(TLS):31OCT75-1287
COOK, R.M. GREEK PAINTED POTTERY.
(2ND ED)
R. HIGGINS, 39:AUG73-149
C. KING, 124:APR-MAY74-403
COOK, S. FORM PHOTOGRAPH.*
S. CURTIS, 148:SPRING72-85
COOK, S. SIGNS OF LIFE.
A. CLUYSENAAR, 565:VOL14#4-75
COOK, T. VAGRANT ALCOHOLICS.
L. TAYLOR, 617(TLS):26SEP75-1102
COOKE, A.B. & J.R. VINCENT. LORD
CARLINGFORD'S JOURNAL.
M. ROSE, 637(VS):MAR74-319
COOKE, J. NEW ROAD.
J. KAVANAGH, 617(TLS):10OCT75-1217
COOKE, K. A.C. BRADLEY & HIS INFLU-
ENCE IN TWENTIETH-CENTURY SHAKE-
SPEARE CRITICISM.*
R.A. FOAKES, 175:AUTUMN72-107
J-B. FORT, 189(EA):JUL-SEP73-355
G.K. HUNTER, 677:VOL4-279
K. MUIR, 541(RES):AUG73-371
COOKE, M.G., ED. MODERN BLACK NOV-
ELISTS.*
B. KING, 529(QQ):SPRING73-141
COOKSON, C. THE GLASS VIRGIN.
E.M. EWING, 441:11MAY75-10
COOKSON, W. - SEE POUND, E.
COOLHAAS, W.P., ED. GENERALE MISSI-
VEN VAN GOUVERNEURS-GENERAAL EN
RADEN AAN HEREN XVII DER VERENIGDE
OOSTINDISCHE COMPAGNIE. (VOLS 1-5)
C.R. BOXER, 617(TLS):28NOV75-1423
COOMBES, H. EDWARD THOMAS.
W.A. SUTTON, 598(SOR):SUMMER75-691

COOPE, G. & OTHERS. A WITTGENSTEIN
WORKBOOK.
J.J.F., 543:SEP72-154
COOPE, R. SALOMON DE BROSSE & THE
DEVELOPMENT OF THE CLASSICAL STYLE
IN FRENCH ARCHITECTURE FROM 1565 TO
1630.
M. GREENHALGH, 46:JUL73-64
COOPER, D. THE DEAD OF WINTER.
A. MACLEAN, 617(TLS):25APR75-445
COOPER, D. THE GULLIBILITY GAP.*
N. SHRAPNEL, 617(TLS):7FEB75-147
COOPER, D. - SEE LAPORTE, G.
COOPER, I.S. THE VICTIM IS ALWAYS
THE SAME.*
P.B. MEDAWAR, 453:23JAN75-17
COOPER, J. EMILY.
617(TLS):31OCT75-1297
COOPER, J. MAPS & WINDOWS.
H. VENDLER, 441:6APR75-4
COOPER, J.L. GRASSHOPPER SUMMER.
M. LEVIN, 441:24AUG75-28
COOPER, L. THE CHINESE LANGUAGE FOR
BEGINNERS.
H-C. CHENG, 399(MLJ):NOV73-384
COOPER, P.S.A. CORRECT YOUR ENG-
LISH. (2ND ED)
P.H. FRIES, 399(MLJ):JAN-FEB74-82
COOPER, R. & J. FREUND. MODERN ENG-
LISH FOR GERMAN STUDENTS. (VOL 1)
A. GEIGER, 353:15JUL73-98
COOPER, S.M., JR. THE SONNETS OF
ASTROPHEL & STELLA.
J. ROBERTSON, 179(ES):FEB72-66
COOPER, W. - SEE MC KAY, C.
COOPERMAN, S. CANNIBALS.*
M. ANDRÉ, 529(QQ):AUTUMN73-471
COOVER, J. & R. COLVIG. MEDIEVAL &
RENAISSANCE MUSIC ON LONG-PLAYING
RECORDS: SUPPLEMENT, 1962-71.
T. WALKER, 415:JUL74-571
COPE, J.I. THE THEATER & THE DREAM.
A. BARTON, 401(MLQ):DEC74-420
D.A. SAMUELSON, 568(SCN):WINTER74-
77
COPELAND, W. FIVE HOURS FROM ISFA-
HAN.
N. CALLENDAR, 441:22JUN75-16
COPERNICUS, N. ON THE REVOLUTIONS.
D.J. BRYDEN, 135:MAR73-214
COPI, I.M. THE THEORY OF LOGICAL
TYPES.*
J. CORCORAN & J. RICHARDS, 486:
JUN73-319
D.L. GROVER, 482(PHR):APR74-281
COPLESTON, F. A HISTORY OF PHILOSO-
PHY. (VOL 9)
C. SMITH, 617(TLS):10OCT75-1216
COPLESTON, F. FRIEDRICH NIETZSCHE.
U. SIMON, 617(TLS):6JUN75-623
COPLESTON, F.C. RELIGION & PHILOSO-
PHY.
A. KENNY, 617(TLS):7FEB75-145
COPPEL, A. THE LANDLOCKED MAN.
L. CONTINI, 617(TLS):18APR75-417
J. MELLORS, 362:24APR75-547
COPPER, B. THE VAMPIRE IN LEGEND,
FACT & ART.
C. FRAYLING, 364:JUN/JUL74-98
CORBETT, E.P.J. CLASSICAL RHETORIC
FOR THE MODERN STUDENT. (2ND ED)
J.R. MC NALLY, 480(P&R):SPRING73-
125

CORBETT, P.B. PETRONIUS.
D. MULROY, 122:JUL73-229
CORBIÈRE, T. THE CENTENARY COR-
BIÈRE.
M. TURNELL, 617(TLS):14FEB75-165
CORCORAN, T.H. - SEE SENECA
CORD, W.O. - SEE ROMERO, J.R.
DE CORDEMOY, G. A PHILOSOPHICALL
DISCOURSE CONCERNING SPEECH...
(1668) [&] A DISCOURSE WRITTEN TO
A LEARNED FRIER...(1670).
K.L. WINEGARDNER, 568(SCN):SPRING-
SUMMER74-20
CORDEN, W.M. TRADE POLICY & ECONOM-
IC WELFARE.
I.F. PEARCE, 617(TLS):7FEB75-144
CORDER, E. THE BITE.
N. CALLENDAR, 441:31AUG75-12
CORDER, J.W., M. CHESSER & L. KAYE.
MORE THAN A CENTURY.
W. GARD, 584(SWR):SPRING74-V
CORDER, S.P. INTRODUCING APPLIED
LINGUISTICS.
F. GOMES DE MATOS, 351(LL):JUN74-
143
C. JAMES, 399(MLJ):NOV74-353
CORDER, S.P. & E. ROULET, EDS. THE-
ORETICAL LINGUISTIC MODELS IN
APPLIED LINGUISTICS.
G.C. LEPSCHY, 402(MLR):JUL74-596
COREA, N.J. A CLEANER BREED.
M. LEVIN, 441:9FEB75-14
CORINA, M. TRUST IN TOBACCO.
T.C. BARKER, 617(TLS):8AUG75-895
CORKE, H. IN OUR INFANCY.
J. CAREY, 362:2OCT75-451
P. KEATING, 617(TLS):24OCT75-1254
CORLISS, R. TALKING PICTURES.*
P. FRENCH, 617(TLS):28FEB75-221
CORMIER, R.J. & U.T. HOLMES, EDS.
ESSAYS IN HONOR OF LOUIS FRANCIS
SOLANO.*
S.C. ASTON, 208(FS):APR74-178
CORN, W.M. THE ART OF ANDREW WYETH.
J.R. MELLOW, 441:7DEC75-82
CORNEILLE, P. CINNA.
M. WAGNER, 207(FR):0CT72-247
CORNEILLE, P. HORACE. (I. MC FAR-
LANE, ED)
H.T. BARNWELL, 208(FS):JUL74-323
CORNEILLE, P. SURÉNA, GÉNÉRAL DES
PARTHES.* (J. SANCHEZ, ED)
J-P. RYNGAERT, 557(RSH):0CT-DEC73-
658
CORNEILLE, P. THÉÂTRE COMPLET.
(VOL 1) (G. COUTON, ED)
P.J. YARROW, 208(FS):JUL74-321
CORNEILLE, T. & D. DE VISÉ. LA
DEVINERESSE.* (P.J. YARROW, ED)
F.R. FREUDMANN, 208(FS):JUL74-324
CORNER, P. FASCISM IN FERRARA 1915-
1925.
M. CLARK, 617(TLS):12SEP75-1028
CORNGOLD, S. THE COMMENTATOR'S
DESPAIR.
S. HUTCHINS, 584(SWR):WINTER74-108
CORNMAN, J.W. MATERIALISM & SENSA-
TIONS.
B. AUNE, 482(PHR):JUL73-410
L. HOLBOROW, 479(PHQ):APR73-178
DE CORNUÄLLE, H. - SEE UNDER HELDRIS
DE CORNUÄLLE

CORNWELL, H.J.C. FORTY YEARS OF
CALEDONIAN LOCOMOTIVES, 1882-1922.
617(TLS):28FEB75-232
CORRIGAN, B. - SEE ALFIERI, V.
CORRIGAN, F. GEORGE THOMAS OF SOHO.
G. DAVID, 189(EA):0CT-DEC73-501
CORRIGAN, R., ED. TRAGEDY.
D. RITCHEY, 583:WINTER73-200
CORRINGHAM, M. I, JANE AUSTEN.
G. THOMAS, 175:SUMMER72-72
CORSINI, G. L'INSTITUZIONE LETTER-
ARIA.
617(TLS):31OCT75-1294
CORSTIUS, J.C.B. HET POËTISCH PRO-
GRAMMA VAN TACHTIG.
R.G. COLLMER, 149:SEP74-253
CORTÁZAR, J. ALL FIRES THE FIRE.*
B. ALLEN, 249(HUDR):SPRING74-119
CORTÁZAR, J. OCTAEDRO.
J.T. BOORMAN, 617(TLS):15AUG75-925
CORTÁZAR, J. ULTIMO ROUND.
W.L. SIEMENS, 268:JAN75-74
CORTELAZZO, M. L'INFLUSSO LINGUIS-
TICO GRECO A VENEZIA.*
H.&R. KAHANE, 545(RPH):FEB74-356
J. KRAMER, 72:BAND211HEFT3/6-453
"HERNAN CORTES: LETTERS FROM MEXICO."
(A.R. PAGDEN, ED & TRANS)
A.B. EDWARDS, 37:APR73-40
CORTÉS DÍAZ, L. FAMILIA Y SOCIEDAD
EN CARTAGENA.
C. GUILLÉN, 37:MAY73-42
BARON CORVO [FREDERICK ROLFE]. VEN-
ICE LETTERS. THE ARMED HANDS &
OTHER STORIES & PIECES. COLLECTED
POEMS.
J. SYMONS, 617(TLS):3JAN75-4
CORY, D. THE CIRCE COMPLEX.
N. CALLENDAR, 441:23MAR75-35
COSER, L. GREEDY INSTITUTIONS.
R. COLES, 31(ASCH):SPRING75-314
COSER, L.A., ED. THE IDEA OF SOCIAL
STRUCTURE.
A. WHITMAN, 441:8NOV75-25
COSGRAVE, P. THE PUBLIC POETRY OF
ROBERT LOWELL.
L. CASPER, 613:WINTER73-536
G.S. LENSING, 295:FEB74-708
COSTA, R.H. MALCOLM LOWRY.*
M. GRIFFITH, 651(WHR):SUMMER74-274
A.J. POTTINGER, 295:FEB74-711
COSTA-AMIC, B., ED. ALBUM DE ORO DE
LA POESIA MEXICANA.
P. JOHNSON, 399(MLJ):SEP-0CT73-302
DA COSTA RAMALHO, A. ESTUDOS SOBRE
A ÉPOCA DO RENASCIMENTO.
E. GLASER, 240(HR):WINTER73-112
COSTAMAGNA, G. IL NOTAIO A GENOVA
TRA PRESTIGIO E POTERE.
A. MOLHO, 551(RENQ):SPRING73-53
COSTANTINI, C. ARE ALL ITALIANS
LOUSY LOVERS?
M. LEVIN, 441:23NOV75-53
COSTANZO, M. CRITICA E POETICA DEL
PRIMO SEICENTO.*
D. CONRIERI, 228(GSLI):VOL150FASC
469-137
COSTE, G. CHAUX VIVE.
F-E. DORENLOT, 207(FR):APR73-1045
DE COSTER, C.C. BIBLIOGRAFÍA CRÍT-
ICA DE JUAN VALERA.
J.L. BROOKS, 86(BHS):JAN73-90

COSTINETT, S. ADVANCED READINGS & CONVERSATIONS.
L.H. COLTHARP, 399(MLJ):NOV74-374
COTEANU, I. OÙ EN SONT LA PHILOLOGIE ET LA LINGUISTIQUE ROUMAINES?
G.F. MEIER, 682(ZPSK):BAND26HEFT 1/2-191
COTEANU, I. & L. WALD, EDS. SISTEMELE LIMBII.
T. PAVEL, 353:15JAN73-126
COTNER, R.C. THE APPORTIONMENT CASES.
J.E. FORTENBERRY, 577(SHR):FALL73-456
COTT, J. - SEE STOCKHAUSEN, K.
COTTÉ, S. CLAUDE LORRAIN.
M. CORMACK, 39:AUG73-152
COTTER, J.F. INSCAPE.*
J.E. CHAMBERLIN, 249(HUDR):SPRING74-133
M. SMITH, 577(SHR):FALL73-436
COTTLE, T.J. A FAMILY ALBUM.
442(NY):7APR75-138
COTTON, J. BRITISH POETRY SINCE 1965.
D. CHAMBERS, 503:SUMMER73-103
COTTON, J. OLD MOVIES.
A. CLUYSENAAR, 565:VOL14#1-70
COTTRELL, A. PORTRAIT OF NATURE.
B. DIXON, 617(TLS):25JUL75-846
COTTRELL, A.P. WILHELM MÜLLER'S LYRICAL SONG-CYCLES.*
I.F., 191(ELN):SEP73(SUPP)-151
N. REEVES, 220(GL&L):JAN74-155
COTTRELL, L. UP IN A BALLOON.
617(TLS):14FEB75-177
COTTRELL, R.D. BRANTÔME.
J.B. ATKINSON, 551(RENQ):SPRING73-54
COUCH, W.T. THE HUMAN POTENTIAL.
639(VQR):AUTUMN74-CLII
COULLING, S. MATTHEW ARNOLD & HIS CRITICS.
J. HOLLOWAY, 617(TLS):8AUG75-897
COULSON, J. & OTHERS - SEE "THE OXFORD ILLUSTRATED DICTIONARY"
COUNCIL, N. WHEN HONOUR'S AT THE STAKE.
R.P. WHEELER, 301(JEGP):OCT74-545
COUNTS, C. POTTERY WORKSHOP.
S. PETERSON, 139:OCT73-64
COUNTS, D.R. A GRAMMAR OF KALIAI-KOVE.
A.M. STEVENS, 353:15AUG73-127
COUPE, W.A., ED. A SIXTEENTH-CENTURY GERMAN READER.
M. EBERT, 406:SUMMER74-173
J.L. FLOOD, 220(GL&L):OCT73-82
COUPER, J.M. LOOKING FOR A WAVE.
M. LEVIN, 441:5OCT75-48
COUPERIE, P. PARIS THROUGH THE AGES.* (FRENCH TITLE: PARIS AU FIL DU TEMPS.)
N. MILLER, 576:MAR73-67
COURDURIÉ, M. LA DETTE DES COLLECTIVITÉS PUBLIQUES DE MARSEILLE AU XVIIIE SIÈCLE.
W. SCOTT, 617(TLS):5SEP75-1001
COURLANDER, H., ED. A TREASURY OF AFRICAN FOLKLORE.
P. ADAMS, 61:MAR75-145
COURSE, E. THE RAILWAYS OF SOUTHERN ENGLAND: SECONDARY & BRANCH LINES.
617(TLS):7FEB75-149

DE COURTENAY, J.B. - SEE UNDER BAUDOUIN DE COURTENAY, J.
COURTÈS, F. LA RAISON ET LA VIE.
F. DUCHESNEAU, 154:DEC73-700
COURTHION, P. SOUTINE.
A. WERNER, 127:WINTER73/74-164
COURTINE, R.J. MADAME MAIGRET'S RECIPES.
R.A. SOKOLOV, 441:7DEC75-7
COURTNEY, E. A MOUSE RAN UP MY NIGHTIE.
617(TLS):3JAN75-18
COUSINS, E.H., ED. PROCESS THEOLOGY.
W.E.M., 543:SEP72-155
COUSINS, N. - SEE BROWN, J.M.
COUSTEAU, J-Y. & P. DIOLÉ. THE WHALE. DOLPHINS.
J.Z. YOUNG, 453:17JUL75-3
COUSTILLAS, P. - SEE GISSING, G.
COUSTILLAS, P. & C. PARTRIDGE, EDS. GISSING: THE CRITICAL HERITAGE.
B.H., 155:SEP73-191
J. KORG, 189(EA):OCT-DEC73-485
J. WOLFF, 177(ELT):VOL16#3-232
COUTANCHE, A. THE MEMOIRS OF LORD COUTANCHE. (H.R.S. POCOCK, COMP)
617(TLS):11JUL75-781
COUTANT, V. - SEE THEOPHRASTUS
COUTON, G. - SEE CORNEILLE, P.
COUTON, G. & J. JEHASSE - SEE PASCAL, B.
COUTURAT, L. DE L'INFINI MATHÉMATIQUE.
R. BLANCHÉ, 542:OCT-DEC73-477
COVA, P.V. I "PRINCIPIA HISTORIAE" E LE IDEE STORIOGRAFICHE DI FRONTONE.
S.I. OOST, 122:JAN73-77
COVATTA, A. THOMAS MIDDLETON'S CITY COMEDIES.
S. WIGLER, 568(SCN):WINTER74-76
COVENEY, J. & S.J. MOORE. GLOSSARY OF FRENCH & ENGLISH MANAGEMENT TERMS.
H. PARKER, 75:2/1973-98
COVENTRY, F. THE HISTORY OF POMPEY THE LITTLE. (R.A. DAY, ED)
P. ROGERS, 617(TLS):20JUN75-688
COVER, R.M. JUSTICE ACCUSED.
R. DWORKIN, 617(TLS):5DEC75-1437
COWAN, J.C. D.H. LAWRENCE'S AMERICAN JOURNEY.*
K. WIDMER, 594:WINTER73-547
COWAN, L. THE SOUTHERN CRITICS.
M.I. CARLSON, 584(SWR):SPRING74-217
COWAN, W. WORKBOOK IN COMPARATIVE RECONSTRUCTION.
R.W.P. BRASINGTON, 297(JL):FEB73-186
H.M. HOENIGSWALD, 215(GL):VOL13#2-99
269(IJAL):OCT73-273
COWASJEE, S. GOODBYE TO ELSA.*
A. MITCHELL, 102(CANL):AUTUMN74-86
COWELL, F.R. VALUES IN HUMAN SOCIETY.
P. DUBOIS, 542:APR-JUN73-218
COWIE, M.A. & M.L., EDS. THE WORKS OF PETER SCHOTT (1460-1490). (VOL 2)
E.S. FIRCHOW, 406:SUMMER74-200
W. SCHWARZ, 220(GL&L):APR74-259

COWIE, P., ED. INTERNATIONAL FILM
GUIDE 1973.
A.H. MARILL, 200:JUN-JUL73-369
COWLEY, A. THE CIVIL WAR.* (A.
PRITCHARD, ED)
R.B. HINMAN, 568(SCN):WINTER74-80
102(CANL):SUMMER74-124
COWLEY, M. A SECOND FLOWERING.*
M. BEEBE, 27(AL):MAY74-223
K. MC SWEENEY, 529(QQ):WINTER73-
671
COWLING, M. THE IMPACT OF HITLER.
R. BLAKE, 617(TLS):25JUL75-839
S. KOSS, 362:25SEP75-407
COX, B.S. CRUCES OF "BEOWULF."*
G. BOURQUIN, 189(EA):APR-JUN73-221
C. CLARK, 179(ES):AUG73-403
COX, C.B. & R. BOYSON, EDS. BLACK
PAPER 1975.
I. MC INTYRE & OTHERS, 362:24APR
75-533
COX, C.B. & A.E. DYSON, EDS. THE
TWENTIETH CENTURY MIND.
295:FEB74-365
COX, C.B. & A.E. DYSON, EDS. THE
TWENTIETH CENTURY MIND. (VOL 2)
G.D. SHEPS, 255(HAB):SUMMER73-207
COX, H. THE SEDUCTION OF THE SPIR-
IT.*
J.D. MARGOLIS, 651(WHR):SPRING74-
186
COX, L.S. FIGURATIVE DESIGN IN
"HAMLET."
A.C. DESSEN, 301(JEGP):OCT74-549
S.J. GREENBLATT, 676(YR):SPRING74-
447
COX, R.G., ED. THOMAS HARDY: THE
CRITICAL HERITAGE.*
J.C. MAXWELL, 447(N&Q):MAR73-109
COX, R.L. BETWEEN EARTH & HEAVEN.
P.N. SIEGEL, 570(SQ):SPRING73-232
COX, R.M. THE REV. JOHN BOWLE.
F. PIERCE, 86(BHS):JUL73-295
COX, R.W. & H.K. JACOBSON, EDS. THE
ANATOMY OF INFLUENCE.
J. BARROS, 529(QQ):WINTER73-662
COYAUD, M. LINGUISTIQUE ET DOCU-
MENTATION.
K. WINN, 430(NS):APR73-236
COYSH, A.W. THE ANTIQUE BUYER'S
DICTIONARY OF NAMES.
G. WILLS, 39:AUG73-152
COYSH, A.W. & J. KING. BUYING AN-
TIQUES REFERENCE BOOK. BUYING AN-
TIQUES GENERAL GUIDE.
G. WILLS, 39:AUG73-152
COZARINSKY, E. BORGES Y EL CINE.
617(TLS):7MAR75-245
CRADDOCK, J.R. & Y. MALKIEL - SEE
GEORGES, E.S.
CRADDOCK, P.B. - SEE GIBBON, E.
CRAFT, R. STRAVINSKY.*
E. LUTYENS, 607:JUN73-45
M. PETERSON, 470:MAY74-24
CRAGG, K. THE EVENT OF THE QUR'ĀN.
S. VAHIDUDDIN, 273(IC):APR73-175
CRAIG, A.M. & D.H. SHIVELY, EDS.
PERSONALITY IN JAPANESE HISTORY.
G.K. GOODMAN, 318(JAOS):JAN-MAR73-
93
CRAIG, C. C.M. WIELAND AS THE OR-
IGINATOR OF THE MODERN TRAVESTY IN
GERMAN LITERATURE.
D. VAN ABBE, 220(GL&L):OCT73-88

CRAIG, D. A DEAD LIBERTY.
617(TLS):21FEB75-184
CRAIG, D. THE REAL FOUNDATIONS.*
L. LERNER, 131(CL):SUMMER74-260
CRAIG, F.W.S., ED. BRITISH GENERAL
ELECTION MANIFESTOS 1900-1974.
N. SHRAPNEL, 617(TLS):31OCT75-1281
CRAIG, J. ALL G.O.D.'S CHILDREN.
M. LEVIN, 441:22JUN75-12
CRAIG, J. THE CLEARING.
M. MILLER, 617(TLS):2MAY75-473
CRAIG, J. HOW FAR BACK CAN YOU GET?
S. ATHERTON, 268:JAN75-83
R.D. CUFF, 99:MAR75-39
CRAIG, K. SALESTALK.
D.M. DAY, 157:SPRING73-84
CRAIG, R.B. THE BRACERO PROGRAM.
P. KELSO, 50(ARQ):SPRING73-76
CRAIK, W.A. THE BRONTË NOVELS.*
H.H. KÜHNELT, 430(NS):JUN73-347
CRAIK, W.A. ELIZABETH GASKELL & THE
ENGLISH PROVINCIAL NOVEL.
S. GILL, 617(TLS):11APR75-396
CRAIN, W.L. - SEE DE BALZAC, H.
CRAMER, T., ED. "LOHENGRIN."*
D.E. LE SAGE, 402(MLR):APR74-451
CRAMPTON, E. A HANDBOOK OF THE
THEATRE. (2ND ED)
J.C. TREWIN, 157:SPRING73-75
CRANE, E., ED. HONEY.
A. VIDLER, 617(TLS):3OCT75-1122
CRANE, F. EXTANT MEDIEVAL MUSICAL
INSTRUMENTS.*
E.A. BOWLES, 589:APR74-324
CRANE, H. & OTHERS. LETTERS OF HART
CRANE & HIS FAMILY.* (T.S.W. LEW-
IS, ED)
C. TOMLINSON, 617(TLS):24JAN75-78
CRANE, J.S., COMP. ROBERT FROST.
C. EVANS, 617(TLS):5SEP75-1002
CRANE, M., ED. SHAKESPEARE'S ART.
C. HOY, 569(SR):SPRING74-363
CRANE, S. THE WORKS OF STEPHEN
CRANE.* (VOL 6) (F. BOWERS, ED)
J.J. KIRSCHKE, 396(MODA):WINTER74-
105
CRANE, S.E. WHITE SILENCE.
J. MARKUS, 127:SPRING74-278
CRANSTON, M. POLITICS & ETHICS.
M. ROSHWALD, 484(PPR):SEP73-119
CRANSTON, M., ED. PROPHETIC POLI-
TICS.
P.R. ROBBINS, 529(QQ):SUMMER73-314
CRASHAW, R. THE COMPLETE POETRY OF
RICHARD CRASHAW. (G.W. WILLIAMS,
ED)
J.R. MULDER, 551(RENQ):AUTUMN73-
382
"RICHARD CRASHAW." (M. CAYLEY, ED)
J.D. JUMP, 148:SUMMER72-187
CRASTER, E. THE HISTORY OF ALL
SOULS COLLEGE LIBRARY.* (E.F.
JACOB, ED)
N. BARKER, 78(BC):SPRING73-95
J. DURKAN, 354:SEP73-259
CRASTRE, V. ANDRÉ BRETON.
M.A. CAWS, 207(FR):DEC72-420
CRATON, M. SINEWS OF EMPIRE.
R. ANSTEY, 617(TLS):28MAR75-340
CRAWFORD, D.J. KERKEOSIRIS.
J.G. GRIFFITHS, 123:NOV74-249
CRAWFORD, D.W. KANT'S AESTHETIC
THEORY.
P.D. GUYER, 311(JP):13FEB75-77

CRAWFORD, I.V. THE COLLECTED POEMS.
S.R. MAC GILLIVRAY, 102(CANL):
SUMMER74-116
CRAWFORD, M. WALTZ ACROSS TEXAS.
C. LEHMANN-HAUPT, 441:1MAR75-23
CRAWFORD, M.H. ROMAN REPUBLICAN
COINAGE.
M. GRANT, 617(TLS):20JUN75-690
CRAWFORD, R. AMERICAN STUDIES &
AMERICAN MUSICOLOGY.
A.R. SCHRAMM, 187:SEP75-483
CRAWFURD, J. A DESCRIPTIVE DICTION-
ARY OF THE INDIAN ISLANDS & ADJA-
CENT COUNTRIES.
J.M. ECHOLS, 318(JAOS):JUL-SEP73-
391
C.S. GRAY, 293(JAST):FEB73-367
CRAWLEY, H. THE GODDAUGHTER.
J. MILLER, 617(TLS):25JUL75-821
CRAY, E., ED. THE EROTIC MUSE.
J.E. KELLER, 582(SFQ):MAR73-79
CREAN, J.E., JR. & K.L. BERGHAHN.
KRITISCHE GESPRÄCHE.
R.J. RUNDELL, 399(MLJ):APR73-223
CREAN, J.E., JR. & P. MOLLENHAUER.
BRIEFE AUS DEUTSCHLAND.
W. NEUBAUER, 221(GQ):JAN73-139
"CREATIVE CAMERA INTERNATIONAL YEAR
BOOK 1975."
M. HAWORTH-BOOTH, 617(TLS):10JAN
75-28
CREEL, H.G. THE ORIGINS OF STATE-
CRAFT IN CHINA.* (VOL 1)
B.B. BLAKELEY, 244(HJAS):VOL33-238
CREELEY, R. A DAY BOOK.*
M.G. PERLOFF, 659:WINTER75-84
CREELEY, R. THE GOLD DIGGERS &
OTHER STORIES.
J.G., 502(PRS):SPRING73-91
CREELEY, R. A QUICK GRAPH.*
295:FEB74-468
CREIGHTON, D. TOWARDS THE DISCOVERY
OF CANADA.*
P.A. BUCHNER, 150(DR):AUTUMN73-552
102(CANL):SUMMER73-125
CRÉMAZIE, O. POÉSIES. (O. CONDE-
MINE, ED)
L.S. RODEN, 529(QQ):SUMMER73-313
DE CRENNE, H. - SEE UNDER HÉLISENNE
DE CRENNE
CRESCI, G.F. A RENAISSANCE ALPHABET.
F.R. COWELL, 89(BJA):SUMMER73-316
CRESSWELL, M.J. LOGICS & LANGUAGES.
S. READ, 518:MAY74-1
M.K. RENNIE, 63:DEC74-277
CRESWELL, J. BRITISH ADMIRALS OF
THE EIGHTEENTH CENTURY.
D.A. BAUGH, 481(PQ):JUL73-343
CREUZER, F. BRIEFE FRIEDRICH CREU-
ZERS AN SAVIGNY (1799-1850). (H.
DAHLMANN, ED)
F. LASSERRE, 182:VOL26#15/16-513
E.A. PHILIPPSON, 301(JEGP):OCT74-
599
CREWS, F. OUT OF MY SYSTEM.
C. LEHMANN-HAUPT, 441:24OCT75-41
P. ROAZEN, 99:DEC75/JAN76-59
R. TOWERS, 441:21DEC75-15
CREWS, H. THE GYPSY'S CURSE.*
J.L. HALIO, 598(SOR):AUTUMN75-942
N. HEPBURN, 362:6FEB75-189
E. KORN, 617(TLS):24JAN75-73
CRIADO, E.L. - SEE UNDER LORENZO
CRIADO, E.

CRICHTON, M. THE GREAT TRAIN ROB-
BERY.
P. ANDREWS, 441:22JUN75-4
P.D. JAMES, 617(TLS):26DEC75-1544
C. LEHMANN-HAUPT, 441:10JUN75-43
L.E. SISSMAN, 442(NY):4AUG75-89
E. WEEKS, 61:JUL75-80
CRICHTON SMITH, I. GOODBYE, MR.
DIXON.
E. MORGAN, 617(TLS):17JAN75-48
CRICHTON SMITH, I. LOVE POEMS &
ELEGIES.* HAMLET IN AUTUMN.
T. EAGLETON, 565:VOL14#1-65
CRICHTON SMITH, I. THE NOTEBOOKS OF
ROBINSON CRUSOE.
A. THWAITE, 617(TLS):23MAY75-552
CRICK, B. CRIME, RAPE & GIN.
A. RYAN, 617(TLS):28MAR75-331
CRICK, J. ROBERT LOWELL.
G. PEARSON, 617(TLS):4JUL75-719
CRICKMAY, C.H. THE WORK OF THE
RIVER.
K. DUNHAM, 617(TLS):15AUG75-929
CRINITI, N. BIBLIOGRAFIA CATILIN-
ARIA.
J-C. DUMONT, 555:VOL47FASC1-156
D.A. MALCOLM, 123:MAR74-154
E.J. PARRISH, 124:MAY73-479
CRINITI, N. L'EPIGRAFE DI ASCULUM
DI GN. POMPEO STRABONE.
J-C. DUMONT, 555:VOL47FASC1-180
M.P. MC HUGH, 124:OCT72-116
B. RAWSON, 122:JAN74-63
CRINITI, N. - SEE PASSERINI, A.
CRINÒ, A.M. - SEE MAGALOTTI, L.
CRIPE, H. THOMAS JEFFERSON & MUSIC.
639(VQR):SUMMER74-CVIII
CRIPER, C. & P. LADEFOGED. LINGUIS-
TIC COMPLEXITY IN UGANDA.
315(JAL):VOL11PT2-102
CRIPPS, D. ELIZABETH OF THE SEALED
KNOT.
R.H. HILL, 617(TLS):7NOV75-1339
"LES CRISES DE LA PENSÉE SCIENTIF-
IQUE DANS LE MONDE ACTUEL."
R. BLANCHÉ, 542:JUL-SEP73-356
CRISPIN, R.K. & J. PROGRESS IN
SPANISH.
F.M. WALTMAN, 238:DEC73-1135
CRISTIN, C. AUX ORIGINES DE L'HIS-
TOIRE LITTÉRAIRE.*
E. SHOWALTER, JR., 131(CL):SUMMER
74-263
M. VERANI, 557(RSH):OCT-DEC73-659
"CRITICAL ESSAYS ON MILTON FROM
ELH."
G.J. SCHIFFHORST, 577(SHR):WINTER
73-90
CROCCO, A. ANTITRADIZIONE E METO-
DOLOGIA FILOSOFICA IN ABELARDO.
F. ALESSIO, 548(RCSF):JAN-MAR73-
111
CROCE, A. THE FRED ASTAIRE & GINGER
ROGERS BOOK.
S.J. COHEN, 290(JAAC):SUMMER74-573
E. SIMPSON, 200:FEB73-111
CROCE, E. LA PATRIA NAPOLETANA.
F. DONINI, 617(TLS):11JUL75-782
CROCHET, P.H. & T.R. KING. A PRO-
GRAM ON SUPPORTING MATERIAL.
T.L. ATTAWAY, 583:FALL73-101

CROCKER, L.G., ED. ANTHOLOGIE DE LA LITTÉRATURE FRANÇAISE DU XVIIIE SIÈCLE.
D. MEDLIN, 399(MLJ):JAN-FEB73-48
W. WRAGE, 207(FR):FEB73-688
CROCKER, L.G. JEAN-JACQUES ROUSSEAU. (VOL 2)
A. KNODEL, 173(ECS):SPRING74-363
CROCKER, L.G. ROUSSEAU'S "SOCIAL CONTRACT."
O. FELLOWS, 207(FR):FEB73-612
CROCKETT, D. A NARRATIVE OF THE LIFE OF DAVID CROCKETT OF THE STATE OF TENNESSEE. (J.A. SHACKFORD & S.J. FOLMSBEE, EDS)
W. GARD, 584(SWR):SPRING74-V
CROFT, K. READINGS ON ENGLISH AS A SECOND LANGUAGE.*
C.A. TUCKER, 399(MLJ):SEP-OCT74-301
CROFT-COOKE, R. THE UNRECORDED LIFE OF OSCAR WILDE.
G.A. CEVASCO, 177(ELT):VOL16#1-85
CROHMĂLNICEANU, O.S. LITERATURA ROMÂNĂ ŞI EXPRESIONISMUL.
H.M. PĂULINI, 52:BAND8HEFT3-352
CROIX, A. NANTES ET LE PAYS NANTAIS AU XVIE SIÈCLE.
R.J. KNECHT, 617(TLS):6JUN75-630
CROKER, T.C. & S. CLIFFORD. LEGENDS OF KERRY.
M.N. COUGHLIN, 159(DM):SUMMER73-115
CROMPTON, L. SHAW THE DRAMATIST.*
H. SERGEANT, 175:AUTUMN72-114
CRONIN, V. LOUIS & ANTOINETTE.
A. WHITMAN, 441:19JAN75-16
442(NY):3MAR75-97
CROOK, J.M. THE BRITISH MUSEUM.*
S. BAYLAY, 576:DEC73-338
CROOK, J.M. THE GREEK REVIVAL.
B. READ, 135:MAR73-215
D. WATKIN, 46:JUL73-63
CROOK, J.M., ED. VICTORIAN ARCHITECTURE.*
P.F. NORTON, 576:MAR73-75
CROOK, J.M. - SEE EASTLAKE, C.L.
CROOK, J.M. & M.H. PORT. THE HISTORY OF THE KING'S WORKS. (VOL 6)
A.H. GOMME, 617(TLS):26SEP75-1109
CROSBIE, S.K. A TACIT ALLIANCE.*
639(VQR):AUTUMN74-CXLVII
CROSBY, J. AN AFFAIR OF STRANGERS.
J. BARNES, 617(TLS):26DEC75-1544
A. BROYARD, 441:28MAY75-45
N. CALLENDAR, 441:10AUG75-10
M. LASKI, 362:25DEC75&1JAN76-893
CROSBY, S.M. THE APOSTLE BAS-RELIEF AT SAINT-DENIS.*
J. BECKWITH, 39:SEP73-238
A. BORG, 589:JAN74-106
CROSS, A.G. N.M. KARAMZIN.*
I. RADEZKY, 574(SEEJ):FALL72-341
CROSS, C. - SEE SYLVESTER, A.J.
CROSS, M. & R. BOTHWELL, EDS. POLICY BY OTHER MEANS.
F.F. THOMPSON, 255:FALL73-313
CROSS, R.K. FLAUBERT & JOYCE.*
B.F. BART, 149:SEP74-251
D. O'CONNELL, 295:FEB74-679
CROSSLEY-HOLLAND, K. THE RAINGIVER.*
A. CLUYSENAAR, 565:VOL14#2-62

CROSSMAN, R. THE DIARIES OF A CABINET MINISTER. (VOL 1)
LORD GEORGE-BROWN, 362:11DEC75-804
E. HEATH, 362:11DEC75-802
CROSSON, F.J., ED. HUMAN & ARTIFICIAL INTELLIGENCE.
M.A. BODEN, 84:MAR73-61
CROW, C.M. PAUL VALÉRY.*
K. WEINBERG, 149:SEP74-261
C.G. WHITING, 207(FR):MAY73-1232
CROW, J. - SEE "LES QUINZE JOYES DE MARIAGE"
CROW, J.A. THE EPIC OF LATIN AMERICA.* (REV)
F.C. HAYES, 37:MAR73-37
CROWE, J. CROOKED SHADOWS.
N. CALLENDAR, 441:3AUG75-24
CROWE, S. & OTHERS. THE GARDENS OF MUGHUL INDIA.
B.D.H. MILLER, 463:AUTUMN73-316
CROWELL, N.B. A READER'S GUIDE TO ROBERT BROWNING.*
K. MC SWEENEY, 529(QQ):WINTER73-643
CROWLEY, E.T., ED. NEW ACRONYMS & INITIALISMS: 1972.
K.B. HARDER, 424:JUN73-122
CROWLEY, E.T. & R.C. THOMAS, EDS. REVERSE ACRONYMS & INITIALISMS DICTIONARY.
K.B. HARDER, 424:MAR73-52
CROWLEY, J.E. THIS SHEBA, SELF.
W. LETWIN, 617(TLS):13JUN75-672
CROWTHER, J. FIREBASE.
V. CUNNINGHAM, 617(TLS):4JUL75-732
CROWTHER, J.G. THE CAVENDISH LABORATORY 1874-1974.
J. NORTH, 617(TLS):3JAN75-6
CROWTHER, S. JOURNAL OF AN EXPEDITION UP THE NIGER & TSHADDA RIVERS IN 1854.
A.H.M. KIRK-GREENE, 69:OCT73-365
CROWTHER, S. & J.C. TAYLOR. THE GOSPEL ON THE BANKS OF THE NIGER.
A.H.M. KIRK-GREENE, 69:OCT73-365
CROXFORD, L. SOLOMON'S FOLLY.*
R. LIDDELL, 362:16JAN75-94
CROYDEN, M. LUNATICS, LOVERS & POETS.
639(VQR):SUMMER74-CVII
CROZIER, B. DE GAULLE.*
J. COLTON, 639(VQR):SUMMER74-467
J.F. SWEETS, 579(SAQ):AUTUMN74-566
CROZIER, B. A THEORY OF CONFLICT.
442(NY):31MAR75-99
"CRUCIAL AMERICAN ELECTIONS."
639(VQR):SUMMER74-XCIII
CRUCIANI, F. IL TEATRO DEL CAMPIDOGLIO E LE FESTE ROMANE DEL 1513, CON LA RICOSTRUZIONE ARCHITETTONICA DEL TEATRO DI ARNALDO BRUSCHI.
B. MITCHELL, 276:SPRING73-101
CRUICKSHANK, C. THE GERMAN OCCUPATION OF THE CHANNEL ISLANDS.
W. HALEY, 617(TLS):11JUL75-781
CRUICKSHANK, D.W. - SEE CALDERÓN DE LA BARCA, P.
CRUICKSHANK, J., ED. FRENCH LITERATURE & ITS BACKGROUND. (VOL 6)
295:FEB74-366
CRUMLEY, J. THE WRONG CASE.
N. CALLENDAR, 441:14SEP75-39

CRUNDEN, R.M. FROM SELF TO SOCIETY,
1919-1941.
295:FEB74-366
CRUNICAN, P. PRIESTS & POLITICIANS.
J. SAYWELL, 99:APR/MAY75-15
CRUTCHLEY, B. - SEE MORISON, S.
VAN DER CRUYSSE, D. LE PORTRAIT
DANS LES "MÉMOIRES" DU DUC DE
SAINT-SIMON.
H. HIMELFARB, 535(RHL):NOV-DEC73-
1070
B.L.O. RICHTER, 481(PQ):JUL73-576
M. WALLAS, 208(FS):OCT74-454
DE LA CRUZ, V. FERNÁN GONZÁLEZ.
617(TLS):23MAY75-573
CRYMES, R. & OTHERS. DEVELOPING
FLUENCY IN ENGLISH.
R.L. LIGHT, 351(LL):DEC74-307
CRYSTAL, D. THE ENGLISH TONE OF
VOICE.
G. BROWN, 617(TLS):28NOV75-1404
CRYSTAL, D. LINGUISTICS.*
T.P. DOBSON, 140(CR):#15-82
R.C. NAREMORE, 480(P&R):FALL73-253
G. SCHELSTRAETE, 179(ES):JUN72-286
CRYSTAL, D. PROSODIC SYSTEMS & IN-
TONATION IN ENGLISH.
O. LINDSTRÖM, 179(ES):JUN73-249
L. LIPKA, 38:BAND91HEFT3-378
K. WODARZ-MAGDICS, 353:1JAN73-117
CRYSTAL, D. & D. DAVY. INVESTIGAT-
ING ENGLISH STYLE.*
N.E. ENKVIST, 179(ES):APR72-181
CSAPODI, C. & K. CSAPODI-GÁRDONYI.
BIBLIOTHECA CORVINIANA.
J. BACKHOUSE, 90:MAR73-169
CUCCIA, S. LA LOMBARDIA ALLA FINE
DELL'ANCIEN RÉGIME.
E.B., 228(GSLI):VOL150FASC469-153
CUDDIHY, J.M. THE ORDEAL OF CIVIL-
ITY.
A. BROYARD, 441:2JAN75-31
CUÉNOT, C. C'E QUE TEILHARD A
VRAIMENT DIT.
J. LANGLOIS, 154:SEP73-556
CUESTA, P.V. & M. MENDES DA LUZ -
SEE UNDER VÁZQUEZ CUESTA, P. & M.
MENDES DA LUZ
"PAUL CUFFE: BLACK AMERICA & THE
AFRICAN RETURN." (S.H. HARRIS, ED)
F.J. MILLER, 432(NEQ):MAR74-168
CULLEN, G. THE CONCISE TOWNSCAPE.
R. GAZZARD, 46:FEB73-146
CULLEN, P. SPENSER, MARVELL, & REN-
AISSANCE PASTORAL.*
D.M. FRIEDMAN, 551(RENQ):SPRING73-
78
W.C. JOHNSON, 179(ES):FEB73-68
G.J. SCHIFFHORST, 577(SHR):SPRING
73-224
CULLEN, T. THE PROSTITUTES' PADRE.
E.S. TURNER, 617(TLS):31OCT75-1300
CULLER, J. STRUCTURALIST POETICS.
D.L. GREENBLATT, 113:FALL74-73
A. LAVERS, 617(TLS):1AUG75-878
D. MAY, 362:20MAR75-379
CULLINAN, E. THE TIME OF ADAM.
J.H. HARKEY, 573(SSF):WINTER73-106
CUMMINGS, E.E. COMPLETE POEMS:
1913-1962.*
W.G.R., 502(PRS):FALL73-280

CUMMINGS, E.E. SELECTED LETTERS OF
E.E. CUMMINGS. (F.W. DUPEE & G.
STADE, EDS)
J. GLOVER, 565:VOL14#1-63
CUMMINGS, R.M., ED. SPENSER: THE
CRITICAL HERITAGE.
W.C. JOHNSON, 179(ES):OCT73-511
CUNHA, G.M. & D.G. CONSERVATION OF
LIBRARY MATERIALS.* (VOL 1) (2ND
ED)
I.P. COLLIS, 325:OCT73-678
CUNHA, G.M. & D.G. CONSERVATION OF
LIBRARY MATERIALS. (VOL 2) (2ND ED)
I.P. COLLIS, 325:OCT73-678
J.C. WRIGHT, 14:OCT73-555
CUNHA, G.M. & N.P. TUCKER, EDS.
LIBRARY & ARCHIVES CONSERVATION.
J.C. WRIGHT, 14:OCT73-555
CUNLIFFE, B. FISHBOURNE.
D.E. KIBBE, 124:SEP72-56
CUNNINGHAM, I.C. - SEE HERODAS
"IMOGEN CUNNINGHAM: PHOTOGRAPHS."
90:MAR73-199
CUNNINGHAM, J.V. THE COLLECTED
POEMS & EPIGRAMS.*
H. SERGEANT, 175:SUMMER72-75
CURI, F. METODO; STORIA; STRUTTURE.
M.E. BROWN, 290(JAAC):SPRING74-439
CURL, J.S. THE VICTORIAN CELEBRA-
TION OF DEATH.*
J. MAASS, 576:MAR73-78
CURLE, A. MYSTICS & MILITANTS.
W. ECKHARDT, 255(HAB):WINTER73-48
CURLEY, C. THE COMING PROFIT IN
GOLD.
B.G. MALKIEL, 441:26JAN75-19
CURRAN, C.E. CATHOLIC MORAL THEOL-
OGY IN DIALOGUE.
R.J. TAPIA, 613:AUTUMN73-433
CURRAN, C.P. JAMES JOYCE REMEMBER-
ED.
P. SWINDEN, 148:SPRING72-91
CURRAN, D.J. - SEE GROVES, H.M.
CURRAN, S. SHELLEY'S "CENCI."*
A.H. ELLIOTT, 447(N&Q):AUG73-310
CURRAN, S. & J.A. WITTREICH, JR.,
EDS. BLAKE'S SUBLIME ALLEGORY.*
I.H. CHAYES, 591(SIR):SPRING74-155
D.R. FAULKNER, 676(YR):SUMMER74-
590
F. SANDLER, 651(WHR):AUTUMN74-389
CURRENT-GARCIA, E., WITH D.B. HAT-
FIELD - SEE TUGGLE, W.O.
CURREY, C.B. CODE NUMBER 72.
F. MC DONALD, 656(WMQ):JAN74-150
CURRY, H.B. FOUNDATIONS OF MATHE-
MATICAL LOGIC.
W. CRAIG, 316:MAR73-149
CURRY, K. SOUTHEY.
K. WALKER, 617(TLS):11JUL75-756
CURRY-LINDAHL, K. LET THEM LIVE.
D.A. CHANT, 529(QQ):WINTER73-630
CURTI, C. - SEE SALONIUS
CURTIN, P.D. ECONOMIC CHANGE IN
PRECOLONIAL AFRICA.
J.D. FAGE, 617(TLS):17OCT75-1240
CURTIS, A. THE PATTERN OF MAUGHAM.*
G. EWART, 364:APR/MAY74-132
CURTIS, A. SWEELINCK'S KEYBOARD
MUSIC.
A. BROWN, 179(ES):APR72-160
CURTIS, A.R. CRISPIN IER.
C. ABRAHAM, 207(FR):APR73-1010

CURTIS, E.S. IN A SACRED MANNER WE
LIVE.* PORTRAITS FROM NORTH AMERI-
CAN INDIAN LIFE.*
  G. WOODCOCK, 102(CANL):SPRING73-97
CURTIS, J.R. WORDSWORTH'S EXPERI-
MENTS WITH TRADITION.*
  S. GILL, 541(RES):FEB73-99
CURTIS, L.P., ED. THE HISTORIAN'S
WORKSHOP.
  R.H.C., 125:OCT73-95
CURTIS, R. DEATH IN THE CREASE.
  N. CALLENDAR, 441:26JAN75-23
CURTIS, T. WALK DOWN A WELSH WIND.
  H. SERGEANT, 175:AUTUMN73-121
CURTIUS, E.R. ESSAYS ON EUROPEAN
LITERATURE.
  J.E. CHAMBERLIN, 249(HUDR):AUTUMN
  74-451
  G.T. DAVENPORT, 569(SR):SPRING74-
  XXXIII
CURWEN, S. THE JOURNAL OF SAMUEL
CURWEN, LOYALIST.* (A. OLIVER, ED)
  M. FREIBERG, 432(NEQ):DEC73-653
  L.F.S. UPTON, 255:FALL73-311
CUSANO, N. OPERE FILOSOFICHE.
(G.F. VESCOVINI, ED)
  G. SANTINELLO, 548(RCSF):OCT-DEC
  73-461
CUSHING, F.H. ZUÑI BREADSTUFF.
  J.D. GREEN, 453:29MAY75-31
CUSHNER, N.P. SPAIN IN THE PHILIP-
PINES.
  E. WICKBERG, 293(JAST):AUG73-755
CUSSLER, C. ICEBERG.
  M. LEVIN, 441:28SEP75-37
CUTLER, M.G. EVOCATIONS OF THE
EIGHTEENTH CENTURY IN FRENCH POETRY
1800-1869.* (FRENCH TITLE: EVOCA-
TIONS DU DIX-HUITIÈME SIÈCLE DANS
LA POÉSIE FRANÇAISE 1800-1869.)
  P. BRADY, 546(RR):MAR74-139
  E. SOUFFRIN, 208(FS):JAN74-88
  J-L. STEINMETZ, 535(RHL):SEP-OCT
  73-902
CUTT, W.T. MESSAGE FROM ARKMAE.
  F. FRAZER, 102(CANL):AUTUMN74-116
CUTTINO, G.P. ENGLISH DIPLOMATIC
ADMINISTRATION. (2ND ED)
  J.R. MADDICOTT, 382(MAE):1974/1-99
CUVILLIER, A. MANUEL DE SOCIOLOGIE.
(VOL 3)
  D. MERLLIÉ, 542:JAN-MAR73-53
CUVILLIER, A. SOCIOLOGIE ET PROB-
LÈMES ACTUELS.
  C. SCHUWER, 542:JAN-MAR73-58
CUYLER, L. THE EMPEROR MAXIMILIAN I
& MUSIC.
  N. DAVISON, 410(M&L):JAN74-110
CYPORYN, D. THE BLUEGRASS SONGBOOK.
  J. GRIFFITH, 292(JAF):APR-JUN73-
  196
CYRUS, S. EL CUENTO NEGRISTA SUD-
AMERICANO.
  M.A. LUBIN, 263:APR-JUN74-176

DABNEY, L.M. THE INDIANS OF YOKNA-
PATAWPHA.
  J. EARLY, 584(SWR):SUMMER74-326
  R.A. MILUM, 27(AL):JAN75-598
DABNEY, V., ED. THE PATRIOTS.
  P-L. ADAMS, 61:DEC75-118

DACOS, N. LA DÉCOUVERTE DE LA DOMUS
AUREA ET LA FORMATION DES GROTES-
QUES À LA RENAISSANCE.*
  T. YUEN, 54:JUN73-301
D'ADAMO, G.C. GIACOMO LEOPARDI.
  V.A.S., 275(IQ):SPRING74-110
DAEMMRICH, H.S. THE SHATTERED SELF.
  B. ELLING, 399(MLJ):SEP-OCT74-285
  J.M. MC GLATHERY, 301(JEGP):OCT74-
  601
DAEMMRICH, H.S. & D.H. HAENICKE,
EDS. THE CHALLENGE OF GERMAN LIT-
ERATURE.*
  H.W. REICHERT, 221(GQ):MAY73-465
DAHL, L. LINGUISTIC FEATURES OF
THE STREAM-OF-CONSCIOUSNESS TECH-
NIQUES OF JAMES JOYCE, VIRGINIA
WOOLF & EUGENE O'NEILL.
  P.J. DE VOOGD, 433:JAN73-110
DAHL, L. NOMINAL STYLE IN THE
SHAKESPEAREAN SOLILOQUY.
  B. CARSTENSEN, 430(NS):JAN73-50
  R.W. ZANDVOORT, 179(ES):AUG72-357
DAHLBERG, E. BECAUSE I WAS FLESH.
  H. LEIBOWITZ, 31(ASCH):SUMMER75-
  473
DAHLMANN, H. - SEE CREUZER, F.
DAHRENDORF, R. THE NEW LIBERTY.
  J. GOULD, 617(TLS):8AUG75-894
DAICHES, D. A THIRD WORLD.
  295:FEB74-367
DAILY, J.E. & M.S. MYERS. CATALOGU-
ING FOR LIBRARY TECHNICAL ASSIS-
TANTS. (2ND ED)
  C. CAUGHLIN, 503:AUTUMN73-145
"THE DAILY MIRROR OLD CODGERS LITTLE
BLACK BOOK."
  617(TLS):13JUN75-660
DAKYNS, J.R. THE MIDDLE AGES IN
FRENCH LITERATURE, 1851-1900.
  A. CHANDLER, 382(MAE):1974/3-321
  J.M. KIDMAN, 67:MAY74-106
  P.C. SMITH, 446:SPRING-SUMMER74-
  182
DALAT, J. MONTESQUIEU MAGISTRAT 1.
  D.L. SCHALK, 481(PQ):JUL73-556
D'ALBERTI, S. GIUSEPPE ANTONIO
BORGESE.
  A. RUFINO, 276:WINTER73-603
DALBOR, J.B. BEGINNING COLLEGE
SPANISH.
  R.W. HATTON, 238:MAY73-525
DALBOR, J.B. SPANISH PRONUNCIATION.*
  M.P. STANLEY, 238:MAR73-194
DALBY, D., ED. LANGUAGE & HISTORY
IN AFRICA.*
  P. ALEXANDRE, 69:JAN73-81
DALE, A.M. METRICAL ANALYSES OF
TRAGIC CHORUSES.* (VOL 1)
  M. GRIFFITH, 123:NOV74-211
  R.P. WINNINGTON-INGRAM, 303:VOL93-
  240
D'ALELIO, E. & M. DUFAU. EN AVANT.
  P.V. CONROY, JR., 207(FR):DEC72-
  461
  F.J. GREENE, 399(MLJ):SEP-OCT73-
  284
DALESKI, H.M. DICKENS & THE ART OF
ANALOGY.*
  L. LANE, JR., 594:SPRING73-125
DALEY, R. STRONG WINE RED AS BLOOD.
  M. LEVIN, 441:20APR75-29
DALLAS, K., COMP. SONGS OF TOIL.
  F. HOWES, 415:MAY74-391

DALLA VALLE, D. LA FRATTURA.
J-P. CHAUVEAU, 535(RHL):JUL-AUG73-680
G. HAINSWORTH, 208(FS):JUL74-320
D'ALLONNES, O.R. - SEE UNDER REVAULT D'ALLONNES, O.
DALRYMPLE, M. & H.H. GOLDSTONE. HISTORY PRESERVED.
E. HOAGLAND, 441:1JUN75-3
DALTON, L. DON'T GIVE UP ON AN AGING PARENT.
R.M. HENIG, 441:14SEP75-12
DALTON, M. ANDREI SINIAVSKII & JULII DANIEL'.
D. BROWN, 574(SEEJ):WINTER73-467
DALTON, M. A.K. TOLSTOY.
J. PADRO, 574(SEEJ):FALL72-346
DALVEN, R. ANNA COMNENA.
C. HEAD, 589:JUL74-554
DALY, L. JAMES JOYCE & THE MULLINGAR CONNECTION.
J.S. ATHERTON, 617(TLS):12DEC75-1483
DALZELL, R.F., JR. DANIEL WEBSTER & THE TRIAL OF AMERICAN NATIONALISM, 1843-1852.*
H.D. MOSER, 432(NEQ):SEP73-473
VAN DAM, J. SYNTAX DER DEUTSCHEN SPRACHE.
C. SOETEMAN, 433:JUL73-310
DAMIEN, P. LETTRE SUR LA TOUTE-PUISSANCE DIVINE. (A. CANTIN, ED & TRANS)
G. CONSTABLE, 589:OCT74-718
DAMIENS, S. AMOUR ET INTELLECT CHEZ LÉON L'HÉBREU.*
T.A. PERRY, 400(MLN):MAR73-421
DAMON, S.F. A BLAKE DICTIONARY.
T.A. BIRRELL, 179(ES):JUN72-263
DAMONTE, M. FONDO ANTICO SPAGNOLO DELLA BIBLIOTECA UNIVERSITARIA DI GENOVA.
C. STERN, 545(RPH):FEB74-443
DAMROSCH, L., JR. SAMUEL JOHNSON & THE TRAGIC SENSE.*
P.K. ALKON, 481(PQ):JUL73-529
L. BRAUDY, 191(ELN):MAR74-224
D. GREENE, 405(MP):MAY74-443
J.A. HAY, 67:MAY74-87
F.W. HILLES, 676(YR):AUTUMN73-104
C.J. RAWSON, 175:SUMMER73-76
H.D. WEINBROT, 173(ECS):SUMMER74-505
DANA, D. - SEE MISTRAL, G.
DANANDJAJA, J. AN ANNOTATED BIBLIOGRAPHY OF JAVANESE FOLKLORE.
J.H. BRUNVAND, 292(JAF):APR-JUN73-198
W.H. JANSEN, 582(SFQ):MAR73-81
DANBY, M. THE BEST OF FRIENDS.
M. HOPE, 617(TLS):14FEB75-157
DANDEKAR, K. & V. BHATE. PROSPECTS OF POPULATION CONTROL.
S. CHANDRASEKHAR, 293(JAST):AUG73-724
ĐẶNG PHU'O'NG-NGHI. LES INSTITUTIONS PUBLIQUES DU VIỆT-NAM AU XVIIIE SIÈCLE.*
G.D. MEILLON, 182:VOL26#19-684
DANIEL, G. A HUNDRED & FIFTY YEARS OF ARCHAEOLOGY. (REV)
617(TLS):31OCT75-1313
DANIEL, G. - SEE ALEXANDER, J.

DANIEL, J. THE SIEGE.
D. WILSON, 617(TLS):24JAN75-73
DANIEL, N. THE ARABS & MEDIAEVAL EUROPE.
C.F. BECKINGHAM, 617(TLS):22AUG75-948
DANIEL, W.W. A NATIONAL SURVEY OF THE UNEMPLOYED.
D. METCALF, 617(TLS):7FEB75-144
DANIEL, Y. PRISON POEMS.
A. CLUYSENAAR, 565:VOL14#1-70
DANIELL, J.R. EXPERIMENT IN REPUBLICANISM.*
R. MIDDLETON, 173(ECS):SPRING74-368
DANIELL, R. A SEXUAL TOUR OF THE DEEP SOUTH.
H. VENDLER, 441:7SEP75-6
DANIELS, D. GHOST SONG. ILLUSION AT HAVEN'S EDGE.
E.M. EWING, 441:11MAY75-10
DANIELS, G. THE ART OF BREGUET.
R. REIF, 441:26JUL75-21
DANIELS, G. THE UNHANDY HANDYMAN'S BOOK.
P. BRACKEN, 441:27APR75-31
DANIELS, J. THE GENTLEMANLY SERPENT. (R. HILTON, ED)
N.K. BURGER, 441:11MAY75-38
DANIELS, J.R. FIREGOLD.
M. LEVIN, 441:2NOV75-54
DANIELS, M.F., COMP. WYNDHAM LEWIS.
E.F. FREIVOGEL, 14:APR73-243
DANIELS, R.L. V.N. TATISHCHEV.
P. SCHENCK, 173(ECS):SPRING74-374
DANIELS, R.V., ED. THE RUSSIAN REVOLUTION.
R.C. ELWOOD, 550(RUSR):JUL73-330
W.H. HILL, 104:WINTER73-556
DANIELSEN, N. DIE FRAGE.
R. HIERSCHE, 72:BAND211HEFT3/6-402
DANIELSEN, D. & R. HAYDEN. USING ENGLISH.*
A. HILFERTY, 399(MLJ):SEP-OCT74-302
DANKOWSKI, W. DIE ENTSTEHUNG DES VERWALTUNGSBEGRIFFS.
U. RICKEN, 682(ZPSK):BAND26HEFT6-728
DANSEL, M. LANGAGE ET MODERNITÉ CHEZ TRISTAN CORBIÈRE.
M. TURNELL, 617(TLS):14FEB75-165
DANTCHEV, P. CRITIQUE DE L'ESTHETIQUE.
270:VOL23#4-81
DANTE ALIGHIERI. DANTE'S "INFERNO."* (M. MUSA, ED & TRANS)
A.L. PELLEGRINI, 399(MLJ):MAR74-137
DANTE ALIGHIERI. LA DIVINA COMMEDIA. (G. GIACALONE, ED)
H. RHEINFELDER, 430(NS):MAR73-178
DANTE ALIGHIERI. LA DIVINA COMMEDIA. (C.H. GRANDGENT, ED; REV BY C.S. SINGLETON)
R.J. DI PIETRO, 399(MLJ):JAN-FEB74-81
DANTE ALIGHIERI. THE DIVINE COMEDY: INFERNO.* THE DIVINE COMEDY: PURGATORIO.* (BOTH ED & TRANS BY C.S. SINGLETON)
D.S. CARNE-ROSS, 453:1MAY75-3

DANTE ALIGHIERI. THE DIVINE COMEDY:
PARADISO. (C.S. SINGLETON, ED &
TRANS)
  D.S. CARNE-ROSS, 453:1MAY75-3
  C. GRAYSON, 617(TLS):29AUG75-974
DANTE ALIGHIERI. NUOVE LETTURE
DANTESCHE. (VOLS 4&5)
  P. ZOCCOLA, 228(GSLI):VOL150FASC
  470/471-447
DA PONTE, L. MEMORIE E ALTRI SCRIT-
TI. (C. PAGNINI, ED)
  400(MLN):JAN73-165
MADAME D'ARBLAY - SEE BURNEY, C.
DARBY, H.C. & H. FULLARD, EDS. NEW
CAMBRIDGE MODERN HISTORY ATLAS.
  C.R. BOXER, 617(TLS):17JAN75-50
DARÍO, R. SUS MEJORES PÁGINAS.*
(R. GULLÓN, ED)
  L. MONGUIÓ, 399(MLJ):JAN-FEB73-72
DARIUS, A. DANCE NAKED IN THE SUN.
  J. ARMSTRONG, 151:DEC73-105
DARLING, F. & A. THAILAND.
  J.A. HAFNER, 293(JAST):MAY73-562
D'ARMS, J.H. ROMANS ON THE BAY OF
NAPLES.*
  F.A. SULLIVAN, 122:JUL73-225
  A.M. WARD, 124:MAY73-477
DARROCH, S.J. OTTOLINE.
  R. BROWNSTEIN, 441:21DEC75-7
DASGUPTA, A.K. ECONOMIC THEORY &
THE DEVELOPING COUNTRIES.
  M. MC QUEEN, 617(TLS):1AUG75-871
DA SILVA, Z.S. BEGINNING SPANISH.
(3RD ED)
  M. BIERLING, 351(LL):JUN74-171
DA SILVA, Z.S. & L.C. DE MORELOS,
EDS. VOCES DE MANAÑA.
  R. ANDERSON, 399(MLJ):SEP-OCT74-
  290
DASSONVILLE, M. RONSARD.* (VOL 2)
  F. JOUKOVSKY, 535(RHL):JUL-AUG73-
  677
DATER, J. & J. WELPOTT. WOMEN &
OTHER VISIONS.
  H. KRAMER, 441:7DEC75-86
D'AUBIGNÉ, A. LES TRAGIQUES.*
(I.D. MC FARLANE, ED)
  R.J. FINK, 551(RENQ):AUTUMN73-352
DAUMAL, R. LE CONTRE-CIEL [SUIVI
DE] LES DERNIÈRES PAROLES DU
POÈTE.*
  R. BERCHAN, 207(FR):OCT72-204
D'AUREVILLY, J.B. - SEE UNDER BARBEY
D'AUREVILLY, J.
DAUS, D. DER AVANTGARDISMUS RAMÓN
GÓMEZ DE LA SERNAS.
  H. ROGMANN, 72:BAND211HEFT1/3-242
DAUSTER, F. XAVIER VILLAURRUTIA.*
  M.H. FORSTER, 399(MLJ):DEC73-440
DAVARAS, C. DIE STATUE AUS ASTRIT-
SI.
  J. BOARDMAN, 123:NOV74-310
DAVAU, M., M. COHEN & M. LALLEMAND.
DICTIONNAIRE DU FRANÇAIS VIVANT.
  M.A. LUBIN, 263:JAN-MAR74-76
DAVE, H.T. THE LIFE & PHILOSOPHY OF
SHREE SWAMINARAYAN (1781-1830).
(L. SHEPARD, ED)
  A.M. PIATIGORSKY, 617(TLS):24OCT75-
  1273
DAVENANT, W. SIR WILLIAM DAVENANT'S
"GONDIBERT."* (D.F. GLADISH, ED)
  E. MACKENZIE, 541(RES):AUG73-336

DAVENANT, W. THE SHORTER POEMS, &
SONGS FROM THE PLAYS & MASQUES.*
(A.M. GIBBS, ED)
  S. ORGEL, 551(RENQ):WINTER73-534
DAVENPORT, F.G., JR. THE MYTH OF
SOUTHERN HISTORY.
  J.R. MILLICHAP, 577(SHR):WINTER73-
  96
  J.G. WATSON, 295:FEB74-420
  A.W. WONDERLEY, 582(SFQ):JUN73-139
DAVES, C.W. - SEE "SAMUEL BUTLER
1612-1680: CHARACTERS"
DAVEY, F. ARCANA.
  M. ANDRÉ, 529(QQ):WINTER73-658
  L. ROGERS, 102(CANL):AUTUMN74-121
DAVEY, F. EARLE BIRNEY.
  M.J. EDWARDS, 102(CANL):SPRING73-
  115
DAVEY, F. FROM THERE TO HERE.
  M. DIXON, 99:FEB75-37
DAVEY, F. KING OF SWORDS.
  L. ROGERS, 102(CANL):AUTUMN74-121
DAVEY, N.K. NETSUKE.
  M.S. NEWSTEAD, 617(TLS):24JAN75-92
DAVIAU, D.G. & J.B. JONES - SEE
SCHNITZLER, A. & R. AUERNHEIMER
DAVID, C., W. WITTKOWSKI & L. RYAN.
KLEIST UND FRANKREICH. (W. MÜLLER-
SEIDEL, ED)
  J. VOISINE, 549(RLC):JUL-SEP73-480
DAVID, E. FRENCH PROVINCIAL COOK-
ING.
  J.A.E. LOUBÈRE, 207(FR):OCT72-184
DAVID, P. - SEE TS'AO CHAO
DAVID, P.A. TECHNICAL CHOICE, INNO-
VATION & ECONOMIC GROWTH.
  S. ENGERMAN, 617(TLS):18JUL75-811
DAVID, P.A. & OTHERS. RECKONING
WITH SLAVERY.
  T.L. HASKELL, 453:2OCT75-33
"DE DAVID À DELACROIX."
  F. HASKELL, 617(TLS):21MAR75-297
DAVIDSON, D. & G. HARMAN. SEMANTICS
OF NATURAL LANGUAGE.
  J.L., 543:MAR73-531
DAVIDSON, D. & J. HINTIKKA, EDS.
WORDS & OBJECTIONS.*
  R.E. GRANDY, 482(PHR):JAN73-99
DAVIDSON, D. & A. TATE. THE LITER-
ARY CORRESPONDENCE OF DONALD DAVID-
SON & ALLEN TATE. (J.T. FAIN &
T.D. YOUNG, EDS)
  G. CORE, 598(SOR):WINTER75-226
  J.H. JUSTUS, 578:SPRING75-124
DAVIE, D. COLLECTED POEMS 1950-
1970.*
  T. EAGLETON, 565:VOL14#2-74
  D. GREENE, 529(QQ):WINTER73-601
  M. SCHMIDT, 148:SPRING73-81
DAVIE, D. THOMAS HARDY & BRITISH
POETRY.*
  S.M. GILBERT, 637(VS):JUN74-438
  J. GLOVER, 565:VOL14#4-62
  B.G. HORNBACK, 191(ELN):MAR74-233
  M. KIRKHAM, 627(UTQ):WINTER74-174
  J.M.P., 134(CP):FALL73-87
  R. PREYER, 72:BAND211HEFT1/3-131
  C.B. WHEELER, 579(SAQ):SUMMER74-
  409
  H. WITEMEYER, 651(WHR):SUMMER74-
  277
DAVIES, C. PERMISSIVE BRITAIN.
  N. SHRAPNEL, 617(TLS):2MAY75-488

DAVIES, D.K., ED. RACE RELATIONS IN
RHODESIA.
J.P. BARBER, 617(TLS):26DEC75-1546
DAVIES, D.W. & E.S. WRIGLEY, EDS.
A CONCORDANCE TO THE ESSAYS OF
FRANCIS BACON.
J. STEPHENS, 568(SCN):FALL74-60
DAVIES, G.C. WORLD WAR I AEROPLANES.
617(TLS):31JAN75-121
DAVIES, G.E. HER NAME LIKE THE
HOURS.
A. MACLEAN, 617(TLS):23MAY75-552
DAVIES, J.C., ED. CATALOGUE OF MAN-
USCRIPTS IN THE LIBRARY OF THE HON-
ORABLE SOCIETY OF THE INNER TEMPLE.
J.F. PRESTON, 14:JUL73-407
DAVIES, J.K. ATHENIAN PROPERTIED
FAMILIES 600-300 B.C.
R.J. LENARDON, 121(CJ):APR/MAY74-
379
DAVIES, J.P., JR. DRAGON BY THE
TAIL.*
W. BARBER, 50(ARQ):SPRING73-88
DAVIES, K.G., ED. DOCUMENTS OF THE
AMERICAN REVOLUTION, 1770-1783.*
(VOLS 1-3)
M. JENSEN, 656(WMQ):OCT74-683
DAVIES, L. FRANCK.*
J. COCKSHOOT, 410(M&L):JAN74-103
DAVIES, M. PRISONERS OF SOCIETY.
T. MORRIS, 617(TLS):7FEB75-147
DAVIES, M. THE TIMES WE HAD. (P.
PFAU & K.S. MARX, EDS)
R. SCHICKEL, 441:7DEC75-90
DAVIES, M. ROGIER VAN DER WEYDEN.*
L. CAMPBELL, 39:JUL73-61
DAVIES, N. WHITE EAGLE, RED STAR.
W. JEDRZEJEWICZ, 497(POLR):VOL18
#3-95
V. MASTNY, 104:SUMMER73-275
A. PARRY, 550(RUSR):APR73-196
DAVIES, R. HONEYSUCKLE GIRL.
N. HEPBURN, 362:21AUG75-254
C. PETERS, 617(TLS):22AUG75-951
DAVIES, R. HUNTING STUART & OTHER
PLAYS.
W.H. NEW, 102(CANL):WINTER74-104
J. NOONAN, 529(QQ):AUTUMN73-466
G. WHITEHEAD, 150(DR):SPRING73-165
DAVIES, R. THE MANTICORE.
P. BARCLAY, 102(CANL):SPRING73-113
A. BEVAN, 150(DR):SPRING73-163
D.O. SPETTIGUE, 529(QQ):SUMMER73-
304
DAVIES, R. WORLD OF WONDERS.
C. BISSELL, 99:DEC75/JAN76-30
DAVIES, R. - SEE KAVAN, A.
DAVIES, S.G. JAMES JOYCE.
J.S. ATHERTON, 617(TLS):12DEC75-
1483
DAVIES, W. - SEE THOMAS, D.
DAVIES, W.D. THE GOSPEL & THE LAND.
P. ALEXANDER, 617(TLS):25APR75-464
DAVIES, W.J.K. THE ROMNEY, HYTHE &
DYMCHURCH RAILWAY.
617(TLS):4JUL75-737
DAVIN, D. BREATHING SPACES.
P. CAMPBELL, 617(TLS):24OCT75-1255
DAVIN, D. CLOSING TIMES.
M. AMORY, 617(TLS):11JUL75-752
442(NY):25AUG75-88
DAVIS, A.F. AMERICAN HEROINE.
K.O. MORGAN, 617(TLS):13JUN75-648

DAVIS, A.L., ED. CULTURE, CLASS, &
LANGUAGE VARIETY.
J. APPLEBY, 35(AS):SPRING-SUMMER
71-158
DAVIS, A.L., R.I. MC DAVID, JR. &
V.G. MC DAVID, EDS. A COMPILATION
OF THE WORK SHEETS OF THE LINGUIS-
TIC ATLAS OF THE UNITED STATES &
CANADA & ASSOCIATED PROJECTS. (2ND
ED)
A.R. DUCKERT, 35(AS):FALL-WINTER
72-278
W. VIERECK, 38:BAND91HEFT1-107
DAVIS, A.R. TU FU.*
T.P. NIELSON, 352(LE&W):VOL16#3-
1064
DAVIS, A.Y. ANGELA DAVIS.* (BRIT-
ISH TITLE: AN AUTOBIOGRAPHY.)
K. KYLE, 362:1MAY75-587
K. MINOGUE, 617(TLS):7NOV75-1318
H.M. PACHTER, 231:AUG75-83
DAVIS, B.H. A PROOF OF EMINENCE.
R. HALSBAND, 173(ECS):SPRING74-370
F.W. HILLES, 676(YR):AUTUMN73-104
DAVIS, D. ART & THE FUTURE.
A. BERLEANT, 290(JAAC):SUMMER74-
570
DAVIS, D.B. THE PROBLEM OF SLAVERY
IN THE AGE OF REVOLUTION 1770-1823.
G.M. FREDRICKSON, 453:16OCT75-38
D. MAC LEOD, 617(TLS):5SEP75-995
J.H. PLUMB, 441:9FEB75-1
DAVIS, G.N. GERMAN THOUGHT & CUL-
TURE IN ENGLAND 1710-1770.*
U. WEISSTEIN, 221(GQ):MAR73-282
DAVIS, H. - SEE CONGREVE, W.
DAVIS, H.E. LATIN AMERICAN THOUGHT.
W.F. COOPER, 263:APR-JUN73-184
DAVIS, J.G. YEARS OF THE HUNGRY
TIGER.
M. LEVIN, 441:26JAN75-27
DAVIS, J.W., ED. VALUE & VALUATION.
R.E. CARTER, 154:JUN73-346
DAVIS, L.B. IMMIGRANTS, BAPTISTS &
THE PROTESTANT MIND IN AMERICA.
W.G. MC LOUGHLIN, 432(NEQ):DEC73-
644
DAVIS, L.J. WALKING SMALL.*
V. GLENDINNING, 617(TLS):20JUN75-
689
DAVIS, M. THE IMAGE OF LINCOLN IN
THE SOUTH.*
F.N. BONEY, 219(GAR):FALL73-425
L.C. KEATING, 582(SFQ):DEC73-409
DAVIS, M. TELL THEM WHAT'S-HER-
NAME CALLED.
N. CALLENDAR, 441:13APR75-30
DAVIS, M.C. THE NEAR WOODS.
442(NY):24FEB75-142
DAVIS, N., ED. NON-CYCLE PLAYS &
FRAGMENTS.
G.H.V. BUNT, 179(ES):FEB73-60
DAVIS, N., ED. PASTON LETTERS &
PAPERS OF THE FIFTEENTH CENTURY.*
(PT 1)
D.C. BAKER, 191(ELN):DEC73-128
DAVIS, N.Z. SOCIETY & CULTURE IN
EARLY MODERN FRANCE.
T. RADD, 617(TLS):21NOV75-1387
DAVIS, P.W. MODERN THEORIES OF LAN-
GUAGE.
D.S. ROOD, 399(MLJ):NOV74-361

DAVIS, R. THE RISE OF THE ATLANTIC
ECONOMIES.
  C.R. BOXER, 656(WMQ):OCT74-694
DAVIS, R.B. LITERATURE & SOCIETY IN
EARLY VIRGINIA, 1608-1840.*
  E.H. CADY, 579(SAQ):AUTUMN74-572
  A.C. LAND, 569(SR):SUMMER74-LIX
  H. PETTER, 656(WMQ):OCT74-685
  639(VQR):WINTER74-XXII
DAVIS, R.M., ED. STEINBECK.
  D.G. DARNELL, 577(SHR):FALL73-449
DAVIS, R.W. POLITICAL CHANGE & CON-
TINUITY 1760-1885.
  R.W. GREAVES, 481(PQ):JUL73-344
DAVIS, T. JOHN NASH.
  R. EMERSON, 135:AUG73-316
DAVIS, W.R. IDEA & ACT IN ELIZA-
BETHAN FICTION.
  C.C. MISH, 570(SQ):WINTER73-100
DAVIS, W.R. - SEE CAMPION, T.
DAVIS-WEYER, C. EARLY MEDIEVAL ART
300-1150.
  J. BECKWITH, 39:SEP73-238
DAVISON, D., ED. EIGHTEENTH-CENTURY
ENGLISH VERSE.
  566:AUTUMN73-35
DAVISON, J.M. SEVEN ITALIC TOMB-
GROUPS FROM NARCE.
  G.F. VELLEK, 124:SEP-OCT73-52
DAVISON, N.J. EDUARDO BARRIOS.*
  M.A. SALGADO, 241:MAY73-77
DAVISON, P. HALF REMEMBERED.
  639(VQR):SPRING74-XLI
DAVISON, P. WALKING THE BOUNDAR-
IES.*
  J. ATLAS, 491:FEB75-295
  R. GARFITT, 364:AUG/SEP74-113
DAVISSON, W.L. & J. HARPER. EURO-
PEAN ECONOMIC HISTORY. (VOL 1)
  J.A.O. LARSEN, 122:OCT73-298
DAVY, A. ÉTHIOPIE D'HIER ET D'AU-
JOURD'HUI.
  J. VANDERLINDEN, 69:OCT73-361
DAVY, M-M., ED. ENCYCLOPÉDIE DES
MYSTIQUES.
  J. BRUNO, 98:MAY73-417
DAWIDOWICZ, L.S. THE WAR AGAINST
THE JEWS 1933-1945.
  I. HOWE, 441:20APR75-1
  C. LEHMANN-HAUPT, 441:12JUN75-41
DAWKINS, J. - SEE DE BRACH, P.
DAWSON, C., ED. MATTHEW ARNOLD, THE
POETRY: THE CRITICAL HERITAGE.*
  P. HONAN, 402(MLR):JUL74-627
  J.D. JUMP, 148:WINTER73-379
DAWSON, D. CEREMONIAL.
  L. ROGERS, 102(CANL):AUTUMN74-121
DAWSON, R. AN INTRODUCTION TO CLAS-
SICAL CHINESE.*
  O. ŠVARNÝ, 353:15MAR73-105
DAY, A.C. FORTRAN TECHNIQUES WITH
SPECIAL REFERENCE TO NON-NUMERICAL
APPLICATIONS.
  V.H. YNGVE, 269(IJAL):OCT73-267
DAY, A.G. ROBERT D. FITZ GERALD.
  C.M. TIFFIN, 71(ALS):MAY75-99
DAY, A.G. & E.C. KNOWLTON, JR.
V. BLASCO IBÁÑEZ.
  R.A. CARDWELL, 402(MLR):JUL74-684
  A. KENWOOD, 67:MAY74-133
DAY, D. MALCOLM LOWRY.*
  R.H. COSTA, 131(CL):FALL74-354
  M. GRIFFITH, 651(WHR):SUMMER74-274
  R.W.B. LEWIS, 639(VQR):SUMMER74-
    441   [CONTINUED]

[CONTINUING]
  W.H. NEW, 102(CANL):SUMMER74-100
  J. RUSSELL, 396(MODA):SPRING74-211
  J. SOMMERFIELD, 364:JUN/JUL74-139
  569(SR):WINTER74-VI
DAY, F.P. ROCKBOUND.
  H. HORWOOD, 296:VOL3#4-85
DAY, J.W. RUM OWD BOYS.
  617(TLS):21FEB75-204
DAY, R. DAY BY DAY.
  B. WENHAM, 362:90CT75-482
DAY, R.A. - SEE COVENTRY, F.
DAZAI, O. NO LONGER HUMAN.
  Y. HIJIYA, 145(CRIT):VOL15#3-34
DEAL, B.H. WAITING TO HEAR FROM
WILLIAM.
  M. LEVIN, 441:50CT75-48
DEAN, B. MIND'S EYE. (VOL 2)
  E. SHORTER, 157:SUMMER73-75
DEAN, W., WITH H. GOREY. "MO."
  A. HELLER, 61:DEC75-116
  M.S. KENNEDY, 441:16NOV75-18
DEANE, P. THUCYDIDES' DATES 465-
431 B.C.*
  C.W. FORNARA, 24:SUMMER74-187
  M.L. LANG, 124:MAY73-469
DEARDEN, R.F., P.H. HIRST & R.S.
PETERS, EDS. EDUCATION & THE DE-
VELOPMENT OF REASON.
  M. ATHERTON, 311(JP):27FEB75-104
  A.J. WATT, 63:MAY74-82
DEARING, V.A., WITH C.E. BECKWITH -
SEE GAY, J.
DEBBASCH, C. L'UNIVERSITÉ DÉSORI-
ENTÉE.
  W.W. THOMAS, 207(FR):FEB73-647
DEBENEDETTI, G. IL ROMANZO DEL
NOVECENTO.
  400(MLN):JAN73-167
DEBICKI, A.P. DÁMASO ALONSO.*
  M-L. GAZARIAN, 546(RR):MAR74-154
  J. GONZÁLEZ MUELA, 399(MLJ):JAN-
  FEB73-69
  E.L. RIVERS, 240(HR):SPRING73-451
  P. SÁENZ, 241:SEP73-85
  I.R. WARNER, 86(BHS):APR73-185
DEBLUÉ, V. ANIMA NATURALITER IRON-
ICA.*
  J.L.S., 191(ELN):SEP73(SUPP)-131
  K.S. WEIMAR, 221(GQ):SEP73-165
DEBON, G. & CHOU CHÜN-SHAN. LOB DER
NATURTREUE.
  M. LOEHR, 57:VOL35#3-297
DEBRAY, R. LA CRITIQUE DES ARMES.
  W. LAQUEUR, 617(TLS):1AUG75-862
DEBRAY-RITZEN, P. LA SCOLASTIQUE
FREUDIENNE.
  Y. BRÈS, 542:JAN-MAR73-35
DEBRÉ, M. THE IMAGE OF THE JEW IN
FRENCH LITERATURE FROM 1800 TO
1908.
  K. BIEBER, 207(FR):OCT72-189
  G. NAKAM, 535(RHL):MAR-JUN73-544
DEBUS, A.G., ED. MEDICINE IN
SEVENTEENTH CENTURY ENGLAND.
  C. WEBSTER, 617(TLS):14MAR75-283
DEBUSSCHER, G. EDWARD ALBEE.
  205(FMLS):APR73-212
DÉCAUDIN, M., ED. GUILLAUME APOLLI-
NAIRE 9.
  H. BÉHAR, 535(RHL):JAN-FEB73-152
DECKER, D.M. LUIS DURAND.*
  C.M. TATUM, 238:MAY73-508

DECOIN, D. ABRAHAM DE BROOKLYN.
  Y. GUERS-VILLATE, 207(FR):DEC72-
  436
DÉCSY, G. DIE LINGUISTISCHE STRUK-
TUR EUROPAS.
  E.H. YARRILL, 182:VOL26#15/16-537
DECTER, M. LIBERAL PARENTS, RADICAL
CHILDREN.
  A. BROYARD, 441:17JUN75-37
  J. O'REILLY, 441:22JUN75-23
  442(NY):11AUG75-87
DEELY, J.N. THE TRADITION VIA HEI-
DEGGER.
  J.D.C., 543:SEP72-156
DEES, A. ETUDE SUR L'ÉVOLUTION DES
DÉMONSTRATIFS EN ANCIEN ET EN MOYEN
FRANÇAIS.
  F.R. HAMLIN, 545(RPH):AUG73-92
  R. POSNER, 361:VOL31#1-82
  G. PRICE, 208(FS):OCT74-497
DEESON, A.F.L., ED. THE COLLECTOR'S
ENCYCLOPEDIA OF ROCKS & MINERALS.
  617(TLS):28FEB75-232
DE FELICE, R. INTERVISTA SUL FASC-
ISMO. (M.A. LEDEEN, ED) MUSSOLINI
IL DUCE. (VOL 4)
  D. MACK SMITH, 617(TLS):31OCT75-
  1278
DEFOE, D. A GENERAL HISTORY OF THE
PYRATES. (M. SCHONHORN, ED)
  J.P. HUNTER, 481(PQ):JUL73-483
DEGENHART, B. & A. SCHMITT. CORPUS
DER ITALIENISCHEN ZEICHNUNGEN 1300-
1450.* (PT 1)
  M. SALMI, 54:DEC73-625
DE GEORGE, R.T. A GUIDE TO PHILO-
SOPHICAL BIBLIOGRAPHY & RESEARCH.
  J.H., 543:MAR73-533
DE GEORGE, R.T. & M. FERNANDE, EDS.
THE STRUCTURALISTS.
  W.G., 543:MAR73-533
DEGLER, C.N. THE OTHER SOUTH.*
  C.B. DEW, 639(VQR):SPRING74-307
DEGO, G. LO STILE DI UN AMORE.
  K. BOSLEY, 617(TLS):31OCT75-1308
DEGUY, M. FIGURATIONS.
  R. VERNIER, 207(FR):OCT72-206
DEGUY, M. POÈMES 1960-1970.
  C.A. HACKETT, 208(FS):JUL74-358
DE HARVEN, E. SUIVEZ LA PISTE.
  P. SIEGEL, 207(FR):FEB73-683
DEHENNIN, E. CÁNTICO DE JORGE
GUILLÉN.
  P.R. OLSON, 546(RR):MAR73-156
DE LA DEHESA, R.P. - SEE UNDER PÉREZ
DE LA DEHESA, R.
DEHN, W. DING UND VERNUNFT.
  L.D. WELLS, 221(GQ):JAN73-99
DEHOUSSE, F. SAINTE-BEUVE.
  J. JOSET, 556(RLV):1973/2-184
DEIGHTON, L. ELEVEN DECLARATIONS OF
WAR.
  G. LYONS, 441:13APR75-5
DEIGHTON, L. SPY STORY.*
  N. CALLENDAR, 441:31AUG75-12
  G. LYONS, 441:13APR75-5
DEIGHTON, L. YESTERDAY'S SPY.
  A. BROYARD, 441:90CT75-45
  L. FINGER, 617(TLS):13JUN75-643
  M. LASKI, 362:20NOV75-684
  P. THEROUX, 441:5OCT75-7
  442(NY):17NOV75-196

DEINDORFER, R.G. LIFE IN LOWER
SLAUGHTER.
  A. BROYARD, 441:22APR75-39
DEINHARD, H. MEANING & EXPRESSION.
  J.C. WACKER, 290(JAAC):WINTER74-
  234
DEININGER, J. DER POLITISCHE WIDER-
STAND GEGEN ROM IN GRIECHENLAND
217-86 V. CHR.*
  J.K. ANDERSON, 121(CJ):FEB/MAR74-
  272
  J. BRISCOE, 123:NOV74-258
  R.M. ERRINGTON, 313:VOL63-249
  F.M. WASSERMANN, 124:FEB73-304
VON DEL-NEGRO, W. KONVERGENZEN IN
DER GEGENWARTSPHILOSOPHIE UND DIE
MODERNE PHYSIK.
  R. BLANCHÉ, 542:JUL-SEP73-355
DELAGE, M-J. - SEE CAESARIUS OF AR-
LES
DELANO, A. SLIP-UP.
  D. GODDARD, 441:26OCT75-8
DELANY, S. CHAUCER'S "HOUSE OF
FAME."*
  L. ELDREDGE, 255:FALL73-325
  J-M. STEADMAN, 382(MAE):1974/3-289
DELANY, S.R. DHALGREN.
  G. JONAS, 441:16FEB75-27
DELAS, D. - SEE RIFFATERRE, M.
DELASANTA, R. THE EPIC VOICE.
  E.R. GREGORY, 568(SCN):FALL74-50
DELATTRE, P. & OTHERS. LES EXER-
CICES STRUCTURAUX, POUR QUOI FAIRE?
  N.A. POULIN, 207(FR):OCT72-250
DE LAURA, D.J. HEBREW & HELLENE IN
VICTORIAN ENGLAND.*
  M.J. SVAGLIC, 405(MP):NOV73-229
DELAVENAY, E. D.H. LAWRENCE.
  W. WALSH, 189(EA):JUL-SEP73-327
  K. WIDMER, 594:WINTER73-547
DELAVENAY, E. D.H. LAWRENCE & ED-
WARD CARPENTER.
  R. BEARDS, 295:FEB74-697
DELBANCO, N. FATHERING.
  P-M. SPACKS, 249(HUDR):SUMMER74-
  293
DELBANCO, N. SMALL RAIN.
  A. BROYARD, 441:3MAR75-23
  J.R. FRAKES, 441:16MAR75-26
  442(NY):18AUG75-83
DELBOUILLE, P. GENÈSE, STRUCTURE ET
DESTIN D'"ADOLPHE."*
  I.W. ALEXANDER, 402(MLR):APR74-415
  J. CRUICKSHANK, 208(FS):JAN74-82
  M. LEHTONEN, 439(NM):1973/1-175
DELCOMBRE, M. LE FRANÇAIS PAR LE
CINÉMA.
  P. SILBERMAN, 399(MLJ):NOV73-364
DELEDALLE, G. L'IDÉE D'EXPÉRIENCE
DANS LA PHILOSOPHIE DE JOHN DEWEY.
  G. DICKER, 321:WINTER73-309
  P. DUBOIS, 542:APR-JUN73-219
DELÉRY, S.D.L.S. NAPOLEON'S SOL-
DIERS IN AMERICA.
  J. SCHUELER, 207(FR):APR73-1088
DELEU, J. VIYĀHAPANNATTI (BHAGA-
VAI).
  E. STEINKELLNER, 318(JAOS):JUL-SEP
  73-382
DELEULE, P. - SEE HUME, D.
DELEUZE, G. & F. GUATTARI. ANTI-
OEDIPE.
  Y. BRÈS, 542:JAN-MAR73-40

DELEUZE, G. & F. GUATTARI. KAFKA.
A. THORLBY, 617(TLS):21NOV75-1393
VAN DELFT, L. LA BRUYÈRE MORALISTE.
J. LAFOND, 535(RHL):JAN-FEB73-125
D.C. POTTS, 208(FS):JAN74-71
S.F. RENDALL, 400(MLN):MAY73-860
H.C. ROTH, 207(FR):OCT72-153
DELIBES, M. LA MORTAJA.*
J.W. DÍAZ, 241:JAN73-86
DELIBES, M. SMOKE ON THE GROUND.*
L.T.L., 502(PRS):SUMMER73-185
DELIBES, M. USA Y YO. (F.L. GOR-
DON, ED)
E.M. MALINAK, 399(MLJ):SEP-OCT73-
299
DE LISSER, H.G. JANE'S CAREER.
M.G. COOKE, 454:FALL73-93
DELLA CORTE, F. LA MAPPA DELL'EN-
EIDE.
N. HORSFALL, 313:VOL63-306
J. PERRET, 555:VOL47FASC1-159
DELLA CORTE, F. OPUSCULA.
J. ANDRÉ, 555:VOL47FASC2-380
DELLA CORTE, F. LA PRESENZA CLAS-
SICA.
A. ERNOUT, 555:VOL47FASC1-192
P.G. WALSH, 123:MAR74-165
DELLEY, G. L'ASSOMPTION DE LA
NATURE DANS LA LYRIQUE FRANÇAISE
DE L'ÂGE BAROQUE.
D.L. RUBIN, 546(RR):MAR74-126
DELLINGER, D. MORE POWER THAN WE
KNOW.
E. LANGER, 441:15JUN75-7
DELMAN, D. ONE MAN'S MURDER.
N. CALLENDAR, 441:11MAY75-26
M. LASKI, 362:25DEC75&1JAN76-893
DEL MAR, N. RICHARD STRAUSS.* (VOL
3)
P. GELLHORN, 607:#104-38
DELMAS, C. LE SCHOONER.
G.H. BAUER, 207(FR):OCT72-207
DELOCHE, J., ED. VOYAGE EN INDE DU
COMTE DE MODAVE, 1773-76.
R.E. EMMERICK, 182:VOL26#11/12-443
DELOFFRE, F. - SEE DE MARIVAUX,
P.C.D.
DELON, P. LES EMPLOYÉS.
J-A. BOUR, 207(FR):FEB73-641
DELTEIL, Y. LA FIN TRAGIQUE DU
VOYAGE DE VICTOR HUGO EN 1843.*
P. GEORGEL, 535(RHL):NOV-DEC73-
1090
DE LUCCA, J., ED. REASON & EXPERI-
ENCE.
L.G. MILLER, 154:SEP73-539
DELVAILLE, B. LA SAISON PERDUE.
S.G. STARY, 207(FR):MAR73-852
DELVING, M. BORED TO DEATH.
N. CALLENDAR, 441:2NOV75-51
DEMARIS, O. THE DIRECTOR.
M. MILLER, 441:23NOV75-4
DEMATS, P. - SEE HÉLISENNE DE CRENNE
DEMBO, L.S. & C.N. PONDROM, EDS.
THE CONTEMPORARY WRITER.
J.D. BELLAMY, 454:FALL73-75
DEMÉLIER, J. LE RÊVE DE JOB.
C.S. BROSMAN, 207(FR):MAR73-853
DEMERSON, G. LA MYTHOLOGIE CLAS-
SIQUE DANS L'OEUVRE LYRIQUE DE LA
"PLÉIADE."
M.J. BAKER, 207(FR):APR73-1007
F. JOUKOVSKY, 545(RPH):FEB74-436
[CONTINUED]

[CONTINUING]
J.C. LAPP, 399(MLJ):SEP-OCT73-287
I. SILVER, 551(RENQ):SPRING73-57
DEMETRIO Y RADAZA, F. - SEE BERNAR-
DO, G.A.
DEMETZ, P. POSTWAR GERMAN LITERA-
TURE.*
D. LATIMER, 577(SHR):FALL73-458
DEMETZ, P., T. GREENE & L. NELSON,
JR., EDS. THE DISCIPLINES OF CRIT-
ICISM.
H.H.H. REMAK, 131(CL):WINTER73-68
DEMIÉVILLE, P., COMP & TRANS. EN-
TRETIENS DE LIN-TSI.
L. HURWITZ, 293(JAST):NOV72-132
DEMING, B. WASH US & COMB US.
C. BROOKE, 376:JAN73-165
DEMING, R.H. CEREMONY & ART.
J.B. BROADBENT, 617(TLS):25JUL75-
836
DEMMER, J. FRANZ KAFKA, DER DICHTER
DER SELBSTREFLEXION.
H. REISS, 182:VOL26#10-348
DEMOLON, P. LE VILLAGE MÉROVINGIEN
DE BREBIÈRES (VI-VII SIÈCLES).
G.T. BEECH, 589:APR74-326
DEMOSTHENES. SIX PRIVATE SPEECHES.
(L. PEARSON, ED)
D.M. MAC DOWELL, 123:NOV74-291
J.R. MC NALLY & R.C. GASCOYNE,
124:SEP-OCT73-45
DEMUS, O. ROMANESQUE MURAL PAINT-
ING.*
C. NORDENFALK, 54:SEP73-441
DE MYLIUS, J.E. SIGURD HOEL -
BEFRIEREN I FUGLEHAM.
A. TVINNEREIM, 172(EDDA):1973/3-
177
DENBIGH, K.G. AN INVENTIVE UNIVERSE.
S. CLARK, 617(TLS):6JUN75-631
DEN BOER, J. TRYING TO COME APART.
K. SKINNER, 134(CP):FALL73-89
DEN BOER, W. SOME MINOR ROMAN HIS-
TORIANS.
C.E.V. NIXON, 487:WINTER73-407
DENCH, G. MALTESE IN LONDON.
C.S. FENTON, 617(TLS):7NOV75-1341
DENECKE, L. JACOB GRIMM UND SEIN
BRUDER WILHELM.*
R.M., 191(ELN):SEP73(SUPP)-127
DENEEF, A.L. "THIS POETICK LITUR-
GIE."
J.B. BROADBENT, 617(TLS):25JUL75-
836
DENG, F.M. THE DINKA & THEIR SONGS.
G. MOORE, 617(TLS):11APR75-395
DENHAM, P., ED. THE EVOLUTION OF
CANADIAN LITERATURE IN ENGLISH,
1945-70.
C. THOMAS, 102(CANL):SPRING74-86
DENHAM, R.B., COMP. NORTHROP FRYE.
A.A., 102(CANL):SUMMER74-128
DENIEL, R. CROYANCES RELIGIEUSES ET
VIE QUOTIDIENNE.
H.J. FISHER, 69:APR73-162
DENIS, M. DU SYMBOLISME AU CLASSI-
CISME. (O. REVAULT D'ALLONNES, ED)
P-M.S., 542:JAN-MAR73-112
DENISOFF, R.S. GREAT DAY COMING.
M. PETERSON, 470:MAY74-24
DENISOFF, R.S. SING A SONG OF
SOCIAL SIGNIFICANCE.
G. BLUESTEIN, 292(JAF):JUL-SEP73-
302

DENISOFF, R.S. SONGS OF PROTEST,
WAR & PEACE.
H.L. LANDY, 187:SEP75-496
DENISON, E.F. ACCOUNTING FOR UNITED
STATES ECONOMIC GROWTH 1929-1969.
P. DEANE, 617(TLS):18JUL75-811
DENISON, M. OVERTURE & BEGINNERS.
I. BROWN, 157:WINTER73-85
DENIZ, G. ADREDE.
K. MÜLLER-BERGH, 263:JAN-MAR74-71
DENKER, H. THE PHYSICIANS.
M. LEVIN, 441:30MAR75-21
DENKLER, H. RESTAURATION UND REVO-
LUTION.
R.C. COWEN, 301(JEGP):JUL74-411
DENLINGER, K. & L. SHAPIRO. ATH-
LETES FOR SALE.
M. WATKINS, 441:12OCT75-44
DENNIS, C. A HOUSE OF MY OWN.
H. VENDLER, 441:6APR75-4
DENNIS, J. GRANT WOOD.
J.R. MELLOW, 441:7DEC75-80
DENNIS, J.V. A COMPLETE GUIDE TO
BIRD FEEDING.
R. CARAS, 441:7DEC75-93
DENOEU, F. FRENCH CULTURAL READER.
G.R. DANNER, 207(FR):MAR73-880
D. O'CONNELL, 399(MLJ):SEP-OCT73-
287
DENSMORE, F. THE AMERICAN INDIANS
& THEIR MUSIC.
M. PETERSON, 470:JAN73-33
DENT, A. THE HORSE THROUGH FIFTY
CENTURIES OF CIVILIZATION.
O. LATTIMORE, 617(TLS):7FEB75-130
DENTICE DI ACCADIA, C.M. PREILLUM-
INISMO E DEISMO IN INGHILTERRA.
G. CARABELLI, 548(RCSF):JAN-MAR73-
111
DE PAUW, L.G., WITH C.B. BICKFORD &
L.M. SIEGEL, EDS. DOCUMENTARY HIS-
TORY OF THE FIRST FEDERAL CONGRESS
OF THE UNITED STATES OF AMERICA,
MARCH 4, 1789-MARCH 3, 1791.* (VOL
1)
B. HENRY, 14:JUL73-415
DE PORTE, M.V. NIGHTMARES & HOBBY-
HORSES.
M. HODGART, 617(TLS):28MAR75-328
D'ERAMO, L. L'OPERE DI IGNAZIO
SILONE.
B. MOLONEY, 402(MLR):APR74-433
A. TRALDI, 276:WINTER73-604
DERLETH, A. THE CHRONICLES OF SOLAR
PONS.
M. YOUNG, 441:2FEB75-21
DER NERSESSIAN, S. ARMENIAN MANU-
SCRIPTS IN THE WALTERS ART GALLERY.
P. BROWN & S. MAC CORMACK, 453:
20FEB75-19
DE ROBERTIS, D., ED. IL CODICI
CHIGIANO L.V. 176.
C. GRAYSON, 617(TLS):31OCT75-1302
DE ROSA, P. JESUS WHO BECAME CHRIST.
F.R. BARRY, 617(TLS):15AUG75-926
DEROZIER, A. MANUEL JOSEF QUINTANA
ET LA NAISSANCE DU LIBÉRALISME EN
ESPAGNE.
P-J. GUINARD, 549(RLC):JAN-MAR73-
159
DERRETT, J.D.M. A CRITIQUE OF MOD-
ERN HINDU LAW.
L. ROCHER, 293(JAST):NOV72-202

DERRICK, L. THE HELLBOMB FLIGHT.
N. CALLENDAR, 441:28SEP75-38
DERRY, J.W. CHARLES JAMES FOX.*
D. SPRING, 481(PQ):JUL73-345
DERWING, B.L. TRANSFORMATIONAL
GRAMMAR AS A THEORY OF LANGUAGE
ACQUISITION.
J.D. MC CAWLEY, 320(CJL):FALL74-
177
DESAN, W. THE PLANETARY MAN.
W. GERBER, 258:JUN73-302
J.E. HANSEN, 484(PPR):MAR74-447
DESANTI, D. UN METIER DE CHIEN.
J.P. GOLLUB, 207(FR):APR73-1046
DESANTI, D. LES SOCIALISTES DE
L'UTOPIE.
J.S.P., 191(ELN):SEP73(SUPP)-69
DESANTI, D. FLORA TRISTAN.
S. DEBOUT, 98:JAN73-81
DESBOROUGH, V.R.D. THE GREEK DARK
AGES.
G. HUXLEY, 303:VOL93-252
C.G. STARR, 24:WINTER74-414
DESCARTES, R. DISCOURS DE LA MÉTH-
ODE.
M. WAGNER, 207(FR):OCT72-247
DESCHAMPS, H. HISTOIRE DE LA TRAITE
DES NOIRS DE L'ANTIQUITÉ À NOS
JOURS.
J.D. FAGE, 69:APR73-158
DESCHAMPS, H. L'AFRIQUE NOIRE PRÉ-
COLONIALE.
C. SCHUWER, 542:JAN-MAR73-91
DESCHARNES, R. & J-F. CHABRUN.
AUGUSTE RODIN.
J. DE CASO, 39:JUL73-68
DESCOTES, M. MOLIÈRE ET SA FORTUNE
LITTÉRAIRE.*
C.N. SMITH, 208(FS):JAN74-67
DESCOTES, M. LE PUBLIC DE THÉÂTRE
ET SON HISTOIRE.
C. SCHUWER, 542:JAN-MAR73-80
DESCRAINS, J. BIBLIOGRAPHIE DES
OEUVRES DE JEAN-PIERRE CAMUS, ÉVÊ-
QUE DE BELLEY (1584-1652).*
E. GOICHOT, 535(RHL):JAN-FEB73-124
DESHPANDE, V.H. INDIAN MUSICAL
TRADITIONS.*
B. WADE, 187:SEP75-496
DESHUSSES, J. LE GRAND SOIR.*
P.J. JOHNSON, 207(FR):MAY73-1238
DE SILVA, D. - SEE UNDER STERNLICHT,
S.
DESJARDINS, J., ED. GAEOMEMPHIONIS
CANTALIENSIS SATYRICON 1628.
L.V. RYAN, 551(RENQ):SUMMER73-215
DE SOLA, R. & D. A DICTIONARY OF
COOKING.
M.F.K. FISHER, 442(NY):10NOV75-183
DESPINIS, G.I. SYMBOLE STE MELETE
TOY ERGOY TOY AGORAKRITOY.
J.M. COOK, 303:VOL93-264
DESSAIN, C.S. & T. GORNALL - SEE
NEWMAN, J.H.
DESSAINTES, M. RECHERCHE LINGUIS-
TIQUE ET ENSEIGNEMENT.
S.E. COTÉ, 207(FR):OCT72-251
DESSEN, A.C. JONSON'S MORAL COMEDY.
J.A. BARISH, 405(MP):AUG73-80
S.F. STATON, 551(RENQ):AUTUMN73-
373
DESSI, G. THE FORESTS OF NORBIO.
H. MITGANG, 441:3AUG75-20

DESSOIR, M. AESTHETICS & THEORY OF
ART.*
  E.A. LIPPMAN, 414(MQ):JAN73-139
DE STEFANIS CICCONE, S. LA QUES-
TIONE DELLA LINGUA NEI PERIODICI
LETTERARI DEL PRIMO '800.*
  M.P., 228(GSLI):VOL15OFASC470/471-
476
DESTLER, I.M. PRESIDENTS, BUREAU-
CRATS, & FOREIGN POLICY.*
  G.S. SMITH, 529(QQ):SPRING73-112
DESVIGNES-PARENT, L. MARIVAUX ET
L'ANGLETERRE.*
  R. MIKLAUS, 189(EA):APR-JUN73-243
DETIENNE, M. LES JARDINS D'ADONIS.*
  D.E. EICHHOLZ, 123:NOV74-233
DETIENNE, M. & J-P. VERNANT. LES
RUSES DE L'INTELLIGENCE.
  H. LLOYD-JONES, 617(TLS):16MAY75-
534
DETWEILER, R. JOHN UPDIKE.
  R. HAUGH, 385(MQR):FALL75-473
DEUTSCH, E. & J.A.B. VAN BUITENEN.
A SOURCE BOOK OF ADVAITA VEDĀNTA.
  R. BROOKS, 485(PE&W):OCT73-551
  D. LORENZEN, 293(JAST):NOV72-174
DEUTSCH, H.C. HITLER & HIS GENER-
ALS.*
  639(VQR):AUTUMN74-CXLVI
DEUTSCH, M. THE RESOLUTION OF CON-
FLICT.
  639(VQR):SPRING74-LVIII
"THE DEVELOPMENT OF A REVOLUTIONARY
MENTALITY."
  B.W. LABAREE, 656(WMQ):APR74-332
DEVERSON, J. & K. LINDSAY. VOICES
FROM THE MIDDLE CLASS.
  N. SHRAPNEL, 617(TLS):15AUG75-915
DEVINE, A.M. THE LATIN THEMATIC
GENITIVE SINGULAR.*
  M. LEUMANN, 343:BAND17HEFT2-173
  G. SERBAT, 555:VOL47FASC1-149
DE VITIS, A.A. ANTHONY BURGESS.
  J. CULLINAN, 295:FEB74-552
DEVLIN, D.D., ED. WALTER SCOTT.
  T.R. DALE, 125:OCT73-82
DEVLIN, P. TOO PROUD TO FIGHT.*
  N. BLIVEN, 442(NY):7APR75-135
  C.E. WYZANSKI, JR., 61:MAY75-89
DE VOTO, B. THE LETTERS OF BERNARD
DE VOTO. (W. STEGNER, ED)
  B. ALLEN, 441:27APR75-10
  E. WEEKS, 61:MAY75-101
DEVOTO, D. INTRODUCCIÓN AL ESTUDIO
DE DON JUAN MANUEL Y EN PARTICULAR
DE EL CONDE LUCANOR.
  R.B. TATE, 402(MLR):JUL74-671
DE VRIES, P. THE GLORY OF THE
HUMMINGBIRD.*
  E. KORN, 617(TLS):21FEB75-185
  J. MELLORS, 362:20FEB75-253
  E. WEEKS, 61:JAN75-87
DE VRIES, P. MRS. WALLOP.
  J-C. FIELD, 556(RLV):1973/1-89
DEWALHENS, P. ABÉCÉDAIRE POUR
SAXOPHONE. TOMBEAUX. CYMBALUM
MUNDI.
  M. CRANSTON, 207(FR):OCT72-209
DEWDNEY, C. A PALAEOZOIC GEOLOGY OF
LONDON, ONTARIO.
  P. STEVENS, 628:SPRING74-101

DEWEY, G. RELATIVE FREQUENCY OF
ENGLISH SPELLINGS.
  R.M. WILLIAMS, 35(AS):SPRING-
SUMMER71-152
DEWEY, J. JOHN DEWEY: THE EARLY
WORKS. (VOLS 4&5) (J.A. BOYDSTON,
GENERAL ED)
  J. GOUINLOCK, 484(PPR):SEP73-131
DE WOLF, L.H. RESPONSIBLE FREEDOM.
  R.P.M., 543:SEP72-158
DEXTER, C. LAST BUS TO WOODSTOCK.
  N. CALLENDAR, 441:9NOV75-55
  P.D. JAMES, 617(TLS):26SEP75-1079
DEYERMOND, A.D. EPIC POETRY & THE
CLERGY.*
  W. METTMANN, 72:BAND211HEFT3/6-469
DEYERMOND, A.D. A LITERARY HISTORY
OF SPAIN: THE MIDDLE AGES.* (R.O.
JONES, ED)
  I.D. HENRY, 399(MLJ):NOV73-377
  C. SMITH, 86(BHS):JAN73-75
  J.M. SOBRÉ, 131(CL):FALL74-358
  400(MLN):MAR73-507
DEYGLUN, M-C. JUSTE À CÔTÉ D'ELLE.
  A. POKORNY, 296:VOL4#1-184
DEZSŐ, L. & P. HAJDÚ, EDS. THEORET-
ICAL PROBLEMS OF TYPOLOGY & THE
NORTHERN EURASIAN LANGUAGES.
  G. ALTMANN, 343:BAND16HEFT2-213
  F.J. OINAS, 104:FALL73-418
DHAENENS, J. LE DESTIN D'ORPHÉE.
  W. BEAUCHAMP, 546(RR):MAY73-220
  M. BOWIE, 208(FS):JUL74-339
DHARAMPAL. INDIAN SCIENCE & TECH-
NOLOGY IN THE EIGHTEENTH CENTURY.
  D. PINGREE, 293(JAST):NOV72-178
DHARMARĀJA ADHVARIN. VEDĀNTAPARIB-
HĀṢĀ. (S.S. SURYANARAYANA SASTRI,
ED & TRANS)
  L. ROCHER, 318(JAOS):JUL-SEP73-375
D'HARNONCOURT, A. & K. MC SHINE,
EDS. MARCEL DUCHAMP.*
  B. GOLD, 31(ASCH):WINTER74/75-142
D'HAUSSY, A. "POLY-OLBION" OU L'AN-
GLETERRE VUE PAR UN ÉLISABÉTHAIN.*
  J. BUXTON, 189(EA):JUL-SEP73-356
D'HOLBACH, T. LE BON SENS, OU IDÉES
NATURELLES OPPOSEES AUX IDÉES SUR-
NATURELLES. (J. DUPRUN, ED)
  P. CHARBONNEL, 535(RHL):NOV-DEC73-
1083
  M.H. WADDICOR, 208(FS):OCT74-472
D'HONDT, J. DE HEGEL À MARX.*
  R. CHAMPAGNE, 154:DEC73-741
D'HULST, R-A. JORDAENS DRAWINGS.
  G. MARTIN, 617(TLS):28NOV75-1427
DIAMOND, E. THE TIN KAZOO.
  J. LEONARD, 441:11OCT75-35
DÍAZ, A.C. & N.I. IORILLO. CONVER-
SACIÓN Y CONTROVERSIA.
  J.B. FERNÁNDEZ, 399(MLJ):APR74-216
DIAZ, F. & L. GUERCI - SEE GALIANI,
F.
DÍAZ, G.V. - SEE UNDER VERDÍN DÍAZ,
G.
DÍAZ, J.S. - SEE UNDER SIMÓN DÍAZ,
J.
DÍAZ, J.W. ANA MARÍA MATUTE.
  O.P. FERRER, 399(MLJ):NOV73-375
  M.E.W. JONES, 238:SEP73-735
DÍAZ, L.C. - SEE UNDER CORTÉS DÍAZ,
L.

DÍAZ-PLAJA, G. AL FILO DEL NOVECI-
ENTOS.
  M.J. MC CARTHY, 86(BHS):JUL73-304
DÍAZ-PLAJA, G. A HISTORY OF SPANISH
LITERATURE.
  A.V. EBERSOLE, 241:JAN73-90
DIB, M. FORMULAIRES.
  K. BIEBER, 207(FR):MAR73-854
DIB, M. OMNEROS.
  G. MARTIN, 617(TLS):10OCT75-1209
DIBBS, P. SIBERIA & THE PACIFIC.
  R.H. FISHER, 550(RUSR):JUL73-314
DI BENEDETTO, V. EURIPIDE.
  R. HAMILTON, 124:MAY73-465
DIBON, P. INVENTAIRE DE LA CORRES-
PONDANCE D'ANDRÉ RIVET (1595-1650).
  P.J.S. WHITMORE, 208(FS):OCT74-446
"DICCIONARIO RUSO-ESPAÑOL DE LA
CIENCIA Y DE LA TÉCNICA."
  W., 75:4/1973-191
DI CESARE, M.A. THE ALTAR & THE
CITY.
  C. MACLEOD, 617(TLS):11JUL75-757
DICK, B.F. THE HELLENISM OF MARY
RENAULT.*
  L.S. GORDON, 295:FEB74-764
DICK, P.K. FLOW MY TEARS, THE
POLICEMAN SAID.
  G. JONAS, 441:20JUL75-10
  P. PURSER, 362:29MAY75-715
DICK, P.K. THE MAN IN THE HIGH
CASTLE.
  E. KORN, 617(TLS):23MAY75-554
  P. PURSER, 362:29MAY75-715
DICK, S. - SEE MOORE, G.
DICKASON, O.P. INDIAN ARTS IN CAN-
ADA.
  J. BONELLIE, 73:SUMMER74-36
DICKENS, A.G. THE AGE OF HUMANISM
& REFORMATION.
  J.K. SOWARDS, 551(RENQ):WINTER73-
  460
DICKENS, C. A CHRISTMAS CAROL - THE
PUBLIC READING VERSION.* (P. COL-
LINS, ED)
  S. MONOD, 189(EA):JUL-SEP73-373
DICKENS, C. CHARLES DICKENS: THE
PUBLIC READINGS. (P. COLLINS, ED)
  J. CAREY, 362:20NOV75-677
DICKENS, C. THE LIFE & ADVENTURES
OF NICHOLAS NICKLEBY.
  E.M. BRENNAN, 155:SEP73-187
DICKENS, C. THE MYSTERY OF EDWIN
DROOD.* (M. CARDWELL, ED)
  B.F. FISHER 4TH, 445(NCF):SEP73-
  229
  T.A. SHIPPEY, 354:SEP73-255
  H.P. SUCKSMITH, 677:VOL4-326
  A. WILSON, 155:JAN73-48
DICKENS, C. THE OLD CURIOSITY SHOP.
(A. EASSON, ED)
  R.L. PATTEN, 155:JAN73-54
DICKENS, C. THE POSTHUMOUS PAPERS
OF THE PICKWICK CLUB. (R.L. PAT-
TEN, ED)
  R. TRICKETT, 155:MAY73-119
"CHARLES DICKENS: THE J.F. DEXTER
COLLECTION."
  P. COLLINS, 617(TLS):5DEC75-1464
DICKENS, C., JR. DICKENS'S DICTION-
ARY OF LONDON, 1879.
  J.G., 155:SEP73-189

DICKENS, M. LAST YEAR WHEN I WAS
YOUNG.
  617(TLS):3JAN75-5
DICKENS, P. NIGHT ACTION.
  617(TLS):18APR75-424
"DICKENS STUDIES ANNUAL." (VOL 1)
(R.B. PARTLOW, JR., ED)
  T.J. CRIBB, 541(RES):MAY73-230
  H. SERGEANT, 175:SPRING72-29
"DICKENS STUDIES ANNUAL." (VOL 2)
(R.B. PARTLOW, JR., ED)
  S.V. DANIELS, 255(HAB):SPRING73-
  148
  S.F. PICKERING, JR., 219(GAR):
  FALL73-455
  G.B. TENNYSON, 445(NCF):JUN73-115
DICKERMAN, E.H. BELLIÈVRE & VILLE-
ROY.
  J.H.M. SALMON, 551(RENQ):WINTER73-
  485
DICKIE, G. AESTHETICS.
  C. LYAS, 89(BJA):WINTER73-81
  B.N. MORTON, 290(JAAC):FALL73-115
DICKIE, G. ART & THE AESTHETIC.
  D. CARRIER, 311(JP):18DEC75-823
DICKINSON, G.L. THE AUTOBIOGRAPHY
OF G. LOWES DICKINSON. (D. PROCTOR,
ED)
  C. MORRIS, 111:26OCT73-21
DICKINSON, H.T. WALPOLE & THE WHIG
SUPREMACY.
  H. HORWITZ, 566:AUTUMN73-41
DICKINSON, P. THE LIVELY DEAD.
  A. BROYARD, 441:4AUG75-17
  N. CALLENDAR, 441:2NOV75-51
  M. LASKI, 362:5JUN75-748
  617(TLS):11JUL75-784
DICKSON, B. HOME SAFELY TO ME.
  R. WILLMOT, 296:VOL4#3-161
DICKSON, G.R., ED. COMBAT SF.
  G. JONAS, 441:14SEP75-22
DICKSON, K.A. - SEE BRECHT, B.
DICKSON, L. RADCLYFFE HALL AT THE
WELL OF LONELINESS.
  A. FREEDMAN, 99:DEC75/JAN76-60
  C. SYKES, 617(TLS):1AUG75-864
DICKSTEIN, M. KEATS & HIS POETRY.*
  W.H. EVERT, 141:SPRING72-194
  H.H. HINKEL, 219(GAR):FALL73-432
"DICTIONARY OF CANADIAN BIOGRAPHY."
(VOL 3) (F.G. HALPENNY, GENERAL ED)
  H.S. FERNS, 617(TLS):30MAY75-605
  D. MIQUELON, 99:APR/MAY75-35
DIDEROT, D. DIDEROT'S LETTERS TO
SOPHIE VOLLAND. (P. FRANCE, ED &
TRANS)
  E.B. HILL, 400(MLN):MAY73-883
  A. KNODEL, 173(ECS):FALL73-97
DIDEROT, D. SALONS. (VOL 1) (J.
SEZNEC & J. ADHÉMAR, EDS)
  A. BROOKNER, 617(TLS):3OCT75-1139
DIDION, J. PLAY IT AS IT LAYS.
(FRENCH TITLE: MARIA AVEC ET SANS
RIEN.)
  P-Y. PETILLON, 98:OCT73-902
DIECKMANN, L. GOETHE'S "FAUST."*
  U.K. GOLDSMITH, 399(MLJ):DEC73-435
  H. HENEL, 406:FALL74-301
DIECKMANN, L. HIEROGLYPHICS.
  J.H. SUMMERS, 191(ELN):MAR74-238
DIEFENBAKER, J.G. "I NEVER SAY ANY-
THING PROVOCATIVE." (M. WENTE, ED)
ONE CANADA.
  J.L. GRANATSTEIN, 99:DEC75/JAN76-
  32

DIEGO, G. MANUEL MACHADO, POETA.
G. BROTHERSTON, 617(TLS):23MAY75-
559
DIEKMANN, E. DIE SUBSTANTIVBILDUNG
MIT SUFFIXEN IN DEN FABLIAUX.
G. INEICHEN, 260(IF):BAND77HEFT
2/3-340
DIENER, G. GOETHES "LILA."
A. LUBOS, 133:1973/3-276
DIENER, H. DIE GROSSEN REGISTERSER-
IEN IM VATIKANISCHEN ARCHIV (1378-
1523).
L.E. BOYLE, 589:JUL74-556
DIÉNY, J-P. AUX ORIGINES DE LA
POÉSIE CLASSIQUE EN CHINE.
F.A. WESTBROOK, 318(JAOS):JAN-MAR
73-80
DIERICKX, J. GLOSSAIRE DE L'ANGLAIS
DU JOURNALISME.
G-F. MEIER, 682(ZPSK):BAND26HEFT
3/4-416
DIESING, P. PATTERNS OF DISCOVERY
IN THE SOCIAL SCIENCES.*
A. MC LAUGHLIN, 486:MAR73-133
DIETRICH, E.L. & OTHERS. DIE HOCH-
KULTUREN IM ZEICHEN DER WELTRELIG-
IONEN. (PT 1)
J. DUCHESNE-GUILLEMIN, 182:VOL26
#11/12-435
DIETRICH-BADER, F. WANDLUNGEN DER
DRAMATISCHEN BAUFORM VOM 16. JAHR-
HUNDERT BIS ZUR FRÜHAUFKLÄRUNG.
P-J. MANNING, 406:SPRING74-96
DIETRICHSON, J.W. THE IMAGE OF MONEY
IN THE AMERICAN NOVEL OF THE GILDED
AGE.*
P. GOETSCH, 38:BAND91HEFT1-135
DIETZ, B., ED. THE PORT & TRADE OF
EARLY ELIZABETHAN LONDON.
J.R. SEWELL, 325:OCT73-674
DIETZ, D.T. THE AUTO SACRAMENTAL &
THE PARABLE IN SPANISH GOLDEN AGE
LITERATURE.
R.W. LISTERMAN, 399(MLJ):NOV74-366
DIEZ DE MEDINA, F. EL GUERRILLERO
Y LA LUNA.
J.A. HERNÁNDEZ, 263:JUL-SEP74-306
DIGBY, J. THE STRUCTURE OF BIFOCAL
DISTANCE.
J. FULLER, 617(TLS):7NOV75-1327
"THE DIGESTER SYSTEM OF WASTE TREAT-
MENT & DISPOSAL."
W.J. MC GUINNESS, 505:FEB73-114
DIGGINS, J.P. MUSSOLINI & FASCISM.*
L. BARZINI, 617(TLS):30CT75-1130
DIGGLE, J. & F.R.D. GOODYEAR - SEE
HOUSMAN, A.E.
DIHLE, A. HOMER-PROBLEME.
M.W. EDWARDS, 24:SPRING74-68
VAN DIJK, T.A. MODERNE LITERATUUR-
TEORIE, EEN EKSPERIMENTELE INLEID-
ING.*
J.J.A. MOOIJ, 204(FDL):SEP73-222
VAN DIJK, T.A. SOME ASPECTS OF
TEXT GRAMMARS.
R. BROWN, 113:FALL73-155
J.G. KOOIJ, 204(FDL):SEP73-207
P.F. SCHMITZ, 204(FDL):SEP73-216
DIJKSTRA, B. THE HIEROGLYPHICS OF A
NEW SPEECH.
G. VAN CROMPHOUT, 179(ES):FEB73-78

DIKAIOS, P. ENKOMI EXCAVATIONS
1948-1958. (VOL 2)
J. BOARDMAN, 123:MAR74-123
DIL, A.S. - SEE FISHMAN, J.A.
DIL, A.S. - SEE GREENBERG, J.H.
DIL, A.S. - SEE LAMBERT, W.E.
DILKE, C. THE SLY SERVANT.
C. PETERS, 617(TLS):19SEP75-1041
DILKE, O.A.W. THE ANCIENT ROMANS.
617(TLS):21MAR75-320
DILLARD, A. PILGRIM AT TINKER
CREEK.*
H. CARRUTH, 639(VQR):AUTUMN74-637
DILLARD, J.L. ALL-AMERICAN ENGLISH.
C. LEHMANN-HAUPT, 441:1MAY75-39
W. SAFIRE, 441:11MAY75-4
M.K. SPEARS, 453:17JUL75-34
DILLARD, J.L. BLACK ENGLISH.*
J.L. FUNKHOUSER, 128(CE):FEB74-625
DILLARD, R.H.W., G. GARRETT & J.R.
MOORE, EDS. THE SOUNDER FEW.*
J. ELLIS, 577(SHR):FALL73-453
DILLER, E. A MYTHIC JOURNEY.
D.P. DENEAU, 268:JUL75-178
DILLER, H. KLEINE SCHRIFTEN ZUR
ANTIKEN LITERATUR.* (H-J. NEWIGER
& H. SEYFFERT, EDS)
P. CHANTRAINE, 555:VOL47FASC2-316
F.M. COMBELLACK, 122:APR73-151
F.F. SCHWARZ, 52:BAND8HEFT3-313
DILLER, H-J. REDEFORMEN DES ENG-
LISCHEN MISTERIENSPIELS.
W. HABICHT, 72:BAND211HEFT1/3-117
DILLER, K.C. GENERATIVE GRAMMAR,
STRUCTURAL LINGUISTICS, & LANGUAGE
TEACHING.
D.W. FOSTER, 399(MLJ):JAN-FEB73-43
M.H. GERTNER, 238:MAY73-524
J.W. NEY, 608:MAR74-91
J.R. SHAWL, 221(GQ):JAN73-134
DILLINGHAM, W.B. AN ARTIST IN THE
RIGGING.*
K. WIDMER, 594:SPRING73-117
DILLISTONE, F.W. CHARLES RAVEN.
F.R. BARRY, 617(TLS):2MAY75-474
M. STOCKWOOD, 362:10APR75-483
DILLON, F. THE PILGRIMS.
M.M. MINTZ, 441:30NOV75-50
DILLON, M., ED & TRANS. THERE WAS
A KING IN IRELAND.
J.H. BRUNVAND, 292(JAF):APR-JUN73-
197
DILLON, M.L. THE ABOLITIONISTS.
617(TLS):13JUN75-680
DILMAN, I. INDUCTION & DEDUCTION.*
C. LYAS, 518:JAN74-1
DI LORENZO, R.E. - SEE DUFFETT, T.
DILTS, M.R. - SEE HERAKLEIDES
DIM, J. RECOLLECTIONS OF A ROTTEN
KID.
M. LEVIN, 441:23FEB75-38
DIMARAS, C.T. A HISTORY OF MODERN
GREEK LITERATURE.*
R.C. CLARK, 544:FALL74-138
DIMBLEBY, J. RICHARD DIMBLEBY.
B. WENHAM, 362:90CT75-482
AD-DĪN FAZLULLĀH, R. - SEE UNDER
RASHĪD AD-DĪN FAZLULLĀH
DINESEN, T. MY SISTER, ISAK DINE-
SEN. (DANISH TITLE: TANNE.)
E. BREDSDORFF, 617(TLS):240CT75-
1269

DINGLE, H. SCIENCE AT THE CROSS-
ROADS.
  H.L. ARMSTRONG, 486:JUN73-318
DINKELACKER, W. ORTNIT-STUDIEN.
  M. DELBOUILLE, 182:VOL26#21/22-789
DINSDALE, T. PROJECT WATER HORSE.
  L.H. MATTHEWS, 617(TLS):26DEC75-
  1542
DIOGENES. DIOGENES OF OENOANDA:
THE FRAGMENTS. (C.W. CHILTON, ED
& TRANS)
  P. DE LACY, 124:OCT72-110
  G.L. KONIARIS, 24:FALL74-308
  É. DES PLACES, 555:VOL47FASC1-141
  F.H. SANDBACH, 123:MAR74-135
  M.F. SMITH, 303:VOL93-234
DION, G-M. DEVINETTES DU RWANDA
IBISAKUZO.
  J. BEATTIE, 69:OCT73-379
DIONYSIUS VON ALEXANDRIEN. DAS ER-
HALTENE WERK. (W.A. BIENERT, ED
& TRANS)
  A. KEMMER, 182:VOL26#1/2-16
DI ORIO, D.M., COMP. LECONTE DE
LISLE.
  A. FAIRLIE, 208(FS):OCT74-476
DI PIETRO, R.J. LANGUAGE STRUCTURES
IN CONTRAST.*
  S. BELASCO, 399(MLJ):SEP-OCT73-292
  T.G. BROWN, 207(FR):MAR73-890
  L.G. KELLY, 320(CJL):SPRING74-94
DIRLMEIER, F. DAS SERBOKROATISCHE
HELDENLIED UND HOMER.
  M.M. WILLCOCK, 123:MAR74-125
DISCH, T.M., ED. THE NEW IMPROVED
SUN.
  G. JONAS, 441:26OCT75-49
DISCHNER, G. URSPRUNGE DER RHEIN-
ROMANTIK IN ENGLAND.
  B.C.H., 191(ELN):SEP73(SUPP)-10
DISRAELI, B. DISRAELI'S REMINIS-
CENCES. (H.M. & M. SWARTZ, EDS)
  H.C.G. MATTHEW, 617(TLS):28NOV75-
  1406
  P. WHITEHEAD, 362:4DEC75-762
DISRAELI, B. LOTHAIR. (V. BOGDAN-
OR, ED)
  W. HALEY, 617(TLS):28NOV75-1406
DITTMANN, U. SPRACHBEWUSSTSEIN UND
REDEFORMEN IM WERK THOMAS MANNS.*
  I. MITTENZWEI, 224(GRM):BAND23
  HEFT2-242
DITTMAR, N. SOZIOLINGUISTIK.
  M. CLYNE, 67:MAY74-129
DITTMER, K. & OTHERS. DIE HOCHKUL-
TUREN IM ZEICHEN DER WELTRELIGION-
EN. (PT 2)
  J. DUCHESNE-GUILLEMIN, 182:VOL26
  #11/12-435
DITTRICH-ORLOVIUS, G. ZUM VERHÄLT-
NIS VON ERZÄHLUNG UND REFLEXION IN
"REINFRIED VON BRAUNSCHWEIG."
  D.H. GREEN, 402(MLR):JAN74-220
DIVĀKARA, S. - SEE UNDER SIDDHASENA
DIVĀKARA
DIVOMLIKOFF, L. THE TRAITOR.*
  B.M. COHEN, 584(SWR):SUMMER74-334
DIX, C. THE CAMARGUE.
  617(TLS):26DEC75-1547
DIXIT, K.K. - SEE GANDHI, V.R.
DIXMIER, E. & M. L'ASSIETTE AU
BEURRE.
  D. JOHNSON, 617(TLS):21MAR75-296

DIXON, N. GEORGIAN PISTOLS.
  N. HALL, 135:MAY73-62
DIXON, N.F. SUBLIMINAL PERCEPTION.
  A.J. WEIR, 478:JUL73-121
DIXON, P. RHETORIC.*
  D.R. HEISEY, 124:OCT72-114
DIXON, P. THE WORLD OF POPE'S
SATIRES.
  I. SIMON, 179(ES):JUN72-258
DIXON, R.M.W. & J. GODRICH. RECORD-
ING THE BLUES.
  N. COHEN, 292(JAF):JAN-MAR73-79
DMITRIEV, L.A. DIE HEILIGENLEGENDEN
DES RUSSISCHEN NORDENS ALS LITERA-
TURDENKMALER DES XIII.-XVII. JAHR-
HUNDERTS.
  D. TSCHIŽEWSKIJ, 72:BAND211HEFT
  2/3-474
DMYTRYSHYN, B. USSR: A CONCISE HIS-
TORY.* (BRITISH TITLE: A CONCISE
HISTORY OF THE USSR.) (2ND ED)
  M. KATZ, 104:SUMMER73-268
DOBAI, J. DIE KUNSTLITERATUR DES
KLASSIZISMUS UND DER ROMANTIK IN
ENGLAND. (VOL 1)
  N. PEVSNER, 617(TLS):21MAR75-310
DOBELL, P.C. CANADA'S SEARCH FOR
NEW ROLES.
  102(CANL):SUMMER73-127
DOBIE, K.L. & OTHERS. A FATAL TREE.
  A. CLUYSENAAR, 565:VOL14#1-70
DOBLER, B. ICEPICK.
  C.D.B. BRYAN, 441:19JAN75-34
DÖBLIN, A. BRIEFE.* (H. GRABER,
ED)
  E. BOA, 182:VOL26#5/6-160
DOBSON, E.J., ED. THE ENGLISH TEXT
OF THE ANCRENE RIWLE.
  B. COTTLE, 301(JEGP):APR74-239
  M.L. SAMUELS, 382(MAE):1974/1-78
DOCKER, J. AUSTRALIAN CULTURAL
ELITES.
  J. COLMER, 71(ALS):MAY75-107
DOCKSTADER, F.J. INDIAN ART IN
NORTH AMERICA.
  J. VASTOKAS, 255(HAB):SUMMER73-199
DOCTOROW, E.L. RAGTIME.
  P. ADAMS, 61:AUG75-88
  C. LEHMANN-HAUPT, 441:8JUL75-35
  R. SALE, 453:7AUG75-21
  G. STADE, 441:6JUL75-1
  442(NY):28JUL75-79
DODDS, D.W. NAPOLEON'S LOVE CHILD.
  617(TLS):4APR75-380
VON DODERER, H. DIE WIEDERKEHER DER
DRACHEN.* (W. SCHMIDT-DENGLER, ED)
  E. KRISPYN, 221(GQ):MAR73-291
DODGE, B., ED & TRANS. THE FIHRIST
OF AL-NADIM.
  M.A-R. KHAN, 273(IC):APR73-178
DODGE, E.S., ED. THIRTY YEARS OF
THE AMERICAN NEPTUNE.
  D.B. LITTLE, 432(NEQ):DEC73-639
DODGSON, J.M. THE PLACE-NAMES OF
CHESHIRE.* (PTS 1-3)
  G. KRISTENSSON, 179(ES):FEB73-92
DODGSON, J.M. THE PLACE-NAMES OF
CHESHIRE.* (PT 4)
  B. COTTLE, 541(RES):MAY73-193
DODSWORTH, M., ED. THE SURVIVAL OF
POETRY.
  W. DAVIES, 447(N&Q):APR73-157

DODWELL, C.R. PAINTING IN EUROPE:
800 TO 1200.
  T.S.R. BOASE, 90:JAN73-46
DOEHRINGER, S., D.G. MITTEN & A.
STEINBERG, EDS. ART & TECHNOLOGY.
  R. HIGGINS, 39:MAR73-319
DOELLE, E. EXPERIMENT UND TRADITION
IN DER PROSA VIRGINIA WOOLFS.
  F. STADTFELD, 38:BAND91HEFT4-555
DOERFER, G., WITH OTHERS. KHALAJ
MATERIALS.
  R. DANKOFF, 318(JAOS):OCT-DEC73-
  571
DOERFLINGER, W.M. SONGS OF THE
SAILOR & LUMBERMAN.
  G. BLUESTEIN, 292(JAF):OCT-DEC73-
  409
DOHERTY, T. THE ANATOMICAL WORKS OF
GEORGE STUBBS.
  Q. BELL, 453:30OCT75-26
  H. KRAMER, 441:29JUN75-6
DOHNAL, B. PŘEKLADATEL A BÁSNÍK.*
  W. ARNDT, 574(SEEJ):FALL73-330
DOI, T. THE ANATOMY OF DEPENDENCE.
  KUMAKURA MASAYA, 285(JAPQ):APR-JUN
  74-206
DOIGNON, J. HILAIRE DE POITIERS
AVANT L'EXIL.
  P. LANGLOIS, 555:VOL47FASC2-360
DOLAN, J.R. ENGLISH ANCESTRAL NAMES.
  M.M. BRYANT, 424:MAR73-53
DOLEŽEL, L. NARRATIVE MODES IN
CZECH LITERATURE.
  A. FRENCH, 67:MAY74-140
  R.B. PYNSENT, 575(SEER):OCT74-616
DOLEŽELOVÁ-VELINGEROVÁ, M. & J.I.
CRUMP - SEE "BALLAD OF THE HIDDEN
DRAGON"
DOLGE, A. PIANOS & THEIR MAKERS.
  F. DAWES, 415:AUG74-659
DOLGOFF, S., ED. THE ANARCHIST COL-
LECTIVES.
  G. WOODCOCK, 31(ASCH):SUMMER75-512
DOLGORUKAYA, N.B. DAS JOURNAL. (A.
SCHMÜCKER, ED)
  G. BARRATT, 575(SEER):OCT74-611
DOLGUN, A., WITH P. WATSON. ALEXAN-
DER DOLGUN'S STORY.
  P. ADAMS, 61:JUN75-94
  A. BROYARD, 441:19JUN75-39
  S. MALOFF, 441:25MAY75-2
  H. MUCHNIC, 453:18SEP75-25
  442(NY):19MAY75-119
DOLINER, R. FOR LOVE OR MONEY.
  M. LEVIN, 441:19JAN75-36
DÖLLE, E. EXPERIMENT UND TRADITION
IN DER PROSA VIRGINIA WOOLFS.
  J. GUIGUET, 189(EA):JUL-SEP73-338
  A. MAACK, 430(NS):JAN73-53
  K. SCHWANK, 72:BAND211HEFT1/3-169
DOLMAN, J., JR. & R.K. KNAUB. THE
ART OF PLAY PRODUCTION. (3RD ED)
  H.C. TEDFORD, 583:SUMMER74-412
DOLSON, H. PLEASE OMIT FUNERAL.
  N. CALLENDAR, 441:26OCT75-54
DOMANDI, A.K., ED. MODERN GERMAN
LITERATURE.
  F.S. LAMBASA, 406:SUMMER74-178
DOMERGUE, L. JOVELLANOS À LA SOCI-
ÉTÉ ÉCONOMIQUE DES AMIS DEL PAYS DE
MADRID (1778-1795).
  J. NADAL-FARRERAS, 86(BHS):JUL73-
  299

DOMHOFF, G.W. THE BOHEMIAN GROVE &
OTHER RETREATS.*
  A. HACKER, 453:1MAY75-9
DOMÍNGUEZ ORTIZ, A. THE GOLDEN AGE
OF SPAIN 1516-1659.*
  I.A.A. THOMPSON, 86(BHS):JUL73-289
DOMÍNGUEZ ORTIZ, A. LA SOCIEDAD
ESPAÑOLA EN EL SIGLO XVII. (VOL 2)
  P.A. LINEHAN, 86(BHS):JAN73-84
DOMINIC, Z. & J.S. GILBERT. FREDER-
ICK ASHTON.
  J. ANDERSON, 151:DEC73-104
DOMMANGET, M. LA JACQUERIE.
  B. BRAUDE, 207(FR):OCT72-188
DOMMEN, A.J. CONFLICT IN LAOS.
  M. LEIFER, 293(JAST):NOV72-121
DOMVILLE, E., ED. A CONCORDANCE TO
THE PLAYS OF W.B. YEATS.
  R.D., 179(ES):AUG73-405
  M.J. SIDNELL, 529(QQ):SUMMER73-298
DONALD, D.H. - SEE BELLARD, A.
DONALDSON, E.T. SPEAKING OF CHAU-
CER.*
  R.D., 179(ES):FEB73-97
DONALDSON, F. EDWARD VIII.*
  P. JOHNSON, 441:18MAY75-24
  R.R. LINGEMAN, 441:26JUN75-43
DONALDSON, I. THE WORLD UPSIDE-
DOWN.*
  A. BARTON, 184(EIC):JUL72-296
DONALDSON, S. POET IN AMERICA: WIN-
FIELD TOWNLEY SCOTT.*
  H.G. MC CURDY, 219(GAR):SPRING73-
  132
DONALDSON, W. BOTH THE LADIES & THE
GENTLEMEN.
  W. FEAVER, 617(TLS):9MAY75-503
DONDIS, D.A. A PRIMER OF VISUAL
LITERACY.
  T.K. KITAO, 290(JAAC):SPRING74-445
DONELLI, F. DICTAMEN.
  270:VOL23#4-85
DONIACH, N.S., ED. THE OXFORD ENG-
LISH-ARABIC DICTIONARY OF CURRENT
USAGE.
  S.A. HANNA, 399(MLJ):MAR74-144
  K.I.H. SEMAAN, 318(JAOS):OCT-DEC73-
  570
DONINGTON, R. THE INTERPRETATION OF
EARLY MUSIC.
  J.E. GARDINER, 617(TLS):7MAR75-259
  S. SADIE, 415:OCT74-847
DONINGTON, R. A PERFORMER'S GUIDE
TO BAROQUE MUSIC.*
  B. LAM, 410(M&L):APR74-215
DONIS, M. CLOUD EIGHT.
  M. LEVIN, 441:25MAY75-13
DONLEAVY, J.E. GEORGE MOORE.
  R.M. SCOTTO, 637(VS):JUN74-447
DONNE, J. DEATH'S DUEL. (G. KEYNES,
ED)
  R.K. TURNER, JR., 568(SCN):SPRING-
  SUMMER74-6
DONNE, J. IGNATIUS HIS CONCLAVE.
(T.S. HEALY, ED)
  G.A.E. PARFITT, 447(N&Q):MAY73-184
"JOHN DONNE'S HOLOGRAPH OF 'A LETTER
TO THE LADY CAREY & MRS. ESSEX
RICHE'." (H. GARDNER, ED)
  R.K. TURNER, JR., 568(SCN):SPRING-
  SUMMER74-5

DONNELLY, J., ED. LOGICAL ANALYSIS
& CONTEMPORARY THEISM.
H.A.D., 543:SEP72-159
A. FLEW, 258:MAR73-141
G. GILLAN, 484(PPR):MAR74-445
K.E. YANDELL, 613:AUTUMN73-434
DONNELLY, J.S., JR. THE LAND & THE
PEOPLE OF NINETEENTH-CENTURY CORK.
J. LEE, 617(TLS):17OCT75-1244
DONNO, E.S. - SEE MARVELL, A.
DONOGHUE, D. EMILY DICKINSON.
A. EASSON, 447(N&Q):SEP73-345
DONOGHUE, D., ED. SEVEN AMERICAN
POETS FROM MAC LEISH TO NEMEROV.
T. BYROM, 617(TLS):12DEC75-1478
DONOGHUE, D., ED. JONATHAN SWIFT.*
P. DANCHIN, 179(ES):JUN73-293
P. ROBERTS, 447(N&Q):NOV73-430
DONOGHUE, D. - SEE YEATS, W.B.
DONOHUE, J.W., JR. DRAMATIC CHARAC-
TER IN THE ENGLISH ROMANTIC AGE.*
N. DENNY, 541(RES):AUG73-357
F. ZAIC, 38:BAND91HEFT4-535
DONOHUE, J.W., JR., ED. THE THEAT-
RICAL MANAGER IN ENGLAND & AMERICA.
A.C. SPRAGUE, 179(ES):DEC73-587
DONOHUE-GAUDET, M-L. LE VOCALISME
ET LE CONSONANTISME FRANÇAIS.*
F. CARTON, 207(FR):OCT72-252
DONOSO, J. THE OBSCENE BIRD OF
NIGHT.* (SPANISH TITLE: EL OB-
SCENO PÁJARO DE LA NOCHE.)
R. CHRIST, 473(PR):3/1974-484
DONOVAN, M.J. THE BRETON LAY.
J. FRAPPIER, 545(RPH):NOV73-244
DONSKOV, A. THE CHANGING IMAGE OF
THE PEASANT IN 19TH CENTURY RUSSIAN
DRAMA.
K. SANINE, 182:VOL26#9-290
I. VAHROS, 574(SEEJ):WINTER72-477
DOOB, L.W. PATTERNING OF TIME.
P.T.D., 543:JUN73-750
DOOB, P.B.R. NEBUCHADNEZZAR'S
CHILDREN.*
R. EDWARDS, 651(WHR):SUMMER74-286
639(VQR):AUTUMN74-CXXVI
DOOLEY, P.K. PRAGMATISM AS HUMAN-
ISM.
D. CWI, 319:OCT75-538
VAN DOORN, J.A.A. & W.J. HENDRIX.
ONTSPORING VAN GEWELD.
W.H. FREDERICK, 293(JAST):MAY73-
568
DORÉ, G. THE RARE & EXTRAORDINARY
HISTORY OF HOLY RUSSIA.*
D. THOMAS, 135:OCT73-144
DORÉ, G. & B. JERROLD. LONDON.
K. GARLICK, 39:FEB73-201
DORE, R. BRITISH FACTORY - JAPANESE
FACTORY.
SUMIYA MIKIO, 285(JAPQ):OCT-DEC74-
400
DOREN, D.M. WINDS OF CRETE.
G. CADOGAN, 617(TLS):3OCT75-1157
DOREY, T.A. CICERO.
L.J. FRIEDMAN, 545(RPH):AUG73-117
DOREY, T.A., ED. ERASMUS.*
D.F. HEIMANN, 121(CJ):APR/MAY74-
371
DOREY, T.A. & D.R. DUDLEY. ROMAN
DRAMA. LATIN HISTORIANS.
L.J. FRIEDMAN, 545(RPH):AUG73-117

DOREY, T.A. & D.R. DUDLEY. ROME
AGAINST CARTHAGE.*
A.H. MC DONALD, 123:NOV74-251
DORFMAN, D. BLAKE IN THE NINETEENTH
CENTURY.
H.B. DE GROOT, 179(ES):AUG73-398
DORFMAN, E. THE NARREME IN THE MED-
IEVAL ROMANCE EPIC.*
P. DAMON, 545(RPH):NOV73-240
M.A. PEI, 546(RR):JAN74-54
DORFMAN, J. - SEE VEBLEN, T.
DORFMÜLLER, K., ED. QUELLENSTUDIEN
ZUR MUSIK, WOLFGANG SCHMIEDER ZUM
70. GEBURTSTAG.
H. BRUNNER, 680(ZDP):BAND92HEFT3-
466
DORIGO, W. LATE ROMAN PAINTING.
J. BECKWITH, 39:SEP73-238
DORION, H., ED. LES NOMS DE LIEUX
ET LE CONTACT DES LANGUES/PLACE
NAMES & LANGUAGE CONTACT.
K.B. HARDER & C.M. ROTHRAUFF, 424:
SEP73-201
D'ORLÉANS, C. - SEE UNDER CHARLES
D'ORLÉANS
D'ORMESSON, J. THE GLORY OF THE
EMPIRE. (FRENCH TITLE: LA GLOIRE
DE L'EMPIRE.)
W. BEAUCHAMP, 441:19JAN75-34
S.G. STARY, 207(FR):FEB73-665
DORN, B. BEITRÄGE ZUR GESCHICHTE
DER KAUKASISCHEN LÄNDER UND VÖLKER,
AUS MORGENLÄNDISCHEN QUELLEN.
A.W. FISHER, 104:WINTER73-544
DORN, G.M. LATIN AMERICA, SPAIN &
PORTUGAL.
G.H. GREEN, 86(BHS):OCT73-385
DORN, K. DIE ERLÖSUNGSTHEMATIK BEI
EUGENE O'NEILL.
G. HOFFMANN, 38:BAND91HEFT2-265
DORNBERG, J. THE NEW TSARS.
A. PARRY, 550(RUSR):APR73-211
DORRA, H. ART IN PERSPECTIVE.
M. HERBAN 3D, 127:SPRING74-272
DÖRRIE, H. - SEE OVID
DORSINVILLE, M. CALIBAN WITHOUT
PROSPERO.
G. MOORE, 617(TLS):19SEP75-1068
DORSON, R.M., ED. AFRICAN FOLKLORE.
S. SCHMIDT, 196:BAND14HEFT1/2-157
DORSON, R.M. AMERICA IN LEGEND.*
639(VQR):SUMMER74-CV
DORSON, R.M. AMERICAN FOLKLORE &
THE HISTORIAN.*
R. BAUMAN, 292(JAF):APR-JUN73-184
DORSON, R.M. BLOODSTOPPERS & BEAR-
WALKERS.
R. BAUMAN, 292(JAF):APR-JUN73-194
DORSON, R.M. THE BRITISH FOLKLOR-
ISTS.
V. NEWALL, 292(JAF):JUL-SEP73-299
DORSON, R.M., ED. BUYING THE WIND.
J.H. BRUNVAND, 292(JAF):JUL-SEP73-
314
DORSON, R.M. FOLKLORE.
J.H. BRUNVAND, 292(JAF):JUL-SEP73-
314
DORSON, R.M., ED. FOLKLORE & FOLK-
LIFE.
J.H. BRUNVAND, 650(WF):JUL73-211
N. MC LEOD, 187:JAN75-145
DORSON, R.M., ED. FOLKLORE & TRA-
DITIONAL HISTORY.
A. BRUFORD, 595(SCS):VOL18-149

DORSON, R.M., ED. PEASANT CUSTOMS
& SAVAGE MYTHS.
  V. NEWALL, 292(JAF):JUL-SEP73-299
DORST, J. THE LIFE OF BIRDS.
  W.H. THORPE, 617(TLS):31JAN75-106
VAN DORSTEN, J., ED. TEN STUDIES IN
ANGLO-DUTCH RELATIONS.
  S.T. BINDOFF, 617(TLS):28NOV75-
  1429
VAN DORSTEN, J.A. THE RADICAL ARTS.
  T.A. BIRRELL, 179(ES):OCT72-458
  R.L. COLIE, 551(RENQ):SPRING73-74
DOSMAN, E.J. INDIANS.
  J.L. ELLIOTT, 150(DR):SPRING73-181
DOS PASSOS, J. CENTURY'S EBB.
  M. COWLEY, 441:9NOV75-6
  442(NY):8DEC75-197
DOS PASSOS, J. THE FOURTEENTH
CHRONICLE. (T. LUDINGTON, ED)
  H.A. LARRABEE, 432(NEQ):SEP74-464
  W.B. RIDEOUT, 27(AL):NOV74-408
  G. STADE, 473(PR):3/1974-476
DOSTOEVSKY, A. DOSTOEVSKY. (B.
STILLMAN, ED & TRANS)
  S. MALOFF, 441:21DEC75-6
  V.S. PRITCHETT, 453:30OCT75-8
  G. STEINER, 442(NY):13OCT75-169
DOSTOEVSKY, F.M. THE ADOLESCENT.*
(A.R. MAC ANDREW, TRANS) NETOCHKA
NEZVANOVA.* (A. DUNNIGAN TRANS)
  J. GLAD, 574(SEEJ):FALL72-343
DOSTOEVSKY, F.M. THE GAMBLER [WITH
THE] DIARY OF POLINA SUSLOVA.*
(E. WASIOLEK, ED; V. TERRAS, TRANS)
  L. KOEHLER, 104:FALL73-426
  G.D. LIVERMORE, JR., 574(SEEJ):
  FALL73-334
  R.V. ZUCKERMAN, 573(SSF):SPRING73-
  215
DOTTI, U. - SEE PETRARCH
DOTTIN, G. - SEE MARGUERITE DE
NAVARRE
DOTY, G.G. & J. ROSS. LANGUAGE &
LIFE IN THE U.S.A. (VOLS 1&2) (3RD
ED)
  H.S. MADSEN, 399(MLJ):SEP-OCT74-
  303
DOUBLEDAY, N.F. HAWTHORNE'S EARLY
TALES.*
  L.B. LEVY, 191(ELN):SEP73-68
DOUBROVSKY, S. THE NEW CRITICISM
IN FRANCE.
  639(VQR):SUMMER74-LXXXI
DOUBROVSKY, S. & OTHERS. L'EN-
SEIGNEMENT DE LA LITTÉRATURE.
  R. MERKER, 399(MLJ):SEP-OCT74-273
DOUCHIN, J-L. LE SENTIMENT DE L'AB-
SURDE CHEZ GUSTAVE FLAUBERT.
  C. GOTHOT-MERSCH, 535(RHL):SEP-OCT
  73-919
DOUGHTIE, E., ED. LYRICS FROM ENG-
LISH AIRS 1596-1622.*
  D. GREER, 410(M&L):JAN74-108
  D. LINDLEY, 447(N&Q):MAY73-188
  F.W. STERNFELD, 541(RES):FEB73-73
DOUGHTY, R.W. FEATHER FASHIONS &
BIRD PRESERVATION.
  S.M. NEWTON, 617(TLS):24OCT75-1260
DOUGLAS, C.L. THUNDER ON THE GULF.
  W. GARD, 584(SWR):WINTER74-98
DOUGLAS, E. APOSTLES OF LIGHT.*
  W. SULLIVAN, 569(SR):WINTER74-138
DOUGLAS, H. CHARLES EDWARD STUART.
  617(TLS):31OCT75-1313

DOUGLAS-HAMILTON, I. & O. AMONG THE
ELEPHANTS.
  M. BOORER, 362:20MAR75-370
  G. CORBET, 617(TLS):2MAY75-475
  S. HEMPSTONE, 441:19OCT75-18
  B. RENSBERGER, 441:22AUG75-29
DOVER, K.J. ARISTOPHANIC COMEDY.*
  W.E. FOREHAND, 399(MLJ):SEP-OCT73-
  278
  J. HENDERSON, 5:VOL1#3-530
  D.M. MAC DOWELL, 123:MAR74-27
  T. MC EVILLEY, 24:FALL74-293
DOVER, K.J. GREEK POPULAR MORALITY
IN THE TIME OF PLATO & ARISTOTLE.
  M.F. BURNYEAT, 362:8MAY75-621
  H. LLOYD-JONES, 617(TLS):14MAR75-
  273
DOVER, K.J. LYSIAS & THE "CORPUS
LYSIACUM."
  R.C. ROSS, 121(CJ):OCT/NOV72-82
DOVER, K.J. - SEE THEOCRITUS
DOVHALEVŠKYJ, M. POETYKA.
  D. TSCHIŽEWSKIJ, 72:BAND211HEFT
  3/6-479
DOW, H.J. THE ART OF ALEX COLVILLE.*
  102(CANL):SUMMER73-125
DOW, S. CONVENTIONS IN EDITING.
  D.E. SAMUEL, 121(CJ):DEC73/JAN74-
  174
DOW, S. & J. CHADWICK. THE CAM-
BRIDGE ANCIENT HISTORY. (REV)
(VOL 2, CHAPTER 13)
  A.M. DAVIES, 318(JAOS):JUL-SEP73-
  389
DOWDEN, W.S. JOSEPH CONRAD.*
  D.C. YELTON, 599:SPRING73-245
DOWER, J.W. THE ELEMENTS OF JAPAN-
ESE DESIGN.
  R.L. BACKUS, 318(JAOS):JUL-SEP73-
  420
DOWER, J.W. - SEE NORMAN, E.H.
DOWLING, J. - SEE BUERO VALLEJO, A.
DOWLING, J. - SEE FERNÁNDEZ DE MORA-
TÍN, L.
DOWLING, J. & R. ANDIOC - SEE FER-
NÁNDEZ DE MORATÍN, L.
DOWLING, J.C. LEANDRO FERNÁNDEZ DE
MORATÍN.
  J.H.R. POLT, 400(MLN):MAR73-464
  P. REGALADO DE KERSON, 399(MLJ):
  NOV73-376
  481(PQ):JUL73-557
DOWN, A. CHICHESTER EXCAVATIONS II.
  B. CUNLIFFE, 617(TLS):2MAY75-477
DOWNER, L.J., ED & TRANS. LEGES
HENRICI PRIMI.
  E. JOHN, 589:JUL74-556
DOWNES, D.A. THE TEMPER OF VICTOR-
IAN BELIEF.
  A.J. HARTLEY, 150(DR):SPRING73-185
  T. VARGISH, 637(VS):SEP73-124
DOWNEY, G. & A.F. NORMAN - SEE
THEMISTIUS
DOWNIE, R.S. ROLES & VALUES.*
  R.F. ATKINSON, 483:APR73-188
  R. BROWN, 482(PHR):OCT73-520
  P. DUBOIS, 542:OCT-DEC73-485
DOWNS, R.C.S. GOING GENTLY.
  P. CAMPBELL, 617(TLS):21FEB75-185
  N. HEPBURN, 362:27FEB75-285
DOWSE, R.E., ED. THE SOCIALIST
IDEAL.
  S. KOSS, 617(TLS):9MAY75-515

DOYLE, A.C. SHERLOCK HOLMES COL-
LECTED EDITION.
C. JAMES, 453:20FEB75-15
DOYLE, A.C. THE WHITE COMPANY. SIR
NIGEL.
P. KEATING, 617(TLS):19DEC75-1503
DOYLE, E.M. & V.H. FLOYD, EDS.
STUDIES IN INTERPRETATION.
W.C. FORREST, 290(JAAC):SPRING74-
437
DOYLE, J.F., ED. EDUCATIONAL JUDG-
MENTS.
R. SCHWARTZ, 311(JP):27FEB75-106
A.J. WATT, 63:AUG74-180
DOYLE, P.A. LIAM O'FLAHERTY.
354:SEP73-265
DOYLE, W. THE PARLEMENT OF BORDEAUX
& THE END OF THE OLD REGIME 1771-
1790.
J. MC MANNERS, 617(TLS):14MAR75-
281
DOYLE, W. & A. CURTIS, EDS. THE
OFFICIAL DIRECTORY OF THE CITY OF
NEW YORK 1974-1975.
F. FERRETTI, 441:11MAY75-20
DOYNO, V.A. - SEE BARNES, B.
DRABBLE, M. ARNOLD BENNETT.*
W. PRITCHARD, 364:OCT/NOV74-127
DRABBLE, M. THE REALMS OF GOLD.
A. BROYARD, 441:31OCT75-37
L. DICKSTEIN, 441:16NOV75-5
D.A.N. JONES, 362:25SEP75-411
E. KORN, 617(TLS):26SEP75-1077
C. RICKS, 453:27NOV75-42
DRAHT, V.H. WAS WOLLEN DIE DEUT-
SCHEN?
J.K. FUGATE, 221(GQ):MAR73-303
DRAKE, S. - SEE GALILEO GALILEI
DRAKE, S.A. OLD LANDMARKS & HISTOR-
IC PERSONAGES OF BOSTON.
L.C. KEATING, 582(SFQ):DEC73-410
"DRAMA IN EDUCATION." (VOL 2) (J.
HODGSON & M. BANHAM, EDS)
C. WILLIAMS, 157:AUTUMN73-77
DRANE, J.W. PAUL, LIBERTINE OR
LEGALIST?
F.R. BARRY, 617(TLS):5DEC75-1468
DRAPER, R.P., ED. D.H. LAWRENCE:
THE CRITICAL HERITAGE.*
S. GILL, 447(N&Q):JUN73-240
"THE DRAWINGS OF MERVYN PEAKE."*
H. BROGAN, 617(TLS):4APR75-354
DRESSLER, W. EINFÜHRUNG IN DIE
TEXTLINGUISTIK.
H.W. KIRKWOOD, 297(JL):SEP73-368
DREW, E. WASHINGTON JOURNAL.
R. MANNING, 61:OCT75-106
W.V. SHANNON, 441:14SEP75-3
DREW, P. THE POETRY OF BROWNING.*
J.C. MAXWELL, 447(N&Q):JUL73-269
D. ROLL-HANSEN, 179(ES):OCT72-469
DREW, P. THIRD GENERATION.
505:MAR73-128
DREW, W. THE WABENO FEAST.
A. APPENZELL, 102(CANL):AUTUMN73-
95
DREW-BEAR, A. RHETORIC IN BEN JON-
SON'S MIDDLE PLAYS.
C.A. ASP, 568(SCN):SPRING-SUMMER
74-14
DREWAL, M.T. & G. JACKSON. SOURCES
ON AFRICAN & AFRICAN-RELATED DANCE.
A.P. MERRIAM, 187:MAY75-307

DREXLER, R. THE COSMOPOLITAN GIRL.
P. ADAMS, 61:APR75-100
C. LEHMANN-HAUPT, 441:21APR75-33
S. SANBORN, 441:30MAR75-4
DREYER, P. A GARDENER TOUCHED WITH
GENIUS.
S.J. GOULD, 441:16NOV75-6
DRISCOLL, P. THE WHITE LIE ASSIGN-
MENT.
N. CALLENDAR, 441:14DEC75-30
DRISKELL, L.V. & J.T. BRITTAIN. THE
ETERNAL CROSSROADS.
P.M. BROWNING, JR., 659:SPRING75-
260
C.M. HEGARTY, 573(SSF):WINTER73-
117
M.D. ORVELL, 295:FEB74-732
DRIVER, C., ED. THE GOOD FOOD GUIDE
1975.
P. CARNEGY, 617(TLS):30MAY75-607
DRIVER, S.N. ANNA AKHMATOVA.
D. WHITE, 574(SEEJ):SUMMER73-236
DRONKE, P. POETIC INDIVIDUALITY IN
THE MIDDLE AGES.*
T. STEMMLER, 38:BAND91HEFT1-113
DROSDOFF, D. EL GOBIERNO DE LAS
VACAS (1933-1956).
A. ARIBE, 37:JUN-JUL73-37
VON DROSTE-HÜLSHOFF, A. GEISTLICHES
JAHR IN LEIDERN AUF ALLE SONN- UND
FESTTAGE. (K.S. KEMMINGHAUSEN & W.
WOESLER, EDS)
G. HÄNTZSCHEL, 224(GRM):BAND23HEFT
4-483
G. RODGER, 220(GL&L):APR74-269
DROT, J-M. LES TEMPS DES DÉSILLU-
SIONS OU LE RETOUR D'ULYSSE MAN-
CHOT.
L. JONES, 207(FR):OCT72-211
DROWDOWSKI, G. & OTHERS - SEE "DER
GROSSE DUDEN"
DRUHE, D.N. RUSSO-INDIAN RELATIONS,
1466-1917.
S.K. GUPTA, 550(RUSR):JAN73-96
DRUMMOND, A.L. & J. BULLOCH. THE
CHURCH IN VICTORIAN SCOTLAND 1843-
1874.
E. PLAYFAIR, 617(TLS):22AUG75-937
DRUMMOND, I. THE POWER OF THE BUG.
N. CALLENDAR, 441:9FEB75-16
DRUMMOND, I.M. IMPERIAL ECONOMIC
POLICY 1917-1939.
N. HILLMER, 99:JUN75-43
DRURY, A. THE PROMISE OF JOY.
R. JONES, 617(TLS):10OCT75-1217
G. LYONS, 441:16MAR75-24
DRURY, M.O. THE DANGER OF WORDS.
483:OCT73-408
DRUTMAN, I. - SEE FLANNER, J.
DRYDEN, J. ALL FOR LOVE.* (D.M.
VIETH, ED)
P. LEGOUIS, 189(EA):JUL-SEP73-369
DRYDEN, J. AURENG-ZEBE.* (F.M.
LINK, ED)
P. LEGOUIS, 189(EA):JUL-SEP73-370
DRYDEN, J. A CHOICE OF DRYDEN'S
VERSE. (W.H. AUDEN, ED)
C.T.P., 566:AUTUMN73-35
DRYDEN, J. JOHN DRYDEN: SELECTED
CRITICISM.* (J. KINSLEY & G.
PARFITT, EDS)
R. LONSDALE, 447(N&Q):MAY73-197

DRYDEN, J. THE WORKS OF JOHN DRY-
DEN.* (VOL 2) (H.T. SWEDENBERG,
JR., ED)
  P. HARTH, 481(PQ):JUL73-492
  W. MYERS, 677:VOL4-291
DRYDEN, J. THE WORKS OF JOHN DRY-
DEN.* (VOL 17) (S.H. MONK, ED)
  P. LEGOUIS, 189(EA):JUL-SEP73-367
DUBARLE, D. & A. DOZ. LOGIQUE ET
DIALECTIQUE.*
  C. MUGLER, 555:VOL47FASC2-329
DUBÉ, M. UN MATIN COMME LES AUTRES.
  E.J. TALBOT, 207(FR):DEC72-439
DUBÉ, M. TEXTES ET DOCUMENTS. DE
L'AUTRE CÔTÉ DU MUR. LE TEMPS DES
LILAS.
  M. DORSINVILLE, 102(CANL):SUMMER74-
  90
DUBÉ, M. THE WHITE GEESE.
  C. BRISSENDEN, 102(CANL):WINTER74-
  111
DUBE, W-D. THE EXPRESSIONISTS.
  F. WHITFORD, 592:MAR73-144
DU BELLAY, J. POÉSIES. DEFFENCE ET
ILLUSTRATION DE LA LANGUE FRANCOYSE.
  M. DEGUY, 98:MAR73-215
DUBERMAN, M. BLACK MOUNTAIN.*
  H. LOMAS, 364:DEC74/JAN75-81
  D.E. WHISNANT, 579(SAQ):SPRING74-
  277
DUBILLARD, R. OLGA MA VACHE.
  G. CRAIG, 617(TLS):14MAR75-284
DUBOIS, C-G. MYTHE ET LANGAGE AU
SEIZIÈME SIÈCLE.*
  F. JOUKOVSKY, 545(RPH):FEB74-436
DU BOIS, D.G. ...AND BID HIM SING.
  M. LEVIN, 441:29JUN75-28
  442(NY):9JUN75-127
DUBOIS, E.T. - SEE ROTROU, J.
DUBOIS, J. & OTHERS. DICTIONNAIRE
DE LINGUISTIQUE.
  E. BERNÁRDEZ, 202(FMOD):JUN73-403
DUBOIS, J. & OTHERS, EDS. DICTION-
NAIRE DU FRANÇAIS CONTEMPORAIN.*
(SPÉCIAL ENSEIGNEMENT)
  H-W. BRANN, 207(FR):OCT72-239
DUBOIS, J. & OTHERS. RHÉTORIQUE
POÉTIQUE.
  D. BOUVEROT, 209(FM):JUL73-312
DUBOIS, P. LANGAGE ET MÉTAPHYSIQUE
DANS LA PHILOSOPHIE ANGLAISE CON-
TEMPORAINE.
  W.H. WALSH, 182:VOL26#7/8-193
DU BOIS, W.E.B. THE CORRESPONDENCE
OF W.E.B. DU BOIS. (VOL 1) (H.
APTHEKER, ED)
  676(YR):SUMMER74-VIII
DUBOS, R. A GOD WITHIN.*
  J.W. MEEKER, 262:AUTUMN73-347
DUBOS, R. GIOVANNI SANTI, PEINTRE
ET CHRONIQUEUR À URBIN, AU XVE
SIÈCLE.
  I. CHENEY, 551(RENQ):AUTUMN73-336
  M. KEMP, 90:MAR73-185
DU BOULAY, F.R.H. & C. BARRON, EDS.
THE REIGN OF RICHARD II.*
  A.G. DYSON, 325:OCT73-664
DUBUISSON, P. ATLAS LINGUISTIQUE ET
ETHNOGRAPHIQUE DU CENTRE. (VOL 1)
  D. MC MILLAN, 182:VOL26#1/2-18
DUBUS, A. SEPARATE FLIGHTS.
  G. GODWIN, 441:24AUG75-24

DUCHAC, R. SOCIOLOGIE ET PSYCHOLO-
GIE.
  C. SCHUWER, 542:JAN-MAR73-59
DUCHÊNE, F. THE CASE OF THE HELMET-
ED AIRMAN.*
  E. CALLAN, 295:APR74-1055
DUCHESNEAU, F. L'EMPIRISME DE LOCKE.
  J-W. YOLTON, 319:JUL75-410
DUCKETT, E. MEDIEVAL PORTRAITS FROM
EAST & WEST.
  J-C. POULIN, 255(HAB):WINTER73-68
DUCKWORTH, A.M. THE IMPORTANCE OF
THE ESTATE.*
  J.E.J., 191(ELN):SEP73(SUPP)-30
DUCKWORTH, C. ANGELS OF DARKNESS.
  295:FEB74-448
DUCKWORTH, G.E. VERGIL & CLASSICAL
HEXAMETER POETRY.
  J.P. POE, 121(CJ):DEC73/JAN74-172
DUCLOS, C. CORRESPONDANCE DE
CHARLES DUCLOS (1704-1772). (J.
BRENGUES, ED)
  R. NIKLAUS, 535(RHL):JUL-AUG73-705
DU COLOMBIER, P. LES CHANTIERS DES
CATHÉDRALES.
  A. REINLE, 182:VOL26#11/12-419
DUCROT, O. & T. TODOROV. DICTION-
NAIRE ENCYCLOPÉDIQUE DES SCIENCES
DU LANGAGE.
  J-M. KLINKENBERG, 209(FM):JAN73-74
DUDA, D. INNENARCHITEKTUR SYRISCHER
STADTHÄUSER DES 16.-18. JAHRHUN-
DERTS.
  L. GOLVIN, 182:VOL26#21/22-830
DUDBRIDGE, G. THE HSI-YU CHI.*
  A-R. DAVIS, 302:JAN73-165
DUDLEY, D.R. LUCRETIUS.
  L.J. FRIEDMAN, 545(RPH):AUG73-117
DUDLEY, D.R., ED. NERONIANS &
FLAVIANS.
  E. JENKINSON, 313:VOL63-300
DUDLEY, E. & M.E. NOVAK, EDS. THE
WILD MAN WITHIN.*
  R.J. QUINONES, 579(SAQ):AUTUMN74-
  565
DUFF, C. THE BASIS & ESSENTIALS OF
SPANISH. (REV)
  R.J. QUIRK, 399(MLJ):APR73-229
DUFF, D. VICTORIA TRAVELS.
  R.C. TOBIAS, 637(VS):DEC73-211
DUFF, J.D. - SEE JUVENAL
DUFFETT, T. THREE BURLESQUE PLAYS
OF THOMAS DUFFETT. (R.E. DI LOREN-
ZO, ED)
  R.D. HUME, 481(PQ):JUL73-496
  F.T. MASON, 568(SCN):FALL74-59
DUFFY, C. THE ARMY OF FREDERICK THE
GREAT.
  617(TLS):21MAR75-320
DUFFY, J.J. - SEE MARSH, J.
DUFFY, M. CAPITAL.
  N. HEPBURN, 362:2OCT75-453
  J. MILLER, 617(TLS):19SEP75-1041
DUFOUR, A. "LES VIES DES FEMMES
CÉLÈBRES," PAR ANTOINE DUFOUR.*
(G. JEANNEAU, ED)
  J.B. ATKINSON, 551(RENQ):SPRING73-
  54
DUFOURNET, J. VILLON ET SA FORTUNE
LITTÉRAIRE.*
  E. BALMAS, 535(RHL):SEP-OCT73-882
DUFRENNE, M. THE PHENOMENOLOGY OF
AESTHETIC EXPERIENCE.
  M.C. AUFHAUSER, 311(JP):30JAN75-49

DUFRESNE, G. THE CALL OF THE WHIP-
POORWILL.
C. BRISSENDEN, 102(CANL):WINTER74-
111
DUFT, J. NOTKER DER ARZT.
B.H. HILL, JR., 589:OCT74-722
DUGAN, A. POEMS 4.
J. ATLAS, 491:FEB75-295
D. DAVIE, 453:6MAR75-10
R. LATTIMORE, 249(HUDR):AUTUMN74-
465
DUGAS, A. & OTHERS, EDS. CAHIERS DE
LINGUISTIQUE DE L'UNIVERSITÉ DU
QUÉBEC. (NO. 1)
M.E. LONG, 207(FR):MAR73-892
DUIGNAN, P., ED. GUIDE TO RESEARCH
& REFERENCE WORKS ON SUB-SAHARAN
AFRICA.
J.A. CASADA, 14:APR73-247
DUITS, C. PTAH HOTEP.*
W.V. GUGLI, 207(FR):DEC72-440
DUKAS, P. CORRESPONDANCE DE PAUL
DUKAS. (G. FAVRE, ED)
G.W. HOPKINS, 415:FEB74-133
R. MYERS, 410(M&L):JAN74-113
DUKE, B.C. JAPAN'S MILITANT TEACH-
ERS.
NAGAI MICHIO, 285(JAPQ):JAN-MAR74-
98
DÜLL, R., ED & TRANS. DAS ZWÖLFTAF-
ELGESETZ. (4TH ED)
W.B. TYRRELL, 124:MAR73-352
DULLES, F.R. AMERICAN POLICY TOWARD
COMMUNIST CHINA.*
L.H.D. GORDON, 293(JAST):NOV72-150
VAN DÜLMEN, R. - SEE ANDREAE, J.V.
DUMAS [FILS], A. LA DAME AUX CAM-
ÉLIAS. (R. CLARK, ED)
F. BASSAN, 446:FALL-WINTER73/74-86
DUMAS, A. ALEXANDRE DUMAS' "GEOR-
GES." (W.N. RIVERS, J.F. MATHEUS
& M. BELATECHE, EDS)
R.J. FULTON, 207(FR):MAR73-884
DUMAS, H. ARK OF BONES.* (E.B.
REDMOND, ED)
442(NY):6JAN75-81
DUMAS, H. PLAY EBONY PLAY IVORY.
(E.B. REDMOND, ED)
J. LESTER, 441:19JAN75-10
DUMAS-DUBOURG, F. LE TRÉSOR DE
FÉCAMP ET LE MONNAYAGE EN FRANCIE
OCCIDENTALE PENDANT LA SECONDE
MOITIÉ DU XE SIÈCLE.
M. MATE, 589:JAN74-114
DUMAZEDIER, J. SOCIOLOGY OF LEI-
SURE.
A. CLAYRE, 617(TLS):28FEB75-229
"DUMBARTON OAKS PAPERS, NO. 25."
J.D. HOWARD-JOHNSTON, 303:VOL93-
275
"DUMBARTON OAKS PAPERS, NO. 28."
A.M. BRYER, 617(TLS):17OCT75-1245
DUMBAUGH, W. WILLIAM BLAKE'S VISION
OF AMERICA.
M.F. SCHULZ, 173(ECS):FALL73-120
DUMÉZIL, G. THE DESTINY OF THE WAR-
RIOR.*
M.J. DRESDEN, 318(JAOS):JUL-SEP73-
370
DUMÉZIL, G. MYTHE ET ÉPOPÉE. (VOLS
1&3)
J. BROUGH, 617(TLS):3JAN75-19

DUMÉZIL, G. MYTHE ET ÉPOPÉE. (VOL
2)
J. BROUGH, 617(TLS):3JAN75-19
M.J. DRESDEN, 318(JAOS):JUL-SEP73-
370
DUMMETT, M. FREGE.
J.E.J. ALTHAM, 111:23NOV73-53
DUMONT, L. HOMO HIERARCHICUS.
P. KOLENDA, 318(JAOS):JAN-MAR73-
120
DUMONT, L. RELIGION, POLITICS &
HISTORY IN INDIA.
P. KOLENDA, 318(JAOS):JAN-MAR73-
121
B. STEIN, 293(JAST):NOV72-172
DUMOULIN, H., ED. BUDDHISMUS DER
GEGENWART.
J. CHING, 485(PE&W):JUL73-404
DUNBAR, J. J.M. BARRIE.*
R.L. OAKMAN, 588:JUL-OCT73-120
DUNCAN, G.I.O. THE HIGH COURT OF
DELEGATES.
E. WELCH, 325:OCT73-669
DUNCAN, I. "YOUR ISADORA."* (F.
STEEGMULLER, ED)
P. BEER, 617(TLS):31JAN75-113
M. DRABBLE, 362:6FEB75-185
A. KISSELGOFF, 441:11JAN75-27
DUNCAN, J.E. MILTON'S EARTHLY PARA-
DISE.*
L. BABB, 141:FALL73-380
A.B. GIAMATTI, 405(MP):MAY74-438
M.A. RADZINOWICZ, 551(RENQ):WINTER
73-535
G. STACY, 568(SCN):SPRING-SUMMER
74-2
DUNCAN, R.L. DRAGONS AT THE GATE.
N. CALLENDAR, 441:23NOV75-52
DUNCAN-JONES, K. - SEE SIDNEY, P.
DUNCAN-JONES, R. THE ECONOMY OF THE
ROMAN EMPIRE.
K. HOPKINS, 617(TLS):21FEB75-201
DUNDES, A., ED. MOTHER WIT FROM THE
LAUGHING BARREL.
S. STERN, 650(WF):OCT73-287
DUNDES, A. & A. FALASSI. LA TERRA
IN PIAZZA.
P. BURKE, 617(TLS):31OCT75-1290
DUNDY, E. THE INJURED PARTY.*
J. MELLORS, 364:JUN/JUL74-135
VAN DEN DUNGEN, P.M.H. THE PUNJAB
TRADITION.
J.A. CASADA, 637(VS):DEC73-230
DUNLAP, J.R. THE BOOK THAT NEVER
WAS.*
J. CHRISTIAN, 90:FEB73-125
DUNLOP, I. THE SHOCK OF THE NEW.
D. FARR, 39:APR73-437
B. LANG, 290(JAAC):SPRING74-434
P. OVERY, 592:MAR73-140
DUNLOP, J.B. STARETZ AMVROSY.
H.A. STAMMLER, 550(RUSR):JUL73-331
DUNMORE, S. COLLISION.
N. CALLENDAR, 441:3AUG75-24
DUNN, D. THE HAPPIER LIFE.*
A. CLUYSENAAR, 565:VOL14#1-70
J. PARISI, 491:JUL75-219
H. SERGEANT, 175:AUTUMN73-121
DUNN, D. LOVE OR NOTHING.
R. FULLER, 617(TLS):31JAN75-107
R. GARFITT, 364:FEB/MAR75-106
DUNN, D. TERRY STREET.
J. PARISI, 491:JUL75-219

DUNN, E.C., T. FOTITCH & B.M. PEEB-
LES, ED. THE MEDIEVAL DRAMA & ITS
CLAUDELIAN REVIVAL.*
  B.M. CRAIG, 188(ECR):SPRING73-85
  J. DE LABRIOLLE, 549(RLC):JAN-MAR
  73-163
DUNN, J. THE POLITICAL THOUGHT OF
JOHN LOCKE.
  H. LABOUCHEIX, 189(EA):JAN-MAR73-
  103
DUNN, J.D.G. JESUS & THE SPIRIT.
  R.P.C. HANSON, 617(TLS):5DEC75-
  1467
DUNN, N. TEAR HIS HEAD OFF HIS
SHOULDERS.*
  D. DURRANT, 364:AUG/SEP74-144
DUNN, T.A., ED. SCOTTISH SHORT
STORIES 1975.
  R. GARFITT, 617(TLS):26SEP75-1077
DUNNE, J.S. A SEARCH FOR GOD IN
TIME & MEMORY.
  U. SIMON, 617(TLS):15AUG75-926
DUNNETT, R. THE TRINOVANTES.
  S. FRERE, 617(TLS):12SEP75-1017
DUNNING, J.H., ED. ECONOMIC ANALY-
SIS & THE MULTINATIONAL ENTERPRISE.
  M.D. STEUER, 617(TLS):18APR75-433
DUNNING, R.W., ED. A HISTORY OF THE
COUNTY OF SOMERSET. (VOL 3)
  G.E. MINGAY, 617(TLS):11APR75-390
DUNSTAN, G.R., ED. DUTY & DISCERN-
MENT.
  F.R. BARRY, 617(TLS):24OCT75-1273
DUPEE, F.W. & G. STADE - SEE CUM-
MINGS, E.E.
DU PLESSIS, S.I.M. THE COMPATIBIL-
ITY OF SCIENCE & PHILOSOPHY IN
FRANCE, 1840-1940.
  C.R. THOMAS, 484(PPR):SEP73-126
DUPRE, L. THE OTHER DIMENSION.*
  J.K. MC CORMACK, 613:SUMMER73-311
DUPRÉ, Y. CHÉLÉE OU LA PASSION
SELON SAINTE-CATHERINE.
  R. WILLMOT, 296:VOL3#4-94
DUPRIEZ, B. L'ETUDE DES STYLES.
(2ND ED)
  P. LARTHOMAS, 209(FM):APR73-198
DUPRUN, J. - SEE D'HOLBACH, T.
DUQUETTE, J-P. FLAUBERT OU L'ARCHI-
TECTURE DU VIDE.
  A.M.G. BOURGEOIS, 207(FR):MAR73-
  835
  205(FMLS):APR73-212
DURAC, J. A MATTER OF TASTE.
  617(TLS):17OCT75-1245
DURÁN, G. & M., EDS. VIVIR HOY.
  M.C. ANDRADE, 399(MLJ):SEP-OCT74-
  292
DURÁN, M. LUIS DE LEÓN.
  E.L. RIVERS, 400(MLN):MAR73-428
DURANT, W. & A. THE AGE OF NAPOLEON.
  J.H. PLUMB, 441:26OCT75-2
MADAME DE DURAS. OLIVIER OU LE
SECRET. (D. VIRIEUX, ED)
  E. CONSTANS, 535(RHL):JAN-FEB73-
  140
  A. FAIRLIE, 208(FS):JAN74-86
  J.S.P., 191(ELN):SEP73(SUPP)-80
DURAS, M. L'AMOUR.
  J.P. GOLLUB, 207(FR):APR73-1047
DURCEY, M. THE FIRST SPASMODIC
CHOLERA EPIDEMIC IN YORK, 1832.
  617(TLS):14FEB75-167

DURDEN, K. A FINE & PEACEFUL KING-
DOM.
  C. LEHMANN-HAUPT, 441:25APR75-39
DÜRER, A. DIARY OF HIS JOURNEY TO
THE NETHERLANDS 1520-1521.
  C. WHITE, 39:DEC73-518
"ALBRECHT DÜRER: MASTER PRINTMAK-
ER."*
  A.W. BINET, 551(RENQ):AUTUMN73-338
DURGNAT, R. JEAN RENOIR.*
  D. BROMWICH, 441:13APR75-22
  G. MILLAR, 362:28AUG75-284
DURGNAT, R. THE STRANGE CASE OF
ALFRED HITCHCOCK.*
  D. BROMWICH, 441:13APR75-22
DURKHEIM, E. LE SOCIALISME.
  D. MERLLIÉ, 542:JAN-MAR73-65
DURKHEIM, E. & M. MAUSS. PRIMITIVE
CLASSIFICATION.
  C. SCHUWER, 542:JAN-MAR73-91
DUROCHER, L., WITH E. LINN. NICE
GUYS FINISH LAST.
  J. FLAHERTY, 441:17AUG75-7
  C. LEHMANN-HAUPT, 441:4JUN75-43
DUROZOI, G. BECKETT.
  H.P. ABBOTT, 399(MLJ):SEP-OCT73-
  281
  H. PULS, 430(NS):JUL73-396
  P.H. SOLOMON, 207(FR):APR73-1026
  205(FMLS):APR73-212
DURRANT, G. WILLIAM WORDSWORTH.
  M.F. SCHULZ, 173(ECS):SPRING74-378
DURRANT, G. WORDSWORTH & THE GREAT
SYSTEM.
  C. CLARKE, 447(N&Q):FEB73-66
  M.F. SCHULZ, 173(ECS):SPRING74-378
DURRANT, M. THE LOGICAL STATUS OF
"GOD."
  S. BROWN, 518:MAY74-3
DURRELL, L. MONSIEUR.*
  A. BROYARD, 441:10JAN75-43
  J.D. O'HARA, 441:2FEB75-4
  P. VANSITTART, 364:FEB/MAR75-130
  E. WEEKS, 61:FEB75-120
  M. WOOD, 453:6MAR75-17
DURRELL, M. DIE SEMANTISCHE ENT-
WICKLUNG DER SYNONYMIK FÜR "WAR-
TEN."
  C.T. CARR, 402(MLR):OCT74-907
DURRY, M-J. EDEN.
  L. RIÈSE, 207(FR):APR73-1049
DURSO, J. & OTHERS. THE SPORTS
FACTORY.
  M. WATKINS, 441:12OCT75-44
DURUY, V. THE WORLD OF THE GREEKS.
  H.A. POHLSANDER, 124:MAY73-482
DURZAK, M., ED. HERMANN BROCH.
  E.F. GEORGE, 182:VOL26#5/6-163
  C.S. MERRILL, 406:SUMMER74-183
DURZAK, M. POESIE UND RATIO.*
  J. GLENN, 221(GQ):SEP73-158
DUŠANIĆ, S. ARKADSKI SAVEZ IV VEKA.
  J.A.O. LARSEN, 122:JUL73-224
DUSINBERRE, J. SHAKESPEARE & THE
NATURE OF WOMEN.
  A. BARTON, 617(TLS):24OCT75-1259
DÜSING, W. SCHILLERS IDEE DES
ERHABENEN.
  K.L. BERGHAHN, 406:WINTER74-401
DUSSART-DEBÈFVE, S. DIE SPRACHE DER
PREDIGTEN JOHANNES TAULERS NACH DER
WIENER HANDSCHRIFT NR. 2744.
  H. WELLMANN, 657(WW):MAR/APR73-140

DUSSLER, L. RAPHAEL.*
  L. BECHERUCCI, 90:JUL73-469
DUTENS, V-L. ORIGINE DES DÉCOUVERTS
  ATTRIBUÉES AUX MODERNES. (2ND ED)
  C. LIMOGES, 154:JUN73-380
DUTTON, B. - SEE DE BERCEO, G.
DUȚU, A. CĂRȚILE DE ÎNȚELEPCIUNE ÎN
  CULTURA ROMÂNĂ.*
  A. CIORANESCU, 549(RLC):OCT-DEC73-
  632
DUȚU, A. ESEU ÎN ISTORIA MODELELOR
  UMANE.
  J. AMSLER, 549(RLC):OCT-DEC73-624
DUȚU, A. & P. CERNOVODEANU, EDS.
  DIMITRIE CANTEMIR.
  E. TAPPE, 575(SEER):OCT74-631
DU VAL, F.A. & L.M. WIEDERHOLUNG
  UND FORTSETZUNG.
  S. BAUSCHINGER, 399(MLJ):MAR73-139
DUVAL, P. FOUR DECADES.*
  M. WILLIAMSON, 96:FEB/MAR73-86
DUVIGNAUD, J. L'EMPIRE DU MILIEU.
  N.L. GOODRICH, 207(FR):DEC72-441
DUVIGNAUD, J. LA SOCIOLOGIE.
  D. MERLLIÉ, 542:JAN-MAR73-53
DUVIGNAUD, J. THE SOCIOLOGY OF ART.
  R.J. LONGHURST, 89(BJA):SUMMER73-
  301
DUYTSCHAEVER, J. JAMES JOYCE.*
  A.M.L. KNUTH, 433:JAN73-109
DVORNIK, F. BYZANTINE MISSIONS
  AMONG THE SLAVS.*
  H.G. LUNT, 574(SEEJ):SUMMER72-269
  A. MOURATIDES, 104:SPRING74-156
DWOSKIN, S. FILM IS...
  R. COMBS, 617(TLS):28FEB75-221
DWYER, D.J., ED. ASIAN URBANIZATION.
  J. GOTTMANN, 617(TLS):17JAN75-58
  R. MURPHEY, 302:JAN73-190
DWYER, D.J., ED. THE CITY AS A CEN-
  TRE OF CHANGE IN ASIA.
  J. GOTTMANN, 617(TLS):17JAN75-58
DWYER, W.W.G. A STUDY OF WEBSTER'S
  USE OF RENAISSANCE NATURAL & MORAL
  PHILOSOPHY.
  C.K. SPIVACK, 568(SCN):FALL74-57
DWYER-JOYCE, A. THE MOONLIT WAY.
  M. LEVIN, 441:23FEB75-38
DYCE, A. THE REMINISCENCES OF ALEX-
  ANDER DYCE. (R.J. SCHRADER, ED)
  B.C.H., 191(ELN):SEP73(SUPP)-29
DYCE, J.R. PATRICK WHITE AS PLAY-
  WRIGHT.
  J.F. BURROWS, 71(ALS):MAY75-105
DYCK, J. - SEE NEUMARK, G.
DYCK, J.W. BORIS PASTERNAK.*
  D.L. PLANK, 574(SEEJ):SPRING73-85
  R.D.B. THOMSON, 575(SEER):JAN74-
  150
DYKHUIZEN, G. THE LIFE & MIND OF
  JOHN DEWEY.*
  P.F. BOLLER, JR., 584(SWR):SPRING
  74-197
DYKMANS, M. LES SERMONS DE JEAN
  XXII SUR LA VISION BÉATIFIQUE.
  B. SMALLEY, 382(MAE):1974/1-52
DYOS, H.J. & M. WOLFF, EDS. THE
  VICTORIAN CITY.*
  A. WELSH, 637(VS):JUN74-419
DYSON, A.E. BETWEEN TWO WORLDS.
  H. PESCHMANN, 175:SUMMER72-73
DYSON, A.E. THE INIMITABLE DICKENS.*
  L. LANE, JR., 594:SPRING73-125

EADIE, J.W., ED. THE CONVERSION OF
  CONSTANTINE.
  P. KERESZTES, 124:SEP72-51
EAGLE, D., WITH J. HAWKINS - SEE
  "THE OXFORD ILLUSTRATED DICTIONARY"
EAGLETON, T. EXILES & ÉMIGRÉS.
  295:FEB74-470
EAGLETON, T. MYTHS OF POWER.
  P. BEER, 362:13MAR75-348
EAGLETON, T.F. WAR & PRESIDENTIAL
  POWER.
  G.E. REEDY, 441:12JAN75-4
EAGLY, R.V. THE STRUCTURE OF CLASS-
  ICAL ECONOMIC THEORY.
  S. HOLLANDER, 617(TLS):1AUG75-870
EAMES, D. FAMILY STYLE.
  M. LEVIN, 441:28DEC75-20
EAMES, E.R. BERTRAND RUSSELL'S
  THEORY OF KNOWLEDGE.
  H. RUJA, 484(PPR):MAR74-440
EAMES, J.D. THE MGM STORY.
  R. SCHICKEL, 441:7DEC75-88
EAMES, W. EARLY NEW ENGLAND CATE-
  CHISMS.
  C. ISRAEL, 568(SCN):WINTER74-91
EARL, G.W. THE EASTERN SEAS.
  N. TARLING, 302:JUL73-268
EARLE, J.B.F. BLACK TOP.
  J. BUTT, 617(TLS):16MAY75-530
EARLE, P.G. PROPHET IN THE WILDER-
  NESS.*
  H. CASTILLO, 238:SEP73-738
  H. RODRÍGUEZ-ALCALÁ, 240(HR):SUM-
  MER73-580
EARLE, W. THE AUTOBIOGRAPHICAL
  CONSCIOUSNESS.
  K.R.M., 543:JUN73-751
EARLY, J. THE MAKING OF "GO DOWN,
  MOSES."*
  T. HELLER & C. CYGANOWSKI, 50(ARQ):
  SPRING73-78
  J.G. WATSON, 454:SPRING74-285
EARLY, R. THE JEALOUS EAR.
  639(VQR):WINTER74-VIII
EARLY, R. POWERS & DOMINATIONS.
  442(NY):24FEB75-140
"EARLY AMERICAN BOOKBINDINGS FROM
  THE COLLECTION OF MICHAEL PAPAN-
  TONIO."
  R.J. ROBERTS, 354:SEP73-253
EASSON, A. - SEE DICKENS, C.
EASSON, R.R. & R.N. ESSICK, EDS.
  WILLIAM BLAKE: BOOK ILLUSTRATOR.
  (VOL 1)
  I.H. CHAYES, 591(SIR):SPRING74-155
EAST, W.G., O.H.K. SPATE & C.A.
  FISHER, EDS. THE CHANGING MAP OF
  ASIA.
  J.E. SPENCER, 293(JAST):AUG73-683
EASTLAKE, C.L. A HISTORY OF THE
  GOTHIC REVIVAL. (J.M. CROOK, ED)
  P.F. NORTON, 576:MAR73-75
EASTLAKE, W. DANCERS IN THE SCALP
  HOUSE.
  P-L. ADAMS, 61:OCT75-110
  B. HANNAH, 441:12OCT75-43
EASTMAN, L.E. THE ABORTIVE REVOLU-
  TION.
  R. TERRILL, 441:15JUN75-10
EASTON, M. AUBREY & THE DYING
  LADY.*
  H. MAAS, 135:FEB73-138
  L. ORMOND, 90:FEB73-127

EATES, M. PAUL NASH.
  C. HARRISON, 592:NOV73-203
EATON, C.E. THE GIRL FROM IPANEMA.*
  L.T. LEMON, 502(PRS):SUMMER73-183
EATON, C.E. ON THE EDGE OF THE
  KNIFE.*
  J. DITSKY, 577(SHR):WINTER73-102
EATON, D. THE LETTERS OF DANIEL
  EATON TO THE THIRD EARL OF CARDI-
  GAN, 1725-1732. (J. WAKE & D.C.
  WEBSTER, EDS)
  C.J. RAWSON, 175:SPRING73-29
  H.L. SNYDER, 481(PQ):JUL73-347
  W.A. SPECK, 447(N&Q):NOV73-433
EATON, L.K. AMERICAN ARCHITECTURE
  COMES OF AGE.*
  D.J. COOLIDGE, 432(NEQ):JUN73-301
EAVES, R.G. HENRY VIII'S SCOTTISH
  DIPLOMACY, 1513-1524.*
  H.C. RANDALL, 577(SHR):SPRING73-
  230
EAVES, T.C.D. & B.D. KIMPEL. SAMUEL
  RICHARDSON.*
  M.C. BATTESTIN, 599:SPRING73-233
  G. BULLOUGH, 175:SUMMER72-70
  R. PAULSON, 594:SPRING73-110
  C. PONS, 189(EA):JUL-SEP73-296
  P. ROGERS, 447(N&Q):JUN73-234
EAYRS, J. IN DEFENCE OF CANADA.
  R.A. PRESTON, 529(QQ):SPRING73-123
EBERHART, M.G. DANGER MONEY.
  N. CALLENDAR, 441:9MAR75-24
EBERHART, R. FIELDS OF GRACE.*
  T. EAGLETON, 565:VOL14#2-74
  R.J. SMITH, 598(SOR):SPRING75-464
EBERLE, R.A. NOMINALISTIC SYSTEMS.*
  M. JUBIEN, 482(PHR):OCT73-540
EBERSOLE, F.B. THINGS WE KNOW.*
  E.B. GREENWOOD, 206:NOV73-601
EBY, C. "THAT DISGRACEFUL AFFAIR,"
  THE BLACK HAWK WAR.
  639(VQR):SPRING74-XLVIII
ECCLES, W.J. FRANCE IN AMERICA.*
  J.S. PRITCHARD, 529(QQ):SUMMER73-
  293
  102(CANL):SUMMER73-126
ECK, W. SENATOREN VON VESPASIAN BIS
  HADRIAN.*
  C.P. JONES, 24:SPRING74-89
  W.C. MC DERMOTT, 124:FEB73-303
  S.I. OOST, 122:APR73-154
ECKE, T.Y-H. CHINESE CALLIGRAPHY.
  J. HAY, 463:SPRING73-84
ECKERT, E.K. THE NAVY DEPARTMENT IN
  THE WAR OF 1812.
  C. MC KEE, 656(WMQ):OCT74-696
ECKMANN, J. CHAGATAY MANUAL.
  G.F. MEIER, 682(ZPSK):BAND26HEFT
  3/4-416
ECKMANN, J. THE DĪVĀN OF GADĀ'Ī.
  J.M. KELLY, 318(JAOS):JUL-SEP73-
  362
"ECLECTIC EVE."
  J. ZEMENS, 73:SUMMER74-38
ECO, U. EINFÜHRUNG IN DIE SEMIOTIK.
  M. RAUPACH, 430(NS):SEP73-497
ECONOMOU, G.D. THE GODDESS NATURA
  IN MEDIEVAL LITERATURE.*
  D.W. ROBERTSON, JR., 131(CL):
  SUMMER74-263
EDDINS, D. YEATS.*
  R.J. FINNERAN, 295:FEB74-835
  M. ROSE, 637(VS):MAR74-319
  J. RUNNELS, 125:OCT73-100

EDEL, L. HENRY JAMES.* (VOL 5:
  THE MASTER, 1901-1916.)
  M. ALLOTT, 541(RES):AUG73-365
  D. FLOWER, 184(EIC):JAN73-85
  R.S. MOORE, 579(SAQ):SPRING74-261
  295:FEB74-661
EDEL, L. - SEE JAMES, H.
EDEL, L. - SEE WILSON, E.
EDELMAN, M. DISRAELI RISING.
  S. MAITLAND, 362:6MAR75-318
  E.S. TURNER, 617(TLS):7MAR75-241
EDELSTEIN, L. & I.G. KIDD - SEE
  "POSIDONIUS"
EDEN, D. WINTERWOOD.
  E.M. EWING, 441:11MAY75-10
EDEN, M. CONQUEST BEFORE AUTUMN.
  A. APPENZELL, 102(CANL):AUTUMN73-
  95
EDGAR, I.I. SHAKESPEARE, MEDICINE
  & PSYCHIATRY.*
  M.W. BUNDY, 570(SQ):SUMMER73-336
EDGAR, W.B. - SEE PRINGLE, R.
EDGEWORTH, M. CASTLE RACKRENT [&]
  THE ABSENTEE.
  B. RUDDICK, 148:WINTER73-378
EDGEWORTH, M. MARIA EDGEWORTH: LET-
  TERS FROM ENGLAND, 1813-1844.* (C.
  COLVIN, ED)
  F.H.A. MICKLEWRIGHT, 447(N&Q):
  AUG73-312
  S. MONOD, 189(EA):APR-JUN73-228
EDIE, J.M., F.H. PARKER & C.O.
  SCHRAG, EDS. PATTERNS OF THE LIFE-
  WORLD.*
  W. HOROSZ, 484(PPR):SEP73-122
EDMANN, E. & G-B. DAHLBERG. URBAN-
  ISATION IN SWEDEN.
  P. HALL, 46:JAN73-79
EDMONDS, R. SOVIET FOREIGN POLICY
  1962-73.
  E. LUTTWAK, 617(TLS):21NOV75-1384
EDMONDSON, M. & A.D. COHEN. THE
  WOMEN OF WATERGATE.
  M.S. KENNEDY, 441:16NOV75-18
EDMONSON, M.S. LORE.
  E. ORING, 650(WF):OCT73-284
EDSON, C., ED. INSCRIPTIONES GRAE-
  CAE. (VOL 10, PT 2, FASC 1)
  M. VICKERS, 303:VOL93-242
EDSON, J.S. A SUPPLEMENT TO ORGAN
  PRELUDES.
  A. BOND, 415:DEC74-1048
EDWARDS, A. FLAWED WORDS & STUBBORN
  SOUNDS.*
  C. GAMER, 513:SPRING-SUMMER73-146
EDWARDS, A. JUDY GARLAND.
  C. LEHMANN-HAUPT, 441:12MAR75-39
  J. SEELYE, 231:JUN75-84
EDWARDS, C.T. PUBLIC FINANCES IN
  MALAYA & SINGAPORE.
  D.R. SNODGRASS, 293(JAST):NOV72-
  213
EDWARDS, G. - SEE CALDERÓN DE LA
  BARCA, P.
EDWARDS, I.E.S., C.J. GADD & N.G.L.
  HAMMOND, EDS. THE CAMBRIDGE AN-
  CIENT HISTORY. (VOL 1, PT 1) (3RD
  ED)
  C. ROEBUCK, 124:FEB73-305
EDWARDS, I.E.S., C.J. GADD & N.G.L.
  HAMMOND, EDS. THE CAMBRIDGE AN-
  CIENT HISTORY. (VOL 1, PT 2) (3RD
  ED)
  J. BOARDMAN, 123:MAR74-152
                          [CONTINUED]

EDWARDS, I.E.S., C.J. GADD & N.G.L.
HAMMOND, EDS. THE CAMBRIDGE AN-
CIENT HISTORY. (VOL 1, PT 2) (3RD
ED) [CONTINUING]
   J.D. MUHLY, 124:FEB73-307
   J.D. MUHLY, 318(JAOS):OCT-DEC73-
   576
EDWARDS, J. THE GREAT AWAKENING.
(C.C. GOEN, ED)
   E.M. GRIFFIN, 481(PQ):JUL73-498
   W.J. SCHEICK, 613:SUMMER73-309
EDWARDS, J. PERSONA NON GRATA.
   A. ANGELL, 617(TLS):3JAN75-18
EDWARDS, M., ED. FRENCH POETRY NOW.
   J. WEIGHTMAN, 362:11SEP73-348
EDWARDS, M. LA TRAGÉDIE RACINIENNE.
   I. BARKO, 67:MAY74-108
EDWARDS, M. & E. HOOVER. THE CHAL-
LENGE OF BEING SINGLE.
   A. NELSON, 441:6JUL75-4
EDWARDS, M.J., ED. THE EVOLUTION OF
CANADIAN LITERATURE IN ENGLISH
1867-1914.
   C. THOMAS, 102(CANL):SPRING74-86
EDWARDS, P. SHAKESPEARE & THE CON-
FINES OF ART.
   J.B. FORT, 189(EA):JAN-MAR73-87
   R. WARREN, 447(N&Q):APR73-154
EDWARDS, R.B. FREEDOM, RESPONSIBIL-
ITY & OBLIGATION.
   M. ADAM, 542:APR-JUN73-219
EDWARDS, S. REBEL!*
   P.F. BOLLER, JR., 584(SWR):SUMMER
   74-321
EDWARDS, S. GEORGE SAND.
   R. MERKER, 399(MLJ):SEP-OCT73-285
EDWARDS, T.R. IMAGINATION & POWER.*
   B.C.H., 191(ELN):SEP73(SUPP)-26
   R.W. UPHAUS, 141:WINTER74-73
   295:FEB74-390
EFRON, A. "DON QUIXOTE" & THE DUL-
CINEATED WORLD.*
   J.J. ALLEN, 241:SEP73-79
   E. SARMIENTO, 400(MLN):MAR73-444
EGAMI, N., T. ESAKA & K. AMAKASU.
THE BEGINNINGS OF JAPANESE ART.
   S. SITWELL, 39:DEC73-516
EGAN, M. HENRY JAMES: THE IBSEN
YEARS.
   G.B. TENNYSON, 445(NCF):SEP73-242
EGERTON, J. THE AMERICANIZATION OF
DIXIE.*
   R.F. DURDEN, 639(VQR):AUTUMN74-625
EGGAN, F. SOCIAL ORGANIZATION OF
THE WESTERN PUEBLOS.
   W. GARD, 584(SWR):WINTER74-98
EGGEBRECHT, H.H., ED. HANDWÖRTER-
BUCH DER MUSIKALISCHEN TERMINOLO-
GIE. (PT 2)
   J.A. WESTRUP, 410(M&L):APR74-240
EGGEBRECHT, H.H. & M. LÜTOLF, EDS.
STUDIEN ZUR TRADITION IN DER MUSIK.
   M. CARNER, 410(M&L):OCT74-494
EGGENSCHWILER, D. THE CHRISTIAN
HUMANISM OF FLANNERY O'CONNOR.*
   P.M. BROWNING, JR., 659:SPRING75-
   260
EGGERS, H., ED. DER VOLKSNAME
DEUTSCH.✝
   B. JEGERS, 221(GQ):NOV73-654
EGGERS, H. & OTHERS. ELEKTRONISCHE
SYNTAXANALYSE DER DEUTSCHEN GEGEN-
WARTSSPRACHE.
   F. GRUCZA, 353:15JUL73-102
                           [CONTINUED]

[CONTINUING]
   W. LENDERS, 680(ZDP):BAND92HEFT1-
   150
EGLER, A. DIE SPANIER IN DER LINKS-
RHEINISCHEN PFALZ 1620-32.
   A. GERLICH, 182:VOL26#13/14-507
EGLETON, C. SKIRMISH.
   N. CALLENDAR, 441:12OCT75-47
EGLI-HEGGLIN, A. LE THÈME DU
"TOTUM SIMUL" DANS L'OEUVRE DE
PAUL CLAUDEL.
   J.F. ERWIN, JR., 546(RR):MAR74-142
EHLE, J. THE CHANGING OF THE GUARD.
   A. BROYARD, 441:7JAN75-37
   M. LEVIN, 441:6APR75-16
EHLERS, J. HUGO VON ST. VIKTOR.
   R. FOLZ, 182:VOL26#19-687
EHMANN, W. PERFORMANCE PRACTICE OF
BACH'S MOTETS.
   W. EMERY, 415:AUG74-661
EHRE, M. OBLOMOV & HIS CREATOR.*
   639(VQR):SUMMER74-LXXXI
EHRENBERG, V. MAN, STATE & DEITY.
   O. MURRAY, 617(TLS):17JAN75-64
EHRENKREUTZ, A.S. SALADIN.
   H.E. MAYER, 589:OCT74-724
EHRENPREIS, I. JONATHAN SWIFT.
   P. ROBERTS, 447(N&Q):NOV73-430
EHRENZWEIG, A. THE PSYCHOANALYSIS
OF ARTISTIC VISION & HEARING.
   617(TLS):18JUL75-806
EHRISMANN, G. - SEE VON TRIMBERG, H.
EHRLICH, M. THE REINCARNATION OF
PETER PROUD.*
   N. CALLENDAR, 441:30MAR75-24
EHRLICH, M-F. L'APPRENTISSAGE VER-
BAL.
   H. JÖRG, 182:VOL26#19-641
EHRLICH, P.R. & A.H. THE END OF
AFFLUENCE.*
   B.G. MALKIEL, 441:26JAN75-19
EHRLICH, S. WEIHNACHT.
   J. KOPPENSTEINER, 221(GQ):JAN73-
   143
EIBEL, D. KAYAK SICKNESS.
   D. BESSAI, 102(CANL):SPRING74-124
EIBL, K. DIE SPRACHSKEPSIS IM WERK
GUSTAV SACKS.
   G. LOOSE, 221(GQ):MAR73-271
EICHHORN, H. DER STRUKTURWANDEL IM
GELDUMLAUF FRANKENS ZWISCHEN 1437
UND 1610.
   F. SPOONER, 182:VOL26#23/24-886
EICHHORN, W. HELDENSAGEN AUS DEM
UNTEREN YANGTSE-TAL (WU-YÜEH CH'UN-
CH'IU).
   K. TIETZE, 318(JAOS):APR-JUN73-212
EICHNER, H., ED. "ROMANTIC" & ITS
COGNATES.*
   M.I. BAYM, 613:WINTER73-534
   R.A. FOAKES, 149:DEC74-348
   F. JORDAN, 529(QQ):WINTER73-642
   W.T.S., 191(ELN):SEP73(SUPP)-164
   E. SHAFFER, 402(MLR):JUL74-610
EICHNER, H. FRIEDRICH SCHLEGEL.*
   M.H., 191(ELN):SEP73(SUPP)-157
EIGELDINGER, M. LA MYTHOLOGIE SOL-
AIRE DANS L'OEUVRE DE RACINE.
   B. CHÉDOZEAU, 535(RHL):SEP-OCT73-
   891
EIGNER, L. SELECTED POEMS. (S.
CHARTERS & A. WYATT, EDS)
   M. PERLBERG, 491:JUN75-172

EIKHENBAUM, B. O POEZII.
J-L. BACKÈS, 98:MAR73-237
EIKHENBAUM, B. THE YOUNG TOLSTOI.
A.F. ZWEERS, 104:WINTER74-588
EINBOND, B.L. SAMUEL JOHNSON'S
ALLEGORY.*
J.T. BOULTON, 179(ES):APR73-177
EINHARD. VITA KAROLI MAGNI. (E.S.
FIRCHOW & E.H. ZEYDEL, EDS & TRANS)
J.W. BINNS, 402(MLR):OCT74-838
EIS, G. FORSCHUNGEN ZUR FACHPROSA.*
V. GÜNTHER, 182:VOL26#9-284
EISELEY, L. ALL THE STRANGE HOURS.
P-L. ADAMS, 61:DEC75-118
W. STAFFORD, 441:23NOV75-36
A. WHITMAN, 441:18DEC75-43
EISELEY, L. THE INNOCENT ASSASSINS.
B. HOWARD, 491:APR75-44
P. RAMSEY, 569(SR):SPRING74-400
EISENDRATH, C.R. THE UNIFYING MOM-
ENT.
D.F.D., 543:DEC72-356
A.H. JOHNSON, 154:DEC73-721
EISENMANN, F. DIE SATZKONJUNKTIONEN
IN GESPROCHENER SPRACHE.
H-W. ROYE, 182:VOL26#19-672
EISLER, C. THE SEEING HAND.
442(NY):15DEC75-155
EISLER, L. MORALS WITHOUT MYSTERY.
L.B. CEBIK, 219(GAR):WINTER73-594
EISNER, E.W. EDUCATING ARTISTIC
VISION.
P. MEESON, 89(BJA):SPRING73-198
EISNER, L.H. MURNAU.
D. MARTIN, 200:NOV73-561
EISNER, S. THE TRISTAN LEGEND.
R.E. ROBERTS, 545(RPH):FEB74-414
EITNER, L. GERICAULT'S "RAFT OF THE
MEDUSA."
A. FORGE, 592:JUL-AUG73-50
G. LEVITINE, 56:WINTER73-421
M. ROSENTHAL, 135:JUN73-152
EKELÖF, G. SELECTED POEMS.*
J. DITSKY, 577(SHR):SUMMER73-346
Y.L. SANDSTROEM, 563(SS):WINTER74-
85
EKSTEINS, M. THE LIMITS OF REASON.
E.K. BRAMSTED, 617(TLS):10OCT75-
1182
ELDRIDGE, C.C. ENGLAND'S MISSION.
639(VQR):SUMMER74-XCVI
ELEY, L. TRANSZENDENTALE PHÄNOMEN-
OLOGIE UND SYSTEMTHEORIE DER
GESELLSCHAFT.
S.L. HART, 484(PPR):JUN74-617
ELEY, L. - SEE HUSSERL, E.
ELGEY, G. THE OPEN WINDOW.
N. ROBERTS, 617(TLS):4JUL75-741
ELGIN, S.H. WHAT IS LINGUISTICS?
J.S. FALK, 320(CJL):FALL74-171
M.C. FULLER, 399(MLJ):APR74-207
ELIADE, M. LE SACRÉ ET LE PROFANE.
C. SCHUWER, 542:JAN-MAR73-101
ELIASON, N.E. THE LANGUAGE OF
CHAUCER'S POETRY.*
C.A. OWEN, JR., 589:OCT74-727
ELIOT, T.S. SELECTED PROSE OF T.S.
ELIOT. (F. KERMODE, ED)
H. KENNER, 441:9NOV75-40
ELIOT, T.S. THE WASTE LAND.* (V.
ELIOT, ED)
W. EMPSON, 184(EIC):OCT72-417
J. PRESS, 189(EA):JAN-MAR73-80

ELKHADEM, S. AJNIHA MIN RASAS.
F. MOUSSA-MAHMOUD, 268:JAN75-69
ELKIN, P.K. THE AUGUSTAN DEFENCE OF
SATIRE.
M. CORDNER, 566:SPRING74-91
J.A. HAY, 67:MAY74-89
W. KINSLEY, 255:FALL73-331
D. NOKES, 402(MLR):JAN74-152
R. PAULSON, 301(JEGP):JAN74-125
C.J. RAWSON, 175:SUMMER73-75
E. ROSENHEIM, JR., 401(MLQ):JUN74-
201
ELKIN, S. SEARCHES & SEIZURES.*
B. ALLEN, 249(HUDR):SPRING74-119
ELKINS, R.E. MANOBO-ENGLISH DIC-
TIONARY.
J.L. FISCHER, 215(GL):VOL13#1-41
ELKINS, S. & E. MC KITRICK, EDS.
THE HOFSTADTER AEGIS.
D.H. DONALD, 31(ASCH):SUMMER75-508
ELLEDGE, S. & D. SCHIER, EDS. THE
CONTINENTAL MODEL. (REV)
H.T. BARNWELL, 208(FS):APR74-196
ELLENBOGEN, G. THE NIGHT UNSTONES.*
K.S. BYER, 219(GAR):SPRING73-110
ELLIN, S. STRONGHOLD.
N. CALLENDAR, 441:2MAR75-17
ELLIOT, A. THE BLOOM HIGH WAY.
E. BUTSCHER, 109:FALL/WINTER73/74-
131
ELLIOT, R. MYTHE ET LÉGENDE DANS
LE THÉÂTRE DE RACINE.*
B. CHÉDOZEAU, 535(RHL):SEP-OCT73-
891
ELLIOTT, B. & R. GOULDING. WRITE IF
YOU GET WORK.
T. HISS, 441:30NOV75-28
M. JANEWAY, 61:DEC75-118
ELLIOTT, G.P. CONVERSIONS.
395:FEB74-470
ELLIOTT, J. HEAVEN ON EARTH.
G. CLIFFORD, 617(TLS):7MAR75-241
S. MAITLAND, 362:6MAR75-318
ELLIOTT, J.L., ED. NATIVE PEOPLES.
R. LANDES, 529(QQ):SPRING73-116
ELLIOTT, R.C. THE SHAPE OF UTOPIA.*
J. GRADY, 447(N&Q):FEB75-80
ELLIOTT, S.L. GOING.
A. BROYARD, 441:5FEB75-37
T. LE CLAIR, 441:9FEB75-6
442(NY):10MAR75-119
ELLIOTT, W.E.Y. THE RISE OF GUARD-
IAN DEMOCRACY.
W. VAN ALSTYNE, 441:27APR75-6
ELLIS, G.M. - SEE "BOSO'S LIFE OF
ALEXANDER III"
ELLIS, J. & R. MOORE. SCHOOL FOR
SOLDIERS.*
M. HOWARD, 617(TLS):9MAY75-511
E.S. TURNER, 362:24APR75-538
ELLIS, J.J. THE NEW ENGLAND MIND IN
TRANSITION.*
N.S. FIERING, 656(WMQ):APR74-314
639(VQR):WINTER74-XXIV
ELLIS, J.M. KLEIST'S "PRINZ FRIED-
RICH VON HOMBURG."*
D.H. CROSBY, 221(GQ):SEP73-148
ELLIS, J.M. SCHILLER'S KALLIAS-
BRIEFE & THE STUDY OF HIS AESTHETIC
THEORY.
K.L. BERGHAHN, 406:WINTER74-401
ELLIS, J.M. THE THEORY OF LITERARY
CRITICISM.
G.S. ROUSSEAU, 617(TLS):5SEP75-985

106

ELLIS, J.R. & R.D. MILNS, EDS &
TRANS. THE SPECTRE OF PHILIP.*
D. KOONCE, 124:FEB73-303
ELLIS, K. CRITICAL APPROACHES TO
RUBÉN DARIO.
617(TLS):23MAY75-559
ELLIS, M. THE ADORATION OF THE
HANGED MAN.
A. MASSIE, 617(TLS):10OCT75-1217
ELLIS, P.B. HELL OR CONNAUGHT!
T.C. BARNARD, 617(TLS):25APR75-451
ELLIS, R.S. FOUNDATION DEPOSITS IN
ANCIENT MESOPOTAMIA.
G. VAN DRIEL, 318(JAOS):JAN-MAR73-
67
ELLISON, H. DEATHBIRD STORIES.
P. ADAMS, 61:MAR75-145
G. JONAS, 441:23MAR75-32
ELLISON, M. SUPPORT FOR SECESSION.
C.D. RICE, 637(VS):DEC73-233
ELLMANN, R. GOLDEN CODGERS.*
D.J. GORDON, 676(YR):SPRING74-424
M. MUDRICK, 249(HUDR):SUMMER74-303
569(SR):WINTER74-VIII
639(VQR):SPRING74-XLI
ELLMANN, R. ULYSSES ON THE LIFFEY.*
A. GOLDMAN, 541(RES):MAY73-242
R. GOTTFRIED, 454:SPRING74-277
C. HANSON, 148:SUMMER72-191
R.M. KAIN, 191(ELN):SEP73-74
A. MAC GILLIVRAY, 613:WINTER73-541
H. SERGEANT, 175:AUTUMN72-114
T.F. STALEY, 598(SOR):SUMMER75-725
295:FEB74-681
ELLMANN, R. - SEE JOYCE, J.
ELLMANN, R. & R. O'CLAIR, EDS. THE
NORTON ANTHOLOGY OF MODERN POETRY.
V. YOUNG, 249(HUDR):WINTER74/75-
597
ELLRODT, R. L'INSPIRATION PERSON-
NELLE ET L'ESPRIT DU TEMPS CHEZ LES
POÈTES MÉTAPHYSIQUES ANGLAIS. (PT
1, VOLS 1&2) (2ND ED)
E. MINER, 568(SCN):SPRING-SUMMER74-
8
ELLSWORTH, S.G. DEAR ELLEN.
D. BITTON, 651(WHR):AUTUMN74-398
ELLWOOD, R.S., JR. RELIGIOUS &
SPIRITUAL GROUPS IN MODERN AMERICA.
E. JORSTAD, 109:SPRING/SUMMER74-
150
ELON, A. HERZL.
A. KAZIN, 441:23FEB75-6
R.F. SHEPARD, 441:16MAY75-29
ELON, A. & S. HASSAN. BETWEEN ENE-
MIES.*
B. AVISHAI, 453:23JAN75-34
442(NY):13JAN75-94
ELON, F., D. HALPERN & G. MAYER.
TREBLE POETS 2.
J. FULLER, 617(TLS):7NOV75-1327
VAN ELS, T.J.M. THE KASSEL MANU-
SCRIPT OF BEDE'S "HISTORIA ECCLESI-
ASTICA GENTIS ANGLORUM" & ITS OLD
ENGLISH MATERIAL.*
O. ARNGART, 597(SN):VOL45#1-173
A.F. BERINGAUSE, 424:MAR73-51
J.D.A. OGILVY, 191(ELN):DEC73-121
EL JAFFAR, R.J. NOVEL TO ROMANCE.
R. MOORE, 268:JAN75-92
ELSEN, A.E. ORIGINS OF MODERN
SCULPTURE.
D. FARR, 617(TLS):25APR75-460

ELSEN, A.E. THE SCULPTURE OF HENRI
MATISSE.
C. GOLDSTEIN, 56:WINTER73-419
ELSOM, J. EROTIC THEATRE.*
C. BARLAS, 214:VOL6#24-107
A. SEYMOUR, 364:APR/MAY74-102
ELTON, G.R. POLICY & POLICE.
J.W. O'MALLEY, 377:JUL74-121
ELVERSON, V.T. & M.A. MC LANAHAN,
COMPS. A COOKING LEGACY.
R.A. SOKOLOV, 441:7DEC75-78
ELVIN, L. THE HARRISON STORY.*
P. WILLIAMS, 415:NOV74-950
ELWERT, W.T. LA POESIA LIRICA ITAL-
IANA DEL SEICENTO.
A.N. MANCINI, 400(MLN):JAN73-125
ELWERT, W.T. STUDIEN ZU DEN ROMAN-
ISCHEN SPRACHEN UND LITERATUREN.
(VOL 1)
G. COSTA, 545(RPH):NOV73-256
ELWERT, W.T. STUDIEN ZU DEN ROMAN-
ISCHEN SPRACHEN UND LITERATUREN.
(VOL 4)
D. RIEGER, 224(GRM):BAND23HEFT4-
497
ELWIN, M. LORD BYRON'S FAMILY.
(P. THOMSON, ED)
P. CONRAD, 617(TLS):29AUG75-962
R. MITCHISON, 362:23OCT75-548
ELWITT, S. THE MAKING OF THE THIRD
REPUBLIC.
J.P.T. BURY, 617(TLS):5SEP75-1001
ELWOOD, R. & R. SILVERBERG, EDS.
EPOCH.
G. JONAS, 441:14DEC75-28
ELY, D. MR. NICHOLAS.*
S. MAITLAND, 362:6MAR75-318
EMBREE, A.T. INDIA'S SEARCH FOR
NATIONAL IDENTITY.
R.W. JONES, 293(JAST):NOV72-180
EMBREE, L.E., ED. LIFE-WORLD & CON-
SCIOUSNESS.*
W. HOROSZ, 484(PPR):SEP73-122
EMECHETA, B. SECOND-CLASS CITIZEN.
M. JOHNSON, 617(TLS):31JAN75-102
M. LEVIN, 441:14SEP75-42
EMELINA, J. LES VALETS ET LES SER-
VANTES DANS LE THÉÂTRE COMIQUE EN
FRANCE DE 1610 À 1700.
P. FRANCE, 617(TLS):8AUG75-889
EMENEAU, M.B. TODA SONGS.*
F.A. DE CARO, 292(JAF):JAN-MAR73-
76
E.P. HAMP, 269(IJAL):JAN73-61
EMERSON, E., ED. MAJOR WRITERS OF
EARLY AMERICAN LITERATURE.*
H. PARKER, 173(ECS):SUMMER74-514
EMERSON, E.H. CAPTAIN JOHN SMITH.
R.E. AMACHER, 577(SHR):SPRING73-
220
R.B. DAVIS, 551(RENQ):WINTER73-487
EMERSON, J. A WEEK AS ANDREA BEN-
STOCK.
M. LEVIN, 441:19OCT75-46
EMERSON, R.W. THE JOURNALS & MIS-
CELLANEOUS NOTEBOOKS OF RALPH WALDO
EMERSON. (VOL 10) (M.M. SEALTS,
JR., ED)
W. STAEBLER, 27(AL):NOV74-400
639(VQR):SUMMER74-LXXXV
EMERSON, W. DIARIES & LETTERS OF
WILLIAM EMERSON, 1743-1776. (A.F.
EMERSON, ED)
T.B. ADAMS, 432(NEQ):JUN73-314

EMERY, L.F. BLACK DANCE IN THE
UNITED STATES FROM 1619 TO 1970.*
O. MAYNARD, 151:APR73-104
EMIG, J.A., J.T. FLEMING & H.M.
POPP, EDS. LANGUAGE & LEARNING.
(2ND ED)
R.J. SCHOLES, 660(WORD):DEC70-410
EMMANUEL, P. AUTOBIOGRAPHIES.
E. KUSHNER, 207(FR):APR73-1050
EMMANUEL, P. BAUDELAIRE.*
E.L. GANS, 188(ECR):WINTER73-366
EMMEL, H. GESCHICHTE DES DEUTSCHEN
ROMANS.* (VOL 1)
L.E. KURTH, 301(JEGP):APR74-308
EMMEL, T.C. BUTTERFLIES.
H.E. EVANS, 441:7DEC75-92
EMMER, P.C. ENGELAND, NEDERLAND,
AFRIKA EN DE SLAVENHANDEL IN DE
NEGENTIENDE EEUW.
C.R. BOXER, 617(TLS):28NOV75-1423
EMMERICK, R.E. SAKA GRAMMATICAL
STUDIES.
R.M. HARRIS, 353:15JUL73-109
EMMERSON, G.S. A SOCIAL HISTORY OF
SCOTTISH DANCE.*
T.M. FLETT, 595(SCS):VOL18-136
EMMERSON, J.K. ARMS, YEN & POWER.*
R. HALLORAN, 285(JAPQ):JUL-SEP73-
346
EMRICH, D. FOLKLORE ON THE AMERICAN
LAND.
R.M. DORSON, 650(WF):APR73-141
W.H. JANSEN, 292(JAF):APR-JUN73-
187
EMRICH, D., COMP. THE HODGEPODGE
BOOK.
C.W. JOYNER, 292(JAF):OCT-DEC73-
410
VON EMS, R. DER GUOTE GÊRHART.
(2ND ED) (J.A. ASHER, ED)
J.S. GROSECLOSE, 406:SUMMER74-216
EMY, H.V. LIBERALS, RADICALS &
SOCIAL POLITICS 1892-1914.
P. STANSKY, 637(VS):MAR74-330
ENCRENAZ, O. & J. RICHER. VIVANTE
ÉTOILE.
N. RINSLER, 208(FS):OCT74-475
G. SCHAEFFER, 535(RHL):NOV-DEC73-
1095
"ENCYCLOPEDIA LITUANICA." (VOLS 1&2)
V.J. ZEPS, 574(SEEJ):SPRING73-115
ENDERTON, H.B. A MATHEMATICAL IN-
TRODUCTION TO LOGIC.
J.R. SHOENFIELD, 316:JUN73-340
ENDO, S. WONDERFUL FOOL.*
J. MELLORS, 364:APR/MAY74-135
ENDRES, M. THE APPLICABILITY OF
WORD FIELD THEORY TO THE INTELLEC-
TUAL VOCABULARY IN GOTTFRIED VON
STRASSBURG'S "TRISTAN."
G.F. JONES, 400(MLN):APR73-623
ENDRES, M. WORD FIELD & WORD CON-
TENT IN MIDDLE HIGH GERMAN.
W.T.H. JACKSON, 406:SUMMER74-193
ENDZELĪNS, J. JĀNIS ENDZELĪNS' COM-
PARATIVE PHONOLOGY & MORPHOLOGY OF
THE BALTIC LANGUAGES.
A. GĀTERS, 343:BAND16HEFT2-222
V.J. ZEPS, 350:SEP74-586
LORD ENERGLYN. THROUGH THE CRUST OF
THE EARTH.
K. DUNHAM, 617(TLS):3JAN75-7

VAN DER ENG, J. & J.M. MEIJER.
"THE BROTHERS KARAMAZOV" BY F.M.
DOSTOEVSKIJ.
T. PACHMUSS, 574(SEEJ):SUMMER72-
231
ENGEL, B.A. & C.N. ROSENTHAL, EDS &
TRANS. FIVE SISTERS.
A. KELLY, 453:17JUL75-20
ENGEL, M. THE HONEYMAN FESTIVAL.
JOANNE.
L. BURTON & D. MORLEY, 99:SEP75-57
ENGEL, M. MONODROMOS.
A. THOMAS, 102(CANL):SUMMER74-79
ENGEL, M. ONE WAY STREET.
J. MELLORS, 362:23JAN75-126
S. MILLAR, 617(TLS):24JAN75-73
ENGEL, M., ED. USES OF LITERATURE.*
R. MACKSEY, 400(MLN):DEC73-1337
ENGEL, S.M. WITTGENSTEIN'S DOCTRINE
OF THE TYRANNY OF LANGUAGE.*
R.A. SHINER, 154:MAR73-161
ENGELBERG, E. THE UNKNOWN DIS-
TANCE.*
N.A. FURNESS, 402(MLR):OCT74-836
H.W. PUPPE, 406:WINTER74-431
ENGELS, H.W. GEDICHTE UND LIEDER
DEUTSCHER JAKOBINER.*
G. CARR, 402(MLR):APR74-460
J. HERMAND, 406:WINTER74-438
ENGELS, J., COMP. STUDIES IN "PAT-
ERSON."
S. FERGUSON, 219(GAR):SUMMER73-291
ENGELSING, R. DER BÜRGER ALS LESER.
W.H. BRUFORD, 617(TLS):10OCT75-
1209
ENGELSING, R., ED. DEUTSCHE BÜCHER-
PLAKATE DES 17. JAHRHUNDERTS.
H-J. KOPPITZ, 182:VOL26#15/16-516
ENGEN, R.K. WALTER CRANE AS A BOOK
ILLUSTRATOR.
617(TLS):28FEB75-222
ENGLAND, R. WALLS OF MALTA.
E. HAPPOLD, 46:JUL73-64
ENGLE, H-L.N. & P. - SEE MAO TSE-
TUNG
ENGLEKIRK, J.E. & OTHERS, EDS. AN
ANTHOLOGY OF SPANISH AMERICAN LIT-
ERATURE. (2ND ED)
M.A. SALGADO, 238:MAY73-533
ENGLER, R. - SEE DE SAUSSURE, F.
ENGLISH, H.E., B.W. WILKINSON & H.C.
EASTMAN. CANADA IN A WIDER ECONOM-
IC COMMUNITY.
G. TEEPLE, 529(QQ):SUMMER73-274
ENGLISH, J. - SEE HUSSERL, E.
"ENGLISH LITERATURE 1660-1800: A
BIBLIOGRAPHY OF MODERN STUDIES."*
(VOLS 5&6) (G.S. ALLEMAN & OTHERS,
COMPS)
H.C. WOODBRIDGE, 517(PBSA):JAN-MAR
74-83
ENGUÍDANOS, M. - SEE BORGES, J.L.
ENKVIST, N.E. LINGUISTIC STYLIS-
TICS.
M. STEINMANN, JR., 290(JAAC):WIN-
TER74-222
ENNAN, E. & G. WIEGELMANN, EDS.
FESTSCHRIFT MATTHIAS ZENDER.
B. GUNDA, 203:SUMMER73-170
ENOCH, P. HABET USHMA. (PT 2)
W. CHOMSKY, 399(MLJ):MAR74-144
ENRIGHT, D.J. DAUGHTERS OF EARTH.
A. CLUYSENAAR, 565:VOL14#1-70

ENRIGHT, D.J. SAD IRES.
  J. BAYLEY, 362:20NOV75-681
ENRIGHT, D.J. SHAKESPEARE & THE
STUDENTS.
  J. BAYLEY, 184(EIC):JUL72-283
  M. HINMAN, 570(SQ):SUMMER73-337
ENRIGHT, D.J. THE TERRIBLE SHEARS.*
  H. VENDLER, 441:6APR75-4
ENSINK, J. & P. GAEFFKE, EDS. INDIA
MAJOR.
  M.J. DRESDEN, 318(JAOS):OCT-DEC73-
  600
ENSLIN, T. ETUDES.
  J. HOPPER, 661:SUMMER73-113
ENSLIN, T. VIEWS.
  P. RAMSEY, 569(SR):SPRING74-397
ENSMINGER, D. RURAL INDIA IN TRAN-
SITION.
  R.W. VOLCKMANN, 293(JAST):FEB73-
  346
ENSOR, A. MARK TWAIN & THE BIBLE.
  W.R. PATRICK, 577(SHR):SPRING73-
  221
ENTERLINE, J.R. VIKING AMERICA.*
  H. BESSASON, 255(HAB):SPRING73-123
ENTHOVEN, J-P. - SEE COMTE, A.
ENTRALGO, P.L. - SEE LAÍN ENTRALGO,
P.
"ENTRETIENS SUR L'ANTIQUITÉ CLASS-
IQUE."* (VOL 15: LUCAIN.) (O. REV-
ERDIN, ED)
  F.M. WASSERMANN, 121(CJ):APR/MAY
  74-380
EOFF, S.H. & N. RAMÍREZ. COMPOSI-
CIÓN-CONVERSACIÓN.
  H.B. RAYMOND, 238:DEC73-1144
  L. SOTO-RUIZ, 238:SEP73-755
  I.E. STANISLAWCZYK, 238:SEP73-754
EPHRON, N. CRAZY SALAD.
  A. BROYARD, 441:27JUN75-39
  A. NELSON, 441:13JUL75-5
EPP, F.H. MENNONITES IN CANADA,
1786-1920.
  H. PALMER, 99:DEC75/JAN76-42
EPSTEIN, D.G. BRASÍLIA.
  J.E. BURCHARD, 639(VQR):WINTER74-
  138
EPSTEIN, D.M. NO VACANCIES IN HELL.
  J.J. MC GANN, 491:OCT74-44
  M. MADIGAN, 385(MQR):SPRING75-220
  P. RAMSEY, 569(SR):SPRING74-404
  639(VQR):SUMMER74-LXXXV
EPSTEIN, E.J. BETWEEN FACT & FIC-
TION.
  M. JANEWAY, 61:NOV75-122
  J. FALLOWS, 441:2NOV75-5
EPSTEIN, E.J. NEWS FROM NOWHERE.
  I. DILLIARD, 639(VQR):WINTER74-121
  W.L. MILLER, 676(YR):WINTER74-305
EPSTEIN, E.L. THE ORDEAL OF STEPHEN
DEDALUS.*
  A. GOLDMAN, 541(RES):MAY73-242
  D. HAYMAN, 141:FALL72-401
EPSTEIN, F.T. GERMANY & THE EAST.
(R.F. BYRNES, ED)
  J.W. HIDEN, 575(SEER):OCT74-633
  R.G. WESSON, 550(RUSR):OCT73-451
  D. WILSON, 575(SEER):OCT74-634
EPSTEIN, J. DIVORCED IN AMERICA.*
(BRITISH TITLE: DIVORCE.)
  E. TENNANT, 362:3APR75-453
EPSTEIN, L. P.D. KIMERAKOV.
  D. BROMWICH, 441:10AUG75-6

EPSTEIN, W.H. JOHN CLELAND.
  D.J. ENRIGHT, 617(TLS):4APR75-352
EPTON, N. VICTORIA & HER DAUGHTERS.
  R.C. TOBIAS, 637(VS):DEC73-211
ERART, J. LES POÉSIES DE JEHAN
ERART. (T. NEWCOMBE, ED)
  L.M. PATERSON, 382(MAE):1974/3-284
"ÉRASME, L'ALSACE ET SON TEMPS."
  J. CHOMARAT, 535(RHL):NOV-DEC73-
  1057
ERATH, W. DIE DICHTUNG DES LYGDA-
MUS.
  A. ERNOUT, 555:VOL47FASC1-161
  E.J. KENNEY, 123:MAR74-138
ERBSE, H. BEITRÄGE ZUM VERSTÄNDNIS
DER "ODYSSEE."
  F.M. COMBELLACK, 122:OCT74-299
ERBSE, H., ED. SCHOLIA GRAECA IN
HOMERI ILIADEM (SCHOLIA VETERA).
(VOL 2)
  F.M. COMBELLACK, 122:OCT74-298
  G.L. KONIARIS, 24:WINTER74-410
  S. WEST, 123:NOV74-190
ERDMAN, D.V. & J.E. GRANT, EDS.
BLAKE'S VISIONARY FORMS DRAMATIC.*
  D. HIRST, 541(RES):FEB73-95
  M. PRAZ, 179(ES):OCT73-516
  M.F. SCHULZ, 173(ECS):FALL73-120
ERDMAN, D.V., WITH D.K. MOORE - SEE
BLAKE, W.
ERDMANN, J.E. PHILOSOPHIE DER NEU-
ZEIT, DER DEUTSCHE IDEALISMUS.
  R. MALTER, 342:BAND64HEFT2-268
ERDMANN, K. DIE KUNST IRANS ZUR
ZEIT DER SASSANIDEN.
  P. HARPER, 57:VOL35#1/2-172
ERICKSON, C. INVISIBLE IMMIGRANTS.
  H. MALCHOW, 637(VS):SEP73-106
  W.W. WASSON, 14:JUL73-418
ERICKSON, C.T. THE ANGLO-NORMAN
TEXT OF "LE LAI DU COR."
  J.B. BESTON, 67:NOV74-236
ERIKSON, E.H. GANDHI'S TRUTH.
  F. WYLIE, 293(JAST):MAY73-526
ERIKSON, E.H. LIFE HISTORY & THE
HISTORICAL MOMENT.
  M. BERMAN, 441:30MAR75-1
  F. CREWS, 453:16OCT75-9
ERLER, A. & E. KAUFMANN, EDS. HAND-
WÖRTERBUCH ZUR DEUTSCHEN RECHTSGE-
SCHICHTE. (LIEFERUNGEN 8&9)
  H. WOLF, 657(WW):JAN/FEB73-71
ERLER, A. & E. KAUFMANN, WITH W.
STAMMLER, EDS. HANDWÖRTERBUCH ZUR
DEUTSCHEN RECHTSGESCHICHTE. (VOL 1)
  R. SCHMIDT-WIEGAND, 680(ZDP):BAND
  92HEFT2-313
ERNST, G. EINFÜHRUNGSKURS ITALIEN-
ISCH.* (2ND ED)
  B. WINKLEHNER, 430(NS):APR73-237
ERNST, J.A. MONEY & POLITICS IN
AMERICA 1755-1775.
  S. BRUCHEY, 656(WMQ):OCT74-673
  J.A. SCHUTZ, 432(NEQ):SEP74-489
  639(VQR):SPRING74-XLV
ERNY, P. LES 1ERS PAS DANS LA VIE
DE L'ENFANT D'AFRIQUE NOIRE.
  E. DAMMANN, 182:VOL26#3/4-78
ERPEL, F. DIE SELBSTBILDNISSE VIN-
CENT VAN GOGHS. (REV)
  R. PICKVANCE, 90:MAR73-177
ERREN, M. - SEE ARATUS
ERRINGTON, R.M. THE DAWN OF EMPIRE.
  C.G. STARR, 124:SEP-OCT73-51

ERTÉ. THINGS I REMEMBER.
G. ANNAN, 617(TLS):12SEP75-1014
ERWIN, E. THE CONCEPT OF MEANING-
LESSNESS.*
E.R. MAC CORMAC, 486:JUN73-324
ESCARPIT, R. BOGEN OG LAESEREN.
H. BOLL-JOHANSEN, 172(EDDA):1973/4-
253
VON ESCHENBACH, W. WILLEHALM. (6TH
ED) (K. LACHMANN, ED) WILLEHALM,
TITUREL. (W.J. SCHRÖDER & G. HOL-
LANDT, EDS)
W.S. LIPTON, 221(GQ):NOV73-651
ESCHENBURG, R. ÖKONOMISCHE THEORIE
DER GENOSSENSCHAFTLICHEN ZUSAMMEN-
ARBEIT.
G. ASCHHOFF, 182:VOL26#9-280
ESCHKER, W., ED & TRANS. MAZEDON-
ISCHE VOLKSMÄRCHEN.
E. ETTLINGER, 203:SPRING73-81
V. MILAK, 196:BAND14HEFT1/2-160
ESHLEMAN, C. COILS.
M.G. PERLOFF, 659:WINTER75-84
ESKENAZI, G. THE FASTEST SPORT.
M. RICHLER, 441:5JAN75-6
ESPANTOSO FOLEY, A. OCCULT ARTS &
DOCTRINE IN THE THEATER OF JUAN
RUIZ DE ALARCÓN.
O. BRENES, 400(MLN):MAR73-453
ESPINOSA, A.M., JR., R.L. FRANKLIN
& K.A. MUELLER. CULTURA HISPÁNICA.
R.V. TESCHNER, 399(MLJ):SEP-OCT74-
291
ESPINOZA, G. LOS CORTEJOS DEL
DIABLO.
E. ECHEVARRÍA, 238:SEP73-741
ESPY, W.R. AN ALMANAC OF WORDS AT
PLAY.
A. WHITMAN, 441:6DEC75-27
ESSLER, W.K. INDUKTIVE LOGIK.
A. MERCIER, 182:VOL26#30-716
ESSLER, W.K. WISSENSCHAFTSTHEORIE.
A. MERCIER, 182:VOL26#11/12-389
ESSLIN, M. BRECHT.
H. GLADE, 221(GQ):MAY73-454
ESSLIN, M. THE PEOPLED WOUND.*
S.H. GALE, 114(CHIR):VOL25#1-177
K.T. VON ROSADOR, 72:BAND211HEFT
1/3-164
J.M. WARNER, 295:FEB74-748
ESTERMANN, C. A VIDA ECONOMICA DOS
BANTOS DO SUDOESTE DE ANGOLA.
A.C. EDWARDS, 69:APR73-178
ESTÈVE, M., ED. ÉTUDES BERNANO-
SIENNES, 11. ÉTUDES BERNANOSIENNES,
12.
R.J. NORTH, 208(FS):APR74-227
ESTRADA, F.L. - SEE UNDER LÓPEZ
ESTRADA, F.
"ESTUDIOS SOBRE GUSTAVO ADOLFO
BÉCQUER."
J.H. HARTSOOK, 402(MLR):APR74-442
ETCHERELLI, C. A PROPOS DE CLÉ-
MENCE.
Y. GUERS-VILLATE, 207(FR):DEC72-
442
ETHEREGE, G. LETTERS OF SIR GEORGE
ETHEREGE.* (F. BRACHER, ED)
639(VQR):AUTUMN74-CXXXI
ETMEKJIAN, J. & R.J. CAEFER. SPOKEN
& WRITTEN FRENCH IN REVIEW.
B. EBLING, 207(FR):MAY73-1260
H.L. ROBINSON, 399(MLJ):DEC73-444

ETS, M.H. ROSA - THE LIFE OF AN
ITALIAN IMMIGRANT.
E.S. FALBO, 275(IQ):SPRING74-67
ETTINGHAUSEN, H. FRANCISCO DE QUE-
VEDO & THE NEOSTOIC MOVEMENT.
R.M. PRICE, 402(MLR):JAN74-204
"ETUDES BAUDELAIRIENNES II."
R.T. CARGO, 207(FR):MAY73-1229
"ÉTUDES BERNANOSIENNES." (VOLS 11
& 12)
C. LEPINEUX, 535(RHL):NOV-DEC73-
1114
D.W. STEEDMAN, 207(FR):DEC72-426
"ÉTUDES CLAUDÉLIENNES NO. 7."
A. BLANC, 535(RHL):JAN-FEB73-155
"ÉTUDES MONGOLES." (CAHIER 2) (E.
LOT-FALCK & OTHERS, EDS)
D.M. FARQUHAR, 244(HJAS):VOL33-260
"ETUDES PROUSTIENNES 2."
M. MEIN, 617(TLS):18APR75-436
EULER, L. & T. MAYER. THE EULER-
MAYER CORRESPONDENCE (1751-1755).
(E.G. FORBES, ED)
G. CARABELLI, 548(RCSF):JAN-MAR73-
113
EURIPIDES. ANDROMACHE. (P.T.
STEVENS, ED)
P. CHANTRAINE, 555:VOL47FASC1-131
EURIPIDES. THE "BACCHAE" BY EURIP-
IDES.* (G.S. KIRK, ED & TRANS)
D.S. CARNE-ROSS, 5:VOL1#3-538
EURIPIDES. IPHIGENEIA IN TAURIS.*
(R. LATTIMORE, TRANS) HIPPOLYTOS.*
(R. BAGG, TRANS)
G.E. DIMOCK, JR., 676(YR):SUMMER
74-573
EURIPIDES. TROADES. (W. BIEHL, ED)
P. CHANTRAINE, 555:VOL47FASC1-130
L. GOLDEN, 124:APR73-428
EUSTATHIUS. EUSTATHII ARCHIEPISCOPI
THESSALONICENSIS "COMMENTARII AD
HOMERI ILIADEM PERTINENTES." (VOL
1) (M. VAN DER VALK, ED)
F.M. COMBELLACK, 122:JAN73-72
N.G. WILSON, 123:NOV74-188
EVANIER, D. THE SWINGING HEADHUNT-
ER.
L. VERNON, 102(CANL):AUTUMN74-115
EVANS, D. THE POLITICS OF TRADE.
G. BARRACLOUGH, 453:7AUG75-24
D. ROBERTSON, 617(TLS):17JAN75-54
EVANS, E. - SEE TERTULLIAN
EVANS, E.N. THE PROVINCIALS.
639(VQR):SPRING74-XLVIII
EVANS, G. THE LIFE OF BEETLES.
G.E.J. NIXON, 617(TLS):3OCT75-1122
EVANS, G.E. THE DAYS THAT WE HAVE
SEEN.
P. HORN, 617(TLS):19DEC75-1512
J. MAPPLEBECK, 362:17JUL75-93
EVANS, G.L. - SEE UNDER LLOYD EVANS,
G.
EVANS, H., B. JACKMAN & M. OTTAWAY.
WE LEARNED TO SKI.
W.F. BUCKLEY, JR., 441:9NOV75-4
EVANS, J. MONASTIC ICONOGRAPHY IN
FRANCE FROM THE RENAISSANCE TO THE
REVOLUTION.*
K. BERGER, 551(RENQ):SPRING73-38
EVANS, J.A.S. PROCOPIUS.
J.W. BARKER, 589:APR74-330
A. CAMERON, 313:VOL63-298

EVANS, M. SPENSER'S ANATOMY OF
HEROISM.*
  H. BOYD, 180(ESA):SEP73-108
  W.C. JOHNSON, 179(ES):AUG72-354
EVANS, P. THE EARLY TROPE REPERTORY
OF SAINT MARTIAL DE LIMOGES.*
  S. FULLER, 317:SPRING73-155
EVENSON, N. TWO BRAZILIAN CAPITALS.
  J.E. BURCHARD, 639(VQR):WINTER74-
  138
EVERETT, B. DONNE.
  H. SERGEANT, 175:SPRING73-28
EVERETT, B. - SEE SHAKESPEARE, W.
EVERETT, T.H. 101 FLOWERING HOUSE
PLANTS ANYONE CAN GROW.
  J. CANADAY, 441:13APR75-16
EVERS, H-D. MONKS, PRIESTS & PEAS-
ANTS.
  D.K. SWEARER, 318(JAOS):OCT-DEC73-
  604
EVERSON, W.K. CLASSICS OF THE
HORROR FILM.
  E. KORN, 617(TLS):28FEB75-220
EVERSON, W.K. A PICTORIAL HISTORY
OF THE WESTERN FILM.
  M. TORME, 441:19OCT75-6
EVITTS, W.J. A MATTER OF ALLEGI-
ANCES.
  W.R. BROCK, 617(TLS):13JUN75-649
EVOE - SEE UNDER KNOX, E.V.
EVOLA, J. LE YOGA TANTRIQUE.
  A. BHARATI, 485(PE&W):JAN-APR73-
  265
EWART, G., Z. GHOSE & B.S. JOHNSON.
PENGUIN MODERN POETS 25.
  J. FULLER, 617(TLS):21FEB75-187
EWEN, D. THE NEW ENCYCLOPEDIA OF
THE OPERA.
  J.A. WESTRUP, 410(M&L):APR74-242
EXLEY, F. A FAN'S NOTES.
  R. SALE, 453:26JUN75-37
EXLEY, F. PAGES FROM A COLD ISLAND.
  A. KAZIN, 441:20APR75-4
  C. LEHMANN-HAUPT, 441:11APR75-41
  R. SALE, 453:26JUN75-37
EYCHENNE, E. DRUGSTORE.
  L. RIÈSE, 207(FR):FEB73-658
EYKMAN, C. GESCHICHTSPESSIMISMUS
IN DER DEUTSCHEN LITERATUR DES
ZWANZIGSTEN JAHRHUNDERTS.*
  N. RITTER, 221(GQ):JAN73-96
"EYRBYGGJA SAGA." (H. PÁLSSON & P.
EDWARDS, TRANS)
  K. HUME, 301(JEGP):OCT74-576
EZORSKY, G., ED. PHILOSOPHICAL PER-
SPECTIVES ON PUNISHMENT.
  J. KLEINIG, 63:MAY74-79
EŽOV, I.S. & E.I. ŠAMURIN. RUSSKAJA
POÈZIJA XX VEKA.
  E. BRISTOL, 574(SEEJ):SPRING73-82

FABER, R. FRENCH & ENGLISH.
  C.H. SISSON, 617(TLS):7NOV75-1321
FABER, R. NOVALIS.
  D.B. SANFORD, 221(GQ):NOV73-616
VON FABER DU FAUR, C. GERMAN BAR-
OQUE LITERATURE. (VOL 2)
  M.G. FLAHERTY, 222(QR):NOV73-321
MADAME FABIA. THE BOOK OF FORTUNE
TELLING.
  C. TENNANT, 617(TLS):17JAN75-50

FABIAN, J. JAMAA.
  R.G. WILLIS, 69:APR73-163
FABRE, M. THE UNFINISHED QUEST OF
RICHARD WRIGHT.
  B. JACKSON, 27(AL):NOV74-412
FÀBREGAS, X. ÀNGEL GUIMERÀ, LES
DIMENSIONS D'UN MITE.
  A. YATES, 86(BHS):OCT73-417
FABVRE, B. RACINES MONTAGNAISES.
  J. HEWSON, 269(IJAL):JUL73-191
FACKENHEIM, E.L. THE RELIGIOUS
DIMENSION IN HEGEL'S THOUGHT.
  A. QUINTON, 453:29MAY75-34
  W.H. WALSH, 479(PHQ):JAN73-77
FAENSEN, H. & V. IVANOV. EARLY
RUSSIAN ARCHITECTURE.
  T. TALBOT-RICE, 617(TLS):28MAR75-
  330
FAFOURNOUX, L. L'ABBAYE DE GRAND
VENT.
  B.J. BUCKNALL, 207(FR):DEC72-444
FAGG, W., ED. THE LIVING ARTS OF
NIGERIA.*
  K.P. KENT, 2:SPRING74-84
  R.M. QUINN, 50(ARQ):WINTER73-366
  M.A. TWINING, 292(JAF):OCT-DEC73-
  409
FAHERTY, W.B. DREAM BY THE RIVER.
  J.B. MC GLOIN, 377:NOV74-180
FÄHNDERS, W., H. KARRENBROCK & M.
RECTOR - SEE JUNG, F.
FÄHNDERS, W. & M. RECTOR. LINKSRAD-
IKALISMUS UND LITERATUR.
  P. LABANYI, 617(TLS):25JUL75-855
FAIDIT, U. THE "DONATZ PROENSALS"
OF UC FAIDIT. (J.H. MARSHALL, ED)
  F.M. CHAMBERS, 545(RPH):AUG73-83
DU FAIL, N. - SEE UNDER NOËL DU FAIL
DE LA FAILLE, J.B. THE WORKS OF
VINCENT VAN GOGH. (REV)
  R. PICKVANCE, 90:MAR73-174
FAIN, J.T. & T.D. YOUNG - SEE DAVID-
SON, D. & A. TATE
FAINLIGHT, R. THE REGION'S VIO-
LENCE.
  R. LATTIMORE, 249(HUDR):AUTUMN74-
  470
FAIR, C. THE NEW NONSENSE.
  442(NY):24FEB75-143
FAIRBANK, J.K., ED. THE MISSIONARY
ENTERPRISE IN CHINA & AMERICA.
  M. FREEDMAN, 617(TLS):13JUN75-671
FAIRBANKS, H.G. LOUISE IMOGEN
GUINEY.
  A.W. WILLIAMS, 432(NEQ):DEC73-647
FAIRBROTHER, N. THE NATURE OF LAND-
SCAPE DESIGN.
  G. JELLICOE, 617(TLS):20JUN75-703
FAIRFAX, G. THE ARCHITECTURE OF
HONOLULU.
  J.M. NEIL, 576:DEC73-347
FAIRFIELD, R. COMMUNES USA.
  N.A. BRITTIN, 577(SHR):SUMMER73-
  350
FAIRLEY, J. THE LION RIVER.
  L.F.R. WILLIAMS, 617(TLS):6JUN75-
  632
FAIRLIE, H. THE KENNEDY PROMISE.
  H.B. GOW, 396(MODA):SPRING74-210
FAIRMAN, H.W., ED & TRANS. THE TRI-
UMPH OF HORUS.
  639(VQR):AUTUMN74-CXXX
FAISANO, G. "LES TRAGIQUES."
  S. BORTON, 207(FR):FEB73-605

FAIZ, F.A. POEMS BY FAIZ.
A. SCHIMMEL, 318(JAOS):OCT-DEC73-
568
FAJEN, F. ÜBERLIEFERUNGSGESCHICHT-
LICHE UNTERSUCHUNGEN ZU DEN "HALIE-
UTIKA" DES OPPIAN.
D.F. JACKSON, 121(CJ):OCT/NOV72-80
FALCK, C. BACKWARDS INTO THE SMOKE.
J. MARTIN, 491:MAY75-103
FALEN, J.E. ISAAC BABEL.
V.D. MIHAILOVICH, 268:JUL75-188
FALK, J.D. JOHANN DANIEL FALKS
BEARBEITUNG DES AMPHITRYON-STOFFES.*
(H. SEMBDNER, ED)
I.F., 191(ELN):SEP73(SUPP)-149
N.H. SMITH, 182:VOL26#5/6-167
J. VOISINE, 549(RLC):JUL-SEP73-480
W. WITTKOWSKI, 406:SPRING74-102
FALK, S.J. QAJAR PAINTINGS.
P.N. ALLEN, 463:WINTER73-439
FALKIRK, R. BLACKSTONE & THE
SCOURGE OF EUROPE.
N. CALLENDAR, 441:5JAN75-24
FALKUS, M.E. THE INDUSTRIALIZATION
OF RUSSIA, 1700-1914.
A. KAHAN, 575(SEER):APR74-292
FALLON, P. POEMS.
J. MONTAGUE, 617(TLS):4JUL75-718
FALQUE, E. VOYAGE ET TRADITION.
M. LAFFRANQUE, 542:JAN-MAR73-81
FÄLT, G. TRES PROBLEMAS DE CONCOR-
DANCIA VERBAL EN EL ESPAÑOL MODER-
NO.
J.C. DAVIS, 238:DEC73-1139
FANKHAUSER, G. VERFREMDUNG ALS
STILMITTEL VOR UND BEI BRECHT.
R. MANTLE, 220(GL&L):JUL74-329
FANSELAU, R. DIE ORGEL IM WERK
EDWARD ELGARS.
C. KENT, 415:AUG74-661
FANSHAWE, D. AFRICAN SANCTUS.
J. BLACKING, 617(TLS):15AUG75-917
FANTHAM, E. COMPARATIVE STUDIES IN
REPUBLICAN LATIN IMAGERY.
F.O. COPLEY, 124:SEP-OCT73-43
"BARRY FANTONI."
G. MELLY, 362:5JUN75-738
FARAGO, L. AFTERMATH.*
H. FRAENKEL, 617(TLS):26SEP75-1106
H. TREVOR-ROPER, 362:18SEP75-383
FARB, P. WORD PLAY.*
M.A.K. HALLIDAY, 617(TLS):24JAN75-
89
FARGHER, R. LIFE & LETTERS IN
FRANCE: THE EIGHTEENTH CENTURY.
P.V. CONROY, JR., 399(MLJ):DEC73-
437
M. DELON, 535(RHL):SEP-OCT73-896
W.G. MOORE, 402(MLR):JAN74-180
FARIQ, K.A. A HISTORY OF ARABIC
LITERATURE.
M.A. MU'ID KHAN, 273(IC):OCT73-357
FARIS, R. THE PASSIONATE EDUCATORS.
W.R. YOUNG, 99:APR/MAY75-38
FARLEY, T. THE LAST SPACEMAN.
D. BESSAI, 99:JUL75-36
FARLEY-HILLS, D., ED. ROCHESTER:
THE CRITICAL HERITAGE.
P. LEGOUIS, 189(EA):JUL-SEP73-371
FARMER, B.H. AGRICULTURAL COLONIZA-
TION IN INDIA SINCE INDEPENDENCE.
M. DESAI, 617(TLS):31JAN75-119

FARMER, D.H., ED. THE RULE OF ST.
BENEDICT.
G. STORMS, 179(ES):APR72-153
FARMILOE, D. AND SOME IN FIRE.
F. TIMLECK, 198:WINTER75-126
R. WILLMOT, 296:VOL4#3-161
FARMILOE, D. BLUE IS THE COLOUR OF
DEATH.
L. GASPARINI, 102(CANL):AUTUMN73-
112
FARNHAM, W. THE SHAKESPEAREAN GRO-
TESQUE.*
A.L. FRENCH, 179(ES):JUN73-282
FARR, F. FAIR ENOUGH.
442(NY):4AUG75-90
FARR, F. O'HARA.*
S.N. GREBSTEIN, 27(AL):MAR74-123
FARR, R. THE ELECTRONIC CRIMINAL.
M. MACKINTOSH, 617(TLS):26SEP75-
1096
FARRELL, J.T. JUDITH & OTHER STOR-
IES.
W. PEDEN, 569(SR):FALL74-712
FARRELL, R.B. A DICTIONARY OF GER-
MAN SYNONYMS. (2ND ED)
G.M. BONNIN, 564:OCT73-265
R.L. JONES, 399(MLJ):DEC73-433
E. MASON, 402(MLR):APR74-446
FARRELL, R.T. BEOWULF, SWEDES &
GEATS.
A.J. DEVERSON, 67:MAY74-79
T.A. SHIPPEY, 402(MLR):JAN74-144
FARRELL, W. THE LIBERATED MAN.*
S. CLARKSON, 99:SEP75-63
L. MC MURTRY, 441:5JAN75-6
FARRERAS, J.N. - SEE UNDER NADAL
FARRERAS, J.
FARSON, R. BIRTHRIGHTS.*
I. GLASSER, 231:FEB75-118
AL FARUGI, I.R., ED. HISTORICAL
ATLAS OF THE RELIGIONS OF THE
WORLD.
P. HEBBLETHWAITE, 617(TLS):30CT75-
1159
FARWELL, B. QUEEN VICTORIA'S LITTLE
WARS.
B.D. GOOCH, 637(VS):DEC73-217
FASANO, G. "LES TRAGIQUES" - UN'
EPOPEA DELLA MORTE.*
I.D. MC FARLANE, 402(MLR):JAN74-
175
FASOLD, R.W. TENSE MARKING IN BLACK
ENGLISH.
R.K.S. MACAULAY, 350:DEC74-758
FASOLD, R.W. & R.W. SHUY, EDS.
TEACHING STANDARD ENGLISH IN THE
INNER CITY.
R.B. LE PAGE, 353:15DEC73-119
FASSKE, H., H. JENTSCH & S. MICHALK,
EDS. SORBISCHER SPRACHATLAS. (VOL
4)
G. STONE, 575(SEER):JUL74-451
FASTEAU, M.F. THE MALE MACHINE.*
L. MC MURTRY, 441:5JAN75-6
FATHY, H. ARCHITECTURE FOR THE
POOR.
M. SAFDIE, 453:11DEC75-56
FAUCHEREAU, S. THÉOPHILE GAUTIER.
J. SOJCHER, 98:MAR73-285
FAULHABER, C. LATIN RHETORICAL
THEORY IN THIRTEENTH & FOURTEENTH
CENTURY CASTILE.
K. WHINNOM, 402(MLR):JAN74-198

FAULK, O.B. DESTINY ROAD.
W. GARD, 584(SWR):WINTER74-98
FAULK, O.B. TOMBSTONE MYTH & REAL-
ITY.
E. LARSEN, 109:FALL/WINTER73/74-
127
FAULKNER, D. THIS LIVING REEF.
P. ADAMS, 61:APR75-100
FAULKNER, G. PRINCE OF DUBLIN
PRINTERS. (R.E. WARD, ED)
E.A. BLOOM, 402(MLR):APR74-377
G.P. TYSON, 481(PQ):JUL73-332
FAULKNER, N. THE JADE BOX.
E.M. EWING, 441:11MAY75-10
FAULKNER, R.O. THE ANCIENT EGYPTIAN
PYRAMID TEXTS. SUPPLEMENT OF HIER-
OGLYPHIC TEXTS.
D.B. REDFORD, 318(JAOS):JAN-MAR73-
77
FAUQUENOY, M.S. ANALYSE STRUCTURALE
DU CRÉOLE GUYANAIS.
D. TAYLOR, 350:JUN74-380
FAUQUET, B. LE SCEPTICISME SELON
HEGEL.
F. CAUJOLLE-ZASLAWSKY, 542:OCT-DEC
73-461
DU FAUR, C.V. - SEE UNDER VON FABER
DU FAUR, C.
FAUROT, R.M. JEROME K. JEROME.
S. MONOD, 617(TLS):25APR75-444
FAUSOLD, M.L. & G.T. MAZUZAN, EDS.
THE HOOVER PRESIDENCY.
617(TLS):13JUN75-680
FAUST, I. A STAR IN THE FAMILY.
R.R. LINGEMAN, 441:3JUL75-29
G. MILLSTEIN, 441:30MAR75-13
FAUST, J.L. THE NEW YORK TIMES
BOOK OF HOUSE PLANTS.
J. CANADAY, 441:13APR75-16
FAUST, R. TOMBS OF BLUE ICE.
N. CALLENDAR, 441:11MAY75-26
FAUSTI, R.P. & E.L. MC GLONE. UNDER-
STANDING ORAL COMMUNICATION.
C.R. GRUNER, 583:SUMMER74-410
FAVERO, G.P.B. CORPUS PALLADIANUM.
(VOL 5: LA VILLA EMO DI FANZOLO.)
M.N. ROSENFELD, 576:DEC73-335
P. SCHNEIDER, 98:APR73-318
F.J.B. WATSON, 39:MAY73-531
FAVRE, G. - SEE DUKAS, P.
FAWCETT, T. THE RISE OF ENGLISH
PROVINCIAL ART.
E. ADAMS, 617(TLS):17JAN75-60
FAWDRY, K. EVERYTHING BUT ALF GAR-
NETT.
M. WARNOCK, 362:6FEB75-187
FAY, P.B. & J.L. GRIGSBY, EDS. JOU-
FROI DE POITIERS.
G.R. MELLOR, 382(MAE):1974/1-68
FAYE, J.P. ISKRA [SUIVI DE] CIRQUE.
S. MAX, 207(FR):MAY73-1239
FAYE, J-P. THÉORIE DU RÉCIT.* LAN-
GAGES TOTALITAIRES.*
D. TEYSSEIRE, 98:NOV73-1038
FAYOLLE, R. SAINTE-BEUVE ET LE
XVIIIE SIÈCLE OU COMMENT LES RÉVO-
LUTIONS ARRIVENT.
J.I. DONOHOE, JR., 446:SPRING-SUM-
MER74-100
FAYT, R. & OTHERS. BIBLIOGRAPHIE
DES ÉCRIVAINS FRANÇAIS DE BELGIQUE,
1881-1960.* (VOL 4)
J. REHBEIN, 72:BAND211HEFT1/3-233
FEATHER, J. - SEE WEBSTER, J.

FEAVER, W. THE ART OF JOHN MARTIN.
D. THOMAS, 362:25DEC75&1JAN76-892
FECHNER, J-U., ED. DAS DEUTSCHE
SONETT.
H-J. SCHLÜTTER, 190:BAND67HEFT2-
212
FEDDEN, R. & R. JOEKES, COMPS. THE
NATIONAL TRUST GUIDE.
A. CLIFTON-TAYLOR, 135:OCT73-143
FEDER, L. ANCIENT MYTH IN MODERN
POETRY.*
P.P. MATSEN, 122:JUL73-220
B. QUINN, 613:SUMMER73-307
FEDYSHYN, O.S. GERMANY'S DRIVE TO
THE EAST & THE UKRAINIAN REVOLU-
TION, 1917-1918.*
J.W. HIDEN, 575(SEER):JAN74-145
FEELEY, K. FLANNERY O'CONNOR.*
P.M. BROWNING, JR., 659:SPRING75-
260
FEFERMAN, S. THE NUMBER SYSTEMS.
W.E. GOULD, 316:MAR73-151
FEHLING, D. DIE WIEDERHOLUNGSFIGU-
REN UND IHR GEBRAUCH BEI DEN
GRIECHEN VOR GORGIAS.
M. LANDFESTER, 260(IF):BAND77HEFT
2/3-330
FEHLING, F.L. & OTHERS. ELEMENTARY
GERMAN. (3RD ED)
E.K. NEUSE, 221(GQ):MAY73-489
FEHLMANN, G. SOMERVILLE ET ROSS -
TÉMOINS DE L'IRLANDE D'HIER.
A. DEDIO, 179(ES):OCT73-518
FEHN, K. DIE ZENTRALÖRTLICHEN FUNK-
TIONEN FRÜHER ZENTREN IN ALTBAYERN.
K. REINDEL, 182:VOL#15/16-560
FEHR, K. GOTTFRIED KELLER.
B.G. THOMAS, 406:FALL74-309
FEHRENBACH, E. WANDLUNGEN DES DEUT-
SCHEN KAISERGEDANKENS 1871-1918.
M. STERNE, 182:VOL26#5/6-174
FEIBLEMAN, J.K. COLLECTED POEMS.
S.C. FELDMAN, 598(SOR):AUTUMN75-
957
FEIBLEMAN, J.K. MORAL STRATEGY.
P. DUBOIS, 542:OCT-DEC73-485
FEIBLEMAN, J.K. SCIENTIFIC METHOD.
M.B., 543:MAR73-534
M. BRADIE, 486:SEP73-467
FEICH, H. - SEE HEIDEGGER, M.
FEIGL, H., W. SELLARS & K. LEHRER,
EDS. NEW READINGS IN PHILOSOPHICAL
ANALYSIS.
W.G., 543:JUN73-751
FEILCHENFELDT, K. VARNHAGEN VON
ENSE ALS HISTORIKER.
J.L.S., 191(ELN):SEP73(SUPP)-160
FEILER, L. - SEE SHKLOVSKY, V.
FEINBERG, J. DOING & DESERVING.*
P.S. ÅRDAL, 154:DEC73-734
FEINER, J. & L. VISCHER, EDS. THE
COMMON CATECHISM.
F.R. BARRY, 617(TLS):18JUL75-812
FEINSTEIN, E. CHILDREN OF THE ROSE.
S. CLAPP, 617(TLS):25APR75-445
J. MELLORS, 362:24APR75-547
FEIST, A. CRIME AT THE CEDARS.
D.M. DAY, 157:SPRING73-84
FEIWEL, G.R. THE SOVIET QUEST FOR
ECONOMIC EFFICIENCY.
G.E. SCHROEDER, 550(RUSR):JAN73-88
FEIX, I. & E. SCHLANT. LITERATUR
UND UMGANGSSPRACHE.*
S. GLINSKY, 221(GQ):SEP73-185

113

FELDMAN, B. & R.D. RICHARDSON, EDS.
THE RISE OF MODERN MYTHOLOGY, 1680-
1860.
  R. ACKERMAN, 322(JHI):JAN-MAR73-
  147
  G.K. GRESSETH, 292(JAF):OCT-DEC73-
  407
  R. SLOTKIN, 31(ASCH):SPRING75-330
  191(ELN):SEP73(SUPP)-10
FELDMAN, I. LOST ORIGINALS.*
  H. TAYLOR, 385(MQR):WINTER75-92
FELDMAN, L.D. & M.D. GOLDRICK, EDS.
POLITICS & GOVERNMENT OF URBAN
CANADA. (2ND ED)
  D.C. ROWAT, 529(QQ):SUMMER73-284
FELDMAN, L.H. - SEE PSEUDO-PHILO
FELDMAN, S.D. THE MORALITY-PATTERN-
ED COMEDY OF THE RENAISSANCE.*
  F. LAGARDE, 189(EA):JAN-MAR73-91
FELDMANN, H. DIE FIABE CARLO GOZ-
ZIS.*
  R. RIZZO, 52:BAND8HEFT2-211
FELDMEIER, E. - SEE RIEDEL, F.J.
FELLINI, F. QUATTRO FILM.
  G. NOWELL-SMITH, 617(TLS):31OCT75-
  1311
FELLINI, F., WITH T. GUERRA. AMAR-
CORD.
  G. NOWELL-SMITH, 617(TLS):31OCT75-
  1311
FELLMAN, M. THE UNBOUNDED FRAME.*
  J. MYERSON, 432(NEQ):DEC74-636
FELLOWS, J. THE FAILING DISTANCE.
  G. WILLS, 453:7AUG75-6
FELLOWS, O. & D. GUIRAGOSSIAN, EDS.
DIDEROT STUDIES X. DIDEROT STUDIES
XII.
  S.J. GENDZIER, 546(RR):NOV73-308
FELLOWS, O.E. & S.F. MILLIKEN. BUF-
FON.
  J. ROGER, 546(RR):MAR74-136
FELLOW, O.E. & N.L. TORREY, EDS.
THE AGE OF ENLIGHTENMENT. (2ND ED)
  B.N. MORTON, 207(FR):DEC72-459
FELLTHAM, O. THE POEMS OF OWEN
FELLTHAM 1604?-1668. (T-L. PEB-
WORTH & C.J. SUMMERS, EDS)
  D. BUSH, 568(SCN):FALL74-47
FELMAN, S. LA "FOLIE" DANS L'OEUVRE
ROMANESQUE DE STENDHAL.*
  K. RINGGER, 224(GRM):BAND23HEFT4-
  501
  M. TILLETT, 208(FS):APR74-209
FELPERIN, H. SHAKESPEAREAN RO-
MANCE.*
  C. HOY, 569(SR):SPRING74-363
  G. LAMBIN, 189(EA):JUL-SEP73-353
  N. RABKIN, 401(MLQ):JUN74-187
FELTON, F. THOMAS LOVE PEACOCK.
  H. MILLS, 637(VS):JUN74-449
  G. THOMAS, 175:AUTUMN73-118
FEMLING, J. BACKYARD.
  N. CALLENDAR, 441:24AUG75-27
FENGER, H. THE HEIBERGS.* (F.J.
MARKER, ED & TRANS)
  R-M.G. OSTER, 399(MLJ):NOV73-382
  P. VINTEN-JOHANSEN, 563(SS):SUM-
  MER74-294
FENN, C. HO CHI MINH.
  639(VQR):SUMMER74-XC

"TÖNNIES FENNE'S LOW GERMAN MANUAL
OF SPOKEN RUSSIAN, PSKOV 1607."*
(VOLS 1&2) (L.L. HAMMERICH & OTHERS,
EDS)
  B. PANZER, 343:BAND16HEFT1-93
  V.A. TUMINS, 574(SEEJ):SPRING73-
  101
FENNELL, J., ED. NINETEENTH-CENTURY
RUSSIAN LITERATURE.
  B. BILOKUR, 399(MLJ):NOV74-369
  R. FREEBORN, 575(SEER):APR74-277
FENNER, T. LEIGH HUNT & OPERA CRIT-
ICISM.
  R.E. AYCOCK, 414(MQ):APR73-314
FENSTERMAKER, V. SANTA-BABY.
  M. LEVIN, 441:30NOV75-62
FENTON, A. THE VARIOUS NAMES OF
SHETLAND.
  D. MURISON, 595(SCS):VOL18-148
FENTON, J. TERMINAL MORAINE.*
  A. CLUYSENAAR, 565:VOL14#1-70
FENWICK, H. THE CHATEAUX OF FRANCE.
  617(TLS):31OCT75-1313
FENYO, M.D. HITLER, HORTHY, & HUN-
GARY.*
  P. IGNOTUS, 617(TLS):14FEB75-163
FERGUSON, A.D. & OTHERS - SEE PUSH-
KAREV, S.
FERGUSON, C.A. LANGUAGE STRUCTURE
& LANGUAGE USE.
  R.A. HUDSON, 315(JAL):VOL11PT1-91
FERGUSON, E.J. - SEE MORRIS, R.
FERGUSON, J. A COMPANION TO GREEK
TRAGEDY.
  J.M. CONANT, 399(MLJ):DEC73-442
FERGUSON, J. UTOPIAS OF THE CLASSI-
CAL WORLD.
  M.I. FINLAY, 617(TLS):11JUL75-757
FERGUSON, J. THE YORUBAS OF NIGERIA.
  J. GOODY, 69:JAN73-82
FERGUSON, J.P. THE PHILOSOPHY OF
DR. SAMUEL CLARKE & ITS CRITICS.
  D.D. RAPHAEL, 617(TLS):4JUL75-736
FERGUSON, M.E. CHINA MEDICAL BOARD
& PEKING UNION MEDICAL COLLEGE.
  M.B. BULLOCK, 293(JAST):AUG73-689
FERGUSON, S. THE POETRY OF RANDALL
JARRELL.*
  P.L. MARIANI, 295:FEB74-671
FERGUSON, S. TO THE PLACE OF SHELLS.
  R. DINNAGE, 617(TLS):19SEP75-1065
  J. MELLORS, 362:7AUG75-189
FERGUSON-LEES, J., Q. HOCKLIFFE & K.
ZWEERES, EDS. A GUIDE TO BIRD
WATCHING IN EUROPE.
  617(TLS):7NOV75-1342
FERGUSSON, A. THE SACK OF BATH.
  G. ALLEN, 45:SEP73-41
FERGUSSON, J. BALLOON TYTLER.
  J. BRUCE, 481(PQ):JUL73-385
FERLINGHETTI, L. OPEN EYE, OPEN
HEART.
  M.G. PERLOFF, 659:WINTER75-84
  639(VQR):SPRING74-LVII
FERM, B. FALSE IDOLS.
  M. LEVIN, 441:9FEB75-14
FERMAN, E.L., ED. THE BEST FROM
FANTASY & SCIENCE FICTION.
  E. KORN, 617(TLS):8AUG75-903
FERMAN, E.L. & B.N. MALZBERG, EDS.
FINAL STAGE.
  G. JONAS, 441:14DEC75-29

FERNANDES/J.C. OATES. THE POISONED
KISS.
  P. ADAMS, 61:SEP75-85
  E. POCHODA, 441:31AUG75-6
FERNANDEZ, D. L'ARBRE JUSQU'AUX
RACINES.
  A. MARISSEL, 207(FR):DEC72-445
FERNÁNDEZ-ARMESTO, F. FERDINAND &
ISABELLA.
  A. PAGDEN, 617(TLS):22AUG75-948
FERNÁNDEZ-SHAW, C.M. PRESENCIA ES-
PAÑOLA EN LOS ESTADOS UNIDOS.*
  G. DE ZÉNDEGUI, 37:JUN-JUL73-36
FERNANDEZ ARENAS, J. MOZARABIC
ARCHITECTURE.
  505:MAY73-134
FERNÁNDEZ DE MORATÍN, L. LA COMEDIA
NUEVA. (J. DOWLING, ED)
  J.H.R. POLT, 400(MLN):MAR73-464
FERNÁNDEZ DE MORATÍN, L. LA COMEDIA
NUEVA (J. DOWLING, ED) [TOGETHER
WITH] EL SÍ DE LAS NIÑAS. (R.
ANDIOC, ED)
  J.H.R. POLT, 400(MLN):MAR73-464
FERNÁNDEZ MÉNDEZ, E. LE PRIMITIVIS-
ME HAÏTIEN/THE HAITIAN PRIMITIVISM/
EL PRIMITIVISMO HAITIANO.
  J.H. DE AYOROA, 37:MAY73-41
FERNEA, E.W. A STREET IN MARRAKECH.
  A. BROYARD, 441:27OCT75-27
FÉRON, J. LA CINQUIÈME SAISON.
  M. SAKHAROFF, 207(FR):APR73-1051
FERRAND, F. - SEE PARMENTIER, J.
FERRAR, H. JOHN OSBORNE.
  A.C. EDWARDS, 397(MD):DEC73-394
FERRARI, E.L. - SEE UNDER LAFUENTE
FERRARI, E.
FERRARI, S. - SEE BOIARDO, M.M.
FERRARO, R.M. GIUDIZI CRITICI E
CRITERI ESTETICI NEL "POETICES LIB-
RI SEPTEM" (1561) DI GIULIO CESARE
SCALIGERO RISPETTO ALLA TEORIA LET-
TERARIA DEL RINASCIMENTO.
  D. DALLA VALLE, 549(RLC):OCT-DEC73-
  631
FERRAROTTI, F. LA SOCIOLOGIA COME
PARTECIPAZIONE.
  E. NAMER, 542:JAN-MAR73-110
FERRARS, E. THE CUP & THE LIP.
  617(TLS):12DEC75-1477
FERRELL, R.K. T.S. ELIOT & THE
TONGUES OF FIRE.
  295:FEB74-584
FERRER BENIMELI, J.A. LA MASONERÍA
ESPAÑOLA EN EL SIGLO XVIII.
  P. DEACON, 617(TLS):23MAY75-557
FERRERO, D.D. - SEE UNDER DE BERNAR-
DI FERRERO, D.
FERRES, A. EN EL SEGUNDO HEMISFER-
IO.
  T.R. FRANZ, 238:SEP73-736
FERRIS, W.R., JR. MISSISSIPPI BLACK
FOLKLORE.*
  D. EVANS, 650(WF):JAN73-59
FERRO, M. THE GREAT WAR 1914-1918.
  A. WHEATCROFT, 111:23NOV73-54
FERRON, J. DU FOND DE MON ARRIÈRE
CUISINE.
  B. GODARD, 296:VOL3#4-96
FERRON, J. TALES FROM THE UNCERTAIN
COUNTRY.*
  J. REID, 102(CANL):WINTER73-124

FERRONI, G. "MUTAZIONE" E "RISCON-
TRO" NEL TEATRO DI MACHIAVELLI/E
ALTRI SAGGI SULLA COMMEDIA DEL
CINQUECENTO.
  C.W., 275(IQ):FALL-WINTER73(VOL17
  #66)-66
FERRUCCI, F. IL CAPPELLO DI PANAMA.
  B. MERRY, 270:VOL23#4-87
FEST, J.C. HITLER.*
  639(VQR):AUTUMN74-CXXXVIII
FETHERLING, D. HUGH GARNER.*
  G. WOODCOCK, 102(CANL):WINTER74-95
FETJÖ, F. A HISTORY OF THE PEOPLES
DEMOCRACIES.
  A. GYORGY, 104:SPRING74-162
FETSCHER, I. LA FILOSOFIA POLITICA
DI ROUSSEAU.
  G. MANFREDI, 548(RCSF):JUL-SEP73-
  348
FETZER, J.F. ROMANTIC ORPHEUS.
  617(TLS):6JUN75-623
DU FEU, P. LET'S HEAR IT FOR THE
LONG-LEGGED WOMEN.
  W. FEAVER, 617(TLS):24JAN75-78
FEUCHTWANGER, E.J. GLADSTONE.
  H.C.G. MATTHEW, 617(TLS):21NOV75-
  1390
FEUERSTEIN, G. & J. MILLER. YOGA
& BEYOND.
  P.J. WILL, 293(JAST):NOV72-175
FEUSTEL, R. TECHNIK DER STEINZEIT.
  M-R. SAUTER, 182:VOL26#17/18-614
FEVRAL'SKIJ, A. PERVAJA SOVETSKAJA
P'ESA, "MISTERIJA-BUFF" V.V. MAJA-
KOVSKOGO. VSTREČI S MAJAKOVSKIM.
  M.L. HOOVER, 574(SEEJ):SUMMER72-
  240
FÉVRIER, P-A. ART DE L'ALGERIE
ANTIQUE.
  K.M.D. DUNBABIN, 313:VOL63-289
FFRENCH BLAKE, R.L.V. THE CRIMEAN
WAR.
  B.D. GOOCH, 637(VS):DEC73-217
FIACC, P., ED. THE WEARING OF THE
BLACK.
  R. FULLER, 617(TLS):17JAN75-50
FICINO, M. THE LETTERS OF MARSILIO
FICINO. (VOL 1)
  C.B. SCHMITT, 617(TLS):17OCT75-
  1232
FICKELSON, M. UNE SOIRÉE CHEZ
AZERBACH.
  N. GREENE, 207(FR):OCT72-212
FIEDLER, L.A. THE STRANGER IN
SHAKESPEARE.*
  C.H. POLLACK, 529(QQ):SUMMER73-301
FIELD, A., COMP. THE COMPLECTION OF
RUSSIAN LITERATURE.*
  S. MONAS, 574(SEEJ):FALL72-356
FIELD, C. & D.C. HAMLEY. FICTION
IN THE MIDDLE SCHOOL.
  617(TLS):31JAN75-103
FIELD, G.W. HERMANN HESSE.*
  K.J. FICKERT, 295:FEB74-642
FIELD, J. ENGLISH FIELD-NAMES.
  B. COTTLE, 541(RES):AUG73-317
  C.M. ROTHRAUFF, 424:SEP73-199
FIELD, P.J.C. ROMANCE & CHRONICLE.*
  W. MATTHEWS, 589:JAN74-114
  E. REISS, 599:SPRING73-236
FIELD, S. & M.P. LEVITT. BLOOMSDAY.
  295:FEB74-682
FIELD, W.H.W. - SEE VIDAL, R.

FIELDING, G. NEW QUEENS FOR OLD.
M. PAGE, 573(SSF):FALL73-433
FIELDING, H. JOSEPH ANDREWS [&]
SHAMELA. (A. HUMPHREYS, ED)
B. RUDDICK, 148:WINTER73-378
FIELDING, H. THE JACOBITE'S JOURNAL
& RELATED WRITINGS. (W.B. COLEY,
ED)
G. CURTIS, 617(TLS):12SEP75-1029
FIELDING, H. MISCELLANIES BY HENRY
FIELDING, ESQ. (VOL 1) (H.K. MIL-
LER, ED)
D. BROOKS, 148:AUTUMN73-287
T. DAVIS, 354:DEC73-351
R. PAULSON, 481(PQ):JUL73-501
FIELDING, J. THE BEST OF FRIENDS.
H. ROSENGARTEN, 102(CANL):AUTUMN
73-92
FIELDING, R. THE AMERICAN NEWSREEL
1911-1967.
J.R. PARISH, 200:APR73-236
L.C. WAFFEN, 14:OCT73-561
FIELDING, S. THE ADVENTURES OF
DAVID SIMPLE. (M. KELSALL, ED)
J. DULCK, 189(EA):JAN-MAR73-104
FIELDS, B. REALITY'S DARK DREAM.
H.B. DE GROOT, 179(ES):OCT72-466
FIELDS, J. A CRY OF ANGELS.*
J. YARDLEY, 569(SR):SUMMER74-537
FIELDS, K. SUNBELLY.*
R.B. SHAW, 491:SEP75-352
T. STEELE, 598(SOR):SPRING75-482
FIETZ, L. MENSCHENBILD UND ROMAN-
STRUKTUR IN ALDOUS HUXLEYS IDEEN-
ROMANEN.*
P. GOETSCH, 179(ES):JUN73-300
I. HANTSCH, 72:BAND211HEFT1/3-172
FIEVE, R.R. MOODSWING.
M. SCARF, 441:28DEC75-4
FIFOOT, R. A BIBLIOGRAPHY OF EDITH,
OSBERT & SACHEVERELL SITWELL.*
(2ND ED)
B.C. BLOOMFIELD, 354:MAR73-76
FIGGE, H.H. GEISTERKULT, BESESSEN-
HEIT UND MAGIE IN DER UMBANDA-
RELIGION BRASILIENS.
R. BASTIDE, 182:VOL26#10-378
FIGUEIREDO, W. AQUI RIO-GENTE.
S. BACIU, 263:OCT-DEC74-464
FILENE, P.G. HIM/HER/SELF.
P. ADAMS, 61:MAY75-103
J. O'REILLY, 441:4MAY75-6
FILLEUL, N. LES THÉÂTRES DE GAIL-
LON. (F. JOUKOVSKY, ED)
K.M. HALL, 402(MLR):APR74-401
I.D. MC FARLANE, 208(FS):APR74-190
D. MÉNAGER, 535(RHL):JAN-FEB73-123
FILLIOZAT, V. L'ÉPIGRAPHIE DE
VIJAYANAGAR DU DÉBUT À 1377.
O. VON HINÜBER, 182:VOL26#9-311
FILLMORE, C.J. & D.T. LANGENDOEN,
EDS. STUDIES IN LINGUISTIC SEMAN-
TICS.*
R.I. BINNICK, 215(GL):VOL13#3-162
R.M. KEMPSON, 297(JL):FEB73-120
"FINAL REPORT BY THE WATERGATE SPE-
CIAL PROSECUTION FORCE."
K. SALE, 453:11DEC75-5
FINAS, L. LA CRUE.
J-C. ENGELSTEIN, 98:DEC73-1075
FINBERG, H.P.R., ED. THE AGRARIAN
HISTORY OF ENGLAND & WALES.* (VOL
1, PT 2)
J.A. RAFTIS, 589:JUL74-559

FINCH, C. NORMAN ROCKWELL'S AMERICA.
E. HOAGLAND, 441:7DEC75-86
FINCH, J.D. INTRODUCTION TO LEGAL
THEORY.
R. GOEDECKE, 321:SPRING73-73
FINCH, P. HAULIN'.
N. CALLENDAR, 441:23NOV75-52
FINCH, R. & E. JOLIAT. FRENCH INDI-
VIDUALIST POETRY 1686-1760.*
S. MENANT, 535(RHL):NOV-DEC73-1075
D.W. WELCH, 402(MLR):APR74-406
FINDLATER, R. LILIAN BAYLIS.
R. BRYDEN, 617(TLS):6JUN75-616
J. ELSOM, 362:22MAY75-684
FINDLAY, J.N. ASCENT TO THE ABSO-
LUTE.*
W.H. WALSH, 393(MIND):APR73-300
FINDLAY, J.N. MEINONG'S THEORY OF
OBJECTS & VALUES. (2ND ED)
K. LAMBERT, 262:SUMMER73-221
FINDLAY, J.N. PLATO.
I.M. CROMBIE, 518:OCT74-3
FINE, B. THE STRANGLEHOLD OF THE
I.Q.
C. LEHMANN-HAUPT, 441:17DEC75-37
FINE, P.M. VAUVENARGUES & LA ROCHE-
FOUCAULD.
A. LEVI, 617(TLS):25APR75-446
FINE, R. BOBBY FISCHER'S CONQUEST
OF THE WORLD CHESS CHAMPIONSHIP.
617(TLS):17JAN75-65
FINEGAN, J. ENCOUNTERING NEW TESTA-
MENT MANUSCRIPTS.
H.F.D. SPARKS, 617(TLS):5DEC75-
1467
FINEMAN, D.A. - SEE MORGANN, M.
FINER, S.E., ED. ADVERSARY POLITICS
& ELECTORAL REFORM.
K. LINDSAY, 617(TLS):19DEC75-1526
FINES, J. & R. VERRIER. THE DRAMA
OF HISTORY.
617(TLS):17JAN75-65
DE FINETTI, B. PROBABILITY, INDUC-
TION & STATISTICS.
H.E. KYBURG, JR., 486:SEP73-451
FINGARETTE, H. THE MEANING OF CRIM-
INAL INSANITY.
J.F. MC HARG, 479(PHQ):JUL73-279
FINGARETTE, H. SELF-DECEPTION.
L. CODE & J. KING-FARLOW, 154:
SEP73-502
A.R. DRENGSON, 154:MAR73-142
FINGER, F.L. CATALOGUE OF THE IN-
CUNABULA IN THE ELMER BELT LIBRARY
OF VINCIANA.*
C. FAHY, 354:MAR73-68
FINGER, H., ED. INTERPRETATION ZU
IRVING, MELVILLE UND POE.
K. OLTMANN, 430(NS):JUL73-389
FINGERHUT, K-H. STANDORTBESTIMMUN-
GEN.
J.L.S., 191(ELN):SEP73(SUPP)-131
FINK, H. AMERIKANISMEN IM WORT-
SCHATZ DER DEUTSCHEN TAGESPRESSE.
A. HELLER, 430(NS):APR73-232
FINK, R.O. ROMAN MILITARY RECORDS
ON PAPYRUS.*
C.M. WELLS, 24:SPRING74-87
FINKE, U., ED. FRENCH NINETEENTH
CENTURY PAINTING & LITERATURE.*
D. ASHTON, 54:SEP73-469
FINKEL, D. A MOTE IN HEAVEN'S EYE.
H. VENDLER, 441:7SEP75-6

FINKENSTAEDT, T., E. LEISI & D.
WOLFF. A CHRONOLOGICAL ENGLISH
DICTIONARY LISTING 80,000 WORDS IN
ORDER OF THEIR EARLIEST KNOWN OC-
CURRENCE.
  R. DEROLEZ, 179(ES):APR72-144
FINLAY, J.L. CANADA IN THE NORTH
ATLANTIC TRIANGLE.
  A. SMITH, 99:NOV75-34
FINLAY, J.L. SOCIAL CREDIT.
  J.A. EAGLE, 529(QQ):AUTUMN73-478
FINLEY, M.I. LES ANCIENS GRECS.
  P. GAUTHIER, 555:VOL47FASC1-122
FINLEY, M.I. THE ANCIENT ECONOMY.*
  W.R. CONNOR, 5:VOL1#4-731
  A. MOMIGLIANO, 453:16OCT75-36
  S.I. OOST, 114(CHIR):VOL25#4-147
  639(VQR):SPRING74-LVIII
FINLEY, M.I. DEMOCRACY ANCIENT &
MODERN.*
  H.A. DEANE, 639(VQR):WINTER74-127
  A. MOMIGLIANO, 453:16OCT75-36
FINLEY, M.I. EARLY GREECE.
  N.C. SCOUFOPOULOS, 121(CJ):FEB/
  MAR74-251
  E. VERMEULE, 122:APR73-145
FINLEY, M.I. THE USE & ABUSE OF
HISTORY.
  A. ANDREWES, 617(TLS):28MAR75-335
  A. MOMIGLIANO, 453:16OCT75-36
FINNEGAN, R. ORAL LITERATURE IN
AFRICA.*
  G. CALAME-GRIAULE, 315(JAL):VOL11
  PT1-100
  D.J. CROWLEY, 292(JAF):JAN-MAR73-
  78
FINNERAN, R.J. THE PROSE FICTION OF
W.B. YEATS.
  G. HOUGH, 617(TLS):14FEB75-160
FINNERAN, R.J. - SEE STEPHENS, J.
FINNEY, H.S. FAIR EXCHANGE.
  H. D'AVIGDOR-GOLDSMID, 617(TLS):
  28MAR75-344
FINOCCHIARO, M.A. HISTORY OF SCI-
ENCE AS EXPLANATION.*
  H. LONGINO, 319(APR75-279
FIORE, P.A., ED. JUST SO MUCH HONOR.
  E.F. DANIELS, 568(SCN):WINTER74-72
  J. GRUNDY, 677:VOL4-285
  H. SERGEANT, 175:SPRING73-28
  J.M. WALLACE, 551(RENQ):SUMMER73-
  238
FIRCHOW, E.S. & E.H. ZEYDEL - SEE
EINHARD
FIRCHOW, P. ALDOUS HUXLEY.*
  D.J. DOOLEY, 529(QQ):WINTER73-652
  R. HOPE, 541(RES):AUG73-375
  P. VITOUX, 402(MLR):APR74-392
  H.H. WATTS, 295:FEB74-651
"FIRE PROTECTION THROUGH MODERN
BUILDING CODES."
  E.W. FOWLER, 505:FEB73-108
FIRENZUOLA, A. LE NOVELLE. (E.
RAGNI, ED)
  D.D., 275(IQ):FALL-WINTER73(VOL17
  #66)-65
FIRESTONE, O.J. THE PUBLIC PERSUAD-
ER.
  W. SCHÄFER, 182:VOL26#3/4-83
FIRPO, M. PIETRO BIZZARRI.
  E. SPIVAKOVSKY, 551(RENQ):AUTUMN
  73-319
"THE FIRST ONE HUNDRED."
  K.J. PIKE, 14:JUL73-412

"THE FIRST SUPPLEMENT TO THE BROCK
BIBLIOGRAPHY OF PUBLISHED CANADIAN
PLAYS."
  G.W., 102(CANL):WINTER74-128
"THE FIRST VOTYAK GRAMMAR."
  B. SCHULZE, 682(ZPSK):BAND26HEFT6-
  729
FIRTH, J. BRITISH BANKING OVERSEAS.
  J.R. EWER, 399(MLJ):SEP-OCT74-298
FIRTH, J.J.F. - SEE ROBERT OF FLAM-
BOROUGH
FIRTH, S. THE URBANIZATION OF
SOPHIA FIRTH.
  F.W. WATT, 99:SEP75-65
FISCH, H. HAMLET & THE WORD.*
  H. JENKINS, 677:VOL4-273
  J.H. JONES, 551(RENQ):AUTUMN73-370
  R.E. LYNCH, 125:JUN74-378
FISCHER, E. AN OPPOSING MAN.
  H.M. PACHTER, 231:AUG75-83
  P. VANSITTART, 364:JUN/JUL74-121
FISCHER, F. WAR OF ILLUSIONS.
  P. WINDSOR, 362:29MAY75-718
FISCHER, F.W. MAX BECKMANN.
  F. WHITFORD, 592:JUL-AUG73-58
FISCHER, H. GEORG BÜCHNER.
  M.B. BENN, 402(MLR):OCT74-929
  M. BRÄNDLE, 67:MAY74-118
FISCHER, H., ED. ENGLISCHE BAROCK-
GEDICHTE, ENGLISCH UND DEUTSCH.
  A. ASSMANN, 72:BAND211HEFT3/6-436
FISCHER, H., ED. ENGLISH SATIRICAL
POETRY FROM JOSEPH HALL TO PERCY B.
SHELLEY.
  P. MICHEL-MICHOT, 556(RLV):1973/6-
  563
  H.O., 430(NS):AUG73-449
FISCHER, J. VITAL SIGNS, U.S.A.
  R. CASSIDY, 441:11MAY75-36
FISCHER, L. THE ROAD TO YALTA.
  G.A. MORGAN, 550(RUSR):JAN73-77
FISCHER, L. & OTHERS. UNTERSUCHUN-
GEN ZUR SPRACHE KANTS, MIT ZAHL-
REICHEN ABBILDUNGEN UND TABELLEN.
  E.F. RITTER, 481(PQ):JUL73-534
FISCHER, T. BEWUSSTSEINSDARSTELLUNG
IM WERK VON JAMES JOYCE.
  W. FÜGER, 329(JJQ):FALL74/WINTER
  75-188
FISCHER, W. GRAMMATIK DES KLASSIS-
CHEN ARABISCH.
  H. GÄTJE, 343:BAND17HEFT2-219
FISCHER-GALATI, S., ED. MAN, STATE,
& SOCIETY IN EAST EUROPEAN HISTORY.
  T. STOIANOVICH, 104:SUMMER73-273
FISCHLER, S. SLASHING!
  M. RICHLER, 441:5JAN75-6
FISH, P.G. THE POLITICS OF FEDERAL
JUDICIAL ADMINISTRATION.
  639(VQR):SPRING74-XLVIII
FISH, R.L. THE MEMOIRS OF SCHLOCK
HOMES.
  M. YOUNG, 441:2FEB75-21
FISH, R.L. TROUBLE IN PARADISE.
  N. CALLENDAR, 441:6APR75-18
FISH, S.E. SELF-CONSUMING ARTI-
FACTS.*
  B. BASHFORD, 128(CE):FEB74-614
  R.A. FOAKES, 175:AUTUMN73-114
  J. FRANK, 191(ELN):JUN74-306
  S.K. HENINGER, JR., 579(SAQ):
  SPRING74-272
  J.H. SUMMERS, 401(MLQ):DEC74-403
                              [CONTINUED]

FISH, S.E. SELF-CONSUMING ARTI-
FACTS.* [CONTINUING]
  H. SUSSMAN, 400(MLN):DEC73-1329
  R.W. UPHAUS, 290(JAAC):SUMMER74-
  572
FISH, S.E., ED. SEVENTEENTH-CENTURY
PROSE.*
  F. COSTA, 189(EA):OCT-DEC73-478
FISHER, J. WATCHING BIRDS. (REV
BY J. FLEGG)
  617(TLS):4APR75-380
FISHER, J.E. SYLLOGE NUMMORUM GRAE-
CORUM. (PT 1)
  A.J. FRANK, 121(CJ):DEC73/JAN74-
  187
FISHER, J.R. GOVERNMENT & SOCIETY
IN COLONIAL PERU.
  P.T. BRADLEY, 86(BHS):APR73-192
FISHER, L. PRESIDENTIAL SPENDING
POWER.
  R. LEKACHMAN, 441:16NOV75-3
FISHER, L. & W. THE MOSCOW GOURMET.
  S.F. STARR, 441:19JAN75-28
FISHMAN, J.A., ED. ADVANCES IN THE
SOCIOLOGY OF LANGUAGE. (VOL 2)
  R.A. HUDSON, 315(JAL):VOL11PT3-95
FISHMAN, J.A. LANGUAGE IN SOCIOCUL-
TURAL CHANGE. (A.S. DIL, ED)
  L. TAYLOR, 351(LL):JUN74-155
FISHMAN, J.A. NATIONAL LANGUAGES &
LANGUAGES OF WIDER COMMUNICATION IN
THE DEVELOPING NATIONS.
  315(JAL):VOL11PT2-99
FISHMAN, J.A. THE SOCIOLOGY OF LAN-
GUAGE.
  M.C. SHAPIRO, 399(MLJ):SEP-OCT74-
  283
FISHMAN, W.J. EAST END JEWISH RADI-
CALS 1875-1914.
  C. ABRAMSKY, 617(TLS):20JUN75-694
  E.S. TURNER, 362:13FEB75-219
FISK, B. STRAWBERRY JAM.
  D.M. DAY, 157:AUTUMN73-86
FISK, R. THE POINT OF NO RETURN.
  D. ANDERSON, 362:18DEC75-837
FISKE, R. ENGLISH THEATRE MUSIC IN
THE EIGHTEENTH CENTURY.*
  J. HERBAGE, 410(M&L):JAN74-91
FISTIÉ, P. SOUS-DÉVELOPPEMENT ET
UTOPIE AU SIAM.
  R. LUCCHINI, 182:VOL26#3/4-85
FISZEL, H. EINFÜHRUNG IN DIE THE-
ORIE DER PLANWIRTSCHAFT.
  G. KIRSCH, 182:VOL26#13/14-476
FISZMAN, J.R. REVOLUTION & TRADI-
TION IN PEOPLE'S POLAND.
  W.F. TULASIEWICZ, 575(SEER):OCT74-
  623
FITCH, B.T., ED. ALBERT CAMUS 2.
  I.H. WALKER, 208(FS):JAN74-108
FITCH, B.T., ED. ALBERT CAMUS 3.
  G.H. BAUER, 207(FR):FEB73-634
  G. BRÉE, 535(RHL):JAN-FEB73-160
FITCH, B.T. & P.C. HOY, EDS. ALBERT
CAMUS 1. (PT 2)
  I.H. WALKER, 208(FS):JAN74-108
FITZ, J. LES SYRIENS À INTERCISA.
  J.T. CUMMINGS, 124:APR-MAY74-409
FITZGERALD, C.P. THE SOUTHERN EX-
PANSION OF THE CHINESE PEOPLE.
  A. LAMB, 302:JUL73-266
  L.E. WILLIAMS, 293(JAST):NOV72-140
  A. WOODSIDE, 244(HJAS):VOL33-282

FITZ GERALD, F. FIRE IN THE LAKE.*
  D.G. MARR, 293(JAST):MAY73-564
FITZGERALD, F.S. & H. OBER. AS
EVER, SCOTT FITZ.* (M.J. BRUCCOLI,
WITH J.M. ATKINSON, EDS)
  L. CASPER, 613:WINTER73-539
FITZGERALD, F.S. & M. PERKINS. DEAR
SCOTT/DEAR MAX. (J. KUEHL & J.R.
BRYER, EDS)
  A. MARGOLIES, 295:FEB74-601
FITZGERALD, P. EDWARD BURNE-JONES.
  R. DAVIES, 617(TLS):12DEC75-1487
  D.A.N. JONES, 362:20NOV75-683
FITZGERALD, S. CHINA & THE OVERSEAS
CHINESE.
  R.J. COUGHLIN, 302:JUL73-267
  G.E. JOHNSON, 293(JAST):AUG73-696
FITZ GIBBON, C. THE GOLDEN AGE.
  S. CLARK, 617(TLS):4APR75-353
  J. MELLORS, 362:24APR75-547
FITZSIMMONS, T., ED & TRANS. JAP-
ANESE POETRY NOW.*
  M. BROCK, 285(JAPQ):JAN-MAR74-101
  E.D. SAUNDERS, 352(LE&W):VOL16#3-
  1090
FITZWILLIAM, J. ANYWAY, THIS PAR-
TICULAR SUNDAY.
  S. KENNEDY, 617(TLS):7MAR75-241
  J. MELLORS, 362:24APR75-547
FLACELIÈRE, R. & E. CHAMBRY - SEE
PLUTARCH
FLADELAND, B. MEN & BROTHERS.
  J.E. MOONEY, 432(NEQ):JUN74-318
FLAGG, J.S. "PROMETHEUS UNBOUND" &
"HELLAS."
  P.H. BUTTER, 677:VOL4-314
"THE JAMES MONTGOMERY FLAGG POSTER
BOOK."
  J-C. SUARES, 441:5OCT75-22
FLAHERTY, D.H. PRIVACY IN COLONIAL
NEW ENGLAND.*
  D.G. ALLEN, 432(NEQ):MAR73-140
FLAM, J.D. - SEE MATISSE, H.
FLANNER, J. LONDON WAS YESTERDAY.
  (I. DRUTMAN, ED)
  A. BROYARD, 441:22MAY75-43
FLANNER, J. PARIS WAS YESTERDAY.
  (I. DRUTMAN, ED)
  H.W. BRANN, 207(FR):MAR73-874
FLASCHE, H., ED. CALDERÓN DE LA
BARCA.
  H.T. OOSTENDORP, 433:OCT73-402
FLASCHE, H., ED. HACIA CALDERÓN.*
  H.T. OOSTENDORP, 433:OCT73-402
  J.H. PARKER, 240(HR):AUTUMN73-702
  A.G. REICHENBERGER, 86(BHS):OCT73-
  399
  B.W. WARDROPPER, 546(RR):MAR73-158
FLASCHE, H., ED. LITTERAE HISPANAE
ET LUSITANAE.
  F. KARLINGER, 430(NS):MAR73-179
FLATHMAN, R.E. POLITICAL OBLIGATION.
  W.N. NELSON, 482(PHR):APR74-266
FLAUBERT, G. CORRESPONDANCE, I
(JANVIER 1830 À AVRIL 1851). (J.
BRUNEAU, ED)
  B.F. BART, 446:SPRING-SUMMER74-192
  A. FAIRLIE, 208(FS):JAN74-97
  C. ROSEN, 453:15MAY75-15
FLAUBERT, G. THE FIRST SENTIMENTAL
EDUCATION. (D. GORMAN, TRANS)
  P. BRADY, 207(FR):APR73-1052

118

FLAUBERT, G. FLAUBERT IN EGYPT.
(F. STEEGMULLER, ED & TRANS)
676(YR):AUTUMN73-XV
FLAUBERT, G. MADAME BOVARY.* (C.
GOTHOT-MERSCH, ED)
R. DEBRAY-GENETTE, 535(RHL):NOV-
DEC73-1091
FLEGG, J. - SEE FISHER, J.
FLEIG, K. ALVAR AALTO.
C. BONNEFOI, 98:APR73-342
FLEIG, K., ED. ALVAR AALTO.
J-M. RICHARDS, 617(TLS):1AUG75-868
FLEISHMAN, A. THE ENGLISH HISTORI-
CAL NOVEL: WALTER SCOTT TO VIRGINIA
WOOLF.*
W. DARBY, 141:SUMMER72-299
J-A. DIBBLE, 454:SPRING74-280
J-E-J., 191(ELN):SEP73(SUPP)-27
H-J. MÜLLENBROCK, 430(NS):SEP73-
502
FLEMING, J. HOW TO LIVE DANGEROUS-
LY.
N. CALLENDAR, 441:13APR75-30
FLEMING, J. TOO LATE! TOO LATE! THE
MAIDEN CRIED.
617(TLS):11JUL75-784
FLEMING, J., H. HONOUR & N. PEVSNER.
THE PENGUIN DICTIONARY OF ARCHITEC-
TURE. (2ND ED)
45:APR73-70
FLEMING, K. & A.T. THE FIRST TIME.
A. BROYARD, 441:2SEP75-35
A. COCKBURN, 453:11DEC75-28
FLEMING, T. 1776.
P. ADAMS, 61:SEP75-85
A. WHITMAN, 441:80CT75-45
FLEMMING, B., ED. TÜRKISCHE HAND-
SCHRIFTEN. (PT 1)
J. STEWART-ROBINSON, 318(JAOS):
JUL-SEP73-421
FLETCHER, A. THE TRANSCENDENTAL
MASQUE.*
J-H. ADAMSON, 597(SN):VOL45#2-452
M-M. BYARD, 551(RENQ):AUTUMN73-380
E-A-J. HONIGMANN, 541(RES):FEB73-
75
FLETCHER, B. A HISTORY OF ARCHITEC-
TURE. (REV BY J. PALMES)
J-M. RICHARDS, 617(TLS):25JUL75-
845
FLETCHER, C. BENEATH THE SURFACE.
P. ABRAMS, 617(TLS):21MAR75-318
FLETCHER, D. A LOVABLE MAN.*
N. CALLENDAR, 441:9MAR75-24
FLETCHER, D. A RESPECTABLE WOMAN.
617(TLS):11JUL75-784
FLETCHER, G. & P. THE POETICAL
WORKS OF GILES & PHINEAS FLETCHER.
(F-S. BOAS, ED)
J-J. YOCH, JR., 568(SCN):SPRING-
SUMMER74-9
FLETCHER, I., ED. MEREDITH NOW.*
B-F. FISHER 4TH, 594:SUMMER73-258
M. HARRIS, 72:BAND211HEFT1/3-128
J. WILT, 637(VS):DEC73-239
FLETCHER, I. - SEE PLARR, V.
FLETCHER, J., ED. FORCES IN MODERN
FRENCH DRAMA.
205(FMLS):OCT73-407
FLETCHER, J. CLAUDE SIMON & FICTION
NOW.
J. STURROCK, 617(TLS):30CT75-1151
FLETCHER, L. SILVER.
G-M. WILSON, 135:DEC73-296

FLETCHER, M. U.S.: WOMEN.
W-H. PRITCHARD, 441:18MAY75-36
FLETCHER, W.C. THE RUSSIAN ORTHODOX
CHURCH UNDERGROUND, 1917-1970.
P. CALL, 104:WINTER73-558
FLEW, A. AN INTRODUCTION TO WESTERN
PHILOSOPHY.*
D-A. ROHATYN, 258:JUN73-308
FLEXNER, J.T. GEORGE WASHINGTON.
(VOL 1)
617(TLS):13JUN75-680
FLINT, F.C. AMY LOWELL.
A. EASSON, 447(N&Q):SEP73-345
FLINT, R.W. - SEE MARINETTI, F.T.
FLOOD, P. PETER OLIVI'S RULE COM-
MENTARY.
L. HÖDL, 182:VOL26#23/24-843
FLORENCE, R. MARX'S DAUGHTERS.
J. DASH, 441:20JUL75-18
A. KELLY, 453:17JUL75-20
FLORENNE, Y. - SEE BAUDELAIRE, C.
FLORES, A., ED. APROXIMACIONES A
PABLO NERUDA.
R. PRING-MILL, 617(TLS):19SEP75-
1068
FLORES, A., ED. APROXIMACIONES A
CÉSAR VALLEJO.
K. SCHWARTZ, 238:DEC73-1128
DE FLORES, J. GRIMALTE Y GRADISSA.
(P. WALEY, ED)
N-G. ROUND, 402(MLR):JAN74-200
205(FMLS):OCT73-407
FLORES, J.M. POETRY IN EAST GER-
MANY.*
M-L. CAPUTO-MAYR, 295:FEB74-422
J. GLENN, 141:WINTER72-85
FLÓREZ, L. LAS "APUNTACIONES CRÍT-
ICAS" DE CUERVO Y EL ESPAÑOL BOGO-
TANO CIEN AÑOS DESPUÉS.
A. PARDO V., 263:OCT-DEC74-471
DE FLORIBAN, C.G. - SEE UNDER GUIT-
TARD DE FLORIBAN, C.
FLORIDA, R.E. VOLTAIRE & THE SOCIN-
IANS.
H. MASON, 617(TLS):30MAY75-594
FLORISOONE, M. DICTIONNAIRE DES
CATHÉDRALES DE FRANCE.
R-H. BLOCH, 207(FR):APR73-1085
FLOTTES, P. VIGNY ET SA FORTUNE
LITTÉRAIRE.*
M. SHAW, 208(FS):APR74-210
FLOWER, J.E., ED. FRANCE TODAY.*
N. HAMPSON, 208(FS):JAN74-115
FLOWER, J.E. INTENTION & ACHIEVE-
MENT.
J. COLLIGNON, 546(RR):NOV73-319
FLOWER, J.E. - SEE MAURIAC, F.
FLÛTRE, L.F. LE MOYEN PICARD D'AP-
RÈS LES TEXTES LITTÉRAIRES DU TEMPS
(1560-1660).
F. CARTON, 207(FR):OCT72-141
FLYNN, G. MANUEL TAMAYO Y BAUS.
G-E. MAZZEO, 399(MLJ):SEP-OCT74-
290
FLYNN, G. SOR JUANA INÉS DE LA
CRUZ.
P-L. FERNÁNDEZ GIMÉNEZ, 263:OCT-
DEC74-465
E-B. MARSHALL, 399(MLJ):JAN-FEB73-
74
G. SABÀT DE RIVERS, 400(MLN):MAR
73-460
K. SCHWARTZ, 238:DEC73-1126

119

FORREST, D.W. FRANCIS GALTON.
P. MEDAWAR, 617(TLS):24JAN75-83
S. MINOGUE, 362:13FEB75-220
FORREST, J. THE GLORY OF THE LILIES.
G. LAMBIN, 189(EA):APR-JUN73-247
"FORSCHUNGEN ZUR OSTEUROPÄISCHE GE-
SCHICHTE."
M. RAEFF, 104:WINTER73-545
FORSSMANN, W. EXPERIMENTS ON MYSELF.
L.K. ALTMAN, 441:7FEB75-35
M.G. MICHAELSON, 441:2FEB75-5
FORSTER, E.M. ASPECTS OF THE NOVEL.
(O. STALLYBRASS, ED)
D. DONOGHUE, 617(TLS):31JAN75-103
FORSTER, E.M. THE LIFE TO COME.
E. HANQUART, 189(EA):APR-JUN73-237
D. SALTER, 364:FEB/MAR75-5
FORSTER, E.M. MAURICE.*
J.C. FIELD, 556(RLV):1973/1-84
E. HANQUART, 189(EA):APR-JUN73-236
FORSTER, E.M. TWO CHEERS FOR DEMOC-
RACY. (M.O. STALLYBRASS, ED)
E. HANQUART, 189(EA):APR-JUN73-238
FORSTER, F. GRILLPARZERS THEORIE
DER DICHTUNG UND DES HUMORS.
W. DÜSING, 680(ZDP):BAND92HEFT2-
297
FORSTER, L. JANUS GRUTER'S ENGLISH
YEARS.
W. BIESTERFELD, 182:VOL26#11/12-
410
FORSTER, L. THE ICY FIRE.*
C. SCHAAR, 179(ES):AUG72-356
FORSTER, L. THE POET'S TONGUES.*
I. SIMON, 556(RLV):1973/3-286
FORSTER, R. THE HOUSE OF SAULX-
TAVANES.*
O. RANUM, 173(ECS):SUMMER74-512
FORSYTH, F. THE DAY OF THE JACKAL.
L.T.L., 502(PRS):FALL73-278
P. WOLFE, 628:SPRING74-5
FORSYTH, F. THE SHEPHERD.
T.J. BINYON, 617(TLS):19DEC75-1508
FORSYTH, J. A GRAMMAR OF ASPECT.*
J.A. ANCTIL, 660(WORD):DEC70-416
FORSYTH, J. - SEE VINOKUR, G.O.
FORSYTH, W.H. THE ENTOMBMENT OF
CHRIST.*
H.G. HOFMANN, 54:DEC73-633
FORT, C. THE COMPLETE BOOKS OF
CHARLES FORT.
G. JONAS, 441:14SEP75-26
FORTE, A. THE STRUCTURE OF ATONAL
MUSIC.*
P. GRIFFITHS, 415:OCT74-848
FORTENBAUGH, W.W. ARISTOTLE ON
EMOTION.
D.W. HAMLYN, 617(TLS):16MAY75-535
FOSCOLO, U. GLI APPUNTI PER LE
"LETTERE SCRITTE DALL 'INGHILTER-
RA."
617(TLS):31OCT75-1280
FOSCOLO, U. ON SEPULCHRES.
O. RAGUSA, 276:AUTUMN73-451
FOSKETT, D. A DICTIONARY OF BRITISH
MINIATURE PAINTERS.*
R. EDWARDS, 90:JAN73-48
FOSS, A. IBIZA & MINORCA.
T. LAMBERT, 617(TLS):30MAY75-606
FOSS, M. THE AGE OF PATRONAGE.*
P.J. KORSHIN, 173(ECS):FALL73-101
FOSS, M. UNDREAMED SHORES.*
442(NY):30JUN75-98

FOSSATTI, P. IL DESIGNO IN ITALIA
1945-1972.
T. DEL RENZIO, 592:JUL-AUG73-51
FOSTER, D. THE PURE LAND.
J. BARNES, 617(TLS):23MAY75-577
FOSTER, D.W. CHRISTIAN ALLEGORY IN
EARLY HISPANIC POETRY.
J. SNOW, 238:MAY73-498
FOSTER, D.W. & V.R. LUIS DE GÓN-
GORA.
B.W. WARDROPPER, 568(SCN):SPRING-
SUMMER74-11
FOSTER, D.W. & V.R. RESEARCH GUIDE
TO ARGENTINE LITERATURE.
J.M. FLINT, 86(BHS):JAN73-106
FOSTER, L. & J.W. SWANSON, EDS. EX-
PERIENCE & THEORY.
R. KIRK, 393(MIND):JAN73-153
FOSTER, L.A., COMP. BIBLIOGRAFIJA
RUSSKOJ ZARUBEŽNOJ LITERATURY 1918-
1968.
G. STRUVE, 574(SEEJ):SPRING72-108
FOSTER, S. THEIR SOLITARY WAY.*
H.R. CEDERBERG, 481(PQ):JUL73-385
B.M. STEPHENS, 568(SCN):SPRING-
SUMMER74-23
FOTHERGILL, R.A. PRIVATE CHRONICLES.
R. DINNAGE, 617(TLS):24JAN75-76
DE FOUCAULT, J. - SEE POLYBIUS
FOUCAULT, M. THE BIRTH OF THE CLIN-
IC.*
A.L. ARONSON, 676(YR):SPRING74-473
FOUCAULT, M. L'ORDRE DU DISCOURS.
W.V.E., 543:MAR73-534
FOUCAULT, M. SURVEILLER ET PUNIR.
C. LUCAS, 617(TLS):26SEP75-1090
FOUCAULT, M. - SEE RIVIÈRE, P.
DE FOUCHÉCOUR, C-H. LA DESCRIPTION
DE LA NATURE DANS LA POÉSIE LYRIQUE
PERSANE DU XIE SIÈCLE.
J. CLINTON, 318(JAOS):JAN-MAR73-99
FOUCHER, J-P. - SEE CHRÉTIEN DE
TROYES
FOUGÈRES, M. CHO' QUA'N.
E.J. TALBOT, 207(FR):OCT72-213
FOUGEROT DE MONBRON, L-C. LE COS-
MOPOLITE OU LE CITOYEN DU MONDE
[SUIVI DE] LA CAPITALE DES GAULES
OU LA NOUVELLE BABYLONE.* (R.
TROUSSON, ED)
L. VERSINI, 535(RHL):JUL-AUG73-703
FOULKES, A.P. & E. LOHNER, EDS. DAS
DEUTSCHE DRAMA VON KLEIST BIS
HAUPTMANN.
E. KRISPYN, 399(MLJ):MAR74-147
FOULON, C. - SEE NOËL DU FAIL
FOULON, C-L. LE POUVOIR EN PROVINCE
À LA LIBÉRATION.
R. GRIFFITHS, 617(TLS):29AUG75-965
FOUQUET, D. WORT UND BILD IN DER
MITTELALTERLICHEN TRISTANTRADI-
TION.*
W.K. FRANCKE, 133:1973/3-269
D.H. GREEN, 402(MLR):JAN74-218
P.W. TAX, 406:SUMMER74-189
W.A. TRINDADE, 382(MAE):1974/2-173
FOURCADE, D. - SEE MATISSE, H.
FOURIER, C. DESIGN FOR UTOPIA. (C.
GIDE, ED)
T.A. MITCHELL, 396(MODA):WINTER74-
109
FOURQUET, J. PROLEGOMENA ZU EINER
DEUTSCHEN GRAMMATIK.
G. KOLDE, 260(IF):BAND78-316

FRANK, M. MODERN ENGLISH.
D.L.F. NILSEN, 399(MLJ):SEP-OCT74-
300
FRANK, M. DAS PROBLEM "ZEIT" IN DER
DEUTSCHEN ROMANTIK.
F. GRIES, 406:WINTER74-428
FRANK, R.W., JR. CHAUCER & THE
LEGEND OF GOOD WOMEN.*
J.M. COWEN, 382(MAE):1974/3-291
R.M. WILSON, 175:AUTUMN73-112
FRANK, V. IZBRANNYE STAT'I. (L.
SCHAPIRO, ED)
K. FITZ LYON, 617(TLS):5SEP75-987
FRANK, W. MEMOIRS OF WALDO FRANK.
(A. TRACHTENBERG, ED)
C.E. EISINGER, 27(AL):MAY74-240
639(VQR):WINTER74-XXVI
FRANKE, H. & OTHERS. DIE ENTDECKUNG
DER WELT DURCH EUROPA, DIE SELBST-
BEHAUPTUNG DER ASIATISCHEN KULTUREN,
EUROPA IM ZEICHEN DER RATIONALITÄT.
J. KELLENS, 182:VOL26#11/12-440
FRANKE, H. & OTHERS. DIE EPOCHE DES
MONGOLENSTURMS, DIE FORMATION EUR-
OPAS, DIE NEUEN ISLAMISCHEN REICHE.
P. LECOQ, 182:VOL26#11/12-437
FRANKE, K. DIE LITERATUR DER
DEUTSCHEN DEMOKRATISCHEN REPUBLIC.
P. HUTCHINSON, 220(GL&L):JUL74-334
G. LOOSE, 400(MLN):OCT73-1062
FRANKE, K. & W.R. LANGENBUCHER, EDS.
ERZÄHLER AUS DER DDR.
S. ELKHADEM, 268:JAN75-90
FRANKFURT, H.G. DEMONS, DREAMERS,
& MADMEN.*
D.H. SANFORD, 482(PHR):JAN73-120
FRANKFURTER, F. FROM THE DIARIES OF
FELIX FRANKFURTER. (J.P. LASH, ED)
M.H. FREEDMAN, 441:31AUG75-4
442(NY):29SEP75-132
FRANKL, P. PRINCIPLES OF ARCHITEC-
TURAL HISTORY.
J.W. RUDD, 290(JAAC):SUMMER74-569
FRANKL, V.E. THE UNCONSCIOUS GOD.
A. BROYARD, 441:26NOV75-27
FRANKLIN, H.B. BACK WHERE YOU CAME
FROM.
B. DE MOTT, 61:AUG75-84
FRANKLIN, H.B. FUTURE PERFECT.
R. ASSELINEAU, 189(EA):JAN-MAR73-
118
FRANKLYN, J. A DICTIONARY OF
RHYMING SLANG.
P. KEATING, 617(TLS):30MAY75-588
FRANOLIĆ, B. LA LANGUE LITTÉRAIRE
CROATE.*
A. ALBIN, 279:VOL16-206
FRANTZ, A. THE ATHENIAN AGORA.
C.G. BOULTER, 124:SEP-OCT73-42
FRANTZ, D.G. TOWARD A GENERATIVE
GRAMMAR OF BLACKFOOT.
I. GODDARD, 350:SEP74-601
FRANZ, G. DIE KIRCHENLEITUNG IN
HOHENLOHE IN DEN JAHRZEHNTEN NACH
DER REFORMATION.
E.W. GRITSCH, 182:VOL26#3/4-124
FRARY, M. & W.A. OWENS. IMPRESSIONS
OF THE BIG THICKET.
C.T. WHALEY, 584(SWR):WINTER74-91
FRASER, A. CROMWELL.*
J. STEPHENS, 568(SCN):WINTER74-80
D. UNDERDOWN, 639(VQR):SPRING74-
317
676(YR):SPRING74-XII

FRASER, A. KING JAMES.
J. HURSTFIELD, 617(TLS):18APR75-
420
A. WHITMAN, 441:30MAR75-16
442(NY):24FEB75-143
FRASER, A., ED. THE LIVES OF THE
KINGS & QUEENS OF ENGLAND.
R. FULFORD, 617(TLS):8AUG75-893
C.L. MEE, JR., 441:7DEC75-42
FRASER, D. THE EVOLUTION OF THE
BRITISH WELFARE STATE.
B.B. GILBERT, 637(VS):JUN74-443
FRASER, D. & H.M. COLE. AFRICAN ART
& LEADERSHIP.*
A. RUBIN, 54:DEC73-650
FRASER, G.M. FLASHMAN IN THE GREAT
GAME.
M. LEVIN, 441:28DEC75-20
R. USBORNE, 617(TLS):28NOV75-1407
FRASER, G.S. LAWRENCE DURRELL.
205(FMLS):APR73-213
FRASER, J. VIOLENCE IN THE ARTS.*
T.J. ROBERTS, 598(SOR):SUMMER75-
685
FRASER, K. WHAT I WANT.
H. CARRUTH, 249(HUDR):SUMMER74-311
FRASER, R. BLACK HORSE TAVERN.
L. SHOHET, 102(CANL):AUTUMN74-107
FRASER, R. THE DARK AGES & THE AGE
OF GOLD.*
R. ELLRODT, 189(EA):OCT-DEC73-473
H.L., 131(CL):FALL73-373
R.J. QUINONES, 401(MLQ):MAR74-78
FRASER, R. THE STRUGGLE OUTSIDE.
S. ATHERTON, 268:JUL75-183
FRASER, R. THE WAR AGAINST POETRY.*
P. BILTON, 179(ES):DEC72-556
FRASER, S. PANDORA.*
P. BARCLAY, 102(CANL):SPRING74-109
FRASER, S.E. & K-L. HSU. CHINESE
EDUCATION & SOCIETY.
R.C., 293(JAST):MAY73-573
FRASER, T.P. LE DUCHAT, FIRST EDI-
TOR OF RABELAIS.
D. COLEMAN, 208(FS):JAN74-58
M. LEVER, 535(RHL):JAN-FEB73-128
FRASER, W.R. REFORMS & RESTRAINTS
IN MODERN FRENCH EDUCATION.
D.F. BRADSHAW, 208(FS):JUL74-374
FRATTI, M. ELEONORA DUSE.
P.T. NOLAN, 160:WINTER72/73-133
FRATTI, M. RACES. (R. HOGAN, ED)
P.T. NOLAN, 160:SPRING73-190
FRAUTSCHI, R.L. & C. BOUYGUES. POUR
ET CONTRE.
B. EBLING, 207(FR):APR73-1080
G.J. HASENAUER, 399(MLJ):JAN-FEB
74-64
FRAUWALLNER, E. THE EARLIEST VINAYA
& THE BEGINNINGS OF BUDDHIST LITER-
ATURE.
C.S. PREBISH, 293(JAST):AUG73-669
FRAYLING, C. - SEE BONAPARTE, N.
FRAYN, M. CONSTRUCTIONS.*
J. BENNETT, 617(TLS):20JUN75-693
FRAYNE, T. THE MAD MEN OF HOCKEY.
M. RICHLER, 441:5JAN75-6
FRÉCAUT, J-M. L'ESPRIT ET L'HUMOUR
CHEZ OVIDE.
J-P. CÈBE, 555:VOL47FASC1-161
FREDEMAN, W.E. - SEE ROSSETTI, W.M.

FREDERIC, L. DAILY LIFE IN JAPAN AT THE TIME OF THE SAMURAI, 1185-1603.
E.P. TSURMI, 529(QQ):WINTER73-637

FREDOUILLE, J-C. TERTULLIEN ET LA CONVERSION DE LA CULTURE ANTIQUE.
P. LANGLOIS, 555:VOL47FASC2-358

FREEBORN, R. THE RISE OF THE RUS-SIAN NOVEL.*
W. ARNDT, 574(SEEJ):WINTER73-448
J. BAYLEY, 575(SEER):APR74-274
H. GIFFORD, 402(MLR):APR74-475

FREEDMAN, J. CROWDING & BEHAVIOR.
J. CHURCH, 441:19OCT75-31
442(NY):24NOV75-195

FREEDMAN, M. AMERICAN DRAMA IN SOCIAL CONTEXT.*
295:FEB74-507

FREEDMAN, M., ED. FAMILY & KINSHIP IN CHINESE SOCIETY.
F.L.K. HSU, 318(JAOS):JAN-MAR73-85

FREEDMAN, M.H. LAWYERS' ETHICS IN AN ADVERSARY SYSTEM.
N. JOHNSTON, 441:28SEP75-5

FREEDMAN, R. THE NOVEL.
442(NY):19MAY75-120

FREELING, N. WHAT ARE THE BUGLES BLOWING FOR?
R. HEPPENSTALL, 617(TLS):26SEP75-1078
M. LASKI, 362:20NOV75-684

FREEMAN, D., ED. BOSTON ARCHITEC-TURE.
N.P., 46:JAN73-80

FREEMAN, D. CREEPS.
A.P. MESSENGER, 102(CANL):WINTER74-101

FREEMAN, D.C., ED. LINGUISTICS & LITERARY STYLE.
J. DORE, 215(GL):VOL13#2-118

FREEMAN, E. THE THEATRE OF ALBERT CAMUS.*
D. KNOWLES, 402(MLR):APR74-424
C.A. VIGGIANI, 399(MLJ):NOV73-361

FREEMAN, G. THE MARRIAGE MACHINE.
J. MELLORS, 362:7AUG75-189
J. MILLER, 617(TLS):4JUL75-714

FREEMAN, J. THE POLITICS OF WOMEN'S LIBERATION.
L. SHERR, 441:5OCT75-38

FREEMAN, M.B. THE SAINT MARTIN EMBROIDERIES.
C.C. MAYER-THURMAN, 54:DEC73-628

FREEMANTLE, B. FACE ME WHEN YOU WALK AWAY.*
N. CALLENDAR, 441:19JAN75-36

FREEMANTLE, B. THE MAN WHO WANTED TOMORROW.
M. LEVIN, 441:14DEC75-31

FREER, C. MUSIC FOR A KING.*
P. CHOSSONNERY, 189(EA):JUL-SEP73-355
J.S. LAWRY, 529(QQ):SUMMER73-302
R.P. LESSENICH, 597(SN):VOL45#2-449
J.C.A. RATHMELL, 551(RENQ):WINTER73-532
H. SERGEANT, 175:SPRING73-28

FREESE, P. DIE INITIATIONSREISE.
A. HELLER, 430(NS):APR73-230
R.D. RUST, 72:BAND211HEFT1/3-174

FREGE, G. CONCEPTUAL NOTATION & RELATED ARTICLES.* (T.W. BYNUM, ED & TRANS)
J. CORCORAN & D. LEVIN, 486:SEP73-454
V.H. DUDMAN, 63:AUG74-177

FREGE, G. NACHGELASSENE SCHRIFTEN UND WISSENSCHAFTLICHER BRIEFWECHSEL. (VOL 1) (H. HERMES, F. KAMBARTEL & F. KAULBACH, EDS) SCHRIFTEN ZUR LOGIK UND SPRACHPHILOSOPHIE. (G. GABRIEL, ED)
M-A. SINACEUR, 98:NOV73-1013

FREGE, G. ON THE FOUNDATIONS OF GEOMETRY & FORMAL THEORIES OF ARITH-METIC.
J. CORCORAN & S. WOOD, 484(PPR):DEC73-283
M.D. RESNIK, 482(PHR):APR73-266

FREI, H. LA GRAMMAIRE DES FAUTES.
F. HELGORSKY, 209(FM):OCT73-423

FREIBERG, M., ED. JOURNALS OF THE HOUSE OF REPRESENTATIVES OF MASSA-CHUSETTS, 1765-1766.* (VOL 42)
L.G. DE PAUW, 14:JAN73-71
J-A. SCHUTZ, 432(NEQ):MAR74-165

FREIBERG, M., ED. JOURNALS OF THE HOUSE OF REPRESENTATIVES OF MASSA-CHUSETTS, 1766. (VOL 43)
J-A. SCHUTZ, 432(NEQ):MAR74-165

FREIDEL, F. FRANKLIN D. ROOSEVELT: LAUNCHING THE NEW DEAL.
J.P. ROCHE, 639(VQR):SPRING74-303

FREIJ, L.W. "TÜRLOSIGKEIT."
G. MÜLLER, 597(SN):VOL45#2-434

FREINET, C. LA MÉTHODE NATURELLE.
H. JÖRG, 182:VOL26#5/6-136

FREMLIN, C. THE LONG SHADOW.
T.J. BINYON, 617(TLS):19DEC75-1508
M. LASKI, 362:20NOV75-684

FRENCH, A., ED & TRANS. THE ATHEN-IAN HALF-CENTURY, 478-431 B.C.*
J. BRISCOE, 123:NOV74-303

FRENCH, A., ED. CZECH POETRY. (VOL 1)
R.B. PYNSENT, 575(SEER):APR74-313

FRENCH, A.L. SHAKESPEARE & THE CRITICS.*
R.A. FOAKES, 175:AUTUMN72-107
P. SWINDEN, 148:WINTER73-375
R. WARREN, 447(N&Q):APR73-151

FRENCH, C.L. SHIBA KŌKAN.
C.R. BOXER, 617(TLS):22AUG75-939

FRENCH, D. LEAVING HOME.*
R.W. BEVIS, 102(CANL):WINTER74-106

FRENCH, H. A SILVER COLLECTORS' GLOSSARY & A LIST OF EARLY AMERICAN SILVERSMITHS & THEIR MARKS.
C. OMAN, 39:FEB73-202

FRENCH, P.J. JOHN DEE.*
W. SHUMAKER, 551(RENQ):SPRING73-68

FREND, W.H.C. THE RISE OF THE MONO-PHYSITE MOVEMENT.*
L.W. BARNARD, 313:VOL63-275

FRENK ALATORRE, M. ENTRE FOLKLORE Y LITERATURA (LÍRICA HISPÁNICA AN-TIGUA).
400(MLN):MAR73-507

FRENK ALATORRE, M. & Y. JIMÉNEZ DE BÁEZ, EDS. COPLAS DE AMOR DEL FOLKLORE MEXICANO.
C. STERN, 545(RPH):FEB74-444

FRENZ, H. & H-J. LANG, EDS. NORD-
AMERIKANISCHE LITERATUR IM DEUT-
SCHEN SPRACHRAUM SEIT 1945.
H. GALINSKY, 301(JEGP):OCT74-604
FRERE-COOK, G. & OTHERS. THE DECOR-
ATIVE ARTS OF THE CHRISTIAN CHURCH.
J. BECKWITH, 39:APR73-436
FRESNAULT-DERUELLE, P. LA BANDE
DESSINÉE.
J-M. KLINKENBERG, 209(FM):JUL73-
307
FREUD, A. INFANTS WITHOUT FAMILIES
& REPORTS ON THE HAMPSTEAD NURSER-
IES 1939-1945.
R. DINNAGE, 617(TLS):18JUL75-795
FREUD, S. COCAINE PAPERS BY SIGMUND
FREUD. (R. BYCK, ED)
N.E. ZINBERG, 453:30OCT75-32
FREUD, S. & C.G. JUNG. THE FREUD/
JUNG LETTERS.* (W. MC GUIRE, ED)
J. CODY, 598(SOR):AUTUMN75-926
J. REED, 99:SEP75-66
FREUDENTHAL, H. LINCOS.
L. NARENS, 316:SEP73-517
FREUND, J. LE NOUVEL ÂGE.
D. MERLLIÉ, 542:JAN-MAR73-99
FREUNDLICH, I. - SEE HINSON, M.
FREUSTIÉ, J. ISABELLE.
J.P. GOLLUB, 207(FR):OCT72-216
FREY, G. PHILOSOPHIE UND WISSEN-
SCHAFT.
R. BLANCHÉ, 542:JUL-SEP73-356
FREY, M. DER KÜNSTLER UND SEIN
WERK BEI W.H. WACKENRODER UND
E.T.A. HOFFMANN.*
P.M. HABERLAND, 221(GQ):NOV73-631
FREYTAG, W. DAS OXYMORON BEI WOLF-
RAM, GOTTFRIED UND ANDERN DICHTERN
DES MITTELALTERS.*
H. ADOLF, 182:VOL26#1/2-21
FRIAR, K., ED & TRANS. MODERN GREEK
POETRY.*
R.C. CLARK, 544:FALL74-142
FRIDAY, N., COMP. MY SECRET GARDEN.
C. BLACKWOOD, 617(TLS):24OCT75-
1258
FRIDH, Å. CONTRIBUTIONS À LA CRIT-
IQUE ET À L'INTERPRÉTATION DES
"VARIAE" DE CASSIODORE.*
P.G. WALSH, 123:MAR74-143
FRIDH, Å. DER SOGENANNTE PROSPEK-
TIVE KONJUNKTIV IM LATEINISCHEN.*
B.I. KNOTT, 123:MAR74-151
FRIED, C. AN ANATOMY OF VALUES.*
J.H. SOBEL, 482(PHR):JAN74-131
FRIED, M. THE WORLD OF THE URBAN
WORKING CLASS.
R.M. JOHNSON, 432(NEQ):JUN74-333
FRIEDE, J. & B. KEEN, EDS. BARTOL-
OMÉ DE LAS CASAS IN HISTORY.
J.H. ELLIOTT, 453:15MAY75-3
FRIEDEN, B.J. & M. KAPLAN. THE
POLITICS OF NEGLECT.
F. POWLEDGE, 441:26OCT75-40
FRIEDENBERG, E.Z. THE DISPOSAL OF
LIBERTY & OTHER INDUSTRIAL WASTES.
B. DE MOTT, 61:OCT75-102
W.C. MC WILLIAMS, 441:12OCT75-31
FRIEDERICH, W. PROBLEME DER SEMAN-
TIK UND SYNTAX DES ENGLISCHEN GER-
UNDIUMS.
A.R. TELLIER, 189(EA):OCT-DEC73-
455

FRIEDLAND, E., P. SEABURY & A. WIL-
DAVSKY. THE GREAT DÉTENTE DISAS-
TER.
J. CHACE, 441:24AUG75-3
FRIEDLAND, M.L., ED. COURTS &
TRIALS.
W.R. CORNISH, 617(TLS):26SEP75-
1101
FRIEDLANDER, I. & N. UZEL. THE
WHIRLING DERVISHES.
A. WEIL, 441:13JUL75-6
FRIEDMAN, B. SMUTS.
J. LEWIN, 617(TLS):21NOV75-1396
FRIEDMAN, B.H. ALMOST A LIFE.
M. LEVIN, 441:24AUG75-28
442(NY):8SEP75-125
FRIEDMAN, B.H. ALFONSO OSSORIO.*
R. HOWARD, 139:APR73-12
FRIEDMAN, B.H. JACKSON POLLOCK.*
D. FREKE, 592:MAR73-144
J. GOLDING, 135:SEP73-69
FRIEDMAN, B.J. ABOUT HARRY TOWNS.*
R. DAVIES, 617(TLS):14FEB75-156
J. MELLORS, 362:20FEB75-253
FRIEDMAN, D.M. MARVELL'S PASTORAL
ART.*
L. POTTER, 179(ES):AUG72-360
FRIEDMAN, J. RETRACKING AMERICA.
M. & S. SOUTHWORTH, 505:NOV73-176
FRIEDMAN, J.B. ORPHEUS IN THE MID-
DLE AGES.*
R.M. WILSON, 402(MLR):APR74-367
FRIEDMAN, M. BURIED ALIVE.
H. WILLIAMS, 364:OCT/NOV74-64
FRIEDMAN, M.J., ED. SAMUEL BECKETT
NOW.
H.P. PRIESSNITZ, 447(N&Q):SEP73-
349
FRIEDMAN, P. AND IF DEFEATED ALLEGE
FRAUD.*
M. GRIFFITH, 573(SSF):WINTER73-116
FRIEDMAN, R.C., R.M. RICHART & R.L.
VANDE WIELE, EDS. SEX DIFFERENCES
IN BEHAVIOR.
S. EDMISTON, 441:13APR75-3
FRIEDMANN, Y. SHAYKH AHMAD SIR-
HINDI.
A. ALI, 273(IC):APR73-184
FRIEDRICH, H. ROMANISCHE LITERA-
TUREN: AUFSÄTZE I - FRANKREICH.
B.L.O. RICHTER, 207(FR):APR73-1032
FRIEDRICH, J. & W. RÖLLIG. PHÖNIZ-
ISCH-PUNISCHE GRAMMATIK. (2ND ED)
J. NAVEH, 318(JAOS):OCT-DEC73-588
FRIEDRICH, P. PROTO-INDO-EUROPEAN
TREES.*
J. & M.J.P. NICHOLS, 545(RPH):AUG
73-79
J. SAFAREWICZ, 353:15OCT73-96
R. SCHMITT, 343:BAND16HEFT1-49
FRIES, H.J. A SIBERIAN JOURNEY.
(W. KIRCHNER, ED)
B. HOLLINGSWORTH, 617(TLS):6JUN75-
632
FRIESE, W. NORDISCHE LITERATUREN
IM 20. JAHRHUNDERT.
G.C. SCHOOLFIELD, 563(SS):FALL74-
435
VON FRISCH, K., WITH O. VON FRISCH.
ANIMAL ARCHITECTURE.*
W.H. THORPE, 617(TLS):3OCT75-1122
FRISKIN, J. & I. FREUNDLICH. MUSIC
FOR THE PIANO.
F. DAWES, 415:AUG74-659

FRISTEDT, S.L. THE WYCLIFFE BIBLE.*
(PT 2)
  V. MURRAY, 541(RES):FEB73-59
FRITH, H.J. WILDLIFE CONSERVATION.
  K. MELLANBY, 617(TLS):14FEB75-175
FRITZ, J. CAST FOR A REVOLUTION.
  J.J. WATERS, 432(NEQ):SEP73-476
VON FRITZ, K. GRUNDPROBLEME DER GE-
SCHICHTE DER ANTIKEN WISSENSCHAFT.*
  F. SOLMSEN, 24:FALL74-314
VON FRITZ, K., ED. PSEUDEPIGRAPH-
ICA I.
  J. PHILIP, 487:WINTER73-414
FRITZ, P. & D. WILLIAMS, EDS. THE
TRIUMPH OF CULTURE.*
  C.P. BARBIER, 402(MLR):JUL74-607
FROBENIUS, L., ED. AFRICAN NIGHTS.
  A.H. CARTER 3D, 352(LE&W):VOL16#3-
  1075
FRODL-KRAFT, E. DIE MITTELALTER-
LICHEN GLASGEMÄLDE IN NIEDERÖSTER-
REICH. (PT 1)
  R. BECKSMANN, 683:BAND36HEFT2/3-
  183
FROHOCK, W.M. THEODORE DREISER.
  R. ASSELINEAU, 189(EA):APR-JUN73-
  247
FROIDEFOND, C. LE MIRAGE ÉGYPTIEN
DANS LA LITTÉRATURE GRECQUE D'HOM-
ÈRE À ARISTOTE.
  É. DES PLACES, 555:VOL47FASC1-120
FROLEC, V., ED. BULGARISCHE VOLKS-
MÄRCHEN.
  M. BOŠKOVIĆ-STULLI, 196:BAND14
  HEFT3-274
FROMENTIN, E. & E. BELTREMIEUX.
GUSTAVE DROUINEAU. (B. WRIGHT, ED)
  G. SAGNES, 535(RHL):SEP-OCT73-918
FROMM, E. THE ANATOMY OF HUMAN
DESTRUCTIVENESS.*
  L.B. HALL, 584(SWR):SPRING74-214
  J. NAUGHTON, 362:13MAR75-347
  P.A. ROBINSON, 473(PR):2/1974-280
FROMM, H. & K. GRUBMÜLLER - SEE
KONRAD VON FUSSESBRUNNEN
FROMRICH, Y. MUSIQUE ET CARICATURE
EN FRANCE AU XIXE SIÈCLE.*
  H. MAC DONALD, 415:JUL74-570
FRONING, H. DITHYRAMBOS UND VASEN-
MALEREI IN ATHEN.*
  R.M. COOK, 123:NOV74-309
FROSCH, T.R. THE AWAKENING OF AL-
BION.*
  P. BROMBERG, 591(SIR):SPRING74-169
  D.R. FAULKNER, 676(YR):SUMMER74-
  590
  639(VQR):SUMMER74-LXXVI
FROSCH-FREIBURG, F. SCHWANKMÄREN
UND FABLIAUX.
  D. BLAMIRES, 402(MLR):APR74-453
  D.H. GREEN, 220(GL&L):APR74-257
FROST, F.J. GREEK SOCIETY.
  S.K. EDDY, 122:APR74-132
FROST, R. ROBERT FROST ON WRITING.
(E. BARRY, ED)
  R. FOSTER, 432(NEQ):SEP74-469
FROST, R. ROBERT FROST: POETRY &
PROSE.* (E.C. LATHEM & L. THOMP-
SON, EDS)
  A. GRADE, 432(NEQ):SEP73-471
FROST, R. & E. FAMILY LETTERS OF
ROBERT & ELINOR FROST.* (A. GRADE,
ED)
  L. ROSENTHAL, 385(MQR):SPRING75-
  229

FROUG, W. THE SCREENWRITER LOOKS AT
THE SCREEN WRITER.
  J.R. PARISH, 200:FEB73-115
"FRÜHE SCHRIFTZEUGNISSE DER MENSCH-
HEIT."
  A. DOSTÁL, 574(SEEJ):WINTER72-497
  W. NAHM, 343:BAND16HEFT1-31
FRUMAN, N. COLERIDGE, THE DAMAGED
ARCHANGEL.*
  J.B. BEER, 541(RES):AUG73-346
  J. COLMER, 677:VOL4-312
  B. COTTLE, 184(EIC):OCT73-413
  A. FLETCHER, 141:SUMMER73-265
  R.A. FOAKES, 175:SPRING73-31
  T. MC FARLAND, 676(YR):WINTER74-
  252
  R. PARK, 89(BJA):SUMMER73-301
  M.F. SCHULZ, 405(MP):MAY74-453
FRUMKINA, R.M. VEROJATNOST' ELEMEN-
TOV TEKSTA I REČEVOE POVEDENIE.
  J. PRŮCHA, 353:1APR73-121
FRUSHELL, R.C. & B.J. VONDER-SMITH,
EDS. CONTEMPORARY THOUGHT ON
EDMUND SPENSER.
  A. FOWLER, 617(TLS):3OCT75-1135
FRUTTERO, C. & F. LUCCENTINI. THE
SUNDAY WOMAN.* (FRENCH TITLE: LA
FEMME DU DIMANCHE.)
  N. KATTAN, 98:DEC73-1147
FRY, A. COME A LONG JOURNEY. HOW A
PEOPLE DIE.
  M. BOWERING, 376:OCT73-137
FRY, D.K. BEOWULF & THE FIGHT AT
FINNSBURH.*
  L. WHITBREAD, 179(ES):JUN72-249
FRY, P.S. BRITISH MEDIEVAL CASTLES.
  617(TLS):26DEC75-1547
FRY, R. LETTERS OF ROGER FRY.* (D.
SUTTON, ED)
  Q. BELL, 90:JAN73-50
  R. EDWARDS, 135:FEB73-112
FRYE, E. THE MARBLE THRESHING
FLOOR.
  L. DURÁN, 415:MAY74-391
FRYE, N. THE STUBBORN STRUCTURE.*
  P. GOETSCH, 430(NS):MAR73-172
FRYE, R.M. SHAKESPEARE.
  L.F. BALL, 570(SQ):SUMMER73-338
FUBINI, M. ROMANTICISMO ITALIANO.
  W.T.S., 191(ELN):SEP73(SUPP)-163
FUCHS, A. MORPHOLOGIE DES VERBS IM
CAHUILLA.*
  R.A. JACOBS, 361:SEP73-128
  S. LILJEBLAD, 269(IJAL):APR73-110
FUCHS, V.R. WHO SHALL LIVE?
  H.J. GEIGER, 441:2MAR75-1
FUEGI, J., ED. BRECHT HEUTE -
BRECHT TODAY.*
  R. MANTLE, 220(GL&L):JAN74-172
FUEGI, J. THE ESSENTIAL BRECHT.
  B.F. DUKORE, 295:FEB74-546
DE FUENTES, Á.G. - SEE UNDER GALMÉS
DE FUENTES, Á.
FUENTES, C. TIEMPO MEXICANO.
  R.M. REEVE, 238:MAY73-509
FUENTES, C. - SEE PAZ, O.
FÜGEN, H.N. DICHTUNG IN DER BÜRGER-
LICHEN GESELLSCHAFT.
  W. GROTHE, 597(SN):VOL45#2-424
FUHRMANN, F. - SEE PLUTARCH
FUHRMANN, J.T. THE ORIGINS OF CAPI-
TALISM IN RUSSIA.*
  W.B. WALSH, 550(RUSR):JAN73-83
FUHRMANS, H. - SEE SCHELLING, F.W.J.

126

FUJIOKA, R. TEA CEREMONY UTENSILS.
S. SITWELL, 39:DEC73-516
FUJITA KŌTATSU. GENSHI JŌDO SHISŌ
NO KENKYŪ.
L. HURVITZ, 318(JAOS):JAN-MAR73-91
FULASS, H. PROBLEMS OF TERMINOLOGY.
315(JAL):VOL11PT2-106
FULCANELLI. LE MYSTÈRE DES CATHÉD-
RALES. (3RD ED)
R.C. CARROLL, 207(FR):OCT72-182
FULFORD, R. - SEE QUEEN VICTORIA
FULGENTIUS. FULGENTIUS THE MYTHOG-
RAPHER. (L.G. WHITBREAD, ED &
TRANS)
R.T. BRUÈRE, 122:APR73-143
FULLER, B. ZEBINA'S MOUNTAIN.
M. LEVIN, 441:8JUN75-16
FULLER, E.L. VISIONS IN STONE.
639(VQR):SUMMER74-CVIII
FULLER, J. CANNIBALS & MISSIONAR-
IES.*
A. CLUYSENAAR, 565:VOL14#1-70
H. SERGEANT, 175:AUTUMN73-121
FULLER, J. POEMS & EPISTLES.
S.C. FELDMAN, 598(SOR):AUTUMN75-
957
FULLER, J. SPACE.
A. NELSON, 441:6JUL75-4
FULLER, J.G. WE ALMOST LOST DETROIT.
M.E. GALE, 441:30NOV75-4
FULLER, R. FROM THE JOKE SHOP.
A. STEVENSON, 362:30OCT75-571
FULLER, R. PROFESSORS & GODS.*
OWLS & ARTIFICERS.
D.E. STANFORD, 598(SOR):SPRING75-
XVII
FULLER, R.B., WITH E.J. APPLEWHITE.
SYNERGETICS.
O.B. HARDISON, JR., 441:29JUN75-4
R. TODD, 61:MAY75-84
FULTON, R. TREE-LINES.
V. YOUNG, 249(HUDR):WINTER74/75-
597
FULWEILER, H.W. LETTERS FROM THE
DARKLING PLAIN.
A. ROPER, 301(JEGP):JUL74-449
M. SMITH, 577(SHR):FALL73-437
"FUND OG FORSKNING." (VOLS 18 & 19)
B.G. FLETCHER HOLT, 78(BC):AUTUMN
73-397
"FUNK & WAGNALLS STANDARD DICTIONARY
OF FOLKLORE, MYTHOLOGY, & LEGEND."
J.H. BRUNVAND, 292(JAF):OCT-DEC73-
411
FUNKE, G. PHÄNOMENOLOGIE - META-
PHYSIK ODER METHODE?
H.E.M.H., 543:DEC72-356
FUNKE, H-G. CRÉBILLON FILS ALS
MORALIST UND GESELLSCHAFTSKRITIKER.
M.D. EBEL, 481(PQ):JUL73-481
FUNNELL, C.E. BY THE BEAUTIFUL SEA.
F. FERRETTI, 441:16NOV75-79
FURBANK, P.N. REFLECTIONS ON THE
WORD "IMAGE."
R. EDGLEY, 184(EIC):JAN72-99
A. MANSER, 321:SPRING73-75
H. PESCHMANN, 175:SUMMER72-73
FURBERG, M. SAYING & MEANING.
W. BERRIMAN, 154:MAR73-159
D. HOLCROFT, 393(MIND):OCT73-626
VON FÜRER-HAIMENDORF, C. HIMALAYAN
TRADERS.
R. NEEDHAM, 617(TLS):1AUG75-869

FURHAMMAR, L. & F. ISAKSSON. POLI-
TICS & FILM.*
J. MELLEN, 295:FEB74-513
FURLONG, W.B. SEASON WITH SOLTI.
J. YOHALEM, 441:19JAN75-31
FURLONG, W.B. SHAW & CHESTERTON.*
F.P.W. MC DOWELL, 295:FEB74-449
FURMAN, E. A CHILD'S PARENT DIES.
G. GORER, 617(TLS):18JUL75-798
FURNEAUX, R. THE ROMAN SIEGE OF
JERUSALEM.
G.M. PAUL, 255(HAB):SUMMER73-201
FURNÉE, E.J. DIE WICHTIGSTEN KON-
SONANTISCHEN ERSCHEINUNGEN DES VOR-
GRIECHISCHEN.
W. DRESSLER, 350:DEC74-736
V.I. GEORGIEV, 343:BAND16HEFT2-164
FURNESS, R.S. EXPRESSIONISM.
I.B. WHYTE, 111:3MAY74-128
FURST, L.R. ROMANTICISM IN PERSPEC-
TIVE.
R. VON TIEDEMANN, 52:BAND8HEFT1-98
FURST, L.R. & P.N. SKRINE. NATURAL-
ISM.*
J. OSBORNE, 220(GL&L):JUL74-325
FURTADO, C. ECONOMIC DEVELOPMENT OF
LATIN AMERICA.
M.H.J. FINCH, 86(BHS):APR73-194
FURULAND, L. FOLKHÖGSKOLAN.
B. BIRKELAND, 172(EDDA):1973/1-58
FURUMARK, A. MYCENAEAN POTTERY.
W. SCHIERING, 182:VOL26#9-304
FUSSELL, E. LUCIFER IN HARNESS.*
A. GELPI, 27(AL):NOV74-405
J.V. HAGOPIAN, 659:SUMMER75-393
639(VQR):SUMMER74-LXXII
FUSSELL, P. THE GREAT WAR & MODERN
MEMORY.
R. EDER, 441:13SEP75-21
M. HOWARD, 617(TLS):5DEC75-1434
F. KERMODE, 441:31AUG75-2
K. MILLER, 453:16OCT75-27
442(NY):200CT75-171
VON FUSSESBRUNNEN, K. - SEE UNDER
KONRAD VON FUSSESBRUNNEN
FÜSSLI, J.H. SÄMTLICHE GEDICHTE.
(M. BIRCHER & K.S. GUTHKE, EDS)
H. BOESCHENSTEIN, 182:VOL26#23/24-
862
FUSSMAN, G. ATLAS LINGUISTIQUE DES
PARLERS DARDES ET KAFIRS.
A. WEIDERT, 182:VOL26#20-729
FYNN. MISTER GOD, THIS IS ANNA.
M. LEVIN, 441:12OCT75-49

GAATONE, D. ETUDE DESCRIPTIVE DU
SYSTÈME DE LA NÉGATION EN FRANÇAIS
CONTEMPORAIN.*
M-L. MOREAU, 556(RLV):1973/2-188
J. POHL, 209(FM):APR73-186
N.C.W. SPENCE, 208(FS):JUL74-368
GABBERT, G., ED. BUDDHISTISCHE
PLASTIK AUS CHINA UND JAPAN.
D. SECKEL, 182:VOL26#17/18-608
GÄBE, L. DESCARTES' SELBSTKRITIK.
R. SPECHT, 536:DEC73-348
GABINSKIJ, M.A. POJAVLENIE I UTRATA
PERVIČNOGO ALBANSKOGO INFINITIVA.
J.S. KOLSTI, 574(SEEJ):WINTER72-
508
GABRIEL, G. - SEE FREGE, G.

GADAMER, H-G. HEGELS DIALEKTIK.
  D.E. CHRISTENSEN, 319:JUL75-416
GADAMER, H-G., ED. STUTTGARTER
HEGEL-TAGE 1970.
  W.H. WALSH, 617(TLS):28MAR75-343
GADD, D. THE LOVING FRIENDS.*
  P. DICKINSON, 364:FEB/MAR75-140
  I. EHRENPREIS, 453:17APR75-9
  P. STANSKY, 441:1JUN75-7
GADDIS, J.L. THE UNITED STATES &
THE ORIGINS OF THE COLD WAR, 1941-
1947.
  G.A. MORGAN, 550(RUSR):JAN73-77
GADDIS, W. J R.
  A. HELLER, 61:NOV75-118
  C. LEHMANN-HAUPT, 441:30OCT75-43
  G. STADE, 441:9NOV75-1
GADNEY, R. THE LAST HOURS BEFORE
DAWN.
  M. AMIS, 617(TLS):17JAN75-48
GAEDE, F. HUMANISMUS, BAROCK, AUF-
KLÄRUNG.*
  J. RIDÉ, 182:VOL26#5/6-164
GAEDE, F. REALISMUS VON BRANT BIS
BRECHT.
  R. GRIMM, 406:SPRING74-97
GAENG, P.A. AN INQUIRY INTO LOCAL
VARIATIONS IN VULGAR LATIN.
  B. LÖFSTEDT, 597(SN):VOL45#1-198
GAENG, P.A. INTRODUCTION TO THE
PRINCIPLES OF LANGUAGE.*
  J. KLAUSENBURGER, 399(MLJ):JAN-FEB
  73-55
  G.K. PULLUM, 353:1SEP73-115
GAETJE, H. KORAN UND KORANEXEGESE.
  I. LICHTENSTADTER, 124:APR73-437
GAGAN, D. THE DENISON FAMILY OF
TORONTO, 1792-1925.*
  G.N. EMERY, 529(QQ):WINTER73-628
GAGE, J. COLOUR IN TURNER.
  G. REYNOLDS, 39:FEB73-196
GAGÉ, J. LE PAGANISME IMPERIAL À
LA RECHERCHE D'UNE THÉOLOGIE VERS
LE MILIEU DU IIIE SIÈCLE.
  W.H.C. FREND, 123:MAR74-166
GAGE, N. THE BOURLOTAS FORTUNE.
  R.R. LINGEMAN, 441:6NOV75-45
  W. SCHOTT, 441:16NOV75-24
DES GAGNIERS, J. L'ACROPOLE D'ATH-
ÈNES.
  D.W. ROLLER, 124:MAR74-298
GAHAGAN, J. INTERPERSONAL & GROUP
BEHAVIOUR.
  I. HUNTER, 617(TLS):6JUN75-629
GAHLEN, B. DER INFORMATIONSGEHALT
DER NEOKLASSISCHEN WACHSTUMSTHEOR-
IE FÜR DIE WIRTSCHAFTSPOLITIK.
  A. HÜFNER, 182:VOL26#10-339
GAHLEN, B. & A.E. OTT, EDS. PROBLEME
DER WACHSTUMSTHEORIE.
  K. MELLEROWICZ, 182:VOL26#13/14-
  478
GAIFFE, F. LE DRAME EN FRANCE AU
XVIIIE SIÈCLE.
  M. LIOURE, 535(RHL):SEP-OCT73-899
GAIGALAS, V.V. ERNEST RENAN & HIS
FRENCH CATHOLIC CRITICS.
  R. GALAND, 207(FR):MAY73-1230
  D. O'CONNELL, 446:FALL-WINTER73/
  74-93
GAIGNEBET, C. LE CARNAVAL.
  P. BURKE, 617(TLS):28MAR75-334

GAILLARD [GALHARD], A. OEUVRES COM-
PLÈTES. (E. NÈGRE, ED & TRANS)
  H. GIORDAN, 535(RHL):NOV-DEC73-
  1055
  L.T. TOPSFIELD, 208(FS):APR74-188
GAINER, B. THE ALIEN INVASION.
  H. MALCHOW, 637(VS):SEP73-106
GAINHAM, S. TO THE OPERA BALL.
  G. ANNAN, 617(TLS):31OCT75-1285
  N. HEPBURN, 362:6NOV75-622
GAIR, J.W. COLLOQUIAL SINHALESE
CLAUSE STRUCTURES.
  J. FILIPSKÝ, 353:1JUL73-104
GAITE, C.M. & A. RUIZ TARAZONA - SEE
UNDER MARTÍN GAITE, C. & A. RUIZ
TARAZONA
GAJECKY, G. & A. BARAN. THE COS-
SACKS IN THE THIRTY YEARS WAR.
(VOL 1)
  J. ROSUMNYJ, 497(POLR):VOL18#3-91
GAJEK, B. HOMO POETA.
  J.F.F., 191(ELN):SEP73(SUPP)-116
  E. STOPP, 402(MLR):JUL74-709
GAL, H. FRANZ SCHUBERT & THE
ESSENCE OF MELODY.*
  M.J.E. BROWN, 415:JUN74-476
GÁL, I. BARTÓKTÓL RADNÓTIIG.*
  J.S. WEISSMANN, 410(M&L):JUL74-335
GALAI, S. THE LIBERATION MOVEMENT
IN RUSSIA 1900-1905.*
  T. EMMONS, 550(RUSR):OCT73-430
  W.E. MOSSE, 575(SEER):JAN74-144
GALAND, R. BAUDELAIRE: POÉTIQUES ET
POÉSIES.*
  A. FAIRLIE, 208(FS):OCT74-477
GALAVARIS, G. THE ILLUSTRATIONS OF
THE LITURGICAL HOMILIES OF GREGORY
NAZIANZENUS.*
  J. BACKHOUSE, 90:MAR73-170
GALBRAITH, J.K. ECONOMICS & THE
PUBLIC PURPOSE.*
  639(VQR):SUMMER74-C
GALBRAITH, J.K. MONEY.
  E.D. GENOVESE, 441:7SEP75-1
  C. LEHMANN-HAUPT, 441:8SEP75-35
  442(NY):20OCT75-172
GALBRAITH, J.S. MACKINNON & EAST
AFRICA, 1878-1895.*
  J.A. CASADA, 637(VS):DEC73-230
GALBRAITH, V.H. DOMESDAY BOOK.
  F. BARLOW, 617(TLS):9MAY75-504
GALE, R.L. PLOTS & CHARACTERS IN
THE WORKS OF MARK TWAIN.
  T. WORTHAM, 445(NCF):MAR74-497
GALERSTEIN, C.L. - SEE LAFORET, C.
GALET, Y. L'ÉVOLUTION DE L'ORDRE
DES MOTS DANS LA PHRASE FRANÇAISE
DE 1600 À 1700.
  Y. LE HIR, 535(RHL):NOV-DEC73-1067
GALHARD, A. - SEE UNDER GAILLARD, A.
GALIANI, F. OPERE. (F. DIAZ & L.
GUERCI, EDS)
  F. VENTURI, 617(TLS):31OCT75-1289
GALILEO GALILEI. TWO NEW SCIENCES,
INCLUDING CENTERS OF GRAVITY &
FORCE OF PERCUSSION. (S. DRAKE, ED
& TRANS)
  I.B. COHEN, 617(TLS):2MAY75-479
GALINSKY, H. AMERIKANISCH-DEUTSCHE
SPRACH- UND LITERATURBEZIEHUNGEN.
  O.C. DEAN, JR., 35(AS):FALL-WINTER
  72-292

GALINSKY, H. WEGBEREITER MODERNER
AMERIKANISCHER LYRIK.
J.G. RIEWALD, 433:JAN73-107
GALINSKY, H. WELCHE AUFGABEN FÜR
FORSCHUNG UND LEHRE STELLT DIE
WELTWEITE AUSBREITUNG DER ENGLIS-
CHEN SPRACHE UND IHRER LITERATUREN?
K. GROSS, 430(NS):JUL73-403
GALISSON, R. INVENTAIRE THÉMATIQUE
ET SYNTAGMATIQUE DU FRANÇAIS FONDA-
MENTAL.*
D.A. DINNEEN, 399(MLJ):MAR74-140
GALLAGHER, D.P. MODERN LATIN AMERI-
CAN LITERATURE.*
L.D. SHAW, 402(MLR):JUL74-689
639(VQR):SUMMER74-LXXX
GALLAGHER, J. TWENTY-FIVE YEARS OF
"THE ARCHERS."
A. HAMILTON, 362:20NOV75-681
GALLAIS, P. PERCEVAL ET L'INITIA-
TION.
E.M. KENNEDY, 382(MAE):1974/3-281
GALLANT, M. THE PEGNITZ JUNCTION.*
D. DURRANT, 364:AUG/SEP74-144
GALLANT, M. LE THÈME DE LA MORT
CHEZ ROGER MARTIN DU GARD.*
G.E. KAISER, 207(FR):APR73-1021
M. RIEUNEAU, 535(RHL):NOV-DEC73-
1112
GALLAS, H. MARXISTISCHE LITERATUR-
THEORIE.
H.D. OSTERLE, 222(GR):MAY73-233
GALLATI, E. JEREMIAS GOTTHELFS
GESELLSCHAFTSKRITIK.
W. JUKER, 182:VOL26#17/18-600
GALLE, J. DIE LATEINISCHE LYRIK
JACOB BALDES UND DIE GESCHICHTE
IHRER ÜBERTRAGUNGEN.
P. SCHÄFFER, 182:VOL26#1/2-24
GALLER, M. & H.E. MARQUESS, COMPS.
SOVIET PRISON CAMP SPEECH.*
G.V. GREBENSCHIKOV, 399(MLJ):SEP-
OCT74-298
N.S. PASHIN, 550(RUSR):APR73-211
GALLET, M. STATELY MANSIONS.
A.D. HYTIER, 207(FR):DEC72-454
GALLICO, P. MRS. 'ARRIS GOES TO
MOSCOW.
M. LEVIN, 441:16MAR75-31
GALLO, E. THE "POETRIA NOVA" & ITS
SOURCES IN EARLY RHETORICAL DOC-
TRINE.*
J.J. MURPHY, 589:JAN74-116
GALLOWAY, D., ED. THE ELIZABETHAN
THEATRE. (VOL 3)
G.F. WALLER, 150(DR):AUTUMN73-573
GALLU, S. "GIVE 'EM HELL HARRY."
P-L. ADAMS, 61:NOV75-124
GALLUS, T. DER NACHKOMME DER FRAU
IN DER ALTLUTHERANISCHEN SCHRIFT-
AUSLEGUNG.
F.F. BRUCE, 182:VOL26#11/12-399
GALMÉS DE FUENTES, Á. HISTORIA DE
LOS AMORES DE PARÍS Y VIANA.*
J.M. SOLA-SOLÉ, 240(HR):AUTUMN73-
698
GAL'PERIN, I.R., ED. BOL'ŠOJ ANGLO-
RUSSKIJ SLOVAR'.
J. GLAD, 574(SEEJ):WINTER73-474
GALPERIN, I.R. STYLISTICS.
H.H. RUDNICK, 599:SPRING73-181

GALSTERER, H. UNTERSUCHUNGEN ZUM
RÖMISCHEN STÄDTEWESEN AUF DER IBER-
ISCHEN HALBINSEL.
D. FISHWICK, 487:WINTER73-418
G.E. RICKMAN, 123:NOV74-276
C.B. RÜGER, 313:VOL63-256
GALT, J. THE MEMBER. (I.A. GORDON,
ED)
B. FERGUSSON, 617(TLS):25JUL75-822
GALTUNG, J. THE EUROPEAN COMMUNITY.
F.A. BEER, 563(SS):FALL74-431
GAMBERALE, L. LA TRADUZIONE IN
GELLIO.
M.E. WELSH, 121(CJ):DEC73/JAN74-
163
GAMBERINI, S. LO STUDIO DELL'ITAL-
IANO IN INGHILTERRA NEL '500 E NEL
'600.*
R. GENDRE, 228(GSLI):VOL150FASC
470/471-459
GAMER-WALLERT, I. FISCHE UND
FISCHKULTE IM ALTEN ÄGYPTEN.
R. HOLTHOER, 318(JAOS):OCT-DEC73-
579
DE GÁMEZ, T., ED. SIMON & SCHUSTER'S
INTERNATIONAL DICTIONARY: ENGLISH-
SPANISH, SPANISH-ENGLISH.
N. DAVISON, 399(MLJ):SEP-OCT74-294
GAMMOND, P., ED. MUSIC HALL SONG-
BOOK.
P. KEATING, 617(TLS):26DEC75-1534
GAMST, F.C. THE QEMANT.
P.T.W. BAXTER, 69:JUL73-272
VON GANDERSHEIM, H. - SEE UNDER
HROTSVITHA VON GANDERSHEIM
GANDHI, I. INDIA.
H. TINKER, 617(TLS):4JUL75-731
GANDHI, V.R. THE SYSTEMS OF INDIAN
PHILOSOPHY. (K.K. DIXIT, ED)
W. HALBFASS, 318(JAOS):JUL-SEP73-
384
GANKOVSKY, Y.V. THE PEOPLES OF PAK-
ISTAN.
R.G. FOX, 293(JAST):FEB73-366
GANS, E.L. THE DISCOVERY OF ILLU-
SION.
J.R. WILLIAMS, 207(FR):DEC72-416
GANS, H.J. POPULAR CULTURE & HIGH
CULTURE.*
D. BROMWICH, 441:23FEB75-16
R. TODD, 61:MAR75-128
442(NY):3MAR75-98
GANZ, A., ED. PINTER.
J.R. BROWN, 397(MD):SEP73-212
GANZ, J.S. RULES.
N. BRETT, 486:SEP73-457
G. SAMPSON, 361:SEP73-160
GANZ, P.F. & W. SCHRÖDER, EDS. PROB-
LEME MITTELHOCHDEUTSCHER ERZÄHLFOR-
MEN.*
D. BLAMIRES, 402(MLR):OCT74-911
R. HOFMEISTER, 221(GQ):SEP73-170
GARBACIK, J., ED. KROSNO. (VOL 1)
P. BUSHKOVITCH, 497(POLR):VOL18#3-
86
GARBATO, L. - SEE BOIARDO, M.M.
GARBER, F. WORDSWORTH & THE POETRY
OF ENCOUNTER.*
B. DARLINGTON, 541(RES):AUG73-384
B. LUPINI, 175:AUTUMN72-111
W.U. OBER, 677:VOL4-306
GARBER, M.B. DREAM IN SHAKESPEARE.
639(VQR):SUMMER74-LXXVI

GARCÍA, C., ED. GRAMÁTICA CASTEL-
LANA POR EL LICENCIADO VILLALÓN.
  D.G. PATTISON, 402(MLR):JUL74-667
GARCÍA, F.O. - SEE UNDER OLMOS GAR-
CÍA, F.
GARCÍA, M., ED. REPERTORIO DE PRÍN-
CIPES DE ESPAÑA Y OBRA POÉTICA DEL
ALCAIDE PEDRO DE ESCAVIAS.
  A. DEYERMOND, 617(TLS):23MAY75-573
GARCÍA, S. LAS IDEAS LITERARIAS EN
ESPAÑA ENTRE 1840 Y 1850.*
  D.A. RANDOLPH, 399(MLJ):MAR73-144
  D.L. SHAW, 86(BHS):JUL73-301
GARCÍA-VIÑO, M. MUNDO Y TRASMUNDO
DE LAS LEYENDAS DE BÉCQUER.*
  R. BROWN, 86(BHS):JAN73-89
  191(ELN):SEP73(SUPP)-175
GARCÍA BARRÓN, C. LA OBRA CRÍTICA Y
LITERARIA DE DON ANTONIO ALCALÁ
GALIANO.*
  J. HERRERO, 86(BHS):APR73-180
GARCÍA DE LEÓN, A. LOS ELEMENTOS
DEL TZOTZIL COLONIAL Y MODERNO.
  L. CAMPBELL, 350:JUN74-394
GARCÍA MÁRQUEZ, G. LEAF STORM &
OTHER STORIES.* ONE HUNDRED YEARS
OF SOLITUDE.
  E. GLOVER, 565:VOL14#4-69
GARCÍA MÁRQUEZ, G. EL OTOÑO DEL
PATRIARCA.
  J. FRANCO, 617(TLS):10OCT75-1172
GARCÍA PAVÓN, F. CUENTOS. (R.
MILLÁN, ED)
  P.W. O'CONNOR, 238:MAY73-531
GARCÍA RIVAS, H. HISTORIA DE LA
LITERATURA MEXICANA. (VOL 1)
  J.S. BRUSHWOOD, 263:APR-JUN74-179
GARCÍA Y BELLIDO, A. IBERISCHE
KUNST IN SPANIEN.
  V.A. HIBBS, 39:JUL73-71
GARDAM, J. BLACK FACES, WHITE FACES.
  V. GLENDINNING, 617(TLS):19SEP75-
  1041
GARDEN, M. LYON ET LES LYONNAIS AU
XVIIIE SIÈCLE.
  O. HUFTON, 617(TLS):6JUN75-630
GARDI, R. AFRICAN CRAFTS & CRAFTS-
MEN.
  G. ATKINS, 89(BJA):WINTER73-91
GARDINER, D. A BOOK OF OCCASIONAL.
  S. SCOBIE, 102(CANL):SPRING73-89
GARDINER, S. EVOLUTION OF THE HOUSE.
  W. FEAVER, 362:26JUN75-852
GÅRDING, E. INTERNAL JUNCTURE IN
SWEDISH.
  G.F. MEIER, 682(ZPSK):BAND26HEFT
  3/4-418
GARDNER, H. THE ARTS & HUMAN DEVEL-
OPMENT.
  J.M. KENNEDY, 290(JAAC):WINTER74-
  228
GARDNER, H., ED. THE FABER BOOK OF
RELIGIOUS VERSE.
  R.L. BRETT, 148:AUTUMN72-284
GARDNER, H., ED. THE NEW OXFORD
BOOK OF ENGLISH VERSE, 1250-1950.*
  M. BOTTRALL, 148:SPRING73-89
  D. DAICHES, 541(RES):NOV73-518
  H. LEVIN, 402(MLR):JAN74-141
  G. WOODCOCK, 569(SR):WINTER74-119
GARDNER, H. RELIGION & LITERATURE.*
  H. PESCHMANN, 175:SPRING72-30

GARDNER, H. THE SHATTERED MIND.
  C. LEHMANN-HAUPT, 441:14FEB75-41
  R.M. RESTAK, 441:2MAR75-23
GARDNER, H. - SEE "JOHN DONNE'S
HOLOGRAPH OF 'A LETTER TO THE LADY
CAREY & MRS. ESSEX RICHE'"
GARDNER, J., ED & TRANS. THE ALLIT-
ERATIVE "MORTE ARTHURE," "THE OWL &
THE NIGHTINGALE," & FIVE OTHER MID-
DLE ENGLISH POEMS.*
  P.H. SALUS, 179(ES):JUN73-275
GARDNER, J. THE CONSTRUCTION OF THE
WAKEFIELD CYCLE.*
  M. STEVENS, 31(ASCH):WINTER74/75-
  151
GARDNER, J. A KILLER FOR A SONG.
  M. LASKI, 362:20MAR75-380
GARDNER, J. THE KING'S INDIAN.*
  T.R. EDWARDS, 453:20FEB75-34
  R. GARFITT, 617(TLS):12DEC75-1477
GARDNER, J. NICKEL MOUNTAIN.*
  P.M. SPACKS, 249(HUDR):SUMMER74-
  288
GARDNER, J. THE RETURN OF MORIAR-
TY.*
  C. JAMES, 453:20FEB75-15
  C. NICOL, 231:FEB75-112
  M. YOUNG, 441:2FEB75-21
GARDNER, J. THE SUNLIGHT DIALOGUES.*
  J.F. MC NATT, 598(SOR):SUMMER75-
  716
GARDNER, M. THE FLIGHT OF PETER
FROMM.
  M. PRICE, 676(YR):AUTUMN73-80
GARDNER, R. THE ADVENTURES OF DON
JUAN.
  D. SUTHERLAND, 473(PR):4/1974-637
GARDNER, W.H. & N.H. MAC KENZIE -
SEE HOPKINS, G.M.
GÁRDONYI, Z. & I. SZELÉNYI - SEE
LISZT, F.
GAREAU, E., ED. CLASSICAL VALUES &
THE MODERN WORLD. (FRENCH TITLE:
VALEURS ANTIQUES ET TEMPS MODERNES)
  D.E. EICHHOLZ, 313:VOL63-310
  H.F. GUITE, 487:WINTER73-410
  R.M. OGILVIE, 123:MAR74-150
GARFIELD, B. DEATH SENTENCE.
  N. CALLENDAR, 441:21DEC75-17
GARFIELD, B. HOPSCOTCH.
  N. CALLENDAR, 441:8JUN75-14
GARFITT, R. WEST OF ELM.
  A. MACLEAN, 617(TLS):23MAY75-552
GARGAN, L. LO STUDIO TEOLOGICO E
LA BIBLIOTECA DEI DOMENICANI A
PADOVA NEL TRE E QUATTROCENTO.*
  F. PURNELL, JR., 551(RENQ):WINTER
  73-465
GARKE, E. THE USE OF SONGS IN ELIZ-
ABETHAN PROSE FICTION.
  M-A. DE KISCH, 189(EA):OCT-DEC73-
  475
GARLAN, Y. WAR IN THE ANCIENT WORLD.
  S. HORNBLOWER, 617(TLS):26SEP75-
  1075
GARLAND, H.B. A CONCISE SURVEY OF
GERMAN LITERATURE.
  W. HOFFMEISTER, 221(GQ):MAR73-252
GARLAND, M. HEBBEL'S PROSE TRAGE-
DIES.
  A.O. BÖNIG, 67:MAY74-119
  U.H. GERLACH, 301(JEGP):JUL74-412
  D. JOST, 182:VOL26#17/18-602

GARLICK, R.   A SENSE OF TIME.
P.E. LEWIS, 565:VOL14#4-52
GARLINGTON, P.   ACES & EIGHTS.
N. CALLENDAR, 441:30NOV75-63
GARLINSKI, J.   FIGHTING AUSCHWITZ.
L. DAWIDOWICZ, 617(TLS):20JUN75-
694
E. DE MAUNY, 362:20FEB75-250
GARNEAU, H.S-D.   OEUVRES.*   (J.
BRAULT & B. LACROIX, EDS)
D.M. HAYNE, 208(FS):JAN74-117
GARNER, F.H. & M. ARCHER.   ENGLISH
DELFTWARE.
G. WILLS, 39:JAN73-110
GARNER, H.   DEATH IN DON MILLS.
N. CALLENDAR, 441:13JUL75-36
GARNER, H.   ONE DAMN THING AFTER
ANOTHER.*
G. WOODCOCK, 102(CANL):WINTER74-95
GARNER, H.M. & M. MEDLEY.   CHINESE
ART IN THREE DIMENSIONAL COLOUR.
B. NEAVE-HILL, 135:JUL73-226
GARNER, S.   HAROLD FREDERIC.
A. EASSON, 447(N&Q):SEP73-345
GARNET, E.   ANGEL.
E. MC NAMARA, 102(CANL):AUTUMN73-
104
GARNET, E.   THE LAST ADVENTURE.
F.W. WATT, 99:JUN75-40
GARNETT, R.G.   CO-OPERATION & THE
OWENITE SOCIALIST COMMUNITIES IN
BRITAIN, 1825-45.
J.F.C. HARRISON, 637(VS):DEC73-227
GARNIER, R.   HIPPOLYTE.   (D.B. WIL-
SON, ED) LE JUIFVES.   (A. SAUN-
DERS, ED)
R. GRIFFITHS, 402(MLR):APR74-397
GARNSEY, P.   SOCIAL STATUS & LEGAL
PRIVILEGE IN THE ROMAN EMPIRE.*
B. BALDWIN, 121(CJ):FEB/MAR74-267
S.I. OOST, 122:APR74-130
GARRARD, J.G., ED.   THE EIGHTEENTH
CENTURY IN RUSSIA.*
M. HEIM, 574(SEEJ):WINTER73-452
GARRETT, B.P.   CANADIAN COUNTRY PRE-
SERVES & WINES.
J.M. COLE, 99:DEC75/JAN76-37
GARRETT, W.D.   THOMAS JEFFERSON
REDIVIVUS.
R.G. WILSON, 576:OCT73-260
GARRIGUE, J.   STUDIES FOR AN ACTRESS
& OTHER POEMS.
L. LIEBERMAN, 676(YR):AUTUMN73-113
P. RAMSEY, 569(SR):SPRING74-403
GARRISON, W.L.   THE LETTERS OF WIL-
LIAM LLOYD GARRISON.*   (VOL 3)
(W.M. MERRILL, ED)
J.E. MOONEY, 432(NEQ):DEC74-614
GARSCHA, K.   HARDY ALS BAROCKDRAMA-
TIKER.
C.N. SMITH, 208(FS):APR74-195
GARSON, B.   ALL THE LIVELONG DAY.
J.R. COLEMAN, 441:5OCT75-16
GÄRTNER, H. - SEE RUFUS OF EPHESUS
GARTNER, L.   MORE NEEDLEPOINT DE-
SIGNS.
B. GUTCHEON, 441:7DEC75-74
GARTON, C.   PERSONAL ASPECTS OF THE
ROMAN THEATRE.
J. PERRET, 555:VOL47FASC2-351
GARVIN, P.L., ED.   METHOD & THEORY
IN LINGUISTICS.*
M. SILVERSTEIN, 215(GL):VOL13#3-
135

GARY, R.   THE ENCHANTERS.
P. ADAMS, 61:JUL75-83
M. LEVIN, 441:21SEP75-34
GARY, R.   LES TRÉSORS DE LA MER
ROUGE.
J. GLASGOW, 207(FR):APR73-1053
DE LA GARZA, M.G. - SEE UNDER GONZÁ-
LEZ DE LA GARZA, M.
GARZILLI, E.   CIRCLES WITHOUT CEN-
TER.
N. DIENGOTT, 141:WINTER74-82
GASCOIGNE, B.   TICKER KHAN.
P. ADAMS, 61:MAY75-103
M. LEVIN, 441:10AUG75-14
R. USBORNE, 617(TLS):4APR75-353
GASCOU, J.   LA POLITIQUE MUNICIPALE
DE L'EMPIRE ROMAIN EN AFRIQUE PRO-
CONSULAIRE DE TRAJAN A SEPTIME-SÉV-
ÈRE.
S.I. OOST, 122:OCT74-305
GASKELL, P.   A NEW INTRODUCTION TO
BIBLIOGRAPHY.*
N. RUSSELL, 541(RES):NOV73-526
A.H. SMITH, 354:DEC73-341
78(BC):SUMMER73-151
GASKELL, P. & R. ROBSON.   THE LIB-
RARY OF TRINITY COLLEGE, 1971.
J. DURKAN, 354:SEP73-259
GASKELL, R.   DRAMA & REALITY.*
J. NORTHAM, 184(EIC):APR73-187
E. POULENARD, 189(EA):APR-JUN73-
246
GASKIN, C.   THE PROPERTY OF A
GENTLEMAN.
P. BEER, 617(TLS):17JAN75-48
GASPARRI, F.   L'ÉCRITURE DES ACTES
DE LOUIS VI, LOUIS VII ET PHILIPPE
AUGUSTE.
G.C., 589:OCT74-773
DE GASPÉ, P.A.   CANADIANS OF OLD.
L. SHOHET, 296:VOL3#4-87
GASS, W.H.   FICTION & THE FIGURES OF
LIFE.*
R. FOSTER, 109:FALL/WINTER73/74-
111
295:FEB74-488
GASS, W.H.   WILLIE MASTERS' LONE-
SOME WIFE.*
P-Y. PÉTILLON, 98:JUL73-596
GASSE, V.   LES RÉGIMES FONCIERS
AFRICAINS ET MALGACHE.
J. VANDERLINDEN, 69:APR73-165
GASSET, J.O. - SEE UNDER ORTEGA Y
GASSET, J.
GASSIER, P.   THE DRAWINGS OF GOYA.*
J. RUSSELL, 441:7DEC75-3
GASSIER, P. & J. WILSON.   GOYA.*
(F. LACHENAL, ED)
P. TROUTMAN, 90:MAY73-330
GASSNER, J. & E. QUINN, EDS.   THE
READER'S ENCYCLOPEDIA OF WORLD
DRAMA.
C.A. CARPENTER, 397(MD):DEC73-396
GASSTER, M.   CHINA'S STRUGGLE TO
MODERNIZE.
D. LOVELACE, 293(JAST):FEB73-323
DE GAST, R.   WESTERN WIND, EASTERN
SHORE.
S. SMITH, 441:7DEC75-95
GASTALDI, U.   STORIA DELL'ANABATTIS-
MO DALLE ORIGINI A MÜNSTER (1525-
1535).
F. PINTACUDA DE MICHELIS,
548(RCSF):JAN-MAR73-99

131

GASTON, P.M. THE NEW SOUTH CREED.
N. LEDERER, 577(SHR):WINTER73-98
GATENBY, R. THE SEASON OF DANGER.
N. CALLENDAR, 441:19JAN75-37
GATHORNE-HARDY, R. - SEE MORRELL, O.
GATTEGNO, C. TEACHING FOREIGN LAN-
GUAGES IN SCHOOLS. (2ND ED)
E.W. STEVICK, 608:SEP74-305
GATTI, H. SHAKESPEARE NEI TEATRI
MILANESI DELL'OTTOCENTO.
J.L. LIEVSAY, 570(SQ):WINTER73-95
GAUCHER-SHULTZ, J. & A. MORALES,
EDS. TRES DRAMAS MEXICANOS EN UN
ACTO.
I. MOLINA, 238:MAR73-186
GAUCHER-SHULTZ, J. & A. MORALES -
SEE CARBALLIDO, E.
GAUDIN, C. - SEE BACHELARD, G.
GAUGER, H-M. WORT UND SPRACHE.*
R.O.U. STRAUCH, 353:15JAN73-116
DE GAULLE, C. MEMOIRS OF HOPE.*
(FRENCH TITLE: MÉMOIRES D'ESPOIR.)
N. HAMPSON, 208(FS):JUL74-362
GAUNT, D.M. SURGE & THUNDER.*
F.M. COMBELLACK, 122:JUL73-232
GAUNT, W. THE GREAT CENTURY OF
BRITISH PAINTING.*
D.V.E., 191(ELN):SEP73(SUPP)-19
GAUNT, W. KENSINGTON & CHELSEA.
617(TLS):9MAY75-504
GAUNT, W. THE RESTLESS CENTURY.*
D. COOMBS, 135:FEB73-138
G. REYNOLDS, 39:FEB73-196
GAUR, A., ED. CATALOGUE OF MALAYA-
LAM BOOKS IN THE BRITISH MUSEUM.
R.E. ASHER, 293(JAST):MAY73-543
K.M.P. VARIAR, 318(JAOS):JUL-SEP
73-387
GAUSE, F. DIE GESCHICHTE DER STADT
KÖNIGSBERG IN PREUSSEN. (VOL 3)
T. KLEIN, 182:VOL26#11/12-425
GAUSTAD, E.S. DISSENT IN AMERICAN
RELIGION.*
639(VQR):SUMMER74-CII
GAUTHIER, M-M. EMAUX DU MOYEN AGE
OCCIDENTAL.
C. OMAN, 39:NOV73-408
GAUTHIER, R.A. ARISTOTE: "L'ÉTHIQUE
À NICOMAQUE." (2ND ED)
J. BARNES, 53(AGP):BAND55HEFT1-79
GAUTHIER, X. SURRÉALISME ET SEXUAL-
ITÉ.
M. BERTRAND, 188(ECR):SUMMER73-166
R.R. HUBERT, 207(FR):FEB73-639
GAUTIER, M-P. CAPTAIN FREDERICK
MARRYAT 1792-1848.
O. WARNER, 189(EA):OCT-DEC73-483
GAUTIER, T. POÉSIES (1830).* (H.
COCKERHAM, ED)
R. CHAMBERS, 67:MAY74-114
GAUTREAU, J. - SEE DE BALZAC, H.
GAWLIKOWSKI, M. MONUMENTS FUNÉR-
AIRES DE PALMYRE.*
M.A.R. COLLEDGE, 313:VOL63-291
GAXOTTE, P. LE NOUVEL INGÉNU, HIS-
TOIRE VÉRITABLE.
J. DAVID, 207(FR):MAY73-1240
GAY, J. THE BEGGAR'S OPERA. (P.E.
LEWIS, ED)
C.T.P., 566:SPRING74-94
GAY, J. POETRY & PROSE. (V.A.
DEARING, WITH C.E. BECKWITH, EDS)
D. GREENE, 617(TLS):6JUN75-614

GAY, P., ED. EIGHTEENTH-CENTURY
STUDIES PRESENTED TO ARTHUR M.
WILSON.
A. KNODEL, 173(ECS):FALL73-100
J. SAREIL, 546(RR):MAR74-135
J.S. SPINK, 208(FS):OCT74-461
GAY, P., ED. THE ENLIGHTENMENT.
566:SPRING74-100
GAY, P. STYLE IN HISTORY.*
J.W. BURROW, 617(TLS):20JUN75-687
GAY-CROSIER, R. RELIGIOUS ELEMENTS
IN THE SECULAR LYRICS OF THE TROUB-
ADOURS.
P. BARRETTE, 207(FR):MAR73-817
W.T.H. JACKSON, 546(RR):MAR74-117
GAY-LUSSAC, B. INTRODUCTION À LA
VIE PROFANE.
M. GIRARD, 207(FR):OCT72-217
GAYLIN, W. PARTIAL JUSTICE.
M.E. GALE, 441:5JAN75-1
GAZARIAN-GAUTIER, M-L. GABRIELA
MISTRAL.
G. DE ZÉNDEGUI, 37:AUG-SEP73-58
GAZI, S. A HISTORY OF CROATIA.
P. AUTY, 617(TLS):18APR75-437
GEACH, P.T. LOGIC MATTERS.*
L. STEVENSON, 479(PHQ):OCT73-365
GEACH, P.T. & A.J.P. KENNY - SEE
PRIOR, A.N.
GEARE, M. OPENING ACCOUNT.
P. CAMPBELL, 617(TLS):5SEP75-998
GEBHARD, D. SCHINDLER.*
T.M. BROWN, 54:JUN73-309
C.W. MOORE, 505:JAN73-132
GECKELER, H. ZUR WORTFELDDISKUS-
SION.
M. SANDMANN, 72:BAND211HEFT1/3-181
GEDDES, G. LETTER OF THE MASTER OF
HORSE.
D. BARBOUR, 150(DR):WINTER73/74-
785
P. STEVENS, 628:SPRING74-109
GEDDES, G. RIVERS INLET.
S. SCOBIE, 102(CANL):SPRING73-89
GEDDES, G. SNAKEROOT.
D. BARBOUR, 150(DR):WINTER73/74-
785
GEDULD, H.M., ED. AUTHORS ON FILM.
N. SILVERSTEIN, 295:FEB74-515
GEELAN, P.J.M. & D.C. TWITCHETT,
EDS. THE TIMES ATLAS OF CHINA.
C.P. FITZGERALD, 617(TLS):7FEB75-
136
R. TERRILL, 441:15JUN75-10
GEERAERTS, J. GANGRENE.
N. HEPBURN, 362:21AUG75-254
M. LEVIN, 441:27APR75-34
J. MILLER, 617(TLS):29AUG75-961
GEERDTS, H.J., ED. LITERATUR DER
DDR IN EINZELDARSTELLUNGEN.
P. HUTCHINSON, 220(GL&L):JUL74-335
G. LOOSE, 400(MLN):OCT73-1062
GEERING, R.G. RECENT FICTION.*
H.W. RHODES, 67:NOV74-233
GEERTZ, C. THE INTERPRETATION OF
CULTURES.
M. DOUGLAS, 617(TLS):8AUG75-886
GEGGIE, M. & P. WHALLEY. NORTHERN
BLIGHTS.
L. GEDMOR, 73:FALL73-44
GÉGOU, F. LETTRE-TRAITÉ DE PIERRE-
DANIEL HUET SUR L'ORIGINE DES
ROMANS [SUIVI DE] LA LECTURE DES
[CONTINUED]

[CONTINUING]
VIEUX ROMANS PAR JEAN CHAPELAIN.
  J. CHUPEAU, 535(RHL):SEP-OCT73-894
GEIGER, A. JUDAISM & ISLAM.
  W.M. BRINNER, 318(JAOS):JAN-MAR73-
  76
GEIGER, W. KLEINE SCHRIFTEN ZUR
INDOLOGIE UND BUDDHISMUSKUNDE.
(H. BECHERT, ED)
  R.E. EMMERICK, 182:VOL26#10-344
GEISMAR, M. RING LARDNER & THE RING
OF FOLLY.
  295:FEB74-696
GELB, B. ON THE TRACK OF MURDER.
  A. BROYARD, 441:3OCT75-29
  F.C. SHAPIRO, 441:2NOV75-6
GELB, I.J. SEQUENTIAL RECONSTRUC-
TION OF PROTO-AKKADIAN.
  V. BUBENIK, 361:VOL31#1-85
GELBER, L. CRISIS IN THE WEST.
  E. LUTTWAK, 617(TLS):21NOV75-1384
GELDNER, F. DIE DEUTSCHEN INKUNA-
BELDRUCKER.* (VOL 2) [ENTRY IN
PREV WAS OF VOLS 1&2]
  C. HUTER, 354:MAR73-68
GELDRICH, H. HEINE UND DER SPANISCH-
AMERIKANISCHE MODERNISMO.*
  O.W. JOHNSTON, 133:1973/3-278
GELFAND, M.I. A NATION OF CITIES.
  F. POWLEDGE, 441:26OCT75-104
GELHAUS, H. DIE PROLOGE DES TERENZ.
  V.J. ROSIVACH, 124:SEP-OCT73-38
GELLATELY, R. THE POLITICS OF ECO-
NOMIC DESPAIR.
  J. NOAKES, 617(TLS):30MAY75-587
GELLIE, G.H. SOPHOCLES.
  G.M. KIRKWOOD, 487:WINTER73-392
GELLINEK, C. DIE DEUTSCHE KAISER-
CHRONIK.*
  E. EGERT, 564:MAR73-73
  P.W. TAX, 133:1973/3-267
GELLINEK, C. HÄUFIGKEITSWÖRTERBUCH
ZUM MINNESANG DES 13. JAHRHUNDERTS.*
  H. TERVOOREN, 680(ZDP):BAND92HEFT
  1-121
GELLINEK, C. KÖNIG ROTHER.
  J.E. HÄRD, 597(SN):VOL45#1-187
GELLINEK, J.L. DIE WELTLICHE LYRIK
DES MARTIN OPITZ.
  G. GILLESPIE, 301(JEGP):JUL74-397
GELLING, M. THE PLACE-NAMES OF
BERKSHIRE. (PT 1)
  K.B. HARDER, 424:DEC73-269
  G.F. JENSEN, 447(N&Q):MAR73-117
GELLING, M., W.F.H. NICOLAISEN & M.
RICHARDS, COMPS. THE NAMES OF
TOWNS & CITIES IN BRITAIN. (W.F.H.
NICOLAISEN, ED)
  T. PYLES, 353:15APR73-122
GELLIUS. A. GELLII "NOCTES ATTI-
CAE." (P.K. MARSHALL, ED)
  M.E. WELSH, 121(CJ):OCT/NOV72-87
GELLNER, E. CONTEMPORARY THOUGHT &
POLITICS.* (I.C. JARVIE & J.
AGASSI, EDS)
  A. FLEW, 518:OCT74-6
GELLNER, E. LEGITIMATION OF BELIEF.
  S. KÖRNER, 617(TLS):4JUL75-736
  S.R. LETWIN, 362:5JUN75-744
GÉLY, C. HUGO ET SA FORTUNE LIT-
TÉRAIRE.
  C. LYONS, 207(FR):OCT72-162
GEMMETT, R.J. - SEE BECKFORD, W.

GENAUER, E. RUFINO TAMAYO.
  J. CANADAY, 441:8FEB75-23
GENDRE, A. RONSARD, POÈTE DE LA
CONQUÊTE AMOUREUSE.*
  B.L.O. RICHTER, 433:OCT73-407
  I. SILVER, 546(RR):MAR74-122
GENDRON, J-D. & G. STRAKA, EDS.
ETUDES DE LINGUISTIQUE FRANCO-
CANADIENNE.
  P. ZUMTHOR, 433:JAN73-105
GENET, J. REFLECTIONS ON THE THEA-
TRE.
  W. DONAHUE, 214:VOL6#23-61
GENETTE, G. FIGURES III.*
  J-A. MOREAU, 98:FEB73-121
GENINASCA, J. ANALYSE STRUCTURALE
DES "CHIMÈRES" DE NERVAL.*
  W. BEAUCHAMP, 546(RR):MAY73-223
  M. SCHAETTEL, 557(RSH):APR-JUN73-
  322
GENNARINI, E. QUESTIONARIO SU "I
PROMESSI SPOSI" E PAGINE DI CRITICA
MANZONIANA. (2ND ED)
  G. PUGLIESE, 399(MLJ):DEC74-432
GENOUVRIER - GRUWEZ. FRANÇAIS ET
EXERCISES STRUCTURAUX AU C.E. 1.
GRAMMAIRE NOUVELLE POUR LE COURS
ÉLÉMENTAIRE 1.
  K. WINN, 430(NS):APR73-234
GENOVESE, E.D. ROLL, JORDAN, ROLL.*
  H. MITGANG, 441:25JAN75-25
  J.R. POLE, 617(TLS):12DEC75-1480
GENSANE, B. L'AUTRE ANGLETERRE.
  H. GODIN, 208(FS):APR74-242
GENT, P. NORTH DALLAS FORTY.
  W. FEAVER, 617(TLS):3JAN75-5
GENTIL, R. TRAINED TO INTRUDE.
  617(TLS):28FEB75-232
GENTILE, G. THE PHILOSOPHY OF ART.*
  H. BREDIN, 89(BJA):WINTER73-83
  M.E. BROWN, 141:SUMMER73-275
GENTILI, V. LE FIGURE DELLA PAZZIA
NEL TEATRO ELISABETTIANO.*
  P.E. BONDANELLA, 179(ES):DEC72-558
GEORGACAS, D.J. THE WATERWAY OF
HELLESPONT & BOSPORUS.
  J-L. PERPILLOU, 555:VOL47FASC1-114
GEORGE, A.G. MILTON & THE NATURE OF
MAN.
  W.B. HUNTER, JR., 568(SCN):FALL74-
  52
GEORGE, C.V.R. SEGREGATED SABBATHS.*
  F.J. MILLER, 432(NEQ):MAR74-168
GEORGE, D.L. & F. STEVENSON - SEE
UNDER LLOYD GEORGE, D. & F. STEVEN-
SON
GEORGE, E.E., ED. FRIEDRICH HÖLDER-
LIN.
  R. HARRISON, 301(JEGP):JAN74-89
GEORGE, H.V. COMMON ERRORS IN LAN-
GUAGE LEARNING.
  J. ARABSKI, 399(MLJ):SEP-OCT73-290
  C.W. STANSFIELD, 238:MAY73-522
GEORGE, R. - SEE BOLZANO, B.
GEORGE, S. ACID DROP.
  P.D. JAMES, 617(TLS):26SEP75-1079
  M. LEVIN, 441:14SEP75-42
"STEFAN GEORGE: LEBEN UND WERKE;
EINE ZEITTAFEL."
  I. JONES, 172(EDDA):1973/2-125
GEORGES, E.S. STUDIES IN ROMANCE
NOUNS EXTRACTED FROM PAST PARTI-
                [CONTINUED]

[CONTINUING]
CIPLES.* (REV BY J.R. CRADDOCK &
Y. MALKIEL)
  R. DE DARDEL, 433:OCT73-404
  J. PURCZINSKY, 350:DEC74-740
  L.F. SAS, 240(HR):SPRING73-464
GEORGI, D. & J. STRUGNELL, EDS. CON-
CORDANCE TO THE CORPUS HERMETICUM.
(FASC 1)
  C.W. MACLEOD, 123:NOV74-294
  L. ROBERTS, 124:DEC73-JAN74-185
GEORGIEV, V.J. ETRUSKISCHE SPRACH-
WISSENSCHAFT. (PT 1)
  A. ERNOUT, 555:VOL47FASC1-148
GEORGIN, R. LES SECRETS DU STYLE.
  M. CHASTAING, 542:JAN-MAR73-113
GERBER, A. GREAT RUSSIAN ANIMAL
TALES.
  A. SOONS, 399(MLJ):JAN-FEB73-66
GERBER, D. DEPARTURE.
  M. MADIGAN, 385(MQR):SPRING75-220
GERBER, D.E., ED. EUTERPE.*
  D. YOUNG, 487:WINTER73-412
GERBER, H.E. & W.E. DAVIS, EDS.
THOMAS HARDY.*
  L.O. JONES, 67:NOV74-228
GERBI, A. THE DISPUTE OF THE NEW
WORLD.
  J.H. ELLIOTT, 453:15MAY75-3
  639(VQR):SPRING74-LIV
GERDTS, W.H. THE GREAT AMERICAN
NUDE.
  P. ADAMS, 61:JAN75-90
  W. FEAVER, 617(TLS):5SEP75-999
  C. ROBINS, 441:16FEB75-6
GERE, C. AMERICAN & EUROPEAN JEWEL-
RY, 1830 TO 1911.
  R. REIF, 441:29DEC75-29
GEREVICH, L. THE ART OF BUDA & PEST
IN THE MIDDLE AGES.
  R. JULLIAN, 182:VOL26#1/2-39
GERHARD, H.P. THE WORLD OF ICONS.
  J. BECKWITH, 39:APR73-436
GERHART, G. THE RUSSIAN'S WORLD.
  S.F. STARR, 441:19JAN75-28
GÉRIN, W. EMILY BRONTE.*
  K.C. ODOM, 594:SPRING73-142
  N. SHERRY, 402(MLR):JUL74-626
  G. THOMAS, 175:SUMMER72-71
  P. THOMSON, 541(RES):MAY73-226
GÉRIN, W. - SEE BRONTE, C.
GERLACH, U.H. HEBBEL-BIBLIOGRAPHIE
1910-1970.
  W. WITTKOWSKI, 301(JEGP):OCT74-603
GERMAIN, F. - SEE DE VIGNY, A.
"GERMANIA ROMANA, III." (H. HINZ,
ED)
  J.C. MANN, 313:VOL63-284
GERMANN, G. GOTHIC REVIVAL IN
EUROPE & BRITAIN.*
  N.P., 46:MAY73-344
GERMANOV, A. LIKE A SIGH.
  270:VOL23#1-21
GERNDT, H. FLIEGENDER HOLLÄNDER UND
KLABAUTERMANN.
  R. GRAMBO, 196:BAND14HEFT1/2-162
GERNDT, H. VIERBERGELAUF.
  I. BAUMER, 182:VOL26#15/16-565
GERNSHEIM, H. JULIA MARGARET CAM-
ERON. (REV)
  H. KRAMER, 441:7DEC75-84

GEROW, E. A GLOSSARY OF INDIAN
FIGURES OF SPEECH.
  R.M. SMITH, 318(JAOS):JUL-SEP73-
  380
GERRATANA, V. - SEE GRAMSCI, A.
GERSCH, H. GEHEIMPOETIK.
  K. HABERKAMM, 182:VOL26#13/14-488
GERSHON, K. LEGACIES & ENCOUNTERS.
  T. EAGLETON, 565:VOL14#1-65
GERSHON, K. MY DAUGHTERS, MY SIS-
TERS.
  A. MACLEAN, 617(TLS):23MAY75-552
GERSON, J.J. HORATIO NELSON LAY &
SINO-BRITISH RELATIONS 1854-1864.
  J.K. LEONARD, 293(JAST):AUG73-685
GERSTEIN, L. NIKOLAI STRAKHOV.*
  H.A. STAMMLER, 574(SEEJ):SPRING72-
  99
GERSTER, G. CHURCHES IN ROCK.*
  G.T. SCANLON, 447(N&Q):MAR73-102
GERT, B. THE MORAL RULES.*
  E.J. BOND, 154:SEP73-486
GERTZ, E. - SEE HARRIS, F.
GERZI, T. NETHERLANDISH DRAWINGS IN
THE BUDAPEST MUSEUM: SIXTEENTH-
CENTURY DRAWINGS.
  C. VAN DE VELDE, 90:JUL73-472
GESCHE, H. - SEE KRAFT, K.
GETTENS, R.J., R.S. CLARKE, JR. &
W.T. CHASE. TWO EARLY CHINESE
BRONZE WEAPONS WITH METEORITIC
IRON BLADES.*
  N. BARNARD, 318(JAOS):OCT-DEC73-
  639
GETTLEMAN, M.E. THE DORR REBELLION.
  P.T. CONLEY, 432(NEQ):MAR74-143
GETTO, G. BAROCCO IN PROSA E IN
POESIA.
  A.N. MANCINI, 400(MLN):JAN73-125
GETTO, G. MANZONI EUROPEO.*
  J. HÖSLE, 52:BAND8HEFT3-348
GETTO, G. & OTHERS. STORIA DELLA
LETTERATURA ITALIANA.
  N.L.F., 275(IQ):SUMMER73-118
GEUDTNER, O. DIE SEELENLEHRE DER
CHALDÄISCHEN ORAKEL.
  E.L. MINAR, JR., 24:WINTER74-423
GEWEHR, W. & W.A. VON SCHMIDT. GER-
MAN REVIEW & READINGS.
  G.R. DIMLER, 399(MLJ):MAR74-147
GEWEHR, W. & W.A. VON SCHMIDT. READ-
ING GERMAN IN THE NATURAL SCIENCES.
  A. BRIEFS, 399(MLJ):APR74-209
GEYMONAT, L. STORIA DEL PENSIERO
FILOSOFICO E SCIENTIFICO. (VOLS
1, 4 & 5)
  B.C.H., 191(ELN):SEP73(SUPP)-13
GEYSSE, A. & E. BAGUÉ, EDS. LOS
AUTORES ESPAÑOLES.
  F. PIERCE, 86(BHS):APR73-166
GHINATTI, F. I GRUPPI POLITICI
ATENIESI FINO ALLE GUERRE PERSIANE.
  M.E. WHITE, 487:AUTUMN73-289
  É. WILL, 555:VOL47FASC2-325
GHISELIN, M.T. THE TRIUMPH OF THE
DARWINIAN METHOD.
  G. BLUM, 486:SEP73-466
GHOSE, S. SOCIALISM & COMMUNISM IN
INDIA.
  M.F. FRANDA, 293(JAST):NOV72-183
GHOSE, Z. THE BEAUTIFUL EMPIRE.
  N. HEPBURN, 362:11DEC75-806
GHOSE, Z. THE VIOLENT WEST.
  A. CLUYSENAAR, 565:VOL14#1-70

GHOSH, S. THE DISINHERITED STATE.
B.M. MORRISON, 293(JAST):AUG73-716
GIACALONE, G. - SEE DANTE ALIGHIERI
GIACOMÁN, H.E., ED. HOMENAJE A
MIGUEL ÁNGEL ASTURIAS.
T.B. IRVING, 263:JAN-MAR74-73
GIAKUMAKIS, G. THE AKKADIAN OF
ALALAH.*
A.D. KILMER, 318(JAOS):JUL-SEP73-
400
GIANAKARIS, C.J. PLUTARCH.*
E.N. O'NEIL, 24:FALL74-296
GIANCOTTI, F. STRUTTURE DELLA
MONOGRAFIA DI SALLUSTIO ET DI
TACITO.
J. HELLEGOUARC'H, 555:VOL47FASC1-
156
GIANETTA, S. THE CAPAC LEGACY.
N. CALLENDAR, 441:5OCT75-47
GIANNETTI, L.D. UNDERSTANDING MOV-
IES.
O. OWOMOYELA, 502(PRS):SPRING73-85
GIANNI, E.M. CONOSCENZA E GIUDIZIO.
E. NAMER, 542:OCT-DEC73-486
GIAZOTTO, R. ANTONIO VIVALDI.
M. ROBINSON, 410(M&L):OCT74-482
GIBBON, E. THE ENGLISH ESSAYS OF
EDWARD GIBBON. (P.B. CRADDOCK, ED)
J.W. JOHNSON, 481(PQ):JUL73-510
GIBBONS, F. DOSSO & BATTISTA DOSSI.*
E. BATTISTI, 54:SEP73-458
"STANLEY GIBBONS: ELIZABETHAN SPEC-
IALIZED CATALOGUE OF MODERN BRITISH
COMMONWEALTH STAMPS."
617(TLS):28FEB75-232
"STANLEY GIBBONS: EUROPE 2 STAMP
CATALOGUE."
617(TLS):28FEB75-232
"STANLEY GIBBONS: EUROPE 3 FOREIGN
STAMP CATALOGUE Q-Z."
617(TLS):21FEB75-204
"STANLEY GIBBONS: OVERSEAS 3 FOR-
EIGN STAMPS CATALOGUE K-O."
617(TLS):21FEB75-204
GIBBS, A.M. SHAW.
F.P.W. MC DOWELL, 295:FEB74-772
GIBBS, A.M. - SEE DAVENANT, W.
GIBBS, M.A. THE ADMIRAL'S LADY.
M. LEVIN, 441:20APR75-29
GIBBS, M.E. WÎPLÎCHEZ WÎBES REHT.
C. LOFMARK, 382(MAE):1974/1-54
GIBBS-SMITH, C. EARLY FLYING MACH-
INES.
617(TLS):17OCT75-1245
GIBBS-SMITH, C.H. FLIGHT THROUGH
THE AGES.*
A. REED, 617(TLS):17JAN75-54
GIBBS-SMITH, C.H. THE REBIRTH OF
EUROPEAN AVIATION 1902-1908.
T.C. BARKER, 617(TLS):16MAY75-530
GIBIAN, G., ED & TRANS. RUSSIA'S
LOST LITERATURE OF THE ABSURD.*
V.D. MIHAILOVICH, 573(SSF):SUMMER
73-299
GIBNEY, F. JAPAN.
E.J. HOBSBAWM, 453:17JUL75-27
GIBSON, G. ELEVEN CANADIAN NOVEL-
ISTS.
A. MAC KINNON, 150(DR):AUTUMN73-
546
GIBSON, I. LA REPRESIÓN NACIONALIS-
TA DE GRANADA EN 1936 Y LA MUERTE
DE FEDERICO GARCÍA LORCA.*
H.F. GRANT, 86(BHS):JUL73-307

GIBSON, R. THE LAND WITHOUT A NAME.
J. CRUICKSHANK, 617(TLS):9MAY75-
509
GIBSON, S. I AM WATCHING.
M. ANDRÉ, 529(QQ):WINTER73-658
GIBSON, W. - SEE TWAIN, M.
GICOVATE, B. SAN JUAN DE LA CRUZ
(ST. JOHN OF THE CROSS).
R.M. ICAZA, 399(MLJ):NOV73-375
R.W. TRUMAN, 402(MLR):APR74-437
GIDE, A. LA SYMPHONIE PASTORALE.
(C. MARTIN, ED)
J. ONIMUS, 557(RSH):APR-JUN73-323
GIDE, C. - SEE FOURIER, C.
GIEDION, S. THE ETERNAL PRESENT.
H. KÜHN, 182:VOL26#19-681
ABBÉ GIERCZYNSKI. LE QUE SAIS-JE
DE MONTAIGNE.
C. FLEURET, 535(RHL):JUL-AUG73-677
GIERSZEWSKI, S. STRUKTURA GOSPODAR-
CZA I FUNKCJE RYNKOWE MNIEJSZYCH
MIAST WOJEWÓDZTWA POMORSKIEGO W
XVI I XVII W.
P. BUSHKOVITCH, 497(POLR):VOL18#3-
86
GIESEMANN, G. KOTZEBUE IN RUSSLAND.
F. STOCK, 52:BAND8HEFT2-218
GIEYSZTOR, A. & OTHERS. HISTOIRE
DE POLOGNE. (S. KIENIEWICZ, ED)
E. NEIDERHAUSER, 104:SUMMER73-274
GIFFEN, L.A. THEORY OF PROFANE
LOVE AMONG THE ARABS.
A. HAMORI, 318(JAOS):OCT-DEC73-568
GIFFORD, D. - SEE HOGG, J.
GIFFORD, D., WITH R.J. SEIDMAN.
NOTES FOR JOYCE.*
R.N. ROSS, 651(WHR):AUTUMN74-394
GIFFORD, T. THE WIND CHILL FACTOR.
M. LEVIN, 441:19JAN75-37
GIGLIOLI, P.P., ED. LANGUAGE &
SOCIAL CONTEXT.
D.L. LAWTON, 399(MLJ):MAR74-150
GIL, A.M. ESPAÑOL CONTEMPORÁNEO.
D.A. KLEIN, 238:MAR73-189
GIL, F. LA LOGIQUE DU NOM.
Y. GAUTHIER, 154:MAR73-183
GILBERT, C., ED. RENAISSANCE ART.
C.H. CLOUGH, 39:MAY73-533
GILBERT, E.L. THE GOOD KIPLING.*
Y. GUÉRIN, 549(RLC):APR-JUN73-356
F. LÉAUD, 189(EA):APR-JUN73-233
G. THOMAS, 175:SUMMER73-80
GILBERT, G.G., ED. THE GERMAN LAN-
GUAGE IN AMERICA.*
T. BYNON, 269(IJAL):OCT73-263
GILBERT, G.G. LINGUISTIC ATLAS OF
TEXAS GERMAN.
T. BYNON, 269(IJAL):OCT73-263
M. CLYNE, 67:MAY74-131
GILBERT, H. AN OFFENSE AGAINST THE
PERSONS.*
N. CALLENDAR, 441:3AUG75-24
GILBERT, M. WINSTON S. CHURCHILL.
(VOL 4)
S. KOSS, 617(TLS):6JUN75-625
K. KYLE, 362:5JUN75-735
GILBERT, M. FLASH POINT.*
N. CALLENDAR, 441:19JAN75-36
GILBERT, M. RUSSIAN HISTORY ATLAS.*
R.P. BROWDER, 50(ARQ):SUMMER73-192
GILBERT, S.M. ACTS OF ATTENTION.*
E. DELAVENAY, 189(EA):JUL-SEP73-
325

[CONTINUED]

135

GILBERT, S.M. ACTS OF ATTENTION.*
[CONTINUING]
  T. MARSHALL, 255(HAB):SUMMER73-233
  N.S. POBURKO, 150(DR):WINTER73/74-
  758
  T. ROGERS, 175:AUTUMN73-119
  R.A. STEIN, 651(WHR):SUMMER74-253
  K. WIDMER, 295:APR74-1044
GILDEA, J., ED. PARTONOPEU DE BLOIS.
  F. KOENIG, 545(RPH):NOV73-250
  H.F. WILLIAMS, 593:SUMMER74-187
GILDER, G. NAKED NOMADS.*
  L. MC MURTRY, 441:5JAN75-6
  442(NY):3MAR75-98
GILDER, G.F. SEXUAL SUICIDE.*
  S. TOTH, 109:SPRING/SUMMER74-127
GILES, P. WATERLOO EXPRESS.
  L. ROGERS, 102(CANL):SUMMER74-121
GILHOOLEY, L. CONTRADICTION & DIL-
EMMA.
  T.R. RYAN, 613:AUTUMN73-418
GILISON, J.M. BRITISH & SOVIET
POLITICS.*
  J.S. RESHETAR, JR., 550(RUSR):
  JUL73-321
GILKES, P. THE DYING LION.
  E. ULLENDORFF, 617(TLS):25APR75-
  462
GILL, A. MALLARMÉ'S POEM "LA CHEVE-
LURE VOL D'UNE FLAMME..."
  R.G. COHN, 535(RHL):NOV-DEC73-1101
GILL, B. HERE AT THE NEW YORKER.
  C. LEHMANN-HAUPT, 441:10FEB75-25
  J. LEONARD, 441:16FEB75-1
  J. RUSSELL, 617(TLS):13JUN75-646
  E. WEEKS, 61:APR75-97
  M. WOOD, 453:15MAY75-13
GILL, B. WAYS OF LOVING.*
  P. FRENCH, 617(TLS):31JAN75-101
  W. PEDEN, 569(SR):FALL74-712
GILL, B. - SEE BARRY, P.
GILL, J.H. - SEE RAMSEY, I.
GILL, R., ED. WILLIAM EMPSON.*
  R. FULLER, 364:AUG/SEP74-127
  M. WOOD, 453:23JAN75-30
GILL, R. HAPPY RURAL SEAT.*
  G.R. HIBBARD, 402(MLR):APR74-390
  G.B. TENNYSON, 445(NCF):JUN73-113
GILL, R. THE SOCIAL CONTEXT OF
THEOLOGY.
  S. BUDD, 617(TLS):5DEC75-1469
GILLAN, G., ED. THE HORIZONS OF THE
FLESH.
  J. O'NEILL, 484(PPR):JUN74-613
GILLE, K.F. "WILHELM MEISTER" IM
URTEIL DER ZEITGENOSSEN.*
  A. KLINGENBERG, 654(WB):6/1973-216
GILLES, A.S., SR. COMANCHE DAYS.
  639(VQR):AUTUMN74-CXXXV
GILLESPIE, G. GERMAN BAROQUE POET-
RY.*
  G. HOFFMEISTER, 221(GQ):MAR73-254
  H. WAGENER, 399(MLJ):MAR73-149
GILLESPIE, G., ED & TRANS. DIE
NACHTWACHEN DES BONAVENTURA.*
  J.L.S., 191(ELN):SEP73(SUPP)-115
GILLHAM, D.G. WILLIAM BLAKE.
  G. THOMAS, 175:AUTUMN73-118
GILLIATT, P. JEAN RENOIR.
  R. SCHICKEL, 441:7DEC75-90
GILLIES, D.A. AN OBJECTIVE THEORY
OF PROBABILITY.
  T.E. WILKERSON, 518:MAY74-5

GILLIS, F.J. & J.W. MINERS, EDS.
OH, DIDN'T HE RAMBLE.
  H.L. LANDY, 187:SEP75-497
GILLIS, J.R. YOUTH & HISTORY.
  T.R. FYVEL, 617(TLS):15AUG75-915
GILLMOR, C.S. COULOMB & THE EVOLU-
TION OF PHYSICS & ENGINEERING IN
EIGHTEENTH-CENTURY FRANCE.
  C. TRUESDELL, 173(ECS):WINTER73/74-
  213
GILLON, E.V., JR. VICTORIAN CEME-
TERY ART.*
  J. MAASS, 576:MAR73-78
GILLON, E.V., JR. & M. GAYLE. CAST-
IRON ARCHITECTURE IN NEW YORK.
  E. HOAGLAND, 441:1JUN75-16
GILLON, E.V., JR. & C. LANCASTER.
VICTORIAN HOUSES.
  639(VQR):SUMMER74-CX
GILLOTT, J. A TRUE ROMANCE.
  N. HEPBURN, 362:2OCT75-453
  J. MILLER, 617(TLS):22AUG75-951
GILMAN, D. A NUN IN THE CLOSET.
  N. CALLENDAR, 441:16MAR75-32
GILMAN, R. THE MAKING OF MODERN
DRAMA.*
  F. KERMODE, 453:1MAY75-20
GILMAN, S. THE SPAIN OF FERNANDO
DE ROJAS.*
  B. DUTTON, 589:OCT74-730
  R.L. KAGAN, 400(MLN):MAR73-410
GILMAN, S.L. FORM UND FUNKTION.
  R. FURNESS, 402(MLR):APR74-469
  T. SCHEUFELE, 400(MLN):APR73-647
GILMORE, M. & S. JOHNSON - SEE
PEAKE, M.
GILSON, E. MATIÈRES ET FORMES.
  C. SCHUWER, 542:JAN-MAR73-113
GIMBUTAS, M. THE SLAVS.
  F.J. OINAS, 574(SEEJ):SPRING72-128
  W.S. VUCINICH, 550(RUSR):JAN73-95
GIMSON, A.C. AN INTRODUCTION TO THE
PRONUNCIATION OF ENGLISH.* (2ND ED)
  K. FAISS, 353:1JAN73-112
  A. WOLLMANN, 38:BAND91HEFT4-499
GINDIN, J. HARVEST OF A QUIET EYE.*
  A.S. LEVITT, 295:FEB74-488
  T. ROGERS, 175:SPRING73-33
  S. SPENCER, 659:SPRING75-249
GINER, S. INITIATION À L'INTELLI-
GENCE SOCIOLOGIQUE.
  C. SCHUWER, 542:JAN-MAR73-61
GINER DE LOS RÍOS, G., A.I. NOLFI &
L.K. NOLFI. POR TIERRAS DE ESPAÑA.
(REV)
  P.W. O'CONNOR, 399(MLJ):MAR73-153
GINGRICH, A. NOTHING BUT PEOPLE.
  295:FEB74-368
GINSBERG, A. ALLEN VERBATIM. (G.
BALL, ED)
  J.M. BRINNIN, 441:2MAR75-4
GINSBERG, E.S. - SEE GRÉVIN, J.
GINSBERG, M. MIND & BELIEF.*
  H.L. ROLSTON, 482(PHR):JUL74-406
GINSBERG, M. - SEE ZAMYATIN, Y.
GINZBURG, C. IL NICODEMISMO.
  T.A. BRADY, JR., 551(RENQ):SUMMER
  73-193
GINZBURG, E.S. JOURNEY INTO THE
WHIRLWIND.
  M.S. SHATZ, 104:SUMMER73-250
GINZBURG, N. DEAR MICHAEL.
  E. TENNANT, 362:20FEB75-253

GINZBURG, N. MAI DEVI DOMANDARMI.
C.S. BOWE, 270:VOL23#2-36
GINZBURG, N. NO WAY.*
J. THOMPSON, 453:23JAN75-39
GINZBURG, N. VITA IMMAGINARIA.
I. QUIGLY, 617(TLS):28MAR75-344
GINZBURG, N. LE VOCI DELLA SERA.
(S. PACIFICI, ED)
C.C. RUGGIERO, 399(MLJ):JAN-FEB73-60
GIOLLI, F. UNGARETTI E ALTRI SCRIT-
TI.
400(MLN):JAN73-171
GIONO, J. OEUVRES ROMANESQUES COM-
PLÈTES. (VOL 1) (R. RICATTE &
OTHERS, EDS)
J. ONIMUS, 557(RSH):JUL-SEP73-500
GIONO, J. OEUVRES ROMANESQUES COM-
PLÈTES.* (VOL 2) (R. RICATTE, WITH
P. CITRON & L. RICATTE, EDS)
J. ONIMUS, 557(RSH):JUL-SEP73-501
GIONO, J. OEUVRES ROMANESQUES COM-
PLÈTES. (VOL 3)
W.D. REDFERN, 617(TLS):18APR75-436
GIONO, J. LES RÉCITS DE LA DEMI-
BRIGADE.
N.L. GOODRICH, 207(FR):APR73-1055
GIORGINI, M.S., WITH C. ROBICHON &
J. LECLANT - SEE UNDER SCHIFF GIOR-
GINI, M., WITH C. ROBICHON & J.
LECLANT
GIOVANNINI, A. UNTERSUCHUNGEN ÜBER
DIE NATUR UND DIE ANFÄNGE DER BUND-
ESSTAATLICHEN SYMPOLITIE IN GRIECH-
ENLAND.
R.B. EGAN, 124:MAY73-483
GIOVANNINI, G. QUESTIONARIO DI
STORIA DELLA FILOSOFIA DA KANT ALL'
ESISTENZIALISMO. (NEW ED)
R. MALTER, 342:BAND64HEFT1-149
GIPPER, H. & H. SCHWARZ. BIBLIO-
GRAPHISCHES HANDBUCH ZUR SPRACH-
INHALTSFORSCHUNG.* (BK 1, PTS 7-13)
C. SOETEMAN, 433:JUL73-308
GIPPER, H. & H. SCHWARZ. BIBLIO-
GRAPHISCHES HANDBUCH ZUR SPRACHIN-
HALTSFORSCHUNG. (BK 1, PT 14)
J. ANDRÉ, 555:VOL47FASC1-148
GIPPIUS, Z.N. - SEE UNDER HIPPIUS,
Z.N.
GIRALDI, G. MORALISTICA FRANCESE.
E. NAMER, 542:OCT-DEC73-487
GIRAUD, J., P. PAMART & J. RIVERAIN.
LES NOUVEAUX MOTS "DANS LE VENT."
P. RICKARD, 617(TLS):25APR75-443
GIRAUD, M. A HISTORY OF FRENCH
LOUISIANA. (VOL 1)
639(VQR):AUTUMN74-CXXXIX
GIRAUD, Y. & M-R. JUNG. LA RENAIS-
SANCE I: 1480-1548.*
D. COLEMAN, 208(FS):JAN74-57
GIRAUDOUX, J. SOUVENIR DE DEUX
EXISTENCES.
C. CAMPOS, 617(TLS):11JUL75-752
GIRDLESTONE, C. LA TRAGÉDIE EN
MUSIQUE (1673-1750) CONSIDÉRÉE
COMME GENRE LITTÉRAIRE.*
N. SUCKLING, 208(FS):OCT74-455
GIROUARD, M. THE VICTORIAN COUNTRY
HOUSE.
P.F. NORTON, 576:MAR73-75

GIROUARD, M. VICTORIAN PUBS.
R. GILBERT, 362:4DEC75-758
J.M. RICHARDS, 617(TLS):19DEC75-
1513
GIROUD, F. I GIVE YOU MY WORD.*
J. NAUGHTON, 362:18SEP75-384
N. ROBERTS, 617(TLS):30CT75-1129
GIROUX, R. - SEE O'CONNOR, F.
GIRVAN, R. BEOWULF & THE SEVENTH
CENTURY.
G. BOURQUIN, 189(EA):APR-JUN73-221
GISSING, G. BORN IN EXILE.
P. COUSTILLAS, 189(EA):JAN-MAR73-
109
GISSING, G. ESSAYS & FICTION.* (P.
COUSTILLAS, ED)
G. LINDOP, 447(N&Q):MAR73-111
GISSING, G. ISABEL CLARENDON. (P.
COUSTILLAS, ED)
S. MONOD, 189(EA):JAN-MAR73-107
GISSING, G. THE ODD WOMEN.
P. COUSTILLAS, 189(EA):JAN-MAR73-
110
GITEAU, M. LE BORNAGE RITUEL DES
TEMPLES BOUDDHIQUES AU CAMBODGE.*
J. WILLIAMS, 318(JAOS):APR-JUN73-
229
GITELMAN, Z.Y. JEWISH NATIONALITY
& SOVIET POLITICS.
W. KOREY, 550(RUSR):OCT73-438
GITTINGS, J. THE WORLD & CHINA
1922-1972.
J.K. FAIRBANK, 453:1MAY75-18
R. HARRIS, 617(TLS):21MAR75-319
R. TERRILL, 441:15JUN75-10
GITTINGS, R. THE YOUNG THOMAS
HARDY.
M. DEAS, 362:17APR75-515
H. GIFFORD, 617(TLS):18APR75-414
I. HOWE, 441:6JUL75-12
M. WOOD, 453:27NOV75-11
442(NY):25AUG75-87
GITTINGS, R. - SEE KEATS, J.
GIUDICE, G. PIRANDELLO.
P. BAILEY, 617(TLS):28FEB75-219
442(NY):26MAY75-120
GIUDICI, G. POESIE SCELTE (1957-
1974).
K. BOSLEY, 617(TLS):31OCT75-1308
GIUFFRIDA, R.T. DAS ADJEKTIV IN
DEN WERKEN NOTKERS.
H. TIEFENBACH, 182:VOL26#11/12-406
GIULIANO, W. BUERO VALLEJO, SASTRE
Y EL TEATRO DE SU TIEMPO.
J. DOWLING, 400(MLN):MAR73-495
M-T. HALSEY, 238:DEC73-1120
DE GIUSTINO, D. CONQUEST OF MIND.
P. COLLINS, 617(TLS):25APR75-455
GIVONE, S., ED. ESTETICHE E POET-
ICHE DEL NOVECENTO.
M. BROWN, 290(JAAC):WINTER74-238
GIVONE, S. LA STORIA DELLA FILOSO-
FIA SECONDO KANT.
W.H. WERKMEISTER, 319:OCT75-535
GJERSTAD, E. EARLY ROME. (PTS 5&6)
E. BIELEFELD, 182:VOL26#17/18-616
GJEVORI, M. FRAZEOLOGJIZMA TË
GJUHËS SHQIPE.
S.E. MANN, 575(SEER):APR74-313
GLADISH, D.F. - SEE DAVENANT, W.

GLADSTONE, W.E. THE GLADSTONE DIAR-
IES. (VOLS 3&4) (M.R.D. FOOT &
H.C.G. MATTHEW, EDS)
S. KOSS, 617(TLS):14MAR75-266
R. MITCHISON, 362:20MAR75-373
GLADSTONE, W.E. THE PRIME MINIS-
TERS' PAPERS: W.E. GLADSTONE.*
(VOL 1) (J. BROOKE & M. SORENSEN,
EDS)
V. CROMWELL, 325:OCT73-673
GLANVILLE, B. THE COMIC.*
M. LEVIN, 441:13APR75-31
P. PELHAM, 364:FEB/MAR75-142
GLASER, H.A. & OTHERS. LITERATUR-
WISSENSCHAFT UND SOZIALWISSEN-
SCHAFTEN.
H.D. OSTERLE, 221(GQ):NOV73-608
GLASKOW, W.G. HISTORY OF THE COS-
SACKS.*
B.W. MENNING, 550(RUSR):APR73-205
GLASS, J.M. REFLECTIONS ON A MOUN-
TAIN SUMMER.*
J. MILLS, 198:WINTER75-118
GLASSCO, J. THE FATAL WOMAN.*
G. WOODCOCK, 606(TAMR):MAR75-93
GLASSCO, J. MONTREAL.
D. BARBOUR, 150(DR):WINTER73/74-
785
R.B. SHAW, 491:APR75-50
GLASSCO, J. SELECTED POEMS.
R.B. SHAW, 491:APR75-50
GLASSER, R. TIME IN FRENCH LIFE &
THOUGHT.
P.C. SMITH, 207(FR):APR73-1036
GLASSTONE, V. VICTORIAN & EDWARD-
IAN THEATRES.
J. RUSSELL, 441:7DEC75-24
GLATT, D. ZUR GESCHICHTLICHEN BE-
DEUTUNG DER MUSIKAESTHETIK EDUARD
HANSLICKS.
J. WEISSMANN, 410(M&L):APR74-230
GLAVIND, J. PYGMALION OG FIGURAN-
TINDEN.
P. VINTEN-JOHANSEN, 563(SS):SUM-
MER74-294
GLAZEBROOK, P. THE EYE OF THE BE-
HOLDER.
S. MILLAR, 617(TLS):28MAR75-329
GLEASON, A. EUROPEAN & MUSCOVITE.*
H.E. BOWMAN, 574(SEEJ):WINTER72-
476
P.P. DUNN, 550(RUSR):JAN73-91
J.D. MORISON, 575(SEER):APR74-317
N.D. ROODKOWSKY, 613:AUTUMN73-420
A. SINEL, 104:WINTER73-550
GLEASON, H.A., JR. LINGUISTISCHE
ASPEKTE DER ENGLISCHEN GRAMMATIK.
(K. WÄCHTLER, ED)
B. CARSTENSEN, 430(NS):JAN73-47
GLEASON, J., WITH A. AWORINDE & J.O.
OGUNDIPE. A RECITATION OF IFA,
ORACLE OF THE YORUBA.
H. DREWAL, 2:SPRING74-85
GLEAVES, R.M. & C.M. VANCE, EDS.
HISPANOAMÉRICA MÁGICA Y MISTERIOSA.
J. KARTCHNER, 399(MLJ):APR74-214
GLENDINNING, N. A LITERARY HISTORY
OF SPAIN: THE EIGHTEENTH CENTURY.*
T.A. SACKETT, 173(ECS):SPRING74-
376
GLENN, J. PAUL CELAN.
E. KRISPYN, 399(MLJ):SEP-OCT74-286

GLENN, J. DEUTSCHES SCHRIFTTUM DER
GEGENWART (AB 1945).*
E. BOA, 402(MLR):APR74-470
E. THURNHER, 133:1973/3-255
GLICK, W. - SEE THOREAU, H.D.
GLICKSBERG, C.I. LITERATURE & SOCI-
ETY.
F. JAMESON, 131(CL):SUMMER73-277
295:FEB74-392
GLICKSBERG, C.I. THE SEXUAL REVOLU-
TION IN MODERN AMERICAN LITERATURE.
295:FEB74-392
GLINZ, H. LINGUISTISCHE GRUNDBE-
GRIFFE UND METHODENÜBERBLICK.*
B. GRÖSCHEL, 361:SEP73-165
GLÖCKNER, E. BEGEGNUNGEN MIT STEFAN
GEORGE: AUS BRIEFEN UND TAGEBÜCHERN
1913-1934.* (F. ADAM, ED)
F.G. CRONHEIM, 402(MLR):OCT74-939
GLORIEUX, P. LA FACULTÉ DES ARTS
ET SES MAÎTRES AU XIIIE SIÈCLE.
P. KIBRE, 589:OCT74-734
GLOVER, B.R. A HISTORY OF SIX SPAN-
ISH VERBS MEANING "TO TAKE, SEIZE,
GRASP."*
J.R. CRADDOCK, 238:MAY73-506
J. GULSOY, 545(RPH):NOV73-231
GLUCK, F.W. & A.B. MORGAN - SEE
HAWES, S.
GLÜCK, L. THE HOUSE ON MARSHLAND.
T. LASK, 441:2AUG75-19
H. VENDLER, 441:6APR75-4
GLUSKI, J., ED. PROVERBS.
205(FMLS):APR73-214
GNÄDIGER, L. EREMETICA.
M.D. LEGGE, 382(MAE):1974/1-61
GNAROWSKI, M. CONCISE BIBLIOGRAPHY
OF ENGLISH-CANADIAN LITERATURE.
L.T.C., 102(CANL):SUMMER74-128
GNAROWSKI, M. - SEE KNISTER, R.
GNEUSS, C. DER SPÄTE TIECK ALS
ZEITKRITIKER.*
W. LILLYMAN, 221(GQ):MAY73-428
J. TRAINER, 220(GL&L):JAN74-153
GOAR, R.J. CICERO & THE STATE RE-
LIGION.
J.R. WEAVER, 124:SEP-OCT73-45
GOCHET, P. ESQUISSE D'UN THÉORIE
NOMINALISTE DE LA PROPOSITION.*
R. BLANCHÉ, 542:JUL-SEP73-357
J. DANEK, 154:SEP73-570
GODBOUT, J. D'AMOUR, P.Q.
J. PIVATO, 102(CANL):AUTUMN74-114
GODBOUT, J. & P. TURGEON. L'INTER-
VIEW.
M. DORSINVILLE, 102(CANL):SUMMER74-
90
GODDEN, G.A. BRITISH POTTERY.
R.L. CHARLES, 617(TLS):2MAY75-493
GODDEN, J. AHMED'S LADY.
V. GLENDINNING, 617(TLS):19SEP75-
1041
N. HEPBURN, 362:11DEC75-806
GODEFROY, V. THE DRAMATIC GENIUS
OF VERDI.
J. WARRACK, 617(TLS):5SEP75-991
GODFREY OF SAINT VICTOR. THE FOUN-
TAIN OF PHILOSOPHY. (E.A. SYNAN,
ED & TRANS)
M. REIDY, 529(QQ):SPRING73-147
GODKIN, E.L. THE GILDED AGE LETTERS
OF E.L. GODKIN. (W. ARMSTRONG, ED)
K.O. MORGAN, 617(TLS):14FEB75-154

GODSON, J. THE RISE & FALL OF THE
DC-10.
R. WITKIN, 441:2MAR75-26
GODWIN, G. THE ODD WOMAN.*
T.R. EDWARDS, 453:20FEB75-34
V. GLENDINNING, 617(TLS):4JUL75-
732
GODWIN, W. DE LA JUSTICE POLITIQUE.
(B. CONSTANT, TRANS; B.R. POLLIN,
ED)
A. FAIRLIE, 208(FS):JAN74-85
B.C. FINK, 149:DEC74-347
102(CANL):SUMMER73-125
GOEBEL, G. POETA FABER.
R.A. SAYCE, 208(FS):JUL74-319
GOEBL, H. DIE NORMANDISCHE UNKUNDEN-
SPRACHE.
H.J. LOPE, 209(FM):JAN73-84
GOEDECKE, W.R. CHANGE & THE LAW.
W.T. BLACKSTONE, 321:WINTER73-315
GOEDICKE, H. THE REPORT ABOUT THE
DISPUTE OF A MAN WITH HIS BA.
L.H. LESKO, 318(JAOS):JAN-MAR73-78
GOEN, C.C. - SEE EDWARDS, J.
GOESSLER, L. - SEE JULIAN
VON GOETHE, J.W. GOETHE'S "DAS
MÄRCHEN." (W. BARTSCHT, TRANS)
J.K. BROWN, 406:SPRING74-107
VON GOETHE, J.W. GOETHES GESPRÄCHE.
(VOL 2) (W. HERWIG, ED)
R. HABEL, 72:BAND211HEFT1/3-105
VON GOETHE, J.W. POETISCHE WERKE.
(VOLS 1-3)
E. BAHR, 221(GQ):SEP73-173
VON GOETHE, J.W. THE SUFFERINGS OF
YOUNG WERTHER.* (H. STEINHAUER,
TRANS)
F.G. RYDER, 221(GQ):NOV73-649
VON GOETHE, J.W. WEST-ÖSTLICHER
DIVAN.
N.H. SMITH, 182:VOL26#17/18-604
GOETHERT, F.W. KATALOG DER ANTIKEN-
SAMMLUNG DES PRINZEN CARL VON
PREUSSEN IM SCHLOSS ZU KLEIN-GLIEN-
ICKE BEI POTSDAM.
J.M. COOK, 123:NOV74-307
GOETSCH, P., ED. ENGLISH DRAMATIC
THEORIES: 20TH CENTURY.
K.T. VON ROSADOR, 72:BAND211HEFT
1/3-151
GOETZ, T.H. TAINE & THE FINE ARTS.
L. WEINSTEIN, 399(MLJ):SEP-OCT74-
276
GOETZMANN, W.H. THE AMERICAN HEGEL-
IANS.
A. QUINTON, 453:12JUN75-39
GOFF, O. THE EYE OF THE PEACOCK.
617(TLS):10OCT75-1174
GOFFMAN, E. FRAME ANALYSIS.
P. ROSENBERG, 441:16FEB75-21
GOFFMAN, E. RELATIONS IN PUBLIC.
M. HICKSON 3D, 186(ETC.):MAR73-100
GÖGELEIN, C. ZU GOETHES BEGRIFF VON
WISSENSCHAFT AUF DEM WEGE DER METH-
ODIK SEINER FARBSTUDIEN.
N.H. SMITH, 182:VOL26#9-292
GOGOL, N.V. THE NOSE. (F. GOTT-
SCHALK, ED) THE GOVERNMENT INSPEC-
TOR. (ADAPTATION BY P. RABY)
M.A. CURRAN, 574(SEEJ):SPRING73-71

GOGUEL, F. MODERNISATION ÉCONOMIQUE
ET COMPORTEMENT POLITIQUE.
J-A. BOUR, 207(FR):FEB73-640
GOHEEN, J.D. & J.L. MOTHERSHEAD, JR.
- SEE LEWIS, C.I.
GÖHRING, H. BA LUBA. (VOL 1) (W.E.
MÜHLMANN & E.W. MÜLLER, EDS)
J. VANSINA, 69:OCT73-364
GOITEIN, S.D., ED & TRANS. LETTERS
OF MEDIEVAL JEWISH TRADERS.
639(VQR):SPRING74-XLI
GOKHALE, G.B., ED. IMAGES OF INDIA.
R.M. SMITH, 318(JAOS):JUL-SEP73-
380
GOLD, D. BELLEVUE.
E. CRAY, 441:6JUL75-11
R.R. LINGEMAN, 441:21JUL75-19
GOLD, H. MY LAST TWO THOUSAND
YEARS.*
A.H. ROSENFIELD, 390:MAR73-70
GOLD, H. SWIFTIE THE MAGICIAN.*
R. BUCKLER, 362:11SEP75-349
V. CUNNINGHAM, 617(TLS):13JUN75-
643
R. SALE, 249(HUDR):WINTER74/75-628
GOLD, J. CHARLES DICKENS.*
A. EASSON, 155:SEP73-190
R.D. MC MASTER, 255(HAB):WINTER73-
56
W. MYERS, 637(VS):SEP73-108
R.L. PATTEN, 445(NCF):JUN73-103
S.F. PICKERING, JR., 219(GAR):
FALL73-455
K. WILSON, 529(QQ):SPRING73-140
GOLD, J., ED. THE STATURE OF DICK-
ENS.*
K.J. FIELDING, 541(RES):FEB73-100
GOLDAMMER, P. - SEE STORM, T.
GOLDBARTH, A. UNDER COVER.
L. HATFIELD, 661:SUMMER73-121
R. MAYES, 448:VOL13#2-99
GOLDBERG, H. JEAN JAURÈS.
R. TREMPÉ, 98:JAN73-71
GOLDBERG, H.E. CAVE DWELLERS &
CITRUS GROWERS.
S.D. GOITEIN, 318(JAOS):OCT-DEC73-
556
GOLDBERG, M. CARLYLE & DICKENS.*
J. CLUBBE, 579(SAQ):AUTUMN74-569
J.A.D., 191(ELN):SEP73(SUPP)-40
K.J. FIELDING, 155:MAY73-111
S. MONOD, 189(EA):JUL-SEP73-373
S.F. PICKERING, JR., 219(GAR):
FALL73-455
E. SHARPLES, 141:SPRING74-180
M. SLATER, 637(VS):MAR74-328
H.P. SUCKSMITH, 402(MLR):OCT74-848
E.M. VIDA, 255(HAB):SUMMER73-227
GOLDEN, H. LONG LIVE COLUMBUS.
A. CORMAN, 441:2MAR75-30
GOLDEN, L., COMP & TRANS. OCHERKI
MUZYKAL'NOI KUL'TURY NARODOV TROPI-
CHESKOI AFRIKI. (D. MIKHAILOV, ED)
B. KRADER, 187:SEP75-487
GOLDEN, M. THE SELF OBSERVED.*
J. GRAY, 529(QQ):SUMMER73-297
R.E. KELLEY, 481(PQ):JUL73-431
C.J. RAWSON, 541(RES):MAY73-250
M.F. SCHULZ, 173(ECS):SPRING74-378
191(ELN):SEP73(SUPP)-64
GOLDER, F.A. RUSSIAN EXPANSION ON
THE PACIFIC 1641-1850.
G.A. LENSEN, 318(JAOS):JUL-SEP73-
407

GOLDFARB, R. JAILS.
R. SHERRILL, 441:29JUN75-3
GOLDHAMER, H. THE FOREIGN POWERS IN
LATIN AMERICA.
G.F.W. YOUNG, 150(DR):SPRING73-177
GOLDING, J. BOCCIONI'S "UNIQUE
FORMS OF CONTINUITY IN SPACE."
C. TISDALL, 592:MAR73-137
GOLDING, J. MARCEL DUCHAMP: THE
BRIDE STRIPPED BARE BY HER BACHE-
LORS, EVEN.*
B. GOLD, 31(ASCH):WINTER74/75-142
R. MAIN, 592:JUL-AUG73-56
GOLDING, R. - SEE CLOSSON, E.
GOLDING, W. THE SCORPION GOD.*
J.R. BAKER, 454:FALL73-62
J.C. FIELD, 556(RLV):1973/1-93
GOLDKNOPF, D. THE LIFE OF THE
NOVEL.*
M.C. CREELMAN, 255(HAB):SPRING73-
145
I. DEER, 290(JAAC):SPRING74-441
R. FOLKENFLIK, 481(PQ):JUL73-431
D. PIZER, 191(ELN):DEC73-153
E.S. RABKIN, 454:SPRING74-271
T. ROGERS, 175:SUMMER73-81
G.B. TENNYSON, 445(NCF):JUN73-111
GOLDMAN, A., ED. JAMES JOYCE.
P. SWINDEN, 148:SPRING72-91
GOLDMAN, A.I. A THEORY OF HUMAN
ACTION.
L. HOLBOROW, 479(PHQ):APR73-180
GOLDMAN, I. ANCIENT POLYNESIAN
SOCIETY.
T.G. HARDING, 318(JAOS):OCT-DEC73-
651
GOLDMAN, J. THE MAN FROM GREEK &
ROMAN.*
617(TLS):11JUL75-784
GOLDMAN, M. SHAKESPEARE & THE ENER-
GIES OF DRAMA.*
R.A. FOAKES, 175:SUMMER73-72
C. HOY, 569(SR):SPRING74-363
GOLDMAN, M.I. THE SPOILS OF PRO-
GRESS.*
I.M. DRUMMOND, 104:WINTER74-614
J.G. TOLPIN, 550(RUSR):APR73-213
GOLDMAN, W. THE GREAT WALDO PEPPER.
M. LEVIN, 441:11MAY75-22
GOLDMANN, L. STRUCTURES MENTALES ET
CRÉATIONS CULTURELLES.
F. GAILLARD, 535(RHL):SEP-OCT73-
929
GOLDNER, N. THE STRAVINSKY FESTIVAL
OF THE NEW YORK CITY BALLET.*
S.J. COHEN, 290(JAAC):WINTER74-243
GOLDSMITH, B. THE STRAW MAN.
A. BROYARD, 441:24APR75-39
GOLDSMITH, M.E. THE MODE & MEANING
OF "BEOWULF."*
G. BOURQUIN, 189(EA):APR-JUN73-221
M. GREEN, 599:WINTER73-64
N. JACOBS, 439(NM):1973/3-551
L. WHITBREAD, 179(ES):DEC72-548
GOLDSMITH, U.K. STEFAN GEORGE.
E. SPEIDEL, 447(N&Q):SEP73-355
GOLDSMITH, V.F. A SHORT TITLE CATA-
LOGUE OF FRENCH BOOKS 1601-1700 IN
THE LIBRARY OF THE BRITISH MUSEUM.
R.A. SAYCE, 354:SEP73-249
GOLDSTEIN, A.D. YOU'RE NEVER TOO
OLD TO DIE.
N. CALLENDAR, 441:12JAN75-18

GOLDSTEIN, B.R. AL-BIṬRŪJĪ: ON THE
PRINCIPLES OF ASTRONOMY.*
D.A. KING, 318(JAOS):OCT-DEC73-566
GOLDSTEIN, I. ISRAEL AT HOME &
ABROAD.
D. BRESLAU, 287:JUN73-28
GOLDSTEIN, J., A. FREUD & A.J. SOL-
NIT. BEYOND THE BEST INTERESTS OF
THE CHILD.*
I. GLASSER, 231:FEB75-118
GOLDSTEIN, R.L. INDIAN WOMEN IN
TRANSITION.
A.D. ROSS, 293(JAST):AUG73-728
GOLDSTONE, H., I. CUMMINGS & T.
CHURCHILL, EDS. POINTS OF DEPAR-
TURE.
C. MORAN, 573(SSF):SUMMER73-293
GOLDSTONE, R.H. THORNTON WILDER.
M. COWLEY, 441:9NOV75-6
GOLDWERT, M. DEMOCRACY, MILITARISM,
& NATIONALISM IN ARGENTINA, 1930-
1966.
D. CARNEIRO, 263:JAN-MAR74-66
GOLDZIHER, I. THE ẒĀHIRĪS, THEIR
DOCTRINE & THEIR HISTORY. (W.
BEHN, ED & TRANS)
J.A. BELLAMY, 318(JAOS):JUL-SEP73-
367
GOLENBOCK, P. DYNASTY.
B.J. PHILLIPS, 441:9NOV75-53
GOLEV, V. UNIVERSE.
270:VOL23#1-12
GOLFIN, J. LES 50 MOTS CLÉS DE LA
SOCIOLOGIE.
D. MERLLIÉ, 542:JAN-MAR73-53
GÖLLER, K.H. GESCHICHTE DER ALTENG-
LISCHEN LITERATUR.*
G. BAUER, 224(GRM):BAND23HEFT1-119
A. CRÉPIN, 189(EA):OCT-DEC73-458
GOL'MAN, M.I. PROBLEMY NOVEISHEI
ISTORII MNR V BURZHUAZNOI ISTORIO-
GRAFII SSHA.
R. ANTE, 293(JAST):NOV72-169
GOLOVIN, B.N. JAZYK I STATISTIKA.
W. LEHFELDT, 353:1MAR73-102
GOLTZ, D. STUDIEN ZUR GESCHICHTE
DER MINERALNAMEN IN PHARMAZIE,
CHEMIE UND MEDIZIN VON DEN ANFÄNGEN
BIS PARACELSUS.
J. ANDRÉ, 182:VOL26#3/4-93
GOM, L. KINDLING.
D. BARBOUR, 529(QQ):SPRING73-141
E. LANCZOS, 648:OCT73-61
GOMBRICH, E.H. L'ART ET L'ILLUSION.
J. WIRTH, 98:MAY73-454
GOMBRICH, E.H. SYMBOLIC IMAGES.*
C.H. CLOUGH, 39:MAY73-533
GOMBRICH, E.H., J. HOCHBERG & M.
BLACK. ART, PERCEPTION & REALITY.
(M. MANDELBAUM, ED)
M.H. BORNSTEIN, 127:SUMMER74-378
M. ROSENTHAL, 135:SEP73-67
M. SAGOFF, 290(JAAC):FALL73-128
D.F. STALKER, 484(PPR):MAR74-450
GOMBRICH, R.F. PRECEPT & PRACTICE.
A.T. KIRSCH, 293(JAST):MAY73-554
D.K. SWEARER, 318(JAOS):OCT-DEC73-
604
GOMBROWICZ, W. A KIND OF TESTA-
MENT.*
E.M. THOMPSON, 497(POLR):VOL18#4-
104

GOMBROWICZ, W. OPERETTA.* THE
MARRIAGE.
  E.J. CZERWINSKI, 574(SEEJ):WINTER
  72-489
GÓMEZ-GIL, O., ED. LITERATURA HIS-
PANOAMERICANA.
  J.A. CHRZANOWSKI, 238:MAR73-188
  E. ECHEVARRIA, 399(MLJ):MAR74-134
GÓMEZ DE LA SERNA, G. ENSAYOS SOBRE
LITERATURA SOCIAL.
  L. HICKEY, 86(BHS):OCT73-411
GOMME, A.W., A. ANDREWES & K.J.
DOVER. A HISTORICAL COMMENTARY ON
THUCYDIDES. (VOL 4)
  M.F. MC GREGOR, 487:WINTER73-395
GOMME, A.W. & F.H. SANDBACH. MENAN-
DER.
  639(VQR):SUMMER74-LXXXI
GÖMÖRI, G. & J. ATLAS - SEE JÓZSEF,
A.
GONČAROV, B.P. ZVUKOVAJA ORGANIZ-
CIJA STIXA I PROBLEMY RIFMY.
  J. BAILEY, 574(SEEJ):SUMMER73-217
GÓNGORA, M. STUDIES IN THE COLONIAL
HISTORY OF SPANISH AMERICA.
  R.A. HUMPHREYS, 617(TLS):14NOV75-
  1351
GONSETH, F. TIME & METHOD.
  V.F. LENZEN, 484(PPR):SEP73-127
GONZÁLEZ, B.B. - SEE UNDER BLANCO
GONZÁLEZ, B.
GONZÁLEZ, J.L. LA GALERÍA.
  M. UGARTE, 238:DEC73-1127
GONZÁLEZ-CRUZ, L.F. PABLO NERUDA Y
EL MEMORIAL DE ISLA NEGRA.
  R. PRING-MILL, 617(TLS):3OCT75-
  1154
GONZÁLEZ-GERTH, M. & G.D. SCHADE,
EDS. RUBÉN DARÍO CENTENNIAL
STUDIES.*
  N. DAVISON, 240(HR):SPRING73-456
GONZÁLEZ DE LA GARZA, M. WALT WHIT-
MAN.
  R. ASSELINEAU, 189(EA):APR-JUN73-
  248
GONZÁLEZ MUELA, J. - SEE MARTÍNEZ DE
TOLEDO, A.
GOOCH, A. DIMINUTIVE, AUGMENTATIVE,
& PEJORATIVE SUFFIXES IN MODERN
SPANISH.*
  A.K. LEVY, 545(RPH):FEB74-406
GOOD, M., ED. PEOPLE PIECES.
  J. PATTERSON, 268:JUL75-185
GOOD, R.C. U.D.I.*
  639(VQR):SUMMER74-CI
GOODALL, V., ED. THE QUEST FOR MAN.
  C.L. MEE, JR., 441:7DEC75-42
  N.S. SUTHERLAND, 617(TLS):26DEC75-
  1542
GOODE, J., ED. THE AIR OF REALITY.*
  T. ROGERS, 175:AUTUMN73-119
  G.B. TENNYSON, 445(NCF):SEP73-242
GOODE, W.J. WORLD REVOLUTION &
FAMILY PATTERNS.
  C. LASCH, 453:13NOV75-33
GOODERS, J. THE GREAT BOOK OF
BIRDS.
  442(NY):15DEC75-156
GOODHEART, E. CULTURE & THE RADICAL
CONSCIENCE.
  D.L. KUBAL, 50(ARQ):WINTER73-361

GOODIN, G., ED. THE ENGLISH NOVEL
IN THE NINETEENTH CENTURY.
  G.M. HARVEY, 150(DR):SUMMER73-339
  A. SMITH, 617(TLS):7MAR75-260
GOODMAN, E. A STUDY OF LIBERTY &
REVOLUTION.
  A. RYAN, 617(TLS):20JUN75-693
GOODMAN, F.D. SPEAKING IN TONGUES.
  W.J. SAMARIN, 350:MAR74-207
GOODMAN, L.E. IBN TUFAYL'S "HAYY
IBN YAQZĀN."
  D.M. DUNLOP, 589:APR74-333
GOODMAN, N. HOLLANDS LEAGUER. (D.S.
BARNARD, JR., ED)
  E. BOURCIER, 189(EA):JAN-MAR73-97
GOODMAN, N. PROBLEMS & PROJECTS.
  J.J.F., 543:SEP72-159
GOODMAN, P. GROWING UP ABSURD.*
(GERMAN TITLE: AUFWACHSEN IM WIDER-
SPRUCH.)
  H. WINDISCHER, 182:VOL26#7/8-199
GOODMAN, S., ED. OUR FIRST FIFTY
YEARS.
  J. PILCH, 287:JUN73-27
GOODSTEIN, R.L. DEVELOPMENT OF
MATHEMATICAL LOGIC.
  J. VAN HEIJENOORT, 482(PHR):JUL73-
  409
  C.F.K., 543:JUN73-752
GOODWIN, G. A HISTORY OF OTTOMAN
ARCHITECTURE.*
  J.W. ALLAN, 463:SPRING73-86
GOODWIN, R.N. THE AMERICAN CONDI-
TION.*
  R. CUFF, 99:AUG75-39
  C.J. FRIEDRICH, 639(VQR):AUTUMN74-
  610
GOODWIN, S. KIN.
  M. LEVIN, 441:22JUN75-10
GOODYEAR, F.R.D. - SEE TACITUS
GOOLAGONG, E., WITH B. COLLINS.
EVONNE!
  J. DURSO, 441:1JUN75-33
GOOLD, G.P. - SEE CATULLUS
GOOSSE, A. FAÇONS DE PARLER: I.
  N.C.W. SPENCE, 208(FS):APR74-235
GOOSSE, M-T. UNE LECTURE DU "LAR-
RON" D'APOLLINAIRE.*
  C. GOTHOT-MERSCH, 535(RHL):SEP-OCT
  73-922
GOPAL, S. JAWAHARLAL NEHRU. (VOL 1)
  N. CHAUDHURI, 617(TLS):14NOV75-
  1346
  J. GRIGG, 362:20NOV75-676
GOPAL, S. - SEE NEHRU, J.
NA GOPALEEN, M. THE POOR MOUTH (AN
BÉAL BOCHT).*
  J. WILLIAMS, 111:3MAY74-129
GORBAČEVIČ, K.S. IZMENENIE NORM
RUSSKOGO LITERATURNOGO JAZYKA.
  D.B. CROCKETT, 574(SEEJ):SPRING73-
  103
GORBATOV, A.V. YEARS OFF MY LIFE.
  M.S. SHATZ, 104:SUMMER73-250
GORDIMER, N. THE CONSERVATIONIST.*
  C. RICKS, 453:26JUN75-13
  P. THEROUX, 441:13APR75-4
  E. WEEKS, 61:APR75-98
  442(NY):12MAY75-141
GORDON, A.L. RONSARD ET LA RHÉTOR-
IQUE.*
  M. GLATIGNY, 535(RHL):SEP-OCT73-
  886
  R.M. HESTER, 207(FR):DEC73-399

141

GORDON, C. THE SHORT FICTION OF
CAROLINE GORDON.* (T.H. LANDESS,
ED)
  J.E. BROWN, 577(SHR):FALL73-452
  J.L. IDOL, JR., 573(SSF):FALL73-
  427
GORDON, C.H. RIDDLES IN HISTORY.*
617(TLS):28FEB75-232
GORDON, F.L. - SEE DELIBES, M.
GORDON, G., ED. BEYOND THE WORDS.
  E. FEINSTEIN, 362:31JUL75-158
  M. MASON, 617(TLS):28FEB75-213
GORDON, G. FAREWELL, FOND DREAMS.
  V. CUNNINGHAM, 617(TLS):28FEB75-
  213
  E. FEINSTEIN, 362:31JUL75-158
GORDON, H.J., JR. HITLER & THE BEER
HALL PUTSCH.*
  R.F. HOPWOOD, 255:FALL73-315
GORDON, I.A. - SEE GALT, J.
GORDON, L.H.D. & F.J. SHULMAN, EDS.
DOCTORAL DISSERTATIONS ON CHINA.
  G.R. NUNN, 293(JAST):NOV72-126
GORDON, M., ED. THE AMERICAN FAMILY
IN SOCIAL-HISTORICAL PERSPECTIVE.
  J.B. ARMSTRONG, 432(NEQ):SEP74-482
  C. LASCH, 453:13NOV75-33
GORDON, R. MYSELF AMONG OTHERS.
295:FEB74-368
GORDON, R. THE SLEEP OF LIFE.
  M. LEVIN, 441:27APR75-34
GORDON, S. UNFINISHED BUSINESS.
442(NY):1SEP75-67
THE GORDONS. CATNAPPED!
  N. CALLENDAR, 441:12JAN75-22
GORE, K. L'IDÉE DE PROGRÈS DANS LA
PENSÉE DE RENAN.*
  R.M. CHADBOURNE, 546(RR):MAY74-232
GOREAU, E.K. INTEGRITY OF LIFE.
  P.S. BERGGREN, 568(SCN):FALL74-58
GORENSTEIN, S. & OTHERS. PREHISPAN-
IC AMERICA.
  N. HAMMOND, 617(TLS):15AUG75-918
GORES, J. HAMMETT.
  N. CALLENDAR, 441:9NOV75-55
  P. FRENCH, 617(TLS):10OCT75-1174
  R.R. LINGEMAN, 441:4SEP75-39
GOREY, H. NADER.
  J. FALLOWS, 441:10AUG75-4
GORKI, M. FRAGMENTS FROM MY DIARY.*
(M. BUDBERG, TRANS)
  L.G. LEIGHTON, 574(SEEJ):FALL73-
  337
GORKI, M. THE LIFE OF A USELESS
MAN.* (M. BUDBERG, TRANS)
  L. KOEHLER, 104:FALL73-427
GORKI, M. ON LITERATURE.
639(VQR):AUTUMN74-CXXVII
GÖRLACH, M. THE SOUTH ENGLISH LEG-
ENDARY, GILTE LEGENDE & GOLDEN
LEGEND.
  N.F. BLAKE, 72:BAND211HEFT3/6-424
GORMAN, T.P., ED. LANGUAGE IN EDU-
CATION IN EASTERN AFRICA.
  K. LEGÈRE, 682(ZPSK):BAND26HEFT6-
  721
GORODECKIJ, B.J. K PROBLEME SEMAN-
TIČESKOJ TIPOLOGII.
  J. MILLER, 297(JL):FEB73-167
GOROSPE, V.R., ED. RESPONSIBLE
PARENTHOOD IN THE PHILIPPINES.
  G.D. NESS, 293(JAST):AUG73-759

GOSCH, M.A. & R. HAMMER. THE LAST
TESTAMENT OF LUCKY LUCIANO.
  C. LEHMANN-HAUPT, 441:28FEB75-37
  T. PLATE, 441:23MAR75-4
GOSE, E. DER GALLO-RÖMISCHE TEMPEL-
BEZIRK IM ALTBACHTAL BEI TRIER.
  E. WIGHTMAN, 487:AUTUMN73-315
GOSE, E.B., JR. IMAGINATION INDULG-
ED.*
  S.M. SMITH, 541(RES):NOV73-510
  295:FEB74-393
GOSLING, J.C.B. PLATO.*
  R.C. CROSS, 518:OCT74-8
  K. SEESKIN & R.E. ALLEN, 311(JP):
  24APR75-221
GOSS, G. HITLER'S DAUGHTER.
  M. LEVIN, 441:12JAN75-16
GOSSE, E. FATHER & SON. (J. HEP-
BURN, ED)
  A. BELL, 617(TLS):24JAN75-79
GOSSEN, G.H. CHAMULAS IN THE WORLD
OF THE SUN.
  E. THOMPSON, 617(TLS):11JUL75-780
GOSSETT, P. - SEE RAMEAU, J-P.
GOSSMAN, L. FRENCH SOCIETY & CUL-
TURE.*
  L.R. FREE, 399(MLJ):DEC73-438
  J. HARDRÉ, 481(PQ):JUL73-432
GÖSSMANN, W. DEUTSCHE KULTURGE-
SCHICHTE IM GRUNDRISS. (4TH ED)
  H.W. PANTHEL, 221(GQ):MAR73-280
GÖSSMANN, W., WITH H.P. KELLER & H.
WALWEI-WIEGELMANN, EDS. GESTÄND-
NISSE.
  J.L.S., 191(ELN):SEP73(SUPP)-132
GOSTELOW, M. A WORLD OF EMBROIDERY.
  B. GUTCHEON, 441:7DEC75-74
GOSZTONY, P. MIKLÓS VON HORTHY,
ADMIRAL UND REICHSVERWESER.
  P. IGNOTUS, 617(TLS):14FEB75-163
GOTESKY, R. PERSONALITY.
  P. DUBOIS, 542:OCT-DEC73-487
GOTH, J. NIETZSCHE UND DIE RHETORIK.
  F. TRAUTMANN, 480(P&R):SPRING73-
  128
GÖTHEL, F., ED. MUSIK IN BAYERN.
(VOL 2)
  J.A. WESTRUP, 410(M&L):APR74-245
GOTHOT-MERSCH, C. - SEE FLAUBERT, G.
GOTKIN, J. & P. TOO MUCH ANGER, TOO
MANY TEARS.
  M.P. DUMONT, 441:23NOV75-46
GOTLIEB, S. THE GOURMET'S CANADA.
  J.M. COLE, 99:DEC75/JAN76-37
GOTOFF, H.C. THE TRANSMISSION OF
THE TEXT OF LUCAN IN THE NINTH
CENTURY.
  G. LUCK, 24:WINTER74-411
  R.A. TUCKER, 124:OCT72-107
GOTSCHALK, F.C. GROWING UP IN TIER
3000.
  G. JONAS, 441:14DEC75-28
GÖTTE, J. & M. - SEE VERGIL
GOTTEHRER, B. THE MAYOR'S MAN.
  S.R. WEISMAN, 441:16MAR75-3
GOTTESMAN, R. & S. BENNETT, EDS.
ART & ERROR.*
  A.C. PARTRIDGE, 180(ESA):MAR73-51
GOTTESMAN, R. & H. GEDULD, EDS.
GUIDEBOOK TO FILM.
  R. CAMPION, 200:MAY73-301
GOTTLIEB, G. EARLY CHILDREN'S BOOKS
& THEIR ILLUSTRATION.
442(NY):29DEC75-56

GOTTLIEB, P. AGENCY.
  D. WILLIAMSON, 296:VOL3#4-99
GOTTSCHALK, F. - SEE GOGOL, N.V.
GOTTSCHALK, H. LEXIKON DER MYTHOLO-
GIE DER EUROPÄISCHEN VÖLKER.
  J. DUCHESNE-GUILLEMIN, 182:VOL26
  #20-755
GOTTSCHED, J.C. SCHRIFTEN ZUR LIT-
ERATUR. (H. STEINMETZ, ED)
  R.P. BAREIKIS, 481(PQ):JUL73-517
GÖTZ, D. & E. BURGSCHMIDT. EINFÜH-
RUNG IN DIE SPRACHWISSENSCHAFT FÜR
ANGLISTEN.
  G. STEIN, 38:BAND91HEFT3-363
GOUGEON, H. GOOD FOOD.
  J.M. COLE, 99:DEC75/JAN76-37
GOUGHER, R.L., ED. INDIVIDUALIZA-
TION OF INSTRUCTION IN FOREIGN LAN-
GUAGES.
  T. ANDERSSON, 238:MAY73-523
GOUHIER, H. RENAN AUTEUR DRAMATIQUE.
  P-M.S., 542:APR-JUN73-231
GOUINLOCK, J. JOHN DEWEY'S PHILOSO-
PHY OF VALUE.
  Y.H. KRIKORIAN, 484(PPR):DEC73-292
GOULART, R. ONE GRAVE TOO MANY.
  N. CALLENDAR, 441:23FEB75-40
GOULD, C. LEONARDO.
  J. RUSSELL, 441:7DEC75-3
GOULD, L. FINAL ANALYSIS.*
  M. MILLER, 617(TLS):10OCT75-1173
GOULET, J. OH'S PROFIT.
  M. LEVIN, 441:9NOV75-54
GOW, A.S., ED & TRANS. THE GREEK
BUCOLIC POETS.
  J.W. VAUGHN, 24:WINTER74-402
GOW, J. A SHORT HISTORY OF GREEK
MATHEMATICS.
  J. STANNARD, 124:DEC73-JAN74-184
GOWRIE, G. A POSTCARD FROM DON GIO-
VANNI.*
  H. MURPHY, 159(DM):AUTUMN/WINTER
  73/74-122
GOYARD-FABRE, S. ESSAI DE CRITIQUE
PHÉNOMÉNOLOGIQUE DU DROIT.
  J-M. GABAUDE, 154:SEP73-576
GOYARD-FABRE, S. NIETZSCHE ET LA
CONVERSION MÉTAPHYSIQUE.
  J-M. GABAUDE, 154:SEP73-577
GOYARD-FABRE, S. LA PHILOSOPHIE DES
LUMIÈRES EN FRANCE.
  J-M. GABAUDE, 154:JUN73-388
GOYEN, W. THE COLLECTED STORIES OF
WILLIAM GOYEN.
  J.C. OATES, 441:16NOV75-4
GOYTISOLO, L. RECUENTO.
  R. BURROWS, 617(TLS):23MAY75-574
GRAB, W. LEBEN UND WERKE NORD-
DEUTSCHER JAKOBINER.
  J. HERMAND, 406:WINTER74-438
GRABER, H. - SEE DÖBLIN, A.
GRABES, H., ED. ELIZABETHAN SONNET
SEQUENCES.
  H.O., 430(NS):AUG73-450
GRACE, J. DOMESTIC SLAVERY IN WEST
AFRICA.
  R. ANSTEY, 617(TLS):1AUG75-880
GRADE, A. - SEE FROST, R. & E.
GRADON, P. FORM & STYLE IN EARLY
ENGLISH LITERATURE.*
  J.J. ANDERSON, 184:SUMMER73-186
  A.J. BLISS, 541(RES):MAY73-197
  D.S. BREWER, 38:BAND91HEFT3-388
                        [CONTINUED]

[CONTINUING]
  B. ROWLAND, 382(MAE):1974/3-286
  P.B. TAYLOR, 179(ES):AUG73-383
  R.M. WILSON, 175:SPRING72-23
  205(FMLS):APR73-213
GRADY, J. SHADOW OF THE CONDOR.
  N. CALLENDAR, 441:21DEC75-17
GRADY, J. SIX DAYS OF THE CONDOR.*
  N. CALLENDAR, 441:30MAR75-24
GRADY, M. SYNTAX & SEMANTICS OF THE
ENGLISH VERB PHRASE.
  F.R. PALMER, 353:1MAR73-110
GRAF, H. OPERA FOR THE PEOPLE.
  A. JACOBS, 415:FEB74-131
GRAF, O. TAO UND JEN.
  J. CHING, 485(PE&W):JUL73-403
GRAF, O.M. REISE IN DIE SOWJET-
UNION 1934.
  P. LABANYI, 617(TLS):25JUL75-855
GRAFF, G. POETIC STATEMENT & CRITI-
CAL DOGMA.*
  R.E. PALMER, 72:BAND211HEFT1/3-83
GRAHAM, A. CONTEMPLATIVE CHRISTIAN-
ITY.
  A.R. VIDLER, 617(TLS):6JUN75-628
GRAHAM, A. THE END OF RELIGION.*
  T. CONNER, 613:SPRING73-148
GRAHAM, D. KEITH DOUGLAS 1920-
1944.*
  K. MILLER, 453:16OCT75-27
  A. ROSS, 364:OCT/NOV74-137
  C. TOMLINSON, 362:9JAN75-59
GRAHAM, F., JR. GULLS.
  R. CARAS, 441:7DEC75-93
GRAHAM, I. GOETHE & LESSING.*
  A.R. SCHMITT, 399(MLJ):SEP-OCT74-
  287
GRAHAM, J. JOHN GRAHAM'S SYSTEM &
DIALECTICS OF ART. (M.E. ALLEN-
TUCK, ED)
  S. BAYLEY, 89(BJA):SPRING73-202
GRAHAM, J. THE RUN TO MORNING.
  N. CALLENDAR, 441:5JAN75-24
GRAHAM, J. & G. GARRETT. THE WRIT-
ER'S VOICE.
  A. MAC KINNON, 150(DR):AUTUMN73-
  546
GRAHAM, P. THE JESUS HOAX.
  K. LEECH, 617(TLS):17JAN75-65
GRAHAM, P. PORTRAIT OF THE AUVERGNE.
  617(TLS):26DEC75-1547
GRAHAM, P.A. COMMUNITY & CLASS IN
AMERICAN EDUCATION, 1865-1918.
  617(TLS):13JUN75-639
GRAHAM, R. & P.H. SMITH, EDS. NEW
APPROACHES TO LATIN AMERICAN HIS-
TORY.
  J. LYNCH, 617(TLS):15AUG75-924
GRAHAM, V.E. & W.M. JOHNSON - SEE
JODELLE, E.
GRAHAM, W. WOMAN IN THE MIRROR.
  617(TLS):11JUL75-784
GRAMSCI, A. LETTERS FROM PRISON.*
  (L. LAWNER, ED)
  M. CLARK, 617(TLS):31OCT75-1280
  A. GAMBLE, 362:21AUG75-252
GRAMSCI, A. QUADERNI DEL CARCERE.
  (V. GERRATANA, ED)
  M. CLARK, 617(TLS):31OCT75-1280
GRAÑA, C. FACT & SYMBOL.*
  S.L. FAISON, JR., 54:MAR73-160
  P. VIRDEN, 89(BJA):WINTER73-87
GRANAROLO, J. D'ENNIUS À CATULLE.*
  E.J. KENNEY, 123:MAR74-137

GRANATSTEIN, J.L. CANADA'S WAR.
H.B. NEATBY, 99:JAN75-43
GRANATSTEIN, J.L. CONSCRIPTION IN
THE SECOND WORLD WAR, 1939-1945.
G.L. COOK, 255(HAB):WINTER73-71
GRANATSTEIN, J.L. & P. STEVENS, EDS.
FORUM.
K. MC SWEENEY, 529(QQ):SPRING73-
152
DE GRANDA, G. TRANSCULTURACIÓN E
INTERFERENCIA LINGÜÍSTICA EN EL
PUERTO RICO CONTEMPORÁNEO (1898-
1968).
R.S. MEYERSTEIN, 545(RPH):FEB74-
411
GRANDGENT, C.H. - SEE DANTE ALIGHI-
ERI
GRANDMAISON, C.L. RÔLES TRADITION-
NELS FÉMININS ET URBANISATION.
R.C. O'BRIEN, 69:JUL73-273
GRANOIEN, N. & M. GREEN - SEE KUZ-
MIN, M.
GRANSDEN, A. HISTORICAL WRITING IN
ENGLAND C. 550 TO C. 1307.
B. SMALLEY, 617(TLS):4APR75-379
GRANSDEN, K.W., ED. TUDOR VERSE
SATIRE.
W. WEISS, 430(NS):JUN73-346
GRANT, C. THE BATTLE OF FONTENOY.
B. HILL, 617(TLS):26DEC75-1543
GRANT, D. WHITE GOATS & BLACK BEES.
C. DAVIDSON, 617(TLS):22AUG75-946
GRANT, E., ED & TRANS. NICOLE
ORESME & THE KINEMATICS OF CIRCULAR
MOTION.*
J. COLEMAN, 382(MAE):1974/1-57
GRANT, J.D. THE PERSONAL MEMOIRS OF
JULIA DENT GRANT. (J.Y. SIMON, ED)
P. ADAMS, 61:MAY75-103
G. VIDAL, 453:18SEP75-6
A. WHITMAN, 441:30MAY75-29
GRANT, J.S., L.A.G. MOSS & J. UNGER,
EDS. CAMBODIA.
M. LEIFER, 293(JAST):NOV72-121
GRANT, J.W. THE CHURCH IN THE CAN-
ADIAN ERA. (VOL 3)
E. LINDSTROM, 529(QQ):SPRING73-144
GRANT, M. THE ANCIENT HISTORIANS.*
M. CHAMBERS, 122:APR73-153
F.M. WASSERMANN, 121(CJ):DEC73/
JAN74-174
GRANT, M., ED. ANCIENT HISTORY
ATLAS.*
W.J. SWITALA, 124:NOV72-185
GRANT, M. CLEOPATRA.
639(VQR):WINTER74-XXVIII
GRANT, M. HEROD THE GREAT.
M. SWAN, 124:MAY73-498
GRANT, M. THE MOBSMEN ON THE SPOT.
N. CALLENDAR, 441:30MAR75-24
GRANT, M. THE ROMAN FORUM.* (FRENCH
TITLE: LE FORUM ROMAIN.)
J.H. D'ARMS, 124:APR73-435
GRANT, M. ROMAN MYTHS.
J. FONTENROSE, 124:NOV72-182
GRANT, M. THE TWELVE CAESARS.
R. SEAGER, 617(TLS):24OCT75-1271
GRANT, W. & D.D. MURISON - SEE "THE
SCOTTISH NATIONAL DICTIONARY"
GRANTHAM, D.W. - SEE BUNCHE, R.J.
"THE GRAPHIC WORK OF M.C. ESCHER."
P. FRESNAULT-DERUELLE, 98:MAY73-
447

GRAPPIN, P. RÉFLEXIONS SUR LES
UNIVERSITÉS FRANÇAISES.
N. HAMPSON, 208(FS):JAN74-116
GRAS, C. ALFRED ROSMER ET LE MOUVE-
MENT RÉVOLUTIONNAIRE INTERNATIONAL.
R. WOHL, 207(FR):DEC72-457
GRASS, G. ANESTHÉSIE LOCALE.
N. KATTAN, 98:APR73-386
GRASS, G. DAVOR. (V. & F. LANGE,
EDS)
R.W. LISTERMAN, 399(MLJ):DEC74-429
GRASS, G. FROM THE DIARY OF A
SNAIL.* (GERMAN TITLE: AUS DEM
TAGEBUCH EINER SCHNECKE.)
J.M. FLORA, 385(MQR):WINTER75-101
270:VOL23#4-82
GRASS, G. KATZ UND MAUS. DIE PLE-
BEJER PROBEN DEN AUFSTAND. (H.F.
BROOKES & C.E. FRAENKEL, EDS OF
BOTH)
J. REDDICK, 220(GL&L):JAN74-177
GRASSÉ, P-P., ED. LAROUSSE ENCYCLO-
PEDIA OF THE ANIMAL WORLD.
A. BROYARD, 441:8DEC75-29
GRASSHOFF, H. & U. LEHMANN, EDS.
STUDIEN ZUR GESCHICHTE DER RUSSI-
CHEN LITERATUR DES 18. JAHRHUNDERTS.
M. RAEFF, 104:SPRING73-118
GRASSI, E. ARTE COME ANTI-ARTE.
M. RIESER, 290(JAAC):SUMMER74-571
GRÄTZER, G. UNIVERSAL ALGEBRA.
K.A. BAKER, 316:DEC73-643
GRAU, S.A. THE WIND SHIFTING WEST.*
W. PEDEN, 569(SR):FALL74-712
GRAUR, A. THE ROMANCE CHARACTER OF
ROMANIAN.
G.F. MEIER, 682(ZPSK):BAND26HEFT
1/2-192
GRAUS, F. & OTHERS. EASTERN & WEST-
ERN EUROPE IN THE MIDDLE AGES.
(G. BARRACLOUGH, ED)
H.G. LUNT, 574(SEEJ):SUMMER72-269
GRAVER, L. CARSON MC CULLERS.
A. EASSON, 447(N&Q):SEP73-345
GRAVES, J.C. THE CONCEPTUAL FOUNDA-
TIONS OF CONTEMPORARY RELATIVITY
THEORY.*
J. DORLING, 482(PHR):APR73-258
GRAVES, R. AT THE GATE.
A. THWAITE, 617(TLS):23MAY75-552
GRAVES, R. COLLECTED POEMS 1975.
R. PADEL, 617(TLS):26DEC75-1537
GRAVES, R.L. COBALT 60.
N. CALLENDAR, 441:24AUG75-27
GRAVINA, G. SCRITTI CRITICI E
TEORICI. (A. QUONDAM, ED)
M. FUBINI, 228(GSLI):VOL150FASC
472-621
GRAWITZ, M. MÉTHODES DES SCIENCES
SOCIALES.
D. MERLLIÉ, 542:JAN-MAR73-53
GRAY, B. STYLE.
J. KELEMEN, 353:1APR73-89
GRAY, C. ARMAND GUILLAUMIN.
G.P. WEISBERG, 127:FALL73-82
GRAY, C. - SEE "HANS RICHTER BY HANS
RICHTER"
GRAY, C.S. CANADIAN DEFENCE PRIOR-
ITIES.*
D. MORTON, 529(QQ):AUTUMN73-457
GRAY, D. RIDE ON A TIGER.
T.J. BINYON, 617(TLS):26DEC75-1544

GRAY, D. THEMES & IMAGES IN THE
MEDIEVAL ENGLISH RELIGIOUS LYRIC.*
S. BROOK, 677:VOL4-249
R.T. DAVIES, 447(N&Q):AUG73-299
T.P. DUNNING, 541(RES):NOV73-467
R.M. WILSON, 175:AUTUMN72-106
GRAY, G.B. THE FORMS OF HEBREW
POETRY.
A.R. MILLARD, 318(JAOS):JUL-SEP73-
398
GRAY, J. A HISTORY OF JERUSALEM.
L.H. FELDMAN, 121(CJ):OCT/NOV73-85
GRAY, J. JOHNSON'S SERMONS.*
C. CHAPIN, 481(PQ):JUL73-529
P.J. KORSHIN, 301(JEGP):JUL74-439
R.B. LOVEJOY, 529(QQ):WINTER73-641
W.J. ONG, 401(MLQ):MAR74-66
C.J. RAWSON, 175:SPRING73-29
C. TRACY, 150(DR):AUTUMN73-574
102(CANL):SUMMER73-126
GRAY, J. THE ROAR OF THE TWENTIES.
J. WARKENTIN, 99:APR/MAY75-36
GRAY, J.F. SETS, RELATIONS, & FUNC-
TIONS.
A. BORGERS, 316:JUN73-341
GRAY, J.M. TENNYSON'S DOPPELGÄNGER,
"BALIN & BALAN."*
D.R. DAVIS, 184(EIC):JAN73-95
GRAY, N. THE SILENT MAJORITY.*
G. WOODCOCK, 401(MLQ):SEP74-331
GRAY, R. FRANZ KAFKA.*
S. CORNGOLD, 141:SUMMER74-270
B. GOLDSTEIN, 301(JEGP):JUL74-416
E. GOLDSTÜCKER, 575(SEER):APR74-
317
W.H. SOKEL, 399(MLJ):SEP-OCT74-286
GRAY, T. THE ORANGE ORDER.
H. SENIOR, 255(HAB):SUMMER73-206
GRAYMONT, B. THE IROQUOIS IN THE
AMERICAN REVOLUTION.*
J.P. REID, 432(NEQ):MAR73-145
GRAYMONT, B. - SEE RICKARD, C.
GRAYSON, C. CINQUE SAGGI SU DANTE.*
M. MARTI, 228(GSLI):VOL150FASC470/
471-411
C.W., 275(IQ):SUMMER73-106
GRAYSON, C. - SEE ALBERTI, L.B.
GRAYSON, L.M. & M. BLISS, EDS. THE
WRETCHED OF CANADA.
W.D. YOUNG, 529(QQ):SPRING73-115
DE GRAZIA, S., ED. MASTERS OF CHIN-
ESE POLITICAL THOUGHT.
T-L. LEE, 396(MODA):SPRING74-216
"GREAT SOVIET ENCYCLOPEDIA."* (VOL
1) (3RD ED) (A.M. PROKHOROV, ED IN
CHIEF)
L.F.S. UPTON, 104:WINTER74-592
G. WALKER, 617(TLS):30MAY75-591
"GREAT SOVIET ENCYCLOPEDIA." (VOLS
2-5) (3RD ED) (A.M. PROKHOROV, ED
IN CHIEF)
G. WALKER, 617(TLS):30MAY75-591
GREAVES, J. WHO'S WHO IN DICKENS.
L. OVERBEEK, 155:JAN73-57
GREAVES, R.L., COMP. AN ANNOTATED
BIBLIOGRAPHY OF JOHN BUNYAN STUD-
IES.
568(SCN):SPRING-SUMMER74-19
GREBANIER, B. THEN CAME EACH ACTOR.
P-L. ADAMS, 61:OCT75-111
GREBE, K. ANTON BRUCKNER IN SELBST-
ZEUGNISSEN UND BILDDOKUMENTEN.
J.S. WEISSMANN, 412:AUG-NOV73-353

GREBE, P., R. KÖSTER & W. MÜLLER,
EDS. BEDEUTUNGSWÖRTERBUCH.
L.E. BRISTER, 399(MLJ):NOV73-379
GREELEY, A.M. WHY CAN'T THEY BE
LIKE US?
H.A. LARRABEE, 432(NEQ):DEC73-643
GREEN, A. ONLY A MINER.*
N. COHEN, 292(JAF):APR-JUN73-191
GREEN, C. & C. MC CREERY. APPARI-
TIONS.
R. HAYNES, 617(TLS):29AUG75-976
GREEN, D. ULYSSES BOUND.*
E. WEBBY, 581:MAR74-95
GREEN, J. JEUNESSE.
R. SPEAIGHT, 617(TLS):7FEB75-146
GREEN, J. LIBERTÉ.
617(TLS):21FEB75-198
GREEN, J. THE OTHER ONE.
M. PRICE, 676(YR):AUTUMN73-80
GREEN, L. CHRONICLE INTO HISTORY.
D.R. KELLEY, 589:APR74-334
J.H. WHITFIELD, 382(MAE):1974/2-
190
GREEN, L.C. LAW & SOCIETY.
W.R. CORNISH, 617(TLS):26SEP75-
1101
GREEN, M. CITIES OF LIGHT & SONS OF
THE MORNING.
M. BYRD, 473(PR):1/1974-132
GREEN, M. HEADS YOU WIN.
D.M. DAY, 157:SUMMER73-80
GREEN, M. THE VON RICHTHOFEN SIS-
TERS.*
P. VANSITTART, 364:FEB/MAR75-141
GREEN, M.J. THE OTHER GOVERNMENT.
J.K. GALBRAITH, 441:18MAY75-4
442(NY):18AUG75-84
GREEN, O.H. THE LITERARY MIND OF
MEDIEVAL & RENAISSANCE SPAIN.*
(J.E. KELLER, ED)
E.S. MORBY, 551(RENQ):SUMMER73-208
J.A. PARR, 240(HR):SPRING74-430
GREEN, P. ALEXANDER THE GREAT.
E.N. BORZA, 122:APR73-139
GREEN, P. THE SHADOW OF THE PARTHE-
NON.
V. ALLEN, 124:MAR74-295
M.L. CLARKE, 123:NOV74-318
GREEN, R. SEXUAL IDENTITY CONFLICT
IN CHILDREN & ADULTS.
I. YOUNG, 617(TLS):21FEB75-203
GREEN, R.L. - SEE CARROLL, L.
GREEN, R.P.H. THE POETRY OF PAULIN-
US OF NOLA.*
A. HUDSON-WILLIAMS, 123:NOV74-298
P.G. WALSH, 313:VOL63-309
GREENAN, R.H. HEART OF GOLD.
C. LEHMANN-HAUPT, 441:14MAR75-43
M. LEVIN, 441:4MAY75-52
GREENBAUM, S. STUDIES IN ENGLISH
ADVERBIAL USAGE.*
W.R. O'DONNELL, 297(JL):SEP73-313
GREENBAUM, S. VERB-INTENSIFIER COL-
LOCATIONS IN ENGLISH.*
A. BRISAU, 179(ES):FEB72-80
GREENBAUM, S. & R. QUIRK. ELICITA-
TION EXPERIMENTS IN ENGLISH.
L. GOOSSENS, 179(ES):OCT72-494
J.W. NEY, 353:15APR73-111
GREENBERG, B.L. THE SPOILS OF AUG-
UST.
R. LATTIMORE, 249(HUDR):AUTUMN74-
466

GREENBERG, J.H. LANGUAGE, CULTURE, & COMMUNICATION. (A.S. DIL, ED)
M. GOODMAN, 269(IJAL):APR73-126
GREENBERG, R.A. & W.B. PIPER - SEE SWIFT, J.
GREENBLATT, S.J. SIR WALTER RALEGH.*
D. FROST, 111:30MAY74-162
L.B. SMITH, 639(VQR):SUMMER74-444
676(YR):WINTER74-XVIII
GREENE, G. BRIGHTON ROCK. IT'S A BATTLEFIELD. ENGLAND MADE ME. OUR MAN IN HAVANA. THE POWER & THE GLORY. THE HEART OF THE MATTER. THE CONFIDENTIAL AGENT. COLLECTED STORIES. A GUN FOR SALE. THE MINISTRY OF FEAR. THE QUIET AMERI-CAN.
R.M. DAVIS, 594:WINTER73-530
GREENE, G. GRAHAM GREENE ON FILM. (J.R. TAYLOR, ED)
R.M. DAVIS, 594:WINTER73-530
N. SILVERSTEIN, 295:FEB74-515
V. YOUNG, 249(HUDR):SUMMER74-245
GREENE, G. THE HONORARY CONSUL.*
W. SULLIVAN, 569(SR):WINTER74-138
GREENE, G., ED. AN IMPOSSIBLE WOMAN.
V. GLENDINNING, 617(TLS):12SEP75-1014
GREENE, G. THE PORTABLE GRAHAM GREENE. (P. STRATFORD, ED)
R.M. DAVIS, 594:WINTER73-530
K. MC SWEENEY, 529(QQ):AUTUMN73-494
GREENE, G. A SORT OF LIFE.*
295:FEB74-368
GREENE, G. - SEE MOOR, D.
GREENE, H., ED. THE FURTHER RIVALS OF SHERLOCK HOLMES.
M. YOUNG, 441:2FEB75-21
GREENE, J. PSYCHOLINGUISTICS.*
R.E. EILERS, 399(MLJ):SEP-OCT74-281
G. KRESS, 307:#2-108
J.L., 543:JUN73-753
GREENE, J. THINKING & LANGUAGE.
I. HUNTER, 617(TLS):6JUN75-629
GREENE, J.C. LA MORTE DI ADAMO.
G. SOLINAS, 548(RCSF):APR-JUN73-210
GREENE, N. ANTONIN ARTAUD, POET WITHOUT WORDS.
E. SELLIN, 295:FEB74-533
GREENE, T.M. RABELAIS.*
J.C. NASH, 188(ECR):WINTER73-364
M. TETEL, 593:SUMMER74-189
GREENFIELD, S.B. THE INTERPRETATION OF OLD ENGLISH POEMS.
A. CRÉPIN, 189(EA):JUL-SEP73-350
J.E. CROSS, 382(MAE):1974/1-42
M.E. GOLDSMITH, 184(EIC):JUL73-298
P. GRADON, 447(N&Q):SEP73-342
B. MITCHELL, 541(RES):AUG73-319
T.A. SHIPPEY, 677:VOL4-242
R.M. WILSON, 175:SPRING73-27
GREENFIELD, S.M. RAMÓN MARÍA DEL VALLE-INCLÁN.
A. SINCLAIR, 402(MLR):JAN74-208
GREENHALGH, P.A.L. THE YEAR OF THE FOUR EMPERORS.
R. SEAGER, 617(TLS):15AUG75-919
GREENHOUGH, T. TIME & TIMOTHY GREN-VILLE.
T.A. SHIPPEY, 617(TLS):8AUG75-903

GREENOUGH, H. LETTERS OF HORATIO GREENOUGH, AMERICAN SCULPTOR. (N. WRIGHT, ED)
M. FRIEDLAENDER, 432(NEQ):MAR74-135
J. MARKUS, 127:SPRING74-278
GREENWAY, D.E., ED. CHARTERS OF THE HONOUR OF MOWBRAY, 1107-1191.
S.D. WHITE, 589:APR74-336
GREENWOOD, E.B. TOLSTOY.
R.F. CHRISTIAN, 617(TLS):7NOV75-1329
GREENWOOD, G. & N. HARPER, EDS. AUSTRALIA IN WORLD AFFAIRS: 1966-1970.
N. MC LACHLAN, 617(TLS):22AUG75-953
GREER, B. SLAMMER.
P. ADAMS, 61:AUG75-89
R. SOKOLOV, 441:14SEP75-41
GREGOR, D.B. ROMAGNOL LANGUAGE & LITERATURE.
T.G. GRIFFITH, 402(MLR):JAN74-189
GREGOR, I. THE GREAT WEB.
J.I.M. STEWART, 617(TLS):18APR75-415
GREGORES, E. & J.A. SUÁREZ - SEE HOCKETT, C.F.
GREGORIUS. MAGISTER GREGORIUS: "NARRACIO DE MIRABILIBUS URBIS ROME." (R.B.C. HUYGENS, ED)
P.G. WALSH, 123:NOV74-307
GREGORY, A. - SEE BURT, C.
GREGORY, B. BRITISH AIRBORNE TROOPS.
617(TLS):31JAN75-121
GREGORY, H. THE HOUSE ON JEFFERSON STREET.
295:FEB74-368
GREGORY, R. & P. HUTCHESSON. THE PARLIAMENTARY OMBUDSMAN.
B. COCKS, 617(TLS):4JUL75-720
GREGORY, R.G. INDIA & EAST AFRICA.*
N.V. RAJKUMAR, 293(JAST):MAY73-544
GREGORY, V. OH BOY, HERE COMES WALT!
M. LEVIN, 441:13JUL75-32
GREIFENHAGEN, A. SCHMUCKARBEITEN IN EDELMETALL. (VOL 1)
R.A. HIGGINS, 303:VOL93-270
GREIMAS, A.J. STRUKTURALE SEMANTIK.
U.L. FIGGE, 343:BAND16HEFT2-136
GREIMAS, A.J. & OTHERS. ESSAIS DE SÉMIOTIQUE POÉTIQUE.
J. CULLER, 208(FS):JUL74-356
J-M. KLINKENBERG, 209(FM):JUL73-300
GREINER, D.J. COMIC TERROR.
W.M. FROHOCK, 584(SWR):SUMMER74-330
I. MALIN, 141:FALL74-347
GREINER, D.J. ROBERT FROST.
P. BEER, 617(TLS):31OCT75-1287
GREINER, K. DIE GLASHÜTTEN IN WÜRT-TEMBERG.
R. SCHNYDER, 182:VOL26#17/18-612
GRENDLER, P.F. CRITICS OF THE ITAL-IAN WORLD (1530-1560).
D. NOLAN, 276:SUMMER73-318
GRENE, M. SARTRE.
G.J. STACK, 484(PPR):JUN74-609

GRENE, N. THE SYNGE MANUSCRIPTS IN
THE LIBRARY OF TRINITY COLLEGE DUB-
LIN.
R. HOGAN, 295:APR74-1031
GREVE, L. BEI TAG.
D. SCRASE, 617(TLS):15AUG75-916
GREVEN, H.A. ELEMENTS OF ENGLISH
PHONOLOGY.
G.F. MEIER, 682(ZPSK):BAND26HEFT
3/4-420
GREVILLE, F. THE REMAINS. (G.A.
WILKES, ED)
R. ELLRODT, 189(EA):JAN-MAR73-87
GREVILLE, F. SELECTED WRITINGS OF
FULKE GREVILLE. (J. REES, ED)
R. ELLRODT, 189(EA):OCT-DEC73-468
J. GRUNDY, 402(MLR):JUL74-619
GRÉVIN, J. CÉSAR.* (E.S. GINSBERG,
ED)
K.M. HALL, 402(MLR):APR74-401
R. ORTALI, 535(RHL):JAN-FEB73-118
C.N. SMITH, 208(FS):JAN74-63
GREY, D. & E.L. - SEE TINGSTEN, H.
GREY, H. TALES FROM THE MOHAVES.
F. GILLMOR, 50(ARQ):SPRING73-83
GREYSMITH, D. RICHARD DADD.
P. ADAMS, 61:JUL75-83
P. ALLDERIDGE, 592:NOV73-204
R. EDWARDS, 39:NOV73-403
GRIBBIN, W. THE CHURCHES MILITANT.*
D.G. MATHEWS, 656(WMQ):JUL74-518
B.M. STEPHENS, 432(NEQ):JUN74-331
GRIBBLE, C.E. MEDIEVAL SLAVIC
TEXTS. (VOL 1)
T. CIZEVSKA, 574(SEEJ):WINTER73-
483
GRIBBLE, C.E. RUSSIAN ROOT LIST.
N.J. BROWN, 575(SEER):APR74-312
GRIDLEY, R.E. BROWNING.
T.J. COLLINS, 637(VS):DEC73-234
P. HONAN, 677:VOL4-328
J. MAYNARD, 85:SPRING73-51
G. THOMAS, 175:SPRING73-32
GRIEDER, J.B. HU SHIH & THE CHINESE
RENAISSANCE.
P.A. KUHN, 318(JAOS):JAN-MAR73-88
GRIER, E. SELECTED POEMS 1955-1970.
D. BARBOUR, 529(QQ):AUTUMN73-472
GRIESBACH, H. DEUTSCHE GRAMMATIK IM
ÜBERBLICK.
E.A. HOPKINS, 399(MLJ):JAN-FEB73-
57
GRIESBACH, H. MODERNE WELT I & II.
E.A. HOPKINS, 399(MLJ):MAR73-145
GRIEST, G.L. MUDIE'S CIRCULATING
LIBRARY & THE VICTORIAN NOVEL.*
B.F. FISHER 4TH, 177(ELT):VOL16#1-
83
GRIEVE, M. & A. SCOTT - SEE MC DIAR-
MID, H.
GRIFFIN, D.H. SATIRES AGAINST MAN.
J.W. JOHNSON, 401(MLQ):DEC74-426
566:SPRING74-95
639(VQR):SUMMER74-LXXVI
GRIFFIN, R. CORONATION OF THE POET.*
L. TERREAUX, 535(RHL):SEP-OCT73-
885
L. WIERENGA, 433:JUL73-307
GRIFFIN, R.A. HIGH BAROQUE CULTURE
& THEATRE IN VIENNA.*
B.W. BROWNING, 568(SCN):SPRING-
SUMMER74-17

GRIFFITH, C.E. THE AFRICAN DREAM.
G. SHEPPERSON, 617(TLS):17OCT75-
1238
GRIFFITH, J. & L.E. MINER, EDS. THE
FIRST LINCOLNLAND CONFERENCE ON DIA-
LECTOLOGY.*
G. KRISTENSSON, 179(ES):JUN72-274
J.B. MC MILLAN, 35(AS):SPRING-SUM-
MER71-159
U. OOMEN, 38:BAND91HEFT1-104
GRIFFITH, J. & L.E. MINER, EDS. THE
SECOND & THIRD LINCOLNLAND CONFER-
ENCES ON DIALECTOLOGY.
J.B. MC MILLAN, 35(AS):SPRING-SUM-
MER71-159
GRIFFITH, J.A.G. PARLIAMENTARY
SCRUTINY OF GOVERNMENT BILLS.
B. COCKS, 617(TLS):10JAN75-30
GRIFFITH, K. THANK GOD WE KEPT THE
FLAG FLYING.
P. GARDNER, 441:14DEC75-12
442(NY):6OCT75-166
GRIFFITHS, N. THE ACADIANS.
J. FINGARD, 150(DR):SUMMER73-366
GRIFFITHS, R. THE DRAMATIC TECH-
NIQUE OF ANTOINE DE MONTCHRESTIEN.
F. CHARPENTIER, 557(RSH):JAN-MAR73-
167
D. ROATEN, 546(RR):JAN73-69
GRIFFITHS, R. RÉVOLUTION À REBOURS.
B. SARRAZIN, 535(RHL):MAR-JUN73-
539
GRIFFITHS, R.A., WITH R.S. THOMAS.
THE PRINCIPALITY OF WALES IN THE
LATER MIDDLE AGES: THE STRUCTURE &
PERSONNEL OF GOVERNMENT. (VOL 1)
R.W. HAYS, 589:JUL74-561
GRIFFITHS, T. OCCUPATIONS & THE
BIG HOUSE.
A. RENDLE, 157:SPRING73-82
GRIGGS, E.L. - SEE COLERIDGE, S.T.
GRIGSON, G. ANGLES & CIRCLES.
R. GARFITT, 364:FEB/MAR75-108
GRIGSON, G. BRITAIN OBSERVED.
W. FEAVER, 617(TLS):25JUL75-847
D.A.N. JONES, 362:30OCT75-575
GRIGSON, G., ED. THE CONCISE ENCY-
CLOPEDIA OF MODERN WORLD LITERA-
TURE. (2ND ED)
295:FEB74-355
GRIGSON, G. THE CONTRARY VIEW.*
P. BAILEY, 364:AUG/SEP74-142
GRIGSON, J. & OTHERS. THE WORLD
ATLAS OF FOOD.
M.F.K. FISHER, 442(NY):10NOV75-189
GRILLANDI, M. INVITO ALLA LETTURA
DI GIORGIO BASSANI.
R. ADAMS, 275(IQ):FALL-WINTER73
(VOL17#66)-72
GRILLO, A. POETICA E CRITICA LET-
TERARIA NELLE BUCOLICHE DI VIR-
GILIO.
J. PERRET, 555:VOL47FASC1-158
GRIMALDI, U.A. & G. BOZZETTI - SEE
UNDER ALFASSIO GRIMALDI, U. & G.
BOZZETTI
GRIMALDI, W.M.A. STUDIES IN THE
PHILOSOPHY OF ARISTOTLE'S RHETORIC.
G.M. LIEGEY, 613:SPRING73-139
GRIMM, R., ED. DEUTSCHE DRAMENTHE-
ORIEN.*
P. GONTRUM, 131(CL):FALL74-365

GRIMM, R. & J. HERMAND, EDS.   EXIL
UND INNERE EMIGRATION.*
  G. STERN, 406:FALL74-325
GRIMM, R. & J. HERMAND - SEE "BASIS"
GRIMM, R. & H. JOST, EDS.   DIE SOG-
ENANNTEN ZWANZIGER JAHRE.
  J.N. HARDIN, 221(GQ):NOV73-613
GRIMSLEY, R.   FROM MONTESQUIEU TO
LACLOS.
  P. FRANCE, 617(TLS):7MAR75-257
GRIMSLEY, R.   SUR L'ORIGINE DU LAN-
GAGE.
  M. CARTWRIGHT, 207(FR):DEC72-402
GRIMSLEY, R. - SEE ROUSSEAU, J-J.
GRIMSTED, P.K.   ARCHIVES & MANU-
SCRIPT REPOSITORIES IN THE USSR:
MOSCOW & LENINGRAD.*
  A.M. SHANE, 574(SEEJ):FALL73-366
GRINDER, J.T. & S.H. ELGIN.   GUIDE
TO TRANSFORMATIONAL GRAMMAR.
  F.H. NUESSEL, JR., 399(MLJ):SEP-
  OCT74-282
  G.D. PRIDEAUX, 320(CJL):FALL74-193
GRINSELL, L., P. RAHTZ & D.P. WIL-
LIAMS.   THE PREPARATION OF ARCHAE-
OLOGICAL REPORTS.
  N. HAMMOND, 617(TLS):18APR75-434
GRINSPOON, L. & P. HEDBLOM.   THE
SPEED CULTURE.
  D.F. MUSTO, 441:18MAY75-34
  N.E. ZINBERG, 453:30OCT75-32
GRISÉ, C. - SEE TRISTAN L'HERMITE, F.
GRITTNER, F.M., ED.   STUDENT MOTI-
VATION & THE FOREIGN LANGUAGE
TEACHER.
  S. HAMILTON, 399(MLJ):SEP-OCT74-
  270
GROB, A.   THE PHILOSOPHIC MIND.*
  R.H. FOGLE, 569(SR):SPRING74-383
  J.A.W. HEFFERNAN, 591(SIR):SUMMER
  74-255
GROENKE, U.   GRUNDZÜGE DER STRUKTUR
DES FINNISCHEN.
  R. AUSTERLITZ, 343:BAND17HEFT2-220
GROJNOWSKI, D. - SEE BÉROUL
GRÖNOSET, D.   ANNA.
  P. ADAMS, 61:APR75-100
GRONOWICZ, A.   THE HOOKMEN.
  T. ALLEN, 497(POLR):VOL18#4-112
GROOM, B.   ON THE DICTION OF TENNY-
SON, BROWNING & ARNOLD.
  D. ROLL-HANSEN, 179(ES):AUG73-404
GROOTEN, J. & G.J. STEENBERGEN.   NEW
ENCYCLOPEDIA OF PHILOSOPHY.   (E.
VAN DEN BOSSCHE, ED & TRANS)
  W.G., 543:JUN73-754
GRÖSCHEL, B.   DIE SPRACHE IVAN
VYSENSKYS.
  H.G. LUNT, 574(SEEJ):WINTER73-491
GROSE, C.   MILTON'S EPIC PROCESS.
  R.L. PEST, 568(SCN):FALL74-51
  639(VQR):AUTUMN74-CXXIV
GROSE, M.W. & D. MC KENNA.   OLD ENG-
LISH LITERATURE.
  A. CRÉPIN, 189(EA):JUL-SEP73-349
GROSMAN, B.A.   POLICE COMMAND.
  R. MARK, 617(TLS):26SEP75-1098
GROSS, F.   VIOLENCE IN POLITICS.
  J.S. ROUCEK, 497(POLR):VOL18#3-97
GROSS, H.   THE CONTRIVED CORRIDOR.
  U. MARGOLIN, 255(HAB):SPRING73-152
GROSS, J., ED.   RUDYARD KIPLING.
  A. SHELSTON, 148:SPRING73-93
  G. THOMAS, 175:SUMMER73-80

GROSS, J.   THE YOUNG MAN WHO WROTE
SOAP OPERAS.
  J. CHARYN, 441:7SEP75-40
GROSS, J. - SEE SEELEY, J.R.
GROSS, M. & A. LENTIN.   INTRODUCTION
TO FORMAL GRAMMARS.
  R.M. SMABY, 297(JL):FEB73-188
GROSS, N. - SEE BARON, S.W. & OTHERS
GROSS, T.L., ED.   THE LITERATURE OF
AMERICAN JEWS.
  S. MOORE, 385(MQR):SUMMER75-358
GROSSBACH, R.   EASY & HARD WAYS OUT.
  A. BROYARD, 441:16JAN75-45
  M. LEVIN, 441:26JAN75-27
GROSSE, E.U.   ALTFRANZÖSISCHER ELE-
MENTARKURS.
  H.D. BORK, 72:BAND211HEFT1/3-193
"DER GROSSE DUDEN."   (VOL 2) (6TH
ED) (G. DROWDOWSKI & OTHERS, EDS)
  J.A. PFEFFER, 221(GQ):MAY73-490
GROSSER, A.   DEUTSCHLANDBILANZ.
  M. EIFLER, 221(GQ):MAY73-485
GROSSER, M.   PAINTER'S PROGRESS.
  M.L. REYNOLDS, 127:FALL73-84
GROSSETESTE, R.   THE MIDDLE ENGLISH
TRANSLATIONS OF ROBERT GROSSE-
TESTE'S "CHÂTEAU D'AMOUR." (K.
SAJAVAARA, ED)
  W. RIEHLE, 38:BAND91HEFT1-119
GROSSMAN, J.   ECHO OF A DISTANT
DRUM.
  P. ADAMS, 61:FEB75-123
GROSSMAN, J.D.   EDGAR ALLAN POE IN
RUSSIA.
  C.L. ANDERSON, 27(AL):MAR74-112
  G. DONCHIN, 575(SEER):APR74-280
GROSSMAN, J.H.   THE BUSINESS OF
LIVING.
  L.C. LEWIN, 441:13APR75-6
GROSSMAN, L.   DOSTOEVSKY.
  M. JONES, 617(TLS):21FEB75-198
  G. STEINER, 442(NY):13OCT75-169
GROSSMAN, M.L.   DADA.*
  E. SELLIN, 295:FEB74-394
GROSSMANN, R.   MEINONG.*
  W. MAYS, 518:OCT74-10
GROTOWSKI, J.   TOWARDS A POOR THE-
ATRE.
  D.A.N. JONES, 617(TLS):18APR75-422
GROULX, L.   MES MÉMOIRES.   (VOLS 1&2)
  R. BONVALET, 102(CANL):WINTER73-
  125
GROUNDS, R.   FERNS.
  617(TLS):26DEC75-1547
GROUSSARD, S.   THE BLOOD OF ISRAEL.
  E. WIESEL, 441:8JUN75-4
GROUT, D.J.   A HISTORY OF WESTERN
MUSIC.   (2ND ED)
  A. JACOBS, 415:JAN74-40
GROVER, P.   HENRY JAMES & THE FRENCH
NOVEL.*
  G.J. BECKER, 27(AL):MAY74-233
GROVES, H.M.   TAX PHILOSOPHERS.
  (D.J. CURRAN, ED)
  A.R. PREST, 617(TLS):22AUG75-952
GRUBBS, H.A.   PAUL VALÉRY.
  D.H. MORRIS 4TH, 577(SHR):WINTER
  73-103
GRUBE, E.J.   ISLAMIC PAINTINGS FROM
THE 11TH TO THE 18TH CENTURY FROM
THE COLLECTION OF HANS P. KRAUS.
  B.W. ROBINSON, 90:JUN73-398

GRUCZA, F. SPRACHLICHE DIAKRISE IM
BEREICH DER AUSDRUCKSEBENE DES
DEUTSCHEN.*
　J. JESZKE, 353:1DEC73-125
GRUEN, E.S. THE LAST GENERATION OF
THE ROMAN REPUBLIC.
　639(VQR):AUTUMN74-CXLVII
GRUEN, J. THE PARTY'S OVER NOW.
　295:FEB74-369
GRUEN, J. THE PRIVATE WORLD OF
BALLET.
　D. HARRIS, 441:4MAY75-4
　A. KISSELGOFF, 441:19JUL75-21
VON DER GRÜN, M. STELLENWEISE GLAT-
TEIS.
　S. ELKHADEM, 268:JAN75-83
　P. PROCHNIK, 617(TLS):22AUG75-950
GRÜNBERG, M. THE WEST-SAXON GOS-
PELS.
　P. MERTENS-FONCK, 179(ES):FEB73-59
VON GRUNEBAUM, G.E. CLASSICAL ISLAM.
　A.A.A. FYZEE, 273(IC):APR73-181
VON GRUNEBAUM, G.E., ED. LOGIC IN
CLASSICAL ISLAMIC CULTURE.
　K. GYEKYE, 318(JAOS):JAN-MAR73-100
GRÜNENWALD, E. LEONHARD KERN.
　C. THEUERKAUFF, 90:MAR73-163
GRUNER, C.R. & OTHERS. SPEECH COM-
MUNICATION IN SOCIETY.
　G.R. KNELLER, 583:SPRING74-304
GRUNER, D. DIE BERBER-KERAMIK AM
BEISPIEL DER ORTE AFIR, MERKALLA,
TAHER, TIBERGUENT UND ROKNIA.
　L. GOLVIN, 182:VOL26#17/18-635
GRUNWALD, S.F.L. A BIOGRAPHY OF
JOHANN MICHAEL MOSCHEROSCH (1601-
1669).*
　K.G. KNIGHT, 220(GL&L):OCT73-84
GRZEGORCZYK, P. INDEX LEXICORUM
POLONIAE.
　H. LEEMING, 575(SEER):JUL74-453
GSELL, O. DAS "JEU DE LA FEUILLÉE"
VON ADAM DE LA HALLE.
　L.R. MUIR, 208(FS):JUL74-311
GSTEIGER, M. FRANZÖSISCHE SYMBOLIS-
TEN IN DER DEUTSCHEN LITERATUR DER
JAHRHUNDERTWENDE (1869-1914).*
　R. BREUGELMANS, 131(CL):SPRING74-
180
　R. FURNESS, 402(MLR):OCT74-935
　K.A. HORST, 52:BAND8HEFT3-351
　R.R. HUBERT, 149:SEP74-254
　A. NIVELLE, 535(RHL):NOV-DEC73-
1102
GUARINO, G.A. - SEE ALBERTI, L.B.
GUATTARI, F. PSYCHANALYSE ET TRANS-
VERSALITÉ.
　Y. BRÈS, 542:JAN-MAR73-40
GUBERMAN, J. THE LIFE OF JOHN
LOTHROP MOTLEY.
　M.F. GUTHEIM, 432(NEQ):DEC74-627
GUDIOL, J. GOYA 1746-1828.
　E. YOUNG, 90:JAN73-43
GUDIOL, J. VELÁZQUEZ 1599-1660.
　T. CROMBIE, 617(TLS):14FEB75-174
　F. HASKELL, 453:2OCT75-14
　J. RUSSELL, 441:7DEC75-3
GUÉHENNO, J. & R. ROLLAND. L'INDÉ-
PENDANCE DE L'ESPRIT.
　R. SPEAIGHT, 617(TLS):12DEC75-1476
GUENTER, C.H. MAX GALAN: HUNTER OF
MEN.
　N. CALLENDAR, 441:31AUG75-12

GUENTHER, H.V. BUDDHIST PHILOSOPHY
IN THEORY & PRACTICE.
　A.C. MC DERMOTT, 485(PE&W):JUL73-
400
　C.S. PREBISH, 293(JAST):FEB73-337
GUÉRIN, D. AUTOBIOGRAPHIE DE JEU-
NESSE.
　P. AUBÉRY, 207(FR):DEC72-458
GUÉRIN, Y. UNE OEUVRE ANGLO-INDI-
ENNE ET SES VISAGES FRANÇAIS.*
　H. GODIN, 208(FS):JUL74-360
GUERINOT, J.V. PAMPHLET ATTACKS ON
ALEXANDER POPE 1711-1744.*
　I. SIMON, 179(ES):DEC72-564
GUEST, B. MOSCOW MANSIONS.*
　P. RAMSEY, 569(SR):SPRING74-394
　H. ZINNES, 109:SPRING/SUMMER74-122
GUEST, H. & L. AND KAJIMA SHOZO, EDS
& TRANS. POST-WAR JAPANESE POETRY.*
　M. BROCK, 285(JAPQ):JAN-MAR74-101
GUEST, T.M. SOME ASPECTS OF HADE-
WIJCH'S POETIC FORM IN THE "STRO-
FISCHE GEDICHTEN."
　P. KING, 617(TLS):28NOV75-1422
DE GUEVARA, J.V. - SEE UNDER VÉLEZ
DE GUEVARA, J.
GUFFEY, G.R. - SEE TRAHERNE, T.
GUGGENHEIM-GRÜNBERG, F. - SEE WELDER-
STEINBERG, A.
GUGLIELMI, A. LA LETTERATURA DEL
RISPARMIO.
　G. ALMANSI, 617(TLS):14FEB75-160
"GUÍA DE LA CIUDAD DE MÉXICO."
　J.A. DABBS, 399(MLJ):JAN-FEB73-75
GUICHARD, A. LES JUIFS.
　J. KOLBERT, 207(FR):OCT72-192
"GUIDE TO MANUSCRIPTS & ARCHIVES IN
THE NEGRO COLLECTION OF TREVOR
ARNETT LIBRARY, ATLANTA UNIVERSITY."
　A.L. NOLEN, 14:JAN73-76
"A GUIDE TO THE NEWSPAPER COLLECTION
OF THE STATE ARCHIVES, NEBRASKA
HISTORICAL SOCIETY."
　A.L. NOLEN, 14:JAN73-76
GUIDUBALDI, E., ED. PSICOANALISI E
STRUTTURALISMO DI FRONTE A DANTE.
　M.M., 228(GSLI):VOL150FASC470/471-
467
GUILD, N. THE LOST & FOUND MAN.
　N. CALLENDAR, 441:21DEC75-16
GUILDS, J.C. - SEE SIMMS, W.G.
GUILES, F.L. MARION DAVIES.
　E. ANDERSON, 200:JAN73-47
GUILES, F.L. HANGING ON IN PARA-
DISE.
　S. FARBER, 441:18MAY75-18
　H. MEYERSON, 231:JUL75-90
GUILFORD, C. THE NEW COOK'S COOK-
BOOK.
　M.F.K. FISHER, 442(NY):10NOV75-176
GUILLAUME, G., ED. L'ATLAS LINGUIS-
TIQUE ARMORICAIN ROMAN.
　J. CHAURAND, 209(FM):OCT73-429
GUILLAUME, J. - SEE DE NERVAL, G.
GUILLAUME, J. & C. PICHOIS - SEE
DE NERVAL, G.
GUILLE, F.V. - SEE HUGO, A.
GUILLÉN, C. LITERATURE AS SYSTEM.*
　E. MINER, 141:WINTER72-78
　D. NEWTON-DE MOLINA, 184(EIC):
APR73-179
　E.L. RIVERS, 400(MLN):MAR73-425
　U. SCHULZ-BUSCHHAUS, 52:BAND8
HEFT2-178

GUILLÉN, J. CÁNTICO (1936). (J.M. BLECUA, ED)
K.M. SIBBALD, 86(BHS):JAN73-101
GUILLERMAZ, J. A HISTORY OF THE CHINESE COMMUNIST PARTY, 1921-1949.
P.J. SEYBOLT, 293(JAST):FEB73-319
GUILLOT, O. LE COMTE D'ANJOU ET SON ENTOURAGE AU XIE SIÈCLE.
R.T. COOLIDGE, 589:OCT74-735
GUILLOU, J. & M. VITOLS. LE FRANÇAIS CONTEMPORAIN.
M. WAGNER, 207(FR):OCT72-249
GUINARD, P.J. GUIDE DU THÈME ESPAGNOL.
J. JOSET, 556(RLV):1973/2-187
GUINNESS, D. & J.T. SADLER, JR. MR. JEFFERSON, ARCHITECT.*
45:MAY73-87
505:OCT73-126
GUIRAUD, P. ESSAIS DE STYLISTIQUE.*
S.J. SCHMIDT, 353:1APR73-112
GUIRAUD, P. LES GROS MOTS.
E. PARTRIDGE, 617(TLS):28NOV75-1414
GUIRAUD, P. LE JARGON DE VILLON OU LE GAI SAVOIR DE LA COQUILLE.* LE TESTAMENT DE VILLON OU LE GAI SAVOIR DE LA BASOCHE.
M. BUTOR, 98:MAR73-195
GUIRAUD, P. PATOIS ET DIALECTES FRANÇAIS.
F.M. JENKINS, 545(RPH):NOV73-226
G.F. MEIER, 682(ZPSK):BAND26HEFT 3/4-419
A. VALDMAN, 207(FR):MAR73-886
GUIRAUD, P. SEMIOLOGY.* (FRENCH TITLE: LA SÉMIOLOGIE.)
A. REY, 361:OCT73-257
617(TLS):24JAN75-88
GUIRAUD, P. STRUCTURES ETYMOLOGIQUES DU LEXIQUE FRANÇAIS.
H.G. SCHOGT, 353:1FEB73-126
GUIRAUD, P. LA VERSIFICATION.
H. NAIS, 209(FM):JAN73-85
GUITTARD DE FLORIBAN, C. JOURNAL DE CÉLESTIN GUITTARD DE FLORIBAN. (R. AUBERT, ED)
N. HAMPSON, 617(TLS):2MAY75-481
GUIZOT, F. HISTORICAL ESSAYS & LECTURES.* (S. MELLON, ED)
R.H. KEYSERLINGK, 255(HAB):SPRING 73-128
GULDBECK, P.E. THE CARE OF HISTORICAL COLLECTIONS.
J.C. WRIGHT, 14:OCT73-555
GULLASON, T.A., ED. STEPHEN CRANE'S CAREER.
R.C. PIERLE, 577(SHR):SPRING73-223
GULLIVER, P.H. NEIGHBOURS & NETWORKS.
R.G. ABRAHAMS, 69:JUL73-270
"GULLIVERIANA III."
566:AUTUMN73-37
GULLÓN, R. TÉCNICAS DE GALDÓS.*
T.R. FRANZ, 238:MAY73-502
GULLÓN, R. UNA POÉTICA PARA ANTONIO MACHADO.
J.F. CIRRE, 238:MAR73-177
GULLÓN, R. - SEE DARÍO, R.
GUMBERT, J.P. & M.J.M. DE HAAN, EDS. ESSAYS PRESENTED TO G.I. LIEFTINCK.
K.W. HUMPHREYS, 354:DEC73-345

GUMILEV, N.S. SELECTED WORKS OF NIKOLAI S. GUMILEV.* (B. RAFFEL & A. BURAGO, EDS & TRANS)
J.F. HENDRY, 104:FALL73-429
G. IVASK, 574(SEEJ):SUMMER73-235
H.W. TJALSMA, 550(RUSR):APR73-208
GUMMERE, J.F., M.M. FORBES & P.L. MAC KENDRICK. LATIN READER 1&2.
M. SCHUMACHER, 124:MAY73-488
GUMPERZ, J.J. & E. HERNANDEZ CH. COGNITIVE ASPECTS OF BILINGUAL COMMUNICATION.
315(JAL):VOL11PT2-101
GUNBY, D.C. WEBSTER: THE WHITE DEVIL.
F. LAGARDE, 189(EA):JAN-MAR73-94
GUNDERSHEIMER, W.L. FERRARA.*
639(VQR):SPRING74-LIV
GUNDERSHEIMER, W.L. - SEE SABADINO DEGLI ARIENTI, G.
GUNDERT, H. DIALOG UND DIALEKTIK.
F. LASSERRE, 182:VOL26#5/6-169
GUNDOLF, F. BRIEFE UND KARTEN VON FRIEDRICH GUNDOLF 1906-31 AN ELSE LIMMER-LEUCHS. (F. USINGER, ED)
E. BOA, 182:VOL26#1/2-34
GUNDY, E. NAKED IN A PUBLIC PLACE.
M. LEVIN, 441:5OCT75-48
GUNDY, H.P. THE SPREAD OF PRINTING: CANADA.
R. CAVE, 503:SPRING73-46
E.J. DEVEREUX, 354:DEC73-356
K. MC SWEENEY, 529(QQ):AUTUMN73-499
G.L. PARKER, 255(HAB):SUMMER73-243
L.S. THOMPSON, 263:JAN-MAR74-64
GUNKEL, R. & H.D. TIESEMA. PRAKTISCHE DEUTSCHE SYNTAX.
J.J. BRAAKENBURG, 433:OCT73-410
GUNN, J. ALTERNATE WORLDS.
M. WOOD, 453:2OCT75-3
GUNN, P. NORMANDY.
S. PAKENHAM, 617(TLS):3OCT75-1157
GUNN, T. MOLY [&] MY SAD CAPTAINS.*
R. OLIVER, 598(SOR):SUMMER75-708
GUNN, T. TO THE AIR.*
R. OLIVER, 598(SOR):SUMMER75-708
R.B. SHAW, 491:SEP75-352
GUNNARSON, K-A. LE COMPLÉMENT DE LIEU DANS LE SYNTAGME NOMINAL.
K.J. DANELL, 597(SN):VOL45#1-202
GUNNELL, B. THE CASHEW-NUT GIRL.
J. MELLORS, 364:APR/MAY74-135
GUNSTON, B. THE PHILATELIST'S COMPANION.
617(TLS):4APR75-380
GUNTHER, A.E. A CENTURY OF ZOOLOGY AT THE BRITISH MUSEUM.
L.H. MATTHEWS, 617(TLS):2MAY75-475
GÜNTHER, H. GRUNDPHÄNOMENE UND GRUNDBEGRIFFE DES AFRIKANISCHEN UND AFRO-AMERIKANISCHEN TANZES.
A.M. DAUER, 187:MAY75-308
GÜNTHER, H. STRUKTUR ALS PROZESS.
R.B. PYNSENT, 575(SEER):APR74-315
GUPTA, P.S. IMPERIALISM & THE BRITISH LABOUR MOVEMENT, 1914-1964.
A.J.P. TAYLOR, 617(TLS):4JUL75-720
GUREWITCH, M. COMEDY.
M. HODGART, 617(TLS):26SEP75-1093
GURGĀNĪ, F.U. VIS & RAMIN. (G. MORRISON, TRANS)
J.A. BELLAMY, 318(JAOS):JUL-SEP73-367

GURIK, R. THE HANGED MAN.
C. BRISSENDEN, 102(CANL):WINTER74-111
GURNEY, J. CRUSADE IN SPAIN.
T.C. WORSLEY, 364(AUG/SEP74-139
GURR, A. THE SHAKESPEAREAN STAGE
1574-1642.*
P. EDWARDS, 447(N&Q):APR73-146
M. MINCOFF, 179(ES):AUG73-387
GURR, E. POPE.*
G. MIDGLEY, 447(N&Q):NOV73-432
GURVITCH, G. THE SOCIAL FRAMEWORKS
OF KNOWLEDGE.
R.M. GOODRIDGE, 262:SUMMER73-231
GUSDORF, G. LES SCIENCES HUMAINES
ET LA PENSÉE OCCIDENTALE. (VOLS
4&5)
R. MERCIER, 557(RSH):JAN-MAR73-153
GUSTAFSON, J.M. CAN ETHICS BE
CHRISTIAN?
F.R.B., 617(TLS):5DEC75-1468
GUSTAFSON, R. FIRE ON STONE.*
M.T. LANE, 198:WINTER75-106
L. SANDLER, 606(TAMR):NOV74-89
GUSTAFSON, R. SELECTED POEMS.
D. BARBOUR, 529(QQ):AUTUMN73-472
C.X. RINGROSE, 102(CANL):AUTUMN73-82
GUSTAFSON, R. THEME & VARIATIONS
FOR SOUNDING BRASS.
C.X. RINGROSE, 102(CANL):AUTUMN73-82
S. SCOBIE, 255(HAB):SUMMER73-240
"GUTENBERG JAHRBUCH 1971." "GUTEN-
BERG JAHRBUCH 1972." (H. WIDMANN,
ED OF BOTH)
H.G. GÖPFERT, 680(ZDP):BAND92HEFT
4-636
GUTHEIM, F. ALVAR AALTO.
C. BONNEFOI, 98:APR73-342
GUTHKE, K.S. DAS DEUTSCHE BÜRGER-
LICHE TRAUERSPIEL.
C.P. MAGILL, 220(GL&L):APR74-263
GUTHKE, K.S. DIE MYTHOLOGIE DER
ENTGÖTTERTEN WELT.*
M. BELLER, 52:BAND8HEFT2-207
H. MEYER, 149:DEC74-345
J. MILFULL, 67:MAY74-128
GUTHMAN, W.H. MARCH TO MASSACRE.
A. BROYARD, 441:20JAN75-25
GUTHRIE, A.B., JR. THE LAST VALLEY.
M. LEVIN, 441:12OCT75-49
GUTHRIE, A.B., JR. WILD PITCH.
T.W. FORD, 649(WAL):SPRING&SUMMER
73-75
GUTHRIE, T. ACTING.
I.W., 214:VOL6#21-127
GUTHRIE, W.K.C. A HISTORY OF GREEK
PHILOSOPHY.* (VOL 3)
R.E. ALLEN, 121(CJ):DEC73/JAN74-168
GUTHRIE, W.K.C. A HISTORY OF GREEK
PHILOSOPHY. (VOL 4)
G. VLASTOS, 617(TLS):12DEC75-1474
GUTHRIE, W.K.C. THE SOPHISTS.
J.V. BROWN, 154:SEP73-530
GUTKIND, P.C.W., ED. THE PASSING OF
TRIBAL MAN IN AFRICA.
V.L. GROTTANELLI, 69:OCT73-367
GUTMAN, H.G. SLAVERY & THE NUMBERS
GAME.
T.L. HASKELL, 453:20CT75-33

GUTMANN, J., ED. NO GRAVEN IMAGES.
L. GOLOMBEK, 318(JAOS):JUL-SEP73-401
GUTTENPLAN, S., ED. MIND & LANGU-
AGE.
P.F. STRAWSON, 617(TLS):21NOV75-1383
GUTTERIDGE, B. OLD DAMSON-FACE.
R. FULLER, 617(TLS):15AUG75-916
GUTTERIDGE, D. BORDERLANDS.
M.T. LANE, 198:SUMMER75-121
GUTTERIDGE, D. BUS-RIDE.
G. NOONAN, 99:FEB75-38
GUTTERIDGE, D. COPPERMINE.*
D. BARBOUR, 150(DR):WINTER73/74-785
P. STEVENS, 628:SPRING74-106
GUTTERIDGE, D. SAYING GRACE.
S. SCOBIE, 255(HAB):SUMMER73-240
GUTTERIDGE, L. FRATRICIDE IS A GAS.
E. KORN, 617(TLS):22AUG75-951
GUTTERIDGE, W.F. MILITARY RÉGIMES
IN AFRICA.
S. ANDRESKI, 617(TLS):17OCT75-1239
GUTTMANN, A. THE JEWISH WRITER IN
AMERICA.*
M.F. SCHULZ, 295:FEB74-425
GUTWIRTH, M. JEAN RACINE.*
B. CHÉDOZEAU, 535(RHL):SEP-OCT73-893
GUTWIRTH, M. STENDHAL.
R.M. CHADBOURNE, 399(MLJ):SEP-OCT
73-285
K.G. MC WATTERS, 402(MLR):APR74-417
M. SACHS, 207(FR):APR73-1014
GUTWIRTH, M., M. GUTWIRTH & J.P.
SPIELMAN, JR., EDS. SOURCES ET
REFLETS DE L'HISTOIRE DE FRANCE.
J. GREENLEE, 207(FR):FEB73-682
GUY, A. & OTHERS. LE TEMPS ET LA
MORT DANS LA PHILOSOPHIE CONTEMPOR-
AINE D'AMÉRIQUE LATINE.
H. WAGNER, 53(AGP):BAND55HEFT1-113
GUYAN, A. CONVERSATIONS WITH A
GOLLIWOG.
A. RENDLE, 157:SPRING73-82
GUYOTAT, P. EDEN, EDEN, EDEN.
J. ALTER, 207(FR):MAR73-856
GUZZO, A. L'ARTE.
E. NAMER, 542:JAN-MAR73-116
GWALTNEY, F.I. DESTINY'S CHICKENS.
639(VQR):WINTER74-VIII
GWILLIAM, K.M. & P.J. MACKIE. ECO-
NOMICS & TRANSPORT POLICY.
T.C. BARKER, 617(TLS):12DEC75-1496
GWYN, J. THE ENTERPRISING ADMIRAL.
G.E. MINGAY, 617(TLS):9MAY75-505
GYARMATHI, S. AFFINITAS LINGUAE
HUNGARICAE CUM LINGUIS FENNICAE
ORIGINIS GRAMMATICE DEMONSTRATE
NEC NON VOCABULARIA DIALECTORUM
TATARICARUM ET SLAVICARUM CUM HUN-
GARICA COMPARATA.
G.F. MEIER, 682(ZPSK):BAND26HEFT
3/4-421
GYATSO, T. THE BUDDHISM OF TIBET &
THE KEY TO THE MIDDLE WAY.
A. PIATIGORSKY, 617(TLS):30CT75-1159
GYATSO, T. THE OPENING OF THE
WISDOM-EYE.
J.D. WILLIS, 485(PE&W):JAN-APR73-261

GYBBON-MONYPENNY, G.B., ED. "LIBRO
DE BUEN AMOR" STUDIES.*
  D. EISENBERG, 241:JAN73-77
GZOWSKI, P. PETER GZOWSKI'S BOOK
ABOUT THIS COUNTRY IN THE MORNING.
  D. CAMERON, 99:JUN75-46

H.D. HERMETIC DEFINITION.*
  J. GLOVER, 565:VOL14#3-22
  W.G.R., 502(PRS):FALL73-279
  R.J. SMITH, 598(SOR):SPRING75-464
  H. ZINNES, 109:SPRING/SUMMER74-122
H.D. TRIBUTE TO FREUD.
  W. GASS, 453:17APR75-3 [& CONT IN]
    453:15MAY75-9
  J. GLOVER, 565:VOL14#3-22
  C. JACKSON, 148:SPRING73-95
H.D. TRILOGY.*
  H. CARRUTH, 249(HUDR):SUMMER74-308
H.R. "MYTHOMYSTES" 1632.
  D.W. HAWKINS, 568(SCN):WINTER74-74
HAACK, S. DEVIANT LOGIC.
  P.F. STRAWSON, 617(TLS):9MAY75-502
VAN DEN HAAG, E. POLITICAL VIOLENCE
& CIVIL DISOBEDIENCE.
  J.M. LALLEY, 396(MODA):WINTER74-87
VAN DEN HAAG, E. PUNISHING CRIMI-
NALS.
  A. BROYARD, 441:18NOV75-41
HAAGE, B. DER TRAKTAT "VON DREIER-
LEI WESEN DER MENSCHEN."
  W. SCHMITT, 597(SN):VOL45#1-189
HAAKONSEN, D., ED. CONTEMPORARY
APPROACHES TO IBSEN.
  189(EA):JAN-MAR73-120
HAAKONSEN, D. & OTHERS, EDS. IBSEN-
ÅRBOK 1972.
  S.A. AARNES, 172(EDDA):1973/6-382
HAARDER, A. BEOWULF.
  T. SHIPPEY, 617(TLS):29AUG75-974
HAAS, A.M. NIM DIN SELBES WAR.
  J.E. CREAN, JR., 221(GQ):SEP73-144
HAAS, E. IN AMERICA.
  E. HOAGLAND, 441:7DEC75-86
  E. DE MARÉ, 617(TLS):12DEC75-1481
HAAS, G. ESSAY.*
  W. EMMERICH, 221(GQ):JAN73-113
HAAS, J.L. VENDETTA.
  N. CALLENDAR, 441:24AUG75-27
HAAS, M.R. THE PREHISTORY OF LAN-
GUAGES.
  C.V.J. RUSS, 297(JL):FEB73-190
HAAS, V. DER KULT VON NERIK.
  C. CARTER, 318(JAOS):JAN-MAR73-65
HAAS, W., ED. ALPHABETS FOR ENG-
LISH.*
  R.D., 179(ES):APR73-199
  J. MOUNTFORD, 297(JL):FEB73-177
HAAS, W. PHONO-GRAPHIC TRANSLATION.*
  R.D., 179(ES):APR73-199
  J. MOUNTFORD, 297(JL):FEB73-177
HABERLAND, P.M. THE DEVELOPMENT OF
COMIC THEORY IN GERMANY DURING THE
EIGHTEENTH CENTURY.
  C.P. MAGILL, 220(GL&L):OCT73-88
HABERMAS, J. ERKENNTNIS UND INTER-
ESSE.* (2ND ED)
  R. GEUSS, 311(JP):18DEC75-810
HABERMAS, J. KNOWLEDGE & HUMAN
INTERESTS.*
  R. GEUSS, 311(JP):18DEC75-810
                      [CONTINUED]

[CONTINUING]
  R.E. INNIS, 258:DEC73-555
  E. VALLANCE, 479(PHQ):APR73-170
HABERMAS, J. & N. LUHMANN. THEORIE
DER GESELLSCHAFT ODER SOZIALTECH-
NOLOGIE.
  J.N. KAUFMANN, 154:MAR73-184
HABICHT, W., ED. ENGLISH & AMERICAN
STUDIES IN GERMAN.
  H. OPPEL, 430(NS):AUG73-450
HABICHT, W. STUDIEN ZUR DRAMENFORM
VOR SHAKESPEARE.
  H-J. DILLER, 179(ES):APR73-169
HACK, B. & M. KLEISS - SEE BROCH, H.
& D. BRODY
HACKER, M. PRESENTATION PIECE.
  B. HOWARD, 491:APR75-44
  R. LATTIMORE, 249(HUDR):AUTUMN74-
  467
  M.G. PERLOFF, 659:WINTER75-84
  C. RICKS, 441:12JAN75-2
HACKER, P.M.S. INSIGHT & ILLUSION.*
  J.F.M. HUNTER, 258:JUN73-295
  J.E. LLEWELYN, 262:WINTER73-431
HACKETT, F. AMERICAN RAINBOW.
  295:FEB74-369
HACKFORTH, N. "AND THE NEXT OB-
JECT..."
  F. DILLON, 617(TLS):25JUL75-820
HACKING, I. A CONCISE INTRODUCTION
TO LOGIC.
  A. BORGERS, 316:JUN73-341
HACKING, I. THE EMERGENCE OF PROBA-
BILITY.
  L.J. COHEN, 617(TLS):5SEP75-993
HADDAD, C.A. THE MOROCCAN.
  N. CALLENDAR, 441:28DEC75-20
HADDAD, R.M. SYRIAN CHRISTIANS IN
MUSLIM SOCIETY.
  M. MOOSA, 318(JAOS):OCT-DEC73-563
HADFIELD, J., ED. THE SATURDAY
BOOK 34.
  S. SMITH, 441:7DEC75-95
HADINGHAM, E. CIRCLES & STANDING
STONES.
  P. ADAMS, 61:JUL75-83
HADJIOANNOU, K. HĒ ARCHAIA KYPROS
EIS TAS HELLĒNIKAS PĒGAS. (VOL 1)
  H.W. CATLING, 303:VOL93-253
  T.B. MITFORD, 123:NOV74-304
HADLICH, R.L. A TRANSFORMATIONAL
GRAMMAR OF SPANISH.*
  P. BEADE, 350:MAR74-177
HAGER, F-P., ED. ETHIK UND POLITIK
DES ARISTOTELES.
  G.E. NIX, 124:APR-MAY74-395
HAGER, R.E. LÉON BLOY ET L'EVOLU-
TION DU CONTE CRUEL: "SES HISTOIRES
DÉSOBLIGEANTES."
  J. DECOTTIGNIES, 557(RSH):JAN-MAR
  73-161
HAGERTY, F. MAKE YOUR OWN ANTIQUES.
  B. GUTCHEON, 441:7DEC75-74
HAGGARD, W. THE KINSMEN.*
  N. CALLENDAR, 441:16FEB75-16
HAGGARD, W. THE SCORPION'S TAIL.
  N. CALLENDAR, 441:14DEC75-30
HAGIWARA SAKUTARŌ. FACE AT THE BOT-
TOM OF THE WORLD & OTHER POEMS.*
  D.K. SHULTS, 502(PRS):SUMMER73-174

HAGSTRÖM, T., COMP. SVENSK LITTERA-
TURHISTORISK BIBLIOGRAFI INTILL ÅR
1900. (PTS 1-4)
  R.C. ELLSWORTH, 517(PBSA):JAN-MAR
  74-87
HAHL, W. REFLEXION UND ERZÄHLUNG.*
  D. KAFITZ, 680(ZDP):BAND92HEFT4-
  582
HAHN, E. LORENZO.
  M. GREEN, 441:21SEP75-7
  442(NY):29SEP75-131
HAHN, E.A. NAMING-CONSTRUCTIONS IN
SOME INDO-EUROPEAN LANGUAGES.*
  F. BADER, 555:VOL47FASC2-304
  D.J. TAYLOR, 121(CJ):FEB-MAR74-277
HAHN, W.G. THE POLITICS OF SOVIET
AGRICULTURE 1960-1970.
  M. MC CAULEY, 575(SEER):APR74-309
  P.M. RAUP, 550(RUSR):OCT73-436
HAHNLOSER-INGOLD, M. DAS ENGLISCHE
THEATER UND BERT BRECHT.*
  R. HALBRITTER, 38:BAND91HEFT1-138
  K. SPINNER, 179(ES):JUN73-304
HAIDU, P. LION-QUEUE-COUPÉE.
  C.E. PICKFORD, 382(MAE):1974/2-167
  V.R. ROSSMAN, 546(RR):MAR74-120
HAIG, S. MADAME DE LAFAYETTE.*
  W.O. GOODE, 400(MLN):MAY73-852
  L.D. JOINER, 207(FR):FEB73-606
HAIG-BROWN, R. RETURN TO THE RIVER.
A RIVER NEVER SLEEPS.
  H. HENKIN, 441:29JUN75-20
HAIGH, C. REFORMATION & RESISTANCE
IN TUDOR LANCASHIRE.
  J.J. SCARISBRICK, 617(TLS):18APR
  75-420
HAILE, H.G. ARTIST IN CHRYSALIS.
  A. GILLIES, 301(JEGP):OCT74-595
HAILEY, A. THE MONEYCHANGERS.
  P. ANDREWS, 441:18MAY75-40
  C. LEHMANN-HAUPT, 441:28JUL75-25
LORD HAILSHAM. THE DOOR WHEREIN I
WENT.
  K. KYLE, 362:20NOV75-678
  LORD LAMBTON, 617(TLS):10OCT75-
  1170
HAIN, P. RADICAL REGENERATION.
  J. GOULD, 362:16OCT75-519
HAINES, J. THE STONE HARP.*
  S. UTZ, 598(SOR):SPRING75-478
HAINING, P., ED. THE FUTURE MAKERS.
  S. CLARK, 617(TLS):8AUG75-903
HAINING, P. GHOSTS.
  R. HAYNES, 617(TLS):4APR75-354
HAINING, P., ED. THE PENNY DREADFUL.
  P. KEATING, 617(TLS):7FEB75-135
HAINING, P., ED. THE SHERLOCK
HOLMES SCRAPBOOK.*
  G. EWART, 364:APR/MAY74-140
  C. JAMES, 453:20FEB75-15
  C. NICOL, 231:FEB75-112
  M. YOUNG, 441:2FEB75-21
HAINSWORTH, J.B., ED. TITULI DORICI
ED IONICI.
  R. SCHMITT, 343:BAND17HEFT2-207
HAIR, D.S. BROWNING'S EXPERIMENTS
WITH GENRE.*
  T.J. COLLINS, 637(VS):DEC73-234
  B. LITZINGER, 191(ELN):JUN74-312
  K. MC SWEENEY, 529(QQ):WINTER73-
  643
  102(CANL):SUMMER73-126
HAISLIP, J. NOT EVERY YEAR.*
  A.A. JOHNSON, 134(CP):SPRING73-91

HAKKARAINEN, H.J. STUDIEN ZUM CAM-
BRIDGER CODEX T-S.10.K.22.* (VOLS
1&2)
  H. PENZL, 343:BAND16HEFT2-198
HAKUIN. THE ZEN MASTER HAKUIN: SEL-
ECTED WRITINGS. (P.B. YAMPOLSKY,
TRANS)
  H.B. EARHART, 318(JAOS):OCT-DEC73-
  626
HÁLA, B., M. ROMPORTL & P. JANOTA,
EDS. PROCEEDINGS OF THE SIXTH
INTERNATIONAL CONGRESS OF PHONETIC
SCIENCES.
  G.F. MEIER, 682(ZPSK):BAND26HEFT
  3/4-444
HALBAUER, S. RUSSISCH-DEUTSCHES
WÖRTERBUCH FÜR NATURWISSENSCHAFTLER
UND INGENIEURE.
  E.W., 75:3/1973-146
HALBERSTAM, D. HO.
  302:JUL73-269
HALDEMAN, J. THE FOREVER WAR.
  M. LEVIN, 441:23MAR75-33
HALE, D.G. THE BODY POLITIC.
  P.M. KENDALL, 551(RENQ):WINTER73-
  516
  L. ROUX, 189(EA):JAN-MAR73-90
HALE, J. RADIO POWER.
  G. JACKSON, 362:31JUL75-157
HALE, J.R., ED. RENAISSANCE VENICE.
  F. CHIAPPELLI, 275(IQ):FALL-WINTER
  73(VOL17#66)-63
HALE, N. MARY CASSATT.
  P. ADAMS, 61:SEP75-85
  J. RUSSELL, 441:31AUG75-7
HALE, N.A. - SEE SCHATOFF, M.
HALÉVY, D. THE END OF THE NOTABLES.
(A. SILVERA, ED)
  D. JOHNSON, 617(TLS):21FEB75-193
HALEY, J. & L. HOFFMANN. TECHNIQUES
OF FAMILY THERAPY.
  E. FIRST, 453:20FEB75-8
HALEY, K.H.D. THE DUTCH IN THE
SEVENTEENTH CENTURY.*
  J. TROMP, 202(FMOD):JUN73-421
HALFMANN, U. DER AMERIKANISCHE
"NEW CRITICISM."
  A. HELLER, 430(NS):APR73-228
HALFMANN, U. "UNREAL REALISM."*
  G. HOFFMANN, 38:BAND91HEFT2-264
HALIBURTON, G.M. THE PROPHET HARRIS.
  H.W. TURNER, 69:JUL73-278
HALKETT, J.G. MILTON & THE IDEA OF
MATRIMONY.*
  G. BULLOUGH, 175:SPRING72-24
HALKHOREE, P. CALDERÓN DE LA BARCA:
EL ALCALDE DE ZALAMEA.
  M. WILSON, 402(MLR):JUL74-681
HALL, A. THE MANDARIN CYPHER.
  N. CALLENDAR, 441:26OCT75-54
  442(NY):15SEP75-132
  617(TLS):17OCT75-1225
HALL, C.S. & R.E. LIND. DREAMS,
LIFE & LITERATURE.
  S. ABRAMS, 221(GQ):MAR73-267
HALL, D. A BLUE WING TILTS AT THE
EDGE OF THE SEA.
  R. GARFITT, 617(TLS):29AUG75-960
HALL, D.D. THE FAITHFUL SHEPHERD.*
  D.B. RUTMAN, 432(NEQ):JUN73-310
  B.M. STEPHENS, 568(SCN):SPRING-
  SUMMER74-23
HALL, J.B. THE HUNT WITHIN.
  639(VQR):SUMMER74-LXXXIV

153

HALL, J.C. ROUSSEAU.
D.O. THOMAS, 518:JAN74-4
HALL, J.W. & J.P. MASS, EDS. MEDI-
EVAL JAPAN.
C. DUNN, 617(TLS):30MAY75-592
HALL, K.M. & C.N. SMITH - SEE DE LA
TAILLE, J.
HALL, M. THE ARTISTS OF NORTHUMBRIA.
D. THOMAS, 135:NOV73-221
HALL, M.W. BROADCAST JOURNALISM.
R. GARAY, 583:SPRING74-300
HALL, O. THE ADELITA.
M. LEVIN, 441:9NOV75-54
HALL, P. URBAN & REGIONAL PLANNING.
B. ROBSON, 617(TLS):25APR75-461
HALL, R. A HUME BIBLIOGRAPHY.*
R.J.G., 543:MAR73-535
HALL, R. STANLEY.*
E. WEEKS, 61:MAR75-140
HALL, R. THE WELL OF LONELINESS.
A. FREEDMAN, 99:DEC75/JAN76-60
HALL, R.A., JR. ESSENTIALS OF ENG-
LISH PHRASE- & CLAUSE-STRUCTURE IN
DIAGRAMS WITH COMMENTARY.
S. GREENBAUM, 353:1JAN73-122
HALL, R.A., JR. LA STRUTTURA DELL'-
ITALIANO.*
G. LEPSCHY, 545(RPH):FEB74-375
HALL, R.T. THE MORALITY OF CIVIL
DISOBEDIENCE.
S.C., 543:SEP72-160
HALL, S. - SEE ADLEMAN, B.
HALL, T.H. OLD CONJURING BOOKS.
P.H. MUIR, 78(BC):WINTER73-539
P. WALLIS, 354:DEC73-349
A. WILLIAM, 503:SUMMER73-101
HALL WILLIAMS, J.E. CHANGING PRIS-
ONS.
S. MC CONVILLE, 617(TLS):26SEP75-
1105
HALLAHAN, W.H. THE ROSS FORGERY.*
N. CALLENDAR, 441:27APR75-29
HALLANDER, L.G. OLD ENGLISH VERBS
IN -SIAN.
G. BOURQUIN, 189(EA):JUL-SEP73-346
HALLBERG, P. HALLDÓR LAXNESS.
P. SCHACH, 563(SS):SUMMER74-291
DE LA HALLE, A. - SEE UNDER ADAM DE
LA HALLE
HALLE, M. & S.J. KEYSER. ENGLISH
STRESS.
D. INGRAM, 255(HAB):SPRING73-133
HALLETT, G. WITTGENSTEIN'S DEFINI-
TION OF MEANING AS USE.
W.A.F., 543:SEP72-160
HALLETT, R. AFRICA SINCE 1875.
S.J. WALKER, 31(ASCH):WINTER74/75-
157
HALLIBURTON, D. EDGAR ALLAN POE.*
C.L. ANDERSON, 579(SAQ):AUTUMN74-
568
R. ASSELINEAU, 189(EA):OCT-DEC73-
497
HALLIDAY, F. ARABIA WITHOUT SUL-
TANS.
R.M. BURRELL, 617(TLS):7FEB75-132
HALLIDAY, J. A POLITICAL HISTORY OF
JAPANESE CAPITALISM.
E.J. HOBSBAWM, 453:17JUL75-27
HALLIDAY, M.A.K. LEARNING HOW TO
MEAN.
P.H. MATTHEWS, 617(TLS):29AUG75-
975

HALLO, W.W. & W.K. SIMPSON. THE
ANCIENT NEAR EAST.
A.K. GRAYSON & D.B. REDFORD,
318(JAOS):OCT-DEC73-575
HALLPIKE, C.R. THE KONSO OF ETHI-
OPIA.
H. BLACKHURST, 69:JUL73-271
HALLS, G. THE VOICE OF THE CRAB.*
D. DURRANT, 364:FEB/MAR75-134
HALPENNY, F.G. - SEE "DICTIONARY OF
CANADIAN BIOGRAPHY"
HALPERIN, J., ED. JANE AUSTEN.
V.S. PRITCHETT, 453:17JUL75-26
HALPERIN, J. EGOISM & SELF-DISCOV-
ERY IN THE VICTORIAN NOVEL.
M. MASON, 617(TLS):16MAY75-542
HALPERIN-DONGHI, T. POLITICS, ECO-
NOMICS & SOCIETY IN ARGENTINA IN
THE REVOLUTIONARY PERIOD.
D. BRADING, 617(TLS):5SEP75-1000
HALPERN, D. TRAVELING ON CREDIT.*
G. MALANGA, 491:SPRING75-162
M.G. PERLOFF, 659:WINTER75-84
HALPERT, I.D. & E. VON NARDROFF. IN
WORT UND SCHRIFT.*
R.J. RUNDELL, 399(MLJ):JAN-FEB74-
69
HALSBAND, R. LORD HERVEY.*
H.M. JONES, 385(MQR):SPRING75-236
G. NIEDHART, 182:VOL26#17/18-625
C.A. PAGLIA, 566:SPRING74-89
639(VQR):SUMMER74-XCII
HALSBAND, R. - SEE MONTAGU, M.W.
HALSEY, M.T. ANTONIO BUERO VALLEJO.
R.L. NICHOLAS, 399(MLJ):APR74-215
HAM, R., ED. THEATRE PLANNING.
J. MIELZINER, 397(MD):DEC73-393
HAMBLIN, C.L. FALLACIES.
G. ENGLEBRETSEN, 154:MAR73-151
J-G. ROSSI, 53(AGP):BAND55HEFT1-91
HAMBLOCH, H. ALLGEMEINE ANTHROPO-
GEOGRAPHIE.
E. WINKLER, 182:VOL26#11/12-445
HAMBURGER, J. LA PUISSANCE ET LA
FRAGILITÉ.
J-C. POLACK, 98:JUL73-659
HAMBURGER, M., ED. EAST GERMAN
POETRY.*
T. EAGLETON, 565:VOL14#3-66
B. FALKENBERG, 473(PR):4/1974-630
R. SIEBURTH, 565:VOL14#4-32
HAMBURGER, M. OWNERLESS EARTH.*
T. EAGLETON, 565:VOL14#3-74
HAMBURGER, M. TRAVELLING I-V.
T. EAGLETON, 565:VOL14#3-66
HAMBURGER, M. - SEE BÜCHNER, G.
HAMBY, A.L. BEYOND THE NEW DEAL.*
D. CAUTE, 617(TLS):13JUN75-657
HAMILTON, A. ALEXANDER HAMILTON: A
BIOGRAPHY IN HIS OWN WORDS. (M-J.
KLINE, ED)
639(VQR):SPRING74-XL
HAMILTON, A. THE PAPERS OF ALEXAN-
DER HAMILTON. (VOLS 14&15) (H.C.
SYRETT, ED)
F. MC DONALD, 656(WMQ):OCT74-678
HAMILTON, A. THE PAPERS OF ALEXAN-
DER HAMILTON.* (VOLS 16&17) (H.C.
SYRETT, ED)
W.E.A. BERNHARD, 579(SAQ):SUMMER
74-404
F. MC DONALD, 656(WMQ):OCT74-678

HAMILTON, A. THE PAPERS OF ALEXAN-
DER HAMILTON. (VOLS 18&19) (H.C.
SYRETT, ED)
  F. MC DONALD, 656(WMQ):OCT74-678
  639(VQR):SPRING74-XLV
HAMILTON, C.D. PABLO NERUDA.
  R. PRING-MILL, 617(TLS):19SEP75-
  1068
HAMILTON, D. THE DIARY OF SIR DAVID
HAMILTON 1709-1714. (P. ROBERTS,
ED)
  C. PROBYN, 617(TLS):24OCT75-1253
HAMILTON, I. A POETRY CHRONICLE.*
  J. GLOVER, 565:VOL14#4-62
  H. SERGEANT, 175:AUTUMN73-121
HAMILTON, K.G. JOHN DRYDEN & THE
POETRY OF STATEMENT.
  C. LINDQUIST, 599:SPRING73-223
HAMILTON, V. M.C. HIGGINS, THE
GREAT.
  F. GIBB, 617(TLS):23MAY75-577
HAMILTON, W. MY QUEEN AND I.
  A. FORBES, 617(TLS):31JAN75-108
  J.P. MACKINTOSH, 362:30JAN75-155
HAMILTON-PATERSON, J. OPTION THREE.
  D. ABSE, 617(TLS):28FEB75-214
HAMLYN, D.W. THE THEORY OF KNOW-
LEDGE.
  M.A. STEWART, 483:JUL73-298
HAMMACHER, A.M. MAGRITTE.*
  E. COWLING, 617(TLS):7NOV75-1323
HAMMARSTRÖM, G. LINGUISTISCHE EIN-
HEITEN IM RAHMEN DER MODERNEN
SPRACHWISSENSCHAFT.
  D. KASTOVSKY, 38:BAND91HEFT3-366
HAMMER, F. THEONOME ANTHROPOLOGIE?
  J.H. NOTA, 484(PPR):DEC73-298
HAMMER, R. PLAYBOY'S ILLUSTRATED
HISTORY OF CRIME.
  T. PLATE, 441:23MAR75-4
HAMMERICH, L.L. & OTHERS - SEE "TÖN-
NIES FENNE'S LOW GERMAN MANUAL OF
SPOKEN RUSSIAN, PSKOV 1607"
HAMMETT, D. THE CONTINENTAL OP.*
(S. MARCUS, ED)
  P. ADAMS, 61:FEB75-122
  P. FRENCH, 617(TLS):10OCT75-1174
  R. SALE, 453:6FEB75-20
HAMMOND, D. & A. JABLOW. THE AFRICA
THAT NEVER WAS.*
  N. LEDERER, 577(SHR):SPRING73-228
HAMMOND, G.P., ED. A GUIDE TO THE
MANUSCRIPT COLLECTIONS OF THE BAN-
CROFT LIBRARY. (VOL 2)
  H.P. BEERS, 14:JUL73-410
  D.M. SZEWCZYK, 517(PBSA):JUL-SEP
  74-342
HAMMOND, N., ED. MESOAMERICAN ARCH-
AEOLOGY.
  G.H.S. BUSHNELL, 617(TLS):12SEP75-
  1016
HAMPE, R. SPERLONGA UND VERGIL.
  A.G. MC KAY, 487:SUMMER73-206
HAMPSHIRE, A.C. ON HAZARDOUS SER-
VICE.
  617(TLS):21FEB75-204
HAMPSHIRE, A.C. THE ROYAL NAVY
SINCE 1945.
  617(TLS):26DEC75-1547
HAMPSHIRE, S. FREEDOM OF MIND &
OTHER ESSAYS.*
  483:JAN73-100
HAMPSON, N. THE FRENCH REVOLUTION.
  G. LEWIS, 617(TLS):3OCT75-1133

HAMPSON, N. THE LIFE & OPINIONS OF
MAXIMILIEN ROBESPIERRE.
  D. JOHNSON, 617(TLS):7FEB75-127
HAMSHERE, C. THE BRITISH IN THE
CARIBBEAN.
  J.J. TE PASKE, 656(WMQ):APR74-334
HAMSUN, K. THE WANDERER.
  H. KELLER, 617(TLS):5DEC75-1439
  J.D. O'HARA, 441:27JUL75-6
HAN, P. - SEE DE LA TAILLE, J.
HAN, W. - SEE UNDER WU HAN
HANCOCK, R.N. TWENTIETH CENTURY
ETHICS.
  617(TLS):12DEC75-1482
HANCOCK, W.K. DISCOVERING MONARO.
  M. AUROUSSEAU, 381:SEP73-335
HANCOCKS, M. SEDAN CHAIRS & SPAT-
TERDASHES.
  P. BEER, 617(TLS):17JAN75-48
HAND, W.D., ED. AMERICAN FOLK LEG-
END.*
  D.M. HINES, 650(WF):OCT73-290
HANDKE, P. THE GOALIE'S ANXIETY AT
THE PENALTY KICK. SHORT LETTER,
LONG FAREWELL.* THE INNERWORLD OF
THE OUTERWORLD OF THE INNERWORLD.
  F. KERMODE, 453:1MAY75-20
HANDKE, P. A SORROW BEYOND DREAMS.
  F. KERMODE, 453:1MAY75-20
  M. WOOD, 441:27APR75-1
  442(NY):12MAY75-142
HANDKE, P. DIE STUNDE DER WAHREN
EMPFINDUNG.
  J. WHITE, 617(TLS):10OCT75-1208
HANDL, J. THE MORALIA OF 1596.
(A.B. SKEI, ED)
  M. LEFKOWITZ, 551(RENQ):SUMMER73-
  202
HANDLER, J.S. A GUIDE TO SOURCE
MATERIALS FOR THE STUDY OF BAR-
BADOS HISTORY 1627-1834.
  E.A. CARSON, 325:OCT73-679
HANDLER, J.S. THE UNAPPROPRIATED
PEOPLE.
  639(VQR):AUTUMN74-CXLII
HANDY, W.C. BLUES. (REV BY J.
SILVERMAN)
  M. PETERSON, 470:JAN74-34
HANDY, W.J. MODERN FICTION.
  295:FEB74-490
HANF, B. & J. FULLER. A BESTIARY.
  A. MACLEAN, 617(TLS):23MAY75-552
HANFMANN, G.M.A. LETTERS FROM SAR-
DIS.
  E. BIELEFELD, 182:VOL26#13/14-500
HANGIN, J.G. A CONCISE ENGLISH-
MONGOLIAN DICTIONARY.
  P. AALTO, 353:15MAR73-121
HANHAM, A. RICHARD III & HIS EARLY
HISTORIANS 1483-1535.
  G.R. ELTON, 617(TLS):10OCT75-1179
HANI, J. - SEE PLUTARCH
HANKE, J.W. MARITAIN'S ONTOLOGY OF
THE WORK OF ART.
  F.J. KOVACH, 290(JAAC):SPRING74-
  425
HANKE, L. ALL MANKIND IS ONE.
  J.H. ELLIOTT, 453:15MAY75-3
  A. PAGDEN, 617(TLS):5SEP75-1000
HANKINS, J.E. SOURCE & MEANING IN
SPENSER'S ALLEGORY.*
  R.A. FOAKES, 175:SUMMER72-67
  R.O. IREDALE, 541(RES):FEB73-63
                          [CONTINUED]

155

HANKINS, J.E. SOURCE & MEANING IN
SPENSER'S ALLEGORY.* [CONTINUING]
  J.B. LUDWIG, 141:WINTER73-86
  J. REES, 677:VOL4-258
HANKS, L.M. RICE & MAN.
  P. WHEATLEY, 293(JAST):FEB73-368
HANLEY, J. A WOMAN IN THE SKY.*
  J. YARDLEY, 569(SR):SUMMER74-537
HANLEY, T.O. THE AMERICAN REVOLU-
TION & RELIGION.*
  W.S. ROBINSON, 481(PQ):JUL73-351
HANNAH, B. STRIVING TOWARDS WHOLE-
NESS.
  G. THOMAS, 175:AUTUMN73-118
HANNAH, D. "ISAK DINESEN" & KAREN
BLIXEN.
  G. CUBBIN, 402(MLR):JUL74-711
  E.O. JOHANNESSON, 301(JEGP):JAN74-
  107
HANNAH, W.H. BOBS.
  B.D. GOOCH, 637(VS):DEC73-217
HANNAS, L. THE ENGLISH JIGSAW PUZ-
ZLE 1760-1890.
  P.H. MUIR, 78(BC):AUTUMN73-393
HANNAY, A. MENTAL IMAGES.*
  V.C. ALDRICH, 484(PPR):SEP73-128
  V. HOPE, 479(PHQ):JUL73-268
  G.B. MATTHEWS, 482(PHR):APR74-252
  J.D. RABB, 154:MAR73-164
HANSEN, E.V. THE ATTALIDS OF PER-
GAMON. (2ND ED)
  P. GAUTHIER, 555:VOL47FASC2-336
HANSEN, J. TROUBLE MAKER.
  N. CALLENDAR, 441:28DEC75-21
  M. LASKI, 362:5JUN75-748
  617(TLS):11 JUL75-784
HANSEN, T.L., E.J. WILKINS & J.G.
  ENOS. LE FRANÇAIS VIF: LEVEL 1.
  N.A. POULIN, 207(FR):MAY73-1266
HANSEN, W.F. THE CONFERENCE SE-
QUENCE.*
  F.M. COMBELLACK, 122:OCT74-300
  J.B. HAINSWORTH, 123:NOV74-286
  W. MC LEOD, 487:SPRING73-92
  P. VIVANTE, 124:MAR73-358
HANSON, A.T. GRACE & TRUTH.
  F.R. BARRY, 617(TLS):3OCT75-1159
HANSON, K.O. THE UNCORRECTED
WORLD.*
  G. BURNS, 584(SWR):WINTER74-103
  J.N. MORRIS, 249(HUDR):SPRING74-
  112
HANSON, N.R. WHAT I DO NOT BELIEVE
& OTHER ESSAYS. (S. TOULMIN & H.
WOOLF, EDS)
  M.B., 543:MAR73-536
HANSTEIN, H. STUDIEN ZUR ENTWICK-
LUNG VON IONESCOS THEATER.
  H. PLOCHER, 224(GRM):BAND23HEFT4-
  503
  C.A. PRENDERGAST, 208(FS):JUL74-
  353
HAPP, H. HYLE.*
  Z.P. AMBROSE, 124:MAR73-358
  P.M. HUBY, 123:MAR74-44
MUSHIR-UL-HAQ. ISLAM IN SECULAR
INDIA.
  B. TYABJI, 273(IC):JUL73-275
HARAMATI, S. CHAPTERS IN THE TEACH-
ING OF THE HEBREW LANGUAGE.
  J. KABAKOFF, 399(MLJ):DEC74-431
HARAMATI, S. WAYS OF TEACHING HEB-
REW TO ADULTS. [IN HEBREW]
  J.A. REIF, 399(MLJ):APR74-213

HARARI, J.V. STRUCTURALISTS &
STRUCTURALISMS.
  A. ABEL, 399(MLJ):JAN-FEB74-65
  J. CULLER, 208(FS):JUL74-357
HARBAGE, A. SHAKESPEARE WITHOUT
WORDS, & OTHER ESSAYS.*
  J. BRITTON, 613:SUMMER73-306
  R.A. FOAKES, 175:SUMMER73-72
  C. HOY, 569(SR):SPRING74-363
HARBAUGH, W.H. LAWYER'S LAWYER.*
  J.W. HOWARD, JR., 639(VQR):SPRING
  74-299
  R.M. IRELAND, 432(NEQ):SEP74-475
HARCOURT, F. - SEE MADAME DE LA TOUR
DU PIN
HARCOURT, P. A FAIR EXCHANGE.
  617(TLS):11 JUL75-784
HARDER, R. & OTHERS. PLOTINS SCHRIF-
TEN. (VOL 6)
  A.H. ARMSTRONG, 123:MAR74-133
HARDIE, C. THE GEORGICS.
  A.G. MC KAY, 124:FEB74-225
HARDIE, M. WATERCOLOUR PAINTING IN
BRITAIN. (VOLS 1-3) (D. SNELGROVE,
J. MAYNE & B. TAYLOR, EDS)
  A. STALEY, 54:MAR73-154
HARDIN, C.M. PRESIDENTIAL POWER &
ACCOUNTABILITY.
  639(VQR):AUTUMN74-CL
HARDIN, G. EXPLORING NEW ETHICS
FOR SURVIVAL.
  H.G. CLASSEN, 529(QQ):SPRING73-125
HARDING, G. THEY KILLED SITTING
BULL.
  R. GARFITT, 364:JUN/JUL74-111
HARDING, J. GOUNOD.
  L. DAVIES, 410(M&L):JAN74-106
HARDING, J. LOST ILLUSIONS.
  R. HEPPENSTALL, 617(TLS):24JAN75-
  80
HARDING, J. ERIK SATIE.
  W. MELLERS, 617(TLS):7NOV75-1334
HARDING, L.V. THE DRAMATIC ART OF
FERDINAND RAIMUND & JOHANN NESTROY.
  K. SEGAR, 617(TLS):30CT75-1148
HARDING, R.E.M. THE PIANO-FORTE.
  F. DAWES, 415:AUG74-659
HARDINGE, G., ED. WINTER'S CRIMES 7.
  T.J. BINYON, 617(TLS):19DEC75-1508
HARDISON, O.B., JR., ED. THE QUEST
FOR THE IMAGINATION.*
  S.R. SUTHERLAND, 89(BJA):WINTER73-
  85
HARDISON, O.B., JR. TOWARD FREEDOM
& DIGNITY.*
  R. BUFFINGTON, 569(SR):WINTER74-
  147
HARDOUIN, P.J. LE GRAND ORGUE DE
NOTRE-DAME DE PARIS.
  P. WILLIAMS, 415:NOV74-950
HARDWICK, C.D. FAITH & OBJECTIVITY.
  E.T.L., 543:JUN73-755
HARDWICK, C.S. LANGUAGE LEARNING IN
WITTGENSTEIN'S LATER PHILOSOPHY.
  R. BLANCHÉ, 542:JUL-SEP73-358
  G. NUCHELMANS, 361:OCT73-275
HARDWICK, E. SEDUCTION & BETRAYAL.*
  S. RUDIKOFF, 249(HUDR):WINTER
  74/75-615
HARDWICK, M. A LITERARY ATLAS &
GAZETTEER OF THE BRITISH ISLES.
  J. COTTON, 503:AUTUMN73-142

HARDWICK, M. & M. THE CHARLES
DICKENS ENCYCLOPEDIA.
L.C.S., 155:SEP73-186
HARDY, A. THE BIOLOGY OF GOD.
J. NAUGHTON, 362:24JUL75-125
T.S. TORRANCE, 617(TLS):29AUG75-
976
HARDY, B. THE ART OF DICKENS.
P. GOETSCH, 430(NS):FEB73-117
HARDY, B. THE EXPOSURE OF LUXURY.*
R.A. COLBY, 445(NCF):DEC73-356
L.P., 502(PRS):SUMMER73-186
T. ROGERS, 175:SPRING73-33
S.M. SMITH, 89(BJA):WINTER73-93
J.I.M. STEWART, 155:MAY73-128
M.G. SUNDELL, 594:FALL73-402
HARDY, B. THE MORAL ART OF DICKENS.*
L. LANE, JR., 594:SPRING73-125
HARDY, F. BUT THE DEAD ARE MANY.
E. KORN, 617(TLS):1AUG75-865
HARDY, J.E. KATHERINE ANNE PORTER.*
R.S. MOORE, 27(AL):NOV74-411
HARDY, J.P. REINTERPRETATIONS.*
G. BULLOUGH, 175:SPRING72-24
HARDY, P. THE MUSLIMS OF BRITISH
INDIA.
A. AHMAD, 318(JAOS):OCT-DEC73-564
HARDY, T. ONE RARE FAIR WOMAN.*
(E. HARDY & F.B. PINION, EDS)
D. KRAMER, 301(JEGP):JAN74-138
B. LUPINI, 175:SUMMER73-68
R.C. SCHWEIK, 177(ELT):VOL16#2-135
HARDY, T. UNDER THE GREENWOOD TREE.
FAR FROM THE MADDING CROWD. THE
RETURN OF THE NATIVE. THE TRUMPET-
MAJOR. THE MAYOR OF CASTERBRIDGE.
THE WOODLANDERS. TESS OF THE
D'URBERVILLES. JUDE THE OBSCURE.
F. KERMODE, 362:2JAN75-28
HARE, R.M. APPLICATIONS OF MORAL
PHILOSOPHY.*
J. DONNELLY, 258:DEC73-595
P. DUBOIS, 542:OCT-DEC73-488
M.H.R., 543:JUN73-756
R. SCRUTON, 483:OCT73-395
HARE, R.M. ESSAYS ON THE MORAL CON-
CEPTS.
J. DONNELLY, 258:DEC73-595
P. DUBOIS, 542:OCT-DEC73-488
W.G., 543:MAR73-536
R. SCRUTON, 483:OCT73-395
HARE, R.M. ESSAYS ON THE PHILOSO-
PHICAL METHOD.*
R. SCRUTON, 483:OCT73-395
HARE, R.M. PRACTICAL INFERENCES.
R. BLANCHÉ, 542:JUL-SEP73-359
H. KHATCHADOURIAN, 484(PPR):JUN74-
605
R. SCRUTON, 483:OCT73-395
"HARE HUNTING."
617(TLS):30MAY75-608
HARGRAVE, L. CLARA REEVE.
R.R. LINGEMAN, 441:23JUL75-35
L. STONE, 441:27JUL75-7
HARGREAVES, J.D. WEST AFRICA PAR-
TITIONED. (VOL 1)
A.E. ATMORE, 617(TLS):17OCT75-1241
HARGREAVES, R. SUPERPOWER.*
H. LOMAS, 364:AUG/SEP74-130
HARGREAVES-MAWDSLEY, W.N. OXFORD
IN THE AGE OF JOHN LOCKE.
M.A. STEWART, 566:AUTUMN73-39

HARICH, W. JEAN PAULS REVOLUTIONS-
DICHTUNG.
P. LABANYI, 617(TLS):8AUG75-905
HARICH-SCHNEIDER, E. A HISTORY OF
JAPANESE MUSIC.*
L. DURÁN, 410(M&L):JAN74-93
W.P. MALM, 414(MQ):OCT73-645
HARINGTON, D. THE ARCHITECTURE OF
THE ARKANSAS OZARKS.
D. WAKEFIELD, 441:2NOV75-53
HARJAN, G. JAN PARANDOWSKI.
F.J. CORLISS, JR., 399(MLJ):JAN-
FEB73-65
HARL, M., WITH G. DORIVAL. LA
CHAÎNE PALESTINIENNE SUR LE PSAUME
118.
É. DES PLACES, 555:VOL47FASC2-344
HARLAN, L.R. & OTHERS - SEE WASHING-
TON, B.T.
HARLE, J.C. GUPTA SCULPTURE.
D. BARRETT, 617(TLS):25APR75-460
HARLFINGER, D. DIE TEXTGESCHICHTE
DER PSEUDO-ARISTOTELISCHEN SCHRIFT
PERI ATOMŌN GRAMMŌN.*
F. LASSERRE, 182:VOL26#3/4-121
HARLOW, C.G. & J. REDMOND, EDS. THE
YEAR'S WORK IN ENGLISH STUDIES.*
(VOL 48)
R. HABENICHT, 570(SQ):SPRING73-237
HARLOW, R. SCANN.*
A. THOMAS, 102(CANL):SPRING73-114
HARMAN, R.A. - SEE MORLEY, T.
HARMER, J.B. VICTORY IN LIMBO.
W. PRITCHARD, 617(TLS):17OCT75-
1226
HARMER, R.M. AMERICAN MEDICAL
AVARICE.
H.J. GEIGER, 441:14DEC75-7
HARMON, M., ED. J.M. SYNGE.
J.R. MULRYNE, 677:VOL4-337
H. PYLE, 541(RES):AUG73-368
HARMON, S. A GIRL LIKE ME.
M. LEVIN, 441:27JUL75-11
HARMON, W. LEGION: CIVIC CHORUSES.*
P. RAMSEY, 569(SR):SPRING74-402
HARMONIUS. IOANNIS HARMONII MARSI:
"COMOEDIA STEPHANIUM." (W. LUDWIG,
ED & TRANS)
F. LASSERRE, 182:VOL26#3/4-123
I.D. MC FARLANE, 402(MLR):APR74-
398
P. PASCAL, 551(RENQ):WINTER73-500
P.G. WALSH, 123:MAR74-144
HARMS, W. HOMO VIATOR IN BIVIO.
R. HOFMEISTER, 221(GQ):NOV73-620
HARO, R.P. LATIN AMERICANA RESEARCH
IN THE UNITED STATES & CANADA.
E.J. MULLEN, 399(MLJ):NOV73-373
HARPAZ, É. - SEE CONSTANT, B.
HARPER, D. THE PATCHWORK MAN.
N. CALLENDAR, 441:7SEP75-39
HARPER, G.M. THE MINGLING OF HEAVEN
& EARTH.
F.S.L. LYONS, 617(TLS):10OCT75-
1187
HARPER, G.M. YEATS'S GOLDEN DAWN.
"GO BACK TO WHERE YOU BELONG."
G. HOUGH, 617(TLS):14FEB75-160
HARPER, H.M., JR. & C. EDGE, EDS.
THE CLASSIC BRITISH NOVEL.*
A. WRIGHT, 454:FALL73-86
295:FEB74-471

HARPER, M.S. DEBRIDEMENT.*
  L. LIEBERMAN, 676(YR):AUTUMN73-113
HARPER, M.S. SONG: I WANT A WIT-
NESS.
  M. PERLBERG, 491:JUN75-172
HARPER, R. THE EXISTENTIAL EXPERI-
ENCE.
  E.T.L., 543:JUN73-757
HARRAUER, H. A BIBLIOGRAPHY TO THE
CORPUS TIBULLIANUM.*
  R.J. BALL, 124:OCT72-105
  E.J. KENNEY, 123:MAR74-138
  E.N. O'NEIL, 122:OCT73-313
HARRÉ, R. THE PRINCIPLES OF SCIEN-
TIFIC THINKING.* THE PHILOSOPHIES
OF SCIENCE.
  E.H. MADDEN, 543:JUN73-723
HARRÉ, R. - SEE WAISMANN, F.
HARRÉ, R. & P.F. SECORD. THE EX-
PLANATION OF SOCIAL BEHAVIOUR.*
  A. RYAN, 479(PHQ):OCT73-374
HARRELL, J.G. & A. WIERZBIANSKA,
EDS. AESTHETICS IN TWENTIETH-CEN-
TURY POLAND.
  M. RIESER, 319:OCT75-546
HARRIMAN, W.A. & E. ABEL. SPECIAL
ENVOY TO CHURCHILL & STALIN, 1941-
1946.
  R. EDER, 441:29NOV75-25
  D. YERGIN, 441:23NOV75-5
  442(NY):8DEC75-197
HARRINGTON-MÜLLER, D. DER FORT-
SCHRITTSKLUB IM ABGEORDNETENHAUS
DES ÖSTERREICHISCHEN REICHSRATS
1873-1910.
  P. PULZER, 575(SEER):APR74-295
HARRIOTT, R. POETRY & CRITICISM
BEFORE PLATO.
  J.M. LUCCIONI, 189(EA):APR-JUN73-
  241
HARRIS, A. & A. SÉDOUY. VOYAGE
À L'INTÉRIEUR DU PARTI COMMUNISTE.
  D. JOHNSON, 617(TLS):22AUG75-942
HARRIS, B.F., ED. AUCKLAND CLASSI-
CAL ESSAYS PRESENTED TO E.M. BLAIK-
LOCK.
  S.I. OOST, 122:JUL73-233
  S.F. WILTSHIRE, 124:FEB73-313
HARRIS, C. REINHARD LETTAU & THE
USE OF THE GROTESQUE.
  P. PROCHNIK, 220(GL&L):JUL74-333
HARRIS, D. - SEE CERNUDA, L.
HARRIS, F. THE SHORT STORIES OF
FRANK HARRIS. (E. GERTZ, ED)
  C. DAVIDSON, 617(TLS):31OCT75-1301
HARRIS, H., ED. JOHN CREASEY'S
MYSTERY BEDSIDE BOOK 1976.
  T.J. BINYON, 617(TLS):26DEC75-1544
HARRIS, H.A. SPORT IN GREECE &
ROME.
  B. BALDWIN, 487:AUTUMN73-313
  P. MAC KENDRICK, 24:WINTER74-413
  J.E. REXINE, 124:DEC73-JAN74-183
HARRIS, H.S. HEGEL'S DEVELOPMENT.
  Q. LAUER, 258:DEC73-581
  M.J. PERRY, 479(PHQ):APR73-163
HARRIS, J. SIR WILLIAM CHAMBERS,
KNIGHT OF THE POLAR STAR.
  D. IRWIN, 90:MAR73-189
  D. STILLMAN, 54:MAR73-152
HARRIS, J. HERMÈS OU RECHERCHES
PHILOSOPHIQUES SUR LA GRAMMAIRE
                    [CONTINUED]

[CONTINUING]
UNIVERSELLE. (A. JOLY, ED)
  J. LAVÉDRINE, 189(EA):APR-JUN73-
  218
HARRIS, J. UNEMPLOYMENT & POLITICS.
  M. ROSE, 637(VS):MAR74-319
HARRIS, J. & A. LÉVÊQUE. INTERMEDI-
ATE CONVERSATIONAL FRENCH. (3RD ED)
  B.M. POHORYLES, 207(FR):FEB73-689
HARRIS, J.W. SPANISH PHONOLOGY.
  J.R. CRADDOCK, 353:1AUG73-83
HARRIS, L. UPTON SINCLAIR.
  A. KOPKIND, 441:2NOV75-4
HARRIS, M. HATTER FOX.
  S. MAITLAND, 362:13FEB75-222
HARRIS, P. ADLAI: THE SPRINGFIELD
YEARS.
  M. HARRIS, 441:31AUG75-4
HARRIS, R. THE DOUBLE SNARE.
  617(TLS):17JAN75-49
HARRIS, R. SYNONYMY & LINGUISTIC
ANALYSIS.
  S.J. NOREN, 484(PPR):DEC73-288
HARRIS, S.H. - SEE "PAUL CUFFE"
HARRIS, T. BLACK SUNDAY.
  N. CALLENDAR, 441:2FEB75-14
  C. LEHMANN-HAUPT, 441:9JAN75-39
HARRIS, W. COMPANIONS OF THE DAY &
NIGHT.
  L. JAMES, 617(TLS):10OCT75-1217
HARRIS, W.V. ROME IN ETRURIA &
UMBRIA.
  R.G. LEWIS, 313:VOL63-247
  R.E.A. PALMER, 124:DEC73-JAN74-182
  E.T. SALMON, 24:SUMMER74-191
  F.W. WALBANK, 123:MAR74-92
HARRIS, Z.S. PAPERS IN STRUCTURAL
& TRANSFORMATIONAL LINGUISTICS.*
  G.C. LEPSCHY, 353:15JUN73-126
HARRISON, A.R.W. THE LAW OF ATHENS:
PROCEDURE.
  P.J. RHODES, 123:MAR74-86
HARRISON, B. FORM & CONTENT.*
  H.A. LEWIS, 518:MAY74-7
HARRISON, C. THE TOPLESS TULIP
CAPER.
  N. CALLENDAR, 441:27JUL75-17
HARRISON, C.Y. GENERALS DIE IN BED.
  J.L. GRANATSTEIN, 99:APR/MAY75-35
HARRISON, F., ED. TIME, PLACE &
MUSIC.
  L. DURÁN, 410(M&L):OCT74-487
  T.L. DWORSKY, 187:MAY75-308
HARRISON, F.R. DEDUCTIVE LOGIC &
DESCRIPTIVE LANGUAGE.
  T.G.N., 543:MAR73-537
HARRISON, H. STAR SMASHERS OF THE
GALAXY RANGERS.
  J. HAMILTON-PATERSON, 617(TLS):
  7MAR75-260
HARRISON, J. OUR KNOWLEDGE OF
RIGHT & WRONG.
  R.F. ATKINSON, 393(MIND):JUL73-468
  S.W. BLACKBURN, 483:JUL73-296
  D. GAUTHIER, 154:JUN73-344
HARRISON, J. & P. LASLETT. THE LIB-
RARY OF JOHN LOCKE.
  D. BERMAN, 447(N&Q):OCT73-397
HARRISON, J.A., ED. CHINA: ENDURING
SCHOLARSHIP.
  S. UHALLEY, JR., 485(PE&W):JUL73-
  401
HARRISON, J.A. THE CHINESE EMPIRE.
  E-T.Z. SUN, 293(JAST):NOV72-129

HARRISON, J.A. THE FOUNDING OF THE
RUSSIAN EMPIRE IN ASIA & AMERICA.*
C.S. GOODRICH, 318(JAOS):JUL-SEP
73-416
HARRISON, J.P. THE LONG MARCH TO
POWER.
J. CH'EN, 293(JAST):AUG73-693
HARRISON, M. THE LONDON OF SHERLOCK
HOLMES. IN THE FOOTSTEPS OF SHER-
LOCK HOLMES.
C. JAMES, 453:20FEB75-15
HARRISON, M. THE LONDON THAT WAS
ROME.
P. SALWAY, 123:MAR74-155
HARRISON, M. & B. WATERS. BURNE-
JONES.
C. NEVE, 592:NOV73-210
HARRISON, R. ON WHAT THERE MUST BE.
P. HACKER, 617(TLS):14FEB75-176
HARRISON, R. REX.*
A. BROYARD, 441:22JAN75-43
HARRISON, R. ROSE.
A. BROYARD, 441:17OCT75-39
A. FORBES, 617(TLS):26SEP75-1084
C. SEEBOHM, 441:12OCT75-7
HARRISON, R. - SEE "THE SONG OF
ROLAND"
HARRISON, S. POOR MEN'S GUARDIANS.
W. HALEY, 617(TLS):3JAN75-17
HARRISON, S. THE YOUNG PERSON'S
GUIDE TO PLAYING THE PIANO. (2ND
ED)
F. DAWES, 415:FEB74-135
HARRISS, J. THE TALLEST TOWER.
P. ADAMS, 61:MAY75-104
P. GOLDBERGER, 441:24MAY75-21
HARRISSON, T. & B. THE PREHISTORY
OF SABAH.
M. BROOKE, 60:NOV-DEC74-74
W.G. SOLHEIM 2D, 293(JAST):AUG73-
746
W.G. SOLHEIM 2D, 302:JAN73-181
HARSDÖRFFER, G.P. FRAUENZIMMER GE-
SPRÄCHSPIELE. (PTS 5&6) (I. BÖTT-
CHER, ED)
G. WEYDT, 222(GR):JAN73-67
HART, C., COMP. A CONCORDANCE TO
"FINNEGANS WAKE." (REV)
J. VAN VOORHIS, 329(JJQ):SPRING75-
340
HART, C. JAMES JOYCE'S "ULYSSES."
P. SWINDEN, 148:SPRING72-91
HART, C. & D. HAYMAN, EDS. JAMES
JOYCE'S "ULYSSES."
G. ECKLEY, 659:AUTUMN75-504
R. ELLMANN, 617(TLS):30CT75-1118
R.M. KAIN, 329(JJQ):SPRING75-323
HART, E.L. - SEE NICHOLS, J.
HART, H.L.A. PUNISHMENT & RESPONSI-
BILITY.*
I. THALBERG, 321:SPRING73-65
HART, J.E. FLOYD DELL.
295:FEB74-575
HART, P., ED. THOMAS MERTON, MONK.
P. HEBBLETHWAITE, 617(TLS):26SEP
75-1107
HART, P. ORPHEUS IN THE NEW WORLD.
M. PETERSON, 470:MAY74-33
HART, R. ENGLISH LIFE IN THE NINE-
TEENTH CENTURY.
R.C. TOBIAS, 637(VS):DEC73-210
HART, T.R. - SEE VICENTE, G.
HART-DAVIS, D. PETER FLEMING.*
B. GUTTERIDGE, 364:FEB/MAR75-127

HARTFORD, H. YOU ARE WHAT YOU WRITE.
D. THOMAS, 362:24JUL75-124
HARTH, D. PHILOLOGIE UND PRAKTISCHE
PHILOSOPHIE.*
W. SCHWARZ, 220(GL&L):APR74-255
HARTH, E. CYRANO DE BERGERAC & THE
POLEMICS OF MODERNITY.*
A.M. BEICHMAN, 546(RR):MAR74-128
HARTLEY, L.P. THE GO-BETWEEN.
M.A. MOAN, 145(CRIT):VOL15#2-27
HARTLEY, L.P. THE HARNESS ROOM.
J.C. FIELD, 556(RLV):1973/1-90
HARTMAN, G.H. BEYOND FORMALISM.*
B. PEDERSEN, 52:BAND8HEFT1-116
J.N. RIDDEL, 131(CL):SPRING73-178
P. TOMLINSON, 184(EIC):APR72-206
HARTMAN, G.H. THE FATE OF READING.
D. DONOGHUE, 617(TLS):22AUG75-934
R. POIRIER, 441:20APR75-21
HARTMAN, G.H., ED. NEW PERSPECTIVES
ON COLERIDGE & WORDSWORTH.*
G. THOMAS, 175:AUTUMN73-118
HARTMAN, S.S. & C-M. EDSMAN, EDS.
MYSTICISM.
E. STEINKELLNER, 318(JAOS):JUL-SEP
73-383
HARTMANN VON AUE. DAS KLAGEBÜCHLEIN
HARTMANNS VON AUE UND DAS ZWEITE
BÜCHLEIN. (L. WOLFF, ED)
B. NAUMANN, 220(GL&L):APR74-257
HARTMANN, K. DIE MARXSCHE THEORIE.
H.B. ACTON, 53(AGP):BAND55HEFT3-
343
A.W. WOOD, 543:SEP72-118
HARTMANN, P. & H. VERNAY, EDS.
SPRACHWISSENSCHAFT UND ÜBERSETZEN.
B. CARSTENSEN, 430(NS):JAN73-46
HARTMANN, R.R.K. & F.C. STORK. THE
DICTIONARY OF LANGUAGE & LINGUIS-
TICS.
E.P. HAMP, 269(IJAL):JUL73-198
J. KLAUSENBURGER, 399(MLJ):SEP-
OCT74-280
HARTMANN, W. DIE FUNKTION DES UR-
SPRÜNGLICH RELIGIÖSEN WORTGUTES IN
DER HEUTIGEN DEUTSCHEN UMGANGS-
SPRACHE.
M. KAEMPFERT, 680(ZDP):BAND92HEFT
2-278
HARTNOLL, P., ED. THE CONCISE OX-
FORD COMPANION TO THE THEATRE.
J.C. TREWIN, 157:SPRING73-75
HARTT, F. THE DRAWINGS OF MICHELAN-
GELO.
C. GOULD, 39:MAR73-317
P. JOANNIDES, 90:MAY73-332
HARTUNG, A.E., ED. A MANUAL OF THE
WRITINGS IN MIDDLE ENGLISH 1050-
1500.* (VOL 3)
D. PEARSALL, 382(MAE):1974/1-87
R.M. WILSON, 402(MLR):JAN74-146
HARTVIGSON, H.H. ON THE INTONATION
& POSITION OF THE SO-CALLED SEN-
TENCE MODIFIERS IN PRESENT-DAY ENG-
LISH.*
M. SCHUBIGER, 179(ES):APR72-175
HARTWIG, J. SHAKESPEARE'S TRAGI-
COMIC VISION.*
C.V. WILLIAMS, 577(SHR):SUMMER73-
340
HARVEY, J. THE MEDIAEVAL ARCHITECT.
A. CLIFTON-TAYLOR, 135:APR73-293
L.R. SHELBY, 589:APR74-340
HARVEY, J. THE MUSIC OF STOCKHAUSEN.
R. TOOP, 617(TLS):20JUN75-702

HAVENS, G.R. FREDERICK J. WAUGH,
AMERICAN MARINE PAINTER.
  M.S. YOUNG, 39:APR73-439
HAVENS, T.R.H. FARM & NATION IN
MODERN JAPAN.
  G.C. ALLEN, 617(TLS):11APR75-405
HAWES, S. THE MINOR POEMS. (F.W.
GLUCK & A.B. MORGAN, EDS)
  A. LATHAM, 617(TLS):11APR75-391
HAWKE, D.F. PAINE.*
  E. FONER, 453:15MAY75-42
HAWKE, D.F. BENJAMIN RUSH, REVOLU-
TIONARY GADFLY.*
  R.E. AMACHER, 577(SHR):WINTER73-94
HAWKES, J., ED. ATLAS OF ANCIENT
ARCHAEOLOGY.
  G. DANIEL, 617(TLS):30MAY75-603
HAWKES, J. DEATH, SLEEP & THE TRAV-
ELER.*
  W.M. FROHOCK, 584(SWR):SUMMER74-
  330
  J.L. HALIO, 598(SOR):AUTUMN75-942
  M. MASON, 617(TLS):14FEB75-156
  J. MELLORS, 362:20FEB75-253
  639(VQR):AUTUMN74-CXX
HAWKEY, R. & R. BINGHAM. WILD CARD.*
  617(TLS):7MAR75-241
HAWKINS, H. BETWEEN HARVARD &
AMERICA.
  D. LEAB, 432(NEQ):JUN73-323
HAWKINS, H. LIKENESSES OF TRUTH IN
ELIZABETHAN & RESTORATION DRAMA.*
  J.I. COPE, 301(JEGP):JAN74-119
  R.A. FOAKES, 175:SUMMER73-72
  R.D. HUME, 481(PQ):JUL73-435
HAWKINS, J.N. - SEE CH'IEN CHUN-JUI
HAWTHORN, J.M. IDENTITY & RELATION-
SHIP.
  J. GLOVER, 565:VOL14#4-62
HAWTHORNE, N. THE AMERICAN NOTE-
BOOKS.* (C.M. SIMPSON, ED)
  A. TURNER, 579(SAQ):SPRING74-280
VON HAXTHAUSEN, A. STUDIES ON THE
INTERIOR OF RUSSIA.* (S.F. STARR,
ED)
  G.E. SNOW, 550(RUSR):APR73-214
HAY, D., P. LINEBAUGH & E.P. THOMP-
SON. ALBION'S FATAL TREE.
  R. MITCHISON, 362:13NOV75-656
HAY, G. DARSTELLUNG DES MENSCHEN-
HASSES IN DER DEUTSCHEN LITERATUR
DES 18. UND 19. JAHRHUNDERTS.
  N. RITTER, 221(GQ):NOV73-637
HAYAKAWA, S.I., ED. MODERN GUIDE TO
SYNONYMS.*
  H.W. BRANN, 207(FR):FEB73-693
HAYDN, H. WORDS & FACES.*
  P. ZIEGLER, 617(TLS):20JUN75-699
HAYES, J. THE DRAWINGS OF THOMAS
GAINSBOROUGH.*
  J. GAGE, 56:SPRING-SUMMER73-106
  D. STILLMAN, 481(PQ):JUL73-413
HAYES, J. GAINSBOROUGH AS PRINT-
MAKER.*
  P. CONISBEE, 90:MAY73-333
  J. GAGE, 56:SPRING-SUMMER73-106
HAYES, J. ROWLANDSON: WATERCOLOURS
& DRAWINGS.*
  R. EDWARDS, 39:MAR73-314
  P. WALCH, 481(PQ):JUL73-414
HAYES, J.R., ED. COGNITION & THE
DEVELOPMENT OF LANGUAGE.
  L. BLOOM, 350:JUN74-398
  M-L. MOREAU, 556(RLV):1973/5-473

HAYES, P.L. THE LIMPING HERO.
  295:FEB74-398
HAYLES, B. SPRING AT BROOKFIELD.
  A. HAMILTON, 362:20NOV75-681
HAYMAN, D. ULYSSES.*
  R. HARRISON, 219(GAR):FALL73-432
HAYMAN, R., ED. THE GERMAN THEATRE.
  A. VIVIS, 617(TLS):8AUG75-888
HAYMAN, R. EUGÈNE IONESCO.*
  C.A. PRENDERGAST, 208(FS):JUL74-
  353
HAYMAN, R. JOHN OSBORNE.
  P.M. ARMATO, 160:SPRING73-189
HAYMAN, R. PLAYBACK.
  N. MARSHALL, 157:AUTUMN73-74
HAYMAN, R. THE SET-UP.*
  A. SEYMOUR, 364:APR/MAY74-102
  214:VOL6#24-115
HAYNES, J. SABON GARI.
  R. GARFITT, 364:DEC74/JAN75-104
HAYNES, R.F. THE AWESOME POWER.
  639(VQR):SPRING74-L
HAYNES, S. LAND OF THE CHIMAERA.
  J. MELLAART, 617(TLS):10JAN75-40
HAYS, D.G., ED. READINGS IN AUTO-
MATIC LANGUAGE PROCESSING.
  G.F. MEIER, 682(ZPSK):BAND26HEFT
  3/4-422
HAYS, H.R., ED. 12 SPANISH AMERICAN
POETS.
  W.G. REGIER, 502(PRS):SUMMER73-177
HAYTER, A. HORATIO'S VERSION.
  R.A. FOAKES, 175:AUTUMN72-107
HAZAZ, H. GATES OF BRONZE.
  T. LASK, 441:5OCT75-46
HAZELTON, N. WHAT SHALL I COOK
TODAY?
  R.A. SOKOLOV, 441:7DEC75-78
HAZERA, L.D.L. - SEE UNDER DE LEÓN
HAZERA, L.
HAZO, S. QUARTERED.
  J. PARISI, 491:JUL75-219
HAZZARD, S. DEFEAT OF AN IDEAL.
  M. MANDELBAUM, 676(YR):AUTUMN73-
  151
HEAD, C. JUSTINIAN II OF BYZAN-
TIUM.*
  G. DOWNEY, 589:JAN74-118
HEADEY, B. BRITISH CABINET MINIS-
TERS.
  B. TREND, 617(TLS):17JAN75-55
HEADLEY, J.M. - SEE MORE, T.
HEADY, E.O., ED. ECONOMIC MODELS &
QUANTITATIVE METHODS FOR DECISIONS
& PLANNING IN AGRICULTURE.
  F. DOVRING, 104:WINTER74-613
HEALD, T. DEADLINE.
  N. CALLENDAR, 441:9NOV75-55
HEALEY, G.H. - SEE JOYCE, S.
HEALY, T.S. - SEE DONNE, J.
HEANEY, S. NORTH.
  C.C. O'BRIEN, 362:25SEP75-404
  A. THWAITE, 617(TLS):1AUG75-866
HEANEY, S. WINTERING OUT.*
  A. CLUYSENAAR, 565:VOL14#2-62
  H. MURPHY, 159(DM):WINTER/SPRING
  73-118
  H. SERGEANT, 175:AUTUMN73-121
HEARNDEN, A. EDUCATION IN THE TWO
GERMANIES.
  M. MC CAULEY, 617(TLS):12SEP75-
  1028
HEARON, S. HANNAH'S HOUSE.
  M. LEVIN, 441:15JUN75-26

HEATH, C. JOSEPH & THE GOTHS.
A. BARNES, 617(TLS):14NOV75-1349
HEATH, D.B. HISTORICAL DICTIONARY
OF BOLIVIA.
E. ECHEVARRÍA, 263:JAN-MAR74-77
HEATH, E. SAILING.
D. THOMAS, 362:27NOV75-729
HEATH, S. THE NOUVEAU ROMAN.*
M.P. LEVITT, 295:FEB74-426
L.S. ROUDIEZ, 546(RR):NOV74-315
HEATH, S.B. TELLING TONGUES.
N.A. MC QUOWN, 350:SEP74-607
HEATH, W. WORDSWORTH & COLERIDGE.*
C. RAINE, 447(N&Q):FEB73-69
HEATHCOTE, T.A. THE INDIAN ARMY.
617(TLS):10JAN75-41
HEATON, J.M. THE EYE.
J.M. KENNEDY, 290(JAAC):FALL73-127
HEBDEN, M. A PRIDE OF DOLPHINS.
P. ADAMS, 61:MAR75-146
N. CALLENDAR, 441:13APR75-30
HÉBERT, A. LES ENFANTS DU SABBAT.
P. FRANCE, 617(TLS):10OCT75-1208
HÉBERT, A. THE SILENT ROOMS.
A. RASPA, 296:VOL4#3-173
HECHINGER, F.M. & G. GROWING UP IN
AMERICA.
G. LICHTENSTEIN, 441:22NOV75-27
H. MAYER, 441:9NOV75-35
HECHT, R. SIGNPOSTS.
P.D. MORROW, 649(WAL):FALL73-153
HECHT, W., ED. BRECHT-DIALOG 1968.
C.L. HART-NIBBRIG, 657(WW):MAY/JUN
73-215
HECHT, W. - SEE BRECHT, B.
HECK, E. DER BEGRIFF RELIGIO BEI
THOMAS VON AQUIN.
W.C. SMITH, 589:APR74-342
HECKMAIR, A. MY LIFE AS A MOUNTAIN-
EER.
N. MORIN, 617(TLS):16MAY75-544
HECKSCHER, A. ALIVE IN THE CITY.*
H. CARRUTH, 249(HUDR):WINTER74/75-
621
639(VQR):SUMMER74-LXXXIX
HEDĀYETULLĀH, M. SAYYID AHMAD.
A. AHMAD, 318(JAOS):JUL-SEP73-361
HEDGES, J. FUNERAL RITES.
N. CALLENDAR, 441:26JAN75-23
HEDLEY, O. QUEEN CHARLOTTE.
G. CURTIS, 617(TLS):25APR75-451
HEDRICK, B.C., J.C. KELLEY & C.L.
RILEY, EDS. THE CLASSIC SOUTHWEST.
W. GARD, 584(SWR):SPRING74-V
HEENEY, A. THINGS THAT ARE CAESAR'S.
102(CANL):SUMMER73-127
HEER, N.W. POLITICS & HISTORY IN
THE SOVIET UNION.*
G. ENTEEN, 104:WINTER73-561
HEESE, G. & H. WEGENER, EDS. ENZY-
KLOPÄDISCHES HANDBUCH DER SONDER-
PÄDAGOGIK UND IHRER GRENZGEBIETE.
G. LINDNER, 682(ZPSK):BAND26HEFT
3/4-409
HEGARTY, W. YOU CAN'T GET THERE
FROM HERE.
V. GLENDINNING, 617(TLS):7NOV75-
1338
HEGEL, G.W.F. FILOSOFIA DELLO
SPIRITO JENESE. (G. CANTILLO, ED)
M. DEL VECCHIO, 548(RCSF):JAN-MAR
73-116

HEGEL, G.W.F. HEGEL'S SCIENCE OF
LOGIC. (A.V. MILLER, TRANS)
A. QUINTON, 453:29MAY75-34
HEGEL, G.W.F. LECTURES ON THE PHIL-
OSOPHY OF WORLD HISTORY: INTRODUC-
TION. (H.B. NISBET, TRANS)
P. GARDINER, 617(TLS):22AUG75-938
HEGEL, G.W.F. DES MANIÈRES DE TRAI-
TER SCIENTIFIQUEMENT DU DROIT NAT-
UREL. (B. BOURGEOIS, ED & TRANS)
LE DROIT NATUREL. (A. KAAN, ED &
TRANS)
F. MARKOVITS, 98:JUL73-636
HEGEL, R. NINETEENTH-CENTURY HIS-
TORIANS OF NEW HAVEN.
B.F. TOLLES, JR., 432(NEQ):MAR73-
152
HEGER, H. DAS LEBENSZEUGNIS WAL-
THERS VON DER VOGELWEIDE.*
M. CURSCHMANN, 222(GR):MAR73-150
HEICK, W.H. & R. GRAHAM, EDS. HIS
OWN MAN.
C. BERGER, 99:APR/MAY75-40
HEIDEGGER, M. HEGEL'S CONCEPT OF
EXPERIENCE.
A. QUINTON, 453:29MAY75-34
HEIDEGGER, M. NIETZSCHE.
P. LACOUE-LABARTHE, 98:JUN73-487
HEIDEGGER, M. ON TIME & BEING.
J.D.C., 543:JUN73-757
HEIDEGGER, M. POETRY, LANGUAGE,
THOUGHT.*
M. MORTON, 154:JUN73-372
HEIDEGGER, M. SCHELLING'S ABHAND-
LUNG ÜBER DAS WESEN DER MENSCHLICH-
EN FREIHEIT (1809). (H. FEICH, ED)
P.J. MC CORMICK, 154:MAR73-129
HEIDELMEYER, W. DAS SELBSTBESTIM-
MUNGSRECHT DER VÖLKER.
A-R. WERNER, 182:VOL26#23/24-845
HEIDENREICH, C. HURONIA.*
F.C. INNES, 628:SPRING74-99
HEIDENREICH, R. & H. JOHANNES. DAS
GRABMAL THEODERICHS ZU RAVENNA
(DEUTSCHES ARCHÄOLOGISCHES INSTI-
TUT).
R. KRAUTHEIMER, 54:JUN73-288
HEIDUK, F. DIE DICHTER DER GALANTEN
LYRIK.*
E.A. METZGER, 133:1973/3-272
HEIKAL, M. THE ROAD TO RAMADAN.
P. WINDSOR, 362:12JUN75-789
HEIKE, G. SPRACHLICHE KOMMUNIKATION
UND LINGUISTISCHE ANALYSE.
F.G. DROSTE, 353:15JAN73-122
HEIKE, G. ZUR PHONOLOGIE DER STADT-
KOLNER MUNDART.
H. RICHTER, 343:BAND16HEFT1-101
HEILBRON, J.L. H.G.J. MOSELEY.
J. NORTH, 617(TLS):3JAN75-6
HEILMAN, R.B. THE GHOST ON THE
RAMPARTS & OTHER ESSAYS IN THE
HUMANITIES.
R. BUFFINGTON, 569(SR):WINTER74-
147
639(VQR):AUTUMN74-CLII
HEILMAN, R.B. THE ICEMAN, THE AR-
SONIST, & THE TROUBLED AGENT.
H.F. FOLLAND, 651(WHR):SUMMER74-
270
C. HOY, 219(GAR):FALL73-435
J.P. SISK, 131(CL):SUMMER74-266
J.L. STYAN, 385(MQR):WINTER75-111
639(VQR):WINTER74-XVII

HEIN, J. FERDINAND RAIMUND.
I. FINDLAY, 221(GQ):NOV73-635
HEIN, J. SPIEL UND SATIRE IN DER
KOMÖDIE JOHANN NESTROYS.
I. FINDLAY, 221(GQ):SEP73-156
HEINE, H. BEITRÄGE ZUR DEUTSCHEN
IDEOLOGIE. (H. MAYER, ED)
J.L.S., 191(ELN):SEP73(SUPP)-136
HEINE, H. SÄMTLICHE SCHRIFTEN.
(VOL 3) (K. PÖRNBACHER, ED)
J.L.S., 191(ELN):SEP73(SUPP)-130
HEINE, H. SÄMTLICHE WERKE: DÜSSEL-
DORFER AUSGABE.* (VOL 6) (J. HER-
MAND, ED)
S. ATKINS, 301(JEGP):JUL74-406
HEINE, H. WERKE. (VOL 1) (S. AT-
KINS, ED)
R.C. FIGGE, 301(JEGP):JUL74-409
HEINE, R. TRANSZENDENTALPOESIE.
617(TLS):18JUL75-809
HEINER, H-J. DAS GANZHEITSDENKEN
FRIEDRICH SCHLEGELS.*
R. PAULIN, 402(MLR):APR74-461
HEINRICHS, H. AUDIO-VISUELLE PRAXIS
IN WORT UND BILD.
K. OLTMANN, 430(NS):JUL73-382
HEINS, E.L. - SEE KUNST, J.
HEINSIUS, D. ON PLOT IN TRAGEDY.*
(P.R. SELLIN & J.J. MC MANMON,
TRANS)
J.M. STEADMAN, 551(RENQ):SPRING73-
62
HEINTZE, B. - SEE NTARA, S.J.
VON HEINTZE, H. ROMAN ART.
R. HIGGINS, 39:AUG73-150
HEINZLE, J. STELLENKOMMENTAR ZU
WOLFRAMS "TITUREL."*
P. SALMON, 182:VOL26#7/8-215
HEISE, E.T. FRENCH FOR REVIEW.
(2ND ED)
B.P. EDMONDS, 207(FR):APR73-1077
HEISE, H-J. UNDERSEAS POSSESSIONS.
A. CLUYSENAAR, 565:VOL14#4-75
HEISENBERG, W. ACROSS THE FRONTIERS.
639(VQR):SUMMER74-CIV
HEISSENBÜTTEL, H. DAS DURCHHAUEN
DES KOHLHAUPTS.
J. WHITE, 617(TLS):3OCT75-1146
HEISSIG, W., ED. MONGOLEIREISE ZUR
SPAETEN GOETHEZEIT.
H. SERRUYS, 318(JAOS):OCT-DEC73-
648
HEISSIG, W., WITH C. BAWDEN, COMPS.
CATALOGUE OF MONGOL BOOKS, MANU-
SCRIPTS & XYLOGRAPHS.
L. HAMBIS, 182:VOL26#20-705
HEITMANN, K. DER IMMORALISMUS-
PROZESZ GEGEN DIE FRANZÖSISCHE LIT-
ERATUR IM 19. JAHRHUNDERT.
A. BLOCH, 546(RR):JAN73-76
J. BOISSEL, 535(RHL):NOV-DEC73-
1098
HEIZER, R.F. & M.A. WHIPPLE, EDS.
THE CALIFORNIA INDIANS. (2ND ED)
E.P. HAMP, 269(IJAL):JAN73-60
HEKLER, A. GREEK & ROMAN PORTRAITS.
R. HIGGINS, 39:AUG73-150
HELBIG, G. & W. SCHENKEL. WÖRTER-
BUCH ZUR VALENZ UND DISTRIBUTION
DEUTSCHER VERBEN. (2ND ED)
M.S. KIRCH, 399(MLJ):SEP-OCT74-289
K. TARVAINEN, 439(NM):1973/4-760

HELBIG, L.F. DER EINZELNE UND DIE
GESELLSCHAFT IN GOETHES "WAHLVER-
WANDTSCHAFTEN."
H.J. GEERDTS, 654(WB):3/1973-190
R. GERULAITIS, 406:FALL74-306
HELBLING, R.E. & A.M.L. BARNETT.
INTRODUCTION AU FRANÇAIS ACTUEL.
J.W. ZDENEK, 399(MLJ):DEC74-424
HELCK, W. ÄGYPTOLOGIE AN DEUTSCHEN
UNIVERSITÄTEN.
M. HEERMA VAN VOSS, 318(JAOS):
JUL-SEP73-403
HELCK, W. DIE LEHRE DES DW3-ḤTJJ.
E.F. WENTE, 318(JAOS):JUL-SEP73-
397
HELD, S. WEAVING.
E. AUVIL, 139:DEC73-59
HELD, V., K. NIELSEN & C. PARSONS,
EDS. PHILOSOPHY & POLITICAL AC-
TION.
W.G., 543:DEC72-357
HELDRIS DE CORNUÄLLE. LE ROMAN DE
SILENCE. (L. THORPE, ED)
A.H. DIVERRES, 382(MAE):1974/1-71
HÉLIN, M. LA LITTÉRATURE LATINE AU
MOYEN AGE.
J. ANDRÉ, 555:VOL47FASC2-378
HÉLISENNE DE CRENNE. "LES ANGOYSSES
DOULOUREUSES QUI PROCÈDENT D'A-
MOURS," ROMAN (1538). (PT 1) (P.
DEMATS, ED)
F. JOUKOVSKY, 545(RPH):FEB74-436
HELLEBRAND, N. LONDONERS.
617(TLS):10JAN75-41
HELLEGOUARC'H, J. - SEE SALLUST
HELLER, E. FRANZ KAFKA.
I. PARRY, 617(TLS):28FEB75-231
W. PHILLIPS, 441:12OCT75-20
HELLER, E. & J. BORN - SEE KAFKA, F.
HELLER, J. SOMETHING HAPPENED.*
R. SALE, 249(HUDR):WINTER74/75-623
HELLER, L.G. THE DEATH OF THE AMER-
ICAN UNIVERSITY.
R. BUFFINGTON, 569(SR):WINTER74-
147
HELLER, R. & N. WILLATT. THE EURO-
PEAN REVENGE.
P. JOHNSON, 362:23OCT75-550
HELLMAN, L. PENTIMENTO.*
J. SYMONS, 364:AUG/SEP74-137
HELLMANN, D.C. JAPAN & EAST ASIA.
IMAZU HIROSHI, 285(JAPQ):JUL-SEP73-
344
J.W. WHITE, 293(JAST):AUG73-711
HELLMANN, M.W. FÜRST, HERRSCHER UND
FÜRSTENGEMEINSCHAFT.
M.G. SCHOLZ, 680(ZDP):BAND92HEFT3-
450
HELLMANN, W. DAS GESCHICHTSDENKEN
DES FRÜHEN THOMAS MANN (1906-1918).
H. HATFIELD, 301(JEGP):JAN74-93
HELLMICH, A. KLANG UND ERLÖSUNG.
H. WETZEL, 406:SUMMER74-198
HELLSTROM, W. ON THE POEMS OF
TENNYSON.
G. JOSEPH, 219(GAR):WINTER73-607
H. KOZICKI, 141:FALL73-374
H. SERGEANT, 175:SUMMER73-78
HELLWEGE, J. ZUR GESCHICHTE DER
SPANISCHEN REITERMILIZEN.
A.W. LOVETT, 182:VOL26#9-314
HELLWIG, G. KENNEN SIE DIE NEUESTEN
WÖRTER.
E. PASTOR, 556(RLV):1973/3-279

HELM, E. FRANZ LISZT IN SELBSTZEUG-
NISSEN UND BILDDOKUMENTEN.
J.S. WEISSMANN, 412:AUG-NOV73-353
HELM, P. THE VARIETIES OF BELIEF.
A.J. MC KAY, 478:JUL73-127
HELMAN, E. JOVELLANOS Y GOYA.
I.M. ZAVALA, 240(HR):SUMMER73-573
VON HELMHOLTZ, H. SELECTED WRITINGS
OF HERMANN VON HELMHOLTZ. (R.
KAHL, ED)
M. LOWE, 84:DEC73-413
HELMHOLZ, R.H. MARRIAGE LITIGATION
IN MEDIEVAL ENGLAND.
R. HILL, 617(TLS):4APR75-379
HELPRIN, M. A DOVE OF THE EAST.
A. HELLER, 61:OCT75-108
D. WAKEFIELD, 441:2NOV75-52
HELSTROM, J. & M.S. METZ. LE FRAN-
ÇAIS À DÉCOUVRIR. (3RD ED)
R.S. DISICK, 207(FR):MAR73-879
HELWIG, D. THE BEST NAME OF
SILENCE.*
M. ANDRÉ, 529(QQ):AUTUMN73-471
D. EVERARD, 102(CANL):SPRING74-110
G. MC WHIRTER, 376:APR73-235
HELWIG, D. & J. HARCOURT, EDS. 72,
NEW CANADIAN STORIES.
S.E. MC MULLIN, 102(CANL):WINTER
74-116
P. MORLEY, 529(QQ):AUTUMN73-468
E.R. ZIETLOW, 376:OCT73-141
HELWIG, D. & J. HARCOURT, EDS. 73:
NEW CANADIAN STORIES.* [SHOWN IN
PREV UNDER TITLE]
B. LEVER, 296:VOL4#1-190
HELWIG, D. & B. MILLER. A BOOK
ABOUT BILLIE.
D. BAILEY, 529(QQ):SPRING73-99
HELYAR, J., ED. GILBERT & SULLIVAN.
C. KLEINHANS, 637(VS):SEP73-117
HEMENWAY, A.M. ABBY HEMENWAY'S VER-
MONT. (B.C. MORRISSEY, ED)
R.C. BARRET, 432(NEQ):JUN74-315
HEMINGWAY, E. THE FIFTH COLUMN, &
FOUR STORIES OF THE SPANISH CIVIL
WAR.
J.A. GERTZMAN, 573(SSF):SPRING73-
224
HEMINGWAY, E. ERNEST HEMINGWAY'S
APPRENTICESHIP. (M.J. BRUCCOLI, ED)
295:FEB74-637
HEMINGWAY, E. THE NICK ADAMS STOR-
IES.* (P. YOUNG, ED)
R.M. DAVIS, 577(SHR):SPRING73-215
J.A. GERTZMAN, 573(SSF):SUMMER73-
297
HEMLOW, J., WITH C.D. CECIL & A.
DOUGLAS - SEE BURNEY, F.
HEMLOW, J. & A. DOUGLAS - SEE BUR-
NEY, F.
HEMMINGS, F.W.J. CULTURE & SOCIETY
IN FRANCE 1848-1898.*
C. DUCKWORTH, 402(MLR):JAN74-184
R.B. GRANT, 546(RR):MAY74-233
HEMPEL, C.G. ELÉMENTS D'ÉPISTÉMOLO-
GIE.
R. BLANCHÉ, 542:JUL-SEP73-359
HEMPEL, W. ÜBERMUOT DIU ALTE...*
F.W. VON KRIES, 221(GQ):MAR73-265
HEMPFER, K.W. TENDENZ UND ÄSTHETIK.
U. SCHULZ-BUSCHHAUS, 72:BAND211
HEFT1/3-87

HEMSCHEMEYER, J. I REMEMBER THE
ROOM WAS FILLED WITH LIGHT.*
F. MORAMARCO, 651(WHR):WINTER74-89
639(VQR):SPRING74-LVII
HENDERSON, E.J.A., ED. THE INDIS-
PENSABLE FOUNDATION.
V.A. FROMKIN, 215(GL):VOL13#1-26
HENDERSON, G. EARLY MEDIEVAL.
E.C. FERNIE, 90:NOV73-748
G. ZARNECKI, 39:JUN73-623
HENDERSON, G.P. THE REVIVAL OF
GREEK THOUGHT 1620-1830.
A.N. ATHANASSAKIS, 124:FEB74-245
HENDERSON, H.B., 3D. VERSIONS OF
THE PAST.*
P. SHAW, 31(ASCH):SUMMER75-496
L. ZIFF, 617(TLS):7MAR75-242
HENDERSON, J.A. THE FIRST AVANT-
GARDE (1887-1894).*
E.C. JACQUART, 207(FR):MAY73-1231
D. KNOWLES, 208(FS):JAN74-100
M.G. ROSE, 399(MLJ):NOV73-363
HENDERSON, M. DANTE GABRIEL ROSSET-
TI.
R. EDWARDS, 39:NOV73-403
HENDERSON, P. WILLIAM MORRIS.
R. EDWARDS, 39:NOV73-403
HENDERSON, P. SWINBURNE.*
I. FLETCHER, 617(TLS):21NOV75-1380
HENDIN, H. THE AGE OF SENSATION.
C. LEHMANN-HAUPT, 441:22SEP75-37
S. SANBORN, 441:5OCT75-3
HENDRICKS, G. ALBERT BIERSTADT.
P. ADAMS, 61:MAR75-144
HENDRICKS, G. EADWEARD MUYBRIDGE.
E. DE MARÉ, 617(TLS):11JUL75-759
G. MILLAR, 362:28AUG75-284
HENDY, P. EUROPEAN & AMERICAN
PAINTINGS IN THE ISABELLA STEWART
GARDNER MUSEUM.
D. SUTTON, 617(TLS):21MAR75-302
HENGEL, M. JUDAISM & HELLENISM.
J. BOWKER, 617(TLS):5SEP75-1006
HENKE, A. DIE WESTLICHEN LEHNWÖRTER
IN DER POLNISCHEN SPRACHE.
B. FRANOLIĆ, 353:1OCT73-106
HENLE, G. THREE SPHERES.
M. PETERSON, 470:NOV72-46
HENN, T.R. THE LIVING IMAGE.*
R.A. FOAKES, 175:AUTUMN72-107
A. LEGGATT, 529(QQ):SPRING73-134
HENNEMAN, J.B. ROYAL TAXATION IN
FOURTEENTH CENTURY FRANCE.*
F.L. CHEYETTE, 589:JAN74-119
HENNESSY, J.P. - SEE UNDER POPE HEN-
NESSY, J.
HENNING, U. & H. KOLB, EDS. MEDIAE-
VALIA LITTERARIA.
C. BAIER, 220(GL&L):OCT73-69
HENRETTA, J.A. THE EVOLUTION OF
AMERICAN SOCIETY, 1700-1815.
M. EGNAL, 656(WMQ):JUL74-510
HENRETTA, J.A. "SALUTARY NEGLECT."*
M. FREIBERG, 432(NEQ):MAR73-134
I.K. STEELE, 481(PQ):JUL73-352
HENRI, F. BLACK MIGRATION.
T. ROSENGARTEN, 441:30MAR75-18
HENRIOT, J. LA CONDITION VOLONTAIRE.
M. ADAM, 542:OCT-DEC73-489
HENRY, A. MÉTONYMIE ET MÉTAPHORE.
D. BOUVEROT, 209(FM):APR73-202
S. ULLMANN, 208(FS):APR74-236

HENRY, A. LES OEUVRES D'ADENET LE
ROI.* (VOL 5)
  W.G. VAN EMDEN, 208(FS):APR74-181
HENRY, C.L. FRENCH STUDY-AIDS.
  P. SILBERMAN, 399(MLJ):APR73-227
HENRY, D.P. MEDIEVAL LOGIC & META-
PHYSICS.*
  I. BOH, 589:JUL74-563
HENRY, J. THE PAPERS OF JOSEPH
HENRY.* (VOL 1) (N. REINGOLD, ED)
  L.J. CAPPON, 14:OCT73-551
HENRY, P., ED. CLASSICS OF SOVIET
SATIRE. (VOL 1)
  L. KOEHLER, 104:FALL73-432
HENRY, P. ON THE TRACK.*
  S. CURTIS, 148:SPRING72-85
HENRY, P. & H-R. SCHWYZER - SEE
PLOTINUS
HENSHEL, R.L. & R.A. SILVERMAN, EDS.
PERCEPTION IN CRIMINOLOGY.
  617(TLS):26SEP75-1100
HENSING, D. ZUR GESTALTUNG DER
WIENER GENESIS.
  J.S. GROSECLOSE, 406:SPRING74-99
  B. MURDOCH, 402(MLR):JUL74-696
HENSLEY, J.L. SONG OF CORPUS JURIS.
  N. CALLENDAR, 441:9FEB75-16
HENTENRYK, G.K-V. - SEE UNDER
KURGAN-VAN HENTENRYK, G.
HENTSCHKE, A.B. POLITIK UND PHILOS-
OPHIE BEI PLATO UND ARISTOTELES.
  P.M. HUBY, 123:MAR74-132
HEPBURN, J. - SEE GOSSE, E.
HEPP, N. DEUX AMIS D'HOMÈRE AU
XVIIE SIÈCLE.
  R. ZUBER, 535(RHL):JUL-AUG73-690
HEPP, N. HOMÈRE EN FRANCE AU XVIIE
SIÈCLE.
  M. FUMAROLI, 535(RHL):JUL-AUG73-
643
  R.C. KNIGHT, 208(FS):OCT74-447
HEPP, N. - SEE PELLISSON, P. & C.
FLEURY
HEPWORTH, B., ED. EDWARD YOUNG
(1683-1765).
  R. FULLER, 617(TLS):10OCT75-1209
HERAKLEIDES. HERACLIDIS LEMBI EX-
CERPTA POLITIARUM.* (M.R. DILTS,
ED & TRANS)
  F.D. CAIZZI, 548(RCSF):OCT-DEC73-
476
  K.H. KINZL, 124:MAY73-497
HERBERT, F. THE BEST OF FRANK HER-
BERT. (A. WELLS, ED)
  E. KORN, 617(TLS):8AUG75-903
HERBERT, I. WINTER'S TALE.
  A. ROSS, 364:AUG/SEP74-117
HERBERT, K. GREEK & LATIN INSCRIP-
TIONS IN THE BROOKLYN MUSEUM.
  R.K. SHERK, 124:DEC73-JAN74-181
HERBERT, R.L. DAVID: BRUTUS.
  M. ROSENTHAL, 135:APR73-291
HERBORT, W. & OTHERS. DER LAND-
KREIS WIEDENBRÜCK (REGIERUNGSBEZIRK
DETMOLD).
  P. VOSSELER, 182:VOL26#21/22-828
HERBST, P.G. BEHAVIOURAL WORLDS.
  R. KALIN, 529(QQ):AUTUMN73-486
HERBST, P.G. SOCIO-TECHNICAL DE-
SIGN.
  617(TLS):28FEB75-229
HERDE, H. JOHANN GEORG HAMANN.*
  E.F. RITTER, 481(PQ):JUL73-521

HERDE, JÜRGEN, H. DIE TARENTINISCHEN
TERRAKOTTEN DES 6. BIS 4. JAHRHUN-
DERTS V. CHR. IM ANTIKENMUSEUM
BASEL.
  R.M. COOK, 123:MAR74-159
HERDING, K. PIERRE PUGET.
  T. HODGKINSON, 90:SEP73-614
HERDING, O. - SEE WIMPFELING, J. &
B. RHENANUS
HERFURTH, G., J. HENNIG & L. HUTH.
TOPOGRAPHIE DER GERMANISTIK.
  R.H. THOMAS, 402(MLR):APR74-474
HERINGER, H-J. DEUTSCHE SYNTAX.*
  J.J. BRAAKENBURG, 433:OCT73-411
  H.W. FELTKAMP, 361:DEC73-333
  O. LUDWIG, 343:BAND16HEFT1-80
HERINGER, H-J. FORMALE LOGIK UND
GRAMMATIK.
  G.F. MEIER, 682(ZPSK):BAND26HEFT
1/2-195
  C.V.J. RUSS, 402(MLR):OCT74-905
HERINGTON, C.J. THE AUTHOR OF THE
"PROMETHEUS BOUND."*
  J. PERADOTTO, 121(CJ):FEB/MAR74-
258
  S.V. TRACY, 122:OCT73-305
HERINGTON, C.J. THE OLDER SCHOLIA
ON THE "PROMETHEUS BOUND."
  E.W. WHITTLE, 303:VOL93-224
  N.G. WILSON, 123:NOV74-287
HERIOT, A. THE CASTRATI IN OPERA.
  S. TROTTER, 362:2OCT75-454
HERIVEL, J. JOSEPH FOURIER.
  P. HEIMANN, 617(TLS):25JUL75-846
HERKOMMER, H. ÜBERLIEFERUNGSGE-
SCHICHTE DER "SÄCHSISCHEN WELT-
CHRONIK."
  F.W. VON KRIES, 589:OCT74-738
HERLIN, H. COMMEMORATIONS.
  M. IRWIN, 617(TLS):21NOV75-1379
  R.R. LINGEMAN, 441:3SEP75-31
  E. PAWEL, 441:21SEP75-5
  442(NY):6OCT75-164
HERM, G. THE PHOENICIANS.
  B.H. WARMINGTON, 617(TLS):3OCT75-
1158
HERMAN, V. & J.E. ALT, EDS. CABINET
STUDIES.
  B. TREND, 617(TLS):7NOV75-1324
HERMAND, J. VON MAINZ NACH WEIMAR
(1793-1919).
  H. ELEMA, 433:OCT73-417
HERMAND, J. STÄNKER UND WEISMACHER.
  H-J. MODLMAYR, 402(MLR):APR74-473
HERMAND, J. UNBEQUEME LITERATUR.*
  T.E. CARTER, 220(GL&L):JUL74-332
HERMAND, J. - SEE HEINE, H.
HERMERÉN, G. REPRESENTATION & MEAN-
ING IN THE VISUAL ARTS.
  F.D. MARTIN, 290(JAAC):FALL73-130
  P. SOMVILLE, 542:JAN-MAR73-117
HERMES, H. EINFÜHRUNG IN DIE MATHE-
MATISCHE LOGIK. (2ND ED)
  E. ENGELER, 316:SEP73-518
HERMES, H., F. KAMBARTEL & F. KAUL-
BACH - SEE FREGE, G.
HERMODSSON, E. KULTUR I BOTTEN.
  R-M.G. OSTER, 563(SS):FALL74-454
HERN, N. PETER HANDKE.*
  C.N. GENNO, 564:JUN73-165
  S. GOOCH, 214:VOL6#21-109

HERNADI, P. BEYOND GENRE.
 S. LANSER, 406:FALL74-330
 W. MARTIN, 131(CL):SPRING74-174
 D. NEWTON-DE MOLINA, 402(MLR):
 JAN74-134
 E.L. RIVERS, 400(MLN):DEC73-1333
HERNANDEZ, M. & B. DE OTERO. SELEC-
TED POEMS.
 W.G. REGIER, 502(PRS):SUMMER73-177
HERODAS. MIMIAMBI.* (I.C. CUNNING-
HAM, ED)
 G. GIANGRANDE, 123:MAR74-33
 G.L. KONIARIS, 124:FEB73-298
 D.N. LEVIN, 24:WINTER74-403
"THE HEROIN TRAIL."
 C.H. ROLPH, 617(TLS):16MAY75-532
HERON, R. SCOTLAND DELINEATED.
 J.A. SMITH, 617(TLS):22AUG75-937
HERRAND VON WILDONIE. THE TALES &
SONGS OF HERRAND VON WILDONIE.
(J.W. THOMAS, TRANS)
 B. NAUMANN, 220(GL&L):APR74-258
DE HERRERA, G.A. - SEE UNDER ALONSO
DE HERRERA, G.
HERRERO, J. LOS ORÍGENES DEL PENSA-
MIENTO REACCIONARIO ESPAÑOL.*
 K. SCHWARTZ, 238:MAR73-175
 I.M. ZAVALA, 400(MLN):MAR73-467
HERRING, G.C., JR. AID TO RUSSIA
1941-1946.
 J.N. HAZARD, 550(RUSR):OCT73-429
HERRING, J. BROWNING'S OLD SCHOOL-
FELLOW.*
 T.J. COLLINS, 637(VS):DEC73-234
HERRIOT, P. ATTRIBUTES OF MEMORY.
 R.A. KENNEDY, 617(TLS):25APR75-450
HERRLITZ, W. HISTORISCHE PHONOLOGIE
DES DEUTSCHEN.* (PT 1)
 I. GUENTHERODT, 133:1973/1-93
 U. SCHEUERMANN, 260(IF):BAND77HEFT
 2/3-348
 N.T.J. VOORWINDEN, 433:JAN73-96
HERRMANN, F., ED. THE ENGLISH AS
COLLECTORS.*
 A.C. SEWTER, 90:FEB73-125
HERRMANN, H.P. NATURNACHAHMUNG UND
EINBILDUNGSKRAFT.
 J.L. GELLINEK, 221(GQ):SEP73-142
HERRMANN, J. ZWISCHEN HRADSCHIN UND
VINETA.
 D.S. COOPER, 574(SEEJ):WINTER72-
 510
HERRMANN, K-J. DAS TUSKULANER
PAPSTTUM (1012-46).
 R. FOLZ, 182:VOL26#20-765
HERRMANN, L. TURNER.
 J. RUSSELL, 441:7DEC75-20
 D. THOMAS, 362:25DEC75&1JAN76-892
HERSEY, G.L. HIGH VICTORIAN GOTHIC.*
 M. GIROUARD, 46:MAR73-210
 P.F. NORTON, 576:MAR73-75
 P. THOMPSON, 637(VS):SEP73-113
HERSEY, J. MY PETITION FOR MORE
SPACE.*
 T.A. SHIPPEY, 617(TLS):16MAY75-529
HERSEY, J. THE PRESIDENT.
 G. WILLS, 453:16OCT75-18
HERSEY, J., ED. THE WRITER'S
CRAFT.*
 639(VQR):SUMMER74-LXXII
HERVÁS, J.M.R. - SEE UNDER ROLDÁN
HERVÁS, J.M.

HERWEGH, G. FRÜHE PUBLIZISTIK 1837-
1841.
 W. FEUDEL, 654(WB):6/1973-220
"GEORG HERWEGH: ÜBER LITERATUR UND
GESELLSCHAFT (1837-1841)." (A.
ZIEGENGEIST, ED)
 W. FEUDEL, 654(WB):6/1973-220
HERWIG, W. - SEE VON GOETHE, J.W.
HERZEN, A. MY PAST & THOUGHTS.
 (D. MACDONALD, ED)
 L. SCHAPIRO, 617(TLS):3JAN75-2
HERZOG, A. EARTHSOUND.
 M. LEVIN, 441:14DEC75-31
HERZOG, C. THE WAR OF ATONEMENT.
 M. BELL, 362:10JUL75-60
 B. COLLIER, 441:50CT75-20
 J. FERON, 441:15NOV75-25
HERZOG, V. IRONISCHE ERZÄHLFORMEN
BEI CONRAD FERDINAND MEYER, DARGE-
STELLT AM "JÜRG JENATSCH."*
 P. SCHIMMELPFENNIG, 221(GQ):NOV73-
 641
 W.D. WILLIAMS, 220(GL&L):JAN74-158
HERZOG, Y. A PEOPLE THAT DWELLS
ALONE. (M. LOUVISH, ED)
 L. KOCHAN, 617(TLS):1AUG75-867
HESCHEL, A.J. THE INSECURITY OF
FREEDOM.
 W.G., 543:MAR73-537
HESELTINE, H., ED. THE PENGUIN BOOK
OF AUSTRALIAN VERSE.
 D.J. O'HEARN, 381:MAR73-94
HESELTINE, J.E., ED. THE OXFORD
BOOK OF FRENCH PROSE.*
 P. MÉNARD, 545(RPH):FEB74-440
HESELTINE, N. MADAGASCAR.
 M. BLOCH, 69:APR73-172
HESS, G. DEUTSCH-LATEINISCHE NAR-
RENZUNFT.*
 J. IJSEWIJN, 52:BAND8HEFT3-331
HESS, H. GEORGE GROSZ.*
 442(NY):27JAN75-104
HESS, H. PICTURES AS ARGUMENTS.
 S. BANN, 617(TLS):25APR75-460
HESS, R., M. FRAUENRATH & G. SIEBE-
MANN. LITERATURWISSENSCHAFTLICHES
WÖRTERBUCH FÜR ROMANISTEN.*
 F. VAN ROSSUM-GUYON, 535(RHL):NOV-
DEC73-1118
HESS, T.B. WILLEM DE KOONING DRAW-
INGS.*
 C. HARRISON, 592:MAR73-139
HESS, T.B. & E.C. BAKER, EDS. ART
& SEXUAL POLITICS.
 M. MOTHERSILL, 290(JAAC):SPRING74-
 435
 C.G. VOPAT, 59(ASOC):SPRING-SUM-
MER74-157
HESS, T.B. & L. NOCHLIN, EDS. WOMAN
AS SEX OBJECT.
 C.G. VOPAT, 59(ASOC):SPRING-SUM-
MER74-157
HESSE, H. STORIES OF FIVE DECADES.*
(T. ZIOLKOWSKI, ED)
 D.P. DENEAU, 573(SSF):FALL73-425
HESSE, H. & T. MANN. THE HESSE/MANN
LETTERS. (A. CARLSSON & V. MICH-
ELS, EDS)
 R. CRAFT, 453:12JUN75-19
 442(NY):28JUL75-80
HESSE, H.R. GOTT IN PERSON.
 C.L. HART-NIBBRIG, 657(WW):MAY/JUN
 73-213

HESSE, M. THE STRUCTURE OF SCIEN-
TIFIC INFERENCE.*
  R. HILPINEN, 311(JP):4SEP75-485
  D. PAPINEAU, 111:30MAY74-167
HESSE-FINK, É. ÉTUDES SUR LE THÈME
DE L'INCESTE DANS LA LITTÉRATURE
FRANÇAISE.
  B. DIDIER, 535(RHL):NOV-DEC73-1117
HESSEN, R. STEEL TITAN.
  R.C. ALBERTS, 441:28DEC75-16
HESTER, R.M. A PROTESTANT BAROQUE
POET, PIERRE POUPO.
  J. PINEAUX, 535(RHL):SEP-OCT73-889
HEUBNER, H. - SEE TACITUS
HEUER, F. DARSTELLUNG DER FREIHEIT.
  K.L. BERGHAHN, 406:WINTER74-401
DE HEUSCH, L. LE ROI IVRE OU
L'ORIGINE DE L'ETAT. (VOL 1)
  J. VANSINA, 69:OCT73-379
HEWER, H.R. BRITISH SEALS.
  L.H. MATTHEWS, 617(TLS):7MAR75-258
HEWETT, C.A. ENGLISH CATHEDRAL CAR-
PENTRY.* CHURCH CARPENTRY.
  Q. HUGHES & D.T. YEOMANS,
  617(TLS):29AUG75-964
HEWETT, D. THE CHAPEL PERILOUS.*
  A.A. PHILLIPS, 381:JUN73-189
HEWITT, D. THE APPROACH TO FICTION.
  G. CLIFFORD, 541(RES):NOV73-524
  T. ROGERS, 175:SPRING73-33
  G.B. TENNYSON, 445(NCF):JUN73-113
HEWITT, J. OUT OF MY TIME.
  R. GARFITT, 617(TLS):29AUG75-960
HEXTER, J.H. DOING HISTORY.
  L.B. CEBIK, 219(GAR):FALL73-427
HEXTER, J.H. THE HISTORY PRIMER.
  A. EZERGAILIS, 676(YR):WINTER74-
  296
HEXTER, J.H. THE VISION OF POLITICS
ON THE EVE OF THE REFORMATION.
  C. MORRIS, 111:30MAY74-163
VON HEYDEBRAND, R. EDUARD MÖRIKES
GEDICHTWERK.
  S. PRAWER, 402(MLR):OCT74-927
  O.G. REINHARDT, 67:MAY74-117
VON HEYDEBRAND, R. & K.G. JUST, EDS.
WISSENSCHAFT ALS DIALOG.
  H. ELEMA, 433:OCT73-420
HEYDENREICH, T. TADEL UND LOB DER
SEEFAHRT.*
  J.M. CONANT, 124:MAY73-495
HEYDON, P.N. & P. KELLEY - SEE
BROWNING, E.B.
HEYEN, W. NOISE IN THE TREES.
  J. PARISI, 491:JUL75-219
  M. WATERS, 398:WINTER75-284
HEYER, G. MY LORD JOHN.
  P-L. ADAMS, 61:DEC75-118
  R.M. FRANKLIN, 617(TLS):21NOV75-
  1379
HEYERDAHL, T. FATU-HIVA.*
  R.R. LINGEMAN, 441:29AUG75-25
  P. SNOW, 617(TLS):6JUN75-632
  R. TRUMBULL, 441:21SEP75-10
HEYM, S. THE QUEEN AGAINST DEFOE.*
  J. MELLORS, 362:18SEP75-386
  J. WILLETT, 617(TLS):4JUL75-732
HEYWOOD, C., ED. PERSPECTIVES ON
AFRICAN LITERATURE.
  B. SSENSALO, 2:WINTER74-79
HEZLET, A. THE ELECTRON & SEA
POWER.
  617(TLS):8AUG75-906
HIBBARD, G.R. - SEE SHAKESPEARE, W.

HIBBARD, H. CARLO MADERNO & ROMAN
ARCHITECTURE 1580-1630.*
  M.D. ROSS, 551(RENQ):SUMMER73-199
HIBBERD, J. A STRETCH OF THE IMAGI-
NATION.*
  A.A. PHILLIPS, 381:JUN73-189
HIBBERT, C. DAILY LIFE IN VICTORIAN
ENGLAND.
  442(NY):15DEC75-155
HIBBERT, C. THE DRAGON WAKES.
  E. LE FEVOUR, 318(JAOS):JAN-MAR73-
  89
HIBBERT, C. GEORGE IV, REGENT &
KING: 1811-1830.
  J. CLIVE, 231:DEC75-96
HIBBERT, C. THE HOUSE OF MEDICI.
(BRITISH TITLE: THE RISE & FALL OF
THE HOUSE OF MEDICI.)
  C.H. CLOUGH, 617(TLS):24JAN75-91
  A. WHITMAN, 441:22MAR75-29
HIBBERT, C. THE PERSONAL HISTORY OF
SAMUEL JOHNSON.*
  L. BASNEY, 651(WHR):WINTER74-79
  C. LAMONT, 541(RES):FEB73-92
HICK, J. GOD & THE UNIVERSE OF
FAITHS.*
  D. BASTOW, 518:MAY74-8
HICK, J., ED. TRUTH & DIALOGUE.
  A. KENNY, 617(TLS):7FEB75-145
HICKEY, K. THE LIGHT OF OTHER
DAYS.*
  H. KRAMER, 441:7DEC75-84
  T. TANNER, 364:APR/MAY74-118
HICKMAN, P. SILHOUETTES.
  F. PICKERING, 617(TLS):4JUL75-715
HICKS, G. GRANVILLE HICKS IN THE
NEW MASSES. (J.A. ROBBINS, ED)
  D. DILLON, 584(SWR):SUMMER74-332
HICKS, G.L. & G. MC NICOLL. TRADE &
GROWTH IN THE PHILIPPINES.
  M.E. ABEL, 293(JAST):FEB73-384
HICKS, J. THE CRISIS IN KEYNESIAN
ECONOMICS.
  H.G. JOHNSON, 617(TLS):7FEB75-139
HICKS, J.B. & K.G. MILLER. AUF
DEUTSCH BITTE.
  G.R. DIMLER, 399(MLJ):JAN-FEB74-70
HIDDLESTON, J.A. MALRAUX.
  CHENG LOK CHUA, 651(WHR):AUTUMN74-
  392
HIERNAUX, J. THE PEOPLE OF AFRICA.
  C.D. DARLINGTON, 617(TLS):17OCT75-
  1230
HIERSCHE, R. FERDINAND DE SAUSSURES
LANGUE-PAROLE-KONZEPTION UND SEIN
VERHÄLTNIS ZU DURKHEIM UND VON DER
GABELENTZ.
  E.F.K. KOERNER, 343:BAND17HEFT2-
  125
HIERSCHE, R. DIE SPRACH HOMERS IM
LICHTE NEUER FORSCHUNGEN.
  P. WATHELET, 343:BAND17HEFT2-208
HIGDON, H. THE CRIME OF THE CEN-
TURY.
  P-L. ADAMS, 61:NOV75-124
HIGGINS, A. THE BALCONY OF EUROPE.*
  H. MURPHY, 159(DM):AUTUMN72-117
HIGGINS, G.V. A CITY ON A HILL.
  P. ADAMS, 61:MAY75-103
  R. DAVIES, 617(TLS):8AUG75-902
  C. LEHMANN-HAUPT, 441:14MAR75-43
  C. LYDON, 441:30MAR75-4
HIGGINS, G.V. COGAN'S TRADE.*
  N. CALLENDAR, 441:27APR75-28

HIGGINS, G.V. THE FRIENDS OF RICH-
ARD NIXON.
M.H. FREEDMAN, 441:26OCT75-28
HIGGINS, J. THE EAGLE HAS LANDED.
T.J. BINYON, 617(TLS):19DEC75-1508
M. LEVIN, 441:17AUG75-23
HIGGINS, J. A PRAYER FOR THE
DYING.*
N. CALLENDAR, 441:30MAR75-24
HIGGINS, J.A. F. SCOTT FITZGERALD.
H.G. HEYMANN, 573(SSF):WINTER73-
114
HIGGS, E.S., ED. PALAEOECONOMY.
M. WALKER, 617(TLS):14MAR75-282
HIGHAM, C. THE FILMS OF ORSON
WELLES.
M. GOLDSTEIN, 295:APR74-1050
HIGHET, G. THE SPEECHES IN VERGIL'S
"AENEID."
D.O. ROBSON, 487:WINTER73-416
HIGHFILL, P.H., JR., K.A. BURNIM &
E.A. LANGHANS. A BIOGRAPHICAL DIC-
TIONARY OF ACTORS, ACTRESSES, MUSI-
CIANS, DANCERS, MANAGERS & OTHER
STAGE PERSONNEL IN LONDON, 1660-
1800.* (VOLS 1&2)
J.A. WESTRUP, 410(M&L):JUL74-340
HIGHSMITH, P. THE ANIMAL-LOVER'S
BOOK OF BEASTLY MURDER.
G. ANNAN, 617(TLS):11JUL75-784
M. LASKI, 362:20NOV75-684
HIGHTOWER, J. EAT YOUR HEART OUT.
F. CERRA, 441:29SEP75-35
HIGMAN, F.M. - SEE CALVIN, J.
HIGONNET, P.L-R. PONT-DE-MONTVERT.*
H. GODIN, 208(FS):OCT74-501
HIKMET, N. THE DAY BEFORE TOMMOROW.
A. CLUYSENAAR, 565:VOL14#1-70
HILDEBRANDT, R. NONSENSE-ASPEKT DER
ENGLISCHEN KINDERLITERATUR.
R. NOLL-WIEMANN, 430(NS):SEP73-511
R. WINKLER, 38:BAND91HEFT1-142
HILDER, G. DER SCHOLASTISCHE WORT-
SCHATZ BEI JEAN DE MEUN.*
B. FOSTER, 208(FS):OCT74-442
HILDICK, W. BRACKNELL'S LAW.
N. CALLENDAR, 441:6JUL75-14
HILEN, A. - SEE LONGFELLOW, H.W.
HILEY, M. FRANK SUTCLIFFE.*
H. KRAMER, 441:7DEC75-84
HILGER, M.I. TOGETHER WITH THE
AINU, A VANISHING PEOPLE.
E. NORBECK, 318(JAOS):APR-JUN73-
229
HILL, C. CHANGE & CONTINUITY IN
SEVENTEENTH CENTURY ENGLAND.
J.H. HEXTER, 617(TLS):24OCT75-1250
HILL, C. JACKDAW.
P.D. JAMES, 617(TLS):26SEP75-1079
HILL, C., ED. LESEN MIT GEWINN.
J. KOPPENSTEINER, 399(MLJ):SEP-
OCT73-297
HILL, D.R. - SEE AL-JAZARĪ, B.I.A.
HILL, F. VICTORIAN LINCOLN.
G.E. MINGAY, 617(TLS):14FEB75-170
HILL, H. MARK TWAIN.
J.S. TUCKEY, 27(AL):MAR74-116
T. WORTHAM, 445(NCF):MAR74-501
HILL, L.A. PREPOSITIONS & ADVERBIAL
PARTICLES.*
J. POSTHUMUS, 179(ES):OCT72-476
HILL, M.S. & J.B. ALLEN, EDS. MOR-
MONISM & AMERICAN CULTURE.
D. BITTON, 651(WHR):SUMMER74-290

HILL, P. THE OCCUPATIONS OF MIG-
RANTS IN GHANA.
R. LAWSON, 69:OCT73-358
HILL, P. RURAL HAUSA.
A.H.M. KIRK-GREENE, 315(JAL):VOL11
PT3-92
HILL, P.P. WILLIAM VANS MURRAY,
FEDERALIST DIPLOMAT.*
J. GODECHOT, 182:VOL26#20-759
HILL, R. AN APRIL SHROUD.
M. LASKI, 362:20NOV75-684
J. STRATFORD, 617(TLS):15AUG75-913
HILL, R.L. KING OF WHITE LADY.
N. CALLENDAR, 441:28DEC75-21
HILL, S. THE COLD COUNTRY, & OTHER
PLAYS FOR RADIO.
F. DILLON, 362:15MAY75-653
HILL, S. IN THE SPRINGTIME OF THE
YEAR.*
J. MELLORS, 364:JUN/JUL74-135
HILL, T.E. THE CONCEPT OF MEANING.*
R.W. NEWELL, 479(PHQ):OCT73-363
HILL, W.S. RICHARD HOOKER.
J. FEATHER, 447(N&Q):MAY73-189
HILL, W.S., ED. STUDIES IN RICHARD
HOOKER.
H.C. COLE, 568(SCN):SPRING-SUMMER
74-19
G.W. WILLIAMS, 579(SAQ):SPRING74-
280
HILLARY, E. NOTHING VENTURE, NOTH-
ING WIN.
D. THOMAS, 362:10APR75-484
C.S. WREN, 441:17AUG75-6
HILLEN, H.J. - SEE LIVY
HILLERMAN, T. THE GREAT TAOS BANK
ROBBERY & OTHER INDIAN COUNTRY
AFFAIRS.
W. GARD, 584(SWR):SPRING74-V
HILLGARTH, J.N. RAMON LULL & LULL-
ISM IN FOURTEENTH CENTURY FRANCE.
H.F., 543:MAR73-538
C.H. LOHR, 589:JAN74-121
M. PEREIRA, 548(RCSF):APR-JUN73-
207
M. REEVES, 382(MAE):1974/2-188
HILLIER, B. AUSTERITY/BINGE.
R. BLYTHE, 362:10JUL75-59
P. FRENCH, 617(TLS):4JUL75-712
HILLIER, J., COMP. THE HARARI COL-
LECTION OF JAPANESE PAINTINGS &
DRAWINGS. (VOLS 1&2)
W. WATSON, 90:APR73-256
HILLMAN, B. ROLY POLY.
D.M. DAY, 157:WINTER73-89
HILLMANN, H. BILDLICHKEIT DER DEUT-
SCHEN ROMANTIK.
G. KLUGE, 680(ZDP):BAND92HEFT2-286
HILLS, D. THE WHITE PUMPKIN.
M. BELL, 362:4DEC75-752
HILSMAN, R. THE CROUCHING FUTURE.
442(NY):3FEB75-95
HILTON, A.M. LOGIC, COMPUTING MACH-
INES, & AUTOMATION.
R.F. BARNES, JR., 316:JUN73-341
HILTON, J.B. NO BIRDS SANG.
T.J. BINYON, 617(TLS):19DEC75-1508
HILTON, R. LA AMÉRICA LATINA DE
AYER Y DE HOY.
D.F. BROWN, 399(MLJ):MAR73-153
HILTON, R. - SEE DANIELS, J.
HILTON, T. THE PRE-RAPHAELITES.*
K. ROBERTS, 90:FEB73-126

HIMELICK, R. ERASMUS & THE SEAMLESS
COAT OF JESUS.
  E.J. DEVEREUX, 551(RENQ):WINTER73-
  461
HIMES, C. BLACK ON BLACK.*
  R. DAVIES, 617(TLS):25APR75-445
  G.E. KENT, 114(CHIR):VOL25#3-73
HIMLY, F.J. ATLAS DES VILLES MÉDI-
ÉVALES D'ALSACE.
  J.C. RUSSELL, 589:JAN74-124
HIMMELFARB, G. ON LIBERTY & LIBER-
ALISM.*
  L. WIESELTIER, 31(ASCH):SPRING75-
  336
HIMMELHEBER, G. BIEDERMEIER FUR-
NITURE.*
  R. REIF, 441:29DEC75-29
HIMMELMANN, N. ARCHÄOLOGISCHES ZUM
PROBLEM DER GRIECHISCHEN SKLAVEREI.
  O. MURRAY, 123:MAR74-153
HINCKFUSS, I. THE EXISTENCE OF
SPACE & TIME.
  D.H. MELLOR, 617(TLS):5SEP75-993
HINCKLE, W., 3D. IF YOU HAVE A
LEMON, MAKE LEMONADE.*
  L. CHARLTON, 441:15MAR75-25
HIND, R.J. HENRY LABOUCHERE & THE
EMPIRE, 1880-1905.
  M. ROSE, 637(VS):MAR74-319
HINDE, T. OUR FATHER.
  R. DAVIES, 617(TLS):100CT75-1173
  J. MELLORS, 362:90CT75-485
HINDLE, G.B. PROVISION FOR THE
RELIEF OF THE POOR IN MANCHESTER
1754-1826.
  617(TLS):100CT75-1215
HINDLEY, J.R., B. LERCHER & J.P.
SELDIN. INTRODUCTION TO COMBINA-
TORY LOGIC.
  H. BARENDREGT, 316:SEP73-518
HINDUS, M., ED. WALT WHITMAN: THE
CRITICAL HERITAGE.
  A. EASSON, 447(N&Q):JUL73-273
HINE, D. THE HOMERIC HYMNS & THE
BATTLE OF THE FROGS & THE MICE.*
  T.N. WINTER, 502(PRS):SUMMER73-170
HINE, D. RESIDENT ALIEN.
  R. PADEL, 617(TLS):15AUG75-916
HINES, T.S. BURNHAM OF CHICAGO.*
  R. BANHAM, 617(TLS):13JUN75-652
HINGLEY, R. - SEE CHEKHOV, A.
HINKLEY, E. MAZZINI.
  A.W. SALOMONE, 275(IQ):SPRING74-97
HINMAN, C. - SEE SHAKESPEARE, W.
HINMAN, C. & F. BOWERS. TWO LEC-
TURES ON EDITING.
  R. KNOWLES, 570(SQ):SPRING73-242
HINSON, M. GUIDE TO THE PIANIST'S
REPERTOIRE.* (I. FREUNDLICH, ED)
  H. FERGUSON, 410(M&L):JAN74-107
HINTIKKA, J. LOGIC, LANGUAGE-GAMES
& INFORMATION.*
  R. BLANCHÉ, 542:OCT-DEC73-477
HINTIKKA, J. TIME & NECESSITY.*
  D.D.C. BRAINE, 518:OCT74-14
HINTON, H.C. THE BEAR AT THE GATE.
  R.L. WALKER, 550(RUSR):APR73-189
VON HINÜBER, O. - SEE LÜDERS, H.
HINZ, H. - SEE "GERMANIA ROMANA, III"
HIONIDES, H. & J. GUNDERSON - SEE
KALOKYRIS, K.

HIONIDES, N.P. SYMBOLE EIS TEN
STEMMATIKEN KAI TEN TAXINOMESIN
TON CHEIROGRAPHON TOY ARISTOPHAN-
OYS.
  K.J. DOVER, 123:NOV74-290
HIPPIUS, Z.N. INTELLECT & IDEAS IN
ACTION. (T. PACHMUSS, ED)
  A. LEVIN, 104:WINTER74-589
HIPPIUS, Z.N. NOVYYE LYUDI. CHOR-
TOVA KUKLA.
  I. KIRILLOVA, 575(SEER):APR74-316
HIPPIUS, Z.N. SELECTED WORKS OF
ZINAIDA HIPPIUS.* (T. PACHMUSS,
ED & TRANS)
  J. BROOKS, 550(RUSR):JUL73-332
  L. KOEHLER, 104:WINTER73-563
  V.D. MIHAILOVICH, 573(SSF):FALL73-
  433
HIPPIUS, Z.N. STIXOTVORENIJA I
POÉMY.* (T. PACHMUSS, ED)
  O. MATICH, 574(SEEJ):SPRING73-84
HIPPOCRATES. HIPPOCRATE. (VOL 6,
PT 2) (R. JOLY, ED & TRANS)
  E.B. LEVINE, 124:FEB74-242
HIRSCH, D.H. REALITY & IDEA IN THE
EARLY AMERICAN NOVEL.
  J.T. FLANAGAN, 179(ES):DEC73-610
HIRSCH, F. & D. GORDON. NEWSPAPER
MONEY.
  W. HALEY, 617(TLS):8AUG75-895
HIRSCH, W. PLATONS WEG ZUM MYTHOS.*
  N. GULLEY, 123:NOV74-290
  T.M. ROBINSON, 124:OCT72-112
HIRSCHI, A. & J. PETIT - SEE BARBEY
D'AUREVILLY, J.
HIRSCHMEIER, J. & T. YUI. THE DEV-
ELOPMENT OF JAPANESE BUSINESS 1600-
1973.
  E.J. HOBSBAWM, 453:17JUL75-27
HIRST, P.H. KNOWLEDGE & THE CURRIC-
ULUM.
  M. WARNOCK, 617(TLS):28MAR75-343
HIRST, P.Q. DURKHEIM, BERNARD &
EPISTEMOLOGY.
  C. MADGE, 617(TLS):30MAY75-593
"THE HISTORY OF THE SAILING SHIP."
  S. SMITH, 441:7DEC75-95
HITCHMAN, J. SUCH A STRANGE LADY.
  P-L. ADAMS, 61:DEC75-118
  G. ANNAN, 362:30JAN75-157
  L. BERNIKOW, 441:9NOV75-51
  P. GREEN, 617(TLS):28FEB75-223
HITOSHI, A., S. KAZUKO & T. SHUNTARO
- SEE UNDER ANZAI HITOSHI, SHIRAI-
SHI KAZUKO & TANIKAWA SHUNTARO
HJELMSLEV, L. LANGUAGE.
  B. CARSTENSEN, 430(NS):JAN73-49
HO, L. - SEE UNDER LI HO
HO TING-JUI. A COMPARATIVE STUDY OF
MYTHS & LEGENDS OF FORMOSAN ABORIG-
INES.
  A. YEN, 318(JAOS):OCT-DEC73-646
HOA, N-D. VIETNAMESE-ENGLISH STU-
DENT DICTIONARY.
  K. GREGERSON, 361:DEC73-358
HOAD, M.J. - SEE WILLIS, A.J.
HOAGLAND, J. SOUTH AFRICA.
  T.M. SHAW, 150(DR):SPRING73-183
HOBAN, R. TURTLE DIARY.
  N. HEPBURN, 362:27MAR75-421
  J. MILLER, 617(TLS):21MAR75-293
HOBBES, T. LE CORPS POLITIQUE. (S.
SORBIÈRE, TRANS; L. ROUX, ED)
  C. EYER, 568(SCN):FALL74-61

HOBBES, T. DE HOMINE (TRAITÉ DE
L'HOMME). (P-M. MAURIN, ED & TRANS)
H.W.S., 319:OCT75-547
HOBBES, T. LÉVIATHAN.* (F. TRI-
CAUD, ED & TRANS)
H. LABOUCHEIX, 189(EA):JAN-MAR73-
102
HOBHOUSE, H. THOMAS CUBITT, MASTER
BUILDER.*
G.L. HERSEY, 637(VS):SEP73-120
P.F. NORTON, 576:MAR73-75
HOBHOUSE, H. LOST LONDON.
G.L. HERSEY, 637(VS):SEP73-120
505:MAY73-134
VAN HOBOKEN, A. JOSEPH HAYDN. (VOL
2)
A. TYSON, 415:AUG74-657
HOBSBAUM, P. A THEORY OF COMMUNICA-
TION.*
P. LE BRUN, 541(RES):FEB73-111
H. PESCHMANN, 175:SUMMER72-73
HOBSBAWM, E.J. REVOLUTIONARIES.
P. DEMETZ, 676(YR):WINTER74-291
HOBSON, F.C., JR. SERPENT IN EDEN.
H. BEAVER, 617(TLS):13JUN75-679
G.C., 569(SR):SUMMER74-LXII
C. WILSON, 396(MODA):FALL74-423
639(VQR):AUTUMN74-CXXII
HOBSON, G.D. LES RELIURES À LA FAN-
FARE. (2ND ED) (A.R.A. HOBSON, ED)
B.L.O. RICHTER, 207(FR):FEB73-636
HOBSON, L.Z. CONSENTING ADULT.
J. BARNES, 617(TLS):5SEP75-998
M. DUBERMAN, 441:6JUL75-5
HOBSON, P. VENUS & HER PREY.
V. GLENDINNING, 617(TLS):24OCT75-
1255
HOCHMAN, B. ANOTHER EGO.
A.C. HEATH, 295:FEB74-698
HOCKETT, C.F. CURSO DE LINGÜÍSTICA
MODERNA. (E. GREGORES & J.A. SUÁR-
EZ, EDS & TRANS)
R.A. HALL, JR., 215(GL):VOL13#1-75
HOCKETT, C.F. - SEE BLOOMFIELD, L.
HOCKING, M. THE BRIGHT DAY.
N. HEPBURN, 362:3JUL75-30
C. PETERS, 617(TLS):4JUL75-732
HOCKS, R.A. HENRY JAMES & PRAGMA-
TISTIC THOUGHT.
J. SEARLE, 617(TLS):5SEP75-990
HODDINOTT, R.F. BULGARIA IN ANTI-
QUITY.
R. BROWNING, 617(TLS):15AUG75-918
HODGE, E.C. LITTLE HODGE. (MAR-
QUESS OF ANGLESEY, ED)
B.D. GOOCH, 637(VS):DEC73-217
HODGE, J.A. ONLY A NOVEL.*
J.E.J., 191(ELN):SEP73(SUPP)-30
HODGES, C.W. SHAKESPEARE'S SECOND
GLOBE.*
639(VQR):SPRING74-LX
HODGSON, J. & M. BANHAM - SEE "DRAMA
IN EDUCATION"
HODGSON, M.G.S. THE VENTURE OF
ISLAM.
C. GEERTZ, 453:11DEC75-18
W.M. WATT, 617(TLS):5DEC75-1469
442(NY):2JUN75-110
HODIN, J.P. EMILIO GRECO: SCULPTURE
& DRAWINGS.
D. HALL, 39:JAN73-110
HODIN, J.P. MODERN ART & THE MODERN
MIND.
S. BAYLEY, 89(BJA):SPRING73-196

HODIN, J.P. EDVARD MUNCH.
R. WOODFIELD, 89(BJA):WINTER73-89
HODNETT, E. MARCUS GHEERAERTS THE
ELDER.
E. WATERHOUSE, 54:SEP73-458
HODNETT, G. & P.J. POTICHNYJ. THE
UKRAINE & THE CZECHOSLOVAK CRISIS.
I. MYHUL, 104:SPRING74-167
HODSON, J.H. THE ADMINISTRATION OF
ARCHIVES.
F.B. EVANS, 14:OCT73-543
F. RANGER, 325:APR73-620
"HODSON'S BOOKSELLERS, PUBLISHERS &
STATIONERS DIRECTORY, 1855."
D. CHAMBERS, 503:AUTUMN72-170
HOEFER, H. TYPOLOGIE IM MITTELALTER.
D.H. GREEN, 220(GL&L):APR74-256
F.P. PICKERING, 402(MLR):APR74-450
HOEKSTRA, A. THE SUB-EPIC STAGE OF
THE FORMULAIC TRADITION.
F.M. COMBELLACK, 122:JAN73-71
HOENIG, G. REAPER.
R. BRAGONIER, JR., 441:7SEP75-37
HOERDER, D. SOCIETY & GOVERNMENT
1760-1780.
A. KULIKOFF, 656(WMQ):JUL74-513
HOERNLE, A.F.R., ED. MANUSCRIPT
REMAINS OF BUDDHIST LITERATURE
FOUND IN EASTERN TURKESTAN.
W. THOMAS, 260(IF):BAND78-249
HOERSTER, N. UTILITARISTISCHE ETHIK
UND VERALLGEMEINERUNG.
G.J. HUGHES, 393(MIND):APR73-304
HOESCH, F. DER GESTUS DES ZEIGENS.
G. BENDA, 406:SPRING74-104
HOEST, S. REDEN UND BRIEFE.* (F.
BARON, ED & TRANS)
M.L. BAEUMER, 406:SUMMER74-214
F. RÄDLE, 52:BAND8HEFT3-328
E.G. SCHWIEBERT, 551(RENQ):AUTUMN
73-312
VOM HOFE, G. DIE ROMANTIKKRITIK
SÖREN KIERKEGAARDS.
W. HOF, 224(GRM):BAND23HEFT4-493
VON HOFE, H. KULTUR UND ALLTAG.
J.J. MULLIGAN, 399(MLJ):MAR74-146
HOFFENBERG, J. THE DESPERATE AD-
VERSARIES.
M. LEVIN, 441:14DEC75-32
HOFFMAN, A. UNWANTED MEXICAN AMERI-
CANS IN THE GREAT DEPRESSION.
W. GARD, 584(SWR):SPRING74-V
HOFFMAN, A. & R. SNYDER. KITSILANO
YOU.
D. HARRON, 99:DEC75/JAN76-57
HOFFMAN, D. THE CENTER OF ATTEN-
TION.*
R. HOWARD, 491:MAR75-354
R. LATTIMORE, 249(HUDR):AUTUMN74-
461
M.K. SPEARS, 598(SOR):SUMMER75-695
HOFFMAN, D. POE POE POE POE POE POE
POE POE.*
R. ASSELINEAU, 189(EA):OCT-DEC73-
499
H. GOLEMBA, 141:FALL72-407
C. KRETZOI, 598(SOR):SUMMER75-702
J. SALZBERG, 191(ELN):DEC73-143
HOFFMAN, L-F. LA PRATIQUE DU FRAN-
ÇAIS PARLÉ.
A. CAPRIO, 399(MLJ):NOV74-356
HOFFMAN, M. CROCKERY COOKERY.
A. NELSON, 441:6JUL75-4

HOFFMAN, R.J.S. THE MARQUIS.
H. BUTTERFIELD, 617(TLS):10OCT75-
1193
P.D.G. THOMAS, 656(WMQ):JUL74-498
HOFFMANN, D. THE ARCHITECTURE OF
JOHN WELLBORN ROOT.
R. CHAFEE, 127:SUMMER74-376
HOFFMANN, E.T.A. LEBENS-ANSICHTEN
DES KATERS MURR NEBST FRAGMENTAR-
ISCHER BIOGRAPHIE DES KAPELLMEIS-
TERS JOHANNES KREISLER IN ZUFÄLLI-
GEN MAKULATURBLÄTTERN. (H.
STEINECKE, ED)
S.P.S., 191(ELN):SEP73(SUPP)-144
HOFFMANN, E.T.A. THREE MÄRCHEN OF
E.T.A. HOFFMANN. (C.E. PASSAGE,
TRANS)
S.P.S., 191(ELN):SEP73(SUPP)-143
HOFFMANN, H., WITH A.E. RAUBITSCHEK.
EARLY CRETAN ARMORERS.
A.M. SNODGRASS, 303:VOL93-263
HOFFMANN, H-C., W. KRAUSE & W. KIT-
LITSCHKA. DAS WIENER OPERNHAUS.
J. MAASS, 576:DEC73-339
HOFFMANN, H.G. & F. SCHMIDT. ENG-
LISH GRAMMAR EXERCISES.
P.H. FRIES, 399(MLJ):JAN-FEB74-82
HOFFMANN, K. DER INJUNKTIV IM VEDA.*
J. HAUDRY, 260(IF):BAND77HEFT2/3-
302
HOFFMANN, M. MEIN WEG MIT MELCHIOR
LECHTER.
D. JOST, 182:VOL26#10-365
HOFFMANN-BECKING, G. NORMAUFBAU UND
METHODE.
E.J. COHN, 182:VOL26#17/18-583
HOFFMEISTER, G., ED. EUROPÄISCHE
TRADITION UND DEUTSCHER LITERATUR-
BAROCK.
E. LUNDING, 301(JEGP):OCT74-586
HOFFMEISTER, G. DIE SPANISCHE DIANA
IN DEUTSCHLAND.
G. DÜNNHAUPT, 406:FALL74-298
HÖFLER, O. HOMUNCULUS - EINE SATIRE
AUF A.W. SCHLEGEL.*
K. MOMMSEN, 400(MLN):OCT73-1049
HOFMAN, H.F. TURKISH LITERATURE.
(SECTION 3, PT 1)
E. BIRNBAUM, 318(JAOS):APR-JUN73-
239
HOFMANN, D., WITH W. LANGE & K. VON
SEE - SEE KUHN, H.
HOFMANN, D., WITH W. SANDERS, EDS.
GEDENKSCHRIFT FÜR WILLIAM FOERSTE.
S.E. BELLAMY, 221(GQ):SEP73-177
HOFMANN, W. GUSTAV KLIMT.*
C.E. SCHORSKE, 453:11DEC75-39
VON HOFMANNSTHAL, H. & R. BEER-
HOFMANN. BRIEFWECHSEL. (E. WEBER,
ED)
E.E. THEOBALD, 406:SPRING74-74
VON HOFMANNSTHAL, H. & R. STRAUSS.
DER ROSENKAVALIER. (W. SCHUH, ED)
W.H. PERL, 221(GQ):JAN73-119
VON HOFMANNSTHAL, H. & A. WILDGANS.
BRIEFWECHSEL.* (N. ALTENHOFER, ED)
M.E. GILBERT, 402(MLR):JAN74-229
P. GOFF, 133:1973/3-286
HOFSTADTER, A. AGONY & EPITAPH.*
G. STAHL, 290(JAAC):SUMMER74-561
HOFSTADTER, R. AMERICA AT 1750.*
W.S. ROBINSON, 481(PQ):JUL73-353
HOGAN, R. - SEE FRATTI, M.

HOGARTH, W. ENGRAVINGS BY HOGARTH.
(S. SHESGREEN, ED)
566:SPRING74-100
HOGE, J.O. - SEE TENNYSON, E.
HOGE, J.O. & C. OLNEY - SEE NORTON,
C.
HOGG, A.H.A. HILL-FORTS OF BRITAIN.
617(TLS):21NOV75-1397
HOGG, I. & J. WEEKS. MILITARY
SMALL ARMS OF THE TWENTIETH CENTURY.
617(TLS):31JAN75-121
HOGG, I.V. A HISTORY OF ARTILLERY.
617(TLS):26DEC75-1543
HOGG, J. THE THREE PERILS OF MAN.
(D. GIFFORD, ED)
T. DALE, 588:APR74-253
HOGG, R. STANDING BACK.
D. BARBOUR, 102(CANL):WINTER74-117
G. MC WHIRTER, 376:APR73-237
HOGGART, R. ON CULTURE & COMMUNICA-
TION.
A.B. KERNAN, 473(PR):2/1974-306
HÖGSTRAND, O. THE DEBT.
N. CALLENDAR, 441:9FEB75-16
HOHENBERG, J. FREE PRESS, FREE
PEOPLE.
P. MANGELSDORF, 50(ARQ):WINTER73-
367
HOHENBERG, J. THE PULITZER PRIZES.*
J. EPSTEIN, 617(TLS):13JUN75-650
HOHENDAHL, P.U., ED. BENN - WIRKUNG
WIDER WILLEN.*
S. PRAWER, 220(GL&L):JUL74-326
HOHENDAHL, P.U. LITERATURKRITIK UND
ÖFFENTLICHKEIT.
P. LABANYI, 617(TLS):25JUL75-855
HOHL-SCHROETER, C. EIN FREMDER ZU
HAUSE.
H. WEBER, 182:VOL26#11/12-413
DE HOJEDA, D. LA CRISTIADA. (F.
PIERCE, ED)
R.M. PRICE, 86(BHS):APR73-173
HOLBROOK, C.A. THE ETHICS OF JONA-
THAN EDWARDS.
R.A. DELATTRE, 432(NEQ):MAR74-155
HOLBROOK, D. GUSTAV MAHLER & THE
COURAGE TO BE.
S. WALSH, 362:27NOV75-730
HOLBROOK, D. DYLAN THOMAS.*
J. BERNARD, 189(EA):APR-JUN73-240
B. FELDMAN, 597(SN):VOL45#2-454
H. PESCHMANN, 175:SUMMER73-83
HOLDEN, A. THE ST. ALBANS POISONER.
C. RYCROFT, 617(TLS):26SEP75-1104
HOLDEN, D. GREECE WITHOUT COLUMNS.*
D.M. NICOL, 123:MAR74-163
HOLDEN, M. THE COUNTRY OVER.
A. MACLEAN, 617(TLS):1AUG75-866
A. STEVENSON, 362:30OCT75-571
HOLDEN, U. ENDLESS RACE.
J. MILLER, 617(TLS):8AUG75-902
HOLLAND, N. WATCHER IN THE SHADOW.
D.M. DAY, 157:WINTER73-89
HOLLAND, N.N. 5 READERS READING.
A. STORR, 617(TLS):18JUL75-801
HOLLAND, N.N. POEMS IN PERSONS.
L.W. HYMAN, 290(JAAC):WINTER74-226
HOLLAND, S. THE SOCIALIST CHALLENGE.
D. MARQUAND, 617(TLS):26SEP75-
1095
P. OPPENHEIMER, 362:31JUL75-155
D. TAVERNE, 362:24JUL75-122

HOLTON, M. CYLINDER OF VISION.*
  J.C. ROWE, 50(ARQ):AUTUMN73-278
HOLWAY, J. VOICES FROM THE GREAT
  BLACK BASEBALL LEAGUES.
  B.J. PHILLIPS, 441:9NOV75-52
HOLYFIELD, F. THE SOUTHERN MOUN-
  TAINS.
  639(VQR):SPRING74-LXII
HOLZNER, B. REALITY CONSTRUCTION IN
  SOCIETY.
  J.O. WISDOM, 488:SEP73-257
HOMANN, H. STUDIEN ZUR EMBLEMATIK
  DES 16. JAHRHUNDERTS.*
  P.M. DALY, 301(JEGP):JAN74-78
  J.M. STEADMAN, 131(CL):FALL74-364
HOME, J. DOUGLAS. (G.D. PARKER,
  ED)
  A. RENDLE, 157:SPRING73-82
"HOMENAJE A ANTONIO TOVAR OFRECIDO
  POR SUS DISCÍPULOS, COLEGAS Y
  AMIGOS."
  F. VON LOCHNER-HÜTTENBACH, 343:
    BAND17HEFT2-150
HOMEYER, H. HROTSVITHAE OPERA.
  P. STOTZ, 182:VOL26#23/24-881
HOMO, L. ROME IMPÉRIALE ET L'URBAN-
  ISME DANS L'ANTIQUITÉ. (2ND ED)
  M.A.R. COLLEDGE, 123:NOV74-274
HONDERICH, T., ED. ESSAYS ON FREE-
  DOM OF ACTION.
  R.L. FRANKLIN, 63:MAY74-76
HONE, J. THE DANCING WAITERS.
  E.S. TURNER, 362:14AUG75-220
HONE, J. THE SIXTH DIRECTORATE.
  A. BROYARD, 441:26AUG75-29
  M. LASKI, 362:20NOV75-684
  D. WILSON, 617(TLS):26SEP75-1078
HONEY, J. A TOUCH OF TABBY.
  D.M. DAY, 157:SPRING73-84
HONEYBOURNE, M.B., ED. LONDON
  TOPOGRAPHICAL RECORD.
  617(TLS):17JAN75-63
HONIG, D. BASEBALL WHEN THE GRASS
  WAS REAL.
  C. LEHMANN-HAUPT, 441:24JUL75-33
HONIG, E. CALDERÓN & THE SEIZURES
  OF HONOR.*
  C.A. JONES, 402(MLR):JUL74-679
HONIG, E. FOUR SPRINGS.*
  J.P. WHITE, 50(ARQ):SUMMER73-191
HÖNNIGHAUSEN, L. PRÄRAPHAELITEN UND
  FIN DE SIÈCLE.
  H-W. LUDWIG, 38:BAND91HEFT4-550
HONOUR, H. THE NEW GOLDEN LAND.
  A. BROYARD, 441:16DEC75-43
HOOD, G. A HISTORY OF MUSIC IN NEW
  ENGLAND.
  M. PETERSON, 470:JAN73-33
HOOD, H. THE GOVERNOR'S BRIDGE IS
  CLOSED.*
  M. WOLFE, 102(CANL):AUTUMN74-102
HOOD, H. YOU CAN'T GET THERE FROM
  HERE.*
  R. LEITOLD, 150(DR):SPRING73-169
  P.A. MORLEY, 529(QQ):SPRING73-138
  R. SMITH, 102(CANL):AUTUMN73-100
HOOD, R., ED. CRIME, CRIMINOLOGY &
  PUBLIC POLICY.
  R. CROSS, 617(TLS):21FEB75-182
HOOD, R. TO THE ARCTIC BY CANOE,
  1819-1821. (C.S. HOUSTON, ED)
  R. HALL, 99:JUN75-38
  A. STEPHENSON, 617(TLS):21FEB75-
    202

HOOD, S. THE MINOANS.*
  K. BRANIGAN, 303:VOL93-262
  T.W. JACOBSEN, 124:OCT72-117
HOOD, T. THE LETTERS OF THOMAS
  HOOD. (P.F. MORGAN, ED)
  A.J. HARTLEY, 150(DR):WINTER73/74-
    786
VAN HOOFF, A.J.L. PAX ROMANA.
  S.I. OOST, 122:APR73-155
HOOK, S., ED. LANGUAGE & PHILOSOPHY.
  V. MIHAILESCU-URECHIA, 353:1SEP73-
    99
HOOKER, M.B., ED. READINGS IN MALAY
  ADAT LAWS.
  R. MC KINLEY, 293(JAST):NOV72-208
HOOPES, D.F. THE AMERICAN IMPRES-
  SIONISTS.*
  D. FLOWER, 432(NEQ):DEC73-634
HOOPES, T. THE DEVIL & JOHN FOSTER
  DULLES.*
  N.A. GRAEBNER, 639(VQR):SPRING74-
    295
  F. MORLEY, 396(MODA):SUMMER74-332
  D. YERGIN, 676(YR):SUMMER74-605
HOPE, A.D. DUNCIAD MINOR.*
  J.M. PURCELL, 134(CP):SPRING73-74
HOPE, C. CAPE DRIVES.*
  R. GARFITT, 364:OCT/NOV74-119
HOPE, J. A RIVER FOR THE LIVING.
  E. ABBEY, 441:12OCT75-24
HOPE, T.E. LEXICAL BORROWING IN
  THE ROMANCE LANGUAGES.*
  N.L. CORBETT, 405(MP):AUG73-66
  R.J. DI PIETRO, 361:SEP73-121
HOPE-BROWN, M. MUSIC WITH EVERY-
  THING.
  F. DAWES, 415:MAR74-221
HOPKINS, G.M. THE POEMS OF GERARD
  MANLEY HOPKINS. (4TH ED) (W.H.
  GARDNER & N.H. MAC KENZIE, EDS)
  G.A.M. JANSSENS, 179(ES):DEC72-569
HOPKINS, J. A COMPANION TO THE
  STUDY OF ST. ANSELM.
  D.P. HENRY, 482(PHR):OCT74-547
  J. LECLERCQ, 382(MAE):1974/3-270
  B. WARD, 589:OCT74-742
HOPKINS, J. & L. RIMPOCHE, WITH A.
  KLEIN - SEE NÄGÄRJUNA & THE SEVENTH
  DALAI LAMA
HOPKINSON, C. A BIBLIOGRAPHY OF THE
  WORKS OF GIUSEPPE VERDI, 1813-1901.
  (VOL 1)
  J. BUDDEN, 410(M&L):JUL74-345
  A. PORTER, 415:APR74-305
HOPPER, R.J. THE ACROPOLIS.
  B.A. SPARKES, 303:VOL93-267
"HORA DE ESPAÑA." (NO. 23)
  A. TERRY, 617(TLS):9MAY75-519
HORAS, P.A. JÓVENES DESVIADOS Y
  DELINCUENTES.
  A. RODRÍGUEZ KAUTH, 37:APR73-39
HORECKÝ, J., P. SGALL & M. TĚŠITEL-
  OVÁ, EDS. PRAGUE STUDIES IN MATHE-
  MATICAL LINGUISTICS. (VOL 4)
  B. BRAINERD, 104:WINTER74-583
HORGAN, P. APPROACHES TO WRITING.
  639(VQR):WINTER74-XXVII
HORGAN, P. LAMY OF SANTA FE.
  P-L. ADAMS, 61:OCT75-111
  M. ROGIN, 441:5OCT75-42

HORKHEIMER, M. NOTIZEN 1950 BIS
1969 UND DÄMMERUNG: NOTIZEN IN
DEUTSCHLAND. (W. BREDE, ED) AUS
DER PUBERTÄT. (A. SCHMIDT, ED)
M. JAY, 617(TLS):4JUL75-722
HÖRMANN, H. PSYCHOLINGUISTICS.*
W. BELLIN, 297(JL):FEB73-192
M-L. MOREAU, 556(RLV):1973/5-476
S.R. ROCHESTER, 320(CJL):SPRING74-
98
HÖRMANN, H. PSYCHOLOGIE DER SPRACHE.
W. ABRAHAM, 343:BAND16HEFT2-215
HORN, D.D. SING TO ME OF HEAVEN.
W.K. MC NEIL, 292(JAF):JAN-MAR73-
73
HORN, M., ED. THE DIRTY THIRTIES.
W.D. YOUNG, 529(QQ):SPRING73-115
HORN, P. THE RISE & FALL OF THE
VICTORIAN SERVANT.
B. HARRISON, 617(TLS):28NOV75-1404
HORN, P. THE VICTORIAN COUNTRY
CHILD.
P. HOLLIS, 617(TLS):14FEB75-170
HORNBACK, B.G. THE METAPHOR OF
CHANCE.*
P.J. CASAGRANDE, 141:SUMMER72-305
HORNBACK, B.G. "NOAH'S ARKITEC-
TURE."*
B.H., 155:MAY73-129
R.D. MC MASTER, 445(NCF):JUN73-107
HORNEY, A.W. - SEE MANN, T.
HORNSEY, R. GOING IN.
D. BARBOUR, 529(QQ):SPRING73-141
HORNUNG, E. DER EINE UND DIE VIEL-
EN.
D. MUELLER, 318(JAOS):JUL-SEP73-
400
HORNUNG, E.W. RAFFLES: THE AMATEUR
CRACKSMAN. RAFFLES: THE BLACK MASK.
P. KEATING, 617(TLS):20JUN75-692
HOROVITZ, J. LAW & LOGIC.
L.C. BECKER, 185:OCT73-89
A. MERCIER, 182:VOL26#5/6-135
HORRY, R.N. PAUL CLAUDEL & SAINT-
JOHN PERSE.*
L. AVILA, 188(ECR):SPRING73-91
R. LITTLE, 208(FS):JAN74-102
Y. SCALZITTI, 405(MP):NOV73-235
H.M. WATSON, 399(MLJ):NOV73-363
TER HORST, J.F. GERALD FORD & THE
FUTURE OF THE PRESIDENCY.*
G. WILLS, 453:16OCT75-18
HORTON, L. SAMUEL BELL MAXEY.
W. GARD, 584(SWR):SUMMER74-V
HORTSCHANSKY, K. PARODIE UND ENT-
LEHNUNG IM SCHAFFEN CHRISTOPH WIL-
LIBALD GLUCKS.
F. STERNFELD, 410(M&L):OCT74-491
HORVAT, B. BUSINESS CYCLES IN
YUGOSLAVIA.*
L.M. KOWAL, 104:WINTER74-616
HORVATH, M.K., COMP. A DOUKHOBOR
BIBLIOGRAPHY.
C. CANT, 575(SEER):JAN74-154
HORWARD, D.D. THE FRENCH REVOLUTION
& NAPOLEON COLLECTION AT FLORIDA
STATE UNIVERSITY.
J.A. DABBS, 446:SPRING-SUMMER74-
183
HORWITZ, J. NATURAL ENEMIES.
A. BROYARD, 441:3JUN75-37
J. MILLER, 617(TLS):24OCT75-1255
R. SOKOLOV, 441:14SEP75-41
442(NY):23JUN75-107

HORWOOD, H. WHITE ESKIMO.
H. ROSENGARTEN, 102(CANL):AUTUMN
73-92
HOSFORD, R.E. & C.S. MOSS, EDS. THE
CRUMBLING WALLS.
G. TRASLER, 617(TLS):26SEP75-1091
HOSKING, G.A. THE RUSSIAN CONSTITU-
TIONAL EXPERIMENT.
M. SZEFTEL, 575(SEER):APR74-296
HOSKINS, J.W. EARLY & RARE POLONICA
OF THE 15TH-17TH CENTURIES IN
AMERICAN LIBRARIES.
L. KUKULSKI, 497(POLR):VOL18#3-90
J.J. MACIUSZKO, 574(SEEJ):FALL73-
347
HÖSLE, J. PIETRO ARETINOS WERK.
H.W. WITTSCHIER, 72:BAND211HEFT1/3-
216
HÖSLE, J., ED. TEXTE ZUM ANTIPET-
RARKISMUS.
G. COSTA, 545(RPH):NOV73-256
HOSTETLER, J.A. HUTTERITE SOCIETY.
R.M. KANTER, 441:23MAR75-14
HOSTLER, J. LEIBNIZ'S MORAL PHILOS-
OPHY.
G.H.R. PARKINSON, 617(TLS):30MAY
75-594
HOSTOWIEC, P. - SEE UNDER STEMPOW-
SKI, J.
HOTOPF, W.H.N. LANGUAGE, THOUGHT &
COMPREHENSION.
E.B. GREENWOOD, 206:NOV73-607
HOUGAN, J. DECADENCE.
P. HAMILL, 441:30NOV75-32
HOUGH, G. STYLE & STYLISTICS.
J.R. BENNETT, 179(ES):FEB73-85
HOUGH, G.A., 3D. STRUCTURES OF MOD-
IFICATION IN CONTEMPORARY AMERICAN
ENGLISH.
H.V. KING, 361:OCT73-273
HOUGH, J., JR. THE GUARDIAN.
M. LEVIN, 441:23FEB75-38
L.E. SISSMAN, 442(NY):4AUG75-90
HOUGH, R. CAPTAIN BLIGH & MR.
CHRISTIAN.
H.M. BARBER, 481(PQ):JUL73-354
HOUGH, R. - SEE QUEEN VICTORIA
HOUGHTON, W.E., ED THE WELLESLEY
INDEX TO VICTORIAN PERIODICALS,
1824-1900. (VOL 2)
R.D. ALTICK, 445(NCF):SEP73-239
R.A. COLBY, 405(MP):MAY74-455
D. DEERING, 637(VS):SEP73-101
H.W. MC CREADY, 255(HAB):SPRING73-
143
HOUIS, M. ANTHROPOLOGIE LINGUIS-
TIQUE DE L'AFRIQUE NOIRE.
J.N. GREEN, 208(FS):JUL74-370
HOURANI, A.H. & S.M. STERN, EDS.
THE ISLAMIC CITY.
H. NIERMAN, 551(RENQ):AUTUMN73-303
M.L. SWARTZ, 318(JAOS):APR-JUN73-
237
HOUSEHOLD, G. RED ANGER.
N. CALLENDAR, 441:30NOV75-63
W. FEAVER, 617(TLS):22AUG75-951
442(NY):1SEP75-68
HOUSEHOLDER, F.W. LINGUISTIC SPECU-
LATIONS.*
R.A. HUDSON, 307:#2-105
HOUSEMAN, J. RUN-THROUGH.
M. GOLDSTEIN, 295:APR74-1050
J. HAMILTON, 157:SUMMER73-76

174

HOUSMAN, A.E. THE CLASSICAL PAPERS
OF A.E. HOUSMAN. (J. DIGGLE &
F.R.D. GOODYEAR, EDS)
  C.J. FORDYCE, 123:MAR74-149
HOUSMAN, A.E. THE LETTERS OF A.E.
HOUSMAN.* (H. MAAS, ED)
  J.W. STEVENSON, 295:FEB74-645
  P.F. WIDDOWS, 122:APR73-136
"HOUSMAN SOCIETY JOURNAL." (NO. 1)
  617(TLS):3JAN75-10
HOUSSER, F.B. A CANADIAN ART MOVE-
MENT.
  A. DAVIS, 99:SEP75-65
HOUSTON, C.S. - SEE HOOD, R.
HOUSTON, J. THE WHITE DAWN.
  C. ROSS, 102(CANL):AUTUMN73-113
HOUSTON, J.P. THE DEMONIC IMAGINA-
TION.*
  A. FAIRLIE, 208(FS):JUL74-336
HOUSTON, J.P. FICTIONAL TECHNIQUE
IN FRANCE: 1802-1927.*
  A. FAIRLIE, 208(FS):JUL74-336
  L.D. JOINER, 399(MLJ):APR74-208
  D.W. LAWRENCE, 150(DR):SUMMER73-
  375
  L.A. UFFENBECK, 446:SPRING-SUMMER
  74-181
  P.M. WETHERILL, 402(MLR):OCT74-879
HOUWINK TEN CATE, P.H.J. THE REC-
ORDS OF THE EARLY HITTITE EMPIRE
(C. 1450-1380 B.C.).
  E. NEU, 260(IF):BAND77HEFT2/3-279
HOVANNISIAN, R.G. THE REPUBLIC OF
ARMENIA.* (VOL 1)
  W.H. HILL, 104:WINTER73-557
  P. KENEZ, 550(RUSR):OCT73-435
HOVEN, R. STOÏCISME ET STOÏCIENS
FACE AU PROBLÈME DE L'AU-DELÀ.
  A.A. LONG, 123:NOV74-232
  C. MUGLER, 555:VOL47FASC2-334
  L. ROBERTS, 124:MAR73-362
"HOW IT WORKS & HOW TO FIX IT."
  P. BRACKEN, 441:27APR75-31
HOWARD, B. THE MANIPULATOR.
  D. JEWISON, 102(CANL):SPRING74-122
HOWARD, C. MARK THE SPARROW.
  M. LEVIN, 441:27JUL75-14
HOWARD, C. SUMMIT KILL.
  M. LEVIN, 441:30MAR75-21
HOWARD, D.R. - SEE POPE INNOCENT III
HOWARD, D.R. & C.K. ZACHER, EDS.
CRITICAL STUDIES OF "SIR GAWAIN &
THE GREEN KNIGHT."
  P.B. TAYLOR, 179(ES):APR72-154
HOWARD, E.J. MR. WRONG.
  R. DINNAGE, 617(TLS):11JUL75-753
  J. MELLORS, 362:18SEP75-386
HOWARD, H. TREBLE CROSS.
  617(TLS):11JUL75-784
HOWARD, J. A DIFFERENT WOMAN.
  S. RUDIKOFF, 249(HUDR):SPRING74-
  150
HOWARD, M. BEFORE MY TIME.
  P. ADAMS, 61:MAR75-144
  D. GRUMBACH, 441:19JAN75-5
  C. LEHMANN-HAUPT, 441:3JAN75-25
  442(NY):3FEB75-93
HOWARD, M.S. JONATHAN CAPE, PUB-
LISHER.*
  295:FEB74-370
HOWARD, P. LONDON'S RIVER.
  P. METCALF, 617(TLS):7NOV75-1341
HOWARD, R., ED. PREFERENCES.*
  J. ATLAS, 491:OCT74-52

HOWARD, R. TWO-PART INVENTIONS.
  C. RICKS, 441:23FEB75-6
HOWARD, R.R. THE DARK GLASS.*
  M. GREENE, 219(GAR):WINTER73-601
HOWARD-HILL, T.H. RALPH CRANE &
SOME SHAKESPEARE FIRST FOLIO COM-
EDIES.
  J. FEATHER, 447(N&Q):APR73-148
HOWARD-HILL, T.H., ED. OXFORD
SHAKESPEARE CONCORDANCES: KING
JOHN,* LOVE'S LABOUR'S LOST,* A
MIDSUMMER NIGHT'S DREAM,* MUCH ADO
ABOUT NOTHING.*
  R.L. WIDMANN, 570(SQ):SUMMER73-338
HOWARD-HILL, T.H., ED. OXFORD
SHAKESPEARE CONCORDANCES: RICHARD
II, RICHARD III, HENRY IV PART 1,
HENRY IV PART 2, HENRY V, HENRY VI
PART 3, HENRY VIII.
  G.W. WILLIAMS, 551(RENQ):AUTUMN73-
  366
HOWARD-HILL, T.H., ED. SHAKESPEAR-
IAN BIBLIOGRAPHY & TEXTUAL CRITI-
CISM.*
  R. KNOWLES, 570(SQ):AUTUMN73-478
HOWARTH, D. MANCHESTER MADNESS.
  S. CURTIS, 148:SPRING72-85
HOWARTH, H. THE TIGER'S HEART.
  B.S. FIELD, JR., 570(SQ):SUMMER73-
  341
HOWARTH, P. PLAY UP & PLAY THE
GAME.
  W. ALLEN, 150(DR):WINTER73/74-755
HOWARTH, S. HANDBOOK OF EASY GARDEN
PLANTS.
  C. SYKES, 617(TLS):7MAR75-258
HOWARTH, W.D. & M. THOMAS, EDS.
MOLIÈRE: STAGE & STUDY.
  M. GUTWIRTH, 400(MLN):MAY73-866
HOWARTH, W.D. & C.L. WALTON. EXPLI-
CATIONS.*
  R. GIBSON, 402(MLR):JAN74-164
  P.H. NURSE, 208(FS):JAN74-114
  G. STRICKLAND, 184(EIC):JUL72-320
HOWATCH, S. THE SHROUDED WALLS.
  E.M. EWING, 441:11MAY75-10
HOWE, C. EMPLOYMENT & ECONOMIC
GROWTH IN URBAN CHINA 1949-1957.
  J. WONG, 302:JAN73-172
HOWE, F. FIRST MARRIAGE.
  M. LEVIN, 441:2MAR75-22
HOWE, F. & E. BASS, EDS. NO MORE
MASKS!*
  F. MORAMARCO, 651(WHR):WINTER74-88
  M.G. PERLOFF, 659:WINTER75-84
  R.E. SEBENTHALL, 59(ASOC):SPRING-
  SUMMER74-165
HOWE, H.S., JR. ELECTRONIC MUSIC
SYNTHESIS.
  R. MACONIE, 617(TLS):9MAY75-506
HOWE, I. THE CRITICAL POINT.*
  G.C., 569(SR):FALL74-XCVI
  639(VQR):AUTUMN74-CXXII
HOWE, R. COOKING FROM THE HEART OF
EUROPE.
  617(TLS):7NOV75-1342
HOWE, R. & A.L. SIMON. DICTIONARY
OF GASTRONOMY.
  M.F.K. FISHER, 442(NY):10NOV75-184
HOWE, W.H. THE BUTTERFLIES OF NORTH
AMERICA.
  H.E. EVANS, 441:7DEC75-92
HOWELL, B. THE RED FOX.*
  D. WYNAND, 376:APR73-239

HOWELL, G., ED. IN VOGUE.
 D. DE MARLY, 617(TLS):12DEC75-1491
HOWELL, W.S. EIGHTEENTH-CENTURY
BRITISH LOGIC & RHETORIC.*
 G.A. HAUSER, 480(P&R):SPRING73-119
 R.S. POMEROY, 173(ECS):SPRING74-
 353
 W.R. WINTEROWD, 599:SPRING73-207
HOWELLS, W.D. W.D. HOWELLS AS
CRITIC. (E.H. CADY, ED)
 G. ARMS, 27(AL):JAN75-589
HOWES, A.B., ED. STERNE: THE CRITI-
CAL HERITAGE.*
 L. HARTLEY, 569(SR):FALL74-LXXXVI
HOWES, F. THE MUSIC OF WILLIAM
WALTON. (2ND ED)
 H. OTTAWAY, 415:JAN74-42
HOWLETT, J. THE CHRISTMAS SPY.
 617(TLS):10OCT75-1174
HØYBYE, P. SCHLÜSSEL ZUR ARABISCHEN
SPRACHE BESONDERS FÜR ROMANISTEN.
 C. LÓPEZ-MORILLAS, 545(RPH):AUG73-
 129
HOYLE, F. NICOLAUS COPERNICUS.
 639(VQR):WINTER74-XXIX
HOYLE, F. & G. INTO DEEPEST SPACE.
 J. HAMILTON-PATERSON, 617(TLS):
 14MAR75-284
HOYLES, J. THE WANING OF THE REN-
AISSANCE, 1640-1740.*
 J.L. DELAPLAIN, 481(PQ):JUL73-390
HOYT, E.P. THE MUTINY ON THE
"GLOBE."
 P. ADAMS, 61:SEP75-85
HRABAL, B. THE DEATH OF MR. BALTIS-
BERGER.
 P. ADAMS, 61:FEB75-122
 T. LASK, 441:50OCT75-46
"HROLF GAUTREKSSON: A VIKING RO-
MANCE." (H. PÁLSSON & P. EDWARDS,
TRANS)
 M. CHESNUTT, 382(MAE):1974/1-94
 T.F. HOAD, 447(N&Q):JUL73-264
 G. JOHNSTON, 529(QQ):SPRING73-146
HROTSVITHA VON GANDERSHEIM. WERKE
IN DEUTSCHER ÜBERTRAGUNG.
 B. NAGEL, 301(JEGP):JUL74-391
 P. STOTZ, 182:VOL26#23/24-882
HRUBÝ, A. DER "ACKERMANN" UND
SEINE VORLAGE.*
 D. BLAMIRES, 402(MLR):JAN74-222
HSIA, A. HERMANN HESSE UND CHINA.
 T. ZIOLKOWSKI, 617(TLS):26SEP75-
 1108
HSIAO TSO-LIANG. CHINESE COMMUNISM
IN 1927.
 J. CH'EN, 293(JAST):AUG73-693
HSÜ CHIN-HSIUNG. THE MENZIES COL-
LECTION OF SHANG DYNASTY ORACLE
BONES. (VOL 1)
 KAN LAO, 318(JAOS):JUL-SEP73-411
 S.L. MICKEL 2D, 293(JAST):FEB73-
 312
HSU, F.L.K. IEMOTO.
 E.J. HOBSBAWM, 453:17JUL75-27
HSÜ, I.C.Y. THE RISE OF MODERN
CHINA.
 P. KUHN, 318(JAOS):OCT-DEC73-643
HSÜEH, C-T., ED. REVOLUTIONARY
LEADERS OF MODERN CHINA.
 R.B. ROSEN, 293(JAST):NOV72-151
HSÜN, L. - SEE UNDER LU HSÜN
HU, J.Y.H. TS'AO YU.
 J. FAUROT, 352(LE&W):VOL16#3-1056

HUBBARD, P.M. THE GRAVEYARD.
 N. CALLENDAR, 441:15JUN75-25
 617(TLS):11JUL75-784
HUBBARD, R.H., ED. THOMAS DAVIES
IN EARLY CANADA.
 K. MC SWEENEY, 529(QQ):AUTUMN73-
 499
 G. WOODCOCK, 102(CANL):SPRING73-97
HUBER, B. & J-C. STEINEGGER - SEE
PROUVE, J.
HUBERMAN, E.L. THE POETRY OF EDWIN
MUIR.*
 E.W. MELLOWN, 295:FEB74-725
HUBERT, R.R. & J.D., EDS. ANTHOLO-
GIE DE LA POÉSIE FRANÇAISE DU
VINGTIÈME SIÈCLE.
 A. BALAKIAN, 207(FR):MAR73-875
HÜBINGER, P.E. DIE LETZTEN WORTE
PAPST GREGORS VII.
 R. FOLZ, 182:VOL26#11/12-426
HÜBINGER, P.E. THOMAS MANN, DIE
UNIVERSITÄT BONN UND DIE ZEITGE-
SCHICHTE.
 T.J.R., 617(TLS):10OCT75-1207
HUBMANN, F., COMP. THE JEWISH FAM-
ILY ALBUM.
 617(TLS):20JUN75-695
HÜBSCHER, A. DENKER GEGEN DEN
STROM.
 E. HELLER, 617(TLS):10OCT75-1167
HÜBSCHER, A. - SEE SCHOPENHAUER, A.
HUCULAK, M. WHEN RUSSIA WAS IN
AMERICA.
 G.R. BARRATT, 104:WINTER73-549
HUDDLESTON, R.D. THE SENTENCE IN
WRITTEN ENGLISH.*
 K. SØRENSEN, 179(ES):FEB73-88
HUDEN, D.P. USA THROUGH BOOKS.
 K. OLTMANN, 430(NS):FEB73-116
HUDER, W. - SEE KAISER, G.
HUDSON, Λ.B. PADJU EPAT.
 C. CUNNINGHAM, 293(JAST):AUG73-752
HUDSON, D. MUNBY, MAN OF TWO
WORLDS.
 G.B. TENNYSON, 445(NCF):DEC73-371
HUDSON, H. THE LISTENER & OTHER
STORIES.
 P. SCHLUETER, 573(SSF):SPRING73-
 213
HUDSON, K. & A. NICHOLLS, EDS. THE
DIRECTORY OF MUSEUMS.
 D. SUTTON, 617(TLS):30MAY75-602
HUDSON, L. HUMAN BEINGS.
 R. DINNAGE, 617(TLS):30OCT75-1119
HUDSON, P. THE WEST RIDING WOOL
TEXTILE INDUSTRY.
 S. POLLARD, 617(TLS):10OCT75-1215
HUDSON, R. THREATENED BIRDS OF
EUROPE.
 617(TLS):21NOV75-1397
HUDSON, R.A. ENGLISH COMPLEX SEN-
TENCES.
 R.B. LONG, 128(CE):FEB74-618
HUDSON, W.D. A PHILOSOPHICAL AP-
PROACH TO RELIGION.
 A. KENNY, 617(TLS):7FEB75-145
HUFFAKER, C. ONE TIME, I SAW MORN-
ING COME HOME.
 M. LEVIN, 441:23FEB75-39
HUFFMAN, C.C. "CORIOLANUS" IN
CONTEXT.
 J.W. VELZ, 125:JUN74-381

HUFFMAN, F.E., WITH IM PROUM, EDS.
INTERMEDIATE CAMBODIAN READER.
J.M. JACOB, 293(JAST):MAY73-563
HUFTON, O.H. THE POOR OF EIGHTEENTH-
CENTURY FRANCE, 1750-1789.
R. BRIGGS, 617(TLS):23MAY75-553
R. DARNTON, 453:2OCT75-17
HUGE, E. POESIE UND REFLEXION IN
DER ÄSTHETIK DES FRÜHEN FRIEDRICH
SCHLEGEL.
D. HARTH, 224(GRM):BAND23HEFT4-486
R. PAULIN, 402(MLR):APR74-461
HUGGETT, F.E. HOW IT HAPPENED.
R.C. TOBIAS, 637(VS):DEC73-210
HUGGETT, R. THE TRUTH ABOUT "PYG-
MALION."
F.P.W. MC DOWELL, 295:FEB74-772
HUGGINS, N.I. HARLEM RENAISSANCE.*
O. CARGILL, 295:FEB74-370
HUGGLER, P. HIRTENLEBEN UND HIRTEN-
KULTUR IM WAADTLÄNDER JURA.
H. GERNDT, 182:VOL26#1/2-58
HUGHES, A. MANUSCRIPT ACCIDENTALS.
A.E. PLANCHART, 308:FALL73-326
HUGHES, C. SWITZERLAND.
J. STEINBERG, 617(TLS):2MAY75-486
HUGHES, D.R. & E. KALLEN. THE ANAT-
OMY OF RACISM.
H. TROPER, 99:APR/MAY75-21
HUGHES, G. MILLSTONE GRIT.
J. MAPPLEBECK, 362:20MAR75-374
HUGHES, G. TOWARDS THE SUN.*
S. CURTIS, 148:SPRING72-85
HUGHES, G. & C. BARDA. THE SCULP-
TURE OF DAVID WYNNE 1968-1974.
D. FARR, 617(TLS):21MAR75-314
HUGHES, G.E. & M.J. CRESSWELL. AN
INTRODUCTION TO MODAL LOGIC.
R. BLANCHÉ, 542:JUL-SEP73-360
HUGHES, H.S. CONSCIOUSNESS & SOCI-
ETY.
A-L. LEROY, 542:JAN-MAR73-65
HUGHES, H.S. THE SEA CHANGE.*
L. KRIEGER, 441:23FEB75-27
HUGHES, J.B. ARTE Y SENTIDO DE MAR-
TÍN FIERRO.
P.G. EARLE, 240(HR):SPRING73-457
HUGHES, J.D. ECOLOGY IN ANCIENT
CIVILIZATIONS.
617(TLS):22AUG75-954
HUGHES, L. THE DRAMA'S PATRONS.*
L.B. FALLER, 405(MP):AUG73-90
HUGHES, P. GEORGE WOODCOCK.
F. COGSWELL, 102(CANL):AUTUMN74-93
HUGHES, P. & D. WILLIAMS, EDS. THE
VARIED PATTERN.*
P.J.S. WHITMORE, 402(MLR):APR74-
366
HUGHES, Q. MILITARY ARCHITECTURE.
S. PEPPER, 617(TLS):23MAY75-569
HUGHES, R. THE WOODEN SHEPHERDESS.*
W. SULLIVAN, 569(SR):WINTER74-138
HUGHES, S. FAMOUS MOZART OPERAS.
(2ND ED) FAMOUS PUCCINI OPERAS.
(2ND ED)
M. PETERSON, 470:MAY73-15
HUGHES, T. CROW.*
S. UTZ, 598(SOR):SPRING75-478
HUGHES, T. SELECTED POEMS 1957-
1967.*
R. WEBER, 159(DM):WINTER/SPRING73-
132
639(VQR):SPRING74-LVII

HUGHEY, R. JOHN HARINGTON OF STEP-
NEY, TUDOR GENTLEMAN.*
E.D. PENDRY, 677:VOL4-260
HÜGLI, A. DIE ERKENNTNIS DER SUB-
JEKTIVITÄT UND DIE OBJEKTIVITÄT DES
ERKENNENS BEI SØREN KIERKEGAARD.
H. DEUSER, 182:VOL26#20-720
HUGLO, M. LES TONAIRES.*
R.L. CROCKER, 317:FALL73-490
K. LEVY, 589:JAN74-125
HUGO, A. LE JOURNAL D'ADÈLE HUGO.
(F.V. GUILLE, ED)
W.T. SECOR, 446:SPRING-SUMMER74-
186
HUGO, J. & J. MOUTON - SEE BOUR-
GOINT, J.
HUGO, L. BERNARD SHAW - PLAYWRIGHT
& PREACHER.*
W. KLUGE, 72:BAND211HEFT1/3-155
HUGO, R. THE LADY IN KICKING HORSE
RESERVOIR.*
K. JACOBSON, 448:VOL13#2-83
L. LIEBERMAN, 676(YR):AUTUMN73-113
HUGO, R. WHAT THOU LOVEST WELL,
REMAINS AMERICAN.
H. VENDLER, 441:7SEP75-6
HUIE, W.B. IN THE HOURS OF NIGHT.
C. LYDON, 441:26OCT75-46
HULL, F., ED. HANDLIST OF KENT
COUNTY COUNCIL RECORDS, 1889-1945.
M. COOK, 325:OCT73-676
HULL, P.L., ED. THE CAPTION OF
SEISIN OF THE DUCHY OF CORNWALL
(1337).
J.T. ROSENTHAL, 325:OCT73-668
HUMBLE, R. MARCO POLO.
C.L. MEE, JR., 441:7DEC75-38
VON HUMBOLDT, W. LINGUISTIC VARIA-
BILITY & INTELLECTUAL DEVELOPMENT.*
R.D., 179(ES):APR72-191
W.K. PERCIVAL, 269(IJAL):OCT73-255
HUME, D. ABRÉGÉ DU TRAITÉ DE LA
NATURE HUMAINE. (P. DELEULE, ED &
TRANS)
G. BRYKMAN, 542:APR-JUN73-221
HUME, I.N. ALL THE BEST RUBBISH.
639(VQR):AUTUMN74-CLVIII
HUME, R.D. DRYDEN'S CRITICISM.*
F.L. HUNTLEY, 405(MP):AUG73-89
P. MORGAN, 179(ES):AUG73-393
HUMMERT, P.A. BERNARD SHAW'S MARX-
IAN ROMANCE.*
E. REUBEN, 637(VS):MAR74-340
J.L. WISENTHAL, 572:SEP73-133
HUMPHREY, B., ED. ESSAYS ON JOHN
COWPER POWYS.
H. WEBER, 182:VOL26#10-350
HUMPHREYS, A. - SEE FIELDING, H.
HUMPHREYS, C. A WESTERN APPROACH TO
ZEN.
L. HURVITZ, 293(JAST):AUG73-663
HUNDSNURSCHER, F. NEUERE METHODEN
DER SEMANTIK.*
R. BARTSCH, 133:1973/1-88
U. SCHEUERMANN, 260(IF):BAND77HEFT
2/3-348
HUNDSNURSCHER, F. DAS SYSTEM DER
PARTIKELVERBEN MIS AUS IN DER
GEGENWARTSSPRACHE.
G.F. MEIER, 682(ZPSK):BAND26HEFT
3/4-424
HUNN, D. GOODWOOD.
H. D'AVIGDOR-GOLDSMID, 617(TLS):
10OCT75-1184

HUNT, B. & M. PRIME TIME.
L.C. LEWIN, 441:13APR75-6
HUNT, D. ON THE SPOT.
G. JACKSON, 617(TLS):10OCT75-1170
HUNT, E.H. COUNTERFEIT KILL.
N. CALLENDAR, 441:29JUN75-30
HUNT, E.H. WASHINGTON PAYOFF.
N. CALLENDAR, 441:27APR75-29
HUNT, J., WITH P. HARBISON. IRISH
MEDIEVAL FIGURE SCULPTURE, 1200-
1600.*
P. BROWN & S. MAC CORMACK, 453:
20FEB75-19
HUNT, J.D., ED. ENCOUNTERS.
C. SALVESEN, 541(RES):MAY73-247
HUNT, M. SEXUAL BEHAVIOR IN THE
1970S.
P.A. ROBINSON, 473(PR):4/1974-626
HUNT, R. & R. CAMPBELL. K.C. IRV-
ING.*
R.I. MC ALLISTER, 150(DR):WINTER
73/74-771
HUNTER, A. GENTLY IN THE HIGHLANDS.
A. BROYARD, 441:22FEB75-25
N. CALLENDAR, 441:22JUN75-18
HUNTER, E. STREETS OF GOLD.
442(NY):13JAN75-90
HUNTER, G.K. & S.K., EDS. JOHN WEB-
STER.
W. SANDERS, 184(EIC):APR72-182
HUNTER, W.B., C.A. PATRIDES & J.H.
ADAMSON. BRIGHT ESSENCE.*
R.M. FRYE, 551(RENQ):SUMMER73-242
R.E.C. HOUGHTON, 447(N&Q):MAY73-
191
D.T. MACE, 541(RES):MAY73-210
SISTER MARGARET TERESA, 613:SPRING
73-124
E.A. PHILLIPS, 124:SEP72-54
HUNTFORD, R. SEA OF DARKNESS.
M. LEVIN, 441:16NOV75-76
HUNTINGTON, D.C. ART & THE EXCITED
SPIRIT.
F. MURPHY, 432(NEQ):SEP73-485
HUNTLEY, F.L. JEREMY TAYLOR & THE
GREAT REBELLION.
C.A. PATRIDES, 551(RENQ):SPRING73-
88
HÜPPAUF, B., ED. LITERATURGESCHICH-
TE ZWISCHEN REVOLUTION UND REAK-
TION.
W. DIETZE, 654(WB):8/1973-181
HUPPÉ, B.F. THE WEB OF WORDS.*
M. GREEN, 599:WINTER73-64
HUPPERT, H. SINNEN UND TRACHTEN.
M. RESO, 654(WB):7/1973-183
HURD, D. VOTE TO KILL.
T.J. BINYON, 617(TLS):19DEC75-1508
HURST, C. FACING YOU.
P. STEVENS, 628:SPRING74-101
HURST, J. NASHVILLE'S GRAND OLE
OPRY.
J. HARRISON, 441:30NOV75-22
HURSTFIELD, J. FREEDOM, CORRUPTION,
& GOVERNMENT IN ELIZABETHAN ENG-
LAND.
639(VQR):SUMMER74-XCVI
HURT, J. AELFRIC.
M.R. GODDEN, 382(MAE):1974/1-46
J.C. POPE, 589:APR74-344
A. SMITH, 255(HAB):SUMMER73-221
R.D. STEVICK, 301(JEGP):JAN74-111
HURT, J. CATILINE'S DREAM.*
E. SPRINCHORN, 397(MD):SEP73-208

HURTADO DE MENDOZA, D. GUERRA DE
GRANADA. (B. BLANCO GONZÁLEZ, ED)
R.B. TATE, 86(BHS):JAN73-80
HURTIG, B., COMP. MASTERPIECES OF
NETSUKE ART.
R. BUSHELL, 60:MAY-JUN74-70
HUS, A. VULCI ETRUSQUE ET ETRUSCO-
ROMAINE.
A. LENGYEL, 54:MAR73-140
F.R.S. RIDGWAY, 313:VOL63-283
HUSAIN, A. BRITISH INDIA'S RELA-
TIONS WITH THE KINGDOM OF NEPAL,
1857-1947.
T. RICCARDI, JR., 318(JAOS):JUL-
SEP73-393
HÜSCHEN, H., ED. MUSICAE SCIENTIAE
COLLECTANEA.
J.A. WESTRUP, 410(M&L):APR74-244
HUSMANN, H., ED. DIE MELODIEN DER
JAKOBITISCHEN KIRCHE.
E. NEUBAUER, 182:VOL26#20-748
HUSSELMAN, E.M. PAPYRI FROM KARA-
NIS. (3RD SER)
P.J. PARSONS, 123:MAR74-147
HUSSERL, E. PHILOSOPHIE DE L'ARITH-
MÉTIQUE. (J. ENGLISH, ED & TRANS)
548(RCSF):JAN-MAR73-118
HUSSERL, E. PHILOSOPHIE DER ARITH-
METIK.* (L. ELEY, ED)
E-H.W. KLUGE, 154:MAR73-147
HUSSEY, E. THE PRESOCRATICS.
R.K. SPRAGUE, 122:APR74-161
HUSSEY, M. THE WORLD OF SHAKESPEARE
& HIS CONTEMPORARIES.*
R.A. FOAKES, 175:SUMMER72-67
HUSSEY, S.S. CHAUCER.*
D.S. BREWER, 541(RES):FEB73-61
D. MEHL, 38:BAND91HEFT2-249
R.M. WILSON, 175:SPRING72-23
HUSSON, G. - SEE LUCIAN
HUSSON, J. & B. TORESSE. BEAUX
LIVRES, BELLES LECTURES, GUIDE
PÉDAGOGIQUE.
H. RÜCK, 430(NS):SEP73-507
HUTCHENS, J.K. & G. OPPENHEIMER,
EDS. THE BEST IN THE WORLD.*
S. DONALDSON, 569(SR):SUMMER74-527
HUTCHINGS, P.A.E. KANT'S ABSOLUTE
VALUE.
W.H. WERKMEISTER, 319:APR75-261
HUTCHINS, W.J. THE GENERATION OF
SYNTACTIC STRUCTURES FROM A SEMAN-
TIC BASE.
D.G. LOCKWOOD, 35(AS):SPRING-
SUMMER71-156
HUTCHISON, R.A. VESCO.
A. COCKBURN, 453:20MAR75-21
HUTH, A. SUN CHILD.
V. GLENDINNING, 617(TLS):21MAR75-
293
N. HEPBURN, 362:27MAR75-421
HUTH, H. LACQUER OF THE WEST.
F. WATSON, 54:JUN73-305
HUTT, A. FOURNIER, THE COMPLEAT
TYPOGRAPHER.
R. MC LEAN, 135:APR73-292
VON HUTTEN, U. DEUTSCHE SCHRIFTEN.*
(P. UKENA, ED)
T.W. BEST, 221(GQ):MAY73-481
HUWS, D. NOTH.*
P.E. LEWIS, 565:VOL14#4-52
HUXLEY, A. PLANT & PLANET.*
H. BORLAND, 441:23NOV75-44

HUXLEY, E. FLORENCE NIGHTINGALE.
442(NY):28APR75-140
HUXLEY, F. THE WAY OF THE SACRED.*
I.M. LEWIS, 617(TLS):14FEB75-173
HUYGENS, R.B.C. - SEE GREGORIUS
HYAMS, E. TERRORISTS & TERRORISM.
R. EDER, 441:14DEC75-6
J.R. REBER, 617(TLS):22AUG75-953
HYDE, G.E. THE PAWNEE INDIANS.
W. GARD, 584(SWR):SUMMER74-V
HYDE, H.M. OSCAR WILDE.
J. ATLAS, 441:21DEC75-6
HYDE, J.K. BENJAMIN FONDANE.
P. DUBOIS, 542:APR-JUN73-222
HYDE, M. THE IMPOSSIBLE FRIEND-
SHIP.*
F.W. HILLES, 676(YR):AUTUMN73-104
E.L. RUHE, 401(MLQ):JUN74-207
M. WAINGROW, 481(PQ):JUL73-470
HYDE, R. PRINTED MAPS OF VICTORIAN
LONDON 1851-1900.
P. METCALF, 617(TLS):8AUG75-904
HYDE, V. AN INTRODUCTION TO THE
LUISEÑO LANGUAGE. (R.W. LANGACKER,
ED)
J. HEATH, 269(IJAL):JAN73-59
HYDEN, G., R. JACKSON & J. OKUMU,
EDS. DEVELOPMENT ADMINISTRATION.
L. MAIR, 69:APR73-166
HYDER, C.K. - SEE SWINBURNE, A.C.
HYLDGAARD-JENSEN, K., ED. DEUTSCHE
LYRIC VON GOETHE BIS ENZENSBERGER.
E. PASTOR, 556(RLV):1973/4-383
HYMAN, L.M. A PHONOLOGICAL STUDY OF
FE? FE? -BAMILEKE.
J. VOORHOEVE, 315(JAL):VOL11PT3-84
HYMAN, L.W. THE QUARREL WITHIN.*
R.H. SUNDELL, 568(SCN):SPRING-
SUMMER74-1
HYMAN, S.E. IAGO.*
R.A. FOAKES, 175:SUMMER72-67
B. SPIVACK, 570(SQ):SUMMER73-342
HYMES, D., ED. PIDGINIZATION &
CREOLIZATION OF LANGUAGES.
E.P. HAMP, 269(IJAL):APR73-130
L. TODD, 361:SEP73-136
P. TRUDGILL, 297(JL):FEB73-193
A. VALDMAN, 399(MLJ):JAN-FEB73-53
"HYMNS OF GURU NANAK." (K. SINGH,
TRANS)
293(JAST):NOV72-227
HYNES, S. EDWARDIAN OCCASIONS.
J.B. BATCHELOR, 677:VOL4-334
J. GLOVER, 565:VOL14#3-22
B. KIELY, 159(DM):SUMMER73-103
G. THOMAS, 175:SUMMER73-80
295:FEB74-472
569(SR):WINTER74-VIII
HYNES, S., ED. GRAHAM GREENE.
R.M. DAVIS, 594:WINTER73-530
HYPPOLITE, J. STUDIES ON MARX &
HEGEL.
A. QUINTON, 453:29MAY75-34
HYSLOP, L.B., ED. BAUDELAIRE AS A
LOVE POET & OTHER ESSAYS.*
W.T. BANDY, 207(FR):OCT72-163
HYSLOP, L.B. HENRY BECQUE.
M.J. FRIEDMAN, 207(FR):FEB73-617
J.L. GREEN, 399(MLJ):SEP-OCT73-284

IATRIDES, J.O. REVOLT IN ATHENS.*
H.C. CLIADAKIS, 104:SPRING74-138

IBÁÑEZ, F.S. - SEE UNDER SOPEÑA
IBÁÑEZ, F.
IBN ABĪ D-DUNYĀ. THE NOBLE QUALI-
TIES OF CHARACTER. (J.A. BELLAMY,
ED)
E. WAGNER, 182:VOL26#11/12-414
IBN AL-JAWZI. KITĀB AL-QUSSĀS WAL
MUDHAKKIRIN. (M.L. SWARTZ, ED &
TRANS)
M.A. MU'ID KHAN, 273(IC):JUL73-280
IBN 'ARABĪ. SUFIS OF ANDALUSIA.
(R.W.J. AUSTIN, TRANS)
A.G. CHEJNE, 318(JAOS):OCT-DEC73-
558
IBN BATTUTA. THE TRAVELS OF IBN
BATTUTA, A.D. 1325-1354. (VOL 3)
(H.A.R. GIBB, TRANS)
K.A. LUTHER, 293(JAST):FEB73-340
IBN FARTUA, A. HISTORY OF THE FIRST
TWELVE YEARS OF THE REIGN OF MAI
ALOOMA OF BORNU.
A.H.M. KIRK-GREENE, 69:OCT73-356
IBN KAMMŪNA. SA'D B. MANṢŪR IBN
KAMMŪNA'S EXAMINATION OF THE IN-
QUIRIES INTO THE THREE FAITHS.*
(M. PERLMANN, ED & TRANS)
M.E. MARMURA, 154:MAR73-166
IBN TUFAYL. HAYY IBN YAQZĀN. (L.E.
GOODMAN, TRANS)
A.A.A. FYZEE, 273(IC):OCT73-356
G.F. HOURANI, 318(JAOS):JUL-SEP73-
364
ICHIRO, H. JAPANESE RELIGION.
H.P. VARLEY, 529(QQ):AUTUMN73-490
ICKSTADT, H. DICHTERISCHE ERFAHRUNG
UND METAPHERNSTRUKTUR.
H. PRIESSNITZ, 72:BAND211HEFT1/3-
150
G. VAN CROMPHOUT, 179(ES):DEC73-
604
IDLE, E. "HELLO SAILOR."
F. PIKE, 617(TLS):21MAR75-293
IGGERS, G.G. & K. VON MOLTKE - SEE
VON RANKE, L.
IGLAUER, E. DENISON'S ICE ROAD.
E. WEEKS, 61:FEB75-121
IGNATOW, D. FACING THE TREE. THE
NOTEBOOKS OF DAVID IGNATOW. (R.J.
MILLS, JR., ED) DAVID IGNATOW:
SELECTED POEMS. (R. BLY, ED)
T. LASK, 441:4MAY75-46
IGWE, G.E. & M.M. GREEN. IGBO LAN-
GUAGE COURSE. (BK 3)
F.D.D. WINSTON, 315(JAL):VOL11
PT3-100
IHIMAERA, W. WHANAU.
M. MILLER, 617(TLS):7MAR75-260
IHWE, J. LINGUISTIK IN DER LITERA-
TURWISSENSCHAFT.
W.J.M. BRONZWAER, 307:#3-121
IHWE, J., ED. LITERATURWISSENSCHAFT
UND LINGUISTIK.* (VOL 1)
L.I. SOUDEK, 221(GQ):SEP73-179
IJSEWIJN, J. & E. KESSLER, EDS.
ACTA CONVENTUS NEO-LATINI LOVANIEN-
SIS.
F. LASSERRE, 182:VOL26#20-756
IKELER, A.A. PURITAN TEMPER & TRANS-
CENDENTAL FAITH.*
M. BAUMGARTEN, 125:OCT73-98
J.A.D., 191(ELN):SEP73(SUPP)-41
E. SHARPLES, 141:SPRING74-180
E.M. VIDA, 637(VS):DEC73-225

179

IONESCO, E. THE HERMIT.*
  E. KORN, 617(TLS):18JUL75-793
IONESCO, E. MACBETT.
  R.C. LAMONT, 207(FR):MAR73-858
IONESCO, E. PRÉSENT PASSÉ PASSÉ
  PRÉSENT.
  R.C. LAMONT, 207(FR):MAR73-857
"EUGENE IONESCO PLAYS." (VOL 9)
  A. RENDLE, 157:WINTER73-87
IORIZZO, L.J. & S. MONDELLO. THE
  ITALIAN-AMERICANS.
  E.S. FALBO, 275(IQ):SPRING74-67
"IRAN SOCIETY SILVER JUBILEE SOUVE-
  NIR (1944-69)."
  R. AKBAR, 273(IC):OCT73-365
IREDALE, D. ENJOYING ARCHIVES.
  L. RAPPORT, 14:OCT73-553
IRELAND, G.W. ANDRÉ GIDE.
  W.W. HOLDHEIM, 546(RR):JAN74-69
  D. MOUTOTE, 535(RHL):JAN-FEB73-159
IRESON, J.C. IMAGINATION IN FRENCH
  ROMANTIC POETRY.
  R. CHAMBERS, 535(RHL):SEP-OCT73-
  913
IRMER, D. ZUR GENEALOGIE DER JÜN-
  GEREN DEMOSTHENESHANDSCHRIFTEN.
  N.G. WILSON, 123:NOV74-292
IRMSCHER, H.D. ADALBERT STIFTER.*
  G.H. HERTLING, 182:VOL26#7/8-219
IRONSIDE, J. JANEY.
  T. DEL RENZIO, 592:JUL-AUG73-52
IRSFELD, J.H. COMING THROUGH.
  M. LEVIN, 441:26OCT75-56
IRVINE, W. & P. HONAN. THE BOOK,
  THE RING, & THE POET.*
  C.D.L. RYALS, 301(JEGP):OCT74-561
  639(VQR):SUMMER74-XCII
IRVING, R.E.M. CHRISTIAN DEMOCRACY
  IN FRANCE.
  D. JOHNSON, 617(TLS):2MAY75-481
IRVING, R.E.M. THE FIRST INDOCHINA
  WAR.
  E. O'BALLANCE, 617(TLS):24OCT75-
  1268
IRVING, W. WASHINGTON IRVING, JOUR-
  NALS & NOTEBOOKS.* (VOL 1 ED BY N.
  WRIGHT; VOL 3 ED BY W.A. REICHART)
  MAHOMET & HIS SUCCESSORS.* (H.A.
  POCHMANN & E.N. FELTSKOG, EDS)
  O. ÖVERLAND, 179(ES):JUN73-295
IRWIN, D. - SEE WINCKELMANN, J.J.
IRWIN, D. & F. SCOTTISH PAINTERS AT
  HOME & ABROAD, 1700-1900.
  D.A.N. JONES, 362:30OCT75-575
IRWIN, G. SAMUEL JOHNSON.*
  C.J. RAWSON, 175:AUTUMN72-110
IRWIN, J. & M. HALL. INDIAN PAINTED
  & PRINTED FABRICS. (VOL 1)
  D.K. DOHANIAN, 293(JAST):FEB73-340
ISAACS, H.R. IDOLS OF THE TRIBE.
  442(NY):8SEP75-125
ISAACS, H.R., ED. STRAW SANDALS.
  S. ELKHADEM, 268:JAN75-86
  639(VQR):AUTUMN74-CXXII
ISAACSON, P. THE AMERICAN EAGLE.
  C.L. MEE, JR., 441:7DEC75-46
ISAJEVYČ, J.D. DŽERELA Z ISTORIJI
  UKRAJINSKOJI KULTURY DOBY FEODAL-
  IZMU.
  D. TSCHIŽEWSKIJ, 72:BAND211HEFT
  1/3-248
ISELY, R.K. A STRANGE CODE OF JUS-
  TICE.
  N. CALLENDAR, 441:5JAN75-84

ISENBERG, H. DAS DIREKTE OBJEKT IM
  SPANISCHEN.
  R.G. KEIGHTLEY, 297(JL):FEB73-204
ISER, W. THE IMPLIED READER.
  F. KERMODE, 617(TLS):11JUL75-751
ISHERWOOD, R.M. MUSIC IN THE SER-
  VICE OF THE KING.
  H.M.C. PURKIS, 255:FALL73-309
  J. RUSHTON, 410(M&L):APR74-224
ISHIGURO, H. LEIBNIZ'S PHILOSOPHY
  OF LOGIC & LANGUAGE.*
  J. HOSTLER, 483:OCT73-406
ISLAM, R. INDO-PERSIAN RELATIONS.
  A. AHMAD, 318(JAOS):JAN-MAR73-103
  J.F. RICHARDS, 293(JAST):NOV72-198
  H.K. SHERWANI, 273(IC):APR73-180
ISLAM, S. KIPLING'S "LAW."
  D.A.N. JONES, 362:25DEC75&1JAN76-
  890
ISOARD, J. LOS ÉCRIVAINS MARSEIL-
  LAIS DE LANGUE PROVENÇALE.
  J. CANTERA, 202(FMOD):NOV72/FEB73-
  175
ISRAEL, P. HUSH MONEY.*
  617(TLS):10OCT75-1174
ISRAILEVICH, E.E., COMP. ENGLISH-
  RUSSIAN GENERAL ECONOMIC & FOREIGN
  TRADE DICTIONARY.
  J. KAYALOFF, 550(RUSR):OCT73-450
ISSACHAROFF, M. J-K. HUYSMANS DE-
  VANT LA CRITIQUE EN FRANCE (1874-
  1960).*
  A. ARTINIAN, 546(RR):JAN73-81
ISSAYEV, M. FOR YOU THERE IS NO
  REST.
  270:VOL23#4-80
ISSELS, J. CANCER.
  H. MILLER, 362:31JUL75-154
"ISSLEDOVANIJA PO POETIKE I STILIS-
  TIKE."
  D. TSCHIŽEWSKIJ, 72:BAND211HEFT
  1/3-253
ITO, T. THE JAPANESE GARDEN.
  M. HILLIER, 89(BJA):SUMMER73-310
ITOH, T. AN APPROACH TO NATURE.
  S. SITWELL, 39:AUG73-148
ITOH, T. THE CLASSIC TRADITION IN
  JAPANESE ARCHITECTURE.
  S. SITWELL, 39:AUG73-148
  R. WEMISCHNER, 44:MAR73-22
ITOH, T. TRADITIONAL DOMESTIC ARCH-
  ITECTURE OF JAPAN.
  C. DRESSER, 592:MAR73-145
ITZKOFF, S.W. ERNST CASSIRER.
  J. BLARER, 486:SEP73-463
ITZKOWITZ, N. & M. MOTE, EDS &
  TRANS. MUBADELE.
  E. BIRNBAUM, 318(JAOS):APR-JUN73-
  242
  A.W. FISHER, 104:SPRING73-122
IVANOFF, P. MAYA.
  E. THOMPSON, 617(TLS):12SEP75-1017
IVANOV, Y., ED. A TREASURY OF RUS-
  SIAN SHORT STORIES.
  I. NAGURSKI, 574(SEEJ):SUMMER72-
  235
IVANOV-RAZUMNIK, R.V. THE MEMOIRS
  OF IVANOV-RAZUMNIK.
  M.S. SHATZ, 104:SUMMER73-250
IVASK, G. & H.W. TJALSMA, EDS. AN-
  THOLOGIE DER PETERSBURGER DICHTUNG
  DER ZEIT DES AKMEISMUS.
  D. TSCHIŽEWSKIJ, 72:BAND211HEFT
  3/6-479

JACOBS, D.M. THE UFO CONTROVERSY IN AMERICA.
A.C. CLARKE, 441:27JUL75-4
C.H. GIBBS-SMITH, 617(TLS):19SEP 75-1047
JACOBS, H. & J. ROELANDS. INDISCH A B C.
W.H. FREDERICK, 293(JAST):MAY73-568
JACOBS, J. WILHELM MEISTER UND SEINE BRÜDER.
N.H. SMITH, 182:VOL26#10-353
JACOBS, N. MODERNIZATION WITHOUT DEVELOPMENT.
M. SMITHIES, 302:JAN73-187
JACOBS, R. & G. SKELTON - SEE WAGNER, R.
JACOBS, R.A. & P.S. ROSENBAUM, EDS. READINGS IN ENGLISH TRANSFORMATIONAL GRAMMAR.*
D. FORMAN, 399(MLJ):JAN-FEB73-55
JACOBS, R.A. & P.S. ROSENBAUM. TRANSFORMATIONS, STYLE & MEANING.*
R.E. CALLARY, 599:SPRING73-177
S.D. FINNEGAN, 186(ETC.):SEP73-326
JACOBSEN, J. THE SHADE-SELLER.
J. MARTIN, 491:MAY75-103
JACOBSON, C.G. SOVIET STRATEGY - SOVIET FOREIGN POLICY.
D.R. JONES, 104:WINTER74-610
JACOBSON, D. INKLINGS.
E. GLOVER, 565:VOL14#4-69
JACOBSON, H. OVID'S HEROIDES.
O. LYNE, 617(TLS):7MAR75-254
JACOBSON, H.S. - SEE NIKITENKO, A.
JACOBSON, R. THE LONDON DIALECT OF THE LATE FOURTEENTH CENTURY.
K. FAISS, 353:15APR73-108
B. SUNDBY, 179(ES):JUN73-308
JACOBSON, R. REVERBERATIONS.
J. YOHALEM, 441:19JAN75-31
JACOBSON, S. STUDIES IN ENGLISH TRANSFORMATIONAL GRAMMAR.
K. SØRENSEN, 179(ES):DEC73-619
JACOBY, H. THE BUREAUCRATIZATION OF THE WORLD.
639(VQR):SUMMER74-C
JACOBY, N.H. CORPORATE POWER & SOCIAL RESPONSIBILITY.*
J.J. CORSON, 639(VQR):SUMMER74-478
JACOBY, R. SOCIAL AMNESIA.
W. GASS, 453:17APR75-3 [& CONT IN] 453:15MAY75-9
JACOMUZZI, A. IL PALINSESTO DELLA RETORICA E ALTRI SAGGI DANTESCHI.
M.M., 228(GSLI):VOL150FASC470/471-470
DI JACOPO, M. MARIANO DI JACOPO DETTO IL TACCOLA: LIBER TERTIUS DE INGENEIS AC EDIFITIIS NON USITATIS. (J.H. BECK, ED)
J. BACKHOUSE, 90:MAR73-170
JACOT, M. THE LAST BUTTERFLY.*
H. PORTER, 296:VOL3#4-89
JACQUART, J. LA CRISE RURALE EN ILE-DE-FRANCE 1550-1670.
D. PARKER, 617(TLS):1AUG75-877
JACQUES, G. "LE LYS DANS LA VALLÉE."
M. LE YAOUANC, 535(RHL):NOV-DEC73-1090
JACQUES, G. - SEE DE BALZAC, H.
JACQUES, J.M. - SEE MENANDER
JACQUET-GORDON, H. - SEE PIANKOFF, A.

JACQUOT, J. & E. KONIGSON, EDS. LES FÊTES DE LA RENAISSANCE. (VOL 3)
P. BURKE, 617(TLS):10OCT75-1210
JAEHRLING, J. DIE PHILOSOPHISCHE TERMINOLOGIE NOTKERS DES DEUTSCHEN IN SEINER UBERSETZUNG DER ARISTO-TELISCHEN "KATEGORIEN."
G. CUBBIN, 220(GL&L):OCT73-75
JAFFÉ, H.L.C. VORDEMBERGE-GILDEWART.
L. MOHOLY, 90:JUN73-404
JAFFE, I.B. JOHN TRUMBULL.
J. RUSSELL, 441:7DEC75-24
JAFFE, R. FAMILY SECRETS.*
E. DUNDY, 617(TLS):8AUG75-902
JAFFIN, D. EMPTIED SPACES.
M. MADIGAN, 385(MQR):SPRING75-220
JAGER, R. THE DEVELOPMENT OF BER-TRAND RUSSELL'S PHILOSOPHY.
R. BLANCHÉ, 542:JUL-SEP73-361
C.J. KOEHLER, 319:JUL75-421
H. RUJA, 484(PPR):MAR74-440
P. SHAW, 478:JUL73-123
JÄGER, S. DER KONJUNKTIV IN DER DEUTSCHEN SPRACHE DER GEGENWART.
B.J. KOEKKOEK, 221(GQ):MAR73-240
JAGO, R.P., ED. HARRAP'S CONCISE FRENCH & ENGLISH DICTIONARY.
H.W. BRANN, 207(FR):APR73-1081
JAIN, R.K. SOUTH INDIANS ON THE PLANTATION FRONTIER IN MALAYA.*
C.E. GLICK, 318(JAOS):APR-JUN73-252
JAIN, S.C. INDIAN MANAGER.
M.R. GOODALL, 293(JAST):NOV72-188
JAIRAZBHOY, N.A. THE RAGS OF NORTH INDIAN MUSIC.*
J. BECKER, 293(JAST):FEB73-338
JAIRAZBHOY, R.A. FOREIGN INFLUENCE IN ANCIENT INDIA.
Z.Y. ALI KHAN, 273(IC):JUL73-282
JAKÓBIEC, M., ED. LITERATURA ROSY-JSKA.
Z. FOLEJEWSKI, 574(SEEJ):SPRING73-67
JAKOBSON, A. KONEC TRAGEDII.
V. TERRAS, 574(SEEJ):FALL73-336
JAKOBSON, L. & V. PRAKASH, EDS. METROPOLITAN GROWTH.
J. GOTTMANN, 617(TLS):17JAN75-58
JAKOBSON, L. & V. PRAKASH, EDS. UR-BANIZATION & NATIONAL DEVELOPMENT.
M.R. HOLLNSTEINER, 293(JAST):NOV 72-210
JAKOBSON, R. SELECTED WRITINGS.* (VOL 2)
M. SHAPIRO, 260(IF):BAND78-193
JAL, P. - SEE LIVY
JAMES I OF SCOTLAND. THE KINGIS QUAIR.* (J. NORTON-SMITH, ED)
D. FOX, 447(N&Q):NOV73-425
W. WEISS, 38:BAND91HEFT2-257
JAMES I OF SCOTLAND. THE KINGIS QUAIR OF JAMES STEWART. (M.P. MC DIARMID, ED)
D. FOX, 447(N&Q):NOV73-425
JAMES, A.W. STUDIES IN THE LANGUAGE OF OPPIAN OF CILICIA.
J-L. PERPILLOU, 555:VOL47FASC1-147
JAMES, C. THE FATE OF FELICITY FARK IN THE LAND OF THE MEDIA.
J. VAIZEY, 362:30OCT75-580
JAMES, C. THE IMPERIAL HOTEL.
R.G. WILSON, 576:OCT73-262

JAMES, C. THE METROPOLITAN CRITIC.*
W. PRITCHARD, 364:AUG/SEP74-147
JAMES, D.C. THE YEARS OF MAC AR-
THUR. (VOL 2)
M. BLUMENSON, 441:11MAY75-34
JAMES, E.A. DANIEL DEFOE'S MANY
VOICES.
D. BLEWETT, 481(PQ):JUL73-484
A. WRIGHT, 402(MLR):JAN74-151
JAMES, E.D. PIERRE NICOLE, JANSEN-
IST & HUMANIST.
A. LEVI, 208(FS):JUL74-326
JAMES, H. HENRY JAMES: LETTERS.
(VOL 1) (L. EDEL, ED)
P. ADAMS, 61:FEB75-123
Q. ANDERSON, 617(TLS):9MAY75-498
L. GRAVER, 441:19JAN75-1
A. KAZIN, 453:23JAN75-12
D. MAY, 362:24APR75-536
V.S. PRITCHETT, 442(NY):17MAR75-
121
JAMES, H. HENRY JAMES: LETTERS.
(VOL 2) (L. EDEL, ED)
I. HOWE, 441:19OCT75-2
JAMES, H. THE PRIVATE LIFE [DANS
SELECTED STORIES]. "LA VIE PRI-
VÉE," [DANS] "L'IMAGE DANS LE
TAPIS." (M. CANAVAGGIA, TRANS)
CARNETS.
A. GREEN, 98:MAY73-391
JAMES, H. THE TALES OF HENRY
JAMES.* (VOL 1) (M. AZIZ, ED)
F.G. ATKINSON, 67:NOV74-230
JAMES, H. THEORY OF FICTION: HENRY
JAMES. (J.E. MILLER, JR., ED)
295:FEB74-665
JAMES, M.R. - SEE PSEUDO-PHILO
JAMES, P.D. THE BLACK TOWER.
N. CALLENDAR, 441:23NOV75-52
M. LASKI, 362:5JUN75-748
617(TLS):11JUL75-784
JAMES, T. LETTERS TO A STRANGER.*
639(VQR):WINTER74-XIV
JAMESON, F. MARXISM & FORM.*
P. CAPPON, 104:WINTER74-592
J. CULLER, 402(MLR):JUL74-599
H.D. OSTERLE, 221(GQ):NOV73-660
JAMESON, F. THE PRISON-HOUSE OF
LANGUAGE.*
F.C. FERGUSON, 473(PR):2/1974-310
JAMIESON, E. ENGLISH EMBOSSED BIND-
INGS 1825-1850.
G. BARBER, 78(BC):AUTUMN73-389
P. MORGAN, 447(N&Q):FEB73-62
JAMMES, F. MÉMOIRES.
T.A. SHEALY, 207(FR):FEB73-659
JANERT, K.L. ABSTÄNDE UND SCHLUSS-
VOKALVERZEICHNUNGEN IN AŚOKA-IN-
SCHRIFTEN.
J. FILLIOZAT, 182:VOL26#13/14-456
JANERT, K.L. - SEE KÖHLER, H-W.
JANERT, K.L., R. SELLHEIM & H.
STRIEDL. SCHRIFTEN UND BILDER.
J. FILLIOZAT, 182:VOL26#13/14-452
JANIK, A. & S. TOULMIN. WITTGEN-
STEIN'S VIENNA.*
483:OCT73-408
639(VQR):WINTER74-XXX
JANKUHN, H. DIE PASSIVE BEDEUTUNG
MEDIALER FORMEN UNTERSUCHT AN DER
SPRACHE HOMERS.*
V. LEINIEKS, 121(CJ):FEB/MAR74-271

JANNACO, C. & U. LIMENTANI, EDS.
STUDI SECENTESCHI. (VOL 10)
A.N. MANCINI, 400(MLN):JAN73-125
JANNACO, C. & U. LIMENTANI, EDS.
STUDI SECENTESCHI. (VOL 11)
R.A., 228(GSLI):VOL15OFASC470/471-
473
JANNACONE, P. WALT WHITMAN'S POETRY
& THE EVOLUTION OF RHYTHMIC FORMS &
WALT WHITMAN'S THOUGHT & ART.
G.M. WHITE, 646(WWR):SEP73-120
JANNINI, P.A. LE AVANGUARDIE LET-
TERARIE NELL'IDEA CRITICA DI GUIL-
LAUME APOLLINAIRE.*
O. RAGUSA, 207(FR):FEB73-622
JANNUZI, F.T. AGRARIAN CRISIS IN
INDIA.
M. DESAI, 617(TLS):31JAN75-119
JANSEN, F.J.B. & P.M. MITCHELL, EDS.
ANTHOLOGY OF DANISH LITERATURE.*
J.E. ANDERSON, 529(QQ):AUTUMN73-
473
F. JENSEN, 399(MLJ):MAR73-148
JANSEN, H.M. A CRITICAL ACCOUNT OF
THE WRITTEN & ARCHAEOLOGICAL
SOURCES' EVIDENCE CONCERNING THE
NORSE SETTLEMENTS IN GREENLAND.
E. HAUGEN, 589:OCT74-743
JANSOHN, H. HERBERT MARCUSE.
S. DECLOUX, 182:VOL26#13/14-459
JANSON, T. THE SUMMER BOOK.
P. ADAMS, 61:JUN75-95
JARAUSCH, K.H. THE ENIGMATIC CHAN-
CELLOR.
D.A.T. STAFFORD, 529(QQ):WINTER73-
636
JARCEVA, V.N., ED. ENGEL'S I JAZY-
KOZNANIE.
E. ALBRECHT & K. KRÜGER, 682(ZPSK):
BAND26HEFT3/4-390
JARDINE, L. FRANCIS BACON.
B. VICKERS, 617(TLS):20JUN75-700
JAREÑO, E. - SEE TIRSO DE MOLINA
JARNÉS BERGUA, E. TRES PASOS EN
FALSO.
L.M. PERRY, 399(MLJ):SEP-OCT73-300
JARRATT, E. & V. THE COMPLETE BOOK
OF PASTA.
617(TLS):30MAY75-607
JARRELL, R. THE COMPLETE POEMS.
H. SERGEANT, 175:SUMMER72-75
JARRELL, R. JEROME.
295:FEB74-673
JARRELL, R. POETRY & THE AGE.
D.J. ENRIGHT, 362:23JAN75-124
JARRELL, R. THE THIRD BOOK OF CRIT-
ICISM.
D.J. ENRIGHT, 362:23JAN75-124
R. PADEL, 617(TLS):21FEB75-188
JARRETT, D. ENGLAND IN THE AGE OF
HOGARTH.
442(NY):3FEB75-94
JARVIE, I.C. CONCEPTS & SOCIETY.
Q. GIBSON, 63:MAY74-74
A.R. LOUCH, 262:SPRING73-127
W.G. RUNCIMAN, 488:MAR73-91
E. VALLANCE, 479(PHQ):OCT73-372
JARVIE, I.C. & J. AGASSI - SEE GELL-
NER, E.
JARVIS, R.C. COLLECTED PAPERS ON
THE JACOBITE RISINGS.
S.P. ANDERSON, 325:APR73-613

JASEN, D.A. P.G. WODEHOUSE.
  G. MIKES, 617(TLS):19SEP75-1063
  R.M. STROZIER, 441:27APR75-23
JASENAS, M. A HISTORY OF THE BIBLI-
OGRAPHY OF PHILOSOPHY.
  J.F. GUIDO, 517(PBSA):OCT-DEC74-
  453
JASINSKI, B.W. L'ENGAGEMENT DE
BENJAMIN CONSTANT.
  P. DEGUISE, 535(RHL):JAN-FEB73-138
  R.B. GRANT, 207(FR):DEC72-410
JASINSKI, R. DEUX ACCÈS À LA BRUY-
ÈRE.
  W.G. MOORE, 208(FS):JAN74-72
  P. SAINTONGE, 207(FR):OCT72-152
  L. VAN DELFT, 535(RHL):NOV-DEC73-
  1068
JASMIN, C. ET PUIS TOUT EST SILENCE.
  R. SUTHERLAND, 102(CANL):WINTER73-
  114
JASON, P.K. - SEE NIN, A.
JASPERS, K. PHILOSOPHY. (VOL 2)
  J.D.C., 543:SEP72-161
JASZI, A. ENTZWEIUNG UND VEREINI-
GUNG.
  H. HENNING, 301(JEGP):APR74-290
JAULIN, R. LA PAIX BLANCHE.
  M. LAFFRANQUE, 542:JAN-MAR73-73
JAVAREK, V., ED. SERBO-CROATIAN
READER.
  C. HAWKESWORTH, 575(SEER):OCT74-
  629
JAWORSKA, W. GAUGUIN & THE PONT-
AVEN SCHOOL.*
  J.I. DANIEC, 497(POLR):VOL18#3-100
JAY, B. ROBERT DEMACHY 1859-1936.
  E. DE MARÉ, 617(TLS):7FEB75-148
JAY, M. THE DIALECTICAL IMAGINA-
TION.*
  R.J. BERNSTEIN, 390:AUG-SEP73-55
  D. HOWARD, 473(PR):3/1974-464
JAY, P., ED. THE GREEK ANTHOLOGY.
  R. PYBUS, 565:VOL14#4-57
JAY, S. THE JET ENGINE.
  J.R. EWER, 399(MLJ):SEP-OCT74-298
JAYAWARDENA, V.K. THE RISE OF THE
LABOR MOVEMENT IN CEYLON.
  P. PEEBLES, 293(JAST):MAY73-552
JAYAWICKRAMA, N.A. - SEE VĀCISSARA-
THERA
JAYNE, R. THE SYMBOLISM OF SPACE &
MOTION IN THE WORKS OF RAINER MARIA
RILKE.
  E. SCHWARZ, 401(MLQ):DEC74-434
AL-JAZARĪ, B.I.A. THE BOOK OF KNOW-
LEDGE OF INGENIOUS MECHANICAL DE-
VICES (KITĀB FĪ MA 'RIFAT AL-ḤIYAL
AL-HANDASIYYA) BY IBN AL-RAZZĀZ AL-
JAZARĪ.* (D.R. HILL, ED & TRANS)
  H. ELKHADEM, 182:VOL26#23/24-833
JEAN DU PRIER. JEHAN DU PRIER DIT
LE PRIEUR: "LE MYSTÈRE DU ROY AD-
VENIR."* (A. MEILLER, ED)
  L.R. MILLS, 546(RR):JAN74-56
JEAN, M. - SEE ARP, J.
JEAN, R. LA FEMME ATTENTIVE.
  W.D. REDFERN, 617(TLS):31JAN75-120
JEANNEAU, G. - SEE DUFOUR, A.
JEAUNEAU, É. - SEE SCOT, J.
JEBB, R.C. - SEE SOPHOCLES
JEFFARES, A.N. THE CIRCUS ANIMALS.*
  R. FRÉCHET, 189(EA):OCT-DEC73-487

JEFFARES, A.N., ED. SCOTT'S MIND &
ART.
  T.R. DALE, 125:OCT73-82
JEFFARES, A.N. & A.S. KNOWLAND. A
COMMENTARY ON THE COLLECTED PLAYS
OF W.B. YEATS.
  F.S.L. LYONS, 617(TLS):10OCT75-
  1187
JEFFERSON, A. THE LIFE OF RICHARD
STRAUSS.*
  J. COCKSHOOT, 410(M&L):APR74-233
JEFFERSON, L. THESE ARE MY SISTERS.
  A.L. BARKER, 362:8MAY75-622
JEFFERY, B., ED. CHANSON VERSE OF
THE EARLY RENAISSANCE.*
  H.M. BROWN, 551(RENQ):SUMMER73-201
  G. DOTTIN, 535(RHL):JUL-AUG73-676
  P. KUNSTMANN, 207(FR):MAR73-820
  R.A. SAYCE, 354:MAR73-79
  N. WILKINS, 208(FS):JUL74-313
  D. WILSON, 402(MLR):JUL74-636
JEFFREY, C. THE OTHER ARK.
  D.M. DAY, 157:WINTER73-89
JEFFREY, R.C. FORMAL LOGIC.
  SIBAJIBAN, 316:DEC73-646
JĒGERS, B. LATVIEŠU TRIMDAS IZDE-
VUMU BIBLIOGRAFIJA 1940-1960.
  (VOL 2)
  V.J. ZEPS, 574(SEEJ):FALL73-365
JEHASSE, J. & L. LA NÉCROPOLE PRÉ-
ROMAINE D'ALÉRIA (1960-68).
  S. MARTIN-KILCHER, 182:VOL26#13/14-
  501
JELAVICH, B. THE OTTOMAN EMPIRE,
THE GREAT POWERS, & THE STRAITS
QUESTION, 1870-1887.
  M.S. ANDERSON, 575(SEER):APR74-294
JELENSKI, C. & D. DE ROUX, EDS.
GOMBROWICZ.
  L. IRIBARNE, 574(SEEJ):SPRING73-93
JELLICOE, G. & S. THE LANDSCAPE OF
MAN.
  C.L. MEE, JR., 441:7DEC75-42
  J.M. RICHARDS, 617(TLS):21NOV75-
  1395
JENCKS, C. LE CORBUSIER & THE
TRAGIC VIEW OF ARCHITECTURE.*
  639(VQR):SUMMER74-CX
JENCKS, C. MODERN MOVEMENTS IN
ARCHITECTURE.*
  R.F. JORDAN, 46:OCT73-273
  R. OLIVER, 45:OCT73-43
JENCKS, C. & OTHERS. INEQUALITY.*
  P. ROSENBERG, 473(PR):3/1974-487
JENCKS, C. & N. SILVER. ADHOCISM.
  S.E. COHEN, 44:JUN73-6
  S. DAVIS, 505:APR73-141
JENKINS, B. BRITAIN & THE WAR FOR
THE UNION. (VOL 1)
  M. HURST, 617(TLS):24OCT75-1261
JENKINS, C. ANDRÉ MALRAUX.
  F-E. DORENLOT, 399(MLJ):MAR74-141
JENKINS, D. THE BRITISH.
  P. HEBBLETHWAITE, 617(TLS):5DEC75-
  1465
JENKINS, D.H. & H.V. WILSON. HOUSE
PLANTS FOR EVERY WINDOW.
  J. CANADAY, 441:13APR75-16
JENKINS, E. DR. GULLY'S STORY.
  R.C. TOBIAS, 637(VS):DEC73-212
JENKINS, E. THE MYSTERY OF KING
ARTHUR.
  C.L. MEE, JR., 441:7DEC75-38

JENKINS, S. LANDLORDS TO LONDON.
F.M.L. THOMPSON, 617(TLS):5SEP75-
988
JENNER, P.N. SOUTHEAST ASIAN LITER-
ATURES IN TRANSLATION.
H.C. WOODBRIDGE, 399(MLJ):NOV74-
369
JENNINGS, E. GROWING-POINTS.
R. FULLER, 617(TLS):4JUL75-718
A. STEVENSON, 362:30OCT75-571
JENNINGS, F. THE INVASION OF
AMERICA.
M.M. MINTZ, 441:30NOV75-50
JENNINGS, G. THE TERRIBLE TEAGUE
BUNCH.
M. LEVIN, 441:8JUN75-16
JENS, I. DICHTER ZWISCHEN RECHTS
UND LINKS.*
H. FETTING, 654(WB):1/1973-187
JENSEN, F. FROM VULGAR LATIN TO OLD
PROVENÇAL.
J. CANTERA, 202(FMOD):NOV72/FEB73-
181
JENSEN, F. THE ITALIAN VERB.*
R.J. DI PIETRO, 399(MLJ):APR73-221
JENSEN, G.F. SCANDINAVIAN SETTLE-
MENT NAMES IN YORKSHIRE.
M. GELLING, 447(N&Q):APR73-144
JENSEN, H. MOTIVATION & THE MORAL
SENSE IN FRANCIS HUTCHESON'S ETHI-
CAL THEORY.*
D.F. NORTON, 154:JUN73-336
P.R., 543:MAR73-538
C. WALTON, 481(PQ):JUL73-527
JENSEN, H.J. & M.R. ZIRKER, JR.,
EDS. THE SATIRIST'S ART.*
M. JOHNSON, 481(PQ):JUL73-437
W. KINSLEY, 255:FALL73-331
R. PAULSON, 677:VOL4-294
JENSEN, J.S. SUBJONCTIF ET HYPOTAXE
EN ITALIEN.*
T.G. GRIFFITH, 402(MLR):JAN74-188
A. STEFINLONGO, 545(RPH):MAY74-521
JENSEN, O. THE AMERICAN HERITAGE
HISTORY OF RAILROADS IN AMERICA.
C.L. MEE, JR., 441:7DEC75-46
JENYNS, S. JAPANESE POTTERY.
J.E. KIDDER, JR., 54:DEC73-619
JENYNS, S. LATER CHINESE PORCELAIN.
FONG CHOW, 57:VOL35#1/2-170
JERROLD, D. THE BEST OF MR. PUNCH.*
(R.M. KELLY, ED)
A. EASSON, 447(N&Q):MAR73-104
JERROLD, D. MRS. CAUDLE'S CURTAIN
LECTURES.
M. SLATER, 617(TLS):14FEB75-156
JERSILD, P.C. THE ANIMAL DOCTOR.
D. WAKEFIELD, 441:16NOV75-25
JESSEL, G., WITH J. AUSTIN. THE
WORLD I LIVED IN.
T. HISS, 441:23NOV75-8
JEUNE, S. MUSSET ET SA FORTUNE
LITTÉRAIRE.*
M. SHAW, 208(FS):APR74-220
S. VIERNE, 535(RHL):SEP-OCT73-916
JEWELL, H.M. ENGLISH LOCAL ADMINIS-
TRATION IN THE MIDDLE AGES.
W.O. AULT, 589:JUL74-567
JHABVALA, R.P. AN EXPERIENCE OF
INDIA.*
D. RUBIN, 293(JAST):NOV72-190
JHABVALA, R.P. HEAT & DUST.
B. ALLEN, 617(TLS):7NOV75-1325
D.A.N. JONES, 362:13NOV75-655

JHABVALA, R.P. TRAVELERS.
B. ALLEN, 569(SR):WINTER74-XII
JIMÉNEZ, J.R. DIARIO DE UN POETA
RECIENCASADO. (A. SÁNCHEZ BAR-
BUDO, ED)
R.A. CARDWELL, 86(BHS):APR73-183
JIMÉNEZ, M.R. - SEE UNDER RAMÍREZ
JIMÉNEZ, M.
JINGOES, S.J. A CHIEF IS A CHIEF BY
THE PEOPLE. (J. & C. PERRY, COMPS)
L. MAIR, 617(TLS):12DEC75-1497
JODELLE, E. LE RECUEIL DES INSCRIP-
TIONS, 1558. (V.E. GRAHAM & W.M.
JOHNSON, EDS)
N. MILLER, 54:DEC73-640
JOHANNSEN, R.W. STEPHEN A. DOUGLAS.*
676(YR):AUTUMN73-XII
JOHANSEN, J.D. OM FORTOLKNINGSSITU-
ATIONEN.
A. FJELDSTAD, 172(EDDA):1973/3-173
JOHANSEN, P. & H. VON ZUR MÜHLEN.
DEUTSCH UND UNDEUTSCH IM MITTELAL-
TERLICHEN UND FRÜHNEUZEITLICHEN
REVAL.
D. KIRBY, 575(SEER):APR74-284
JOHN OF GARLAND. JOHANNES DE GAR-
LANDIA: DE MENSURABILI MUSICA.*
(E. REIMER, ED)
W. WAITE, 308:FALL73-320
J.A. WESTRUP, 410(M&L):APR74-243
JOHN, A. & OTHERS - SEE JONES, J.
JOHN, B. SUPREME FICTIONS.
J.P. RUSSO, 617(TLS):10OCT75-1186
JOHN, E. ZUR DIALEKTIK DES SOZIALEN,
NATIONALEN UND INTERNATIONALEN IN
DER KULTURENTWICKLUNG.
R. RINDFLEISCH, 654(WB):2/1973-188
JOHN, V.P. & OTHERS. EARLY CHILD-
HOOD BILINGUAL EDUCATION.
B. SPOLSKY, 399(MLJ):JAN-FEB73-43
JOHNS, E., ED. THEATRE REVIEW '73.
W. LUCAS, 157:WINTER73-92
JOHNSEN, C. MAN - THE INDIVISIBLE.
R. FORSMAN, 154:JUN73-353
JOHNSON, B. CONRAD'S MODELS OF
MIND.*
N. SHERRY, 637(VS):MAR74-336
C.T. WATTS, 541(RES):MAY73-239
JOHNSON, B.S. CHRISTIE MALRY'S OWN
DOUBLE ENTRY.*
E. GLOVER, 565:VOL14#4-69
M. PRICE, 676(YR):SUMMER74-554
JOHNSON, B.S. SEE THE OLD LADY
DECENTLY.
P. ADAMS, 61:AUG75-89
V. CUNNINGHAM, 617(TLS):2MAY75-473
E. FEINSTEIN, 362:31JUL75-158
D.K. MANO, 441:10AUG75-6
442(NY):22SEP75-131
JOHNSON, B.S., WITH M. BAKEWELL &
G. GORDON, EDS. YOU ALWAYS REMEM-
BER THE FIRST TIME.
D.J. ENRIGHT, 617(TLS):3OCT75-1141
JOHNSON, C. COMMUNIST CHINA & LATIN
AMERICA, 1959-1967.
A.P.L. LIU, 318(JAOS):APR-JUN73-
221
JOHNSON, C. FAITH & THE GOOD THING.
A. GOTTLIEB, 441:12JAN75-6
JOHNSON, D. REGENCY REVOLUTION.
P. ZIEGLER, 617(TLS):24JAN75-72

JOHNSON, D. THE SHADOW KNOWS.*
P. ADAMS, 61:JAN75-90
R. DINNAGE, 617(TLS):6JUN75-617
T.R. EDWARDS, 453:20FEB75-34
L.E. SISSMAN, 442(NY):3MAR75-97
JOHNSON, D.B., A. KASPIN & M.W.
KOSTRUBA, EDS. EYEWITNESS.
R.G. JONES, 399(MLJ):MAR73-146
J. PADRO, 574(SEEJ):SPRING72-118
JOHNSON, E. SIR WALTER SCOTT.*
T.R. DALE, 125:OCT73-82
JOHNSON, E.A.J. THE FOUNDATIONS OF
AMERICAN ECONOMIC FREEDOM.
H.J. HENDERSON, 656(WMQ):APR74-330
JOHNSON, H.G., ED. THE NEW MERCAN-
TILISM.
E. ROLL, 617(TLS):18APR75-432
JOHNSON, H.L. - SEE ALTAMIRANO, I.M.
JOHNSON, I. EMANUEL SWEDENBORG.
L.P. WESSELL, JR., 399(MLJ):JAN-
FEB73-59
JOHNSON, J.H., J. SALT & P.A. WOOD,
EDS. HOUSING & THE MIGRATION OF
LABOUR IN ENGLAND & WALES.
617(TLS):10JAN75-41
"JOHN G. JOHNSON COLLECTION: CATA-
LOGUE OF FLEMISH & DUTCH PAINTINGS."
90:MAY73-348
JOHNSON, J.W. & D. STOCK. THE
CIRCLE OF SEASONS.
639(VQR):AUTUMN74-CLVIII
JOHNSON, L. THE DEVIL, THE GARGOYLE
& THE BUFFOON.
295:FEB74-431
JOHNSON, L. HIGHLIFE FOR CALIBAN.
J. POVEY, 2:SUMMER74-86
JOHNSON, M., COMP. RECORDS OF THE
UNITED STATES MARINE CORPS: RECORD
GROUP 127.
D.B. GRACY 2D, 14:APR73-249
JOHNSON, M. VIRGINIA WOOLF.
L.D. BLOOM, 454:SPRING74-255
JOHNSON, M. & W.J. HEYNEN, COMPS.
RECORDS OF THE HYDROGRAPHIC OFFICE:
RECORD GROUP 37.
D.B. GRACY 2D, 14:APR73-249
JOHNSON, M.L. THE NEW JOURNALISM.
295:FEB74-371
JOHNSON, M.W. LET'S GO PLAY AT THE
ADAMS'.*
N. CALLENDAR, 441:27APR75-29
P.M. SPACKS, 249(HUDR):SUMMER74-
283
JOHNSON, P. FORM & TRANSFORMATION
IN MUSIC & POETRY OF THE ENGLISH
RENAISSANCE.*
D. ARNOLD, 677:VOL4-257
M-A. DE KISCH, 189(EA):OCT-DEC73-
461
R.P. MACCUBBIN, 301(JEGP):JUL74-
425
J.L. PALLISTER, 568(SCN):SPRING-
SUMMER74-9
JOHNSON, P. POPE JOHN XXIII.
J. BOSSY, 362:5JUN75-744
JOHNSON, P.H. THE GOOD LISTENER.
E. ABEEL, 441:28SEP75-30
A. DUCHÊNE, 617(TLS):20JUN75-689
J. MELLORS, 362:19JUN75-821
442(NY):3NOV75-171
JOHNSON, P.H. IMPORTANT TO ME.*
E. JANEWAY, 441:14SEP75-18
S. SECKER, 617(TLS):3JAN75-18
442(NY):21APR75-144

JOHNSON, P.H. A SUMMER TO DECIDE.
A. DUCHÊNE, 617(TLS):2MAY75-473
442(NY):30JUN75-98
JOHNSON, R. MAN'S PLACE.*
C. DUNCAN, 150(DR):AUTUMN73-567
M. KIRKHAM, 529(QQ):WINTER73-646
M.K. SPEARS, 27(AL):MAR74-120
G. WOODCOCK, 569(SR):FALL74-685
JOHNSON, R. & P. - SEE DE MONTHER-
LANT, H.
JOHNSON, R.B. HENRY DE MONTHERLANT.
D.H. MORRIS 4TH, 577(SHR):WINTER
73-103
JOHNSON, R.F. THE ROYAL GEORGE.
D.W. JACKSON, 447(N&Q):NOV73-436
JOHNSON, R.S. MESSIAEN.
D. ARNOLD, 362:3JUL75-29
W. MELLERS, 617(TLS):12SEP75-1030
JOHNSON, R.S. MORE'S "UTOPIA."
M-A. DE KISCH, 189(EA):OCT-DEC73-
459
JOHNSON, S. THE HISTORY OF RASSE-
LAS, PRINCE OF ABISSINIA. (G.
TILLOTSON & B. JENKINS, EDS)
I. DONALDSON, 447(N&Q):NOV73-431
JOHNSON, S. A JOURNEY TO THE WEST-
ERN ISLANDS OF SCOTLAND.* (M. LAS-
CELLES, ED)
J.T. BOULTON, 179(ES):APR73-177
C. LAMONT, 541(RES):FEB73-92
P. ROGERS, 447(N&Q):NOV73-434
JOHNSON, S. LIFE OF SAVAGE.* (C.
TRACY, ED)
J.T. BOULTON, 447(N&Q):JUN73-227
JOHNSON, S. THE RAMBLER.* (W.J.
BATE & A.B. STRAUSS, EDS)
W. GAUGER, 38:BAND91HEFT2-260
C.J. RAWSON, 184(EIC):JUL72-303
JOHNSON, T. HOMING SIGNALS.
G. HITCHCOCK, 651(WHR):AUTUMN74-
404
JOHNSON, U. ANNIVERSARIES. (VOL 1)
C. LEHMANN-HAUPT, 441:24FEB75-23
E. PAWEL, 441:23FEB75-4
JOHNSON, V., S.H. ORMEROD & F.
STADTFELD. ERZÄHLT ES MIR.
L. GILBERT, 399(MLJ):JAN-FEB73-57
JOHNSON, W.R. LUXURIANCE & ECONOMY.
U. HEIBGES, 24:SPRING74-75
M. WINTERBOTTOM, 123:MAR74-70
JOHNSTON, G. HAPPY ENOUGH.*
D.G. JONES, 102(CANL):WINTER74-81
S. SCOBIE, 529(QQ):SUMMER73-310
JOHNSTON, H.J.M. BRITISH EMIGRATION
POLICY, 1815-1830.
H. MALCHOW, 637(VS):SEP73-106
JOHNSTON, J. HOW MANY MILES TO
BABYLON?*
J. MELLORS, 364:JUN/JUL74-135
JOHNSTON, J. WILDERNESS WOMEN.*
C. THOMAS, 99:DEC75/JAN76-43
JOHNSTON, R.C. & D.D.R. OWEN, EDS.
TWO OLD FRENCH GAUVAIN ROMANCES.
J.A. BURROW, 382(MAE):1974/2-168
D. EVANS, 447(N&Q):DEC73-470
N.J. LACY, 399(MLJ):SEP-OCT74-274
JOHNSTON, W. CHRISTIAN ZEN.*
R. WEBER, 613:SPRING73-146
JOHNSTON, W.M. THE AUSTRIAN MIND.*
M. ERMARTH, 125:OCT73-91
A.D. KLARMANN, 406:FALL74-328
JOHNSTON, W.M. THE FORMATIVE YEARS
OF R.G. COLLINGWOOD.
L. RUBINOFF, 154:MAR73-135

JOISTEN, C. CONTES POPULAIRES DU
DAUPHINÉ.
  J. CHOCHEYRAS, 549(RLC):JUL-SEP73-
485
JOLLY, W.P. SIR OLIVER LODGE.
  C. DAVIDSON, 617(TLS):7FEB75-146
JOLY, A. - SEE HARRIS, J.
JOLY, A. - SEE THUROT, F.
JOLY, R. - SEE HIPPOCRATES
JONAS, G. CITIES.*
  F.W. WATT, 99:JUN75-40
JONAS, K.W., ED. DEUTSCHE WELTLIT-
ERATUR.
  L.R. FURST, 131(CL):SPRING73-181
  A.F. GOESSL, 406:WINTER74-425
JONAS, K.W. DIE THOMAS-MANN-LITERA-
TUR.* (VOL 1)
  W.V. BLOMSTER, 406:FALL74-312
  W. GROTHE, 597(SN):VOL45#1-192
  H. LEHNERT, 301(JEGP):JAN74-92
  E. SCHIFFER, 399(MLJ):JAN-FEB74-70
JONAS, O. - SEE SCHENKER, H.
JONAS, P. LES SYSTÈMES COMPARATIFS
À DEUX TERMES EN ANCIEN FRANÇAIS.
  B. FOSTER, 208(FS):APR74-239
JONDORF, G. ROBERT GARNIER & THE
THEMES OF POLITICAL TRAGEDY IN THE
SIXTEENTH CENTURY.*
  F. HIGMAN, 402(MLR):APR74-403
JONES, A. HOPE SHOULD ALWAYS.
  W. PEDEN, 569(SR):FALL74-712
639(VQR):WINTER74-X
JONES, A.H.M. THE CITIES OF THE
EASTERN ROMAN PROVINCES. (2ND ED
REV BY M. AVI-YONAH & OTHERS)
  E.W. GRAY, 123:NOV74-271
  E. WILL, 555:VOL47FASC2-338
JONES, A.H.M. THE CRIMINAL COURTS
OF THE ROMAN REPUBLIC & PRINCIPATE.
  P.A. BRUNT, 123:NOV74-265
  R. SEAGER, 313:VOL63-312
  W.B. TYRRELL, 124:MAY73-476
JONES, A.H.M., J.R. MARTINDALE & J.
MORRIS. THE PROSOPOGRAPHY OF THE
LATER ROMAN EMPIRE.* (VOL 1)
  J.F. MATTHEWS, 123:MAR74-97
  S.I. OOST, 122:JAN74-70
JONES, B. FOR MAD MARY.
  R. GARFITT, 364:DEC74/JAN75-101
JONES, B. POEMS & A FAMILY ALBUM.
  A. CLUYSENAAR, 565:VOL14#1-70
JONES, B. & B.L. HAWES. STEP IT
DOWN.
  B. SUTTON-SMITH, 292(JAF):JUL-SEP
73-307
JONES, B. & B. HOWELL. POPULAR
ARTS OF THE FIRST WORLD WAR.
  D. KUNZLE, 54:DEC73-646
JONES, C.P. PLUTARCH & ROME.*
  J. BRISCOE, 123:NOV74-202
  H. MARTIN, JR., 124:NOV72-180
  L. PEARSON, 24:SUMMER74-204
JONES, D. EPOCH & ARTIST.
  D. BLAMIRES, 148:AUTUMN73-285
JONES, D. MISS LIBERTY, MEET CRAZY
HORSE!
  P.D. MORROW, 649(WAL):FALL73-153
JONES, D. THE SLEEPING LORD & OTHER
FRAGMENTS.*
  P. ADAMS, 61:FEB75-123
  R. GARFITT, 364:AUG/SEP74-108
  J. MATTHIAS, 491:JAN75-233
JONES, D. - SEE THOMAS, D.

JONES, D.G. BUTTERFLY ON ROCK.*
  P. GOETSCH, 447(N&Q):MAR73-105
JONES, E. POPE & DULNESS.
  P. ROBERTS, 447(N&Q):NOV73-430
JONES, E. SCENIC FORM IN SHAKE-
SPEARE.*
  J. WILDERS, 184(EIC):JAN73-76
JONES, E., ED. STORIES FOR OUR
TIME.
  K. OLTMANN, 430(NS):JUL73-391
JONES, E. & J. LLOYD. THE RIPPER
FILE.
  P.D. JAMES, 617(TLS):11APR75-394
JONES, E.A. VOICES OF NÉGRITUDE.
  M. COOK, 207(FR):DEC72-427
JONES, E.L. AGRICULTURE & THE IN-
DUSTRIAL REVOLUTION.
  M. HAVINDEN, 617(TLS):18APR75-421
JONES, G. CORREGIDORA.
  C. LEHMANN-HAUPT, 441:21APR75-33
  R. SOKOLOV, 441:25MAY75-21
  J. UPDIKE, 442(NY):18AUG75-80
JONES, G. KINGS, BEASTS, & HEROES.*
  R. BROMWICH, 541(RES):NOV73-465
  A. CRÉPIN, 189(EA):JUL-SEP73-350
  R. FRANK, 255(HAB):SUMMER73-220
  N. JACOBS, 382(MAE):1974/2-144
  B. RAW, 447(N&Q):NOV73-429
  R.M. WILSON, 175:SPRING73-27
JONES, G.F. SPÄTES MITTELALTER
[1300-1450].*
  E. THURNHER, 133:1973/3-255
JONES, G.F. & A. DEMAITRE - SEE "LA
CHANSON DE ROLAND"
JONES, G.S. OUTCAST LONDON.*
  A. WELSH, 155:MAY73-123
JONES, G.W. - SEE MATHER, C.
JONES, H.E. KANT'S PRINCIPLE OF
PERSONALITY.*
  R.F. ATKINSON, 479(PHQ):OCT73-357
  J.G. MURPHY, 482(PHR):JUL73-388
  M.E. WILLIAMS, 154:JUN73-342
JONES, H.M. THE AGE OF ENERGY.*
  H.F. SMITH, 376:OCT73-138
JONES, H.M. REVOLUTION & ROMANTI-
CISM.*
  A.O. ALDRIDGE, 27(AL):JAN75-582
  P. CONRAD, 617(TLS):23MAY75-550
  S. PAUL, 385(MQR):SPRING75-216
  M. PECKHAM, 591(SIR):FALL74-359
  M.D. PETERSON, 639(VQR):SUMMER74-
451
  N. PETTIT, 432(NEQ):SEP74-461
JONES, J. THE GYPSIES OF GRANADA.
(TEXT BY A. JOHN & OTHERS)
  E.F. STANTON, 582(SFQ):MAR73-83
JONES, J. WW II.
  M. BLUMENSON, 441:12OCT75-26
  C. LEHMANN-HAUPT, 441:10SEP75-37
JONES, J.A. POPE'S COUPLET ART.*
  I. SIMON, 179(ES):JUN72-258
JONES, J.W. THE SHATTERED SYNTHE-
SIS.*
  J.M. BUMSTED, 656(WMQ):JUL74-524
  D. LEVIN, 639(VQR):WINTER74-148
JONES, K. & OTHERS. OPENING THE
DOOR.
  S. BUDD, 617(TLS):30OCT75-1119
JONES, M. JUSTICE & JOURNALISM.
  O. MILTON, 617(TLS):7FEB75-147
JONES, M. MR. ARMITAGE ISN'T BACK
YET.
  J.C. FIELD, 556(RLV):1973/1-89

JONES, M. THE PURSUIT OF HAPPINESS.
V. CUNNINGHAM, 617(TLS):7NOV75-
1325
N. HEPBURN, 362:11DEC75-806
JONES, N. & I. SCHERFF. ENGLISH
PHRASAL VERBS.
K. FAISS, 353:1JAN73-119
JONES, P., ED. IMAGIST POETRY.*
J. GLOVER, 565:VOL14#3-22
JONES, P. THE RESCUE.
D.M. DAY, 157:WINTER73-89
JONES, R. RATNOSE.
E. MORGAN, 617(TLS):7MAR75-241
JONES, R. THE THEME OF LOVE IN THE
"ROMANS D'ANTIQUITÉ."*
P. HAIDU, 589:APR74-350
A.R. PRESS, 402(MLR):OCT74-861
JONES, R.B. THAI TITLES & RANKS.
A.G. EPSTEIN, 293(JAST):FEB73-374
JONES, R.G. LANGUAGE & PROSODY OF
THE RUSSIAN FOLK EPIC.
J. BAILEY, 574(SEEJ):FALL73-324
JONES, R.G., ED. POETRY OF WALES
1930-1970.
N. THOMAS, 617(TLS):30MAY75-596
JONES, R.O. A LITERARY HISTORY OF
SPAIN: THE GOLDEN AGE; PROSE &
POETRY.
G.A. DAVIES, 86(BHS):JUL73-291
C.B. JOHNSON, 551(RENQ):WINTER73-
507
J.M. SOBRÉ, 131(CL):FALL74-358
400(MLN):MAR73-507
JONES, R.O. - SEE DEYERMOND, A.D.
JONES, R.W. URBAN POLITICS IN INDIA.
617(TLS):30CT75-1126
JONES, V.L., A.H. EAKLE & M.H.
CHRISTENSEN. GENEALOGICAL RESEARCH.
(REV)
J.C. PARKER, 14:APR73-252
JONES, W.D. THE AMERICAN PROBLEM IN
BRITISH DIPLOMACY, 1841-1861.*
639(VQR):AUTUMN74-CXLII
JONES, W.D. & A.B. ERICKSON. THE
PEELITES, 1846-1857.
D.C. MOORE, 637(VS):SEP73-118
JONES, W.G. WILLIAM HEINESEN.
J.F. WEST, 617(TLS):11APR75-406
JONG, E. FEAR OF FLYING.*
D. DURRANT, 364(AUG/SEP74-144
P.M. SPACKS, 249(HUDR):SUMMER74-
283
JONG, E. HALF-LIVES.*
M.G. PERLOFF, 659:WINTER75-84
JONG, E. LOVEROOT.
A. BROYARD, 441:11JUN75-43
H. VENDLER, 441:7SEP75-6
DE JONG, L. HET KONINKRIJK DER
NEDERLANDEN IN DE TWEEDE WEREL-
DOORLOG. (VOLS 1-6)
K.W. SWART, 617(TLS):28NOV75-1428
JONGELING, B. A CLASSIFIED BIBLIO-
GRAPHY OF THE FINDS IN THE DESERT
OF JUDAH 1958-1969.
S.A. KAUFMAN, 318(JAOS):JUL-SEP73-
397
JONKE, L. HRVATSKI KNJIŽEVNI JEZIK
19. I 20. STOLJEĆA.
R. DUNATOV, 574(SEEJ):SUMMER72-264
JONSON, B. EPICOENE.* (E. PAR-
TRIDGE, ED)
J.J. YOCH, JR., 568(SCN):SPRING-
SUMMER74-16

JONSON, B. EVERY MAN IN HIS HUMOUR.*
(G.B. JACKSON, ED)
J. GURY, 549(RLC):JAN-MAR73-157
M. MINCOFF, 179(ES):DEC72-557
JOORAT, S.A. CATALOGUE OF WESTERN
MANUSCRIPTS ON MEDICINE & SCIENCE
IN THE WELLCOME HISTORICAL MEDICAL
LIBRARY. (VOL 2)
W. LE FANU, 78(BC):WINTER73-543
JOOST, N. & A. SULLIVAN. D.H. LAW-
RENCE & "THE DIAL."
S. GILL, 447(N&Q):JUN73-240
JOOST, N. & A. SULLIVAN, EDS. TO-
WARD THE MODERN.
295:FEB74-371
JORAVSKY, D. & G. HAUPT - SEE MEDVE-
DEV, R.A.
JORDAN, D. BLACK ACCOUNT.
T.J. BINYON, 617(TLS):19DEC75-1508
JORDAN, P. A FALSE SPRING.
J. DURSO, 441:1JUN75-32
JORDAN, R. BERENICE.
P. GREEN, 617(TLS):17JAN75-64
JORDAN, R.D. THE TEMPLE OF ETER-
NITY.*
D.G. DONOVAN, 577(SHR):SUMMER73-
341
R. WILCHER, 677:VOL4-288
JORDAN, W.D. THE WHITE MAN'S BUR-
DEN.*
R.E. LUKER, 432(NEQ):DEC74-616
JORDAN, W.K. EDWARD VI.
A.B. FERGUSON, 551(RENQ):SPRING73-
65
JØRGENSEN, A., ED. ISAK DINESEN,
STORYTELLER.
T.R. WHISSEN, 563(SS):SUMMER74-296
JORGENSEN, J.G. SALISH LANGUAGE &
CULTURE.
H. LANDAR, 353:15MAY73-123
JORGENSEN, P.A. OUR NAKED FRAILTIES.
J.B. FORT, 189(EA):OCT-DEC73-467
J.C. MAXWELL, 551(RENQ):AUTUMN73-
372
H. OPPEL, 430(NS):SEP73-499
JOSEPH, B.L. SHAKESPEARE'S EDEN.*
F.J. LEVY, 551(RENQ):AUTUMN73-363
JOSEPH, J. ROSE IN THE AFTERNOON.
A. MACLEAN, 617(TLS):23MAY75-552
A. STEVENSON, 362:30OCT75-571
JOSEPH, M.K. INSCRIPTION ON A
PAPER DART.
A. MACLEAN, 617(TLS):23MAY75-552
JOSEY, A. LEE KUAN YEW. (2ND ED)
M. OSBORNE, 293(JAST):NOV72-216
JOSHI, S.D., WITH J.A.F. ROODBERGEN
- SEE "PATAÑJALI'S 'VYĀKARAṆA-
MAHĀBHĀṢYA'"
JOSIPOVICI, G. MOBIUS THE STRIP-
PER.*
J. MELLORS, 362:9JAN75-61
JOSIPOVICI, G. THE PRESENT.
A. DUCHÊNE, 617(TLS):4JUL75-714
W. FEAVER, 362:14AUG75-221
JOSIPOVICI, G. THE WORLD & THE
BOOK.*
D. LODGE, 148:SUMMER72-171
H. PESCHMANN, 175:SUMMER72-73
R.W. UPHAUS, 141:WINTER74-73
295:FEB74-472
JOUHANDEAU, M. ORFÈVRE ET SORCIER.
M. TURNELL, 617(TLS):28MAR75-344

JOUKOVSKY, F. ORPHÉE ET SES DIS-
CIPLES DANS LA POÉSIE FRANÇAISE ET
NÉO-LATINE DU XVIE SIÈCLE.*
C. NELSON, 551(RENQ):AUTUMN73-347
JOUKOVSKY, F. - SEE FILLEUL, N.
"JOURNAL DE L'ANNÉE: 1ER JUILLET
1970 - 30 JUIN 1971."
W.W. THOMAS, 207(FR):MAY73-1271
"JOURNAL OF ARABIC LITERATURE."
(VOLS 1-3)
J.A. BELLAMY, 318(JAOS):JUL-SEP73-
369
"THE JOY OF CRAFTS."
B. GUTCHEON, 441:7DEC75-74
JOYCE, J. FINNEGANS WAKE.
J.S. ATHERTON, 617(TLS):12DEC75-
1483
JOYCE, J. SELECTED LETTERS OF JAMES
JOYCE. (R. ELLMANN, ED)
I. HOWE, 441:23NOV75-3
C. LEHMANN-HAUPT, 441:15DEC75-29
JOYCE, S. THE COMPLETE DUBLIN
DIARY OF STANISLAUS JOYCE. (G.H.
HEALEY, ED)
295:FEB74-683
JOYES, C. MONET AT GIVERNY.
F. CRICHTON, 617(TLS):21NOV75-1382
JÓZSEF, A. SELECTED POEMS & TEXTS.
(G. GÖMÖRI & J. ATLAS, EDS)
R. GARFITT, 364:JUN/JUL74-108
J. MARTIN, 491:MAY75-103
JUCKER, H., ED. SONNTAGE MIT LAT-
EINISCHER LITERATUR.
C.J. MATZKE, 124:MAR73-354
JUDD, D. PALMERSTON.
J. RIDLEY, 617(TLS):5DEC75-1436
JUDEN, B. TRADITIONS ORPHIQUES ET
TENDANCES MYSTIQUES DANS LE ROMAN-
TISME FRANÇAIS (1800-1855).*
F.P. BOWMAN, 402(MLR):JUL74-645
A. KIES, 549(RLC):JAN-MAR73-158
JUDSON, W. COLD RIVER.
M. LEVIN, 441:16FEB75-12
JUHÁSZ, J. PROBLEME DER INTERFER-
ENZ.*
E. MARTINS, 353:1APR73-94
J.D. SIMONS, 104:FALL73-418
JUILLAND, A., ED. LINGUISTIC STUD-
IES PRESENTED TO ANDRÉ MARTINET ON
THE OCCASION OF HIS SIXTIETH BIRTH-
DAY.* (VOLS 1&2)
G. INEICHEN, 260(IF):BAND77HEFT2/3-
266
J. KRÁMSKÝ, 353:1MAY73-109
JUIN, H. CHARLES NODIER.
S.F. BELL, 446:FALL-WINTER73/74-90
J. DECOTTIGNIES, 535(RHL):SEP-OCT
73-910
JUKIC, I. THE FALL OF YUGOSLAVIA.
R.K. KINDERSLEY, 617(TLS):24JAN75-
74
JULIA, D. ÉTUDE ÉPIGRAPHIQUE ET
ICONOGRAPHIQUE DES STÈLES FUNÉR-
AIRES DE VIGO.
J.M.C. TOYNBEE, 313:VOL63-277
JULIA, D. LA QUESTION DE L'HOMME ET
LE FONDEMENT DE LA PHILOSOPHIE.
P. BAUMANNS, 53(AGP):BAND55HEFT3-
341
JULIAN. KAISER JULIAN DER ABTRÜN-
NIGE, DIE BRIEFE. (L. GOESSLER,
ED & TRANS)
M.J. COSTELLOE, 124:MAY74-484

JULIARD, P. PHILOSOPHIES OF LANGU-
AGE IN EIGHTEENTH-CENTURY FRANCE.*
J. LEVITT, 353:1JAN73-78
G. NUCHELMANS, 361:SEP73-172
S.N. ROSENBERG, 207(FR):OCT72-253
JULIUSBURGER, S. BEGINNINGS.
M. LEVIN, 441:5JAN75-21
JULLIAN, P. D'ANNUNZIO.*
R. HASTINGS, 402(MLR):JAN74-194
JULLIAN, P. THE SYMBOLISTS.*
C. NEVE, 592:NOV73-210
JULLIAN, P. THE TRIUMPH OF ART
NOUVEAU.*
P. CONRAD, 617(TLS):18JUL75-805
JUMP, J.D., ED. BYRON.
E.E.B., 191(ELN):SEP73(SUPP)-39
P. CONRAD, 617(TLS):29AUG75-962
G. THOMAS, 175:SPRING73-32
JUNEAU, M. CONTRIBUTION À L'HIS-
TOIRE DE LA PRONONCIATION FRANÇAISE
AU QUÉBEC.*
H-M. MILITZ, 682(ZPSK):BAND26HEFT
6-727
N.A. POULIN, 399(MLJ):NOV74-355
JUNG, F. JOE FRANK ILLUSTRIERT DIE
WELT. DIE EROBERUNG DER MASCHINEN.
(W. FÄHNDERS, H. KARRENBROCK & M.
RECTOR, EDS OF BOTH)
H. DENKLER, 406:SUMMER74-181
JUNG, M-R. ÉTUDES SUR LE POÈME AL-
LÉGORIQUE EN FRANCE AU MOYEN ÂGE.*
A.R. PRESS, 402(MLR):JAN74-166
JUNG, R. LICHTENBERG-BIBLIOGRAPHIE.
H. THOMKE, 182:VOL26#19-677
JUNG-EN, L. - SEE UNDER LIU JUNG-EN
JUNGE, H-D. MESSEN, STEUERN, REGELN.
75:4/1973-191
JUNGHANNS, K. BRUNO TAUT - 1880-
1938.
R. BLETTER, 576:OCT73-255
JUNGRAITHMAYR, W., ED. DAS HISTOR-
ISCHE MUSEUM ALS AUFGABE.
E. ETTLINGER, 203:SUMMER73-172
JUNKER, E.W. ZWISCHEN NAHE UND
RHEIN.
F.G. CRONHEIM, 402(MLR):OCT74-939
JUNKER, H. DRAMA UND "PSEUDO-
DRAMA."*
R.N. COE, 402(MLR):APR74-426
JÜRGENS, H. POMPA DIABOLI.
W.H.C. FREND, 123:NOV74-306
JURGENSEN, M. MAX FRISCH: DIE
ROMANE.
G. HILLEN, 301(JEGP):JAN74-97
H. MAC LEAN, 564:OCT73-270
JUST, K.G. VON DER GRÜNDERZEIT BIS
ZUR GEGENWART.
H. REISS, 182:VOL26#13/14-495
JUST, W. NICHOLSON AT LARGE.
C. LEHMANN-HAUPT, 441:24SEP75-45
C. LYDON, 441:26OCT75-46
JUSTICE, D. DEPARTURES.*
I. EHRENPREIS, 453:16OCT75-3
J.J. MC GANN, 491:OCT74-44
J.N. MORRIS, 249(HUDR):SPRING74-
115
A. OSTROFF, 651(WHR):SUMMER74-292
P. RAMSEY, 569(SR):SPRING74-398
639(VQR):SPRING74-LVI
JÜTTNER, S. GRUNDTENDENZEN DER
THEATERKRITIK VON FRIEDRICH-MEL-
CHIOR GRIMM (1753-1773).*
W.D. HOWARTH, 208(FS):JAN74-81

JUVENAL. SATIRES. (NEW ED) (J.D. DUFF, ED)
J.G. GRIFFITH, 123:MAR74-140

KA-TZETNIK 135633. HOUSE OF DOLLS.
PIEPEL. HOUSE OF LOVE. STAR
ETERNAL.
A. RUDOLF, 565:VOL14#4-28
KAAN, A. - SEE HEGEL, G.W.F.
KAČALA, J. DOPLNOK V SLOVENČINE.
W. BROWNE, 574(SEEJ):FALL72-381
KACHRU, B.B. A REFERENCE GRAMMAR OF
KASHMIRI.
R.M. HARRIS, 353:1JUL73-106
KACZEROWSKY, K. BÜRGERLICHE ROMAN-
KUNST IM ZEITALTER DES BAROCK.
P. SKRINE, 402(MLR):JUL74-702
KADLEC, J. LEBEN UND SCHRIFTEN DES
PRAGER MAGISTERS ADALBERT RANKONIS
DE ERICINIO.
O. ODLOZILIK, 589:JAN74-127
DE KADT, E. - SEE MEDVEDEV, R.A.
KADUSHIN, C. THE AMERICAN INTELLEC-
TUAL ELITE.*
P. STEINFELS, 231:JAN75-80
KAEL, P. THE CITIZEN KANE BOOK.
M. GOLDSTEIN, 295:APR74-1050
A.H. MARILL, 200:JUN-JUL73-370
214:VOL6#24-114
KAEL, P. DEEPER INTO MOVIES.
R. MAYNE, 617(TLS):24OCT75-1256
KAEMPFERT, M. SÄKULARISATION UND
NEUE HEILIGKEIT.*
J. LEAMAN, 402(MLR):APR74-462
P. PÜTZ, 680(ZDP):BAND92HEFT4-608
W.D. WILLIAMS, 220(GL&L):APR74-271
H. WINGLER, 182:VOL26#15/16-522
KAFKA, F. BRIEFE AN OTTLA UND DIE
FAMILIE.
I. PARRY, 617(TLS):28FEB75-231
KAFKA, F. LETTERS TO FELICE.* (GER-
MAN TITLE: BRIEFE AN FELICE.) (E.
HELLER & J. BORN, EDS)
639(VQR):WINTER74-XXVIII
KAFKA, F. OEUVRES COMPLÈTES. (M.
ROBERT, ED)
G. DELEUZE & F. GUATTARI, 98:NOV73-
1046
KAGAN, D. THE ARCHIDAMIAN WAR.
P. GREEN, 617(TLS):29AUG75-972
KAGAN, D. THE OUTBREAK OF THE PELO-
PONNESIAN WAR.
S.K. EDDY, 122:OCT73-308
KAGAN, R.L. STUDENTS & SOCIETY IN
EARLY MODERN SPAIN.
H. KAMEN, 617(TLS):23MAY75-556
KAGARLITSKY, Y. CHTO TAKOYE FAN-
TASTIKA?
B. RULLKÖTTER, 617(TLS):25JUL75-
857
KAHANE, M. THE STORY OF THE JEWISH
DEFENSE LEAGUE.
H. GOLD, 441:8JUN75-4
KAHL, K. JOHANN NESTROY ODER DER
WIENERISCHE SHAKESPEARE.
K. SEGAR, 617(TLS):30OCT75-1148
KAHL, R. - SEE VON HELMHOLTZ, H.
KAHLER, E. THE GERMANS.* (R. & R.
KIMBER, EDS)
639(VQR):AUTUMN74-CXLVI

KAHLER, E. THE INWARD TURN OF NAR-
RATIVE.*
P. STEVICK, 131(CL):WINTER74-85
KAHMEN, V. ART HISTORY OF PHOTOG-
RAPHY.
H. KRAMER, 441:7DEC75-5
KAHN, E.J., JR. THE CHINA HANDS.
J. LELYVELD, 441:5OCT75-4
R. TRUMBULL, 441:28NOV75-41
442(NY):13OCT75-177
KAHN, H.L. MONARCHY IN THE EMPER-
OR'S EYES.*
PEI HUANG, 318(JAOS):APR-JUN73-210
KAHN, J., ED. OPEN AT YOUR OWN RISK.
442(NY):10NOV75-195
KAHN, J. LA PARTICIPATION.
J-A. BOUR, 207(FR):FEB73-642
KAHN, K. HILLBILLY WOMEN.
M.P. GODDIN, 109:FALL/WINTER73/74-
129
KAHN, L. & D.D. HOOK, EDS. STIMMEN
AUS DEUTSCHEN LANDEN.
H. HOIVIK, 399(MLJ):APR73-224
KAIMO, M. THE CHORUS OF GREEK DRAMA
WITHIN THE LIGHT OF THE PERSON &
NUMBER USED.
W.M. CALDER 3D, 122:APR74-158
KAINZ, F. PSYCHOLOGIE DER SPRACHE.
(VOL 2)
J. PRŮCHA, 353:1JAN73-94
KAINZ, F. PSYCHOLOGIE DER SPRACHE.*
(VOL 5, PT 2)
B. CARSTENSEN, 430(NS):JAN73-45
G.F. MEIER, 682(ZPSK):BAND26HEFT
3/4-428
KAISER, F.B. DIE RUSSISCHE JUSTIZ-
REFORM VON 1864.*
M. RAEFF, 550(RUSR):JUL73-318
KAISER, G. WERKE, AUSGABE IN SECHS
BÄNDEN. (VOLS 1-3)
G-C. TUNSTALL, 399(MLJ):MAR73-142
KAISER, G. WERKE, AUSGABE IN SECHS
BÄNDEN. (VOLS 4&5) (W. HUDER, ED)
G-C. TUNSTALL, 399(MLJ):APR74-212
KAISER, G. WERKE, AUSGABE IN SECHS
BÄNDEN. (VOL 6) (W. HUDER, ED)
W. PAULSEN, 301(JEGP):JAN74-94
G.C. TUNSTALL, 399(MLJ):APR74-212
KAISER, G.R. PROUST-MUSIL-JOYCE.
T. ZIOLKOWSKI, 131(CL):WINTER74-87
KAKRIDIS, J.T. HOMER REVISITED.*
J.T. HOOKER, 303:VOL93-220
KAKRIDIS, J.T. MELETES KAI ARTHRA.*
H. LLOYD-JONES, 123:MAR74-164
KALB, M. & B. KISSINGER.*
D. STAIRS, 99:NOV75-32
KALECHOFSKY, R. GEORGE ORWELL.
A. DE VITIS, 651(WHR):SUMMER74-281
KALINOWSKI, G. LA LOGIQUE DES
NORMES.
R. BLANCHÉ, 542:JUL-SEP73-361
KALLICH, M. THE ASSOCIATION OF
IDEAS & CRITICAL THEORY IN EIGHT-
EENTH-CENTURY ENGLAND.*
I. SIMON, 179(ES):APR73-176
KALLICH, M. HORACE WALPOLE.*
R.R. REA, 577(SHR):SUMMER73-344
KALM, P. TRAVELS INTO NORTH AMER-
ICA. (R.M. SARGENT, ED)
S.W. JACKMAN, 432(NEQ):SEP73-479
KALOKYRIS, K. THE BYZANTINE WALL
PAINTINGS OF CRETE. (H. HIONIDES
& J. GUNDERSON, EDS)
A. BRYER, 617(TLS):21MAR75-315

KALOUS, M. CANNIBALS & TONGO PLAY-
ERS OF SIERRA LEONE.
B.E. HARRELL-BOND, 617(TLS):17OCT
75-1228
KAMBER, G. MAX JACOB & THE POETICS
OF CUBISM.*
S.J. COLLIER, 208(FS):APR74-224
B. DIJKSTRA, 295:FEB74-658
J. GOLDING, 90:SEP73-616
KAMINSKY, M. WHAT'S INSIDE YOU IT
SHINES OUT OF YOU.
P. ZWEIG, 441:9FEB75-5
KAMMEN, M. PEOPLE OF PARADOX.*
H.B. GOW, 396(MODA):SPRING74-205
KAMMEN, M. - SEE BECKER, C.L.
KÄMPER, D. STUDIEN ZUR INSTRUMEN-
TALEN ENSEMBLEMUSIK DES 16. JAHR-
HUNDERTS IN ITALIEN.
C. MAC CLINTOCK, 317:SPRING73-161
KANAPATHY, V. THE MALAYSIAN ECON-
OMY.
G.D. NESS, 293(JAST):AUG73-746
KANDEL, L. WORD ALCHEMY.
M.G. PERLOFF, 659:WINTER75-84
KÄNDLER, K. DRAMA UND KLASSENKAMPF.*
J.H. REID, 182:VOL26#3/4-103
KANE, G. & E.T. DONALDSON - SEE
"PIERS PLOWMAN: THE B VERSION"
KANE, H. LUST OF POWER.
N. CALLENDAR, 441:9MAR75-22
KANG, S.T. SUMERIAN ECONOMIC TEXTS
FROM THE DREHEM ARCHIVE.
J. RENGER, 318(JAOS):JUL-SEP73-404
KANIN, G. HOLLYWOOD.*
J. HOUSEMAN, 617(TLS):24OCT75-1256
"KANJI KANJI."
R.L. BROWN, 270:VOL23#2-40
KANNGIESSER, S. ASPEKTE DER SYN-
CHRONEN UND DIACHRONEN LINGUISTIK.
W. BLÜMEL, 343:BAND16HEFT2-117
KANT, I. CRITICA DEL GIUDIZIO. (A.
PLEBE, ED)
K. OEDINGEN, 342:BAND64HEFT1-148
KANT, I. CRITICA DELLA RAGION PURA
(ESTRATTI). (G. BONTADINI, ED &
TRANS)
K. OEDINGEN, 342:BAND64HEFT1-146
KANT, I. GESAMMELTE SCHRIFTEN.
(VOL 28, 2ND HALF)
C. CESA, 548(RCSF):OCT-DEC73-476
KANT, I. IL GIUDIZIO ESTETICO. (A.
NEGRI, ED)
K. OEDINGEN, 342:BAND64HEFT1-148
KANT, I. KANT'S POLITICAL WRIT-
INGS.* (H. REISS, ED)
W.H.W., 319:OCT75-548
KANT, I. LETTRES SUR LA MORALE ET
LA RELIGION.* (J-L. BRUCH, ED &
TRANS)
V.C., 154:SEP73-581
KANT, I. LEZIONI DI ETICA. (A.
GUERRA, TRANS)
K. OEDINGEN, 342:BAND64HEFT1-147
KANT, I. MÉTAPHYSIQUE DES MOEURS.
(PT 1) (A. PHILONENKO, TRANS)
J. KOPPER, 342:BAND64HEFT1-146
KANT, I. LA RELIGIONE ENTRO I
LIMITI DELLA SOLA RAGIONE. (A.
POGGI, ED & TRANS)
K. OEDINGEN, 342:BAND64HEFT1-147
KANT, I. ZUM EWIGEN FRIEDEN. (T.
VALENTINER, ED)
R. MALTER, 342:BAND64HEFT2-272

KANTOR, M. VALLEY FORGE.
P-L. ADAMS, 61:NOV75-126
M. LEVIN, 441:19OCT75-45
KANZOG, K. PROLEGOMENA ZU EINER
HISTORISCH-KRITISCHEN AUSGABE DER
WERKE HEINRICH VON KLEISTS.
I.F., 191(ELN):SEP73(SUPP)-148
KAPFERER, B. STRATEGY & TRANSACTION
IN AN AFRICAN FACTORY.
M. PEIL, 69:OCT73-362
KAPLAN, C.A. THE WARSAW DIARY OF
CHAIM A. KAPLAN. (A.I. KATSH, ED
& TRANS)
A.J. RAWICK, 287:JUL-AUG73-30
KAPLAN, F. MIRACLES OF RARE DE-
VICE.*
H. SERGEANT, 175:SUMMER73-78
KAPLAN, H. DEMOCRATIC HUMANISM &
AMERICAN LITERATURE.*
J.C. STUBBS, 445(NCF):SEP73-232
295:FEB74-398
KAPLAN, J. LINCOLN STEFFENS.*
T. COOLEY, 27(AL):JAN75-592
K.O. MORGAN, 617(TLS):4JUL75-710
KAPLAN, J.M. "LA NEUVAINE DE CYTH-
ÈRE:" UNE DÉMARMONTÉLISATION DE
MARMONTEL.*
J. RENWICK, 208(FS):OCT74-471
KAPLAN, S. THE BLACK PRESENCE IN
THE ERA OF THE AMERICAN REVOLUTION,
1770-1800.
W.M. BILLINGS, 432(NEQ):SEP74-485
639(VQR):SPRING74-XLII
KAPLOW, J. THE NAMES OF KINGS.
R. DARNTON, 453:20CT75-17
KAPPELER, A. IVAN GROZNYJ IM
SPIEGEL DER AUSLÄNDISCHEN DRUCK-
SCHRIFTEN SEINER ZEIT.
H.F. GRAHAM, 104:WINTER74-594
KARA, G. CHANTS D'UN BARDE MONGOL.
J.C. STREET, 318(JAOS):APR-JUN73-
228
KARANFILOV, E. BULGARES.
270:VOL23#3-60
KARKOSCHKA, E. NOTATION IN NEW
MUSIC.*
T.D. DUNN, 308:SPRING73-168
KARL, F.R. THE ADVERSARY LITERA-
TURE.
R. MOORE, 268:JUL75-191
KARLIN, W. & OTHERS, EDS. FREE FIRE
ZONE.
J.H., 502(PRS):FALL73-281
KARLINGER, F. & G. DE FREITAS, EDS &
TRANS. BRASILIANISCHE MÄRCHEN.
E. ETTLINGER, 203:SPRING73-81
KARLINSKY, S. - SEE CHEKHOV, A.
KARLSSON, H. STUDIER ÖVER BÅTNAMN,
SÄRSKILT NAMN PÅ BACKEBÅTAR OCH
BANKSKUTOR FRÅN 1700-TALETS BOHUS-
LÄN.
B. KRESS, 682(ZPSK):BAND26HEFT1/2-
168
M. NOLSØE, 260(IF):BAND78-332
KARMAY, S.G., ED & TRANS. THE
TREASURY OF GOOD SAYINGS.
J. BLOFELD, 302:JUL73-259
T.V. WYLIE, 244(HJAS):VOL33-297
KARMEL, I. AN ESTATE OF MEMORY.
R.E. ROSS, 502(PRS):SUMMER73-171
KARNEIN, A. - SEE CAPELLANUS, A.
KARNOW, S. MAO & CHINA.
J.C. HSIUNG, 293(JAST):AUG73-691

KAROL, K.S. THE SECOND CHINESE
REVOLUTION.
J.K. FAIRBANK, 453:1MAY75-18
R. TERRILL, 441:15JUN75-10
KAROW, O., ED & TRANS. MÄRCHEN AUS
VIETNAM.
E. ETTLINGER, 203:SPRING73-81
KARSEN, S.P. JAIME TORRES BODET.
E.J. MULLEN, 238:SEP73-740
KARSTIEN, H. INFIXE IM INDOGERMAN-
ISCHEN (GEKÜRZTE FASSUNG).
O. SZEMERÉNYI, 343:BAND17HEFT2-145
KARTOMI, M.J. MATJAPAT SONGS IN
CENTRAL & WEST JAVA.
H. SUSILO, 187:SEP75-484
KARUNAKARAN, K. THE KOLLIMALAI
TAMIL DIALECT.
H.F. SCHIFFMAN, 318(JAOS):JUL-SEP
73-387
KARUNATILAKE, H.N.S. ECONOMIC DEV-
ELOPMENT IN CEYLON.
W.H. WRIGGINS, 293(JAST):MAY73-548
KASACK, W. DER STIL KONSTANTIN
GEORGIEVIČ PAUSTOVSKIJS.*
V.D. MIHAILOVICH, 574(SEEJ):FALL73-
340
KASCHNITZ, M.L. EIN LESEBUCH, 1964-
1974.
S.S. PRAWER, 617(TLS):12DEC75-1495
KASDAGLIS, E.C. - SEE SEFERIS, G.
KASHAP, S.P., ED. STUDIES IN SPIN-
OZA.*
483:APR73-199
KASHIKAR, C.G. - SEE "ŚRAUTAKOŚA"
KASSEL, R. DER TEXT DER ARISTOTEL-
ISCHEN RHETORIK.
S. BERNARDINELLO, 303:VOL93-225
F. TRAUTMANN, 124:SEP-OCT73-47
KASTENBAUM, R. & R. AISENBERG. THE
PSYCHOLOGY OF DEATH.
C. RICKS, 617(TLS):18JUL75-790
KASTLE, H. CROSS COUNTRY.
N. CALLENDAR, 441:4MAY75-55
KÄSTNER, E. FRIEDRICH DER GROSSE
UND DIE DEUTSCHE LITERATUR.
F. STOCK, 52:BAND8HEFT3-340
KATIČIĆ, R. A CONTRIBUTION TO THE
GENERAL THEORY OF COMPARATIVE LIN-
GUISTICS.*
C.S. LEONARD, JR., 399(MLJ):SEP-
OCT73-294
KATO, S. FORM STYLE TRADITION.*
M. MEDLEY, 39:NOV73-408
KATSH, A.I. - SEE KAPLAN, C.A.
KATZ, A. THE POLITICS OF ECONOMIC
REFORM IN THE SOVIET UNION.
R.W. CAMPBELL, 550(RUSR):JUL73-319
KATZ, H.M. LOVE & MARRIAGE.
M. LEVIN, 441:31AUG75-13
KATZ, J., ED. STEPHEN CRANE IN
TRANSITION.*
D. PIZER, 594:SUMMER73-261
KATZ, J., ED. PROOF. (VOL 3)
G.T. TANSELLE, 617(TLS):8AUG75-904
KATZ, J. RESISTANCE AT CHRISTIANA.
639(VQR):AUTUMN74-CXLII
KATZ, J.J. THE UNDERLYING REALITY
OF LANGUAGE & ITS PHILOSOPHICAL
IMPORT.
S.P. STICH, 482(PHR):APR74-259
KATZ, J.L. LINGUISTIC PHILOSOPHY.
G. SAMPSON, 297(JL):SEP73-366

KATZ, N. & N. MILTON, EDS. WOMEN
OF THE THIRD WORLD.
J. MILLER, 617(TLS):9MAY75-501
KATZMAN, A. MY NAME IS MARY...
M. LEVIN, 441:16MAR75-31
KAUF, R. & D.C. MC CLUNEY, JR., EDS.
PROBEN DEUTSCHER PROSA.
E. WEBER, 399(MLJ):MAR73-140
KAUFFMANN, S., WITH B. HENSTELL, EDS.
AMERICAN FILM CRITICISM: FROM THE
BEGINNINGS TO CITIZEN KANE.
T.J. ROSS, 114(CHIR):VOL25#1-180
KAUFFMANN, C.M. ROMANESQUE MANU-
SCRIPTS 1066-1190.
W. OAKESHOTT, 617(TLS):22AUG75-949
KAUFFMANN, H. GIOVANNI LORENZO
BERNINI.
H. HIBBARD, 56:WINTER73-414
KAUFMAN, L., B. FITZGERALD & T.
SEWELL. MOE BERG.
C. LEHMANN-HAUPT, 441:12FEB75-37
J. SCHWARTZ, 441:30MAR75-20
KAUFMAN, S. GOLD COUNTRY.
J.J. MC GANN, 491:OCT74-44
P. RAMSEY, 569(SR):SPRING74-397
KAUFMAN, T. EL PROTO-TZELTAL-TZOT-
ZIL.
L. CAMPBELL, 350:JUN74-394
KAUFMANN, H., ED. POSITIONEN DER
DDR-LITERATURWISSENSCHAFT.
J. WHITE, 617(TLS):19SEP75-1068
KAUFMANN, W., ED. HEGEL'S POLITICAL
PHILOSOPHY.
A. QUINTON, 453:12JUN75-39
KAUFMANN, W. WITHOUT GUILT & JUS-
TICE.
D.B. KUSPIT, 484(PPR):DEC73-294
KAUSHIK, D. THE INDIAN OCEAN.
S.P. COHEN, 293(JAST):FEB73-358
KAVAN, A. JULIA & THE BAZOOKA.*
(R. DAVIES, ED)
J. ROBINSON, 441:11MAY75-47
442(NY):28APR75-139
KAVAN, A. WHO ARE YOU? MY SOUL IN
CHINA. (R. DAVIES, ED)
E. KORN, 617(TLS):16MAY75-529
KAVANAGH, J.F. & I.G. MATTINGLY,
EDS. LANGUAGE BY EAR & BY EYE.
F. SMITH, 350:DEC74-762
KAVANAGH, P. A PATRICK KAVANAGH
ANTHOLOGY. (E.R. PLATT, ED)
J. JORDAN, 159(DM):AUTUMN/WINTER
73/74-122
KAVANAGH, T.M. THE VACANT MIRROR.
G. MAY, 546(RR):JAN74-66
KAVEESHWAR, G.W. THE ETHICS OF THE
GITĀ.
L. STERNBACH, 318(JAOS):JUL-SEP73-
378
KAVENAGH, W.K., ED. FOUNDATIONS OF
COLONIAL AMERICA.
L.R. GERLACH, 656(WMQ):APR74-327
KAWABATA, Y. BEAUTY & SADNESS.
A. BROYARD, 441:21FEB75-29
A.G. MOJTABAI, 441:2MAR75-3
R. SCRUTON, 617(TLS):3OCT75-1125
E. WEEKS, 61:MAR75-142
442(NY):17MAR75-125
KAWAHITO, K. THE JAPANESE STEEL
INDUSTRY.
T.R. KERSHNER, 293(JAST):FEB73-328

KAWIN, B.F. TELLING IT AGAIN & AGAIN.*
P. HARCOURT, 255(HAB):SPRING73-134
295:FEB74-473
KAYE, C. COMMUNISM IN INDIA.
P. OLDENBURG, 293(JAST):AUG73-722
KAYE, E. - SEE MATTEI, M.
KAYSER, W. & H. GRONEMEYER. MAX BROD.*
E. BOA, 402(MLR):APR74-470
KAZAN, E. THE UNDERSTUDY.*
J. BARNES, 617(TLS):15AUG75-913
R. BUCKLER, 362:11SEP75-349
G. LYONS, 441:12JAN75-6
442(NY):27JAN75-102
KAZANTZAKIS, H. NIKOS KAZANTZAKIS.
P. MACKRIDGE, 617(TLS):25JUL75-856
KAZANTZAKIS, N. JOURNEYING.
P. ADAMS, 61:MAR75-145
442(NY):31MAR75-100
KAZIN, A. BRIGHT BOOK OF LIFE.*
T. COLSON, 268:JAN75-71
D.B. GRAHAM, 594:FALL73-404
A.H. ROSENFELD, 390:NOV73-68
S. SPENCER, 659:SPRING75-249
KEALEY, E.J. ROGER OF SALISBURY.
M. ALTSCHUL, 589:APR74-351
R. BRENTANO, 377:JUL74-116
D.H. FARMER, 382:1974/2-207
KEAN, P.M. CHAUCER & THE MAKING OF ENGLISH POETRY.
M.W. BLOOMFIELD, 382(MAE):1974/2-193
R.T. DAVIES, 541(RES):MAY73-199
R.M. WILSON, 175:AUTUMN72-106
KEARNEY, P.J. THE OLYMPIA PRESS 1953-65.
617(TLS):7NOV75-1330
KEARNEY, R.N. TRADE UNIONS & POLITICS IN CEYLON.
W.H. WRIGGINS, 393(JAST):MAY73-548
KEAST, W.R., ED. SEVENTEENTH CENTURY ENGLISH POETRY.* (REV)
P. LEGOUIS, 189(EA):OCT-DEC73-472
KEATING, L.C. JOACHIM DU BELLAY.
R. GRIFFIN, 207(FR):APR73-1006
M.S. WHITNEY, 399(MLJ):SEP-OCT73-281
KEATING, L.C. ANDRÉ MAUROIS.
D.H. MORRIS 4TH, 577(SHR):WINTER 73-103
KEATING, L.C. ETIENNE PASQUIER.
M-C. WRAGE, 399(MLJ):DEC74-419
KEATING, L.C. & R.O. EVANS - SEE BORGES, J.L., WITH E.Z. DE TORRES
KEATING, P.J. - SEE MORRISON, A.
KEATS, J. LETTERS OF JOHN KEATS. (R. GITTINGS, ED)
J.C. MAXWELL, 447(N&Q):FEB73-77
KEAY, C., ED. AMERICAN POSTERS OF THE TURN OF THE CENTURY.
J.R. MELLOW, 441:7DEC75-82
KEDOURIE, E. ARABIC POLITICAL MEMOIRS & OTHER STUDIES.
G.E. WHEELER, 617(TLS):10JAN75-30
KEEGAN, M. WE CAN STILL HEAR THEM CLAPPING.
P. SHOWERS, 441:19OCT75-7
KEELEY, E. & P. BIEN, EDS. MODERN GREEK WRITERS.*
R.C. CLARK, 544:FALL74-147
M.P. LEVITT, 295:FEB74-431
P. MACKRIDGE, 131(CL):SUMMER73-263

KEEN, B. THE AZTEC IMAGE IN WESTERN THOUGHT.*
J.L. PHELAN, 551(RENQ):WINTER73-489
KEENAN, E.L. THE KURBSKII-GROZNYI APOCRYPHA.*
H.W. DEWEY, 574(SEEJ):SUMMER72-223
W.F. RYAN, 402(MLR):JUL74-716
S.A. ZENKOVSKY, 550(RUSR):JUL73-299
KEENE, D., WITH R. TYLER, EDS. 20 PLAYS OF THE NŌ THEATER.*
R.N. MC KINNON, 293(JAST):NOV72-154
KEENE, H.G. - SEE BEALE, T.W.
KEENER, F.M. ENGLISH DIALOGUES OF THE DEAD.
566:SPRING74-97
KEENER, F.M. AN ESSAY ON POPE.
C. RAWSON, 617(TLS):14MAR75-275
KEEP, D. HISTORY THROUGH STAMPS.
617(TLS):25APR75-465
KEESEY, R.E. MODERN PARLIAMENTARY PROCEDURE.
M.C. MORRISON, 583:SUMMER74-413
KEIFETZ, N. THE SENSATION.
M. LEVIN, 441:20APR75-29
KEIL, E-E. & J. TALÉNS, EDS & TRANS. POESÍA EXPRESIONISTA.
M.J.G., 202(FMOD):JUN73-411
KEIL, G. DER "KURZE HARNTRAKTAT" DES BRESLAUER "CODEX SALERNITANUS" UND SEINE SIPPE.* DER UROGNOSTISCHE PRAXIS IN VOR- UND FRÜHSALERNITANISCHER ZEIT.
W. SCHMITT, 597(SN):VOL45#1-191
KEILER, A.R. A PHONOLOGICAL STUDY OF THE INDO-EUROPEAN LARYNGEALS.
R. ANTTILA, 215(GL):VOL13#2-109
F.O. LINDEMAN, 260(IF):BAND78-237
KEILER, A.R., ED. A READER IN HISTORICAL & COMPARATIVE LINGUISTICS.
W.L. BALLARD, 35(AS):FALL-WINTER 71-254
E.P. HAMP, 269(IJAL):JUL73-200
KEISLER, H.J. MODEL THEORY FOR INFINITARY LOGIC.
E.G.K. LÓPEZ-ESCOBAR, 316:SEP73-522
KEITH, W.J. - SEE ROBERTS, C.G.D.
KEITH-SMITH, B., ED. ERMAHNENDE AUSDEUTUNGEN.
205(FMLS):APR73-212
KELEMAN, S. LIVING YOUR DYING.
G. LUCE, 441:5JAN75-18
KELEMAN, S. YOUR BODY SPEAKS ITS MIND.
A. BROYARD, 441:23OCT75-43
KELLER, A.C. - SEE RABELAIS, F.
KELLER, H.H. GERMAN ROOT LEXICON.
B.W. GILLETTE, 399(MLJ):SEP-OCT74-284
KELLER, J.E. ALFONSO X, EL SABIO.
J.A. MADRIGAL, 577(SHR):WINTER73-105
E. PUPO-WALKER, 202(FMOD):NOV72/FEB73-172
KELLER, J.E. - SEE GREEN, O.H.
KELLER, O. WILHELM HEINSES ENTWICKLUNG ZUR HUMANITÄT.
D.G. LITTLE, 402(MLR):OCT74-920
C.P. MAGILL, 220(GL&L):APR74-264
R. TERRAS, 301(JEGP):JAN74-87

KELLEY, A.C. & J.G. WILLIAMSON.
LESSONS FROM JAPANESE DEVELOPMENT.
G.C. ALLEN, 617(TLS):11APR75-405
KELLEY, A.V. THE NOVELS OF VIRGINIA
WOOLF.
A. FLEISHMAN, 594:WINTER73-559
639(VQR):SUMMER74-LXXIII
KELLEY, B.M. YALE.
J.D. HOEVELER, JR., 432(NEQ):SEP
74-467
R. MC CAUGHEY, 617(TLS):19SEP75-
1047
KELLEY, D. - SEE BAUDELAIRE, C.
KELLEY, D.M. WHY CONSERVATIVE
CHURCHES ARE GROWING.
E. JORSTAD, 109:SPRING/SUMMER74-
150
KELLEY, D.R. FRANÇOIS HOTMAN.
M. WIBEL, 182:VOL26#19-690
KELLEY, E.S. THE DEVIL'S HAND.
J. MILLER, 617(TLS):7FEB75-129
KELLEY, M. - SEE MILTON, J.
KELLING, H-W. THE IDOLATRY OF POET-
IC GENIUS IN GERMAN GOETHE CRITI-
CISM.
K. THOENELT, 221(GQ):NOV73-622
KELLING, H-W. & M.H. FOLSOM. WIE
MAN'S SAGT UND SCHREIBT.
B. ELLING, 399(MLJ):JAN-FEB74-71
KELLMAN, M.C. PLANT GEOGRAPHY.
617(TLS):7MAR75-261
KELLNER, H-J. DIE RÖMER IN BAYERN.
M. HASSALL, 313:VOL63-313
KELLOGG, A.L. CHAUCER, LANGLAND,
ARTHUR.*
B. RAW, 447(N&Q):NOV73-437
R.M. WILSON, 677:VOL4-245
KELLOGG, G. THE VITAL TRADITION.
295:FEB74-399
KELLOGG, R. ANALYZING CHILDREN'S
ART.
J.S. KEEL, 186(ETC.):MAR73-104
KELLY, H.A. DIVINE PROVIDENCE IN
THE ENGLAND OF SHAKESPEARE'S HIS-
TORIES.*
R.E. BURKHART, 179(ES):JUN73-286
KELLY, J.N.D. JEROME.
D. CUPITT, 362:30OCT75-571
KELLY, M. REMINISCENCES.
S. TROTTER, 362:20OCT75-454
KELLY, R.J., COMP. JOHN BERRYMAN.*
W. KEEP, 134(CP):SPRING73-86
KELLY, R.M. DOUGLAS JERROLD.
C. KENT, 529(QQ):SUMMER73-318
KELLY, R.M. - SEE JERROLD, D.
KELSALL, M. - SEE FIELDING, S.
KEMAL, Y. THE LEGEND OF ARARAT.
D.A.N. JONES, 617(TLS):5SEP75-998
KEMELMAN, H. TUESDAY THE RABBI
SAW RED.*
N. CALLENDAR, 441:30MAR75-24
KEMMINGHAUSEN, K.S. & W. WOESLER -
SEE VON DROSTE-HÜLSHOFF, A.
KEMP, J.A. - SEE WALLIS, J.
KEMPNER, T., K. MACMILLAN & K. HAWK-
INS. BUSINESS & SOCIETY.
M. BEESLEY, 617(TLS):8AUG75-895
KENDAL, W. JUST GIN.
R. MC CARTHY, 150(DR):WINTER73/74-
773
KENDALL, A. BENJAMIN BRITTEN.
J. WARRACK, 415:FEB74-132

KENDALL, D.G. & OTHERS, EDS. THE
PLACE OF ASTRONOMY IN THE ANCIENT
WORLD.
J. NORTH, 617(TLS):15AUG75-921
KENDALL, P.M. & V. ILARDI, EDS &
TRANS. DISPATCHES WITH RELATED
DOCUMENTS OF MILANESE AMBASSADORS
IN FRANCE & BURGUNDY, 1450-1483.
(VOL 1)
D.E. QUELLER, 551(RENQ):SUMMER73-
188
KENDALL, P.M. & V. ILARDI, EDS &
TRANS. DISPATCHES WITH RELATED
DOCUMENTS OF MILANESE AMBASSADORS
IN FRANCE & BURGUNDY, 1450-1483.
(VOL 2)
D.E. QUELLER, 551(RENQ):WINTER73-
479
KENDLE, J.E. THE ROUND TABLE MOVE-
MENT & IMPERIAL UNION.
A.D. GILBERT, 99:OCT75-35
KENDRICK, G. BICYCLE TYRE IN A TALL
TREE.
R. GARFITT, 364:FEB/MAR75-110
KENDRICK, G. EROSIONS.*
S. CURTIS, 148:SPRING72-85
KENEALLY, T. BLOOD RED, SISTER
ROSE.*
N. HEPBURN, 362:6FEB75-189
A.G. MOJTABAI, 441:9FEB75-7
442(NY):10FEB75-115
KENEALLY, T. GOSSIP FROM THE FOR-
EST.
A. DUCHÊNE, 617(TLS):19SEP75-1041
D.A.N. JONES, 362:13NOV75-655
"KENKYUSHA'S NEW JAPANESE-ENGLISH
DICTIONARY." (4TH ED) (KOH MASUDA,
ED)
KUNIMOTO YOSHIRŌ, 285(JAPQ):OCT-
DEC74-402
KENNAN, G.F. MEMOIRS, 1950-1963.*
T.T. HAMMOND, 550(RUSR):APR73-193
R.D. SCHULZINGER, 50(ARQ):AUTUMN73-
281
KENNEDY, A. THE DOMINO PRINCIPLE.
N. CALLENDAR, 441:21DEC75-16
KENNEDY, A.K. SIX DRAMATISTS IN
SEARCH OF A LANGUAGE.
D.A.N. JONES, 617(TLS):28FEB75-219
KENNEDY, B., ED & TRANS. MUSKETS,
CANNON BALLS & BOMBS.
G.F. SCHEER, 441:6APR75-3
KENNEDY, D. (OCHANKUGAHE) RECOLLEC-
TIONS OF AN ASSINIBOINE CHIEF.
(J.R. STEVENS, ED)
R. LANDES, 529(QQ):SPRING73-116
KENNEDY, D. THE TORTILLA BOOK.
R.A. SOKOLOV, 441:7DEC75-78
KENNEDY, E.C., ED. THE NEGRITUDE
POETS.
J. SLATER, 441:30NOV75-56
KENNEDY, E.C. & V.J. HECKLER. THE
CATHOLIC PRIEST IN THE UNITED
STATES.
W.A. BARRY, 613:AUTUMN73-430
KENNEDY, E.S. & D. PINGREE. THE
ASTROLOGICAL HISTORY OF MĀSHĀʾAL-
LĀH.
P. KUNITZSCH, 318(JAOS):OCT-DEC73-
565

KENNEDY, G. THE ART OF RHETORIC IN
THE ROMAN WORLD: 300 B.C. - A.D.
300.*
  M.A. HAWORTH, 377:MAR74-48
  M.H. MC CALL, JR., 124:MAR74-304
  D. OCHS, 480(P&R):SUMMER73-186
KENNEDY, G. QUINTILIAN.*
  R. JOHNSON, 122:JUL73-230
KENNEDY, J.J. A PSYCHOLOGY OF PIC-
TURE PERCEPTION.
  M.S. LINDAUER, 290(JAAC):WINTER74-
232
KENNEDY, J.M. & J.A. REITHER, EDS.
A THEATRE FOR SPENSERIANS.
  G.F. WALLER, 150(DR):AUTUMN73-571
KENNEDY, P.M. THE SAMOAN TANGLE.
  E.W. EDWARDS, 617(TLS):7FEB75-133
KENNEDY, R. A BOY AT THE HOGARTH
PRESS.
  T. ROGERS, 175:AUTUMN73-119
KENNEDY, R.L. STUDIES IN TIRSO, 1.
  D. MOIR, 617(TLS):23MAY75-575
KENNEDY, S. MURPHY'S BED.
  R. COHN, 295:FEB74-537
KENNEDY, X.J. EMILY DICKINSON IN
SOUTHERN CALIFORNIA.*
  R. LATTIMORE, 249(HUDR):AUTUMN74-
464
KENNELLY, B. SALVATION, THE STRAN-
GER.
  F. HARVEY, 159(DM):WINTER/SPRING
73-115
KENNER, H. A HOMEMADE WORLD.
  T.R. EDWARDS, 441:9FEB75-21
  C. LEHMANN-HAUPT, 441:4FEB75-37
  M. WOOD, 453:17APR75-15
KENNER, H. THE POUND ERA.*
  D. BARBOUR, 529(QQ):AUTUMN73-450
  G. BURNS, 584(SWR):WINTER74-103
  D. DAVIE, 148:SPRING73-51
  R. ELLIS, 148:WINTER72-381
  H. PESCHMANN, 175:SPRING73-35
KENNER, H. A READER'S GUIDE TO SAM-
UEL BECKETT.
  L. GRAVER, 473(PR):4/1974-622
639(VQR):WINTER74-XVII
KENNEY, E.J. THE CLASSICAL TEXT.
  N. BARKER, 617(TLS):15AUG75-927
KENNEY, E.J. - SEE LUCRETIUS
KENNY, A. THE ANATOMY OF THE SOUL.*
  J.M. COOPER, 311(JP):20NOV75-765
  A. FLEW, 518:MAY74-10
KENNY, A. WITTGENSTEIN.
  A. PALMER, 518:JAN74-6
KENNY, H.A. LITERARY DUBLIN.*
  R.M. KAIN, 329(JJQ):FALL74/WINTER
75-185
  R. O'DRISCOLL, 99:JUL75-39
KENNY, S.S. - SEE STEELE, R.
KENT, A. SIGNAL - CLOSE ACTION!
  M. LEVIN, 441:5JAN75-21
KENT, A. & H. LANCOUR, WITH W.Z.
NASRI, EDS. ENCYCLOPEDIA OF LIB-
RARY & INFORMATION SCIENCE. (VOL 8)
  C.W. EVANS, 517(PBSA):JAN-MAR74-81
KENT, H.S.K. WAR & TRADE IN NORTH-
ERN SEAS.
  H. BUSZELLO, 182:VOL26#17/18-626
KENT, M. EL INGLÉS QUE LOS NIÑOS
NECESITAN. (2ND ED)
  K. SUTHERLAND, 399(MLJ):NOV74-372
KENT, R. - SEE BLAKE, H.
KENWORTHY, B.J. - SEE SUDERMANN, H.

KENYON, K.M. PALESTINE IN THE TIME
OF THE EIGHTEENTH DYNASTY.
  M. ARTZY, 318(JAOS):JUL-SEP73-399
KENYON, M. MR. BIG.
  617(TLS):20JUN75-692
KENYON, M. THE SHOOTING OF DAN
MC GREW.
  N. CALLENDAR, 441:21SEP75-41
KEPPEL, C. MADAM, YOU MUST DIE.
  P. BEER, 617(TLS):17JAN75-48
KEPPLER, C.F. THE LITERATURE OF THE
SECOND SELF.*
  D.R. DAVIS, 184(EIC):JAN73-95
  295:FEB74-399
KER, N.R. RECORDS OF ALL SOULS
COLLEGE LIBRARY 1437-1600.*
  N. BARKER, 78(BC):SPRING73-95
  J. DURKAN, 354:SEP73-259
KERES, P. PRACTICAL CHESS ENDINGS.
  617(TLS):7MAR75-261
KERKER, A. ERNST JÜNGER - KLAUS
MANN.
  617(TLS):6JUN75-623
KERMAN, C.E. CREATIVE TENSION.
  A. CURLE, 617(TLS):7FEB75-128
KERMODE, F. THE CLASSIC.
  H. KENNER, 441:9NOV75-40
  C. LEHMANN-HAUPT, 441:30SEP75-41
  442(NY):10NOV75-193
KERMODE, F. D.H. LAWRENCE.*
  E. DELAVENAY, 189(EA):JUL-SEP73-
325
  K. WIDMER, 594:WINTER73-547
KERMODE, F. SHAKESPEARE, SPENSER,
DONNE.*
  R. ELLRODT, 189(EA):OCT-DEC73-463
  W.C. JOHNSON, 179(ES):AUG73-388
KERMODE, F. - SEE ELIOT, T.S.
KERMODE, F. & J. HOLLANDER, EDS.
THE OXFORD ANTHOLOGY OF ENGLISH
LITERATURE.*
  J.M. PATRICK, 568(SCN):FALL74-48
  N. TALBOT, 67:MAY74-98
KERN, E. EXISTENTIAL THOUGHT & FIC-
TIONAL TECHNIQUE.
  G.M. HYDE, 447(N&Q):SEP73-350
  E. MOROT-SIR, 546(RR):NOV73-319
KERN, P.C. ZUR GEDANKENWELT DES
SPÄTEN HOFMANNSTHAL.*
  H.K. DOSWALD, 222(GR):JAN73-61
KERR, H. MEDIUMS, & SPIRIT-RAPPERS,
& ROARING RADICALS.*
  E.H. CADY, 445(NCF):MAR74-491
  D.K. KIRBY, 432(NEQ):JUN73-331
  J.N. SATTERWHITE, 219(GAR):FALL73-
463
KERR, W. THE SILENT CLOWNS.
  C. LEHMANN-HAUPT, 441:11DEC75-43
  W. MARKFIELD, 441:23NOV75-1
  442(NY):29DEC75-56
KERSHAW, I., ED. BOLTON PRIORY REN-
TALS & MINISTERS' ACCOUNTS, 1473-
1539.
  J.T. ROSENTHAL, 325:APR73-611
KERST, G. JACOB MECKEL, SEIN LEBEN,
SEIN WIRKEN IN DEUTSCHLAND UND
JAPAN.
  E.L. PRESSEISEN, 318(JAOS):APR-
JUN73-225
KERTZ, W. & OTHERS, EDS. DAS UNTER-
NEHMEN ERDMANTEL.
  P. VOSSELER, 182:VOL26#7/8-252

KESAVAN, K.V. JAPAN'S RELATIONS
WITH SOUTHEAST ASIA, 1952-60.
MARUYAMA SHIZUO, 285(JAPQ):JUL-SEP
74-304
MASASHI NISHIHARA, 293(JAST):AUG
73-738
KESSLER, C. THE ACQUISITION OF SYN-
TAX IN BILINGUAL CHILDREN.
K. CONNORS, 350:JUN74-413
KESSLER, E. IMAGES OF WALLACE
STEVENS.*
D.L. EDER, 295:FEB74-794
KESSLER, M. SAILING TOO FAR.
J. LOGAN, 398:SPRING75-89
H. ZINNES, 109:SPRING/SUMMER74-154
KESTEN, H. - SEE ROTH, J.
KESTING, M. ENTDECKUNG UND DESTRUK-
TION.
W. LOCKEMANN, 221(GQ):MAY73-474
KETCHUM, R.M. DECISIVE DAY.
G.F. SCHEER, 441:6APR75-26
KETCHUM, W.C., JR. A TREASURY OF
AMERICAN BOTTLES.
G. WARD & R. STROZIER, 441:7DEC75-
94
KETELSEN, U-K. VON HEROISCHEM SEIN
UND VÖLKISCHEM TOD.
C.L. HART-NIBBRIG, 657(WW):MAY/JUN
73-217
KEUDEL, U. POETISCHE VORLÄUFER UND
VORBILDER IN CLAUDIANS DE CONSULATU
STILICHONIS.*
H.H. HUXLEY, 124:FEB73-301
KEULEN, H. UNTERSUCHUNGEN ZU PLA-
TONS "EUTHYDEM."
É. DES PLACES, 555:VOL47FASC1-133
KEVE, P.W. PRISON LIFE & HUMAN
WORTH.
A.E. BOTTOMS, 617(TLS):26SEP75-
1100
KEYES, K., JR. LIVING LOVE.
R. WANDERER, 186(ETC.):SEP73-321
KEYES, R.S. & K. MIZUSHIMA. THE
THEATRICAL WORLD OF OSAKA PRINTS.*
R.H. LEARY, 60:SEP-OCT74-75
KEYNES, G. A BIBLIOGRAPHY OF DR.
JOHN DONNE, DEAN OF ST. PAUL'S.
M. HUNTER, 78(BC):WINTER73-547
KEYNES, G. BLAKE STUDIES.* (2ND
ED)
J.B. BEER, 447(N&Q):AUG73-305
D. HIRST, 541(RES):FEB73-95
M.F. SCHULZ, 173(ECS):FALL73-120
KEYNES, G. JOHN EVELYN. (2ND ED)
D.I.B. SMITH, 179(ES):DEC72-563
KEYNES, G. - SEE BROOKE, R.
KEYNES, G. - SEE DONNE, J.
KEYNES, G. - SEE WILSON, M.
KEYNES, M., ED. ESSAYS ON JOHN MAY-
NARD KEYNES.
N. ANNAN, 617(TLS):2MAY75-469
J.C.R. DOW, 617(TLS):2MAY75-471
D. PROCTOR, 617(TLS):2MAY75-472
P. STANSKY, 441:1JUN75-7
J. VAIZEY, 362:20MAR75-369
VON KEYSERLING, E. WELLEN.
A.W. WONDERLEY, 221(GQ):MAR73-294
KEYSSAR, A. MELVILLE'S "ISRAEL
POTTER."
R. BERGSTROM, 502(PRS):SPRING73-80
KEZICH, T. SVEVO E ZENO.
400(MLN):JAN73-169

KHAN, I.A. GOVERNMENT IN RURAL
INDIA.
G.E. SUSSMAN, 293(JAST):NOV72-184
KHAN, M.M.R. THE PRIVACY OF THE
SELF.
A. STORR, 617(TLS):24JAN75-75
KHAN, S.A. WRITINGS & SPEECHES OF
SIR SYED AHMAD KHAN. (S. MOHAMMAD,
ED)
M.H. CASE, 293(JAST):AUG73-714
KHARMS, D. & A. VVEDENSKY. RUSSIA'S
LOST LITERATURE OF THE ABSURD.
C. BROWN, 574(SEEJ):FALL73-338
KHATCHADOURIAN, H. THE CONCEPT OF
ART.*
W. CHARLTON, 89(BJA):SPRING73-191
KHERDIAN, D., ED. VISIONS OF AMERI-
CA BY THE POETS OF OUR TIME.
G.L.N., 502(PRS):FALL73-277
KHLEBNIKOV, V.V. SOBRANIYE SOCHI-
NENIY. (V. MARKOV, ED)
R.D.B. THOMSON, 575(SEER):JUL74-
462
KHODOROVICH, T., ED. ISTORIYA BOL-
EZNI LEONIDA PLYUSHCHA.
B.W. HUDSON, 617(TLS):18APR75-425
KHOI, L.T., ED. L'ENSEIGNEMENT EN
AFRIQUE TROPICALE.
S. MILBURN, 69:OCT73-360
KHOLSHEVNIKOV, V.Y., ED. TEORIYA
STIKHA.
R.D.B. THOMSON, 492:#9-113
KHOO KAY KIM. THE WESTERN MALAY
STATES 1850-1873.
C.S. GRAY, 293(JAST):MAY73-557
KHOURI, M.A. POETRY & THE MAKING OF
MODERN EGYPT (1882-1922).
S.J. ALTOMA, 318(JAOS):JAN-MAR73-
107
KHOURY, A-T. LES THÉOLOGIENS BYZAN-
TINS ET L'ISLAM.
J. KRITZECK, 318(JAOS):JAN-MAR73-
96
KHRUSHCHEV, N.S. KHRUSHCHEV REMEM-
BERS: THE LAST TESTAMENT.* (S.
TALBOTT, ED & TRANS)
A.H. BROWN, 617(TLS):31JAN75-115
KIÇI, G. & H. ALIKO. FJALOR
ANGLISHT-SHQIP.
E.P. HAMP, 574(SEEJ):FALL72-384
KICKNOSWAY, F. A MAN IS A HOOK.
TROUBLE.
T. PETROSKY, 398:SPRING75-90
KIDDER, E. EARLY BUDDHIST JAPAN.
C.J. KILEY, 244(HJAS):VOL33-294
KIDDER, J.E. PREHISTORIC JAPANESE
ARTS: JŌMON POTTERY.
D.F. MC CALLUM, 57:VOL35#3-298
KIDDER, R.M. DYLAN THOMAS.*
639(VQR):WINTER74-XVI
KIDEL, B. A FLAWED ESCAPE.
442(NY):17FEB75-106
KIDEL, B. THE INCIDENT IS CLOSED.
J. BARNES, 617(TLS):2MAY75-492
J. MELLORS, 362:13MAR75-349
KIEFER, F. GENERATIVE MORPHOLOGIE
DES NEUFRANZÖSISCHEN.
W. RETTIG, 72:BAND211HEFT1/3-189
K. WINN, 430(NS):JUL73-401
KIEFFER, R. ESSAIS DE MÉTHODOLOGIE
NÉO-TESTAMENTAIRE.
J. SANDYS-WUNSCH, 124:MAY73-475

KIELHOLZ, J. WILHELM HEINRICH WACK-
ENRODER.
 J.F.F., 191(ELN):SEP73(SUPP)-161
KIELY, R. THE ROMANTIC NOVEL IN
ENGLAND.
 D.R. DEAN, 125:OCT73-97
 R.A. DONOVAN, 191(ELN):JUN74-309
 P. FAULKNER, 402(MLR):APR74-380
 A. WELSH, 445(NCF):DEC73-351
 191(ELN):SEP73(SUPP)-28
KIENIEWICZ, S. - SEE GIEYSZTOR, A.
 & OTHERS
KIERNAN, B. CRITICISM.
 L. CANTRELL, 71(ALS):MAY75-101
 H.W. RHODES, 67:NOV74-233
KIERNAN, B. IMAGES OF SOCIETY &
NATURE.*
 M. WILDING, 677:VOL4-333
KIERNAN, T. THE MIRACLE AT COOGAN'S
BLUFF.
 J. FLAHERTY, 441:17AUG75-7
 C. LEHMANN-HAUPT, 441:24JUL75-33
KIESLINGER, A. DIE STEINE DER
WIENER RINGSTRASSE.
 J. MAASS, 576:DEC73-339
 W. WEYRES, 182:VOL26#7/8-227
KIEVE, J.L. THE ELECTRIC TELEGRAPH
IN THE U.K.
 S. GELBAND, 637(VS):JUN74-445
KILCHENMANN, R.J. DIE KURZGESCHICH-
TE.
 R. BREMER, 433:JUL73-298
KILGALLIN, T. LOWRY.*
 D. WATMOUGH, 102(CANL):SPRING74-
 116
KILGORE, D.E. A RANGER LEGACY.
 W. GARD, 584(SWR):WINTER74-98
KILLICK, B. BENEATH THE DOME.
 S. KENNEDY, 617(TLS):23MAY75-577
KILLION, R. & C. WALLER, EDS. SLAV-
ERY TIME.
 J.W. BLASSINGAME, 219(GAR):WINTER
 73-584
KILLON, R.G. & C.T. WALLER, EDS. A
TREASURY OF GEORGIA FOLKLORE.
 W.H. JANSEN, 582(SFQ):JUN73-140
KILPATRICK, W. IDENTITY & INTIMACY.
 A. BROYARD, 441:21OCT75-41
KILROY, J. THE "PLAYBOY" RIOTS.
 R. HOGAN, 295:APR74-1031
KILSON, M. AFRICAN URBAN KINSMEN.
 K. LITTLE, 617(TLS):17OCT75-1242
KIM, H.C., ED. THE GOSPEL OF NICO-
DEMUS.
 M. GÖRLACH, 72:BAND211HEFT3/6-426
KIM, K.K. - SEE UNDER KHOO KAY KIM
KIMBALL, A.G. CRISIS IN IDENTITY &
CONTEMPORARY JAPANESE NOVELS.
 S. GOLDSTEIN, 50(ARQ):AUTUMN73-284
KIMBALL, J.P. THE FORMAL THEORY OF
GRAMMAR.
 R. SUSSEX, 67:MAY74-143
KIMBALL, S.B., ED. SLAVIC-AMERICAN
IMPRINTS.*
 J.B. RUDNYCKYJ, 574(SEEJ):SPRING
 73-114
KIMBER, R. & R. - SEE KAHLER, E.
KIMBROUGH, R. SIR PHILIP SIDNEY.
 D.G. DONOVAN, 577(SHR):FALL73-440
 W. NELSON, 551(RENQ):SPRING73-76
KIMMEL, A.S., ED. THE OLD PROVENÇAL
EPIC "DAUREL ET BETON."
 P. BARRETTE, 207(FR):MAR73-817
 W. ROTHWELL, 402(MLR):JUL74-634

KINCAID, J.R. DICKENS & THE RHETOR-
IC OF LAUGHTER.*
 K.J. FIELDING, 541(RES):FEB73-100
 S. MONOD, 189(EA):APR-JUN73-231
 W. MYERS, 637(VS):SEP73-108
 E.F. QUIRK, 301(JEGP):APR74-260
 P. SCHLICKE, 155:JAN73-51
 H.P. SUCKSMITH, 677:VOL4-323
 G. THOMAS, 175:SUMMER72-71
KING, A. BRITISH MEMBERS OF PARLIA-
MENT.
 B. TREND, 617(TLS):28MAR75-331
KING, A. & H. NORTH - SEE CAPLAN, H.
KING, C. THE CECIL KING DIARY 1970-
1974.
 J. GRIGG, 362:16OCT75-514
 LORD LAMBTON, 617(TLS):7NOV75-1324
KING, E. PETERBOROUGH ABBEY 1086-
1310.*
 M. CHIBNALL, 382(MAE):1974/2-208
KING, F. THE NEEDLE.
 N. HEPBURN, 362:2OCT75-453
 M. JOHNSON, 617(TLS):12SEP75-1013
KING, H. PARADIGM RED.
 N. CALLENDAR, 441:15JUN75-24
KING, I. & C. THURMAN, WITH W.W.
LYNCH. SHE'S A COP ISN'T SHE?
 N. CALLENDAR, 441:30NOV75-63
KING, J.C. - SEE NOTKER DER DEUTSCHE
KING, K.J. PAN-AFRICANISM & EDUCA-
TION.
 S. MILBURN, 69:APR73-179
KING, L.L. THE OLD MAN & LESSER
MORTALS.*
 S. DONALDSON, 569(SR):SUMMER74-527
KING, P. THE IDEOLOGY OF ORDER.*
 M.T. DALGARNO, 518:OCT74-17
KING, P. MULTATULI.
 L. GILLET, 556(RLV):1973/6-565
KING, P.D. LAW & SOCIETY IN THE
VISIGOTHIC KINGDOM.
 J. RILEY-SMITH, 382(MAE):1974/1-
 100
KING, R.A., JR. - SEE BROWNING, R.
KING, R.D. HISTORICAL LINGUISTICS &
GENERATIVE GRAMMAR.*
 O.W. ROBINSON & F. VAN COETSEM,
 361:VOL31#4-331
KING, T.J. SHAKESPEAREAN STAGING,
1599-1642.*
 P. EDWARDS, 447(N&Q):APR73-146
 R.D. ERLICH, 160:FALL72-70
KING, T.R. A PROGRAM ON THE PROCESS
OF COMMUNICATION.
 T.L. ATTAWAY, 583:FALL73-101
"THE KINGDOM INTERLINEAR TRANSLATION
OF THE GREEK SCRIPTURES."
 T.N. WINTER, 121(CJ):APR/MAY74-375
KINGHORN, A.M. THE CHORUS OF
HISTORY.
 W.C. JOHNSON, 125:JUN74-391
KINGHORN, A.M., ED. THE MIDDLE
SCOTS POETS.
 P.S. MACAULAY, 179(ES):OCT73-501
 A.A. MACDONALD, 433:JAN73-107
 J.S. SIMON, 189(EA):OCT-DEC73-458
KINGSLEY, B. THE BLACK ANGEL.
 E.M. EWING, 441:11MAY75-10
KINGSLEY, H. THE HILLYARS & THE
BURTONS.
 H.W. RHODES, 67:NOV74-233

198

KINKEAD-WEEKES, M. SAMUEL RICHARD-
SON.*
  I. KONIGSBERG, 301(JEGP):OCT74-552
  D. MEHL, 182:VOL26#10-355
KINNAMON, K. THE EMERGENCE OF RICH-
ARD WRIGHT.*
  M. FABRE, 189(EA):OCT-DEC73-491
  D.B. GIBSON, 454:SPRING74-283
  B. JACKSON, 579(SAQ):SUMMER74-409
  E. MARGOLIES, 295:FEB74-831
  C.W. SCRUGGS, 50(ARQ):AUTUMN73-286
KINNELL, G. THE AVENUE BEARING THE
INITIAL OF CHRIST INTO THE NEW
WORLD.
  J. ATLAS, 491:FEB75-295
  T. COMITO, 398:AUTUMN75-189
  C. RICKS, 441:12JAN75-2
  V. YOUNG, 249(HUDR):WINTER74/75-
  597
KINNELL, G. THE BOOK OF NIGHTMARES.
  W.M. RANSOM, 114(CHIR):VOL25#1-189
KINNEY, A.F. TITLED ELIZABETHANS.
  568(SCN):FALL74-61
KINOSHITA, N. PILLAR OF FIRE.
  J.A. O'BRIEN, 352(LE&W):VOL16#4-
  1253
KINSELLA, T. NOTES FROM THE LAND OF
THE DEAD & OTHER POEMS.*
  D. BROMWICH, 491:JAN75-229
KINSELLA, T. - SEE "THE TAIN"
KINSEY, T.E. - SEE CICERO
KINSLEY, J. & H., EDS. DRYDEN: THE
CRITICAL HERITAGE.
  P. MORGAN, 179(ES):AUG73-393
KINSLEY, J. & G. PARFITT - SEE DRY-
DEN, J.
KINVIG, R.H. THE ISLE OF MAN.
  F. KERMODE, 617(TLS):17OCT75-1235
KIRBY, G. - SEE BALDWIN, J.
KIRBY, I.M. DIOCESE OF BRISTOL: A
CATALOGUE OF THE RECORDS OF THE
BISHOPS & ARCHDEACONS & OF THE
DEAN & CHAPTER.
  D.M. OWEN, 325:OCT73-675
KIRBY, R.G. MEXICAN LANDSCAPE
ARCHITECTURE.
  45:APR73-70
  505:MAR73-128
KIRBY, T.A. & W.J. OLIVE, EDS.
ESSAYS IN HONOR OF ESMOND LINWORTH
MARILLA.
  R. ELLRODT, 189(EA):OCT-DEC73-460
KIRCHHEIM, A. TRAGIK UND KOMIK IN
SHAKESPEARES "TROILUS & CRESSIDA,"
"MEASURE FOR MEASURE" UND "ALL'S
WELL THAT ENDS WELL."
  G. MÜLLER-SCHWEFE, 551(RENQ):WIN-
  TER73-528
KIRCHNER, W. - SEE FRIES, H.J.
KIRK, D. WIDER WAR.
  M. LEIFER, 293(JAST):NOV72-121
KIRK, E.D. THE DREAM THOUGHT OF
"PIERS PLOWMAN."*
  D.C. FOWLER, 405(MP):MAY74-393
  J. LAWLOR, 402(MLR):APR74-369
  B. RAW, 447(N&Q):NOV73-437
KIRK, G.S. MYTH.*
  R. ACKERMAN, 322(JHI):JAN-MAR73-
  147
  E.B. HOLTSMARK, 121(CJ):DEC73/JAN
  74-185
  M.H. JAMESON, 122:APR74-148
KIRK, G.S. - SEE EURIPIDES

KIRK, H.L. PABLO CASALS.*
  S. WALSH, 362:24APR75-539
KIRK, I. PROFILES IN RUSSIAN RESIS-
TANCE.
  J. LABER, 441:25MAY75-5
KIRK, M. ALL OTHER PERILS.
  N. CALLENDAR, 441:6JUL75-14
KIRK, R. DESERT.
  W. GARD, 584(SWR):WINTER74-98
KIRK-GREENE, A.H. & P. NEWMAN, EDS
& TRANS. WEST AFRICAN TRAVELS &
ADVENTURES.
  M. LAST, 69:OCT73-365
KIRKCONNELL, W. AWAKE THE COURTEOUS
ECHO.
  617(TLS):22AUG75-954
KIRKENDALE, W. L'ARIA DI FIORENZA,
ID EST IL BALLO DEL GRAN DUCA.*
  P. WEISS, 414(MQ):JUL73-474
KIRKNESS, W.J. LE FRANÇAIS DU THÉ-
ÂTRE ITALIEN.*
  G.B. DANIELS, 399(MLJ):SEP-OCT73-
  280
KIRKPATRICK, J. - SEE IVES, C.E.
KIRKUP, J. HEAVEN, HELL & HARA-KIRI.
  J-P. LEHMANN, 617(TLS):11APR75-405
KIRKWOOD, G.M. EARLY GREEK MONODY.*
  J. RUSSO, 5:VOL1#4-707
KIRKWOOD, J. SOME KIND OF HERO.
  R.A. SOKOLOV, 441:28SEP75-36
KIRSCH, A.C. JACOBEAN DRAMATIC
PERSPECTIVES.*
  J.I. COPE, 301(JEGP):JAN74-119
  C.R. FORKER, 191(ELN):MAR74-217
  M. HATTAWAY, 541(RES):AUG73-330
  A.F. MAROTTI, 405(MP):FEB74-328
  D.A. SAMUELSON, 568(SCN):WINTER74-
  77
  A. WERTHEIM, 551(RENQ):AUTUMN73-
  375
KIRSOP, W. BIBLIOGRAPHIE MATÉRIELLE
ET CRITIQUE TEXTUELLE.*
  F. BASSAN, 207(FR):OCT72-140
KIRST, H.H. A TIME FOR TRUTH.*
  617(TLS):3JAN75-5
KIRSTEIN, L. FLESH IS HEIR.
  A. GOLDMAN, 617(TLS):12DEC75-1477
KIRSTEIN, L. ELIE NADELMAN.
  S. SCHWARTZ, 442(NY):20OCT75-154
KIRSTEIN, L. THE NEW YORK CITY
BALLET.
  M. CLARKE, 617(TLS):9MAY75-507
  S.J. COHEN, 290(JAAC):WINTER74-243
KIRSTEIN, L. NIJINSKY DANCING.
  D. HARRIS, 441:23NOV75-6
  A. KISSELGOFF, 441:13DEC75-25
KIRSTEN, M., ED. YOUTH WRITES 1973
& 1974.
  S.E. LEE, 581:MAR74-92
KIRTLEY, B.F. A MOTIF-INDEX OF TRA-
DITIONAL POLYNESIAN NARRATIVES.
  R.E. MITCHELL, 650(WF):JAN73-57
KIRWAN, A.L. THE MUSIC OF LINCOLN
CATHEDRAL.
  W. SHAW, 415:JAN74-38
KIRWAN, C. - SEE ARISTOTLE
KISH, G. ECONOMIC ATLAS OF THE
SOVIET UNION.
  M. MC CAULEY, 575(SEER):JAN74-156
KISPERT, R.J. OLD ENGLISH.
  J.B. TRAHERN, JR., 215(GL):VOL13
  #2-123

KISS, S. LES TRANSFORMATIONS DE LA
STRUCTURE SYLLABIQUE EN LATIN TAR-
DIF.*
  B. LÖFSTEDT, 343:BAND17HEFT1-90
KISSANE, J.D. ALFRED TENNYSON.
  S. MONOD, 577(SHR):FALL73-443
KISSINGER, H.A. LE CHEMIN DE LA
PAIX.
  C. ZORGBIBE, 98:OCT73-949
KITCHEN, P. A MOST UNSETTLING PER-
SON.
  P.B. CHECKLAND, 617(TLS):24OCT75-
  1260
  P.N. FURBANK, 362:4SEP75-317
KITE, V.J. GOVERNMENT REPORTS,
1971-2.
  J.B. CHILDS, 517(PBSA):APR-JUN74-
  193
KITMAN, M. THE COWARD'S ALMANAC.
  M.S. KENNEDY, 441:3AUG75-10
KIUCHI SHINZŌ & TANABE KEN'ICHI,
EDS. KŌIKI CHŪSHIN TOSHI.
  J.D. EYRE, 293(JAST):FEB73-330
KIVIMAA, K. ASPECTS OF STYLE IN
T.S. ELIOT'S "MURDER IN THE CATHED-
RAL."
  K. SMIDT, 179(ES):APR72-193
KIVIMAA, K. & L. LEHTO. THE GREAT
VOWEL SHIFT - A COMBINATORY CHANGE?*
  F. CERCIGNANI, 179(ES):APR73-168
KIVY, P. SPEAKING OF ART.
  J-J. DAETWYLER, 182:VOL26#21/22-
  777
KIVY, P. - SEE REID, T.
KIZER, C. MIDNIGHT WAS MY CRY.
  K.S. BYER, 219(GAR):SPRING73-110
  P.D. MORROW, 649(WAL):FALL73-153
KJELLÉN, A. BELLMAN SOM BOHEM OCH
PARODIKER.
  J. MESSENGALE, 563(SS):SUMMER74-
  301
KJELLMER, G. CONTEXT & MEANING.
  N.E. ENKVIST, 597(SN):VOL45#2-439
  U. FRIES, 72:BAND211HEFT3/6-423
  R.M. HOGG, 361:VOL31#1-79
KJETSAA, G. YEVGENY BARATYNSKY.
  A.B. MC MILLIN, 575(SEER):JUL74-
  460
KJETSAA, G. LEKSIKA STIKHOTVORENIY
LERMONTOVA.
  A.B. MC MILLIN, 575(SEER):APR74-
  314
KLAJN, I. INFLUSSI INGLESI NELLA
LINGUA ITALIANA.
  H. DIAMENT, 275(IQ):SUMMER73-98
  G.C. LEPSCHY, 402(MLR):JUL74-650
KLANE, R. FIRE SALE.
  M. LEVIN, 441:30NOV75-62
KLASS, P.J. UFOS EXPLAINED.
  P. ADAMS, 61:FEB75-122
  A.C. CLARKE, 441:27JUL75-4
KLAUA, D. KONSTRUKTIVE ANALYSIS.
  B.H. MAYOH, 316:MAR73-154
KLAUS, G. SPRACHE DER POLITIK.
  H. HARNISCH, 682(ZPSK):BAND26HEFT
  1/2-154
KLAW, S. THE GREAT AMERICAN MEDI-
CINE SHOW.
  H.J. GEIGER, 441:14DEC75-7
KLEE, P. PAUL KLEE NOTEBOOKS.*
  (VOL 2) (J. SPILLER, ED)
  N. LYNTON, 592:NOV73-211

KLEEMANN, G. DIE ORGELMACHER UND
IHR SCHAFFEN IM EHEMALIGEN HERZOG-
TUM WÜRTTEMBERG.
  H.M. BALZ, 182:VOL26#21/22-805
KLEENE, S.C. INTRODUCTION TO META-
MATHEMATICS.
  H.B. ENDERTON, 316:JUN73-333
KLEIBER, W. OTFRID VON WEISSENBURG.
  H. KRATZ, 133:1973/3-262
KLEIN, E. A COMPREHENSIVE ETYMOLO-
GICAL DICTIONARY OF THE ENGLISH
LANGUAGE.*
  A. MOULIN, 556(RLV):1973/4-382
  P.A.M. SEUREN, 433:OCT73-423
KLEIN, H.G. & P. CEAUŞESCU. EINFÜH-
RUNG IN DIE RUMÄNISCHE SPRACHE.
  I. RONCA, 72:BAND211HEFT3/6-448
KLEIN, K.W. THE PARTISAN VOICE.*
  L.T. TOPSFIELD, 382(MAE):1974/3-
  278
KLEIN, L.A. PORTRAIT DE LA JUIVE
DANS LA LITTÉRATURE FRANÇAISE.
  D. GOITEIN, 546(RR):MAR74-149
KLEIN, M. THE PSYCHO-ANALYSIS OF
CHILDREN. (REV WITH A. STRACHEY &
H.A. THORNER) NARRATIVE OF A CHILD
ANALYSIS.
  J. PADEL, 617(TLS):18JUL75-798
KLEIN, N. LOVE & OTHER EUPHEMISMS.
  H. ANDERSON, 573(SSF):SPRING73-223
KLEIN, R. SYMMACHUS.*
  S.I. OOST, 122:APR73-155
KLEIN, W. PARSING.
  P.O. SAMUELSDORFF, 343:BAND16HEFT
  2-217
KLEINER, S. WIENNERISCHES WELTTHE-
ATER.
  R. WAGNER-RIEGER, 683:BAND36HEFT1-
  82
KLEINSCHNIEDER, M. GOETHES NATUR-
STUDIEN.
  G. SEEL, 53(AGP):BAND55HEFT3-350
KLEINSTÜCK, J. WIRKLICHKEIT UND
REALITÄT.
  H.H. RUDNICK, 133:1973/1-68
KLEISS, W. ZENDAN-I SULEIMAN.
  W. SCHIRMER, 182:VOL26#7/8-235
KLEIVAN, I. WHY IS THE RAVEN BLACK?
  R. GRAMBO, 196:BAND14HEFT1/2-163
KLIMA, G.J. THE BARABAIG.
  P. SPENCER, 69:JAN73-90
KLIMA, U. UNTERSUCHUNGEN ZU DEM
BEGRIFF SAPIENTIA VON DER REPUBLI-
KANISCHEN ZEIT BIS TACITUS.
  J. HELLEGOUARC'H, 555:VOL47FASC2-
  357
KLIMENKO, A.P. VOPROSY PSIXOLING-
VISTIČESKOGO IZUČENIJA SEMANTIKI.
  J. PRŮCHA, 353:15SEP73-109
KLIN, E. DIE HERMENEUTISCHE UND
KRITISCHE LEISTUNG FRIEDRICH SCHLE-
GELS IN DEN ROMANTISCHEN KRISEN-
JAHREN.
  J.D. SIMONS, 104:FALL73-434
KLINCK, C.F. & R.E. WATTERS, EDS.
CANADIAN ANTHOLOGY. (NEW ED)
  G.W., 102(CANL):AUTUMN74-125
KLINE, M.B. BEYOND THE LAND ITSELF.
  P. GOETSCH, 447(N&Q):MAR73-105
KLINE, M-J. - SEE HAMILTON, A.
KLINE, P. SCENES TO PERFORM.
  J. VAN DER POLL, 583:FALL73-95

KLINE, T.J. ANDRÉ MALRAUX & THE
METAMORPHOSIS OF DEATH.*
  CHENG LOK CHUA, 651(WHR):AUTUMN74-
392
KLINGENBERG, A. GOETHES ROMAN "WIL-
HELM MEISTERS WANDERJAHRE."
  H.J. GEERDTS, 654(WB):5/1973-178
KLINGENBERG, H. RUNENSCHRIFT -
SCHRIFTDENKEN - RUNENINSCHRIFTEN.
  H-J. GRAF, 72:BAND211HEFT1/3-91
KLINGENDER, F. ANIMALS IN ART &
THOUGHT TO THE END OF THE MIDDLE
AGES.* (E. ANTAL & J. HARTHAN,
EDS)
  J. BECKWITH, 39:APR73-436
  W.N. CLARKE, 258:MAR73-153
KLINKOWITZ, J. & J. SOMER, EDS.
INNOVATIVE FICTION.
  J.W. STEVENSON, 573(SSF):SPRING73-
211
KLINKOWITZ, J. & J. SOMER. THE
VONNEGUT STATEMENT.
  R. DAVIES, 617(TLS):21FEB75-187
  R.B. HAUCK, 27(AL):MAY74-242
AF KLINTBERG, B. SVENSKA FOLKSÄG-
NER.
  R. GRAMBO, 196:BAND14HEFT3-271
KLOCKARS, C.B. THE PROFESSIONAL
FENCE.*
  G.V. HIGGINS, 617(TLS):25JUL75-827
  E.S. TURNER, 362:10JUL75-60
KLOEPFER, R. & U. OOMEN. SPRACH-
LICHE KONSTITUENTEN MODERNER DICH-
TUNG.
  A.W.G. EIJGENDAAL, 204(FDL):DEC73-
293
  J-C-C-K. KIEFER, 535(RHL):JUL-AUG
73-717
  N. SCHWAB-BAKMAN, 557(RSH):JAN-MAR
73-175
KLONSKY, M., ED. THE FABULOUS EGO.*
442(NY):6JAN75-82
KLOSS, H. LES DROITS LINGUISTIQUES
DES FRANCO-AMÉRICAINS AUX ETATS-
UNIS.*
  J. BEZOU, 207(FR):OCT72-197
KLOSSOWSKI, P. UN SI FUNESTE DÉSIR.
NIETZSCHE ET LE CERCLE VICIEUX.
  M. BROC-LAPEYRE, 98:JUN73-530
KLOSTY, J., ED. MERCE CUNNINGHAM.
  D. HARRIS, 441:4MAY75-4
KLOTZ, G. INDIVIDUUM UND GESELL-
SCHAFT IM ENGLISCHEN DRAMA DER
GEGENWART.
  G. WALCH, 654(WB):10/1973-187
KLOTZ, H. DIE FRÜHWERKE BRUNELLES-
CHIS UND DIE MITTELALTERLICHE TRA-
DITION.
  H. LORENZ, 683:BAND36HEFT2/3-200
KLUCKHOHN, C. INITIATION À L'ANTH-
ROPOLOGIE.
  C. SCHUWER, 542:JAN-MAR73-71
KLUGE, E-H.W. THE PRACTICE OF
DEATH.
  C. RICKS, 617(TLS):18JUL75-790
KLUGER, P. A NEEDLEPOINT GALLERY OF
PATTERNS FROM THE PAST.
  B. GUTCHEON, 441:7DEC75-74
KLÜVER, J. & F.O. WOLF, EDS. WISSEN-
SCHAFTSKRITIK UND SOZIALISTISCHE
PRAXIS.
  S. PROKOP, 654(WB):1/1973-176
KLUXEN, K. GESCHICHTE ENGLANDS.
  B. LENZ, 38:BAND91HEFT2-276

KLYMASZ, R.B. AN INTRODUCTION TO
THE UKRANIAN-CANADIAN IMMIGRANT
FOLKSONG CYCLE. THE UKRANIAN WIN-
TER FOLKSONG CYCLE IN CANADA.
  D. COELHO, 292(JAF):JAN-MAR73-74
KNABE, P-E. SCHLÜSSELBEGRIFFE DES
KUNSTTHEORETISCHEN DENKENS IN
FRANKREICH.
  H. SCKOMMODAU, 72:BAND211HEFT1/3-
230
KNAP, A.H. WILD HARVEST.
  J.M. COLE, 99:DEC75/JAN76-37
KNAPP, B.L. JEAN COCTEAU.
  D.H. MORRIS 4TH, 577(SHR):WINTER
73-103
KNAPP, F.P. RENNEWART.*
  H. SCHANZE, 680(ZDP):BAND92HEFT1-
128
KNAPP, J.G. TORTURED SYNTHESIS.*
  B.C. BACH, 613:SPRING73-128
KNAPP-TEPPERBERG, E-M. ROBERT
CHALLES "ILLUSTRES FRANÇOISES."*
  H.R. PICARD, 535(RHL):JUL-AUG73-
693
KNAPPERT, J. SWAHILI ISLAMIC POETRY.
  J.W.T. ALLEN, 315(JAL):VOL11PT1-95
KNAUTH, P. A SEASON IN HELL.
  W. SCHOTT, 441:16MAR75-4
KNEF, H. THE VERDICT.
  A. BROYARD, 441:30DEC75-23
KNEŽEVIĆ, A. HOMOPHONE UND HOMO-
GRAMME IN DER SCHRIFTSPRACHE DER
KROATEN UND SERBEN.
  W.W. DERBYSHIRE, 574(SEEJ):SPRING
73-105
"KNIGA: ISSLEDOVANIYA I MATERIALY."
(VOLS 24 & 25)
  J.S.G. SIMMONS, 78(BC):SUMMER73-
253
KNIGHT, D., ED. ORBIT 16.
  G. JONAS, 441:29JUN75-25
KNIGHT, D. TWO NOVELS.
  J. HAMILTON-PATERSON, 617(TLS):
7MAR75-260
KNIGHT, D.M. NATURAL SCIENCE BOOKS
IN ENGLISH, 1600-1900.
  J.T. ALLANSON, 354:JUN73-167
KNIGHT, F. BEETHOVEN & THE AGE OF
REVOLUTION.
  J. COCKSHOOT, 410(M&L):JAN74-103
KNIGHT, M. HONEST TO MAN.
  G.R. DUNSTAN, 617(TLS):18APR75-435
KNIGHT, R.C. - SEE RACINE, J.
KNIGHT, S.K. THE JOURNAL OF MADAM
KNIGHT.
  M.J. DOWD, 14:OCT73-563
  C. FENNELLY, 432(NEQ):MAR73-154
KNIGHT, W.F.J. ELYSION.
  C.B. PASCAL, 122:APR74-127
KNIGHT, W.F.J. ROMAN VERGIL. (REV)
  A.G. MC KAY, 124:FEB74-225
KNIGHTLEY, P. THE FIRST CASUALTY.
  A. COCKBURN, 453:11DEC75-28
  M. JANEWAY, 61:NOV75-123
  H. THOMAS, 362:4DEC75-752
  G. WILLS, 441:14SEP75-1
442(NY):27OCT75-167
KNIGHTS, L.C. PUBLIC VOICES.*
  K. THOMAS, 541(RES):MAY73-208
KNIPPING, J.B. ICONOGRAPHY OF THE
COUNTER REFORMATION IN THE NETHER-
LANDS.
  S. SCHAMA, 617(TLS):21MAR75-301

KNISTER, R. SELECTED STORIES OF
RAYMOND KNISTER. (M. GNAROWSKI, ED)
  D. LIVESAY, 102(CANL):AUTUMN74-79
  R. MANE, 189(EA):OCT-DEC73-493
KNOBLOCH, E. BEYOND THE OXUS.
  O. GRABAR, 293(JAST):FEB73-333
KNOBLOCH, E. DIE WORTWAHL IN DER
ARCHAISIERENDEN CHRONIKALISCHEN
ERZÄHLUNG.
  H.R. KLIENEBERGER, 402(MLR):JAN74-
  228
KNOEPFLMACHER, U.C. LAUGHTER &
DESPAIR.*
  W.E. MESSENGER, 136:VOL5#3-70
  H.P. SUCKSMITH, 677:VOL4-319
  V.L. TOLLERS, 651(WHR):SPRING74-
  184
KNOLL, P.W. THE RISE OF THE POLISH
MONARCHY.*
  K. GÓRSKI, 575(SEER):APR74-283
  R.C. HOFFMANN, 589:JUL74-573
KNOPF, K. ENGLISH PRONUNCIATION
EXERCISES.
  S. & J. MC DONOUGH, 430(NS):SEP73-
  498
KNOTT, J.R., JR. MILTON'S PASTORAL
VISION.*
  J. FRANK, 405(MP):AUG73-87
  A.J. SMITH, 541(RES):FEB73-76
KNOWLES, D., C.N.L. BROOKE & V. LON-
DON. THE HEADS OF RELIGIOUS HOUSES,
ENGLAND & WALES, 940-1216.*
  B.D. HILL, 589:JUL74-575
KNOWLES, J. SPREADING FIRES.*
  R. SALE, 249(HUDR):WINTER74/75-624
KNOWLSON, J. UNIVERSAL LANGUAGE
SCHEMES IN ENGLAND & FRANCE 1600-
1800.
  V. SALMON, 617(TLS):28NOV75-1403
KNOWLTON, E.C., JR. - SEE DE SÁ DE
MENESES, F.
KNOX, B. RALLY TO KILL.
  N. CALLENDAR, 441:21SEP75-42
KNOX, E.C., ED. RENCONTRES.
  J. GREENLEE, 207(FR):MAR73-877
KNOX, E.V. [EVOE] IN MY OLD DAYS.
  R. USBORNE, 617(TLS):11APR75-396
KNOX, J. THE HIGHLANDS & HEBRIDES
IN 1786.
  J.A. SMITH, 617(TLS):22AUG75-937
KNOX, O. AN ITALIAN DELUSION.
  R. USBORNE, 617(TLS):4JUL75-713
KOBEL, E. HUGO VON HOFMANNSTHAL.*
  W. NEHRING, 221(GQ):MAY73-436
KOBLER, J. ARDENT SPIRITS.
  M. EGREMONT, 617(TLS):16MAY75-533
KOBS, J. KAFKA.* (U. BRECH, ED)
  M. PASLEY, 220(GL&L):JAN74-170
KOBYSH, V. VZRYV STAL NEIZBEZHEN.
  B. MURPHY, 617(TLS):4APR75-375
KOCH, H. SCHILLER UND SPANIEN.
  N.H. SMITH, 182:VOL26#23/24-865
KOCH, K. THE ART OF LOVE.
  A. SAROYAN, 441:28SEP75-16
KOCH, K. A CHANGE OF HEARTS.*
  639(VQR):WINTER74-XVI
KOCH, R.A. JOACHIM PATINIR.
  K.G. BOON, 54:JUN73-297
KOCH, W.A. TAXOLOGIE DES ENGLISCHEN.
  E. STANDOP, 38:BAND91HEFT1-87
KOCHER, P.H. MASTER OF THE MIDDLE
EARTH.
  D.M. MILLER, 295:FEB74-806

KOCKELMANS, J.J., ED & TRANS. ON
HEIDEGGER & LANGUAGE.
  S.L. BARTKY, 484(PPR):MAR74-442
  J.D.C., 543:SEP72-162
KOEHLER, L. ANTON ANTONOVIČ DEL'VIG.
  B. DEES, 574(SEEJ):SPRING72-95
  T. EEKMAN, 279:VOL16-208
KOENIG, T. THE PHILOSOPHY OF
GEORGES BASTIDE.
  H. JONES, 154:JUN73-376
KOEPKE, W. DIE DEUTSCHEN.
  J. KOPPENSTEINER, 399(MLJ):APR73-
  224
KOERNER, E.F.K. BIBLIOGRAPHIA
SAUSSUREANA 1870-1970.
  P. WUNDERLI, 343:BAND17HEFT2-117
KOERTGE, R. THE FATHER-POEMS.
  M. MADIGAN, 385(MQR):SPRING75-220
  A. OSTROFF, 651(WHR):SUMMER74-302
KOESTERMANN, E. - SEE SALLUST
KOESTLER, A. THE CALL GIRLS.*
  C.P. CROWLEY, 628:FALL73-119
KOESTLER, A. THE ROOTS OF COINCI-
DENCE.*
  W. HOLTZ, 454:WINTER74-190
KOFMAN, S. NIETZSCHE ET LA MÉTA-
PHORE.
  R. LAPORTE, 98:JUN73-514
KOFOS, E. GREECE & THE EASTERN
CRISIS 1875-1878.
  C.M. WOODHOUSE, 617(TLS):14NOV75-
  1367
KOGAWA, J. A CHOICE OF DREAMS.
  L. SANDLER, 606(TAMR):NOV74-89
KOH MASUDA - SEE "KENKYUSHA'S NEW
JAPANESE-ENGLISH DICTIONARY"
KOHL, H. HALF THE HOUSE.
  E.Z. FRIEDENBERG, 453:27NOV75-30
KOHL, W.L. FRENCH NUCLEAR DIPLOM-
ACY.*
  J.C. CAIRNS, 207(FR):MAY73-1272
KOHLER, B. DER VERTRAG ÜBER DIE
NICHTVERBREITUNG VON KERNWAFFEN
UND DAS PROBLEM DER SICHERHEITS-
GARANTIEN.
  A-R. WERNER, 182:VOL26#11/12-402
KÖHLER, H-W. ŚRAD-DHĀ- IN DER VED-
ISCHEN UND ALTBUDDHISTISCHEN LITER-
ATUR. (K.L. JANERT, ED)
  R.E. EMMERICK, 182:VOL26#20-734
KOHN, R.H. EAGLE & SWORD.
  M.M. MINTZ, 441:30NOV75-51
  453:16OCT75-41
KÖHNKEN, A. DIE FUNKTION DES MYTHOS
BEI PINDAR.
  M.M. WILLCOCK, 123:NOV74-191
KÖHRING, K.H. & J.T. MORRIS. IN-
STANT ENGLISH.
  R. AHRENS, 430(NS):MAR73-180
KOJ, P. DIE FRÜHE REZEPTION DER
FAZETIEN POGGIOS IN FRANKREICH.*
  B.L.O. RICHTER, 207(FR):DEC72-396
KOJECKÝ, R. T.S. ELIOT'S SOCIAL
CRITICISM.*
  G.H. BANTOCK, 148:SPRING73-37
  M. DODSWORTH, 184(EIC):JUL73-310
  H. PESCHMANN, 175:SPRING73-35
KOJÈVE, A. INTRODUCTION TO THE
READING OF HEGEL.* (A. BLOOM, ED)
  A. QUINTON, 453:29MAY75-34 [& CONT
  IN] 453:12JUN75-39
KOKOSCHKA, O. MY LIFE.*
  E. WEEKS, 61:JAN75-87

202

KOLAKOWSKI, L. & S. HAMPSHIRE, EDS.
THE SOCIALIST IDEA.
  J. DUNN, 362:9JAN75-58
  K. MINOGUE, 617(TLS):21MAR75-307
KOLARI, V. & J. SUONSYRJÄ, COMPS.
POLITICAL HISTORY OF THE SCANDINAV-
IAN COUNTRIES & FINLAND IN THE 19TH
& 20TH CENTURIES.
  J.E.O. SCREEN, 575(SEER):APR74-318
KOLB, A.   EAST ASIA.
  B. BOXER, 293(JAST):NOV72-125
KOLB, E. & J. HASLER, EDS.   FEST-
SCHRIFT RUDOLF STAMM.*
  G. KUMS, 179(ES):DEC73-608
KOLB, F.   LITERARISCHE BEZIEHUNGEN
ZWISCHEN CASSIUS DIO, HERODIAN UND
DER HISTORIA AUGUSTA.
  J.H. OLIVER, 24:SUMMER74-179
KOLB, P. - SEE PROUST, M.
KOLGUSCHKIN, A.N.   LINGVISTIKA V
VOENNOM DELE.
  K. KRÜGER, 682(ZPSK):BAND26HEFT
  3/4-402
KÖLLERSTRÖM, O.   THE ACTUAL & THE
REAL.
  H.A. WILLIAMS, 617(TLS):28MAR75-
  345
KOLNEDER, W.   DAS BUCH DER VIOLINE.*
  A.H. KING, 182:VOL26#9-299
KOLNEDER, W.   MELODIETYPEN BEI VIV-
ALDI.
  M. TALBOT, 415:AUG74-662
KOLODIN, I.   THE INTERIOR BEETHOVEN.
  A. TYSON, 453:29MAY75-14
KOLODNY, A.   THE LAY OF THE LAND.
  W. MARTIN, 165:FALL75-227
KÖLSCH, N.   FRANKREICH IN DER DEUT-
SCHEN PRESSE.
  G. SCHWEIG, 430(NS):AUG73-454
KOLSTOE, O.P.   COLLEGE PROFESSORING.
  M. IVINS, 441:7SEP75-32
KÖLVER, B., ED.   TEXTKRITISCHE UND
PHILOLOGISCHE UNTERSUCHUNGEN ZUR
RĀJATARAÑGIṆĪ DES KALHAṆA.
  J. FILLIOZAT, 182:VOL26#13/14-457
KOMAR, A.J.   THEORY OF SUSPENSIONS.*
  C.H., 414(MQ):APR73-320
KOMINES, A.D.   FACSIMILES OF DATED
PATMIAN CODICES.
  N.G. WILSON, 123:MAR74-145
KONARSKI, S. & OTHERS, EDS.   MATER-
IAŁY DO BIOGRAFII, GENEALOGII I
HERALDYKI POLSKIEJ.   (VOLS 4&5)
  S. BÖBR-TYLINGO, 104:SPRING74-157
KÖNIG, H.   HEINRICH MANN.*
  K. THOENELT, 400(MLN):OCT73-1058
  J.J. WHITE, 402(MLR):OCT74-941
KÖNIG, R.   SOCIOLOGIE.
  D. MERLLIÉ, 542:JAN-MAR73-53
KÖNIGOVÁ, M., M. LUDVÍKOVÁ & J.
KRAUS.   PĚTIJAZYČNÝ SLOVNIK Z KVAN-
TITATIVNÍ LINGVISTIKY.
  J. KRÁMSKÝ, 353:1AUG73-82
KONING, H.   THE PETERSBURG-CANNES
EXPRESS.
  N. CALLENDAR, 441:24AUG75-27
  442(NY):9JUN75-126
KONJETZKY, K.   POEM VOM GRÜNEN ECK.
  M. HAMBURGER, 617(TLS):6JUN75-623
KONKIN, S.S., ED.   PROBLEMY POETIKI
I ISTORII LITERATURY.
  M.V. JONES, 617(TLS):25JUL75-857

KONRAD VON FUSSESBRUNNEN.   DIE KIND-
HEIT JESU.   (H. FROMM & K. GRUB-
MÜLLER, EDS)
  L. WOLFF, 301(JEGP):JUL74-393
KONRAD, A.N.   OLD RUSSIA & BYZAN-
TIUM.*
  R.W.F. POPE, 574(SEEJ):WINTER73-
  484
KONRÁD, G.   THE CASE WORKER.*
  R. DINNAGE, 617(TLS):31JAN75-101
  N. HEPBURN, 362:6FEB75-189
  M. PRICE, 676(YR):SUMMER74-554
  P.M. SPACKS, 249(HUDR):SUMMER74-
  288
  639(VQR):SUMMER74-LXXXII
KONUŠ, J.J.   SLOVAK-ENGLISH PHRASE-
OLOGICAL DICTIONARY.
  Z.P. MEYERSTEIN, 574(SEEJ):SPRING
  73-109
KONVITZ, M.R., ED.   THE RECOGNITION
OF RALPH WALDO EMERSON.*
  J.W.H., 502(PRS):SPRING73-93
KOOIJ, J.G.   AMBIGUITY IN NATURAL
LANGUAGE.
  D.L.F. NILSEN, 206:NOV73-595
  A.M. ZWICKY, 361:SEP73-95
KOOLISH, L.   JOURNEYS ON THE LIVING.
  P. SAVERY, 181:AUTUMN73-120
KOONTZ, D.R.   AFTER THE LAST RACE.
  N. CALLENDAR, 441:12JAN75-18
KOOP, A.J. & HOGITARŌ INADA.   MEIJI
BENRAN.
  L.R.H. SMITH, 463:SUMMER73-203
KÖPECZI, B.   LA FRANCE ET LA HONGRIE
AU DÉBUT DU XVIIIE SIÈCLE.*
  H. DURANTON, 535(RHL):NOV-DEC73-
  1077
KOPMAN, H.M.   RECONTRES WITH THE
INANIMATE IN PROUST'S "RECHERCHE."
  L.B. PRICE, 188(ECR):SUMMER73-178
KOPPERMAN, R.   MODEL THEORY & ITS
APPLICATION.
  A. ROBINSON, 316:DEC73-647
KOPS, B.   PARTNERS.
  E. KORN, 617(TLS):28MAR75-329
  J. MELLORS, 362:24APR75-547
KORDA, M.   POWER!
  R. REEVES, 441:21SEP75-4
KORDON, B.   LOS NAVEGANTES.
  G. FIGUEIRA, 263:JUL-SEP74-307
KORFF, F.W.   DIASTOLE UND SYSTOLE.
  H.R. KLIENEBERGER, 657(WW):JAN/FEB
  73-68
KORIZES, C.   TO AFTARCHIKO KATHES-
TOS.
  G. YANNOPOULOS, 617(TLS):14NOV75-
  1367
KORN, F.   ELEMENTARY STRUCTURES
RECONSIDERED.
  G.C. RUMP, 182:VOL26#5/6-185
KORNBLUM, W.   BLUE COLLAR COMMUNITY.
  A.H. RASKIN, 441:15FEB75-27
KÖRNER, A.   DIE WIENER JAKOBINER.
  G. CARR, 402(MLR):APR74-459
  J. HERMAND, 406:WINTER74-438
  H. SCHEEL, 182:VOL26#15/16-562
KÖRNER, S.   CATEGORICAL FRAMEWORKS.
  M. HOLLIS, 393(MIND):JUL73-457
KÖRNER, S.   THE PHILOSOPHY OF MATHE-
MATICS.
  J. VUILLEMIN, 542:JUL-SEP73-333

KORNWOLF, J.D. M.H. BAILLIE SCOTT &
THE ARTS & CRAFTS MOVEMENT.*
R. BANHAM, 46:JAN73-79
P.F. NORTON, 576:MAR73-75
H. SCHAEFER, 54:JUN73-307
KOROLENKO, V.G. THE HISTORY OF MY
CONTEMPORARY.* (TRANS & ABRIDGED
BY N. PARSONS)
R.F. BYRNES, 550(RUSR):APR73-215
N.M. KOLB-SELETSKI, 574(SEEJ):
SPRING73-81
KOROL'KOVA, A.N. RUSSKIE NARODNYE
SKAZKI. (E.V. POMERANCEVA, ED)
M. BOŠKOVIĆ-STULLI, 196:BAND14
HEFT3-279
KOROTKOV, N.N. OSNOVNYE OSOBENNOSTI
MORFOLOGIČESKOGO STROJA KITAJSKOGO
JAZYKA.
O. ŠVARNÝ, 353:15MAR73-106
KORS, A.C. & E. PETERS, EDS. WITCH-
CRAFT IN EUROPE 1100-1700.
L.F. BARMANN, 613:SUMMER73-314
R. CAVENDISH, 203:AUTUMN73-259
R.H. WEST, 219(GAR):SPRING73-137
KORSAKAS, K. & K. DOVEIKA, EDS.
LIETUVIŲ LITERATŪROS KRITIKA: 1547-
1917. (VOL 1)
R. ŠILBAJORIS, 574(SEEJ):SUMMER73-
241
KORSHIN, P.J. FROM CONCORD TO DIS-
SENT.*
J. FREEHAFER, 566:SPRING74-95
KORSHIN, P.J., ED. STUDIES IN
CHANGE & REVOLUTION.*
W. VON KOPPENFELS, 72:BAND211HEFT
3/6-432
KORT, W.A. SHRIVEN SELVES.
L.S. CUNNINGHAM, 613:AUTUMN73-422
KORTH, E.H. SPANISH POLICY IN COL-
ONIAL CHILE.
R. SOUTHERN, 86(BHS):JUL73-319
KORTNER, P. BREAKFAST WITH A STRAN-
GER.
J. BARNES, 617(TLS):5SEP75-998
KORZENIEWSKI, D. HIRTENGEDICHTE AUS
NERONISCHER ZEIT.
F.R.D. GOODYEAR, 123:NOV74-297
KOSAKIEWICZ, S. BERNARDO BELLOTTO.
M. LEVEY, 90:SEP73-615
KOSÁRY, D. BEVEZETÉS MAGYARORSZÁG
TÖRTÉNETÉNEK FORRÁSAIBA ES IRODAL-
MÁBA. (VOL 1)
L. PÉTER, 575(SEER):OCT74-605
KOSCH, W. & B. BERGER, EDS. DEUT-
SCHES LITERATUR-LEXIKON. (VOLS 2-4)
(3RD ED)
H. WEBER, 182:VOL26#21/22-798
KOSCHATZKY, W. & A. STROBL. DÜRER
DRAWINGS IN THE ALBERTINA.
C. WHITE, 39:DEC73-518
KOSCHORRECK, W. DIE HEIDELBERGER
BILDERHANDSCHRIFT DES SACHSENSPIE-
GELS.
G.W. RADIMERSKY, 221(GQ):MAR73-295
KOSINSKI, J. COCKPIT.
P. ADAMS, 61:SEP75-85
J. BAUMBACH, 441:10AUG75-3
E. KORN, 617(TLS):29AUG75-961
R.R. LINGEMAN, 441:15AUG75-39
C. RICKS, 453:27NOV75-42
KOSINSKI, J. THE DEVIL TREE.*
E. BUTSCHER, 109:FALL/WINTER73/74-
131
[CONTINUED]

[CONTINUING]
J. KLINKOWITZ, 114(CHIR):VOL25#1-
172
L.T. LEMON, 502(PRS):SUMMER73-183
P. STEVICK, 473(PR):2/1974-302
KOSOK, H. SEAN O'CASEY.*
G. AHRENDS, 72:BAND211HEFT1/3-158
K.P.S. JOCHUM, 301(JEGP):JAN74-144
H. RASCHE, 182:VOL26#23/24-867
KOSS, S. NON-CONFORMITY & MODERN
BRITISH POLITICS.
E. BOYLE, 617(TLS):19SEP75-1044
P. WHITEHEAD, 362:25SEP75-408
KOSSMAN, E.H. & A.F. MELLINK, EDS.
TEXTS CONCERNING THE REVOLT OF THE
NETHERLANDS.
G.N. PARKER, 617(TLS):6JUN75-630
KOST, K., ED. MUSAIOS, "HERO UND
LEANDER."*
F.F. SCHWARZ, 52:BAND8HEFT2-184
KOSTELANETZ, R., ED. BREAKTHROUGH
FICTIONEERS.
W. PEDEN, 569(SR):FALL74-712
KOSTELANETZ, R. THE END OF INTELLI-
GENT WRITING.*
J.W. ALDRIDGE, 385(MQR):SUMMER75-
346
B. DE MOTT, 61:FEB75-112
KOSTER, R.M. THE DISSERTATION.
C. LEHMANN-HAUPT, 441:12SEP75-27
D. WAKEFIELD, 441:2NOV75-52
KOSTIĆ, V. KULTURNE VEZE IZMEĐU
JUGOSLOVENSKIH ZEMALJA I ENGLESKE
DO 1700 GODINE.
C. HAWKESWORTH, 575(SEER):JUL74-
465
KOSTOMAROV, V. RUSSKIJ JAZYK DLJA
VSEX.
A.K. DONCHENKO, 574(SEEJ):SPRING73-
96
KŌTATSU, F. - SEE UNDER FUJITA KŌT-
ATSU
KOTELOVA, N.Z. & J.S. SOROKIN, EDS.
NOVYE SLOVA I ZNAČENIJA.
K.A. KLEIN, 574(SEEJ):WINTER73-477
KOTHARI, R., ED. CASTE IN INDIAN
POLITICS.
M.S.A. RAO, 293(JAST):MAY73-531
KOTTANNER, H. DIE DENKWÜRDIGKEITEN
DER HELENE KOTTANNERIN (1439-1440).
(K. MOLLAY, ED)
B.L. SPAHR, 133:1973/2-185
KOTZIN, M.C. DICKENS & THE FAIRY
TALE.*
R.D. MC MASTER, 445(NCF):JUN73-107
W. MYERS, 637(VS):SEP73-108
H. STONE, 155:MAY73-121
KOTZWINKLE, W. SWIMMER IN THE SEC-
RET SEA.
M. LEVIN, 441:2NOV75-54
KOUBOURLIS, D.J. SOVIET ACADEMY
"GRAMMAR," PHONOLOGY & MORPHOLOGY.
G.L. HARRIS, 574(SEEJ):WINTER73-
479
KOUDELKA, J. GYPSIES.
H. KRAMER, 441:7DEC75-86
KOUMANDAREAS, M. VIOTECHNÍA YALI-
KŌN.
P. MACKRIDGE, 617(TLS):14NOV75-
1368
KOURY, M.J. ARMS FOR TEXAS.
W. GARD, 584(SWR):WINTER74-98

KOUSSER, J.M. THE SHAPING OF SOUTH-
ERN POLITICS.
  J. WHITE, 617(TLS):13JUN75-679
KOUTAISSOFF, E. THE SOVIET UNION.*
  G. KALBOUSS, 574(SEEJ:WINTER72-513
KOVAČEVIC, I. FACT INTO FICTION.
  P. KEATING, 617(TLS):22AUG75-947
KOYRÉ, A. & I.B. COHEN, WITH A.
WHITMAN. ISAAC NEWTON'S PHILOSOPH-
IAE NATURALIS PRINCIPIA MATHEMAT-
ICA.
  P. WALLIS, 354:DEC73-350
KOZAKIEWICZ, S. BERNARDO BELLOTTO.
  J.G. LINKS, 39:JAN73-107
KOZELKA, P. DIRECTING.
  J. VAN DER POLL, 583:FALL73-95
KOZIOL, H. HANDBUCH DER ENGLISCHEN
WORTBILDUNGSLEHRE. (2ND ED)
  R.W.Z., 179(ES):AUG73-402
KOZLOFF, M. CUBISM/FUTURISM.
  W.C. WEES, 141:FALL74-349
KOZLOFF, M. JASPER JOHNS.
  W. RUBIN, 54:SEP73-471
KOZŁOWSKA, H. FORMENNEUTRALISIERUNG
IM NOMINALEN BEREICH DER DEUTSCHEN
SPRACHE.
  H.W. SCHALLER, 343:BAND16HEFT1-83
KOZOL, J. THE NIGHT IS DARK & I AM
FAR FROM HOME.
  V. GORNICK, 441:2NOV75-8
  442(NY):27OCT75-167
KRA, P. RELIGION IN MONTESQUIEU'S
"LETTRES PERSANES."*
  C.J. BEYER, 546(RR):MAY73-235
KRABIEL, K-D. JOSEPH VON EICHEN-
DORFF.*
  J.F.F., 191(ELN):SEP73(SUPP)-122
KRAFT, C.H. & M.G. INTRODUCTORY
HAUSA.
  D.H. LOSSE, 399(MLJ):SEP-OCT74-268
KRAFT, H. - SEE SCHILLER, F.
KRAFT, K. DER "RATIONALE" ALEXAN-
DER. (REV) (H. GESCHE, ED)
  A.B. BOSWORTH, 303:VOL93-256
  C.I. REID, 487:SUMMER73-205
KRAFT, K. DAS SYSTEM DER KAISER-
ZEITLICHEN MÜNZPRÄGUNG IN KLEIN-
ASIEN.
  M. PRICE, 124:MAR74-310
KRAFT, K. & J. BLEICKEN - SEE ZIEG-
LER, J.
KRAFT, W.S. SO SIND DIE DEUTSCHEN I.
  K.O. ANDERSON, 399(MLJ):APR74-210
KRAGH-JACOBSEN, S. & OTHERS. THE-
ATRE RESEARCH STUDIES II.
  S.J. COHEN, 290(JAAC):SUMMER74-573
KRAHE, H. EINLEITUNG IN DAS VER-
GLEICHENDE SPRACHSTUDIUM.* (W.
MEID, ED)
  F. BADER, 555:VOL47FASC1-110
  G.B. FORD, JR., 353:15OCT73-89
  W. THOMAS, 260(IF):BAND78-225
KRAHL, S. & J. KURZ. KLEINES WÖR-
TERBUCH DER STILKUNDE.
  G.F. MEIER, 682(ZPSK):BAND26HEFT
  3/4-433
KRAILSHEIMER, A.J., ED. THE CONTI-
NENTAL RENAISSANCE, 1500-1600.
  S.F.R. & T.R.H., 131(CL):WINTER74-
  95
  P. WALEY, 86(BHS):APR73-170

KRAMER, H. THE AGE OF THE AVANT-
GARDE.*
  W. FEAVER, 364:JUN/JUL74-125
  L.G. KATZ, 249(HUDR):SPRING74-145
KRAMER, K.D. THE CHAMELEON & THE
DREAM.
  T.G. WINNER, 574(SEEJ):SPRING73-79
KRÄMER, P. DIE PRÄSENSKLASSEN DES
GERMANISCHEN SCHWACHEN VERBUMS.
  I. DAL, 343:BAND17HEFT1-96
  D.R. MC LINTOCK, 220(GL&L):OCT73-
  67
KRAMMER, J. ÖDÖN VON HORVÁTH.
  H. JARKA, 680(ZDP):BAND92HEFT4-621
KRAMNICK, I. - SEE LORD BOLINGBROKE
KRAMSKY, J. THE ARTICLE & THE CON-
CEPT OF DEFINITENESS IN LANGUAGE.
  R.A. HUDSON, 361:DEC73-355
KRANZ, G. - SEE LEWIS, C.S.
KRAPOTH, H. DICHTUNG UND PHILOSO-
PHIE.
  J.J. WHITE, 220(GL&L):JAN74-168
KRATOCHVÍL, P. THE CHINESE LANGUAGE
TODAY.
  O. ŠVARNÝ, 353:15MAR73-109
KRATOCHVÍL, P. - SEE LU HSÜN
KRAUSE, D. - SEE O'CASEY, S.
KRAUSE, G. CORNEILLE - RACINE.
  J. THIEL, 430(NS):MAR73-173
KRAUSE, J.H. THE NATURE OF ART.
  J.S. KEEL, 186(ETC.):MAR73-104
KRAUSS, E.S. JAPANESE RADICALS RE-
VISITED.
  R. STORRY, 617(TLS):12SEP75-1027
KRAUSS, R.E. TERMINAL IRON WORKS.*
  C. GOLDSTEIN, 56:WINTER73-419
KRAUSS, W. LITERATUR DER FRANZÖSIS-
CHEN AUFKLÄRUNG.
  W.H. BARBER, 208(FS):OCT74-464
KRAUSZ, M., ED. CRITICAL ESSAYS ON
THE PHILOSOPHY OF R.G. COLLING-
WOOD.*
  P. DUBOIS, 542:APR-JUN73-222
KRAUTHEIMER, R. GHIBERTI'S BRONZE
DOORS.*
  P. CANNON-BROOKES, 39:FEB73-202
KRAUTHEIMER, R., WITH T. KRAUTHEIM-
ER-HESS. LORENZO GHIBERTI.
  P. CANNON-BROOKES, 39:FEB73-202
KRECH, H. & OTHERS, EDS. WÖRTERBUCH
DER DEUTSCHEN AUSSPRACHE.
  B.J. KOEKKOEK, 399(MLJ):MAR73-145
KREEGER, L., ED. THE LARGE GROUP.
  P. HALMOS, 617(TLS):25JUL75-832
KREITLER, H. & S. PSYCHOLOGY OF
THE ARTS.*
  M. BORNSTEIN, 290(JAAC):FALL73-123
KREJČÍ, J. SOCIAL CHANGE & STRATIF-
ICATION IN POSTWAR CZECHOSLOVAKIA.*
  V.V. KUSIN, 575(SEER):OCT74-637
KREMEN, M.R. THE IMAGINATION OF THE
RESURRECTION.
  I.H.C., 191(ELN):SEP73(SUPP)-34
  J.B. VICKERY, 295:FEB74-400
KREMER, E.J. & E.A. SYNAN, EDS.
DEATH BEFORE BIRTH.
  V. HUNTER, 99:APR/MAY75-25
KRENKEL, W. - SEE LUCILIUS
KRENN, H. DIE SPRACHWISSENSCHAFT-
LICHE FRAGE DER SEMANTIK UND FUNK-
TION, ERÖRTERT AN DEN GEGEBENHEITEN
                              [CONTINUED]

[CONTINUING]
DER CONSECUTIO TEMPORUM IM ITALIEN-
ISCHEN.
G.F. MEIER, 682(ZPSK):BAND26HEFT
1/2-197
KRENN, H. & K. MÜLLNER. BIBLIOGRA-
PHIE ZUR TRANSFORMATIONSGRAMMATIK.*
H. PÜTZ & W. THÜMMEL, 260(IF):
BAND77HEFT2/3-377
"KRESGE'S CATALOG."
S. SMITH, 441:7DEC75-95
KREUGER, J.R. & E.D. FRANCIS, EDS.
CHEREMIS-CHUVASH LEXICAL RELATION-
SHIPS.
G.F. MEIER, 682(ZPSK):BAND26HEFT
1/2-190
KREUZER, I. ENTFREMDUNG UND ANPAS-
SUNG.
S. MANDEL, 399(MLJ):JAN-FEB74-71
KREYCHE, R.J. THE BETRAYAL OF WIS-
DOM.
G.D., 543:JUN73-758
KRIEGEL, L. EDMUND WILSON.
W. ALEXANDER, 141:FALL72-397
KRIEGER, L. AN ESSAY ON THE THEORY
OF ENLIGHTENED DESPOTISM.
J. DUNN, 617(TLS):26DEC75-1535
KRIEGER, M. THE CLASSIC VISION.*
295:FEB74-473
KRIKORIAN, Y.H. RECENT PERSPECTIVES
IN AMERICAN PHILOSOPHY.
H.W.S., 319:OCT75-549
KRIKORIAN, Y.V. THE PURSUIT OF
IDEALS.
S.L. HART, 321:FALL73-239
KRISCH, H. GERMAN POLITICS UNDER
SOVIET OCCUPATION.
D.C. WATT, 617(TLS):8AUG75-892
KRISCHER, T. FORMALE KONVENTIONEN
DER HOMERISCHEN EPIK.
F.M. COMBELLACK, 122:OCT73-307
H.G. EDINGER, 124:MAY73-464
J.B. HAINSWORTH, 123:NOV74-285
KRISHNA, D., D.C. MATHUR & A.P. RAO,
EDS. MODERN LOGIC.
D. SHARMA & S. SINHA, 485(PE&W):
JUL73-409
KRISHNA, G. THE SECRET OF YOGA.
W.C., 543:JUN73-758
KRISHNAMURTI, B. KOṆḌA OR KŪBI.
K. DE VREESE, 318(JAOS):OCT-DEC73-
597
KRISHNAN, T.V.K. - SEE UNDER KUNHI
KRISHNAN, T.V.
KRISPYN, E. GÜNTER EICH.*
J. GLENN, 399(MLJ):SEP-OCT73-298
S. PRAWER, 220(GL&L):JUL74-333
KRISTELLER, P.O., ED-IN-CHIEF. CAT-
ALOGUS TRANSLATIONUM ET COMMENTARI-
ORUM. (VOL 2)
B.B. BOYER, 551(RENQ):SUMMER73-181
KRISTJÁNSSON, J. UM FÓSTBRAEÐRA-
SÖGU.
P. SCHACH, 301(JEGP):OCT74-574
KRIUKELIENĖ, O. & E. STANEVIČIENĖ.
LIETUVIŲ KALBOTYRA 1965-1968.
W.R. SCHMALSTIEG, 574(SEEJ):SUMMER
72-273
KROEBER, K. STYLES IN FICTIONAL
STRUCTURE.*
W.A. MADDEN, 594:FALL73-406
B. MENIKOFF, 599:SPRING73-238
G.B. TENNYSON, 141:SPRING72-192
E. WIKBORG, 179(ES):DEC73-597

KROESEN, J.M.C. DE SAGA VAN EGIL
ZOON VAN SKALLA-GRÍM.
T. HOMAN, 433:JAN73-95
KROETSCH, R. BADLANDS.
R.H. RAMSEY, 99:DEC75/JAN76-54
KROETSCH, R. GONE INDIAN.
R.M. BROWN, 102(CANL):SUMMER74-103
KROETSCH, R., J. BACQUE & P. GRAVEL.
CREATION.
L. ROGERS, 102(CANL):WINTER73-119
KROLL, J. IN THE TEMPERATE ZONE.*
J. PARISI, 491:JUL75-219
KROLL, J.H. ATHENIAN BRONZE ALLOT-
MENT PLATES.
J.J. KEANEY, 124:MAR74-312
KROLOW, K. GESAMMELTE GEDICHTE 2.
M. HAMBURGER, 617(TLS):5SEP75-1004
KRÖMER, W. DIE FRANZÖSISCHE NOVELLE
IM 19. JAHRHUNDERT.
O. WIRTZ, 430(NS):JUL73-397
KRONENBERG, A. LOGIK UND LEBEN.
P. ERNY, 182:VOL26#7/8-251
KRONENBERGER, L. THE EXTRAORDINARY
MR. WILKES.*
G. CURTIS, 617(TLS):24JAN75-72
639(VQR):SUMMER74-XCII
KROÓ, G. A GUIDE TO BARTÓK.
N. CHADWICK, 410(M&L):JUL74-334
KROOK, D. ELEMENTS OF TRAGEDY.
E. POULENARD, 189(EA):APR-JUN73-
245
D.D. RAPHAEL, 447(N&Q):FEB73-63
KRUEGER, J.R., WITH F. ADELMAN - SEE
POZDNEYEV, A.M.
KRÜGER, H-J., ED. ARCHIVALISCHE
FUNDSTÜCKE ZU DEN RUSSISCH-DEUT-
SCHEN BEZIEHUNGEN.
M. RAEFF, 104:WINTER74-597
KRUSE, H.H. MARK TWAIN'S "LIFE ON
THE MISSISSIPPI."
A. HELLER, 430(NS):APR73-231
KRUSE, J.A. HEINES HAMBURGER ZEIT.
G. HÄNTZSCHEL, 680(ZDP):BAND92
HEFT4-606
J.L.S., 191(ELN):SEP73(SUPP)-134
KRUSZEWSKI, Z.A. THE ODER-NEISSE
BOUNDARY & POLAND'S MODERNIZATION.
A. MATEJKO, 104:SPRING74-168
KRYZYTSKI, S. THE WORKS OF IVAN
BUNIN.
D.J. RICHARDS, 575(SEER):JAN74-133
KRZYWON, E.J. HEINRICH HEINE UND
POLEN.
J.L.S., 191(ELN):SEP73(SUPP)-134
KRZYŻANOWSKI, J.R. WŁADYSLAW STAN-
ISŁAW REYMONT.
Z. FOLEJEWSKI, 104:WINTER74-591
M.G. LEVINE, 497(POLR):VOL18#3-99
S. SANDLER, 574(SEEJ):FALL73-348
KU, P. - SEE UNDER PAN KU
KUBACH, H.E. ROMANESQUE ARCHITEC-
TURE.
J. RUSSELL, 441:7DEC75-3
KUBAL, D.L. OUTSIDE THE WHALE.
D. SMYER, 50(ARQ):WINTER73-370
KUBLER, G. PORTUGUESE PLAIN ARCHI-
TECTURE.
R.C. SMITH, 90:JUL73-472
KUBY, L. AN UNCOMMON POET FOR THE
COMMON MAN.
J. FULLER, 617(TLS):24OCT75-1259
KUCZYNSKI, J. GESTALTEN UND WERKE.
R. SCHOBER, 654(WB):11/1973-184

KUDSZUS, W. SPRACHVERLUST UND SINN-
WANDEL.
   F. ASPETSBERGER, 680(ZDP):BAND92
   HEFT2-294
KUEHL, J. & J.R. BRYER - SEE FITZ-
GERALD, F.S. & M. PERKINS
KUEHN, D. TAKEOVERS & THE THEORY OF
THE FIRM.
   B. HINDLEY, 617(TLS):10OCT75-1215
KUEN, H. ROMANISTISCHE AUFSÄTZE.
   H.J. SIMON, 430(NS):JAN73-57
KUFNER, H.L. KONTRASTIVE PHONOLOGIE
DEUTSCH-ENGLISCH.
   A. WOLLMANN, 38:BAND91HEFT1-99
KUHL, E.P. STUDIES IN CHAUCER &
SHAKESPEARE.*
   R.T. DAVIES, 447(N&Q):JAN73-30
KUHLMANN, S. KNAVE, FOOL, & GENIUS.*
   K.S. LYNN, 27(AL):MAR74-115
   T. WORTHAM, 445(NCF):MAR74-502
   639(VQR):WINTER74-XXII
KÜHLWEIN, W., ED. LINGUISTICS IN
GREAT BRITAIN.* (VOL 1)
   E.F.K. KOERNER, 72:BAND211HEFT1/3-
   108
   A. WOLLMANN, 38:BAND91HEFT1-84
KÜHLWEIN, W., ED. LINGUISTICS IN
GREAT BRITAIN.* (VOL 2)
   G. FEUERSTEIN, 430(NS):APR73-239
   A. WOLLMANN, 38:BAND91HEFT1-84
KUHN, D. LA POÉTIQUE DE FRANÇOIS
VILLON.
   R.L. COON, 207(FR):OCT72-145
KUHN, H. DAS ALTE ISLAND.*
   J. HARRIS, 563(SS):WINTER74-73
KUHN, H. KLEINE SCHRIFTEN.* (VOLS
1-3) (D. HOFMANN, WITH W. LANGE &
K. VON SEE, EDS)
   H. UECKER, 680(ZDP):BAND92HEFT3-
   444
KUHN, P.A. REBELLION & ITS ENEMIES
IN LATE IMPERIAL CHINA.
   I.C.Y. HSU, 318(JAOS):JUL-SEP73-
   408
KUHN, R., ED. L'ESPRIT MODERNE DANS
LA LITTÉRATURE FRANÇAISE.
   W.W. KIBLER, 207(FR):MAR73-882
   L. LE SAGE, 399(MLJ):SEP-OCT73-282
KUHN, S.M. & J. REIDY, EDS. MIDDLE
ENGLISH DICTIONARY.* (PTS H1-5 &
I1-2)
   B. SUNDBY, 179(ES):DEC72-551
KUHN, T.S. LA STRUCTURE DES RÉVOLU-
TIONS SCIENTIFIQUES.
   R. BLANCHÉ, 542:JUL-SEP73-362
KÜHN, W. GÖTTERSZENEN BEI VERGIL.
   R. HORNSBY, 124:SEP72-44
KÜHNE, C. & H. OTTEN. DER ŠAUŠGA-
MUWA-VERTRAG.
   G. NEUMANN, 260(IF):BAND78-243
KUHNS, R. STRUCTURES OF EXPERI-
ENCE.* (BRITISH TITLE: LITERATURE
& PHILOSOPHY.)
   L. MACKEY, 258:DEC73-565
KUKENHEIM, L. GRAMMAIRE HISTORIQUE
DE LA LANGUE FRANÇAISE: LES SYN-
TAGMES.
   P.F. DEMBOWSKI, 545(RPH):AUG73-86
KUKI, S. - SEE UNDER SHUZO KUKI
KUKLICK, B. JOSIAH ROYCE.
   H.A. LARRABEE, 432(NEQ):MAR73-129
   J.K. ROTH, 319:JUL75-419

KULKARNI, A.R. MAHARASHTRA IN THE
AGE OF SHIVAJI.
   N.K. WAGLE, 293(JAST):MAY73-520
KULKARNI, E.D., ED. PARAMĀNANDĪ-
YANĀMAMĀLĀ OF MAKARANDADĀSA. (PT 2)
   R. ROCHER, 318(JAOS):JUL-SEP73-381
KUMARASWAMI RAJA, N. POST-NASAL
VOICELESS PLOSIVES IN DRAVIDIAN.*
   K.V. ZVELEBIL, 318(JAOS):JAN-MAR
   73-119
KUMIN, M. THE DESIGNATED HEIR.*
   J. BARNES, 617(TLS):9MAY75-501
   J.L. HALIO, 598(SOR):AUTUMN75-942
KUMIN, M. HOUSE, BRIDGE, FOUNTAIN,
GATE.
   H. VENDLER, 441:7SEP75-6
KUMIN, M. UP COUNTRY.*
   J.N. MORRIS, 249(HUDR):SPRING74-
   113
   P. RAMSEY, 569(SR):SPRING74-403
"KIPTON KUMLER: PHOTOGRAPHS."
   H. KRAMER, 441:7DEC75-86
KUNER, M.C. THORNTON WILDER.*
   295:FEB74-823
KUNHI KRISHNAN, T.V. CHAVAN & THE
TROUBLED DECADE.
   B. BUENO DE MESQUITA, 293(JAST):
   FEB73-355
KUNISCH, N., ED. ANTIKEN DER SAMM-
LUNG JULIUS C. UND MARGOT FUNCKE.
   B.A. SPARKES, 303:VOL93-271
KUNITZ, S. A KIND OF ORDER, A KIND
OF FOLLY.
   T. LASK, 441:16NOV75-61
KUNITZ, S. THE TERRIBLE THRESHOLD.*
   R. GARFITT, 364:FEB/MAR75-112
KUNNE-IBSCH, E. DIE STELLUNG NIET-
ZSCHES IN DER ENTWICKLUNG DER MOD-
ERNEN LITERATURWISSENSCHAFT.
   H. BLUHM, 301(JEGP):APR74-301
   E. SCHAPER, 89(BJA):SPRING73-193
KUNST, J. MUSIC IN JAVA. (3RD ED)
(E.L. HEINS, ED)
   J. BECKER, 187:MAY75-310
   N. SORRELL, 415:JUL74-570
KUNZE, K. STUDIEN ZUR LEGENDE DER
HEILIGEN MARIA AEGYPTIACA IM
DEUTSCHEN SPRACHGEBIET.*
   H. VAN DER VOLK, 433:JAN73-99
KUNZE, R. WITH THE VOLUME TURNED
DOWN.
   R. GARFITT, 364:JUN/JUL74-107
KUNZE, S. DON GIOVANNI VOR MOZART.
   P. BRANSCOMBE, 410(M&L):JUL74-331
KUNZLE, D. THE EARLY COMIC STRIP.
   639(VQR):SUMMER74-CVIII
KUPER, L. RACE, CLASS & POWER.
   M. BANTON, 617(TLS):7FEB75-128
KÜPPER, H. WÖRTERBUCH DER DEUTSCHEN
UMGANGSSPRACHE. (VOL 6) AM A...
DER WELT.
   M. KAEMPFERT, 680(ZDP):BAND92HEFT
   1-156
KURASZKIEWICZ, W., ED. WYRAZY POL-
SKIE W SŁOWNIKU ŁACIŃSKO-POLSKIM
JANA MĄCZYNSKIEGO.*
   H. LEEMING, 575(SEER):JUL74-453
KURATH, H. STUDIES IN AREA LINGUIS-
TICS.
   R.I. MC DAVID, JR., 35(AS):FALL-
   WINTER72-285
KURELEK, W. O TORONTO.
   R. LEVIN, 73:WINTER74-43

KYOZO, T. SELECTED POEMS.
R. GARFITT, 364:JUN/JUL74-110
KYTZLER, B., ED & TRANS. ROMA
AETERNA.
R.J.S., 570(SQ):SUMMER73-351

L.M. [I. BAKER] KATHERINE MANSFIELD:
THE MEMORIES OF L.M.
A. ALPERS, 255(HAB):WINTER73-58
LAAGE, K.E., ED. SCHRIFTEN DER
THEODOR-STORM-GESELLSCHAFT.
(SCHRIFT 18/1969)
E. MC INNES, 220(GL&L):JAN74-161
LAAGE, K.E., ED. SCHRIFTEN DER
THEODOR-STORM-GESELLSCHAFT.
(SCHRIFT 19)
J.U. TERPSTRA, 433:OCT73-419
LAAGE, K.E., ED. SCHRIFTEN DER
THEODOR-STORM-GESELLSCHAFT.
(SCHRIFT 21/1972)
J. DE CORT, 556(RLV):1973/3-285
LAAGE, K.E. - SEE STORM, T.
LAAGE, K.E. - SEE STORM, T. & E.
SCHMIDT
LABAN, R. A LIFE FOR DANCE. (L.
ULLMANN, ED & TRANS)
M. CLARKE, 617(TLS):8AUG75-889
LABARGE, M.W. HENRY V.
G. HOLMES, 617(TLS):7NOV75-1339
LABARRE, A. HISTOIRE DU LIVRE.
G. BARBER, 447(N&Q):MAR73-116
LABARRE, A. LE LIVRE DANS LA VIE
AMIÉNOISE DU SEIZIÈME SIÈCLE.
R.A. SAYCE, 354:MAR73-69
LABEDZ, L., ED. SOLZHENITSYN.*
R. RAMSEY, 295:FEB74-782
LABEDZ, L., ED. SOLZHENITSYN. (EN-
LARGED ED)
N.J. ANNING, 575(SEER):OCT74-613
LABORDE, A.M. L'ESTHETIQUE CIR-
CÉENNE.
H.F. MAJEWSKI, 546(RR):JAN73-69
DE LA BRUYERE, J. LES CARACTÈRES.
M. WAGNER, 207(FR):OCT72-247
LACAN, J. DE LA PSYCHOSE PARANOÏ-
AQUE DANS SES RAPPORTS AVEC LA
PERSONNALITÉ, SUIVI DE PREMIERS
ÉCRITS SUR LA PARANOÏA.
A. LAVERS, 617(TLS):18JUL75-797
LACASSIN, F. & G. SIGAUX, EDS.
SIMENON.
R. COBB, 617(TLS):17JAN75-53
LACEY, R. SIR WALTER RALEGH.*
T.K. RABB, 453:3APR75-31
L.B. SMITH, 639(VQR):SUMMER74-444
LACH, F. - SEE SCHWITTERS, K.
LACHENAL, F. - SEE GASSIER, P. & J.
WILSON
LACHMANN, K. - SEE VON ESCHENBACH,
W.
LACHMANN, L.M. THE LEGACY OF MAX
WEBER.
T. BURGER, 529(QQ):SPRING73-145
LACKEY, D. - SEE RUSSELL, B.
LACORTE, C. KANT.*
M. BARALE, 342:BAND64HEFT1-120
LACROIX, J. LE PERSONNALISME COMME
ANTI-IDÉOLOGIE.
M. ADAM, 542:OCT-DEC73-491

LACY, N.J., ED. A MEDIEVAL FRENCH
MISCELLANY.
P. HAIDU, 399(MLJ):DEC73-428
G. MERMIER, 207(FR):MAY73-1218
LADEFOGED, P. PRELIMINARIES TO LIN-
GUISTIC PHONETICS.*
L.F. BROSNAHAN, 297(JL):SEP73-339
H. ROGERS, 320(CJL):FALL74-205
LADEFOGED, P. THREE AREAS OF EXPER-
IMENTAL PHONETICS.
J.W. LEWIS, 179(ES):FEB72-76
LADOO, H.S. NO PAIN LIKE THIS BODY.
D. BESSAI, 102(CANL):SUMMER74-106
LADOO, H.S. YESTERDAYS.*
P. SUCH, 606(TAMR):OCT74-78
LADU, T.T. WHAT MAKES THE FRENCH
FRENCH.
J.D. ANDERSON, 399(MLJ):DEC74-417
LAERMANN, K. EIGENSCHAFTSLOSIGKEIT.*
J.J. WHITE, 220(GL&L):JUL74-330
MADAME DE LAFAYETTE. LA PRINCESSE
DE CLÈVES.
M. WAGNER, 207(FR):OCT72-247
MADAME DE LAFAYETTE. LA PRINCESSE
DE CLÈVES. (P.H. NURSE, ED)
G. HAINSWORTH, 208(FS):JAN74-69
LAFOND, J. LES VITRAUX DE L'EGLISE
SAINT-OUEN DE ROUEN. (VOL 1)
R. BECKSMANN, 683:BAND36HEFT2/3-
177
J. HAYWARD, 54:JUN73-293
LAFONT, R. RENAISSANCE DU SUD.
A.V. ROCHE, 546(RR):MAR73-152
DE LA FONTAINE, J. FABLES CHOISIES.
M. WAGNER, 207(FR):OCT72-247
LA FONTAINE, J.S. CITY POLITICS.
V. PONS, 69:OCT73-355
LAFORET, C. UN NOVIAZGO. (C.L.
GALERSTEIN, ED)
I. FINE, 399(MLJ):APR74-216
LA FOUNTAINE, G. TWO MINUTE WARN-
ING.
N. CALLENDAR, 441:9FEB75-16
LA FRANCE, M. A READING OF STEPHEN
CRANE.*
S. COOPERMAN, 529(QQ):SUMMER73-305
J.C. ROWE, 50(ARQ):AUTUMN73-278
E. SOLOMON, 594:SPRING73-144
E. STONE, 295:FEB74-571
LAFUENTE FERRARI, E. EL GRECO.
F. HASKELL, 453:2OCT75-14
LAGANE, R. - SEE DE VAUGELAS, C.F.
LAGARDE, A. & L. MICHARD, WITH J.
MONFÉRIER. LES GRANDS AUTEURS
FRANÇAIS.*
E.L. DUTHIE, 208(FS):JAN74-113
J.T. JOHNSON, JR., 399(MLJ):NOV73-
364
LAGARRIGUE, G. - SEE SALVIEN DE MAR-
SEILLE
LAGERGREN, D. MISSION & STATE IN
THE CONGO.
F.B. WELBOURN, 69:OCT73-356
LAGERKVIST, P. EVENINGLAND/AFTON-
LAND. (W.H. AUDEN & L. SJÖBERG,
TRANS)
P-L. ADAMS, 61:OCT75-110
LAGERROTH, U-B. & G. LINDSTRÖM, EDS.
PERSPEKTIV PÅ "FRØKEN JULIE."
T. NAESS, 172(EDDA):1973/4-255
LAGO, M.M. & K. BECKSON - SEE BEER-
BOHM, M. & W. ROTHENSTEIN

209

LANDON, H.C.R. HAYDN.*
M. PETERSON, 470:MAR74-30
LANDOW, G.P. THE AESTHETIC & CRITI-
CAL THEORIES OF JOHN RUSKIN.*
C.T. DOUGHERTY, 54:MAR73-157
J. UNRAU, 179(ES):JUN73-297
LANDSMAN, C. DISCOURSE & ITS PRE-
SUPPOSITIONS.
R.B., 543:MAR73-539
LANDWEHR, J. EMBLEM BOOKS IN THE
LOW COUNTRIES 1554-1949.* ROMEYN
DE HOOGHE (1645-1708) AS BOOK
ILLUSTRATOR.
S.H.A. BRUNTJEN, 90:AUG73-547
LANDY, J. THE ARCHITECTURE OF MIN-
ARD LAFEVER.
R.G. WILSON, 576:OCT73-260
LANE, A. LATER ISLAMIC POTTERY.
R. ETTINGHAUSEN, 57:VOL35#1/2-165
LANE, A.E. AN ADEQUATE RESPONSE.
F. GARBER, 301(JEGP):JUL74-454
H. PESCHMANN, 175:SUMMER73-83
J.N. WYSONG, 529(QQ):AUTUMN73-484
LANE, D. POLITICS & SOCIETY IN THE
USSR.
B. HARASYMIW, 104:WINTER73-558
LANE, D. & G. KOLANKIEWICZ, EDS.
SOCIAL GROUPS IN POLISH SOCIETY.
Z. BAUMAN, 575(SEER):APR74-306
LANE, F.C. VENICE, A MARITIME RE-
PUBLIC.*
J. HALE, 617(TLS):28FEB75-210
LANE, J. HEIRS OF SQUIRE HARRY.
P. BEER, 617(TLS):17JAN75-48
LANE, P. BEWARE THE MONTHS OF
FIRE.*
F.W. WATT, 99:JUN75-40
LANG, B. & F. WILLIAMS, EDS. MARX-
ISM & ART.*
L.H. LEGTERS, 550(RUSR):JUL73-322
M. RADER, 290(JAAC):FALL73-118
LANG, H-J., ED. DER AMERIKANISCHE
ROMAN.
T. WORTHAM, 445(NCF):MAR74-502
LANG, P.H. CRITIC AT THE OPERA.
M. PETERSON, 470:NOV72-46
"V.R. LANG: POEMS & PLAYS."
S. BINGHAM, 441:26OCT75-24
P. DAVISON, 61:NOV75-120
LANGACKER, R.W. SPRACHE UND IHRE
STRUKTUR.
N.C.W. SPENCE, 208(FS):OCT74-495
LANGACKER, R.W. - SEE HYDE, V.
LANGBAUM, R. THE MODERN SPIRIT.*
P. TOMLINSON, 184(EIC):APR72-206
LANGBEHN-ROHLAND, R. ZUR INTERPRE-
TATION DER ROMANE DES DIEGO DE SAN
PEDRO.
F. MÁRQUEZ VILLANUEVA, 240(HR):
AUTUMN73-693
LANGE, R.A. THE PHONOLOGY OF
EIGHTH-CENTURY JAPANESE.
J.M. UNGER, 320(CJL):FALL74-217
LANGE, V. & F. - SEE GRASS, G.
LANGE, V. & H-G. ROLOFF, EDS. DICH-
TUNG - SPRACHE - GESELLSCHAFT.
A.F. GOESSL, 406:SUMMER74-212
LANGE, W-D. EL FRAILE TROBADOR.*
R. AF GEIJERSTAM, 86(BHS):APR73-
167
LANGE, W-D. & H.J. WOLF, EDS. PHIL-
OLOGISCHE STUDIEN FÜR JOSEPH M.
PIEL.
D. MESSNER, 430(NS):JAN73-55

LANGEN, A. DER WORTSCHATZ DES
DEUTSCHEN PIETISMUS.
M. KAEMPFERT, 680(ZDP):BAND92HEFT
2-278
"LANGENSCHEIDT POCKET GERMAN DIC-
TIONARY."
H. LEDERER, 399(MLJ):MAR74-131
"LANGENSCHEIDTS GROSSWÖRTERBUCH
ENGLISCH-DEUTSCH." (H. MESSINGER,
ED)
A.L. LLOYD, 399(MLJ):JAN-FEB74-72
A. MOULIN, 556(RLV):1973/3-281
H.R. STERN, 35(AS):FALL-WINTER71-
284
"LANGENSCHEIDTS HANDWÖRTERBUCH SPAN-
ISCH." (PT 1 BY H. MÜLLER & G.
HAENSCH, PT 2 BY E. ALVAREZ PRADA)
J. JOSET, 556(RLV):1973/6-567
H. SCHNEIDER, 430(NS):JUN73-343
"LANGENSCHEIDT'S NEW COLLEGE GERMAN
DICTIONARY." (NEW ED) (H. MESSIN-
GER, ED)
J. EICHHOFF, 406:SPRING74-90
H. LEDERER, 399(MLJ):MAR74-131
LANGER, P.F. COMMUNISM IN JAPAN.
N.B. THAYER, 293(JAST):NOV72-160
LANGER, S.K. MIND. (VOL 2)
J.M.O. WHEATLEY, 529(QQ):WINTER73-
660
LANGER, W.L., ED. THE NEW ILLUSTRAT-
ED ENCYCLOPEDIA OF WORLD HISTORY.
S. SMITH, 441:7DEC75-95
LANGEVIN, A. DUST OVER THE CITY.
R. MOORE, 268:JAN75-85
L. SHOHET, 296:VOL3#4-87
LANGFELDT, G. GÅTEN VIDKUN QUIS-
LING.
J.M. HOBERMAN, 563(SS):SUMMER74-
289
LANGFORD, G. FAULKNER'S REVISION OF
"SANCTUARY."
T. HELLER, 50(ARQ):WINTER73-365
LANGFORD, J.J. GALILEO, SCIENCE &
THE CHURCH. (REV)
A.M. PATERSON, 551(RENQ):SUMMER73-
195
LANGFORD, P. THE EXCISE CRISIS.
J. CARSWELL, 617(TLS):24OCT75-1253
LANGFORD, P. THE FIRST ROCKINGHAM
ADMINISTRATION, 1765-1766.
P.D.G. THOMAS, 656(WMQ):JUL74-498
LANGFORD, W.M. THE MEXICAN NOVEL
COMES OF AGE.
J. SOMMERS, 399(MLJ):JAN-FEB73-73
LANGHOLF, V. DIE GEBETE BEI EURIP-
IDES UND DIE ZEITLICHE FOLGE DER
TRAGÖDIEN.
D. BAIN, 123:MAR74-25
LANGHORNE, E. NANCY ASTOR & HER
FRIENDS.*
639(VQR):AUTUMN74-CXXXIV
LANGLAND, J., T. ACZEL & L. TIKOS,
EDS & TRANS. POETRY FROM THE RUS-
SIAN UNDERGROUND.
R. LATTIMORE, 249(HUDR):AUTUMN74-
473
LANGLAND, W. PIERS PLOWMAN: THE
PROLOGUE & PASSUS I-VII OF THE B
TEXT AS FOUND IN BODLEIAN MS. LAUD
MISC. 581.* (J.A.W. BENNETT, ED)
S.S. HUSSEY, 402(MLR):JAN74-146
H. PHILLIPS, 382(MAE):1974/2-197
S. WENZEL, 589:OCT74-745

LANGLOIS, W.G., ED. THE PERSISTENT
VOICE.
  R.R. BOLGAR, 402(MLR):JUL74-633
LANGO, J.W. WHITEHEAD'S ONTOLOGY.*
  A.H. JOHNSON, 154:DEC73-721
LANGOSCH, K. LITERATUR UND SPRACHE
IM EUROPÄISCHEN MITTELALTER.
  F. LASSERRE, 182:VOL26#20-758
LANGSETH-CHRISTENSEN, L. & C.S.
SMITH. THE COMPLETE KITCHEN GUIDE.
  M.F.K. FISHER, 442(NY):10NOV75-182
LANGSTAFF, J. & C. SHIMMY SHIMMY
COKE-CA-POP!
  M. PETERSON, 470:JAN74-34
LÅNGSTRÖM, T. SVENSKA FORDONSTER-
MER.
  B. KRESS, 682(ZPSK):BAND26HEFT1/2-
  169
"A LANGUAGE-TEACHING BIBLIOGRAPHY."
(2ND ED)
  D.S. BLAIR, 180(ESA):MAR73-48
  C.C. HOFFMEISTER, 399(MLJ):JAN-FEB
  73-47
  N.C.W. SPENCE, 208(FS):OCT74-493
"LE LANGUES DE SPÉCIALITÉ, ANALYSE
LINGUISTIQUE ET RECHERCHE PÉDAGOG-
IQUE, ACTES DU STAGE DE SAINT-
CLOUD 23-30 NOVEMBRE 1967."
  R.J. STEINER, 207(FR):APR73-1093
LANHAM, R.A. STYLE.*
  K. CHERRY, 569(SR):FALL74-LXXIV
  D. HYMES, 113:SPRING74-87
LANHAM, R.A. "TRISTRAM SHANDY."
  L. HARTLEY, 569(SR):FALL74-LXXXVI
  M. LOVERSO, 150(DR):AUTUMN73-589
  J. MC MASTER, 401(MLQ):SEP74-322
  639(VQR):SUMMER74-LXXVI
LANIER, S.E. HIERO'S JOURNEY.
  S. CLARK, 617(TLS):8AUG75-903
LANLY, A., ED. FICHES DE PHILOLOGIE
FRANÇAISE.
  B. FOSTER, 208(FS):OCT74-499
"L'ANNÉE BALZACIENNE 1971."
  B. VANNIER, 400(MLN):MAY73-895
"L'ANNÉE BALZACIENNE 1972."
  B. VANNIER, 400(MLN):MAY73-901
"L'ANNÉE BALZACIENNE 1973."
  B. VANNIER, 400(MLN):MAY73-912
LANNOY, R. THE SPEAKING TREE.
  B. STEIN, 293(JAST):NOV72-171
LANSBURY, C. ELIZABETH GASKELL.
  M. JACOBUS, 617(TLS):14NOV75-1352
LANT, G.G. KRATKIJ SLOVAR' DREVNE-
RUSSKOGO JAZYKA (XI-XVII VEKOV).
  G. HÜTTL-WORTH, 574(SEEJ):FALL72-
  366
LANZINGER, K., ED. AMERICANA-
AUSTRIACA.
  H.O., 430(NS):AUG73-452
LAPASSADE, G. & R. LOURAU. CLEFS
POUR LA SOCIOLOGIE.
  D. MERLLIÉ, 542:JAN-MAR73-53
LAPIE, P-O. DE LÉON BLUM À DE
GAULLE.
  R. WOHL, 207(FR):APR73-1084
LAPIERRE, D. & L. COLLINS. Ô JÉR-
USALEM.
  H.H. WEINBERG, 207(FR):MAR73-859
LAPORTE, G. SUNSHINE AT MIDNIGHT.
(D. COOPER, ED & TRANS)
  L. BERNIKOW, 441:9NOV75-51

LAPP, J.C. THE ESTHETICS OF NEGLI-
GENCE.*
  J.D. BAIRD, 208(FS):OCT74-451
  D. BEYERLE, 72:BAND211HEFT1/3-226
  J-P. COLLINET, 557(RSH):APR-JUN73-
  318
  N. GROSS, 400(MLN):MAY73-862
  O. DE MOURGUES, 402(MLR):JUL74-640
LAQUEUR, W. A HISTORY OF ZIONISM.*
  M.S. CHERTOFF, 287:MAY73-37
LAQUEUR, W. WEIMAR.*
  C. LEHMANN-HAUPT, 441:27JAN75-23
  C.E. SCHORSKE, 441:26JAN75-1
LAQUEUR, W. & G.L. MOSSE, EDS. HIS-
TORIANS IN POLITICS.
  E.H. CARR, 617(TLS):7MAR75-246
LARBAUD, V. LE COEUR DE L'ANGLE-
TERRE, SUIVI DE LUIS LOSADA. (F.
WEISSMAN, ED)
  H. GODIN, 208(FS):APR74-225
LARGE, B. MARTINU.
  D. ARNOLD, 362:3JUL75-29
LARGE, S.S. THE YUAIKAI, 1912-1919.
  KOZO YAMAMURA, 293(JAST):AUG73-704
LARGEAULT, J. ENQUÊTE SUR LE NOMI-
NALISME.
  A. THOMSON, 479(PHQ):OCT73-360
LARKIN, B.D. CHINA & AFRICA 1949-
1970.
  G.T. YU, 293(JAST):AUG73-699
LARKIN, P. HIGH WINDOWS.*
  C. BEDIENT, 441:12JAN75-3
  R. GARFITT, 364:OCT/NOV74-111
  R. MURPHY, 453:15MAY75-30
LARKIN, P., ED. THE OXFORD BOOK OF
TWENTIETH-CENTURY ENGLISH VERSE.*
  D. DAICHES, 541(RES):NOV73-518
  T. EAGLETON, 565:VOL14#3-74
  F. SCARFE, 189(EA):OCT-DEC73-443
  R. SKELTON, 376:JUL73-5
  G. WOODCOCK, 569(SR):WINTER74-119
LARNER, J. CULTURE & SOCIETY IN
ITALY, 1290-1420.*
  W.M. BOWSKY, 551(RENQ):AUTUMN73-
  307
LARNEUIL, M. LE VAUTOUR ET L'EN-
FANT.
  J-A. BOUR, 207(FR):MAY73-1244
LAROCHE, E. CATALOGUE DES TEXTES
HITTITES.
  H. BERMAN, 318(JAOS):JUL-SEP73-401
LAROCQUE, P-A. RUINES.
  R. WILLMOT, 296:VOL3#4-94
LARRAZABAL, J.S. AIR WAR OVER
SPAIN.
  617(TLS):25APR75-465
LARSEN, J.P. HANDEL'S MESSIAH.
(2ND ED)
  M. PETERSON, 470:MAY73-18
LARSON, C. MATTHEW'S HAND.
  N. CALLENDAR, 441:12JAN75-22
LARSON, J.J. REASON & EXPERIENCE.
  P.L. FARBER, 173(ECS):FALL73-105
"L'ART DU LIVRE À L'IMPRIMERIE
NATIONALE."
  N. BARKER, 617(TLS):2MAY75-491
LARTIGUE, J.H. DIARY OF A CENTURY.
(R. AVEDON, ED)
  K.R., 90:MAR73-199
LARY, N.M. DOSTOEVSKY & DICKENS.*
  M. GREENE, 575(SEER):APR74-315
  S. MONOD, 189(EA):OCT-DEC73-484
  R.A. PEACE, 402(MLR):APR74-478
  E. WASIOLEK, 637(VS):MAR74-342

DE LAS CASAS, B. IN DEFENSE OF THE
INDIANS. (S. POOLE, ED & TRANS)
J.H. ELLIOTT, 453:15MAY75-3
LASCELLES, M. NOTIONS & FACTS.
C.J. RAWSON, 175:SUMMER73-75
LASCELLES, M. - SEE JOHNSON, S.
LASH, J.P. - SEE FRANKFURTER, F.
LASIĆ, S. SUKOB NA KNJIŽEVNOJ
LJEVICI 1928-1952.
V. BUBRIN, 104:FALL73-433
LASKI, M. GEORGE ELIOT & HER WORLD.
M. ALLOTT, 402(MLR):APR74-387
LASLETT, J.H.M. & S.M. LIPSET, EDS.
FAILURE OF A DREAM?
K.W. MC NAUGHT, 99:OCT75-34
LASLETT, P. THE WORLD WE HAVE LOST.
C. LASCH, 453:13NOV75-33
LASLETT, P., W.G. RUNCIMAN & Q.
SKINNER, EDS. PHILOSOPHY, POLITICS
& SOCIETY. (4TH SER)
A.W. SPARKES, 63:MAY74-80
LASLETT, P. & R. WALL, EDS. HOUSE-
HOLD & FAMILY IN PAST TIME.
T. KNORR, 182:VOL26#3/4-88
C. LASCH, 453:13NOV75-33
LASOCKI, A-M. SIMONE DE BEAUVOIR
OU L'ENTREPRISE DE VIVRE.
A. FABRE-LUCE, 535(RHL):NOV-DEC73-
1117
LASS, R. APPROACHES TO ENGLISH
HISTORICAL LINGUISTICS.
E.P. HAMP, 269(IJAL):JUL73-200
LASSERRE, F. - SEE STRABO
"LAST MINUTE SKETCHES."
D.M. DAY, 157:SPRING73-84
LÁSZLÓ, F. DIE PARALLELVERSION DER
MANUSMRTI IM BHAVIṢYAPURĀṆA.
L. STERNBACH, 318(JAOS):OCT-DEC73-
607
LÁSZLÓ, G. THE ART OF THE MIGRATION
PERIOD.
D.M. WILSON, 617(TLS):18APR75-434
DE LA TAILLE, J. JEAN DE LA TAILLE,
DRAMATIC WORKS.* (K.M. HALL & C.N.
SMITH, EDS)
H.H. KALWIES, 207(FR):APR73-1008
I.D. MC FARLANE, 208(FS):APR74-192
R. PASCH, 72:BAND211HEFT1/3-222
205(FMLS):APR73-213
LATHAM, A. CRAZY SUNDAYS.*
J.W. TUTTLETON, 295:FEB74-602
LATHAM, L. IDENTITY CRISIS.
N. CALLENDAR, 441:12OCT75-47
LATHAM, R.E., ED. DICTIONARY OF
MEDIEVAL LATIN FROM BRITISH SOURCES.
(FASC 1)
617(TLS):20JUN75-690
LATHEM, E.C. & L. THOMPSON - SEE
FROST, R.
LATHEN, E. BY HOOK OR BY CROOK.
N. CALLENDAR, 441:22JUN75-16
P.D. JAMES, 617(TLS):26DEC75-1544
M. LASKI, 362:20NOV75-684
LATHEN, E. MURDER AGAINST THE
GRAIN.
N. CALLENDAR, 441:25MAY75-16
MADAME DE LA TOUR DU PIN. MEMOIRS
OF MADAME DE LA TOUR DU PIN. (F.
HARCOURT, ED & TRANS)
M. O'NEILL-KARCH, 207(FR):OCT72-
175

LATTANZI, A.D. & M. DEBAE, COMPS.
LA MINIATURE ITALIENNE DU XE AU
XVIE SIÈCLE.
J. BACKHOUSE, 90:MAR73-167
LAU, D.C. - SEE "MENCIUS"
LAUB, F. ESCHATOLOGISCHE VERKÜNDI-
GUNG UND LEBENSGESTALTUNG NACH
PAULUS.
F.F. BRUCE, 182:VOL26#10-332
LAUER, Q. HEGEL'S IDEA OF PHILOSO-
PHY.*
V. GOUREVITCH, 258:MAR73-150
A. QUINTON, 453:29MAY75-34
LAUF, D.I. DAS ERBE TIBETS.
S. KRAMRISCH, 57:VOL35#4-377
LAUFER, R. LESAGE OU LE MÉTIER DE
ROMANCIER.*
H. COULET, 535(RHL):JUL-AUG73-696
P. STEWART, 188(ECR):SUMMER73-175
LAUFER, R. - SEE LESAGE, A-R.
LAUFHÜTTE, H. WIRKLICHKEIT UND
KUNST IN GOTTFRIED KELLERS ROMAN
"DER GRÜNE HEINRICH."*
D.F. MERRIFIELD, 221(GQ):JAN73-124
LAUGAA, M., ED. LECTURES DE MADAME
DE LAFAYETTE.
P.H. NURSE, 208(FS):OCT74-450
S. TIEFENBRUN, 207(FR):OCT72-151
LAUGHTON, B. PHILIP WILSON STEER.*
W. BARON, 90:JAN73-49
LAUGHLIN, C.D., JR. & E.G. D'AQUILI.
BIOGENETIC STRUCTURALISM.
C.H. WADDINGTON, 453:7AUG75-30
LAUGIER, J-L. TACITE.
J-C. DUMONT, 555:VOL47FASC1-167
LAUMER, K. FAT CHANCE.
N. CALLENDAR, 441:30MAR75-24
LAUMONIER, P. - SEE LONG, M.
LAUNAY, M. JEAN-JACQUES ROUSSEAU
ÉCRIVAIN POLITIQUE (1712-1762).
G. MANFREDI, 548(RCSF):OCT-DEC73-
468
R. MERCIER, 557(RSH):JUL-SEP73-495
J.S. SPINK, 208(FS):OCT74-465
LAUNAY, M. - SEE ROUSSEAU, J-J.
LAURENCE, D.H. - SEE SHAW, G.B.
LAURENCE, M. THE DIVINERS.*
L. BURTON & D. MORLEY, 99:SEP75-57
P. GOTLIEB, 606(TAMR):OCT74-80
M. JOHNSON, 617(TLS):10JAN75-29
B. MICKLEBURGH, 198:WINTER75-111
A. THOMAS, 102(CANL):AUTUMN74-89
LAURENCE, M. THE FIRE-DWELLERS.
L. BURTON & D. MORLEY, 99:SEP75-57
LAURENSON, D.T. & A. SWINGEWOOD.
THE SOCIOLOGY OF LITERATURE.*
T. EAGLETON, 541(RES):NOV73-529
LAURENT, V. LE CORPUS DES SCEAUX DE
L'EMPIRE BYZANTIN. (VOL 3)
N. OIKONOMIDÈS, 589:OCT74-746
LAURENT, V. LES "MÉMOIRES" DU GRAND
ECCLÉSIARQUE DE L'EGLISE DE CON-
STANTINOPLE SYLVESTRE SYROPOULOS
SUR LE CONCILE DE FLORENCE (1438-
39).
O. KRESTEN, 182:VOL26#1/2-53
LAURENTI, J.L. BIBLIOGRAFÍA DE LA
LITERATURA PICARESCA.
H.C. WOODBRIDGE, 399(MLJ):MAR74-
136
LAURENTIN, R. LIBERATION, DEVELOP-
MENT, & SALVATION.
E.W. RANLY, 613:WINTER73-543

213

LAURIE, H.C.R. TWO STUDIES IN
CHRÉTIEN DE TROYES.
  A.H. DIVERRES, 205(FMLS):JUL73-298
  E. KENNEDY, 208(FS):OCT74-437
  M. MARCY, 405(MP):MAY74-407
  P. NYKROG, 589:APR74-353
LAURY, J.R. & R. LAW. HANDMADE TOYS
& GAMES.
  B. GUTCHEON, 441:7DEC75-74
LAUSBERG, H. ROMANISCHE SPRACHWIS-
SENSCHAFT. (VOL 1, 3RD ED; VOLS
2&3, 2ND ED)
  H-E. KELLER, 260(IF):BAND78-278
LAUSBERG, H. DAS SONETT "LES GREN-
ADES" VON PAUL VALÉRY.
  J. SCHMIDT-RADEFELDT, 72:BAND211
  HEFT3/6-472
COMTE DE LAUTRÉAMONT & G. NOUVEAU.
OEUVRES COMPLÈTES. (P-O. WALZER,
ED)
  L. FORESTIER, 535(RHL):JUL-AUG73-
  718
LAUWERYS, J. & G. TAYLOR, EDS. EDU-
CATION AT HOME & ABROAD.
  617(TLS):21FEB75-204
LAVER, J. VICTORIANA.
  R. REIF, 441:29DEC75-29
LAVERACK, M.S. & H. BLACKLER, EDS.
FAUNA & FLORA OF ST. ANDREWS BAY.
  617(TLS):10JAN75-41
LAVERS, A. - SEE BARTHES, R.
LAVERY, P., ED. RECREATIONAL
GEOGRAPHY.
  T.P. BAYLISS-SMITH, 617(TLS):25APR
  75-461
LAVIN, M. COLLECTED STORIES.
  R.V. ZUCKERMAN, 573(SSF):WINTER73-
  105
LAVIN, M. A MEMORY & OTHER STORIES.
  569(SR):WINTER74-XIII
LAVIN, M.A. PIERO DELLA FRANCESCA:
THE FLAGELLATION.*
  B. COLE, 90:NOV73-749
  C. GOULD, 39:JUL73-70
  J.B. MYERS, 139:JUN73-8
LAVIS, G. "LES CHANSONS" DE BLONDEL
DE NESLE.
  A. FOULET, 545(RPH):AUG73-135
  R.M. PENSOM, 208(FS):JUL74-308
LAVOTHA, Ö. STUDIEN ZU DEM UNGAR-
ISCHEN POTENTIALSUFFIX "HAT/HET."
  T. KESZTYÜS, 343:BAND16HEFT1-114
LAVRIN, J. A PANORAMA OF RUSSIAN
LITERATURE.
  A.K. LOJKINE, 67:MAY74-138
  A.B. MC MILLIN, 575(SEER):APR74-
  275
  D.J. RICHARDS, 402(MLR):JUL74-712
LAW, S. & OTHERS. BLUE CROSS.*
  J. RIDGEWAY, 31(ASCH):WINTER74/75-
  160
LAWLER, J.R. THE LANGUAGE OF FRENCH
SYMBOLISM.
  W.V. GUGLI, 599:SPRING73-214
LAWLER, J.R. THE POET AS ANALYST.
  J.M. COCKING, 617(TLS):18JUL75-809
LAWNER, L. - SEE GRAMSCI, A.
LAWRENCE, A.W. GREEK & ROMAN SCULP-
TURE.
  R. HIGGINS, 39:AUG73-150
  R. HOPE-SIMPSON, 255(HAB):SPRING73-
  120

LAWRENCE, B. COLERIDGE & WORDS-
WORTH IN SOMERSET.
  M.F. SCHULZ, 173(ECS):SPRING74-378
LAWRENCE, D.H. THE COMPLETE POEMS
OF D.H. LAWRENCE. (V. DE SOLA
PINTO & F.W. ROBERT, EDS)
  E. DELAVENAY, 189(EA):JUL-SEP73-
  320
LAWRENCE, D.H. THE QUEST FOR RANA-
NIM.* (G.J. ZYTARUK, ED)
  P.S. MACAULAY, 179(ES):OCT72-473
LAWRENCE, D.H. JOHN THOMAS & LADY
JANE.*
  E.J. HINZ, 529(QQ):SPRING73-137
  K. WIDMER, 594:WINTER73-547
LAWRENCE, D.H. MOVEMENTS IN EURO-
PEAN HISTORY. (2ND ED)
  E. DELAVENAY, 189(EA):JUL-SEP73-
  323
LAWRENCE, H. YORKSHIRE POTS & POT-
TERIES.
  617(TLS):7FEB75-144
LAWRENCE, J. UNDER ONE ROOF.
  M. LEVIN, 441:12OCT75-49
LAWRENCE, M.S. WRITING AS A THINK-
ING PROCESS.
  K.O. ASTON, 399(MLJ):SEP-OCT74-302
LAWRENCE, R. MOTIVE & INTENTION.
  J.A. FULTON, 258:DEC73-575
  R.A. GORMAN, 484(PPR):DEC73-289
LAWRENCE, V.B. MUSIC FOR PATRIOTS
POLITICIANS & PRESIDENTS.
  G. WARD & R. STROZIER, 441:7DEC75-
  94
LAWRENSON, H. STRANGER AT THE
PARTY.
  A. BROYARD, 441:10APR75-43
  J. O'REILLY, 441:20APR75-14
LAWRY, J.S. SIDNEY'S TWO "ARCAD-
IAS."*
  A.C. HAMILTON, 529(QQ):SPRING73-
  132
  R.A. LANHAM, 191(ELN):MAR74-215
  N. LINDHEIM, 255(HAB):SUMMER73-225
  R.W.Z., 179(ES):FEB73-98
LAWS, G.M., JR. THE BRITISH LITER-
ARY BALLAD.
  A.B. FRIEDMAN, 191(ELN):JUN74-319
LAWSON, A. PATRICK WHITE.
  L. CANTRELL, 71(ALS):MAY75-101
  H.W. RHODES, 67:NOV74-233
LAWSON, J. LECTURES CONCERNING ORA-
TORY BY JOHN LAWSON. (E.N. CLAUS-
SEN & K.R. WALLACE, EDS)
  V.M. BEVILACQUA, 124:FEB74-247
LAWSON, R.M. THE CHANGING ECONOMY
OF THE LOWER VOLTA.
  R.W. WYLLIE, 69:JAN73-88
LAWTON, D. CLASS, CULTURE & THE
CURRICULUM.
  617(TLS):17OCT75-1245
LAWTON, H.W. TÉRENCE EN FRANCE AU
XVIe SIÈCLE.
  C.N. SMITH, 208(FS):JUL74-315
LAX, E. ON BEING FUNNY.
  R.R. LINGEMAN, 441:9JUL75-41
  M. RICHLER, 441:1JUN75-4
LAXALT, R. IN A HUNDRED GRAVES.
  H.J. NUWER, 649(WAL):SPRING&SUMMER
  73-83
LAXER, R.M., ED. (CANADA) LTD.*
  C.L. BROWN-JOHN, 628:SPRING74-93

LAYTON, I. ENGAGEMENTS. (S. MAYNE, ED)
  J. CHRISTY, 102(CANL):SPRING74-126
  B. KURTH, 376:APR73-229
  K. MC SWEENEY, 529(QQ):SUMMER73-325
LAYTON, I. LOVERS & LESSER MEN.
  K. MC SWEENEY, 529(QQ):SUMMER73-325
  C.X. RINGROSE, 150(DR):SPRING73-160
  P. STEVENS, 628:SPRING74-102
LAYTON, I. THE POLE-VAULTER.*
  L. SANDLER, 606(TAMR):NOV74-89
  F.W. WATT, 99:JUN75-40
LAZAR, M., ED & TRANS. LE JUGEMENT DERNIER (LO JUTGAMEN GENERAL).
  F.M. CHAMBERS, 545(RPH):FEB74-422
  L.T. TOPSFIELD, 208(FS):JUL74-313
LAZARSFELD, P. QU'EST-CE QUE LA SOCIOLOGIE?
  D. MERLLIÉ, 542:JAN-MAR73-53
LAZARUS, A.L. & OTHERS. A SUIT OF FOUR.
  M. MARCUS, 502(PRS):FALL73-273
LAZERSON, M. ORIGINS OF THE URBAN SCHOOL.
  H.P. SEGAL, 432(NEQ):MAR73-150
LAZITCH, B. & M.M. DRACHKOVITCH. LENIN & THE COMINTERN.* (VOL 1)
  S. HOOK, 550(RUSR):JAN73-1
  G. STERN, 575(SEER):JUL74-476
LEA, K. THE POETIC POWERS OF REPETITION.
  F. MC COMBIE, 447(N&Q):MAR73-119
LEAB, D.J. FROM SAMBO TO SUPERSPADE.
  A.H., 441:9NOV75-44
LEACH, C. THE PHEASANT SHOOT.
  M. JOHNSON, 617(TLS):20JUN75-704
  J. MELLORS, 362:19JUN75-821
LEACH, D.E. ARMS FOR EMPIRE.
  W.J. ECCLES, 656(WMQ):JUL74-501
  I.D. GRUBER, 432(NEQ):MAR74-148
LEACH, J. BRIGHT PARTICULAR STAR.*
  H. KOSOK, 447(N&Q):MAR73-107
LEACOCK, S. THE SOCIAL CRITICISM OF STEPHEN LEACOCK. (A. BOWKER, ED)
  C. BALLSTADT, 102(CANL):AUTUMN74-105
LEACROFT, R. THE DEVELOPMENT OF THE ENGLISH PLAYHOUSE.
  J.C. TREWIN, 157:AUTUMN73-71
LEAKE, J.A. THE GEATS OF "BEOWULF."
  G. BOURQUIN, 189(EA):APR-JUN73-221
LEAKEY, F.W. BAUDELAIRE & NATURE.*
  C. SCOTT, 447(N&Q):MAR73-108
LEAKEY, L.S.B. BY THE EVIDENCE.*
  K. KYLE, 362:7AUG75-188
  D. ROE, 617(TLS):21NOV75-1396
  J. UPDIKE, 442(NY):24MAR75-110
  J.Z. YOUNG, 453:29MAY75-18
LEAL, L. BREVE HISTORIA DE LA LITERATURA HISPANOAMERICANA.*
  L. PEARSON, 399(MLJ):JAN-FEB74-77
LEAL, L., ED. CUENTISTAS HISPANO-AMERICANOS DEL SIGLO VEINTE.
  J.R. AYORA, 399(MLJ):MAR74-134
LEAL, L. MÉXICO. (REV)
  C.F. WHITMER, 238:MAR73-190
LEAR, E. LEAR IN THE ORIGINAL.
  V. GLENDINNING, 617(TLS):14NOV75-1353
  442(NY):24NOV75-196

LEAR, W. DOWN THE RABBIT HOLE.
  S. SECKER, 617(TLS):16MAY75-544
"THE LEARNING SOCIETY."
  E.F. SHEFFIELD, 529(QQ):AUTUMN73-434
LEARY, L. - SEE TUCKER, N.
LEARY, L. - SEE TWAIN, M.
LEASE, B. THAT WILD FELLOW JOHN NEAL & THE AMERICAN LITERARY REVOLUTION.*
  D.J. MAC MILLAN, 255(HAB):SUMMER73-237
  C.C. NICKELS, 432(NEQ):JUN73-315
  G.B. TENNYSON, 445(NCF):SEP73-245
LEASKA, M.A. VIRGINIA WOOLF'S "LIGHTHOUSE."*
  J. GUIGUET, 189(EA):JUL-SEP73-338
LEASOR, J. GREEN BEACH.
  B. COLLIER, 441:17AUG75-12
  D. THOMAS, 362:13MAR75-349
LEASURE, R. BLACK MOUNTAIN.
  M. LEVIN, 441:120CT75-49
LEAVIS, F.R. LETTERS IN CRITICISM.* (J. TASKER, ED)
  R. FULLER, 364:AUG/SEP74-127
LEAVIS, F.R. THE LIVING PRINCIPLE.
  P.N. FURBANK, 362:30OCT75-577
  R. SCRUTON, 617(TLS):17OCT75-1231
  R. TOWERS, 441:21DEC75-15
LEAVIS, F.R. & Q.D. DICKENS THE NOVELIST.*
  L. LANE, JR., 594:SPRING73-125
LEBECK, A. THE "ORESTEIA."*
  M. MC CALL, 24:FALL74-288
  J. PERADOTTO, 124:NOV72-167
  M.J. SMETHURST, 122:APR74-162
  E.W. WHITTLE, 123:MAR74-16
LEBEN, B.C. ERNEST RENAN ET SA SOEUR HENRIETTE.
  K. GORE, 208(FS):APR74-222
LEBLANC, H. & W.A. WISDOM. DEDUCTIVE LOGIC.
  Y. GAUTHIER, 154:DEC73-743
LEBOIS, A. FABULEUX NERVAL.
  W. BEAUCHAMP, 546(RR):MAY73-218
LE BONNIEC, H. - SEE OVID
LE BONNIEC, H. - SEE PLINY
LEBOWITZ, N. HUMANISM & THE ABSURD IN THE MODERN NOVEL.
  G.B. TENNYSON, 445(NCF):JUN73-113
LEBOYER, F. BIRTH WITHOUT VIOLENCE.
  A. RICH, 453:20CT75-25
  J. WILSON, 441:22JUN75-7
LEBRA, J.C. JUNGLE ALLIANCE.
  G.K. GOODMAN, 293(JAST):MAY73-542
  MARUYAMA SHIZUO, 285(JAPQ):JAN-MAR73-110
LEBRETON-SAVIGNY, M. VICTOR HUGO ET LES AMÉRICAINS, 1825-1885.
  J-A. BÉDÉ, 207(FR):FEB73-616
LE BRUN, J. BOSSUET.*
  H.F. BROOKS, 207(FR):OCT72-154
  T. GOYET, 535(RHL):JUL-AUG73-688
LE BRUN, J. LES OPUSCULES SPIRITUELS DE BOSSUET.
  H.F. BROOKS, 207(FR):OCT72-154
LEBRUN, Y. CAN & MAY IN PRESENT-DAY ENGLISH.
  R.D. EAGLESON, 353:15APR73-101
LECALDANO, E. LE ANALISI DEL LINGUAGGIO MORALE.
  E. NAMER, 542:APR-JUN73-223

215

LECHLER, H.J. & F. UNGERER, EDS.
MODERN LIFE. (AUSGABE A4/B3)
T.L. WULLEN, 430(NS):MAY73-285
LECHLITNER, R. A CHANGING SEASON.
H. TAYLOR, 385(MQR):WINTER75-92
H. ZINNES, 109:SPRING/SUMMER74-122
LECHNER, J. EL COMPROMISO EN LA
POESÍA ESPAÑOLA DEL SIGLO XX.
(PT 1)
P. ILIE, 240(HR):WINTER73-79
LECKE, B., ED. FRIEDRICH SCHILLER.
K.L. BERGHAHN, 406:WINTER74-401
LECLAIRE, J. FRANCIS BRETT YOUNG.
C.P. SNOW, 189(EA):JAN-MAR73-110
LECLANT, J. INVENTAIRE BIBLIOGRA-
PHIQUE DES ISIACA.
R.E. WITT, 313:VOL63-272
LECLERC, F. ALLEGRO.
L. SHOHET, 296:VOL3#4-87
LECLERC, I. THE NATURE OF PHYSICAL
EXISTENCE.*
P. DUBOIS, 542:JUL-SEP73-363
A.H. JOHNSON, 154:DEC73-714
J.D. NORTH, 479(PHQ):OCT73-362
B. WILSHIRE, 258:SEP73-435
LECLERC, I., ED. THE PHILOSOPHY OF
LEIBNIZ & THE MODERN WORLD.*
J. HOSTLER, 483:OCT73-406
LE CLÉZIO, J.M.G. THE GIANTS.
J. STURROCK, 441:23NOV75-18
LE CLÉZIO, J.M.G. HAÏ.
M. CAGNON, 207(FR):FEB73-661
LECOMBER, B. TURN KILLER.
N. CALLENDAR, 441:14SEP75-39
LECONTE DE LISLE, C.M. ARTICLES,
PRÉFACES, DISCOURS.* (E. PICH, ED)
R. JOUANNY, 535(RHL):JAN-FEB73-151
LECOURT, D. BACHELARD OU LE JOUR
ET LA NUIT.
J. CULLER, 617(TLS):28FEB75-230
LECOURT, D. POUR UNE CRITIQUE DE
L'ÉPISTÉMOLOGIE.
R. BLANCHÉ, 542:JUL-SEP73-365
LECOURT, D. - SEE BACHELARD, G.
LEDDERHOSE, L. DIE SIEGELSCHRIFT
(CHUAN-SHU) IN DER CH'ING-ZEIT.*
T. LAWTON, 318(JAOS):APR-JUN73-207
LEDEEN, M.A. - SEE DE FELICE, R.
LEDERER, H. REFERENCE GRAMMAR OF
THE GERMAN LANGUAGE.
G.F. CARR, 353:15JUL73-92
LEDÉSERT, R.P.L. & M. - SEE MANSION,
J.E.
LEDKOVSKY, M. THE OTHER TURGENEV.
R. FREEBORN, 575(SEER):JUL74-459
J.B. WOODWARD, 574(SEEJ):WINTER73-
456
LEDUC, V. MAD IN PURSUIT.
295:FEB74-372
LEE, A. TIME.
H. VENDLER, 441:7SEP75-6
LEE, A.A. THE GUEST-HALL OF EDEN.*
N.E. ELIASON, 405(MP):NOV73-187
P.O.E. GRADON, 447(N&Q):JAN73-26
M. LARÈS, 189(EA):JAN-MAR73-86
B. MITCHELL, 541(RES):MAY73-195
E.S. SKLAR, 141:FALL73-371
L. WHITBREAD, 179(ES):AUG73-381
R.M. WILSON, 175:AUTUMN72-106
LEE, B. LOVE & WHISKEY.
T. HENDRY, 99:MAR75-32
A. MOTYER, 150(DR):AUTUMN73-579

LEE, D. CIVIL ELEGIES & OTHER
POEMS.
A. SCHROEDER, 102(CANL):WINTER73-
102
LEE, L. I CAN'T STAY LONG.
R. BLYTHE, 362:20NOV75-680
LEE, O.H. - SEE UNDER OEY HONG LEE
LEE, P.H., ED & TRANS. LIVES OF
EMINENT KOREAN MONKS.
K.H.J. GARDINER, 302:JAN73-174
LEE, S.E. ANCIENT CAMBODIAN SCULP-
TURE.
G. TARR, 293(JAST):AUG73-753
LEE, V. QUEST FOR A PUBLIC.
A. DEMAITRE, 207(FR):DEC72-428
M. GUGGENHEIM, 160:SPRING73-191
LEECH, C. THE DRAMATIST'S EXPERI-
ENCE.*
F. LAGARDE, 189(EA):APR-JUN73-244
LEECH, C. - SEE SHAKESPEARE, W.
LEECH, C. & J.M.R. MARGESON, EDS.
SHAKESPEARE 1971.*
W. BLISSETT, 627(UTQ):WINTER74-191
D. CRAWLEY, 529(QQ):WINTER73-639
R. SCHULER, 376:APR73-231
A.R. YOUNG, 150(DR):SPRING73-195
LEECH, G.N. A LINGUISTIC GUIDE TO
ENGLISH POETRY.*
R. FOWLER, 492:#9-116
LEECH, G.N. TOWARDS A SEMANTIC DES-
CRIPTION OF ENGLISH.*
F.G.A.M. AARTS, 179(ES):AUG73-347
LEEMING, G. & S. TRUSSLER. THE
PLAYS OF ARNOLD WESKER.
R. AHRENS, 72:BAND211HEFT1/3-166
LEES-MILNE, J. ANCESTRAL VOICES.
A. FORBES, 617(TLS):10OCT75-1190
A. QUINTON, 362:4DEC75-749
"LEF, I & II." "NOVYJ LEF, I & II."
E.F. COHEN, 574(SEEJ):FALL72-349
LE FANU, J.S. GHOST STORIES & MYS-
TERIES. (E.F. BLEILER, ED) BEST
GHOST STORIES OF J.S. LE FANU.
(E.F. BLEILER, ED) UNCLE SILAS.
J. SULLIVAN, 441:21SEP75-40
LEFÈVRE, E. DIE EXPOSITIONSTECHNIK
IN DEN KOMÖDIEN DES TERENZ.
P.G.M. BROWN, 313:VOL63-301
LEFKOWITZ, M. - SEE SHIRLEY, J. &
OTHERS
LEFLER, H.T. & W.S. POWELL. COLON-
IAL NORTH CAROLINA.
J.J. NADELHAFT, 656(WMQ):JUL74-507
639(VQR):SPRING74-XLIV
LEFORT, C. LE TRAVAIL DE L'OEUVRE
MACHIAVEL.
P. HOCHART, 98:JUL73-600
LEFORT, C. - SEE MERLEAU-PONTY, M.
LE GALL, B. - SEE DE SENANCOUR, E.P.
LEGEZA, I.L. A DESCRIPTIVE & ILLUS-
TRATED CATALOGUE OF THE MALCOLM
MAC DONALD CHINESE CERAMICS IN THE
GULBENKIAN MUSEUM OF ART & ARCHAE-
OLOGY, SCHOOL OF ORIENTAL STUDIES,
UNIVERSITY OF DURHAM.*
M. MEDLEY, 463:SPRING73-86
LEGGE, D. AN INTRODUCTION TO PSY-
CHOLOGICAL SCIENCE.
I. HUNTER, 617(TLS):6JUN75-629
LEGGE, J.D. SUKARNO.
S. SLOAN, 293(JAST):AUG73-749
LEGGET, R.F. RAILROADS OF CANADA.
P.B. WAITE, 150(DR):WINTER73/74-
764

LEGGETT, B.J. HOUSMAN'S LAND OF
LOST CONTENT.*
J.W. STEVENSON, 295:FEB74-645
LE GOFF, J. & P. NORA, EDS. FAIRE
DE L'HISTOIRE.
E. KEDOURIE, 617(TLS):7MAR75-238
LEGOUIS, P. ASPECTS DU XVIIE
SIÈCLE.*
K. MUIR, 402(MLR):JUL74-622
E. SHOWALTER, JR., 131(CL):SUMMER
74-268
LEGOUIS, P., WITH E.E. DUNCAN-JONES
- SEE MARVELL, A.
LE GUERN, M. SÉMANTIQUE DE LA MÉTA-
PHORE ET DE LA MÉTONYMIE.
K. WINN, 430(NS):JUL73-402
LE GUILLOU, L. - SEE DE LAMENNAIS,
F.R.
LE GUIN, U. THE DISPOSSESSED.
J. HAMILTON-PATERSON, 617(TLS):
20JUN75-704
G. JONAS, 441:26OCT75-48
M. WOOD, 453:20OCT75-3
LE GUIN, U. ROCANNON'S WORLD. PLAN-
ET OF EXILE. CITY OF ILLUSIONS.
THE LEFT HAND OF DARKNESS. THE
LATHE OF HEAVEN. A WIZARD OF
EARTHSEA. THE TOMBS OF ATUAN. THE
FARTHEST SHORE.
FANTASTES, 111:23NOV73-43
LE GUIN, U. THE WIND'S TWELVE QUAR-
TERS.
P-L. ADAMS, 61:DEC75-118
LEHISTE, I. CONSONANT QUANTITY &
PHONOLOGICAL UNITS IN ESTONIAN.
G.F. MEIER, 682(ZPSK):BAND26HEFT
3/4-434
LEHISTE, I. SUPRASEGMENTALS.*
K. WODARZ-MAGDICS, 353:1NOV73-126
LEHMANN, E. NORSK-ISLENDSK SAMTALE-
BOK/NORSK-ÍSLENZK SAMTALSORĐABÓK.
S.R. SMITH, 563(SS):SPRING74-190
LEHMANN, G., ED. COMIC AUSTRALIAN
VERSE.
G.A.W., 581:MAR74-101
LEHMANN, J. VIRGINIA WOOLF & HER
WORLD.
M. DRABBLE, 362:18SEP75-382
LEHMANN, P. THE TRANSFIGURATION OF
POLITICS.
P. HEBBLETHWAITE, 617(TLS):5SEP75-
1006
LEHMANN, P.L. MEDITATIONEN UM
STEFAN GEORGE.
I. JONES, 172(EDDA):1973/2-125
LEHMANN, W.C. HENRY HOME, LORD
KAMES, & THE SCOTTISH ENLIGHTEN-
MENT.*
G. CARABELLI, 548(RCSF):APR-JUN73-
222
LEHMANN, W.P. DESCRIPTIVE LINGUIS-
TICS.
R. FINK, 320(CJL):SPRING74-89
E.A. HOPKINS, 399(MLJ):JAN-FEB74-
60
LEHMANN, W.P. PROTO-INDO-EUROPEAN
SYNTAX.
R.G.G. COLEMAN, 617(TLS):29AUG75-
975
LEHMANN, W.P., T.J. O'HARE & C.
COBET. GERMAN.
B.J. SNYDER, 399(MLJ):APR73-225

LEHMANN-HAUPT, H., ED. THE GÖTTIN-
GEN MODEL BOOK.
H. BOBER, 589:APR74-354
LEHNERT, M. RÜCKLAUFIGES WÖRTERBUCH
DER ENGLISCHEN GEGENWARTSSPRACHE.
R. DEROLEZ, 179(ES):APR72-150
LEHNING, A., ED. MICHEL BAKOUNINE
ET SES RELATIONS AVEC SERGEJ NEČ-
AEV, 1870-1872.
S. LUKASHEVICH, 574(SEEJ):FALL72-
344
LEHRER, A. & K., EDS. THEORY OF
MEANING.
G.F. MEIER, 682(ZPSK):BAND26HEFT
1/2-201
S.J. NOREN, 484(PPR):JUN74-604
LEHTONEN, J. ASPECTS OF QUANTITY IN
STANDARD FINNISH.
G.F. MEIER, 682(ZPSK):BAND26HEFT
3/4-435
LEIBFRIED, E. KRITISCHE WISSEN-
SCHAFT VOM TEXT.*
K-H. GÖTTERT, 680(ZDP):BAND92HEFT
2-268
LEIBNIZ, G.W. SÄMTLICHE SCHRIFTEN
UND BRIEFE. (PT 1, VOL 8) (G.
SCHEEL, K. MÜLLER & G. GERBER, EDS)
H. DUCHHARDT, 182:VOL26#20-706
LEIBOWITZ, R. SCHOENBERG ET SON
ÉCOLE. QU'EST-CE QUE LA MUSIQUE
DE DOUZE SONS? INTRODUCTION À LA
MUSIQUE DE DOUZE SONS. L'ARTISTE
ET SA CONSCIENCE. L'EVOLUTION DE
LA MUSIQUE DE BACH À SCHOENBERG.
HISTOIRE DE L'OPÉRA. SCHOENBERG.
LE COMPOSITEUR ET SON DOUBLE. LES
FANTÔMES DE L'OPÉRA.
M-P. PHILIPPOT, 98:OCT73-934
LEIBRICH, L. THOMAS MANN.
T-J.R., 617(TLS):10OCT75-1207
LEICHTY, E. THE OMEN SERIES ŠUMMA
IZBU.
W. HEIMPEL, 318(JAOS):OCT-DEC73-
585
LEIDERER, R., ED. ZWÖLF MINNEREDEN
DES CGM 270.
P. GRUNDLEHNER, 406:FALL74-297
A. MASSER, 182:VOL26#20-736
B. NAUMANN, 220(GL&L):APR74-258
LEIGH, J. NO MAN'S LAND.
P. CAMPBELL, 617(TLS):1AUG75-865
N. HEPBURN, 362:21AUG75-254
LEIGH, R.A. - SEE ROUSSEAU, J-J.
LEIGHTON, A.C. TRANSPORT & COMMUNI-
CATION IN EARLY MEDIEVAL EUROPE,
A.D. 500-1100.
L. WHITE, JR., 589:JUL74-577
LEINER, J. LE DESTIN LITTÉRAIRE DE
PAUL NIZAN ET SES ÉTAPES SUCCES-
SIVES.*
J-A. BÉDÉ, 546(RR):MAY73-240
M. REBÉRIOUX, 535(RHL):SEP-OCT73-
927
J. STEEL, 402(MLR):JAN74-187
LEISHMAN, J.B. MILTON'S MINOR
POEMS. (G. TILLOTSON, ED)
D.A. ROBERTS, 551(RENQ):SPRING73-
89
LEITCH, M. STAMPING GROUND.
R. FOSTER, 617(TLS):4JUL75-714
N. HEPBURN, 362:3JUL75-30
LEITNER, B. THE ARCHITECTURE OF
LUDWIG WITTGENSTEIN.
M. PROUDFOOT, 111:3MAY74-137

LEJEUNE, M. MÉMOIRES DE PHILOLOGIE
MYCÉNIENNE. (2ND SER)
  P. CHANTRAINE, 555:VOL47FASC1-120
  A. HEUBECK, 343:BAND16HEFT2-168
LEJEUNE, M. PHONÉTIQUE HISTORIQUE
DU MYCÉNIEN ET DU GREC ANCIEN.
  A. HEUBECK, 343:BAND17HEFT2-157
  B. NEWTON, 350:DEC74-738
LEJEUNE, P. L'AUTOBIOGRAPHIE EN
FRANCE.
  F.P. BOWMAN, 207(FR):APR73-1034
LEJEUNE, R. & J. STIENNON. THE
LEGEND OF ROLAND IN THE MIDDLE AGES.
  J. FOLDA, 54:DEC73-621
LELCHUK, A. MIRIAM AT THIRTY-FOUR.*
  J. BARNES, 617(TLS):20JUN75-704
LEM, S. CYBÉRIADA.
  J.M. PURCELL, 573(SSF):SUMMER73-
  298
LEM, S. THE FUTUROLOGICAL CONGRESS.
THE CYBERIAD.
  E. KORN, 617(TLS):5DEC75-1439
LEM, S. MEMOIRS FOUND IN A BATH-
TUB.* THE INVINCIBLE.
  R.K. WILSON, 574(SEEJ):FALL73-351
LEMAITRE, G. JEAN GIRAUDOUX.
  P. NEWMAN-GORDON, 399(MLJ):JAN-FEB
  74-66
LEMARCHAND, E. DEATH ON DOOMSDAY.
  N. CALLENDAR, 441:23MAR75-35
LEMARIÉ, J. - SEE CHROMATIUS
LE MASTERS, E.E. BLUE COLLAR ARIS-
TOCRATS.
  M.P. DUMONT, 441:18MAY75-5
LEMAY, J.A.L. MEN OF LETTERS IN
COLONIAL MARYLAND.*
  M.J. COLACURCIO, 481(PQ):JUL73-439
  R.B. DAVIS, 579(SAQ):SPRING74-278
  P.L. MARAMBAUD, 165:WINTER75-340
  H. PARKER, 173(ECS):FALL73-110
LEMBACH, K. DIE PFLANZEN BEI THEO-
KRIT.
  G. GIANGRANDE, 123:MAR74-32
LEMERLE, P. LE PREMIER HUMANISME
BYZANTIN.*
  A. MOFFATT, 303:VOL93-271
LEMERLE, P., A. GUILLOU & N. SVOR-
ONOS, EDS. ACTES DE LAVRA.* (PT 1)
  R. BROWNING, 303:VOL93-274
LEMMER, M. - SEE SCHERNBERG, D.
LEMMON, S.M. FRUSTRATED PATRIOTS.
  639(VQR):SPRING74-XLII
LEMMON, S.M., ED. THE PETTIGREW
PAPERS.* (VOL 1)
  W.M. FOWLER, JR., 14:APR73-240
LEMONS, J.S. THE WOMAN CITIZEN.
  A.F. SCOTT, 579(SAQ):SUMMER74-406
LENDERS, W. ALLGEMEINE GRUNDLAGEN
DER LINGUISTISCHEN DATENVERARBEI-
TUNG.
  G.F. MEIER, 682(ZPSK):BAND26HEFT6-
  722
LENDVAI, E. BÉLA BARTÓK.
  B. FENNELLY, 308:FALL73-330
  J.S. WEISSMANN, 607:SEP73-47
LENSEN, G.A. THE STRANGE NEUTRAL-
ITY.*
  J.K. EMMERSON, 550(RUSR):APR73-204
  J.J. STEPHAN, 293(JAST):FEB73-326
LENSEN, G.A. - SEE KUTAKOV, L.L.
LENSEN, G.A. - SEE POUTIATINE, O.
LENT, J. PHILIPPINE MASS COMMUNICA-
TIONS BEFORE 1811 AFTER 1966.
  B. NUSSBAUM, 293(JAST):MAY73-571

LENTIN, L. APPRENDRE À PARLER/À
L'ENFANT DE MOINS DE SIX ANS/OU?
QUAND? COMMENT?
  J. POHL, 556(RLV):1973/3-283
LENTZEN, M. STUDIEN ZUR DANTE-EXE-
GESE CRISTOFORO LANDINOS MIT EINEM
ANHANG BISHER UNVERÖFFENTLICHER
BRIEFE UND REDEN.
  S. PRETE, 52:BAND8HEFT2-194
LENTZEN, M. - SEE LANDINO, C.
LENZ, F.W. & G.C. GALINSKY - SEE
TIBULLUS
DE LEÓN, A.G. - SEE UNDER GARCÍA DE
LEÓN, A.
LÉON, M. L'ACCENTUATION DES PRONOMS
PERSONNELS EN FRANÇAIS STANDARD.*
  F. CARTON, 209(FM):OCT73-431
LÉON, P. & OTHERS, EDS. PROBLÈMES
DE L'ANALYSE TEXTUELLE.
  J. CULLER, 402(MLR):OCT74-829
LÉON, P., F. CROUZET & R. GASCON,
EDS. L'INDUSTRIALISATION EN EUROPE
AU XIXE SIÈCLE.
  F. TREMEL, 182:VOL26#17/18-591
LÉON, P.R., ED. RECHERCHES SUR LA
STRUCTURE PHONIQUE DU FRANÇAIS CAN-
ADIEN.*
  A. VALDMAN, 207(FR):FEB73-690
DE LEÓN HAZERA, L. LA NOVELA DE LA
SELVA HISPANOAMERICANA.
  G. FIGUEIRA, 263:APR-JUN74-177
LEONARD, G. THE ULTIMATE ATHLETE.
  A. BROYARD, 441:12AUG75-33
LEONARD, J. BLACK CONCEIT.
  B. ALLEN, 249(HUDR):SPRING74-119
LEONARD, J. THIS PEN FOR HIRE.
  B. DE MOTT, 61:FEB75-111
LEONARDO DA VINCI. THE LITERARY
WORKS OF LEONARDO DA VINCI. (3RD
ED) (J.P. RICHTER, ED)
  C. GOULD, 39:FEB73-202
LEONOV, L.M. RANNIYE RASSKAZY.
  R.D.B. THOMSON, 575(SEER):JUL74-
  470
LEOPARDI, G. SCRITTI FILOLOGICI
(1817-1832). (G. PACELLA & S.
TIMPANARO, EDS)
  N.J. PERELLA, 276:SPRING73-103
LEOPOLD, J.H. THE ALMANUS MANU-
SCRIPT.*
  B.S. HALL, 589:JAN74-128
LEOPOLD, R. EGON SCHIELE.
  C.E. SCHORSKE, 453:11DEC75-39
"L'ÉPOQUE PHANARIOTE."
  C. MANGO, 617(TLS):14NOV75-1367
LEPROHON, P. THE ITALIAN CINEMA.
  R. CAMPION, 200:APR73-235
  B.L., 275(IQ):SUMMER73-119
LERCH, W. PROBLEME DER SCHREIBUNG
BEI SCHWEIZERDEUTSCHEN MUNDART-
SCHRIFTSTELLERN.*
  W. SCHENKER, 343:BAND16HEFT2-221
  E.H. YARRILL, 182:VOL26#7/8-213
LERMAN, E. ARMED LOVE.*
  G. BURNS, 584(SWR):WINTER74-104
  P. RAMSEY, 569(SR):SPRING74-404
LERMAN, R. CALL ME ISHTAR.
  T. EDWARDS, 473(PR):3/1974-469
LERNER, A., ED. THE HIRSHHORN
MUSEUM & SCULPTURE GARDEN.
  D. COOPER, 453:29MAY75-9
LERNER, L. A.R.T.H.U.R.
  A. MACLEAN, 617(TLS):23MAY75-552

LERNER, L. THE USES OF NOSTALGIA.*
J. BARRELL, 541(RES):NOV73-522
J. BUXTON, 402(MLR):OCT74-832
LERNER, R.E. THE HERESY OF THE FREE
SPIRIT IN THE LATER MIDDLE AGES.
E.L. MC LAUGHLIN, 589:OCT74-747
LEROY, M. LES GRANDS COURANTS DE LA
LINGUISTIQUE MODERNE.* (2ND ED)
E.F.K. KOERNER, 215(GL):VOL13#1-54
G.C. LEPSCHY, 297(JL):FEB73-196
H.J. NEUHAUS, 343:BAND16HEFT2-209
W. ZWANENBURG, 433:JAN73-105
LESAGE, A-R. LE DIABLE BOITEUX.*
(R. LAUFER, ED)
J. ALTER, 546(RR):MAY73-236
LESKY, A. DIE TRAGISCHE DICHTUNG
DER HELLENEN. (3RD ED)
G. RONNET, 555:VOL47FASC2-332
LESKY, E. & OTHERS, EDS. DIE AUF-
KLÄRUNG IN OST- UND SÜDOSTEUROPA.
P. PETSCHAUER, 481(PQ):JUL73-393
LESLAU, W. AMHARIC TEXTBOOK.
E. HAMMERSCHMIDT, 343:BAND17HEFT2-
222
LESLIE, A. FRANCIS CHICHESTER.
M. RICHEY, 617(TLS):10OCT75-1184
LESLIE, D. THE INCREDIBLE DUCHESS.
P. BEER, 617(TLS):17JAN75-48
LESLIE, J. THE DEVIL & MRS. DEVINE.
E.M. EWING, 441:11MAY75-10
LESLIE, J.K. SPANISH FOR CONVERSA-
TION. (3RD ED)
F.G. VINSON, 399(MLJ):MAR73-151
LESLIE, K. THE POEMS OF KENNETH
LESLIE.
A.R. SHUCARD, 102(CANL):WINTER73-
115
LESOBRE, J. & H. SOMMER. LEXIQUE
D'ASSURANCE ET DE RÉASSURANCE
ANGLAIS/AMÉRICAIN - FRANÇAIS/ENG-
LISH-AMÉRICAN-FRENCH.
E.I.S., 75:3/1973-145
LÉSOUALC'H, T. LA VIE VITE.
F-E. DORENLOT, 207(FR):FEB73-662
LESSING, D. THE GRASS IS SINGING.
R. DINNAGE, 453:17JUL75-38
LESSING, D. THE HABIT OF LOVING.
J.L. HALIO, 598(SOR):AUTUMN75-942
LESSING, D. THE MEMOIRS OF A SUR-
VIVOR.*
R. DINNAGE, 453:17JUL75-38
M. HOWARD, 441:8JUN75-1
C. LEHMANN-HAUPT, 441:2JUN75-23
P. MC CALLUM, 99:DEC75/JAN76-56
J. MELLORS, 362:23JAN75-126
442(NY):2JUN75-109
LESSING, D. THE SUMMER BEFORE THE
DARK.*
K. MC SWEENEY, 529(QQ):WINTER73-
666
LESSING, G.E. LAOCOON.
T. TODOROV, 98:JAN73-26
LESSING, G.E., M. MENDELSSOHN & C.F.
NICOLAI. LESSING, MENDELSSOHN,
NICOLAI: BRIEFWECHSEL ÜBER DAS
TRAUERSPIEL. (J. SCHULTE-SASSE, ED)
R.K. ANGRESS, 406:FALL74-299
"LESSING YEARBOOK II, 1970."* (G.
STERN, G. MERKEL & J. GLENN, EDS)
P. HERNADI, 399(MLJ):NOV73-381
"LESSING YEARBOOK III."* (G. STERN,
G. MERKEL & J. GLENN, EDS)
L.P. WESSELL, JR., 399(MLJ):NOV73-
381

"LESSING YEARBOOK IV, 1972."
E. BAHR & R.G. KUNGER, 399(MLJ):
MAR74-148
LESTZ, G.S. AMISH BELIEFS, CUSTOMS
& DISCIPLINE.
M.A. MOOK, 292(JAF):OCT-DEC73-405
LESURE, F. L'OPÉRA CLASSIQUE FRAN-
ÇAIS.*
D. HEARTZ, 415:APR74-303
LESY, M. WISCONSIN DEATH TRIP.*
T. TANNER, 364:APR/MAY74-118
LESZL, W. LOGIC & METAPHYSICS IN
ARISTOTLE.*
A.R. LACEY, 393(MIND):JAN73-143
LESZNAI, L. BARTÓK.*
N. CHADWICK, 410(M&L):JAN74-114
P. GRIFFITHS, 415:FEB74-132
LETHABY, W.R. ARCHITECTURE, MYSTI-
CISM & MYTH.
S. BAYLEY, 617(TLS):23MAY75-569
LEUBE, E. DIE "CELESTINA."
D.S. SEVERIN, 545(RPH):FEB74-443
LEUBE, E. FORTUNA IN KARTHAGO.*
D.J.A. ROSS, 208(FS):JAN74-55
LEUBE, E. & L. SCHRADER, EDS. INTER-
PRETATION UND VERGLEICH.
E. KERN, 131(CL):WINTER74-80
R. PAGEARD, 549(RLC):OCT-DEC73-627
LEUBE-FEY, C. BILD UND FUNKTION DER
"DOMPNA" IN DER LYRIK DER TROBADORS.
J.H. MARSHALL, 208(FS):OCT74-439
LEVAS, S. SIBELIUS.
412:MAY73-175
LEVENSON, C. STILLS.*
A. CLUYSENAAR, 565:VOL14#1-70
LEVENSON, J.R. REVOLUTION & COSMO-
POLITANISM.*
D. MERWIN, 318(JAOS):OCT-DEC73-645
LEVENSTON, E.A. ENGLISH FOR IS-
RAELIS.
F. DUBIN, 399(MLJ):SEP-OCT73-306
LEVER, C. GOLDSMITHS & SILVERSMITHS
OF ENGLAND.
J.F. HAYWARD, 617(TLS):11APR75-407
LEVER, J.W. THE TRAGEDY OF STATE.*
S.G. PUTT, 175:SPRING72-26
LEVERTOV, D. FOOTPRINTS.*
M.G. PERLOFF, 659:WINTER75-84
LEVERTOV, D. THE FREEING OF THE
DUST.
D. IGNATOW, 441:30NOV75-54
LEVERTOV, D. THE POET IN THE
WORLD.*
H. CARRUTH, 249(HUDR):AUTUMN74-475
639(VQR):AUTUMN74-CXXXI
LEVESON, M. - SEE SEGAL, P.
LEVEY, M. PAINTING AT COURT.*
D. THOMSON, 90:APR73-257
LEVEY, M. & W.G. KALNEIN. ART &
ARCHITECTURE OF THE EIGHTEENTH
CENTURY IN FRANCE.
J. CAILLEUX, 90:SEP73-610
LEVI, A.H.T., ED. HUMANISM IN
FRANCE AT THE END OF THE MIDDLE
AGES & IN THE EARLY RENAISSANCE.*
J.C. LAIDLAW, 208(FS):OCT74-443
P.S. LEWIS, 447(N&Q):MAY73-190
LÉVI-STRAUSS, C. DU MIEL AUX CEN-
DRES.
C. SCHUWER, 542:JAN-MAR73-78
"LEVIATÁN: REVISTA MENSUAL DE HECHOS
E IDEAS." (NOS. 1-26)
P. PRESTON, 617(TLS):10OCT75-1204

LEVIN, D.N. APOLLONIUS' ARGONAUTICA
RE-EXAMINED.* (VOL 1)
G. GIANGRANDE, 123:MAR74-36
LEVIN, H. GROUNDS FOR COMPARISON.
C.S. BROWN, 131(CL):SPRING73-161
D. NEWTON-DE MOLINA, 402(MLR):
APR74-359
295:FEB74-474
LEVIN, K. LUCAS SAMARAS.
J.R. MELLOW, 441:7DEC75-80
LEVIN, M., ED. LOVE STORIES.
H. BEVINGTON, 441:21DEC75-18
LEVIN, M. THE SETTLERS.
H. FISCH, 390:JAN73-71
LEVIN, R. THE MULTIPLE PLOT IN ENG-
LISH RENAISSANCE DRAMA.*
R.V. HOLDSWORTH, 541(RES):FEB73-65
D. MEHL, 38:BAND91HEFT4-523
S. SCHOENBAUM, 551(RENQ):SUMMER73-
224
LEVIN, S. THE INDO-EUROPEAN & SEM-
ITIC LANGUAGES.*
G.M. MESSING, 122:OCT73-301
O. SZEMERÉNYI, 215(GL):VOL13#2-101
LEVINE, A. PROPHECY IN BRIDGEPORT
& OTHER POEMS.*
J.H., 502(PRS):FALL73-278
LEVINE, B. THE DISSOLVING IMAGE.*
E. MACKENZIE, 447(N&Q):SEP73-359
LEVINE, D.N. GREATER ETHIOPIA.
E. ULLENDORFF, 617(TLS):25APR75-
462
LEVINE, H.S. HITLER'S FREE CITY.
F.L. CARSTEN, 575(SEER):APR74-305
LEVINE, I.D. EYEWITNESS TO HISTORY.
A. PARRY, 550(RUSR):OCT73-437
LEVINE, J.P. CREATION & CRITICISM.
A. WILDE, 295:FEB74-608
LEVINE, P. 1933.
G. HITCHCOCK, 651(WHR):AUTUMN74-
408
R. HOWARD, 491:MAR75-354
R. MAZZOCCO, 453:3APR75-20
V. YOUNG, 249(HUDR):WINTER74/75-
597
LEVINE, P. THEY FEED THEY LION.*
J. ANDERSON, 502(PRS):SUMMER73-181
A. HELMS, 473(PR):1/1974-151
LEVINE, S. EDGAR POE.*
G.B. TENNYSON, 445(NCF):SEP73-245
LEVINSON, C. CAPITAL, INFLATION, &
THE MULTINATIONALS.
R.L. HEILBRONER, 453:20MAR75-6
LEVINSON, C. L'INFLATION MONDIALE
ET LES FIRMES MULTINATIONALES.
A. FINKIELKRAUT, 98:DEC73-1118
LEVISON, A. THE WORKING-CLASS MA-
JORITY.
A. KEYSSAR, 617(TLS):17OCT75-1233
LEVISON, M., R.G. WARD & J.W. WEBB.
THE SETTLEMENT OF POLYNESIA.
617(TLS):10JAN75-40
LEVITT, P.M. A STRUCTURAL APPROACH
TO THE ANALYSIS OF DRAMA.
E. TÖRNQVIST, 597(SN):VOL45#1-180
LEVY, D. & S. REUBEN. THE CHESS
SCENE.
617(TLS):7MAR75-261
LEVY, E. JAMES WELDON JOHNSON.
H. JARRETT, 27(AL):JAN75-593
LEVY, F.J. - SEE BACON, F.
LEVY, H.L. CLAUDIAN'S "IN RUFINUM."
J. ANDRÉ, 555:VOL47FASC1-152
J.W. EADIE, 124:SEP72-43

LEVY, J.E. CESAR CHAVEZ.
F. CARNEY, 453:13NOV75-39
W. GRIFFITH, 441:9NOV75-10
LEVY, L.W. AGAINST THE LAW.
M.E. GALE, 441:27APR75-6
LEVY, M. LOVECRAFT.
R. ASSELINEAU, 189(EA):JUL-SEP73-
376
LEVY, P. QUELQUES ASPECTS DE LA
PENSÉE D'UN MATHÉMATICIEN.
R. BLANCHÉ, 542:JUL-SEP73-365
LEVY, R.S. THE DOWNFALL OF THE
ANTI-SEMITIC POLITICAL PARTIES IN
IMPERIAL GERMANY.
F.L. CARSTEN, 617(TLS):21NOV75-
1392
LEWALD, H.E., ED. THE CRY OF HOME.*
D. SCHIER, 109:FALL/WINTER73/74-
135
295:FEB74-433
LEWALSKI, B.K. DONNE'S "ANNIVERSAR-
IES" & THE POETRY OF PRAISE.
J. BROADBENT, 617(TLS):19SEP75-
1040
P.A. PARRISH, 141:FALL74-339
A. STEIN, 401(MLQ):SEP74-317
639(VQR):AUTUMN74-CXXVI
LEWALSKI, B.K. - SEE COLIE, R.L.
LEWALSKI, B.K. & A.J. SABOL, EDS.
MAJOR POETS OF THE EARLIER SEVEN-
TEENTH CENTURY.*
R. ELLRODT, 189(EA):OCT-DEC73-478
LEWES, G.H. RANTHORPE. (B. SMAL-
LEY, ED)
P. CONRAD, 617(TLS):9MAY75-520
LEWIS, A. IONESCO.
B.L. KNAPP, 399(MLJ):SEP-OCT74-275
LEWIS, A.A. THE MOUNTAIN ARTISANS
QUILTING BOOK.
F. PETTIT, 139:DEC73-58
LEWIS, A.H. MURDER BY CONTRACT.
B.A. FRANKLIN, 441:9NOV75-28
LEWIS, B. HISTORY.
442(NY):9JUN75-127
LEWIS, B.I. GEORGE GROSZ.*
F.L. BORCHARDT, 406:SUMMER74-185
LEWIS, C.I. COLLECTED PAPERS OF
CLARENCE IRVING LEWIS.* (J.D. GO-
HEEN & J.L. MOTHERSHEAD, JR., EDS)
J. CEDERBLOM, 319:JAN75-119
LEWIS, C.S. STORIES BY C.S. LEWIS.
(G. KRANZ, ED)
K. OLTMANN, 430(NS):JUL73-388
LEWIS, D. COUNTERFACTUALS.*
J.J.C. SMART, 63:AUG74-174
LEWIS, H.D. THE SELF & IMMORTALITY.
A. FLEW, 518:MAY74-12
LEWIS, H.D. & R.L. SLATER. THE
STUDY OF RELIGIONS.
C.S.J. WHITE, 318(JAOS):OCT-DEC73-
624
LEWIS, J. THE LEFT BOOK CLUB.
295:FEB74-372
LEWIS, J.W. A CONCISE PRONOUNCING
DICTIONARY OF BRITISH & AMERICAN
ENGLISH.
E.L. TIBBITTS, 399(MLJ):MAR74-139
M. VIEL, 189(EA):APR-JUN73-217
LEWIS, J.W. A GUIDE TO ENGLISH PRO-
NUNCIATION.
H-W. WODARZ, 353:15APR73-125

LEWIS, J.W., ED. PARTY LEADERSHIP
& REVOLUTIONARY POWER IN CHINA.
E. WICKBERG, 318(JAOS):JAN-MAR73-
86
LEWIS, M. & L. WALLACE STEGNER.
M. BUCCO, 649(WAL):FALL73-159
LEWIS, M.B. SENTENCE ANALYSIS IN
MODERN MALAY.*
H. ROFÉ, 302:JAN73-177
LEWIS, N. THE SICILIAN SPECIALIST.
N. CALLENDAR, 441:16FEB75-13
LEWIS, P.E. - SEE GAY, J.
LEWIS, R. MARGARET THATCHER.
LORD HILL, 362:4SEP75-315
LORD LAMBTON, 617(TLS):5SEP75-984
LEWIS, R.W.B. EDITH WHARTON.
Q. ANDERSON, 441:31AUG75-1
K. CLARK, 617(TLS):19DEC75-1502
I. EHRENPREIS, 453:13NOV75-4
R.R. LINGEMAN, 441:27AUG75-29
R. TODD, 61:NOV75-114
LEWIS, T. JACK CARTER & THE LAW.
M. LEVIN, 441:9NOV75-54
LEWIS, T. JACK CARTER'S LAW.
617(TLS):21FEB75-184
LEWIS, T.S.W. - SEE CRANE, H. &
OTHERS
LEWIS, W.S. - SEE WALPOLE, H.
LEWIS, W.S. & OTHERS - SEE WALPOLE,
H.
LEWY, C. - SEE BROAD, C.D.
LEWY, G. RELIGION & REVOLUTION.*
639(VQR):AUTUMN74-CLII
"LEXICON MEDIAE ET INFIMAE LATINI-
TATIS POLONORUM." (VOL 3, FASC 5
& 6)
J. ANDRÉ, 555:VOL47FASC2-378
"A LEXICON TO THE GLORY OF GOD,
GREEK-RUSSIAN (18TH CENTURY)."
H. LEEMING, 575(SEER):JAN74-149
LEYDA, J. DIANYING: ELECTRIC SHAD-
OWS.*
R.C. CROIZIER, 293(JAST):MAY73-501
LEYDA, S.D. "THE SERPENT IS SHUT
OUT FROM PARADISE."
P.H. BUTTER, 677:VOL4-314-
"THE J.C. LEYENDECKER POSTER BOOK."
J-C. SUARES, 441:5OCT75-22
LEYMARIE, J., ED. THE GRAPHIC WORKS
OF THE IMPRESSIONISTS.*
R. PICKVANCE, 135:APR73-292
LEYS, C. UNDERDEVELOPMENT IN KENYA.
M. TWADDLE, 617(TLS):26DEC75-1545
LEYS, S. OMBRES CHINOISES.
W. JENNER, 617(TLS):25APR75-448
LEYTON, E. DYING HARD.
P. NEARY, 99:NOV75-33
LEZAMA LIMA, J. POESÍA COMPLETA.
LA CANTIDAD HECHIZADA.
G. BROTHERSTON, 617(TLS):15AUG75-
925
L'HERMITE, F.T. - SEE UNDER TRISTAN
L'HERMITE, F.
LI HO. THE POEMS OF LI HO (791-
817). (J.D. FRODSHAM, TRANS)
LI CHI, 318(JAOS):JAN-MAR73-79
LI YU-NING. THE INTRODUCTION OF
SOCIALISM INTO CHINA.*
E. WICKBERG, 318(JAOS):APR-JUN73-
220
LI-FU, C. - SEE UNDER CHEN LI-FU
LIACI, M.T. - SEE LANDINO, C.
LIAN, P.C. - SEE UNDER PANG CHENG
LIAN

LIBANIUS. SELECTED WORKS. (VOL 1)
(A.F. NORMAN, ED & TRANS)
W.M. CALDER 3D, 122:JAN73-74
LIBERMAN, E.G. ECONOMIC METHODS &
THE EFFECTIVENESS OF PRODUCTION.*
I.M. DRUMMOND, 104:WINTER74-615
LIBMAN, L. AND MUSIC AT THE CLOSE.
M. PETERSON, 470:NOV73-21
LICHET, R. ROUSSEAU, LA VIE ET
L'OEUVRE. ECRIRE À TOUT LE MONDE.
P. SILBERMAN, 399(MLJ):NOV73-364
"ALEXIS LICHINE'S NEW ENCYCLOPEDIA
OF WINE & SPIRITS."* (BRITISH
TITLE: LICHINE'S ENCYCLOPAEDIA OF
WINES & SPIRITS.)
T. ASPLER, 362:25DEC75&1JAN76-891
LICHTHEIM, G. FROM MARX TO HEGEL &
OTHER ESSAYS.*
A. QUINTON, 453:12JUN75-39
LIDA, C.E. & I.M. ZAVALA, EDS. LA
REVOLUCIÓN DE 1868.*
L.E. DAVIS, 131(CL):SUMMER73-268
M.C. SUÁREZ-MURIAS, 238:MAR73-176
LIDDELL, R. CAVAFY.
P. BEER, 362:16JAN75-93
J. MERRILL, 453:17JUL75-12
A. ROSS, 364:FEB/MAR75-143
LIDDIARD, J. ISAAC ROSENBERG.
K. MILLER, 453:16OCT75-27
W.W. ROBSON, 617(TLS):29AUG75-958
D. THOMAS, 362:4SEP75-318
LIDZ, T. THE ORIGIN & TREATMENT OF
SCHIZOPHRENIC DISORDERS.
J.K. WING, 617(TLS):19SEP75-1064
LIEB, I.C. THE FOUR FACES OF MAN.
P. GUNTER, 577(SHR):SUMMER73-348
C. HARTSHORNE, 258:MAR73-131
LIEBER, T.M. ENDLESS EXPERIMENTS.*
G.B. TENNYSON, 445(NCF):SEP73-247
LIEBERMAN, L. THE OSPREY SUICIDES.*
J.R. CARPENTER, 491:DEC74-166
LIEBESCHUETZ, J.H.W.G. ANTIOCH.
J-P. CALLU, 555:VOL47FASC2-370
M.A.R. COLLEDGE, 123:MAR74-95
T.E. GREGORY, 124:MAR73-376
B. LEVICK, 313:VOL63-270
J. SONGSTER, 613:WINTER73-545
LIEBMAN, M. LENINISM UNDER LENIN.
A. ULAM, 617(TLS):10OCT75-1195
LIEBMANN-FRANKFORT, T. LA FRONTIÈRE
ORIENTALE DANS LA POLITIQUE EXTÉR-
IEURE DE LA RÉPUBLIQUE ROMAINE DE-
PUIS LE TRAITÉ D'APAMÉE JUSQU'À LA
FIN DES CONQUÊTES ASIATIQUES DE
POMPÉE (189/8-63).
J-C. DUMONT, 555:VOL47FASC1-183
LIEBNER, J. MOZART ON THE STAGE.
P. BRANSCOMBE, 410(M&L):JUL74-339
LIEHR, R. STADTRAT UND STÄDTISCHE
OBERSCHICHT VON PUEBLA AM ENDE DER
KOLONIALZEIT (1787-1810).
F. TICHY, 182:VOL26#20-762
LIEVSAY, J.L. VENETIAN PHOENIX.
C. BAZERMAN, 568(SCN):WINTER74-82
LIEVSAY, J.L. - SEE TUVILL, D.
LIFTON, B.J. TWICE BORN.
J. WHEDON, 441:2NOV75-38
LIFTON, R.J. & E. OLSON. LIVING &
DYING.*
C. RICKS, 617(TLS):18JUL75-790
LIGETI, L. MONUMENTS PRÉCLASSIQUES
1, XIIIE ET XIVE SIÈCLES.
D.M. FARQUHAR, 244(HJAS):VOL33-251

LILES, B.L. AN INTRODUCTORY TRANS-
FORMATIONAL GRAMMAR.*
  G. HELBIG, 353:15NOV73-123
LILIA, S.R.C. CLEMENT OF ALEXAN-
DRIA.
  E. DES PLACES, 555:VOL47FASC1-142
LILLA, S.R.C. CLEMENT OF ALEXANDRIA.
  C.C. RICHARDSON, 124:MAR73-360
LILLO, B. TRES CUENTOS. (R. MIL-
LAN, ED)
  D.R. MC KAY, 399(MLJ):SEP-OCT73-
  302
LILLY, M. SICKERT.*
  W. BARON, 90:FEB73-128
LIMA, J.L. - SEE UNDER LEZAMA LIMA,
  J.
LIMA, R. AN ANNOTATED BIBLIOGRAPHY
OF RAMON DEL VALLE-INCLAN.
  M.A. SALGADO, 517(PBSA):JAN-MAR74-
  84
LIN, J.C. MODERN CHINESE POETRY.*
  A. PALANDRI, 352(LE&W):VOL16#3-
  1066
  M. ROBERTSON, 293(JAST):FEB73-314
LIND, L. THE LEARNING MACHINE.
  M. KATZ, 99:APR/MAY75-16
LINDBECK, A. SWEDISH ECONOMIC POL-
ICY.
  B. THOMAS, 617(TLS):22AUG75-952
LINDBECK, J.M.H., ED. CHINA: MANAGE-
MENT OF A REVOLUTIONARY SOCIETY.*
  E. WICKBERG, 318(JAOS):OCT-DEC73-
  641
LINDBERG, J.D. - SEE WEISE, C.
LINDEMANN, J.W.R. OLD ENGLISH PRE-
VERBAL "GE-": ITS MEANING.
  E.G. STANLEY, 38:BAND91HEFT4-493
LINDENBERGER, H. GEORG TRAKL.
  T. FIEDLER, 131(CL):WINTER74-82
LINDERMAN, G.F. THE MIRROR OF WAR.
  L. ZIFF, 617(TLS):25APR75-453
LINDOP, A.E. THE SELF-APPOINTED
SAINT.
  P.D. JAMES, 617(TLS):26SEP75-1079
LINDOP, G. - SEE "THOMAS CHATTERTON"
LINDQUIST, E. AN IMMIGRANT'S TWO
WORLDS.
  P. VINTEN-JOHANSEN, 563(SS):WINTER
  74-86
LINDSAY, J. BLAST-POWER & BALLIS-
TICS.
  G.E.R. LLOYD, 617(TLS):17JAN75-64
LINDSAY, J. A HISTORY OF THE NORTH
WALES SLATE INDUSTRY.
  617(TLS):7NOV75-1342
LINDSAY, J. WILLIAM MORRIS.
  D.A.N. JONES, 362:20NOV75-683
  E. PENNING-ROWSELL, 617(TLS):
  30CT75-1124
LINDSAY, J. ORIGINS OF ASTROLOGY.
  J.G. GRIFFITHS, 123:NOV74-315
  B.A. PEARSON, 124:SEP72-57
  R. SCRANTON, 122:APR74-164
LINDSAY, R.O. & J. NEU. MAZARIN-
ADES.*
  H. CARRIER, 549(RLC):JUL-SEP73-472
LINE, L., ED. THE PLEASURE OF BIRDS.
  R. CARAS, 441:7DEC75-93
LINEHAN, P. THE SPANISH CHURCH &
THE PAPACY IN THE THIRTEENTH CEN-
TURY.*
  R.A. FLETCHER, 86(BHS):JUL73-283
LINGARD, J. A PROPER PLACE.
  M. LEVIN, 441:23NOV75-54

"LINGUISTIQUE: LISTE MONDIALE DES
PERIODIQUES SPECIALISES."
  C.V.J. RUSS, 402(MLR):JUL74-596
LINK, E.M. THE BOOK OF SILVER.
  G.M. WILSON, 135:DEC73-296
LINK, F.H. EUGENE O'NEILL UND DIE
WIEDERGEBURT DER TRAGODIE AUS DEM
UNBEWUSSTEN.
  G. HOFFMANN, 38:BAND91HEFT2-265
LINK, F.M. - SEE DRYDEN, J.
LINK, J. ARTISTISCHE FORM UND AS-
THETISCHER SINN IN PLATENS LYRIK.
  H. HENEL, 301(JEGP):APR74-296
LINKS, J.G. TOWNSCAPE PAINTING &
DRAWING.*
  J. HAYES, 90:MAR73-187
  H. HUTH, 54:MAR73-159
LINLEY, J. ARCHITECTURE OF MIDDLE
GEORGIA: THE OCONEE AREA.
  E.R. DE ZURKO, 219(GAR):SUMMER73-
  298
  J. HNEDAK, 576:OCT73-261
LINSTRUM, D. SIR JEFFRY WYATVILLE,
ARCHITECT TO THE KING.
  D. HINTON, 135:JUL73-227
  J. LEES-MILNE, 39:JUN73-625
  D. WATKIN, 46:JUL73-63
LIOURE, M. L'ESTHETIQUE DRAMATIQUE
DE PAUL CLAUDEL.
  H.T. NAUGHTON, 188(ECR):SPRING73-
  89
LIPCHITZ, J., WITH H.H. ARNASON.
MY LIFE IN SCULPTURE.*
  W. TUCKER, 592:MAR73-143
LIPMAN, J. AMERICAN PRIMITIVE
PAINTING.
  T. CRAIG, 592:JUL-AUG73-55
LIPMAN, M., ED. CONTEMPORARY AES-
THETICS.
  J.F. O'LEARY, 290(JAAC):SPRING74-
  427
LIPMAN, M. HARRY STOTTLEMEIER'S
DISCOVERY.
  A. QUINTON, 617(TLS):4APR75-358
LIPP, S. & S.E., EDS. HISPANOAMERI-
CA VISTA POR SUS ENSAYISTAS.
  D.F. BROWN, 399(MLJ):JAN-FEB73-67
LIPPARD, L.R., ED. SIX YEARS.*
  R.H. FUCHS, 592:NOV73-205
LIPPINCOTT, D. TREMOR VIOLET.
  M. LEVIN, 441:10AUG75-14
LIPSCHUTZ, I.H. SPANISH PAINTING &
THE FRENCH ROMANTICS.
  J. BRUNEAU, 131(CL):FALL74-367
  J.S.P., 191(ELN):SEP73(SUPP)-71
  J. SEZNEC, 208(FS):APR74-204
LIPSET, S.M. & D. RIESMAN. EDUCA-
TION & POLITICS AT HARVARD.
  R. MC CAUGHEY, 617(TLS):19SEP75-
  1047
LIPSYTE, R. SPORTSWORLD.
  A. BROYARD, 441:24NOV75-39
  R. KAHN, 441:9NOV75-4
  G. WILLS, 453:300CT75-3
LIPTON, L. INDEPENDENT FILM-MAKING.
  M. LE GRICE, 592:MAR73-145
LISCANO, J. PANORAMA DE LA LITERA-
TURA VENEZOLANA ACTUAL.
  R.L.F. DURAND, 263:OCT-DEC74-467
LISH, G., ED. THE SECRET LIFE OF
OUR TIMES.*
  W. PEDEN, 569(SR):FALL74-712
  W. WEATHERS, 584(SWR):WINTER74-94

DE LISLE, C.M.L. - SEE UNDER LECONTE
DE LISLE, C.M.
LIST, S. NOBODY MAKES ME CRY.
  P. ADAMS, 61:SEP75-85
  M. LEVIN, 441:17AUG75-23
LISTER, R. BRITISH ROMANTIC ART.
  R. EDWARDS, 39:JUL73-65
  M. ROSENTHAL, 135:JUL73-228
LISTER, R. SAMUEL PALMER.
  W. FEAVER, 617(TLS):21MAR75-304
  D. THOMAS, 362:20MAR75-372
LISTER, R. - SEE PALMER, S.
LISZT, F. NEUE AUSGABE SÄMTLICHER
WERKE/NEW LISZT EDITION. (SER 1,
VOLS 1&2) (Z. GÁRDONYI & I. SZEL-
ÉNYI, EDS)
  P. FRIEDHEIM, 317:SPRING73-171
"LITERARISCHE ZEITSCHRIFTEN UND
JAHRBÜCHER 1880-1970."
  J.K. KING, 406:WINTER74-435
LITMAN, T.A. LE SUBLIME EN FRANCE
(1660-1714).
  J. LETTS, 481(PQ):JUL73-441
LITSKY, F. SUPERSTARS.
  R. SMITH, 441:7DEC75-34
LITTELL, R. SWEET REASON.*
  D. WILSON, 617(TLS):2MAY75-492
LITTLE, A.M.G. ROMAN PERSPECTIVE
PAINTING & THE ANCIENT STAGE.
  J. HILTON, 313:VOL63-278
  S. LATTIMORE, 124:NOV72-187
LITTLE, J.S. EURODOLLARS.
  K. COONEY, 441:26JAN75-10
  442(NY):31MAR75-100
LITTLE, K. URBANIZATION AS A SOCIAL
PROCESS.
  J.C. MITCHELL, 617(TLS):14FEB75-
  172
LITTLE, L. PARTHIAN SHOT.
  M. LEVIN, 441:11MAY75-22
LITTLE, R. SAINT-JOHN PERSE.
  205(FMLS):APR73-213
LITTLETON, C.S. THE NEW COMPARATIVE
MYTHOLOGY.
  J. BROUGH, 617(TLS):3JAN75-19
LITTLEWOOD, J.E. HOW TO PLAY THE
MIDDLE GAME IN CHESS.
  617(TLS):31JAN75-121
LITVINOFF, E. BLOOD ON THE SNOW.
  J. MELLORS, 362:13MAR75-349
  J. MILLER, 617(TLS):14MAR75-269
LITVINOFF, E. A DEATH OUT OF SEA-
SON.*
  E. GLOVER, 565:VOL14#4-69
LITVINOFF, E. JOURNEY THROUGH A
SMALL PLANET.
  E. GLOVER, 565:VOL14#2-36
LITVINOFF, E., ED. SOVIET ANTI-
SEMITISM.
  J. MILLER, 617(TLS):18APR75-425
LITVINOV, P., COMP. THE TRIAL OF
THE FOUR.* (P. REDDAWAY, ED)
  D.V. POSPIELOVSKY, 550(RUSR):OCT
  73-441
LITVINSKIY, B.A. DREVNIE KOTCHEV-
NIKI "KRICHI MIRA."
  R. GHIRSHMAN, 57:VOL35#4-374
LITZ, A.W., ED. ELIOT IN HIS TIME.*
  P. GRAY, 111:23NOV73-55
  R. KIRK, 569(SR):FALL74-698
  D.E.S. MAXWELL, 402(MLR):OCT74-850
  639(VQR):WINTER74-XVI

LITZ, A.W. INTROSPECTIVE VOYAGER.*
  J. BAIRD, 191(ELN):DEC73-151
  G. MC FADDEN, 295:FEB74-796
  SISTER MAURA, 613:WINTER73-535
LITZ, A.W., ED. MAJOR AMERICAN
SHORT STORIES.
  617(TLS):30MAY75-601
LITZINGER, B. & D. SMALLEY, EDS.
BROWNING: THE CRITICAL HERITAGE.*
  J.C. MAXWELL, 447(N&Q):JUL73-269
LIU, A.P.L. COMMUNICATIONS &
NATIONAL INTEGRATION IN COMMUNIST
CHINA.*
  C.K. LEUNG, 302:JAN73-171
LIU JUNG-EN, ED & TRANS. SIX YÜAN
PLAYS.
  J.I. CRUMP, 352(LE&W):VOL16#3-1059
  S.H. WEST, 293(JAST):FEB73-313
LIU, W-C. & I.Y. LO, EDS. SUNFLOWER
SPLENDOR.
  D. LATTIMORE, 441:21DEC75-1
LIUNGMAN, C.G. WHAT IS IQ?
  C. LEHMANN-HAUPT, 441:17DEC75-37
LIVERMORE, H.V. THE ORIGINS OF
SPAIN & PORTUGAL.
  D.W. LOMAX, 86(BHS):OCT73-385
  J.F. POWERS, 589:APR74-358
LIVESAY, D. COLLECTED POEMS.
  T. MARSHALL, 529(QQ):WINTER73-655
  C.X. RINGROSE, 150(DR):SPRING73-
  171
  R. SKELTON, 102(CANL):AUTUMN73-77
LIVESAY, D. A WINNIPEG CHILDHOOD.*
  D. STEPHENS, 102(CANL):SPRING74-93
LIVESEY, H. THE PROFESSORS.
  M. IVINS, 441:7SEP75-32
LIVINGS, H. THAT THE MEDALS & THE
BATON BE PUT ON VIEW.
  617(TLS):10OCT75-1192
LIVINGS, H. THIS JOCKEY DRIVES
LATE NIGHTS.
  A. RENDLE, 157:SPRING73-82
LIVINGSTON, C.H., WITH F.R. LIVING-
STON & R.H. IVY, JR. - SEE DE VIG-
NEULLES, P.
LIVINGSTONE, L. TEMA Y FORMA EN
LAS NOVELAS DE AZORÍN.*
  S. BACARISSE, 86(BHS):OCT73-408
  M. DE SERVODIDIO, 546(RR):MAR73-
  152
LIVY. TITE-LIVE, "HISTOIRE RO-
MAINE." (VOL 21) (P. JAL, ED &
TRANS)
  J.P. PACKARD, 124:FEB73-301
LIVY. TITUS LIVIUS, "DER UNTERGANG
DES MAKEDONISCHEN REICHES." (H.J.
HILLEN, ED & TRANS)
  K. GRIES, 124:MAR74-309
LIXFELD, H. GOTT UND TEUFEL ALS
WELTSCHÖPFER.
  D. WARD, 221(GQ):MAY73-458
L.JUNG, M. ENGLISH DENOMINAL ADJEC-
TIVES.*
  D. KASTOVSKY, 38:BAND91HEFT4-505
  F.R. PALMER, 353:1JUN73-121
LLEÓ, C. PROBLEMS OF CATALAN PHON-
OLOGY.
  J. GULSOY, 240(HR):AUTUMN73-711
LLERENA, J.A. MADRE NATURALEZA.
HEBRA DE TIEMPO.
  A. CARRIÓN, 263:JUL-SEP74-308
LLEWELLYN, R. GREEN, GREEN MY
VALLEY NOW.
  M. LEVIN, 441:14SEP75-42

LOGAN, G.E. INDIVIDUALIZED FOREIGN
LANGUAGE LEARNING.
  R.S. DISICK, 399(MLJ):SEP-OCT74-
  271
  A.N. SMITH, JR., 399(MLJ):SEP-OCT
  74-267
LOGAN, J. THE ANONYMOUS LOVER.*
  J.R. CARPENTER, 491:DEC74-166
  M. MADIGAN, 385(MQR):SPRING75-220
  M.G. PERLOFF, 659:WINTER75-84
  P. RAMSEY, 569(SR):SPRING74-397
  J.K. ROBINSON, 598(SOR):SUMMER75-
  668
LOGAN, O. CULTURE & SOCIETY IN
VENICE: 1470 TO 1790.
  J.B. MYERS, 139:JUN73-8
LOGAN, P. MAKING A CURE.
  E. TRIMMER, 203:WINTER73-344
LOHIA, S. - SEE "THE MONGOL TALES OF
THE 32 WOODEN MEN"
LOHNER, E., ED. STUDIEN ZUM WEST-
ÖSTLICHEN DIVAN.
  H. BLUHM, 400(MLN):APR73-625
LOHNER, E. - SEE TIECK, L., F.
SCHLEGEL & A.W. SCHLEGEL
LOHNES, W.F.W. & F.W. STROTHMANN.
GERMAN. (SHORTER ED)
  C. GELLINEK, 221(GQ):MAR73-302
LOHR, T. THE MECHANICS OF THE MIND.
  J.F., 543:SEP72-162
LOI, M. ROSEAUX SUR LE MUR.
  J-L. BACKÈS, 549(RLC):OCT-DEC73-
  643
  G. GADOFFRE, 208(FS):APR74-240
LOIZOS, P. THE GREEK GIFT.
  P.G. POLYVIOU, 617(TLS):25JUL75-
  856
DE LOLLIS, C. SCRITTORI DI FRANCIA.
(G. CONTINI & V. SANTOLI, EDS)
  D. DALLA VALLE, 549(RLC):JUL-SEP73-
  468
LOMAS, H. PRIVATE & CONFIDENTIAL.
  R. GARFITT, 364:DEC74/JAN75-105
LOMBARD, A. RUMÄNSK GRAMMATIK.
  J. KRAMER, 72:BAND211HEFT3/6-451
LOMBARD, C. FRENCH ROMANTICISM ON
THE FRONTIER.
  J.S.P., 191(ELN):SEP73(SUPP)-13
LOMBARDI, O. LA NARRATIVA ITALIANA
NELLE CRISI DEL NOVECENTO.
  P.R. BALDINI, 275(IQ):SPRING74-111
LOMBARDO, A. LETTURA DEL MACBETH.
  S. ROSSI, 570(SQ):SPRING73-233
LOMTEV, T.P. PREDLOŽENIE I EGO
GRAMMATIČESKIE KATEGORII.
  W. GIRKE, 72:BAND211HEFT1/3-250
"LONDON IN COLOUR."
  90:MAR73-199
LONDRES, A. AU BAGNE; L'HOMME QUI
S'ÉVADA. DANTE N'AVAIT RIEN VU;
CHEZ LES FOUS. LE JUIF ERRANT EST
ARRIVÉ. LES PÊCHEURS DE PERLES.
  W.D. REDFERN, 617(TLS):10OCT75-
  1202
LONERGAN, B.J.F. METHOD IN THEOLOGY.
  W.F.J. RYAN, 613:SPRING73-141
LONG, C.C. THE ROLE OF NEMESIS IN
THE STRUCTURE OF SELECTED PLAYS BY
EUGENE O'NEILL.
  G. HOFFMANN, 38:BAND91HEFT2-265
LONG, J.H., ED. MUSIC IN ENGLISH
RENAISSANCE DRAMA.*
  B. PATTISON, 179(ES):JUN72-254

LONG, J.H. SHAKESPEARE'S USE OF
MUSIC.
  J.P. CUTTS, 141:WINTER73-72
  P.J. SENG, 551(RENQ):SUMMER73-234
  M. SHAPIRO, 414(MQ):APR73-310
  F. STERNFELD, 410(M&L):APR74-228
LONG, M. AT THE PIANO WITH DEBUSSY.
  A. BUSH, 607:SEP73-43
LONG, M. AT THE PIANO WITH RAVEL.*
(P. LAUMONIER, ED)
  G.W. HOPKINS, 415:SEP74-752
  R. NICHOLS, 410(M&L):OCT74-486
"THE LONG DEBATE ON POVERTY."
  G.B. TENNYSON, 445(NCF):DEC73-371
LONGACKER, R.W. FUNDAMENTALS OF
LINGUISTIC ANALYSIS.
  E. BERNÁRDEZ, 202(FMOD):JUN73-421
LONGFELLOW, H.W. THE LETTERS OF
HENRY WADSWORTH LONGFELLOW.* (VOLS
3&4) (A. HILEN, ED)
  L. BUELL, 432(NEQ):JUN73-296
LONGFORD, E. THE ROYAL HOUSE OF
WINDSOR.*
  R. FULFORD, 617(TLS):7MAR75-256
LONGFORD, E. WELLINGTON: PILLAR OF
STATE.*
  N. THOMPSON, 637(VS):JUN74-437
LONGHURST, C. LAS NOVELAS HISTÓRI-
CAS DE PÍO BAROJA.
  617(TLS):23MAY75-571
LONGLEY, M. AN EXPLODED VIEW.*
  H. MURPHY, 159(DM):AUTUMN/WINTER
  73/74-119
LONGMAN, W. TOKENS OF THE EIGH-
TEENTH CENTURY CONNECTED WITH BOOK-
SELLERS & BOOKMAKERS.
  D. CHAMBERS, 503:AUTUMN72-166
LONGMATE, N. THE GI'S. MILESTONES
IN WORKING-CLASS HISTORY.
  E.S. TURNER, 362:27NOV75-728
LONGO, O. SCHOLIA BYZANTINA IN
SOPHOCLIS OEDIPUM TYRANNUM.
  N.G. WILSON, 123:MAR74-19
LONGO, O. - SEE SOPHOCLES
LONGRIGG, R. THEIR PLEASING SPORT.
  R. USBORNE, 617(TLS):14FEB75-157
LONGSTREET, S. WE ALL WENT TO PARIS.
  H.W. BRANN, 207(FR):APR73-1083
LONGWORTH, P. THE RISE & FALL OF
VENICE.
  P. BURKE, 617(TLS):28FEB75-211
LOOGMAN, A. SWAHILI GRAMMAR & SYN-
TAX.
  E.A. GREGERSEN, 660(WORD):DEC70-
  421
LOPATE, P. BEING WITH CHILDREN.
  E.Z. FRIEDENBERG, 453:27NOV75-30
  V. GORNICK, 441:2NOV75-8
LOPE DE VEGA - SEE UNDER DE VEGA, L.
LÓPEZ, M.C. - SEE UNDER COFIÑO
LÓPEZ, M.
LÓPEZ ESTRADA, F. RUBÉN DARÍO Y LA
EDAD MEDIA.*
  G. BROTHERSTON, 86(BHS):OCT73-419
  E.U. IRVING, 238:SEP73-740
LÓPEZ ESTRADA, F. - SEE DE VEGA, L.
& C. DE MONROY
LÓPEZ MORALES, H. ESTUDIOS SOBRE
EL ESPAÑOL DE CUBA.
  V. HONSA, 238:DEC73-1125
  J.G. SIMÓN, 400(MLN):MAR73-503
LÓPEZ SERRANO, M. LA ENCUADERNACIÓN
ESPAÑOLA.
  A. HOBSON, 617(TLS):19DEC75-1524

225

LOPREATO, J. ITALIAN AMERICANS.
E.S. FALBO, 275(IQ):SPRING74-67
LORAINE, P. WRONG MAN IN THE MIRROR.
M. LEVIN, 441:2NOV75-54
LORANT, A. ORIENTATIONS ÉTRANGÈRES
CHEZ ANDRÉ MALRAUX.
G.H. BAUER, 207(FR):OCT72-169
J. DALE, 208(FS):JAN74-108
LORCH, M.D.P. - SEE UNDER DE PANIZZA
LORCH, M.
LORD, G. THE SPIDER & THE FLY.
N. CALLENDAR, 441:23MAR75-35
LORD, M. HAL PORTER.*
H.W. RHODES, 67:NOV74-233
LORDE, A. THE NEW YORK HEAD SHOP &
MUSEUM.
H. VENDLER, 441:7SEP75-6
LORE, P. WHO KILLED THE PIE MAN?
N. CALLENDAR, 441:3AUG75-24
LORENCINI, A. LA COMPARAISON ET LA
MÉTAPHORE DANS GERMINAL D'EMILE
ZOLA.
J. TAMINE, 209(FM):JUL73-310
LORENTZ, H.A. A VIEW OF CHINESE
RUGS FROM THE SEVENTEENTH TO THE
TWENTIETH CENTURY.
J. MAILEY, 57:VOL35#3-295
LORENTZ, P. LORENTZ ON FILM.
R. SCHICKEL, 441:7DEC75-90
LORENZO CRIADO, E. LENGUA Y VIDA
ESPAÑOLAS: CURSO ELEMENTAL. LENGUA
Y VIDA ESPAÑOLAS: CURSO MEDIO.
I. MOLINA, 238:DEC73-1132
LORTZ, R. CHILDREN OF THE NIGHT.
M. LEVIN, 441:19JAN75-36
LOSADA, B. POETAS GALLEGOS CONTEM-
PORÁNEOS.
270:VOL23#3-68
LOSEE, J. A HISTORICAL INTRODUCTION
TO THE PHILOSOPHY OF SCIENCE.
J. GIEDYMIN, 84:SEP73-307
LOSMAN, B. NORDEN OCH REFORMKONSIL-
IERNA 1408-49.
V. NIITEMAA, 182:VOL26#7/8-239
LOT-FALCK, E. & OTHERS - SEE "ÉTUDES
MONGOLES"
LOTCHIN, R.W. SAN FRANCISCO, 1846-
1856.
639(VQR):AUTUMN74-CLVI
LOTMAN, I.M. STRUKTURA KHUDOZHEST-
VENNOGO SLOVO.
P.M. AUSTIN, 104:FALL73-419
LOTMAN, I.M. STRUKTURA KHUDOZHEST-
VENNOGO TEKSTA.
R.L. CHAPPLE, 104:WINTER74-585
G. DE MALLAC, 550(RUSR):JAN73-98
LOTMAN, J.M. VORLESUNGEN ZU EINER
STRUKTURALEN POETIK. DIE STRUKTUR
LITERARISCHER TEXTE.
M. OLSEN, 462(OL):VOL28#1-83
LOTT, R.E. LANGUAGE & PSYCHOLOGY
IN "PEPITA JIMÉNEZ."*
J.L. BROOKS, 86(BHS):JAN73-90
C. DE COSTER, 240(HR):SPRING73-446
LOTTMAN, E. SUMMERSEA.
M. LEVIN, 441:19OCT75-46
LOUBERE, J.A.E. THE NOVELS OF
CLAUDE SIMON.
J. STURROCK, 617(TLS):3OCT75-1151
LOUGH, A.G. JOHN MASON NEALE -
PRIEST EXTRAORDINARY.
N. MASTERMAN, 617(TLS):26DEC75-
1531

LOUGH, J. THE CONTRIBUTORS TO THE
"ENCYCLOPÉDIE."
R. MERCIER, 557(RSH):OCT-DEC73-662
M.H. WADDICOR, 208(FS):APR74-198
LOUGH, J. THE "ENCYCLOPÉDIE."
H. BROWN, 207(FR):FEB73-610
M. CARDY, 188(ECR):SUMMER73-176
F.A. KAFKER, 141:SUMMER73-280
A. VARTANIAN, 322(JHI):APR-JUN73-
303
A.M. WILSON, 399(MLJ):DEC73-425
LOUGH, J. THE "ENCYCLOPÉDIE" IN
EIGHTEENTH-CENTURY ENGLAND & OTHER
STUDIES.*
R. SHACKLETON, 447(N&Q):JAN73-39
400(MLN):MAY73-880
LOUIS-DAVID, A. - SEE TYRRELL, G.
LOURIE, D., ED. ELEVEN CONTEMPORARY
AMERICAN INDIAN POETS.
V. YOUNG, 249(HUDR):WINTER74/75-
597
LOUVISH, M. - SEE HERZOG, Y.
LOUX, M.J., ED. UNIVERSALS & PAR-
TICULARS.
W. DE V., 543:DEC72-358
LOVE, F.W.D. & L.J. HONIG. OPTIONS
& PERSPECTIVES.
V.E. HANZELI, 399(MLJ):SEP-OCT74-
281
LOVE, H., ED. RESTORATION LITERA-
TURE.*
C. BENTLEY, 67:MAY74-92
R.A. FOAKES, 175:AUTUMN73-114
H. HAWKINS, 541(RES):MAY73-213
P. LEGOUIS, 189(EA):OCT-DEC73-479
E. MINER, 481(PQ):JUL73-442
W. MYERS, 677:VOL4-290
205(FMLS):APR73-215
LOVECRAFT, H.P. & W. CONOVER. LOVE-
CRAFT AT LAST.
P. ADAMS, 61:JUL75-83
LOVEJOY, D.S. THE GLORIOUS REVOLU-
TION IN AMERICA.*
J. APPLEBY, 432(NEQ):JUN73-294
LOVETT, R.W. AMERICAN ECONOMIC &
BUSINESS HISTORY INFORMATION
SOURCES.
M.H. FISHBEIN, 14:APR73-251
LOW, A. AUGUSTINE BAKER.
D.M. SCHMITTER, 551(RENQ):AUTUMN
73-327
G. SITWELL, 447(N&Q):MAY73-187
LOWANCE, M.I., JR. INCREASE MATHER.
D. WEBER, 165:FALL75-229
LOWBURY, E. THE NIGHT WATCHMAN.
A. THWAITE, 617(TLS):7NOV75-1327
LOWDEN, D. BELLMAN & TRUE.
N. CALLENDAR, 441:7SEP75-39
M. LASKI, 362:20MAR75-380
LOWE, E.A. PALAEOGRAPHICAL PAPERS,
1907-1965.* (L. BIELER, ED)
K.W. HUMPHREYS, 354:DEC73-346
LOWE, J. CERVANTES: TWO NOVELAS
EJEMPLARES.*
R.A. DAY, 238:DEC73-1135
P.N. DUNN, 86(BHS):JUL73-293
LOWE, R. & J. BRIGHT. ROBERT LOWE:
SPEECH ON THE REPRESENTATION OF THE
PEOPLE BILL & THE REDISTRIBUTION OF
SEATS BILL, MAY 1ST, 1866/JOHN
BRIGHT: SPEECH ON REFORM (XI), LON-
DON, DEC. 4TH, 1866. (H. VIEBROCK,
ED)
A.J. FARMER, 182:VOL26#5/6-155

LOWE, T.L., J.J. MULLIGAN & A.H.
WEGENER. MODERN COLLEGE GERMAN.
K.T. BEAN, 399(MLJ):DEC73-434
LOWELL, R. THE DOLPHIN.*
P. RAMSEY, 569(SR):SPRING74-400
J.K. ROBINSON, 598(SOR):SUMMER75-
668
H. VENDLER, 61:JAN75-68
M. WATTERLOND, 661:SPRING74-96
LOWELL, R. HISTORY.* FOR LIZZIE &
HARRIET.*
J.K. ROBINSON, 598(SOR):SUMMER75-
668
H. VENDLER, 61:JAN75-68
LOWELL, R.T.S. NEW PRIEST IN CON-
CEPTION BAY.
H. HORWOOD, 296:VOL4#1-178
LOWENHEIM, F.L., H.D. LANGLEY & M.
JONAS - SEE ROOSEVELT, F.D. & W.S.
CHURCHILL
LOWENSTEIN, E. BIBLIOGRAPHY OF
AMERICAN COOKERY BOOKS, 1742-1860.
M.F. GUTHEIM, 432(NEQ):JUN73-317
LÖWENSTEIN, J.I. VISION UND WIRK-
LICHKEIT.
A. TARTAKOWER, 182:VOL26#7/8-195
LOWER, A.R.M. GREAT BRITAIN'S WOOD-
YARD.
W.L. MORTON, 529(QQ):WINTER73-616
LOWRY, M. OCTOBER FERRY TO GABRI-
OLA.* (M. LOWRY, ED)
J.C. FIELD, 556(RLV):1973/1-83
LOWTHER, P. MILK STONE.
D. BESSAI, 99:JUL75-36
A. RAVEL, 198:SPRING75-116
LOYN, H.R., ED. A WULFSTAN MANU-
SCRIPT, CONTAINING INSTITUTES, LAWS
& HOMILIES, B.M. COTTON NERO A.1.
G. STORMS, 179(ES):OCT73-497
LU HSÜN. SELECTED STORIES OF LU
HSÜN.
S.P. CHONG, 268:JUL75-187
LU HSÜN. THREE STORIES. (P. KRAT-
OCHVÍL, ED)
S. O'HARROW, 399(MLJ):SEP-OCT73-
305
LU YU. THE OLD MAN WHO DOES AS HE
PLEASES. (B. WATSON, TRANS)
V. YOUNG, 249(HUDR):AUTUMN74-416
639(VQR):SPRING74-LVIII
LUARD, E. THE CONTROL OF THE SEA-
BED.
A.M. RENDEL, 617(TLS):17JAN75-55
LUARD, N. THE ROBESPIERRE SERIAL.
A. BROYARD, 441:22FEB75-25
N. CALLENDAR, 441:6APR75-18
617(TLS):21FEB75-184
LUARD, N. TRAVELLING HORSEMAN.
T.J. BINYON, 617(TLS):19DEC75-1508
DE LUBAC, H. THE ETERNAL FEMININE.
D. GRAY, 613:AUTUMN73-427
LUBACHKO, I.S. BELORUSSIA UNDER
SOVIET RULE, 1917-1957.*
W. SUKIENNICKI, 550(RUSR):APR73-
210
LUBBOCK, B. THE BEST OF SAIL.
S. SMITH, 441:7DEC75-95
LUBIENIECKI, S. HISTORIA REFORMA-
TIONIS POLONICAE.
W. WEINTRAUB, 551(RENQ):WINTER73-
476
LUBLINSKAYA, A.D. FRENCH ABSOLUT-
ISM: THE CRUCIAL PHASE, 1620-1629.
F.L. FORD, 207(FR):DEC72-453

LUBLINSKY, V.S., ED. TEXTES NOU-
VEAUX DE LA CORRESPONDANCE DE VOL-
TAIRE.
C. MERVAUD, 535(RHL):JAN-FEB73-136
LUCAS, J. ARNOLD BENNETT.
W. HALEY, 617(TLS):21FEB75-188
LUCAS, J. - SEE AUSTEN, J.
LUCAS, J. & P. CRITCH. LIFE IN THE
OCEANS.
L.H. MATTHEWS, 617(TLS):7MAR75-258
LUCAS, J.R. THE CONCEPT OF PROBA-
BILITY.*
J.P. DAY, 479(PHQ):JAN73-83
LUCAS, J.R. THE FREEDOM OF THE
WILL.*
G. ROBINSON, 393(MIND):APR73-306
LUCAS, J.R. A TREATISE ON TIME &
SPACE.
A. MATTHEW, 518:JAN74-10
A. MERCIER, 182:VOL26#13/14-460
LUCAS, R. FRIEDA LAWRENCE.
V. WHITE, 584(SWR):WINTER74-V
K. WIDMER, 594:WINTER73-547
639(VQR):WINTER74-XXVI
LUCAS, T.E. ELDER OLSON.*
R.E. AMACHER, 141:FALL73-366
R.E. AMACHER, 577(SHR):SUMMER73-
347
LUCE, J.V. HOMER & THE HEROIC AGE.
P-L. ADAMS, 61:DEC75-118
442(NY):22SEP75-132
LUCIAN. LUCIAN VON SAMOSATA, "SÄMT-
LICHE WERKE." (C-M. WIELAND, ED)
M.D. MACLEOD, 123:MAR74-134
LUCIAN. LUCIANUS. "SCYTHARUM COL-
LOQUIA." (E. STEINDL, ED)
P. CHANTRAINE, 555:VOL47FASC1-145
LUCIAN. LUCIEN, LE NAVIRE OU LES
SOUHAITS.* (G. HUSSON, ED & TRANS)
L. CASSON, 24:SPRING74-73
F. JOUAN, 555:VOL47FASC2-340
LUCIE-SMITH, E. THE BURNT CHILD.
H. SPURLING, 617(TLS):8AUG75-890
LUCIE-SMITH, E. SYMBOLIST ART.*
T. LASK, 55:NOV72-17
LUCILIUS. SATIREN. (W. KRENKEL,
ED & TRANS)
A-S. GRATWICK, 313:VOL63-302
D-C. WHITE, 122:JAN73-36
LUCINI, G.P. LIBRI E COSE SCRITTE.
(G. VIAZZI, ED) PER UNA POETICA
DEL SIMBOLISMO. (G. VIAZZI, ED)
IL VERSO LIBERO-PROPOSTA. (M.
BRUSCIA, ED)
M-C., 228(GSLI):VOL150FASC469-155
LUCIUS, H. LA LITTÉRATURE "VISION-
NAIRE" EN FRANCE DU DÉBUT DU XVIE
AU DEBUT DU XIXE SIÈCLE.
J. DECOTTIGNIES, 557(RSH):JAN-MAR
73-157
LUCK, R. GOTTFRIED KELLER ALS LIT-
ERATURKRITIKER.*
K.T. LOCHER, 221(GQ):MAY73-441
LUCKYJ, G.S-N., ED. MODERN UKRAIN-
IAN SHORT STORIES.
L. KOEHLER, 104:WINTER73-566
LUCRETIUS. DE RERUM NATURA.* (BK
3) (E.J. KENNEY, ED)
J.P. ELDER, 24:SUMMER74-167
M-F. SMITH, 123:NOV74-204
LÜDERS, H. KLEINE SCHRIFTEN. (O.
VON HINÜBER, ED)
J. FILLIOZAT, 182:VOL26#17/18-598
LUDINGTON, T. - SEE DOS PASSOS, J.

LUZI, M. VICISSITUDINE E FORMA.
G. ALMANSI, 617(TLS):24JAN75-89
LUZURIAGA, G. DEL REALISMO AL EX-
PRESIONISMO.
L.F. LYDAY, 399(MLJ):SEP-OCT73-303
LYALL, G. JUDAS COUNTRY.
N. CALLENDAR, 441:14SEP75-39
617(TLS):11JUL75-784
LYCURGUS. ORATIO IN LEOCRATEM CUM
CETERARUM LYCURGI ORATIONUM FRAG-
MENTIS POST C. SCHEIBE ET F. BLASS.
(N.C. CONOMIS, ED)
P. CHANTRAINE, 555:VOL47FASC1-135
LYDON, J.F. THE LORDSHIP OF IRELAND
IN THE MIDDLE AGES.
D.W. CASHMAN, 589:JUL74-579
LYLE, K.L. FAIR DAY, & ANOTHER
STEP BEGUN.
639(VQR):AUTUMN74-CXX
LYNAM, S. HUMANITY DICK.
R. FOSTER, 617(TLS):18JUL75-794
J. HORGAN, 362:10JUL75-61
LYNCH, O. THE POLITICS OF UNTOUCH-
ABILITY.
M. JUERGENSMEYER, 293(JAST):MAY73-
532
LYNDON, R.C. NOTES ON LOGIC.
J.C. SHEPHERDSON, 316:DEC73-644
LYNES, R. GOOD OLD MODERN.*
B. SCHWARTZ, 59(ASOC):SUMMER-FALL
74-327
LYNGSTAD, A. & S. IVAN GONCHAROV.
T.L. AMAN, 550(RUSR):APR73-215
C.A. MOSER, 104:FALL73-425
G. ROSENSHIELD, 574(SEEJ):SPRING73-
75
LYNN, E.C. TIRED DRAGONS.
505:MAR73-128
LYNN, K.S. VISIONS OF AMERICA.
W.G. HEATH, JR., 432(NEQ):JUN74-
309
LYON, B. HENRI PIRENNE.
C. CIPOLLA, 617(TLS):3OCT75-1127
LYON, R.C. - SEE SANTAYANA, G.
LYON, T.J. JOHN MUIR.
M. BUCCO, 649(WAL):FALL73-159
LYONS, A. ALL GOD'S CHILDREN.
N. CALLENDAR, 441:14SEP75-39
LYONS, B.G. VOICES OF MELANCHOLY.*
L. BABB, 551(RENQ):SPRING73-72
R.A. FOAKES, 175:SUMMER72-67
LYONS, C.R. HENRIK IBSEN.*
J. MCFARLANE, 301(JEGP):JAN74-103
E. SPRINCHORN, 397(MD):SEP73-208
LYONS, C.R. SHAKESPEARE & THE AM-
BIGUITY OF LOVE'S TRIUMPH.
G. SALGĀDO, 677:VOL4-270
LYONS, J. NOAM CHOMSKY.*
T.P. DOBSON, 140(CR):#15-82
LYONS, J. INTRODUCTION TO THEORETI-
CAL LINGUISTICS.
W. HAAS, 297(JL):FEB73-71
LYONS, J., ED. NEW HORIZONS IN
LINGUISTICS.*
C.E. BAZELL, 297(JL):FEB73-198
R.D., 179(ES):APR72-191
T.P. DOBSON, 140(CR):#15-82
A. TRAILL, 180(ESA):MAR73-53
LYONS, J.B. JAMES JOYCE & MEDICINE.
F.L. WALZL, 329(JJQ):FALL74/WINTER
75-192
LYONS, N. FISHING WIDOWS.*
H. HENKIN, 441:29JUN75-20

LYOTARD, J-F. DISCOURS, FIGURE.
G. LIPOVETSKY, 98:JUL73-615
LYTLE, A. A WAKE FOR THE LIVING.
N.K. BURGER, 441:13JUL75-14
442(NY):15SEP75-131
LYTTELTON, A. THE SEIZURE OF POWER.*
G. GERSH, 396(MODA):FALL74-432
D.D. ROBERTS, 639(VQR):WINTER74-
133
LYTTELTON, M. BAROQUE ARCHITECTURE
IN CLASSICAL ANTIQUITY.
J.B. WARD-PERKINS, 617(TLS):4APR
75-378

MAAS, H. - SEE HOUSMAN, A.E.
MAAS, P. KING OF THE GYPSIES.
P. ANDREWS, 441:9NOV75-29
C. LEHMANN-HAUPT, 441:28OCT75-37
MAAS, P. & C.A. TRYPANIS, EDS.
SANCTI ROMANI MELODI CANTICA, CAN-
TICA DUBIA.
J. GROSDIDIER DE MATONS, 555:VOL
47FASC1-96
MABBOTT, J.D. JOHN LOCKE.
J.J. JENKINS, 518:JAN74-12
MABBOTT, T.O. - SEE POE, E.A.
MABEY, D. BREADLINES.
M. PRINGLE, 362:25DEC75&1JAN76-891
MABOGUNJE, A.L. & J. OMER-COOPER.
OWU IN YORUBA HISTORY.
R. SMITH, 69:JAN73-83
MABRO, R. THE EGYPTIAN ECONOMY
1952-1972.
C. ISSAWI, 617(TLS):6JUN75-620
MC ARTHUR, D.G.M. LES CONSTRUCTIONS
VERBALES DU FRANÇAIS CONTEMPORAIN.*
N.C.W. SPENCE, 208(FS):JAN74-120
MACAULAY, K. THE HISTORY OF ST.
KILDA.
J.A. SMITH, 617(TLS):22AUG75-937
MC AULAY, S. CATCH RIDES.
A. BROYARD, 441:6AUG75-35
N. KLEIN, 441:13JUL75-30
MACAULAY, T.B. THE LETTERS OF THOM-
AS BABINGTON MACAULAY.* (VOLS 1&2)
(T. PINNEY, ED)
H.R. TREVOR-ROPER, 453:16OCT75-30
MC BAIN, E. BREAD.
N. CALLENDAR, 441:19JAN75-37
MC BAIN, E. HAIL TO THE CHIEF.*
N. CALLENDAR, 441:27JUL75-18
MC BAIN, E. WHERE THERE'S SMOKE.
N. CALLENDAR, 441:12OCT75-47
MACBEATH, I. POWER SHARING IN
INDUSTRY.
D.A. ELLIOTT, 617(TLS):4JUL75-742
MAC BETH, G. IN THE HOURS WAITING
FOR THE BLOOD TO COME.
R. GARFITT, 617(TLS):29AUG75-960
MAC BETH, G. THE SAMURAI.
G. LYONS, 441:10AUG75-10
MAC BETH, G. SHRAPNEL.*
T. EAGLETON, 565:VOL14#3-74
MAC BETH, G. THE TRANSFORMATION.
P. BAILEY, 617(TLS):7FEB75-129
J. MELLORS, 362:20FEB75-253
MC BRIDE, J. & M. WILMINGTON. JOHN
FORD.
G. MILLAR, 362:28AUG75-284
MC CABE, J. LAUREL & HARDY.
R. SCHICKEL, 441:7DEC75-88

MC CAFFERY, S. DR. SADHU'S MUFFINS.
F.W. WATT, 99:JUN75-40
MC CAFFREY, A. TO RIDE PEGASUS.
J. HAMILTON-PATERSON, 617(TLS):
14MAR75-284
MC CAGG, W. JEWISH NOBLES & GENI-
USES IN MODERN HUNGARY.
A. KATZ, 497(POLR):VOL18#4-101
MAC CAIG, N. THE WHITE BIRD.*
A. CLUYSENAAR, 565:VOL14#4-75
MAC CAIG, N. THE WORLD'S ROOM.
R. GARFITT, 364:FEB/MAR75-109
A. THWAITE, 617(TLS):23MAY75-552
MC CALL, D. JACK THE BEAR.*
639(VQR):AUTUMN74-CXX
MC CALL, D.F. & N.R. BENNETT, EDS.
ASPECTS OF WEST AFRICAN ISLAM.
H.J. FISHER, 69:JUL73-274
MC CALL, D.K. THE THEATRE OF JEAN-
PAUL SARTRE.*
H.T. MASON, 447(N&Q):SEP73-348
MC CALL, M.H., JR., ED. AESCHYLUS.
M.J. SMETHURST, 124:NOV72-170
MC CALL, M.H., JR. ANCIENT RHETORI-
CAL THEORIES OF SIMILE & COMPARI-
SON.
M.R. LEFKOWITZ, 121(CJ):FEB/MAR74-
268
MAC CALLUM, H. - SEE WOODHOUSE,
A.S.P.
MC CARRY, C. THE TEARS OF AUTUMN.
N. CALLENDAR, 441:23MAR75-35
MC CARTHY, C. CHILD OF GOD.
R. BUCKLER, 362:1MAY75-590
R. FOSTER, 617(TLS):25APR75-445
639(VQR):SPRING74-LVI
MC CARTHY, C. INNER COMPANIONS.
T. LASK, 441:16NOV75-61
MC CARTHY, E.V. THE PIED PIPER OF
HELFENSTEIN.
N. CALLENDAR, 441:28DEC75-20
MAC CARTHY, F. ALL THINGS BRIGHT &
BEAUTIFUL.*
P. OWEN, 89(BJA):WINTER73-89
MC CARTHY, M. BIRDS OF AMERICA.*
J.C. FIELD, 556(RLV):1973/1-88
MC CARTHY, P. CÉLINE.
R. COBB, 617(TLS):25JUL75-818
MC CARTHY, P., COMP. RALPH J. RIV-
ERS, U.S. REPRESENTATIVE TO CON-
GRESS FROM ALASKA, 1959-1966; AN
INVENTORY OF HIS CONGRESSIONAL PAP-
ERS IN THE ARCHIVES & MANUSCRIPT
COLLECTIONS OF THE ELMER E. RAS-
MUSON LIBRARY, UNIVERSITY OF ALASKA.
A.L. NOLEN, 14:JAN73-76
MC CAUGHEY, R.A. JOSIAH QUINCY,
1772-1864.
R.V. SPARKS, 432(NEQ):DEC74-605
MACCHIA, G. LA LETTERATURA FRAN-
CESE.
N. MANN, 208(FS):JUL74-373
L. PERTILE, 546(RR):MAR74-116
MC CLELLAN, C. THE GIRL WHO MARRIED
A BEAR.
E.K. MARANDA, 292(JAF):APR-JUN73-
190
MC CLELLAN, E. TWO JAPANESE NOVEL-
ISTS.*
M. RYAN, 318(JAOS):JAN-MAR73-90
MC CLELLAND, C.E. THE GERMAN HIS-
TORIANS & ENGLAND.*
J.A. MOSES, 125:OCT73-88

MC CLELLAND, D. THE UNKINDEST CUTS.
R. CAMPION, 200:APR73-233
MC CLELLAND, I.L. BENITO JERÓNIMO
FEIJÓO.*
H.B. HALL, 86(BHS):OCT73-404
MC CLELLAND, I.L. SPANISH DRAMA OF
PATHOS, 1750-1808.*
P.P. ROGERS, 546(RR):JAN74-72
MC CLELLAND, V.A. ENGLISH ROMAN
CATHOLICS & HIGHER EDUCATION 1830-
1903.
S. GILLEY, 637(VS):JUN74-443
MC CLINTOCK, D. THE WILD FLOWERS OF
GUERNSEY.
617(TLS):17OCT75-1245
MC CLINTOCK, R. MAN & HIS CIRCUM-
STANCES.*
W.J. KILGORE, 484(PPR):SEP73-118
MC CLOY, H. MINOTAUR COUNTRY.
N. CALLENDAR, 441:11MAY75-26
MC CLUNG, N.L. IN TIMES LIKE THESE.
W.P. WARD, 529(QQ):WINTER73-626
MC CLURE, J. SNAKE.
T.J. BINYON, 617(TLS):19DEC75-1508
M. LASKI, 362:25DEC75&1JAN76-893
MACCOBY, E.E. & C.N. JACKLIN. PSY-
CHOLOGY OF SEX DIFFERENCES.
S. EDMISTON, 441:13APR75-3
MC COLLOM, W.G. THE DIVINE AVERAGE.*
R.D. HUME, 290(JAAC):SPRING74-438
MAC COMBIE, J. THE PRINCE & THE
GENIE.
A.E. CARTER, 207(FR):DEC72-419
L.D. JOINER, 188(ECR):WINTER73-367
MC CONNELL, F.D. THE CONFESSIONAL
IMAGINATION.
J. WORDSWORTH, 617(TLS):14NOV75-
1352
MC CONNELL, J. A VOCABULARY ANALY-
SIS OF GADDA'S "PASTICCIACCIO."
R.J. DI PIETRO, 399(MLJ):MAR74-137
G.C. LEPSCHY, 402(MLR):OCT74-892
MC CORMACK, J.R., ED. GUI DE NAN-
TEUIL: CHANSON DE GESTE.*
E. RUHE, 439(NM):1973/2-364
MC CORMICK, J. AMERICAN LITERATURE:
1919-1932.
M. TERRIER, 189(EA):JAN-MAR73-117
MC CORMICK, J. THE MIDDLE DISTANCE.
295:FEB74-372
MC COURT, J. MAWRDEW CZGOWCHWZ.
P. ADAMS, 61:APR75-100
C. LEHMANN-HAUPT, 441:20FEB75-37
G. WILLS, 453:1MAY75-36
J. YOHALEM, 441:26JAN75-6
MC COY, E. WE LEARN RUSSIAN.
C. WALKER, 574(SEEJ):SPRING73-100
MC COY, E., WITH R.L. MAKINSON.
FIVE CALIFORNIA ARCHITECTS.
P. GOLDBERGER, 441:19APR75-29
MC COY, G. ARCHIVES OF AMERICAN
ART: A DIRECTORY OF RESOURCES.
M.F. DANIELS, 14:JUL73-403
MC CULLERS, C. THE MORTGAGED HEART.*
(M.G. SMITH, ED)
R. PHILLIPS, 573(SSF):WINTER73-109
MC CULLOUGH, C. STRANGER IN CHINA.*
R. DIAL, 150(DR):AUTUMN73-576
MC CULLY, H. NOBODY EVER TELLS YOU
THESE THINGS ABOUT FOOD & DRINK.
M.F-K. FISHER, 442(NY):10NOV75-183
MC CULLY, H. WASTE NOT, WANT NOT.
R.A. SOKOLOV, 441:7DEC75-78

MAC CURDY, R.R., ED.   SPANISH DRAMA
OF THE GOLDEN AGE.*
  W.C. MC CRARY, 551(RENQ):SPRING73-
  59
MAC CURDY, R.R. - SEE DE ROJAS ZOR-
  RILLA, F.
MC CUTCHAN, P.   BEWARE, BEWARE THE
BIGHT OF BENIN.
  M. LEVIN, 441:13APR75-31
MC DANIEL, J.N.   THE FICTION OF
PHILIP ROTH.
  S. PINSKER, 659:SUMMER75-386
MAC DERMOT, V.   THE CULT OF THE SEER
IN THE ANCIENT MIDDLE EAST.
  K.M. BRIGGS, 203:SPRING73-79
MC DERMOTT, J.   SETH EASTMAN'S
MISSISSIPPI.
  639(VQR):SPRING74-LXII
MC DIARMID, H.   THE HUGH MC DIARMID
ANTHOLOGY.* (M. GRIEVE & A. SCOTT,
EDS)
  A. CLUYSENAAR, 565:VOL14#2-62
MC DIARMID, M.P. - SEE JAMES I OF
SCOTLAND
MC DONAGH, E.   GIFT & CALL.
  D. CUPITT, 617(TLS):6JUN75-628
MACDONALD, A.W., ED & TRANS.   MATÉR-
IAUX POUR L'ÉTUDE DE LA LITTÉRATURE
POPULAIRE TIBÉTAINE.   (VOL 2)
  T.V. WYLIE, 244(HJAS):VOL33-286
MAC DONALD, C.   AMPUTATIONS.*
  M.G. PERLOFF, 659:WINTER75-84
MC DONALD, D. - SEE ADDISON, J. & R.
STEELE
MACDONALD, D. - SEE HERZEN, A.
MAC DONALD, D.C., ED.   GOVERNMENT &
POLITICS OF ONTARIO.
  POLITICUS, 99:JUL75-4
MC DONALD, G.   FLETCH.
  N. CALLENDAR, 441:16FEB75-13
MAC DONALD, H.   AEROFLOT.
  E.C. SHEPHERD, 617(TLS):8AUG75-900
MC DONALD, J.   THE GAME OF BUSINESS.
  L. SLOANE, 441:10MAY75-27
MAC DONALD, J.D.   THE DREADFUL LEMON
SKY.
  J. HARRISON, 441:23FEB75-32
  442(NY):7APR75-139
MAC DONALD, J.D.   THE TURQUOISE
LAMENT.*
  617(TLS):10OCT75-1174
MAC DONALD, M.   THE SYMPHONIES OF
HAVERGAL BRIAN.* (VOL 1)
  A. WHITTALL, 410(M&L):OCT74-484
MACDONALD, M.   THE WORLD FROM ROUGH
STONES.
  M. LEVIN, 441:13JUL75-32
MAC DONALD, R.H., ED.   THE LIBRARY
OF DRUMMOND OF HAWTHORNDEN.
  D. JAVITCH, 551(RENQ):WINTER73-530
  J.H.P. PAFFORD, 447(N&Q):OCT73-396
MAC DONALD, S. - SEE UNDER SILIS NA
CEAPAICH
MACDONALD, T.   THE WHITE LANES OF
SUMMER.
  F. PICKERING, 617(TLS):25JUL75-833
MC DONALD, W.A. & G.R. RAPP.   THE
MINNESOTA MESSENIA EXPEDITION.
  J. BOARDMAN, 123:NOV74-308
MC DOUGAL, S.Y.   EZRA POUND & THE
TROUBADOUR TRADITION.
  J. MAZZARO, 141:WINTER74-85
  W.G.R., 502(PRS):FALL73-276
  J. SAVILLE, 27(AL):MAY74-235

MAC DOUGALL, A.K., ED.   THE PRESS.
  186(ETC.):SEP73-323
MC DOUGALL, B.S.   THE INTRODUCTION
OF WESTERN LITERARY THEORIES INTO
MODERN CHINA, 1919-1925.*
  H.C. CHUANG, 141:SPRING73-182
  L.O-F. LEE, 302:JAN73-168
  D. MEI, 293(JAST):NOV72-144
MC DOWELL, R.B.   THE CHURCH OF IRE-
LAND 1869-1969.
  D. JENKINS, 617(TLS):17OCT75-1244
MC DOWELL, R.B. & J.A. WOODS - SEE
BURKE, E.
MACE, C.A.   SELECTED PAPERS.   (M.
MACE, ED)
  A. FLEW, 479(PHQ):OCT73-371
MACE, C.E.   TWO SPANISH-QUICHÉ
DANCE-DRAMAS OF RABINAL.*
  D. GIFFORD, 86(BHS):JAN73-104
MACEBUH, S.   JAMES BALDWIN.
  617(TLS):13JUN75-666
MACEK, E.   BIBLIOGRAFIE ČESKÉ BELE-
TRIE A LITERÁRNÍ VĚDY: METODICKA
PŘÍRUČKA.
  D. SHORT, 575(SEER):OCT74-615
MC ELROY, B.   SHAKESPEARE'S MATURE
TRAGEDIES.
  N. COUNCIL, 301(JEGP):JUL74-433
  S.J. GREENBLATT, 676(YR):SPRING74-
  447
  C. HOY, 569(SR):SPRING74-363
  639(VQR):SUMMER74-LXXVII
MC ELROY, D.   MAKING IT SIMPLE.
  M.L. ROSENTHAL, 441:28DEC75-18
MC ELROY, J.   LOOKOUT CARTRIDGE.
  G. STADE, 441:2FEB75-3
MC ELWEE, W.   THE ART OF WAR.
  M. CARVER, 617(TLS):6JUN75-619
MC EWAN, I.   FIRST LOVE, LAST RITES.
  P. ADAMS, 61:JUL75-83
  G. ANNAN, 617(TLS):16MAY75-529
  N. HEPBURN, 362:5JUN75-746
  M. MEWSHAW, 441:28SEP75-32
MAC EWEN, G.   THE ARMIES OF THE
MOON.
  R. GUSTAFSON, 102(CANL):WINTER73-
  105
MAC EWEN, G.   MAGIC ANIMALS.
  M.T. LANE, 198:SPRING75-127
  S. NAMJOSHI, 99:APR/MAY75-62
MAC EWEN, G.   NOMAN.
  L. ROGERS, 102(CANL):AUTUMN73-110
  E.R. ZIETLOW, 376:OCT73-141
MC EWEN, G.D.   THE ORACLE OF THE
COFFEE HOUSE.*
  A. PAILLER, 189(EA):JUL-SEP73-372
  P. ROGERS, 481(PQ):JUL73-497
MC FADDEN, D.   INTENSE PLEASURE.*
  R. GUSTAFSON, 102(CANL):WINTER73-
  105
MC FADDEN, M.   BACHELOR FATHERHOOD.
  A. NELSON, 441:6JUL75-4
MC FARLAND, J.D.   KANT'S CONCEPT OF
TELEOLOGY.
  J.J. MAC INTOSH, 479(PHQ):JAN73-76
  A. SAVILE, 393(MIND):OCT73-618
MC FARLAND, T.   COLERIDGE & THE PAN-
THEIST TRADITION.*
  H.B. DE GROOT, 179(ES):DEC73-600
  J.E. SCHLANGER, 542:APR-JUN73-223

MC FARLAND, T. SHAKESPEARE'S PAS-
TORAL COMEDY.*
  L. DANSON, 191(ELN):JUN74-299
  C. HOY, 569(SR):SPRING74-363
  N. RABKIN, 401(MLQ):JUN74-187
  H. SMITH, 551(RENQ):WINTER73-524
  E.M. WAITH, 301(JEGP):JAN74-117
MC FARLANE, I. - SEE CORNEILLE, P.
MC FARLANE, I.D. - SEE D'AUBIGNÉ, A.
MC FARLANE, K.B. HANS HEMLING.*
  (E. WIND, WITH G.L. HARRISS, EDS)
  C.D. CUTTLER, 54:JUN73-296
MC FARLANE, K.B. LANCASTRIAN KINGS
& LOLLARD KNIGHTS.
  J.M.W. BEAN, 589:JUL74-582
  V.J. SCATTERGOOD, 382(MAE):1974/2-
  210
MACFARLANE, K.H. TRISTAN CORBIÈRE
DANS "LES AMOURS JAUNES."
  M. TURNELL, 617(TLS):19SEP75-1068
MC GAHERN, J. THE LEAVETAKING.
  J. JEBB, 617(TLS):10JAN75-29
  M. LEVIN, 441:2FEB75-10
  J. MELLORS, 362:23JAN75-126
MC GANN, J.J. SWINBURNE.*
  T.A.J. BURNETT, 114(CHIR):VOL25#1-
  185
  B.A. INMAN, 50(ARQ):SPRING73-92
  K. MC SWEENEY, 255(HAB):SPRING73-
  140
  W.G.R., 502(PRS):FALL73-276
  M.B. RAYMOND, 191(ELN):DEC73-146
  H. SERGEANT, 175:SUMMER73-78
  F.J. SYPHER, JR., 636(VP):SUMMER
  73-173
  M. TIMKO, 579(SAQ):SUMMER74-414
  639(VQR):WINTER74-XX
MC GANN, J.J. - SEE BULWER-LYTTON,
  E.G.
MC GARRITY, J. ONCE A JOLLY BLACK
MAN.
  R. BUCKLER, 617(TLS):31JAN75-102
MC GEE, T.G. THE URBANIZATION PRO-
CESS IN THE THIRD WORLD.
  CHAN KOK ENG, 302:JAN73-189
MC GIFFERT, M. - SEE SHEPARD, T.
MC GINN, M. FRY THE LITTLE FISHES.
  A. MACLEAN, 617(TLS):4JUL75-732
MC GINNIS, D. AFTER THE DEATH OF
AN ELDER KLALLAM.
  P. GOW, 134(CP):SPRING73-90
MC GIVERN, J.S. YOUR NAME & COAT-
OF-ARMS.
  E.B. VEST, 424:JUN73-123
MC GIVERN, W.P. NIGHT OF THE JUGG-
LER.
  N. CALLENDAR, 441:8JUN75-12
MC GLONE, E.L. & R.P. FAUSTI. IN-
TRODUCTORY READINGS IN ORAL COMMUN-
ICATION.
  C.R. GRUNER, 583:SUMMER74-410
MC GRADY, D. JORGE ISAACS.
  P. JOHNSON, 399(MLJ):SEP-OCT74-293
MC GRADY, M. THE KITCHEN SINK
PAPERS.
  O. BEAN, 441:14DEC75-4
MC GRATH, D.F., ED. BOOKMAN'S
PRICE INDEX. (VOL 6)
  J.R. PAYNE, 517(PBSA):APR-JUN74-
  192
MC GREGOR, R.S. OUTLINE OF HINDI
GRAMMAR.
  P.E. HOOK, 293(JAST):NOV72-170
                            [CONTINUED]

[CONTINUING]
  H.J. VERMEER, 343:BAND17HEFT2-203
  M.C. SHAPIRO, 399(MLJ):DEC74-427
MAC GREGOR, S. THE SINNER.*
  M. MAC DOUGALL, 588:APR74-256
MC GREW, J.H. - SEE "STURLUNGA SAGA"
MC GUINNESS, B.F., T. NYBERG & G.H.
VON WRIGHT - SEE WITTGENSTEIN, L.
MC GUIRE, W. - SEE FREUD, S. & C.G.
JUNG
MACHADO, A. SOLEDADES; GALERÍAS;
OTROS POEMAS. (G. RIBBANS, ED)
  617(TLS):23MAY75-576
MACHADO, C.D. - SEE RANGEL, A.
MACHADO, M. ANTOLOGÍA. (E. MIRÓ,
ED)
  G. BROTHERSTON, 617(TLS):23MAY75-
  559
MACHADO DE ASSIS, J.M. COUNSELOR
AYRES' MEMORIAL. (H. CALDWELL,
TRANS)
  A.I. BAGBY, JR., 263:APR-JUN74-180
DE MACHAUT, G. LA LOUANGE DES
DAMES.* (N. WILKINS, ED)
  D. EVANS, 447(N&Q):MAY73-200
MACHIAVELLI, N. LEGAZIONI, COMMIS-
SARIE, SCRITTI DI GOVERNO. (VOL 1)
(F. CHIAPPELLI, ED)
  H. BUTTERFIELD, 551(RENQ):AUTUMN
  73-314
MC HUGH, J. THE MOTHER OF JESUS IN
THE NEW TESTAMENT.
  E.L. MASCALL, 617(TLS):18JUL75-812
MC HUGH, R., ED. JACK B. YEATS: A
CENTENARY GATHERING.
  R. HOGAN, 295:APR74-1031
MC HUGH, R. & P. EDWARDS, EDS. JON-
ATHAN SWIFT 1667-1967.
  P. DANCHIN, 179(ES):APR72-166
MC INERNEY, M. PEADER O'DONNELL.
  G. Ó TUATHAIGH, 617(TLS):18APR75-
  424
MC INERNY, R. GATE OF HEAVEN.
  M. LEVIN, 441:8JUN75-20
MAC INNES, H. CLIMB TO THE LOST
WORLD.
  617(TLS):7FEB75-149
MAC INNES, H. THE SNARE OF THE
HUNTER.*
  N. CALLENDAR, 441:30MAR75-24
MAC INNIS, D.E. RELIGIOUS POLICY &
PRACTICE IN COMMUNIST CHINA.
  R.C., 293(JAST):FEB73-386
MC INTOSH, C. THE CHOICE OF LIFE.*
  S.M. TAVE, 401(MLQ):DEC74-428
MC INTOSH, J. THOREAU AS ROMANTIC
NATURALIST.
  S. PAUL, 301(JEGP):JUL74-458
MC INTOSH, L., T.V. RAMOS & R. MOR-
ALES GOULET. ADVANCING IN ENGLISH.
  D. DANIELSON, 399(MLJ):JAN-FEB73-
  77
MAC INTYRE, A. AGAINST THE SELF-
IMAGES OF THE AGE.
  A. MONTEFIORE, 393(MIND):APR73-311
  483:JAN73-100
MAC INTYRE, A., ED. HEGEL.
  A. QUINTON, 453:29MAY75-34
MC INTYRE, J., COMP. MIND IN THE
WATERS.*
  J.Z. YOUNG, 453:17JUL75-3
  442(NY):14JUL75-100
MAC ISAAC, S. FREUD & ORIGINAL SIN.
  G. HOROWITZ, 99:APR/MAY75-53

232

MC LAREN, J., ED. TOWARDS A NEW
AUSTRALIA.
C.A. HUGHES, 381:MAR73-112
MC LAUCHLAN, J. NOSTROMO.
S. PINSKER, 136:VOL5#2-84
MC LAUCHLAN, J. SHAKESPEARE: OTHEL-
LO.
R.A. FOAKES, 175:SUMMER72-67
MC LAUGHLIN, B.L. DIDEROT ET L'AM-
ITIÉ.
G. MAY, 546(RR):JAN74-66
M.A. SIMONS, 400(MLN):MAY73-886
MC LAUGHLIN, R. & P. FORAN. NOTHING
TO REPORT.
N. CALLENDAR, 441:20JUL75-26
MC LAURIN, A. VIRGINIA WOOLF.
L.D. BLOOM, 454:SPRING74-255
A. FLEISHMAN, 594:WINTER73-559
J. GUIGUET, 189(EA):JUL-SEP73-338
T. ROGERS, 175:AUTUMN73-119
S.M. SMITH, 89(BJA):AUTUMN73-415
MACLEAN, A. CIRCUS.
M. LEVIN, 441:14SEP75-42
617(TLS):6JUN75-617
MACLEAN, A.A. NORTH BRITISH ALBUM.
617(TLS):21NOV75-1397
MACLEAN, A.D., ED. WINTER'S TALES
21.
D. LODGE, 617(TLS):26DEC75-1533
MACLEAN, F. TO THE BACK OF BEYOND.
J. ZORN, 441:7SEP75-4
442(NY):4AUG75-91
MC LEAN, R. VICTORIAN BOOK DESIGN &
COLOUR PRINTING.* (2ND ED)
A.B., 155:MAY73-125
D. CHAMBERS, 503:SPRING73-49
P.H. MUIR, 78(BC):SUMMER73-243
MC LEAN, S.K. THE "BÄNKELSANG" &
THE WORK OF BERTOLT BRECHT.
R. GRIMM, 406:FALL74-318
MC LEAVE, H. ONLY GENTLEMEN CAN
PLAY.*
617(TLS):7FEB75-129
MAC LEISH, A. THE GREAT AMERICAN
FOURTH OF JULY PARADE.
E. WEEKS, 61:JUN75-94
MAC LEISH, A. THE MIDDLE ENGLISH
SUBJECT-VERB CLUSTER.*
R. NAGUCKA, 353:15JUN73-121
MC LEISH, J. SOVIET PSYCHOLOGY.
E. MARTIN, 617(TLS):12DEC75-1493
MC LELLAN, D. KARL MARX.*
A. RYAN, 617(TLS):1AUG75-875
MC LELLAN, D. THE THOUGHT OF KARL
MARX.
R. BLACK, 393(MIND):OCT73-623
D-H. RUBEN, 479(PHQ):JAN73-79
MC LEMORE, R.A., ED. A HISTORY OF
MISSISSIPPI.
L. CAMPBELL, 9(ALAR):OCT73-273
MC LEOD, A.L. THE PATTERN OF NEW
ZEALAND CULTURE.
S.B. LILJEGREN, 439(NM):1973/2-354
MC LEOD, A.L. - SEE SMUTS, J.C.
MC LEOD, H. CLASS & RELIGION IN THE
LATE VICTORIAN CITY.
D. MARTIN, 617(TLS):14FEB75-170
MACLEOD, R. STYLE & SOCIETY.
P.F. NORTON, 576:MAR73-75
MC LEVY, J. THE CASEBOOK OF A VIC-
TORIAN DETECTIVE. (G. SCOTT-MON-
CRIEFF, ED)
P. KEATING, 617(TLS):25JUL75-826

MC LOGHLAN, D. THE LAST HEADLANDS.
A. CLUYSENAAR, 565:VOL14#2-62
MC MAHON, J.C. HUMANS BEING.
T.R.F., 543:SEP72-165
MC MANAWAY, J.G. STUDIES IN SHAKE-
SPEARE, BIBLIOGRAPHY & THEATER.
M. MINCOFF, 179(ES):JUN72-254
MC MANUS, E.J. BLACK BONDAGE IN THE
NORTH.
L.W. BROWN, 656(WMQ):APR74-337
F.J. MILLER, 432(NEQ):MAR74-168
MC MASTER, J. THACKERAY: THE MAJOR
NOVELS.*
J.I.M. STEWART, 155:MAY73-128
G. THOMAS, 175:SUMMER72-71
K. WILSON, 529(QQ):SUMMER73-317
MACMILLAN, D.S., ED. CANADIAN BUSI-
NESS HISTORY.
A.G. GREEN, 529(QQ):AUTUMN73-461
MACMILLAN, H. AT THE END OF THE
DAY: 1961-1963.*
M. MANDELBAUM, 676(YR):SUMMER74-
599
MACMILLAN, H. THE PAST MASTERS.
J.P. MACKINTOSH, 362:20NOV75-679
MACMILLAN, W.M. MY SOUTH AFRICAN
YEARS.
J. LEWIN, 617(TLS):26DEC75-1545
MC MILLIN, S., ED. RESTORATION &
EIGHTEENTH-CENTURY COMEDY.
566:AUTUMN73-38
MAC MULLEN, R. ROMAN SOCIAL RELA-
TIONS, 50 B.C. TO A.D. 284.*
639(VQR):AUTUMN74-CL
MC MURTRY, L. TERMS OF ENDEARMENT.
P-L. ADAMS, 61:NOV75-126
C. LEHMANN-HAUPT, 441:22OCT75-49
R. TOWERS, 441:19OCT75-4
442(NY):27OCT75-166
MACNAB, I. THE 42ND YEAR OF MRS.
CHARLES PRESCOTT.
M. LEVIN, 441:31AUG75-13
MC NALLY, R.T. CHAADAYEV & HIS
FRIENDS.*
J.B. GEBHARD, 574(SEEJ):SPRING73-
72
L. SCHAPIRO, 575(SEER):JAN74-142
E.C. THADEN, 550(RUSR):JAN73-93
MC NALLY, R.T. & R. FLORESCU. IN
SEARCH OF DRACULA.
C. FRAYLING, 364:JUN/JUL74-100
B.F. KIRTLEY, 292(JAF):OCT-DEC73-
400
MAC NAMARA, D.E.J. & M. RIEDEL, EDS.
POLICE.
M. CAIN, 617(TLS):26SEP75-1102
MC NAMARA, E. DIVING FOR THE BODY.
C.G. LIMAN, 198:FALL75-143
S. SCOBIE, 198:SUMMER75-106
F.W. WATT, 99:JUN75-40
MC NAMARA, E. HARD WORDS.
D. BARBOUR, 529(QQ):SPRING73-141
MC NAMARA, E. PASSAGES & OTHER
POEMS.
C.G. LIMAN, 198:FALL75-143
G. MC WHIRTER, 376:APR73-236
MC NAMARA, J.A. GILLES AYCELIN.
G.T. BEECH, 377:NOV74-175
T.S.R. BOASE, 382(MAE):1974/3-319
MC NAUGHT, K. & D.J. BERCUSON. THE
WINNIPEG STRIKE: 1919.
R. ALLEN, 99:APR/MAY75-28

234

MC NAUGHTON, W. THE BOOK OF SONGS.*
E.G. PULLEYBLANK, 293(JAST):NOV72-
134
C.H. WANG, 352(LE&W):VOL16#3-1069
MC NAUGHTON, W., ED. CHINESE LITER-
ATURE.
V. YOUNG, 249(HUDR):AUTUMN74-416
MC NEAL, R.H. BRIDE OF THE REVOLU-
TION.
B. FARNSWORTH, 550(RUSR):JUL73-324
MC NEAL, R.H., GENERAL ED. RESOLU-
TIONS & DECISIONS OF THE COMMUNIST
PARTY OF THE SOVIET UNION.
A. BROWN, 617(TLS):14NOV75-1350
MC NEAL, R.H., ED. RUSSIA IN TRAN-
SITION, 1905-1914.
D. SENESE, 104:WINTER74-603
MC NEIL, F. THE RIM OF THE PARK.
D. BESSAI, 102(CANL):SPRING74-124
MAC NEILL, D. BY COMMAND OF THE
VICEROY.
M. LEVIN, 441:14DEC75-33
MC NEILL, J.T. THE CELTIC CHURCHES.
P. BROWN & S. MAC CORMACK, 453:
20FEB75-19
MC NEILL, W.H. THE SHAPE OF EURO-
PEAN HISTORY.*
639(VQR):AUTUMN74-CXLIII
MC NEILL, W.H. VENICE: THE HINGE OF
EUROPE, 1081-1797.*
F. BRAUDEL, 617(TLS):28FEB75-210
MC NERNEY, R.F., JR. - SEE O'LEARY,
D.F.
MC NICHOL, S. VIRGINIA WOOLF: "TO
THE LIGHTHOUSE."
J. GUIGUET, 189(EA):JUL-SEP73-338
MC NICKLE, D. INDIAN MAN.
K. YOUNG, 649(WAL):FALL73-161
MC NICOL, D. A PRIMER OF SIGNAL
DETECTION THEORY.
L.L. CUDDY, 255(HAB):WINTER73-49
MC NULTY, R. - SEE ARIOSTO, L.
MC PEEK, J.A.S. THE BLACK BOOK OF
KNAVES & UNTHRIFTS IN SHAKESPEARE
& OTHER RENAISSANCE AUTHORS.
C. CAMDEN, 570(SQ):SPRING73-238
MC PHEE, J. PIECES OF THE FRAME.
E. HOAGLAND, 441:22JUN75-3
C. LEHMANN-HAUPT, 441:18JUN75-33
MC PHEE, J. THE SURVIVAL OF THE
BARK CANOE.
C. LEHMANN-HAUPT, 441:27NOV75-31
R. TODD, 61:DEC75-114
MACPHERSON, C.B. DEMOCRATIC THEORY.
M.T. DALGARNO, 518:JAN74-15
MAC PHERSON, M. THE POWER LOVERS.
J. O'REILLY, 441:30NOV75-8
MC PHERSON, S. RADIATION.*
J. MARTIN, 491:MAY75-103
MC PHERSON, T. THE ARGUMENT FROM
DESIGN.
M. PATERSON, 154:DEC73-733
G. SLATER, 479(PHQ):JUL73-283
MC PHERSON, T. PHILOSOPHY & RELIG-
IOUS BELIEF.
D. BASTOW, 518:OCT74-20
A. KENNY, 617(TLS):7FEB75-145
MC PHERSON, T. SOCIAL PHILOSOPHY.*
R.F. ATKINSON, 483:APR73-188
MC QUEEN, I. SHERLOCK HOLMES DETEC-
TED.*
C. JAMES, 453:20FEB75-15

MAC QUEEN, J., ED. BALLATTIS OF
LUVE.*
P.S. MACAULAY, 179(ES):FEB73-65
A.A. MACDONALD, 433:OCT73-427
MACREADY, W.C. - SEE "LORD BYRON:
WERNER, A TRAGEDY"
MACRÍ, O. ENSAYO DE MÉTRICA SINTAG-
MÁTICA (EJEMPLOS DEL "LIBRO DE
BUEN AMOR" Y DEL "LABERINTO" DE
JUAN DE MENA).
D.C. CLARKE, 240(HR):WINTER73-92
MAC SHANE, F., ED. FORD MADOX FORD:
THE CRITICAL HERITAGE.
295:FEB74-606
MC SHANE, P. RANDOMNESS, STATISTICS
& EMERGENCE.
B. BRIER, 486:SEP73-468
MAC SKIMMING, R. FORMENTERA.
F. SUTHERLAND, 102(CANL):WINTER74-
121
MAC STIOFAIN, S. MEMOIRS OF A REV-
OLUTIONARY.
K. KYLE, 362:16OCT75-518
MACURA, P. RUSSIAN-ENGLISH DICTION-
ARY OF ELECTROTECHNOLOGY & ALLIED
SCIENCES.
H.K. ZALUCKY, 574(SEEJ):SUMMER72-
257
MC WHIRTER, G. BODYWORKS.
M. BAXTER, 99:DEC75/JAN76-48
MC WHIRTER, G. CATALAN POEMS.*
F. DAVEY, 102(CANL):WINTER73-118
MC WILLIAMS, J.P., JR. POLITICAL
JUSTICE IN A REPUBLIC.
J.F. BEARD, 27(AL):MAR74-110
R.E. SPILLER, 445(NCF):DEC73-362
MC WILLIAMS, W.C. THE IDEA OF FRA-
TERNITY IN AMERICA.*
H.B. GOW, 396(MODA):FALL74-424
MC WILLIAMS-TULLBERG, R. WOMEN AT
CAMBRIDGE.
B. HARRISON, 617(TLS):28NOV75-1404
MĄCZYŃSKI, I. LEXICON LATINO-POLON-
ICUM, REGIOMONTI BORUSSIAE, 1564.
(R. OLESCH, ED)
H. LEEMING, 575(SEER):JUL74-452
MADDEN, D. CASSANDRA SINGING.
S. PINSKER, 145(CRIT):VOL15#2-15
MADDEN, D., ED. NATHANAEL WEST.
J. MARTIN, 27(AL):NOV74-410
MADDEN, L., ED. ROBERT SOUTHEY:
THE CRITICAL HERITAGE.
K.C., 191(ELN):SEP73(SUPP)-61
J. RAIMOND, 189(EA):OCT-DEC73-482
MADDOW, B. EDWARD WESTON: FIFTY
YEARS.*
M. HAWORTH-BOOTH, 617(TLS):11JUL
75-759
MADDOX, J. BEYOND THE ENERGY
CRISIS.
P. HOBDAY, 362:14AUG75-220
MADDOX, R.J. THE NEW LEFT & THE
ORIGINS OF THE COLD WAR.*
T.H. ETZOLD, 396(MODA):WINTER74-96
"MADE IN AMERICA: PRINTMAKING 1760-
1860."
A. FERN, 127:SPRING74-274
MADELUNG, A.M.A. THE LAXDAELA SAGA.*
P. SCHACH, 406:WINTER74-422
MADGE, C. & B. WEINBERGER. ART
STUDENTS OBSERVED.
A. DEWDNEY, 592:JUL-AUG73-52
MADISON, C.A. IRVING TO IRVING.
L.D. RUBIN, 617(TLS):2MAY75-491

"JAMES MADISON: A BIOGRAPHY IN HIS OWN WORDS." (M.D. PETERSON, ED)
 639(VQR):SUMMER74-LXXXVIII
"MADRID: CUADERNOS DE LA CASA DE LA CULTURA." (NO. 1-3)
 A. TERRY, 617(TLS):9MAY75-519
MADSEN, A. BORDERLINES.
 N. CALLENDAR, 441:5OCT75-47
MADSEN, B.D. - SEE REID, A.J.
MAE, V. THURSDAYS & EVERY OTHER SUNDAY OFF.
 J.G., 502(PRS):FALL73-277
MAEGAARD, J. STUDIEN ZUR ENTWICK-LUNG DES DODEKAPHONEN SATZES BEI ARNOLD SCHÖNBERG.
 M. CARNER, 410(M&L):JUL74-351
MAETZKE, G. & M. CRISTOFANI, EDS. NUOVE LETTURE DI MONUMENTI ETRUSCHI DOPO IL RESTAURO.
 A. LENGYEL, 54:MAR73-140
MAGALANER, M. THE FICTION OF KATH-ERINE MANSFIELD.
 R.S. KENNEDY, 295:FEB74-719
 C.R. THOMAS, 573(SSF):FALL73-430
MAGALOTTI, L. RELAZIONI D'INGHIL-TERRA 1668 E 1688. (A.M. CRINÒ, ED)
 D. NOLAN, 402(MLR):JUL74-664
MAGEE, B., ED. MODERN BRITISH PHILOSOPHY.*
 J. DONNELLY, 258:MAR73-143
 C.K. GRANT, 393(MIND):JUL73-456
MAGEE, B. KARL POPPER.*
 483:OCT73-409
MAGEE, D. INFINITE RICHES.
 J.M. EDELSTEIN, 517(PBSA):JUL-SEP 74-341
MAGEE, J. NORTHERN IRELAND.
 G. Ó TUATHAIGH, 617(TLS):18APR75-424
MAGEE, W. URBAN GORILLA.
 A. CLUYSENAAR, 565:VOL14#4-75
MAGGS, B.D. BOOKBINDING IN GREAT BRITAIN.
 A. HOBSON, 617(TLS):19DEC75-1524
MAGIDOFF, R. YEHUDI MENUHIN. (REV BY H. RAYNOR)
 A. BLYTH, 415:APR74-307
MAGNER, J.E., JR. JOHN CROWE RAN-SOM.*
 G. MC FADDEN, 295:FEB74-761
 T.D. YOUNG, 219(GAR):SUMMER73-275
MAGNER, T.F. INTRODUCTION TO THE CROATIAN & SERBIAN LANGUAGE.
 R. BUGARSKI, 574(SEEJ):FALL72-368
 M. SURDUCKI, 104:FALL73-397
MAGNER, T.F. SOVIET DISSERTATIONS FOR ADVANCED DEGREES IN RUSSIAN LITERATURE & SLAVIC LINGUISTICS, 1934-1962.
 J.J. DOSSICK, 574(SEEJ):SPRING72-133
MAGNER, T.F. & L. MATEJKA. WORD ACCENT IN MODERN SERBO-CROATIAN.*
 W. BROWNE, 574(SEEJ):WINTER72-503
 E.T. PURCELL, 104:WINTER74-584
MAGNY, C-E. THE AGE OF THE AMERICAN NOVEL.*
 295:FEB74-476
MAGOFFIN, R. FAIR DINKUM MATILDA.
 F.T. MACARTNEY, 581:MAR74-80
MAGRIS, C. LONTANO DA DOVE.
 I.H. SOLBRIG, 133:1973/3-281

MAGRUDER, J.S. AN AMERICAN LIFE.*
 K. KYLE, 362:27FEB75-283
 J. VAIZEY, 617(TLS):16MAY75-532
MAGUIRE, J.H. MARY HALLOCK FOOTE.
 M. BUCCO, 649(WAL):FALL73-159
MAGUIRE, R.A., ED. GOGOL FROM THE TWENTIETH CENTURY.
 A. DE JONGE, 617(TLS):7MAR75-251
"A MAGYARORSZÁGI NYELVTUDOMÁNY BIB-LIOGRÁFIÁJA."
 G.F. MEIER, 682(ZPSK):BAND26HEFT 1/2-170
MAHANEY, W.E. JOHN WEBSTER. DECEP-TION IN JOHN WEBSTER'S PLAYS.
 C.K. SPIVACK, 568(SCN):FALL74-57
MAHER, J.T. THE TWILIGHT OF SPLEN-DOR.
 P. GOLDBERGER, 441:30NOV75-48
MAHFOUZ, N. AL-KARNAK.
 S. ELKHADEM, 268:JAN75-81
MAHMOUDIAN, M. LES MODALITÉS NOMIN-ALES EN FRANÇAIS.*
 N.C.W. SPENCE, 208(FS):JAN74-120
 M. TUŢESCU, 353:15JUL73-113
MAHMUD, S. HUERTO PALESTINO.
 J. CANTERA, 202(FMOD):JUN73-405
MAHN, L.H. ZUR MORPHOLOGIE UND SE-MANTIK ENGLISCHER VERBEN AUF -IFY MIT BERÜCKSICHTIGUNG FRANZÖSISCHER UND DEUTSCHER ENTSPRECHUNGEN.
 E. BURGSCHMIDT, 38:BAND91HEFT1-102
MAHON, D. ECCLESIASTES.*
 S. CURTIS, 148:SPRING72-85
MAHON, D. LIVES.*
 A. CLUYSENAAR, 565:VOL14#1-70
MAHON, D. THE SNOW PARTY.
 A. THWAITE, 617(TLS):7NOV75-1327
MAHON, J.K. THE WAR OF 1812.
 C.B. BROOKS, 656(WMQ):JAN74-160
 J.H. SCHROEDER, 432(NEQ):SEP73-478
MAHONEY, I. MADAME CATHERINE.
 P. ADAMS, 61:AUG75-88
 J. O'REILLY, 441:20JUL75-4
MAHOWALD, M.B. AN IDEALISTIC PRAG-MATISM.
 N.L., 543:JUN73-759
MAIER, J. & R.W. WEATHERHEAD - SEE TANNENBAUM, F.
MAIER, P. FROM RESISTANCE TO REVO-LUTION.*
 R. MIDDLETON, 173(ECS):SPRING74-368
MAIERÙ, A. TERMINOLOGIA LOGICA DELLA TARDA SCOLASTICA.
 C.B. SCHMITT, 319:JAN75-99
MAILER, N. THE FIGHT.
 P. ADAMS, 61:SEP75-85
 C. LEHMANN-HAUPT, 441:14JUL75-23
 G. WILLS, 453:30OCT75-3
 M. WOOD, 441:27JUL75-1
 442(NY):11AUG75-86
MAILER, N. MARILYN.*
 R. BOWERS, 200:DEC73-621
 L. HUDSON, 617(TLS):24JAN75-77
MAILER, N. THE PRISONER OF SEX.*
 295:FEB74-403
MAILHOT, L. LA LITTÉRATURE QUÉBEC-OISE.*
 A.A., 102(CANL):AUTUMN74-128
MAILLET, A. LES CRASSEUX.* LA SAGOUINE.
 M. DORSINVILLE, 102(CANL):SUMMER74-90

MAIN, J.T. THE SOVEREIGN STATES,
1775-1783.
L.G. DE PAUW, 656(WMQ):APR74-319
MAINER, J-C. - SEE MARTÍN-SANTOS, L.
MAINSTONE, R. DEVELOPMENTS IN
STRUCTURAL FORM.
P. STEADMAN, 617(TLS):3OCT75-1153
MAINWARING, M. - SEE TURGENEV, I.S.
MAISONNEUVE, J. PSYCHOSOCIOLOGIE
DES AFFINITÉS.
M. CHASTAING, 542:JAN-MAR73-89
MAJENDIE, V.D. & C.O. BROWN. MILI-
TARY BREECH-LOADING RIFLES.
617(TLS):7FEB75-149
MAJEWSKI, H.F. THE PREROMANTIC
IMAGINATION OF L-S. MERCIER.
G. BOLLÈME, 535(RHL):NOV-DEC73-
1086
J. GILLET, 549(RLC):OCT-DEC73-640
M. GSTEIGER, 149:DEC74-339
H.T. PATTERSON, 208(FS):JUL74-333
MAJOR, A. L'ÉPOUVANTAIL.
F.M. MACRI, 296:VOL3#4-95
MAJOR, C. REFLEX & BONE STRUCTURE.
T. LASK, 441:30NOV75-61
MAJSTRAK, M. & H. ROSSMANN. BIBLIO-
GRAPHIE DER INTERPRETATIONEN.
W. REAL, 430(NS):JUN73-344
MAKINSON, D. ASPECTOS DE LA LÓGICA
MODAL.
F.G. ASENJO, 316:JUN73-330
MAKINSON, D.C. TOPICS IN MODERN
LOGIC.
R. BLANCHÉ, 542:OCT-DEC73-478
E. MARTIN, 63:AUG74-178
MAKKAI, V.B., ED. PHONOLOGICAL
THEORY.
M.H. GERTNER, 238:DEC73-1131
MAKULU, H.F. EDUCATION, DEVELOPMENT
& NATION BUILDING IN INDEPENDENT
AFRICA.
S. MILBURN, 69:APR73-167
MALAGOLI, L. L'ANTI-OTTOCENTO.
V.A.S., 275(IQ):FALL-WINTER73(VOL
17#66)-70
MALAGOLI, L. SEICENTO ITALIANO E
MODERNITÀ.
A.N. MANCINI, 276:SUMMER73-321
V.S., 275(IQ):SUMMER73-110
MALAMUD, B. REMBRANDT'S HAT.*
L.T. LEMON, 502(PRS):FALL73-270
R. WINEGARTEN, 390:OCT73-76
MALCOLM, N. PROBLEMS OF MIND.*
J. DONNELLY, 258:JUN73-305
MALCOLMSON, R.W. POPULAR RECREA-
TIONS IN ENGLISH SOCIETY 1700-1850.
566:SPRING74-98
MALE, D.A. APPROACHES TO DRAMA.
J. ALLEN, 157:WINTER73-86
MAŁECKI, J.M. ZWIĄZKI HANDLOWE
MIAST POLSKICH Z GDAŃSKIEM W XVI I
PIERWSZEJ POŁOWIE XVII WIEKU.
P. BUSHKOVITCH, 497(POLR):VOL18#3-
86
DE MALHERBE, F. OEUVRES.* (A.
ADAM, ED)
M. SIMON, 535(RHL):NOV-DEC73-1061
MALICET, M. - SEE CLAUDEL, P.
MALIK, H., ED. IQBAL.*
M.N. PEARSON, 318(JAOS):APR-JUN73-
250
MALING, A. BENT MAN.
N. CALLENDAR, 441:12OCT75-47
MALIPIERO, G.F. - SEE SOGRAFI, A.S.

MALKIEL, Y. ESSAYS ON LINGUISTIC
THEMES.*
M. BALABAN, 353:1MAR73-91
MALKIEL, Y. LINGUISTICA GENERALE,
FILOLOGIA ROMANZA, ETIMOLOGIA.*
C. SCHWARZE, 260(IF):BAND78-296
MALKIEL, Y. PATTERNS OF DERIVATION-
AL AFFIXATION IN THE CABRANIEGO
DIALECT OF EAST-CENTRAL ASTURIAN.*
J. PURCZINSKY, 350:MAR74-185
R. ST. CLAIR, 353:15OCT73-116
MALKOFF, K. CROWELL'S HANDBOOK OF
CONTEMPORARY AMERICAN POETRY.*
27(AL):MAY74-244
MALLARMÉ, S. CORRESPONDANCE, IV.
(H. MONDOR & L.J. AUSTIN, EDS)
E. SOUFFRIN, 208(FS):OCT74-480
MALLE, L. LE SOUFFLE AU COEUR.
B. KAY, 207(FR):OCT72-219
MALLEA, E. TRISTE PIEL DEL UNIVER-
SO.
M.I. LICHTBLAU, 238:SEP73-739
MALLET-JORIS, F. THE UNDERGROUND
GAME.
M. ENGEL, 441:24AUG75-16
442(NY):29SEP75-131
MALLO, J. & J. RODRÍGUEZ-CASTELLANO.
ESPAÑA. (2ND ED)
H.R. STONE, 238:MAY73-534
MALLORY, D. TARGET MANHATTAN.
N. CALLENDAR, 441:14SEP75-39
MALLOY, R.L. TRAVEL GUIDE TO THE
PEOPLE'S REPUBLIC OF CHINA.
J.A. & J.L. COHEN, 441:5OCT75-5
MALMBERG, B. LES DOMAINES DE LA
PHONÉTIQUE.*
A. MALÉCOT, 361:SEP73-125
MALMBERG, B. PHONÉTIQUE FRANÇAISE.*
D.C. WALKER, 545(RPH):AUG73-131
MALMSTRÖM, G. MENNESKEHJERTETS
VERDEN.
E.M. ELLESTAD, 563(SS):WINTER74-80
MALOF, J. A MANUAL OF ENGLISH
METERS.
R.A. NAGER, 599:SPRING73-189
MALONE, D. JEFFERSON THE PRESIDENT:
SECOND TERM, 1805-1809.*
R.B. MORRIS, 639(VQR):SUMMER74-459
MALONEY, G.A. RUSSIAN HESYCHASM.
N. GORODETZKY, 575(SEER):OCT74-626
MALONEY, W.C. A SKETCH OF THE HIS-
TORY OF KEY WEST, FLORIDA.
E.C. WILLIAMSON, 9(ALAR):JUL73-231
MALORY, T. WORKS. (2ND ED)
K.H. GÖLLER, 38:BAND91HEFT1-121
MALORY, T. THE WORKS OF SIR THOMAS
MALORY.* (2ND ED) (E. VINAVER, ED)
K.H. GÖLLER, 38:BAND91HEFT1-121
MALRAUX, A. LES CHÊNES QU'ON ABAT...
F-E. DORENLOT, 207(FR):OCT72-220
MALRAUX, A. LAZARE.
C. RICKS, 617(TLS):18JUL75-790
MALRAUX, A. ORAISONS FUNÈBRES.
F-E. DORENLOT, 207(FR):FEB73-663
MALRAUX, A. LE TRIANGLE NOIR.
F-E. DORENLOT, 207(FR):APR73-1024
MALTBY, W.S. THE BLACK LEGEND IN
ENGLAND.
D. JENSEN, 551(RENQ):AUTUMN73-322
D.W. LOMAX, 86(BHS):OCT73-394
MALZBERG, B. THE DAY OF THE BURN-
ING. THE SODOM & GOMORRAH BUSI-
NESS.
G. JONAS, 441:12JAN75-33

MALZBERG, B. UNDERLAY.
R. SALE, 249(HUDR):WINTER74/75-628
MALZBERG, B.N. GUERNICA NIGHT.
J.C. OATES, 441:21SEP75-18
MAMATEY, V.S. & R. LUŽA, EDS. A
HISTORY OF THE CZECHOSLOVAK REPUB-
LIC, 1918-1948.*
F.L. CARSTEN, 575(SEER):OCT74-619
639(VQR):SPRING74-LIV
MAMPEL, S. DIE SOZIALISTISCHE VER-
FASSUNG DER DEUTSCHEN DEMOKRATIS-
CHEN REPUBLIK. (3RD ED)
G. STRICKRODT, 182:VOL26#7/8-205
DE MAN, P. BLINDNESS & INSIGHT.*
F. GARBER, 131(CL):SUMMER74-276
J.C. SHERWOOD, 648:OCT73-56
J. TERRASSE, 549(RLC):OCT-DEC73-
620
MANACH, J. TEORÍA DE LA FRONTERA.
E. ARDURA, 37:MAR73-36
MANCALL, M. RUSSIA & CHINA.*
R. QUESTED, 302:JAN73-176
MANCINI, A.N. IL ROMANZO NEL SEI-
CENTO.*
M. CAPUCCI, 402(MLR):JAN74-191
MANCUSI-UNGARO, H.R., JR. MICHELAN-
GELO: THE BRUGES MADONNA & THE PIC-
COLOMINI ALTAR.*
C. GOULD, 39:MAR73-317
P. JOANNIDES, 90:MAY73-332
R.E. STONE, 551(RENQ):AUTUMN73-340
DE MANDACH, A. CHRONIQUE DITE
SAINTONGEAISE.
D. MC MILLAN, 208(FS):OCT74-440
MANDEL, A. LE PÉRIPLE.
J. SOJCHER, 98:MAY73-482
MANDEL, E. CRUSOE.
M. ANDRÉ, 529(QQ):WINTER73-658
C. LEVENSON, 102(CANL):AUTUMN74-91
P. STEVENS, 628:SPRING74-105
MANDEL, E., ED. POETS OF CONTEMPOR-
ARY CANADA 1960-1970.
M. ANDRÉ, 529(QQ):WINTER73-658
W.H. NEW, 102(CANL):SPRING73-123
MANDEL, E. STONY PLAIN.
C. LEVENSON, 102(CANL):AUTUMN74-91
P. STEVENS, 628:SPRING74-105
MANDEL, O. SIMPLICITIES.
V. YOUNG, 249(HUDR):WINTER74/75-
597
MANDEL, O., ED. THREE CLASSIC DON
JUAN PLAYS.
J.J. YOCH, JR., 568(SCN):SPRING-
SUMMER74-16
MANDEL, S. GROUP 47.
D.P. DENEAU, 268:JAN75-91
E. TRAHAN, 399(MLJ):DEC74-430
MANDELBAUM, D.G. HUMAN FERTILITY IN
INDIA.
C. MADGE, 617(TLS):14FEB75-172
MANDELBAUM, M. HISTORY, MAN, &
REASON.*
E.M. LOUDFOOT, 479(PHQ):APR73-168
L. POMPA, 262:AUTUMN73-323
J.B. SCHNEEWIND, 482(PHR):OCT74-
528
MANDELBAUM, M. - SEE GOMBRICH, E.H.,
J. HOCHBERG & M. BLACK
MANDELSTAM, N. CHAPTER 42 [TOGETHER
WITH] MANDELSTAM, O. THE GOLDFINCH
& OTHER POEMS. (D. RAYFIELD, TRANS)
J. BAINES, 402(MLR):OCT74-954
J. BAINES, 575(SEER):JUL74-441

MANDELSTAM, N. HOPE ABANDONED.*
(RUSSIAN TITLE: VTORAIA KNIGA.)
G. DAVENPORT, 249(HUDR):SUMMER74-
298
J. LUDWIG, 473(PR):3/1974-455
G. STRUVE, 550(RUSR):OCT73-425
P. VANSITTART, 364:JUN/JUL74-121
MANDELSTAM, N. HOPE AGAINST HOPE.*
M.S. SHATZ, 104:SUMMER73-250
MANDELSTAM, N. MOZART & SALIERI.
L. KOEHLER, 104:WINTER73-564
MANDELSTAM, O. COMPLETE POETRY OF
OSIP EMILIEVICH MANDELSTAM.* (B.
RAFFEL & A. BURAGO, TRANS; S.
MONAS, ED)
J. BAINES, 402(MLR):OCT74-954
J. BAINES, 575(SEER):JUL74-441
639(VQR):WINTER74-XVI
MANDELSTAM, O. OSIP MANDEL'SHTAM,
SELECTED POEMS.* (D. MC DUFF,
TRANS)
J. BAINES, 402(MLR):OCT74-954
J. BAINES, 575(SEER):JUL74-441
H. VENDLER, 441:7SEP75-6
MANDELSTAM, O. THE PROSE OF OSIP
MANDELSTAM. (C. BROWN, TRANS)
G. DAVENPORT, 249(HUDR):SUMMER74-
296
MANDELSTAM, O. SELECTED POEMS.*
(C. BROWN & W.S. MERWIN, TRANS)
J. BAINES, 402(MLR):OCT74-954
J. BAINES, 575(SEER):JUL74-441
G. DAVENPORT, 249(HUDR):SUMMER74-
300
M.G. LEVINE, 473(PR):3/1974-462
639(VQR):SPRING74-LVIII
MANDEL'ŠTAM, O. STIXOTVORENIJA.
A. KLIMOV, 574(SEEJ):WINTER73-465
MANDELSTAM, O. - ALSO SEE UNDER
MANDELSTAM, N.
VAN MANDER, K. DEN GRONDT DER EDEL
VRY SCHILDER-CONST.
E. ZIMMERMANN, 182:VOL26#11/12-421
MANDER, R. & J. MITCHENSON. BRITISH
MUSIC HALL.
C. DAVIDSON, 617(TLS):21MAR75-292
MANDER, R. & J. MITCHENSON. PANTO-
MIME.
617(TLS):21FEB75-204
MANDEVILLE, B. A MODEST DEFENCE OF
PUBLICK STEWS (1724).
566:SPRING74-98
MANDILARAS, B.G. STUDIES IN THE
GREEK LANGUAGE.
M. ALEXIOU, 123:NOV74-301
P. MACKRIDGE, 402(MLR):JAN74-239
MANDILARAS, B.G. THE VERB IN THE
GREEK NON-LITERARY PAPYRI.
J.A.L. LEE, 67:NOV74-223
MANE, R. HENRY ADAMS ON THE ROAD TO
CHARTRES.*
E.S. BODZIN, 529(QQ):SPRING73-136
H.F. SMITH, 376:OCT73-138
MANET, E. EUX OU LA PRISE DU POU-
VOIR.
F. TONELLI, 207(FR):OCT72-222
MANFRED, F. LORD GRIZZLY. CONQUER-
ING HORSE. SCARLET PLUME. RIDERS
OF JUDGMENT. KING OF SPADES.
M. JONES, 441:16FEB75-6
MANGANELLI, G. A E B.
G. ALMANSI, 617(TLS):31OCT75-1305
MANGIONE, J. THE DREAM & THE DEAL.*
D. YANNELLA, 295:FEB74-373

MANGUIN, P-Y. LES PORTUGAIS SUR LES
CÔTES DU VIÊT-NAM ET DU CAMPĀ.
P. VOSSELER, 182:VOL26#10-382
MANKIEWICZ, F. U.S. V. RICHARD M.
NIXON.
H. MITGANG, 441:24MAR75-29
MANN, D., ED. A CONCORDANCE TO THE
PLAYS OF WILLIAM CONGREVE.
J.M.P., 568(SCN):FALL74-60
G.W. STONE, JR., 566:AUTUMN73-31
MANN, J. CAPTIVE AUDIENCE.
617(TLS):10OCT75-1174
MANN, J. CHAUCER & MEDIEVAL ESTATES
SATIRE.
A. BALDWIN, 111:26OCT73-25
P.M. KEAN, 382(MAE):1974/3-296
MANN, J. A PLACE WITH TWO FACES.
E.M. EWING, 441:11MAY75-10
MANN, K. KATIA MANN: UNWRITTEN MEM-
OIRS. (GERMAN TITLE: MEINE UNGE-
SCHRIEBENEN MEMOIREN.) (E. VON
PLESSEN & M. MANN, EDS)
P. ADAMS, 61:JUL75-83
R. CRAFT, 453:12JUN75-19
T.J. REED, 617(TLS):3JAN75-18
442(NY):1SEP75-68
MANN, O., ED. CHRISTLICHE DICHTER
IM 20. JAHRHUNDERT.
P. PROCHNIK, 182:VOL26#10-360
MANN, P. DOG DAY AFTERNOON.
N. CALLENDAR, 441:2MAR75-17
MANN, T. BRIEFE AN OTTO GRAUTOFF
1894-1901 UND IDA BOY-ED 1903-1928.
(P. DE MENDELSSOHN, ED) GESAMMELTE
WERKE. (VOL 13)
T.J.R., 617(TLS):10OCT75-1207
MANN, T. DOCTOR FAUSTUS. THE STORY
OF A NOVEL.
R. CRAFT, 453:7AUG75-18
MANN, T. DER TOD IN VENEDIG.* (A.W.
HORNEY, ED)
P.H. ZOLDESTER, 221(GQ):MAR73-297
MANN, T. DER TOD IN VENEDIG.*
(T.J. REED, ED)
E.A. WIRTZ, 220(GL&L):JAN74-166
P.H. ZOLDESTER, 221(GQ):MAR73-297
MANN, T. & E. KAHLER. AN EXCEPTION-
AL FRIENDSHIP.
R. CRAFT, 453:12JUN75-19
442(NY):28JUL75-80
MANN, T. & K. KERÉNYI. MYTHOLOGY &
HUMANISM.
R. CRAFT, 453:12JUN75-19
442(NY):28JUL75-80
MANNHEIMER, M. THE GENERATIONS IN
MEREDITH'S NOVELS.
D. ROLL-HANSEN, 172(EDDA):1973/1-
56
J. WILT, 637(VS):DEC73-239
MANNING, O. THE RAIN FOREST.*
E. FEINSTEIN, 364:OCT/NOV74-134
MANNING, S.B. DICKENS AS SATIRIST.*
T.J. CRIBB, 541(RES):MAY73-230
L. LANE, JR., 594:SPRING73-125
MANSELL, D. THE NOVELS OF JANE
AUSTEN.
C.J. RAWSON, 175:AUTUMN73-116
MANSERGH, N. THE IRISH QUESTION
1840-1921. (NEW ED)
617(TLS):21NOV75-1397
MANSION, J.E., COMP. NEW STANDARD
FRENCH & ENGLISH DICTIONARY.* (PT
1: FRENCH-ENGLISH.) (R.P.L. & M.
[CONTINUED]

[CONTINUING]
LEDÉSERT, EDS)
E. WOODS, 402(MLR):OCT74-851
MANSUY, M., ED. POSITIONS ET OPPOS-
ITIONS SUR LE ROMAN CONTEMPORAIN.*
N. BAILEY, 402(MLR):OCT74-881
MANTELL, M. JOHNSON, GRANT, & THE
POLITICS OF RECONSTRUCTION.
639(VQR):SPRING74-XLVI
MANUEL, F.E. THE RELIGION OF ISAAC
NEWTON.
P.M. RATTANSI, 617(TLS):20JUN75-
700
MANUEL, J. DON JUAN MANUEL: "LIBRO
DE LOS ESTADOS." (R.B. TATE & I.R.
MACPHERSON, EDS)
R. HIGHFIELD, 617(TLS):24JAN75-91
MANVELL, R. CHAPLIN.
G. MILLAR, 362:28AUG75-284
MANVELL, R. FILMS OF THE SECOND
WORLD WAR.
R. MAYNE, 617(TLS):28FEB75-220
MANVELL, R. SHAKESPEARE & THE FILM.*
R.H. BALL, 570(SQ):AUTUMN73-479
MANZALAOUI, M., ED. ARABIC WRITING
TODAY: THE SHORT STORY.*
T.J. LE GASSICK, 318(JAOS):JUL-
SEP73-361
MANZITTI, C. VALERIO CASTELLO.
E. YOUNG, 39:JUL73-66
MANZONI, A. ALESSANDRO MANZONI'S
"I PROMESSI SPOSI." (P. MAZZAMUTO,
ED)
R. DE LA NOVAL, 399(MLJ):NOV73-368
MANZONI, A. SCRITTI LINGUISTICI.
(F. MONTEROSSO, ED)
F. FORTI, 228(GSLI):VOL150FASC472-
631
MANZONI, C. L'EPISTEMOLOGIA DI
EMILE MEYERSON.
R. BLANCHÉ, 542:JUL-SEP73-366
MAO TSE-TUNG. CHAIRMAN MAO TALKS TO
THE PEOPLE. (S. SCHRAM, ED)
J.K. FAIRBANK, 453:1MAY75-18
MAO TSE-TUNG. THE POEMS OF MAO TSE-
TUNG.* (W. BARNSTONE, WITH KO
CHING-PO, EDS & TRANS)
A. CLUYSENAAR, 565:VOL14#2-62
E. MC CRORIE, 134(CP):FALL73-90
MAO TSE-TUNG. POEMS OF MAO TSE-
TUNG. (H-L.N. & P. ENGLE, EDS &
TRANS)
V. YOUNG, 249(HUDR):AUTUMN74-423
MAPP, A.J., JR. THE GOLDEN DRAGON.
J. GARDNER, 231:APR75-104
MARABOTTINI, A. POLIDORO DA CARA-
VAGGIO.
R. KULTZEN, 54:DEC73-637
"MARAGTAS SYMPOSIUM."
D.V. HART, 293(JAST):MAY73-572
MARAN, L.R. BURMESE & JINGPHO.
J.A. MATISOFF, 293(JAST):AUG73-741
MARANA, G.P. LETTERS WRIT BY A
TURKISH SPY. (A.J. WEITZMAN, ED)
L. DESVIGNES, 549(RLC):APR-JUN73-
345
R. LONSDALE, 447(N&Q):MAY73-197
MARANDA, E.K. & P. STRUCTURAL MOD-
ELS IN FOLKLORE & TRANSFORMATIONAL
ESSAYS.
K.L. COTHRAN, 292(JAF):JAN-MAR73-
66

MARANDA, P. & E.K., EDS. STRUCTURAL
ANALYSIS OF ORAL TRADITION.*
  B.N. COLBY, 297(JL):FEB73-202
MARBÁN, E. EL TEATRO ESPAÑOL MEDI-
EVAL Y DEL RENACIMIENTO.
  J.A. PARR, 238:DEC73-1118
MARCEL, G. TRAGIC WISDOM & BEYOND.
  D.S. ROBINSON, 484(PPR):JUN74-602
MARC'HADOUR, G. THE BIBLE IN THE
WORKS OF ST. THOMAS MORE. (PTS 2-5)
  W.L. GODSHALK, 551(RENQ):SUMMER73-
  210
  M-A. DE KISCH, 189(EA):JAN-MAR73-
  92
MARC'HADOUR, G., ED. MOREANA.
(VOLS 31&32)
  L. MILES, 551(RENQ):SUMMER73-212
MARCHAND, H. THE CATEGORIES & TYPES
OF PRESENT-DAY ENGLISH WORD-FORMA-
TION.* (2ND ED)
  G.F. MEIER, 682(ZPSK):BAND26HEFT
  3/4-436
MARCHAND, L.A. - SEE LORD BYRON
MARCHANT, W. THE PRIVILEGE OF HIS
COMPANY.
  P. ADAMS, 61:MAY75-103
  H. FRANKEL, 441:22JUN75-32
  N. SHRAPNEL, 617(TLS):19DEC75-1506
MARCHEL, L. WITH ALL MY LOVE, I
HATE YOU.
  D.M. DAY, 157:WINTER73-89
MARCHI, G.P. CONCORDANZE VERGHIANE.
  400(MLN):JAN73-166
MARCHIONE, M. & S.E. SCALIA - SEE
BOINE, G. & G. PREZZOLINI
MARCONI, S.M. - SEE UNDER MOSCHINI
MARCONI, S.
MARCOS MORÍN, F. APROXIMACIÓN A LA
GRAMÁTICA ESPAÑOLA.
  A. YLLERA, 202(FMOD):JUN73-412
MARCUCCI, S. ASPETTI EPISTEMOLOGICI
DELLA FINALITÀ IN KANT.
  W.H. WERKMEISTER, 319:JUL75-415
MARCUS, A. THE MOON IS A MARRYING
EYE.
  R. MOORE, 661:SUMMER73-105
MARCUS, F.H. FILM & LITERATURE.
  J. MELLEN, 295:FEB74-518
MARCUS, G. MYSTERY TRAIN.
  J. ROCKWELL, 441:14JUN75-25
MARCUS, G.J. HEART OF OAK.
  J. WATERMAN, 362:30OCT75-581
MARCUS, H.G. THE LIFE & TIMES OF
MENELIK II.
  E. ULLENDORFF, 617(TLS):25APR75-
  462
MARCUS, H.G. THE MODERN HISTORY OF
ETHIOPIA & THE HORN OF AFRICA.
  J.A. CASADA, 14:APR73-247
MARCUS, P.L. YEATS & THE BEGINNING
OF THE IRISH RENAISSANCE.*
  R.J. FINNERAN, 295:FEB74-835
MARCUS, S. - SEE HAMMETT, D.
MARCUSE, H. COUNTERREVOLUTION &
REVOLT.*
  D.F.D., 543:DEC72-359
MARDER, H. FEMINISM & ART.
  J. GUIGUET, 189(EA):JUL-SEP73-338
MARDON, E.G. THE NARRATIVE UNITY OF
THE CURSOR MUNDI.
  J.O. FICHTE, 597(SN):VOL45#2-446

DE LA MARE, A., COMP. CATALOGUE OF
THE COLLECTION OF MEDIEVAL MANU-
SCRIPTS BEQUEATHED TO THE BODLEIAN
LIBRARY BY JAMES P.R. LYELL.*
  N. BARKER, 78(BC):SPRING73-95
  K.W. HUMPHREYS, 354:JUN73-162
DE MARE, E. THE LONDON DORE SAW.
  M. GIROUARD, 46:MAY73-344
  D. THOMAS, 135:OCT73-144
DE LA MARE, W. THE COMPLETE POEMS
OF WALTER DE LA MARE.
  H. SERGEANT, 175:SUMMER72-75
MAREIN, S. CREATING RUGS & WALL
HANGINGS.
  B. GUTCHEON, 441:7DEC75-74
MAREIN, S. OFF THE LOOM.
  D. SMITH, 139:APR74-13
MAREK, G.R. TOSCANINI.
  D. HENAHAN, 441:1APR75-39
  M. STEINBERG, 441:30MAR75-7
MAREN-GRIESBACH, M. METHODEN DER
LITERATURWISSENSCHAFT.*
  W. FENDEL, 430(NS):MAR73-181
MAREŠ, F.V. DIACHRONISCHE PHONOLO-
GIE DES UR- UND FRÜHSLAVISCHEN.
  L.R. MICKLESEN, 574(SEEJ):FALL72-
  365
MARESCA, T.E. EPIC TO NOVEL.
  M. IRWIN, 617(TLS):12SEP75-1029
MARETT, R.R. PSYCHOLOGY & FOLK-LORE.
  W.H. JANSEN, 582(SFQ):JUN73-142
MARG, W. HOMER ÜBER DIE DICHTUNG.
(2ND ED)
  F.M. COMBELLACK, 122:JUL73-233
  M.M. WILLCOCK, 123:MAR74-125
MARGARET, DUCHESS OF ARGYLL. FORGET
NOT.
  A. FORBES, 617(TLS):19DEC75-1510
MARGARY, H., ED. A MAP OF THE COUN-
TY OF ESSEX BY J. CHAPMAN & P.
ANDRE, 1777.
  R. HYDE, 325:APR73-622
MARGETSON, S. THE LONG PARTY.
  A. FORBES, 617(TLS):19DEC75-1510
MARGHIERI, C. AMATI ENIGMI.
  F. DONINI, 617(TLS):21FEB75-188
MARGOLIN, J-C. BACHELARD.
  J. CULLER, 617(TLS):28FEB75-230
MARGOLIOUTH, H.M. - SEE MARVELL, A.
MARGOLIS, J., ED. FACT & EXISTENCE.
  R. BLANCHÉ, 542:OCT-DEC73-478
MARGOLIS, J. VALUES & CONDUCT.
  A. BROADIE, 479(PHQ):JAN73-89
  G.R. GRICE, 393(MIND):JUL73-467
  J.D. WALLACE, 482(PHR):JAN73-117
MARGOLIS, J.D. T.S. ELIOT'S INTEL-
LECTUAL DEVELOPMENT, 1922-1939.*
  M. DODSWORTH, 184(EIC):JUL73-310
  P.G. ELLIS, 541(RES):AUG73-369
MARGUERITE DE NAVARRE. CHANSONS
SPIRITUELLES.* (G. DOTTIN, ED)
  D. WILSON, 402(MLR):APR74-400
MARI, P. HENRI DUTILLEUX.
  G.W. HOPKINS, 415:NOV74-947
MARIANI, G. IL PRIMO MARINETTI.*
PREISTORIA DEL FUTURISMO.
  J-P. DE NOLA, 549(RLC):APR-JUN73-
  357
MARIANI, P.L. A COMMENTARY ON THE
COMPLETE POEMS OF GERARD MANLEY
HOPKINS.*
  M. SMITH, 577(SHR):FALL73-434
MARIAS, J. GENERATIONS.
  F.A., 543:DEC72-358

MARIÁTEGUI, J.C. SEVEN INTERPRETIVE
ESSAYS ON PERUVIAN REALITY.*
  M. DEAS, 617(TLS):18APR75-422
MARICHAL, J. - SEE AZAÑA, M.
DE MARICHAL, S.S. - SEE UNDER SAL-
INAS DE MARICHAL, S.
MARINATOS, S. LIFE & ART IN PRE-
HISTORIC THERA.
  R.M. COOK, 123:NOV74-308
MARINER, D. OPERATION SCORPIO.
  M. LEVIN, 441:23MAR75-34
MARINETTI, F.T. MARINETTI: SELECTED
WRITINGS. (R.W. FLINT, ED)
  K.D. ANTONELLI, 275(IQ):SPRING74-
  112
  J.S. RUSKAMP, 114(CHIR):VOL25#3-
  177
  C. TISDALL, 592:MAR73-137
MARION, S. HAUT FAITS DU CANADA
FRANÇAIS RELEVES ET COMMENTES PAR
DES ANGLOPHONES.
  J.S. PRITCHARD, 529(QQ):SUMMER73-
  293
MARISSEL, A. CHANTS POUR VARSOVIE
ET AUTRES POEMES.
  C. FRANÇOIS, 207(FR):OCT72-223
DE MARIVAUX, P.C.D. OEUVRES DE
JEUNESSE. (F. DELOFFRE, ED)
  R. MERCIER, 557(RSH):JAN-MAR73-168
MARK, T.C. SPINOZA'S THEORY OF
TRUTH.
  W. HARVEY, 319:JAN75-105
  M.D. WILSON, 311(JP):16JAN75-22
MARKANDAYA, K. TWO VIRGINS.*
  D. DURRANT, 364:AUG/SEP74-144
  J. FLETCHER, 268:JAN75-80
MARKELS, J. THE PILLAR OF THE
WORLD.
  J.W. VELZ, 570(SQ):WINTER73-98
MARKER, F.J. - SEE FENGER, H.
MARKLE, J.B. FIGHTERS & LOVERS.
  S.D. WARNER, 27(AL):JAN75-601
MARKLE, M.K. & T.R. KING. A PROGRAM
ON SPEECH PREPARATION.
  T.L. ATTAWAY, 583:FALL73-101
MARKMAN, A.M. & E.R. STEINBERG, EDS.
ENGLISH THEN & NOW.
  J.L. ERICKSON, 215(GL):VOL13#2-128
MARKOV, V. - SEE KHLEBNIKOV, V.V.
MARKS, C. FROM THE SKETCHBOOKS OF
THE GREAT ARTISTS.
  D.A. COVI, 579(SAQ):SPRING74-279
  T. LASK, 55:NOV72-16
MARKS, C. PILGRIMS, HERETICS, &
LOVERS.
  C.D. HEYMANN, 441:13JUL75-7
MARKS, E.R. - SEE SAINTE-BEUVE, C-A.
MARKS, F.W., 3D. INDEPENDENCE ON
TRIAL.
  P.A. VARG, 656(WMQ):JUL74-517
  639(VQR):SPRING74-XLV
MARKS, G.A. & C.B. JOHNSON. HARRAP'S
ENGLISH-FRENCH DICTIONARY OF SLANG
& COLLOQUIALISMS.
  R. MAYNE, 617(TLS):30MAY75-588
MARKUS, R.A. CHRISTIANITY IN THE
ROMAN WORLD.
  W.H.C. FREND, 617(TLS):29AUG75-977
MARKUS, R.A. SAECULUM.
  J. DILLON, 121(CJ):FEB/MAR74-265
  H.I. MARROU, 182:VOL26#9-273

MARKUSHEVICH, A.I. & OTHERS, EDS.
AL'MANAKH BIBLIOFILA.
  J.S.G. SIMMONS, 78(BC):WINTER73-
  544
MARKUSHEVICH, A.I. & OTHERS, EDS.
KNIGA I GRAFIKA.
  J.S.G. SIMMONS, 78(BC):SPRING73-
  107
MARLATT, D. VANCOUVER POEMS.
  D. HELWIG, 102(CANL):SPRING74-118
MARLOW, D. I LOVED YOU WEDNESDAY.
  M. LEVIN, 441:18MAY75-50
MARLOW, J. THE UNCROWNED QUEEN OF
IRELAND.
  C. SEEBOHM, 441:20JUL75-4
  A. WHITMAN, 441:26JUL75-21
MARLOWE, C. THE COMPLETE WORKS OF
CHRISTOPHER MARLOWE.* (F. BOWERS,
ED)
  K. MUIR, 301(JEGP):JUL74-428
MARLOWE, D.J. OPERATION DEATHMAKER.
  N. CALLENDAR, 441:30MAR75-24
MARLOWE, J. CECIL RHODES.
  J.A. CASADA, 637(VS):DEC73-230
MARMONTEL, J-F. MARMONTEL: MÉMOIRES.
(J. RENWICK, ED)
  A.D. HYTIER, 481(PQ):JUL73-553
  J. LOUGH, 208(FS):OCT74-469
MARONITIS, D.N. ANEMOSKALA KAI
SIMADOURES.
  P.L., 617(TLS):14NOV75-1366
MAROT, C. LES ÉPIGRAMMES.* (C.A.
MAYER, ED)
  F. CHARPENTIER, 557(RSH):JAN-MAR
  73-166
MAROT, J. RECUEIL. (A. SAUNDERS,
ED)
  R. GRIFFITHS, 402(MLR):APR74-397
MAROTHY, J. MUSIC & THE BOURGEOIS.
  K.P. ETZKORN, 187:JAN75-147
  R. MIDDLETON, 410(M&L):OCT74-476
MAROWITZ, C. CONFESSIONS OF A COUN-
TERFEIT CRITIC.
  A. SEYMOUR, 364:APR/MAY74-102
MAROWITZ, C. A LONDON THEATRE NOTE-
BOOK 1958-71.
  C. BARLAS, 214:VOL6#24-110
MARQUES, A.H.R.D. - SEE UNDER DE
OLIVEIRA MARQUES, A.H.R.
MARQUET, G. L'OEIL DE DÉODAT.
  M.G. ROSE, 207(FR):FEB73-664
MARQUET, J-F. LIBERTÉ ET EXISTENCE.
  F. MARTI, 319:APR75-263
MÁRQUEZ, G.G. - SEE UNDER GARCÍA
MÁRQUEZ, G.
MARR, D.G. VIETNAMESE ANTICOLONIAL-
ISM, 1885-1925.
  F.J. CORLEY, 613:SPRING73-157
MARRAS, A. INTENTIONALITY, MIND, &
LANGUAGE.
  W.G., 543:MAR73-542
  N.J. MOUTAFAKIS, 484(PPR):JUN74-
  614
MARRAST, R. JOSÉ DE ESPRONCEDA.
  C. IRANZO DE EBERSOLE, 241:JAN73-
  85
MARRIC, J.J. GIDEON'S FOG.
  442(NY):6JAN75-83
MARRIOTT, J. A SPECIAL ILLNESS.
  S. CURTIS, 148:SPRING72-85
MARRUS, M.R. THE POLITICS OF ASSIM-
ILATION.
  K. BIEBER, 207(FR):OCT72-189
  D.B. GOLDEY, 208(FS):JUL74-361

241

MARSDEN, E.W. GREEK & ROMAN ARTIL-
LERY.
  G.R. WATSON, 123:NOV74-243
MARSH, J. COLERIDGE'S AMERICAN
DISCIPLES. (J.J. DUFFY, ED)
  L. LEARY, 432(NEQ):DEC74-620
  W.E. WILLIAMS, 27(AL):NOV74-398
MARSHALL, A. FOUR SUNDAY SUITS.
  M. LEVIN, 441:30NOV75-62
MARSHALL, D.C. THE ENGLISH YOU
NEED (EL INGLÉS QUE USTED NECES-
ITA). (4TH ED REV BY C.M. BOYLE)
  K. SUTHERLAND, 399(MLJ):NOV74-372
MARSHALL, J. RAIL FACTS & FEATS.
  442(NY):13JAN75-95
MARSHALL, J.H. - SEE ADAM DE LA
HALLE
MARSHALL, J.H. - SEE FAIDIT, U.
MARSHALL, J.H. - SEE VIDAL, R.
MARSHALL, P.K. - SEE GELLIUS
MARSHALL, R.L. THE COMPOSITIONAL
PROCESS OF J.S. BACH.*
  P. BRAINARD, 317:FALL73-483
MARSHALL, T. THE EARTH-BOOK.
  L. HICKS, 99:APR/MAY75-62
  G. MC WHIRTER, 198:SPRING75-132
MARSHALL, T. MAGIC WATER.
  F. DAVEY, 102(CANL):WINTER73-118
MARSHALL, T. THE PSYCHIC MARINER.*
  E. DELAVENAY, 189(EA):JUL-SEP73-
  320
MARSHALLSAY, D. OFFICIAL PUBLICA-
TIONS.
  J.B. CHILDS, 517(PBSA):APR-JUN74-
  193
MARSHBURN, J.H. MURDER & WITCHCRAFT
IN ENGLAND, 1550-1640.
  R.H. WEST, 219(GAR):SPRING73-137
MARTEL, B. LA PSYCHOLOGIE DE GON-
SALVE D'ESPAGNE.
  N. PALLINI, 548(RCSF):APR-JUN73-
  235
MARTENS, G. VITALISMUS UND EXPRES-
SIONISMUS.
  A. VIVIANI, 680(ZDP):BAND92HEFT4-
  611
MARTENS, G. & H. ZELLER, EDS. TEXTE
UND VARIANTEN.
  R. FOLTER, 301(JEGP):JAN74-98
  W.F. HUNTER, 86(BHS):OCT73-398
MARTIN, A. ONE MAN, HURT.
  A. BROYARD, 441:14MAY75-35
  R. PIRSIG, 441:8JUN75-27
MARTIN, C. FULL FATHOM FIVE.
  K.R. ANDREWES, 617(TLS):3OCT75-
  1158
  P. GARDNER, 441:14DEC75-12
  442(NY):15DEC75-154
MARTIN, C. THE GREAT CHRISTIAN CEN-
TURIES TO COME.
  F.R. BARRY, 617(TLS):25APR75-464
MARTIN, C. - SEE GIDE, A.
MARTIN, D. THE TASK.
  R. FOSTER, 617(TLS):26SEP75-1077
MARTIN, F.D. ART & THE RELIGIOUS
EXPERIENCE.*
  R.A. OAKES, 484(PPR):MAR74-444
MARTIN, G. THE DURHAM REPORT &
BRITISH POLICY.*
  W. ORMSBY, 150(DR):WINTER73/74-772
MARTIN, G. NATIONAL GALLERY CATA-
LOGUES: THE FLEMISH SCHOOL CA.
1600-CA. 1900.
  M. JAFFÉ, 54:SEP73-462

MARTIN, G.D., ED & TRANS. ANTHOLOGY
OF CONTEMPORARY FRENCH POETRY.*
  T. GREENE, 207(FR):APR73-1037
MARTIN, H.H. RALPH MC GILL, REPOR-
TER.*
  E.H. METHVIN, 396(MODA):FALL74-421
MARTIN, J.H. LOVE'S FOOLS.*
  S. BARNEY, 589:APR74-362
  D. EISENBERG, 400(MLN):MAR73-408
  S.G. NICHOLS, JR., 131(CL):SPRING
  73-171
MARTIN, J.K. MEN IN REBELLION.
  J.J. WATERS, 656(WMQ):JAN74-149
MARTIN, J.S. RAGNARQK.*
  E.A. PHILIPPSON, 301(JEGP):APR74-
  277
MARTIN, L. & L. MARCH, EDS. URBAN
SPACE & STRUCTURES.
  R. OLIVER, 45:JUL73-41
MARTIN, M. A HALF-CENTURY OF ELIOT
CRITICISM.
  295:FEB74-584
  354:JUN73-173
MARTIN, M-L. KIMBANGU.
  M. SINGLETON, 617(TLS):5DEC75-1469
MARTIN, P. SHAKESPEARE'S SONNETS.*
  S. BOOTH, 401(MLQ):MAR74-82
  R.A. FOAKES, 175:SUMMER73-72
MARTIN, R. INTERNATIONAL DICTIONARY
OF FOOD & COOKING.
  M.F.K. FISHER, 442(NY):10NOV75-182
MARTIN, R. RECHERCHES SUR LES
AGRONOMES LATINS ET LEUR CONCEP-
TIONS ÉCONOMIQUES ET SOCIALES.*
  P.N. LOCKHART, 124:MAR73-366
MARTIN, R.B. THE TRIUMPH OF WIT.
  A. BELL, 617(TLS):11APR75-396
MARTIN, R.L., ED. THE PARADOX OF
THE LIAR.
  K. JONES, 393(MIND):APR73-308
MARTIN, S.E. & Y-S.C. LEE, WITH E.C.
HORNE. BEGINNING KOREAN.
  B. LEWIN, 353:15MAR73-92
MARTIN, T.L., JR. MALICE IN BLUN-
DERLAND.
  L.C. MILAZZO, 584(SWR):WINTER74-
  110
MARTIN, W. THE "NEW AGE" UNDER
ORAGE.
  N.C. DE NAGY, 72:BAND211HEFT1/3-
  141
MARTIN, W. - SEE ORAGE, A.R.
MARTIN-JENKINS, C. ASSAULT ON THE
ASHES.
  G. SCOTT, 362:24JUL75-126
MARTÍN-SANTOS, L. TIEMPO DE DES-
TRUCCIÓN. (J-C. MAINER, ED)
  J. CHAPMAN, 617(TLS):23MAY75-574
MARTÍN GAITE, C. & A. RUIZ TARAZONA.
OCHO SIGLOS DE POESÍA GALLEGA.
  A. ADELL, 270:VOL23#3-70
MARTINDALE, A. THE RISE OF THE
ARTIST IN THE MIDDLE AGES & EARLY
RENAISSANCE.*
  R.M. QUINN, 50(ARQ):SPRING73-79
MARTINET, A. EVOLUTION DES LANGUES
ET RECONSTRUCTION.
  S. ULLMAN, 617(TLS):23MAY75-568
MARTINET, A., ED. LA LINGÜÍSTICA.
  E. BERNÁRDEZ, 202(FMOD):JUN73-403
MARTINET, A. LA PRONONCIATION DU
FRANÇAIS CONTEMPORAIN. (2ND ED)
  A. CLASSE, 208(FS):OCT74-492
  A. VALDMAN, 350:SEP74-582

MARTINET, A. & H. WALTER. DICTION-
NAIRE DE LA PRONONCIATION FRANÇAISE
DANS SON USAGE RÉEL.
  R.L. POLITZER, 399(MLJ):DEC74-418
MARTINEZ-ALIER, V. MARRIAGE, CLASS
& COLOUR IN NINETEENTH-CENTURY CUBA.
  L. WHITEHEAD, 617(TLS):14MAR75-270
MARTÍNEZ CARRERAS, J.U. - SEE ALONSO
DE HERRERA, G.
MARTÍNEZ DE TOLEDO, A. ARCIPRESTE
DE TALAVERA O CORBACHO. (J. GONZA-
LEZ MUELA, ED)
  E. VON RICHTHOFEN & J.I. CHICOY-
  DABÁN, 240(HR):AUTUMN73-695
MARTÍNEZ NADAL, R. LORCA'S "THE
PUBLIC."
  617(TLS):23MAY75-576
MARTÍNEZ PELÁEZ, S. LA PATRIA DEL
CRIOLLO.
  T.B. IRVING, 263:APR-JUN74-170
MARTINO, A. GESCHICHTE DER DRAMA-
TISCHEN THEORIEN IN DEUTSCHLAND IM
18. JAHRHUNDERT. (VOL 1)
  M.L. BAEUMER, 406:SUMMER74-206
MARTINS, E. STUDIEN ZUR FRAGE DER
LINGUISTISCHEN INTERFERENZ.
  F. ABEL, 430(NS):AUG73-453
  J. JUHÁSZ, 680(ZDP):BAND92HEFT1-
  143
MARTINS DE OLIVEIRA, D. MANANTIAL.
  G. FIGUEIRA, 263:APR-JUN74-181
MARTINSON, H., G. EKELÖF & T. TRANS-
TRÖMER. FRIENDS, YOU DRANK SOME
DARKNESS. (R. BLY, ED & TRANS)
  M. MEYER, 617(TLS):31OCT75-1287
  H. VENDLER, 441:7SEP75-6
MARTY, F., W. PORTER & E. STEWART.
VIVRE EN FRANCE.
  J. GREENLEE, 207(FR):OCT72-242
MARTY, S. HEADWATERS.*
  A. SAFARIK, 606(TAMR):1STQTR74-86
MARTZ, L.L., ED. ENGLISH SEVEN-
TEENTH-CENTURY VERSE. (VOL 1)
  J. POST, 568(SCN):FALL74-49
MARTZ, L.L. THE WIT OF LOVE.*
  J.B. BROADBENT, 447(N&Q):MAY73-193
  L. POTTER, 179(ES):DEC73-591
MARTZ, W.T. JOHN BERRYMAN.
  A. EASSON, 447(N&Q):SEP73-345
MARUYAMA, M. STUDIES IN THE INTEL-
LECTUAL HISTORY OF TOKUGAWA JAPAN.
  W.G. BEASLEY, 617(TLS):22AUG75-939
MARVELL, A. THE COMPLETE POEMS.
(E.S. DONNO, ED)
  T. HAYES, 568(SCN):FALL74-47
MARVELL, A. THE POEMS & LETTERS OF
ANDREW MARVELL.* (H.M. MARGOLIOUTH,
ED; 3RD ED REV BY P. LEGOUIS, WITH
E.E. DUNCAN-JONES)
  H. CASTROP, 72:BAND211HEFT3/6-433
  E.S. DONNO, 551(RENQ):SPRING73-95
  P. MALEKIN, 597(SN):VOL45#2-453
  I. SIMON, 556(RLV):1973/6-564
MARVELL, A. THE REHEARSAL TRANS-
PROS'D [&] THE REHEARSAL TRANS-
PROS'D THE SECOND PART.* (D.I.B.
SMITH, ED)
  H. CASTROP, 72:BAND211HEFT3/6-435
  T.R. CLEARY, 376:JAN73-162
  W. VON KOPPENFELS, 38:BAND91HEFT4-
  530

MARX, K. CRITIQUE OF HEGEL'S "PHIL-
OSOPHY OF RIGHT."* (J. O'MALLEY,
ED)
  Z.A. PELCZYNSKI, 220(GL&L):JAN74-
  152
MARX, K. EARLY WRITINGS. (L. COL-
LETTI, ED)
  A. RYAN, 617(TLS):28MAR75-342
MARX, K. GRUNDRISSE.
  A. FINKIELKRAUT, 98:DEC73-1118
MARX, K. SULLA RELIGIONE. (L. PAR-
INETTO, ED)
  F. PINTACUDA DE MICHELIS,
  548(RCSF):JAN-MAR73-115
MARX, K. & F. ENGELS. COLLECTED
WORKS. (VOL 1)
  D. MC LELLAN, 617(TLS):10JAN75-25
MARX, K. & F. ENGELS. DIE RUSSISCHE
KOMMUNE. (M. RUBEL, ED)
  H. HIRSCH, 182:VOL26#9-315
MARX, W. HEGELS PHÄNOMENOLOGIE DES
GEISTES.
  D.E. CHRISTENSEN, 319:JAN75-115
  W. FLACH, 53(AGP):BAND55HEFT1-100
MARX, W. HEIDEGGER & THE TRADI-
TION.*
  M. MURRAY, 482(PHR):APR73-252
MARX, W. REASON & WORLD.
  A.G., 543:DEC72-360
MARSZALEK, J.F., JR. COURT-MARTIAL.
  L.M. SIMMS, JR., 432(NEQ):SEP73-
  475
MARZAC, N. - SEE DE CIBOULE, R.
MASANI, Z. INDIRA GANDHI.
  H. TINKER, 617(TLS):4JUL75-731
MASARYK, T.G. THE MEANING OF CZECH
HISTORY.* (R. WELLEK, ED)
  639(VQR):AUTUMN74-CXLVI
MASELLA, A.B. ORLANDO IL CURIOSO.
  J. NARDIELLO, 399(MLJ):SEP-OCT74-
  295
MASER, W. ADOLF HITLER.*
  A. WAHL, 182:VOL26#17/18-628
  639(VQR):SUMMER74-LXXXIX
MASHECK, J., ED. MARCEL DUCHAMP IN
PERSPECTIVE.
  B. GOLD, 31(ASCH):WINTER74/75-142
MASI, A. RICERCHE SULLA "RES PRI-
VATA" DEL "PRINCEPS."
  R. VILLERS, 555:VOL47FASC1-190
MASING, I. A. BLOK'S "THE SNOW
MASK."
  L. VOGEL, 574(SEEJ):WINTER73-459
MASINTON, C.G. CHRISTOPHER MAR-
LOWE'S TRAGIC VISION.*
  M. HATTAWAY, 677:VOL4-266
  N. RABKIN, 301(JEGP):OCT74-543
MASOLIVER, P.A. ORIGEN Y PRIMEROS
AÑOS (1616-34) DE LA CONGREGACIÓN
CISTERCIENSE DE LA CORONA DE ARAGÓN.
  C.M. BATTLE, 182:VOL26#17/18-631
MASON, B.A. NAKOKOV'S GARDEN.
  A. DE JONGE, 617(TLS):16MAY75-526
MASON, H. VOLTAIRE.
  W.H. BARBER, 617(TLS):25APR75-446
MASON, H.A. EDITING WYATT.
  J. DAALDER, 184(EIC):OCT73-399
MASON, H.A. SHAKESPEARE'S TRAGEDIES
OF LOVE.
  J. BAYLEY, 184(EIC):JUL72-283
  M. GRIVELET, 189(EA):OCT-DEC73-465
  H. HAWKINS, 541(RES):NOV73-473

244

MATTEI, M. LETTRES À THÉOPHILE
GAUTIER ET À LOUIS DE CORMENIN.
(E. KAYE, ED)
J.G. LOWIN, 207(FR):MAY73-1228
MATTER, H., ED. DIE LITERATUR ÜBER
THOMAS MANN.*
W. GROTHE, 597(SN):VOL45#1-192
K.W. JONAS, 406:SPRING74-83
H. LEHNERT, 301(JEGP):JAN74-92
E. NÜNDEL, 657(WW):MAR/APR73-142
MATTES, J. DER WAHNSINN IM GRIECH-
ISCHEN MYTHOS UND IN DER DICHTUNG
BIS ZUM DRAMA DES FÜNFTEN JAHRHUN-
DERTS.*
E.B. HOLTSMARK, 121(CJ):OCT/NOV72-
81
MATTESINI, F. PIETRO PANCRAZI TRA
AVANGUARDIA E TRADIZIONE.
P.A.T., 228(GSLI):VOL150FASC470/
471-477
MATTEUCCI, A.M. CARLO FRANCESCO
DOTTI E L'ARCHITETTURA BOLOGNESE
DEL SETTECENTO.
A. ROWAN, 90:MAR73-188
MATTHEWS, C.M. PLACE NAMES OF THE
ENGLISH-SPEAKING WORLD.*
K.B. HARDER, 424:JUN73-112
MATTHEWS, D., ED. KEYBOARD MUSIC.
M. PETERSON, 470:MAY74-24
MATTHEWS, D.J. & C. SHACKLE, EDS &
TRANS. AN ANTHOLOGY OF CLASSICAL
URDU LOVE LYRICS.*
M.S. ALI BAIG, 273(IC):OCT73-364
A. SCHIMMEL, 318(JAOS):OCT-DEC73-
569
MATTHEWS, G.M., ED. KEATS: THE
CRITICAL HERITAGE.*
S.M.S., 191(ELN):SEP73(SUPP)-51
MATTHEWS, H.C.G. THE LIBERAL IM-
PERIALISTS.
P. STANSKY, 637(VS):MAR74-330
MATTHEWS, H.L. REVOLUTION IN CUBA.
K.H. SILVERT, 441:7SEP75-5
MATTHEWS, H.L. A WORLD IN REVOLU-
TION.
J.F. THORNING, 613:SPRING73-158
MATTHEWS, J. PICTURES OF THE JOUR-
NEY BACK.*
J.M. FLORA, 385(MQR):WINTER75-101
MATTHEWS, J. WESTERN ARISTOCRACIES
& IMPERIAL COURT A.D. 364-425.
J.J. WILKES, 617(TLS):2MAY75-476
MATTHEWS, J.H. SURREALISM & FILM.*
M. KUSHNIR, 295:FEB74-520
N. WATANABE, 207(FR):FEB73-630
MATTHEWS, J.H. SURREALIST POETRY IN
FRANCE.
M. BERTRAND, 188(ECR):SUMMER73-166
MATTHEWS, K. MEMORIES OF A MOUNTAIN
WAR.
H.C. CLIADAKIS, 104:SPRING74-138
MATTHEWS, P.H. INFLECTIONAL MOR-
PHOLOGY.
W. ABRAHAM, 343:BAND17HEFT2-200
MATTHEWS, S.R. INTERWOVEN.
W. GARD, 584(SWR):SUMMER74-V
MATTHEWS, T.S. GREAT TOM.*
J.E. BRESLIN, 639(VQR):AUTUMN74-
632
R. FULLER, 364:OCT/NOV74-135
R. KIRK, 569(SR):FALL74-698
MATTHEWS, W., ED. AMERICAN DIARIES
IN MANUSCRIPT, 1580-1954.
639(VQR):AUTUMN74-CXXXV

MATTHIESSEN, P. FAR TORTUGA.
A. BROYARD, 441:6MAY75-43
T.R. EDWARDS, 453:7AUG75-34
R. STONE, 441:25MAY75-1
E. WEEKS, 61:JUN75-92
442(NY):19MAY75-118
MATVEJEVITCH, P. LA POÉSIE DE
CIRCONSTANCE.*
D.J. MOSSOP, 208(FS):APR74-244
MAUCH, U. GESCHEHEN "AN SICH" UND
VORGANG OHNE URHEBERBEZUG IM MODER-
NEN FRANZÖSISCH.
L. ZAWADOWSKI, 545(RPH):AUG73-96
MAUGENDRE, L.A. LA RENAISSANCE
CATHOLIQUE AU DÉBUT DU XXE SIÈCLE.
(VOL 6)
G.E. GINGRAS, 207(FR):APR73-1016
MAUGEY, A. POÉSIE ET SOCIÉTÉ AU
QUÉBEC (1937-1970).
L. MAILHOT, 102(CANL):WINTER73-121
MAULE, H. SCOBIE.
R. CLOGG, 617(TLS):14NOV75-1362
MAURENS, J. - SEE DE VOLTAIRE, F.M.A.
MAURER, C.B. CALL TO REVOLUTION.*
G. STERN, 400(MLN):APR73-636
P.F. WILKINSON, 628:FALL73-115
MAURER, F. DICHTUNG UND SPRACHE
DES MITTELALTERS.* (2ND ED)
H. KRATZ, 133:1973/1-77
H. MARTIN, 406:FALL74-296
MAURER, F., ED. DIE RELIGIÖSEN
DICHTUNGEN DES 11. UND 12. JAHR-
HUNDERTS.* (VOL 3)
W.G. CUNLIFFE, 221(GQ):SEP73-155
MAURER, F. - SEE WALTHER VON DER
VOGELWEIDE
MAURIAC, C. ANDRÉ BRETON.
N. OXENHANDLER, 207(FR):DEC72-421
MAURIAC, C. THE OTHER DE GAULLE.*
J. COLTON, 639(VQR):SUMMER74-467
B.H. SMITH, 396(MODA):SUMMER74-325
MAURIAC, F. UN ADOLESCENT D'AUTRE-
FOIS. (J.E. FLOWER, ED)
M. SCOTT, 208(FS):OCT74-485
205(FMLS):APR73-213
MAURIAC, F. LA PHARISIENNE.*
(A.M.C. WILCOX, ED)
R.J. NORTH, 208(FS):JUL74-347
MAURICIUS. ARTA MILITARĂ. (H.
MIHĂESCU, ED)
E. TRAPP, 260(IF):BAND78-260
MAURIN, P-M. - SEE HOBBES, T.
DE MAURO, T. - SEE DE SAUSSURE, F.
MAURO, W. INVITO ALLA LETTURA DI
FENOGLIO.
B. MERRY, 402(MLR):APR74-431
MAURO DE VASCONCELOS, J. CHUVA
CRIOULA.
M. SILVERMAN, 238:DEC73-1122
MAUROIS, A. THE WORLD OF MARCEL
PROUST.
442(NY):7APR75-139
"MAURUS OF SALERNO TWELFTH-CENTURY
'OPTIMUS PHYSICUS,' WITH HIS COM-
MENTARY ON THE PROGNOSTICS OF
HIPPOCRATES." (M.H. SAFFRON, TRANS)
J.M. RIDDLE, 589:JAN74-153
MAUSER-GOLLER, K. DIE RELATIVE
CHRONOLOGIE DES NEOLITHIKUMS IN
SÜDWESTDEUTSCHLAND UND DER SCHWEIZ.
P. SCHRÖTER, 182:VOL26#9-307
MAUTNER, F.H. LICHTENBERG.
E. SCHWARZ, 131(CL):WINTER73-75

MAUTNER, F.H. NESTROY.
  K. SEGAR, 617(TLS):3OCT75-1148
MAUTNER, F.H. - SEE NESTROY, J.
MAUVILLON, É. TRAITÉ GÉNÉRAL DU
  STILE AVEC UN TRAITÉ PARTICULIER DU
  STILE ÉPISTOLAIRE.
  P. LARTHOMAS, 209(FM):OCT73-416
MAVES, C. SENSUOUS PESSIMISM.*
  D.K. KIRBY, 432(NEQ):MAR74-173
  G. MELCHIORI, 402(MLR):OCT74-849
  G.B. TENNYSON, 445(NCF):SEP73-242
MAVRODES, G.I. BELIEF IN GOD.
  M.R. HAGAN, 480(P&R):SUMMER73-191
MAW, J. KISWAHILI KUSOMEA CERTIFI-
  CATE.
  J.J. CHRISTIE, 315(JAL):VOL11PT3-
  96
MAW, J. SOCIO-LINGUISTIC PROBLEMS
  & POTENTIALITIES OF EDUCATION
  THROUGH A FOREIGN LANGUAGE.
  315(JAL):VOL11PT2-104
MAXIMOV, V. THE SEVEN DAYS OF CREA-
  TION.
  E. MORGAN, 617(TLS):13JUN75-643
  J. RUBENSTEIN, 441:23FEB75-10
MAXSEIN, A. PHILOSOPHIA CORDIS.
  S. DECLOUX, 182:VOL26#3/4-68
MAXWELL, J.C. - SEE URE, P.
MAXWELL, N. WITCH DOCTOR'S APPREN-
  TICE.
  A. GOTTLIEB, 441:6APR75-7
MAXWELL, R. THE MINUS MAN.
  N. CALLENDAR, 441:6APR75-18
MAXWELL, R. NEW BRITISH ARCHITEC-
  TURE.
  R. OLIVER, 45:JUL73-41
MAXWELL, R.S., COMP. RECORDS OF THE
  BUREAU OF INSULAR AFFAIRS: RECORD
  GROUP 350.
  D.B. GRACY 2D, 14:APR73-249
MAXWELL-HYSLOP, K.R. WESTERN ASIAT-
  IC JEWELLERY C. 3000-612 B.C.
  I. PEILLON, 182:VOL26#17/18-618
"CATHERINE MAY: AN INDEXED REGISTER
  OF HER CONGRESSIONAL PAPERS, 1959-
  1970, IN THE WASHINGTON STATE UNI-
  VERSITY LIBRARY."
  K.J. PIKE, 14:JUL73-411
MAY, E.R. "LESSONS" OF THE PAST.*
  639(VQR):SPRING74-L
MAY, E.R. & J.C. THOMSON, JR., EDS.
  AMERICAN-EAST ASIAN RELATIONS.*
  W. LAFEBER, 293(JAST):AUG73-679
MAY, J.R. TOWARD A NEW EARTH.*
  R.B. HAUCK, 125:JUN74-373
  S. MALONEY, 219(GAR):FALL73-447
  T. ROGERS, 175:SUMMER73-81
  295:FEB74-403
MAY, K.M. ALDOUS HUXLEY.
  R. ASHLEY, 141:WINTER74-90
  R. HOPE, 541(RES):AUG73-375
  T. ROGERS, 175:SUMMER73-81
  P. VITOUX, 402(MLR):APR74-392
MAY, R. A COMPANION TO THE THEATRE.
  214:VOL6#24-114
MAY, R. THE COURAGE TO CREATE.
  A. BROYARD, 441:10NOV75-31
MAY, R. PAULUS.
  M. ELLMANN, 676(YR):SUMMER74-602
  639(VQR):AUTUMN74-CXXXIV
MAYAKOVSKY, V. WI THE HAILL VOICE.
  A. CLUYSENAAR, 565:VOL14#1-70

MAYASOVA, N.A. OLD RUSSIAN EMBROID-
  ERY.
  M. CHAMOT, 39:DEC73-514
MAYER, C.A. - SEE MAROT, C.
MAYER, D.M. ANGELICA KAUFFMAN, R.A.,
  1741-1807.
  D. THOMAS, 135:JUL73-228
MAYER, H. - SEE HEINE, H.
MAYER, J. MISCHFORMEN BAROCKER
  ERZÄHLKUNST.*
  B.L. SPAHR, 222(GR):NOV73-318
MAYER, M. THE BANKERS.
  D. HAPGOOD, 441:26JAN75-2
  N. VON HOFFMAN, 453:6MAR75-6
  C. LEHMANN-HAUPT, 441:1JAN75-15
  442(NY):27JAN75-104
"TOBIAS MAYER'S 'OPERA INEDITA'."
  (E.G. FORBES, TRANS)
  G. CARABELLI, 548(RCSF):JAN-MAR73-
  113
MAYEROFF, M. ON CARING.
  W.N. CLARKE, 258:MAR73-152
  C. WELCH, 321:SUMMER73-158
MAYFIELD, S. EXILES FROM PARADISE.*
  295:FEB74-604
MAYHEAD, R. WALTER SCOTT.
  G. THOMAS, 175:SUMMER73-80
MAYHEW, C. & M. ADAMS. PUBLISH IT
  NOT...
  M. BELL, 362:14AUG75-219
MAYHEW, D.R. THE ELECTORAL CONNEC-
  TION.
  P. FOTHERINGHAM, 617(TLS):1AUG75-
  876
MAYNARD, J. LOOKING BACK.
  C. TENNANT, 617(TLS):18APR75-418
MAYNE, S. - SEE LAYTON, I.
MAYO, A.P. - SEE UNDER PORQUERAS
  MAYO, A.
MAYO, P.E. THE ROOTS OF IDENTITY.
  K.O. MORGAN, 617(TLS):31JAN75-116
MAYOR, A.H. GOYA: 67 DRAWINGS.
  F. HASKELL, 453:2OCT75-14
MAYOUX, J-J. ENGLISH PAINTING FROM
  HOGARTH TO THE PRE-RAPHAELITES.
  D.A.N. JONES, 362:30OCT75-575
  J. RUSSELL, 441:7DEC75-20
MAYOUX, J-J. L'HUMOUR ET L'ABSURDE.
  A. FAIRLIE, 208(FS):OCT74-489
MAYRHOFER, M. KURZGEFASSTES ETYMOL-
  OGISCHES WÖRTERBUCH DES ALTINDIS-
  CHEN. (PTS 23 & 24)
  T. BURROW, 343:BAND17HEFT2-154
MAYRHOFER, M. A SANSKRIT GRAMMAR.
  O. VON HINÜBER, 343:BAND17HEFT1-
  103
MAYS, W. & S.C. BROWN, EDS. LIN-
  GUISTIC ANALYSIS & PHENOMENOLOGY.
  M. HOLLIS, 483:JAN73-95
  E. MATTHEWS, 479(PHQ):APR73-172
  P. MEW, 159(DM):AUTUMN/WINTER
  73/74-116
MAZAL, O. EUROPÄISCHE EINBANDKUNST
  AUS MITTELALTER UND NEUZEIT.
  A. HOBSON, 617(TLS):19DEC75-1524
MAZAL, O. - SEE ARISTAENETUS
MAZENOT, G. LA LIKOUALA-MOSSAKA,
  HISTOIRE DE LA PÉNÉTRATION DU HAUT-
  CONGO, 1878-1920.
  C. COQUERY-VIDROVITCH, 69:OCT73-
  368

MAZLISH, B. JAMES & JOHN STUART
MILL.
  G. HIMMELFARB, 617(TLS):23MAY75-
  565
  R.R. LINGEMAN, 441:25JUL75-29
  P. ROSENBERG, 441:6APR75-25
  A. RYAN, 453:29MAY75-4
MAZO, J.H. DANCE IS A CONTACT SPORT.
  L. SCHWARZBAUM, 441:26JAN75-5
MAZONOWICZ, D. VOICES FROM THE
STONE AGE.
  T.G.E. POWELL, 617(TLS):15AUG75-
  918
MAZOUR, A.G. WOMEN IN EXILE.
  L. SCHAPIRO, 617(TLS):26DEC75-1539
MAZOUR, A.G. THE WRITING OF HISTORY
IN THE SOVIET UNION.*
  S.H. BARON, 104:SUMMER73-262
  R.T. FISHER, JR., 550(RUSR):JUL73-
  320
MAZRUI, A.A. ISLAM & THE ENGLISH
LANGUAGE IN EAST & WEST AFRICA.
  315(JAL):VOL11PT2-103
MAŽVYDAS, M. THE OLD LITHUANIAN
CATECHISM OF MARTYNAS MAŽVYDAS
(1547). (G.B. FORD, JR., ED &
TRANS)
  A. BAMMESBERGER, 343:BAND16HEFT1-
  95
  D. ROBINSON, 279:VOL16-193
MAZZACANE, A. SCIENZA, LOGICA E
IDEOLOGIA NELLA GIURISPRUDENZA
TEDESCA DEL SEC. XVI.
  C. VASOLI, 548(RCSF):JAN-MAR73-92
MAZZAMUTO, P. - SEE MANZONI, A.
MAZZARO, J. WILLIAM CARLOS WIL-
LIAMS: THE LATER POEMS.*
  W. STAFFORD, 141:SPRING74-183
  L.W. WAGNER, 659:SUMMER75-378
MAZZARO, J. TRANSFORMATIONS IN THE
RENAISSANCE ENGLISH LYRIC.*
  J.S. LAWRY, 529(QQ):SUMMER73-302
MAZZOLANI, L.S. THE IDEA OF THE
CITY IN ROMAN THOUGHT.
  O. MURRAY, 447(N&Q):FEB73-79
MAZZOLI, G. SENECA E LA POESIA.
  N.T. PRATT, 24:SUMMER74-177
MEAD, G.H. L'ESPRIT, LE SOI ET LA
SOCIÉTÉ.
  C. SCHUWER, 542:JAN-MAR73-90
MEAD, M. RUTH BENEDICT.*
  J. BERNSTEIN, 442(NY):3FEB75-92
MEADE, R. GAYLORD'S BADGE.
  M. LEVIN, 441:9NOV75-54
MEADOWS, A.J. SCIENCE & CONTROVER-
SY.*
  L.G. WILSON, 637(VS):SEP73-114
MEADOWS, D.H. & OTHERS. THE LIMITS
TO GROWTH.*
  D.A. CHANT, 529(QQ):AUTUMN73-478
MEAKER, G.H. THE REVOLUTIONARY LEFT
IN SPAIN, 1914-1923.
  J. FUSI, 617(TLS):29AUG75-966
MEBANE, J. THE POOR MAN'S GUIDE TO
TRIVIA COLLECTING.
  G. WARD & R. STROZIER, 441:7DEC75-
  94
MEDEA, A. & K. THOMPSON. AGAINST
RAPE.
  G. SADLER, 617(TLS):20JUN75-692
DE MEDINA, F.D. - SEE UNDER DIEZ DE
MEDINA, F.

MEDINA, J.T. INTRODUCTION TO SPAN-
ISH LITERATURE.
  L. FONTANELLA, 399(MLJ):NOV74-367
MEDLEY, M. YÜAN PORCELAIN & STONE-
WARE.
  J. ADDIS, 617(TLS):2MAY75-493
MEDLIN, V.D., ED. THE RUSSIAN
REVOLUTION.
  D. SENESE, 104:WINTER74-603
MEDVEDEV, R.A. LET HISTORY JUDGE.*
  (D. JORAVSKY & G. HAUPT, EDS)
  D. LA BELLE, 104:SUMMER73-269
MEDVEDEV, R.A. ON SOCIALIST DEMO-
CRACY. (E. DE KADT, ED & TRANS)
  N. BLIVEN, 442(NY):22SEP75-127
  S.F. COHEN, 441:13JUL75-1
  R.R. LINGEMAN, 441:17JUL75-33
MEE, C.L., JR. MEETING AT POTSDAM.
  C. COCKBURN, 441:9MAR75-1
  C. LEHMANN-HAUPT, 441:9APR75-47
  K.G.M. ROSS, 617(TLS):21NOV75-1385
  A.J.P. TAYLOR, 231:MAY75-90
MEEROPOL, R. & M. WE ARE YOUR SONS.
  L. BRAUDY, 441:25MAY75-6
  C. LEHMANN-HAUPT, 441:23MAY75-41
MEETHAM, A.R. & R.A. HUDSON, EDS.
ENCYCLOPAEDIA OF LINGUISTICS, IN-
FORMATION & CONTROL.
  H. KRENN, 597(SN):VOL45#2-404
MEGAW, J.V.S. ART OF THE EUROPEAN
IRON AGE.
  H.L. THOMAS, 54:SEP73-440
MEGGS, B. THE MATTER OF PARADISE.
  N. CALLENDAR, 441:8JUN75-10
MEGGS, B. SATURDAY GAMES.*
  P.D. JAMES, 617(TLS):26SEP75-1079
MEHENDALE, M.A. SOME ASPECTS OF
INDO-ARYAN LINGUISTICS.*
  A.S. KAYE, 353:1JUL73-112
  L.A. SCHWARZSCHILD, 318(JAOS):
  OCT-DEC73-613
MEHL, D. DIE MITTELENGLISCHEN ROM-
ANZEN DES 13. UND 14. JAHRHUN-
DERTS.*
  G.H.V. BUNT, 179(ES):APR72-157
MEHL, R. LES ATTITUDES MORALES.
  M. ADAM, 542:OCT-DEC73-492
MEHLINGER, H.D. & J.M. THOMPSON.
COUNT WITTE & THE TSARIST GOVERN-
MENT IN THE 1905 REVOLUTION.*
  J. KEEP, 550(RUSR):JAN73-79
MEHLMAN, J. A STRUCTURAL STUDY OF
AUTOBIOGRAPHY.
  J. STURROCK, 617(TLS):18JUL75-806
MEHRA, P. THE YOUNGHUSBAND EXPEDI-
TION.
  R.W. WINKS, 318(JAOS):APR-JUN73-
  232
MEHRING, F. WERKAUSWAHL.
  P. LABANYI, 617(TLS):25JUL75-855
MEHROTRA, S.R. THE EMERGENCE OF
THE INDIAN NATIONAL CONGRESS.
  S.A. KOCHANEK, 293(JAST):FEB73-350
MEHTA, J.L. THE PHILOSOPHY OF MAR-
TIN HEIDEGGER.
  J.D.C., 543:JUN73-760
MEID, V. - SEE VON ZESEN, P.
MEID, W. DICHTER UND DICHTKUNST IM
ALTEN IRLAND.
  H. BIRKHAN, 343:BAND16HEFT1-103
MEID, W. DAS GERMANISCHE PRÄTERI-
TUM.*
  A. BAMMESBERGER, 38:BAND91HEFT2-
  245

MEID, W. - SEE KRAHE, H.
MEIER, A. & E. RUDWICK. CORE.*
N. MILLS, 676(YR):AUTUMN73-146
MEIER, P. LA PENSÉE UTOPIQUE DE
WILLIAM MORRIS.
D. LEDUC-FAYETTE, 542:APR-JUN73-
225
MEIJER, H.R. BANG WEER.
R. MEIJER, 617(TLS):28NOV75-1420
MEIJER, M.J. MARRIAGE LAW & POLICY
IN THE CHINESE PEOPLE'S REPUBLIC.*
D.C. BUXBAUM, 293(JAST):AUG73-699
MEIJER, R.P. LITERATURE OF THE LOW
COUNTRIES.*
J. TROMP, 202(FMOD):JUN73-419
MEILLER, A., ED. LA PACIENCE DE
JOB, MYSTÈRE ANONYME DU XVE
SIÈCLE.
S.R. ALFONSI, 207(FR):FEB73-602
MEILLER, A. - SEE JEAN DU PRIER
MEILLET, A. GENERAL CHARACTERISTICS
OF THE GERMANIC LANGUAGES.*
R.D., 179(ES):APR72-190
MEINECKE, D., ED. ÜBER PAUL CELAN.
K. WEISSENBERGER, 221(GQ):MAY73-
467
MEINECKE, D. WORT UND NAME BEI
PAUL CELAN.*
J.K. LYON, 221(GQ):JAN73-127
MEINEL, H. A COURSE IN SCIENTIFIC
GERMAN.
S. BAUSCHINGER, 399(MLJ):JAN-FEB
74-72
MEINTJES, J. PRESIDENT PAUL KRUGER.
P. WARWICK, 617(TLS):17OCT75-1243
MEIR, C. THE BALLADS & SONGS OF
W.B. YEATS.
G. HOUGH, 617(TLS):14FEB75-160
MEIR, G. MY LIFE.
A. ELON, 441:30NOV75-5
442(NY):10NOV75-190
MEISEL, J. WORKING PAPERS ON CAN-
ADIAN POLITICS. (REV)
J.A. LAPONCE, 529(QQ):AUTUMN73-456
MEISEL, J.M. EINFÜHRUNG IN DIE
TRANSFORMATIONELLE SYNTAX.
P. BLUMENTHAL, 72:BAND211HEFT1/3-
192
MEISEL, P. THOMAS HARDY.*
J.O. BAILEY, 125:OCT73-99
D. KRAMER, 445(NCF):DEC73-347
B. LUPINI, 175:SUMMER73-68
J.K. ROBINSON, 295:FEB74-628
B. SANKEY, 219(GAR):WINTER73-616
R.C. SCHWEIK, 177(ELT):VOL16#2-135
MEISS, M. FRENCH PAINTING IN THE
TIME OF JEAN DE BERRY.
J.J.G. ALEXANDER, 617(TLS):21MAR75-
309
MEISS, M. THE GREAT AGE OF FRESCO.
J. SCHULZ, 90:MAR73-184
MEISS, M. & E.W. KIRSCH - SEE "THE
VISCONTI HOURS"
MEISSNER, B., ED. SOCIAL CHANGE IN
THE SOVIET UNION.*
R.G. WESSON, 550(RUSR):JUL73-333
MEJEAN, S. LA CHANSON SATIRIQUE
PROVENÇALE AU MOYEN-AGE.
R. EHNERT, 439(NM):1973/2-366
MEJER, G. U ISTOKOV REVOLJUCII.
H.A. STAMMLER, 574(SEEJ):FALL73-
342

MEJÍA SÁNCHEZ, E. & F. GUILLÉN, EDS.
EL ENSAYO ACTUAL LATINOAMERICANO.
R. ESQUENAZI-MAYO, 263:JAN-MAR74-
71
MELANDER, I. THE POETRY OF SYLVIA
PLATH.*
I. LINDBLAD, 597(SN):VOL45#2-457
"MÉLANGES D'ESTHETIQUE ET DE SCIENCE
DE L'ART OFFERTS À ARSÈNE SOREIL."
P-M.S., 542:APR-JUN73-234
"MÉLANGES D'HISTOIRE DU XVIE SIÈCLE
OFFERTS À HENRI MEYLAN."
R.D. LINDER, 551(RENQ):SUMMER73-
191
MELANI, N. MOTIVI TRADIZIONALI E
FANTASIA DEL "DIVERTISSEMENT" NEL
TEATRO DI FLORENT CARTON DANCOURT
(1661-1725).
A. BLANC, 535(RHL):JAN-FEB73-127
MELCHIOR, I. SLEEPER AGENT.
N. CALLENDAR, 441:23NOV75-52
MELCHIOR DE MOLÈNES, C. L'EUROPE
DE STRASBOURG.
P. REYNERS, 189(EA):OCT-DEC73-500
MELDAU, R. SCHULSYNONYMIK DER DEUT-
SCHEN SPRACHE.
R.W. LISTERMAN, 399(MLJ):APR74-212
MELDAU, R. & J. LEYTON. THE LITTLE
ENGLAND BOOK. (5TH ED)
P.H. FRIES, 399(MLJ):JAN-FEB74-82
MELDAU, R. & R.J. TAYLOR. DEUTSCHE
ÜBERSETZUNGSBEISPIELE ZUR ENGLIS-
CHEN SPRACHLEHRE. (8TH ED)
P.H. FRIES, 399(MLJ):JAN-FEB74-82
MELDRUM, J. THE SEMONOV IMPULSE.
M. LASKI, 362:25DEC75&1JAN76-893
617(TLS):10OCT75-1174
MELETINSKI, E.M. & S.N. NEKLYUDOV,
EDS. TIPOLOGICHESKIE ISSLEDOVANIJA
PO FOLKLORU.
B. OGIBENIN, 617(TLS):12SEP75-1033
MELGUNOV, S.P. THE BOLSHEVIK SEIZ-
URE OF POWER. (ED & ABRIDGED BY
S.G. PUSHKAREV WITH B.S. PUSHKAREV)
A.E. ADAMS, 550(RUSR):OCT73-440
MELLEN, J. VOICES FROM THE JAPANESE
CINEMA.
M. WOOD, 453:12JUN75-36
MELLEN, P. JEAN CLOUET.*
C. SCHAEFER, 54:JUN73-298
MELLERS, W. TWILIGHT OF THE GODS.*
R. MIDDLETON, 410(M&L):JUL74-337
MELLERT-HOFFMANN, G. UNTERSUCHUNGEN
ZUR "IPHIGENIE IN AULIS" DES EURIP-
IDES.
W.T. MAC CARY, 121(CJ):DEC73/JAN74-
171
MELLGREN, L. & M. WALKER. NO MOON
ON FRIDAY. (H. SCHÜTT, ED)
K. OLTMANN, 430(NS):JUL73-387
MELLINKOFF, R. THE HORNED MOSES IN
MEDIEVAL ART & THOUGHT.*
M. STOKSTAD, 292(JAF):OCT-DEC73-
397
MELLON, S. - SEE GUIZOT, F.
MELLOR, A.K. BLAKE'S HUMAN FORM
DIVINE.
D.R. FAULKNER, 676(YR):SUMMER74-
590
MELLOR, D.H. THE MATTER OF CHANCE.*
R.N. GIERE, 536:JUN73-149
I. LEVI, 482(PHR):OCT73-524
J.L. MACKIE, 479(PHQ):JAN73-85
[CONTINUED]

MELLOR, D.H. THE MATTER OF CHANCE.*
[CONTINUING]
  A.C. MICHALOS, 486:MAR73-141
  A. MORTON, 154:MAR73-154
MELLOR, R.E.H. COMECON.*
  R.E. KANET, 104:SUMMER73-280
MELLORS, J. SHOTS IN THE DARK.*
  C. HOPE, 364:DEC74/JAN75-123
MELLOW, J.R. CHARMED CIRCLE.*
  639(VQR):SUMMER74-LXXXVIII
MELLOWN, E.W. A DESCRIPTIVE CATA-
LOGUE OF THE BIBLIOGRAPHIES OF 20TH
CENTURY BRITISH WRITERS.
  295:FEB74-357
  354:SEP73-266
MELMAN, S. THE PERMANENT WAR ECON-
OMY.
  J. FALLOWS, 441:26JAN75-3
MELTZER, B. & D. MICHIE, EDS. MACH-
INE INTELLIGENCE. (VOLS 5&6)
  M.A. BODEN, 84:MAR73-61
MEMMI, A. JEWS & ARABS.
  A.E. SHAPIRO, 441:21DEC75-5
  442(NY):8DEC75-199
MENANDER. THE PLAYS OF MENANDER.
  (L. CASSON, ED & TRANS)
  P.G.M. BROWN, 123:MAR74-128
  E. KEULS, 124:SEP72-47
MENANDER. LA SAMIENNE. (J.M.
JACQUES, ED & TRANS)
  C. DEDOUSSI, 303:VOL93-228
MÉNARD, P. MANUEL D'ANCIEN FRAN-
ÇAIS. (VOL 3)
  P.F. DEMBOWSKI, 545(RPH):AUG73-86
MÉNARD, P. LE RIRE ET LE SOURIRE
DANS LE ROMAN COURTOIS EN FRANCE
AU MOYEN ÂGE (1150-1250).*
  P. HAIDU, 546(RR):JAN73-54
  F. LYONS, 382(MAE):1974/3-283
"MENCIUS."* (D.C. LAU, TRANS)
  F.C. GRAMLICH, 318(JAOS):APR-JUN73-
  209
MENDELOFF, H. A MANUAL OF COMPARA-
TIVE ROMANCE LINGUISTICS.*
  J.L. BUTLER, 545(RPH):FEB74-372
  R. DE DARDEL, 433:JUL73-305
MENDELSON, E. - SEE AUDEN, W.H.
DE MENDELSSOHN, P. S. FISCHER UND
SEIN VERLAG.
  T.J. REED, 402(MLR):APR74-464
DE MENDELSSOHN, P. DER ZAUBERER.
  (VOL 1)
  T.J. REED, 617(TLS):10OCT75-1206
DE MENDELSSOHN, P. - SEE MANN, T.
MENDÈS FRANCE, P. FACE TO FACE
WITH ASIA.
  639(VQR):SUMMER74-CI
MÉNDEZ, E.F. - SEE UNDER FERNÁNDEZ
MÉNDEZ, E.
MENDILOW, A.A. & A. SHALVI. THE
WORLD & ART OF SHAKESPEARE.
  J. HASLER, 179(ES):OCT72-459
DE MENDOZA, D.H. - SEE UNDER HURTADO
DE MENDOZA, D.
MENDOZA, P.M.D. - SEE UNDER DE USAN-
DIZAGA Y MENDOZA, P.M.
MENEN, A. FONTHILL.*
  M. IRWIN, 617(TLS):4JUL75-713
MENEN, A. THE NEW MYSTICS.
  P. HEBBLETHWAITE, 617(TLS):3JAN75-
  20
DE MENESES, F.D. - SEE UNDER DE SÁ
DE MENESES, F.

MENGER, R. DAS REGAL.
  S. JEANS, 410(M&L):JAN74-95
MENGES, K. KRITISCHE STUDIEN ZUR
WERTPHILOSOPHIE HERMANN BROCHS.
  E. BOA, 402(MLR):JAN74-231
MENKE, H. DIE TIERNAMEN IN "VAN
DEN VOS REINAERDE."
  D. LE SAGE, 402(MLR):JUL74-701
MENNEMEIER, F.N. FRIEDRICH SCHLEG-
ELS POESIEBEGRIFF, DARGESTELLT
ANHAND DER LITERATURKRITISCHEN
SCHRIFTEN.*
  M.H., 191(ELN):SEP73(SUPP)-157
  D. HARTH, 224(GRM):BAND23HEFT4-486
  R. PAULIN, 402(MLR):APR74-461
MENYUK, P. THE ACQUISITION & DEVEL-
OPMENT OF LANGUAGE.
  E.P. HAMP, 269(IJAL):JUL73-199
MERCADIER, G. - SEE DE CADALSO, J.
MERCER, P. SYMPATHY & ETHICS.*
  M. MIDGLEY, 483:OCT73-399
  C.B. STEWART, 154:MAR73-124
  C.C.W. TAYLOR, 482(PHR):OCT73-537
MERCIER, L-S. L'AN DEUX MILLE
QUATRE CENT QUARANTE.* (R. TROUS-
SON, ED)
  I. PATERSON, 402(MLR):APR74-414
  L.C. ROSENFIELD, 207(FR):OCT72-159
MERCIER, V. THE NEW NOVEL FROM
QUENEAU TO PINGET.*
  M.P. LEVITT, 295:FEB74-434
MEREDITH, G. THE LETTERS OF GEORGE
MEREDITH.* (C.L. CLINE, ED)
  F. LÉAUD, 189(EA):JAN-MAR73-65
MEREDITH, W. HAZARD, THE PAINTER.
  J.M. BRINNIN, 441:21SEP75-39
MÉRIMÉE, P. NOTES DE VOYAGES.
  (P-M. AUZAS, ED)
  P. SALOMON, 535(RHL):JAN-FEB73-143
MERK, F., WITH L.B. MERK. SLAVERY
& THE ANNEXATION OF TEXAS.*
  R.N. CURRENT, 579(SAQ):SPRING74-
  274
  J.H. SCHROEDER, 432(NEQ):JUN74-324
MERKEL, I. BAROCK.*
  E. THURNHER, 133:1973/3-255
MERKELBACH, R. & H. VAN THIEL, EDS.
LATEINISCHES LESEHEFT ZUR EINFÜH-
RUNG IN PALÄOGRAPHIE UND TEXTKRIT-
IK.
  J.J. KEANEY, 124:MAR74-306
MERLEAU-PONTY, M. PHENOMENOLOGY,
LANGUAGE & SOCIOLOGY. (J. O'NEILL,
ED)
  C. SMITH, 617(TLS):4JUL75-736
MERLEAU-PONTY, M. THE PROSE OF THE
WORLD. (C. LEFORT, ED)
  J.P. MALL, 399(MLJ):NOV74-360
MERMIER, G. & Y. BOILLY-WIDMER. EX-
PLICATION DE TEXTE.
  J.C. EVANS, 399(MLJ):DEC73-439
  M.R. MORRIS, 207(FR):MAR73-885
MERRIAM, A.P. AN AFRICAN WORLD.
  J. LA FONTAINE, 617(TLS):17OCT75-
  1229
MERRILL, J. BRAVING THE ELEMENTS.*
  T. EAGLETON, 565:VOL14#3-66
  W.G.R., 502(PRS):FALL73-277
MERRILL, W.M. - SEE GARRISON, W.L.
MERRIMAN, J.D. THE FLOWER OF KINGS.
  D. PEARSALL, 402(MLR):OCT74-839
"THE MERRY ADVENTURES OF ROBIN HOOD."
  G. TYLER, 157:AUTUMN73-75
MERSMANN, H. - SEE MOZART, J.C.W.A.

MERTENS, J. & OTHERS. ORDONA. (VOL 3)
  A. HUS, 555:VOL47FASC1-187
MERTENS, V. DAS PREDIGTBUCH DES PRIESTERS KONRAD.
  I. MEINERS, 680(ZDP):BAND92HEFT3-457
  H.B. WILLSON, 402(MLR):JUL74-698
MERTZ, H. PALE INK.
  A.A. RICKETT, 651(WHR):SUMMER74-282
MERTZ, R. & B. TWO THOUSAND YEARS IN ROME.
  R.M. OGILVIE, 123:NOV74-267
MERWICK, D. BOSTON PRIESTS, 1848-1910.
  W.L. JOYCE, 432(NEQ):DEC73-637
MERWIN, W.S. (ASIAN FIGURES).*
  E. ENGELBERG, 598(SOR):SPRING75-440
MERWIN, W.S. WRITINGS TO AN UNFINISHED ACCOMPANIMENT.*
  P. RAMSEY, 569(SR):SPRING74-397
MESA-LAGO, C., ED. REVOLUTIONARY CHANGE IN CUBA.
  W.F. BARBER, 529(QQ):SPRING73-119
MESAROVIC, M. & E. PESTEL. MANKIND AT THE TURNING POINT.
  W. BECKERMAN, 617(TLS):12SEP75-1027
  J. NAUGHTON, 362:27MAR75-418
  E. ROTHSCHILD, 453:26JUN75-31
MESERVE, W.J. ROBERT E. SHERWOOD.
  J.M. WARE, 295:FEB74-778
MESNARD, J. - SEE PASCAL, B.
MESNARD, J. & OTHERS. LES "PENSÉES" DE PASCAL ONT TROIS CENTS ANS.
  A.D. SELLSTROM, 207(FR):MAR73-826
MESSBARGER, P.R. FICTION WITH A PAROCHIAL PURPOSE.
  R.J. CUNNINGHAM, 613:SPRING73-134
MESSINGER, H. - SEE "LANGENSCHEIDTS GROSSWÖRTERBUCH ENGLISCH-DEUTSCH"
MESSMANN, F.J. RICHARD PAYNE KNIGHT.
  J. GAGE, 617(TLS):25APR75-459
MESTRE, A. ILUSTRACIÓN Y REFORMA DE LA IGLESIA.
  G.E. MAZZEO, 241:SEP73-84
METCALF, G.J. & H.S. SCHULTZ, EDS. DEUTSCHE BEITRÄGE ZUR GEISTIGEN ÜBERLIEFERUNG. (VOL 6)
  H.A. HARTWIG, 221(GQ):NOV73-628
METCALF, J. GOING DOWN SLOW.
  J.R. LEITOLD, 150(DR):SUMMER73-367
  P. MORLEY, 102(CANL):AUTUMN73-102
  P.A. MORLEY, 529(QQ):SPRING73-138
METCALF, J. THE TEETH OF MY FATHER.
  A. BRENNAN, 198:SPRING75-123
  B. CAMERON, 99:AUG75-36
METCALF, P. VICTORIAN LONDON.*
  S. BAYLAY, 576:DEC73-347
  H. HOBHOUSE, 46:OCT73-273
METCALF, T.R., ED. MODERN INDIA.
  P. WALLACE, 318(JAOS):JAN-MAR73-124
METTAS, O. LES TECHNIQUES DE LA PHONÉTIQUE INSTRUMENTALE ET L'INTONATION.*
  A.W. GRUNDSTROM, 207(FR):OCT72-255
METTKE, H., ED. ALTDEUTSCHE TEXTE.
  M.O. WALSHE, 220(GL&L):OCT73-76

METTKE, H. MITTELHOCHDEUTSCHE GRAMMATIK. (3RD ED)
  M.O. WALSHE, 220(GL&L):OCT73-76
METZ, L.C. PAT GARRETT.
  W. GARD, 584(SWR):SUMMER74-V
METZ, R. CBS.
  K. COONEY, 441:17AUG75-4
  R.R. LINGEMAN, 441:19AUG75-37
METZGER, B.M. A TEXTUAL COMMENTARY OF THE GREEK NEW TESTAMENT.
  M. RISSI, 24:FALL74-295
METZGER, M.M. & E.A. STEFAN GEORGE.*
  I. JONES, 172(EDDA):1973/2-125
  M. WINKLER, 399(MLJ):SEP-OCT73-296
MEYER, B. DIE BILDUNG DER EIDGENOSSENSCHAFT IM 14. JAHRHUNDERT.
  H.S. OFFLER, 182:VOL26#5/6-180
MEYER, C.F. SÄMTLICHE WERKE. (VOLS 1-3, 8, 13 & 14) (H. ZELLER & A. ZÄCH, EDS)
  H. HENEL, 190:BAND67HEFT3/4-391
MEYER, C.S., ED. SIXTEENTH CENTURY ESSAYS & STUDIES. (VOL 2)
  R. PINEAS, 551(RENQ):WINTER73-477
MEYER, E. - SEE "PAUSANIAS FÜHRER DURCH OLYMPIA"
MEYER, F.S., ED. BREATHES THERE THE MAN.
  J.M. LALLEY, 396(MODA):SUMMER74-307
MEYER, F.S. A HANDBOOK OF ORNAMENT. (T. BIRKS, ED)
  S. JERVIS, 617(TLS):30MAY75-590
MEYER, H. DIE KUNST DES ERZÄHLENS.
  H. ADOLF, 400(MLN):OCT73-1039
MEYER, H. NATÜRLICHER ENTHUSIASMUS.
  S. ATKINS, 301(JEGP):APR74-288
MEYER, H. THE POETICS OF QUOTATION IN THE EUROPEAN NOVEL.
  B. ROUSE, 599:SPRING73-184
MEYER, H.C. THE LONG GENERATION.
  639(VQR):SPRING74-LI
MEYER, I.S., ED. THE HEBREW EXERCISES OF GOVERNOR WILLIAM BRADFORD.
  N. PETTIT, 432(NEQ):JUN74-321
MEYER, K., WITH OTHERS. BIBLIOGRAPHIE ZUR OSTEUROPÄISCHEN GESCHICHTE.
  M. RAEFF, 104:WINTER73-544
  J.S.G. SIMMONS, 575(SEER):JAN74-147
MEYER, K.M., ED. DETROIT ARCHITECTURE.*
  M.B. LAPPING, 576:OCT73-262
MEYER, L.B. EXPLAINING MUSIC.
  E. SAMS, 415:FEB74-133
  J.A. WESTRUP, 410(M&L):JAN74-89
DE MEYER, M. LE CONTE POPULAIRE FLAMAND.
  F.C. AMELINCKX, 582(SFQ):JUN73-145
MEYER, N. THE SEVEN-PER-CENT SOLUTION.*
  P. FRENCH, 617(TLS):21FEB75-184
  C. JAMES, 453:20FEB75-15
  C. NICOL, 231:FEB75-112
  M. YOUNG, 441:2FEB75-21
MEYER, N. TARGET PRACTICE.*
  617(TLS):12DEC75-1477
MEYER, U., ED. CONCEPTUAL ART.*
  R.J. SCLAFANI, 290(JAAC):SPRING74-443
MEYER-BAER, K. MUSIC OF THE SPHERES & THE DANCE OF DEATH.
  R. GRAMBO, 196:BAND14HEFT3-282

MEYER-TASCH, P.C. KORPORATIVISMUS
UND AUTORITARISMUS.
F. GILLIARD, 182:VOL26#21/22-786
MEYERS, E.M. JEWISH OSSUARIES.
Y.L. HOLMES, 318(JAOS):JUL-SEP73-
402
MEYERS, J. FICTION & THE COLONIAL
EXPERIENCE.
T. ROGERS, 175:SUMMER73-81
MEYERS, J. PAINTING & THE NOVEL.
D. MAY, 617(TLS):19SEP75-1066
MEYERSTEIN, R.S. FUNCTIONAL LOAD.*
H. KUČERA, 350:MAR74-169
H.J. NEUHAUS, 343:BAND16HEFT2-133
MEYNELL, F. MY LIVES.*
295:FEB74-375
MEYNELL, L. BURLINGTON SQUARE.
M. LEVIN, 441:13APR75-31
MEYNELL, L. DON'T STOP FOR HOOKY
HEFFERMAN.
617(TLS):11JUL75-784
MEYNET, R. L'ECRITURE ARABE EN
QUESTION.
H.K. SHERWANI, 273(IC):OCT73-355
MEYRAT, W. DAS SCHWEIZERISCHE BUND-
ESARCHIV VON 1798 BIS ZUR GEGENWART.
E. POSNER, 14:JUL73-406
MIANNAY, R. - SEE ROLLINAT, M.
MICEWSKI, A. ROMAN DMOWSKI.
S. DĄBROWSKI, 497(POLR):VOL18#4-
110
MICHA, H. VOLTAIRE D'APRÈS SA COR-
RESPONDANCE AVEC MADAME DENIS.
P. CONLON, 481(PQ):JUL73-590
MICHAEL, H.N. - SEE OKLADNIKOV, A.P.
MICHAEL, I., ED. THE POEM OF THE
CID.
A. DEYERMOND, 617(TLS):30OCT75-1127
MICHAEL, I. THE TREATMENT OF CLAS-
SICAL MATERIAL IN THE "LIBRO DE
ALEXANDRE."*
L. ALONSO, 400(MLN):MAR73-399
MICHAEL, W.F. DAS DEUTSCHE DRAMA
DES MITTELALTERS.*
D. BRETT-EVANS, 564:MAR73-75
MICHAELIS, R.F. ANTIQUE PEWTER OF
THE BRITISH ISLES.
G.M. WILSON, 135:APR73-290
MICHAELIS-JENA, R. THE BROTHERS
GRIMM.*
W.F.H. NICOLAISEN, 292(JAF):
JUL-SEP73-295
MICHAELS, B. THE SEA KING'S DAUGH-
TER.
M. LEVIN, 441:23NOV75-54
MICHAELS, L. I WOULD HAVE SAVED
THEM IF I COULD.
A. HELLER, 61:OCT75-108
I. HOWE, 453:13NOV75-42
C. LEHMANN-HAUPT, 441:30JUL75-31
T.R. EDWARDS, 441:3AUG75-1
P. ZWEIG, 231:SEP75-68
MICHALOS, A.C. THE POPPER-CARNAP
CONTROVERSY.
K.M., 543:SEP72-166
R.H. VINCENT, 154:JUN73-365
MICHAUX, H. ECUADOR.
J.S. RUSKAMP, 114(CHIR):VOL25#3-
177
MICHAUX, H. MOMENTS.* MISÉRABLE
MIRACLE. L'INFINI TURBULENT. CON-
NAISSANCE PAR LES GOUFFRES. LES
GRANDES ÉPREUVES DE L'ESPRIT.
[CONTINUED]

[CONTINUING]
EMERGENCES-RÉSURGENCES.
C. MOUCHARD, 98:OCT73-869
MICHEL, N. ICI COMMENCE.
J. PIEL, 98:DEC73-1148
MICHEL, P. BLAISE DE MONLUC.
R.D. COTTRELL, 207(FR):MAR73-821
MICHEL-MICHOT, P. WILLIAM SANSOM.
T. STEINMANN, 573(SSF):SUMMER73-
292
MICHELMAN, C. THE BLACK SASH OF
SOUTH AFRICA.
A. DELIUS, 617(TLS):17OCT75-1243
MICHELSON, H. CHARLIE O.
J. DURSO, 441:1JUN75-34
MICHELSON, P. THE EATER.
D.S. LENFEST, 114(CHIR):VOL25#4-
129
M.G. PERLOFF, 659:WINTER75-84
MICIŃSKA, A. - SEE WITKIEWICZ, S.I.
MICKEL, E.J., JR. THE ARTIFICIAL
PARADISES IN FRENCH LITERATURE.*
(VOL 1)
J.S.P., 191(ELN):SEP73(SUPP)-71
MICLĂU, P. LE SIGNE LINGUISTIQUE.
E.F.K. KOERNER, 353:1DEC73-123
MIDDENDORF, J.H., ED. ENGLISH WRIT-
ERS OF THE EIGHTEENTH CENTURY.*
P. ROGERS, 541(RES):MAY73-216
MIDDLEBROOK, D.W. WALT WHITMAN &
WALLACE STEVENS.
L. BECKETT, 617(TLS):7MAR75-243
MIDDLEMAS, K. CABORA BASSA.
D. BIRMINGHAM, 617(TLS):7NOV75-
1328
MIDDLETON, B.C. THE RESTORATION OF
LEATHER BINDINGS.*
D. CHAMBERS, 503:SPRING73-49
MIDDLETON, D. CAN AMERICA WIN THE
NEXT WAR?
R. EDER, 441:1NOV75-27
C. JOHNSON, 441:26OCT75-26
MIDDLETON, S. DISTRACTIONS.
G. CLIFFORD, 617(TLS):17OCT75-1225
J. MELLORS, 362:9OCT75-485
MIDDLETON, T. A CHASTE MAID IN
CHEAPSIDE. (R.B. PARKER, ED)
R. DAVRIL, 189(EA):OCT-DEC73-476
MIDELFORT, H.C.E. WITCH HUNTING IN
SOUTHWESTERN GERMANY, 1562-1684.*
676(YR):WINTER74-XVI
MIDGLEY, G. THE LIFE OF ORATOR
HENLEY.
A. BOWER, 566:AUTUMN73-40
MIERAU, F. REVOLUTION UND LYRIK.
S. SCHLENSTEDT, 654(WB):10/1973-
178
MIES, P. BEETHOVEN'S SKETCHES.
A. TYSON, 617(TLS):21FEB75-186
MIGEL, P. THE BALLERINAS.
A. PAGE, 290(JAAC):FALL73-136
MIGEOD, F.W.H. THE LANGUAGES OF
WEST AFRICA.
P.E.H. HAIR, 315(JAL):VOL11PT2-95
MIGNER, K. THEORIE DES MODERNEN
ROMANS.
H. STEINECKE, 52:BAND8HEFT1-106
MIGNOT, X. RECHERCHES SUR LE SUF-
FIXE "-TĒS," "-TĒTOS" (-TĀS,
-TĀTOS) DES ORIGINES À LA FIN DU
IVE SIÈCLE AVANT J-C.
V. LEINIEKS, 124:MAR73-377
MIGOZZI, J. CAMBODGE.
R. LUCCHINI, 182:VOL26#23/24-848

251

MIGUE, J-L. & G. BELANGER. THE
PRICE OF HEALTH.
  M.C. BROWN, 99:JAN75-42
DE MIGUEL, A. SOCIOLOGÍA DEL
FRANQUISMO.
  P. PRESTON, 617(TLS):4JUL75-740
MIGUEZ BONINO, J. REVOLUTIONARY
THEOLOGY COMES OF AGE.
  P. HEBBLETHWAITE, 617(TLS):5SEP75-
  1006
MIHĂESCU, H. - SEE MAURICIUS
MIHAILOVICH, V.D., ED. MODERN
SLAVIC LITERATURES.* (VOL 1)
  D. FANGER, 574(SEEJ):WINTER73-451
MIKASINOVICH, B., D. MILIVOJEVIĆ &
V.D. MIHAILOVICH, EDS. INTRODUC-
TION TO YUGOSLAV LITERATURE.
  M.P. COOTE, 574(SEEJ):FALL73-346
MIKES, G. SWITZERLAND FOR BEGINNERS.
  T.R. FYVEL, 617(TLS):2MAY75-486
MIKHAIL, E.H. A BIBLIOGRAPHY OF
MODERN IRISH DRAMA, 1899-1970.
  J.R. MULRYNE, 677:VOL4-337
MIKHAIL, E.H. SEAN O'CASEY.
  H. KOSOK, 430(NS):MAY73-286
  M.J. SIDNELL, 397(MD):JUN73-108
MIKHAIL, E.H. J.M. SYNGE.
  617(TLS):10OCT75-1187
MIKHAILOV, D. - SEE GOLDEN, L.
MIKKOLA, E. DIE ABSTRAKTION.
  J. UNTERMANN, 343:BAND16HEFT1-60
MIKO, S.J. TOWARD "WOMEN IN LOVE."*
  A.E. AUSTIN, 141:WINTER73-79
  E. DELAVENAY, 189(EA):JUL-SEP73-
  322
  V. MAHON, 541(RES):MAY73-246
  K. WIDMER, 295:APR74-1044
MIKROGIANNAKIS, E.I. DYNASTEIA
ANTIPATRIDŌN.
  J. BRISCOE, 123:NOV74-305
MILBURN, G., ED. TEACHING HISTORY
IN CANADA.
  C. KARR, 255:FALL73-312
MILES, D.H. HOFMANNSTHAL'S NOVEL
"ANDREAS."*
  T.P. BALDWIN, 406:SPRING74-80
  T. SCHEUFELE, 400(MLN):APR73-643
MILES, J. POETRY & CHANGE.
  D. DONOGHUE, 617(TLS):25APR75-442
MILES, J. TO ALL APPEARANCES.
  D. DONOGHUE, 617(TLS):25APR75-442
  H. VENDLER, 441:6APR75-4
MILES, J. & T. MORRIS. OPERATION
NIGHTFALL.
  N. CALLENDAR, 441:20APR75-27
MILES, J.C. HOUSE NAMES AROUND THE
WORLD.
  L. DUNKLING, 424:MAR73-50
MILES, K. AMBRIDGE SUMMER.
  A. HAMILTON, 362:20NOV75-681
MILES, R. THE FICTION OF SEX.
  G. CLIFFORD, 617(TLS):22AUG75-947
MILES, T.R. RELIGIOUS EXPERIENCE.
  R. NASH, 154:DEC73-732
  G. SLATER, 479(PHQ):JUL73-283
MILGATE, W. - SEE BALD, R.C.
MILGRAM, S. OBEDIENCE TO AUTHOR-
ITY.*
  639(VQR):SUMMER74-CIV
MILHAUD, D. MA VIE HEUREUSE.*
  C. PALMER, 415:NOV74-947
MILIBAND, R. & J. SAVILLE, EDS. THE
SOCIALIST REGISTER 1973.*
  J. DUNN, 362:9JAN75-58

MILIN, G. - SEE NOËL DU FAIL
MILIUTIN, N.A. SOTSGOROD.
  C. COOKE, 617(TLS):12DEC75-1492
MILL, J.S. THE COLLECTED WORKS OF
JOHN STUART MILL. (VOLS 14-17: THE
LATER LETTERS OF JOHN STUART MILL,
1849-1873.) (F.E MINEKA & D.N.
LINDLEY, EDS)
  C.R. SANDERS, 579(SAQ):SPRING74-
  270
  J.B. SCHNEEWIND, 637(VS):DEC73-238
  L.W. SUMNER, 482(PHR):OCT74-504
  676(YR):AUTUMN73-VIII
MILL, J.S. A SYSTEM OF LOGIC.
(J.M. ROBSON, ED)
  J.L. MACKIE, 617(TLS):7MAR75-257
MILLÁN, R. LECTURAS DEL SUBURBIO.
  L.C. PÉREZ, 399(MLJ):JAN-FEB73-67
MILLÁN, R. - SEE GARCÍA PAVÓN, F.
MILLÁN, R. - SEE LILLO, B.
MILLAND, R. WIDE-EYED IN BABYLON.*
  G. MILLAR, 362:27MAR75-419
MILLAR, B. THE DRIFTERS.
  M. PETERSON, 470:JAN74-33
MILLAR, G. THE BRUNEVAL RAID.*
  B. COLLIER, 441:17AUG75-12
DE MILLE, A. SPEAK TO ME, DANCE
WITH ME.
  D. VAUGHAN, 151:SEP73-90
"MILLE."* [CIRCOLO LINGUISTICO FLOR-
ENTINO]
  C. DE SIMONE, 343:BAND16HEFT1-115
MILLER, A. THE ANNEXATION OF A
"PHILOSOPHE."
  G. DULAC, 535(RHL):NOV-DEC73-1081
  R.J. ELLRICH, 207(FR):FEB73-611
  J.R. LOY, 546(RR):NOV74-313
  R. NIKLAUS, 208(FS):JUL74-328
MILLER, B. ROBERT BROWNING.
  639(VQR):WINTER74-XXVI
MILLER, D.M. THE NET OF HEPHAESTUS.
  R.S., 543:SEP72-166
MILLER, E.H. MELVILLE.
  R. TODD, 61:DEC75-114
  A. TRACHTENBERG, 441:14DEC75-23
MILLER, E.L. GOD & REASON.
  J.K. ROTH, 319:JAN75-125
MILLER, G.M., ED. BBC PRONOUNCING
DICTIONARY OF BRITISH NAMES.*
  I. SIMON, 556(RLV):1973/6-571
MILLER, H. AMBULANCE.
  M. LEVIN, 441:23NOV75-54
MILLER, H. BLACK SPRING.
  R. DAVIES, 617(TLS):17JAN75-50
MILLER, H., ED. MANAGEMENT & THE
WORKING ENVIRONMENT.
  D.A. ELLIOTT, 617(TLS):4JUL75-742
MILLER, H. THE NIGHTMARE NOTEBOOK.
  J. MARTIN, 441:14SEP75-7
MILLER, H. & W. FOWLIE. LETTERS OF
HENRY MILLER & WALLACE FOWLIE.
  J. MARTIN, 441:14SEP75-7
MILLER, H.K. - SEE FIELDING, H.
MILLER, H.K., E. ROTHSTEIN & G.S.
ROUSSEAU, EDS. THE AUGUSTAN
MILIEU.*
  H. ERSKINE-HILL, 541(RES):FEB73-89
  B. FABIAN, 173(ECS):FALL73-112
MILLER, H.R. A SPIRITUAL DIVORCE.
  M. LEVIN, 441:13APR75-32
MILLER, J. POPERY & POLITICS IN
ENGLAND, 1660-1688.
  N.C. PEARSE, 568(SCN):WINTER74-81
  G. REEDY, 173(ECS):SPRING74-372

252

MILLER, J. UNWRITTEN HISTORY.
W. KITTREDGE, 448:VOL13#2-80
MILLER, J.E., JR. - SEE JAMES, H.
MILLER, K. COCKBURN'S MILLENNIUM.
N. PHILLIPSON, 617(TLS):31OCT75-
1286
H. TREVOR-ROPER, 362:30OCT75-574
MILLER, M. PLAIN SPEAKING.*
D. CAUTE, 617(TLS):13JUN75-657
MILLER, M. THE SICILIAN COLONY
DATES: STUDIES IN CHRONOGRAPHY, I.
M.L. LANG, 122:JAN73-64
MILLER, M. THE THALASSOCRACIES.
A.S. BENJAMIN, 124(APR-MAY74-396
C.G. STARR, 122:JAN74-71
MILLER, M.H. ERNIE.
P. YOUNG, 441:27APR75-16
"THE MAX MILLER BLUE BOOK."
P. KEATING, 617(TLS):17OCT75-1224
MILLER, N. & R. AYA, EDS. NATIONAL
LIBERATION.
D. CALLAWAY, 293(JAST):MAY73-508
MILLER, P.L. THE RING OF WORDS.
M. PETERSON, 470:MAY73-15
MILLER, R.A. JAPANESE & THE OTHER
ALTAIC LANGUAGES.*
P.F. WELLS, 67:MAY74-141
MILLER, S. BURGFRIEDEN UND KLASSEN-
KAMPF.
P. PULZER, 617(TLS):12SEP75-1028
MILLER, V.B. A VERY DEADLY GAME.
N. CALLENDAR, 441:25MAY75-16
MILLER, W.C. AN ARMED AMERICA.*
J.T. FLANAGAN, 179(ES):AUG73-400
MILLER, W.R. UTO-AZTECAN COGNATE
SETS.
G.F. MEIER, 682(ZPSK):BAND26HEFT
3/4-438
MILLGATE, M. THOMAS HARDY.*
D. KRAMER, 301(JEGP):JAN74-138
R.C. SCHWEIK, 177(ELT):VOL16#2-135
MILLINGTON, R. THE STRANGE WORLD OF
THE CROSSWORD.
617(TLS):24JAN75-82
MILLMAN, R.N. THE MAKING OF THE
SCOTTISH LANDSCAPE.
R.E. GLASSCOCK, 617(TLS):31OCT75-
1286
MILLON, R. URBANIZATION AT TEOTI-
HUACÁN, MEXICO. (VOL 1)
N. HAMMOND, 617(TLS):11JUL75-780
MILLS, J. THE LAND OF IS.
T.E. TAUSKY, 102(CANL):WINTER74-
119
MILLS, J. ONE JUST MAN.
G. BURNSIDE, 441:16FEB75-4
442(NY):24MAR75-115
MILLS, J. REPORT TO THE COMMISSION-
ER.
N. CALLENDAR, 441:27APR75-29
MILLS, L.R., ED. L'HISTOIRE DE BAR-
LAAM ET JOSAPHAT.
B.M. CRAIG, 399(MLJ):DEC74-422
MILLS, M., ED. LYBEAUS DESCONUS.
A.S.G. EDWARDS, 179(ES):JUN72-251
MILLS, M., ED. SIX MIDDLE ENGLISH
ROMANCES.
R.M. WILSON, 402(MLR):OCT74-839
MILLS, N. AMERICAN & ENGLISH FIC-
TION IN THE NINETEENTH CENTURY.
M.D. BELL, 591(SIR):FALL74-371
MILLS, R.J., JR. - SEE IGNATOW, D.
MILLUM, T. IMAGES OF WOMAN.
P. WHITEHEAD, 362:22MAY75-683

MILLY, J. LES PASTICHES DE PROUST.
PROUST ET LE STYLE.
P. LARTHOMAS, 209(FM):APR73-196
MILNE, C. THE ENCHANTED PLACES.
P. ADAMS, 61:MAY75-103
P. GREEN, 617(TLS):4APR75-358
MILOJCIC-V. ZUMBUSCH, J. & V. MILOJ-
CIC. DIE DEUTSCHEN AUSGRABUNGEN
AUF DER OTZAKI-MAGULA IN THESSALIEN.
(PT 1)
M.S.F. HOOD, 303:VOL93-261
MILOSZ, C. SELECTED POEMS.*
V. YOUNG, 249(HUDR):WINTER74/75-
597
MILTNER, V. THEORY OF HINDU SYNTAX.
R. ROCHER, 318(JAOS):JUL-SEP73-382
MILTON, J. COMPLETE PROSE WORKS OF
JOHN MILTON. (VOL 4) (D.M. WOLFE,
ED)
M. FIXLER, 541(RES):FEB73-79
MILTON, J. COMPLETE PROSE WORKS OF
JOHN MILTON. (VOL 5, PT 1 ED BY
F. FOGLE; VOL 5, PT 2 ED BY P.W.
BLACKFORD)
M. FIXLER, 541(RES):FEB73-79
R. LEJOSNE, 189(EA):JAN-MAR73-101
D.A. ROBERTS, 551(RENQ):SPRING73-
89
MILTON, J. COMPLETE PROSE WORKS OF
JOHN MILTON. (VOL 6) (M. KELLEY,
ED)
W.B. HUNTER, JR., 568(SCN):SPRING-
SUMMER74-2
MILTON, J. PARADISE LOST. (BKS 1&2
ED BY C.A. PATRIDES; BK 9 ED BY R.
SYFRET; BK 10 ED BY C.A. PATRIDES)
THE MINOR POEMS IN ENGLISH. (D.
BUSH, ED)
R.E.C. HOUGHTON, 541(RES):NOV73-
488
MILTON, J.R., ED. CONVERSATIONS
WITH FRANK WATERS.
C. BANGS, 448:VOL13#2-96
MILWARD, P. SHAKESPEARE'S RELIG-
IOUS BACKGROUND.
E.D. MACKERNESS, 402(MLR):OCT74-
842
K. MUIR, 401(MLQ):JUN74-199
MINADEO, R. THE LYRE OF SCIENCE.
D.H. KELLY, 131(CL):WINTER73-94
MINAMI, H. PSYCHOLOGY OF THE JAPAN-
ESE PEOPLE.
R.G. FLERSHEM, 529(QQ):WINTER73-
639
J. SEWARD, 285(JAPQ):JAN-MAR73-107
H. WAGATSUMA, 293(JAST):NOV72-161
MINCHINTON, W. DEVON AT WORK.
617(TLS):7MAR75-261
MINDSZENTY, J. MEMOIRS.
W.F. BUCKLEY, JR., 441:20APR75-6
J.M. CAMERON, 453:18SEP75-3
G. MIKES, 617(TLS):21MAR75-294
P. WINDSOR, 362:20MAR75-378
MINEAR, R.H. VICTOR'S JUSTICE.*
K. STEINER, 293(JAST):AUG73-708
MINEKA, F.E. & D.N. LINDLEY - SEE
MILL, J.S.
MINEO, N. DANTE.
B.L., 275(IQ):FALL-WINTER73(VOL17
#66)-62
MINER, E. THE CAVALIER MODE FROM
JONSON TO COTTON.*
W. KERRIGAN, 141:FALL72-390
[CONTINUED]

MINER, E. THE CAVALIER MODE FROM JONSON TO COTTON.* [CONTINUING]
P.J. KORSHIN, 405(MP):NOV73-204
P. LEGOUIS, 189(EA):JUL-SEP73-362
J.H. MC CABE, 613:SPRING73-122
MINER, E., ED. JOHN DRYDEN.*
P. LEGOUIS, 189(EA):JUL-SEP73-366
MINER, E., ED. ENGLISH CRITICISM IN JAPAN.
R.D., 179(ES):AUG73-406
E.D. PENDRY, 677:VOL4-240
MINER, E. THE METAPHYSICAL MODE FROM DONNE TO COWLEY.*
T.A. BIRRELL, 179(ES):FEB73-71
MINER, E., ED. SEVENTEENTH-CENTURY IMAGERY.
M.C. BRADBROOK, 551(RENQ):WINTER73-542
R. ELLRODT, 189(EA):JAN-MAR73-95
R.P. LESSENICH, 597(SN):VOL45#1-182
K.J. SEMON, 599:SPRING73-202
MINGAZZINI, P. GREEK POTTERY PAINTING.
R. HIGGINS, 39:AUG73-150
MINISSI, N. PHONOLOGISCHE THEORIE UND ERGEBNISSE DER EXPERIMENTALEN PHONETIK.
G.F. MEIER, 682(ZPSK):BAND26HEFT 1/2-205
MINOGUE, K.R. THE CONCEPT OF A UNIVERSITY.
R. BUFFINGTON, 569(SR):WINTER74-147
483:OCT73-409
MINOT, S. CROSSINGS.
J.D. O'HARA, 441:26OCT75-50
MINOVI, M. & I. AFSHAR - SEE RASHĪD AD-DĪN RASHĪDĪYAH
MINSHALL, M. GUILT-EDGED.
R. LEWIN, 362:4DEC75-760
MINTON, C.E. JUAN OF SANTO NIÑO.
W. GARD, 584(SWR):WINTER74-98
MINTS, Z.G. - SEE SOLOVIEV, V.
MINTY, J. LAKE SONGS & OTHER FEARS.
R. LATTIMORE, 249(HUDR):AUTUMN74-468
J. SYLVESTER, 661:SPRING74-103
MINUCHIN, S. FAMILIES & FAMILY THERAPY.
E. FIRST, 453:20FEB75-8
MIRGELER, A. REVISION DER EUROPÄISCHEN GESCHICHTE.
M. ROUCHÉ, 182:VOL26#7/8-242
MIRÓ, E. - SEE MACHADO, M.
MIRSKY, M.J. THE SECRET TABLE.
T. LE CLAIR, 441:18MAY75-6
MISCHEL, T., ED. COGNITIVE DEVELOPMENT & EPISTEMOLOGY.
W. EASTMAN, 154:SEP73-541
V.J. MC GILL, 484(PPR):SEP73-112
MISCOLL-RECKERT, I.J. KLOSTER PETERSHAUSEN ALS BISCHÖFLICH-KONSTANZISCHES EIGENKLOSTER.
R. FOLZ, 182:VOL26#11/12-428
MISHIMA, Y. THE DECAY OF THE ANGEL.*
V. GLENDINNING, 617(TLS):24JAN75-73
MISHIMA, Y. RUNAWAY HORSES.*
B. ALLEN, 249(HUDR):SPRING74-119
J. MELLORS, 364:APR/MAY74-135
MISHIMA, Y. THE TEMPLE OF DAWN.*
B. ALLEN, 249(HUDR):SPRING74-119
639(VQR):SPRING74-LVI
MISHIMA, Y. & G. BOWNAS, EDS. NEW WRITING IN JAPAN.
M. BROCK, 285(JAPQ):JAN-MAR74-101
MISKIMIN, A. - SEE "SUSANNAH"
MISS READ. FARTHER AFIELD.
M. LEVIN, 441:16MAR75-30
MISTRAL, G. SELECTED POEMS OF GABRIELA MISTRAL.* (D. DANA, ED & TRANS)
M-L. GAZARIAN, 238:MAR73-183
MITCHELL, A. LABOUR IN IRISH POLITICS 1890-1930.
J. LEE, 617(TLS):11JUL75-758
MITCHELL, A. WARTIME.
442(NY):23JUN75-108
MITCHELL, B. THE JUSTIFICATION OF RELIGIOUS BELIEF.*
I.M. CROMBIE, 518:MAY74-14
MITCHELL, B. THE PRICE OF INDEPENDENCE.
P.D. NELSON, 656(WMQ):OCT74-692
G.F. SCHEER, 441:6APR75-28
E. WRIGHT, 617(TLS):13JUN75-663
639(VQR):AUTUMN74-CXLII
MITCHELL, D. GUSTAV MAHLER: THE WUNDERHORN YEARS.
S. WALSH, 362:27NOV75-730
MITCHELL, D.W. A HISTORY OF RUSSIAN & SOVIET SEA POWER.
J. ERICKSON, 617(TLS):25JUL75-823
MITCHELL, E.D. & J. WHITE, EDS. PSYCHIC EXPLORATION.
P. GROSE, 441:23AUG75-19
MITCHELL, E.J., ED. DIALOGUE ON WORLD OIL.
G. BARRACLOUGH, 453:7AUG75-23
MITCHELL, G. CONVENT ON STYX.
P.D. JAMES, 617(TLS):26DEC75-1544
MITCHELL, J. DEATH & BRIGHT WATER.*
N. CALLENDAR, 441:2FEB75-14
MITCHELL, J. THOMAS HOCCLEVE.*
M. ANDREW, 179(ES):OCT73-508
MITCHELL, J. SMEAR JOB.
M. LASKI, 362:25DEC75&1JAN76-893
MITCHELL, J.G. LOSING GROUND.
E. ABBEY, 441:20JUL75-6
MITCHELL, K. WANDERING RAFFERTY.
D. JEWISON, 102(CANL):SPRING74-122
MITCHELL, M. & OTHERS. FIRST CREE-READING BOOK.
H.C. WOLFART, 269(IJAL):OCT73-272
MITCHELL, R.E. PUPIL, PARENT & SCHOOL.
R.W. WILSON, 293(JAST):FEB73-324
MITCHELL, W.O. THE VANISHING POINT.*
H. ROSENGARTEN, 102(CANL):SUMMER 74-109
MITCHELL, W.S. - SEE DE VEGA, L.
MITCHELL, Y. COLETTE.
442(NY):8DEC75-198
MITCHISON, N. ALL CHANGE HERE.
M. WARNOCK, 362:19JUN75-820
MITCHISON, N. SOLUTION THREE.
T.A. SHIPPEY, 617(TLS):5DEC75-1438
MITFORD, J. THE AMERICAN PRISON BUSINESS.
M. DEAS, 362:20FEB75-250
T. PARKER, 617(TLS):21FEB75-184
MITFORD, J. KIND & USUAL PUNISHMENT.*
676(YR):SPRING74-VIII

MITFORD, T., ED. THE INSCRIPTIONS
OF KOURION.
  R.S. BAGNALL & T. DREW-BEAR, 487:
  SUMMER73-99 [& CONT IN] 487:AUT-
  UMN73-213
MITSCH, E. THE ART OF EGON SCHIELE.
  C.E. SCHORSKE, 453:11DEC75-39
MITTEN, D.G., J.G. PEDLEY & J.A.
  SCOTT, EDS. STUDIES PRESENTED TO
  GEORGE M.A. HANFMANN.
  R. HIGGINS, 54:SEP73-441
MITTENZWEI, I. DIE SPRACH ALS
  THEMA.
  J. VAN LENTE, 221(GQ):MAY73-434
MITTENZWEI, W. BRECHTS VERHÄLTNIS
  ZUR TRADITION.
  K. KÄNDLER, 654(WB):10/1973-166
MITTINS, W.H. & OTHERS. ATTITUDES
  TO ENGLISH USAGE.*
  L. GOOSSENS, 179(ES):APR72-179
MITTLER, E. DIE UNIVERSITÄTSBIBLIO-
  THEK FREIBURG I. BR. 1795-1823.
  J.L. FLOOD, 354:DEC73-355
MIYASHITA, K. MÖRIKES VERHÄLTNIS ZU
  SEINEN ZEITGENOSSEN.
  R. POHL, 680(ZDP):BAND92HEFT4-601
MIYOSHI, M. ACCOMPLICES OF SI-
  LENCE.*
  I. SCHUSTER, 268:JUL75-181
  639(VQR):AUTUMN74-CXXVII
MIZENER, A. THE SADDEST STORY.
  M. COHEN, 295:FEB74-606
MIZRAHI, H. BAY SHISHIM HOKHMA.
  E. SCHOENFELD, 196:BAND14HEFT1/2-
  168
MIZUNO, S. ASUKA BUDDHIST ART:
  HORYU-JI.
  M. MEDLEY, 617(TLS):11APR75-407
MIZUO, H. EDO PAINTING: SOTATSU &
  KORIN.
  C. DRESSER, 592:JUL-AUG73-59
  S. SITWELL, 39:AUG73-148
MLADENOV, M.S. IXTIMANSKIJAT GOVOR.
  T.J. BUTLER, 574(SEEJ):FALL72-380
MLIKOTIN, A.M. GENRE OF THE "INTER-
  NATIONAL NOVEL" IN THE WORKS OF
  TURGENEV & HENRY JAMES.
  R. FREEBORN, 575(SEER):JUL74-459
MOBERLY, R.B. THREE MOZART OPERAS.
  R. CRAFT, 453:27NOV75-16
"MOBILE HOMES."
  R. CASSIDY, 441:12JAN75-28
MOCCIA, D. LA VOCE DI DANTE.
  R.A., 275(IQ):SPRING74-104
MÓCSY, A. PANNONIA & UPPER MOESIA.
  J.M.C. TOYNBEE, 617(TLS):10JAN75-
  40
MODIANO, P. VILLA TRISTE.
  D. LEITCH, 617(TLS):12DEC75-1477
MOE, K. & T. STEMLAND, EDS. NORD-
  NORGE I PROSA OG LYRIKK.
  Å.H. LERVIK, 172(EDDA):1973/4-256
MOEHS, T.E. GREGORIUS V, 996-9.
  R. FOLZ, 182:VOL26#20-764
MOELLEKEN, W.W., ED. LIEBE UND EHE.
  C. BAIER, 220(GL&L):OCT73-79
  F. URBANEK, 221(GQ):JAN73-132
MOELLER, J. & OTHERS. BLICKPUNKT
  DEUTSCHLAND.
  R.E. WOOD, 399(MLJ):NOV74-363
MOFFATT, G. MISS PINK AT THE EDGE
  OF THE WORLD.
  617(TLS):4APR75-353

MOFFETT, K. JULES OLITSKI.
  J. ELDERFIELD, 592:NOV73-206
MOGGRIDGE, D.E., ED. KEYNES.
  H.G. JOHNSON, 617(TLS):7FEB75-139
MOGUŠ, M. FONOLOŠKI RAZVOJ HRVAT-
  SKOGA JEZIKA.
  A. ALBIN, 574(SEEJ):FALL72-375
MOHAMMAD, S. - SEE KHAN, S.A.
MOHANTY, J.N. THE CONCEPT OF INTEN-
  TIONALITY.*
  R.J. DEVETTERE, 258:DEC73-583
MOHR, H. WILHELM HEINSE.
  M. POITZSCH, 406:SUMMER74-202
VON MOHRENSCHILDT, D., ED. THE RUS-
  SIAN REVOLUTION OF 1917.
  D.R. JONES, 104:SUMMER73-268
MOIGNET, G. GRAMMAIRE DE L'ANCIEN
  FRANÇAIS.
  J. KLAUSENBURGER, 399(MLJ):DEC74-
  425
MOISEEVA, G.N. LOMONOSOV I DREVNE-
  RUSSKAJA LITERATURA.
  J.G. GARRARD, 574(SEEJ):SUMMER73-
  225
MOISÉS, M., ED. A LITERATURA BRAS-
  ILEIRA ATRAVÉS DOS TEXTOS.
  M.L. DANIEL, 399(MLJ):JAN-FEB73-62
VON MOISY, S. UNTERSUCHUNGEN ZUR
  ERZÄHLWEISE IN STATIUS' "THEBAIS."
  F. DELARUE, 555:VOL47FASC1-165
MOIX, T. MÓN MASCLE.
  A. ADELL, 270:VOL23#2-44
MOJTABAI, A.G. MUNDOME.*
  J. YARDLEY, 569(SR):SUMMER74-537
MOLDENHAUER, J.J. - SEE THOREAU,
  H.D.
MOLE, J. THE INSTRUMENTS.*
  S. CURTIS, 148:SPRING72-85
MOLE, J. A PARTIAL LIGHT.
  A. THWAITE, 617(TLS):7NOV75-1327
VAN DER MOLEN, S.J. PROFIEL VAN EEN
  WATERLAND.
  C.R. BOXER, 617(TLS):28NOV75-1423
DE MOLÈNES, C.M. - SEE UNDER MEL-
  CHIOR DE MOLÈNES, C.
MOLES, A.A. LE KITSCH, L'ART DU
  BONHEUR.
  A. GIGUÈRE, 154:SEP73-566
MOLHO, A. & J.A. TEDESCHI, EDS.
  RENAISSANCE STUDIES IN HONOR OF
  HANS BARON.
  G.A. BRUCKER, 551(RENQ):AUTUMN73-
  297
MOLHO, R. L'ORDRE ET LES TÉNÈBRES,
  OU LA NAISSANCE D'UN MYTHE DU
  XVIIE SIÈCLE CHEZ SAINTE-BEUVE.
  R. MERCIER, 557(RSH):JAN-MAR73-172
MOLIÈRE, J·B·P· LES FOURBERIES DE
  SCAPIN.* (J.T. STOKER, ED)
  C.N. SMITH, 208(FS):JAN74-67
DE MOLINA, T. - SEE UNDER TIRSO DE
  MOLINA
MOLINARI, C. THEATRE THROUGH THE
  AGES.
  R. SOUTHERN, 617(TLS):8AUG75-888
  G. WARD & R. STROZIER, 441:7DEC75-
  94
MOLINARO, J.A., ED. PETRARCH TO
  PIRANDELLO.
  A.L. LEPSCHY, 402(MLR):JUL74-654
DE MOLINOS, M. GUÍA ESPIRITUAL
  SEGUIDA DE LA DEFENSA DE LA CON-
  TEMPLACIÓN. (J.A. VALENTE, ED)
  J.M. COHEN, 617(TLS):28MAR75-345

MOLLAY, K. - SEE KOTTANNER, H.
MOLLENHAUER, K. & OTHERS. EVANGEL-
ISCHE JUGENDARBEIT IN DEUTSCHLAND.
N.M. BEATTIE, 182:VOL26#5/6-141
MÖLLER, G. PRAKTISCHE STILLEHRE.
G.F. MEIER, 682(ZPSK):BAND26HEFT6-
724
MØLLER, S. MALTE-BRUNS LITTERAERE
KRITIK OG DENS PLADS I TRANSFORMA-
TIONPROCESSEN MELLEM KLASSICISME
OG ROMANTIK I FRANSK LITTERATURHIS-
TORIE 1800-1826.
K. TOGEBY, 597(SN):VOL45#2-410
MØLLER, S. - SEE BRUUN, M.C.
MOLLICA, A., D. STEFOFF & E. MOLLICA,
EDS. FLEURS DE LIS.
L.R. POLLY, 399(MLJ):DEC74-421
MOLLOY, S. LA DIFFUSION DE LA LIT-
TÉRATURE HISPANO-AMÉRICAINE EN
FRANCE AU XXE SIÈCLE.
M.G. BERG, 131(CL):SPRING74-187
MOLNAR, T. GOD & THE KNOWLEDGE OF
REALITY.
H.M. CURTLER, 396(MODA):SUMMER74-
322
MOLYNEUX, M. LEGAL PROBLEMS.
J.R. EWER, 399(MLJ):SEP-OCT74-298
MOMADAY, N.S. ANGLE OF GEESE &
OTHER POEMS.*
J. FINLAY, 598(SOR):SUMMER75-658
R.B. SHAW, 491:SEP75-352
MOMIGLIANO, A. THE DEVELOPMENT OF
GREEK BIOGRAPHY.
A.J. PODLECKI, 124:MAY73-466
F. WEHRLI, 24:SUMMER74-184
MOMMSEN, H., D. PETZINA & B. WEIS-
BROD, EDS. INDUSTRIELLES SYSTEM
UND POLITISCHE ENTWICKLUNG IN DER
WEIMARER REPUBLIK.
P. PULZER, 617(TLS):12SEP75-1028
MONACO, G. IL LIBRO DEI LUDI. (2ND
ED)
J. PERRET, 555:VOL47FASC2-355
MONACO, G. - SEE PLAUTUS
MONAS, S. - SEE MANDELSTAM, O.
DE MONBRON, L-C.F. - SEE UNDER FOU-
GEROT DE MONBRON, L-C.
"LE MONDE AUTOUR DE 1492."
R.H. BLOCH, 207(FR):MAR73-872
"LE MONDE DE M.C. ESCHER."
P. FRESNAULT-DERUELLE, 98:MAY73-
447
MONDELLI, R.J. & P. FRANÇOIS.
FRENCH CONVERSATIONAL REVIEW GRAM-
MAR. (3RD ED)
G.R. DANNER, 207(FR):DEC72-467
MONDOR, H. & L.J. AUSTIN - SEE MAL-
LARMÉ, S.
MONEY, J. & P. TUCKER. SEXUAL SIG-
NATURES.
L. WOLFE, 441:4MAY75-6
MONEY, K. FONTEYN.*
J. ROCKWELL, 441:19JAN75-32
"THE MONGOL TALES OF THE 32 WOODEN
MEN." (S. LOHIA, TRANS)
G. KARA, 318(JAOS):JAN-MAR73-93
MONGRÉDIEN, G. RECUEIL DES TEXTES
ET DES DOCUMENTS DU XVIIE SIÈCLE
RELATIFS À CORNEILLE.
R. HORVILLE, 557(RSH):OCT-DEC73-
657

MONGRÉDIEN, G. & J. ROBERT. DIC-
TIONNAIRE BIOGRAPHIQUE DES COMÉD-
IENS FRANÇAIS DU XVIIE SIÈCLE.
(SUPPLEMENT)
M. LEVER, 535(RHL):NOV-DEC73-1065
MONK, J.D. INTRODUCTION TO SET
THEORY.
J.R. SHOENFIELD, 316:MAR73-151
MONK, S.H. - SEE DRYDEN, J.
MÖNKE, H. DAS FUTURUM DER POLNIS-
CHEN VERBA.
R.D. STEELE, 574(SEEJ):SPRING73-
107
MONOD, J. CHANCE & NECESSITY.*
(FRENCH TITLE: LE HASARD ET LA
NÉCESSITÉ.)
W. HOLTZ, 454:WINTER74-190
MONOGATARI, O. - SEE UNDER OCHIKUBO
MONOGATARI
MONRO, H. THE AMBIVALENCE OF BER-
NARD MANDEVILLE.
R. TUCK, 617(TLS):5SEP75-983
MONROE, J.T. ISLAM & THE ARABS IN
SPANISH SCHOLARSHIP (SIXTEENTH CEN-
TURY TO THE PRESENT).
R. HITCHCOCK, 86(BHS):OCT73-387
MONROE, M. MY STORY.
G. MILLAR, 362:4DEC75-754
MONSKY, M. LOOKING OUT FOR NO. 1.
N. CALLENDAR, 441:16MAR75-32
MONTAGU, M.W. THE SELECTED LETTERS
OF LADY MARY WORTLEY MONTAGU. (R.
HALSBAND, ED)
R. LONSDALE, 447(N&Q):MAY73-197
MONTAGUE, J., ED. THE FABER BOOK OF
IRISH VERSE.*
K. MILLER, 453:15MAY75-40
MONTAGUE, J. THE ROUGH FIELD.
A. CLUYSENAAR, 565:VOL14#3-70
D. MAHON, 376:JUL73-132
D.E.S. MAXWELL, 148:SUMMER73-180
MONTAGUE, R. FORMAL PHILOSOPHY.*
(R.H. THOMASON, ED)
T. PARSONS, 311(JP):10APR75-196
DE MONTAIGNE, M. DU REPENTIR. (R.A.
SAYCE, ED)
R. GRIFFITHS, 402(MLR):APR74-397
MONTALE, E. DIARIO DEL '71 E DEL
'72.
F. FORTINI, 617(TLS):31OCT75-1308
DE MONTALEMBERT, C. CORRESPONDANCE
INÉDITE, 1852-1870.
R.C. CARROLL, 207(FR):OCT72-180
DE MONTCHRESTIEN, A. ANTOINE DE
MONTCHRESTIEN: TWO TRAGEDIES. (C.N.
SMITH, ED)
G. JONDORF, 208(FS):APR74-194
R. PASCH, 72:BAND211HEFT1/3-221
MONTEFIORE, A., ED. NEUTRALITY &
IMPARTIALITY.
K. MINOGUE, 617(TLS):2MAY75-487
MONTEILHET, A. THAMAR.
S.S. WEINER, 207(FR):APR73-1058
MONTELL, W.L. THE SAGA OF COE
RIDGE.*
N. LEDERER, 577(SHR):WINTER73-98
MONTENEGRO, T.H. TUBERCULOSE E LIT-
ERATURA.* (2ND ED)
M. GANDOLFO, 37:JUN-JUL73-39
MONTER, B.H. KOZ'MA PRUTKOV.
M. DALTON, 574(SEEJ):SUMMER73-228
S.D. GRAHAM, 575(SEER):JAN74-132
MONTERO, X.A. - SEE UNDER ALONSO
MONTERO, X.

MONTERROSO, A. THE BLACK SHEEP &
OTHER FABLES.
J.G., 502(PRS):SPRING73-93
MONTEROSSO, F. - SEE MANZONI, A.
MONTESINOS, J.F. GALDŌS. (VOL 3)
E. RODGERS, 402(MLR):OCT74-905
MONTEVECCHI, A. MACHIAVELLI.
K.O., 275(IQ):SUMMER73-108
MONTEVERDI, C. LETTERE, DEDICHE E
PREFAZIONI. (D. DE' PAOLI, ED)
D. ARNOLD, 410(M&L):APR74-235
D. STEVENS, 617(TLS):9MAY75-507
MONTGOMERY, E.D., JR. "LE CHASTOIE-
MENT D'UN PÈRE À SON FILS."*
N.L. CORBETT, 545(RPH):AUG73-135
MONTGOMERY, M. FUGITIVE.*
W. LEAMON, 598(SOR):WINTER75-233
MONTGOMERY, M. THE REFLECTIVE JOUR-
NEY TOWARD ORDER.
A.C. LABRIOLA, 219(GAR):FALL73-445
DE MONTHERLANT, H. LE CARDINAL
D'ESPAGNE. (R. & P. JOHNSON, EDS)
L. BECKER, 399(MLJ):APR73-227
DE MONTHERLANT, H. LA MARÉE DU
SOIR.
H. KOPS, 207(FR):OCT72-225
DE MONTHERLANT, H. TOUS FEUX ÉTE-
INTS.
J. CRUICKSHANK, 617(TLS):12SEP75-
1032
MONTY, J.R. LES ROMANS DE L'ABBÉ
PRÉVOST.*
R.L. FRAUTSCHI, 546(RR):MAR74-131
MOODIE, T.D. THE RISE OF AFRIKANER-
DOM.
J. LEWIN, 617(TLS):17OCT75-1243
MOODY, A.D., ED. "THE WASTE LAND"
IN DIFFERENT VOICES.
G. HOUGH, 617(TLS):1AUG75-866
MOODY, C. SOLZHENITSYN.*
N.J. ANNING, 575(SEER):OCT74-613
P. ROSSBACHER, 574(SEEJ):FALL73-
341
MOODY, H.L.B. THE TEACHING OF LIT-
ERATURE IN DEVELOPING COUNTRIES.
E. QUENON-PAQUES, 556(RLV):1973/3-
282
MOODY, R. LILLIAN HELLMAN.*
J. COAKLEY, 295:FEB74-632
MOODY, R.E., ED. THE SALTONSTALL
PAPERS, 1607-1815. (VOL 1)
R.S. DUNN, 432(NEQ):MAR74-137
W.M. FOWLER, JR., 14:APR73-240
MOON, H.K. ALEJANDRO CASONA, PLAY-
WRIGHT.
E.L. PLACER, 593:FALL74-285
MOON, H.K. SPANISH LITERATURE.
M.M. DÍAZ, 238:MAR73-192
E. ECHEVARRÍA, 399(MLJ):NOV73-374
MOONEY, M.M. - SEE CATLIN, G.
MOOR, D. AN IMPOSSIBLE WOMAN. (G.
GREENE, ED)
A.L. BARKER, 362:25SEP75-406
DE MOOR, J.C. NEW YEAR WITH CANAAN-
ITES & ISRAELITES.
D. MARCUS, 318(JAOS):OCT-DEC73-589
MOORCOCK, M. THE HOLLOW LANDS.
V. GLENDINNING, 617(TLS):10OCT75-
1217
MOORE, A.K. CONTESTABLE CONCEPTS OF
LITERARY CRITICISM.
M. EATON, 113:FALL73-166
MOORE, B., ED. BLACK THEOLOGY.*
617(TLS):10JAN75-41

MOORE, B. CATHOLICS.*
J.M. FLORA, 385(MQR):WINTER75-101
M. PRICE, 676(YR):AUTUMN73-80
R. SMITH, 102(CANL):AUTUMN73-100
MOORE, B. THE GREAT VICTORIAN COL-
LECTION.
K. DOBBS, 99:OCT75-37
T.R. EDWARDS, 453:7AUG75-34
P. FRENCH, 617(TLS):17OCT75-1225
C. LEHMANN-HAUPT, 441:2JUN75-23
J. MELLORS, 362:30OCT75-582
L.E. SISSMAN, 442(NY):4AUG75-89
P. THEROUX, 441:29JUN75-2
E. WEEKS, 61:JUL75-81
MOORE, C., G. ALLEN & D. LYNDON.
THE PLACE OF HOUSES.
P. GOLDBERGER, 441:28JAN75-37
MOORE, C.M. ÜBER DEUTSCHLAND.
205(FMLS):APR73-214
MOORE, D.L., ED. LORD BYRON ACCOUNTS
RENDERED.*
W. MAXWELL, 442(NY):31MAR75-86
MOORE, F.T. & OTHERS. EXPORT PROS-
PECTS FOR THE REPUBLIC OF VIETNAM.
P.F. BELL, 293(JAST):NOV72-220
MOORE, G. CONFESSIONS OF A YOUNG
MAN.* (S. DICK, ED)
H.E. GERBER, 255(HAB):WINTER73-59
E. GILCHER, 177(ELT):VOL16#1-81
L. ORMOND, 677:VOL4-332
MOORE, G. THE JOURNAL OF GILES
MOORE. (R. BIRD, ED)
M. BOND, 325:APR73-614
MOORE, G. THE SCHUBERT SONG CYCLES.
D. ARNOLD, 362:1MAY75-588
W. GRUNER, 617(TLS):12SEP75-1030
MOORE, H.T. THE PRIEST OF LOVE.
M. MUDRICK, 249(HUDR):AUTUMN74-425
MOORE, J.M., ED. ARISTOTLE & XENO-
PHON ON DEMOCRACY & OLIGARCHY.
V. EHRENBERG, 617(TLS):16MAY75-534
MOORE, J.R. MASKS OF LOVE & DEATH.*
H.H. WATTS, 295:FEB74-838
MOORE, L.H., JR. ROBERT PENN WAR-
REN & HISTORY.*
E.M. KERR, 295:FEB74-812
MOORE, P., ED. 1976 YEARBOOK OF
ASTRONOMY.
617(TLS):26DEC75-1547
MOORE, R. A QUESTION OF SURVIVAL.
K.S. BYER, 219(GAR):SPRING73-110
J. DITSKY, 577(SHR):SPRING73-227
MOORE, T. NOUVEAUMANIA.
L. EISENBERG, 441:26OCT75-44
MOORE, T.W. EDUCATIONAL THEORY.
617(TLS):7MAR75-261
MOORE, W.G. THE CLASSICAL DRAMA OF
FRANCE.*
H.T. BARNWELL, 402(MLR):JAN74-176
L. GOSSMAN, 207(FR):FEB73-608
J. MOREL, 557(RSH):OCT-DEC73-655
J-P. RYNGAERT, 535(RHL):NOV-DEC73-
1066
MOOREHEAD, L. - SEE STARK, F.
MOOREY, P.R.S. ANCIENT PERSIAN
BRONZES.
J.E. CURTIS, 617(TLS):24JAN75-92
MOORMAN, C. KINGS & CAPTAINS.*
F.M. COMBELLACK, 122:JAN73-70
E. REISS, 125:JUN74-370
MOORMAN, M. - SEE WORDSWORTH, W. & D.
MOORMAN, M. & A.G. HILL - SEE WORDS-
WORTH, W. & D.

MORAES, D. THE TEMPEST WITHIN.
B.M. MORRISON, 293(JAST):AUG73-716
MORAES, F. & E. HOWE, EDS. INDIA.
617(TLS):21FEB75-204
MORALES, H.L. - SEE UNDER LÓPEZ
MORALES, H.
MORÁN, F. NOVELA Y SEMIDESARROLLO.
L. HICKEY, 86(BHS):OCT73-411
MORAN, J. PRINTING PRESSES.
D. CHAMBERS, 503:AUTUMN73-146
MORAN, T.H. COPPER IN CHILE.
A. ANGELL, 617(TLS):15AUG75-924
MORAND, P. LES ÉCARTS AMOUREUX.
B. WRIGHT, 617(TLS):31JAN75-120
DE MORATÍN, L.F. - SEE UNDER FERNÁN-
DEZ DE MORATÍN, L.
MORAUD, Y. JUDITH OU L'IMPOSSIBLE
LIBERTÉ.
J. FOX, 208(FS):OCT74-484
MORAUX, P. & D. HARLFINGER, EDS.
UNTERSUCHUNGEN ZUR EUDEMISCHEN
ETHIK.*
J. BARNES, 53(AGP):BAND55HEFT3-334
MORAVEC, F. MASTER OF SPIES.
B. COLLIER, 441:17AUG75-12
V. KUSIN, 617(TLS):11APR75-408
E. DE MAUNY, 362:20FEB75-250
MORAVIA, A. LADY GODIVA & OTHER
STORIES.
R. FOSTER, 617(TLS):20JUN75-704
J. MELLORS, 362:18SEP75-386
MORAVIA, A. WHICH TRIBE DO YOU
BELONG TO?*
N. GORDIMER, 364:OCT/NOV74-53
J. UPDIKE, 442(NY):24MAR75-109
MORAVIA, S. IL RAGAZZO SELVAGGIO
DELL'AVEYRON.
G. GARFAGNINI, 548(RCSF):JAN-MAR
73-113
MORAWSKI, S. L'ABSOLU ET LA FORME.
L. WELCH, 290(JAAC):SPRING74-427
MORE, T. THE COMPLETE WORKS OF ST.
THOMAS MORE.* (VOL 5) (J.M. HEAD-
LEY, ED)
A. NOVOTNY, 182:VOL26#21/22-816
H.C. PORTER, 447(N&Q):OCT73-395
MORE, T. THE COMPLETE WORKS OF ST.
THOMAS MORE.* (VOL 8) (L.A. SCHUS-
TER & OTHERS, EDS)
A. NOVOTNY, 182:VOL26#21/22-816
MOREAU, J. PLOTIN OU LA GLOIRE DE
LA PHILOSOPHIE ANTIQUE.
H. SEIDL, 53(AGP):BAND55HEFT1-86
MOREL, J. JEAN ROTROU DRAMATURGE
DE L'AMBIGÜITÉ.
J. VAN BAELEN, 400(MLN):MAY73-848
MORENZ, S. DIE BEGEGNUNG EUROPAS
MIT ÄGYPTEN.
W.R. BERGER, 52:BAND8HEFT1-84
MORESCHINI, C. - SEE TERTULLIAN
MORETTI, I. & R. STOPPANI. CHIESE
ROMANICHE NEL CHIANTI. CHIESE ROM-
ANICHE IN VALDELSA. CHIESE GOTICHE
NEL CONTADO FIORENTINO. CHIESE
ROMANICHE IN VAL DI CECINA. LA
PIEVE DI SANTA MARIA NOVELLA IN
CHIANTI. I CASTELLI DELL'ANTICA
LEGA DEL CHIANTI. CHIESE ROMANICHE
IN VAL DI PESA E VAL DI GREVE.
U. MIDDELDORF, 90:MAR73-184
MORETTI, M. DUALISMO GRECO E ANTRO-
POLOGIA CRISTIANA.
A.A. DE GENNARO, 319:JAN75-124

MORFORD, M., ED. THE ENDLESS FOUN-
TAIN.
J.F. FLEISCHAUER, 141:FALL73-378
MORFORD, M.P.O. & R.J. LENARDON.
CLASSICAL MYTHOLOGY.
E. PHINNEY, JR., 124:NOV72-183
MORGAN, A. THE CAT CAY WARRANT.
N. CALLENDAR, 441:23FEB75-40
MORGAN, B., ED. CRIME ON THE LINES.
H. GREENE, 362:18SEP75-385
MORGAN, D. SUFFRAGISTS & LIBERALS.
F.M. LEVENTHAL, 617(TLS):19SEP75-
1044
MORGAN, E. GLASGOW SONNETS.
A. CLUYSENAAR, 565:VOL14#3-70
MORGAN, E.S. AMERICAN SLAVERY,
AMERICAN FREEDOM.
J.H. PLUMB, 453:27NOV75-3
P.H. WOOD, 441:21DEC75-4
MORGAN, F. A BOOK OF CHANGE.
J.W. HEALEY, 502(PRS):SPRING73-90
L. LIEBERMAN, 676(YR):SPRING74-453
H. TAYLOR, 385(MQR):WINTER75-92
MORGAN, J.P. THE HOUSE OF LORDS &
THE LABOUR GOVERNMENT, 1964-1970.
E. BOYLE, 362:3JUL75-27
H. D'AVIGDOR-GOLDSMID, 617(TLS):
5SEP75-984
MORGAN, J.S. NOAH WEBSTER.
E.J. MONAGHAN, 441:21SEP75-14
MORGAN, K.O. KEIR HARDIE.
A. BRIGGS, 617(TLS):1AUG75-875
MORGAN, M.M. THE SHAVIAN PLAY-
GROUND.*
J-C. AMALRIC, 189(EA):OCT-DEC73-
486
R. DAVIES, 397(MD):DEC73-401
A.M. GIBBS, 541(RES):MAY73-237
W. KLUGE, 72:BAND211HEFT1/3-155
H. SERGEANT, 175:AUTUMN72-114
M. THOMPSON, 571:SUMMER73-265
A. TURCO, JR., 572:JAN73-30
MORGAN, P. CHILD CARE.
N. TUCKER, 617(TLS):18JUL75-799
MORGAN, P., ED. WARWICKSHIRE PRINT-
ERS' NOTICES, 1799-1866.
W.B. TODD, 447(N&Q):MAR73-115
MORGAN, P.F. - SEE HOOD, T.
MORGAN, R. MONSTER.*
H. ZINNES, 109:SPRING/SUMMER74-122
MORGAN, W.J., ED. NAVAL DOCUMENTS
OF THE AMERICAN REVOLUTION. (VOL 6)
S.G. MORSE, 432(NEQ):DEC74-607
MORGAN-GRENVILLE, G. BARGING INTO
BURGUNDY.
617(TLS):7MAR75-261
MORGANN, M. SHAKESPEARIAN CRITI-
CISM.* (D.A. FINEMAN, ED)
R.A. FOAKES, 175:AUTUMN72-107
J.P. HARDY, 541(RES):NOV73-496
G. MC FADDEN, 481(PQ):JUL73-558
B. VICKERS, 677:VOL4-276
MORGENSTERN, C. THE DAYNIGHT LAMP
& OTHER POEMS.
R. LATTIMORE, 249(HUDR):AUTUMN74-
472
MORGHEN, R. CIVILTÀ MEDIOEVALE AL
TRAMONTO.
S. MORAN, 275(IQ):SUMMER73-103
MORÍN, F.M. - SEE UNDER MARCOS
MORÍN, F.

258

MORRISON, H. & W. EBERHARD. HUA
SHAN - TAOIST MOUNTAIN IN CHINA.
R.H. LEARY, 60:SEP-OCT74-79
MORRISON, J. THE RISE OF THE ARTS
ON THE AMERICAN CAMPUS.
E.L. KAMARCK, 59(ASOC):SUMMER-FALL
74-320
MORRISON, K. ROBERT FROST.*
W.A. SUTTON, 598(SOR):AUTUMN75-937
MORRISON, T. SULA.*
P.M. SPACKS, 249(HUDR):SUMMER74-
283
MORRISSETTE, B. THE NOVELS OF
ROBBE-GRILLET.
A.R. PUGH, 268:JUL75-184
MORRISSEY, B.C. - SEE HEMENWAY, A.M.
MORROW, G.R. - SEE PROCLUS
MORROW, P. BRET HARTE.
M. BUCCO, 649(WAL):FALL73-159
MORSE, D. MOTOWN & THE ARRIVAL OF
BLACK MUSIC.
M. PETERSON, 470:JAN74-33
MORTIER, R. CLARTÉS ET OMBRES DU
SIÈCLE DES LUMIÈRES.
M. DELON, 535(RHL):NOV-DEC73-1073
MORTIMER, M.P., ED. CONTES AFRI-
CAINS.
J. ERICKSON, 399(MLJ):JAN-FEB74-67
MORTIMER, P. THE HOME.
J.C. FIELD, 556(RLV):1973/1-94
MORTIMER, P. ONLY WHEN IT HURTS.
617(TLS):28FEB75-232
MORTON, A. DANGER FOR THE BARON.
R. MOORE, 268:JAN75-82
MORTON, A.Q. & OTHERS. IT'S GREEK
TO THE COMPUTER.*
E.J.W. BARBER, 320(CJL):FALL74-167
E.G. BERRY, 255(HAB):WINTER73-66
J.G. GRIFFITH, 123:MAR74-162
J.T. MC DONOUGH, JR., 124:OCT72-
119
MORTON, B.N. & J. LA PRESSE.
R. MERKER, 399(MLJ):SEP-OCT73-283
MORTON, C. & H. MUNTZ, EDS. THE
"CARMEN DE HASTINGAE PROELIO" OF
GUY BISHOP OF AMIENS.
K.E. CUTLER, 589:APR74-364
MORTON, D. MAYOR HOWLAND.
A. POWELL, 99:APR/MAY75-29
MORTON, D. THE LAST WAR DRUM.
J.L. GRANATSTEIN, 529(QQ):SUMMER
73-295
MORTON, D. & R.H. ROY. TELEGRAMS OF
THE NORTH-WEST CAMPAIGN, 1885.
C.B. KOESTER, 150(DR):WINTER73/74-
766
MORTON, D.E. VLADIMIR NABOKOV.
A. DE JONGE, 617(TLS):16MAY75-526
MORTON, J., ED. BIOLOGICAL & SOCIAL
FACTORS IN PSYCHOLINGUISTICS.
A. DABIJA, 353:15SEP73-112
MORTON, J. IN THE SEA OF STERILE
MOUNTAINS.
H. TROPER, 99:APR/MAY75-21
MORTON, M.J. THE TERRORS OF IDEOL-
OGICAL POLITICS.
R. REINITZ, 656(WMQ):JAN74-156
MORTON, W.L. THE CANADIAN IDENTITY.
C. MILLER, 255(HAB):SUMMER73-210
VON MORUNGEN, H. ABBILDUNGEN ZUR
GESAMTEN HANDSCHRIFTLICHEN ÜBER-
LIEFERUNG. (U. MÜLLER, ED)
G.F. JONES, 221(GQ):MAR73-290

MORWITZ, E. KOMMENTAR ZU DEM WERK
STEFAN GEORGES. KOMMENTAR ZU DEN
PROSA-, DRAMA-, UND JUGEND-DICHTUN-
GEN STEFAN GEORGES.
I. JONES, 172(EDDA):1973/2-125
MOSCATI, S. & OTHERS. AN INTRODUC-
TION TO THE COMPARATIVE GRAMMAR OF
THE SEMITIC LANGUAGES.
J. FELLMAN, 361:OCT73-255
MOSCHINI MARCONI, S. GALLERIE
DELL'ACCADEMIA DI VENEZIA. (VOL 3)
90:MAY73-348
MOSELEY, G.V.H., 3D. THE CONSOLIDA-
TION OF THE SOUTH CHINA FRONTIER.
K.C. SMITH, 293(JAST):AUG73-701
MOSER, C.A. A HISTORY OF BULGARIAN
LITERATURE, 865-1944.*
M. PUNDEFF, 574(SEEJ):SUMMER73-239
MOSER, C.A. IVAN TURGENEV.
R.E. MATLAW, 574(SEEJ):WINTER72-
476
MOSER, H. BRIEFE IN AUSWAHL. (K.
SCHIB, ED)
A. LASSERRE, 182:VOL26#10-374
MOSER, H. DEUTSCHE SPRACHGESCHICHTE.
H. SZKLENAR, 260(IF):BAND77HEFT
2/3-382
MOSER, H., ED. MITTELHOCHDEUTSCHE
SPRUCHDICHTUNG.
U. MÜLLER, 680(ZDP):BAND92HEFT3-
465
MOSER, H., ED. NEUE GRAMMATIKTHE-
ORIEN UND IHRE ANWENDUNG AUF DAS
HEUTIGE DEUTSCH.
G. CUBBIN, 402(MLR):OCT74-908
MOSER, H. & U. MÜLLER - SEE VON WOL-
KENSTEIN, O.
MOSER, H. & J. MÜLLER-BLATTAU, EDS.
DEUTSCHE LIEDER DES MITTELALTERS
VON WALTHER VON DER VOGELWEIDE BIS
ZUM LOCHAMER-LIEDERBUCH.
J.W. THOMAS, 133:1973/3-271
MOSES, S. UNE AFFINITÉ LITTERAIRE.
F.S. LAMBASA, 406:FALL74-316
MOSHIMER, J. THE COMPLETE RUG HOOK-
ER.
B. GUTCHEON, 441:7DEC75-74
MOSKOFF, K. ETHNIKI KAI KOINONIKI
SYNEIDISI STIN ELLADA.
P.J. VATIKIOTIS, 617(TLS):14NOV75-
1366
MOSKOVIČ, V.A. STATISTIKA I SEMAN-
TIKA.
J. VEYRENC, 353:1OCT73-105
MOSLEY, O. MY LIFE.*
J. VINCENT, 617(TLS):4APR75-350
MOSS, H., ED. THE POET'S STORY.*
B. ALLEN, 249(HUDR):SPRING74-119
W.F. CLAIRE, 31(ASCH):WINTER74/75-
156
MOSS, J. PATTERNS OF ISOLATION IN
ENGLISH-CANADIAN FICTION.*
W.H. NEW, 102(CANL):AUTUMN74-83
MOSSÉ, F. MITTELENGLISCHE KURZGRAM-
MATIK.
J.R. SIMON, 189(EA):JUL-SEP73-347
MOSSE, G.L., ED. POLICE FORCES IN
HISTORY.
P.J. STEAD, 617(TLS):26SEP75-1106
MOSSOP, D.J. PURE POETRY.*
R. CHAMPIGNY, 207(FR):OCT72-166
P.J. SIEGEL, 446:SPRING-SUMMER74-
195
205(FMLS):OCT73-408

MOSTAERT, A. MANUAL OF MONGOL AS-
TROLOGY & DIVINATION. (F.W.
CLEAVES, ED)
  G. KARA, 318(JAOS):JAN-MAR73-94
MOSTERT, N. SUPERSHIP.*
  S. BARRACLOUGH, 362:10JUL75-61
MOU TSUNG-SAN. CHIH TE CHIH-CHIAO
YÜ CHUNG-KUO CHE-HSÜEH.
  S-H. LIU, 485(PE&W):JAN-APR73-255
MOULIN, R. & OTHERS. LES ARCHITEC-
TES.
  P. CHARPENTRAT, 98:NOV73-1057
MOULINAS, R. L'IMPRIMERIE, LA LIB-
RAIRIE ET LA PRESSE À AVIGNON AU
XVIIIE SIÈCLE.
  P. FRANCE, 617(TLS):21FEB75-193
MOULY, J. & E. COSTA. EMPLOYMENT
POLICIES IN DEVELOPING COUNTRIES.
  H. MYINT, 617(TLS):22AUG75-952
MOUNT, F. THE MAN WHO RODE AMPER-
SAND.
  N. HEPBURN, 362:20CT75-453
  R. USBORNE, 617(TLS):12SEP75-1013
MOUNT, M.W. AFRICAN ART.
  M. WAHLMAN, 2:SUMMER74-87
MOURELATOS, A.P.D. THE ROUTE OF
PARMENIDES.*
  I. MUELLER, 122:APR74-145
MOURTHÉ, C. AMOUR NOIR.
  R.M. HENKELS, JR., 207(FR):APR73-
1060
MOUSNIER, R. LES INSTITUTIONS DE LA
FRANCE SOUS LA MONARCHIE ABSOLUE
1598-1789. (VOL 1)
  R.J. KNECHT, 617(TLS):30CT75-1133
MOUSSETTE, M. LES PATENTEUX.
  R. HATHORN, 296:VOL4#3-186
MOUTOTE, D. LE JOURNAL DE GIDE ET
LES PROBLÈMES DU MOI (1889-1925).
  G.E. GINGRAS, 207(FR):MAR73-836
MOVIA, G. ALESSANDRO DI AFRODISIA.
  W.E. CHARLTON, 123:MAR74-134
  A.C. LLOYD, 303:VOL93-248
  E.P. MAHONEY, 319:JUL75-402
MOVIA, G. ANIMA E INTELLETTO.
  E.P. MAHONEY, 319:JUL75-402
MOWAT, D. THE OTHERS.
  A. RENDLE, 157:WINTER73-87
MOWAT, F. WAKE OF THE GREAT SEAL-
ERS.*
  D. FLEISHER, 73:WINTER74-41
MOWAT, F. A WHALE FOR THE KILLING.*
  J. POLK, 102(CANL):SUMMER73-120
MOWATT, D.G. FRIDERICH VON HÛSEN.*
  D. BLAMIRES, 402(MLR):JAN74-216
  H. HOMANN, 400(MLN):APR73-615
  J.W. THOMAS, 222(GR):JAN73-72
MOYLES, R.G. COMPLAINTS IS MANY &
VARIOUS BUT THE ODD DIVIL LIKES IT.
  E.J. DEVEREUX, 99:APR/MAY75-37
MOYNIHAN, D.P. COPING.*
  639(VQR):AUTUMN74-CLI
MOYNIHAN, M., ED. A PLACE CALLED
ARMAGEDDON.
  A. BRETT-JAMES, 617(TLS):22AUG75-
936
MOZART, J.C.W.A. DON GIOVANNI. (W.
PLATH & W. REHM, EDS)
  R. CRAFT, 453:30OCT75-11
MOZART, J.C.W.A. LETTERS OF WOLF-
GANG AMADEUS MOZART. (H. MERS-
MANN, ED)
  M. PETERSON, 470:MAY73-15

MTSHALI, O. SOUNDS OF A COWHIDE
DRUM.
  A. CLUYSENAAR, 565:VOL14#2-62
MUCCHIELLI, R. LE MYTHE DE LA CITÉ
IDÉALE.
  D. VICTOROFF, 542:JAN-MAR73-92
MUELA, J.G. - SEE UNDER GONZÁLEZ
MUELA, J.
MUELLER, W.R. CELEBRATION OF LIFE.
  F. SCHNEIDER, 613:WINTER73-538
MÜFFELMANN, F. ALTHOCHDEUTSCH.*
  H. SZKLENAR, 260(IF):BAND78-350
MUGGERIDGE, M. CHRONICLES OF WASTED
TIME.* (VOL 1)
  H.B. GOW, 396(MODA):FALL74-426
MUGGERIDGE, M. JESUS.
  D. CUPITT, 362:25SEP75-405
  P. HEBBLETHWAITE, 617(TLS):12SEP
75-1025
MUGLER, C. - SEE ARCHIMEDES
MÜHLEMANN, S. OMBRES ET LUMIÈRES
DANS L'OEUVRE DE PIERRE CARLET DE
CHAMBLAIN DE MARIVAUX.
  J. SGARD, 535(RHL):JAN-FEB73-133
MÜHLMANN, W.E. & E.W. MÜLLER - SEE
GÖHRING, H.
MUHR, O. DIE PRÄPOSITION "PER" BEI
SALLUST.
  H-O. KRÖNER, 343:BAND16HEFT2-178
MUIR, E. SELECTED LETTERS OF EDWIN
MUIR.* (P.H. BUTTER, ED)
  P. DICKINSON, 364:OCT/NOV74-125
MUIR, H. DON'T CALL IT LOVE.
  G. EWART, 617(TLS):15AUG75-913
  J. MELLORS, 362:7AUG75-189
MUIR, J. A MODERN APPROACH TO ENG-
LISH GRAMMAR.
  R.B. LONG, 128(CE):FEB74-618
  K. SØRENSEN, 179(ES):DEC73-618
  A.R. TELLIER, 189(EA):JUL-SEP73-
347
MUIR, K., ED. SHAKESPEARE SURVEY
24.*
  R.A. FOAKES, 175:SUMMER72-67
  J-B. FORT, 189(EA):JAN-MAR73-88
  R. WARREN, 447(N&Q):APR73-149
  R.W.Z., 179(ES):FEB73-98
MUIR, K., ED. SHAKESPEARE SURVEY
25.
  I. BROWN, 157:SPRING73-73
  P. EDWARDS, 402(MLR):JUL74-621
  R.A. FOAKES, 175:SUMMER73-72
  R.A. FOAKES, 541(RES):AUG73-329
  R.W.Z., 179(ES):FEB73-98
MUIR, K., ED. SHAKESPEARE SURVEY
27.
  S. SCHOENBAUM, 617(TLS):11JUL75-
756
MUIR, K. SHAKESPEARE THE PROFES-
SIONAL.
  R.A. FOAKES, 175:SUMMER73-72
MUIR, K. SHAKESPEARE'S TRAGIC SE-
QUENCE.*
  R.A. FOAKES, 175:SUMMER73-72
  J-B. FORT, 189(EA):JUL-SEP73-354
  D. MEHL, 541(RES):NOV73-477
MUIR, K. & S. SCHOENBAUM, EDS. A
NEW COMPANION TO SHAKESPEARE STUD-
IES.*
  A.L. FRENCH, 179(ES):JUN73-282
  C. LEECH, 551(RENQ):AUTUMN73-364
MUIR, K. & P. THOMSON - SEE WYATT,
T.

MUIR, P.   VICTORIAN ILLUSTRATED
BOOKS.*
   A.B., 155:MAY73-125
   A.H. MAYOR, 54:MAR73-158
   G. REYNOLDS, 39:FEB73-196
MUIRDEN, J.   BEGINNER'S GUIDE TO
ASTRONOMICAL TELESCOPE MAKING.
   617(TLS):8AUG75-906
MUKERJEE, R., ED & TRANS.   THE SONG
OF THE SELF SUPREME.
   L. STERNBACH, 318(JAOS):JUL-SEP73-
   379
MUKHERJEE, B.   WIFE.
   M. LEVIN, 441:8JUN75-17
MUKHERJEE, M.   THE TWICE BORN FIC-
TION.
   G.C. SPIVAK, 454:FALL73-91
   295:FEB74-435
MUKHERJEE, R.   THE SONG OF THE SELF
SUPREME (AṢṬĀVAKRAGĪTĀ).
   W.C. FINLEY, 485(PE&W):JUL73-402
MULDOON, P.   NEW WEATHER.*
   T. EAGLETON, 565:VOL14#3-74
   H. SERGEANT, 175:AUTUMN73-121
MULDROW, G.M.   MILTON & THE DRAMA OF
THE SOUL.*
   P.S. MACAULAY, 179(ES):JUN73-289
MULHAUSER, F.L. - SEE CLOUGH, A.H.
MULKEEN, A.   WILD THYME, WINTER
LIGHTNING.
   G. EWART, 364:APR/MAY74-132
MULL, D.L.   HENRY JAMES'S "SUBLIME
ECONOMY."
   D.K. KIRBY, 432(NEQ):JUN74-342
   V.H. WINNER, 27(AL):MAY74-232
   639(VQR):SUMMER74-LXXIII
MULLER, A.V., ED & TRANS. THE "SPIR-
ITUAL REGULATION" OF PETER THE
GREAT.*
   J.T. ALEXANDER, 481(PQ):JUL73-364
   D.W. EDWARDS, 550(RUSR):OCT73-451
   L.R. LEWITTER, 575(SEER):APR74-288
   M. RAEFF, 104:SUMMER74-327
MÜLLER, G.   STUDIEN ZU ROBERT MUSILS
ROMANEN "DIE VERWIRRUNGEN DES ZÖG-
LINGS TÖRLESS" UND "DER MANN OHNE
EIGENSCHAFTEN."
   C. MELCHINGER, 462(OL):VOL28#1-82
MÜLLER, G.H.   NIGHTMARES & VISIONS.*
   P.M. BROWNING, JR., 659:SPRING75-
   260
MÜLLER, H.   FORMEN MODERNER DEUT-
SCHER LYRIK.
   R.F. AMBACHER, 399(MLJ):SEP-OCT73-
   297
MÜLLER, H., G. HAENSCH & E. ALVAREZ
PRADA - SEE "LANGENSCHEIDTS HAND-
WÖRTERBUCH SPANISCH"
MULLER, H.J.   IN PURSUIT OF RELE-
VANCE.
   L.B. CEBIK, 219(GAR):SPRING73-121
MÜLLER, I.   GESCHICHTE DER ABTEI
DISENTIS VON DEN ANFÄNGEN BIS ZUR
GEGENWART.
   G. ZIMMERMANN, 182:VOL26#17/18-633
VON MÜLLER, I.   HANDBUCH DER ALTER-
TUMSWISSENSCHAFT.   (VOL 12, PTS
2&3)
   E.M. JEFFREYS, 303:VOL93-273
MULLER, J.   DICTIONNAIRE ABRÉGÉ DES
IMPRIMEURS - ÉDITEURS FRANÇAIS DU
SEIZIÈME SIÈCLE.
   R.M. KINGDON, 551(RENQ):SUMMER73-
   189

MÜLLER, K.E.   GESCHICHTE DER ANTIKEN
ETHNOGRAPHIE UND ETHNOLOGISCHEN
THEORIEBILDUNG VON DEN ANFÄNGEN BIS
AUF DIE BYZANTINISCHEN HISTORIOGRA-
PHEN.   (PT 1)
   F. LASSERRE, 182:VOL26#1/2-60
MÜLLER, K-L.   ÜBERTRAGENER GEBRAUCH
VON ETHNIKA IN DER ROMANIA.
   H.J. WOLF, 72:BAND211HEFT3/6-455
MULLER, P.E.   JEWELS IN SPAIN, 1500-
1800.*
   H.L. BLACKMORE, 135:APR73-290
   J. HAYWARD, 54:JUN73-303
MÜLLER, T.   SCULPTURE IN THE NETHER-
LANDS, GERMANY, FRANCE, SPAIN:
1400-1500.*
   W.D. WIXOM, 54:SEP73-456
MÜLLER, U. - SEE VON MORUNGEN, H.
MÜLLER-MARKUS, S.   PROTOPHYSIK.
(PT 1)
   H. MARGENAU, 486:JUN73-326
MÜLLER-SCHOTTE, H.   DER MARITIME
SONDERCHARAKTER DES BRITISCHEN
VOLKES IM SPIEGEL DER ENGLISCHEN
SPRACHE.
   E.O. FINK, 430(NS):JAN73-51
   W. FRIEDERICH, 430(NS):JUL73-400
   M-P. GAUTIER, 189(EA):APR-JUN73-
   216
MÜLLER-SEIDEL, W. - SEE DAVID, C.,
   W. WITTKOWSKI & L. RYAN
MÜLLER-SOLGER, H.   DER DICHTERTRAUM.
   A. PHELAN, 433:OCT73-414
MULLIN, G.W.   FLIGHT & REBELLION.*
   J.W. FROST, 481(PQ):JUL73-362
MUMFORD, L.   FINDINGS & KEEPINGS.
   M. COWLEY, 441:12OCT75-4
MUMFORD, L.   INTERPRETATIONS & FORE-
CASTS: 1922-1972.*
   G.A. PANICHAS, 396(MODA):SUMMER74-
   315
MUNBY, A.N.L.   CONNOISSEURS & MEDI-
EVAL MINIATURES 1750-1850.*
   C. HUTER, 354:DEC73-354
MUNCH, P.A.   THE SONG TRADITION OF
TRISTAN DA CUNHA.
   A. JABBOUR, 650(WF):JAN73-62
MUNCH-PETERSEN, E.   KILDER TIL LIT-
TERATURSØGNING.
   P.M. MITCHELL, 301(JEGP):APR74-274
MUNCY, R.L.   SEX & MARRIAGE IN
UTOPIAN COMMUNITIES.
   J.F.C. HARRISON, 637(VS):DEC73-227
MUNDEN, K.W., ED.   THE AMERICAN FILM
INSTITUTE CATALOG OF MOTION PICTURE
FILMS PRODUCED IN THE UNITED STATES:
FEATURE FILMS, 1921-1930.
   N. SAHLI, 14:JAN73-74
MUNDIS, H.   JESSICA'S WIFE.
   M. LEVIN, 441:25MAY75-13
MUNDLE, C.W.K.   PERCEPTION.*
   J.M. HINTON, 393(MIND):JUL73-459
   D. OLIN, 482(PHR):APR73-246
MUNDSCHAU, H.   SPRECHER ALS TRÄGER
DER "TRADITION VIVANTE" IN DER
GATTUNG "MÄRE."
   D. BLAMIRES, 402(MLR):OCT74-915
MUNGO, R.   RETURN TO SENDER.
   J. ZORN, 441:7SEP75-4
MUNK, A.W.   ROY WOOD SELLARS AS
CREATIVE THINKER & CRITIC.
   N. MELCHERT, 484(PPR):DEC73-286
MUNONYE, J.   A DANCER OF FORTUNE.
   G. CLIFFORD, 617(TLS):24JAN75-73

MUNRO, A. SOMETHING I'VE BEEN MEAN-
ING TO TELL YOU.*
  M. JULIAN, 606(TAMR):OCT74-82
  H. KIRKWOOD, 99:JUN75-42
  J. ORANGE, 296:VOL4#1-194
MUNRO, C. SAILING SHIPS.
  B. GREENHILL, 617(TLS):21FEB75-202
MUNSKE, H.H. DER GERMANISCHE
RECHTSWORTSCHATZ IM BEREICH DER
MISSETATEN. (VOL 1)
  D.H. GREEN, 301(JEGP):JAN74-73
MÜNSTER, R. & H. SCHMID. MUSIK IN
BAYERN. (VOL 1)
  M. CARNER, 415:JUN74-479
  J.A. WESTRUP, 410(M&L):APR74-245
MUNSTERBERG, H. THE ARTS OF CHINA.
  C.N. SPINKS, 302:JAN73-167
MUNTANER, R. CRÓNICA.
  C.L. SOPER, 238:MAR73-172
MÜNTJES, M. BEITRÄGE ZUM BILD DES
DEUTSCHEN IN DER RUSSISCHEN LITERA-
TUR VON KATHARINA BIS AUF ALEXANDER
II.
  P. THIERGEN, 52:BAND8HEFT2-222
MÜNTZER, T. SCRITTI POLITICI. (E.
CAMPI, ED)
  F.P. DE MICHELIS, 548(RCSF):JUL-
  SEP73-359
MURAOKA, K. & OKAMURA. FOLK ARTS &
CRAFTS OF JAPAN.
  S. SITWELL, 39:DEC73-516
MURARI, T. THE NEW SAVAGES.
  S. CLAPP, 617(TLS):22AUG75-951
MURATORI, L.A. DELLA PERFETTA
POESIA ITALIANA. (A. RUSCHIONI, ED)
  M. FUBINI, 228(GSLI):VOL150FASC
  469-146
MURDOCH, B. THE FALL OF MAN IN THE
EARLY MIDDLE HIGH GERMAN BIBLICAL
EPIC.
  D.A. WELLS, 402(MLR):JUL74-694
MURDOCH, I. THE BLACK PRINCE.*
  M. PRICE, 676(YR):AUTUMN73-80
MURDOCH, I. THE SACRED & PROFANE
LOVE MACHINE.*
  B.F. DICK, 569(SR):FALL74-XC
  J. MELLORS, 364:JUN/JUL74-135
  J. UPDIKE, 442(NY):6JAN75-78
MURDOCH, I. THE SOVEREIGNTY OF
GOOD.*
  J. GRIFFIN, 184(EIC):JAN72-74
MURDOCH, I. A WORD CHILD.
  P. ADAMS, 61:SEP75-85
  D. BROMWICH, 441:24AUG75-21
  A. BROYARD, 441:8AUG75-25
  F. KERMODE, 362:17APR75-516
  S. WALL, 617(TLS):18APR75-416
MURIE, O. JOURNEYS TO THE FAR NORTH.
  T.J. LYON, 649(WAL):SPRING&SUMMER
  73-84
MURPHEY, M. OUR KNOWLEDGE OF THE
HISTORICAL PAST.
  R.H.C., 125:OCT73-95
  W. DRAY, 311(JP):18DEC75-805
MURPHY, A.L. THE FIRST FALLS ON
MONDAY.
  J. NOONAN, 529(QQ):AUTUMN73-466
  A. RENDLE, 157:AUTUMN73-81
MURPHY, C.T. A CANDID HISTORY OF
THE VERGILIAN SOCIETY & THE VILLA
VERGILIANA AT CUMAE.
  P.N. LOCKHART, 124:MAR73-353
MURPHY, F. - SEE WINTERS, Y.

MURPHY, G. & M. LEEDS. OUTGROWING
SELF-DECEPTION.
  M.P. DUMONT, 441:13JUL75-10
  C. LEHMANN-HAUPT, 441:4JUL75-21
MURPHY, G.M.H. - SEE OVID
MURPHY, J. PAY ON THE WAY OUT.
  N. CALLENDAR, 441:5OCT75-47
MURPHY, J.B. L.Q.C. LAMAR.*
  W.W. BRADEN, 583:WINTER73-199
MURPHY, J.G. KANT: THE PHILOSOPHY
OF RIGHT.*
  R.A. SCHULTZ, 482(PHR):JAN73-114
MURPHY, J.J. MEDIEVAL RHETORIC.
  T. HUNT, 597(SN):VOL45#2-405
MURPHY, J.J., ED. A SYNOPTIC HIS-
TORY OF CLASSICAL RHETORIC.*
  L.W. ROSENFIELD, 480(P&R):WINTER
  73-61
MURPHY, M. GOLF IN THE KINGDOM.
  P. DICKINSON, 364:DEC74/JAN75-138
MURPHY, P.T. OUR KINDLY PARENT...THE
STATE.
  I. GLASSER, 231:FEB75-118
  S. SCHLOSSMAN, 31(ASCH):AUTUMN75-
  679
MURPHY, R. HIGH ISLAND.
  D. DAVIE, 453:6MAR75-10
  J. MONTAGUE, 617(TLS):4JUL75-718
  A. STEVENSON, 362:30OCT75-571
MURPHY, W.M. THE YEATS FAMILY & THE
POLLEXFENS.
  R. FRÉCHET, 189(EA):APR-JUN73-246
MURPHY, Y. & R.F. WOMEN OF THE FOR-
EST.
  P. RIVIÈRE, 617(TLS):5SEP75-1000
MURRAY, E. THE CINEMATIC IMAGINA-
TION.*
  N. SILVERSTEIN, 295:FEB74-515
MURRAY, F.W. LA IMAGEN ARQUETÍPICA
EN LA POESÍA DE RAMÓN LÓPEZ VELARDE.
  G. BROTHERSTON, 402(MLR):JAN74-210
MURRAY, G. VOLTAIRE'S "CANDIDE."*
  J. SPICA, 535(RHL):SEP-OCT73-897
MURRAY, J. THE FIRST EUROPEAN AGRI-
CULTURE.
  L.S. LESHNIK, 318(JAOS):JUL-SEP73-
  390
MURRAY, P. THE SHAKESPEARIAN SCENE.
  S. VISWANATHAN, 570(SQ):SUMMER73-
  343
MURRAY, R. SELECTED POEMS.
  M.T. LANE, 198:SUMMER75-121
MURRELLS, J. THE BOOK OF GOLDEN
DISCS.
  J. PEEL, 362:24APR75-544
  617(TLS):18APR75-426
MURRIN, M. THE VEIL OF ALLEGORY.
  P. SACCIO, 599:SPRING73-193
MURRY, C.M. I AT THE KEYHOLE.
  P. STANSKY, 441:1JUN75-7
  442(NY):8SEP75-127
MURRY, C.M. ONE HAND CLAPPING.
  J. CARSWELL, 617(TLS):21NOV75-1396
  D.A.N. JONES, 362:16JAN75-90
MURTHY, P.A.N. THE RISE OF MODERN
NATIONALISM IN JAPAN.
  MARUYAMA SHIZUO, 285(JAPQ):JUL-SEP
  74-304
MUSA, M. - SEE DANTE ALIGHIERI
MUSAEUS. MUSÉE: "HÉRO ET LÉANDRE."
(P. ORSINI, ED & TRANS)
  D. HENRY, 122:JUL73-222

MUSCATINE, C. POETRY & CRISIS IN
THE AGE OF CHAUCER.*
  E.T. DONALDSON, 131(CL):SUMMER73-
  262
  R.M. WILSON, 175:AUTUMN73-112
MUSCHG, A. ALBISSERS GRUND.
  G.P. BUTLER, 617(TLS):3JAN75-4
MUSGRAVE, S. ENTRANCE OF THE CELE-
BRANT.
  D. HELWIG, 102(CANL):SPRING74-118
  S. SOLECKI, 529(QQ):SUMMER73-311
MUSGRAVE, S. GRAVE-DIRT & SELECTED
STRAWBERRIES.*
  L. ROGERS, 102(CANL):SUMMER74-121
MUSGROVE, F. ECSTASY & HOLINESS.
  A. CURLE, 617(TLS):21FEB75-203
MUSIL, R. ETHIK UND ÄSTHETIK.
  M-L. ROTH, 462(OL):VOL28#1-78
MUSSO AMBROSI, L.A. BIBLIOGRAFÍA
URUGUAYA SOBRE BRASIL. (2ND ED)
  G. FIGUEIRA, 263:OCT-DEC74-460
MUSSULMAN, J.A. MUSIC IN THE CUL-
TURED GENERATION.*
  M. PETERSON, 470:JAN73-32
MUSTI, D. TENDENZE NELLA STORIOGRA-
FIA ROMANA E GRECA SU ROMA ARCAICA.
  J.M. GLEASON, 121(CJ):APR/MAY74-
  373
MUSUMARRA, C. LA POESIA TRAGICA
ITALIANA NEL RINASCIMENTO.
  P.R. HORNE, 402(MLR):OCT74-889
MUSUMARRA, C. - SEE TEMPIO, D.
MUSURILLO, H., ED & TRANS. THE
ACTS OF THE CHRISTIAN MARTYRS.*
  E.M. SMALLWOOD, 313:VOL63-297
MUTHER, R. GERMAN BOOK ILLUSTRATION
OF THE GOTHIC PERIOD & THE EARLY
RENAISSANCE (1460-1530).
  J.M. EDELSTEIN, 517(PBSA):JAN-MAR
  74-85
MUTHESIUS, S. THE HIGH VICTORIAN
MOVEMENT IN ARCHITECTURE, 1850-
1870.*
  M. GIROUARD, 46:MAR73-210
  J. LEES-MILNE, 39:FEB73-200
  P.F. NORTON, 576:MAR73-75
  P. THOMPSON, 637(VS):SEP73-113
MYATT, F. THE SOLDIER'S TRADE.
  617(TLS):22AUG75-936
MYERS, A.B., ED. THE KNICKERBOCKER
TRADITION. THE WORLDS OF WASHING-
TON IRVING 1783-1859.
  W.L. HEDGES, 165:WINTER75-339
MYERS, M. FRIGATE.
  S. SOLECKI, 99:DEC75/JAN76-54
MYERS, R. THE CROSS OF FRANKENSTEIN.
  E. KORN, 617(TLS):7NOV75-1338
MYERS, R. MODERN FRENCH MUSIC FROM
FAURÉ TO BOULEZ.
  M. PETERSON, 470:MAR73-35
MYERS, W. DRYDEN.*
  D. ISLES, 566:AUTUMN73-29
MYINT, H. SOUTHEAST ASIA'S ECONO-
MY.*
  R.C. RICE, 293(JAST):FEB73-369
MYLNE, V. PRÉVOST: "MANON LESCAUT."
  J.S. SPINK, 208(FS):OCT74-459
MYRA, H. IS THERE A PLACE I CAN
SCREAM?
  H. VENDLER, 441:7SEP75-6

NAAMANI, I.T. ISRAEL.
  A.J. RAWICK, 287:JUN73-28
NABLOW, R.A. A STUDY OF VOLTAIRE'S
LIGHTER VERSE.
  H. MASON, 617(TLS):30MAY75-594
NABOKOV, N. BAGÁZH.
  N. ROREM, 441:28DEC75-6
NABOKOV, V. LOOK AT THE HARLE-
QUINS!*
  E. KORN, 617(TLS):18APR75-417
  P. WINDSOR, 362:24APR75-546
NABOKOV, V. POEMS & PROBLEMS.*
  M.K. HULTQUIST, 502(PRS):FALL73-
  271
  E. SZTEIN, 574(SEEJ):SUMMER72-244
NABOKOV, V. STRONG OPINIONS.*
  P. BAILEY, 364:AUG/SEP74-142
NABOKOV, V. TRANSPARENT THINGS.*
  J. VISWANATHAN, 648:OCT73-59
NABOKOV, V. TYRANTS DESTROYED.
  E. KORN, 617(TLS):21NOV75-1379
  C. LEHMANN-HAUPT, 441:20MAR75-43
  J. MELLORS, 362:20NOV75-685
  T. ROGERS, 441:9MAR75-4
  E. WEEKS, 61:MAR75-144
NACCI, C.N. ALTAMIRANO.*
  M.A. SALGADO, 241:MAY73-77
"NACHLÄSSE UND SAMMLUNGEN."
  J.K. KING, 406:WINTER74-435
NACK, W. BIG RED OF MEADOW STABLE.
  J. DURSO, 441:1JUN75-34
NADA PATRONE, A.M. - SEE DI CLARI,
R.
NADAL, R.M. - SEE UNDER MARTÍNEZ
NADAL, R.
NADAL FARRERAS, J. LA INTRODUCCIÓN
DEL CATASTRO EN GERONA.
  J. CASEY, 86(BHS):JUL73-316
NADEAU, M. THE GREATNESS OF FLAU-
BERT.
  L.D. JOINER, 399(MLJ):SEP-OCT73-
  280
NADVI, M.A.B. - SEE UNDER BARI NADVI,
M.A.
NADWI, S.A.H.A. BASIS OF A NEW
SOCIAL ORDER.
  S. ALI, 273(IC):APR73-183
NADWI, S.A.H.A. THE FOUR PILLARS OF
ISLAM.
  A. ALI, 273(IC):APR73-182
NADWI, S.A.H.A. RECONSTRUCTION OF
INDIAN SOCIETY.
  A. ALI, 273(IC):APR73-185
NAESS, A. THE PLURALIST & POSSIBIL-
IST ASPECT OF THE SCIENTIFIC ENTER-
PRISE.
  N. KOERTGE, 84:SEP73-313
  E. LASZLO, 484(PPR):DEC73-279
NAESS, A. & A. HANNAY, EDS. INVITA-
TION TO CHINESE PHILOSOPHY.
  S-C. HUANG, 485(PE&W):OCT73-546
NAESS, H.S. & S. SKARD, EDS. SCAN-
DINAVIAN AMERICAN INTERRELATIONS.
  A. VAN MARKEN, 301(JEGP):APR74-275
NĀGĀRJUNA & THE SEVENTH DALAI LAMA.
THE PRECIOUS GARLAND & THE SONG OF
THE FOUR MINDFULNESSES. (J. HOP-
KINS & L. RIMPOCHE, WITH A. KLEIN,
EDS & TRANS)
  A. PIATIGORSKY, 617(TLS):3OCT75-
  1159

NAGEL, I. DIE BEZEICHNUNG FÜR "DUMM" UND "VERRUCKT" IM SPANIS-CHEN.*
H. MEIER, 72:BAND211HEFT3/6-465
NAGEL, T. THE POSSIBILITY OF ALTRU-ISM.*
N.L. STURGEON, 482(PHR):JUL74-374
NAGELE, H. DER DEUTSCHE IDEALISMUS IN DER EXISTENTIELLEN KATEGORIE DES HUMORS.
H. MOENKEMEYER, 563(SS):FALL74-441
NAGLER, M.N. SPONTANEITY & TRADI-TION.
G.S. KIRK, 617(TLS):7NOV75-1326
NAGY, G. GREEK DIALECTS & THE TRANSFORMATION OF AN INDO-EUROPEAN PROCESS.*
G.M. MESSING, 122:OCT73-303
K. STRUNK, 260(IF):BAND78-251
NAGY, L. LOVE OF THE SCORCHING WIND.*
R. GARFITT, 364:JUN/JUL74-109
DE NAGY, N.C. THE POETRY OF EZRA POUND. (2ND ED)
W. MARTIN, 179(ES):APR72-171
NAHAL, C. AZADI.
M. LEVIN, 441:18MAY75-50
NAHAL, C. THE NARRATIVE PATTERN IN ERNEST HEMINGWAY'S FICTION.
295:FEB74-635
NAHUM, L. SHADOW 81.
N. CALLENDAR, 441:12OCT75-47
NAIDOO, P. & M. BOLCH. OFFICE PRACTICE. (BK 2)
J.R. EWER, 399(MLJ):SEP-OCT74-298
NAIK, J.A. INDIA, RUSSIA, CHINA & BANGLA DESH.
C.H. ASHTON, 293(JAST):AUG73-720
NAIPAUL, V.S. GUERRILLAS.
A. BROYARD, 441:20NOV75-45
D.A.N. JONES, 617(TLS):12SEP75-1013
K. MILLER, 453:11DEC75-3
P. THEROUX, 441:16NOV75-1
J. VAIZEY, 362:25SEP75-410
442(NY):22DEC75-95
NAIPAUL, V.S. IN A FREE STATE.
J.C. FIELD, 556(RLV):1973/1-93
NAIPAUL, V.S. THE MYSTIC MASSEUR. THE SUFFRAGE OF ELVIRA. A HOUSE FOR MR. BISWAS. MR. STONE & THE KNIGHTS COMPANION. THE MIMIC MEN.
H. BLODGETT, 579(SAQ):SUMMER74-388
NAIPAUL, V.S. THE OVERCROWDED BARRACOON.*
E. GLOVER, 565:VOL14#2-36
K. MC SWEENEY, 529(QQ):AUTUMN73-496
NAKAHARA, J. & R.A. WITTON. DEVEL-OPMENT & CONFLICT IN THAILAND.
C.F. KEYES, 293(JAST):FEB73-376
NAKANO, M. A PHONOLOGICAL STUDY IN THE 'PHAGS-PA SCRIPT & THE MENG-KU TZU-YUN.
KUN CHANG, 318(JAOS):OCT-DEC73-640
NAKATA, Y. THE ART OF JAPANESE CAL-LIGRAPHY.*
S. SITWELL, 39:DEC73-516
NAKOV, A.B. - SEE TARABOUKINE, N.
NAKOVSKI, A. DIMENSION DE LA MORAL CONTEMPORAINE.
270:VOL23#1-14

NALBACH, D. THE KING'S THEATRE 1704-1867.*
J.C. TREWIN, 157:AUTUMN73-71
NAMER, E. LA PHILOSOPHIE ITALIENNE.
M. PINE, 551(RENQ):SPRING73-47
NANCE, J. THE GENTLE TASADAY.
P. ADAMS, 61:JUN75-95
J. KRAMER, 441:1JUN75-1
NANDA, B.R., ED. SOCIALISM IN INDIA.
W.R. BREWER, 293(JAST):MAY73-524
NANDRIS, G. COLLOQUIAL RUMANIAN. (4TH ED)
J.E. ALGEO, 399(MLJ):NOV73-368
NANTET, J. PANORAMA DE LA LITTERA-TURE NOIRE D'EXPRESSION FRANÇAISE.
M-A. GASH, 207(FR):MAR73-873
DI NAPOLI, G. LORENZO VALLA.
J.W. O'MALLEY, 551(RENQ):WINTER73-468
NAQVI, H.K. URBAN CENTRES & INDUS-TRIES IN UPPER INDIA: 1556-1803.
H. SPODEK, 293(JAST):FEB73-342
NARANG, G.C., ED. URDU.
R.N. SRIVASTAVA, 353:1JUL73-73
NARANJO, P. & C. ROLANDO. JUAN MON-TALVO.
A. CARRIÓN, 37:FEB73-42
NARAYAN, R.K. MY DAYS.*
P. MASON, 362:26JUN75-854
NARAYAN, R.K. THE RAMAYANA.
C.G. HOSPITAL, 529(QQ):AUTUMN73-489
NARDI, E. PROCURATO ABORTO NEL MONDO GRECO ROMANO.
E.D. PHILLIPS, 123:NOV74-302
NAREMORE, J. THE WORLD WITHOUT A SELF.*
J. ALEXANDER, 150(DR):SUMMER73-361
S. DICK, 529(QQ):WINTER73-650
A. FLEISHMAN, 594:WINTER73-559
J. GUIGUET, 189(EA):JUL-SEP73-338
NARKISS, B. - SEE ROTH, C.
NASH, J.M. THE AGE OF REMBRANDT & VERMEER.
T. LASK, 55:NOV72-16
G. MARTIN, 39:MAR73-319
J.K. NELSON, 290(JAAC):FALL73-134
NASH, N.R. CRY MACHO.
M. LEVIN, 441:13JUL75-32
NASSAUER, R. THE UNVEILING.
V. GLENDINNING, 617(TLS):2MAY75-473
NATAN, A. & B. KEITH-SMITH, EDS. GERMAN MEN OF LETTERS. (VOL 6)
I.M. KIMBER, 402(MLR):OCT74-917
J. OSBORNE, 220(GL&L):JUL74-326
NATANSON, M. EDMUND HUSSERL.
H.B. HALL, 311(JP):18DEC75-819
J.N. MOHANTY, 319:OCT75-542
NATANSON, M. THE JOURNEYING SELF.
A. HANNAY, 262:SPRING73-111
NATANSON, M. PHENOMENOLOGY, ROLE & REASON.
W. MAYS, 518:OCT74-21
NATHAN, J. MISHIMA.*
F.L. HUNTLEY, 385(MQR):FALL75-480
H. ISHIGURO, 453:11DEC75-48
R. SCRUTON, 617(TLS):11APR75-388
NATHAN, M. & D. ROCHE - SEE THOMAS, D.
NATHAN, N.M.L. THE CONCEPT OF JUS-TICE.
N.J.H. DENT, 479(PHQ):JAN73-90
R. NORMAN, 482(PHR):OCT74-544

NATHAN, R. HEAVEN & HELL & THE
MEGAS FACTOR.
M. LEVIN, 441:31AUG75-13
NAUDEAU, O. LA PENSÉE DE MONTAIGNE
ET LA COMPOSITION DES "ESSAIS."*
R.C. LA CHARITÉ, 546(RR):NOV74-308
NAUEN, F.G. REVOLUTION, IDEALISM &
HUMAN FREEDOM.
M. FOX, 154:SEP73-533
NAUMANN, B. WORTBILDUNG IN DER
DEUTSCHEN GEGENWARTSSPRACHE.*
H. LÖFFLER, 343:BAND17HEFT1-107
C.V.J. RUSS, 402(MLR):OCT74-906
G. STARKE, 682(ZPSK):BAND26HEFT
3/4-467
NAVA, P. BAÚ DE OSSOS.
S. BACIU, 263:JUL-SEP74-310
NAVAGERO, A. LUSUS. (A.E. WILSON,
ED)
G. TOURNOY-THOEN, 568(SCN):WINTER
74-99
NAVARRA, G. CITTÀ SICANE SICULE E
GRECHE NELLA ZONA DI GELA.
P. FREI, 182:VOL26#17/18-621
DE NAVARRE, M. - SEE UNDER MARGUER-
ITE DE NAVARRE
NAVARRE, Y. LADY BLACK.
D. O'CONNELL, 207(FR):DEC72-446
NAVROZOV, L. THE EDUCATION OF LEV
NAVROZOV.
N. BLIVEN, 442(NY):22SEP75-127
H. MUCHNIC, 453:18SEP75-25
H.E. SALISBURY, 441:25MAY75-3
NAWAZ, J.A.S. - SEE UNDER SHAH
NAWAZ, J.A.
NAYLOR, B., L. HALLEWELL & C. STEELE.
DIRECTORY OF LIBRARIES & SPECIAL
COLLECTIONS ON LATIN AMERICA & THE
WEST INDIES.
617(TLS):30MAY75-606
NAZZARO, A. & F.W. LINDSAY, EDS.
RÉALITÉ ET FANTAISIE.
W.W. KIBLER, 207(FR):OCT72-246
N'DIAYE, G. STRUCTURE DU DIALECTE
BASQUE DE MAYA.
J. ANDERSON, 361:DEC73-344
NEAL, G.C. - SEE BLUCK, R.S.
NEALE, B. ASIANS IN NAIROBI.
315(JAL):VOL11PT2-106
NEAMAN, J.S. SUGGESTION OF THE
DEVIL.
H. COX, 441:19OCT75-8
NEAVE, G. HOW THEY FARED.
M. WARNOCK, 362:20FEB75-252
NEBEL, O. ZUGINSFELD.
P. LABANYI, 617(TLS):25JUL75-855
NEČAEVA, V.S. ŽURNAL M·M. I F.M.
DOSTOEVSKIX "VREMJA" 1861-1863.
E. CHANCES, 574(SEEJ):SUMMER73-229
NECTOUX, J-M. - SEE SAINT-SAËNS, C.
& G. FAURÉ
NEDELJKOVIĆ, D-D. ROMAIN ROLLAND ET
STEFAN ZWEIG.
M. MICHAUX, 535(RHL):JUL-AUG73-731
NEEDHAM, J., WITH WANG LING & LU
GWEI-DJEN. SCIENCE & CIVILISATION
IN CHINA.* (VOL 4, PT 3)
J.P. LO, 318(JAOS):OCT-DEC73-636
NEEDHAM, R., ED. RIGHT & LEFT.
R. FIRTH, 617(TLS):21FEB75-190
NEELY, R. THE RIDGWAY WOMEN.
M. LEVIN, 441:20JUL75-23
NEEPER, C. A PLACE BEYOND MAN.
G. JONAS, 441:4MAY75-50

NEGLIA, E.G. PIRANDELLO Y LA DRA-
MÁTICA RIOPLATENSE.
A. ILLIANO, 131(CL):WINTER73-74
NÈGRE, E. - SEE GAILLARD [GALHARD],
A.
NEGRI, A. LA COMUNITÀ ESTETICA IN
KANT.
K. OEDINGEN, 342:BAND64HEFT1-137
NEGRI, A. - SEE KANT, I.
NEGRI, R. LEOPARDI NELLA POESIA
ITALIANA.
W.T. STARR, 276:SPRING73-110
NEHMAD, M. HAGLIMA HAHADASHA SHEL
MULA ABRAHAM.
E. SCHOENFELD, 196:BAND14HEFT1/2-
168
NEHRU, J. SELECTED WORKS OF JAWAH-
ARLAL NEHRU. (VOL 1)(S. GOPAL, ED)
T.A. RUSCH, 293(JAST):MAY73-529
NEIDER, C. EDGE OF THE WORLD.*
L.M. GOULD, 31(ASCH):SPRING75-327
NEIER, A. DOSSIER.
S. BROWNMILLER, 441:26JAN75-4
NEIL, W. CONCISE DICTIONARY OF
RELIGIOUS QUOTATIONS.
617(TLS):30MAY75-604
NEILL, P. MOCK TURTLE SOUP.*
L.T. LEMON, 502(PRS):SUMMER73-183
NEILSON, S. THE POEMS OF SHAW
NEILSON. (REV) (A.R. CHISHOLM, ED)
J.F. BURROWS, 581:MAR74-98
NEISTEIN, J., ED. POESIA BRASILEIRA
MODERNA.
W.M. DAVIS, 399(MLJ):SEP-OCT74-297
NEKRASSOV, V. KIRA GEORGIEVNA.
(H. BLAIR & M. GREENE, ED)
R. BARTHÉLEMY-VOGELS, 556(RLV):
1973/2-186
NELLI, H.S. ITALIANS IN CHICAGO
1880-1930.
E.S. FALBO, 275(IQ):SPRING74-67
NELSON, A.F. THE DEVELOPMENT OF
LESTER WARD'S WORLD VIEW.
P. DUBOIS, 542:APR-JUN73-227
NELSON, A.H. THE MEDIEVAL ENGLISH
STAGE.
A.C. CAWLEY, 617(TLS):17JAN75-51
NELSON, C. THE INCARNATE WORD.
J. STOKES, 128(CE):OCT73-77
NELSON, D.F. PORTRAIT OF THE ART-
IST AS HERMES.*
J. WICH, 224(GRM):BAND23HEFT2-246
NELSON, G. CHANGES OF HEART.
R. HINDMARSH, 72:BAND211HEFT1/3-
147
NELSON, H. CHARLES NODIER.
L.M. PORTER, 446:FALL-WINTER73/74-
88
NELSON, J.G. THE EARLY NINETIES.*
I. FLETCHER, 541(RES):FEB73-103
295:FEB74-376
NELSON, J.G., R.C. SCACE & R. KOURI,
EDS. CANADIAN PUBLIC LAND USE IN
PERSPECTIVE.
H.V. NELLES, 99:JUN75-45
NELSON, L. PROGRESS & REGRESS IN
PHILOSOPHY.
D.P. DRYER, 154:MAR73-127
W. GERBER, 322(JHI):OCT-DEC73-669
N. NATHAN, 536:DEC73-338
NELSON, R.J. IMMANENCE & TRANSCEN-
DENCE.*
J. VAN BAELEN, 400(MLN):MAY73-850

NEMEROV, H. GNOMES & OCCASIONS.*
  H. GILMAN, 114(CHIR):VOL25#1-193
  J.K. ROBINSON, 598(SOR):SUMMER75-
  668
  H. TAYLOR, 385(MQR):WINTER75-92
  639(VQR):WINTER74-XI
NEMEROV, H. REFLEXIONS ON POETRY &
POETICS.*
  R. FOSTER, 109:FALL/WINTER73/74-
  111
NEMILOVA, I.S. RIDDLES OF OLD PIC-
TURES. [IN RUSSIAN]
  M. CHAMOT, 39:DEC73-514
NENCIONI, G. - SEE BOIARDO, M.M.
NENNI, P. I NODI DELLA POLITICA
ESTERA ITALIANA. (D. ZUCARO, ED)
  S. WOOLF, 617(TLS):11JUL75-783
NERSESOVA, M. XOLODNIJ DOM DIKKEN-
SA.
  L. SENELICK, 155:JAN73-56
NERUDA, P. AUFENTHALT AUF ERDEN.
  K. BARCK, 654(WB):10/1973-150
NERUDA, P. THE CAPTAIN'S VERSES.*
(D.D. WALSH, ED & TRANS)
  W.G. REGIER, 502(PRS):SUMMER73-177
  L.A. WALSER, 399(MLJ):JAN-FEB74-80
NERUDA, P. EXTRAVAGARIA.*
  G. BROTHERSTON, 565:VOL14#2-45
NERUDA, P. NEW POEMS (1968-1970).*
(B. BELITT, ED & TRANS)
  G.S. FRASER, 473(PR):2/1974-289
  R.J. SMITH, 598(SOR):SPRING75-464
NERUDA, P. OBRAS COMPLETAS. CON-
FIESO QUE HE VIVIDO. LA ROSA SEP-
ARADA. JARDÍN DE INVIERNO. 2000.
EL CORAZÓN AMARILLO. LIBRO DE LAS
PREGUNTAS. ELEGÍA. DEFECTOS ESCO-
GIDOS. EL MAR Y LAS CAMPANAS.
MAREMOTO.
  R. PRING-MILL, 617(TLS):3OCT75-
  1154
NERUDA, P. SPLENDOR & DEATH OF
JOAQUÍN MURIETA.*
  W.G. REGIER, 502(PRS):SUMMER73-177
NERUDA, P., S. FACIO & A. D'AMICO.
GEOGRAFÍA DE PABLO NERUDA.
  R. PRING-MILL, 617(TLS):3OCT75-
  1154
NERUDA, P. & C. VALLEJO. NERUDA &
VALLEJO: SELECTED POEMS.* (R.
BLY, ED)
  G.S. FRASER, 473(PR):2/1974-289
DE NERVAL, G. AURÉLIA. (P-G. CAS-
TEX, ED)
  L. CELLIER, 535(RHL):NOV-DEC73-
  1093
  M. SCHAETTEL, 557(RSH):APR-JUN73-
  320
DE NERVAL, G. AURÉLIA. (J. GUIL-
LAUME, ED) LETTRES À FRANZ LISZT.
(J. GUILLAUME & C. PICHOIS, EDS)
  A. FAIRLIE, 208(FS):APR74-216
DE NERVAL, G. LES CHIMÈRES. (N.
RINSLER, ED)
  R. CHAMBERS, 67:MAY74-114
  A. FAIRLIE, 208(FS):APR74-217
DE NERVAL, G. "LES CHIMÈRES" DE
NERVAL. (J. GUILLAUME, ED)
  L. CELLIER, 535(RHL):JUL-AUG73-715
DE NERVAL, G. OEUVRES COMPLÉMEN-
TAIRES DE GÉRARD DE NERVAL. (VOLS
3&5) (J. RICHER, ED)
  A. DU BRUCK, 546(RR):JAN73-78

DE NERVAL, G. PANDORA. (J. GUIL-
LAUME, ED)
  M. JEANNERET, 98:NOV73-977
NESBIT, A. & B. NEVIUS, EDS. DICK-
ENS CENTENNIAL ESSAYS.
  H.P. SUCKSMITH, 677:VOL4-325
NESBITT, C. A LITTLE LOVE & GOOD
COMPANY.
  G. ANNAN, 617(TLS):21MAR75-292
  D.A.N. JONES, 362:20MAR75-376
NESS, J.L., ED. LYONEL FEININGER.
  S.B., 617(TLS):12DEC75-1492
NESTROY, J. KOMÖDIEN.* (F.H. MAUT-
NER, ED)
  P. BRANSCOMBE, 220(GL&L):JAN74-157
NETTELBECK, C.W. LES PERSONNAGES
DE BERNANOS ROMANCIER.*
  C.S. BROSMAN, 207(FR):OCT72-167
NEUBAUER, J. BIFOCAL VISION.*
  W. KUDSZUS, 406:SUMMER74-215
  B.N.W., 191(ELN):SEP73(SUPP)-153
  M. WINDER, 220(GL&L):JAN74-154
NEUFELDT, L. A WAY OF WALKING.
  E. LANCZOS, 648:OCT73-61
  M. MADIGAN, 385(MQR):SPRING75-220
NEUGEBAUER, O. & D. PINGREE - SEE
VARÂHAMIHIRA
NEUHAUS, V. TYPEN MULTIPERSPEKTIV-
ISCHEN ERZÄHLENS.
  P. PÜTZ, 52:BAND8HEFT3-311
  M. SWALES, 402(MLR):APR74-467
"BENJAMIN NEUKIRCHS ANTHOLOGIE."
(VOL 3) (A.G. DE CAPUA & E.A. METZ-
GER, EDS)
  P.W. TAX, 221(GQ):MAR73-287
NEUMANN, B. IDENTITÄT UND ROLLEN-
ZWANG.
  H.R. PICARD, 680(ZDP):BAND92HEFT4-
  626
NEUMANN, F. STUDIEN ZUR GESCHICHTE
DER DEUTSCHEN PHILOLOGIE.
  B. PESCHKEN, 564:JUN73-160
  F.P. PICKERING, 402(MLR):APR74-449
  H. SACKER, 220(GL&L):APR74-251
  G. SCHIEB, 654(WB):9/1973-175
NEUMANN, G., J. SCHRÖDER & M. KAR-
NICK. DÜRRENMATT, FRISCH, WEISS.*
  C.L. HART-NIBBRIG, 657(WW):MAY-JUN
  73-214
NEUMARK, G. POETISCHE TAFELN.* (J.
DYCK, ED)
  H-J. LANGE, 52:BAND8HEFT3-333
NEUMEISTER, E. THOMAS MANNS FRÜHE
ERZÄHLUNGEN.
  A.D. LATTA, 406:FALL74-313
NEUREUTER, H.P. DAS SPIEGELMOTIV
BEI CLEMENS BRENTANO.
  J.F.F., 191(ELN):SEP73(SUPP)-117
NEUSER, P-E. ZUM SOG. "HEINRICH VON
MELK."
  R. RUDOLF, 182:VOL26#20-737
NEVANLINNA, S., ED. THE NORTHERN
HOMILY CYCLE. (PT 1)
  K. SAJAVAARA, 439(NM):1973/1-184
NEVIUS, B. IVY COMPTON-BURNETT.
  A. MAACK, 447(N&Q):APR73-160
NEVO, R. TRAGIC FORM IN SHAKE-
SPEARE.*
  G. HOY, 569(SR):SPRING74-363
  M. ROSENBERG, 191(ELN):DEC73-133
  639(VQR):WINTER74-XVII
NEW, M. LAURENCE STERNE AS SATIR-
IST.*
  P. DANCHIN, 179(ES):OCT73-514

267

NEW, W.H. ARTICULATING WEST.
G. GEDDES, 376:APR73-233
G. WARKENTIN, 102(CANL):AUTUMN73-86
NEW, W.H., ED. DRAMATISTS IN CANADA.
C. JOHNSON, 255(HAB):SUMMER73-239
A. LEGGATT, 397(MD):SEP73-215
R. LISTER, 102(CANL):WINTER74-113
NEW, W.H. MALCOLM LOWRY.*
C. THOMAS, 102(CANL):SPRING73-103
"THE NEW YORKER ALBUM OF DRAWINGS 1925-1975."
P-L. ADAMS, 61:DEC75-118
H. KRAMER, 441:2NOV75-35
NEWCOMB, B.H. FRANKLIN & GALLOWAY.*
D.J. ROBERTS, 481(PQ):JUL73-508
NEWCOMBE, T. - SEE ERART, J.
NEWELL, D.M. IF NOTHIN' DON'T HAPPEN.
M. LEVIN, 441:9FEB75-10
NEWELL, R.S. THE POLITICS OF AFGHANISTAN.
L. DUPREE, 293(JAST):NOV72-203
NEWHALL, B. FREDERICK H. EVANS.
M. HAWORTH-BOOTH, 617(TLS):7FEB75-148
NEWHALL, N. P.H. EMERSON.
H. KRAMER, 441:7DEC75-84
NEWIGER, H-J. & H. SEYFFERT - SEE DILLER, H.
NEWLOVE, J. LIES.*
S. SOLECKI, 529(QQ):SUMMER73-311
G. WARKENTIN, 102(CANL):SPRING73-121
NEWMAN, C., ED. TRI-QUARTERLY 26.
W. PEDEN, 569(SR):FALL74-712
NEWMAN, C.J. A RUSSIAN NOVEL.*
D. EVANS, 102(CANL):SUMMER74-104
A. ROBERTSON, 648:OCT73-63
NEWMAN, E. THE MAN LISZT.
R. CRAFT, 453:6FEB75-3
NEWMAN, J. & F. RIKKO. A THEMATIC INDEX TO THE WORKS OF SALAMON ROSSI.
T. WALKER, 415:MAY74-391
NEWMAN, J.H. THE LETTERS & DIARIES OF JOHN HENRY NEWMAN. (VOLS 27 & 28) (C.S. DESSAIN & T. GORNALL, EDS)
M. TREVOR, 617(TLS):15AUG75-926
NEWMAN, L. GATHERING FORCE.
A. GOTTLIEB, 441:5JAN75-10
NEWMAN, L. THE JOHN A. MACDONALD ALBUM.
D. SWAINSON, 99:JUN75-42
NEWMAN, M. & B. BERKOWITZ. HOW TO BE AWAKE & ALIVE.
C. LEHMANN-HAUPT, 441:4JUL75-21
NEWMAN, O. DEFENSIBLE SPACE.
S. KAPLAN, 44:MAY73-8
NEWMAN, W.M. LES SEIGNEURS DE NESLE EN PICARDIE (XIIE-XIIIE SIÈCLE).* LE PERSONNEL DE LA CATHÉDRALE D'AMIENS.
J.F. BENTON, 589:JAN74-135
NEWMAN, W.S. PERFORMANCE PRACTICES IN BEETHOVEN'S PIANO SONATAS.
R. WINTER, 415:SEP74-750
NEWTON, B. THE GENERATIVE INTERPRETATION OF DIALECT.
P. MACKRIDGE, 402(MLR):OCT74-958
NEWTON, R.R. MEDIEVAL CHRONICLES & THE ROTATION OF THE EARTH.
N.H. STENECK, 589:APR74-365

NEWTON, S.M. HEALTH, ART & REASON.
A. HOLLANDER, 617(TLS):3JAN75-12
NEWTON, S.M. RENAISSANCE THEATRE COSTUME.
C.V. WEDGWOOD, 617(TLS):7NOV75-1337
NIALL, B. MARTIN BOYD.*
H.W. RHODES, 67:NOV74-233
NIATUM, D. ASCENDING RED CEDAR MOON.
V. YOUNG, 249(HUDR):WINTER74/75-597
"DAS NIBELUNGENLIED."* (M.S. BATTS, ED)
G.F. JONES, 400(MLN):APR73-619
R.E. WALLBANK, 382(MAE):1974/1-56
NIČEV, A. L'ÉNIGME DE LA CATHARSIS TRAGIQUE DANS ARISTOTE.*
T. BRUNIUS, 290(JAAC):WINTER74-235
H.G. EDINGER, 122:APR73-142
NICHOL, B.P. ABC.
F. DAVEY, 102(CANL):WINTER73-118
NICHOL, B.P. THE MARTYROLOGY.
D. BARBOUR, 102(CANL):SPRING73-93
NICHOL, B.P. MONOTONES.
S. SCOBIE, 102(CANL):SPRING73-89
NICHOLAS OF AUTRECOURT. THE UNIVERSAL TREATISE OF NICHOLAS OF AUTRECOURT. (L.A. KENNEDY, R.E. ARNOLD & A.E. MILLWARD, TRANS)
J.F.W., 543:SEP72-168
NICHOLLS, R. THE PLANT DOCTOR.
J. CANADAY, 441:13APR75-16
NICHOLS, J. MINOR LIVES.* (E.L. HART, ED)
P. ROGERS, 447(N&Q):JUN73-235
NICHOLS, P. ITALIA, ITALIA.*
G. GERSH, 396(MODA):FALL74-432
NICHOLS, R. THE MARROW OF THE WORLD.
F. FRAZER, 102(CANL):AUTUMN74-116
NICHOLS, R. MESSIAEN.
W. MELLERS, 617(TLS):12SEP75-1030
NICHOLS, S.G., JR. & R.B. VOWLES, EDS. COMPARATISTS AT WORK.
S.L. FLAXMAN, 131(CL):WINTER73-91
NICHOLSON, N. A LOCAL HABITATION.*
A. CLUYSENAAR, 565:VOL14#3-70
R. KELL, 148:WINTER73-383
H. SERGEANT, 175:AUTUMN73-121
NICHOLSON, N. WEDNESDAY EARLY CLOSING.
R. BLYTHE, 362:20NOV75-680
S. SECKER, 617(TLS):21NOV75-1396
NICKEL, G., ED. READER ZUR KONTRASTIVEN LINGUISTIK.
V. FRIED, 399(MLJ):MAR74-148
NICKLES, H.G. THE DICTIONARY OF DO'S & DONT'S.
T.M. BERNSTEIN, 441:26APR75-25
NICOÏDSKI, C. LES VOYAGES DE GABRIEL.
E. ZANTS, 207(FR):OCT72-228
NICOL, B.P. LOVE.
D. BARBOUR, 198:SPRING75-121
NICOL, D.M. THE LAST CENTURIES OF BYZANTIUM, 1261-1453.
M. HEPPELL, 575(SEER):JAN74-136
NICOL, E. THE CLAM MADE A FACE.
A.P. MESSENGER, 102(CANL):WINTER74-101
NICOLAISEN, W.F.H. - SEE GELLING, M., W.F.H. NICOLAISEN & M. RICHARDS

NICOLAOU, I. CYPRIOT INSCRIBED
STONES.
J. BOARDMAN, 123:MAR74-160
NICOLL, A. ENGLISH DRAMA, 1900-
1930.
A.P. HINCHLIFFE, 148:AUTUMN73-284
M. JAMIESON, 157:SPRING73-74
NICOLL, J. THE PRE-RAPHAELITES.
K. ROBERTS, 90:FEB73-126
NICOLL, J. ROSSETTI.
D.A.N. JONES, 362:20NOV75-683
NICOLSON, B. COURBET.
R. MAIN, 592:JUL-AUG73-56
NICOLSON, B. JOSEPH WRIGHT OF DERBY.
T.J. MC CORMICK, 54:SEP73-464
NICOLSON, B. & C. WRIGHT. GEORGES
DE LA TOUR.
V. BLOCH, 617(TLS):21MAR75-300
J. CANADAY, 441:8FEB75-23
NICOLSON, I.F. & C.A. HUGHES, EDS.
PACIFIC POLITIES.
B. NUSSBAUM, 293(JAST):MAY73-556
NICOLSON, N. PORTRAIT OF A MARRI-
AGE.*
G.S. HAIGHT, 676(YR):SPRING74-416
S. PICKERING, JR., 569(SR):SPRING
74-XXXI
S. RUDIKOFF, 249(HUDR):SUMMER74-
273
D. TRILLING, 473(PR):1/1974-120
639(VQR):WINTER74-XXVI
NICOLSON, N. & J. TRAUTMANN - SEE
WOOLF, V.
NIDA, E. A SYNOPSIS OF ENGLISH SYN-
TAX.
G.F. MEIER, 682(ZPSK):BAND26HEFT
1/2-206
NIDA, E.A. & C.R. TABER. THE THEORY
& PRACTICE OF TRANSLATION.*
A.K. LOJKINE, 67:MAY74-146
NIDA, E.A. & W.I. WONDERLY. COMMUN-
ICATION ROLE OF LANGUAGES IN MULTI-
LINGUAL SOCIETIES.
315(JAL):VOL11PT2-99
NIDDITCH, P.H. - SEE LOCKE, J.
NIDERST, A. FONTENELLE À LA RECHER-
CHE DE LUI-MÊME 1657-1702.
M.L. PERKINS, 481(PQ):JUL73-506
NIDERST, A., ED. L'AME MATÉRIELLE
(OUVRAGE ANONYME).*
G. MENANT-ARTIGAS, 535(RHL):NOV-
DEC73-1074
J.S. SPINK, 208(FS):JAN74-77
NIEBUHR, R.R. EXPERIENTIAL RELI-
GION.
H.A.D., 543:SEP72-169
NIEH, H-L. SHEN TS'UNG-WEN.
J.C. KINKLEY, 293(JAST):AUG73-687
NIELSEN, K. CONTEMPORARY CRITIQUES
OF RELIGION.*
P.W. GOOCH, 154:JUN73-361
NIELSEN, W.A. THE BIG FOUNDATIONS.
V.S. NAVASKY, 473(PR):1/1974-143
NIEMEIJER, J.W. CORNELIS TROOST
1696-1750.
D. SUTTON, 39:DEC73-522
NIEMEYER, J. GENUGTUUNG DES VER-
LETZTEN DURCH BUSSE.
A. HAEFLIGER, 182:VOL26#23/24-847
NIERAAD, J. STANDPUNKTBEWUSSTSEIN
UND WELTZUSAMMENHANG.
A. MERCIER, 182:VOL26#9-265

NIERENBERG, G.I. THE ART OF NEGOTI-
ATING.
186(ETC.):MAR73-103
NIES, F. GATTUNGSPOETIK UND PUBLIK-
UMSSTRUKTUR.
E.T. DUBOIS, 182:VOL26#10-363
NIETO ALCAIDE, V. LAS VIDRIERAS DE
LA CATEDRAL DE SEVILLA, MADRID.
R. BECKSMANN, 683:BAND36HEFT2/3-
174
NIETZSCHE, F.W. NIETZSCHE WERKE.
(VOL 3, PT 2; VOL 5, PT 2) (G. COL-
LI & M. MONTINARI, EDS)
A. THORLBY, 617(TLS):3JAN75-3
NIEVA, C.S. THIS TRANSCENDING GOD.
P.S. JOLLIFFE, 541(RES):FEB73-60
NIGHTINGALE, F. NOTES ON NURSING.
P.D. JAMES, 617(TLS):9MAY75-517
NIINILUOTO, I. & R. TUOMELA. THEOR-
ETICAL CONCEPTS & HYPOTHETICO-IN-
DUCTIVE INFERENCE.
H.E. KYBURG, JR., 311(JP):4SEP75-
491
LADY NIJŌ. THE CONFESSIONS OF LADY
NIJŌ. (K. BRAZELL, TRANS)
D.J. ENRIGHT, 617(TLS):24OCT75-
1258
NIKIFOROVA, L. RUSSIAN PORCELAIN IN
THE HERMITAGE COLLECTION.
M. CHAMOT, 39:DEC73-514
NIKITENKO, A. THE DIARY OF A RUS-
SIAN CENSOR. (ABRIDGED & TRANS BY
H.S. JACOBSON)
R. HINGLEY, 617(TLS):14NOV75-1350
NIKLAUS, R. A LITERARY HISTORY OF
FRANCE: THE EIGHTEENTH CENTURY,
1715-1789.*
G.R. HAVENS, 546(RR):MAY73-234
NILOV, F.N. ZAPADNAYA BENGALIYA.
T.P. THORNTON, 293(JAST):FEB73-364
NILSEN, D.L.F. ENGLISH ADVERBIALS.
G. SCHELSTRAETE, 179(ES):APR73-199
NIMS, J.F., ED & TRANS. SAPPHO TO
VALÉRY.*
V. YOUNG, 249(HUDR):WINTER74/75-
597
NIN, A. THE DIARY OF ANAÏS NIN.*
(VOL 5: 1947-1955.) (G. STUHLMANN,
ED)
D. DURRANT, 364:OCT/NOV74-131
NIN, A. ANAÏS NIN READER. (P.K.
JASON, ED)
H. ZINNES, 109:FALL/WINTER73/74-
124
NIRENBERG, M. THE RECEPTION OF AM-
ERICAN LITERATURE IN GERMAN PERIOD-
ICALS, 1820-1850.*
G. HOLLYDAY, 221(GQ):MAY73-472
NISBET, A. & B. NEVIUS, EDS. DICK-
ENS CENTENNIAL ESSAYS.*
R. BENNETT, 541(RES):NOV73-508
S.F. PICKERING, JR., 219(GAR):
FALL73-455
NISBET, H.B. GOETHE & THE SCIENTIF-
IC TRADITION.
N. BOYLE, 402(MLR):JUL74-706
H. HENEL, 406:FALL74-305
NISBET, H.B. HERDER & THE PHILOSO-
PHY & HISTORY OF SCIENCE. HERDER
& SCIENTIFIC THOUGHT.
A.R. SCHMITT, 222(GR):MAR73-157

NORES, D. LES CRITIQUES DE NOTRE
TEMPS ET BECKETT.
   J. FOX, 208(FS):JUL74-350
NORMAN, A.F. - SEE LIBANIUS
NORMAN, B. END PRODUCT.
   N. HEPBURN, 362:3JUL75-30
   T.A. SHIPPEY, 617(TLS):8AUG75-903
NORMAN, E.H. ORIGINS OF THE MODERN
JAPANESE STATE. (J.W. DOWER, ED)
   E.J. HOBSBAWM, 453:17JUL75-27
NORMAN, F. DOWN & OUT IN HIGH
SOCIETY.
   W. FEAVER, 617(TLS):26SEP75-1077
NORMAN, K.R., ED & TRANS. THE
ELDERS' VERSES I: THERAGĀTHĀ. THE
ELDERS' VERSES II: THERĪGĀTHĀ.
   W.B. BOLLÉE, 318(JAOS):OCT-DEC73-
   601
NORMAN, R. REASONS FOR ACTIONS.*
   J.E.J. ALTHAM, 483:APR73-192
   P. DUBOIS, 542:OCT-DEC73-493
   D. GAUTHIER, 482(PHR):OCT73-545
NORMAN, V. THE MEDIEVAL SOLDIER.
   N. HALL, 135:APR73-293
NORMAN-BUTLER, B. VICTORIAN ASPIRA-
TIONS.
   N.F. POPE, JR., 637(VS):JUN74-441
NORRIS, L. MOUNTAINS, POLECATS,
PHEASANTS.*
   R. GARFITT, 364:OCT/NOV74-117
NORTH, E. PELICAN RISING.
   G. CLIFFORD, 617(TLS):5SEP75-998
NORTHAM, J. IBSEN.
   F. PAUL, 301(JEGP):JAN74-101
   E. SPRINCHORN, 397(MD):SEP73-208
NORTHAM, J. IBSEN'S DRAMATIC METHOD.
(2ND ED)
   189(EA):JAN-MAR73-120
NORTON, B. & J., EDS. LA PRESSE.
   J. GREENLEE, 207(FR):APR73-1078
NORTON, C. THE LETTERS OF CAROLINE
NORTON TO LORD MELBOURNE. (J.O.
HOGE & C. OLNEY, EDS)
   P. ZIEGLER, 617(TLS):4APR75-377
NORTON, L. - SEE DUC DE SAINT-SIMON
NORTON, M.B. THE BRITISH-AMERICANS.*
   R.M. CALHOON, 432(NEQ):JUN73-284
NORTON-SMITH, J. - SEE JAMES I OF
SCOTLAND
NOSEK, S. KULTURA AMFOR KULISTYCH
W POLSCE.
   P.B. GROSS, 182:VOL26#3/4-115
NOSSACK, H.E. TO THE UNKNOWN HERO.*
THE IMPOSSIBLE PROOF. THE D'ARTHEZ
CASE.
   M. WOOD, 453:18SEP75-56
NOTEHELFER, F.G. KŌTOKU SHŪSUI,
PORTRAIT OF A JAPANESE RADICAL.*
   C. TOTMAN, 318(JAOS):APR-JUN73-225
NÖTHER, I. DIE GEISTLICHEN GRUNDGE-
DANKEN IM ROLANDSLIED UND IN DER
KAISERCHRONIK.
   H. BACKES, 680(ZDP):BAND92HEFT1-
   124
NOTKER DER DEUTSCHE. DIE WERKE NOT-
KERS DES DEUTSCHEN.* (VOL 5) (J.C.
KING, ED)
   E.A. EBBINGHAUS, 400(MLN):APR73-
   612
   E.S. FIRCHOW, 589:JUL74-568
   D. LE SAGE, 402(MLR):OCT74-910
   K. OSTBERG, 382(MAE):1974/2-155

NOTKER DER DEUTSCHE. DIE WERKE NOT-
KERS DES DEUTSCHEN.* (VOL 8A)
(P.W. TAX, ED)
   E.A. EBBINGHAUS, 400(MLN):APR73-
   612
   E.S. FIRCHOW, 589:JUL74-568
   R.T. GIUFFRIDA, 564:MAR73-72
   D. LE SAGE, 402(MLR):OCT74-910
NOTT, K. PHILOSOPHY & HUMAN NATURE.
   G.D., 543:DEC72-361
NOULET, E. LE TON POÉTIQUE.
   P. MOREAU, 535(RHL):JAN-FEB73-161
"NOUVEAU CHOIX D'INSCRIPTIONS
GRECQUES."
   P. CHANTRAINE, 555:VOL47FASC2-327
   D.M. LEWIS, 123:MAR74-148
   J. WILKES, 124:NOV72-171
NOVA, C. THE GEEK.
   C.D.B. BRYAN, 441:21DEC75-19
NOVACK, G. UNDERSTANDING HISTORY.
   S. FINKELSTEIN, 125:OCT73-96
NOVAK, J.D., ED. FACILITIES FOR
SECONDARY SCHOOL SCIENCE TEACHING.
   W.M. RICE, 505:APR73-141
NOVAK, R.A. WILHELM VON HUMBOLDT AS
A LITERARY CRITIC.
   C.L. NOLLENDORFS, 406:FALL74-300
NOVALÍN, J.L.G. EL INQUISIDOR GEN-
ERAL FERNANDO DE VALDÉS (1483-1568).
   D.W. LOMAX, 86(BHS):APR73-169
NOVÁS CALVO, L. MANERAS DE CONTAR.
   R.D. SOUZA, 268:JAN75-67
   G.G. WING, 238:MAR73-183
NOVOZHILOV, V.V. PROBLEMS OF COST-
BENEFIT ANALYSIS IN OPTIMAL PLAN-
NING.
   K. LAL, 104:WINTER74-611
NOWINSKI, J. BARON DOMINIQUE VIVANT
DENON (1747-1825).*
   A. VIELWAHR, 546(RR):MAY73-238
NOWLAN, A. BETWEEN TEARS & LAUGH-
TER.
   A. SHUCARD, 102(CANL):SPRING73-126
   S. SOLECKI, 529(QQ):SUMMER73-311
NOWLAN, A. I'M A STRANGER HERE MY-
SELF.
   S. LAUDER, 99:APR/MAY75-61
   S. SCOBIE, 198:SUMMER75-106
NOWLAN, A. VARIOUS PERSONS NAMED
KEVIN O'BRIEN.*
   F. SUTHERLAND, 102(CANL):SPRING74-
   119
NOWOTNY, K.A. BEITRÄGE ZUR GE-
SCHICHTE DES WELTBILDES (FARBEN UND
WELTRICHTUNGEN).
   S. KRAMRISCH, 57:VOL35#4-375
   G.F. MEIER, 682(ZPSK):BAND26HEFT
   3/4-439
NOXON, J. HUME'S PHILOSOPHICAL DE-
VELOPMENT.
   N. CAPALDI, 319:APR75-259
   A. FLEW, 518:JAN74-16
NOY, D. & Z. KAGAN - SEE "THE YEAR-
BOOK OF THE FOLKLORE ARCHIVES IN
HAIFA"
NOY, D. & M., EDS. FOLKLORE RE-
SEARCH CENTER STUDIES. (VOL 2)
   S. STERN, 292(JAF):JUL-SEP73-313
NOZICK, M. MIGUEL DE UNAMUNO.
   J.W. BUTT, 86(BHS):OCT73-405
   D.L. SHAW, 402(MLR):APR74-443

NOZICK, M. & B.P. PATT, EDS. SPAN-
ISH LITERATURE SINCE THE CIVIL WAR.
E.M. MALINAK, 399(MLJ):NOV74-365
NOZICK, R. ANARCHY, STATE, &
UTOPIA.
M. COHEN, 231:MAR75-92
C. LEHMANN-HAUPT, 441:5AUG75-29
P. SINGER, 453:6MAR75-19
B. WILLIAMS, 617(TLS):17JAN75-46
S.S. WOLIN, 441:11MAY75-31
NTARA, S.J. THE HISTORY OF THE
CHEWA (MBIRI YA ACHEWA). (B.
HEINTZE, ED)
G.C. RUMP, 182:VOL26#19-698
"U NU: SATURDAY'S SON." (U KYAW
WIN, ED)
H. TINKER, 617(TLS):1AUG75-867
NÜBEL, O. POMPEJUS OCCO (1483-
1537).
R. HOWELL, JR. 182:VOL26#23/24-888
NUECHTERLEIN, D. UNITED STATES
NATIONAL INTERESTS IN A CHANGING
WORLD.
D. YERGIN, 676(YR):SUMMER74-605
639(VQR):SPRING74-L
NUMMENMAA, L. THE USES OF "SO,"
"AL SO" & "AS" IN EARLY MIDDLE
ENGLISH.
M. RISSANEN, 439(NM):1973/4-764
NUNTE, G.C., JR. FIREARMS ENCYCLO-
PEDIA.
617(TLS):7FEB75-149
NURSE, P.H. CLASSICAL VOICES.*
Q.M. HOPE, 207(FR):OCT72-150
R.C. KNIGHT, 208(FS):JAN74-66
C.G.S. WILLIAMS, 402(MLR):JAN74-
179
NURSE, P.H. - SEE MADAME DE LAFAY-
ETTE
NUTTALL, A.D. A COMMON SKY.
R.L. ARRINGTON, 569(SR):SPRING74-
XXVI
NWANKWO, N. MY MERCEDES IS BIGGER
THAN YOURS.
D.A.N. JONES, 617(TLS):17OCT75-
1238
442(NY):10NOV75-190
NYE, R. - SEE SWINBURNE, A.C.
NYE, R.B. SOCIETY & CULTURE IN
AMERICA, 1830-1860.*
639(VQR):SUMMER74-XCII
NYKROG, P. LA PENSÉE DE BALZAC DANS
"LA COMÉDIE HUMAINE."
M.G. WORTHINGTON, 545(RPH):NOV73-
228
NYLANDER, C. IONIANS IN PASARGA-
DAE.*
A. FARKAS, 54:MAR73-137
H. GOETZ, 318(JAOS):JUL-SEP73-372
G.M.A. HANFMANN, 182:VOL26#20-750

OAKESHOTT, M. ON HUMAN CONDUCT.
A. RYAN, 362:17APR75-517
J. SHKLAR, 617(TLS):12SEP75-1018
OAKESHOTT, W. SIGENA.
J.F. HEALY, 135:SEP73-68
G. ZARNECKI, 39:JUN73-623
OAKLEY, A. THE SOCIOLOGY OF HOUSE-
WORK. HOUSEWIFE.
S. JACKSON, 617(TLS):28FEB75-232

OAKSEY, J. THE STORY OF MILL REEF.*
A. ROSS, 364:AUG/SEP74-116
OATES, J.C. ANGEL FIRE.*
D. BARBOUR, 150(DR):WINTER73/74-
785
M.G. PERLOFF, 659:WINTER75-84
OATES, J.C. THE ASSASSINS.
J.D. O'HARA, 441:23NOV75-10
OATES, J.C. DO WITH ME WHAT YOU
WILL.*
B. ALLEN, 249(HUDR):SPRING74-119
W. SULLIVAN, 569(SR):WINTER74-138
OATES, J.C. THE EDGE OF IMPOSSIBIL-
ITY.*
295:FEB74-478
OATES, J.C. THE GODDESS & OTHER
WOMEN.*
D. LODGE, 617(TLS):4APR75-353
J. MELLORS, 362:22MAY75-685
OATES, J.C. THE SEDUCTION & OTHER
STORIES.
E. POCHODA, 441:31AUG75-6
OATES, J.C. - SEE UNDER FERNANDES/
J.C. OATES
OATES, S.B. THE FIRES OF JUBILEE.
H. MAYER, 441:5OCT75-12
OATES, W.J. PLATO'S VIEW OF ART.*
V. MENZA, 482(PHR):APR74-272
R.K. SPRAGUE, 122:JAN74-72
Ó BAOILL, C. - SEE SILIS NA CEAPAICH
OBERHELMAN, H.D. ERNESTO SÁBATO.*
M.A. SALGADO, 241:MAY73-77
OBERLEITNER, M. DIE HANDSCHRIFT-
LICHE UEBERLIEFERUNG DER WERKE DES
HEILIGEN AUGUSTINUS. (VOL 1)
P. LANGLOIS, 555:VOL47FASC1-174
OBERTELLO, L. SEVERINO BOEZIO.
J.J.E. GRACIA, 319:OCT75-523
OBEYESEKERE, G., F. REYNOLDS & B.L.
SMITH. THE TWO WHEELS OF DHAMMA.
R.T. BOBILIN, 485(PE&W):JAN-APR73-
259
A.T. KIRSCH, 293(JAST):MAY73-553
OBIECHINA, E. CULTURE, TRADITION &
SOCIETY IN THE WEST AFRICAN NOVEL.
M.M. MAHOOD, 617(TLS):17OCT75-1238
OBNORSKIJ, S.P. & S.G. BARXUDAROV.
XRESTOMATIJA PO ISTORII RUSSKOGO
JAZYKA. (PT 1)
T. CIZEVSKA, 574(SEEJ):WINTER73-
483
OBOLENSKY, A.P. FOOD-NOTES ON
GOGOL.
L.B. TURKEVICH, 550(RUSR):OCT73-
453
OBOLENSKY, D. THE BYZANTINE COMMON-
WEALTH.*
A.E. ALEXANDER, 574(SEEJ):SUMMER
72-270
O'BRIEN, C.C. STATES OF IRELAND.
L.P. CURTIS, JR., 676(YR):AUTUMN
73-137
O'BRIEN, C.C. THE SUSPECTING
GLANCE.*
H. LABOUCHEIX, 189(EA):JAN-MAR73-
106
H. SERGEANT, 175:AUTUMN72-114
J. VINCENT, 184(EIC):APR73-193
O'BRIEN, D. THE CONSCIENCE OF JAMES
JOYCE.
P. SWINDEN, 148:SPRING72-91

O'BRIEN, D.B.C. THE MOURIDES OF
SENEGAL.
J. COPANS, 69:OCT73-366
O'BRIEN, D.B.C. SAINTS & POLITI-
CIANS.
L. MAIR, 617(TLS):1AUG75-880
O'BRIEN, D.J. THE RENEWAL OF AMERI-
CAN CATHOLICISM.
R.J. CUNNINGHAM, 613:AUTUMN73-432
O'BRIEN, D.P. THE CLASSICAL ECONO-
MISTS.
L. ROBBINS, 617(TLS):1AUG75-870
O'BRIEN, F. THE POOR MOUTH.
D. MC CLELLAND, 231:FEB75-116
K. MILLER, 453:1MAY75-31
B. O'DOHERTY, 441:19JAN75-25
J. UPDIKE, 442(NY):1SEP75-65
O'BRIEN, F. STORIES & PLAYS.*
J. WILLIAMS, 111:3MAY74-129
O'BRIEN, F. THE THIRD POLICEMAN.
K. MILLER, 453:1MAY75-31
O'BRIEN, J. CONTEMPORARY FRENCH
LITERATURE.* (L.S. ROUDIEZ, ED)
V.E. GRAHAM, 546(RR):NOV73-312
P. NEWMAN-GORDON, 399(MLJ):JAN-FEB
74-67
295:FEB74-436
O'BRIEN, J. INTERVIEWS WITH BLACK
WRITERS.*
J. KLINKOWITZ, 473(PR):4/1974-634
O'BRIEN, R.J., ED. LINGUISTICS.
R.R. BUTTERS, 35(AS):WINTER69-287
O'BRIEN, T. NORTHERN LIGHTS.
R. SALE, 453:13NOV75-31
O'BRINE, M. NO EARTH FOR FOXES.
N. CALLENDAR, 441:20APR75-28
O'CALLAGHAN, J.F. A HISTORY OF
MEDIEVAL SPAIN.
P. LINEHAN, 617(TLS):7NOV75-1339
OCAMPO, S. LOS DÍAS DE LA NOCHE.
A.W. ASHHURST, 238:MAR73-180
O'CASEY, S. THE LETTERS OF SEAN
O'CASEY. (VOL 1) (D. KRAUSE, ED)
R. GILMAN, 441:16MAR75-1
442(NY):5MAY75-143
OCHIKUBO MONOGATARI. THE TALE OF
THE LADY OCHIKUBO.* (W. WHITE-
HOUSE & E. YANAGISAWA, TRANS)
M. URY, 318(JAOS):JUL-SEP73-410
OCKHAM, WILLIAM OF. SCRIPTUM IN
LIBRUM PRIMUM SENTENTIARUM; ORDI-
NATIO. (VOL 2) (S. BROWN, WITH
G. GÁL, EDS)
K.M., 543:JUN73-775
O'CONNELL, D. THE TEACHINGS OF
SAINT LOUIS.*
R.W. BOYKIN, 207(FR):FEB73-600
O'CONNELL, J. ENDING INSULT TO
INJURY.
D. SANFORD, 441:10AUG75-4
O'CONNOR, A. HE'S SOMEWHERE IN
THERE.
J. MELLORS, 362:23JAN75-126
O'CONNOR, F. FLANNERY O'CONNOR: THE
COMPLETE STORIES.* (R. GIROUX, ED)
J. IDOL, 573(SSF):WINTER73-103
O'CONNOR, F.V., ED. THE NEW DEAL
ART PROJECTS.*
M.S. YOUNG, 39:APR73-441
O'CONNOR, J.J. "AMADIS DE GAULE" &
ITS INFLUENCE ON ELIZABETHAN LITER-
ATURE.*
E.B. PLACE, 240(HR):SPRING73-427

O'CONNOR, P.F. A SEASON FOR UNNAT-
URAL CAUSES.
J.D. O'HARA, 441:26OCT75-50
O'CONNOR, R. HEYWOOD BROUN.
P. KIHSS, 441:1JUL75-27
442(NY):4AUG75-90
O'CONNOR, R.G. FORCE & DIPLOMACY.
G.S. SMITH, 529(QQ):SPRING73-112
O'CONNOR, S.J., JR. HINDU GODS OF
PENINSULAR SIAM.
T. BOWIE, 54:SEP73-440
O'CONNOR, U. BRENDAN.
M. WOHLGELERNTER, 295:FEB74-540
O'CONNOR, U. LIFE STYLES.
M. GIBBON, 159(DM):AUTUMN/WINTER
73/74-123
ODDIE, W. DICKENS & CARLYLE.
J.A.D., 191(ELN):SEP73(SUPP)-41
K.J. FIELDING, 155:MAY73-111
E. SHARPLES, 141:SPRING74-180
M. SLATER, 637(VS):MAR74-328
G.B. TENNYSON, 445(NCF):JUN73-115
ODELL, R. EXHUMATION OF A MURDER.
R. DAVIES, 617(TLS):26SEP75-1097
O'DONNELL, J.H., 3D. SOUTHERN IN-
DIANS IN THE AMERICAN REVOLUTION.
D.H. CORKRAN, 656(WMQ):JUL74-509
O'DONNELL, L. THE BABY MERCHANTS.
N. CALLENDAR, 441:5OCT75-47
O'DRISCOLL, R., ED. THEATRE &
NATIONALISM IN TWENTIETH-CENTURY
IRELAND.
M. BROWN, 529(QQ):SPRING73-129
H. SERGEANT, 175:AUTUMN72-114
O'DRISCOLL, R. & L. REYNOLDS, EDS.
YEATS & THE THEATRE.
F.S.L. LYONS, 617(TLS):10OCT75-
1187
O'DRISCOLL, R. & L. REYNOLDS, EDS.
YEATS STUDIES, NUMBER TWO.
R. HOGAN, 295:APR74-1031
ODUYOYE, M. YORUBA NAMES.
E.C. ROWLANDS, 315(JAL):VOL11PT3-
97
OE, K. A PERSONAL MATTER.
W. FALKE, 145(CRIT):VOL15#3-43
OELLERS, N., ED. SCHILLER - ZEITGE-
NOSSE ALLER EPOCHEN. (PT. 1)
K.L. BERGHAHN, 406:WINTER74-401
H.B. GARLAND, 220(GL&L):JAN74-151
OENSLAGER, D. STAGE DESIGN.
R. SOUTHERN, 617(TLS):8AUG75-888
OESTERBY, M., ED. SLOVAR' AKADEMII
ROSSIYSKOY. (VOL 7)
B. COMRIE, 575(SEER):APR74-311
OETTINGER, K. PHANTASIE UND ER-
FAHRUNG.
M.A. POITZSCH, 221(GQ):JAN73-122
OEY, G.P. A CHECK LIST OF THE VIET-
NAMESE HOLDINGS OF THE WASON COL-
LECTION, CORNELL UNIVERSITY LIBRAR-
IES, AS OF JUNE, 1971.
K. TAYLOR, 293(JAST):FEB73-379
OEY HONG LEE. INDONESIAN GOVERNMENT
& PRESS DURING GUIDED DEMOCRACY.
R.K. PAGET, 293(JAST):MAY73-570
O'FAOLAIN, J. MAN IN THE CELLAR.*
D. DURRANT, 364:OCT/NOV74-131
O'FAOLAIN, J. WOMEN IN THE WALL.
N. HEPBURN, 362:5JUN75-746
L. PULVERTAFT, 617(TLS):4APR75-353
OFFEN, R. CAGNEY.
R. CAMPION, 200:APR73-234

"OFFICIAL MASTER REFERENCE FOR BI-
CENTENNIAL ACTIVITIES."
H. MITGANG, 441:4JAN75-21
OFFORD, M.Y., ED. THE BOOK OF THE
KNIGHT OF THE TOWER.* (W. CAXTON,
TRANS)
A.G. DYSON, 325:APR73-611
K. REICHL, 38:BAND91HEFT4-522
K. SØRENSEN, 179(ES):JUN73-276
R.M. WILSON, 402(MLR):APR74-367
OFFUTT, A. OPERATION SUPER MS.
N. CALLENDAR, 441:26JAN75-23
O'FLAHERTY, J.C. & J.K. KING - SEE
RAABE, W.
OGBURN, C. THE SOUTHERN APPALACH-
IANS.
E. ABBEY, 441:20JUL75-6
OGDEN, M.S. - SEE DE CHAULIAC, G.
OGILVIE, R.M. THE ROMANS & THEIR
GODS IN THE AGE OF AUGUSTUS.
J. FONTENROSE, 122:APR74-154
S.J. SIMON, 121(CJ):OCT/NOV73-92
O'GORMAN, D. DIDEROT THE SATIRIST.*
(FRENCH TITLE: DIDEROT SATIRIQUE.)
D. GUIRAGOSSIAN, 188(ECR):SPRING73-
84
J.R. LOY, 546(RR):MAR74-132
S. MENANT, 535(RHL):NOV-DEC73-1080
N. SUCKLING, 208(FS):JAN74-80
O'GORMAN, F. THE RISE OF PARTY IN
ENGLAND.
H. BUTTERFIELD, 617(TLS):10OCT75-
1193
O'GRADY, D. DESCHOOLING KEVIN
CAREW.
P. CAMPBELL, 617(TLS):22AUG75-951
O'HANLON, T.J. THE IRISH.
R. EDER, 441:13APR75-28
O'HARA, F. SELECTED POEMS. (D.
ALLEN, ED)
G. BURNS, 584(SWR):SPRING74-201
O'HARA, F. STANDING STILL & WALKING
IN NEW YORK. (D. ALLEN, ED)
A. SAROYAN, 441:14DEC75-27
OHKAWA, K. DIFFERENTIAL STRUCTURE
& AGRICULTURE.
G.C. ALLEN, 285(JAPQ):OCT-DEC73-
459
OHKAWA, K. & H. ROSOVSKY. JAPANESE
ECONOMIC GROWTH.
E.J. HOBSBAWM, 453:17JUL75-27
OIKONOMIDÈS, N. LES LISTES DE PRÉS-
ÉANCE BYZANTINES DES IXE ET XE
SIÈCLES.
J.F. HALDON, 182:VOL26#11/12-430
OKAMOTO, Y. THE NAMBAN ART OF JAPAN.
C. DRESSER, 592:JUL-AUG73-59
S. SITWELL, 39:AUG73-148
OKASHA, E. HAND-LIST OF ANGLO-SAXON
NON-RUNIC INSCRIPTIONS.*
R.D. WARE, 589:JUL74-584
O'KEEFFE, T., ED. MYLES.
J. WILLIAMS, 111:3MAY74-129
OKELL, J. A REFERENCE GRAMMAR OF
COLLOQUIAL BURMESE.*
R.B. JONES, 350:MAR74-205
J.A. MATISOFF, 318(JAOS):APR-JUN
73-230
OKLADNIKOV, A.P. YAKUTIA BEFORE ITS
INCORPORATION INTO THE RUSSIAN
STATE.* (H.N. MICHAEL, ED)
E. DUNN, 550(RUSR):APR73-216

OKONJO, U. THE IMPACT OF URBANIZA-
TION ON THE IBO FAMILY STRUCTURE.
G.I. JONES, 69:OCT73-371
OKUN, A.M. EQUALITY & EFFICIENCY.
L. SILK, 441:9AUG75-15
OLBY, R. THE PATH TO THE DOUBLE
HELIX.
V. MC ELHENY, 441:16MAR75-23
OLDERMAN, R.M. BEYOND THE WASTE
LAND.*
L. DITTMAR, 128(CE):FEB74-609
J.T. FLANAGAN, 179(ES):AUG73-405
S. PINSKER, 295:FEB74-492
OLDSON, W.O. THE HISTORICAL & NA-
TIONALISTIC THOUGHT OF NICOLAE
IORGA.
S.D. SPECTOR, 104:WINTER74-607
O'LEARY, D.F. BOLÍVAR & THE WAR OF
INDEPENDENCE. (ABRIDGED) (R.F.
MC NERNEY, JR., ED & TRANS)
J. FISHER, 86(BHS):APR73-195
OLENDORFF, R.R. GOLDEN EAGLE COUN-
TRY.
R. CARAS, 441:7DEC75-92
OLESCH, R. - SEE MĄCZYŃSKI, I.
OLIVA, L.J., ED. CATHERINE THE
GREAT.
J.T. ALEXANDER, 104:SPRING73-112
DE OLIVEIRA, D.M. - SEE MARTINS DE
OLIVEIRA, D.
DE OLIVEIRA MARQUES, A.H.R. DAILY
LIFE IN PORTUGAL IN THE LATE MIDDLE
AGES.
R. HARVEY, 382(MAE):1974/1-92
A.R. MYERS, 86(BHS):JUL73-311
F.M. ROGERS, 589:JAN74-130
OLIVER, A. BENJAMIN CONSTANT.
R.B. GRANT, 207(FR):DEC72-410
OLIVER, A. - SEE CURWEN, S.
OLIVER, D. BOUGAINVILLE.
J. GRIFFIN, 381:DEC73-442
OLIVER, H.J. - SEE SHAKESPEARE, W.
OLIVER, J.H. MARCUS AURELIUS: AS-
PECTS OF CIVIC & CULTURAL POLICY IN
THE EAST.*
E.W. GRAY, 303:VOL93-259
OLIVER, M. WEEKEND MAGAZINE COOK
BOOK.
J.M. COLE, 99:DEC75/JAN76-37
OLIVER, R. POEMS WITHOUT NAMES.*
A.S.G. EDWARDS, 179(ES):DEC72-553
R.H. ROBBINS, 599:FALL73-376
C.S. WRIGHT, 191(ELN):DEC73-121
OLIVOVÁ, V. THE DOOMED DEMOCRACY.*
J.M. BAK, 529(QQ):SPRING73-121
OLLÉ, J.G. AN INTRODUCTION TO BRIT-
ISH GOVERNMENT PUBLICATIONS. (2ND
ED)
J.B. CHILDS, 517(PBSA):APR-JUN74-
193
OLLER, J.W., JR. & J.C. RICHARDS,
EDS. FOCUS ON THE LEARNER.
V.E. HANZELI, 399(MLJ):DEC74-416
E.G. JOINER, 399(MLJ):NOV74-355
OLMOS GARCÍA, F. CERVANTES EN SU
ÉPOCA. (2ND ED)
E.H. FRIEDMAN, 400(MLN):MAR73-448
OLMSTEAD, A.H. THRESHOLD.
442(NY):13OCT75-178
OLNEY, J. METAPHORS OF SELF.*
D. BOWMAN, 402(MLR):JUL74-603
P. HAMILL, 295:FEB74-478
[CONTINUED]

OLNEY, J. METAPHORS OF SELF.*
[CONTINUING]
T. MIDDLEBRO', 529(QQ):SPRING73-
135
A.E. STONE, 131(CL):SPRING73-164
OLNEY, R.J. LINCOLNSHIRE POLITICS
1832-1885.
F. HILL, 637(VS):MAR74-337
OLSEN, H. & P. AMATO, EDS. ATTI:
CONVEGNO DI STUDI SU CORRADO GIA-
QUINTO.
F.R. DIFEDERICO, 54:JUN73-304
OLSEN, J. ALPHABET JACKSON.
M. LEVIN, 441:27APR75-34
OLSEN, T. YONNONDIO.*
S. CLAPP, 617(TLS):10JAN75-29
639(VQR):AUTUMN74-CXX
OLSON, A.G. ANGLO-AMERICAN POLI-
TICS, 1660-1775.*
E.R. SHERIDAN, 656(WMQ):APR74-324
OLSON, C. THE MAXIMUS POEMS. (C.
BOER & G.F. BUTTERICK, EDS) THE
POST OFFICE.
H. CARRUTH, 441:23NOV75-35
OLSON, C. CHARLES OLSON & EZRA
POUND. (C. SEELYE, ED)
H. CARRUTH, 441:23NOV75-35
442(NY):6OCT75-165
OLSON, E. THE THEORY OF COMEDY.
D.D. RAPHAEL, 447(N&Q):FEB73-63
OLSON, J.E. ULZANA.
W. GARD, 584(SWR):WINTER74-98
OLSON, R.E. & A.M. PAUL, EDS. CON-
TEMPORARY PHILOSOPHY IN SCANDINAVIA.
D.S. ROBINSON, 484(PPR):SEP73-125
OLZIEN, O.H. WIRKEN.
H. SCHANZE, 224(GRM):BAND23HEFT2-
249
"OMAGGIO A CLEMENTE REBORA."
400(MLN):JAN73-169
O'MALLEY, J. - SEE MARX, K.
OMAN, C. CAROLINE SILVER.
C. BLAIR, 90:JAN73-47
OMAN, J.C. CULTS, CUSTOMS & SUPER-
STITIONS OF INDIA.
P.G. HIEBERT, 293(JAST):MAY73-536
O'MEARA, P. RHODESIA.
J.P. BARBER, 617(TLS):26DEC75-1546
ONDAATJE, M. RAT JELLY.
P. STEVENS, 529(QQ):WINTER73-656
O'NEILL, E.A. THE ROTTERDAM DELIV-
ERY.
N. CALLENDAR, 441:16NOV75-74
O'NEILL, J. PERCEPTION, EXPRESSION,
& HISTORY.*
S.T. MAYO, 258:MAR73-154
O'NEILL, J. SOCIOLOGY AS A SKIN
TRADE.*
D.E.W. HOLDEN, 529(QQ):AUTUMN73-
487
O'NEILL, J. - SEE MERLEAU-PONTY, M.
O'NEILL, J.C. THE LETTER TO THE
ROMANS.
D. CUPITT, 362:27FEB75-284
O'NEILL, J.P. WORKABLE DESIGN.
M. BANTA, 27(AL):MAY74-231
O'NEILL, K. ANDRÉ GIDE & THE "ROMAN
D'AVENTURE."*
G.E. GINGRAS, 207(FR):MAR73-837
205(FMLS):APR73-214
O'NEILL, P.G. JAPANESE NAMES.
T. CONNOR, 244(HJAS):VOL33-288

ONG, W.J. RHETORIC, ROMANCE, &
TECHNOLOGY.*
H. BABB, 599:SPRING73-173
R.J. BAUER, 577(SHR):WINTER73-88
T.J. FARRELL, 480(P&R):WINTER73-59
ONIMUS, J., ED. LES IDÉOLOGIES DANS
LE MONDE ACTUEL.
M. ADAM, 542:JAN-MAR73-96
ONODA, H. NO SURRENDER.
D.J. ENRIGHT, 362:12JUN75-789
"ONTARIO SINCE 1867."
C. THIBAULT, 99:MAR75-35
ONYEMELUKWE, C.C. ECONOMIC UNDER-
DEVELOPMENT.
H. MYINT, 617(TLS):18APR75-432
OOMEN, U. AUTOMATISCHE SYNTAKTISCHE
ANALYSE.
G.F. MEIER, 682(ZPSK):BAND26HEFT
3/4-440
OPIE, I. & P., EDS. THE OXFORD
BOOK OF CHILDREN'S VERSE.
M. BOTTRALL, 148:AUTUMN73-286
OPITZ, M. GESAMMELTE WERKE.* (VOL
3, PTS 1&2) (G. SCHULZ-BEHREND, ED)
K.F. OTTO, JR., 221(GQ):MAR73-286
OPPÉ, A.P. RAPHAEL.
L. BECHERUCCI, 90:JUL73-469
OPPEL, H. ENGLISCH-DEUTSCHE LITERA-
TURBEZIEHUNGEN.*
L. BORINSKI, 430(NS):SEP73-508
A. CLOSS, 402(MLR):JUL74-689
A. CRÉPIN, 189(EA):OCT-DEC73-458
F. SCHMITT-VON MÜHLENFELS, 52:
BAND8HEFT3-320
OPPEN, G. COLLECTED POEMS.
H. KENNER, 441:190CT75-5
OPPEN, G. SEASCAPE: NEEDLE'S EYE.
M. PERLBERG, 491:JUN75-172
OPPENHEIMER, E.M. GOETHE'S POETRY
FOR OCCASIONS.
W.H. BRUFORD, 617(TLS):18JUL75-809
OPPENHEIMER, J. ON OCCASION.
H. CARRUTH, 249(HUDR):SUMMER74-311
OPPONG, C. MARRIAGE AMONG A MATRI-
LINEAL ELITE.
L. MAIR, 617(TLS):3JAN75-8
"OPUSCULA ATHENIENSIA." (VOL 10)
R.M. COOK, 123:MAR74-160
"OPUSCULA ROMANA." (VOL 7)
A.R. NEUMANN, 182:VOL26#23/24-874
ORAGE, A.R. ORAGE AS CRITIC. (W.
MARTIN, ED)
W. HALEY, 617(TLS):7FEB75-135
ORAM THOMAS, J. THE GIANT-KILLERS.
E. BREDSDORFF, 617(TLS):29AUG75-
965
ORD-HUME, A.W.J.G. CLOCKWORK MUSIC.
G.M. WILSON, 135:NOV73-220
ORDERIC VITALIS. THE ECCLESIASTICAL
HISTORY OF ORDERIC VITALIS.* (VOL
2, BKS 3&4) (M. CHIBNALL, ED &
TRANS)
R.B. PATTERSON, 589:APR74-320
ORDERIC VITALIS. THE ECCLESIASTICAL
HISTORY OF ORDERIC VITALIS.* (VOL
3, BKS 5&6) (M. CHIBNALL, ED &
TRANS)
A.G. DYSON, 325:OCT73-667
R.B. PATTERSON, 589:APR74-320
ORDERIC VITALIS. THE ECCLESIASTICAL
HISTORY OF ORDERIC VITALIS. (VOL
4, BKS 7&8) (M. CHIBNALL, ED)
F. BARLOW, 382(MAE):1974/3-268

ORDERIC VITALIS. THE ECCLESIASTICAL
HISTORY OF ORDERIC VITALIS. (VOL 5,
BKS 9 & 10) (M. CHIBNALL, ED)
  F.R.H. DU BOULAY, 617(TLS):8AUG75-
  901
ORDISH, G. THE YEAR OF THE BUTTER-
FLY.
  P. ADAMS, 61:APR75-100
ORDISH, O. THE THEATRE.
  J.C. TREWIN, 157:SPRING73-75
ORENSTEIN, A. RAVEL.
  D. HENAHAN, 441:30NOV75-40
ORGEL, S. & R. STRONG. INIGO JONES.*
  A.B. KERNAN, 676(YR):SPRING74-434
ORIZET, J. SILENCIEUSE ENTRAVE AU
TEMPS.
  R. CHAMPIGNY, 207(FR):MAR73-863
ORKIN, H. SCUFFLER.*
  E. DUNDY, 617(TLS):20JUN75-704
ORKIN, M.M. SPEAKING CANADIAN ENG-
LISH.
  R.I. MC DAVID, JR., 35(AS):FALL-
  WINTER71-287
ORLANDO, V. GIOVANNI MELI E LA
CULTURA FRANCESE.
  P.R. HORNE, 208(FS):APR74-200
ORMONDE, P. THE MOVEMENT.
  M. LYONS, 381:MAR73-106
ORNSTEIN, J., R.W. EWTON, JR. & T.H.
MUELLER. PROGRAMMED INSTRUCTION &
EDUCATIONAL TECHNOLOGY IN THE LAN-
GUAGE TEACHING FIELD.
  E.A. FRECHETTE, 399(MLJ):JAN-FEB
  73-45
ORNSTEIN, R. A KINGDOM FOR A
STAGE.*
  A.S. CAIRNCROSS, 551(RENQ):SUMMER
  73-232
  J.R. ELLIOTT, JR., 405(MP):MAY74-
  421
  R.D. ERLICH, 160:WINTER72/73-132
  C. HOY, 569(SR):SPRING74-363
  P. TRACI, 141:SUMMER73-281
ORNSTEIN, R.E. THE PSYCHOLOGY OF
CONSCIOUSNESS.*
  W.G., 543:JUN73-761
  E.L. KAMARCK, 59(ASOC):SUMMER-FALL
  74-320
O'ROURKE, P.J. & D. KENNEY, EDS.
NATIONAL LAMPOON 1964 HIGH SCHOOL
YEARBOOK PARODY.
  C. NICOL, 231:APR75-107
OROZ, R. LA LENGUA CASTELLANA EN
CHILE.
  L.B. KIDDLE, 545(RPH):AUG73-104
ORR, D. ITALIAN RENAISSANCE DRAMA
IN ENGLAND BEFORE 1625.*
  B. MITCHELL, 276:SUMMER73-320
ORR, G. BURNING THE EMPTY NESTS.*
  P. NELSON, 109:SPRING/SUMMER74-131
  639(VQR):SPRING74-LVII
ORSINI, P. - SEE COLLUTHUS
ORSINI, P. - SEE MUSAEUS
ORT, D. OFF TO SEE THE WIZARD.
  M. LEVIN, 441:15JUN75-26
ORTALI, R. ENTRE NOUS.
  L.R. POLLY, 399(MLJ):JAN-FEB74-68
ORTEGA Y GASSET, J. PHENOMENOLOGY
& ART.
  453:17APR75-37
ORTIZ, A.D. - SEE UNDER DOMÍNGUEZ
ORTIZ, A.

ORTNER, J.P. MARQUARD HERRGOTT
(1694-1762).
  M.L. FREY, 481(PQ):JUL73-363
ORTON, H. & N. WRIGHT, WITH M.J.
JONES. QUESTIONNAIRE FOR THE IN-
VESTIGATION OF AMERICAN REGIONAL
ENGLISH.
  A.R. DUCKERT, 35(AS):FALL-WINTER
  72-278
ORTZI. HISTORIA DE EUSKADI.
  P. PRESTON, 617(TLS):4JUL75-740
ØRUM, P. SCAPEGOAT.
  P-L. ADAMS, 61:OCT75-110
ØRUM, P. THE WHIPPING-BOY.
  617(TLS):20JUN75-692
ORVELL, M. INVISIBLE PARADE.*
  P.M. BROWNING, JR., 659:SPRING75-
  260
ØRVIK, N. & OTHERS. DEPARTMENTAL
DECISION-MAKING.
  J. BARROS, 529(QQ):WINTER73-662
OSBORN, J.M. YOUNG PHILIP SIDNEY,
1572-1577.*
  N.C. CARPENTER, 219(GAR):SPRING73-
  141
  A.C. HAMILTON, 529(QQ):SPRING73-
  132
  M. HATTAWAY, 175:AUTUMN73-113
  W. NELSON, 551(RENQ):SPRING73-76
  J. REES, 191(ELN):SEP73-57
  J. ROBERTSON, 405(MP):MAY74-418
  R.W.Z., 179(ES):OCT72-495
OSBORNE, C. THE COMPLETE OPERAS OF
VERDI.
  A. PORTER, 415:FEB74-130
OSBORNE, C. THE CONCERT SONG COM-
PANION.
  E. SAMS, 415:NOV74-949
OSBORNE, C. - SEE VERDI, G.
OSBORNE, C. - SEE WAGNER, R.
OSBORNE, H., ED. AESTHETICS.
  M.M. EATON, 290(JAAC):FALL73-120
  R.W. HEPBURN, 89(BJA):AUTUMN73-405
OSBORNE, H., ED. THE OXFORD COMPAN-
ION TO ART.*
  B.S. MYERS, 54:SEP73-473
OSBORNE, J. HANDBUCH DER DEUTSCHEN
LITERATURGESCHICHTE. (VOL 8)
  J.M. MC GLATHERY, 301(JEGP):OCT74-
  598
OSBORNE, J. THE NATURALIST DRAMA IN
GERMANY.*
  S. GOOCH, 214:VOL6#21-109
  H. SCHEUER, 680(ZDP):BAND92HEFT2-
  311
OSBORNE, J. ROMANTIK.*
  E. THURNHER, 133:1973/3-255
OSBORNE, M. RIVER ROAD TO CHINA.
  J. ZORN, 441:7SEP75-4
  442(NY):20OCT75-171
OSBURN, C.B. GUIDE TO FRENCH STUD-
IES: SUPPLEMENT WITH CUMULATIVE
INDEXES.
  H. PEYRE, 399(MLJ):JAN-FEB73-68
  H.C. WOODBRIDGE, 545(RPH):AUG73-
  140
OSBURN, C.B., ED. THE PRESENT STATE
OF FRENCH STUDIES.*
  H. PEYRE, 399(MLJ):JAN-FEB73-49
  H.C. WOODBRIDGE, 545(RPH):AUG73-
  140
OSGOOD, W.E. & L.J. HURLEY. SKI
TOURING.
  J. SAVERCOOL, 441:23MAR75-37

OSMOND, A. SALADIN!
T.J. BINYON, 617(TLS):26DEC75-1544
M. LASKI, 362:25DEC75&1JAN76-893
ØSTBY, A. KNUT HAMSUN.
N.M. KNUTSEN, 172(EDDA):1973/2-121
OSTERGAARD, G. & M. CURRELL. THE
GENTLE ANARCHISTS.
A. PAREL, 293(JAST):MAY73-527
OSTRY, S., ED. CANADIAN HIGHER EDU-
CATION IN THE SEVENTIES.
M. CREET, 529(QQ):SPRING73-92
OSTRY, S. & M.A. ZAIDI. LABOUR
ECONOMICS IN CANADA. (2ND ED)
F.T. DENTON, 529(QQ):SPRING73-126
Ó SÚILLEABHÁIN, S. A HANDBOOK OF
IRISH FOLKLORE.
W.H. JANSEN, 582(SFQ):JUN73-149
O'SULLIVAN, F. THE EGNATIAN WAY.
J.J. WILKES, 313:VOL63-288
O'SULLIVAN, J. & A.M. MECKLER, EDS.
THE DRAFT & ITS ENEMIES.
617(TLS):13JUN75-657
OTERO, C-P. INTRODUCCIÓN A LA LIN-
GÜÍSTICA TRANSFORMACIONAL.
H. LÓPEZ MORALES, 545(RPH):FEB74-
368
OTERO, L. LA SITUACIÓN.
J.A. MARBÁN, 268:JAN75-58
OTIS, B. OVID AS AN EPIC POET.*
(2ND ED)
S. VIARRE, 555:VOL47FASC2-355
OTT, P. ZUR SPRACHE DER JÄGER IN
DER DEUTSCHEN SCHWEIZ.*
R.A. FOWKES, 222(GR):JAN73-68
OTTAWAY, H. VAUGHAN WILLIAMS SYM-
PHONIES.*
A.E.F. DICKINSON, 607:SEP73-47
OTTEN, H. EINE ALTHETHITISCHE ER-
ZÄHLUNG UM DIE STADT ZALPA.
G. NEUMANN, 260(IF):BAND78-245
OTTEN, H. MATERIALIEN ZUM HETHITIS-
CHEN LEXIKON.
V. HAAS, 343:BAND16HEFT2-161
G. NEUMANN, 260(IF):BAND78-242
OTTEN, K. DER ENGLISCHE ROMAN VOM
16. ZUM 19. JAHRHUNDERT.
A. CRÉPIN, 189(EA):OCT-DEC73-458
OTTEN, T. THE DESERTED STAGE.
M.R. BOOTH, 637(VS):SEP73-110
J.E. DEITZ, 50(ARQ):WINTER73-358
OTTO, E. DIE SPRACHE DER ZEITZER
KANZLEIEN IM 16. JAHRHUNDERT.
E. SKÁLA, 680(ZDP):BAND92HEFT1-138
OTTO, K.F., JR. PHILIPP VON ZESEN.
J. BRUCKNER, 220(GL&L):APR74-262
U. MACHÉ, 301(JEGP):JAN74-80
P. SKRINE, 402(MLR):JUL74-702
OUELLET, R. LES RELATIONS HUMAINES
DANS L'OEUVRE DE SAINT-EXUPÉRY.
H. GODIN, 208(FS):JUL74-349
J. ONIMUS, 557(RSH):APR-JUN73-324
OUELLETTE-MICHALSKA, M. LE JEU DES
SAISONS.
R. SUTHERLAND, 102(CANL):WINTER73-
114
OUGHTON, J. TAKING TREE TRAINS.
P. STEVENS, 628:SPRING74-100
OVENDEN, G., ED. THE ILLUSTRATORS
OF ALICE.*
R. MC LEAN, 135:JUN73-152
OVERBECK, J.C. & S. SWINY. TWO
CYPRIOT BRONZE AGE SITES AT KAF-
KALLIA (DHALI).
J. BOUZEK, 182:VOL26#19-683

OVID. METAMORPHOSES. (BK 11)
(G.M.H. MURPHY, ED)
R.J. GARIEPY, JR., 124:MAY73-488
OVID. OVIDE: "LES FASTES."* (VOL
2) (H. LE BONNIEC, ED & TRANS)
F. LASSERRE, 182:VOL26#15/16-557
OVID. P. OVIDII NASONIS "EPISTULAE
HEROIDUM." (H. DÖRRIE, ED)
J. ANDRÉ, 555:VOL47FASC1-150
M.D. REEVE, 123:MAR74-57
OVID. OVID'S HEROIDES. (H.C. CAN-
NON, TRANS)
E.J. KENNEY, 123:MAR74-139
OVIEDO, J.M. MARIO VARGAS LLOSA.*
G. BROTHERSTON, 240(HR):SUMMER73-
589
OWEN, D.D.R., ED. ARTHURIAN RO-
MANCE.*
R. HARRIS, 208(FS):JAN74-52
K. REICHL, 38:BAND91HEFT3-392
OWEN, D.M. ELY RECORDS.
J.E. SAYERS, 325:OCT73-675
OWEN, G. THE WHITE STALLION & OTHER
POEMS.*
K.S. BYER, 219(GAR):SPRING73-110
OWEN, G.D., ED. CALENDAR OF THE
MANUSCRIPTS OF THE MARQUESS OF
SALISBURY, PRESERVED AT HATFIELD
HOUSE. (PT 22)
A.G.R. SMITH, 325:OCT73-671
OWEN, G.E.L., ED. ARISTOTLE ON
DIALECTIC.
R.G. HOERBER, 121(CJ):DEC72/JAN73-
187
OWEN, H. AFTERMATH.
295:FEB74-377
OWEN, J.E. L.T. HOBHOUSE.
A. RYAN, 617(TLS):12SEP75-1019
OWEN, N.G., ED. COMPADRE COLONIAL-
ISM.
T. FRIEND, 293(JAST):NOV72-224
OWEN, R. & T.D. COLE. BEAUTIFUL &
BELOVED.
J. MILLER, 617(TLS):3JAN75-18
OWEN, W.J.B. & J.W. SMYSER - SEE
WORDSWORTH, W.
OWENS, B. OUR KIND OF PEOPLE.
C. LEHMANN-HAUPT, 441:1AUG75-31
OWENS, I. AFTER CLAUDE.
E.R. WIDMER, 59(ASOC):SPRING-SUM-
MER74-153
OWSLEY, H.C., ED. GUIDE TO THE PRO-
CESSED MANUSCRIPTS OF THE TENNESSEE
HISTORICAL SOCIETY.
A.L. NOLEN, 14:JAN73-76
OXFORD, W.H. THE SPEECHES OF FUKU-
ZAWA.
KUMAKURA MASAYA, 285(JAPQ):JUL-SEP
74-301
"THE OXFORD ILLUSTRATED DICTIONARY."
(J. COULSON & OTHERS, EDS; 2ND ED
REV BY D. EAGLE, WITH J. HAWKINS)
M. WARNOCK, 617(TLS):30MAY75-604
"OXFORD LATIN DICTIONARY." (FASC
1&2)
R.R. DYER, 121(CJ):OCT/NOV72-89
"OXFORD LATIN DICTIONARY."* (FASC 3)
E.J. KENNEY, 123:MAR74-88
J.W. POULTNEY, 124:MAY73-496
OXNARD, C.E. UNIQUENESS & DIVERSITY
IN HUMAN EVOLUTION.
J.Z. YOUNG, 453:29MAY75-18

OZ, A. TOUCH THE WATER, TOUCH THE WIND.*
N. HEPBURN, 362:27MAR75-421
J. THOMPSON, 453:23JAN75-39
J. WILLETT, 617(TLS):21MAR75-293
OZ, A. UNTO DEATH.*
J. MC ELROY, 441:26OCT75-4
OZAKI, R.S. THE CONTROL OF IMPORTS & FOREIGN CAPITAL IN JAPAN.
M. BRONFENBRENNER, 293(JAST):FEB 73-329

PÄÄNÄNEN, U. SALLUST'S POLITICO-SOCIAL TERMINOLOGY.
T.F. CARNEY, 487:SUMMER73-198
J. HELLEGOUARC'H, 555:VOL47FASC1-154
A.J. WOODMAN, 313:VOL63-293
PABST, M. TECHNOLOGISCHES WÖRTERBUCH PORTUGIESISCH, DEUTSCH-PORTUGIESISCH, PORTUGIESISCH-DEUTSCH.
E.I.S., 75:3/1973-144
PABST, W., ED. DAS MODERNE FRANZÖSISCHE DRAMA.*
205(FMLS):OCT73-407
PACCAGNINI, G. PISANELLO.
S. LEGOUIX, 135:DEC73-297
PACCHI, A. CARTESIO IN INGHILTERRA.
R.S. WESTFALL, 319:JAN75-103
PACELLA, G. & S. TIMPANARO - SEE LEOPARDI, G.
PACEY, A. THE MAZE OF INGENUITY.
A.R. HALL, 617(TLS):14MAR75-283
PACEY, D. WAKEN, LORDS & LADIES GAY. (F.M. TIERNEY, ED)
B. MITCHELL, 198:SUMMER75-110
PACHMUSS, T. ZINAÏDA HIPPIUS.*
G. IVASK, 574(SEEJ):SPRING72-105
PACHMUSS, T. - SEE HIPPIUS, Z.N.
PÄCHT, O. & J.J.G. ALEXANDER. ILLUMINATED MANUSCRIPTS IN THE BODLEIAN LIBRARY, OXFORD.* (VOL 2)
J. BACKHOUSE, 90:MAR73-168
PÄCHT, O. & J.J.G. ALEXANDER. ILLUMINATED MANUSCRIPTS IN THE BODLEIAN LIBRARY, OXFORD. (VOL 3)
S. HESLOP, 135:JUL73-227
PACI, E. THE FUNCTION OF THE SCIENCES & THE MEANING OF MAN.
I.H. ANGUS, 154:JUN73-359
PACI, F.R. - SEE UNDER ROMANA PACI, F.
PACIFICI, S. THE MODERN ITALIAN NOVEL FROM CAPUANA TO TOZZI.
R. SEVERINO, 399(MLJ):APR74-217
PACIFICI, S. - SEE GINZBURG, N.
PACK, R. NOTHING BUT LIGHT.*
P. NELSON, 109:SPRING/SUMMER74-131
P. RAMSEY, 569(SR):SPRING74-395
PACKARD, S.R. TWELFTH CENTURY EUROPE.
C.N.L. BROOKE, 382(MAE):1974/3-312
PACKARD, W., ED. THE CRAFT OF POETRY.
J.M. BRINNIN, 441:2MAR75-4
PACKENHAM, R.A. LIBERAL AMERICA & THE THIRD WORLD.
D. YERGIN, 676(YR):SUMMER74-605
639(VQR):AUTUMN74-CLI
PACKER, B. CARO.
J. YOHALEM, 441:28DEC75-18

PACKER, J.E. THE INSULAE OF IMPERIAL OSTIA.
R.J. LING, 313:VOL63-279
R. MEIGGS, 123:NOV74-268
PADOAN, G. - SEE DA BIBBIENA, B.D.
PAGANELLI, E. LA POESIA DI DRUMMOND OF HAWTHORNDEN.
L.C. BORELLI, 588:APR74-259
PAGANI, W. REPERTORIO TEMATICO DELLA SCUOLA POETICA SICILIANA.*
J.A. SCOTT, 545(RPH):AUG73-139
PAGDEN, A.R. - SEE "HERNAN CORTES: LETTERS FROM MEXICO"
PAGE, D. FOLKTALES IN HOMER'S "ODYSSEY."*
639(VQR):SUMMER74-LXXXI
PAGE, D., ED. SUPPLEMENTUM LYRICIS GRAECIS.
P. GREEN, 617(TLS):14MAR75-272
PAGE, N. THE LANGUAGE OF JANE AUSTEN.*
C.J. RAWSON, 175:AUTUMN73-116
K. SØRENSEN, 179(ES):DEC73-595
S.I. TUCKER, 541(RES):AUG73-359
A. WRIGHT, 402(MLR):APR74-382
PAGE, P.K. POEMS, SELECTED & NEW, 1942-1973.*
T. INKSTER, 606(TAMR):OCT74-83
PAGE, R.I. AN INTRODUCTION TO ENGLISH RUNES.
J. TURVILLE-PETRE, 382(MAE):1974/3-267
PAGET, J. PARLE OU MEURS.
A.G. RODRIGUEZ, 207(FR):APR73-1063
PAGLIARO, H.E., ED. STUDIES IN EIGHTEENTH-CENTURY CULTURE: RACISM IN THE EIGHTEENTH CENTURY.
566:AUTUMN73-33
PAGNINI, C. - SEE DA PONTE, L.
PÅHLSSON, C. THE NORTHUMBRIAN BURR.
G. KRISTENSSON, 179(ES):DEC73-611
PAIGE, D.D. - SEE POUND, E.
PAINTING, N. FOREVER AMBRIDGE.
A. HAMILTON, 362:20NOV75-681
PAIVIO, A. IMAGERY & VERBAL PROCESSES.
J.T.E. RICHARDSON, 307:#2-116
DE PALACIO, J. MARY SHELLEY DANS SON OEUVRE.*
B. MICHA, 52:BAND8HEFT2-228
PALANDRI, A.J., ED & TRANS. MODERN VERSE FROM TAIWAN.*
M. ROBERTSON, 293(JAST):FEB73-314
PALÉOLOGUE, M. AN AMBASSADOR'S MEMOIRS 1914-1917.*
F.L. CARSTEN, 575(SEER):APR74-300
S. PLOSS, 550(RUSR):OCT73-454
PALEY, G. ENORMOUS CHANGES AT THE LAST MINUTE.*
G. ANNAN, 617(TLS):14FEB75-157
J. MELLORS, 362:22MAY75-685
W. PEDEN, 569(SR):FALL74-712
R. SALE, 249(HUDR):WINTER74/75-628
PALEY, M.D. ENERGY & THE IMAGINATION.*
J. ADLARD, 179(ES):FEB73-74
J.B. BEER, 447(N&Q):FEB73-75
M.F. SCHULZ, 173(ECS):FALL73-120
PALEY, M.D. & M. PHILLIPS, EDS. WILLIAM BLAKE.*
D.R. FAULKNER, 676(YR):SUMMER74-590
R.H. FOGLE, 569(SR):SPRING74-383
[CONTINUED]

PALEY, M.D. & M. PHILLIPS, EDS.
WILLIAM BLAKE.* [CONTINUING]
D. WAGENKNECHT, 591(SIR):SPRING74-
164
639(VQR):SUMMER74-LXXIV
PALLADIO, A. THE FOUR BOOKS OF
ARCHITECTURE.
P. SCHNEIDER, 98:APR73-318
PALLISTER, J.L. THE WORLD VIEW OF
BÉROALDE DE VERVILLE.*
R.J. RINK, 551(RENQ):AUTUMN73-352
PALLOTTINO, M. CIVILTÀ ARTISTICA
ETRUSCO-ITALICA.
D. RIDGWAY, 313:VOL63-313
PALLS, B.P. INTERMEDIATE GREEK
READER & GRAMMAR REVIEW.
J.E. REXINE, 399(MLJ):SEP-OCT74-
271
PALMATIER, R.A., COMP. A GLOSSARY
FOR ENGLISH TRANSFORMATIONAL GRAM-
MAR.
V.E. HANZELI, 399(MLJ):SEP-OCT73-
288
PALMER, C. IMPRESSIONISM IN MUSIC.*
R. NICHOLS, 410(M&L):JAN74-101
PALMER, C. RAVEL.
G.W. HOPKINS, 415:SEP74-752
PALMER, D.J., ED. TENNYSON.
H. SERGEANT, 175:SUMMER73-78
PALMER, F.R. GRAMMAR.*
T.P. DOBSON, 140(CR):#15-82
R.A. HUDSON, 361:SEP73-153
R.C. NAREMORE, 480(P&R):FALL73-253
PALMER, F.R. A LINGUISTIC STUDY OF
THE ENGLISH VERB.
H.U. BOAS, 260(IF):BAND77HEFT2/3-
359
PALMER, H. ANALOGY.
T. MC PHERSON, 518:MAY74-17
PALMER, H.R. SUDANESE MEMOIRS.
A.H.M. KIRK-GREENE, 69:OCT73-356
PALMER, I. TEXTILES IN INDONESIA.
R.C. RICE, 293(JAST):FEB73-372
PALMER, J.J.N. ENGLAND, FRANCE &
CHRISTENDOM, 1377-99.*
G.P. CUTTINO, 589:OCT73-751
PALMER, L. CHANGE LOBSTERS - &
DANCE.
S. HELGESEN, 441:9NOV75-26
PALMER, L.R. DESCRIPTIVE & COMPARA-
TIVE LINGISTICS.
R. ANTTILA, 343:BAND17HEFT2-113
PALMER, L.R. A NEW GUIDE TO THE
PALACE OF KNOSSOS.
J. RAISON, 555:VOL47FASC1-116
PALMER, N.D. ELECTIONS & POLITICAL
DEVELOPMENT.
W.H. MORRIS-JONES, 617(TLS):19DEC
75-1526
PALMER, R. THE BORNU SAHARA &
SUDAN.
A.H.M. KIRK-GREENE, 69:OCT73-356
PALMER, R., ED. THE PAINFUL PLOUGH.*
J.H. BRUNVAND, 292(JAF):JUL-SEP73-
315
PALMER, R.B. & R. HAMERTON-KELLY,
EDS. PHILOMATHES.*
E. ASMIS, 124:NOV72-179
PALMER, R.E. HERMENEUTICS.*
G. FLØISTAD, 262:WINTER73-445
PALMER, R.E., JR. THOMAS WHYTHORNE'S
SPEECH.*
B. SUNDBY, 179(ES):DEC73-605

PALMER, R.E.A. THE ARCHAIC COMMUN-
ITY OF THE ROMANS.*
R.J. ROWLAND, JR., 121(CJ):DEC73/
JAN74-166
PALMER, S. THE LETTERS OF SAMUEL
PALMER. (R. LISTER, ED)
W. FEAVER, 617(TLS):21MAR75-304
PALMER, S.E., JR. & R.R. KING.
YUGOSLAV COMMUNISM & THE MACEDONIAN
QUESTION.*
H.G. LUNT, 574(SEEJ):SPRING72-132
PALMES, J. - SEE FLETCHER, B.
PÁLSSON, H. ART & ETHICS IN "HRAF-
NKEL'S SAGA."*
R.F. ALLEN, 589:JAN74-138
PÁLSSON, H. & P. EDWARDS, EDS &
TRANS. THE BOOK OF SETTLEMENTS:
LANDNÁMABÓK.
T.F. HOAD, 447(N&Q):JUL73-264
PÁLSSON, H. & P. EDWARDS - SEE "EYR-
BYGGJA SAGA"
PÁLSSON, H. & P. EDWARDS - SEE
"HROLF GAUTREKSSON: A VIKING RO-
MANCE"
PAMLÉNYI, E., ED. A HISTORY OF HUN-
GARY.
P. IGNOTUS, 617(TLS):8AUG75-905
PAMLÉNYI, E., ED. SOCIAL-ECONOMIC
RESEARCHES ON THE HISTORY OF EAST-
CENTRAL EUROPE.*
T. SPIRA, 104:SUMMER73-276
PAN KU. COURTIER & COMMONER IN
ANCIENT CHINA. (B. WATSON, TRANS)
C.P. FITZGERALD, 617(TLS):25APR75-
449
PANČENKO, A.M. RUSSKAJA STICHOTVOR-
NAJA KUL'TURA XVII VEKA.
D. TSCHIŽEWSKIJ, 72:BAND211HEFT
1/3-249
PANDEY, K.C. WESTERN AESTHETICS/
COMPARATIVE AESTHETICS. (VOL 2)
T.J. DIFFEY, 89(BJA):SUMMER73-298
W. TATARKIEWICZ, 290(JAAC):SPRING
74-429
LAYMAN P'ANG. THE RECORDED SAYINGS
OF LAYMAN P'ANG.* (R.F. SASAKI, Y.
IRIYA & D.R. FRASER, TRANS)
P. YAMPOLSKY, 318(JAOS):JUL-SEP73-
412
PANG CHENG LIAN. SINGAPORE'S
PEOPLE'S ACTION PARTY.
V.M. FIC, 302:JAN73-186
G.D. NESS, 293(JAST):AUG73-749
PANGLE, T.L. MONTESQUIEU'S PHILOSO-
PHY OF LIBERALISM.
W.B. ALLEN, 319:APR75-256
639(VQR):SUMMER74-CIV
PANICHAS, G.A., ED. THE POLITICS OF
TWENTIETH-CENTURY NOVELISTS.
J. FUEGI, 295:FEB74-403
PANICHAS, G.A. THE REVERENT DISCI-
PLINE.*
R. KIRK, 569(SR):FALL74-698
J.M. LALLEY, 396(MODA):FALL74-415
J. TASKER, 569(SR):FALL74-XCII
DE PANIZZA LORCH, M. - SEE VALLA, L.
PANNONIUS, I.S. GRAMMATICA HUNGARO-
LATINA.
P. AALTO, 353:15JUL73-91
G. HAZAI, 682(ZPSK):BAND26HEFT6-
719
PANOFF, M. & F. L'ETHNOLOGUE ET SON
OMBRE.
C. SCHUWER, 542:JAN-MAR73-72

PANSAERS, C. POINT D'ORGUE PROGRAM-
MATIQUE POUR JEUNE OURANG-OUTANG.
  S. FAUCHEREAU, 98:NOV73-997
PANTŮČKOVÁ, L. W.M. THACKERAY AS A
CRITIC OF LITERATURE.
  D. HAWES, 541(RES):AUG73-361
  S. MONOD, 189(EA):JUL-SEP73-375
  S.M. SMITH, 402(MLR):JAN74-157
PANUPONG, V. - SEE UNDER VICHIN PAN-
UPONG
PANZER, B. & W. THÜMMEL. DIE EIN-
TEILUNG DER NIEDERDEUTSCHEN MUNDAR-
TEN AUF GRUND DER STRUKTURELLEN
ENTWICKLUNG DES VOKALISMUS.
  H.J. GERNENTZ, 682(ZPSK):BAND26
  HEFT6-711
  B.J. KOEKKOEK, 361:SEP73-119
DE' PAOLI, D. - SEE MONTEVERDI, C.
PAOLUCCI, A. FROM TENSION TO TONIC.*
  L. CASPER, 613:SPRING73-133
PAPANOUTSOS, E.P. THE FOUNDATIONS
OF KNOWLEDGE. (J.P. ANTON, ED)
  P. PARRINI, 548(RCSF):APR-JUN73-
  225
PAPARELLI, G. STORIA DELLA "LIRICA"
FOSCOLIANA.
  P.R. BALDINI, 275(IQ):SPRING74-108
PAPER, L.J. THE PROMISE & THE PER-
FORMANCE.
  W.V. SHANNON, 441:28DEC75-2
"PAPER HOUSES."
  R. NORTH, 362:24APR75-542
PAPIČ, M. L'EXPRESSION ET LA PLACE
DU SUJET DANS LES "ESSAIS" DE MON-
TAIGNE.*
  M. WILMET, 209(FM):JAN73-89
PARATORE, E. STUDI SUI "PROMESSI
SPOSI."
  F. FORTI, 228(GSLI):VOL150FASC472-
  628
PARDIES, I-G. DISCOURS DE LA CON-
NOISSANCE DES BESTES. (L.C. ROSEN-
FIELD, ED)
  R.A. WATSON, 319:JUL75-407
PARDUE, P.A. BUDDHISM.*
  A. BLOOM, 485(PE&W):JUL73-407
PARÉ, A. DES MONSTRES ET PRODIGES.*
(J. CÉARD, ED)
  M.T. GNUDI, 551(RENQ):AUTUMN73-354
  I.D. MC FARLANE, 208(FS):APR74-184
  R. MULHAUSER, 207(FR):OCT72-149
  J. ROGER, 535(RHL):JAN-FEB73-120
PAREDES, A. & R. BAUMAN, EDS. TO-
WARDS NEW PERSPECTIVES IN FOLKLORE.
  F.A. DE CARO, 292(JAF):JUL-SEP73-
  312
PAREDES, A. & E.J. STEKERT, EDS.
THE URBAN EXPERIENCE & FOLK TRADI-
TION.
  J.D.A. WIDDOWSON, 203:SPRING73-77
PAREKH, B. & R.N. BERKI, EDS. THE
MORALITY OF POLITICS.
  M. WARNOCK, 479(PHQ):JUL73-282
PARENT, M. COHÉRENCE ET RÉSONANCE
DANS LE STYLE DE "CHARMES" DE PAUL
VALÉRY.*
  M. LECUYER, 546(RR):NOV73-315
  Y. SCALZITTI, 405(MP):AUG73-105
PARET, R. DER KORAN.
  F. ROSENTHAL, 318(JAOS):JUL-SEP73-
  362
PARGETER, E. SUNRISE IN THE WEST.
  P. BEER, 617(TLS):17JAN75-48
PARINETTO, L. - SEE MARX, K.

PARIS, B.J. A PSYCHOLOGICAL AP-
PROACH TO FICTION.
  D.B. KUSPIT, 290(JAAC):WINTER74-
  224
PARIS, J. HAMLET ET PANURGE.
  B. DIDIER, 535(RHL):JAN-FEB73-122
PARISH, J.R. THE PARAMOUNT PRETTIES.
  R.P. CAMPION, 200:MAR73-187
PARISH, J.R. THE SLAPSTICK QUEENS.
  D. MC CLELLAND, 200:DEC73-622
PARISH, J.R. & A.H. MARILL. THE
CINEMA OF EDWARD G. ROBINSON.
  E. ANDERSON, 200:MAR73-186
PARK, J. CHARLIE'S BACK IN TOWN.
  N. CALLENDAR, 441:25MAY75-16
PARK, R. HAZLITT & THE SPIRIT OF
THE AGE.*
  G. THOMAS, 175:SPRING72-27
PARKER, A. STATES OF MIND.
  R. HAYNES, 617(TLS):10OCT75-1216
PARKER, C-A. MR. STUBBS THE HORSE
PAINTER.
  J. HAYES, 90:APR73-256
PARKER, D. FAMILIAR TO ALL.
  R. MITCHISON, 362:31JUL75-156
PARKER, D., ED. SACHEVERELL SITWELL.
  A. BELL, 617(TLS):12DEC75-1479
PARKER, G., ED. THE EVOLUTION OF
CANADIAN LITERATURE IN ENGLISH,
1914-45.
  C. THOMAS, 102(CANL):SPRING74-86
PARKER, G.D. - SEE HOME, J.
PARKER, G.T. MIND CURE IN NEW ENG-
LAND.
  L. BUELL, 432(NEQ):DEC73-630
PARKER, L. THE GUNS OF MAZATLAN.
  N. CALLENDAR, 441:23FEB75-40
PARKER, R. THE COMMON STREAM.
  R. BLYTHE, 362:20FEB75-251
  A. BROYARD, 441:24DEC75-19
PARKER, R.B. - SEE MIDDLETON, T.
PARKER, T. LIGHTHOUSE.
  P. BEER, 617(TLS):9MAY75-513
PARKER, T.H. & F.J. TESKEY, EDS.
THEMES TO EXPLORE.
  A. RENDLE, 157:SPRING73-82
PARKER, W.H. THE SUPERPOWERS.*
  F. SPOONER, 575(SEER):JUL74-474
PARKER, W.R. MILTON.
  H.W. DONNER, 179(ES):APR72-162
PARKIN, D.J. LANGUAGE CHOICE IN TWO
KAMPALA HOUSING ESTATES.
  315(JAL):VOL11PT2-107
PARKIN, F., ED. THE SOCIAL ANALYSIS
OF CLASS STRUCTURE.
  P. ABRAMS, 617(TLS):9MAY75-508
PARKIN, M. UP TIGHT.
  J. MILLER, 617(TLS):7NOV75-1338
PARKINSON, C.N. FIRESHIP.
  M. LEVIN, 441:22JUN75-12
PARKINSON, R. THE HUSSAR GENERAL.
  A. BRETT-JAMES, 617(TLS):6JUN75-
  619
PARKMAN, E. THE DIARY OF EBENEZER
PARKMAN 1703-1782. (PT 1) (F.G.
WALETT, ED)
  M.H. THOMAS, 165:SPRING75-96
PARLAVANTZA-FRIEDRICH, U. TÄUSCH-
UNGSSZENEN IN DEN TRAGÖDIEN DES
SOPHOKLES.
  W.M. CALDER 3D, 122:APR74-159

PARMÉE, D., ED. TWELVE FRENCH
POETS, 1820-1900.
  C.F. COATES, 399(MLJ):SEP-OCT73-
  287
  A.J. WRIGHT, JR., 207(FR):DEC72-
  411
PARMENIUS, S. THE NEW FOUND LAND OF
STEPHEN PARMENIUS. (D.B. QUINN &
N.M. CHESHIRE, EDS & TRANS)
  P.G. ADAMS, 149:SEP74-266
  R.T. BRUÈRE, 122:OCT73-300
  J.B. DALLETT, 551(RENQ):AUTUMN73-
  355
  C. FANTAZZI, 124:SEP-OCT73-55
PARMENTIER, J. OEUVRES POÉTIQUES.*
(F. FERRAND, ED)
  J.J. BEARD, 208(FS):JAN74-59
  D. WILSON, 402(MLR):OCT74-865
PARMET, H.S. EISENHOWER & THE AMER-
ICAN CRUSADES.
  J.R. WAGNER, 50(ARQ):SPRING73-82
PARMING, T. THE COLLAPSE OF LIBERAL
DEMOCRACY & THE RISE OF AUTHORITAR-
IANISM IN ESTONIA.
  J. HIDEN, 617(TLS):12DEC75-1485
PARPOLA, A. & OTHERS. DECIPHERMENT
OF THE PROTO-DRAVIDIAN INSCRIPTIONS
OF THE INDUS CIVILIZATION: A FIRST
ANNOUNCEMENT. PROGRESS IN THE DE-
CIPHERMENT OF THE PROTO-DRAVIDIAN
INDUS SCRIPT. FURTHER PROGRESS IN
THE INDUS SCRIPT DECIPHERMENT.
  V.V. ŠEVOROŠKIN, 353:1JUL73-82
PARRA, N. EMERGENCY POEMS.* (M.
WILLIAMS, ED & TRANS)
  G.S. FRASER, 473(PR):2/1974-289
PARRA, V. DÉCIMAS.
  K. MÜLLER-BERGH, 263:JAN-MAR74-75
PARRET, H. LANGUAGE & DISCOURSE.
  W.O. HENDRICKS, 361:OCT73-270
PARRINDER, P., ED. H.G. WELLS: THE
CRITICAL HERITAGE.
  B. KIELY, 159(DM):SUMMER73-103
"THE MAXFIELD PARRISH POSTER BOOK."
  W. FEAVER, 617(TLS):10JAN75-28
PARRISH, S.M. THE ART OF "THE LYRI-
CAL BALLADS."*
  J.A.W. HEFFERNAN, 591(SIR):SUMMER
  74-255
  S.M. SPERRY, 301(JEGP):JUL74-445
PARRONCHI, A. OPERE GIOVANILI DI
MICHELANGELO.
  A.S. CALARCO, 127:SUMMER74-368
PARRY, B. DELUSIONS & DISCOVERIES.*
  G. CANNON, 318(JAOS):OCT-DEC73-622
  G.B. TENNYSON, 445(NCF):JUN73-114
PARRY, J.H. THE DISCOVERY OF THE
SEA.*
  R. DAVIS, 617(TLS):14NOV75-1351
PARRY, M. THE MAKING OF HOMERIC
VERSE.* (A. PARRY, ED)
  P. CHANTRAINE, 555:VOL47FASC2-318
  J.B. HAINSWORTH, 123:MAR74-12
PARSONS, D. DIRECTORY OF TUNES &
MUSICAL THEMES.
  R. MACONIE, 617(TLS):30MAY75-609
PARSONS, N. - SEE KOROLENKO, V.G.
PARSONS, T. & G.M. PLATT, WITH N.J.
SMELSER. THE AMERICAN UNIVERSITY.*
  R. BUFFINGTON, 569(SR):WINTER74-
  147
PARTINGTON, N. MASTER OF BENGAL.
  M. LEVIN, 441:19JAN75-36
  617(TLS):10JAN75-29

PARTINGTON, N. THE SUNSHINE PATRI-
OT.
  M. LEVIN, 441:28DEC75-20
PARTLOW, R.B., JR. - SEE "DICKENS
STUDIES ANNUAL"
PARTNER, P. THE LANDS OF ST. PETER.
  D. HERLIHY, 589:APR74-368
PARTRIDGE, A.C. ENGLISH BIBLICAL
TRANSLATION.
  G. HAMMOND, 148:WINTER73-361
PARTRIDGE, A.C., ED. THE TRIBE OF
BEN.
  M.T. JONES-DAVIES, 189(EA):JUL-SEP
  73-355
PARTRIDGE, E. - SEE JONSON, B.
PASCAL, B. OEUVRES COMPLÈTES.*
(VOL 3) (J. MESNARD, ED)
  D. DESCOTES, 557(RSH):APR-JUN73-
  314
PASCAL, B. PENSÉES.
  M. WAGNER, 207(FR):OCT72-247
PASCAL, B. PENSÉES DE M. PASCAL SUR
LA RELIGION ET SUR QUELQUES AUTRES
SUJETS.* (G. COUTON & J. JEHASSE,
EDS)
  P. SELLIER, 535(RHL):NOV-DEC73-
  1064
PASCAL, V. THE DISCIPLE & HIS
DEVIL.
  F.P.W. MC DOWELL, 295:FEB74-772
PASCHOUD, F. - SEE ZOSIMUS
PASCOLI, G. LETTERE A MARIO NOVARO
E AD ALTRI AMICI.
  E. SACCONE, 400(MLN):JAN73-156
PASINETTI, L.L. GROWTH & INCOME
DISTRIBUTION.
  R. SOLOW, 617(TLS):14MAR75-277
PASLEY, M., ED. GERMANY.*
  205(FMLS):APR73-213
PASOLINI, P.P. EMPIRISMO ERETICO.
  B.L., 275(IQ):FALL-WINTER73(VOL17
  #66)-73
PASOLINI, P.P. SCRITTI CORSARI. LA
NUOVA GIOVENTÙ.
  B. MERRY, 617(TLS):31OCT75-1311
PASQUALINI, J. - SEE UNDER BAO RUO-
WANG
PASSERINI, A. LINEE DI STORIA
ROMANA IN ETÀ IMPERIALE. (N. CRIN-
ITI, ED)
  J-C. RICHARD, 555:VOL47FASC1-184
PASSERINI, A. STUDI SU CAIO MARIO.
  J. BRISCOE, 313:VOL63-311
PASSERON, R. IMPRESSIONIST PRINTS.*
  T.J. CLARK, 617(TLS):11APR75-401
PASSLER, D. TIME, FORM, & STYLE IN
BOSWELL'S "LIFE OF JOHNSON."*
  J.T. BOULTON, 179(ES):APR73-177
  C. LAMONT, 541(RES):FEB73-92
  R. LONSDALE, 447(N&Q):JUN73-228
  M. RENNER, 599:FALL73-380
PASSMORE, J. THE PERFECTIBILITY OF
MAN.*
  K. BRITTON, 393(MIND):OCT73-631
  A.R. DRENGSON, 154:JUN73-350
PASTORINO, A. LA RELIGIONE ROMANA.
  J-C. RICHARD, 555:VOL47FASC2-368
PASTORINO, A. - SEE AUSONIUS
PATAI, R., ED. ENCYCLOPEDIA OF
ZIONISM & ISRAEL.
  M.I. UROFSKY, 390:APR73-77
PATAI, R. MYTH & MODERN MAN.
  D.R. SKEELS, 292(JAF):APR-JUN73-
  183

"PATAÑJALI'S 'VYĀKARAṆA-MAHĀBHĀṢ-
YA'."* (S.D. JOSHI, WITH J.A.F.
ROODBERGEN, EDS & TRANS)
R. ROCHER, 318(JAOS):JAN-MAR73-114
PATERSON, L.M. TROUBADOURS & ELO-
QUENCE.
P. DRONKE, 617(TLS):12SEP75-1023
PATERSON, R.W.K. THE NIHILISTIC
EGOIST: MAX STIRNER.*
L.S. STEPELEVICH, 321:WINTER73-317
PATON, A. APARTHEID & THE ARCH-
BISHOP.*
639(VQR):AUTUMN74-CXXXV
PATRICK, A. THE MEN OF THE FIRST
FRENCH REPUBLIC.
D. HIGGS, 529(QQ):WINTER73-634
PATRIDES, C.A., ED. APPROACHES TO
"PARADISE LOST."
G.J. SCHIFFHORST, 577(SHR):WINTER
73-90
PATRIDES, C.A., ED. THE CAMBRIDGE
PLATONISTS.*
J. CARLSEN, 179(ES):JUN73-291
PATRIDES, C.A. THE GRAND DESIGN OF
GOD.*
G. BULLOUGH, 175:SUMMER73-74
T.F. DRIVER, 125:JUN74-353
J.L. LIEVSAY, 191(ELN):MAR74-235
G.M. LOGAN, 255:FALL73-306
G.F. WALLER, 150(DR):SPRING73-191
PATRIDES, C.A. - SEE MILTON, J.
PATRONE, A.M.N. - SEE UNDER NADA
PATRONE, A.M.
PATROUCH, J.F., JR. THE SCIENCE
FICTION OF ISAAC ASIMOV.
G. JONAS, 441:12JAN75-32
PATTANAYAK, D.P. ASPECTS OF APPLIED
LINGUISTICS.
J.M. LINDHOLM, 293(JAST):AUG73-725
PATTEN, R.L. - SEE DICKENS, C.
PATTERSON, A.M. HERMOGENES & THE
RENAISSANCE.*
I. CLARK, 599:SPRING73-198
J.F. FLEISCHAUER, 141:SUMMER72-311
D. NEWTON-DE MOLINA, 148:SPRING72-
87
PATTERSON, G. T.S. ELIOT.
K. SMIDT, 179(ES):DEC72-571
295:FEB74-585
PATTERSON, N-L. CANADIAN NATIVE
ART.
R.M. HUME, 99:JUN75-39
PATTERSON, S.E. POLITICAL PARTIES
IN REVOLUTIONARY MASSACHUSETTS.
C.W. AKERS, 432(NEQ):MAR74-120
G.A. BILLIAS, 656(WMQ):APR74-320
PATTISON, W.T. EMILIA PARDO BAZÁN.
D.F. BROWN, 238:MAY73-501
R.E. LOTT, 593:WINTER74-382
PATTON, L. & P. MANN - SEE COLER-
IDGE, S.T.
PÄTZOLD, K. DIE PALAU-SPRACHE UND
IHRE STELLUNG ZU ANDEREN INDONESIS-
CHEN SPRACHEN.
A. CAPELL, 353:15MAR73-122
PAUL OF VENICE. LOGICA MAGNA (TRAC-
TATUS DE SUPPOSITIONIBUS). (A.R.
PERREIAH, ED & TRANS)
K.M., 543:DEC72-362
PAUL, A. KIDS' INDOOR GARDENING.
(D. BROWN, ED)
J. CANADAY, 441:13APR75-7

PAUL, C.B. & R.D. PEPPER. THE IMPOR-
TANCE OF READING ALFRED.
P. GINESTIER, 189(EA):APR-JUN73-
234
PAUL, F. HENRICH STEFFENS.
N.H. SMITH, 182:VOL26#11/12-394
PAUL, H. PRINZIPIEN DER SPRACHGE-
SCHICHTE.
S. KANNGIESSER, 260(IF):BAND78-217
PAUL, R.W. - SEE FOOTE, M.H.
PAUL, S. HART'S BRIDGE.*
B. QUINN, 219(GAR):WINTER73-612
PAULIK, W. PORTUGUÊS PRÁTICO.
J. HORRENT, 556(RLV):1973/6-573
PAULS-EISENBEISS, E. GERMAN PORCE-
LAIN IN THE 18TH CENTURY.
T.H. CLARKE, 135:MAY73-63
PAULSEN, W., ED. DER DICHTER UND
SEINE ZEIT.*
H. SCHEUER, 52:BAND8HEFT1-109
PAULSEN, W., ED. REVOLTE UND EXPER-
IMENT.
J. GLENN, 133:1973/3-286
R.H. THOMAS, 402(MLR):OCT74-944
PAULSON, R. THE ART OF HOGARTH.
D. THOMAS, 362:25DEC75&1JAN76-892
PAULSON, R. HOGARTH.* (VOLS 1&2)
J. SUNDERLAND, 90:AUG73-538
PAULSON, R. ROWLANDSON.*
D.V.E., 191(ELN):SEP73(SUPP)-23
R. EDWARDS, 39:MAR73-314
T. LASK, 55:NOV72-16
"PAUSANIAS FÜHRER DURCH OLYMPIA."
(E. MEYER, ED & TRANS)
J.A. GAERTNER, 124:NOV72-186
PAUTASSO, S. LE FRONTIERE DELLA
CRITICA.
G. ALMANSI, 402(MLR):APR74-365
PAUTRAT, B. VERSIONS DU SOLEIL.*
F. GALICHET, 98:JUN73-545
PAUW, B.A. CHRISTIANITY & XHOSA
TRADITION.
L. MAIR, 617(TLS):7NOV75-1328
PAVESE, C. AMERICAN LITERATURE.*
J.T. FLANAGAN, 179(ES):JUN72-269
PAVEŠIC, S. JEZIČNI SAVJETNIK.
R. DUNATOV, 574(SEEJ):SUMMER72-264
PAVIC, M. ISTORIJA SRPSKE KNJIŽEV-
NOSTI BAROKNOG DOBA, XVII I XVIII
VEK.
N.R. PRIBIC, 574(SEEJ):SPRING73-92
PAVÓN, F.G. - SEE UNDER GARCÍA
PAVÓN, F.
PAWLEY, M. GARBAGE HOUSING.
P. STEADMAN, 617(TLS):19SEP75-1046
PAWLEY, M. FRANK LLOYD WRIGHT,
PUBLIC BUILDINGS.
R.G. WILSON, 576:OCT73-262
PAXTON, J. WORLD LEGISLATURES.
B. COCKS, 617(TLS):19SEP75-1045
PAYNE, D. THE MAN OF ONLY YESTER-
DAY.
J. BROOKS, 441:6APR75-6
E. WEEKS, 231:JUN75-92
PAYNE, F.A. KING ALFRED & BOETHIUS.
K. OTTEN, 38:BAND91HEFT4-517
PAYNE, R. THE LIFE & DEATH OF ADOLF
HITLER.
B.H. SMITH, 396(MODA):SPRING74-219
PAZ, O. ALTERNATING CURRENT.*
J. FRANCO, 617(TLS):7MAR75-245
G. SCHULMAN, 249(HUDR):AUTUMN74-
381

PAZ, O. THE BOW & THE LYRE.*
J. FRANCO, 617(TLS):7MAR75-245
G. SCHULMAN, 249(HUDR):AUTUMN74-
381
639(VQR):SUMMER74-LXXX
PAZ, O. CHILDREN OF THE MIRE.*
R. CHRIST, 473(PR):3/1974-484
J. FRANCO, 617(TLS):7MAR75-245
PAZ, O. EARLY POEMS 1935-1955.
CONFIGURATIONS.
G. SCHULMAN, 249(HUDR):AUTUMN74-
388
PAZ, O. CLAUDE LÉVI-STRAUSS. EL
SIGNO Y EL GARABATO. CONJUNCTIONS
& DISJUNCTIONS.*
J. FRANCO, 617(TLS):7MAR75-245
PAZ, O. LOS SIGNOS EN ROTACIÓN Y
OTROS ENSAYOS. (C. FUENTES, ED)
A. BORINSKY, 400(MLN):MAR73-500
PAZ, O. & OTHERS. IN PRAISE OF
HANDS.
639(VQR):AUTUMN74-CLVIII
PAZI, M. MAX BROD.
H. ZOHN, 221(GQ):MAY73-444
P'BITEK, O., ED & TRANS. THE HORN
OF MY LOVE.
G. MOORE, 617(TLS):21FEB75-204
PEABODY, J.B. - SEE "JOHN ADAMS, A
BIOGRAPHY IN HIS OWN WORDS"
PEACE, R. DOSTOYEVSKY.*
J. FRANK, 574(SEEJ):WINTER72-472
PEACOCK, A. A VERY SPECIAL OCCASION.
D.M. DAY, 157:WINTER73-89
PEACOCK, A. & R. WEIR. THE COMPOSER
IN THE MARKET PLACE.
B. TROWELL, 617(TLS):26DEC75-1530
PEACOCK, R. CRITICISM & PERSONAL
TASTE.
J. CULLER, 402(MLR):JUL74-602
H. MEYER, 149:SEP74-264
PEACOCK, R. HÖLDERLIN.
L. FORSTER, 220(GL&L):APR74-266
PEAKE, M. MERVYN PEAKE: WRITINGS &
DRAWINGS. (M. GILMORE & S. JOHN-
SON, EDS)
H. BROGAN, 617(TLS):4APR75-354
PEAKE, M. SELECTED POEMS.
H. SERGEANT, 175:SUMMER72-75
PEARCE, R.H. HISTORICISM ONCE MORE.
U. BRUMM, 38:BAND91HEFT4-557
PEARCE, T.M. OLIVER LA FARGE.*
K. YOUNG, 649(WAL):FALL73-161
PEARL, J. A JURY OF HIS PEERS.
N. CALLENDAR, 441:21DEC75-17
PEARLMAN, D.D. THE BARB OF TIME.*
D. BARBOUR, 529(QQ):AUTUMN73-450
PEARS, D. QUESTIONS IN THE PHILOSO-
PHY OF MIND.
M.F. BURNYEAT, 617(TLS):22AUG75-
938
PEARS, D. WHAT IS KNOWLEDGE?
P.A. CLARKE, 479(PHQ):APR73-175
PEARS, D.F., ED. BERTRAND RUSSELL.
T. RICHARDS, 479(PHQ):JUL73-261
PEARSALL, D. JOHN LYDGATE.*
A.S.G. EDWARDS, 179(ES):OCT73-504
J.R. SIMON, 189(EA):JUL-SEP73-352
PEARSALL, R. EDWARDIAN POPULAR
MUSIC.
M. HODGART, 617(TLS):5SEP75-991
PEARSALL, R.B. THE LIFE & WRITINGS
OF ERNEST HEMINGWAY.
P. MICHEL, 556(RLV):1973/6-572
W. SCHLEPPER, 182:VOL26#9-294

PEARSON, D. DREW PEARSON DIARIES
1949-1959.* (T. ABELL, ED)
K. KYLE, 362:6FEB75-186
PEARSON, J. EDWARD THE RAKE.
M. EDELMAN, 441:24AUG75-5
PEARSON, L. - SEE DEMOSTHENES
PEARSON, L.B. MIKE. (VOL 1)
H.P. GUNDY, 255(HAB):SPRING73-130
A.R.M. LOWER, 529(QQ):SPRING73-130
102(CANL):SUMMER73-127
PEARSON, M. THE SEALED TRAIN.
442(NY):28APR75-140
PEASE, J.H. & W.H. BOUND WITH THEM
IN CHAINS.
J.E. MOONEY, 432(NEQ):JUN74-318
PEASE, J.H. & W.H. THEY WHO WOULD
BE FREE.
W.L. ROSE, 453:18SEP75-46
A. WHITMAN, 441:18JAN75-33
PEAVY, C.D. GO SLOW NOW.*
R.P. PLAYER, 577(SHR):FALL73-448
PEBWORTH, T-L. & C.J. SUMMERS - SEE
FELLTHAM, O.
PECK, E. & J. SENDEROWITZ, EDS.
PRONATALISM.
L.C. POGREBIN, 441:23FEB75-36
PECK, R. DREAMLAND LAKE.
N. CALLENDAR, 441:23FEB75-40
PECK, R.N. FAWN.
M. LEVIN, 441:2FEB75-12
PEDECH, P. - SEE POLYBIUS
PEDERSEN, O. A SURVEY OF THE AMAL-
GEST.
J. NORTH, 617(TLS):15AUG75-921
PEDERSON, L., ED. A MANUAL FOR DIA-
LECT RESEARCH IN THE SOUTHERN
STATES.
A.R. DUCKERT, 35(AS):FALL-WINTER
72-278
PEDLER, F. THE LION & THE UNICORN
IN AFRICA.
D. JONES, 617(TLS):1AUG75-880
PEEK, W. EPIGRAMME UND ANDERE IN-
SCHRIFTEN AUS LAKONIEN UND ARKADIEN.
D.W. PRAKKEN, 124:FEB74-244
PEEL, B.B. A BIBLIOGRAPHY OF THE
PRAIRIE PROVINCES TO 1953 WITH BIO-
GRAPHICAL INDEX. (2ND ED)
G.W., 102(CANL):SUMMER74-128
PEEL, H.M. LAW OF THE WILD.
617(TLS):31JAN75-121
PEELE, G. THE DRAMATIC WORKS OF
GEORGE PEELE. (VOL 3) (R.M. BEN-
BOW, E.M. BLISTEIN & F.S. HOOK, EDS)
G. BULLOUGH, 179(ES):AUG73-385
M.T. JONES-DAVIES, 189(EA):JUL-SEP
73-358
"GEORGE PEELE." (S. PURCELL, ED)
J.D. JUMP, 148:SUMMER72-187
PÉGUY, C. & ALAIN-FOURNIER. CORRES-
PONDANCE (1910-1914). (Y. REY-
HERME, ED)
H.T. NAUGHTON, 399(MLJ):SEP-OCT74-
276
PEIL, M. THE GHANAIAN FACTORY WORK-
ER.
R.D. GRILLO, 69:OCT73-359
PEIRONE, L. NICCOLÒ MACHIAVELLI.
B.L., 275(IQ):SUMMER73-108
PEITZ, W., ED. DENKEN IN WIDER-
SPRÜCHEN.
H.W. PUPPE, 406:FALL74-327

PEKARSKII, P. NAUKA I LITERATURA V
ROSSII PRI PETRE VELIKOM.
M.J. OKENFUSS, 104:SUMMER74-328
PEKÁRY, T. DIE FUNDMÜNZEN VON VIN-
DONISSA VON HADRIAN BIS ZUM AUS-
GANG DER RÖMERHERRSCHAFT.
R. REECE, 313:VOL63-277
PÉLADEAU, M.B. - SEE TYLER, R.
PELÁEZ, S.M. - SEE UNDER MARTÍNEZ
PELÁEZ, S.
PELC, J. BILD - WORT - ZEICHEN.
D. TSCHIŽEWSKIJ, 72:BAND211HEFT
3/6-477
PELCZYNSKI, Z.A., ED. HEGEL'S POL-
ITICAL PHILOSOPHY.*
R. NORMAN, 393(MIND):OCT73-619
A. QUINTON, 453:12JUN75-39
PELIKAN, J. THE SPIRIT OF EASTERN
CHRISTENDOM (600-1700). (VOL 2)
P. BROWN & S. MAC CORMACK, 453:
20FEB75-19
PELLEGRINI, C., ED. IL BOCCACCIO
NELLA CULTURA FRANCESE.*
J.G. BROMFIELD, 402(MLR):JUL74-631
PELLEGRINI, G.B. GLI ARABISMI NELLE
LINGUE NEOLATINE CON SPECIALE
RIGUARDO ALL'ITALIA.
G.C. LEPSCHY, 402(MLR):JUL74-650
PELLETIER, A. - SEE PHILO
PELLISSON, P. & C. FLEURY. DEUX
AMIS D'HOMÈRE AU XVIIE SIÈCLE. (N.
HEPP, ED)
R.C. KNIGHT, 208(FS):OCT74-447
PELLS, R.H. RADICAL VISIONS & AMER-
ICAN DREAMS.
W.B. RIDEOUT, 27(AL):MAR74-119
PELTERS, W. LESSINGS STANDORT.
N.H. SMITH, 182:VOL26#1/2-28
PELZER, K.J. WEST MALAYSIA & SINGA-
PORE.
P. WHEATLEY, 318(JAOS):OCT-DEC73-
652
PEMBERTSON, R.A., ED. PENGUIN SPAN-
ISH READER.
J.L. BENBOW, 399(MLJ):APR73-230
PEMBLE, J. THE INVASION OF NEPAL.
R. CALLAHAN, 318(JAOS):JAN-MAR73-
124
DE PEÑA, G.S. - SEE UNDER SCHUMACHER
DE PEÑA, G.
PENDLEBURY, J.D.S. THE ARCHAEOLOGY
OF CRETE.
J. RAISON, 555:VOL47FASC2-316
PENDLETON, D. HAWAIIAN HELLGROUND.
N. CALLENDAR, 441:29JUN75-30
PENELHUM, T. PROBLEMS OF RELIGIOUS
KNOWLEDGE.
S.C. BROWN, 393(MIND):JUL73-473
P.W. GOOCH, 154:JUN73-361
PENELHUM, T. RELIGION & RATIONALITY.
H.A.D., 543:JUN73-761
T. MC PHERSON, 393(MIND):OCT73-630
PENFOLD, P.A., ED. MAPS & PLANS IN
THE PUBLIC RECORD OFFICE. (VOL 2)
J. ISRAEL, 617(TLS):30MAY75-603
PENLINGTON, N. THE ALASKA BOUNDARY
DISPUTE.
D.J. HALL, 529(QQ):AUTUMN73-462
PENN, J.M. LINGUISTIC RELATIVITY
VERSUS INNATE IDEAS.
W. LENDERS, 343:BAND17HEFT1-102
PENNANEN, E.V. CONVERSION & ZERO-
DERIVATION IN ENGLISH.
Z., 179(ES):FEB72-89

PENNER, A. THE GIMMICK.
D.E. SCHLESINGER, 207(FR):MAR73-
882
PENNY, R.J. EL HABLA PASIEGA.*
S. FLEISCHMAN, 545(RPH):MAY74-497
PENNYCUICK, J. IN CONTACT WITH THE
PHYSICAL WORLD.*
R.A. JAEGER, 482(PHR):OCT73-534
M. LEARY, 393(MIND):APR73-303
P. WARREN, 484(PPR):JUN74-603
PENROSE, R. MAX ERNST'S "CELEBES."
C.R. BRIGHTON, 89(BJA):SPRING73-
201
"LES 'PENSÉES' DE PASCAL ONT TROIS
CENTS ANS."*
B. CROQUETTE, 557(RSH):APR-JUN73-
316
PENTECOST, H. THE JUDAS FREAK.
N. CALLENDAR, 441:19JAN75-36
PENTECOST, H. TIME OF TERROR.
N. CALLENDAR, 441:3AUG75-24
PEÑUELAS, M.C. LA OBRA NARRATIVA DE
RAMÓN J. SENDER.
C.L. KING, 238:MAY73-504
PEÑUELAS, M.C. & W.E. WILSON. IN-
TRODUCCIÓN A LA LITERATURA ESPAÑ-
OLA.*
L.C. PÉREZ, 238:DEC73-1144
PENZL, H. LAUTSYSTEM UND LAUTWANDEL
IN DEN ALTHOCHDEUTSCHEN DIALEKTEN.*
E.S. FIRCHOW, M. KUELBS & C.B.
ZUCKER, 406:SPRING74-87
T.H. WILBUR, 361:OCT73-261
PENZL, H. METHODEN DER GERMANISCHEN
LINGUISTIK.*
D.S. ROOD, 399(MLJ):APR74-210
P. VALENTIN, 343:BAND17HEFT2-214
J. WEINSTOCK, 301(JEGP):APR74-280
PÉPIN, J. DANTE ET LA TRADITION DE
L'ALLÉGORIE.*
G. MAZZOTTA, 276:WINTER73-590
PÉPIN, J. A FRENCH CHEF COOKS AT
HOME.
R.A. SOKOLOV, 441:7DEC75-7
PÉPIN, J. IDÉES GRECQUES SUR
L'HOMME ET SUR DIEU.
W. BONDESON, 124:FEB74-243
PEPITONE, J., WITH B. STAINBACK.
JOE YOU COULDA MADE US PROUD.
B.J. PHILLIPS, 441:9NOV75-53
PEPPARD, M.B. PATHS THROUGH THE
FOREST.
C.F. BAYERSCHMIDT, 222(GR):JAN73-
56
PEPPERDENE, M.W., ED. THAT SUBTLE
WREATH.
639(VQR):AUTUMN74-CXXVI
PERCIVAL, J. NUREYEV.
A. KISSELGOFF, 441:18OCT75-27
PERCY, W. THE MESSAGE IN THE BOTTLE.
T. LE CLAIR, 441:8JUN75-6
T. NAGEL, 453:18SEP75-54
PEREBYJNIS, V.S. KIL'KISNI TA JAK-
ISNI CHARAKTERYSTYKY SYSTEMY FONEM
SUČASNOJI UKRAJINS'KOJI LITERATUR-
NOJI MOVY.
W. LEHFELDT, 353:15FEB73-115
PEREIRA, M.H.D. - SEE UNDER DA ROCHA
PEREIRA, M.H.
PEREIRA, T.A. - SEE UNDER ALVES
PEREIRA, T.

PESTALOZZI, K. DIE ENTSTEHUNG DES
LYRISCHEN ICH.*
W.G. MÜLLER, 224(GRM):BAND23HEFT1-
121
PETER MARTYR D'ANGHIERA. ACHT DEKA-
DEN ÜBER DIE NEUE WELT. (H. KLING-
ELHÖFER, TRANS)
F. LASSERRE, 182:VOL26#23/24-885
PETER, H. ENTSTEHUNG UND AUSBILDUNG
DER ITALIENISCHEN EISENBAHNTERMIN-
OLOGIE.
R. STEFANINI, 545(RPH):MAY74-527
PETERKIEWICZ, J. THE THIRD ADAM.
L. BLIT, 617(TLS):21NOV75-1378
PETERS, E. THE SHADOW KING.*
R. SOMERVILLE, 551(RENQ):AUTUMN73-
301
PETERS, E.H. HARTSHORNE & NEOCLAS-
SICAL METAPHYSICS.*
R.L.C., 543:JUN73-762
PETERS, F.E. THE HARVEST OF HELLEN-
ISM.*
G.E. KADISH, 124:APR-MAY74-399
S.I. OOST, 122:JAN74-67
PETERS, J-U. TURGENEVS "ZAPISKI
OCHOTNIKA" INNERHALB DER OČERK-
TRADITION DER 40ER JAHRE.
R. FREEBORN, 575(SEER):JUL74-459
PETERS, M. CHARLOTTE BRONTË.*
M. ALLOTT, 301(JEGP):JAN74-130
G.D. HIRSCH, 113:FALL74-95
E.A. KNIES, 445(NCF):DEC73-359
J. MILLGATE, 637(VS):MAR74-343
N. SHERRY, 402(MLR):JUL74-626
PETERS, M. UNQUIET SOUL.
442(NY):4AUG75-91
PETERS, R. THE GIFT TO BE SIMPLE.
M.L. ROSENTHAL, 441:28DEC75-18
PETERS, R.M. BULB MAGIC IN YOUR
WINDOW.
J. CANADAY, 441:13APR75-16
PETERS, R.S. PSYCHOLOGY & ETHICAL
DEVELOPMENT.
B.F. SKINNER, 617(TLS):14MAR75-271
PETERS, R.S. REASON & COMPASSION.
F. SNARE, 63:AUG74-179
PETERS, U. FRAUENDIENST.*
S.M. JOHNSON, 400(MLN):OCT73-1045
PETERSEN, J. HITLER - MUSSOLINI.
A. WAHL, 182:VOL26#19-692
PETERSEN, P. WELCOME TO OBLIVION.
N. CALLENDAR, 441:27JUL75-17
PETERSON, D.L. TIME, TIDE, & TEM-
PEST.
C. HOY, 569(SR):SPRING74-363
K.J. SEMON, 401(MLQ):DEC74-423
PETERSON, E. TRISTAN TZARA, DADA &
SURRATIONAL THEORIST.
A. BALAKIAN, 207(FR):FEB73-627
M. BERTRAND, 188(ECR):SUMMER73-166
M.A. CAWS, 400(MLN):MAY73-922
PETERSON, M.D. - SEE "JAMES MADISON"
PETERSON, R. THE THIRD SECRETARY.*
A.A. PHILLIPS, 381:JUN73-189
PETERSON, W.S., ED. BROWNING INSTI-
TUTE STUDIES. (VOL 2)
M. ROBERTS, 617(TLS):16MAY75-543
PETERSON, W.S. INTERROGATING THE
ORACLE.*
J.C. MAXWELL, 447(N&Q):JUL73-269
PETERSSON, R.T. THE ART OF ECSTASY.*
D. CAROZZA, 276:SPRING73-95
F.J. WARNKE, 551(RENQ):SUMMER73-
241

PETHYBRIDGE, D. SPARE A COPPER FOR
THE GUY.
D.M. DAY, 157:WINTER73-89
PETHYBRIDGE, R. THE SPREAD OF THE
RUSSIAN REVOLUTION.*
P. KENEZ, 550(RUSR):APR73-202
PETIT, J., ED. BARBEY D'AUREVILLY,
5 (1970).
P.J. YARROW, 208(FS):APR74-220
PETIT, J. BERNANOS, BLOY, CLAUDEL,
PÉGUY.
J. JURT, 98:FEB73-168
PETIT, J., ED. PAUL CLAUDEL 7.*
W.H. MATHESON, 207(FR):FEB73-626
PETIT, J. LE PREMIER DRAME DE
CLAUDEL.
J-N. SEGRESTAA, 535(RHL):SEP-OCT
73-924
PETIT, J. - SEE BLOY, L.
PETRARCH. BUCOLICUM CARMEN. (T.G.
BERGIN, ED & TRANS)
C.N.J. MANN, 617(TLS):24JAN75-91
PETRARCH [F. PETRARCA]. LE FAMIL-
IARI.* (BKS 1-4) (U. DOTTI, ED &
TRANS)
D.D., 275(IQ):SUMMER73-104
PETRARCH [F. PETRARCA]. RERUM FAM-
ILIARIUM LIBRI I-VIII. (A.S. BER-
NARDO, TRANS)
N. MANN, 617(TLS):31OCT75-1291
PETRAUSKIENĖ, Z. & P. VALENTELIENĖ.
LIETUVOS TSR MOKSLININKŲ DISERTA-
CIJOS 1945-1968.
W.R. SCHMALSTIEG, 574(SEEJ):SUMMER
72-273
PETRE, D. THE SECRET ORCHARD OF
ROGER ACKERLEY.
R. FULLER, 362:4SEP75-317
PETROCCHI, G. MANZONI LETTERATURA E
VITA.
M. PUCCINI, 275(IQ):SPRING74-89
PETRONE, G. LA BATTUTA A SORPRESA
NEGLI ORATORI LATINI.
M. WINTERBOTTOM, 123:NOV74-218
PETRONIO, G. PARINI E L'ILLUMINISMO
LOMBARDO. (2ND ED)
J.T.S. WHEELOCK, 481(PQ):JUL73-561
PETROSKY, T. WAITING OUT THE RAIN.
J. MAZZARO, 398:SPRING75-94
PETROV, I. BEFORE & AFTER I WAS
BORN.
270:VOL23#1-13
PETROV, Z. PERSONALITIES & DESTIN-
IES.
270:VOL23#1-16
PETTAZZONI, R. RELIGIONE E SOCIETÀ.
E. NAMER, 542:JAN-MAR73-105
PETTER, H. THE EARLY AMERICAN
NOVEL.*
D.A. RINGE, 445(NCF):JUN73-96
PETTIGREW, J. ROBBER NOBLEMEN.
F.G. BAILEY, 617(TLS):30CT75-1126
PETTINATO, G. DAS ALTORIENTALISCHE
MENSCHENBILD UND DIE SUMERISCHEN
UND AKKADISCHEN SCHÖPFUNGSMYTHEN.
J.S. COOPER, 318(JAOS):OCT-DEC73-
581
PETTIT, A.G. MARK TWAIN & THE SOUTH.
J.M. COX, 578:FALL75-144
PETTIT, C.E. THE EXPERTS.
S. FRIEDMAN, 441:4MAY75-3

PETTIT, F.H. HOW TO MAKE WHIRLIGIGS
& WHIMMY DIDDLES & OTHER AMERICAN
FOLKCRAFT OBJECTS.
 M. LYON, 139:APR73-12
PETTIT, H. - SEE YOUNG, E.
PETZOLD, K-E. STUDIEN ZUR METHODE
DES POLYBIOS UND ZU IHRER HISTOR-
ISCHEN AUSWERTUNG.
 F.M. WASSERMANN, 121(CJ):DEC73/
 JAN74-170
VAN PEURSEN, C.A. PHENOMENOLOGY &
ANALYTICAL PHILOSOPHY.
 C.F.B., 543:JUN73-768
 H.L. MEYN, 258:DEC73-592
PEVSNER, N. THE BUILDINGS OF ENG-
LAND: YORKSHIRE; YORK & THE EAST
RIDING.
 D. LINSTRUM, 46:JAN73-80
PEVSNER, N. RUSKIN & VIOLLET-LE-
DUC.
 P.F. NORTON, 576:MAR73-75
PEVSNER, N. SOME ARCHITECTURAL
WRITERS OF THE NINETEENTH CENTURY.
 T. GIBBONS, 89(BJA):SUMMER73-304
 P.F. NORTON, 576:MAR73-75
 B. READ, 135:MAY73-62
 D. WATKIN, 39:JUL73-70
PEVSNER, N. & J.M. RICHARDS, EDS.
THE ANTI-RATIONALISTS. [SEE ALSO
WITH EDS REVERSED]
 L.K. EATON, 505:DEC73-92
PEYRE, H. HUGO.
 D. FESTA-MC CORMICK, 399(MLJ):
 APR74-208
PEYRE, H. MARCEL PROUST.*
 P. KOLB, 546(RR):JAN73-82
PEYRE, H. QU'EST-CE QUE LE ROMAN-
TISME?*
 G. MEAD, 207(FR):DEC72-407
 B. TOLLEY, 402(MLR):OCT74-877
PEYRE, H. QU'EST-CE QUE LE SYMBOL-
ISME?
 A.G. LEHMANN, 617(TLS):18APR75-436
PEYRE, H. & J. SERONDE, EDS. NINE
CLASSIC FRENCH PLAYS.
 E. HARVEY, 399(MLJ):DEC74-419
PEYROT, L. LE ST-ESPRIT ET LE
PROCHAIN RETROUVÉ.
 F.F. BRUCE, 182:VOL26#20-725
PEYTON, M.A. - SEE DE VEGA, L.
PFANKUCH, P., ED. HANS SCHAROUN.
 S. BAYLEY, 617(TLS):21NOV75-1395
PFAU, P. & K.S. MARX - SEE DAVIES,
M.
PFEFFER, J.A. & OTHERS. BASIC SPOK-
EN GERMAN GRAMMAR.
 E. DILLER, 399(MLJ):DEC74-428
PFEFFER, R. NIETZSCHE.
 P. PREUSS, 154:MAR73-134
 H.W. REICHERT, 406:SUMMER74-176
PFEIFER, M. HERMANN-HESSE-BIBLIO-
GRAPHIE.
 J. MILECK, 301(JEGP):JUL74-421
PFEIFFER, M. ELEMENTS OF KURUX
HISTORICAL PHONOLOGY.
 M.B. EMENEAU, 350:DEC74-755
PFISTER, M. LEXIKALISCHE UNTERSUCH-
UNGEN ZU GIRART DE ROUSSILLON.
 G. INEICHEN, 260(IF):BAND78-307
PFORDRESHER, J. - SEE TENNYSON, A.
PHARR, R.D. THE SOUL MURDER CASE.
 M. LEVIN, 441:28SEP75-37

PHÉBUS, G. LIVRE DE CHASSE. (G.
TILANDER, ED)
 J. ANDRÉ, 555:VOL47FASC2-379
 R. ARVEILLER, 209(FM):JUL73-316
 D. EVANS, 382(MAE):1974/1-74
 W. METTMANN, 72:BAND211HEFT1/3-215
PHELPS, G. THE LOW ROADS.
 N. HEPBURN, 362:21AUG75-254
 J. MILLER, 617(TLS):23MAY75-555
PHELPS, G. TRAGEDY OF PARAGUAY.
 R.A. HUMPHREYS, 617(TLS):14MAR75-
 270
PHILBRICK, T. ST. JOHN DE CRÈVE-
COEUR.
 R.E. AMACHER, 577(SHR):SPRING73-
 220
PHILIA, B.I. KOINONIA KAI EXOUSIA
STIN ELLADA.
 P.J. VATIKIOTIS, 617(TLS):14NOV75-
 1366
PHILIP, L.B. THE GHENT ALTARPIECE &
THE ART OF JAN VAN EYCK.
 L. CAMPBELL, 39:JUL73-61
 A. STONES, 589:JAN74-140
 A. TOMLINSON, 135:FEB73-140
PHILIP, M. LECTURES DE LAUTRÉAMONT.
 S.I. LOCKERBIE, 208(FS):OCT74-479
 P.W. NESSELROTH, 207(FR):FEB73-620
PHILIPE, A. ICI, LÀ-BAS, AILLEURS.
 B. WRIGHT, 617(TLS):2MAY75-492
PHILIPPI, P., ED. STUDIEN ZUR GE-
SCHICHTSSCHREIBUNG IM 19. UND 20.
JAHRHUNDERT.
 H. BRAHM, 182:VOL26#1/2-57
PHILIPS, P. SELECT ITALIAN MADRI-
GALS. (J. STEELE, ED)
 J. HAAR, 551(RENQ):AUTUMN73-332
PHILLIPPS, K.C. JANE AUSTEN'S
ENGLISH.
 M. KIRKHAM, 184(EIC):APR72-192
 K. SØRENSEN, 179(ES):AUG72-365
 A. WRIGHT, 402(MLR):APR74-382
PHILLIPS, A.W. TEMAS DEL MODERNISMO
HISPÁNICO Y OTROS ESTUDIOS.
 617(TLS):23MAY75-571
PHILLIPS, C. THE 1940S.
 R.C. ALBERTS, 441:27JUL75-4
 442(NY):15SEP75-131
PHILLIPS, J.R.S. AYMER DE VALENCE,
EARL OF PEMBROKE, 1307-1324.
 B. WILKINSON, 589:OCT74-752
PHILLIPS, J.W. WASHINGTON STATE
PLACE NAMES.
 F.L. UTLEY, 424:DEC73-267
PHILLIPS, K.P. MEDIACRACY.
 P. TRACY, 441:4MAY75-10
PHILLIPS, M. DUNCAN PHILLIPS & HIS
COLLECTION.
 M.S. YOUNG, 39:APR73-441
PHILLIPS, O.H. SHAKESPEARE & THE
LAWYERS.
 R.A. FOAKES, 175:SUMMER73-72
PHILLIPS, R. THE CONFESSIONAL
POETS.
 L.S. DEMBO, 27(AL):NOV74-415
PHILLIPS, R. THE POETIC MODES OF
OCTAVIO PAZ.
 R. PRING-MILL, 617(TLS):4JUL75-719
 F.T. RIESS, 402(MLR):APR74-445
PHILLIPS, R. & O. MÁRQUEZ. VISIONES
DE LATINOAMÉRICA.
 A.W. ASHHURST, 238:MAY73-530

PHILO. PHILON D'ALEXANDRIE, "LEG-
ATIO AD GAIUM." (A. PELLETIER, ED)
C.W. MACLEOD, 123:NOV74-293
PHILOSTRATUS. LIFE OF APOLLONIUS.
(C.P. JONES, TRANS; ED & ABRIDGED
BY G.W. BOWERSOCK)
I. AVOTINS, 487:SPRING73-96
"PHONÉTIQUE ET LINGUISTIQUE ROMANES:
MÉLANGES OFFERTS À M. GEORGES
STRAKA."*
G.F. MEIER, 682(ZPSK):BAND26HEFT
3/4-441
G. ZINK, 209(FM):JAN73-79
PHONG, N.V. LA SOCIÉTÉ VIETNAMIENNE
DE 1882 À 1902 D'APRÈS LES ÉCRITS
DES AUTEURS FRANÇAIS.
A. WOODSIDE, 293(JAST):FEB73-380
PHU'O'NG-NGHI, Đ. - SEE UNDER ĐẶNG
PHU'O'NG-NGHI
PIA, J. SS REGALIA.
S. SONTAG, 453:6FEB75-23
PIAGET, J. EPISTÉMOLOGIE DES SCI-
ENCES DE L'HOMME.
R. BLANCHÉ, 542:JUL-SEP73-367
PIAGET, J. ESSAI DE LOGIQUE OPÉRA-
TOIRE.
R. BLANCHÉ, 542:JUL-SEP73-369
PIAGET, J. STRUCTURALISM.* (FRENCH
TITLE: LE STRUCTURALISME.)
C. ATKINSON, 393(MIND):JUL73-471
PIAGET, J., ED. LES THÉORIES DE LA
CAUSALITÉ.* LES EXPLICATIONS CAUS-
ALES.
R. BLANCHÉ, 542:JUL-SEP73-368
DE PIAGGI, G. SOCIETÀ MILITARE E
MONDO FEMMINILE NELL'OPERA DI
BRANTÔME.
N. CAZAURAN, 535(RHL):NOV-DEC73-
1058
PIANCIOLA, C., ED. IL PENSIERO DI
KARL MARX.
M. CINGOLI, 548(RCSF):APR-JUN73-
239
PIANKOFF, A., ED & TRANS. THE WAN-
DERING OF THE SOUL.* (COMPLETED
BY H. JACQUET-GORDON)
639(VQR):AUTUMN74-CLIII
PIAULT, M-H. HISTOIRE MAWRI.
M. LAST, 69:APR73-171
PICASSO, P. PICASSO ON ART. (D.
ASHTON, ED)
M. VAIZEY, 135:OCT73-144
PICERNO, R.A. - SEE DE VEGA, L.
PICH, E. - SEE LECONTE DE LISLE,
C.M.
PICHOIS, C. & R. PINTARD - SEE
ROUSSEAU, J-J.
PICKARD, R. A COMPANION TO THE
MOVIES.
R. CAMPION, 200:APR73-235
PICKERING, F.P., ED. THE HOLKHAM
BIBLE PICTURE BOOK.
M.D. LEGGE, 402(MLR):JAN74-168
PICKERING, G. CREATIVE MALADY.
M. HURST, 617(TLS):2MAY75-489
PICKERING, W.S.F., ED. DURKHEIM ON
RELIGION.
C. MADGE, 617(TLS):15AUG75-915
PICKFORD, C.E., ED. THE SONG OF
SONGS.*
P. RICKARD, 382(MAE):1974/3-273
PICKFORD, R.W. PSYCHOLOGY & VISUAL
AESTHETICS.*
J. HOGG, 89(BJA):SUMMER73-299

PICKLES, D. THE GOVERNMENT & POLI-
TICS OF FRANCE. (VOL 1)
P. GUIRAL, 182:VOL26#23/24-893
PICKVANCE, R. ENGLISH INFLUENCES ON
VINCENT VAN GOGH.
P. CONRAD, 617(TLS):31JAN75-111
PICOZZI, R. A HISTORY OF TRISTAN
SCHOLARSHIP.*
H. MAYER, 564:MAR73-74
PIDHAINY, O.S. & A.I. THE UKRAINIAN
REPUBLIC IN THE GREAT EAST-EUROPEAN
REVOLUTION.*
O.W. GERUS, 104:SUMMER73-272
PIDMOHYLNY, V. A LITTLE TOUCH OF
DRAMA.
R. HANTULA, 574(SEEJ):SPRING73-90
PIERCE, F. - SEE DE CERVANTES SAAV-
EDRA, M.
PIERCE, F. - SEE DE HOJEDA, D.
PIERCE, R.B. SHAKESPEARE'S HISTORY
PLAYS.*
K. FRIEDENREICH, 125:JUN74-384
J.E. JOHNSON, 551(RENQ):AUTUMN73-
368
PIERCE, R.H. THREE DEMOTIC PAPYRI
IN THE BROOKLYN MUSEUM.
J.D. THOMAS, 123:NOV74-314
PIERCY, M. SMALL CHANGES.
T. EDWARDS, 473(PR):3/1974-469
PIERCY, M. TO BE OF USE.
D. BROMWICH, 491:JAN75-229
M.G. PERLOFF, 659:WINTER75-84
"PIERS PLOWMAN: THE B VERSION."
(G. KANE & E.T. DONALDSON, EDS)
J. BURROW, 617(TLS):21NOV75-1380
PIERSON, J. ROCK-A-BYE.
D.M. DAY, 157:SUMMER73-80
PIERSON, S. MARXISM & THE ORIGINS
OF BRITISH SOCIALISM.
M.J. WIENER, 637(VS):SEP73-112
PIETARINEN, J. LAWLIKENESS, ANALOGY
& INDUCTIVE LOGIC.
R. BLANCHÉ, 542:JUL-SEP73-370
PIETZCKER, C. DIE LYRIK DES JUNGEN
BRECHT.
P. BRADY, 617(TLS):25APR75-458
PIGANIOL, A. SCRIPTA VARIA. (R.
BLOCH & OTHERS, EDS)
J-C. RICHARD, 555:VOL47FASC2-367
PIGASSE, J-P. LA DIFFICULTÉ D'IN-
FORMER.
M. PALMER, 617(TLS):10OCT75-1203
PIGGOTT, P. THE LIFE & MUSIC OF
JOHN FIELD, 1782-1837.*
R. LANGLEY, 410(M&L):APR74-231
PIGNATTI, T. GIORGIONE.
A.R. TURNER, 54:SEP73-457
PIGUET, J-C. L'OEUVRE DE PHILOSO-
PHIE.
C. WELCH, 480(P&R):WINTER73-63
PIIRAINEN, E. GERM. "*FROĐ-" UND
GERM. "*KLŌK-."
J.L. FLOOD, 402(MLR):JAN74-211
PIIRAINEN, I.T. DAS STADTRECHTS-
BUCH VON SILLEIN.
E. SCHWARZ, 343:BAND16HEFT2-194
PIIRAINEN, I.T., ED. ZUR ENTSTEHUNG
DES NEUHOCHDEUTSCHEN.
R.P. EBERT, 406:FALL74-293
PIKE, R. ARISTOCRATS & TRADERS.
A.J.R. RUSSELL-WOOD, 400(MLN):MAR
73-414

288

PILCH, H. ALTENGLISCHE GRAMMATIK.*
ALTENGLISCHER LEHRGANG.*
  M. PERRELET-BRIDGES & P.B. TAYLOR,
  353:15APR73-118
PILCHER, R. THE EMPTY HOUSE.
  M. LEVIN, 441:2MAR75-22
PILCHER, R. THE END OF SUMMER.
  M. LEVIN, 441:20APR75-29
PILKINGTON, A.E. - SEE APOLLINAIRE,
  G.
PILLET, R. FOREIGN LANGUAGE STUDY.
  R.J. GRIFFIN, 351(LL):DEC74-305
  R.C. LAFAYETTE, 399(MLJ):NOV74-375
PILLING, C. IN ALL THE SPACES ON
ALL THE LINES.*
  S. CURTIS, 148:SPRING72-85
PIMLOTT, D.H., K.M. VINCENT & C.E.
MC KNIGHT, EDS. ARCTIC ALTERNA-
TIVES.
  W.C. WONDERS, 529(QQ):AUTUMN73-458
PIMSLEUR, P. SOL Y SOMBRA.
  A. EISENHARDT, 238:MAR73-187
PIMSLEUR, P. & D. BERGER, EDS. EN-
COUNTERS.
  S.W. BRAUN, 351(LL):DEC74-315
PIMSLEUR, P. & T. QUINN, EDS. THE
PSYCHOLOGY OF SECOND LANGUAGE
LEARNING.*
  D.E. BARTLEY, 399(MLJ):APR73-218
  N.C.W. SPENCE, 208(FS):OCT74-494
DU PIN, MADAME D.L.T. - SEE UNDER
MADAME DE LA TOUR DU PIN
PINCHON, J. LES PRONOMS ADVERBIAUX
"EN" ET "Y."
  J. CANTERA, 202(FMOD):JUN73-406
PINDAR. DIE ISTHMISCHEN GEDICHTE.
(VOL 2) (E. THUMMER, ED & TRANS)
  C. SEGAL, 121(CJ):DEC73/JAN74-154
PINEAUX, J. LA POÉSIE DES PROTES-
TANTS DE LANGUE FRANÇAISE (1559-
1598).
  I.D. MC FARLANE, 208(FS):APR74-187
  H. WEBER, 535(RHL):SEP-OCT73-887
PIÑERA, V. EL QUE VINO A SALVARME.
  C.W. BUTLER, 238:MAR73-180
PINERO, A. THE COLLECTED LETTERS OF
SIR ARTHUR PINERO.* (J.P. WEARING,
ED)
  639(VQR):AUTUMN74-CXXXI
PINES, S. AN ARABIC VERSION OF THE
TESTIMONIUM FLAVIANUM & ITS IMPLI-
CATIONS.
  M. MOOSA, 318(JAOS):OCT-DEC73-562
PINGET, R. CETTE VOIX.
  J. STURROCK, 617(TLS):2MAY75-492
PINGET, R. FABLE.*
  R.M. HENKELS, JR., 207(FR):OCT72-
  232
PINGET, R. IDENTITÉ [SUIVI DE] ABEL
ET BELA.*
  J. DECOCK, 207(FR):MAR73-863
PINGET, R. LE RENARD ET LA BOUS-
SOLE.
  J. ALETER, 207(FR):APR73-1064
PINION, F.B. A JANE AUSTEN COMPAN-
ION.
  H. CARNELL, 541(RES):NOV73-533
  C.J. RAWSON, 175:AUTUMN73-116
PINNEY, T. - SEE MACAULAY, T.B.
PINSENT, G. JOHN & THE MISSUS.
  A. BRENNAN, 268:JAN75-73
PINSENT, G. THE ROWDYMAN.*
  A. SCOTT, 296:VOL3#4-98

PINSKER, S. THE SCHLEMIEL AS META-
PHOR.*
  M.J. FRIEDMAN, 295:FEB74-436
PINTO, V.D. & F.W. ROBERT - SEE
UNDER DE SOLA PINTO, V. & F.W.
ROBERT
PIONTEK, H. MÄNNER DIE GEDICHTE
MACHEN.
  R.R. READ, 221(GQ):MAY73-446
PIPER, D., ED. THE GENIUS OF BRIT-
ISH PAINTING.
  J. RUSSELL, 441:7DEC75-20
PIPER, D.G.B. V.A. KAVERIN.*
  H. OULANOFF, 574(SEEJ):SUMMER72-
  236
  M.H. SHOTTON, 402(MLR):APR74-479
PIPER, W.B. THE HEROIC COUPLET.
  G. HEMPHILL, 599:SPRING73-191
  H.W. SAMS, 568(SCN):SPRING-SUMMER
  74-10
PIPES, R. RUSSIA UNDER THE OLD
RÉGIME.
  J. KEEP, 617(TLS):20JUN75-697
  A.B. ULAM, 441:13JUL75-2
  453:17APR75-37
PIPPIDI, D.M., ED. NICOLAS IORGA -
L'HOMME ET L'OEUVRE.
  S.D. SPECTOR, 104:WINTER74-607
PIRA, G., ED. BLACK IS MY FAVORITE
COLOR.
  K. OLTMANN, 430(NS):JUL73-389
PIRES, T. & OTHERS. TRAVEL ACCOUNTS
OF THE ISLANDS (1513-1787).
  A.L. REBER, 293(JAST):NOV72-222
PIROTTI, U. BENEDETTO VARCHI E LA
CULTURA DEL SUO TEMPO.
  M.P., 228(GSLI):VOL150FASC470/471-
  471
PIRSIG, R.M. ZEN & THE ART OF
MOTORCYCLE MAINTENANCE.*
  E. ABBEY, 441:30MAR75-6
  H. LOMAS, 364:DEC74/JAN75-136
DE PISAN, C. THE EPISTLE OF OTHEA.*
(S. SCROPE, TRANS; C.F. BÜHLER, ED)
  K. REICHL, 38:BAND91HEFT4-522
  R.M. WILSON, 402(MLR):APR74-367
PITCAIRNE, A. THE ASSEMBLY. (T.
TOBIN, ED)
  R.D. HUME, 481(PQ):JUL73-562
PITCHER, G. A THEORY OF PERCEP-
TION.*
  L. HOLBOROW, 483:JUL73-300
PITCHER, H. THE CHEKHOV PLAY.*
  L.W. BAILEY, 157:WINTER73-83
PITKIN, H.F. WITTGENSTEIN & JUS-
TICE.
  J. WHELAN, JR., 482(PHR):OCT74-540
PITT, D. & M. SHAW. PORTRAIT OF
NORMANDY.
  617(TLS):4APR75-380
PITTAWAY, A. & B. SCOFIELD. TRADI-
TIONAL ENGLISH COUNTRY CRAFTS & HOW
TO ENJOY THEM TODAY.
  B. GUTCHEON, 441:7DEC75-74
VAN DE PITTE, F.P. KANT AS PHILO-
SOPHICAL ANTHROPOLOGIST.* [FILED
IN PREV UNDER VAN]
  P. LASKA, 488:DEC73-348
  R. MALTER, 342:BAND64HEFT1-127
PITTER, R. END OF DROUGHT.
  P. BEER, 617(TLS):4JUL75-718

PITTOCK, J. THE ASCENDANCY OF
TASTE.
　F.W. HILLES, 676(YR):AUTUMN73-104
　C.T.P., 566:AUTUMN73-37
　C.J. RAWSON, 175:AUTUMN73-116
PITTS, D. THIS CITY IS OURS.
　N. CALLENDAR, 441:19OCT75-47
PIZZORUSSO, A. DA MONTAIGNE A
BAUDELAIRE.*
　J.G. BROMFIELD, 402(MLR):APR74-396
　N. SUCKLING, 208(FS):OCT74-487
PLACE, F. THE AUTOBIOGRAPHY OF
FRANCIS PLACE (1771-1854). (M.
THALE, ED)
　D.V.E., 191(ELN):SEP73(SUPP)-24
PLACE, I., E.L. POPHAM & H.N. FUJ-
ITA. FUNDAMENTAL FILING PRACTICE.
　W. BENEDON, 14:OCT73-565
DES PLACES, É. LA RELIGION GRECQUE.
　J. FONTENROSE, 122:JAN73-66
PLACOLY, V. LA VIE ET LA MORT DE
MARCEL GONSTRAN.
　A. CAPRIO, 207(FR):APR73-1065
PLAIDY, J. THE BASTARD KING.
　P. BEER, 617(TLS):17JAN75-48
PLAIDY, J. MADAME SERPENT.
　M. LEVIN, 441:2MAR75-22
PLAMENATZ, J. IDEOLOGY.
　G.A. COHEN, 479(PHQ):JAN73-92
PLANES, R. - SEE RUSIÑOL, S.
PLANT, A. SELECTED ECONOMIC ESSAYS
& ADDRESSES.
　R. CAVES, 617(TLS):6JUN75-620
PLANT, M.A. DRUGTAKERS IN AN ENG-
LISH TOWN.
　G.M. CARSTAIRS, 617(TLS):25JUL75-
831
PLANT, R. HEGEL.
　A. QUINTON, 453:29MAY75-34 [& CONT
IN] 453:12JUN75-39
PLANTINGA, A. GOD, FREEDOM & EVIL.
　A. KENNY, 617(TLS):5DEC75-1466
PLANTINGA, A. THE NATURE OF NECES-
SITY.
　J.L. MACKIE, 617(TLS):14NOV75-1354
PLARR, V. THE COLLECTED POEMS OF
VICTOR PLARR. (I. FLETCHER, ED)
　W. GOULD, 617(TLS):19SEP75-1040
PLASKOVITIS, S. TO SYRMATOPLEGMA.
　P. MACKRIDGE, 617(TLS):14NOV75-
1368
PLATE, T. CRIME PAYS!
　L. FRANKS, 441:6JUL75-7
PLATER, A. AND A LITTLE LOVE BE-
SIDES.
　A. RENDLE, 157:SUMMER73-79
PLATH, S. THE BELL JAR.*
　M. HARRIS, 648:OCT73-54
　L.R. PRATT, 502(PRS):SPRING73-87
PLATH, S. CROSSING THE WATER.*
　L.R. PRATT, 502(PRS):SPRING73-87
PLATH, S. LETTERS HOME. (A.S.
PLATH, ED)
　M. HOWARD, 441:14DEC75-1
　C. LEHMANN-HAUPT, 441:9DEC75-45
442(NY):22DEC75-95
PLATH, S. WINTER TREES.*
　D. GRANT, 148:SPRING72-92
　L.R. PRATT, 502(PRS):SPRING73-87
　H. SERGEANT, 175:SUMMER72-75
PLATH, W. & W. REHM - SEE MOZART,
J.C.W.A.

PLATO. LACHES & CHARMIDES.* (R.K.
SPRAGUE, ED & TRANS)
　B. MOLLENHAUER, 154:SEP73-582
PLATO. PLATONS, "APOLOGIE DES
SOKRATES." (F.J. WEBER, ED)
　N. GULLEY, 123:MAR74-132
　P. LOUIS, 555:VOL47FASC1-133
PLATO. TIMAEUS & CRITIAS. (H.D.P.
LEE, TRANS)
　D. SIDER, 399(MLJ):NOV73-382
　I. THOMAS, 124:APR-MAY74-397
PLATON, N. ZAKROS.
　R.V. SCHODER, 124:MAR73-374
PLATONOV, S.F. MOSCOW & THE WEST.*
(J.L. WIECZYNSKI, ED & TRANS)
　G. ALEF, 550(RUSR):JAN73-99
　S.L. PARSONS, 104:WINTER73-546
PLATONOV, S.F. THE TIME OF TROU-
BLES.*
　S.L. PARSONS, 104:WINTER73-546
PLATT, E.R. - SEE KAVANAGH, P.
PLATT, K. MATCH POINT FOR MURDER.
　N. CALLENDAR, 441:19OCT75-47
PLATTEL, M.G. UTOPIAN & CRITICAL
THINKING.
　G.D., 543:JUN73-763
PLATZ-WAURY, E., ED. ENGLISH THEOR-
IES OF THE NOVEL III.
　D. MEHL, 72:BAND211HEFT1/3-126
PLAUTUS. PLAUTI "ASINARIA."* (F.
BERTINI, ED)
　A. MANIET, 487:WINTER73-415
PLAUTUS. PLAUTO: CURCULIO. (G.
MONACO, ED)
　E.W. LEACH, 24:FALL74-298
"PLAUTUS IN COMICS."
　S. WEISLOGEL, 124:NOV72-175
"PLAY."
　R. NORTH, 362:24APR75-542
PLAYER, R. LET'S TALK OF GRAVES,
OF WORMS, & EPITAPHS.
　M. LASKI, 362:20MAR75-380
　617(TLS):11APR75-389
PLEBE, A. - SEE KANT, I.
VON PLESSEN, E. & M. MANN - SEE
MANN, K.
DU PLESSIS, S.I. KANTS HYPOTHESIS-
BEGRIFF.
　W. STEINBECK, 342:BAND64HEFT4-511
DU PLESSIS, S.I.M. THE COMPATIBIL-
ITY OF SCIENCE & PHILOSOPHY IN
FRANCE 1840-1940.
　R. BLANCHÉ, 542:JUL-SEP73-370
PLETT, H.F. EINFÜHRUNG IN DIE
RHETORISCHE TEXTANALYSE.
　G. WIGGER, 430(NS):APR73-228
PLINY. PLINE L'ANCIEN, "HISTOIRE
NATURELLE." (BK 18) (H. LE BON-
NIEC, ED & TRANS)
　W.D.E. COULSON, 124:MAR74-308
PLINY. PLINE L'ANCIEN, "HISTOIRE
NATURELLE."* (BK 23) (J. ANDRÉ, ED
& TRANS)
　W.D.E. COULSON, 124:NOV72-173
　J.J. PATERSON, 313:VOL63-294
PLINY. PLINE L'ANCIEN, "HISTOIRE
NATURELLE." (BK 31) (G. SERBAT,
ED & TRANS)
　J. ANDRÉ, 555:VOL47FASC1-151
　W.D.E. COULSON, 124:SEP-OCT73-39
PLINY. PLINE L'ANCIEN, "HISTOIRE
NATURELLE." (BK 37) (E. DE SAINT-
DENIS, ED & TRANS)
　W.D.E. COULSON, 124:SEP-OCT73-39

PLOMER, W. THE AUTOBIOGRAPHY OF
WILLIAM PLOMER.
A. BELL, 617(TLS):10OCT75-1185
PLOMER, W. CELEBRATIONS.*
A. CLUYSENAAR, 565:VOL14#1-70
PLOMLEY, R. DESERT ISLAND DISCS.
F. DILLON, 617(TLS):25JUL75-820
PLOTINUS. PLOTINI OPERA. (VOL 3)
(P. HENRY & H-R. SCHWYZER, EDS)
P.O. KRISTELLER, 311(JP):16JAN75-
21
PLOTKIN, V.Y. THE DYNAMICS OF THE
ENGLISH PHONOLOGICAL SYSTEM.
A.R. JAMES, 343:BAND17HEFT2-194
PLOURDE, M. THE WHITE MAGNET.
D. BARBOUR, 150(DR):WINTER73/74-
785
PLUMB, J.H. THE FIRST FOUR GEORGES.
442(NY):17FEB75-108
PLUMER, J.M. TEMMOKU, A STUDY OF
THE WARE OF CHIEN.*
M. MEDLEY, 39:SEP73-240
D. RHODES, 293(JAST):FEB73-325
M. TREGEAR, 463:WINTER73-438
J. WIRGIN, 302:JUL73-257
PLUMLY, S. GIRAFFE.
J. MARTIN, 491:MAY75-103
PLUTARCH. LIFE OF ALEXANDER. (K.J.
MAIDMENT, TRANS)
I.L. MERKER, 124:MAR73-367
C.B.R. PELLING, 303:VOL93-231
PLUTARCH. MORAL ESSAYS. (R. WARNER,
TRANS; D.A. RUSSELL, ED)
J. DE BOER, 124:SEP72-49
PLUTARCH. OEUVRES MORALES. (VOL 9,
PT 1) (F. FUHRMANN, ED & TRANS)
F.H. SANDBACH, 303:VOL93-233
PLUTARCH. PLUTARQUE, "CONSOLATION À
APOLLONIOS." (J. HANI, ED & TRANS)
T.S. BROWN, 124:SEP-OCT73-48
PLUTARCH. PLUTARQUE, "VIES."*
(VOL 6) (R. FLACELIÈRE & E. CHAM-
BRY, EDS & TRANS)
A.J. GOSSAGE, 303:VOL93-232
G. LACHENAUD, 555:VOL47FASC2-341
POAG, J.F. WOLFRAM VON ESCHENBACH.
S.J. KAPLOWITT, 399(MLJ):APR74-209
F. SHAW, 402(MLR):OCT74-913
POCHMANN, H.A. & E.N. FELTSKOG - SEE
IRVING, W.
POCHODA, E.T. ARTHURIAN PROPAGANDA.*
W. MATTHEWS, 405(MP):AUG73-73
POCOCK, G. CORNEILLE & RACINE.
C.G.S. WILLIAMS, 399(MLJ):NOV74-
357
POCOCK, H.R.S. - SEE COUTANCHE, A.
POCOCK, J.G.A. POLITICS, LANGUAGE
& TIME.
C.N. STOCKTON, 481(PQ):JUL73-399
PODDAR, A. RENAISSANCE IN BENGAL.*
K.K. SARKAR, 318(JAOS):APR-JUN73-
248
PODRO, M. THE MANIFOLD IN PERCEP-
TION.*
K. ASCHENBRENNER, 290(JAAC):FALL
73-121
F.X.J. COLEMAN, 482(PHR):OCT74-536
T.J. DIFFEY, 89(BJA):AUTUMN73-408
M.R. HAIGHT, 479(PHQ):OCT73-380
POE, E.A. COLLECTED WORKS OF EDGAR
ALLAN POE. (VOL 1) (T.O. MABBOTT,
ED)
R.W. BUTTERFIELD, 184(EIC):APR72-
196

POE, E.A. POÈMES. (H. PARISOT,
TRANS)
R. ASSELINEAU, 189(EA):OCT-DEC73-
498
POE, E.A. PROSE ROMANCES.
R. ASSELINEAU, 189(EA):OCT-DEC73-
498
"POEMA DE MIO CID."* (C. SMITH, ED)
B. DUTTON, 589:APR74-380
P.W. ROGERS, 255(HAB):SUMMER73-214
"POEMS OF SOLITUDE." (J. CH'EN & M.
BULLOCK, TRANS)
L.M. ZOLBROD, 352(LE&W):VOL16#3-
1080
"POETRY INTRODUCTION 2."*
R. KELL, 148:SUMMER72-186
H. SERGEANT, 175:SUMMER72-75
"POETRY INTRODUCTION 3."
P. BEER, 617(TLS):7MAR75-243
POGGI, A. - SEE KANT, I.
POGGI, G. IMAGES OF SOCIETY.
E.H. VOLKART, 319:APR75-268
POGGI SALANI, T. IL LESSICO DELLA
"TANCIA" DI MICHELANGELO BUONAR-
ROTI IL GIOVANE.*
V. BRAMANTI, 597(SN):VOL45#1-213
POGREBIN, L.C. GETTING YOURS.
S. HARRIMAN, 441:4MAY75-14
POHL, I. THE IRON AGE NECROPOLIS OF
SORBO AT CERVETERI.
A.R. NEUMANN, 182:VOL26#23/24-878
R.M. OGILVIE, 123:MAR74-160
PÖHLMANN, E. DENKMÄLER ALTGRIECH-
ISCHER MUSIK.
D. FEAVER, 124:FEB73-311
POINTON, M.R. MILTON & ENGLISH ART.*
M. PRAZ, 179(ES):FEB73-73
POIRIER, R. NORMAN MAILER.*
R.F. LUCID, 594:SUMMER73-263
POITELON, J-C., G. RAZAFINTSALAMA &
R. RANDRIANARIVELO. PÉRIODIQUES
MALGACHES DE LA BIBLIOTHÈQUE NATION-
ALE.
M. URBAIN-FAUBLÉE, 69:APR73-178
POITRAS, L. HENRI BOSCO ET LA PAR-
TICIPATION AU MONDE.
K. BIEBER, 207(FR):FEB73-633
POKORNY, J. ALTIRISCHE GRAMMATIK.
(2ND ED)
E. NEU, 260(IF):BAND77HEFT2/3-343
POLAKOFF, K.I. THE POLITICS OF
INERTIA.
639(VQR):SPRING74-XLVI
POŁCZYŃSKA, E. STUDIEN ZUM "SALMAN
UND MOROLF."
U. MEVES, 680(ZDP):BAND92HEFT3-447
POLIAKOV, L. THE ARYAN MYTH.*
H.M. BRACKEN, 319:JUL75-401
POLIAKOV, L. THE HISTORY OF ANTI-
SEMITISM. (VOLS 1&2)
L. KOCHAN, 617(TLS):14MAR75-270
POLIN, R. LA POLITIQUE DE LA SOLI-
TUDE.*
M. ANTOMELLI, 548(RCSF):APR-JUN73-
219
POLITE, C.H. SISTER X & THE VICTIMS
OF FOUL PLAY.
F. BUSCH, 441:23NOV75-24
442(NY):8DEC75-194
POLITIS, L. A HISTORY OF MODERN
GREEK LITERATURE.
R.C. CLARK, 544:FALL74-138
P. MACKRIDGE, 402(MLR):OCT74-959
P.R. THOMAS, 67:NOV74-224

POLITZER, H. GRILLPARZER ODER DAS
ABGRÜNDIGE BIEDERMEIER.
H. SCHMIDT, 406:SUMMER74-174
POLITZER, R.L. & F.N. TEACHING ENG-
LISH AS A SECOND LANGUAGE.*
M. CELCE-MURCIA, 399(MLJ):MAR74-
140
C.A. YORIO, 351(LL):JUN74-151
POLITZER, R.L. & H.N. URRUTIBEHEITY.
PELDAÑOS.
J.L. MARTIN, 238:DEC73-1136
POLITZER, R.L. & L. WEISS. IMPROV-
ING ACHIEVEMENT IN FOREIGN LANGU-
AGE.*
J.W. NEY, 399(MLJ):APR73-217
POLITZER, R.L. & L. WEISS. THE SUC-
CESSFUL FOREIGN LANGUAGE TEACHER.*
J.W. NEY, 399(MLJ):NOV73-383
POLK, J. WILDERNESS WRITERS.
W. DREW, 102(CANL):WINTER74-126
POLK, J.K. CORRESPONDENCE OF JAMES
K. POLK.* (VOL 2) (H. WEAVER &
P.H. BERGERON, EDS)
J.E. MURPHY, 14:OCT73-562
POLLARD, A., ED. CRABBE: THE CRITI-
CAL HERITAGE.
D.V.E., 191(ELN):SEP73(SUPP)-48
POLLARD, E., M.D. HOOPER & N.W.
MOORE. HEDGES.
L. NEWTON, 617(TLS):31JAN75-106
POLLARD, R. & H.B. FROM HUMAN SEN-
TIENCE TO DRAMA.
W.N. WHISNER, 290(JAAC):WINTER74-
237
POLLIN, B.R. DICTIONARY OF NAMES &
TITLES IN POE'S COLLECTED WORKS.*
R. ASSELINEAU, 189(EA):OCT-DEC73-
495
POLLIN, B.R. DISCOVERIES IN POE.*
R. ASSELINEAU, 189(EA):OCT-DEC73-
495
P. MICHEL, 556(RLV):1973/4-382
POLLIN, B.R. GODWIN CRITICISM.*
J. GERRITSEN, 179(ES):APR72-189
POLLIN, B.R. - SEE GODWIN, W.
POLLITT, J.J. ART & EXPERIENCE IN
CLASSICAL GREECE.*
R.M. COOK, 123:MAR74-148
R. HIGGINS, 39:AUG73-149
F. HOOPER, 141:FALL73-365
R. SCRANTON, 54:MAR73-138
POLLITZ, E.A., JR. THE FORTY-FIRST
THIEF.
N. CALLENDAR, 441:10AUG75-14
POLLMANN, L. LA "NUEVA NOVELA" EN
FRANCIA Y EN IBEROAMÉRICA.
G.R. MC MURRAY, 131(CL):SUMMER73-
282
POLLOCK, A. PORTRAIT OF MY VICTOR-
IAN YOUTH.
R.C. TOBIAS, 637(VS):DEC73-214
POLLOCK, D.H. & A.R.M. RITTER. LATIN
AMERICAN PROSPECTS FOR THE 1970S.
F. MEISSNER, 37:JUN-JUL73-36
POLLOCK, J.L. KNOWLEDGE & JUSTIFI-
CATION.
P. HACKER, 617(TLS):9MAY75-502
DE POLNAY, P. SPRING SNOW & ALGY.
P. ADAMS, 61:FEB75-122
POLOMÉ, E.C. MULTILINGUALISM IN AN
AFRICAN URBAN CENTRE.
315(JAL):VOL11PT2-107

POLSON, D. BRIEF EVENING IN CATH-
OLIC HOSPITAL & OTHER POEMS.
D. BARBOUR, 529(QQ):SPRING73-141
POLT, J.H.R. GASPAR MELCHOR DE
JOVELLANOS.*
E.V. COUGHLIN, 238:MAY73-501
POLT, J.H.R. - SEE FORNER Y SEGARRA,
J.P.
POLTORATZKY, N.P., ED. RUSSKAIA
LITERATURA V EMIGRATSII.
H. MUCHNIC, 550(RUSR):OCT73-446
POLYBIUS. POLYBE, "HISTOIRES."*
(BK 2) (P. PÉDECH, ED & TRANS)
P. CHANTRAINE, 555:VOL47FASC1-146
B. FORTE, 124:OCT72-108
POLYBIUS. POLYBE, "HISTOIRES."
(BK 4) (J. DE FOUCAULT, ED & TRANS)
G.M. COHEN, 124:MAR74-296
POLYKOFF, S. DOES SHE...OR DOESN'T
SHE?
L.C. POGREBIN, 441:14SEP75-36
POLYVIOU, P.G. CYPRUS, THE TRAGEDY
& THE CHALLENGE.
R. FLETCHER, 617(TLS):19SEP75-1042
POMERANCEVA, E.V. - SEE KOROL'KOVA,
A.N.
POMEROY, R. THE ICE CREAM CONNEC-
TION.
M. PRINGLE, 362:25DEC75&1JAN76-891
617(TLS):310CT75-1296
POMEROY, S.B. GODDESSES, WHORES,
WIVES & SLAVES.
E. BADIAN, 453:30OCT75-28
E. JANEWAY, 441:7SEP75-35
H. LLOYD-JONES, 617(TLS):26SEP75-
1074
POMFRET, J.E. COLONIAL NEW JERSEY.
D.L. KEMMERER, 656(WMQ):JUL74-505
639(VQR):SPRING74-XLV
POMORSKA, K., ED. FIFTY YEARS OF
RUSSIAN PROSE.*
P. CARDEN, 574(SEEJ):SPRING73-69
W. REWAR, 454:SPRING74-267
POMPA, L. VICO.
A. MOMIGLIANO, 617(TLS):5SEP75-982
POMPER, P. PETER LAVROV & THE RUS-
SIAN REVOLUTIONARY MOVEMENT.*
P. AVRICH, 550(RUSR):JUL73-313
M. KATZ, 104:WINTER73-554
639(VQR):SPRING74-XLI
PONCEAU, A. LE TEMPS DÉPASSÉ.
P-M. SCHUHL, 542:APR-JUN73-233
PONEKDER, E.M. RONALD FIRBANK.
R. ASSELINEAU, 189(EA):OCT-DEC73-
493
PONICSAN, D. THE ACCOMPLICE.
N. CALLENDAR, 441:16MAR75-32
PONTAUT, A. DICTIONNAIRE CRITIQUE
DU THÉÂTRE QUÉBÉCOIS.
L. MAILHOT, 102(CANL):SPRING74-128
PONTE, G. ATTORNO AL SAVONAROLA.
E. BIGI, 228(GSLI):VOL150FASC469-
130
PONTEIL, F. LES BOURGEOIS ET LA
DÉMOCRATIE SOCIALE: 1914-1968.
J.A. GREEN, 207(FR):APR73-1087
PONTING, G.K. WILTSHIRE PORTRAITS.
617(TLS):17OCT75-1245
PONZIO, A. LINGUAGGIO E RELAZIONI
SOCIALI.
E. NAMER, 542:JUL-SEP73-371
POOLE, A. GISSING IN CONTEXT.
B. BERGONZI, 617(TLS):12DEC75-1476
POOLE, S. - SEE DE LAS CASAS, B.

POPA, V. EARTH ERECT.
R. GARFITT, 364:JUN/JUL74-110
H. MURPHY, 159(DM):AUTUMN/WINTER
73/74-121
POPA, V. SELECTED POEMS.
M.P. COOTE, 574(SEEJ):SPRING72-112
POPE, A.U. PERSIAN ARCHITECTURE.
M. LEVEY, 39:AUG73-151
POPE, D. RAMAGE'S PRIZE.*
M. LEVIN, 441:9FEB75-12
POPE, M. THE STORY OF DECIPHERMENT.
J. CHADWICK, 617(TLS):15AUG75-918
POPE, P. HUNT THE FRENCHMAN.
D.M. DAY, 157:WINTER73-89
POPE, W.B. - SEE BARRETT, E.B. &
B.R. HAYDON
POPE-HENNESSY, J. ITALIAN GOTHIC
SCULPTURE. (REV)
T. LASK, 55:NOV72-16
POPE-HENNESSY, J. RAPHAEL.*
L. BECHERUCCI, 90:JUL73-469
POPE-HENNESSY, J. ROBERT LOUIS
STEVENSON.*
J. CLIVE, 231:DEC75-96
K. MILLER, 453:29MAY75-16
A. WHITMAN, 441:13JUN75-43
POPE HENNESSY, J. ANTHONY TROL-
LOPE.*
J. MC MASTER, 529(QQ):SUMMER73-315
POPHAM, A.E. CATALOGUE OF THE DRAW-
INGS OF PARMIGIANINO.* DISEGNI DI
GIROLAMO BEDOLI.
S.J. FREEDBERG, 54:MAR73-148
POPPER, K.R. OBJECTIVE KNOWLEDGE.*
A.F. CHALMERS, 63:MAY74-70
H. RUJA, 484(PPR):DEC73-278
POPPI, A. INTRODUZIONE ALL'ARISTOT-
ELISMO PADOVANO. SAGGI SUL PENSI-
ERO INEDITO DI PIETRO POMPONAZZI.
M. PINE, 551(RENQ):SPRING73-47
"POPULATION, EDUCATION, DEVELOPMENT
IN AFRICA SOUTH OF THE SAHARA."
S. MILBURN, 69:OCT73-362
PORCHER, M-C., ED & TRANS. LA VIŚ-
VAGUNĀDARŚACAMPŪ DE VEŃKAṬĀDHVARIN.
O. VON HINÜBER, 182:VOL26#9-296
PORGES, I. EDGAR RICE BURROUGHS.
J. SEEYLE, 441:26OCT75-36
PÖRKSEN, U. DER ERZÄHLER IM MITTEL-
HOCHDEUTSCHEN EPOS.*
M. CURSCHMANN, 133:1973/2-179
PÖRNBACHER, K. - SEE HEINE, H.
PORQUERAS MAYO, A. TEMAS Y FORMAS
DE LA LITERATURA ESPAÑOLA.
H.P. SCHMIDT, 72:BAND211HEFT1/3-
223
PORTER, A. A MUSICAL SEASON.*
J.R. ELLIOTT, JR., 617(TLS):20JUN
75-702
PORTER, H.C., ED. PURITANISM IN
TUDOR ENGLAND.
R. PINEAS, 551(RENQ):WINTER73-477
PORTER, J.P., ED. HOW THINGS WORK
IN YOUR HOME.
A. RUDER, 441:29JUN75-22
PORTER, M.E. MRS. PORTER'S COOK-
BOOK.
J.M. COLE, 99:DEC75/JAN76-37
PORTER, P. PREACHING TO THE CON-
VERTED.* AFTER MARTIAL.*
T. EAGLETON, 565:VOL14#2-74
PORTER, P. & C. OSBORNE, EDS. NEW
POETRY 1.
J. FULLER, 617(TLS):7NOV75-1327

PORTER, R.J. BRENDAN BEHAN.
A.C. EDWARDS, 397(MD):DEC73-394
PORTER, S. SYLVIA PORTER'S MONEY
BOOK.
L. SLOANE, 441:21JUN75-25
PORTOGHESI, P. L'ECLETTISMO A
ROMA, 1870-1922. ROMA UN'ALTRA
CITTÀ.
S. KOSTOF, 576:OCT73-239
PORTOGHESI, P. ROMA BAROCCA.
J.B. MYERS, 139:JUN73-8
PORTOGHESI, P. ROME OF THE RENAIS-
SANCE.*
J. WILTON-ELY, 39:NOV73-407
PORTWAY, C. THE TIRANA ASSIGNMENT.
N. CALLENDAR, 441:27APR75-29
PÖSCHL, V. HORAZISCHE LYRIK.
F.M. WASSERMANN, 121(CJ):FEB/MAR
74-257
POSER, H. ZUR THEORIE DER MODALBE-
GRIFFE BEI G.W. LEIBNIZ.
A. MERCIER, 182:VOL26#9-263
"POSIDONIUS." (VOL 1) (L. EDELSTEIN
& I.G. KIDD, EDS)
M.E. REESOR, 124:MAR74-297
POSNER, D. ANNIBALE CARRACCI.*
R. WOODFIELD, 89(BJA):SUMMER73-309
POSNER, D. WATTEAU: A LADY AT HER
TOILET.
B. SCOTT, 39:DEC73-521
POSNER, E. ARCHIVES IN THE ANCIENT
WORLD.
L.J. CAPPON, 14:JAN73-67
E. RAWSON, 313:VOL63-265
VAN DER POST, L. JUNG.
P. DAVISON, 61:DEC75-115
VAN DER POST, L. A MANTIS CAROL.
P. BEER, 362:18DEC75-839
POSTAL, B. & H.W. LEVY. AND THE
HILLS SHOUTED FOR JOY.
M.I. UROFSKY, 390:AUG-SEP73-79
POSTAL, P.M. CROSS-OVER PHENOMENA.
J.K. CHAMBERS, 320(CJL):SPRING74-
104
POSTAL, P.M. ON RAISING.
P. MATTHEWS, 617(TLS):14FEB75-165
POSTAN, M.M. FACT & RELEVANCE.
R. GINGER, 529(QQ):SUMMER73-292
"POSTERS OF MUCHA."
J-C. SUARES, 441:5OCT75-22
POSTL, B. DIE BEDEUTUNG DES NIL IN
DER RÖMISCHEN LITERATUR.*
R. CHEVALLIER, 555:VOL47FASC1-169
POSTON, L. & OTHERS. CONTINUING
SPANISH I & II.
D.S. DÍAZ, 238:MAR73-194
N. MAC KINNON, 238:DEC73-1142
POTGIETER, E.J. & C.B. HUET. DE
VOLLEDIGE BRIEFWISSELING VAN E.J.
POTGIETER EN CD. BUSKEN HUET. (J.
SMIT, ED)
P. DE VROOMEN, 204(FDL):SEP73-200
POTHOLM, C.P. & R. DALE, EDS.
SOUTHERN AFRICA IN PERSPECTIVE.*
G.W. HARTWIG, 579(SAQ):SPRING74-
276
T.M. SHAW, 69:OCT73-372
POTOK, C. IN THE BEGINNING.
C. LEHMANN-HAUPT, 441:3DEC75-37
H. NISSENSON, 441:19OCT75-36
442(NY):17NOV75-193
POTTER, E. THE PRESS AS OPPOSITION.
C.R. HILL, 617(TLS):10OCT75-1205

POTTER, K.H., COMP. BIBLIOGRAPHY OF
INDIAN PHILOSOPHIES.*
W.C.C., 543:DEC72-362
POTTER, R. THE ENGLISH MORALITY
PLAY.
R. AXTON, 617(TLS):22AUG75-934
POTTIER, B. GRAMÁTICA DEL ESPAÑOL.*
O.T. MYERS, 545(RPH):FEB74-403
POTTIER, B. PRÉSENTATION DE LA LIN-
GUISTIQUE. GRAMMAIRE DE L'ESPAG-
NOL.
K. TOGEBY, 545(RPH):MAY74-519
POTTINGER, G. ST. MORITZ.
R.R. FEDDEN, 46:FEB73-146
POUILLON, J. FÉTICHES SANS FÉTICH-
ISME.
R. NEEDHAM, 617(TLS):30CT75-1126
POULET, G. LA CONSCIENCE CRITIQUE.
J.G. CLARK, 208(FS):JUL74-355
POULIN, A., JR. IN ADVENT.*
A. PICCIONE, 577(SHR):SPRING73-225
H. TAYLOR, 385(MQR):WINTER75-92
POULTON, D. JOHN DOWLAND.*
D. GREER, 410(M&L):JAN74-99
M. HATTAWAY, 175:AUTUMN73-113
J.H. LONG, 551(RENQ):AUTUMN73-331
POULTON, H.J., WITH M.S. HOWLAND.
THE HISTORIAN'S HANDBOOK.
L. RAPPORT, 14:JAN73-71
POUND, E. EZRA POUND: SELECTED
PROSE, 1909-1965.* (W. COOKSON,
ED)
R. KIRK, 569(SR):FALL74-698
POUND, E. THE SELECTED LETTERS OF
EZRA POUND 1907-1941. (D.D. PAIGE,
ED)
A.P. HINCHLIFFE, 148:SUMMER72-189
POUNDS, N.J.G. AN ECONOMIC HISTORY
OF MEDIEVAL EUROPE.
C. DYER, 617(TLS):30CT75-1160
POUPART, J-M. C'EST PAS DONNÉ À
TOUT LE MONDE D'AVOIR UNE BELLE
MORT.
R. HATHORN, 296:VOL3#4-92
POUTIATINE, O. WAR & REVOLUTION.
(G.A. LENSEN, ED)
W.B. WALSH, 550(RUSR):JAN73-97
POWELL, A. BOOKS DO FURNISH A ROOM.
J.C. FIELD, 556(RLV):1973/1-91
POWELL, A., ED. THE CITY.
I. DAVIES, 99:JAN75-40
POWELL, A. HEARING SECRET HARMON-
IES.
J. BAYLEY, 617(TLS):12SEP75-1010
D. MAY, 362:11SEP75-346
POWELL, A. TEMPORARY KINGS.
M.T. BERNON, 189(EA):OCT-DEC73-489
S. PICKERING, JR., 569(SR):SPRING
74-XXII
POWELL, J.W. DOWN THE COLORADO.
(NOTES BY D.D. FOWLER)
M.S. YOUNG, 39:APR73-439
POWELL, N. FUSELI: THE NIGHTMARE.*
R. EDWARDS, 39:JUN73-619
POWELL, N. THE SACRED SPRING.
C.E. SCHORSKE, 453:11DEC75-39
POWELL, P.W. TREE OF HATE.* (SPAN-
ISH TITLE: ARBOL DE ODIO.)
M. BARRACO MÁRMOL, 37:FEB73-41
POWER, P.F., ED. THE MEANINGS OF
GANDHI.
A. BHARATI, 485(PE&W):JAN-APR73-
267

[CONTINUED]

[CONTINUING]
S.W. CROKER, 293(JAST):FEB73-352
R.M. SMITH, 318(JAOS):JUL-SEP73-
381
POWERS, D., COMP. FIRST PEOPLE
SPEAK.
B. HAMMES, 448:VOL13#2-98
POWERS, D.C. ENGLISH FORMAL SATIRE:
ELIZABETHAN TO AUGUSTAN.
M.R. ZIRKER, JR., 566:AUTUMN73-39
POWERS, J.F. LOOK HOW THE FISH LIVE.
P-L. ADAMS, 61:NOV75-124
A. BROYARD, 441:25SEP75-47
T. MC HALE, 441:2NOV75-14
R. SALE, 453:13NOV75-31
POWERS, L.H., ED. HENRY JAMES'S
MAJOR NOVELS.
R.E. LONG, 432(NEQ):SEP73-489
G.B. TENNYSON, 445(NCF):SEP73-242
POWERS, T. BALITA MULA MAYNILA.
K.J. PIKE, 14:JUL73-411
POWLEDGE, F. MUD SHOW.
E. HOAGLAND, 441:9NOV75-8
442(NY):3NOV75-172
POWLEY, A.E. BROADCAST FROM THE
FRONT.
W.R. YOUNG, 99:APR/MAY75-38
POWNALL, D. AFRICAN HORSE.
V. CUNNINGHAM, 617(TLS):25JUL75-
821
POWNALL, D. THE RAINING TREE WAR.*
D. DURRANT, 364:FEB/MAR75-133
POWYS, J-C. LETTERS 1937-1954.
G. STEINER, 617(TLS):16MAY75-541
POZDNEYEV, A.M. MONGOLIA & THE MON-
GOLS.* (VOL 1) (J.R. KRUEGER, WITH
F. ADELMAN, EDS)
O. LATTIMORE, 318(JAOS):OCT-DEC73-
647
POZZA, N. COMEDIA FAMILIARE.
F. DONINI, 617(TLS):18JUL75-792
POZZA, N. LA PUTINA GRECA.
G-P. BIASIN, 275(IQ):SUMMER73-93
"PRACTICAL RUSSIAN READER."
C. KULESOV, 574(SEEJ):SPRING73-98
PRADER-SCHUCANY, S. ROMANISCH BÜN-
DEN ALS SELBSTÄNDIGE SPRACHLAND-
SCHAFT.
G. FRANCESCATO, 433:JUL73-305
PRADES, J.D. - SEE DE VEGA, L.
"PRAEGER ENCYCLOPEDIA OF ART."
G. LEVITINE, 127:FALL73-72
"PRAGUE STUDIES IN ENGLISH XIV."
C.J.E. BALL, 447(N&Q):MAR73-101
PRANDI, A., ED. INTERPRETAZIONI DEL
RINASCIMENTO.
M.A. DEL TORRE, 548(RCSF):APR-JUN
73-236
PRANG, M. N.W. ROWELL.
D. MORTON, 99:APR/MAY75-12
G. WOODCOCK, 617(TLS):10OCT75-1188
PRASSINOS, G. LA VIE LA VOIX.
F. GALAND, 207(FR):DEC72-448
PRAT, H. L'ESPACE MULTIDIMENSIONNEL.
R. BLANCHÉ, 542:JUL-SEP73-371
PRATHER, R.S. THE SURE THING.
N. CALLENDAR, 441:27JUL75-17
PRATT, J.G. ESP RESEARCH TODAY.
639(VQR):SPRING74-LIX
PRAUSS, G. ERSCHEINUNG BEI KANT.*
H-U. HOCHE, 53(AGP):BAND55HEFT1-96

PRAWER, S., ED. SEVENTEEN MODERN
GERMAN POETS.*
R.F. ABT, 221(GQ):NOV73-647
J.P.J. MAASEN, 433:OCT73-421
PRAWER, S.S. COMPARATIVE LITERARY
STUDIES.*
D.P. SCALES, 67:NOV74-243
PRAZ, M. CALEIDOSCOPIO SHAKESPEAR-
IANO.
S. ROSSI, 570(SQ):SPRING73-233
PRAZ, M. MNEMOSYNE.*
G. BULLOUGH, 179(ES):APR73-193
K. GARLICK, 447(N&Q):AUG73-313
PRECERUTTI-GARBERI, M. FRESCOES
FROM VENETIAN VILLAS.
F.J.B. WATSON, 39:MAY73-531
"PRELIMINARY GUIDE TO THE SMITHSON-
IAN ARCHIVES."
K.J. PIKE, 14:JUL73-411
PRERAU, D.S. COMPUTER PATTERN RE-
COGNITION OF STANDARD ENGRAVED
MUSIC NOTATION.
M. KASSLER, 513:FALL-WINTER72-250
"PRESSE ET POLITIQUE."
D. JOHNSON, 617(TLS):10OCT75-1180
PREST, W.R. THE INNS OF COURT UNDER
ELIZABETH I & THE EARLY STUARTS
1590-1640.
J.S. COCKBURN, 551(RENQ):WINTER73-
484
PRESTON, J. THE CREATED SELF.
S.M. PASSLER, 577(SHR):SUMMER73-
333
PRESTON, R.A., ED. THE INFLUENCE OF
THE UNITED STATES ON CANADIAN DEV-
ELOPMENT.
R.N. KOTTMAN, 529(QQ):WINTER73-622
PRESTON, S. VUILLARD.
S. WHITFIELD, 90:JUN73-403
PRESTON, S. & OTHERS. SIMBARI.
J.R. MELLOW, 441:7DEC75-80
PRESTON, T.R. NOT IN TIMON'S MAN-
NER.
C. RAWSON, 617(TLS):21NOV75-1381
PRETO-RODAS, R.A. FRANCISCO RODRI-
GUES LOBO.
T.F. EARLE, 86(BHS):OCT73-415
PREZZOLINI, G. L'ITALIA FINISCE.
S.E. SCALIA, 276:SPRING73-108
PREZZOLINI, G. LA VOCE.
S. VINALL, 617(TLS):31OCT75-1305
PRIBRAM, K.H. LANGUAGES OF THE
BRAIN.
Z.S. BOND, 320(CJL):SPRING74-79
PRICE, A. OUR MAN IN CAMELOT.
M. LASKI, 362:20NOV75-684
617(TLS):14NOV75-1349
PRICE, C. THEATRE IN THE AGE OF
DAVID GARRICK.
I. BROWN, 157:AUTUMN73-72
PRICE, C. - SEE SHERIDAN, R.B.
PRICE, E.C. THE STATE OF THE UNION.
P. GOW, 648:JUN73-59
PRICE, G. THE FRENCH LANGUAGE.*
W. MAŃCZAK, 439(NM):1973/2-359
PRICE, G. - SEE "THE YEAR'S WORK IN
MODERN LANGUAGE STUDIES"
PRICE, H.H. ESSAYS IN THE PHILOSO-
PHY OF RELIGION.*
S.P. SCHWARTZ, 482(PHR):APR74-283
PRICE, J.G. THE UNFORTUNATE COMEDY.
N. ALEXANDER, 570(SQ):WINTER73-96
PRICE, J.M. FRANCE & THE CHESAPEAKE.
J.J. MC CUSKER, 656(WMQ):JAN74-142

PRICE, L.B., ED. MARCEL PROUST.*
R. BIRN, 131(CL):WINTER74-78
PRICE, M., ED. THE RESTORATION &
EIGHTEENTH CENTURY.
566:AUTUMN73-35
PRICE, P.V. THE TASTE OF WINE.
T. ASPLER, 362:25DEC75&1JAN76-891
PRICE, R. THE SURFACE OF THE EARTH.
P. ADAMS, 61:AUG75-88
R. GILMAN, 441:29JUN75-1
C. LEHMANN-HAUPT, 441:18JUL75-29
C. RICKS, 453:26JUN75-13
442(NY):13OCT75-176
PRICE, R. THINGS IN THEMSELVES.
R. FOSTER, 109:FALL/WINTER73/74-
111
PRICE, R. THE WANDERERS.*
J. LAHR, 617(TLS):30MAY75-585
PRICE, R.F. MIXAIL ŠOLOXOV IN YUGO-
SLAVIA.
V.D. MIHAILOVICH, 574(SEEJ):FALL73-
339
PRICE, V. - SEE BÜCHNER, G.
PRICHARD, I. THE CHRONICLES OF
BUDGEPORE OR SKETCHES OF LIFE IN
UPPER INDIA.
T.G. KESSINGER, 293(JAST):AUG73-
714
PRICKETT, S. COLERIDGE & WORDS-
WORTH, THE POETRY OF GROWTH.
R.H. WELLS, 447(N&Q):FEB73-71
DU PRIER, J. - SEE UNDER JEAN DU
PRIER
PRIEST, C. REAL-TIME WORLD.
J. HAMILTON-PATERSON, 617(TLS):
14MAR75-284
PRIESTLEY, J.B. THE CARFITT CRISIS.
D.A.N. JONES, 617(TLS):6JUN75-617
J. MELLORS, 362:19JUN75-821
PRIESTLEY, J.B. THE PRINCE OF PLEAS-
URE & HIS REGENCY.
G. NIGOT, 189(EA):JAN-MAR73-112
PRIESTLEY, J.B. SALT IS LEAVING.
M. LEVIN, 441:2MAR75-18
442(NY):7APR75-140
PRIESTLEY, M. MUSIC THERAPY IN
ACTION.
A. STORR, 617(TLS):20JUN75-702
PRIMACK, J. & F. VON HIPPEL. ADVICE
& DISSENT.
D. SHAPLEY, 441:29JUN75-4
PRIMMER, A. CICERO NUMEROSUS.
R. JOHNSON, 122:APR73-141
PRINCE, R., ED. TRANCE & POSSESSION
STATES. THE ELECTROENCEPHALOGRAM,
MEDITATION & MYSTICISM.
J. BRUNO, 98:MAY73-417
PRINGLE, R. THE LETTERBOOK OF ROB-
ERT PRINGLE.* (W.B. EDGAR, ED)
K.J. BAUER, 14:JUL73-417
PRINZ, W. DIE ENTSTEHUNG DER GALER-
IE IN FRANKREICH UND ITALIEN.
R.W. BERGER, 54:SEP73-459
PRINZHORN, H. ARTISTRY OF THE MEN-
TALLY ILL.
R. CARDINAL, 592:JUL-AUG73-54
PRIOR, A.N. OBJECTS OF THOUGHT.*
(P.T. GEACH & A.J.P. KENNY, EDS)
L.J. COHEN, 393(MIND):JAN73-127
K. FINE, 482(PHR):JUL73-392
PRITCHARD, A. - SEE COWLEY, A.
PRITCHARD, R.E. D.H. LAWRENCE.*
K. WIDMER, 295:APR74-1044

PRITCHARD, W.H., ED. W.B. YEATS.
I. FLETCHER, 617(TLS):2MAY75-490
PRITCHETT, V.S. BALZAC.
M. BELL, 639(VQR):SUMMER74-447
H.J. HUNT, 208(FS):APR74-211
PRITCHETT, V.S. THE CAMBERWELL
BEAUTY & OTHER STORIES.*
M. HODGART, 453:20MAR75-32
PRITCHETT, V.S. MIDNIGHT OIL.
295:FEB74-377
PRITCHETT, W.K. ANCIENT GREEK MILI-
TARY PRACTICES. (PT 1)
P. GAUTHIER, 555:VOL47FASC2-328
N.G.L. HAMMOND, 303:VOL93-254
A.M. SNODGRASS, 123:NOV74-247
PRITCHETT, W.K. THE CHOISEUL MARBLE.
W.M. CALDER 3D, 122:APR74-156
PRIVITERA, G.A. DIONISO IN OMERO E
NELLA POESIA GRECA ARCAICA.*
F.M. COMBELLACK, 122:APR73-150
J. POLLARD, 303:VOL93-221
PRIZEMAN, J. YOUR HOUSE, THE OUT-
SIDE VIEW.
R. NORTH, 362:24APR75-542
PROBST, G.F., ED. DEUTSCHER HUMOR.
R.J. RUNDELL, 399(MLJ):SEP-OCT73-
298
PROBST, L. OFF CAMERA.
A. BROYARD, 441:26DEC75-29
"PROCEEDINGS OF THE MASSACHUSETTS
HISTORICAL SOCIETY." (VOLS 82&83)
R.E. WELCH, JR., 432(NEQ):MAR74-
150
PROCLUS. A COMMENTARY ON THE FIRST
BOOK OF EUCLID'S "ELEMENTS." (G.R.
MORROW, ED & TRANS)
M. BROWN, 53(AGP):BAND55HEFT1-82
PROCLUS. THÉOLOGIE PLATONICIENNE.
(BK 1) (H.D. SAFFREY & L.G. WESTER-
INK, EDS & TRANS)
W.H. O'NEILL, 122:JUL73-230
PROCTER-GREGG, H., ED. SIR THOMAS
BEECHAM.
R. ANDERSON, 415:AUG74-661
J.A. WESTRUP, 410(M&L):APR74-237
PROCTOR, D. HANNIBAL'S MARCH IN
HISTORY.*
W.V. HARRIS, 24:WINTER74-421
T.J. LUCE, 124:OCT72-122
A.H. MC DONALD, 123:NOV74-252
PROCTOR, D. - SEE DICKINSON, G.L.
PROFFER, C.R., ED. A BOOK OF THINGS
ABOUT VLADIMIR NABOKOV.
A. DE JONGE, 617(TLS):16MAY75-526
PROFFER, C.R., ED & TRANS. SOVIET
CRITICISM OF AMERICAN LITERATURE IN
THE SIXTIES.*
E. WASIOLEK, 574(SEEJ):SUMMER73-
237
PROFFER, C.R. - SEE PUSHKIN, A.
PROFFER, E. - SEE BULGAKOV, M.
PROFFER, E. & C.R. - SEE BULGAKOV,
M.
PROHL, J. HUGO VON HOFMANNSTHAL UND
RUDOLF BORCHARDT.
E.F. GEORGE, 182:VOL26#23/24-869
PROKHOROV, A.M. - SEE "GREAT SOVIET
ENCYCLOPEDIA"
PRONIN, A. BYLINY.
J. BAILEY, 574(SEEJ):SPRING73-89
PRONZINI, B. SNOWBOUND.*
N. CALLENDAR, 441:29JUN75-30

PROSE, F. THE GLORIOUS ONES.*
P.M. SPACKS, 249(HUDR):SUMMER74-
293
PROSSER, E. HAMLET & REVENGE.*
(2ND ED)
J.C. MAXWELL, 447(N&Q):APR73-152
"PROTSESS TSEPNOI REAKTSII."
D.V. POSPIELOVSKY, 550(RUSR):OCT
73-441
PROU, S. THE BERNARDINIS' TERRACE.
M. JOHNSON, 617(TLS):1AUG75-865
J. MELLORS, 362:7AUG75-189
PROU, S. MÉCHAMMENT LES OISEAUX.
B.L. KNAPP, 207(FR):DEC72-449
PROUDFOOT, J. PRO HOCKEY '74-75.
J. SAVERCOOL, 441:23MAR75-37
PROUDFOOT, M. BRITISH POLITICS &
GOVERNMENT 1951-1970.
C.M. WOODHOUSE, 617(TLS):17JAN75-
55
PROUDFOOT, W.B. THE ORIGIN OF STEN-
CIL DUPLICATING.
B. MENKUS, 14:APR73-254
PROUST, J., ED. RECHERCHES NOU-
VELLES SUR QUELQUES ÉCRIVAINS DES
LUMIÈRES.
R. MERCIER, 557(RSH):OCT-DEC73-661
PROUST, M. TEXTES RETROUVÉS. (P.
KOLB, ED)
P. CLARAC, 535(RHL):NOV-DEC73-1112
J. CRUICKSHANK, 208(FS):JUL74-346
S. SULEIMAN, 207(FR):APR73-1020
PROUVE, J. UNE ARCHITECTURE PAR
L'INDUSTRIE. (B. HUBER & J-C.
STEINEGGER, EDS)
H. DAMISCH, 98:APR73-348
PROVENCHER, J. RENÉ LÉVESQUE.
J. LEVITT, 99:OCT75-32
PRUCHA, F.P., ED. AMERICANIZING THE
AMERICAN INDIANS.*
W. GARD, 584(SWR):WINTER74-98
PRUDHOE, J. THE THEATRE OF GOETHE
& SCHILLER.
M. ESSLIN, 157:WINTER73-81
PRUS, B. THE DOLL.*
G. DARRING, 574(SEEJ):FALL72-360
PRŮŠEK, J. DICTIONARY OF ORIENTAL
LITERATURES.
R. DAWSON, 617(TLS):30MAY75-605
PRUSLIN, D.H. AUTOMATIC RECOGNITION
OF SHEET MUSIC.
M. KASSLER, 513:FALL-WINTER72-250
PRUTSKOV, N.I. GLEB USPENSKY.
L. BROM, 574(SEEJ):WINTER72-479
PRYCE-JONES, D. THE ENGLAND COM-
MUNE.
J. MELLORS, 362:20FEB75-253
PRYCE-JONES, D., ED. EVELYN WAUGH
& HIS WORLD.*
W. SULLIVAN, 569(SR):SUMMER74-LV
PRYNNE, J.H. WOUND RESPONSE.
A. MACLEAN, 617(TLS):1AUG75-866
PRZYBYLSKI, R. EROS I TANATOS.
J.T. BAER, 497(POLR):VOL18#4-105
PSEUDO-PHILO. THE "BIBLICAL AN-
TIQUITIES" OF PHILO. (M.R. JAMES,
ED & TRANS; NEW ED BY L.H. FELDMAN)
W.R. SCHOEDEL, 124:SEP72-45
PSICHARI, H. LES CONVERTIS DE LA
BELLE ÉPOQUE.
R. POMEAU, 535(RHL):MAR-JUN73-540

PUCCINI, G. LETTERS OF GIACOMO
PUCCINI. (G. ADAMI, ED; REV BY
M. CARNER)
  617(TLS):10JAN75-39
PUGH, A.R. BALZAC'S RECURRING CHAR-
ACTERS.
  F.W.J. HEMMINGS, 617(TLS):5SEP75-
  1004
PUGH, R. SOME REFLECTIONS OF A
MEDIEVAL CRIMINOLOGIST.
  D.E.C. YALE, 382(MAE):1974/2-212
PUHVEL, J., ED. MYTH & LAW AMONG
THE INDO-EUROPEANS.*
  H. BIEZAIS, 260(IF):BAND78-231
PUIG, M. HEARTBREAK TANGO.
  B. ALLEN, 249(HUDR):SPRING74-119
  R. CHRIST, 473(PR):3/1974-484
PUJALS, E. LA POESÍA INGLESA DEL
SIGLO XX.
  R.G. HAVARD, 402(MLR):JUL74-630
  T. MARCOS OREA, 202(FMOD):JUN73-
  408
DEL PULGAR, F. CLAROS VARONES DEL
CASTILLA.* (R.B. TATE, ED)
  N.G. ROUND, 86(BHS):OCT73-390
  H.R. STONE, 238:MAY73-500
  A. VÁRVARO, 545(RPH):NOV73-261
PULLAN, B. A HISTORY OF EARLY
RENAISSANCE ITALY.
  C.H. CLOUGH, 39:MAY73-533
PULLAN, B. RICH & POOR IN RENAIS-
SANCE VENICE.
  J.C. DAVIS, 551(RENQ):SPRING73-51
PULLAR, P. FRANK HARRIS.
  P. BEER, 362:5JUN75-737
  C. DAVIDSON, 617(TLS):31OCT75-1301
PUPPI, L. CORPUS PALLADIANUM.
(VOL 7: LA VILLA BADOER DI FRATTA
POLESINE.)
  M.N. ROSENFELD, 576:DEC73-335
  F.J.B. WATSON, 39:MAY73-531
PURCELL, S. - SEE "GEORGE PEELE"
PURDY, A. HIROSHIMA POEMS.
  B. CAMERON, 99:JAN75-47
  G. WARKENTIN, 102(CANL):SPRING73-
  121
PURDY, A. IN SEARCH OF OWEN ROBLIN.
  B. CAMERON, 99:JAN75-47
  L. SANDLER, 606(TAMR):MAR75-98
PURDY, A. POEMS FOR ALL THE ANN-
ETTES. ON THE BEARPAW SEA.
  B. CAMERON, 99:JAN75-47
PURDY, A. SELECTED POEMS.*
  P. STEVENS, 102(CANL):WINTER73-99
PURDY, A. SEX & DEATH.
  G. BOWERING, 102(CANL):SUMMER74-95
  B. CAMERON, 99:JAN75-47
  P. STEVENS, 628:SPRING74-104
PURDY, H.L. TRANSPORT COMPETITION
& PUBLIC POLICY IN CANADA.
  J.H. BALDWIN & C.E. LAW, 529(QQ):
  WINTER73-624
VON PÜRKEL, J.U-S. - SEE UNDER
UNGERN-STERNBERG VON PÜRKEL, J.
PURTILL, R.L. LOGIC FOR PHILOSO-
PHERS.*
  F.J. PELLETIER, 154:MAR73-171
PURVES, J.G. & D.A. WEST, EDS. WAR
& SOCIETY IN THE NINETEENTH CENTURY
RUSSIAN EMPIRE.
  G. TOKMAKOFF, 550(RUSR):JUL73-334
PUSHKAREV, S., COMP. A SOURCE BOOK
FOR RUSSIAN HISTORY FROM EARLY
                          [CONTINUED]

[CONTINUING]
TIMES TO 1917. (A.D. FERGUSON &
OTHERS, EDS)
  E.C. THADEN, 550(RUSR):JUL73-312
PUSHKAREV, S.G., COMP. DICTIONARY
OF RUSSIAN HISTORICAL TERMS FROM
THE ELEVENTH CENTURY TO 1917. (G.
VERNADSKY & R.T. FISHER, JR., EDS)
  G. HÜTTL-WORTH, 574(SEEJ):FALL72-
  366
PUSHKAREV, S.G., WITH B.S. PUSHKAREV
- SEE MELGUNOV, S.P.
PUSHKIN, A. THE CRITICAL PROSE OF
ALEXANDER PUSHKIN.* (C.R. PROFFER,
ED & TRANS)
  J.T. SHAW, 574(SEEJ):SPRING72-92
PUSHKIN, A. PUSHKIN ON LITERATURE.*
(T. WOLFF, ED & TRANS)
  H. GIFFORD, 184(EIC):JUL72-313
  J.T. SHAW, 574(SEEJ):SPRING72-92
PUTNAM, H. PHILOSOPHY OF LOGIC.*
  J. CORCORAN, 486:MAR73-131
  L. STEVENSON, 479(PHQ):OCT73-366
PUTNAM, M.C.J. VIRGIL'S PASTORAL
ART.*
  W.R. JOHNSON, 121(CJ):DEC73/JAN74-
  152
PUTNAM, R.D. THE BELIEFS OF POLI-
TICIANS.
  639(VQR):SPRING74-LVIII
PÜTZ, P., ED. THOMAS MANN UND DIE
TRADITION.*
  J.H. PETERSEN, 52:BAND8HEFT1-112
  S.P. SCHER, 680(ZDP):BAND92HEFT4-
  618
PÜTZ, P. DIE ZEIT IM DRAMA.*
  T. KOEBNER, 52:BAND8HEFT2-182
PUZYNA, K. - SEE WITKIEWICZ, S.I.
PYLE, F. "THE WINTER'S TALE."
  W.D. SMITH, 570(SQ):SPRING73-229
PYMAN, A. - SEE BLOK, A.
PYMAN, A. - SEE BULGAKOV, M.
PYMAN, A. - SEE SHVARTS, Y.
PYNCHON, T. GRAVITY'S RAINBOW.*
  J. HENDIN, 231:MAR75-82
  J. MILLS, 529(QQ):WINTER73-648
  M.A. SABRI, 502(PRS):FALL73-269
  P. STEVENS, 376:JUL73-142
PYNCHON, T. V.
  J. HENDIN, 231:MAR75-82
PYROMAGLOU, K. I ETHNIKI ANTI-
STASIS.
  R. CLOGG, 617(TLS):14NOV75-1362
PYTLÍK, R. TOULAVÉ HOUSE.
  W. PROCHAZKA, 574(SEEJ):WINTER72-
  491

QAMBER, A. YEATS & THE NOH.
  A. THWAITE, 617(TLS):25JUL75-837
QUARITSCH, H. STAAT UND SOUVERÄNI-
TÄT. (VOL 1)
  G. POST, 551(RENQ):SPRING73-41
QUARLES, B. ALLIES FOR FREEDOM.
  639(VQR):AUTUMN74-CXLIII
QUARONI, L. IMMAGINE DI ROMA.
  S. KOSTOF, 576:OCT73-239
QUASIMODO, S. DEBIT & CREDIT.
  T. EAGLETON, 565:VOL14#3-66
QUASS, F. NOMOS UND PSEPHISMA.
  S.M. BURSTEIN, 124:FEB74-238
  D.M. LEWIS, 123:NOV74-300

QUAYLE, E. THE COLLECTOR'S BOOK OF
DETECTIVE FICTION.
 J. CARTER, 354:JUN73-168
 J. COTTON, 503:SPRING73-44
 R. MC LEAN, 135:JUN73-152
 D.A. RANDALL, 78(BC):SUMMER73-246
QUEEN, E., ED. ELLERY QUEEN'S
CHRISTMAS HAMPER.
 T.J. BINYON, 617(TLS):19DEC75-1508
QUELLET, H. LES DÉRIVÉS LATINS EN
"-OR."*
 M. FAUST, 260(IF):BAND77HEFT2/3-
 324
QUELLET, R. LES RELATIONS HUMAINES
DANS L'OEUVRE DE SAINT-EXUPÉRY.
 M.A. SMITH, 207(FR):FEB73-632
QUENEAU, R. LE VOYAGE EN GRÈCE.
OULIPO.
 Y. BELAVAL, 98:DEC73-1061
QUENNELL, P. SAMUEL JOHNSON, HIS
FRIENDS & ENEMIES.
 L. BASNEY, 651(WHR):WINTER74-79
 C.J. RAWSON, 175:SPRING73-29
QUENNELL, P., ED. MARCEL PROUST
1871-1922.
 M. BOWIE, 208(FS):JUL74-345
QUEVAL, J. EN SOMME.
 A.J. KNODEL, 207(FR):DEC72-450
DE QUEVEDO, F. OBRA POÉTICA. (J.M.
BLECUA, ED)
 J.O. CROSBY, 240(HR):AUTUMN73-627
QUICK, J. & T. LA BAU. HANDBOOK OF
FILM PRODUCTION.
 200:FEB73-112
QUILTER, D., ED. EL HIDALGO DE LA
MANCHA.
 E.M. MALINAK, 399(MLJ):NOV74-352
QUIMBY, I.M.G., ED. AMERICAN PAINT-
ING TO 1776.*
 J.D. PROWN, 54:MAR73-150
QUINE, W.V. THE ROOTS OF REFERENCE.
 G. HARMAN, 311(JP):17JUL75-388
QUINN, B. EZRA POUND.*
 R. KIRK, 569(SR):FALL74-698
 J. MAZZARO, 141:WINTER74-85
QUINN, D.B. ENGLAND & THE DISCOVERY
OF AMERICA 1481-1620.*
 K.R. ANDREWS, 656(WMQ):OCT74-676
 W.E. WASHBURN, 639(VQR):SUMMER74-
 456
QUINN, D.B., ED. THE HAKLUYT HAND-
BOOK.
 J. ISRAEL, 617(TLS):28MAR75-340
QUINN, D.B. & N.M. CHESHIRE - SEE
PARMENIUS, S.
QUINN, K., ED. APPROACHES TO CATUL-
LUS.*
 D.O. ROSS, JR., 124:MAR74-307
QUINN, K. CATULLUS: AN INTERPRETA-
TION.*
 L.A. MAC KAY, 487:AUTUMN73-300
QUINN, K. - SEE CATULLUS
QUINN, S. WE'RE GOING TO MAKE YOU A
STAR.
 A. COCKBURN, 453:11DEC75-28
 B. DE MOTT, 61:AUG75-86
 E.R. LIPSON, 441:17AUG75-4
QUINTANILHA, F.E.G. - SEE PESSOA, F.
QUINTAVALLE, A.G. PARMIGIANINO,
DISEGNI.
 C. GOULD, 39:JAN73-111
QUINTILIAN. QUINTILIANI INSTITU-
TIONIS ORATORIAE LIBRI DUODECIM.*
(M. WINTERBOTTOM, ED)
 P.K. MARSHALL, 24:SPRING74-80

QUINTING, G. HESITATION PHENOMENA
IN ADULT APHASIC & NORMAL SPEECH.
 P. SCHVEIGER, 353:1NOV73-120
QUINTON, A. THE NATURE OF THINGS.*
 H. LAYCOCK, 154:SEP73-537
QUINTON, A. UTILITARIAN ETHICS.
 D.F. KOCH, 319:JUL75-417
"LES QUINZE JOYES DE MARIAGE."* (J.
CROW, ED)
 F.W. MARSHALL, 382(MAE):1974/3-300
QUIRK, R. THE LINGUIST & THE ENG-
LISH LANGUAGE.
 R.A. HALL, JR., 617(TLS):16MAY75-
 531
QUIRK, R. & OTHERS. A GRAMMAR OF
CONTEMPORARY ENGLISH.*
 R.B. LONG, 128(CE):FEB74-618
 M. RENSKY, 399(MLJ):MAR74-139
 I. SIMON, 556(RLV):1973/5-459
QUIRK, R.E. THE MEXICAN REVOLUTION
& THE CATHOLIC CHURCH, 1910-1929.
 S. POOLE, 377:NOV74-182
QUONDAM, A. - SEE GRAVINA, G.

RAABE, P., ED. INTERNATIONALER AR-
BEITSKREIS FÜR DEUTSCHE BAROCKLIT-
ERATUR.
 E. LUNDING, 301(JEGP):OCT74-591
RAABE, W. ELSE VON DER TANNE.
(J.C. O'FLAHERTY & J.K. KING, EDS
& TRANS)
 R.K. ANGRESS, 406:SPRING74-106
RABAN, J. SOFT CITY.*
 L. BRETT, 364:JUN/ JUL74-129
RABB, T.K. & R.I. ROTBERG, EDS. THE
FAMILY IN HISTORY.
 C. LASCH, 453:13NOV75-33
RABELAIS, F. CONTES CHOISIS. (A.C.
KELLER, ED)
 M.S. WHITNEY, 207(FR):DEC72-465
RABELAIS, F. GARGANTUA. (R. CAL-
DER, WITH M.A. SCREECH, EDS)
 G. DEFAUX, 207(FR):FEB73-602
RABINOWITCH, J. & L.K.D. KRISTOFF,
EDS. REVOLUTION & POLITICS IN
RUSSIA.
 R. PETHYBRIDGE, 575(SEER):APR74-
 303
RABONI, G. CADENZA D'INGANNO.
 F. FORTINI, 617(TLS):31OCT75-1308
RABY, P. - SEE GOGOL, N.V.
RACE, J. WAR COMES TO LONG AN.
 J. RECORD, 302:JAN73-184
RACHELS, J. & F.A. TILLMAN, EDS.
PHILOSOPHICAL ISSUES.
 W.G., 543:DEC72-363
DE RACHEWILTZ, I. PAPAL ENVOYS TO
THE GREAT KHANS.*
 A.S. ATIYA, 589:JAN74-112
DE RACHEWILTZ, I. & M. NAKANO. IN-
DEX TO BIOGRAPHICAL MATERIAL IN
CHIN & YÜAN LITERARY WORKS. (1ST
SER)
 J.T.C. LIU, 318(JAOS):APR-JUN73-
 214
DE RACHEWILTZ, M. DISCRETIONS.
 D. BARBOUR, 529(QQ):AUTUMN73-450
 A.P. HINCHLIFFE, 148:SUMMER72-189
 295:FEB74-378

RACHMAN, S.J. & C. PHILIPS. PSY-
CHOLOGY & MEDICINE.
  N.S. SUTHERLAND, 617(TLS):25APR75-
  450
RACINE, J. ANDROMAQUE.
  M. WAGNER, 207(FR):OCT72-247
RACINE, J. PHÈDRE.* (R.C. KNIGHT,
ED & TRANS)
  H.T. BARNWELL, 208(FS):APR74-197
  M.S. KOPPISCH, 207(FR):MAY73-1221
"LE RACISME DEVANT LA SCIENCE."
  C. SCHUWER, 542:JAN-MAR73-70
RAD, K. LE VENT S'ARRÊTE À SOFIA.
  B. KAY, 207(FR):MAR73-865
RADAZA, F.D. - SEE UNDER DEMETRIO Y
RADAZA, F.
RADCLIFF-UMSTEAD, D. UGO FOSCOLO.*
  O. RAGUSA, 276:AUTUMN73-451
RADCLIFF-UMSTEAD, D., ED. INNOVATION
IN MEDIEVAL LITERATURE.
  N.J. LACY, 207(FR):OCT72-142
RADDATZ, F.J. TRADITIONEN UND TEN-
DENZEN.
  P. HUTCHINSON, 220(GL&L):JUL74-334
  G. LOOSE, 400(MLN):OCT73-1062
RADER, D. BLOOD DUES.*
  H. LOMAS, 364:AUG/SEP74-130
RADER, M., ED. A MODERN BOOK OF
ESTHETICS. (4TH ED)
  A. SHIELDS, 290(JAAC):FALL73-119
RADFORD, J. NORMAN MAILER.
  M. MASON, 617(TLS):8AUG75-891
RADIGUET, R. COUNT D'ORGEL.
  P. BAILEY, 617(TLS):17JAN75-50
RADIN, P. AFRICAN FOLKTALES.
  D.J. CROWLEY, 2:AUTUMN73-84
RADINI TEDESCHI, T. ORAZIONE CON-
TRO FILIPPO MELANTONE.
  A. CORSANO, 548(RCSF):OCT-DEC73-
  465
"A.N. RADIŠČEV UND DEUTSCHLAND."
  M. RAEFF, 104:SPRING73-118
RADITCHKOV, I. ABÉCÉDAIRE EXPLOSIF.
  270:VOL23#1-19
RADKE, G., ED. CICERO EIN MENSCH
SEINER ZEIT.
  J.P.V.D. BALSDON, 313:VOL63-254
RADKE, G., ED. POLITIK UND LITER-
ARISCHE KUNST IM WERK DES TACITUS.
  A.D. CASTRO, 124:FEB74-235
RADLEY, V.L. ELIZABETH BARRETT
BROWNING.
  T.J. COLLINS, 637(VS):DEC73-234
RADLOFF, V.V. SOUTH-SIBERIAN ORAL
LITERATURE, TURKIC TEXTS. (VOL 1)
  G.F. MEIER, 682(ZPSK):BAND26HEFT
  3/4-448
RADNER, L. EICHENDORFF.*
  W.L. HAHN, 221(GQ):MAR73-261
  D.C. RIECHEL, 222(GR):JAN73-77
RADNITZKY, G. CONTEMPORARY SCHOOLS
OF METASCIENCE.* (2ND ED)
  J.N. HATTIANGADI, 125:OCT73-86
RADNOTI, M. CLOUDED SKY.
  T. EAGLETON, 565:VOL14#3-74
RADOFF, M.L. THE STATE HOUSE AT
ANNAPOLIS.
  J. HNEDAK, 576:OCT73-261
RADOMSKI, R. OSTJAKISCHE ORTSNAMEN.
  L. SCHIEFER, 343:BAND16HEFT1-107
RADOSH, R. PROPHETS ON THE RIGHT.
  H. MAYER, 441:20APR75-7
RADT, S. - SEE SCHWYZER, E.

RADVÁNYI, J. HUNGARY & THE SUPER-
POWERS.*
  I. VOLGYES, 104:SPRING74-163
DE RADZITZKY, C. LE COMMUN DES
MORTELS.
  J-G. LINZE, 270:VOL23#3-57
RAE, I. CHARLES CAMERON, ARCHITECT
TO THE COURT OF RUSSIA.*
  K. CRUFT, 46:FEB73-146
RAEFF, M., ED. CATHERINE THE GREAT.
  J.T. ALEXANDER, 104:SPRING73-112
RAFFEL, B., ED & TRANS. RUSSIAN
POETRY UNDER THE TSARS.*
  M. KANDEL, 574(SEEJ):SUMMER72-232
  H.W. TJALSMA, 550(RUSR):APR73-208
RAFFEL, B. & A. BURAGO - SEE GUMI-
LEV, N.S.
RAFROIDI, P. L'IRLANDE ET LE ROMAN-
TISME.
  N.H. MACKENZIE, 529(QQ):SPRING73-
  128
RAGNI, E. - SEE FIRENZUOLA, A.
RAGON, M. HISTOIRE DE LA LITTÉRA-
TURE PROLÉTARIENNE EN FRANCE.
  W.D. REDFERN, 617(TLS):14MAR75-280
RAGONESE, G. L'ALLEGORISMO DELLE
TRE FIERE ED ALTRI STUDI DANTESCHI.
  M.M., 228(GSLI):VOL150FASC469-152
RAGOTZKY, H. STUDIEN ZUR WOLFRAM-
REZEPTION.
  B. WACHINGER, 680(ZDP):BAND92HEFT
  3-452
RAGUSA, O. LUIGI PIRANDELLO.
  G. SINGH, 276:SUMMER73-325
RAHNER, K., ED. ENCYCLOPEDIA OF
THEOLOGY.
  P. HEBBLETHWAITE, 617(TLS):30MAY
  75-605
RAHTZ, P.A., ED. RESCUE ARCHAEOLOGY.
  J. COLES, 617(TLS):21FEB75-187
RAIMONDI, E. POLITICA E COMMEDIA.
  C.W., 275(IQ):FALL-WINTER73(VOL17
  #66)-64
RAIMONDI, E. IL ROMANZO SENZA IDIL-
LIO.
  K. FOSTER, 617(TLS):31OCT75-1293
RAINE, K. DEATH-IN-LIFE & LIFE-IN-
DEATH.
  G. HOUGH, 617(TLS):14FEB75-160
RAINE, K. THE LAND UNKNOWN.
  H. BEVINGTON, 441:12OCT75-5
  V. GLENDINNING, 617(TLS):8AUG75-
  890
  442(NY):13OCT75-178
RAINEY, A. MOSAICS IN ROMAN BRITAIN.
  R. HIGGINS, 39:OCT73-321
RAIS, A. LE MACHINISTE TÊTU.
  S.G. STARY, 207(FR):FEB73-666
RAITH, J. & H. MARCHL. BEISPIEL-
SÄTZE ZUR ENGLISCHEN GRAMMATIK.
(3RD ED)
  P.H. FRIES, 399(MLJ):JAN-FEB74-82
RAITT, A.W. PROSPER MÉRIMÉE.*
  T.G.S. COMBE, 208(FS):APR74-214
  J. GAULMIER, 535(RHL):JUL-AUG73-
  714
  A.S. ROSENTHAL, 207(FR):MAR73-833
RAITT, J. MADAME DE LAFAYETTE &
"LA PRINCESSE DE CLÈVES."*
  C.G.S. WILLIAMS, 399(MLJ):NOV73-
  365
RAJA, N.K. - SEE UNDER KUMARASWAMI
RAJA, N.

VON RANKE, L. THE THEORY & PRAC-
TICE OF HISTORY. (G.G. IGGERS &
K. VON MOLTKE, EDS)
H. LIEBEL, 125:JUN74-359
VON RANKE, L. ÜBER DIE EPOCHEN DER
NEUEREN GESCHICHTE. (T. SCHIEDER &
H. BERDING, EDS)
H.F. YOUNG, 182:VOL26#7/8-244
RANKIN, H.F. FRANCIS MARION.
F.B. WICKWIRE, 656(WMQ):OCT74-693
RANNIT, A. LINE.
P. SAAGPAKK, 270:VOL23#2-34
RANSOM, J.C. BEATING THE BUSHES.
R. FOSTER, 109:FALL/WINTER73/74-
111
T.D. YOUNG, 219(GAR):SUMMER73-275
RANSOME, M., ED. WILTSHIRE RETURNS
TO THE BISHOP'S VISITATION QUERIES,
1783.
M.H. PORT, 447(N&Q):FEB73-60
RANSTRAND, G. POMPONII MELAE DE
CHOROGRAPHIA LIBRI TRES. BEITRÄGE
ZU POMPONIUS MELA.
M.E. MILHAM, 487:SUMMER73-208
RANTAVAARA, I. VIRGINIA WOOLF'S
"THE WAVES."
J. GUIGUET, 189(EA):JUL-SEP73-338
RANUM, O.A. RICHELIEU & THE COUN-
CILLORS OF LOUIS XIII.
A. BOURDE, 182:VOL26#21/22-818
RAO, M.S.A. TRADITION, RATIONALITY,
& CHANGE.
S. VATUK, 293(JAST):MAY73-519
RAO, P.V.R. RED TAPE & WHITE CAP.
M.R. GOODALL, 293(JAST):NOV72-193
RAO, S. & S.D. HOLKAR. COOKING OF
THE MAHARAJAHS.
R.A. SOKOLOV, 441:7DEC75-7
RAO, V.K.R.V. THE NEHRU LEGACY.
W.R. BREWER, 293(JAST):FEB73-355
"RAPE & ITS VICTIMS."
D. JOHNSON, 453:11DEC75-36
RAPER, J.R. WITHOUT SHELTER.
M. FRAZEE, 189(EA):JAN-MAR73-114
W.D. TAYLOR, 295:FEB74-619
RAPHAEL, D.D., ED. BRITISH MORAL-
ISTS 1650-1800.
P. DUBOIS, 542:APR-JUN73-227
RAPHAEL, D.D. PROBLEMS OF POLITICAL
PHILOSOPHY.
J. REES, 483:JAN73-93
RAPHAEL, F. CALIFORNIA TIME.
N. HEPBURN, 362:6NOV75-622
J. SUTHERLAND, 617(TLS):31OCT75-
1285
RAPHAEL, F. RICHARD'S THINGS.
M. LEVIN, 441:26OCT75-55
RAPHAEL, M. THEORIE DES GEISTIGEN
SCHAFFENS AUF MARXISTISCHER GRUND-
LAGE.
P. LABANYI, 617(TLS):25JUL75-855
RAPP, F. L'EGLISE ET LA VIE RELIG-
IEUSE EN OCCIDENT À LA FIN DU MOYEN
AGE.
N. ARONSON, 207(FR):OCT72-177
RAPP, L. & J. MOTHER EARTH'S
HASSLE-FREE INDOOR PLANT BOOK.
J. CANADAY, 441:13APR75-16
"RAPPORT DES ARCHIVES NATIONALES DU
QUÉBEC, 1971." (VOL 49)
T.D.S. BASSETT, 14:JUL73-420

RASCH, W., H. GEULEN & K. HABERKAMM,
EDS. REZEPTION UND PRODUKTION
ZWISCHEN 1570 UND 1730.
G. HOFFMEISTER, 221(GQ):MAY73-462
RASCOE, J. YOURS, & MINE.*
J.M. FLORA, 385(MQR):WINTER75-101
RASHĪD AD-DĪN FAZLULLĀH. AL-WAQFI-
YAH AR-RASHĪDĪYAH. (M. MINOVI & I.
AFSHAR, EDS)
B.G. MARTIN, 318(JAOS):OCT-DEC73-
561
RASKIN, J. OUT OF THE WHALE.
H.M. PACHTER, 231:AUG75-83
M. ROSSMAN, 441:11MAY75-30
RASKIN, M. NOTES ON THE OLD SYS-
TEM.*
G.E. REEDY, 441:12JAN75-4
RASMUSSEN, A-M. THERE WAS ONCE A
TIME.
M.S. KENNEDY, 441:13APR75-26
RASPAIL, J. THE CAMP OF THE SAINTS.
T. LASK, 441:5OCT75-46
R.R. LINGEMAN, 441:13AUG75-33
RASTALL, R., ED. L'ART ET INSTRUC-
TION DE BIEN DANCER (MICHEL TOU-
LOUZE, PARIS).
N. WILKINS, 208(FS):JAN74-56
RATCLIFFE, E.J. THROUGH THE BADGER
GATE.
617(TLS):14FEB75-177
RATH, R. DIE PARTIZIPIALGRUPPE IN
DER DEUTSCHEN SPRACHE DER GEGENWART.
G. HELBIG, 353:1DEC73-107
RATHBONE, J. KILL CURE.
N. CALLENDAR, 441:17AUG75-26
RATHER, D. & G.P. GATES. THE PALACE
GUARD.*
L.J. PAPER, 31(ASCH):WINTER74/75-
164
RATHJEN, F.W. THE TEXAS PANHANDLE
FRONTIER.
L.C. MILAZZO, 584(SWR):SPRING74-
216
RATHJENS, C., C. TROLL & H. UHLIG,
EDS. VERGLEICHENDE KULTURGEOGRA-
PHIE DER HOCHGEBIRGE DES SÜDLICHEN
ASIEN.
M. SCHICK, 182:VOL26#15/16-569
RAUCHE, G.A. TRUTH & REALITY IN
ACTUALITY.
J.J.F., 543:DEC72-364
RAVETZ, J.R. SCIENTIFIC KNOWLEDGE
& ITS SPECIAL PROBLEMS.
A. LYON, 479(PHQ):JUL73-274
J.H. MOOR, 486:SEP73-455
RAVITCH, D. THE GREAT SCHOOL WARS.*
S. RUDIKOFF, 473(PR):4/1974-639
RAWLS, J. A THEORY OF JUSTICE.*
P. DANIELSON, 488:DEC73-331
G.G., 543:JUN73-764
R.M. HARE, 479(PHQ):APR73-144 [&
CONT IN] 479(PHQ):JUL73-241
C.B. MACPHERSON, 488:DEC73-341
T. NAGEL, 482(PHR):APR73-220
P.H. NOWELL-SMITH, 488:DEC73-315
RAWLYK, G.A. NOVA SCOTIA'S MASSA-
CHUSETTS.
J.B. BELL, 432(NEQ):DEC74-625
J. FINGARD, 99:JUN75-46
RAWSKI, E.S. AGRICULTURAL CHANGE &
THE PEASANT ECONOMY OF SOUTH CHINA.
M. ELVIN, 293(JAST):NOV72-141

RAWSON, C.J. HENRY FIELDING & THE
AUGUSTAN IDEAL UNDER STRESS.*
  B. BOYCE, 191(ELN):DEC73-142
  D. BROOKS, 677:VOL4-302
  J.P. HUNTER, 481(PQ):JUL73-504
  P. ROGERS, 148:SUMMER73-187
  A. WILLIAMS, 579(SAQ):SUMMER74-411
RAWSON, C.J. GULLIVER & THE GENTLE
READER.
  W.B. CARNOCHAN, 301(JEGP):APR74-
  247
  P. DIXON, 566:SPRING74-90
RAWSON, C.J. - SEE URE, P.
RAWSON, E. CICERO.
  D.R. SHACKLETON-BAILEY, 617(TLS):
  24OCT75-1271
RAWSON, P. INTRODUCING ORIENTAL
ART.*
  S. MARKBREITER, 60:JUL-AUG74-70
RAY, A. ENGLISH DELFTWARE TILES.
  A. CAIGER-SMITH, 135:NOV73-219
RAY, D. GATHERING FIREWOOD.
  H. VENDLER, 441:6APR75-4
RAY, G.E. WILY WOMEN OF THE WEST.
  J.G., 502(PRS):SUMMER73-186
RAY, G.N. H.G. WELLS & REBECCA
WEST.*
  A. WEST, 231:JAN75-82
RAY, L. LES MÉTAMORPHOSES DU BIO-
GRAPHE [SUIVI DE] LA PAROLE POSSI-
BLE.
  H.A. BOURAOUI, 207(FR):MAY73-1248
RAY, M., M-A. LIOTIER & J.P. CAP-
REMZ. ALM FRENCH LEVEL III. (2ND
ED)
  A. PAPALIA, 399(MLJ):JAN-FEB74-69
RAY, P.C. THE SURREALIST MOVEMENT
IN ENGLAND.*
  A. YOUNG, 148:SPRING73-90
  295:FEB74-405
RAY, R.B. THE INDIANS OF MAINE.
  W.S. HADLOCK, 432(NEQ):MAR73-157
RAY, S. MUSIC OF EASTERN INDIA.
  C.H. CAPWELL, 187:SEP75-489
RAYA, G. - SEE VERGA, G.
RAYAN, K. SUGGESTION & STATEMENT IN
POETRY.
  S. BERGSTEN, 597(SN):VOL45#1-178
  A. RODWAY, 89(BJA):WINTER73-91
  H. SERGEANT, 175:AUTUMN73-121
RAYAPATI, J.P.R. EARLY AMERICAN
INTEREST IN VEDANTA.
  A.R. FERGUSON, 27(AL):MAY74-228
RAYMOND, L. MY LIFE WITH A BRAHMIN
FAMILY.
  A. BHARATI, 318(JAOS):JUL-SEP73-
  388
RAYMOND, M. MÉMORIAL.
  A.J. STEELE, 208(FS):JUL74-371
RAYMOND, M., ED. LA POÉSIE FRAN-
ÇAISE ET LE MANIÉRISME 1546-
1610(?).*
  T.M. GREENE, 551(RENQ):WINTER73-
  513
  O. DE MOURGUES, 208(FS):APR74-185
RAYNOR, H. - SEE MAGIDOFF, R.
MISS READ - SEE UNDER MISS
READ, C.H. & O.M. DALTON. ANTIQUI-
TIES FROM THE CITY OF BENIN & FROM
OTHER PARTS OF WEST AFRICA IN THE
BRITISH MUSEUM.
  F. WILLETT, 2:WINTER74-78
READ, D. EDWARDIAN ENGLAND.
  M. ROSE, 637(VS):MAR74-319

READ, E.A. A CHECKLIST OF BOOKS,
CATALOGUES & PERIODICAL ARTICLES
RELATING TO THE CATHEDRAL LIBRARIES
OF ENGLAND.
  R.C. NORRIS, 447(N&Q):MAR73-116
READ, H., ED. SURREALISM.*
  A. YOUNG, 148:SPRING73-90
READ, J. THE MOORS IN SPAIN & POR-
TUGAL.
  W.M. WATT, 617(TLS):17JAN75-52
READING, P. FOR THE MUNICIPALITY'S
ELDERLY.
  D. ABSE, 617(TLS):28FEB75-214
  A. MACLEAN, 617(TLS):23MAY75-552
READY, S. VIVA! WOMEN'S LIB.
  D.M. DAY, 157:SUMMER73-80
REAL, H.J. UNTERSUCHUNGEN ZUR LU-
KREZ - ÜBERSETZUNG VON THOMAS
CREECH.
  W.B. FLEISCHMANN, 131(CL):WINTER73-
  93
REALE, G. I PROBLEMI DEL PENSICRO
ANTICO DALLE ORIGINI AD ARISTOTELE.
  H. WAGNER, 53(AGP):BAND55HEFT3-349
REANEY, G. GUILLAUME DE MACHAUT.
  D.G. HUGHES, 589:JAN74-142
REANEY, J. MASKS OF CHILDHOOD.
  J. NOONAN, 529(QQ):AUTUMN73-466
REANEY, J. POEMS. (G. WARKENTIN,
ED)
  M. ATWOOD, 102(CANL):SUMMER73-113
  M. ESTOK, 150(DR):SUMMER73-383
REANEY, J. STICKS & STONES.
  S. MARTINEAU, 99:OCT75-36
REARDON, B.P. COURANTS LITTÉRAIRES
GRECS DES IIE ET IIIE SIÈCLES APRÈS
J-C.
  R. DYER, 124:MAY73-490
  É. DES PLACES, 555:VOL47FASC2-339
REARDON, J.J. EDMUND RANDOLPH.
  T. LASK, 441:2APR75-37
REAVER, J.R., COMP. AN O'NEILL CON-
CORDANCE.
  P. LEWTON, 447(N&Q):APR73-159
REBOUL, O. KANT ET LE PROBLÈME DU
MAL.*
  J. KOPPER, 342:BAND64HEFT1-143
  205(FMLS):APR73-214
RÉBUFFAT, G. THE MONT BLANC MASSIF.
  617(TLS):25APR75-465
RECCHIA, V. SISEBUTO DI TOLEDO: IL
"CARMEN DE LUNA."
  P. LANGLOIS, 555:VOL47FASC2-366
"RECERQUES." (NO. 1 & 2)
  S. GINER, 86(BHS):APR73-190
"RECHERCHES SUR LES STRUCTURES SOC-
IALES DANS L'ANTIQUITÉ CLASSIQUE."
  P. GAUTHIER, 555:VOL47FASC1-122
RECHTSCHAFFEN, B. & C. HOMBERGER.
GERMAN FOR RESEARCH: BIOLOGICAL &
PHYSICAL SCIENCES.
  A. BRIEFS, 399(MLJ):JAN-FEB74-73
"RÉCIT ET ROMAN, FORMES DU ROMAN
ANGLAIS DU XVIE AU XXE."
  Y. GUÉRIN, 549(RLC):APR-JUN73-340
RECK, A.J. SPECULATIVE PHILOSOPHY.
  P.M., 543:MAR73-543
RECK, R.D. LITERATURE & RESPONSI-
BILITY.*
  W.A. STRAUSS, 141:WINTER72-83
RÉDA, J. LA TOURNE.
  G. MARTIN, 617(TLS):10OCT75-1209

REDDAWAY, P., ED & TRANS. UNCENSOR-
ED RUSSIA.*
  P.S. GILLETTE, 104:SUMMER73-270
REDDAWAY, P. - SEE LITVINOV, P.
REDDICK, J. THE "DANZIG TRILOGY" OF
GÜNTER GRASS.
  A.F. BANCE, 617(TLS):24OCT75-1270
REDEI, K. NORD-OSTJAKISCHE TEXTE
(KAZYM-DIALEKT) MIT SKIZZE DER
GRAMMATIK.*
  E. SCHIEFER, 343:BAND16HEFT2-224
REDFERN, J. A GLOSSARY OF SPANISH
LITERARY COMPOSITION.
  J. AYORA, 399(MLJ):APR74-214
REDFERN, W.D. PAUL NIZAN.*
  F. JAMESON, 207(FR):FEB73-631
  A. KING, 295:FEB74-729
REDFERN, W.D. - SEE VALLÈS, J.
REDGROVE, P. DR. FAUST'S SEA-SPIRAL
SPIRIT.*
  T. EAGLETON, 565:VOL14#1-65
  H. SERGEANT, 175:AUTUMN73-121
REDGROVE, P. IN THE COUNTRY OF THE
SKIN.
  E. GLOVER, 565:VOL14#4-69
REDGROVE, P. SONS OF MY SKIN.
  P. BEER, 362:20NOV75-682
REDING, J. MENSCHEN IM RUHRGEBIET.
  P. PROCHNIK, 617(TLS):4JUL75-723
REDINGER, R.V. GEORGE ELIOT.
  P. ADAMS, 61:JUL75-83
  G. GODWIN, 441:7SEP75-27
  A. WHITMAN, 441:27SEP75-27
  M. WOOD, 453:27NOV75-11
RED'KIN, V.A. AKCENTOLOGIJA SOVRE-
MENNOGO RUSSKOGO LITERATURNOGO
JAZYKA.
  H.S. COATS, 574(SEEJ):WINTER73-480
REDMON, A. EMILY STONE.*
  A. BROYARD, 441:25FEB75-39
  E. FEINSTEIN, 364:OCT/NOV74-134
REDMOND, E.B. - SEE DUMAS, H.
REDPATH, T. THE YOUNG ROMANTICS &
CRITICAL OPINION 1807-1824.
  J.O. HAYDEN, 141:FALL74-342
REDSHAW, T.D. HEIMAEY.
  J. MONTAGUE, 617(TLS):4JUL75-718
REE, J. DESCARTES.
  A.B. SAVILE, 617(TLS):18APR75-435
REECE, B.R. LEARNING IN THE TENTH
CENTURY.
  R.J. SCHNEIDER, 124:FEB73-314
REED, B. DIESEL-HYDRAULIC LOCOMO-
TIVES OF THE WESTERN REGION.
  617(TLS):21FEB75-204
REED, C.E., ED. THE LEARNING OF
LANGUAGE.
  J.W. NEY, 399(MLJ):JAN-FEB73-46
REED, J. THE BORDER BALLADS.
  H. TRANTER, 67:NOV74-231
REED, J.R. VICTORIAN CONVENTIONS.
  K.J. FIELDING, 617(TLS):3OCT75-
  1161
REED, J.W., JR. FAULKNER'S NARRA-
TIVE.*
  P.R. BROUGHTON, 598(SOR):SUMMER75-
  681
REED, T.J. - SEE MANN, T.
REED, W.L. MEDITATIONS ON THE HERO.
  P. CONRAD, 617(TLS):23MAY75-550
REEDIJK, C., ED. ACTES DU CONGRES
ERASME.
  A. HYMA, 551(RENQ):WINTER73-463

REES, B. PROPHET OF THE WIND.
  A. BARNES, 617(TLS):29AUG75-961
REES, G. BRIEF ENCOUNTERS.
  P. BAILEY, 364:AUG/SEP74-142
REES, J. THE QUEEN OF HEARTS.
  P. BEER, 617(TLS):17JAN75-48
REES, J. - SEE GREVILLE, F.
REES, L. THE MAKING OF AUSTRALIAN
DRAMA.
  T. STURM, 581:JUN74-212
REES, M.A. ALFRED DE MUSSET.*
  G. DELATTRE, 399(MLJ):NOV73-361
REES, R.A. & E.N. HARBERT, EDS.
FIFTEEN AMERICAN AUTHORS BEFORE
1900.*
  R.H. HUDSON, 573(SSF):SPRING73-217
  L.S. LUEDTKE, 173(ECS):WINTER
  73/74-239
REES, T.R. THE TECHNIQUE OF T.S.
ELIOT.
  G. HOUGH, 617(TLS):1AUG75-866
REES-MOGG, W. THE REIGNING ERROR.
  B. GRIFFITHS, 617(TLS):7FEB75-142
  P. OPPENHEIMER, 362:16JAN75-88
REEVE, F.D. THE BLUE CAT.*
  H. TAYLOR, 385(MQR):WINTER75-92
REEVE, F.D. THE BROTHER.
  D. WILSON, 617(TLS):16MAY75-529
REEVE, F.D. WHITE COLOURS.
  F. PIKE, 617(TLS):7MAR75-260
  639(VQR):SPRING74-LV
REEVES, G.M. - SEE COINDREAU, M.E.
REEVES, J. TRIPTYCH.
  P. HAY, 102(CANL):WINTER74-109
REEVES, M. & B. HIRSCH-REICH. THE
"FIGURAE" OF JOACHIM OF FIORE.
  C.H. CLOUGH, 39:MAY73-533
  G. LEFF, 382(MAE):1974/2-185
REEVES, P.D. - SEE SLEEMAN, W.H.
REEVES, R. A FORD, NOT A LINCOLN.
  W.F. BUCKLEY, JR., 441:26OCT75-8
  M. JANEWAY, 61:DEC75-116
  G. WILLS, 453:16OCT75-18
  442(NY):27OCT75-167
REEVES, R.S. & P. ROBINSON. CLASSIC
LINES.
  S. SMITH, 441:7DEC75-95
"REFORM ON CAMPUS."
  R. BUFFINGTON, 569(SR):WINTER74-
  147
REGALADO, N.F. POETIC PATTERNS IN
RUTEBEUF.*
  A.M. COLBY, 207(FR):MAY73-1217
REGEN, F. APULEIUS PHILOSOPHUS
PLATONICUS.*
  J. WHITTAKER, 487:AUTUMN73-314
  T. WINTER, 124:SEP72-50
  R.E. WITT, 123:MAR74-141
REGENSTEIN, L. THE POLITICS OF EX-
TINCTION.
  H. BORLAND, 441:23NOV75-44
"REGLAS DE CATALOGACIÓN ANGLOAMERI-
CANAS."
  A. MORATORIO, 263:JUL-SEP74-303
REGNELL, H., ED. READINGS IN ANA-
LYTICAL PHILOSOPHY.
  R. BLANCHÉ, 542:JUL-SEP73-372
REGULA, M. BEITRÄGE ZUR DEUTSCHEN
SYNTAX IN FORM KRITISCHER BEMERKUN-
GEN ZUR DUDEN-GRAMMATIK (SATZKUNDE).
  J.J. BRAAKENBURG, 433:JAN73-99
REHDER, H. & OTHERS. SPRECHEN UND
LESEN. (REV)
  B.J. KOEKKOEK, 399(MLJ):APR73-222

REHLE, S. & K. GAMBER, EDS. SACRA-
MENTARIUM ARNONIS.
H. BECKER, 182:VOL26#20-727
REHRAUER, G. CINEMA BOOKLIST.
J.R. PARISH, 200:APR73-236
REIBEL, D.A. & S.A. SCHANE, EDS.
MODERN STUDIES IN ENGLISH.
R.C. DOUGHERTY, 206:SEP73-423
K. FAISS, 353:15APR73-104
A.M. ZWICKY, 350:JUN74-367
REICH, R. TALES OF ALEXANDER THE
MACEDONIAN.
F.L. UTLEY, 292(JAF):OCT-DEC73-395
REICH, S. JOHN MARIN.
M.S. YOUNG, 39:APR73-440
REICHARDT, D. LATEINAMERIKANISCHE
AUTOREN.
H. ROGMANN, 72:BAND211HEFT1/3-238
REICHART, W.A. - SEE IRVING, W.
REICHEL-DOLMATOFF, G. SAN AGUSTÍN.
M. STIRLING, 37:APR73-41
REICHENBACH, B.R. THE COSMOLOGICAL
ARGUMENT.
H.F., 543:JUN73-765
REICHENBACH, H. THE DIRECTION OF
TIME.
T. CHAPMAN, 154:DEC73-717
REICHMANN, F. & J. THARPE. BIBLIO-
GRAPHIC CONTROL OF MICROFORMS.
W. SAFFADY, 14:JUL73-404
REID, A.J. LETTERS OF LONG AGO.
(B.D. MADSEN, ED)
D. BITTON, 651(WHR):AUTUMN74-398
REID, B.L. THE MAN FROM NEW YORK.
M. HUGGLER, 182:VOL26#1/2-10
REID, D. A CONCISE HISTORY OF
CANADIAN PAINTING.
P. FLEISHER, 73:WINTER74-43
REID, D.A. SOLDIER-SURGEON. (J.O.
BAYLEN & A. CONWAY, EDS)
B.D. GOOCH, 637(VS):DEC73-217
REID, F. ILLUSTRATORS OF THE
EIGHTEEN SIXTIES.
617(TLS):18JUL75-802
REID, J.H. HEINRICH BÖLL. (VOL 1)
P. PROCHNIK, 617(TLS):31JAN75-120
REID, M. THE SHOUTING SIGNPAINTERS.
F. SUTHERLAND, 102(CANL):SPRING73-
101
REID, R. THE FICTION OF NATHANAEL
WEST.
G. LOCKLIN, 573(SSF):SPRING73-212
REID, R. LOST & FOUND.
K. ROOSEVELT, 441:50CT75-41
REID, R.O. INTRODUCTORY CONCEPTS IN
COMMUNICATION PROCESSES.
T.L. ATTAWAY, 583:FALL73-101
REID, T. LECTURES ON THE FINE ARTS.
(P. KIVY, ED)
W.J. HIPPLE, JR., 290(JAAC):WIN-
TER74-236
D.D. TODD, 319:OCT75-534
REID, T.B.W. THE "TRISTRAN" OF
BEROUL.*
M. HACKETT, 382(MAE):1974/3-275
REIFF, D.D. ARCHITECTURE IN FRE-
DONIA, 1811-1972. WASHINGTON ARCH-
ITECTURE 1791-1861.
J. HNEDAK, 576:OCT73-261
REIGSTAD, P. RÖLVAAG.*
C.D. RUUD, 502(PRS):SUMMER73-172
H.P. SIMONSON, 563(SS):SUMMER74-
301

REILLY, A.P. AMERICA IN CONTEMPOR-
ARY SOVIET LITERATURE.*
E. WASIOLEK, 574(SEEJ):FALL72-357
REILLY, F.E. CHARLES PEIRCE'S
THEORY OF SCIENTIFIC METHOD.
W.A.F., 543:MAR73-544
REILLY, R.J. ROMANTIC RELIGION.*
R. DETWEILER, 295:FEB74-405
J.C. ULREICH, JR., 50(ARQ):SPRING
73-74
REIMAN, D.H., COMP. THE ROMANTICS
REVIEWED.
D.V.E., 191(ELN):SEP73(SUPP)-17
P.F. MORGAN, 301(JEGP):JAN74-129
REIMER, E. - SEE JOHN OF GARLAND
REIN, I.J. RUDY'S RED WAGON.
E.C. GLENN, 583:SUMMER74-409
DE REINCOURT, A. SEX & POWER IN
HISTORY.
J. CORRY, 441:26APR75-25
REINERT, B. DIE LEHRE VOM "TAWAK-
KUL" IN DER KLASSISCHEN SUFIK.
J.A. BELLAMY, 318(JAOS):APR-JUN73-
236
REINERT, H.F. REVIEW TEXT IN GER-
MAN FIRST YEAR.*
C. SHACKELFORD, 399(MLJ):JAN-FEB
73-56
REINERT, O., ED. AUGUST STRINDBERG:
A COLLECTION OF CRITICAL ESSAYS.
R-M.G. OSTER, 399(MLJ):JAN-FEB74-
74
REINGOLD, N. - SEE HENRY, J.
REINHARDT, J.M. FOREIGN POLICY &
NATIONAL INTEGRATION.
F. BUNNELL, 293(JAST):AUG73-751
REINHARDT, K. SOPHOCLE.
G. RONNET, 555:VOL47FASC1-128
REINHARDT, U. DIE BISCHÖFTLICHEN
RESIDENZEN VON CHÂLONS-SUR-MARNE,
VERDUN UND STRASSBURG.
P. LAVEDAN, 182:VOL26#10-368
REINHOLD, H., ED. CHARLES DICKENS.*
C.A. BODELSEN, 179(ES):JUN72-264
REINHOLD, M. HISTORY OF PURPLE AS
A STATUS SYMBOL IN ANTIQUITY.*
H.W. STUBBS, 313:VOL63-267
REINHOLD, M. PAST & PRESENT.
L. FEDER, 122:JUL74-230
D.R. GORDON, 124:SEP-OCT73-56
REININK, A.W. K.P.C. DE BAZEL -
ARCHITECT.
H. SEARING, 576:OCT73-253
REINMUTH, H.S., JR., ED. EARLY STU-
ART STUDIES.
E.R. FOSTER, 551(RENQ):SUMMER73-
221
REISS, E. THE ART OF THE MIDDLE
ENGLISH LYRIC.*
C.A. CONWAY, 255(HAB):SUMMER73-223
R.T. DAVIES, 677:VOL4-246
T.P. DUNNING, 541(RES):NOV73-467
B. RAW, 447(N&Q):NOV73-437
J.I. WIMSATT, 589:APR74-369
REISS, H., ED. GOETHE UND DIE TRA-
DITION.
W.H. BRUFORD, 402(MLR):JUL74-705
REISS, H. - SEE KANT, I.
REISS, J. THE BREATHERS.
H. VENDLER, 441:6APR75-4
REISS, S. AELBERT CUYP.
C. BROWN, 617(TLS):28NOV75-1412
J. RUSSELL, 441:7DEC75-16

REISS, T.J. TOWARD DRAMATIC ILLU-
SION.*
T. LAWRENSON, 402(MLR):JUL74-637
REISSMAN, L. LES CLASSES SOCIALES
AUX ETATS-UNIS.
D. VICTOROFF, 542:JAN-MAR73-90
REITER, J. SYSTEM UND PRAXIS.
S. DECLOUX, 182:VOL26#21/22-779
LORD REITH. THE REITH DIARIES. (C.
STUART, ED)
H. GREENE, 617(TLS):19SEP75-1061
O. WHITLEY, 362:25SEP75-401
REKERS, B. BENITO ARIAS MONTANO
(1527-1598).
R.W. TRUMAN, 402(MLR):JAN74-201
RELA, W. GUÍA BIBLIOGRÁFICA DE LA
LITERATURA HISPANOAMERICANA DESDE
EL SIGLO XIX HASTA 1970.*
D.L. SHAW, 86(BHS):OCT73-418
H.C. WOODBRIDGE, 238:SEP73-737
REMINGTON, R.A. THE WARSAW PACT.
D.E. PIENKOS, 104:SPRING74-163
REMNANT, G.L. A CATALOGUE OF MISER-
ICORDS IN GREAT BRITAIN.
C. HOHLER, 54:JUN73-292
REMY, M. DICTIONNAIRE DU FRANÇAIS
MODERNE.
H.W. BRANN, 207(FR):DEC72-464
REMY, P-J. LE SAC DU PALAIS D'ÉTÉ.
F.C. ST. AUBYN, 207(FR):DEC72-451
RENA, S. THE SEA ROAD WEST.
N. HEPBURN, 362:5JUN75-746
RENARD, R. INTRODUCTION À LA MÉTH-
ODE VERBO-TONALE DE CORRECTION
PHONÉTIQUE.
P.F. CINTAS, 207(FR):OCT72-256
RENAULT, M. THE NATURE OF ALEXAN-
DER.
P-L. ADAMS, 61:NOV75-126
C.L. MEE, JR., 441:7DEC75-38
RENAULT, M. THE PERSIAN BOY.*
J. COAKLEY, 385(MQR):WINTER75-108
RENCHON, H. ÉTUDES DE SYNTAXE DES-
CRIPTIVE.
F.M. JENKINS, 545(RPH):FEB74-386
RENDELL, R. MURDER BEING ONCE DONE.
N. CALLENDAR, 441:27APR75-29
RENDELL, R. SHAKE HANDS FOREVER.
N. CALLENDAR, 441:23NOV75-52
M. LASKI, 362:5JUN75-748
RENDER, L.E. THE MOUNTAINS & THE
SKY.
K. BELL, 99:JUN75-39
RENDLEMAN, D.L. SIGNALS TO THE
BLIND.
C. ITZIN, 448:VOL13#2-101
RENEHAN, R. GREEK TEXTUAL CRITICISM.
H.S. LONG, 121(CJ):OCT/NOV72-84
RENEK, M. LAS VEGAS STRIP.
W. SCHOTT, 441:3AUG75-6
RENFREW, C., ED. BRITISH PREHISTORY.
N. HAMMOND, 617(TLS):14MAR75-282
RENFREW, C. THE EMERGENCE OF CIVIL-
ISATION.
M.S.F. HOOD, 303:VOL93-251
RENFREW, C., ED. THE EXPLANATION OF
CULTURAL CHANGE.
D.H. MELLOR, 111:FEB74-71
RENOIR, J. MY LIFE & MY FILMS.*
B. GILL, 442(NY):25AUG75-83
R. KOENIG, 231:JAN75-86

RENSON, J. LES DÉNOMINATIONS DU
VISAGE EN FRANÇAIS ET DANS LES
AUTRES LANGUES ROMANES.
G. JOCHNOWITZ, 660(WORD):DEC70-433
RENWICK, J., ED. LA DESTINÉE POST-
HUME DE JEAN-FRANÇOIS MARMONTEL
(1723-1799).
R.A. BROOKS, 207(FR):APR73-1012
R. MERCIER, 557(RSH):APR-JUN73-320
M.H. WADDICOR, 208(FS):OCT74-469
481(PQ):JUL73-554
RENWICK, J. - SEE MARMONTEL, J-F.
REPETTO, R.C. TIME IN INDIA'S DEV-
ELOPMENT PROGRAMMES.
A.W. HESTON, 293(JAST):NOV72-192
REPLOGLE, J. AUDEN'S POETRY.*
J.M. LUCCIONI, 189(EA):OCT:DEC73-
488
"REPORT ON TORTURE." [AMNESTY INTER-
NATIONAL]
D. MARTIN, 99:APR/MAY75-50
REPOSIANUS. REPOSIANO, "CONCUBITUS
MARTIS ET VENERIS." (U. ZUCCAREL-
LI, ED & TRANS)
P. LANGLOIS, 555:VOL47FASC2-309
REPPUCCI, G. QUESTIONARIO SU VERGA
E PIRANDELLO E PAGINE DI CRITICA.
G. PUGLIESE, 399(MLJ):DEC74-432
RESCHER, N. THE COHERENCE THEORY OF
TRUTH.
D. MC QUEEN, 518:JAN74-18
RESCHER, N. ESSAYS IN PHILOSOPHICAL
ANALYSIS.*
P. PARRINI, 548(RCSF):JAN-MAR73-
104
RESCHER, N., ED. THE LOGIC OF
DECISION & ACTION.
J.W. GARSON, 316:MAR73-135
RESCHER, N. THE PRIMACY OF PRAC-
TICE.*
E. TELFER, 518:OCT74-24
RESCHER, N. TEMPORAL MODALITIES IN
ARABIC LOGIC.
H. KAMP, 316:JUN73-325
RESCHER, N. WELFARE.*
C. BLAKE, 479(PHQ):OCT73-379
A. ROSENBERG, 154:MAR73-120
RESCHER, N. & M.E. MARMURA, EDS &
TRANS. THE REFUTATION BY ALEXANDER
OF APHRODISIAS OF GALEN'S TREATISE
ON THE THEORY OF MOTION.
M. MAHDI, 318(JAOS):JUL-SEP73-365
RESCHER, N. & A. URQUHART. TEMPORAL
LOGIC.*
P.L. MOTT, 393(MIND):JUL73-461
RESHETAR, J.S., JR. THE SOVIET
POLITY.*
B. HARASYMIW, 104:SUMMER73-278
RESHETOVSKAYA, N. SANYA.
R.R. LINGEMAN, 441:25AUG75-25
442(NY):11AUG75-86
RESTAK, R.M. PREMEDITATED MAN.
G. JONAS, 441:16NOV75-6
RESTALL, R.L. FINCHES & OTHER SEED-
EATING BIRDS.
617(TLS):31OCT75-1313
RESTAN, P. SINTAKSIS VOPROSITEL'-
NOGO PREDLOZHENIYA.
B. COMRIE, 575(SEER):JUL74-457
RÉTAT, P. LE DICTIONNAIRE DE BAYLE
ET LA LUTTE PHILOSOPHIQUE AU XVIIIE
SIÈCLE.
R. MORTIER, 549(RLC):JUL-SEP73-473
J. SOLÉ, 535(RHL):JAN-FEB73-131

REUTER, H.G. DIE LEHRE VOM RITTER-
STAND.*
  H. KOKOTT, 680(ZDP):BAND92HEFT3-
  454
REUTERSWÄRD, P. HIERONYMUS BOSCH.
  M.S. FRINTA, 54:MAR73-145
REVAULT D'ALLONNES, O. - SEE DENIS,
  M.
REVEL, J-F. ON PROUST.*
  L.D. JOINER, 207(FR):MAR73-842
REVERDIN, O. - SEE "ENTRETIENS SUR
L'ANTIQUITÉ CLASSIQUE"
REVERDY, P. SOURCES DU VENT [PRÉ-
CÉDÉ DE] LA BALLE AU BOND.
  R.W. GREENE, 207(FR):FEB73-668
REVERDY, P. LE VOLEUR DE TALAN.
FLAQUES DE VERRE.
  S. FAUCHEREAU, 98:APR73-375
REVOL, E.L. MUTACIONES BRUSCAS.
  G.R. MC MURRAY, 238:DEC73-1122
REXROTH, K. AMERICAN POETRY IN THE
TWENTIETH CENTURY.
  J. HARDIE, 295:FEB74-502
REXROTH, K. NEW POEMS.
  H. LEIBOWITZ, 441:23MAR75-2
REXROTH, K. THE REXROTH READER.
  J. GLOVER, 565:VOL14#1-63
REXROTH, K. & LING CHUNG, EDS &
TRANS. THE ORCHID BOAT.*
  V. YOUNG, 249(HUDR):AUTUMN74-417
REY, J-M. L'ENJEU DES SIGNES.
  E. ESCOUBAS, 98:JUN73-568
DEL REY, L., ED. FANTASTIC SCIENCE-
FICTION ART.
  G. JONAS, 441:14DEC75-29
REY, W.H. ARTHUR SCHNITZLER, "PRO-
FESSOR BERNHARDI."*
  M. SWALES, 220(GL&L):JAN74-163
REY-HERME, Y. - SEE PÉGUY, C. &
ALAIN-FOURNIER
REYBOLD, M. THE INSPECTOR'S OPINION.
  R. SHERRILL, 441:30NOV75-8
DE LOS REYES, R. AN ANALYSIS OF THE
DECORATIVE MOTIFS OF SOME PHILIP-
PINE CULTURAL MINORITIES. PHILIP-
PINE CERAMIC DESIGNS.
  LEE YU-LIN, 60:JAN-FEB74-54
REYNA, R. INTRODUCTION TO INDIAN
PHILOSOPHY.
  E. STEINKELLNER, 318(JAOS):JUL-SEP
  73-383
REYNOLDS, L.D. & N.G. WILSON.
SCRIBES & SCHOLARS.
  N. BARKER, 617(TLS):15AUG75-927
RHEES, R. DISCUSSIONS OF WITTGEN-
STEIN.*
  A. MANSER, 393(MIND):APR73-298
RHEIN, P.H. ALBERT CAMUS.*
  D.H. MORRIS 4TH, 577(SHR):WINTER
  73-103
RHINE, L.E. MIND OVER MATTER.
  G. WILLIAMS, 484(PPR):SEP73-115
RHINEHART, L. MATARI.
  W. FEAVER, 617(TLS):7FEB75-129
RHODES, A. PRINCES OF THE GRAPE.
  E.S. TURNER, 362:14AUG75-220
RHODES, D. CLAY & GLAZES FOR THE
POTTER. (REV)
  J. TROY, 139:JUN73-58
RHODES, E.H. THE PRINCE OF CENTRAL
PARK.
  M. LEVIN, 441:16FEB75-12

RHODES, P.J. THE ATHENIAN BOULE.
  J.A.O. LARSEN, 122:JUL74-229
  R.E. WYCHERLEY, 303:VOL93-255
RHOODIE, N.J., ED. SOUTH AFRICAN
DIALOGUE.
  K. GLASER, 396(MODA):SUMMER74-309
RHYS, J. QUATUOR.
  A. FABRE-LUCE, 98:JUL73-674
RHYS, J. TIGERS ARE BETTER-LOOK-
ING.*
  R. TYLER, 61:JAN75-81
DE RIBADENEIRA, M. HISTORIA DEL
ARCHIPIELAGO Y OTROS REYNOS.
  J.L. PHELAN, 293(JAST):FEB73-381
RIBBANS, G. NIEBLA Y SOLEDAD.*
  J. LÓPEZ-MORILLAS, 402(MLR):JAN74-
  206
  D.L. SHAW, 86(BHS):JAN73-100
RIBBANS, G. - SEE MACHADO, A.
RIBBAT, E. DIE WAHRHEIT DES LEBENS
IM FRÜHEN WERK ALFRED DÖBLINS.*
  G.C. AVERY, 400(MLN):APR73-646
RIBIERO, D. THE AMERICAS & CIVILI-
ZATION.
  J.E. BACHMAN, 37:JUN-JUL73-38
RIBNER, I. WILLIAM SHAKESPEARE.
  A. YAMADA, 570(SQ):SPRING73-231
RIBNER, I. & G.L. KITTREDGE - SEE
SHAKESPEARE, W.
RICARDOU, J. LA PRISE/PROSE DE
CONSTANTINOPLE.
  D.B. RICE, 268:JUL75-106
RICATTE, R. & OTHERS - SEE GIONO, J.
RICATTE, R., WITH P. CITRON & L.
RICATTE - SEE GIONO, J.
RICCARDI, T., JR. A NEPALI VERSION
OF THE VETĀLAPAÑCAVIMŚATI.
  L.A. SCHWARZSCHILD, 318(JAOS):
  OCT-DEC73-615
DE' RICCI, G. CRONACA (1532-1606).
(G. SAPORI, ED)
  M.P., 228(GSLI):VOL150FASC470/471-
  472
RICCI, J. LOS MANIÁTICOS.
  H.E. LEWALD, 241:JAN73-91
RICE, C.D. THE RISE & FALL OF BLACK
SLAVERY.
  442(NY):11AUG75-87
RICE, C.E. AUTHORITY & REBELLION.
  B. DE MARGERIE, 613:SUMMER73-312
RICE, D. & T.T. ICONS & THEIR DAT-
ING.
  R. CORMACK, 617(TLS):14FEB75-174
RICE, D. & T.T. ICONS & THEIR HIS-
TORY.
  P. BROWN & S. MAC CORMACK, 453:
  20FEB75-19
RICE, E.F., JR., ED. THE PREFATORY
EPISTLES OF JACQUES LEFÈVRE D'ETA-
PLES & RELATED TEXTS.
  D. STONE, JR., 207(FR):MAY73-1219
RICE, T.T. ELIZABETH.
  M. RAEFF, 104:SPRING73-122
RICE, V. - SEE BUTLER, B.C.
RICH, A. DIVING INTO THE WRECK.*
  M.G. PERLOFF, 659:WINTER75-84
  J.K. ROBINSON, 598(SOR):SUMMER75-
  668
  P. SAVERY, 181:AUTUMN73-120
RICH, A. POEMS.
  W. CLEMONS, 441:27APR75-5
RICH, A. THE WILL TO CHANGE.
  T. EAGLETON, 565:VOL14#3-66

RICHARD, F.S. HISPANOAMÉRICA MOD-
ERNA.
J.L. WALKER, 238:SEP73-744
RICHARD, J-P. ÉTUDES SUR LE ROMAN-
TISME.
L. CELLIER, 535(RHL):SEP-OCT73-914
RICHARDS, D.A. THE COMING OF WIN-
TER.*
M. BAXTER, 99:DEC75/JAN76-48
R. GIBBS, 296:VOL4#3-166
D. WATMOUGH, 198:WINTER75-121
RICHARDS, D.A.J. A THEORY OF REAS-
ONS FOR ACTION.
P. DUBOIS, 542:OCT-DEC73-494
A. GEWIRTH, 479(PHQ):APR73-182
G.R. GRICE, 482(PHR):JAN74-139
J. NARVESON, 154:MAR73-116
J. WILLIAMSON, 393(MIND):APR73-309
J.W. YOLTON, 488:MAR73-81
RICHARDS, E. THE LEVIATHAN OF
WEALTH.
F.C. MATHER, 637(VS):JUN74-446
RICHARDS, I.A. BEYOND.*
J.P. RUSSO, 617(TLS):2MAY75-480
RICHARDS, I.A. INTERNAL COLLOQUIES.
H. SERGEANT, 175:SUMMER72-75
RICHARDS, I.A. POETRIES.
R. JAKOBSON, 617(TLS):5SEP75-985
RICHARDS, J. & M. POLIQUIN. ENGLISH
THROUGH SONGS.
J.M. DOBSON, 399(MLJ):DEC73-443
RICHARDS, J.M. & N. PEVSNER, EDS.
THE ANTI-RATIONALISTS. [SEE ALSO
WITH EDS REVERSED]
B. READ, 135:NOV73-220
RICHARDS, J.O. PARTY PROPAGANDA UN-
DER QUEEN ANNE.*
H.L. SNYDER, 481(PQ):JUL73-367
RICHARDS, K. & P. THOMSON, EDS. THE
EIGHTEENTH-CENTURY ENGLISH STAGE.*
C.J. RAWSON, 175:SUMMER73-76
P. ROGERS, 148:SUMMER73-187
RICHARDS, K. & P. THOMSON, COMPS.
ESSAYS ON NINETEENTH CENTURY BRIT-
ISH THEATRE.*
E.A. LANGHANS, 570(SQ):AUTUMN73-
481
R. LAWRENCE, 175:SPRING72-32
RICHARDS, M.K. ELLEN GLASGOW'S
DEVELOPMENT AS A NOVELIST.
295:FEB74-621
RICHARDS, S.R., ED. SECRET WRITING
IN THE PUBLIC RECORDS.
J. CARSWELL, 617(TLS):21FEB75-192
RICHARDSON, A. & OTHERS. OUR SECU-
LAR CATHEDRALS.
R. BUFFINGTON, 569(SR):WINTER74-
147
RICHARDSON, A.H., WITH A.S.L. BARNES.
CONSERVATION BY THE PEOPLE.
H.V. NELLES, 99:JUN75-45
RICHARDSON, D.H.S. THE VANISHING
LICHENS.
L. NEWTON, 617(TLS):7MAR75-258
RICHARDSON, J. ENID STARKIE.*
639(VQR):SUMMER74-XCII
RICHARDSON, J. STENDHAL.*
V.S. PRITCHETT, 442(NY):27JAN75-99
G. STRICKLAND, 617(TLS):21FEB75-
198
RICHARDSON, J. VERLAINE.
A.W. RAITT, 402(MLR):JUL74-646
L.A.M. SUMBERG, 207(FR):FEB73-618

RICHARDSON, J.B. METAL MINING.
K. DUNHAM, 617(TLS):14FEB75-175
RICHARDSON, S. PAMELA.
B. RUDDICK, 148:WINTER73-378
RICHARZ, M. DER EINTRITT DER JUDEN
IN DIE AKADEMISCHEN BERUFE.
R. HAUSWIRTH, 182:VOL26#20-707
RICHER, J. LES MANUSCRITS D'"AUR-
ELIA" DE GÉRARD DE NERVAL.
M. FRANÇON, 207(FR):MAR73-834
RICHER, J. NERVAL AU ROYAUME DES
ARCHÉTYPES.
W. BEAUCHAMP, 546(RR):MAY73-219
M. BOWIE, 208(FS):JUL74-339
RICHER, J., ED. NERVAL PAR LES
TÉMOINS DE SA VIE.
B. JUDEN, 208(FS):JAN74-93
T. MARCH, 207(FR):OCT72-161
M. SCHAETTEL, 557(RSH):APR-JUN73-
321
RICHER, J. - SEE DE NERVAL, G.
RICHIE, D. OZU.
E. RHODE, 617(TLS):28FEB75-227
M. WOOD, 453:12JUN75-36
RICHIE, M. LOVING UPWARD.
M. LEVIN, 441:30NOV75-62
RICHLER, M. SHOVELLING TROUBLE.*
D. FETHERLING, 102(CANL):SUMMER73-
118
E. WATERSTON, 255(HAB):SPRING73-
150
RICHLER, M. THE STREET.*
N.L. MAGID, 441:5OCT75-6
442(NY):17NOV75-195
RICHMAN, B. & R. FARMER. LEADERSHIP
GOALS & POWER IN HIGHER EDUCATION.
H. CROWE, 99:APR/MAY75-17
RICHMOND, H.M. SHAKESPEARE'S SEXUAL
COMEDY.*
T.W. CRAIK, 551(RENQ):SUMMER73-231
G. SALGÁDO, 677:VOL4-270
RICHTER, D.H. FABLE'S END.
M. IRWIN, 617(TLS):7NOV75-1329
RICHTER, G.M.A. KOUROI.* (3RD ED)
J. MAXMIN, 5:VOL1#4-740
RICHTER, G.M.A. PERSPECTIVE IN
GREEK & ROMAN ART.
J. BOARDMAN, 447(N&Q):JAN73-40
RICHTER, H. GRIECHENLAND ZWISCHEN
REVOLUTION UND KONTERREVOLUTION
(1936-1946).
R. CLOGG, 617(TLS):14NOV75-1362
RICHTER, H. GRUNDSÄTZE UND SYSTEM
DER TRANSKRIPTION -IPA(G)-.
E.H. YARRILL, 182:VOL26#21/22-793
RICHTER, H. VIRGINIA WOOLF.*
J. GUIGUET, 189(EA):JUL-SEP73-338
F. STADTFELD, 38:BAND91HEFT4-553
"HANS RICHTER BY HANS RICHTER."*
(C. GRAY, ED)
A. WINDSOR, 89(BJA):AUTUMN73-418
RICHTER, J.P. - SEE LEONARDO DA
VINCI
RICHTER, K. LITERATUR UND NATUR-
WISSENSCHAFT.
T.K. THAYER, 481(PQ):JUL73-448
RICHTER, M. GIRALDUS CAMBRENSIS,
THE GROWTH OF THE WELSH NATION.
J.C. RUSSELL, 589:OCT74-754
VON RICHTHOFEN, E. NUEVOS ESTUDIOS
ÉPICOS MEDIEVALES.
M. CHAPLIN, 240(HR):SPRING73-425

VON RICHTHOFEN, E. TRADICIONALISMO
ÉPICO NOVELESCO.
R.B. TATE, 402(MLR):JUL74-670
RICHTMAN, J. ADRIENNE LECOUVREUR.
A. CAPRIO, 207(FR):OCT72-181
RICKARD, C. FIGHTING TUSCARORA.
(B. GRAYMONT, ED)
G.A. BAILEY, 377:NOV74-184
RICKARD, P. - SEE PESSOA, F.
RICKARDS, M. BANNED POSTERS.
R. LEVIN, 73:FALL73-44
RICKMAN, G. ROMAN GRANARIES &
STORE BUILDINGS.*
J.K. ANDERSON, 122:JUL73-234
P. SALWAY, 123:MAR74-116
RICKS, C. TENNYSON.*
J.D. JUMP, 148:AUTUMN72-285
J. KILLHAM, 677:VOL4-318
B.C. SOUTHAM, 541(RES):NOV73-505
G. THOMAS, 175:SPRING73-32
RICKWORD, E. ESSAYS & OPINIONS
1921-31. (A. YOUNG, ED)
E. FEINSTEIN, 362:1MAY75-590
RICO, F. ALFONSO EL SABIO Y LA
GENERAL ESTORIA.
617(TLS):23MAY75-573
RICO, F. LA NOVELA PICARESCA Y EL
PUNTO DE VISTA.*
O.H. GREEN, 240(HR):SPRING73-436
RICO, F. EL PEQUEÑO MUNDO DEL
HOMBRE.*
J.R. CHATHAM, 238:MAY73-498
O.H. GREEN, 240(HR):SPRING73-434
RICOEUR, P. LA MÉTAPHORE VIVE.
G. STEINER, 617(TLS):1AUG75-879
RICOU, L. VERTICAL MAN/HORIZONTAL
WORLD.
H. KREISEL, 102(CANL):SUMMER74-88
E. THOMPSON, 99:JUL75-38
RIDDEL, J.N. THE INVERTED BELL.
L.W. WAGNER, 659:SUMMER75-378
RIDDLE, A. A SINGER & HER SONGS.
(R.D. ABRAHAMS & G. FOSS, EDS)
C.W. JOYNER, 292(JAF):JUL-SEP73-
300
RIDER, A. A SAFE PLACE.
M. LEVIN, 441:6APR75-14
RIDER, F. THE DIALECTIC OF SELF-
HOOD IN MONTAIGNE.
R.L. GILLIN, 568(SCN):FALL74-60
G.P. NORTON, 141:SPRING74-170
S.F.R., 131(CL):WINTER74-91
RIDGWAY, R.S. VOLTAIRE & SENSIBIL-
ITY.
J. GRAY, 150(DR):WINTER73/74-777
W.E. REX, 401(MLQ):SEP74-324
RIDING, L. SELECTED POEMS.
J. ATLAS, 491:FEB75-295
P. AUSTER, 453:7AUG75-36
RIDLER, A. SOME TIME AFTER.
A. CLUYSENAAR, 565:VOL14#1-70
H. SERGEANT, 175:AUTUMN73-121
RIDLEY, J. GARIBALDI.*
R. MITCHISON, 362:2JAN75-27
RIDLEY, J. LORD PALMERSTON.*
R. BULLEN, 325:APR73-618
RIDLEY, M. FAR EASTERN ANTIQUI-
TIES.*
A.J.B. KIDDEL, 463:SUMMER73-204
RIECK, W. JOHANN CHRISTOPH GOTT-
SCHED.
R.P. BAREIKIS, 481(PQ):JUL73-518

RIEDEL, F.J. BRIEFE UBER DAS PUB-
LIKUM. (E. FELDMEIER, ED)
R.R. HEITNER, 301(JEGP):JUL74-401
RIEFENSTAHL, L. THE LAST OF THE
NUBA.*
S. SONTAG, 453:6FEB75-23
RIEFF, P. FELLOW TEACHERS.
F. KERMODE, 617(TLS):13JUN75-638
RIEGER, L. ON THE CONSISTENCY OF
THE GENERALIZED CONTINUUM HYPOTHE-
SIS.
F.R. DRAKE, 316:MAR73-153
VON RIEKHOFF, H. GERMAN-POLISH RE-
LATIONS, 1918-1933.*
V. MASTNY, 104:SPRING74-160
DE RIENCOURT, A. SEX & POWER IN
HISTORY.
E. BADIAN, 453:30OCT75-28
RIESENHUBER, K. DIE TRANSZENDENZ
DER FREIHEIT ZUM GUTEN.
F. PÉREZ RUÍZ, 258:MAR73-144
RIESS, F. THE WORD & THE STONE.
J. LÓPEZ-PACHECO, 255(HAB):SUMMER
73-216
RIESZ, J. DIE SESTINE.
W. MÖNCH, 52:BAND8HEFT2-196
RIEWALD, J.G. REYNIER JANSEN OF
PHILADELPHIA.
T.A. BIRRELL, 433:JUL73-312
J.T. FLANAGAN, 179(ES):OCT72-465
RIEWALD, J.G., ED. THE SURPRISE OF
EXCELLENCE.
S. MONOD, 617(TLS):29AUG75-963
RIFFATERRE, H.B. L'ORPHISME DANS
LA POÉSIE ROMANTIQUE.*
B. JUDEN, 208(FS):APR74-206
RIFFATERRE, M. ESSAIS DE STYLIS-
TIQUE STRUCTURALE.* (D. DELAS, ED
& TRANS)
A. LORIAN, 545(RPH):FEB74-381
M. PIRON, 209(FM):JAN73-77
RIFKIN, S. MC QUAID.*
N. CALLENDAR, 441:27JUL75-18
RIGBY, A. COMMUNES IN BRITAIN.
A. CURLE, 617(TLS):21FEB75-203
RIGGS, D. SHAKESPEARE'S HEROICAL
HISTORIES.*
R.A. FOAKES, 175:SUMMER72-67
R.E. MC GUGAN, 570(SQ):AUTUMN73-
473
J.C. MAXWELL, 447(N&Q):APR73-152
RIGGS, W.G. THE CHRISTIAN POET IN
"PARADISE LOST."*
L. BABB, 141:FALL73-380
J. WEBBER, 301(JEGP):JAN74-124
RIGHINI, V. LINEAMENTI DI STORIA
ECONOMICA DELLA GALLIA CISALPINA.*
G. RICKMAN, 313:VOL63-284
RIGOLOT, F. LES LANGAGES DE RABEL-
AIS.
D. COLEMAN, 208(FS):OCT74-445
V.E. GRAHAM, 207(FR):APR73-1005
RIHA, K. CROSS-READING & CROSS-
TALKING.
R.W. LAST, 402(MLR):JAN74-228
RIIS, J. ALEXANDER L. KIELLAND.
G.C. SCHOOLFIELD, 563(SS):SUMMER
74-297
RIKER, T. & H. ROTTENBERG. THE
GARDENER'S CATALOGUE.
J. CANADAY, 441:13APR75-16
RILEY, P. THE POLITICAL WRITINGS OF
LEIBNIZ.
J. HOSTLER, 483:OCT73-406

RILKE, R.M. DAS TESTAMENT. (E.
ZINN, ED)
    I. PARRY, 617(TLS):16MAY75-541
RILOVA, A.C. & D. SUTHERLAND - SEE
UNDER CENTENO Y RILOVA, A. & D.
SUTHERLAND
RIMBAUD, A. COMPLETE WORKS. (P.
SCHMIDT, TRANS)
    F. BROWN, 231:JUN75-93
RIMBAUD, A. OEUVRES COMPLÈTES. (A.
ADAM, ED)
    M. SCHAETTEL, 557(RSH):JAN-MAR73-
    174
RIMBAUD, A. A SEASON IN HELL [&]
THE ILLUMINATIONS.* (E.R. PESCHEL,
TRANS)
    V.A. LA CHARITÉ, 446:SPRING-SUMMER
    74-198
RIMER, J.T. TOWARDS A MODERN JAPAN-
ESE THEATRE.
    639(VQR):AUTUMN74-CXXVII
RIMINI, R. LA MORTE NEL SALOTTO.
    F. DONINI, 617(TLS):10OCT75-1202
RIMMER, R. THE PREMAR EXPERIMENTS.
    M. LEVIN, 441:28SEP75-37
RINALDI, A. LA MAISON DES ATLANTES.
    E. ZANTS, 207(FR):MAR73-865
RING, E. UP THE COCKNEYS.
    E.S. TURNER, 362:13FEB75-219
RINGE, D.A. THE PICTORIAL MODE.*
    F.M. COLLINS, 594:SPRING73-145
RINK, H. TALES & TRADITIONS OF THE
ESKIMO. DANISH GREENLAND.
    G. JONES, 617(TLS):9MAY75-516
RINSER, L. GRENZÜBERGÄNGE.
    P. PROCHNIK, 617(TLS):25JUL75-855
RINSLER, N. GÉRARD DE NERVAL.
    R. CHAMBERS, 67:MAY74-114
    A. FAIRLIE, 208(FS):APR74-217
RINSLER, N. - SEE DE NERVAL, G.
VON RINTELEN, F-J. CONTEMPORARY GER-
MAN PHILOSOPHY & ITS BACKGROUND.*
    M.S. FRINGS, 321:WINTER73-313
VON RINTELEN, F-J. VALUES IN EURO-
PEAN THOUGHT I.
    C.E. SCHUETZINGER, 484(PPR):DEC73-
    291
    W. TEICHNER, 536:DEC73-346
    W.H. WERKMEISTER, 319:OCT75-546
DEL RÍO, D.A. PÁGINAS DE GLORIA.
    A.A. CARSON, 37:MAR73-39
DE DEL RÍO, E.A., ED. FLORES DEL
ROMANCERO.
    C. SMITH, 240(HR):SUMMER73-559
DE LOS RÍOS, C.A. - SEE UNDER ALONSO
DE LOS RÍOS, C.
DE LOS RÍOS, G.G., A.I. NOLFI & L.K.
NOLFI - SEE UNDER GINER DE LOS
RÍOS, G., A.I. NOLFI & L.K. NOLFI
RIPOLL, C. ARCHIVO JOSÉ MARTÍ. ÍN-
DICE UNIVERSAL DE LA OBRA DE JOSÉ
MARTÍ. "PATRIA:" EL PERIÓDICO DE
JOSÉ MARTÍ; REGISTRO GENERAL, 1892-
1895.
    E. ARDURA, 263:APR-JUN74-168
RIPOSATI, B. M. TERENTI VARRONIS
"DE UITA POPULI ROMANI."
    J. ANDRÉ, 555:VOL47FASC2-349
DE RIQUER, M. GUILLEM DE BERGUEDÀ.
    T.G. BERGIN, 589:APR74-327
    T. NEWCOMBE, 402(MLR):OCT74-864
    F.J. OROZ ARIZCUREN, 72:BAND211
    HEFT1/3-206
    L.T. TOPSFIELD, 208(FS):JUL74-312

RIS, R. DAS ADJEKTIV "REICH" IM
MITTELALTERLICHEN DEUTSCH.
    D.H. GREEN, 402(MLR):JAN74-215
RISATTI, H. NEW MUSIC VOCABULARY.
    R. MACONIE, 617(TLS):7NOV75-1336
RIST, J.M. EPICURUS, AN INTRODUC-
TION.*
    E. ASMIS, 482(PHR):JUL74-413
    W.A.F., 543:MAR73-545
    P.M. HUBY, 479(PHQ):JUL73-260
    J. JOPE, 124:NOV73-118
RIST, J.M. STOIC PHILOSOPHY.*
    P. DE LACY, 121(CJ):DEC72/JAN73-
    185
RISTAT, J. DU COUP D'ETAT EN LIT-
TÉRATURE.
    M. PIERSSENS, 207(FR):MAR73-866
RISTOW, W.W., COMP. À LA CARTE.
    J.M. KINNEY, 14:OCT73-560
RITCHIE, C. THE SIREN YEARS.*
    A. FORBES, 617(TLS):21FEB75-189
RITCHIE, J.M. - SEE STORM, T.
RITSOS, Y. GESTURES.*
    A. CLUYSENAAR, 565:VOL14#1-70
RITSOS, Y. SELECTED POEMS.
    P. LEVI, 617(TLS):18JUL75-809
RITTER, E.F. JOHANN BAPTIST VON
ALXINGER & THE AUSTRIAN ENLIGHTEN-
MENT.
    J.A.A. TER HAAR, 221(GQ):SEP73-153
RITTER, G.A., ED. GESELLSCHAFT,
PARLAMENT UND REGIERUNG.
    P. PULZER, 617(TLS):12SEP75-1028
RITTER, J. HEGEL ET LA RÉVOLUTION
FRANÇAISE.
    R.J.G., 543:DEC72-365
RITTERS, C. PÄDAGOGIK UND INTER-
NATIONALE BEGEGNUNG.
    W. CANZIANI, 182:VOL26#7/8-200
RITTNER, F. DIE WERDENDE JURIS-
TISCHE PERSON.
    R. GANGHOFFER, 182:VOL26#21/22-788
DE LA RIVA, B. - SEE UNDER BONVESIN
DE LA RIVA
RIVAS, H.G. - SEE UNDER GARCÍA
RIVAS, H.
RIVERA, T. "... Y NO SE LO TRAGÓ
LA TIERRA."
    W.H. GONZÁLEZ, 399(MLJ):APR73-229
RIVERO, E.S. EL GRAN AMOR DE PABLO
NERUDA.
    T.A. PÉREZ, 238:DEC73-1123
    F.T. RIESS, 86(BHS):JUL73-322
RIVERS, I. THE POETRY OF CONSERVA-
TISM 1600-1745.*
    C.J. RAWSON, 175:AUTUMN73-116
RIVERS, W.M. SPEAKING IN MANY
TONGUES.
    E.G. JOINER, 399(MLJ):SEP-OCT74-
    269
RIVERS, W.N., J.R. MATHEUS & M.
BELATECHE - SEE DUMAS, A.
RIVETT, R. DAVID RIVETT.
    F.M. BURNET, 381:MAR73-97
RIVIÈRE, C. L'OBJET SOCIAL.
    D. MERLLIÉ, 542:JAN-MAR73-61
RIVIÈRE, P. I, PIERRE RIVIÈRE, HAV-
ING SLAUGHTERED MY MOTHER, MY SIS-
TER, & MY BROTHER...* (FRENCH
TITLE: MOI, PIERRE RIVIÈRE, AYANT
ÉGORGÉ MA MÈRE, MA SOEUR ET MON
FRÈRE...) (M. FOUCAULT, ED)
    P. DELANY, 441:18MAY75-31

RIVKIN, E. THE SHAPING OF JEWISH
HISTORY.
  Y. SHAMIR, 352(LE&W):VOL16#3-1091
DE RIVOYRE, C. BOY.*
  A. GOTTLIEB, 441:5JAN75-12
RIX, B. MY FARCE FROM MY ELBOW.
  N. SHRAPNEL, 617(TLS):19DEC75-1506
RIZESCU, I. PRAVILA RITORULUI
LUCACI.
  H. STEIN, 260(IF):BAND78-304
RIZZA, C. THÉOPHILE GAUTIER,
CRITICO LETTERARIO.*
  G. HAINSWORTH, 208(FS):JAN74-94
  W. LEINER, 207(FR):DEC72-414
RIZZO, F.P. LA REPUBBLICA DI SIRA-
CUSA NEL MOMENTO DI DUCEZIO.
  J. BRISCOE, 123:NOV74-245
RIZZO, J.J. ISAAK SEBASTOKRATOR'S
"PERI TĒS TŌN KAKŌN HYPOSTASEŌS"
(DE MALORUM SUBSISTENTIA).
  D.M. NICOL, 123:MAR74-136
RIZZO, S. IL LESSICO FILOLOGICO
DEGLI UMANISTI.
  G. TOURNOY-THOEN, 568(SCN):WINTER
  74-100
RIZZUTO, A. STYLE & THEME IN REV-
ERDY'S "LES ARDOISES DU TOIT."*
  R.L. ADMUSSEN, 599:SPRING73-227
  P. BROOME, 208(FS):JAN74-106
  G.D. MARTIN, 402(MLR):APR74-422
ROA BASTOS, A. YO EL SUPREMO.
  J. FRANCO, 617(TLS):15AUG75-925
ROACH, H. BLACK AMERICAN MUSIC.
  I.V. JACKSON-BROWN, 187:SEP75-490
ROACH, W., ED. THE CONTINUATIONS
OF THE OLD FRENCH "PERCEVAL" OF
CHRÉTIEN DE TROYES. (VOL 4)
  A.W. THOMPSON, 589:JAN74-143
  B. WOLEDGE, 402(MLR):JUL74-635
ROACHE, J.H. RICHARD EBERHART.*
  R.J. FEIN, 295:FEB74-583
ROADARMEL, G.C., ED & TRANS. A
DEATH IN DELHI.
  C. COPPOLA, 293(JAST):AUG73-726
  S.M. POULOS, 352(LE&W):VOL16#3-
  1077
ROAZEN, P. FREUD & HIS FOLLOWERS.
  R. COLES, 442(NY):14JUL75-96
  W. GASS, 453:17APR75-3 [& CONT IN]
  453:15MAY75-9
  N.G. HALE, JR., 441:12JAN75-23
  C. HANLY, 99:DEC75/JAN76-58
  C. LEHMANN-HAUPT, 441:21JAN75-37
ROBBINS, J.A. - SEE HICKS, G.
ROBE, S.L. AMAPA STORYTELLERS.
  J.R. REYNA, 292(JAF):OCT-DEC73-408
ROBE, S.L. MEXICAN TALES & LEGENDS
FROM VERACRUZ.
  T.L. HANSEN, 292(JAF):JAN-MAR73-81
ROBERT OF FLAMBOROUGH. LIBER POENI-
TENTIALIS.* (J.J.F. FIRTH, ED)
  S. WENZEL, 382(MAE):1974/1-50
ROBERT, J-C. DU CANADA FRANÇAIS AU
QUÉBEC LIBRE.
  G. WOODCOCK, 617(TLS):10OCT75-1188
ROBERT, M. - SEE KAFKA, F.
ROBERTS, B. THE ZULU KINGS.
  P. ADAMS, 61:JUN75-95
  A. WHITMAN, 441:20JUL75-20
ROBERTS, C. THE PLEASANT YEARS:
1947-1972.
  M. BISHOP, 617(TLS):3JAN75-18

ROBERTS, C.G.D. THE HEART OF THE
ANCIENT WOOD.
  T. MURRAY, 296:VOL4#3-158
ROBERTS, C.G.D. SELECTED POETRY &
CRITICAL PROSE. (W.J. KEITH, ED)
  G. WOODCOCK, 102(CANL):SUMMER74-
  113
ROBERTS, D. ARTISTIC CONSCIOUSNESS
& POLITICAL CONSCIENCE.*
  U. WEISSTEIN, 564:JUN73-163
ROBERTS, G. TEMAS EXISTENCIALES EN
LA NOVELA ESPAÑOLA DE POSTGUERRA.
  R.A. CARDWELL, 402(MLR):JUL74-687
ROBERTS, J. THE JUDAS SHEEP.
  N. CALLENDAR, 441:13APR75-30
ROBERTS, J.M. THE MYTHOLOGY OF THE
SECRET SOCIETIES.*
  S.W. JACKMAN, 481(PQ):JUL73-401
  B. JUDEN, 402(MLR):JAN74-183
ROBERTS, K. THE CHALK GIANTS.*
  G. JONAS, 441:14SEP75-22
ROBERTS, L. SANG BRANCH SETTLERS.
  S. WOODRUFF, 187:SEP75-497
ROBERTS, M. MACARTNEY IN RUSSIA.
  I. DE MADARIAGA, 617(TLS):4JUL75-
  716
ROBERTS, M. THE TRADITION OF ROMAN-
TIC MORALITY.
  G.W. SPENCE, 67:MAY74-94
  G. THOMAS, 175:AUTUMN73-118
ROBERTS, N. GEORGE ELIOT.
  J. SEARLE, 617(TLS):3OCT75-1161
ROBERTS, P. THE PSYCHOLOGY OF
TRAGIC DRAMA.
  A. STORR, 617(TLS):6JUN75-616
ROBERTS, P. THEATRE IN BRITAIN.
  W. LUCAS, 157:WINTER73-92
ROBERTS, P. - SEE HAMILTON, D.
ROBERTS, T.J. WHEN IS SOMETHING
FICTION?
  E.S. RABKIN, 454:SPRING74-271
  P. STEVICK, 131(CL):SPRING73-175
ROBERTS, V.M. THE NATURE OF THE
THEATRE.
  C.W. BRADFORD, 583:FALL73-99
ROBERTS, W.D. WHITE JADE.
  M. LEVIN, 441:8JUN75-20
ROBERTSON, C. BATH.
  617(TLS):21NOV75-1397
ROBERTSON, D. SEA SURVIVAL.
  617(TLS):21FEB75-204
ROBERTSON, H. RESERVATIONS ARE FOR
INDIANS.
  102(CANL):AUTUMN73-116
ROBERTSON, H. SALT OF THE EARTH.
  C. BERGER, 99:MAR75-37
ROBERTSON, I., ED. THE BLUE GUIDE
TO SPAIN.
  T. LAMBERT, 617(TLS):30MAY75-606
ROBERTSON, J. PROFIT OR PEOPLE?
  J.D. WOOD, 617(TLS):18APR75-433
ROBERTSON, J. - SEE SIDNEY, P.
ROBERTSON, J. & J. LEWALLEN, EDS.
THE GRASS ROOTS PRIMER.
  J. UNDERWOOD, 441:14DEC75-6
ROBILLARD, R. EARLE BIRNEY.
  C. THOMAS, 102(CANL):SPRING73-103
ROBIN, M. THE RUSH FOR SPOILS.
  102(CANL):AUTUMN73-116
ROBINETTE, G.O. PLANTS/PEOPLE/&
ENVIRONMENTAL QUALITY.
  45:MAY73-87

ROBINSON, C. & R.H. BLETTER. SKY-
SCRAPER STYLE.
W. FEAVER, 362:26JUN75-852
P. GOLDBERGER, 441:2MAR75-6
ROBINSON, E.A.G. & K. GRIFFIN, EDS.
THE ECONOMIC DEVELOPMENT OF BANGLA-
DESH WITHIN A SOCIALIST FRAMEWORK.
A.R. KHAN, 617(TLS):23MAY75-563
ROBINSON, F.G. THE SHAPE OF THINGS
KNOWN.
R.J. BAUER, 568(SCN):SPRING-SUMMER
74-18
A.C. HAMILTON, 529(QQ):SPRING73-
132
N. LEVINE, 551(RENQ):AUTUMN73-359
G.A.E. PARFITT, 89(BJA):SUMMER73-
303
ROBINSON, F.W. & S.G. NICHOLS, JR.,
EDS. THE MEANING OF MANNERISM.
M. WEITZ, 207(FR):MAR73-822
ROBINSON, G.J. - SEE LUKIĆ, S.
ROBINSON, I. CHAUCER & THE ENGLISH
TRADITION.*
P.G. BEIDLER, 276:AUTUMN73-446
D. DAVIE, 184(EIC):OCT72-429
E.T. DONALDSON, 405(MP):MAY74-413
D.K. FRY, 191(ELN):DEC73-123
B. HUPPÉ, 141:WINTER73-69
D. MEHL, 38:BAND91HEFT2-252
M. RIGBY, 541(RES):AUG73-321
R.M. WILSON, 175:AUTUMN72-106
ROBINSON, I. CHAUCER'S PROSODY.*
H. BOYD, 180(ESA):SEP73-106
D.K. FRY, 191(ELN):DEC73-123
C.A. OWEN, JR., 589:JAN74-148
K.C. PHILLIPPS, 179(ES):JUN73-272
ROBINSON, I. THE NEW GRAMMARIANS'
FUNERAL.
J. SEARLE, 617(TLS):21NOV75-1377
ROBINSON, I. THE SURVIVAL OF ENG-
LISH.
B. BERGONZI, 249(HUDR):SPRING74-
140
483:OCT73-409
ROBINSON, J. THE LIFE & TIMES OF
FRANCIE NICHOL OF SOUTH SHIELDS.
F. PICKERING, 617(TLS):25JUL75-833
ROBINSON, J. - SEE VALÉRY, P.
ROBINSON, J. & J. EATWELL. AN IN-
TRODUCTION TO MODERN ECONOMICS.*
M. KING, 111:26OCT73-23
ROBINSON, J.O., COMP. AN ANNOTATED
BIBLIOGRAPHY OF MODERN LANGUAGE
TEACHING.*
J.R. MC KAY, 206:NOV73-599
ROBERTSON, M. & A. FRANTZ. THE PAR-
THENON FRIEZE.
P. LEVI, 617(TLS):6JUN75-618
ROBINSON, T. THE SCHOOL OF MUSICKE
(1603).* (D. LUMSDEN, ED)
J. HAAR, 551(RENQ):AUTUMN73-332
ROBINSON, W.P. RESTRICTED CODES IN
SOCIO-LINGUISTICS & THE SOCIOLOGY
OF EDUCATION.
315(JAL):VOL11PT2-100
DE LA ROBRIE, J. GALERIE DES CHATS
ILLUSTRES.
H. GODIN, 208(FS):APR74-243
ROBRIEUX, P. MAURICE THOREZ.
D. JOHNSON, 617(TLS):22AUG75-942
ROBSON, J.M. - SEE MILL, J.S.

ROBSON, S.O., ED & TRANS. WANGBANG
WIDEYA, A JAVANESE PANJI ROMANCE.
J.M. ECHOLS, 318(JAOS):OCT-DEC73-
623
ROBSON, W.W. MODERN ENGLISH LITERA-
TURE.
F. MC COMBIE, 447(N&Q):MAR73-119
ROBY, K. THE KING, THE PRESS & THE
PEOPLE.
J. GRIGG, 362:27MAR75-419
ROBY, K.E. A WRITER AT WAR.*
O. BROOMFIELD, 150(DR):AUTUMN73-
591
J.G. KENNEDY, 177(ELT):VOL16#2-143
DA ROCHA PEREIRA, M.H. TEMAS CLÁS-
SICOS NA POESIA PORTUGUESA.
G.R. LIND, 72:BAND211HEFT3/6-471
ROCHE, M. PHENOMENOLOGY, LANGUAGE &
THE SOCIAL SCIENCES.
W. MAYS, 518:JAN74-21
ROCHE, M. SISMOS.
P.A. CRANT, 207(FR):MAR73-868
ROCHE, T.W.E. "MINETTE" - HENRIETTA
OF EXETER.
H.M. BARBER, 481(PQ):JUL73-368
ROCHEFORT, C. ENCORE HEUREUX QU'ON
VA VERS L'ÉTÉ.
B. WRIGHT, 617(TLS):3OCT75-1152
ROCHER, G. INTRODUCTION À LA SOCI-
OLOGIE GÉNÉRALE.
D. MERLLIÉ, 542:JAN-MAR73-53
ROCHON, L. LAUTRÉAMONT ET LE STYLE
HOMÉRIQUE.
S.I. LOCKERBIE, 208(FS):OCT74-479
ROCK, D., ED. ARGENTINA IN THE
TWENTIETH CENTURY.
H.S. FERNS, 617(TLS):15AUG75-924
ROCK, J.F. A NA-KHI-ENGLISH ENCY-
CLOPEDIC DICTIONARY.
S.B. SUTTON, 244(HJAS):VOL33-277
ROCKEY, D. PHONETIC LEXICON.
D.K. OLLER, 399(MLJ):DEC74-426
ROCQUE, J. A TOPOGRAPHICAL MAP OF
THE COUNTY OF MIDDLESEX, 1754.
R. HYDE, 325:OCT73-681
RODAS, R.P. - SEE UNDER PESÁNTEZ
RODAS, R.
RODEWALD, D. ROBERT WALSERS PROSA.*
H.L. KAUFMANN, 221(GQ):JAN73-118
RODGERS, C. TIME IN THE NARRATIVE
OF "THE FAERIE QUEENE."
R.F. HILL, 677:VOL4-259
RODGERS, H.I. SEARCH FOR SECURITY.
D. KIRBY, 617(TLS):8AUG75-892
RODGERS, R. MUSICAL STAGES.
M. GUSSOW, 441:12OCT75-8
C. LEHMANN-HAUPT, 441:26SEP75-41
RODGERS, W.R., ED. IRISH LITERARY
PORTRAITS.*
295:FEB74-481
RODI, F. PROVOKATION - AFFIRMATION.
W. DE SCHMIDT, 53(AGP):BAND55HEFT1-
114
RODINI, R.J. ANTONFRANCESCO GRAZ-
ZINI.
A.L. DE GAETANO, 276:WINTER73-594
RODIS-LEWIS, G. L'OEUVRE DE DES-
CARTES.*
E. MOROT-SIR, 207(FR):DEC72-402
R.A. WATSON, 319:JUL75-406
RODNEY, W. JOE BOYLE, KING OF THE
KLONDIKE.
R. BOTHWELL, 99:APR/MAY75-14

RODRIGUEZ, A.G. LE CORYPHÉE.
D. O'CONNELL, 207(FR):APR73-1066
RODRIGUEZ, J. NU-PLASTIC & FANFARE
RED.
E. BALDERSTON, 581:MAR74-86
RODRÍGUEZ-PERALTA, P.W. JOSÉ SANTOS
CHOCANO.
M.A. SALGADO, 241:MAY73-77
RODRÍGUEZ-PUÉRTOLAS, J. DE LA EDAD
MEDIA A LA EDAD CONFLICTIVA.
D. EISENBERG, 400(MLN):MAR73-406
RODRÍGUEZ ALCALÁ, H. HISTORIA DE LA
LITERATURA PARAGUAYA.*
T.E. CASE, 240(HR):SPRING73-461
RODWAY, A. ENGLISH COMEDY.
M. HODGART, 617(TLS):26SEP75-1093
ROEMING, R.F., ED. DEVELOPING
AWARENESS THROUGH POETRY.
Y.G. BARRETT, 399(MLJ):NOV73-366
ROETHEL, H.K. THE BLUE RIDER.
F. WHITFORD, 592:NOV73-212
ROETHLISBERGER-BIANCO, M. CAVALIER
PIETRO TEMPESTA & HIS TIME.*
E. WATERHOUSE, 90:JAN73-46
ROETT, R., ED. BRAZIL IN THE SIX-
TIES.
D. CARNEIRO, 263:APR-JUN74-171
ROETTER, C. PSYCHOLOGICAL WARFARE.
H. GREENE, 617(TLS):10JAN75-26
ROFF, W.R., ED. KELANTAN.
M. FREEDMAN, 617(TLS):1AUG75-869
ROFHEART, M. MY NAME IS SAPPHO.
M. LEVIN, 441:12JAN75-18
ROGER-MARX, C. & S. COTTÉ. DELA-
CROIX.
M. CORMACK, 39:AUG73-152
ROGERS, A.D. THE HOUSING OF OGLE-
THORPE COUNTY, GEORGIA, 1790-1860.
E.R. DE ZURKO, 219(GAR):SUMMER73-
298
ROGERS, C.H. ENCYCLOPEDIA OF CAGE
& AVIARY BIRDS.
R. CARAS, 441:7DEC75-93
ROGERS, F.R. & P. BAENDER - SEE
TWAIN, M.
ROGERS, H.C.B. G.J. CHURCHWARD.
617(TLS):14FEB75-177
ROGERS, K.M. WILLIAM WYCHERLEY.
J. MILHOUS, 481(PQ):JUL73-594
ROGERS, M.F., JR. RANDOLPH ROGERS,
AMERICAN SCULPTOR IN ROME.
W. CRAVEN, 54:MAR73-158
W.H. GERDTS, 127:FALL73-74
ROGERS, N. - SEE SHELLEY, P.B.
ROGERS, P. GRUB STREET.*
E.A. BLOOM, 677:VOL4-296
D. BROOKS, 148:AUTUMN72-286
J.A. HAY, 67:MAY74-91
R. LONSDALE, 184(EIC):JAN73-79
G. MIDGLEY, 541(RES):AUG73-342
A. PAILLER, 189(EA):JUL-SEP73-371
C.J. RAWSON, 175:AUTUMN72-110
A.H. SCOUTEN, 481(PQ):JUL73-450
205(FMLS):APR73-215
ROGERS, R. A PSYCHOANALYTIC STUDY
OF THE DOUBLE IN LITERATURE.*
D.R. DAVIS, 184(EIC):JAN73-95
ROGERS, T. RUPERT BROOKE.
R. LAWRENCE, 175:SPRING72-32
A.S. MONOD, 189(EA):JAN-MAR73-72
H.D. SPEAR, 177(ELT):VOL16#4-309

ROGERS, T. LEICESTER'S GHOST.
(F.B. WILLIAMS, JR., ED)
E. ROSENBERG, 551(RENQ):AUTUMN73-
378
ROGERS, T.F. "SUPERFLUOUS MEN" &
THE POST-STALIN THAW.
R.D.B. THOMSON, 574(SEEJ):WINTER
73-467
ROGERS, T.J. TECHNIQUES OF SOLIP-
SISM.*
H. JARKA, 400(MLN):APR73-635
E. MC INNES, 220(GL&L):JAN74-159
ROGERS, W.E. IMAGE & ABSTRACTION.
R.T. DAVIES, 677:VOL4-246
B. RAW, 447(N&Q):NOV73-437
R.H. ROBBINS, 72:BAND211HEFT3/6-
427
ROGERS, W.W. & R. PRUITT. STEPHEN
F. RENFROE.
W.S. HOOLE, 9(ALAR):JAN73-74
ROGERS, W.W. & R.D. WARD. AUGUST
RECKONING.
639(VQR):SPRING74-XLVIII
ROGGE, W. - SEE ADORNO, T.W. & E.
KRENEK
ROGIN, M.P. FATHERS & CHILDREN.
R. DRINNON, 441:15JUN75-21
W.A. WILLIAMS, 453:7AUG75-38
ROHLFS, G. FROM VULGAR LATIN TO OLD
FRENCH.*
P.A. GAENG, 660(WORD):DEC70-425
R. LESAGE, 320(CJL):SPRING74-96
H.G. SCHOGT, 353:150CT73-115
ROHLFS, G. ROMANISCHE SPRACHGEOGRA-
PHIE.
J. CHAURAND, 209(FM):JUL73-315
H.G. SCHOGT, 353:1SEP73-126
ROHMER, R. EXODUS/U.K.
D. GODFREY, 99:DEC75/JAN76-33
ROHOU, G. LA RADE FORAINE.
C.G. WHITING, 207(FR):MAY73-1249
ROHR, R. FRANZÖSISCHE SYNTAX.
M. SANDMANN, 545(RPH):AUG73-130
ROHRER, C. DER KONJUNKTIV IM GES-
PROCHENEN SCHWEIZER HOCHDEUTSCHEN.
E.H. YARRILL, 182:VOL26#19-675
ROIDER, K.A., JR. THE RELUCTANT
ALLY.
M.L. FREY, 481(PQ):JUL73-368
ROJAS, C. AQUELLARRE.
R.E. LOTT, 238:MAY73-505
DE ROJAS, F. LA CELESTINA. (D.S.
SEVERIN, ED)
617(TLS):23MAY75-576
DE ROJAS ZORRILLA, F. DEL REY
ABAJO, NINGUNO. (R.R. MAC CURDY,
ED)
W.M. WHITBY, 399(MLJ):MAR73-150
ROKEAH, D. RED EARTH.
T. EAGLETON, 617(TLS):28FEB75-214
"DAS ROLANDSLIED DES PFAFFEN KON-
RAD."
G.W. RADIMERSKY, 221(GQ):MAY73-481
ROLDÁN HERVÁS, J.M. ITER AB EMERITA
ASTURICAM.
D.G. BIRD, 313:VOL63-289
ROLFE, F. - SEE UNDER BARON CORVO
ROLIN, D. LES ÉCLAIRS.
E. MARKS, 207(FR):OCT72-233
ROLLE, D. INGENIOUS STRUCTURE.
E.A.J. HONIGMANN, 447(N&Q):DEC73-
473

312

RÖLLEKE, H., ED. DIE ÄLTESTE MÄRCH-
ENSAMMLUNG DER BRÜDER GRIMM.
S.S. PRAWER, 617(TLS):26DEC75-1537
ROLLESTON, J. RILKE IN TRANSITION.*
E. SPEIDEL, 447(N&Q):SEP73-355
ROLLINAT, M. OEUVRES I. (R. MIAN-
NAY, ED)
L. FORESTIER, 535(RHL):NOV-DEC73-
1096
S.I. LOCKERBIE, 208(FS):OCT74-482
R. MERKER, 446:FALL-WINTER73/74-87
J.L. SHEPHERD 3D, 207(FR):DEC72-
418
ROLOFF, D. PLOTIN: DIE GROSSSCHRIFT,
III, 8; V, 8; V, 5; II, 9.*
H. SEIDL, 53(AGP):BAND55HEFT1-88
ROLT, L.T.C. THE POTTERS' FIELD.
J. HATCHER, 617(TLS):7FEB75-144
"ROMA CENTO ANNI FA NELLE FOTOGRAFIE
DEL TEMPO."
S. KOSTOF, 576:OCT73-239
ROMAGNOLI, M. & G.F. THE ROMAGNOLIS'
TABLE.
R.A. SOKOLOV, 441:7DEC75-78
ROMALO, V.G. MORFOLOGIE STRUCTURALA
A LIMBII ROMÂNE.
G. FRANCESCATO, 353:1APR73-126
"LE ROMAN DE MERLIN L'ENCHANTEUR."
(H. DE BRIEL, TRANS)
C.E. PICKFORD, 208(FS):JAN74-53
ROMANA PACI, F. JAMES JOYCE.
P. RECONDO, 202(FMOD):NOV72/FEB73-
176
ROMANELLI, P. TOPOGRAFIA E ARCHEO-
LOGIA DELL'AFRICA ROMANA.
I.M. BARTON, 313:VOL63-290
ROMANINI, A.M. ARNOLFO DI CAMBIO E
LO "STIL NUOVO" DEL GOTICO ITALIANO.
M. WUNDRAM, 54:DEC73-624
ROMANO, R. TRA DUE CRISI.
M.B. BECKER, 551(RENQ):WINTER73-
469
ROMANO, R. & C. VIVANTI, EDS.
STORIA D'ITALIA. (VOLS 1-3)
J.M. ROBERTS, 617(TLS):11JUL75-782
ROMANOS. KONTAKIA OF ROMANOS,
BYZANTINE MELODIST. (VOL 1) (M.
CARPENTER, TRANS)
A.C. BANDY, 124:FEB73-300
ROMBAUER, I.S. & M.R. BECKER. JOY
OF COOKING. (1ST ED)
M.F.K. FISHER, 442(NY):10NOV75-178
ROMBAUER, I.S. & M.R. BECKER. JOY
OF COOKING. (REV)
R.A. SOKOLOV, 441:7DEC75-78
RÖMER, R. DIE SPRACHE DER ANZEIGEN-
WERBUNG.
E. MITTELBERG, 680(ZDP):BAND92HEFT
1-147
ROMERO, J.R. LA VIDA INÚTIL DE PITO
PÉREZ. (W.O. CORD, ED)
M.M. DIAZ, 399(MLJ):JAN-FEB74-78
DE ROMILLY, J. LA LOI DANS LA PEN-
SÉE GRECQUE DES ORIGINES À ARIS-
TOTE.
H. LLOYD-JONES, 303:VOL93-243
M. OSTWALD, 124:APR73-431
DE ROMILLY, J. TIME IN GREEK TRAG-
EDY. (FRENCH TITLE: LE TEMPS DANS
LA TRAGÉDIE GRECQUE.)
R. CRAFT, 453:15MAY75-37
M. TRÉDÉ, 555:VOL47FASC2-331
DE ROMILLY, J. LA TRAGÉDIE GRECQUE.*
D. HENRY & B. WALKER, 122:JAN74-56

RONALD, M.T. A VICTORIAN MASQUE.
617(TLS):16MAY75-536
RONAN, C.A. GALILEO.
I.B. COHEN, 617(TLS):2MAY75-479
RONAY, G. THE DRACULA MYTH.
C. FRAYLING, 364:JUN/JUL74-101
RONBERG, G. THE HOCKEY ENCYCLOPED-
IA.
M. RICHLER, 441:5JAN75-6
RONDEAU, G., ED. CONTRIBUTIONS CAN-
ADIENNES À LA LINGUISTIQUE APPLI-
QUÉE (SOME ASPECTS OF CANADIAN
APPLIED LINGUISTICS).
S. HAMILTON, 399(MLJ):DEC74-418
RONDOLINO, G. DIZIONARIO DEL CINEMA
ITALIANO: 1945-1969.
B.L., 275(IQ):SPRING74-114
RONEN, D. DAHOMEY.
J.D. HARGREAVES, 617(TLS):17OCT75-
1242
RONNIE, A. LOCKLEAR.
S.A. PEEPLES, 200:OCT73-496
DE RONSARD, P. LES OEUVRES DE
PIERRE DE RONSARD.* (VOLS 7&8)
(I. SILVER, ED)
V.E. GRAHAM, 546(RR):MAR74-121
ROOKE, B.E. - SEE COLERIDGE, S.T.
ROOP, D.H. AN INTRODUCTION TO THE
BURMESE WRITING SYSTEM.
L. DEROY, 556(RLV):1973/2-189
R.B. JONES, 293(JAST):NOV72-205
ROOS, P. THE ROCK-TOMBS OF CAUNUS.
(VOL 1)
J. BOARDMAN, 123:NOV74-312
ROOSEVELT, E. & J. BROUGH. A REN-
DEZVOUS WITH DESTINY.
C.L. MEE, JR., 441:19OCT75-16
ROOSEVELT, F.D. & W.S. CHURCHILL.
ROOSEVELT & CHURCHILL. (F.L. LOW-
ENHEIM, H.D. LANGLEY & M. JONAS,
EDS)
M. BELOFF, 617(TLS):13JUN75-654
L.J. HALLE, 441:4MAY75-16
S. KOSS, 362:25SEP75-407
D. MIDDLETON, 441:5APR75-27
ROOT, W.P. STRIKING THE DARK AIR
FOR MUSIC.*
R. BENTLEY, 448:VOL13#2-93
P. NELSON, 109:SPRING/SUMMER74-131
P. RAMSEY, 569(SR):SPRING74-398
ROPER, L.W. F.L.O.*
H. CARRUTH, 249(HUDR):WINTER74/75-
620
ROSA, G.T. - SEE UNDER TITTA ROSA,
G.
ROSALDO, R., ED. CHICANO.
E.H. MAYER, 399(MLJ):SEP-OCT74-294
ROSCI, M. BASCHENIS, BETTERA & CO.*
90:MAY73-348
ROSCOE, A.A. MOTHER IS GOLD.
H. SERGEANT, 175:SPRING72-29
K. TURKINGTON, 180(ESA):MAR73-49
ROSE, C.H. ALONSO NÚÑEZ DE REINOSO.
H. ZIOMEK, 238:MAR73-173
ROSE, K. THE LATER CECILS.
J. GRIGG, 362:10JUL75-58
J. RIDLEY, 617(TLS):11JUL75-755
442(NY):15DEC75-154
ROSE, K.F.C. THE DATE & AUTHOR OF
THE "SATYRICON."*
M.S. SMITH, 313:VOL63-308
ROSE, M. INDUSTRIAL BEHAVIOUR.
D.A. ELLIOTT, 617(TLS):4JUL75-742

313

ROSE, M. SHAKESPEAREAN DESIGN.*
G.M. HARVEY, 150(DR):AUTUMN73-587
C. HOY, 569(SR):SPRING74-363
K. MUIR, 551(RENQ):WINTER73-526
ROSE, P., WITH B. HERTZEL. CHARLIE
HUSTLE.
B.J. PHILLIPS, 441:9NOV75-53
ROSEN, A. RISE UP, WOMEN!
J. GRIGG, 362:6FEB75-188
F.M. LEVENTHAL, 617(TLS):19SEP75-
1044
ROSEN, C. HAVE JUMP SHOT WILL
TRAVEL.
C. LEHMANN-HAUPT, 441:1MAR75-23
M. LEVIN, 441:30MAR75-21
ROSEN, C. ARNOLD SCHOENBERG.
R. CRAFT, 453:18SEP75-50
D. HENAHAN, 441:28DEC75-6
ROSEN, E. THREE COPERNICAN TREAT-
ISES. (3RD ED)
W.D. STAHLMAN, 322(JHI):JUL-SEP73-
483
ROSEN, K., ED. THE MAN TO SEND
RAIN CLOUDS.*
W. GARD, 584(SWR):SPRING74-V
ROSEN, K., ED. VOICES OF THE RAIN-
BOW.
P. ADAMS, 61:AUG75-89
ROSEN, M. POPCORN VENUS.*
S. FARBER, 249(HUDR):WINTER74/75-
571
M. MITCHELL, 141:FALL74-355
ROSEN, R.S. E.T.A. HOFFMANNS "KATER
MURR."*
G. VITT-MAUCHER, 221(GQ):JAN73-105
ROSEN, S. G.W.F. HEGEL.*
M.J. PETRY, 518:OCT74-26
ROSENAU, H. SOCIAL PURPOSE IN ARCH-
ITECTURE.
N. MILLER, 576:MAR73-67
ROSENBAUER, H. BRECHT UND DER BE-
HAVIORISMUS.*
B.A. WOODS, 222(GR):MAY73-239
ROSENBAUM, S.P., ED. THE BLOOMSBURY
GROUP.
A. BELL, 617(TLS):22AUG75-947
I. EHRENPREIS, 453:17APR75-9
P. STANSKY, 441:1JUN75-7
ROSENBAUM, S.P., ED. ENGLISH LITER-
ATURE & BRITISH PHILOSOPHY.*
R.J.G., 543:SEP72-170
R.W. WALLACE, 481(PQ):JUL73-451
483:JAN73-99
ROSENBERG, A. TYSSOT DE PATOT & HIS
WORKS (1655-1738).
D.L. ANDERSON, 568(SCN):WINTER74-
84
A.D. HYTIER, 481(PQ):JUL73-586
ROSENBERG, D. BLUES OF THE SKY.
B. ZAVATSKY, 441:14DEC75-16
ROSENBERG, D. LEAVIN AMERICA.
L. ROGERS, 102(CANL):AUTUMN74-121
ROSENBERG, D. PARIS & LONDON.
S. SCOBIE, 102(CANL):SPRING73-89
ROSENBERG, H. THE DE-DEFINITION OF
ART.*
A. MC CULLOCH, 381:DEC73-482
ROSENBERG, H. THE SCANDINAVIAN HIS
MASTER'S VOICE V-SERIES 1920-1932.
T. WALKER, 415:JUL74-571
ROSENBERG, J.D. THE FALL OF CAMELOT.
G. JOSEPH, 639(VQR):WINTER74-152
H. KOZICKI, 301(JEGP):OCT74-565
R. SALE, 249(HUDR):AUTUMN74-443

ROSENBERG, M. THE MASKS OF "KING
LEAR."*
P. BEMENT, 541(RES):NOV73-471
C. HOY, 569(SR):SPRING74-363
P.N. SIEGEL, 191(ELN):JUN74-297
ROSENBERG, P. CONTRACT ON CHERRY
STREET.
G. LYONS, 441:11MAY75-44
ROSENBERG, P. THE SEVENTH HERO.*
H. KAPLAN, 31(ASCH):SUMMER75-499
ROSENBERG, S. NAKED IS THE BEST
DISGUISE.*
C. JAMES, 453:20FEB75-15
C. NICOL, 231:FEB75-112
M. YOUNG, 441:2FEB75-21
ROSENBERG, S.N. MODERN FRENCH "CE."*
K. TOGEBY, 545(RPH):FEB74-446
ROSENBERGER, F.C., ED. RECORDS OF
THE COLUMBIA HISTORICAL SOCIETY OF
WASHINGTON, D.C., 1971-1972.
639(VQR):SPRING74-LX
ROSENBLAT, Á. LENGUA LITERARIA Y
LENGUA POPULAR EN AMÉRICA.
M. SANDMANN, 545(RPH):FEB74-446
ROSENBLATT, J. BUMBLEBEE DITHYRAMB.
E. MC NAMARA, 102(CANL):AUTUMN73-
104
ROSENBLATT, J. DREAM CRATERS.
F.W. WATT, 99:JUN75-40
ROSENBLOOD, N., ED. SHAW.
R. LAWRENCE, 175:SPRING72-32
F.P.W. MC DOWELL, 295:FEB74-772
ROSENBLUM, R. THE GOOD THIEF.*
617(TLS):11JUL75-784
ROSENBLUM, R. MODERN PAINTING & THE
NORTHERN ROMANTIC TRADITION.
J. RUSSELL, 441:19OCT75-40
D. THOMAS, 362:25DEC75&1JAN76-892
ROSENBLUM, R. TRANSFORMATIONS IN
LATE EIGHTEENTH CENTURY ART.
K. GARLICK, 447(N&Q):JUN73-236
ROSENDORFER, H. DEUTSCHE SUITE.
P. PROCHNIK, 617(TLS):10OCT75-1208
ROSENFELD, A.H. - SEE WHEELWRIGHT,
J.
ROSENFELD, M. EDMOND JALOUX.*
J. KOLBERT, 207(FR):MAY73-1234
ROSENFELDT, N.E. HOLBERGS DANMARKS-
HISTORIE I RUSLAND.
P. RIES, 575(SEER):OCT74-635
ROSENFIELD, L.C. - SEE PARDIES, I-G.
ROSENFIELD, L.W. ARISTOTLE & INFOR-
MATION THEORY.
K.D. FRANDSEN, 480(P&R):SUMMER73-
194
ROSENGARTEN, T. - SEE SHAW, N.
ROSENMEYER, T.G. THE GREEN CABINET.
F.J. FABRY, 568(SCN):FALL74-45
G. LAWALL, 121(CJ):DEC73/JAN74-160
ROSENNE, S. THE LAW OF TREATIES.
A-R. WERNER, 182:VOL26#15/16-527
ROSENSTOCK, G.G. TOWARD A NEW
MORALITY.
P. DUBOIS, 542:OCT-DEC73-494
ROSENSTOCK-HUESSY, E. SPEECH &
REALITY.
R.L. LANIGAN, 480(P&R):SPRING73-
124
ROSENSTONE, R.A. ROMANTIC REVOLU-
TIONARY.
A. KOPKIND, 441:2NOV75-4
ROSENTHAL, B.G. THE IMAGES OF MAN.
R. NEVILLE, 258:SEP73-443

ROSENTHAL, E. THE ILLUMINATIONS OF
THE VERGILIUS ROMANUS.*
L.J. DALY, 377:JUL74-116
ROSENTHAL, F. THE CLASSICAL HERI-
TAGE IN ISLAM.
W.M. WATT, 617(TLS):5DEC75-1469
ROSENTHAL, F. KNOWLEDGE TRIUMPHANT.
R.M. FRANK, 318(JAOS):JAN-MAR73-
108
ROSENTHAL, J.T. THE PURCHASE OF
PARADISE.
J.R. LANDER, 589:OCT74-754
ROSENTHAL, M.L. RANDALL JARRELL.
R. ASSELINEAU, 189(EA):APR-JUN73-
247
ROSENTHAL, M.L. POETRY & THE COMMON
LIFE.
J.M. BRINNIN, 441:2MAR75-4
B. WALLENSTEIN, 659:SUMMER75-397
ROSENTHAL, M.L. THE VIEW FROM THE
PEACOCK'S TAIL.*
H. TAYLOR, 385(MQR):WINTER75-92
ROSIER, J.L., ED. PHILOLOGICAL
ESSAYS IN HONOUR OF HERBERT DEAN
MERITT.
P.H. SALUS, 353:1AUG73-116
ROSKILL, M. VAN GOGH, GAUGUIN & THE
IMPRESSIONIST CIRCLE.*
V.F. JIRAT-WASIUTYNSKI, 127:FALL73-
78
ROSKILL, S. HANKEY.* (VOL 3)
C.P. STACEY, 99:APR/MAY75-47
ROSS, A. OPEN SEA.
R. FULLER, 617(TLS):15AUG75-916
A. STEVENSON, 362:30OCT75-571
ROSS, A.M. WILLIAM HENRY BARTLETT.*
M. BELL, 99:MAR75-34
ROSS, A.S.C. HOW TO PRONOUNCE IT.
C. BARBER, 597(SN):VOL45#1-174
A. WOLLMANN, 38:BAND91HEFT1-98
ROSS, C. EDWARD IV.
R.L. STOREY, 617(TLS):11APR75-390
ROSS, D.J.A. ILLUSTRATED MEDIEVAL
ALEXANDER-BOOKS IN GERMANY & THE
NETHERLANDS.*
J. FOLDA, 54:DEC73-621
W.O. HASSALL, 220(GL&L):OCT73-74
C. HUTER, 354:JUN73-163
ROSS, D.O., JR. BACKGROUNDS TO
AUGUSTAN POETRY.
C. MACLEOD, 617(TLS):7NOV75-1326
ROSS, D.O., JR. STYLE & TRADITION
IN CATULLUS.*
J-D. MINYARD, 121(CJ):OCT/NOV73-88
ROSS, F. THE ALTAR OF EROS.
J. COAKLEY, 385(MQR):WINTER75-108
ROSS, I. POWER WITH GRACE.
P. ADAMS, 61:AUG75-89
ROSS, I.S. LORD KAMES & THE SCOT-
LAND OF HIS DAY.*
G. CARABELLI, 548(RCSF):APR-JUN73-
222
R.L. EMERSON, 319:JAN75-111
J. GRAY, 150(DR):SUMMER73-370
R. MARSH, 481(PQ):JUL73-533
ROSS, J. THEY DON'T DANCE MUCH.
P. FRENCH, 617(TLS):28NOV75-1407
ROSS, J. & D. FREED. THE EXISTEN-
TIALISM OF ALBERTO MORAVIA.
H. LAWTON, 276:WINTER73-606
ROSS, R. OBLIGATION.
A. SCHWARTZ, 311(JP):24APR75-224

ROSS, S. SAWBONES MEMORIAL.
B. DAVIES, 198:SPRING75-130
S. LAUDER, 99:NOV75-37
ROSS, S.D. THE NATURE OF MORAL
RESPONSIBILITY.
R.L. SIMON, 484(PPR):DEC73-290
ROSSANT, C. COOKING WITH COLETTE.
R.A. SOKOLOV, 441:7DEC75-78
ROSSBACH, E. BASKETS AS TEXTILE
ART.
J.L. LARSEN, 139:DEC73-15
ROSSEL, S.H. DEN LITTERAERE VISE I
FOLKETRADITIONEN.
V. ESPELAND, 172(EDDA):1973/1-53
ROSSEL, S.H. SKANDINAVISCHE LITERA-
TUREN 1870-1970.
G.C. SCHOOLFIELD, 563(SS):FALL74-
435
ROSSELLI, R. COMPENDIO DI LOGICA.
E. NAMER, 542:JUL-SEP73-372
ROSSELLI, R. ENTUSIASMO COME CATE-
GORIA MORALE ASSOLUTA.
E. NAMER, 542:OCT-DEC73-495
ROSSEN, R. THREE SCREENPLAYS.
200:FEB73-112
ROSSER, R. THE END OF SOMEONE
ELSE'S RAINBOW.
N. CALLENDAR, 441:30MAR75-24
ROSSET, C. LA LOGIQUE DU PIRE.
F. ARCHAMBAULT, 154:SEP73-567
ROSSETTI, W.M. THE PRB JOURNAL.
(W.E. FREDEMAN, ED)
D.A.N. JONES, 362:15MAY75-651
ROSSI, A.S., ED. THE FEMINIST PAP-
ERS.
676(YR):WINTER74-XXVI
ROSSI, L. TRAJAN'S COLUMN & THE
DACIAN WARS.
G.R. WATSON, 123:MAR74-112
ROSSI, P. LO STORICISMO TEDESCO
CONTEMPORANEO.
A.M., 543:SEP72-170
ROSSI, P. UN SOIR À PISE.
S.G. STARY, 207(FR):OCT72-235
RÖSSING-HAGER, M. SYNTAX UND TEXT-
KOMPOSITION IN LUTHERS BRIEFPROSA.
J.L. FLOOD, 182:VOL26#5/6-153
K. SIMON, 301(JEGP):OCT74-581
ROSSITER, F.R. CHARLES IVES & HIS
AMERICA.
D. HENAHAN, 441:30NOV75-40
ROSSITER, J. THE DEADLY GOLD.
N. CALLENDAR, 441:14DEC75-30
RÖSSLE, W. DIE SOZIALE WIRKLICHKEIT
IN ARTHUR MILLERS "DEATH OF A
SALESMAN."
W. HABICHT, 72:BAND211HEFT1/3-162
ROSSNER, J. LOOKING FOR MR. GOOD-
BAR.
C. BLACKWOOD, 617(TLS):12SEP75-
1012
C. LEHMANN-HAUPT, 441:21MAY75-43
C.E. RINZLER, 441:8JUN75-24
R. TODD, 61:SEP75-84
442(NY):14JUL75-98
ROSSO, C. MONTESQUIEU MORALISTE.*
G. MAY, 207(FR):OCT72-156
G. TONELLI, 319:OCT75-548
ROSSO, C. IL SERPENTE E LA SIRENA.
A. SCAGLIONE, 131(CL):SPRING74-169
ROSTAND, C. LISZT.*
R. CRAFT, 453:6FEB75-3
ROSTEN, L., ED. THE LOOK BOOK.
D. DEMPSEY, 441:7DEC75-96

ROSTENBERG, L. THE MINORITY PRESS &
THE ENGLISH CROWN, 1558-1625.*
L.H. CARLSON, 551(RENQ):WINTER73-
517
M. HUNTER, 78(BC):SPRING73-108
ROSTON, M. THE SOUL OF WIT.
J. BROADBENT, 617(TLS):19SEP75-
1040
ROSTOW, W.W. THE DIFFUSION OF POWER.
W.F. BARBER, 150(DR):SUMMER73-373
ROSTOW, W.W. HOW IT ALL BEGAN.
D. YERGIN, 441:6APR75-2
ROSZAK, T. PONTIFEX.
S. CLARK, 617(TLS):14NOV75-1349
ROSZAK, T. UNFINISHED ANIMAL.
P. HAMILL, 441:30NOV75-32
ROSZAK, T. WHERE THE WASTELAND
ENDS.*
H.G. CLASSEN, 529(QQ):AUTUMN73-488
ROTERMUND, E. AFFEKT UND ARTISTIK.
A.G. DE CAPUA, 301(JEGP):APR74-283
J. SCHMIDT, 182:VOL26#3/4-110
ROTH, B. DIE ROMANISCH-DEUTSCHE
SPRACHGRENZE IM MURTENBIET WÄHREND
DES XV. JAHRHUNDERTS.
U.F. CHEN, 545(RPH):FEB74-397
ROTH, C. JEWISH ART.* (REV BY B.
NARKISS)
C. ABRAMSKY, 592:MAR73-146
ROTH, G.K. FIJIAN WAY OF LIFE.
(2ND ED)
P. SNOW, 617(TLS):21FEB75-204
ROTH, J. BRIEFE 1911-1939. (H.
KESTEN, ED) DER NEUE TAG. (I.
SÜLTEMEYER, ED)
M.L. MARTIN, 221(GQ):MAY73-470
ROTH, J. DIE KAPUZINERGRUFT. (A.F.
BANCE, ED)
205(FMLS):APR73-215
ROTH, M.L. ROBERT MUSIL.
H.W. PUPPE, 406:FALL74-321
ROTH, O. STUDIEN ZUM "ESTRIF DE
FORTUNE ET VERTU" DES MARTIN LE
FRANC.
F. JOUKOVSKY, 545(RPH):NOV73-266
ROTH, P. THE BREAST.*
E. SABISTON, 268:JAN75-27
ROTH, P. THE GREAT AMERICAN NOVEL.*
MY LIFE AS A MAN.*
D. MONAGHAN, 268:JUL75-113
ROTH, P. READING MYSELF & OTHERS.
A. BROYARD, 441:5JUN75-41
R. SALE, 441:25MAY75-7
ROTH, R. SAND IN THE WIND.
V. CUNNINGHAM, 617(TLS):14MAR75-
269
ROTH, R.J., ED. GOD KNOWABLE &
UNKNOWABLE.
J. COLLINS, 258:SEP73-452
R.P. IMBELLI, 613:AUTUMN73-436
ROTHBERG, A. THE HEIRS OF STALIN.*
P.S. GILLETTE, 104:SUMMER73-270
W. LEONHARD, 550(RUSR):JAN73-85
ROTHBERG, A. ALEXANDER SOLZHENIT-
ZYN, THE MAJOR NOVELS.*
V.S. DUNHAM, 574(SEEJ):WINTER72-
486
R. RAMSEY, 295:FEB74-782
ROTHENBERG, J. SHAKING THE PUMPKIN.
L.J. EVERS, 502(PRS):SPRING73-79
ROTHENBERT, A. & B. GREENBERT. THE
INDEX OF SCIENTIFIC WRITINGS ON
CREATIVITY.
617(TLS):30MAY75-609

ROTHKEGEL, A. FESTE SYNTAGMEN.
E.H. YARRILL, 182:VOL26#23/24-855
ROTHMUND, A. DICTÉES ET VERSIONS.
G. SCHWEIG, 430(NS):SEP73-508
ROTHSCHILD, E. PARADISE LOST.*
N. MILLS, 676(YR):SUMMER74-566
ROTHSCHILD, J. EAST CENTRAL EUROPE
BETWEEN THE TWO WORLD WARS. (P.F.
SUGAR & D.W. TREADGOLD, EDS)
H. SETON-WATSON, 617(TLS):2MAY75-
483
ROTHSTEIN, E., ED. LITERARY MONO-
GRAPHS. (VOL 3)
J.B. BELL, 447(N&Q):MAY73-194
ROTHSTEIN, E., ED. LITERARY MONO-
GRAPHS. (VOL 4)
C.J. RAWSON, 447(N&Q):JUN73-237
ROTHSTEIN, E. & R.N. RINGLER, EDS.
LITERARY MONOGRAPHS. (VOL 2)
J.M. STEADMAN, 570(SQ):SUMMER73-
345
ROTIMI, O. KURUNMI.
A. RENDLE, 157:SPRING73-82
ROTONDI, P. THE DUCAL PALACE OF
URBINO.
C.H. CLOUGH, 39:MAY73-533
ROTROU, J. HERCULE MOURANT.* (D.A.
WATTS, ED)
J. MOREL, 535(RHL):SEP-OCT73-890
ROTROU, J. LE VÉRITABLE SAINT GEN-
EST. (E.T. DUBOIS, ED)
H. MATTAUCH, 182:VOL26#3/4-111
ROTTENSTEINER, F. THE SCIENCE FIC-
TION BOOK.
G. JONAS, 441:14DEC75-29
E. KORN, 617(TLS):8AUG75-903
ROTTENSTEINER, F., ED. VIEW FROM
ANOTHER SHORE.*
R.K. WILSON, 574(SEEJ):FALL73-351
ROTTER, P., ED. BITCHES & SAD
LADIES.
N. BALAKIAN, 441:30MAR75-10
A. BROYARD, 441:11FEB75-43
P. GROSSKURTH, 99:SEP75-61
ROTTMANN, L., J. BARRY & B.T. PAQUET,
EDS. WINNING HEARTS & MINDS.*
N. LAVERS, 134(CP):SPRING73-86
RÖTZER, H.G. PICARO - LANDSTÖRTZER
- SIMPLICIUS.
R.T. LLEWELLYN, 220(GL&L):APR74-
260
RÖTZER, H.G. DER ROMAN DES BAROCK
1600-1700.*
P. SKRINE, 402(MLR):JUL74-702
ROUBAUD, J. MONO NO AWARE.* [SHOWN
IN PREV UNDER ROUBARD]
J. GUÉRON, 98:MAR73-255
ROUBINE, J-J. LECTURES DE RACINE.*
R.C. KNIGHT, 208(FS):JAN74-70
ROUDAUT, J., ED. POÈTES ET GRAM-
MAIRIENS AU XVIIIE SIÈCLE.*
S. MENANT, 535(RHL):NOV-DEC73-1075
F.J-L. MOURET, 208(FS):JUL74-334
ROUDIEZ, L.S. FRENCH FICTION TODAY.*
E. MOROT-SIR, 546(RR):NOV74-317
295:FEB74-438
ROUDIEZ, L.S. - SEE O'BRIEN, J.
ROUDIL, J., ED. LES FUEROS D'ALCAR-
AZ ET D'ALARCÓN.
J. GULSOY, 240(HR):SPRING73-347
ROUECHÉ, B. THE CATS.
P.D. JAMES, 617(TLS):26SEP75-1079
ROUECHÉ, B. FERAL.*
P. ADAMS, 61:JAN75-91

ROUECHÉ, B. THE LAST ENEMY.
N. CALLENDAR, 441:28DEC75-21
ROULLET, A. THE EGYPTIAN & EGYP-
TIANIZING MONUMENTS OF IMPERIAL
ROME.
T.T. TINH, 313:VOL63-273
ROULSTONE, M. THE ROYAL HOUSE OF
TUDOR.
617(TLS):28FEB75-232
ROUMAIN, J. BOIS D'ÉBÈNE/EBONY
WOOD.*
K. CONGDON, 37:MAY73-40
ROUMAIN, J. GOUVERNEURS DE LA
ROSÉE.
M. SERRES, 98:JAN73-3
ROUND, N.G. UNAMUNO: "ABEL SÁN-
CHEZ."
J. BUTT, 617(TLS):23MAY75-570
ROUNDELL, J. THOMAS SHOTTER BOYS
1803-1874.
J. GAGE, 617(TLS):7FEB75-148
ROUSE, P., JR. THE GREAT WAGON ROAD
FROM PHILADELPHIA TO THE SOUTH.
J.A. CARUSO, 656(WMQ):JAN74-158
ROUSSEAU, G., ED. PRÉFACES DES
ROMANS QUÉBÉCOIS DU XIXE SIÈCLE.
J. MÉNARD, 535(RHL):NOV-DEC73-1104
ROUSSEAU, G.S., ED. ORGANIC FORM.* →
H. TROWBRIDGE, 173(ECS):WINTER
73/74-234
ROUSSEAU, G.S. & P-G. BOUCÉ, EDS.
TOBIAS SMOLLETT.*
H. AUFFRET, 549(RLC):JUL-SEP73-476
F. FELSENSTEIN, 173(ECS):FALL73-
116
M. IRWIN, 541(RES):NOV73-494
D.K. JEFFREY, 577(SHR):WINTER73-93
J.W. LOOFBOUROW, 613:SPRING73-125
C.J. RAWSON, 175:AUTUMN72-110
ROUSSEAU, J-J. DU CONTRAT SOCIAL.
(R. GRIMSLEY, ED)
205(FMLS):APR73-215
ROUSSEAU, J-J. CORRESPONDANCE COM-
PLÈTE. (VOLS 13 & 14) (R.A. LEIGH,
ED)
E.R. BRIGGS, 402(MLR):APR74-412
ROUSSEAU, J-J. JEAN-JACQUES ENTRE
SOCRATE ET CATON. (C. PICHOIS & R.
PINTARD, EDS)
D.G. CREIGHTON, 207(FR):MAY73-1225
G. MANFREDI, 548(RCSF):JAN-MAR73-
33
M.L. PERKINS, 481(PQ):JUL73-573
M. VERANI, 557(RSH):JUL-SEP73-493
ROUSSEAU, J-J. OEUVRES COMPLÈTES.
(VOLS 2&3) (M. LAUNAY, ED)
R. MERCIER, 557(RSH):JUL-SEP73-494
ROUSSEL, R. THE METAPHYSICS OF
DARKNESS.*
N. SHERRY, 637(VS):MAR74-336
C.T. WATTS, 541(RES):MAY73-239
ROUSSOPOULOS, D. THE POLITICAL
ECONOMY OF THE STATE.
C.L. BROWN-JOHN, 628:SPRING74-93
ROUSSOS, E.N. HÉRAKLEITOS, TA APOS-
PASMATA.
C.J. EMLYN-JONES, 123:MAR74-38
ROUT, L., JR. POLITICS OF THE CHACO
PEACE CONFERENCE, 1935-1939.
D. CARNEIRO, 263:JAN-MAR74-69
ROUTH, F. STRAVINSKY.
617(TLS):7NOV75-1336

ROUX, J. L'ORGANISATION SCIENTIF-
IQUE DE L'ÉCONOMIE NATIONALE. (BKS
1&2) LA MACHINE À GOUVERNER?
W. SCHÄFER, 182:VOL26#3/4-90
ROUX, L. - SEE HOBBES, T.
ROWAN, R. THE FOUR DAYS OF MAYA-
GUEZ.
W. PINCUS, 441:28SEP75-18
ROWBOTHAM, S. HIDDEN FROM HISTORY.
P. ADAMS, 61:MAR75-146
E. LONG, 441:16MAR75-12
ROWE, C.J. THE "EUDEMIAN" & "NICO-
MACHEAN ETHICS."*
C. KIRWAN, 123:MAR74-43
R.K. SPRAGUE, 122:OCT73-315
ROWE, J.G. & W.H. STOCKDALE, EDS.
FLORILEGIUM HISTORIALE.
J.K. GADOL, 551(RENQ):AUTUMN73-295
ROWE, W.W. NABOKOV'S DECEPTIVE
WORLD.
M.K. HULTQUIST, 502(PRS):FALL73-
271
D.B. JOHNSON, 574(SEEJ):SUMMER72-
242
ROWELL, G., ED. VICTORIAN DRAMATIC
CRITICISM.*
H. KOSOK, 447(N&Q):JUL73-278
ROWLAND, B. ANIMALS WITH HUMAN
FACES.
K. VARTY, 617(TLS):8AUG75-901
639(VQR):SPRING74-LX
ROWLAND, B. BLIND BEASTS.*
D. MEHL, 38:BAND91HEFT2-255
E. REISS, 589:JAN74-151
R.M. WILSON, 175:SPRING72-23
ROWLAND, B., ED. CHAUCER & MIDDLE
ENGLISH STUDIES.
E.T. DONALDSON, 617(TLS):28FEB75-
212
ROWLAND, H.S. NO MORE SCHOOL.
A. BROYARD, 441:8APR75-41
ROWLAND, P. THE LAST LIBERAL GOV-
ERNMENTS.
M. ROSE, 637(VS):MAR74-319
ROWLANDS, S. UNCOLLECTED POEMS
(1604?-1617). (F.O. WAAGE, JR.,
ED)
D.M. FRIEDMAN, 551(RENQ):SPRING73-
78
ROWLEY, A., ED. THE BARONS OF EURO-
PEAN INDUSTRY.
N. FAITH, 617(TLS):2MAY75-486
ROWSE, A.L. OXFORD IN THE HISTORY
OF ENGLAND. (BRITISH TITLE: OXFORD
IN THE HISTORY OF THE NATION.)
R. FULFORD, 617(TLS):17OCT75-1244
C.L. MEE, JR., 441:7DEC75-46
ROWSE, A.L. SHAKESPEARE THE MAN.*
I. BROWN, 157:SUMMER73-73
M. HATTAWAY, 175:AUTUMN73-113
A.R. YOUNG, 150(DR):WINTER73/74-
767
ROY, C. POÉSIES.
A. BERGENS, 207(FR):APR73-1067
ROY, E. BRITISH DRAMA SINCE SHAW.
A.N. ATHANASON, 572:JAN73-37
ROY, G. LA RIVIÈRE SANS REPOS.
P. BRADY, 207(FR):APR73-1068
ROY, J. JULIO CORTÁZAR ANTE SU
SOCIEDAD.
W.L. SIEMENS, 268:JUL75-179
ROY, P. & G. GARCIN. LE FRANÇAIS
PRATIQUE I. (2ND ED)
R. MIKUS, 207(FR):DEC72-468

317

ROY, P. & G. GARCIN. LE FRANÇAIS
PRATIQUE II.
  R. MIKUS, 207(FR):MAY73-1269
ROY, S.C. ORAON RELIGION & CUSTOMS.
  E.J. JAY, 293(JAST):MAY73-537
ROY CHAUDHURY, P.C. C.F. ANDREWS.
  J.H. BROOMFIELD, 293(JAST):FEB73-
  351
"ROYAL BOROUGH OF KINGSTON UPON
THAMES: GUIDE TO THE BOROUGH AR-
CHIVES."
  S. BOND, 325:APR73-615
"ROYAL COMMISSION ON ANCIENT & HIS-
TORICAL MONUMENTS OF SCOTLAND."
(ARGYLL: VOL 1, KINTYRE.)
  D. WALKER, 46:JAN73-80
"ROYAL COMMISSION ON BOOK PUBLISH-
ING: BACKGROUND PAPERS." "ROYAL
COMMISSION ON BOOK PUBLISHING: CAN-
ADIAN PUBLISHERS & CANADIAN PUB-
LISHING."
  M. WOLFE, 102(CANL):SUMMER73-108
ROYCE, J.R., ED. TOWARD UNIFICATION
IN PSYCHOLOGY.
  R.F. KITCHENER, 486:SEP73-461
ROYCE, J.R. & W.W. ROZEBOOM, EDS.
THE PSYCHOLOGY OF KNOWING.
  H.F. MOORE, 486:JUN73-322
  C.G. MORGAN, 154:SEP73-544
ROYCE, K. THE WOODCUTTER OPERATION.
  N. CALLENDAR, 441:4MAY75-55
ROZANOV, V. DOSTOEVSKY & THE LEGEND
OF THE GRAND INQUISITOR.*
  M. BANERJEE, 574(SEEJ):WINTER72-
  480
  E. HEINE, 573(SSF):FALL73-434
  R. NEUHÄUSER, 104:FALL73-427
ROZAS, J.M. - SEE DE TASSIS, J. & C.
DE VILLAMEDIANA
ROZOV, N.N. RUSSKAIA RUKOPISNAIA
KNIGA.
  R.W.F. POPE, 104:WINTER74-593
RUBCOVA, E.S. ÈSKIMOSSKO-RUSSKIJ
SLOVAR'.
  T. ULVING, 269(IJAL):JUL73-194
RUBEL, M. - SEE MARX, K. & F. ENGELS
RUBENIUS, A. THE WOMAN QUESTION IN
MRS. GASKELL'S LIFE & WORKS.
  G.B. TENNYSON, 445(NCF):DEC73-370
RUBENS, B. I SENT A LETTER TO MY
LOVE.
  G. CLIFFORD, 617(TLS):25JUL75-821
  J. MELLORS, 362:7AUG75-189
RUBIN, D.L. HIGHER, HIDDEN ORDER.*
  A.J. STEELE, 402(MLR):OCT74-869
RUBIN, J. & B.H. JERNUDD, EDS. CAN
LANGUAGE BE PLANNED?
  A. PIETRZYK, 399(MLJ):APR73-216
RUBIN, J.J. THE HISTORIC WHITMAN.
  G.W. ALLEN, 27(AL):MAY74-224
RUBIN, L.D., JR., ED. THE COMIC
IMAGINATION IN AMERICAN LITERATURE.
  639(VQR):SUMMER74-LXXII
RUBIN, L.D., JR. THE WRITER IN THE
SOUTH.*
  J.M. COX, 569(SR):WINTER74-163
  J.L. DAVIS, 125:OCT73-77
  I. MALIN, 219(GAR):SPRING73-128
  295:FEB74-438
RUBIN, M. UNFINISHED BUSINESS.
  M. LEVIN, 441:4MAY75-53
RUBIN, S. MEDIEVAL ENGLISH MEDI-
CINE.
  C. WELLS, 617(TLS):14MAR75-283

RUBINOFF, L. COLLINGWOOD & THE
REFORM OF METAPHYSICS.*
  D. POLE, 393(MIND):APR73-294
RUBINSTEIN, A. MY YOUNG YEARS.
  F. DAWES, 415:MAR74-220
  J.A. WESTRUP, 410(M&L):JAN74-98
RUBINSTEIN, R.L. MY BROTHER PAUL.
  G. BERGER, 287:JUN73-24
RUBINSTEIN, S.L. WRITING.
  J. BLANKENSHIP, 480(P&R):FALL73-
  255
RUBULIS, A. BALTIC LITERATURE.
  R. AUTY, 447(N&Q):AUG73-317
RUDAT, E.M. LAS IDEAS ESTÉTICAS DE
ESTEBAN DE ARTEAGA.
  R.M. COX, 481(PQ):JUL73-458
RUDD, N., ED. ESSAYS ON CLASSICAL
LITERATURE SELECTED FROM "ARION"
WITH AN INTRODUCTION.
  G.W. WILLIAMS, 123:NOV74-317
RUDE, F. ALOYSIUS BERTRAND.
  J-L. STEINMETZ, 535(RHL):JAN-FEB
  73-146
RUDÉ, G. ROBESPIERRE.
  R. COBB, 362:4SEP75-314
RUDISILL, R. MIRROR IMAGES.
  M.S. YOUNG, 39:JUL73-72
RUDNER, R. & I. SCHEFFLER, EDS.
LOGIC & ART.*
  J.E. LLEWELYN, 479(PHQ):OCT73-367
RUDNICKI, K.S. THE LAST OF THE WAR
HORSES.
  E. DE MAUNY, 362:20FEB75-250
RUDOLPH, E. DAS FINALE SATZGEFÜGE
ALS INFORMATIONSKOMPLEX.
  H. MEIER, 72:BAND211HEFT3/6-458
RUDORFF, R. BELLE EPOQUE.*
  A. POWELL, 39:APR73-438
RUDORFF, R. THE MYTH OF FRANCE.
  J.K. SIMON, 207(FR):OCT72-174
RUDOWSKI, V.A. LESSING'S "AESTHET-
ICA IN NUCE."
  G. HILLEN, 400(MLN):OCT73-1047
  M.M. METZGER, 399(MLJ):JAN-FEB73-
  60
RUDSKOGER, A. PLAIN.
  B. NILSSON, 597(SN):VOL45#1-176
RUETHER, R.R. FAITH & FRATRICIDE.
  D. GOLDSTEIN, 617(TLS):15AUG75-926
RUFER, J. - SEE SCHOENBERG, A.
RUFF, J.L. SHELLEY'S "THE REVOLT OF
ISLAM."
  P.H. BUTTER, 677:VOL4-314
RUFINOS. THE POEMS OF RUFINOS.
(J.M. DRYOFF, TRANS)
  D. BESSAI, 99:JUL75-36
RUFUS OF EPHESUS. RUFI EPHESII
QUAESTIONES MEDICINALES. (H.
GÄRTNER, ED)
  A.E. HANSON, 124:FEB74-237
RUGANDA, J. THE BURDENS.
  A. RENDLE, 157:SUMMER73-79
RUGE, H. ZUR ENTSTEHUNG DER NEU-
GRIECHISCHEN SUBSTANTIVDEKLINATION.
  E. NEU, 260(IF):BAND77HEFT2/3-314
  H. SEILER, 343:BAND16HEFT2-172
RUHE, E. LES "PROUERBES SENEKE" LE
PHILOSOPHE.
  M. JACKSON, 545(RPH):NOV73-252
RUIJGH, C.J. AUTOUR DU "'TE' ÉP-
IQUE."
  P. CHANTRAINE, 555:VOL47FASC2-319

RUIZ, J. LIBRO DE BUEN AMOR. (R.S.
WILLIS, ED & TRANS)
K. ADAMS, 402(MLR):JUL74-677
R. EDWARDS, 141:SPRING73-186
T.R.H., 131(CL):SUMMER74-286
RUIZ RAMÓN, F. HISTORIA DEL TEATRO
ESPAÑOL: SIGLO XX.
T.B. BARCLAY, 397(MD):JUN73-103
RUIZ SALVADOR, A. EL ATENEO CIEN-
TÍFICO, LITERARIO Y ARTÍSTICO DE
MADRID (1835-1885).*
S. GARCÍA CASTAÑEDA, 405(MP):MAY
74-459
RŪĶE-DRAVIŅA, V., ED. DONUM BALTI-
CŪM.
E. HAUZENBERGA-ŠTURMA, 343:BAND16
HEFT1-65
RŪĶE-DRAVIŅA, V. PLACE NAMES IN
KĀUGURI COUNTY, LATVIA.
A. GĀTERS, 343:BAND16HEFT1-96
RUKEYSER, M. BREAKING OPEN.*
J.J. MC GANN, 491:OCT74-44
RUKEYSER, M. THE LIFE OF POETRY.
J.M. BRINNIN, 441:2MAR75-4
"RUKOPISNOE NASLEDIE DREVNEJ. RUSI
PO MATERIALAM PUŠKINSKOGO DOMA."
D. TSCHIŽEWSKIJ, 72:BAND211HEFT
3/6-477
RULE, J. LESBIAN IMAGES.
P. GROSSKURTH, 99:SEP75-61
RUMBELOW, D. THE COMPLETE JACK THE
RIPPER.
P.D. JAMES, 617(TLS):11APR75-394
RUMBLE, T.C. THE BRETON LAYS IN
MIDDLE ENGLISH.
N. JACOBS, 439(NM):1973/2-354
RUMPLER, H. DIE DEUTSCHE POLITIK
DES FREIHERRN VON BEUST 1848-1850.
F. EYCK, 575(SEER):JUL74-472
RUNCIMAN, S. THE ORTHODOX CHURCHES
& THE SECULAR STATE.
M. HEPPELL, 575(SEER):JUL74-477
RUNCIMAN, W.G. A CRITIQUE OF MAX
WEBER'S PHILOSOPHY OF SOCIAL SCI-
ENCE.
J. HEIL, 486:JUN73-317
M. WESTON, 483:APR73-195
P. WINCH, 482(PHR):APR74-263
RUNDLE, B. PERCEPTION, SENSATION,
& VERIFICATION.*
R.W. MILLER, 482(PHR):JUL74-403
G.J. WARNOCK, 479(PHQ):OCT73-369
RUNNALS, G.A., ED. LE MIRACLE DE
L'ENFANT RESSUSCITÉ.
L.R. MUIR, 208(FS):OCT74-442
RUNNALLS, G.A., ED. LE MYSTÈRE DE
SAINT CHRISTOFLE.
P. RICKARD, 382(MAE):1974/3-299
RUO-WANG, B. - SEE UNDER BAO RUO-
WANG
RUOFF, A. GRUNDLAGEN UND METHODEN
DER UNTERSUCHUNG GESPROCHENER
SPRACHE.
H-W. ROYÉ, 182:VOL26#19-669
RUPP, H. & E. STUDER - SEE RANKE, F.
RUPRECHT, E. & D. BÄNSCH, EDS. LIT-
ERARISCHE MANIFESTE DER JAHRHUN-
DERTWENDE 1890-1910.*
C. HILL, 221(GQ):MAY73-448
RUSCH, J. DIE VORSTELLUNG VOM GOL-
DENEN ZEITALTER DER ENGLISCHEN
SPRACHE IM 16., 17. UND 18. JAHR-
[CONTINUED]

[CONTINUING]
HUNDERT.*
A.R. TELLIER, 189(EA):JUL-SEP73-
347
RUSCHIONI, A. INTRODUZIONE AL LEO-
PARDI.
V. POZZI, 275(IQ):SPRING74-109
RUSCHIONI, A. - SEE MURATORI, L.A.
RUSE, G.A. HOUNDSTOOTH.
N. CALLENDAR, 441:13JUL75-36
RUSH, M. & M. SHAW, EDS. THE HOUSE
OF COMMONS: SERVICES & FACILITIES.
617(TLS):28FEB75-232
RUSHDIE, S. GRIMUS.
D. WILSON, 617(TLS):21FEB75-185
RUSHER, W.A. THE MAKING OF THE NEW
MAJORITY PARTY.
M. TOLCHIN, 441:19OCT75-43
RUSHMER, R.F. HUMANIZING HEALTH
CARE.
H.J. GEIGER, 441:14DEC75-7
RUSIÑOL, S. SANTIAGO RUSIÑOL PER
ELL MATEIX. (R. PLANES, ED)
A. YATES, 86(BHS):JUL73-317
RUSKIN, J. RUSKIN IN ITALY.* (H.I.
SHAPIRO, ED)
J.S. DEARDEN, 135:JUN73-150
G.P. LANDOW, 301(JEGP):APR74-264
K. ROBERTS, 90:FEB73-126
RUSKIN, J. THE WINNINGTON LETTERS.
(V.A. BURD, ED)
B.K. HELSINGER, 405(MP):AUG73-98
RUSS, J. THE FEMALE MAN.
G. JONAS, 441:4MAY75-50
RUSSEL, H.D. RARE ETCHINGS BY GIO-
VANNI BATTISTA & GIOVANNI DOMENICO
TIEPOLO.
T. LASK, 55:NOV72-16
RUSSELL, A.J. THE DEVALINO CAPER.
N. CALLENDAR, 441:13JUL75-36
RUSSELL, B. ESSAYS IN ANALYSIS.
(D. LACKEY, ED)
N. GRIFFIN, 63:AUG74-183
RUSSELL, B. LA MÉTHODE SCIENTIFIQUE
EN PHILOSOPHIE.
P. DUBOIS, 542:APR-JUN73-228
RUSSELL, C. THE CRISIS OF PARLIA-
MENTS.
J.M.W. BEAN, 551(RENQ):AUTUMN73-
318
RUSSELL, D. THE TAMARISK TREE.
R. DINNAGE, 617(TLS):1AUG75-864
M. LASKI, 362:17JUL75-92
RUSSELL, D.A. - SEE PLUTARCH
RUSSELL, D.A. & M. WINTERBOTTOM,
EDS. ANCIENT LITERARY CRITICISM.
M.L. CLARKE, 123:MAR74-78
G. KENNEDY, 124:NOV72-178
R.S. KILPATRICK, 255(HAB):SPRING73-
137
RUSSELL, F. A CITY IN TERROR.
N. BLIVEN, 442(NY):30JUN75-97
R. COLES, 453:7AUG75-39
RUSSELL, G.O. THE VOWEL.
I. LEHISTE, 269(IJAL):APR73-123
RUSSELL, I. & J. THE TASKS OF MING
LO.
D.M. DAY, 157:AUTUMN73-86
RUSSELL, J. ANTHONY POWELL.
T.L. ASHTON, 295:FEB74-755
A. MAACK, 447(N&Q):SEP73-352
RUSSELL, J. VUILLARD.
S. WHITFIELD, 90:JUN73-403

RUSSELL, J.B. WITCHCRAFT IN THE
MIDDLE AGES.*
  R. BRIGGS, 617(TLS):3JAN75-13
  R.H. WEST, 219(GAR):SPRING73-137
RUSSELL, J.C. MEDIEVAL REGIONS &
THEIR CITIES.
  J. MUNDY, 589:APR74-371
RUSSELL, L. EVERYDAY LIFE IN COLON-
IAL CANADA.
  K. MC SWEENEY, 529(QQ):AUTUMN73-
  500
RUSSELL, N.H. INDIAN THOUGHTS.
  J. HEYNEN, 448:VOL13#2-96
RUSSELL, P.E., ED. SPAIN.
  W.C. ATKINSON, 402(MLR):OCT74-893
  B. STEEL, 67:NOV74-248
RUSSELL, R. BIRD LIVES!* JAZZ
STYLE IN KANSAS CITY & THE SOUTH-
WEST.
  F.J. GILLIS, 187:MAY75-315
RUSSELL, T. BLACKS, WHITES & BLUES.
  N. COHEN, 292(JAF):JAN-MAR73-80
RUSSELL-WOOD, A.J.R., ED. FROM
COLONY TO NATION.
  617(TLS):21NOV75-1397
"LA RUSSIE ET L'EUROPE XVE-XXE
SIÈCLES."
  M. RAEFF, 104:SPRING73-120
RUSSO, J.P. ALEXANDER POPE.*
  W. KUPERSMITH, 481(PQ):JUL73-565
  P. MC ISAAC, 150(DR):SPRING73-187
  A. SHERBO, 402(MLR):JUL74-623
RUSSU, I.I. ELEMENTE AUTOHTONE ÎN
LIMBA ROMÂNĂ.*
  H. STEIN, 260(IF):BAND78-301
RÜSTER, C. HETHITISCHE KEILSCHRIFT-
PALÄOGRAPHIE.
  G. NEUMANN, 260(IF):BAND78-246
RUSTOMJI, N. ENCHANTED FRONTIERS.
  L.E. ROSE, 293(JAST):NOV72-196
RUTHERFORD, A., ED. BYRON: THE
CRITICAL HERITAGE.*
  T. VON BREMEN, 38:BAND91HEFT1-127
RUTHERFORD, A., ED. COMMONWEALTH.
  W.H. NEW, 102(CANL):WINTER74-87
RUTHVEN, K.K. A GUIDE TO EZRA
POUND'S "PERSONAE" (1926).
  A. LEFEVERE, 179(ES):JUN72-268
RUTLAND, R.A. THE NEWSMONGERS.
  I. DILLIARD, 639(VQR):WINTER74-121
RUTT, R., ED & TRANS. THE BAMBOO
GROVE.*
  D.R. MC CANN, 244(HJAS):VOL33-272
RÜTTEN, R. SYMBOL UND MYTHUS IM
ALTFRANZÖSISCHEN ROLANDSLIED.
  M. WENDT, 430(NS):JAN73-58
RUWET, N. LANGAGE, MUSIQUE, POÉSIE.
  F. EDELINE, 209(FM):JUL73-304
RUYSLINCK, W. GOLDEN OPHELIA.
  R. GARFITT, 617(TLS):5SEP75-998
RYALL, E.W. SECOND TIME ROUND.
  A. CALDER-MARSHALL, 362:10APR75-
  485
RYALS, C.D., WITH J. CLUBBE & B.F.
FISHER, EDS. NINETEENTH-CENTURY
LITERARY PERSPECTIVES.
  M. MASON, 617(TLS):16MAY75-542
RYAN, A. J.S. MILL.
  D.D. RAPHAEL, 617(TLS):15AUG75-914
RYAN, A. THE PHILOSOPHY OF THE
SOCIAL SCIENCES.*
  D. EMMET, 393(MIND):APR73-313
  R.C. STALNAKER, 482(PHR):JAN73-126

RYAN, J. REMEMBERING HOW WE STOOD.
  C. FITZ GIBBON, 617(TLS):10OCT75-
  1186
RYAN, M. THREATS INSTEAD OF TREES.
  J. ATLAS, 491:FEB75-295
  G. HITCHCOCK, 651(WHR):AUTUMN74-
  405
RYAN, R.V.F. & OTHERS. OUR CREE
DICTIONARY.
  H.C. WOLFART, 269(IJAL):OCT73-272
RYDEN, H. GOD'S DOG.
  R. CARAS, 441:8JUN75-30
RYDÉN, M. COORDINATION OF RELATIVE
CLAUSES IN SIXTEENTH CENTURY ENG-
LISH.
  F.G.A.M. AARTS, 361:SEP73-157
  B. CARSTENSEN, 430(NS):APR73-237
  J.R. SIMON, 189(EA):APR-JUN73-219
  R.W.Z., 179(ES):OCT72-494
RYDER, A.J. TWENTIETH-CENTURY GER-
MANY.
  639(VQR):SPRING74-L
RYDER, D.E. CANADIAN REFERENCE
SOURCES.
  R.C. ELLSWORTH, 517(PBSA):JUL-SEP
  74-343
RYDER, R. EDITH CAVELL.
  G. ANNAN, 362:24APR75-539
  K.O. MORGAN, 617(TLS):4APR75-355
RYDER, R.D. VICTIMS OF SCIENCE.
  A. COWEY, 617(TLS):18APR75-419
RYDJORD, J. KANSAS PLACE-NAMES.
  J.H. BRUNVAND, 292(JAF):JUL-SEP73-
  315
  F.L. UTLEY, 424:DEC73-262
RYE, B.R. THE EXPATRIATE.
  M. LEVIN, 441:13JUL75-34
RYGA, G. THE ECSTASY OF RITA JOE &
OTHER PLAYS.
  J. NOONAN, 529(QQ):AUTUMN73-466
RYKEN, L. THE APOCALYPTIC VISION IN
"PARADISE LOST."*
  M-S. RØSTVIG, 179(ES):OCT72-463
RYKWERT, J. ON ADAM'S HOUSE IN
PARADISE.*
  676(YR):AUTUMN73-XVII
RYLE, G. COLLECTED PAPERS BY GIL-
BERT RYLE.*
  J. PASSMORE, 63:DEC74-257
RYMER, T. THE TRAGEDIES OF THE LAST
AGE 1678.
  P.E. PARNELL, 568(SCN):FALL74-59
RYSTEN, F.S.A. FALSE PROPHETS IN
THE FICTION OF CAMUS, DOSTOEVSKY,
MELVILLE & OTHERS.
  295:FEB74-407
RYUM, U. OM ONDT OG GODT FOLK.
  Å-H. LERVIK, 172(EDDA):1973/2-123

DE SÁ DE MENESES, F. THE CONQUEST
OF MALACCA. (E.C. KNOWLTON, JR.,
ED & TRANS)
  W.G. BOLTZ, 545(RPH):MAY74-541
  J.G. DE CASPARIS, 293(JAST):AUG73-
  748
SAAGE, R. EIGENTUM, STAAT UND GE-
SELLSCHAFT BEI IMMANUEL KANT.
  J. KOPPER, 342:BAND64HEFT4-518
SAAKE, H. SAPPHOSTUDIEN.
  M.R. LEFKOWITZ, 124:NOV73-115
SAAKE, H. ZUR KUNST SAPPHOS.
  E.D. FLOYD, 124:NOV73-116

320

SAALMAN, H. HAUSSMANN.
N. MILLER, 576:MAR73-67
SAATRÖWE, J. GENIE UND REFLEXION.
W. STEINBECK, 342:BAND64HEFT4-513
SAAVEDRA, M.D. - SEE UNDER DE CER-
VANTES SAAVEDRA, M.
SABADINO DEGLI ARIENTI, G. ART &
LIFE AT THE COURT OF ERCOLE I
D'ESTE.* (W.L. GUNDERSHEIMER, ED)
L. LOCKWOOD, 551(RENQ):WINTER73-
494
SABATINI, A.G. RAGIONE E TECNICA.
E. NAMER, 542:OCT-DEC73-496
SABIANI, J. "LA BALLADE DU COEUR."
J. VIARD, 535(RHL):MAR-JUN73-537
SABINE, W.H.W. MURDER, 1776 & WASH-
INGTON'S POLICY OF SILENCE.
J. CROWLEY, 150(DR):AUTUMN73-585
SABOURIN, P. LA RÉFLEXION SUR L'ART
D'ANDRÉ MALRAUX.
205(FMLS):APR73-216
SABRI-TABRIZI, G.R. THE "HEAVEN"
& "HELL" OF WILLIAM BLAKE.*
S.H. BRISMAN, 591(SIR):FALL74-365
SACCENTI, M. LIBRI E MASCHERE DEL
SEICENTO ITALIANO.
N.L.F., 275(IQ):SPRING74-107
SACHS, A., ED. STUDIES IN THE
DRAMA.
J. HASLER, 179(ES):JUN72-271
SACHS, V. THE MYTH OF AMERICA.
J. MARTIN, 27(AL):JAN75-584
SACOTO, A. EL INDIO EN EL ENSAYO DE
LA AMÉRICA ESPAÑOLA.*
I. CARVALLO CASTILLO, 263:OCT-DEC
74-469
SACRÉ, J. COEUR ÉLÉGIE ROUGE.
M. NAUDIN, 207(FR):MAY73-1250
SADDLEMYER, A. - SEE SYNGE, J.M.
SADOUL, G. DICTIONARY OF FILMS.
DICTIONARY OF FILM MAKERS. (BOTH
ED & TRANS BY P. MORRIS)
A.H. MARILL, 200:JAN73-46
SAFFIN, N.W. SCIENCE, RELIGION &
EDUCATION IN BRITAIN, 1804-1904.
617(TLS):31JAN75-121
SAFFREY, H.D. & L.G. WESTERINK - SEE
PROCLUS
SAFFRON, M.H. - SEE "MAURUS OF SAL-
ERNO TWELFTH-CENTURY 'OPTIMUS
PHYSICUS'"
SAFIRE, W. BEFORE THE FALL.
C. LEHMANN-HAUPT, 441:18FEB75-27
R.H. ROVERE, 442(NY):19MAY75-116
D. SCHORR, 441:23FEB75-2
R. TODD, 61:JUL75-72
G. WILLS, 453:15MAY75-7
SÄFLUND, M-L. THE EAST PEDIMENT OF
THE TEMPLE OF ZEUS AT OLYMPIA.
J. FREL, 121(CJ):FEB/MAR74-257
"THE SAGA OF TRISTRAM & ÍSÖND." (P.
SCHACH, TRANS)
K.H. OBER, 301(JEGP):OCT74-578
SAGARIN, E. FLAKE OF SNOW.
M. LEVIN, 441:2FEB75-12
SAGARRA, E. TRADITION & REVOLU-
TION.*
D. GEARY, 220(GL&L):OCT73-92
F. STOCK, 52:BAND8HEFT3-349
SAHGAL, N. THE DAY IN SHADOW.
M.E. DERRETT, 293(JAST):AUG73-727
N. HEPBURN, 362:27MAR75-421
M. JOHNSON, 617(TLS):28MAR75-329

SAID, E.W. BEGINNINGS.
R. TOWERS, 441:21DEC75-15
SAINATI, A. STUDI DI LETTERATURA
MEDIEVALE E UMANISTICA.
E. BIGI, 228(GSLI):VOL150FASC470/
471-445
SAINE, T.P. DIE ÄSTHETISCHE THEO-
DIZEE.*
R. BELGARDT, 222(GR):NOV73-317
SAINE, T.P. GEORG FORSTER.
H.L. BACHARACH, 125:OCT73-98
H.R. VAGET, 406:SPRING74-95
ST. CLAIR, L. THE EMERALD TRAP.*
M. LASKI, 362:20NOV75-684
ST. CLAIR, W. THAT GREECE MIGHT
STILL BE FREE.*
D.V.E., 191(ELN):SEP73(SUPP)-39
ST. JOHN-STEVAS, N. - SEE BAGEHOT, W.
DE SAINT-DENIS, E. - SEE PLINY
SAINT-JACQUES, B. STRUCTURAL ANALY-
SIS OF MODERN JAPANESE.
B. EVERSMEYER, 353:15JUL73-94
SAINT-LOUIS, C. & M.A. LUBIN, EDS.
PANORAMA DE LA POÉSIE HAÏTIENNE.
W.J. SMITH, 37:MAY73-40
SAINT-LU, A. LA VERA PAZ.
M. MIQUEL, 263:APR-JUN74-156
SAINT-SAËNS, C. & G. FAURÉ. CAMILLE
SAINT-SAËNS & GABRIEL FAURÉ: COR-
RESPONDANCE. (J-M. NECTOUX, ED)
G.W. HOPKINS, 415:SEP74-751
DUC DE SAINT-SIMON. HISTORICAL MEM-
OIRS, 1691-1709 [&] 1710-1715. (L.
NORTON, ED & TRANS)
B.L.O. RICHTER, 207(FR):FEB73-643
DE STE. CROIX, G.E.M. THE ORIGINS
OF THE PELOPONNESIAN WAR.
W.R. CONNOR, 487:WINTER73-399
SAINTE-BEUVE, C-A. CORRESPONDANCE
GÉNÉRALE. (VOL 16) (J. & A. BON-
NEROT, EDS)
R. MOLHO, 535(RHL):JAN-FEB73-144
SAINTE-BEUVE, C-A. CORRESPONDANCE
GÉNÉRALE. (VOL 17) (J. BONNEROT,
ED)
J. RICHARDSON, 617(TLS):3OCT75-
1150
SAINTE-BEUVE, C-A. LITERARY CRITI-
CISM. (E.R. MARKS, ED & TRANS)
T.H. GOETZ, 446:FALL-WINTER73/74-
91
SAISSELIN, R.G. THE RULE OF REASON
& THE RUSES OF THE HEART.*
V.W. TOPAZIO, 546(RR):JAN73-71
SAITZ, R.L. & D. CARR. SELECTED
READINGS IN ENGLISH FOR STUDENTS OF
ENGLISH AS A SECOND LANGUAGE.*
J. ROSS, 399(MLJ):NOV73-366
SAIYIDAIN, Z. THE REALM OF PERCEP-
TION.
D. BASTOW, 479(PHQ):JUL73-266
SAJAVAARA, K. - SEE GROSSETESTE, R.
SAJÓ, G. - SEE BOETHIUS
SAKHAROV, A.D. MY COUNTRY & THE
WORLD.
R.H. ANDERSON, 441:14NOV75-41
H.J. MORGENTHAU, 441:9NOV75-3
442(NY):22DEC75-96
SAKUTARO, H. - SEE UNDER HAGIWARA
SAKUTARO
SALA, A. & E. DURÁN. CRÍTICA DE LA
IZQUIRDA AUTORITARIA EN CATALUÑA
1967-1974.
P. PRESTON, 617(TLS):4JUL75-740

SALA, G. DAS APRIORI IN DER MENSCH-
LICHEN ERKENNTNIS.
  H. HOLZ, 342:BAND64HEFT4-509
SALAMA, A. SHELLEY'S MAJOR POEMS.
  P.H. BUTTER, 402(MLR):JUL74-624
SALAMAN, R.A. DICTIONARY OF TOOLS.
  P. CARNEGY, 617(TLS):30MAY75-590
SALAMANCA, J.R. EMBARKATION.*
  P.M. SPACKS, 249(HUDR):SUMMER74-
  293
  639(VQR):SUMMER74-LXXXII
SALAMON, F. A COLLECTOR'S GUIDE TO
PRINTS & PRINTMAKERS FROM DÜRER TO
PICASSO.
  M. GREENHALGH, 135:MAY73-64
SALANI, T.P. - SEE UNDER POGGI SAL-
ANI, T.
SALCEDO-BASTARDO, J.L. BOLÍVAR.
  D. BUSHNELL, 263:JUL-SEP74-301
SALE, A. UNDER THE WAR & OTHER
POEMS.
  J. FULLER, 617(TLS):7NOV75-1327
SALE, K. POWER SHIFT.
  M. JANEWAY, 61:DEC75-116
  C. LEHMANN-HAUPT, 441:21NOV75-47
  R. LEKACHMAN, 441:30NOV75-1
SALE, K. SDS.
  N. MILLS, 676(YR):AUTUMN73-146
SALE, R. MODERN HEROISM.*
  W.H. PRITCHARD, 401(MLQ):MAR74-92
SALE, R. THE WHITE BUFFALO.
  M. LEVIN, 441:28DEC75-20
SALGADO, G. EYE-WITNESSES OF SHAKE-
SPEARE.
  A. BARTON, 362:7AUG75-187
SALGADO, M.A. EL ARTE POLIFACÉTICO
DE LA "CARICATURAS LÍRICAS" JUAN-
RAMONIANAS.
  W.H. ROBERTS, 399(MLJ):MAR73-151
SALGADO, S. BREVE HISTORIA DE LA
MÚSICA CULTA EN EL URUGUAY.
  R. STEVENSON, 37:AUG-SEP73-58
SALIFOU, A. LE DAMAGARAM DU SUL-
TANAT DE ZINDER AU XIXE SIÈCLE.
  M.M. HOROWITZ, 69:OCT73-373
SALINAS DE MARICHAL, S. EL MUNDO
POÉTICO DE RAFAEL ALBERTI.*
  C.A. PÉREZ, 546(RR):JAN73-83
SALINGAR, L. SHAKESPEARE & THE TRA-
DITIONS OF COMEDY.
  C.L. BARBER, 617(TLS):8AUG75-889
SALINGER, J.D. THE COMPLETE UNCOL-
LECTED SHORT STORIES OF J.D. SALIN-
GER.
  D. LODGE, 617(TLS):13JUN75-642
SALISBURY, C.Y. RUSSIAN DIARY.*
  S.F. STARR, 441:19JAN75-28
SALISBURY, H.E. THE GATES OF HELL.
  A. ASTRACHAN, 441:2NOV75-16
  R.R. LINGEMAN, 441:27DEC75-15
SALKEY, A., ED. BREAKLIGHT.
  A. CLUYSENAAR, 565:VOL14#2-62
SALLASKA, G. PRIAM'S DAUGHTER.
  P. BEER, 617(TLS):17JAN75-48
SALLMANN, K.G. DIE GEOGRAPHIE DES
ÄLTEREN PLINIUS IN IHREM VERHÄLTNIS
ZU VARRO.
  R. CHEVALLIER, 555:VOL47FASC1-166
  W.D.E. COULSON, 124:MAR73-352
SALLUST. SALLUSTE, "DE CATILINAE
CONIURATIONE (LA CONJURATION DE
CATILINA)." (J. HELLEGOUARC'H, ED)
  D. PETITJEAN, 555:VOL47FASC2-349

SALLUST. C. SALLUSTIUS CRISPUS,
"BELLUM JUGURTHINUM." (E. KOESTER-
MANN, ED)
  M.G. MORGAN, 124:MAY73-478
SALM, P. THE POEM AS PLANT.*
  L.W. KAHN, 222(GR):JAN73-60
  W. LEPPMANN, 131(CL):SUMMER73-278
SALMON, V., ED. THE WORKS OF FRAN-
CIS LODWICK.
  W.F. BOLTON, 297(JL):SEP73-365
  M. DOBROVOLSKY, 320(CJL):SPRING74-
  84
  S. POTTER, 677:VOL4-239
SALOMON, J-J. SCIENCE & POLITICS.*
(FRENCH TITLE: SCIENCE ET POLI-
TIQUE.)
  J. FREUND, 542:JAN-MAR73-93
SALOMON, N. LA VIDA RURAL CASTEL-
LANA EN TIEMPOS DE FELIPE II.
  A. MACKAY, 402(MLR):JUL74-678
SALONIUS. SALONII, "DE EVANGELIO
IOHANNIS;" "DE EVANGELIO MATTHAEI."
(C. CURTI, ED)
  P. LANGLOIS, 555:VOL47FASC1-178
SALSANO, F. TRADIZIONE E MODERNITÀ
NELL'OTTOCENTO.
  W.T.S., 191(ELN):SEP73(SUPP)-164
SALTARELLI, M. A PHONOLOGY OF ITAL-
IAN IN A GENERATIVE GRAMMAR.*
  G. LEPSCHY, 353:1AUG73-109
SALTER, A. & P. WOLF, EDS. THE CAL-
ENDAR OF THE CLAUDE ELLIOTT COLLEC-
TION, 1821-1937.
  A.L. NOLEN, 14:JAN73-76
SALTER, C. NORTHERN SPAIN.
  T. LAMBERT, 617(TLS):30MAY75-606
SALTER, J. LIGHT YEARS.
  A. BROYARD, 441:25JUN75-47
  R. TOWERS, 441:27JUL75-6
SALTER, R. GEORG HEYMS LYRIK.
  H. WOLFSCHÜTZ, 182:VOL26#17/18-606
SALTVEIT, L. - SEE SEIP, D.A.
SALU, H. SEID UMSCHLUNGEN, MILLION-
EN!
  H. NÄGELE, 680(ZDP):BAND92HEFT4-
  595
SALUS, P.H., COMP. PĀṆINI TO POS-
TAL.*
  E.F.K. KOERNER, 206:NOV73-589
SALVADOR, A.R. - SEE UNDER RUIZ SAL-
VADOR, A.
SALVERTE, E. HISTORY OF THE NAMES
OF MEN, NATIONS, & PLACES IN THEIR
CONNECTION WITH THE PROGRESS OF
CIVILIZATION.
  K.B. HARDER, 424:JUN73-120
SALVESEN, C. FLOODSHEAF.
  T. EAGLETON, 617(TLS):28FEB75-214
SALVIEN DE MARSEILLE. OEUVRES.
(VOL 1) (G. LAGARRIGUE, ED)
  J. ANDRÉ, 555:VOL47FASC1-175
SALVUCCI, P. ADAM FERGUSON, SOCIOL-
OGIA E FILOSOFIA POLITICA.
  E. NAMER, 542:JAN-MAR73-63
SAMARAS, Z. THE COMIC ELEMENT OF
MONTAIGNE'S STYLE.*
  R.D. COTTRELL, 546(RR):NOV73-306
SAMARIN, W.J. SANGO.
  A.N. TUCKER, 69:OCT73-363
SAMAY, S. REASON REVISITED.
  J-D.C., 543:JUN73-765
  M.W. HAMILTON, 479(PHQ):APR73-166
  A. KOLNAI, 393(MIND):JUL73-453

SAMBURSKY, S. & S. PINES. THE CON-
CEPT OF TIME IN LATE NEOPLATONISM.
   A.H. ARMSTRONG, 123:NOV74-231
SAMELSON, W. ENGLISH AS A SECOND
LANGUAGE. (PHASE 1)
   Y.A. EL-EZABI, 399(MLJ):NOV74-373
SAMMARTINI, G.B. THE SYMPHONIES OF
G.B. SAMMARTINI. (VOL 1) (B. CHUR-
GIN, ED)
   E.K. WOLF, 317:SPRING73-164
SAMMET, D. DIE SUBSTANTIVBILDUNG
MIT SUFFIXEN BEI CHRESTIEN DE
TROYES.
   G. INEICHEN, 260(IF):BAND77HEFT
   2/3-342
SAMMONS, J.L. ANGELUS SILESIUS.
   K.G. KNIGHT, 220(GL&L):OCT73-87
SAMMONS, J.L. SIX ESSAYS ON THE
YOUNG GERMAN NOVEL.
   R-E.B. JOERES, 406:SUMMER74-175
SAMOFF, J. TANZANIA.
   W. TORDOFF, 617(TLS):17OCT75-1242
SAMONÀ, G.P. IL GATTOPARDO, I
RACONTI, LAMPEDUSA.
   F. DONINI, 617(TLS):31OCT75-1292
SAMPERI, F. THE PREFIGURATION.
   C. CORMAN, 114(CHIR):VOL25#1-195
SAMPSON, A. THE SEVEN SISTERS.
   K. COONEY, 441:19OCT75-1
   F. MC FADZEAN, 617(TLS):26SEP75-
   1083
   442(NY):8DEC75-200
SAMPSON, E.C. E.B. WHITE.
   G.C., 569(SR):FALL74-XCVII
SAMSON, J. AMARNA.
   R.J.L. WYNNE-THOMAS, 135:AUG73-316
SAMUEL, A.E. & OTHERS. DEATH &
TAXES.
   P.S. & E.O. DEROW, 487:SPRING73-80
SAMUEL, R., ED. VILLAGE LIFE &
LABOUR.
   P. HORN, 617(TLS):19DEC75-1512
SAMUELS, C.T. THE AMBIGUITY OF
HENRY JAMES.*
   J-P. TOMPKINS, 295:FEB74-662
SAMUELS, E. & J.N. - SEE ADAMS, H.
SAMUELS, M.L. LINGUISTIC EVOLUTION,
WITH SPECIAL REFERENCE TO ENGLISH.
   R.A. DWYER, 35(AS):FALL-WINTER71-
   278
   R.D. EAGLESON, 67:NOV74-244
   A.R. TELLIER, 189(EA):OCT-DEC73-
   456
SÁNCHEZ, E.M. & F. GUILLÉN - SEE
UNDER MEJÍA SÁNCHEZ, E. & F. GUIL-
LÉN
SANCHEZ, J. - SEE CORNEILLE, P.
SÁNCHEZ-ROMERALO, A. & F. IBARRA,
EDS. ANTOLOGÍA DE AUTORES ESPAÑ-
OLES ANTIGUOS Y MODERNOS. (VOL 1)
   J.A. CROW, 399(MLJ):MAR74-136
SÁNCHEZ BARBUDO, A., ED. MIGUEL DE
UNAMUNO.
   J. BUTT, 617(TLS):23MAY75-570
SÁNCHEZ BARBUDO, A. - SEE JIMÉNEZ,
J.R.
SÁNCHEZ VÁZQUEZ, A. ART & SOCIETY.
   L. BAXANDALL, 59(ASOC):FALL-WINTER
   74-485
SANDARS, J. AN INTRODUCTION TO WAR-
GAMING.
   B. HILL, 617(TLS):26DEC75-1543
SANDBACH, F.H. THE STOICS.
   S. PEMBROKE, 617(TLS):16MAY75-535

SANDBACH, M. - SEE STRINDBERG, A.
SANDELL, R.E., ED. ABSTRACTS OF
WILTSHIRE INCLOSURE AWARDS & AGREE-
MENTS.
   E. KERRIDGE, 325:APR73-616
SANDER, H-D. GESCHICHTE DER SCHÖNEN
LITERATUR IN DER DDR.
   P. HUTCHINSON, 220(GL&L):JUL74-334
SANDER, L. PALÄOGRAPHISCHES ZU DEN
SANSKRITHANDSCHRIFTEN DER BERLINER
TURFANSAMMLUNG.*
   J. FILLIOZAT, 182:VOL26#13/14-454
SANDER, V., ED. IDEOLOGIEKRITISCHE
STUDIEN ZUR LITERATUR: ESSAYS I.
   D.H. MILES, 406:SPRING74-92
SANDERS, E. TALES OF BEATNIK GLORY.
   J. YOHALEM, 441:9NOV75-22
SANDERS, L. THE TOMORROW FILE.
   J. DECK, 441:16NOV75-78
SANDERS, P. MOSHOESHOE.
   L. MAIR, 617(TLS):12DEC75-1497
SANDERS, W. JOHN DONNE'S POETRY.*
   E.R. AMOILS, 180(ESA):MAR73-45
   R.A. FOAKES, 175:SUMMER72-67
   J.H. MC CABE, 613:SPRING73-122
   J.M. MUELLER, 405(MP):FEB74-335
SANDFORD, J. SMILING DAVID.
   C.H. ROLPH, 617(TLS):8AUG75-894
SANDGREN, F., ED. OTIUM ET NEGOTIUM.
   A. FAULKES, 402(MLR):OCT74-834
SANDKÜHLER, H-J. FRIEDRICH WILHELM
JOSEPH SCHELLING.
   M.H., 191(ELN):SEP73(SUPP)-155
SANDLER, I. THE TRIUMPH OF AMERICAN
PAINTING.*
   C.W. MILLARD, 54:JUN73-312
SANDMAN, P.M., D.M. RUBIN & D.B.
SACHSMAN. MEDIA.
   I. DILLIARD, 639(VQR):WINTER74-121
SANDMEL, S. THE ENJOYMENT OF SCRIP-
TURE.
   E.M. MOSELEY, 149:DEC74-341
SANDMEL, S. PHILO'S PLACE IN JUDA-
ISM.
   D.E. GROH, 124:FEB73-299
SANDOZ, E. POLITICAL APOCALYPSE.
   R.A. PEACE, 575(SEER):JAN74-133
SANDULESCU, J. & A. GOTTLIEB. THE
CARPATHIAN CAPER.
   S. ELLIN, 441:20JUL75-14
SANECKI, K. THE COMPLETE BOOK OF
HERBS.
   S. CAMPBELL, 362:2JAN75-31
SANFAÇON, R. L'ARCHITECTURE FLAM-
BOYANTE EN FRANCE.*
   R. BRANNER, 54:JUN73-289
SANGUINETI, E. POESIA ITALIANA DEL
NOVECENTO. (VOL 2)
   L. TOSCHI, 275(IQ):SUMMER73-116
SAN JUAN, E., JR. BALAGTAS: ART &
REVOLUTION.
   L. CASPER, 352(LE&W):VOL16#3-1096
SAN JUAN, E., JR. JAMES JOYCE &
THE CRAFT OF FICTION.
   W. PEDEN, 573(SSF):SPRING73-219
SANKALIA, H.D. SOME ASPECTS OF PRE-
HISTORIC TECHNOLOGY IN INDIA.
   SATYAPRAKASH, 273(IC):OCT73-363
SANKEY, B. A COMPANION TO WILLIAM
CARLOS WILLIAMS'S "PATERSON."*
   S. FERGUSON, 219(GAR):SUMMER73-291
   J. MAZZARO, 141:SUMMER72-302
   L. VEZA, 189(EA):JAN-MAR73-115

SAN MIGUEL, Á. SENTIDO Y ESTRUCTURA
DEL "GUZMÁN DE ALFARACHE" DE MATEO
ALEMÁN.
M.J. THACKER, 86(BHS):OCT73-395
SANSOM, W. A YOUNG WIFE'S TALE.*
N. HEPBURN, 362:6FEB75-189
J. MELLORS, 364:DEC74/JAN75-130
SANTAYANA, G. SANTAYANA ON AMERICA.
(R.C. LYON, ED)
J. LACHS, 154:JUN73-370
DE SANTILLANA, G. & H. VON DECHEND.
HAMLET'S MILL.
H.A.T. REICHE, 121(CJ):OCT/NOV73-
81
SANTINELLO, G. LEON BATTISTA ALBER-
TI.
E. NAMER, 542:JAN-MAR73-119
SANTOLI, V. PHILOLOGIE UND KRITIK.
A.P. COTTRELL, 221(GQ):SEP73-181
SANTOS, E.B. PHILIPPINE WINGS.
J.D. WILLIAMS, 293(JAST):AUG73-761
SANZ, L.T. - SEE UNDER TORMO SANZ,
L.
SANZENBACH, S. LES ROMANS DE PIERRE
JEAN JOUVE.*
M.G. ROSE, 207(FR):MAY73-1235
SAPIR, E. & H. HOIJER. THE PHONOL-
OGY & MORPHOLOGY OF THE NAVAHO
LANGUAGE.
G.F. MEIER, 682(ZPSK):BAND26HEFT
3/4-449
SAPORI, G. - SEE DE' RICCI, G.
SAPPENFIELD, J.A. A SWEET INSTRUC-
TION.*
A.O. ALDRIDGE, 656(WMQ):JUL74-522
M. HALL, 432(NEQ):JUN74-337
"SAPPHIRES & PYRITES."
D.V. HART, 293(JAST):MAY73-572
SAPPLER, P., ED. DAS KÖNIGSSTEINER
LIEDERBUCH: MS GERM. QU. 719 BER-
LIN.*
O. SAYCE, 402(MLR):APR74-454
ŠÁRA, M., J. ŠÁROVÁ & A. BYTEL.
ČEŠTINA PRO CIZINCE.
C.E. TOWNSEND, 574(SEEJ):SUMMER72-
262
SARABIANOV, D. RUSSIAN PAINTING OF
THE LATE 1900S & EARLY 1910S. [IN
RUSSIAN]
M. CHAMOT, 39:DEC73-514
SARAN, P., ED. PERSIAN DOCUMENTS.
(PT 1)
A. AHMAD, 318(JAOS):JUL-SEP73-421
SARASON, B.D. HEMINGWAY & "THE SUN"
SET.
295:FEB74-635
SARDESAI, D.R. & B.D. THESES & DIS-
SERTATIONS ON SOUTHEAST ASIA.
W.R. ROFF, 318(JAOS):JAN-MAR73-96
SARDUY, S. COBRA.
J. CHARYN, 441:9MAR75-18
M., WOOD, 453:20MAR75-27
442(NY):27JAN75-102
SAREIL, J. LES TENCIN.
J. DECOTTIGNIES, 535(RHL):JUL-AUG
73-695
J.N. PAPPAS, 207(FR):FEB73-638
SARGENT, P., ED. WOMEN OF WONDER.
G. JONAS, 441:4MAY75-49
SARGENT, R.M. - SEE KALM, P.
SARGENT, T., ED & TRANS. THE HOM-
ERIC HYMNS.*
639(VQR):WINTER74-XIV

SARGESON, F. MORE THAN ENOUGH.
P. CAMPBELL, 362:29MAY75-718
D. DAVIN, 617(TLS):25JUL75-820
SARIKAKIS, T.C. HRŌMAIOI ARCHONTES
TĒS EPARCHIAS MAKEDONIAS. (VOL 1)
J. BRISCOE, 123:NOV74-263
J.M.R. CORMACK, 313:VOL63-257
SARKAR, J.N. ISLAM IN BENGAL (THIR-
TEENTH TO NINETEENTH CENTURY).
H.K. SHERWANI, 273(IC):OCT73-360
SARKAR, K.K. EARLY INDO-CAMBODIAN
CONTACTS.
P.N. JENNER, 302:JAN73-178
SARKESIAN, S.C., ED. REVOLUTIONARY
GUERRILLA WARFARE.
R. EDER, 441:14DEC75-6
SARMA, E.R.S. - SEE UNDER SREEKRISH-
NA SARMA, E.R.
SARMA, M.V.R. THE HEROIC ARGUMENT.*
G. BULLOUGH, 175:SPRING72-24
SARMA, N. TEXTES SANSCRITS ET
TAMOULS DE THAILANDE.
O. VON HINÜBER, 182:VOL26#10-346
SARMIENTO, A. & F. TORRES. NERUDA.
R. PRING-MILL, 617(TLS):19SEP75-
1068
SARMIENTO, E. CONCORDANCIAS DE LAS
OBRAS POÉTICAS EN CASTELLANO DE
GARCILASO DE LA VEGA.*
D. EISENBERG, 241:JAN73-78
P.E. RUSSELL, 402(MLR):APR74-435
SAROLLI, G.R. PROLEGOMENA ALLA
"DIVINA COMMEDIA."
M. MARTI, 228(GSLI):VOL150FASC470/
471-411
SARRAUTE, N. DO YOU HEAR THEM?*
(FRENCH TITLE: VOUS LES ENTENDEZ?)
M. CAGNON, 207(FR):APR73-1070
E. KORN, 617(TLS):11JUL75-753
L.T. LEMON, 502(PRS):SUMMER73-183
M. PRICE, 676(YR):AUTUMN73-80
SARRAZIN, G. - SEE SCHMIDT, A.
SARTIN, P. LA FEMME LIBÉRÉE?
N. ARONSON, 207(FR):OCT72-178
SARTON, M. COLLECTED POEMS: 1930-
1973.
J. MARTIN, 491:MAY75-103
SARTON, M. CRUCIAL CONVERSATIONS.
D. GRUMBACH, 441:27APR75-4
C. LEHMANN-HAUPT, 441:16JUN75-25
E. WEEKS, 61:JUN75-93
SARTRE, J-P. BETWEEN EXISTENTIALISM
& MARXISM.*
G. LEVINE, 441:23MAR75-25
SARTRE, J-P. L'IDIOT DE LA FAMILLE.*
(VOLS 1&2)
J. CULLER, 402(MLR):APR74-419
A. NABARRA, 154:JUN73-373
SARTRE, J-P. L'IDIOT DE LA FAMILLE.
(VOL 3)
T.H. ADAMOWSKI, 454:WINTER74-182
G. GOOD 454:WINTER74-175
SARTRE, J-P. THE PSYCHOLOGY OF
IMAGINATION.
483:JUL73-307
SASO, M.R. TAOISM & THE RITE OF
COSMIC RENEWAL.
G.W. KENT, 293(JAST):FEB73-311
M. TOPLEY, 302:JUL73-258
SASSETTI, F. LETTERE DA VARI PAESI
(1570-1588). (V. BRAMANTI, ED)
M. POZZI, 228(GSLI):VOL150FASC469-
135

SASTRE, A. MUERTE EN EL BARRIO.
(R. BOWBEER & G. SCHERI, EDS)
F. ANDERSON, 399(MLJ):JAN-FEB74-78
ŚĀSTRĪ, D. APABHRAMŚA BHĀṢĀ AUR
SĀHITYA KI ŚODH PRAVṚTTIYĀ.
E. BENDER, 318(JAOS):JUL-SEP73-396
SASTRI, S.S.S. - SEE UNDER SURYANAR-
AYANA SASTRI, S.S.
SATER, J.E., A.G. RONHOVDE & L.C.
VAN ALLEN. ARCTIC ENVIRONMENT &
RESOURCES.
M.J. DUNBAR, 529(QQ):WINTER73-631
SATO, M. KYOTO CERAMICS.
S. SITWELL, 39:DEC73-516
SAUERLAND, K. DILTHEYS ERLEBNISBE-
GRIFF.
A. CLOSS, 402(MLR):OCT74-936
SAUERLÄNDER, W. GOTHIC SCULPTURE IN
FRANCE, 1140-1270.* (GERMAN TITLE:
GOTISCHE SKULPTUR IN FRANKREICH
1140-1270.)
G. ZARNECKI, 39:JUN73-623
SAUL, O. THE DARK SIDE OF LOVE.*
F. PICKERING, 617(TLS):28MAR75-329
SAUNDERS, A. - SEE GARNIER, R.
SAUNDERS, A. - SEE MAROT, J.
SAUNDERS, J.J. THE HISTORY OF THE
MONGOL CONQUESTS.
L.W. MOSES, 293(JAST):NOV72-167
R.A. PIERCE, 529(QQ):WINTER73-633
A.K. SANDERS, 302:JAN73-175
SAUNDERS, M. THE WALKABOUTS.
D. THOMAS, 362:13FEB75-221
617(TLS):21FEB75-202
DE SAUSSURE, F. CORSO DI LINGUIS-
TICA GENERALE. (3RD ED) (T. DE
MAURO, TRANS)
E.F.K. KOERNER, 545(RPH):AUG73-75
DE SAUSSURE, F. COURS DE LINGUIS-
TIQUE GÉNÉRALE. (T. DE MAURO, ED)
J. ROUDAUT, 98:MAR73-287
DE SAUSSURE, F. COURS DE LINGUIS-
TIQUE GÉNÉRALE.* (FASC 2&3) (R.
ENGLER, ED)
G.C. LEPSCHY, 353:1DEC73-117
SAUTERMEISTER, G. IDYLLIK UND DRA-
MATIK IM WERK FRIEDRICH SCHILLERS.
K.L. BERGHAHN, 406:WINTER74-401
SAUVAGEOT, A. L'ÉDIFICATION DE LA
LANGUE HONGROISE.
R. HETZRON, 297(JL):SEP73-345
E.A. MORAVCSIK, 350:SEP74-599
DE SAUVIGNY, G.D.B. - SEE UNDER DE
BERTIER DE SAUVIGNY, G.
SAVAGE, G. THE LANGUEDOC.
617(TLS):8AUG75-906
SAVAGE, T. A STRANGE GOD.*
R. SALE, 249(HUDR):WINTER74/75-628
SAVARD, J-G. & J. RICHARDS. LES
INDICES D'UTILITÉ DU VOCABULAIRE
FONDAMENTAL FRANÇAIS.*
P.F. CINTAS, 207(FR):FEB73-692
SAVESON, J.E. JOSEPH CONRAD.
B.E. TEETS, 177(ELT):VOL16#3-236
J. WALT, 136:VOL5#3-73
SAVIANE, R. APOCALISSI E MESSIAN-
ISMO NEI ROMANZI DI HERMANN BROCH.
E. BOA, 402(MLR):JAN74-231
SAVIDIS, G. - SEE CAVAFY, C.P.
SAVIDIS, G.P. - SEE SEFERIS, G.
SAVIGNON, S.J. COMMUNICATIVE COM-
PETENCE.
E.D. ALLEN, 238:DEC73-1131
E.G. JOINER, 399(MLJ):MAR74-130

SAVILLE, G. & J. AUSTIN. KING OF
KIRIWINA.
617(TLS):21FEB75-204
SAVILLE, J. THE MEDIEVAL EROTIC
ALBA.*
R.G. COOK, 301(JEGP):JAN74-113
G. GILLESPIE, 131(CL):SPRING74-171
G. MIESZKOWSKI, 529(QQ):AUTUMN73-
479
E. REISS, 579(SAQ):SUMMER74-412
L.T. TOPSFIELD, 402(MLR):JUL74-604
SAW, R.L. AESTHETICS.*
W. CHARLTON, 518:JAN74-23
L.A. REID, 89(BJA):WINTER73-78
E. SCHAPER, 393(MIND):OCT73-628
SAWA, T. ART IN JAPANESE ESOTERIC
BUDDHISM.*
R. POOR, 293(JAST):MAY73-517
SAWYER, J., ED. STUDIES IN AMERICAN
INDIAN LANGUAGES.
W.R. MERRIFIELD, 269(IJAL):APR73-
122
SAXTON, D. & L. LEGENDS & LORE OF
THE PAPAGO & PIMA INDIANS.
W. GARD, 584(SWR):WINTER74-98
SAXTON, M. JAYNE MANSFIELD & THE
AMERICAN FIFTIES.
J. SEELYE, 231:JUN75-84
SAYCE, R.A. THE ESSAYS OF MON-
TAIGNE.*
D.M. FRAME, 546(RR):NOV73-305
S.F. RENDALL, 400(MLN):MAY73-855
205(FMLS):OCT73-408
SAYCE, R.A. - SEE DE MONTAIGNE, M.
SAYER, M. SAMUEL RENN.*
C. CLUTTON, 410(M&L):JUL74-336
P. WILLIAMS, 415:JUN74-479
SAYLES, G.O. THE KING'S PARLIAMENT
OF ENGLAND.
S.B. CHRIMES, 617(TLS):16MAY75-528
SAYLES, J. PRIDE OF THE BIMBOS.
R. SOKOLOV, 441:14SEP75-40
SAYRE, A. ROSALIND FRANKLIN & DNA.
D. SHAPLEY, 441:21SEP75-27
C.P. SNOW, 453:13NOV75-3
SAYRE, E.A. THE CHANGING IMAGE.
N. GLENDINNING, 617(TLS):23MAY75-
558
F. HASKELL, 453:20OCT75-14
SAYRE, N. SIXTIES GOING ON SEVEN-
TIES.*
H. LOMAS, 364:APR/MAY74-124
SBISÀ, M. & J.O. URMSON - SEE
AUSTIN, J.L.
SBORDONE, F. SCRITTI DI VARIA FIL-
OLOGIA.
H. LLOYD-JONES, 123:MAR74-150
SCAGLIONE, A. THE CLASSICAL THEORY
OF COMPOSITION FROM ITS ORIGINS TO
THE PRESENT.
C. MOULTON, 124:MAR73-378
I. WILLI-PLEIN, 343:BAND17HEFT2-
129
M. WINTERBOTTOM, 123:NOV74-299
SCAGLIONE, A.D. "ARS GRAMMATICA."
E.R. LEONARD, 276:SPRING73-100
J. SAFAREWICZ, 353:15OCT73-111
K.D. UITTI, 545(RPH):NOV73-221
SCALAMANDRÈ, R. - SEE FONTAINE, C.
SCALAPINO, R.A. ELITES IN THE
PEOPLE'S REPUBLIC OF CHINA.
J. CH'EN, 293(JAST):AUG73-693

SCALFARI, E. & G. TURANI. RAZZA
PADRONA.
G. REID, 617(TLS):31OCT75-1307
SCAMMELL, M. - SEE SOLZHENITSYN, A.
& OTHERS
SCAMOZZI, O.B. - SEE UNDER BERTOTTI
SCAMOZZI, O.
SCANNELL, D. MOTHER KNEW BEST.*
E.S. TURNER, 362:13FEB75-219
SCARBOROUGH, J. ROMAN MEDICINE.
L.R. LIND, 121(CJ):OCT/NOV72-86
SCARNE, J. SCARNE'S NEW COMPLETE
GUIDE TO GAMBLING. SCARNE ON CARDS.
SCARNE ON DICE.
C. WORDSWORTH, 617(TLS):30MAY75-
608
VON SCARPATETTI, B.M. DIE KIRCHE
UND DAS AUGUSTINER-CHORHERRENSTIFT
ST. LEONHARD IN BASEL (11./12.
JAHRHUNDERT BIS 1525).
R. FOLZ, 182:VOL26#23/24-893
SCARPATI, C. INVITO ALLA LETTURA
DI EUGENIO MONTALE.
C.A. MC CORMICK, 402(MLR):OCT74-
891
SCATTERGOOD, V.J. POLITICS & POETRY
IN THE FIFTEENTH CENTURY, 1399-
1485.
A.S.G. EDWARDS, 589:APR74-372
ŠČERBAK, A.M. SRAVNITEL'NAJA FON-
ETIKA TJURKSKIX JAZYKOV.
N. POPPE, 353:15MAR73-96
SCHAAR, C. MARINO & CRASHAW, "SOS-
PETTO D'HERODE," A COMMENTARY.
J.V. MIROLLO, 551(RENQ):WINTER73-
544
SCHABERT, I., ED. SHAKESPEARE-
HANDBUCH.
E.T. SEHRT, 38:BAND91HEFT3-397
SCHABRAM, H. SUPERBIA.* (PT 1)
L-G. HALLANDER, 597(SN):VOL45#1-
171
SCHACH, P. - SEE "THE SAGA OF TRIS-
TRAM & ÍSÖND"
SCHACHERMEYR, F. PERIKLES.*
S.I. OOST, 122:JAN74-69
SCHACHT, S. THE DICTIONARY OF EX-
CEPTIONS TO RULES OF RUSSIAN GRAM-
MAR.
C.V. CHVANY, 574(SEEJ):SPRING72-
127
SCHACHTER, P. & F.T. OTANES. TAGA-
LOG REFERENCE GRAMMAR.
M.L. FORMAN, 293(JAST):AUG73-760
SCHÄDLER, K.F. AFRICAN ART IN PRI-
VATE GERMAN COLLECTIONS.
H.M. COLE, 2:SUMMER74-87
SCHAEDER, G. THE HEBREW HUMANISM
OF MARTIN BUBER.
D.S. ROBINSON, 484(PPR):DEC73-281
SCHAEFER, H. NINETEENTH CENTURY
MODERN.
D. GEBHARD, 56:SPRING-SUMMER73-108
SCHAEFER, H.W. COMECON & THE POLI-
TICS OF INTEGRATION.*
R.E. KANET, 104:SUMMER73-280
SCHAEFFER, P. TRAITÉ DES OBJETS
MUSICAUX.
C. PRÉVOST, 542:JAN-MAR73-119
SCHAEFFER, S.F. GRANITE LADY.
J. PARISI, 491:JUL75-219
W.H. PRITCHARD, 441:18MAY75-36

SCHAEFFLER, R. RELIGION UND KRIT-
ISCHES BEWUSSTSEIN.
H. DEUSER, 182:VOL26#10-322
SCHAFER, E.H. THE DIVINE WOMAN.
639(VQR):SUMMER74-LXXXI
SCHÄFER, G. DIE EVANGELISCHE LAND-
ESKIRCHE IN WÜRTTEMBERG UND DER
NATIONALSOZIALISMUS.
A. WAHL, 182:VOL26#13/14-509
SCHÄFER, G.M. UNTERSUCHUNGEN ZUR
DEUTSCHSPRACHIGEN MARIENLYRIK DES
12. UND 13. JAHRHUNDERTS.*
O. SAYCE, 402(MLR):JAN74-220
SCHAFER, P., D. RICE & W. BERG, EDS.
POÈMES, PIÈCES, PROSE.
B.P. EDMONDS, 399(MLJ):SEP-OCT74-
274
SCHAFER, S. THE POLITICAL CRIMI-
NAL.*
J. WHITEHILL, 31(ASCH):WINTER74/
75-162
SCHAFF, A. MARXISM & THE HUMAN IN-
DIVIDUAL. (R.S. COHEN, ED)
J. SOMERVILLE, 484(PPR):DEC73-239
SCHALK, F. "PRAEJUDICIUM" IM ROMAN-
ISCHEN.
M. SANDMANN, 545(RPH):AUG73-128
SCHALLER, K. COMENIUS.
D. TSCHIŽEWSKIJ, 72:BAND211HEFT
3/6-477
SCHAMJAKIN, I. DAS BEKENNTNIS.
R. GÖBNER, 654(WB):6/1973-132
SCHAMONI, P. MAX ERNST: MAXIMILI-
ANA.
J.R. MELLOW, 441:7DEC75-2
SCHANE, S.A. GENERATIVE PHONOLOGY.
V.E. HANZELI, 399(MLJ):SEP-OCT74-
278
R. SUSSEX, 67:MAY74-143
SCHANZER, G.O., COMP. RUSSIAN LIT-
ERATURE IN THE HISPANIC WORLD.*
J.S.G. SIMMONS, 402(MLR):JUL74-715
J. WEINER, 574(SEEJ):SUMMER73-237
SCHAPIRO, L. - SEE FRANK, V.
SCHARFE, H. PĀNINI'S METALANGUAGE.
T.S. PAIK, 206:NOV73-581
R. ROCHER, 318(JAOS):JAN-MAR73-112
SCHARFE, H. UNTERSUCHUNGEN ZUR
STAATSRECHTSLEHRE DES KAUṬALYA.
F. WILHELM, 343:BAND17HEFT1-104
SCHARPÉ, J.L. & E. VYNCKE, EDS.
BDINSKI ZBORNIK.
M. HEPPELL, 575(SEER):OCT74-628
SCHARPF, P. EUROPÄISCHE WIRTSCHAFTS-
GEMEINSCHAFT UND DEUTSCHE DEMOKRAT-
ISCHE REPUBLIK.
S. MAMPEL, 182:VOL26#15/16-528
SCHATOFF, M., COMP. HALF A CENTURY
OF RUSSIAN SERIALS, 1917-1968.*
(VOLS 1-3) (N.A. HALE, ED)
J. ROSENSHIELD, 574(SEEJ):FALL72-
387
SCHAU, A. MÄRCHENFORMEN BEI EICHEN-
DORFF.*
D.C. RIECHEL, 222(GR):JAN73-77
SCHÄUBLIN, P. PROBLEME DES ADNOMI-
NALEN ATTRIBUTS IN DER DEUTSCHEN
SPRACHE DER GEGENWART.
E.H. YARRILL, 182:VOL26#23/24-858
SCHAZMANN, P-E. CHARLES DICKENS IN
SWITZERLAND.
155:MAY73-130

SCHEDELMANN, H. DIE GROSSEN BÜCHSEN-
MACHER.
   A.V.B. NORMAN, 39:JUL73-69
SCHEEL, G., K. MÜLLER & G. GERBER -
SEE LEIBNIZ, G.W.
SCHEER, R. AMERICA AFTER NIXON.
   R.L. HEILBRONER, 453:20MAR75-6
SCHEFFLER, I. FOUR PRAGMATISTS.
   C.K. GRANT, 617(TLS):14FEB75-176
SCHEFFLER, I. REASON & TEACHING.
   I. GREGORY, 518:MAY74-20
SCHEFFLER, W. & G. FIEGE, EDS.
BUCHUMSCHLÄGE 1900-50 AUS DER
SMLG. CURT TILLMANN.
   C. VISEL, 182:VOL26#23/24-838
SCHEFOLD, B., ED. FLOATING, REALIGN-
MENT, INTEGRATION.
   A. OCKER, 182:VOL26#23/24-850
SCHEFOLD, K. LA PEINTURE POMPÉIENNE.
   J. LIVERSIDGE, 313:VOL63-279
SCHEICK, W.J. THE WILL & THE WORD.*
   N.S. GRABO, 27(AL):NOV74-397
SCHEIER, C-A. DIE SELBSTENTFALTUNG
DER METHODISCHEN REFLEXION ALS
PRINZIP DER NEUEREN PHILOSOPHIE.
   S. DECLOUX, 182:VOL26#15/16-526
SCHELESNIKER, H. SCHRIFTSYSTEME BEI
DEN SLAVEN.
   E. WEIHER, 343:BAND17HEFT2-212
SCHELLING, F.W.J. BRIEFE UND DOKU-
MENTE.* (VOL 2) (H. FUHRMANS, ED)
   P. PACHET, 182:VOL26#21/22-780
SCHENCK, H.G. GEIST DER EUROPÄIS-
CHEN ROMANTIK.
   R. VON TIEDEMANN, 52:BAND8HEFT1-98
SCHENK, D. STUDIEN ZUR ANAKREON-
TISCHEN ODE IN DER RUSSISCHEN LIT-
ERATUR DES KLASSIZISMUS UND DER
EMPFINDSAMKEIT.
   P.R. HART, 574(SEEJ):FALL73-327
SCHENKER, A.M. BEGINNING POLISH.
(REV)
   J. ARABSKI, 399(MLJ):DEC74-433
   B.W. MAZUR, 575(SEER):OCT74-634
   J. PERELMUTER, 574(SEEJ):FALL73-
   359
SCHENKER, H. ERLÄUTERUNGSAUSGABE
DER LETZTEN SONATEN VON BEETHOVEN.
(ED & REV BY O. JONAS)
   W. DRABKIN, 513:FALL-WINTER73/
   SPRING-SUMMER74-319
SCHEPELERN, P. DEN FORTAELLENDE
FILM.
   S. KJØRUP, 290(JAAC):FALL73-134
SCHERER, J. LE CARDINAL ET L'ORANG-
OUTANG.
   G.B. WALTERS, JR., 207(FR):MAR73-
   830
SCHÉRER, J.C., WITH J.B. WALKER.
INDIANS.
   W. GARD, 584(SWR):SPRING74-V
SCHERF, M. IF YOU WANT A MURDER
WELL DONE.
   N. CALLENDAR, 441:5JAN75-24
SCHERMAN, D.E., ED. LIFE GOES TO
THE MOVIES.
   R. SCHICKEL, 441:7DEC75-6
SCHERNBERG, D. EIN SCHÖN SPIEL VON
FRAU JUTTEN.* (M. LEMMER, ED)
   M. BEARE, 220(GL&L):OCT73-81
SCHERPE, K. WERTHER UND WERTHERWIR-
KUNG.*
   W.D. WETZELS, 191(ELN):SEP73(SUPP)-
   126

SCHEUCH, E.K. & R. MEYERSOHN, EDS.
SOZIOLOGIE DER FREIZEIT.
   H.W. OPASCHOWSKI, 182:VOL26#23/24-
   852
SCHEUER, H. ARNO HOLZ IM LITERARIS-
CHEN LEBEN DES AUSGEHENDEN 19.
JAHRHUNDERTS (1883-1896).
   J.J. WHITE, 402(MLR):OCT74-933
SCHEURLEER, D.F.L. CHINESE EXPORT
PORCELAIN.
   M. TREGEAR, 617(TLS):11APR75-407
SCHEURWEGHS, G. ANALYTICAL BIBLIO-
GRAPHY OF WRITINGS ON MODERN ENG-
LISH MORPHOLOGY & SYNTAX 1877-
1960. (VOLS 3&4)
   B. CARSTENSEN, 430(NS):JAN73-47
SCHEVILL, J. THE BUDDHIST CAR &
OTHER CHARACTERS.
   J.R. CARPENTER, 491:DEC74-166
   F. MORAMARCO, 651(WHR):WINTER74-92
SCHEVILL, W.E., ED. THE WHALE PROB-
LEM.
   L.H. MATTHEWS, 617(TLS):14FEB75-
   175
   J.Z. YOUNG, 453:17JUL75-3
SCHEYER, E. THE CIRCLE OF HENRY
ADAMS.
   H.F. SMITH, 376:OCT73-138
SCHIB, K., ED. DIE RECHTSQUELLEN
DES KANTONS SCHAFFHAUSEN. (PT 1,
VOL 2)
   R. GANGHOFFER, 182:VOL26#5/6-143
SCHIB, K. - SEE MOSER, H.
SCHIBSBYE, K. ORIGIN & DEVELOPMENT
OF THE ENGLISH LANGUAGE. (PT 1)
   T. KISBYE, 597(SN):VOL45#2-437
SCHICK, E.B. METAPHORICAL ORGANI-
CISM IN HERDER'S EARLY WORKS.*
   F. RADANDT, 405(MP):MAY74-448
SCHICKEL, R. THE WORLD OF TENNIS.
   R. SMITH, 441:7DEC75-30
SCHIEDER, T. & H. BERDING - SEE VON
RANKE, L.
SCHIEDERMAIR, H. DAS PHÄNOMEN DER
MACHT UND DIE IDEE DES RECHTS BEI
GOTTFRIED WILHELM LEIBNIZ.
   A. MERCIER, 182:VOL26#3/4-69
SCHIFF GIORGINI, M., WITH C. ROBI-
CHON & J. LECLANT. SOLEB II: LES
NÉCROPOLES.
   A.J. ARKELL, 69:APR73-161
SCHIFFER, S.R. MEANING.*
   B. AUNE, 113:FALL74-85
   R. BLANCHÉ, 542:OCT-DEC73-478
SCHILDT, G. MODERN FINNISH SCULP-
TURE.
   J.B. SMITH, 39:JUL73-71
SCHILLER, A.A. AN AMERICAN EXPERI-
ENCE IN ROMAN LAW.
   W.M. GORDON, 123:MAR74-161
SCHILLER, F. BRIEFWECHSEL ZWISCHEN
SCHILLER UND KÖRNER. (K.L. BERG-
HAHN, ED)
   G.A. WELLS, 301(JEGP):OCT74-597
SCHILLER, F. SCHILLERS WERKE. (VOL
11) (H. KRAFT, ED)
   D.W. SCHUMANN, 301(JEGP):JUL74-402
SCHILLING, E. GERMAN DRAWINGS AT
WINDSOR CASTLE [TOGETHER WITH]
BLUNT, A. SUPPLEMENTS TO THE CATA-
LOGUES OF THE ITALIAN & FRENCH
DRAWINGS.
   M. LEVEY, 90:MAR73-185
   C. WHITE, 39:DEC73-518

SCHILPP, P.A., ED. THE PHILOSOPHY
OF C.I. LEWIS.
  J. CEDERBLOM, 319:JAN75-119
  D. KEYT, 482(PHR):OCT73-491
SCHIMMEL, A., ED. MIRZA GHALIB.
  I. SOLBRIG, 406:SPRING74-101
SCHIMMEL, A. ISLAMIC CALLIGRAPHY.
  L. GOLOMBEK, 318(JAOS):OCT-DEC73-
  572
SCHINDLER, F. & E. THÜRMANN, WITH C.
RIEK, COMPS. BIBLIOGRAPHIE ZUR
PHONETIK UND PHONOLOGIE DES DEUT-
SCHEN.
  W. DRESSLER, 353:1DEC73-97
  G.F. MEIER, 682(ZPSK):BAND26HEFT
  3/4-415
SCHINDLER, M.S. THE SONNETS OF
ANDREAS GRYPHIUS.*
  H. POWELL, 221(GQ):JAN73-92
  K.L. ROOS, 399(MLJ):SEP-OCT73-295
  G.H. SUTTON, 220(GL&L):OCT73-86
SCHINZEL, I. - SEE TACITUS
SCHIPPERS, K. - SEE BONSET, I.K.
SCHIPPOREIT, L. TENSES & TIME
PHRASES IN MODERN GERMAN.
  F. FREUND, 597(SN):VOL45#2-418
SCHIROK, B. DER AUFBAU VON WOLFRAMS
"PARZIVAL."*
  G.F. CARR, 406:SUMMER74-191
  C. LOFMARK, 402(MLR):OCT74-914
SCHLACHTER, W., ED. SYMPOSIUM ÜBER
SYNTAX DER URALISCHEN SPRACHEN 15.-
18. JULI 1969 IN REINHAUSEN BEI
GÖTTINGEN.
  G. LAKÓ, 260(IF):BAND78-358
SCHLAFFER, H. DRAMENFORM UND KLASS-
ENSTRUKTUR.
  J.H. PETERSEN, 680(ZDP):BAND92HEFT
  4-631
SCHLAGER, K., ED. RÉPERTOIRE INTER-
NATIONAL DES SOURCES MUSICALES/IN-
TERNATIONALES QUELLENLEXIKON DER
MUSIK/INTERNATIONAL INVENTORY OF
MUSICAL SOURCES. (SER A/1, VOLS 1&2)
  V. DUCKLES, 317:SPRING73-153
SCHLANT, E. DIE PHILOSOPHIE HERMANN
BROCHS.
  E. BOA, 402(MLR):JAN74-231
  R.A. KAHN, 125:OCT73-101
  J.J. WHITE, 220(GL&L):JAN74-168
SCHLECHTRIEM, P.H. VERTRAGSORDNUNG
UND AUSSERVERTRAGLICHE HAFTUNG.
  P. PADIS, 182:VOL26#15/16-531
SCHLEE, S. A HISTORY OF OCEANOGRA-
PHY.
  P.J.P. WHITEHEAD, 617(TLS):15AUG
  75-929
SCHLEGEL, F. FRIEDRICH SCHLEGEL'S
"LUCINDE" & THE FRAGMENTS.* (P.
FIRCHOW, TRANS)
  H. EICHNER, 221(GQ):MAY73-478
SCHLEGEL, S.A. TIRURAY-ENGLISH LEX-
ICON.*
  J.U. WOLFF, 318(JAOS):APR-JUN73-
  234
SCHLEGEL, W. DER WEINBAU IN DER
SCHWEIZ.
  P. VOSSELER, 182:VOL26#15/16-574
SCHLEINER, W. THE IMAGERY OF JOHN
DONNE'S SERMONS.*
  M.L. WILEY, 551(RENQ):SUMMER73-236
SCHLENK, H. DER BINNENHANDEL DER
DDR.
  M. MC CAULEY, 575(SEER):APR74-320

SCHLESINGER, A.M., JR. THE IMPERIAL
PRESIDENCY.*
  R. EGGER, 639(VQR):SPRING74-289
  H.A. LARRABEE, 432(NEQ):MAR74-132
SCHLESINGER, B., ED. FAMILY PLAN-
NING IN CANADA.
  I. GENTLES, 99:APR/MAY75-22
SCHLESINGER, G. CONFIRMATION & CON-
FIRMABILITY.
  D.H. MELLOR, 617(TLS):14FEB75-176
SCHLESINGER, S. THE NEW REFORMERS.
  M. TOLCHIN, 441:19OCT75-43
SCHLIEBEN-LANGE, B. OKZITANISCHE
UND KATALANISCHE VERBPROBLEME.
  H. MEIER, 72:BAND211HEFT1/3-195
SCHLÖSSER, A. & A-G. KUCKHOFF, EDS.
SHAKESPEARE JAHRBUCH. (VOL 108)
  R.A. FOAKES, 175:AUTUMN72-107
SCHLOTTKE, E. MITTELDEUTSCHLAND.
  H. WOLF, 680(ZDP):BAND92HEFT1-146
SCHLÜSSEL, P. ENTWICKLUNGEN IM EIN-
FLUSSBEREICH DER GROSSSTADT.
  E-D. KOHL, 182:VOL26#5/6-187
SCHMALSTIEG, W.R. & A. KLIMAS.
LITHUANIAN-ENGLISH GLOSSARY OF LIN-
GUISTIC TERMINOLOGY.
  G.B. FORD, JR., 574(SEEJ):FALL72-
  385
SCHMID, W., ED. DIE INTERPRETATION
IN DER ALTERTUMSWISSENSCHAFT.
  R.T. SCOTT, 124:OCT72-113
SCHMID, W.P. DIE PRAGMATISCHE KOM-
PONENTE IN DER GRAMMATIK.
  J. BECHERT, 343:BAND17HEFT2-135
SCHMID, W.P. SKIZZE EINER ALLGE-
MEINEN THEORIE DER WORTARTEN.
  J. BECHERT, 260(IF):BAND78-207
SCHMIDT, A. IL CONCETTO DI NATURA
IN MARX.
  M. CINGOLI, 548(RCSF):APR-JUN73-
  165
SCHMIDT, A. SHAKESPEARE LEXICON &
QUOTATION DICTIONARY. (3RD ED REV
BY G. SARRAZIN)
  K.B. MICHAEL, 570(SQ):AUTUMN73-476
SCHMIDT, A. - SEE HORKHEIMER, M.
SCHMIDT, A. & H. FLEISCHHACKER.
MENSCHEN UND MASCHINEN.
  J.E. CREAN, JR., 399(MLJ):DEC73-
  432
SCHMIDT, A-M. POÈTES DU XVIE SIÈCLE.
  M. DEGUY, 98:MAR73-215
SCHMIDT, D. DIE NAMEN DER RECHTS-
RHEINISCHEN ZUFLÜSSE ZWISCHEN
WUPPER UND LIPPE.
  A. GREULE, 260(IF):BAND78-351
SCHMIDT, E.P. UNION POWER & THE
PUBLIC INTEREST.
  M. PETERSON, 396(MODA):WINTER74-
  104
SCHMIDT, G. AUFKLÄRUNG UND META-
PHYSIK.
  M.S., 543:SEP72-172
SCHMIDT, H. NIKOLAUS LENAU.*
  L.J. RIPPLEY, 221(GQ):SEP73-172
  C.A. SAMMONS, 191(ELN):SEP73(SUPP)-
  150
SCHMIDT, H., ED. PÄDAGOGISCHER
JAHRESBERICHT, TEXTBAND 1971.
  K. OLTMANN, 430(NS):JUL73-380
SCHMIDT, H.J. SATIRE, CARICATURE,
& PERSPECTIVISM IN THE WORKS OF
GEORG BÜCHNER.
  R.C. COWEN, 221(GQ):SEP73-141

SCHMIDT, L. CARVED CUSTOM MASKS OF
THE AUSTRIAN ALPS.
  E. ETTLINGER, 203:SPRING73-81
SCHMIDT, L., ED. HISTORISCHE VOLKS-
LIEDER AUS ÖSTERREICH VOM 15. BIS
ZUM 19. JAHRHUNDERT.*
  E.F. GRAUBART, 301(JEGP):JAN74-77
  B.L. SPAHR, 133:1973/2-185
SCHMIDT, L. VOLKSGESANG UND VOLKS-
LIED.*
  G. HEILFURTH, 680(ZDP):BAND92HEFT
  3-469
SCHMIDT, L. VOLKSKUNDE VON NIEDER-
ÖSTERREICH. (VOL 1)
  E. ETTLINGER, 203:AUTUMN73-260
SCHMIDT, L. VOLKSKUNDE VON NIEDER-
ÖSTERREICH. (VOL 2)
  E. ETTLINGER, 203:WINTER73-346
SCHMIDT, M. DESERT OF THE LIONS.*
  D. GRANT, 148:SPRING72-92
SCHMIDT, M. & G. LINDOP, EDS. BRIT-
ISH POETRY SINCE 1960.
  J. GLOVER, 565:VOL14#2-71
SCHMIDT, O. NEIZVESTNYJ POÈT P.D.
BUTURLIN.
  G. KJETSAA, 574(SEEJ):WINTER73-458
SCHMIDT, V. SPRACHLICHE UNTERSUCH-
UNGEN ZU HERONDAS.*
  J. VAIO, 122:OCT73-310
SCHMIDT, W., ED. SPRACHE UND
IDEOLOGIE.
  G. STARKE, 682(ZPSK):BAND26HEFT6-
  734
SCHMIDT-DENGLER, W. - SEE VON DOD-
ERER, H.
SCHMIDT-KNÄBEL, S. DIE SYNTAX DER
-ANT-FORMEN IM MODERNEN FRANZÖ-
SISCH "ADJECTIF VERBAL," "PARTICIPE
PRÉSENT," UND "GÉRONDIF."
  F.J. HAUSMANN, 72:BAND211HEFT1/3-
  197
  J. SKÖLDBERG, 597(SN):VOL45#1-205
  K. WINN, 430(NS):APR73-235
SCHMITT, C.B. A CRITICAL SURVEY &
BIBLIOGRAPHY OF STUDIES ON RENAIS-
SANCE ARISTOTELIANISM 1958-1969.*
  F. PURNELL, JR., 551(RENQ):WINTER
  73-465
SCHMITT, C.J. SCHAUM'S OUTLINE OF
SPANISH GRAMMAR.
  H.J. FREY, 399(MLJ):MAR74-135
SCHMITT, E. LEXIKALISCHE UNTERSUCH-
UNGEN ZUR ARABISCHEN ÜBERSETZUNG
VON ARTEMIDORS TRAUMBUCH.
  J. PAULINY, 353:1AUG73-127
SCHMITT, L.E., ED. KURZER GRUNDRISS
DER GERMANISCHEN PHILOLOGIE BIS
1500.* (VOL 1)
  P. HESSMANN, 680(ZDP):BAND92HEFT1-
  140
  I.T. PIIRAINEN, 439(NM):1973/3-546
  E. SEEBOLD, 260(IF):BAND78-310
SCHMITT, L.E., ED. KURZER GRUNDRISS
DER GERMANISCHEN PHILOLOGIE BIS
1500. (VOL 2)
  G. GEIL, 343:BAND17HEFT2-217
  I.T. PIIRAINEN, 439(NM):1973/3-546
SCHMITT, L.E. UNTERSUCHUNGEN ZU
ENTSTEHUNG UND STRUKTUR DER "NEU-
HOCHDEUTSCHEN SCHRIFTSPRACHE."
(VOL 1)
  E. SCHRADER, 400(MLN):APR73-607

SCHMITT, W., ED. DEUTSCHE FACHPROSA
DES MITTELALTERS.
  B.D. HAAGE, 680(ZDP):BAND92HEFT3-
  467
SCHMITT-BRANDT, R., ED. DONUM INDO-
GERMANICUM.
  O. SZEMERÉNYI, 343:BAND17HEFT1-86
  W. THOMAS, 260(IF):BAND78-227
SCHMITZ, A. & E., EDS. AN AUGUST
DAY IN RIDGEBURY & OTHER STORIES.
  K. OLTMANN, 430(NS):JUL73-390
SCHMITZ, J. THE ABRA MISSION IN
NORTHERN LUZON, PHILIPPINES: 1598-
1955.
  N.P. CUSHNER, 293(JAST):FEB73-382
SCHMITZ, V.A. GUNDOLF.
  I. JONES, 172(EDDA):1973/2-125
SCHMÜCKER, A. - SEE DOLGORUKAYA,
N.B.
SCHNEEWIND, E.H. - SEE BRENTANO, F.
SCHNEIDER, B. DIE MITTELALTERLICHEN
GRIECHISCH-LATEINISCHEN UEBERSETZ-
UNGEN DER ARISTOTELISCHEN RHETORIK.*
  M.R. DILTS, 124:APR-MAY74-405
  P. LOUIS, 555:VOL47FASC2-346
SCHNEIDER, B.R., JR. THE ETHOS OF
RESTORATION COMEDY.*
  I. DONALDSON, 447(N&Q):DEC73-476
SCHNEIDER, K., ED. EIN LOSBUCH KON-
RAD BOLLSTATTERS AUS CGM 312 DER
BAYERISCHEN STAATSBIBLIOTHEK MÜN-
CHEN.
  E. GRÜNENWALD, 182:VOL26#20-710
SCHNEIDER, M.J. UN AMIGO DEL NORTE.
  G.J. HASENAUER, 399(MLJ):DEC73-432
SCHNEIDER, M.J. LA FAMILIA MARÍN.
  G.J. HASENAUER, 399(MLJ):SEP-OCT
  73-301
SCHNEIDER, R. DIE REISE NACH JARO-
SLAW.
  K.S. PARKES, 617(TLS):3OCT75-1151
SCHNEIDER, R. DIE TRINITÄTSLEHRE IN
DEN "QUODLIBETA" UND "QUAESTIONES
DISPUTATAE" DES JOHANNES VON NEAPEL
O.P. (†1336).
  L. HÖDL, 182:VOL26#13/14-467
  T.K. SCOTT, JR., 589:APR74-376
SCHNEIDER, U. DIE FUNKTION DER
ZITATE IM "ULYSSES" VON JAMES
JOYCE.*
  A.M.L. KNUTH, 433:JAN73-109
SCHNELL, H. KER KIRCHENBAU DES 20.
JAHRHUNDERTS IN DEUTSCHLAND.
  G. BINDING, 182:VOL26#17/18-613
SCHNITZLER, A. PROFESSOR BERNHARDI.
(M. SWALES, ED)
  205(FMLS):JUL73-310
SCHNITZLER, A. & R. AUERNHEIMER.
THE CORRESPONDENCE OF ARTHUR
SCHNITZLER & RAOUL AUERNHEIMER.
(D.G. DAVIAU & J.B. JONES, EDS)
  G.C. AVERY, 400(MLN):OCT73-1057
  R.R. SCHLEIN, 406:SPRING74-79
SCHOBER, R. VON DER WIRKLICHEN WELT
IN DER DICHTUNG.*
  J-R. ARMOGATHE, 557(RSH):OCT-DEC73-
  665
  H.H. WEINBERG, 535(RHL):NOV-DEC73-
  1100
SCHOBERT, H. & F. KAPELLE, KIRCHE,
GNADENBILD.
  B. GUNDA, 203:SUMMER73-171

SCHOCHET, G.J. PATRIARCHALISM IN
POLITICAL THOUGHT.
J.G.A. POCOCK, 617(TLS):26SEP75-
1082
SCHODER, R.V. ANCIENT GREECE FROM
THE AIR.
J.M. COOK, 617(TLS):21FEB75-202
SCHOEDEL, W.R. - SEE ATHENAGORAS
SCHOELL, K. DAS FRANZÖSISCHE DRAMA
SEIT DEM ZWEITEN WELTKRIEG.
M. KRÜGER, 430(NS):MAY73-285
SCHOELLER, B. GELÄCHTER UND SPAN-
NUNG.*
R. GRIMM, 406:SPRING74-91
P. STEINER, 400(MLN):OCT73-1041
SCHOENBAUM, S., ED. RENAISSANCE
DRAMA.* (NEW SER, VOL 3)
N. RABKIN, 677:VOL4-262
SCHOENBAUM, S. WILLIAM SHAKESPEARE.
P. ADAMS, 61:AUG75-88
C.L. BARBER, 453:16OCT75-33
A. BROYARD, 441:20MAY75-41
G. BULLOUGH, 617(TLS):18APR75-427
F. KERMODE, 441:13APR75-1
SCHOENBAUM, S. SHAKESPEARE'S
LIVES.*
M. ECCLES, 551(RENQ):SPRING73-83
M. MINCOFF, 179(ES):AUG73-387
SCHOENBAUM, S. & A.C. DESSEN, EDS.
RENAISSANCE DRAMA. (NEW SER, VOL 4)
A.C. SPRAGUE, 402(MLR):JAN74-147
SCHOENBERG, A. BERLINER TAGEBUCH.
(J. RUFER, ED)
C. ROSEN, 617(TLS):7NOV75-1335
SCHOENBERG, A. STYLE & IDEA. (L.
STEIN, ED)
R. CRAFT, 453:18SEP75-50
D. HENAHAN, 441:28DEC75-6
C. ROSEN, 617(TLS):7NOV75-1335
SCHOLES, R. STRUCTURAL FABULATION.
M. WOOD, 453:20OCT75-3
SCHOLES, R. STRUCTURALISM IN LITER-
ATURE.*
D.L. GREENBLATT, 113:FALL74-73
R. WELLEK, 301(JEGP):JUL74-459
SCHOLZ, B.W., ED & TRANS. CAROLIN-
GIAN CHRONICLES.
S. WEINBERGER, 124:MAR73-375
SCHOLZ, H-J. UNTERSUCHUNGEN ZUR
LAUTSTRUKTUR DEUTSCHER WÖRTER.
E.H. YARRILL, 182:VOL26#13/14-481
SCHOLZ, U.W. STUDIEN ZUM ALTITAL-
ISCHEN UND ALTRÖMISCHEN MARSKULT
UND MARSMYTHOS.*
N. ROBERTSON, 124:FEB73-312
SCHOLZ-BABISCH, M. QUELLEN ZUR GE-
SCHICHTE DES KLEVISCHEN RHEINZOLL-
WESENS VOM 11.-18. JAHRHUNDERT.
P. BRIGHTWELL, 182:VOL26#7/8-246
SCHÖN, E. JAN FRIDEGÅRD OCH FORN-
TIDEN.
C.L. ANDERSON, 563(SS):FALL74-451
SCHÖN, I. NEUTRUM UND KOLLEKTIVUM.
F. BADER, 555:VOL47FASC1-111
B. LÖFSTEDT, 343:BAND16HEFT2-182
SCHÖN, J.F. & S. CROWTHER. JOURNALS
OF THE REV. JAMES FREDERICK SCHÖN
& MR. SAMUEL CROWTHER WHO ACCOMPAN-
IED THE EXPEDITION UP THE NIGER IN
1841.
A.H.M. KIRK-GREENE, 69:OCT73-365
SCHONBERG, H.C. GRANDMASTERS OF
CHESS.*
617(TLS):10JAN75-41

SCHÖNDORF, K.E. DIE TRADITION DER
DEUTSCHEN PSALMENÜBERSETZUNG.
P.W. TAX, 400(MLN):OCT73-1042
SCHÖNFELDT, O., ED. "UND ALLE LIEB-
EN HEINRICH HEINE..."
J.L.S., 191(ELN):SEP73(SUPP)-138
SCHONFIELD, H.J. THE PENTECOST REV-
OLUTION.
G. VERMES, 617(TLS):17JAN75-65
SCHÖNHAAR, R., ED. DIALOG.
E.W. HERD, 67:NOV74-240
SCHONHORN, M. - SEE DEFOE, D.
SCHÖNING, K., ED. NEUES HÖRSPIEL.
A. WEGENER, 221(GQ):SEP73-166
"RUDOLF SCHÖNWALD."
P. VERGO, 90:AUG73-550
SCHOONMAKER, F. ENCYCLOPEDIA OF
WINE. (NEW ED)
T. ASPLER, 362:25DEC75&1JAN76-891
617(TLS):21NOV75-1397
SCHOPENHAUER, A. GESPRÄCHE.* (A.
HÜBSCHER, ED) PARERGA & PARALIPO-
MENA. (E.F.J. PAYNE, TRANS)
E. HELLER, 617(TLS):10OCT75-1167
SCHORN, E. ZERSTÖRTE WIRKLICHKEIT
UND ABSOLUTES SEIN.
D. HAAS, 72:BAND211HEFT1/3-231
SCHOTT, H. PLAYING THE HARPSICHORD.
K. COOPER, 414(MQ):JAN73-137
SCHOTT, J.L. NO LEFT TURNS.
P. ADAMS, 61:JUN75-94
W. HINCKLE, 441:13JUL75-4
SCHRADER, L. SINNE UND SINNESVER-
KNÜPFUNGEN.
B. CIPLIJAUSKAITÉ, 240(HR):WINTER
73-95
SCHRADER, P. TRANSCENDENTAL STYLE
IN FILM.
J.M. PURCELL, 599:SPRING73-211
SCHRADER, R.J. - SEE DYCE, A.
SCHRAG, O.O. EXISTENCE, EXISTENZ &
TRANSCENDENCE.*
R.D. KNUDSEN, 480(P&R):SUMMER73-
196
SCHRAG, P. & D. DIVOKY. THE MYTH OF
THE HYPERACTIVE CHILD.
E.Z. FRIEDENBERG, 453:27NOV75-30
H. MAYER, 441:9NOV75-35
SCHRAM, S. - SEE MAO TSE-TUNG
SCHRECKER, J.E. IMPERIALISM &
CHINESE NATIONALISM.*
E.L. PRESSEISEN, 318(JAOS):OCT-DEC
73-643
SCHREIBER, K. BIBLIOGRAPHIE LAUFEN-
DER BIBLIOGRAPHIEN ZUR ROMANISCHEN
LITERATURWISSENSCHAFT.
D.M. SUTHERLAND, 208(FS):APR74-232
SCHREIBER, W. GUSTAV MAHLER IN
SELBSTZEUGNISSEN UND BILDDOKUMENTEN.
J.S. WEISSMANN, 412:AUG-NOV73-353
SCHREINER, O. A TRACK TO THE
WATER'S EDGE. (H. THURMAN, ED)
G.B. TENNYSON, 445(NCF):DEC73-370
SCHRENK, J. ZUM GRÖSSENINVENTAR
EINER THEORIE DES SATZES.
G.F. MEIER, 682(ZPSK):BAND26HEFT
1/2-208
SCHREY, K., ED. DETECTIVES AT WORK
AGAIN.
K. OLTMANN, 430(NS):JUL73-388
SCHREYL, K.H., WITH D. NEUMEISTER.
JOSEPH MARIA OLBRICH.
N. PEVSNER, 46:MAR73-210

SCHRÖDER, J. ZU DARSTELLUNG UND
FUNKTION DER SCHAUPLÄTZE IN DEN
ARTUSROMANEN HARTMANNS VON AUE.
G.R. DIMLER, 406:SUMMER74-187
SCHRÖDER, J. GOTTHOLD EPHRAIM LES-
SING.
G. HILLEN, 301(JEGP):JAN74-85
J.M. MAYER, 182:VOL26#7/8-222
SCHRÖDER, W., ED. DER NIBELUNGE
LIET UND DIU KLAGE.*
L. OKKEN, 433:JAN73-102
SCHRÖDER, W.A. - SEE CATO
SCHRÖDER, W.J. & G. HOLLANDT - SEE
VON ESCHENBACH, W.
SCHROEDER, A. THE LATE MAN.*
H. ROSENGARTEN, 102(CANL):WINTER
73-111
SCHROEDER, J.H. MR. POLK'S WAR.
D.M. JACOBS, 432(NEQ):DEC74-618
SCHROLL, H.T. HAROLD PINTER.
J.M. WARNER, 295:FEB74-748
SCHUBERT, M.H. - SEE WACKENRODER,
W.H.
SCHUBERT, R. METHODOLOGISCHE UNTER-
SUCHUNGEN AN OZEANISCHEM MYTHENMA-
TERIAL.
P. ERNY, 182:VOL26#7/8-250
SCHUCAN, L. DAS NACHLEBEN VON BAS-
ILIUS MAGNUS' "AD ADOLESCENTES."
G.M. DE DURAND, 182:VOL26#15/16-
548
SCHUCHARD, B. "VALOR."*
R. DE DARDEL, 433:OCT73-403
SCHUCHARDT, W-H. GREEK ART.
R. HIGGINS, 39:AUG73-150
M. ROSENTHAL, 135:JUN73-152
SCHUH, H. 2,000 WÖRTER UND WAS MAN
DAMIT MACHEN KANN.
A.G. PRELLER, 399(MLJ):MAR73-148
SCHUH, W. - SEE VON HOFMANNSTHAL,
H. & R. STRAUSS
SCHULBERG, B. SWAN WATCH.
P. SHOWERS, 441:2NOV75-50
SCHULL, J. EDWARD BLAKE. (VOL 1)
D. MORTON, 99:AUG75-38
SCHULTE-SASSE, J. DIE KRITIK AN DER
TRIVIALLITERATUR SEIT DER AUFKLÄR-
UNG.*
A. KAPPLER, 52:BAND8HEFT1-95
A. WARD, 402(MLR):JAN74-225
SCHULTE-SASSE, J. LITERARISCHE WER-
TUNG.*
R. DAU, 654(WB):12/1973-188
A. KAPPLER, 52:BAND8HEFT1-95
SCHULTE-SASSE, J. - SEE LESSING,
G.E., M. MENDELSSOHN & C.F. NICOLAI
SCHULTHEISS, T., ED. RUSSIAN STUD-
IES, 1941-1958.
W.B. WALSH, 550(RUSR):JUL73-334
SCHULTS, R.L. CRUSADER IN BABYLON.
G. CORE, 219(GAR):WINTER73-599
SCHULTZ, H. PANICS & CRASHES.
B.G. MALKIEL, 441:26JAN75-19
SCHULTZ, S.K. THE CULTURE FACTORY.
J.D. HOEVELER, JR., 432(NEQ):JUN
74-307
SCHULTZE, B. H.G. WELLS UND DER
ERSTE WELTKRIEG.
H-J. MÜLLENBROCK, 430(NS):SEP73-
503
SCHULZ, C.M. PEANUTS JUBILEE.
R.R. LINGEMAN, 441:7DEC75-7

SCHULZ, G., ED. NOVALIS.*
E.E. ROGERS, 221(GQ):MAR73-272
B.N.W., 191(ELN):SEP73(SUPP)-154
SCHULZ, M.F. BLACK HUMOR FICTION OF
THE SIXTIES.*
J. GINDIN, 301(JEGP):JAN74-148
SCHULZ, R.K. THE PORTRAYAL OF THE
GERMAN IN RUSSIAN NOVELS.
N.M. KOLB-SELETSKI, 574(SEEJ):
WINTER72-475
SCHULZ-BEHREND, G., ED. THE GERMAN
BAROQUE.*
H.F. KRAUSSE, 255:FALL73-323
SCHULZ-BEHREND, G. - SEE OPITZ, M.
SCHULZE, E.J. SHELLEY'S THEORY OF
POETRY.
M. SELETZKY, 38:BAND91HEFT1-124
SCHULZE, W. LANDESDEFENSION UND
STAATSBILDUNG.
F.L. CARSTEN, 575(SEER):APR74-287
SCHUMACHER, E.F. SMALL IS BEAUTI-
FUL.*
B.G. MALKIEL, 441:26JAN75-19
SCHUMACHER DE PEÑA, G. LATEINISCH
"CAP(P)ULARE" IM ROMANISCHEN.
U.F. CHEN, 545(RPH):NOV73-216
SCHUMANN, C. & J. BRAHMS. LETTERS
OF CLARA SCHUMANN & JOHANNES
BRAHMS.
E. SAMS, 415:SEP74-751
SCHUPPENHAUER, C. DER KAMPF UM DEN
REIM IN DER DEUTSCHEN LITERATUR DES
18. JAHRHUNDERTS.*
H.J. SCHUELER, 222(GR):JAN73-73
SCHÜPPERT, H. KIRCHENKRITIK IN DER
LATEINISCHEN LYRIK DES 12. UND 13.
JAHRHUNDERTS.
K. LANGOSCH, 182:VOL26#15/16-550
SCHUR, N.W. BRITISH SELF-TAUGHT.
M. PEI, 396(MODA):SPRING74-203
SCHÜRER, E. GEORG KAISER.
B.J. KENWORTHY, 402(MLR):APR74-468
M. KUXDORF, 400(MLN):OCT73-1061
N. RITTER, 406:SUMMER74-179
G.L. TRACY, 564:JUN73-164
SCHURHAMMER, G. FRANCIS XAVIER.*
(VOL 1)
E. BURRUS, 377:NOV74-179
SCHÜRMANN, U. CENTRAL ASIAN RUGS.
M. BEATTIE, 39:MAR73-318
SCHUSTER, I. THEODOR STORM.
L.H.C. THOMAS, 220(GL&L):APR74-270
SCHUSTER, L.A. & OTHERS - SEE MORE,
T.
SCHUSTER-ŠEWC, H. HISTORISCH-ETYMO-
LOGISCHES WÖRTERBUCH DER OBER- UND
NIEDERSORBISCHEN SPRACHE.
I. ŠERÁK, 682(ZPSK):BAND26HEFT
3/4-466
I. ŠERÁK, 682(ZPSK):BAND26HEFT6-
730
SCHÜTH, H. - SEE MELLGREN, L. & M.
WALKER
SCHÜTZ, A. DIE SPRACHLICHE AUFNAHME
UND STILISTISCHE WIRKUNG DES ANG-
LIZISMUS IM FRANZÖSISCHEN, AUFGE-
ZEIGT AN DER REKLAMESPRACHE (1962-
1964).
M. HÖFLER, 430(NS):SEP73-494
SCHÜTZ, J.H. PAUL & THE ANATOMY OF
APOSTOLIC AUTHORITY.
F.R. BARRY, 617(TLS):5DEC75-1468
SCHÜTZEICHEL, R. - SEE FRANCK, J.

SCHWAAB, E.L., ED. TRAVELS IN THE
OLD SOUTH.
639(VQR):SUMMER74-XCVI
SCHWAB, R.N., W.E. REX & J. LOUGH.
INVENTORY OF DIDEROT'S "ENCYCLO-
PEDIE."
R. SHACKLETON, 208(FS):JUL74-330
P. STEWART, 207(FR):DEC72-405
SCHWAB, U. ARBEO LAOSA.
D. LE SAGE, 402(MLR):OCT74-909
SCHWAB, U. DIE STERNRUNE IM WESSO-
BRUNNER GEBET.
H-J. GRAF, 72:BAND211HEFT1/3-98
SCHWAB, U., ED. DAS TIER IN DER
DICHTUNG.
D. LE SAGE, 402(MLR):JUL74-701
SCHWAKE, H.P. KORREKTUREN, ERGÄN-
ZUNGEN UND NACHTRÄGE ZUR "BIBLIO-
GRAPHIE ZUR TRANSFORMATIONSGRAMMA-
TIK."
H. PÜTZ & W. THÜMMEL, 260(IF):
BAND77HEFT2/3-377
SCHWARTLÄNDER, J. DER MENSCH IST
PERSON.
H.K. KOHLENBERGER, 342:BAND64HEFT
2-262
SCHWARTZ, A. A TWISTER OF TWISTS,
A TANGLER OF TONGUES.
J.H. BRUNVAND, 292(JAF):APR-JUN73-
198
SCHWARTZ, B. FROM CONFEDERATION TO
NATION.
639(VQR):SPRING74-XLIV
SCHWARTZ, B.I., ED. REFLECTIONS ON
THE MAY FOURTH MOVEMENT.
A. DIRLIK, 293(JAST):MAY73-514
SCHWARTZ, E. ELECTRONIC MUSIC.*
H.S. HOWE, JR., 513:FALL-WINTER73/
SPRING-SUMMER74-379
SCHWARTZ, E. THE FORMS OF FEELING.*
W.H. CLARK, JR., 290(JAAC):FALL73-
134
SCHWARTZ, K. A NEW HISTORY OF
SPANISH AMERICAN FICTION.
W.P. SCOTT, 219(GAR):SUMMER73-284
J. WALKER, 529(QQ):SUMMER73-306
SCHWARTZ, R.B. SAMUEL JOHNSON & THE
NEW SCIENCE.*
J.T. BOULTON, 179(ES):APR73-177
SCHWARZ, A. MARCEL DUCHAMP.
J.R. MELLOW, 441:7DEC75-2
SCHWARZ, B. MUSIC & MUSICAL LIFE IN
SOVIET RUSSIA, 1917-1970.*
M.H. BROWN, 317:FALL73-498
R. LAYTON, 607:JUN73-44
A.B. MC MILLIN, 575(SEER):JAN74-
135
M. PETERSON, 470:MAR73-35
M. VELIMIROVIĆ, 414(MQ):JAN73-134
SCHWARZ, D.W.H. SACHGÜTER UND
LEBENSFORMEN.
E. STRASSNER, 680(ZDP):BAND92HEFT
3-468
SCHWARZ, E. JOSEPH VON EICHENDORFF.
J.F.F., 191(ELN):SEP73(SUPP)-124
L.R. RADNER, 406:FALL74-308
O. SEIDLIN, 221(GQ):SEP73-150
F. WASSERMANN, 400(MLN):APR73-629
SCHWARZ, E. DAS VERSCHLUCKTE
SCHLUCHZEN.*
H. ADOLF, 400(MLN):APR73-644
J. HERMAND, 131(CL):SPRING74-190
P. SPYCHER, 401(MLQ):MAR74-87

SCHWARZ, G. WAS JESUS WIRKLICH
SAGTE.
F. FORSTER, 172(EDDA):1973/5-318
SCHWARZ, M., ED. VARIÉTÉ DU CONTE
FRANÇAIS.
W.W. KIBLER, 207(FR):MAY73-1265
SCHWARZ, P.P. AURORA.*
D.C. RIECHEL, 222(GR):JAN73-77
SCHWARZ, W.J. DER ERZÄHLER UWE
JOHNSON.*
P. PROCHNIK, 220(GL&L):JUL74-334
SCHWARZ-BART, A. A WOMAN NAMED SOL-
ITUDE.* (FRENCH TITLE: LA MULÂ-
TRESSE SOLITUDE.)
M. HINDUS, 390:MAR73-75
H.H. WEINBERG, 207(FR):APR73-1071
SCHWARZ-BART, S. THE BRIDGE OF
BEYOND.*
S. MAITLAND, 362:13FEB75-222
A. REDMON, 617(TLS):10JAN75-29
SCHWARZE, J. DIE BEURTEILUNG DES
PERIKLES DURCH DIE ATTISCHE KOMÖDIE
UND IHRE HISTORISCHE UND HISTORIO-
GRAPHISCHE BEDEUTUNG.
D.K. SILHANEK, 124:MAR73-357
E. WILL, 555:VOL47FASC1-128
SCHWARZKOPF, U. DIE RECHNUNGSLEGUNG
DES HUMBERT DE PLAINE ÜBER DIE
JAHRE 1448 BIS 1452.
G.H. FICK, 589:APR74-377
SCHWAUSS, M. WÖRTERBUCH DER FLORA
UND FAUNA IN LATEINAMERIKA.
K. GINGOLD, 75:1/1973-47
SCHWED, P. GOD BLESS PAWNBROKERS.
C. LEHMANN-HAUPT, 441:17NOV75-29
SCHWEIKERT, U. JEAN PAULS "KOMET."*
W. KOEPKE, 221(GQ):MAR73-258
SCHWEIKERT, U. - SEE "LUDWIG TIECK"
SCHWEIKLE, G., ED. DICHTER ÜBER
DICHTER IN MITTELHOCHDEUTSCHER
LITERATUR.*
G.J. OONK, 433:OCT73-416
SCHWEIKLE, G. - SEE VON TRIMBERG, H.
SCHWEMMER, O. PHILOSOPHIE DER
PRAXIS.
W. STEINBECK, 342:BAND64HEFT2-265
SCHWIEBERT, E. REMEMBRANCES OF
RIVERS PAST. NYMPHS.
H. HENKIN, 441:29JUN75-18
SCHWITTERS, K. DAS LITERARISCHE
WERK. (VOL 2) (F. LACH, ED)
R. LAST, 617(TLS):28FEB75-231
SCHWOB, A. WEGE UND FORMEN DES
SPRACHAUSGLEICHS IN NEUZEITLICHEN
OST- UND SÜDOSTDEUTSCHEN SPRACHIN-
SELN.
H. WELLMANN, 657(WW):MAR/APR73-141
SCHWOEBEL, R., ED. RENAISSANCE MEN
& IDEAS.
J.K. GADOL, 551(RENQ):AUTUMN73-295
SCHWOERER, L.G. "NO STANDING AR-
MIES."
B. WORDEN, 617(TLS):11APR75-390
SCHWYZER, E. GRIECHISCHE GRAMMATIK
AUF DER GRUNDLAGE VON KARL BRUG-
MANNS GRIECHISCHER GRAMMATIK. (VOL
4) (S. RADT, ED)
G.M. MESSING, 124:APR73-429
SCIARONE, A.G. LA PLACE DE L'ADJEC-
TIF EN ITALIEN MODERNE.
G. LEPSCHY, 353:15OCT73-102
M. SANDMANN, 545(RPH):AUG73-133
SCIASCIA, L. LA CORDA PAZZA.
400(MLN):JAN73-168

SCIASCIA, L. TODO MODO.
P. LLOYD, 617(TLS):14MAR75-284
SCOBEY, J. & N. MYERS. GIFTS FROM
YOUR GARDEN.
S. SMITH, 441:7DEC75-95
SCOBIE, E. BLACK BRITANNIA.
G.E. KENT, 114(CHIR):VOL25#3-73
SCOBIE, J.R. BUENOS AIRES.
A. ANGELL, 617(TLS):25APR75-453
SCOBIE, S. THE ROOMS WE ARE.
P. THOMAS, 198:FALL75-129
SCOFIELD, J., ED. SEVEN NEW VOICES.
A. CLUYSENAAR, 565:VOL14#2-62
SCOLES, E. - SEE CARVAJAL
"SCORINIANA 1517-1967."
P. WEXLER, 574(SEEJ):SPRING72-130
SCORTIA, T.N. & F.M. ROBINSON. THE
PROMETHEUS CRISIS.
M. LEVIN, 441:23NOV75-53
SCOT, J. COMMENTAIRE SUR L'ÉVANGILE
DE JEAN. (É. JEAUNEAU, ED & TRANS)
J.J. CONTRENI, 589:APR74-348
SCOTT, D. JOHN SLOAN.
J.R. MELLOW, 441:7DEC75-82
SCOTT, D.C. SELECTED STORIES OF
DUNCAN CAMPBELL SCOTT. (G. CLEVER,
ED)
R. MANE, 189(EA):OCT-DEC73-493
E. WATERSTON, 102(CANL):SUMMER74-
111
SCOTT, F.R. THE DANCE IS ONE.
A. MUIR, 150(DR):WINTER73/74-781
S. SCOBIE, 529(QQ):WINTER73-654
P. STEVENS, 628:SPRING74-102
SCOTT, G.W. ROBERT HERRICK 1591-
1674.
J.B. BROADBENT, 617(TLS):25JUL75-
836
SCOTT, J.M. BOADICEA.
G. WEBSTER, 617(TLS):9MAY75-504
SCOTT, N.A., JR. THREE AMERICAN
MORALISTS.*
M. MASON, 617(TLS):8AUG75-891
M.F. SCHULZ, 301(JEGP):JUL74-463
SCOTT, N.A., JR. THE WILD PRAYER OF
LONGING.
D.J. CAHILL, 141:SPRING72-203
SCOTT, P. A DIVISION OF THE SPOILS.
J.G. FARRELL, 617(TLS):23MAY75-555
W. SCHOTT, 441:12OCT75-34
SCOTT, R.L. & B.L. BROCK. METHODS
OF RHETORICAL CRITICISM.
O. PETERSON, 583:SUMMER74-416
SCOTT, W. THE JOURNAL OF SIR WALTER
SCOTT. (W.E.K. ANDERSON, ED)
K.C., 191(ELN):SEP73(SUPP)-54
T.R. DALE, 125:OCT73-82
J. KINSLEY, 677:VOL4-308
H-J. MÜLLENBROCK, 72:BAND211HEFT
3/6-440
G.A.M. WOOD, 354:JUN73-165
SCOTT, W.T. THE LITERARY NOTEBOOKS
OF WINFIELD TOWNLEY SCOTT.
H.G. MC CURDY, 219(GAR):SPRING73-
132
SCOTT-BUCCLEUCH, R.L. & M. TELES DE
OLIVEIRA, COMPS. AN ANTHOLOGY OF
BRAZILIAN PROSE.
O. FERNÁNDEZ, 399(MLJ):APR73-031
J. PARKER, 86(BHS):JUL73-323
SCOTT-JAMES, A. SISSINGHURST.
C. SYKES, 617(TLS):25APR75-461
SCOTT-MONCRIEFF, G. - SEE MC LEVY,
J.

SCOTT-SUTHERLAND, C. ARNOLD BAX.*
B. HOPKINS, 607:SEP73-48
"THE SCOTTISH NATIONAL DICTIONARY."
VOL 6, PT 3 THRU VOL 9, PT 2) (W.
GRANT & D.D. MURISON, EDS)
H.H. MEIER, 179(ES):JUN73-306
SCOTUS, J.D. GOD & CREATURES.
D.P. HENRY, 617(TLS):5DEC75-1467
SCRIBNER, H.B. & L.B. STEVENS. MAKE
YOUR SCHOOLS WORK.
J. FEATHERSTONE, 441:7SEP75-2
SCRIVEN, R.C. THE SEASONS OF THE
BLIND.
F. DILLON, 362:6MAR75-315
SCROGGINS, D.C. A CONCORDANCE OF
JOSÉ HERNÁNDEZ' "MARTÍN FIERRO."
P.R. BEARDSELL, 86(BHS):JUL73-321
SCRUTON, R. ART & IMAGINATION.
M. PODRO, 617(TLS):21MAR75-316
SCULLARD, H.H. THE ELEPHANT IN THE
GREEK & ROMAN WORLD.
P. GREEN, 617(TLS):7FEB75-131
SCULLARD, H.H. SCIPIO AFRICANUS.*
M.G. MORGAN, 121(CJ):DEC73/JAN74-
158
SCULLY, A., JR. JAMES DAKIN, ARCHI-
TECT.
639(VQR):SUMMER74-LXXXVIII
SCULLY, V. AMERICAN ARCHITECTURE &
URBANISM.*
W. CREESE, 54:SEP73-470
SCULLY, V. PUEBLO.
R.M. ADAMS, 453:16OCT75-6
SCUPHAM, P. PREHISTORIES.
A. THWAITE, 617(TLS):23MAY75-552
SCUPHAM, P. THE SMALL CONTAINERS.
S. CURTIS, 148:SPRING72-85
SCUPHAM, P. THE SNOWING GLOBE.
A. CLUYSENAAR, 565:VOL14#4-75
SEABORNE, M. THE ENGLISH SCHOOL.*
P.F. NORTON, 576:MAR73-75
SEAGER, R. TIBERIUS.*
B. BALDWIN, 124:MAY73-476
SÉAILLES, A. MAURIAC.
M. HANREZ, 207(FR):MAR73-843
R.B. LANG, 399(MLJ):DEC73-426
M. SCOTT, 208(FS):OCT74-485
205(FMLS):APR73-216
SEALSFIELD, C. CHARLES SEALSFIELD
(KARL POSTL 1793-1864): SÄMTLICHE
WERKE. (K.J.R. ARNDT, ED)
A. WALDENRATH, 406:WINTER74-430
SEALTS, M.M., JR. THE EARLY LIVES
OF MELVILLE.
L. ZIFF, 617(TLS):13JUN75-674
SEALTS, M.M., JR. - SEE EMERSON,
R.W.
SEAMAN, D. THE DEFECTOR.
T.J. BINYON, 617(TLS):26DEC75-1544
SEAMAN, P.D. MODERN GREEK & AMERI-
CAN ENGLISH IN CONTACT.
H. KAHANE, 343:BAND17HEFT2-169
SEAR, W. THE NEW WORLD OF ELECTRON-
IC MUSIC.
P. GRIFFITHS, 415:DEC74-1048
SEARLE, G.R. THE QUEST FOR NATIONAL
EFFICIENCY.
M. ROSE, 637(VS):MAR74-319
SEARLE, J. THE LUCKY STREAK.*
A.A. PHILLIPS, 381:JUN73-189
SEARLE, J.R. SPEECH ACTS.*
B. SIERTSEMA, 353:1JUN73-114

SEARS, D.T.P. THE LARK IN THE CLEAR
AIR.*
  A. MITCHELL, 102(CANL):AUTUMN74-86
  A. POKORNY, 296:VOL3#4-90
SEARS, S. THE NEGATIVE IMAGINATION.
  P. MERCER, 148:WINTER72-383
SEARS, S.W. HOMETOWN, U.S.A.
  E. HOAGLAND, 441:7DEC75-4
SEAVER, J. JEANNETTE'S SECRETS OF
EVERYDAY GOOD COOKING.
  R.A. SOKOLOV, 441:7DEC75-7
SEAY, J. WATER TABLES.
  V.M. BELL, 598(SOR):AUTUMN75-933
  D. HUDDLE, 109:SPRING/SUMMER74-155
SEBEOK, T.A., ED. CURRENT TRENDS IN
LINGUISTICS.* (VOL 5)
  G. CARDONA, 353:1JUL73-40
SEBEOK, T.A., ED. CURRENT TRENDS IN
LINGUISTICS. (VOL 7)
  R.H. ROBINS, 315(JAL):VOL11PT1-92
  H.F.W. STAHLKE, 350:MAR74-195
SEBEOK, T.A. & A. RAMSAY, EDS. AP-
PROACHES TO ANIMAL COMMUNICATION.
  H. HEDIGER, 353:1JAN73-104
SEBOLD, R.P. COLONEL DON JOSÉ
CADALSO.
  J. DOWLING, 400(MLN):MAR73-462
  J.H.R. POLT, 240(HR):AUTUMN73-705
  191(ELN):SEP73(SUPP)-176
SEBOLD, R.P. EL RAPTO DE LA MENTE.
  P. ILIE, 240(HR):WINTER73-106
SECCHI, C.C. GIUSEPPE PARINI.
  V.A.S., 275(IQ):FALL-WINTER73(VOL
  17#66)-68
SECKLER, D. THORSTEIN VEBLEN & THE
INSTITUTIONALISTS.
  D. MAC RAE, 617(TLS):25JUL75-824
  J. VAIZEY, 362:29MAY75-716
SECLER, H. CAHUILLA TEXTS WITH AN
INTRODUCTION.
  G.F. MEIER, 682(ZPSK):BAND26HEFT
  3/4-450
SECO, M. ARNICHES Y EL HABLA DE
MADRID.
  N.P. SACKS, 240(HR):SPRING73-448
"THE LAURA SECORD CANADIAN COOK
BOOK."
  J.M. COLE, 99:DEC75/JAN76-37
SEDLÁČEK, K. DAS GEMEIN-SINO-TIBET-
ISCHE.
  R.A. MILLER, 318(JAOS):OCT-DEC73-
  649
SEDWICK, F. & M.M. AZAÑA. CONVERSA-
CIONES CON MADRILEÑOS.
  J.B. FERNÁNDEZ, 399(MLJ):NOV74-363
VON SEE, K. GERMANISCHE HELDEN-
SAGE.*
  J. HARRIS, 563(SS):SPRING74-185
VON SEE, K. DIE GESTALT DER "HÁVA-
MÁL."*
  J. WILSON, 563(SS):SPRING74-175
SEEBASS, G. BIBLIOGRAPHIA OSIAN-
DRICA.*
  L.W. SPITZ, 551(RENQ):WINTER73-473
SEEBERG, A. CORINTHIAN KOMOS VASES.
  R.M. COOK, 123:MAR74-159
SEEBOLD, E. VERGLEICHENDES UND ETY-
MOLOGISCHES WÖRTERBUCH DER GERMAN-
ISCHEN STARKEN VERBEN.*
  A. BAMMESBERGER, 260(IF):BAND78-
  324
SEEKAMP, H.J., R.C. OCKENDEN & M.
KEILSON, EDS. STEFAN GEORGE.
  F.G. CRONHEIM, 402(MLR):OCT74-939

SEEL, O. VERSCHLÜSSELTE GEGENWART.
  L. RICHARDSON, JR., 124:MAY73-493
  G.W. WILLIAMS, 123:NOV74-316
SEELEY, J.R. THE EXPANSION OF ENG-
LAND. (J. GROSS, ED)
  R. CALLAHAN, 318(JAOS):JUL-SEP73-
  392
SEELYE, C. - SEE OLSON, C.
SEELYE, J. DIRTY TRICKS.*
  639(VQR):SPRING74-LVI
SEFERIS, G. MERES A. (E.C. KASDAG-
LIS, ED) EXI NYHTES STIN AKROPOLI.
(G.P. SAVIDIS, ED)
  R. BEATON, 617(TLS):14NOV75-1364
SEFERIS, G. A POET'S JOURNAL.*
(BRITISH TITLE: DAYS OF 1945-51.)
  A. ROSS, 364:FEB/MAR75-117
  M. SAVVAS, 385(MQR):FALL75-477
SEGAL, C. THE THEME OF THE MUTILA-
TION OF THE CORPSE IN THE "ILIAD."*
  F.M. COMBELLACK, 122:APR73-149
SEGAL, C.P. LANDSCAPE IN OVID'S
"METAMORPHOSES."
  G.K. GALINSKY, 121(CJ):DEC73/JAN
  74-157
SEGAL, E. LOVE STORY.
  B. MERRY, 364:AUG/SEP74-80
SEGAL, P. PHILIP SEGAL: ESSAYS &
LECTURES. (M. LEVESON, ED)
  G. BUTLER, 180(ESA):SEP73-103
SEGALEN, V. RENÉ LEYS.*
  F.C. ST. AUBYN, 207(FR):DEC72-451
SEGARRA, J.P.F. - SEE UNDER FORNER Y
SEGARRA, J.P.
SEGHERS, A. ÜBER KUNSTWERK UND
WIRKLICHKEIT. (S. BOCK, ED)
  W.F. TULASIEWICZ, 220(GL&L):JAN74-
  174
SEGRE, C. LE STRUTTURE E IL TEMPO.
  G. ALMANSI, 617(TLS):1AUG75-879
SEIBERT, J. ALEXANDER DER GROSSE.
  E.N. BORZA, 122:JUL74-232
SEIDEL, M. & R-H. MARIJNISSEN, EDS.
JHERONIMUS BOSCH.
  R. JULLIAN, 182:VOL26#1/2-40
SEIDENBAUM, A. THIS IS CALIFORNIA:
PLEASE KEEP OUT.
  P. SCHRAG, 441:11MAY75-16
SEIDLIN, O. KLASSISCHE UND MODERNE
KLASSIKER.
  E. STOPP, 402(MLR):OCT74-922
SEILER, H. CAHUILLA TEXTS WITH AN
INTRODUCTION.
  S. LILJEBLAD, 269(IJAL):APR73-110
  H-J. PINNOW, 343:BAND16HEFT2-226
SEILERN, A. FLEMISH PAINTINGS &
DRAWINGS AT 56 PRINCES GATE LONDON.
  M. JAFFÉ, 54:SEP73-462
SEIP, D.A. NORWEGISCHE SPRACHGE-
SCHICHTE. (REV & TRANS BY L. SALT-
VEIT)
  H. BECK, 343:BAND17HEFT2-183
  E. HAUGEN, 350:SEP74-575
  E. HAUGEN, 133:1973/3-254
SEITZ, A. SÄMTLICHE SCHRIFTEN.
(VOL 1) (P. UKENA, ED)
  M. WINDER, 220(GL&L):OCT73-80
SEIVER, G. INTRODUCTION TO ROMAN-
IAN.
  J.E. ALGEO, 399(MLJ):NOV73-368
SELA, O. THE BENGALI INHERITANCE.
  N. CALLENDAR, 441:3AUG75-24
  M. LASKI, 362:5JUN75-748

SELA, O. THE KIRIOV TAPES.*
N. CALLENDAR, 441:30MAR75-24
SELBY, J.E. A CHRONOLOGY OF VIR-
GINIA & THE WAR OF INDEPENDENCE,
1768-1783.
639(VQR):SUMMER74-XCIII
SELBY, R. THE PRINCIPLE OF RESERVE
IN THE WRITINGS OF JOHN HENRY CARD-
INAL NEWMAN.
M. TREVOR, 617(TLS):26SEP75-1107
SELDEN, M. THE YENAN WAY IN REVOLU-
TIONARY CHINA.*
LEE NGOK, 302:JUL73-246
SELFRIDGE-FIELD, E. VENETIAN IN-
STRUMENTAL MUSIC FROM GABRIELI TO
VIVALDI.
D. STEVENS, 617(TLS):25JUL75-854
DE SELINCOURT, E. - SEE WORDSWORTH,
W. & D.
SELLARS, J. SAMUEL PALMER.
W. FEAVER, 617(TLS):21MAR75-304
SELLERS, C.C. & M.C. SLOTTEN, WITH
R.A. VINCETT, COMPS. ARCHIVES &
MANUSCRIPT COLLECTIONS OF DICKINSON
COLLEGE.
K.J. PIKE, 14:JUL73-412
SELLIN, P.R. DANIEL HEINSIUS &
STUART ENGLAND.
L. FORSTER, 179(ES):DEC72-560
SELLS, A.L. OLIVER GOLDSMITH.
P. ROGERS, 617(TLS):7FEB75-134
SELTÉN, B. THE ANGLO-SAXON HERITAGE
IN MIDDLE ENGLISH PERSONAL NAMES,
EAST ANGLIA 1100-1399. (VOL 1)
G.F. JENSEN, 447(N&Q):MAY73-199
R.M. WILSON, 402(MLR):APR74-367
SELUCKY, R. CZECHOSLOVAKIA.
A. MATEJKO, 104:SPRING74-166
SELVON, S. MOSES ASCENDING.
V. CUNNINGHAM, 617(TLS):29AUG75-
961
SELWYN, F. CRACKSMAN ON VELVET.*
N. CALLENDAR, 441:19JAN75-37
SELZ, J. EDVARD MUNCH.
P. ADAMS, 61:JAN75-91
SELZ, P. SAM FRANCIS.
J.R. MELLOW, 441:7DEC75-80
SELZER, R. RITUALS OF SURGERY.
W. PEDEN, 569(SR):FALL74-712
SELZNICK, D.O. MEMO FROM DAVID O.
SELZNICK. (R. BEHLMER, ED)
200:JAN73-52
SEMBDNER, H. - SEE FALK, J.D.
SEMENZATO, C. CORPUS PALLADIANUM.
(VOL 1: THE ROTONDA OF ANDREA PAL-
LADIO.)
M.N. ROSENFELD, 576:DEC73-335
F.J.B. WATSON, 39:MAY73-531
SEMMLER, C. DOUGLAS STEWART.
C. HADGRAFT, 71(ALS):OCT75-217
SEN, J.P. THE PROGRESS OF T.S.
ELIOT AS POET & CRITIC.
R. KIRK, 569(SR):FALL74-698
SEN, S.K. A STUDY OF THE METAPHYS-
ICS OF SPINOZA.
R.J. MULVANEY, 319:JUL75-408
SENA, J.F. A BIBLIOGRAPHY OF MELAN-
CHOLY: 1660-1800.
L. BABB, 551(RENQ):SPRING73-72
DE SENANCOUR, E.P. LIBRES MÉDITA-
TIONS: TROISIÈME VERSION.* (B.
LE GALL, ED)
P. THOMPSON, 535(RHL):JUL-AUG73-
709

SENCOURT, R. T.S. ELIOT: A MEMOIR.*
(D. ADAMSON, ED)
A. HOLDER, 295:FEB74-585
SENECA. NATURALES QUAESTIONES.
(T.H. CORCORAN, ED & TRANS)
A.L. MOTTO, 124:MAR74-303
SENG, P.L.F. THE MALAY STATES 1877-
1895.
R.W. WINKS, 318(JAOS):APR-JUN73-
232
SENGLE, F. BIEDERMEIERZEIT. (VOL 2)
H. DENKLER, 680(ZDP):BAND92HEFT4-
597
C.P. MAGILL, 402(MLR):OCT74-926
SEN GUPTA, K.P. THE CHRISTIAN MIS-
SIONARIES IN BENGAL, 1793-1833.
B. SOUTHARD, 293(JAST):FEB73-347
SENIOR, H. ORANGEISM: THE CANADIAN
PHASE.
G.L. COOK, 255(HAB):WINTER73-71
G.N. EMERY, 529(QQ):WINTER73-628
SENN, A.E. DIPLOMACY & REVOLUTION.
E.H. CARR, 617(TLS):8AUG75-900
SENN, A.E. THE RUSSIAN REVOLUTION
IN SWITZERLAND, 1914-1917.*
D.R. JONES, 104:SUMMER73-267
SENN, F., ED. NEW LIGHT ON JOYCE
FROM THE DUBLIN SYMPOSIUM.*
A. GOLDMAN, 541(RES):NOV73-516
T. ROGERS, 175:AUTUMN73-119
295:FEB74-683
SENN, W. STUDIES IN THE DRAMATIC
CONSTRUCTION OF ROBERT GREENE &
GEORGE PEELE.
N. SANDERS, 402(MLR):APR74-370
SENNA, C., ED. THE FALLACY OF I.Q.
A.R. JENSEN, 219(GAR):FALL73-439
SENNETT, R. & J. COBB. THE HIDDEN
INJURIES OF CLASS.
N. MILLS, 676(YR):SUMMER74-566
DE SENS, O. OPERA OMNIA. (R-H.
BAUTIER & M. GILLES, EDS & TRANS)
W. SALMEN, 182:VOL26#21/22-807
SERBAT, G. - SEE PLINY
SEREBRENNIKOV, B.A., ED. OBŠČEE
JAZYKOZNANIE.
E. ISING & OTHERS, 682(ZPSK):BAND
26HEFT1/2-159
SEREBRIAKOV, I.D. OČERKI DREVNEIN-
DIJSKOJ LITERATURY.
L. STERNBACH, 318(JAOS):JUL-SEP73-
378
SERENI, V. UN POSTO DI VACANZA.
F. FORTINI, 617(TLS):31OCT75-1308
SERGE, V. THE CONQUERED CITY.
W. GOODMAN, 441:28DEC75-14
SERGEANT, P.W. WITCHES & WARLOCKS.
617(TLS):31JAN75-117
SERLE, G. FROM DESERTS THE PROPHETS
COME.*
H.P. HESELTINE, 381:JUN73-215
DE LA SERNA, G.G. - SEE UNDER GÓMEZ
DE LA SERNA, G.
SERPER, A. LA MANIÈRE SATIRIQUE DE
RUTEBEUF.
E.M. RUTSON, 382(MAE):1974/2-172
SERPER, A. RUTEBEUF, POÈTE SATIR-
IQUE.*
W. HENDRICKSON, 207(FR):DEC72-395
SERPIERI, A. T.S. ELIOT.
J. WOODRESS, 27(AL):JAN75-596
SERRA, R.A. - SEE UNDER ARAMÓN I
SERRA, R.

SERRALTA, F. LA RENEGADA DE VALLA-
DOLID.
F. LÓPEZ ESTRADA, 240(HR):SPRING
73-445
SERRANO, M.L. - SEE UNDER LÓPEZ
SERRANO, M.
SERRES, M., F. DAGOGNET & A. SINA-
CEUR - SEE COMTE, A.
SERRIN, W. THE COMPANY & THE UNION.
N. MILLS, 676(YR):SUMMER74-566
SERVICE, A. EDWARDIAN ARCHITECTURE
& ITS ORIGINS.
J. BETJEMAN, 617(TLS):19DEC75-1512
SERVIER, J. LES PORTES DE L'ANNÉE.
M. LAFFRANQUE, 542:JAN-MAR73-85
SERVOTTE, H. ENGLISH LITERATURE IN
THE TWENTIETH CENTURY: THE NOVEL.
P. MICHEL-MICHOT, 556(RLV):1973/6-
563
SESHADRI, K. & S.P. JAIN. PANCHAYATI
RAJ & POLITICAL PERCEPTIONS OF EL-
ECTORATE.
B.W. COYER, 293(JAST):AUG73-722
SETH-SMITH, M. STEVE.*
A. ROSS, 364:AUG/SEP74-116
SETTGAST, E.E. & G.F. ANDERSON.
BASIC SPANISH.*
E.M. MALINAK, 399(MLJ):JAN-FEB73-
71
SÈVE, L. MARXISMUS UND THEORIE DER
PERSÖNLICHKEIT.
I. DÖLLING, 654(WB):7/1973-176
SEVERIN, D.S. MEMORY IN "LA CELES-
TINA."*
K. KISH, 545(RPH):NOV73-264
SEVERIN, D.S. - SEE DE ROJAS, F.
SEVERNYAK, S. BETWEEN THE ROSE &
THE LION.
270:VOL23#1-23
SEVERS, J.B., ED. A MANUAL OF THE
WRITINGS ON MIDDLE ENGLISH 1050-
1500. (VOL 2)
A. HUDSON, 382(MAE):1974/2-199
SEWALL, R.B. THE LIFE OF EMILY
DICKINSON.*
J. CODY, 598(SOR):SUMMER75-639
I. EHRENPREIS, 453:23JAN75-3
C.R. LARSON, 31(ASCH):AUTUMN75-681
R. TODD, 61:JAN75-74
442(NY):20JAN75-98
SEWALL, S. THE DIARY OF SAMUEL
SEWALL, 1674-1729.* (M.H. THOMAS,
ED)
639(VQR):SPRING74-XL
SEWARD, D. THE FIRST BOURBON.
H.H. ROWEN, 207(FR):OCT72-198
SEWELL, B. OLIVE CUSTANCE.
M. DAVSON, 362:21AUG75-253
SEWID, J. GUESTS NEVER LEAVE HUN-
GRY.
R. LANDES, 529(QQ):SPRING73-116
N. NEWTON, 102(CANL):WINTER73-122
SEXTON, A. THE AWFUL ROWING TOWARD
GOD.
S.G. AXELROD, 398:AUTUMN75-187
R. MAZZOCCO, 453:3APR75-20
J.C. OATES, 441:23MAR75-3
SEXTON, A. THE DEATH NOTEBOOKS.
H. CARRUTH, 249(HUDR):SUMMER74-311
R. MAZZOCCO, 453:3APR75-20
639(VQR):SUMMER74-LXXXIV

SEXTON, R.J. THE COMPLEX OF YVOR
WINTERS' CRITICISM.*
R. FOSTER, 27(AL):JAN75-599
H. KAYE, 598(SOR):SUMMER75-652
SEYDOUX, M. & M. BIESIEKIERSKI. RÉ-
PERTOIRE DES THÈSES CONCERNANT LES
ÉTUDES SLAVES L'U.R.S.S. ET LES
PAYS DE L'EST EUROPÉEN ET SOUTENUES
EN FRANCE DE 1824 À 1969.
J.J. DOSSICK, 574(SEEJ):SPRING72-
133
SEYERSTED, P. KATE CHOPIN.
M. FRAZEE, 189(EA):JAN-MAR73-119
C. KOCHUYT, 179(ES):APR73-184
SEYERSTED, P. - SEE CHOPIN, K.
SEYMANN, M.R. BASIC SPANISH FOR
HEALTH PERSONNEL.
V.R. FOSTER, 399(MLJ):APR74-213
SEYMOUR, C., JR. EARLY ITALIAN
PAINTINGS IN THE YALE UNIVERSITY
ART GALLERY.
L. VERTOVA, 90:MAR73-159
SEYMOUR, C., JR., ED. MICHELANGELO:
THE SISTINE CHAPEL CEILING.
C. GOULD, 39:JUN73-621
P. JOANNIDES, 90:JUN73-410
J. SHAPLEY, 127:SUMMER74-366
SEYMOUR, C., JR. JACOPO DELLA
QUERCIA, SCULPTOR.
H.W. JANSON, 676(YR):AUTUMN73-91
J. SHAPLEY, 127:SUMMER74-366
SEYMOUR, G. HARRY'S GAME.
T.J. BINYON, 617(TLS):26DEC75-1544
C. LEHMANN-HAUPT, 441:2OCT75-43
P. THEROUX, 441:5OCT75-7
442(NY):17NOV75-196
SEYMOUR, M.C., ED. THE METRICAL
VERSION OF "MANDEVILLE'S TRAVELS."
B.D.H. MILLER, 382(MAE):1974/3-302
SEZGIN, F. GESCHICHTE DES ARABIS-
CHEN SCHRIFTTUMS. (VOLS 3&4)
F. ROSENTHAL, 318(JAOS):APR-JUN73-
235
SEZNEC, J. & J. ADHÉMAR - SEE DID-
EROT, D.
SHAARA, M. THE KILLER ANGELS.*
T. LASK, 441:10MAY75-27
E. WEEKS, 61:APR75-98
SHABAN, M.A. THE 'ABBÂSID REVOLU-
TION.
P.G. FORAND, 318(JAOS):JUL-SEP73-
364
B. TYABJI, 273(IC):JAN73-78
SHACK, W.A. & H-M. MARCOS, EDS.
GODS & HEROES.
G. MOORE, 617(TLS):11APR75-395
SHACKFORD, J.A. & S.J. FOLMSBEE -
SEE CROCKETT, D.
SHACKLETON BAILEY, D.R. CICERO.*
W.C. MC DERMOTT, 124:MAY73-492
H. MUSURILLO, 613:SUMMER73-315
G. PHIFER, 583:SPRING74-303
D. STOCKTON, 123:MAR74-68
SHADBOLT, J. MIND'S I.
D. LIVESAY, 102(CANL):SPRING74-114
G. SMEDMOR, 73:WINTER74-41
SHADBOLT, M. A TOUCH OF CLAY.
D. DAVIN, 617(TLS):3JAN75-5
D. DURRANT, 364:FEB/MAR75-136
SHAH NAWAZ, J.A. FATHER & DAUGHTER.
R.S. WHEELER, 293(JAST):NOV72-199
SHAHAR, D. THE PALACE OF SHATTERED
VESSELS.
T. LASK, 441:21SEP75-38

SHAHĪD, I., ED. THE MARTYRS OF
NAJRAN, NEW DOCUMENTS.
  F. ROSENTHAL, 318(JAOS):OCT-DEC73-
  557
  R.W. THOMSON, 589:APR74-378
SHAKESPEARE, R. THE PSYCHOLOGY OF
HANDICAP.
  I. HUNTER, 617(TLS):6JUN75-629
SHAKESPEARE, W. THE BLACKFRIARS
SHAKESPEARE. (J.L. BARROLL, GEN-
ERAL ED)
  P.K. MESZAROS, 570(SQ):SPRING73-
  231
SHAKESPEARE, W. THE COMPLETE SIGNET
SHAKESPEARE.
  I. BROWN, 157:SPRING73-73
SHAKESPEARE, W. THE COMPLETE WORKS
OF SHAKESPEARE. (I. RIBNER & G.L.
KITTREDGE, EDS)
  S. THOMAS, 570(SQ):SUMMER73-344
SHAKESPEARE, W. THE MERRY WIVES OF
WINDSOR. (H.J. OLIVER, ED)
  T.W. CRAIK, 551(RENQ):SUMMER73-231
  T.H. HOWARD-HILL, 541(RES):FEB73-
  67
SHAKESPEARE, W. MUCH ADO ABOUT
NOTHING.* (C. HINMAN, ED)
  K.B. MICHAEL, 570(SQ):AUTUMN73-476
SHAKESPEARE, W. TIMON OF ATHENS.
(G.R. HIBBARD, ED) ALL'S WELL THAT
ENDS WELL. (B. EVERETT, ED)
  L. DESVIGNES, 549(RLC):APR-JUN73-
  341
SHAKESPEARE, W. THE TWO GENTLEMEN
OF VERONA. (C. LEECH, ED)
  M. MINCOFF, 179(ES):OCT72-461
SHALES, T. & OTHERS. THE AMERICAN
FILM HERITAGE.*
  W.T. MURPHY, 14:JUL73-414
SHALOM, A. R.G. COLLINGWOOD, PHIL-
OSOPHE ET HISTORIEN.
  P. DUBOIS, 542:APR-JUN73-229
SHANAB, R.E.A. & G.J. WEINROTH, EDS.
PRESENT-DAY ISSUES IN PHILOSOPHY.
  W.G., 543:DEC72-367
SHANAMUGAM, S.V. DRAVIDIAN NOUNS.
  H.F. SCHIFFMAN, 318(JAOS):JUL-SEP
  73-386
SHANET, H. PHILHARMONIC.
  D. HENAHAN, 441:17FEB75-19
  J. PEYSER, 441:26JAN75-6
SHANIN, T., ED. THE RULES OF THE
GAME.
  W. SCHÄFER, 182:VOL26#3/4-75
SHANKLAND, P. BYRON OF THE WAGER.
  C. LLOYD, 617(TLS):4APR75-377
SHANNON, B. & G. KALINSKY. THE
BALLPARKS.
  R. SMITH, 441:7DEC75-30
SHANNON, D. DEUCES WILD.
  N. CALLENDAR, 441:6APR75-18
SHANNON, E. THE COOK IN THE KITCHEN.
  M.F.K. FISHER, 442(NY):10NOV75-182
SHANNON, J. COURAGE.
  M. LEVIN, 441:8JUN75-17
SHANNON, R. THE CRISIS OF IMPERIAL-
ISM 1865-1915.
  M. HURST, 617(TLS):14FEB75-158
SHANNON, R.T. GLADSTONE & THE BUL-
GARIAN AGITATION 1876.
  S. KOSS, 617(TLS):22AUG75-941
SHAPERE, D. GALILEO.
  J. NORTH, 617(TLS):11APR75-397

SHAPIRO, D. THE PAGE-TURNER.
  J.J. MC GANN, 491:OCT74-44
  M. MADIGAN, 385(MQR):SPRING75-220
  J.N. MORRIS, 249(HUDR):SPRING74-
  109
SHAPIRO, D., ED. SOCIAL REALISM.
  D.W. CRAWFORD, 290(JAAC):SPRING74-
  432
SHAPIRO, H.I. - SEE RUSKIN, J.
SHAPIRO, H.L. PEKING MAN.
  P. ADAMS, 61:MAR75-145
  J.Z. YOUNG, 453:29MAY75-18
SHAPIRO, K. THE POETRY WRECK.
  A. BROYARD, 441:13MAR75-43
SHAPIRO, M. ASPECTS OF RUSSIAN MOR-
PHOLOGY.
  B.J. DARDEN, 215(GL):VOL13#1-56
SHARMA, B.L. KASHMIR AWAKES.
  R.L. DIAL, 293(JAST):FEB73-361
SHARMA, B.N.K. THE BRAHMASŪTRAS &
THEIR PRINCIPAL COMMENTARIES. (VOL
1)
  G.M.C. SPRUNG, 485(PE&W):JUL73-399
SHARMA, C.H. A MANUAL OF HOMEOPATHY
& NATURAL MEDICINE.
  617(TLS):8AUG75-906
SHARMA, D. THE NEGATIVE DIALECTS OF
INDIA.
  L.O. GOMEZ, 485(PE&W):JAN-APR73-
  251
SHARMA, S.P. INDIA'S BOUNDARY &
TERRITORIAL DISPUTES.
  C.V. CRABB, JR., 293(JAST):FEB73-
  360
SHARP, A. NIGHT MOVES.
  N. CALLENDAR, 441:27JUL75-18
SHARP, G. THE POLITICS OF NONVIO-
LENT ACTION.
  E. GARVER, 185:APR74-266
  A. ROBERTS, 617(TLS):4APR75-357
SHARP, M. THE FAITHFUL SERVANTS.
  M. LEVIN, 441:4MAY75-53
  R. USBORNE, 617(TLS):5SEP75-998
SHARP, T. THE WARTIME ALLIANCE &
THE ZONAL DIVISION OF GERMANY.
  D.C. WATT, 617(TLS):8AUG75-892
SHARPE, L.A., ED. THE OLD PORTU-
GUESE "VIDA DE SAM BERNARDO."
  D.M. ATKINSON, 86(BHS):OCT73-414
  K.S. ROBERTS, 399(MLJ):JAN-FEB73-
  63
SHARPE, T. BLOTT ON THE LANDSCAPE.
  J. MELLORS, 362:19JUN75-821
  R. USBORNE, 617(TLS):23MAY75-555
SHATTUCK, R. MARCEL PROUST.*
  J. BAYLEY, 453:6MAR75-24
  442(NY):3FEB75-95
SHATTUCK, R. - SEE APOLLINAIRE, G.
SHAW, B. ORBITSVILLE.
  J. HAMILTON-PATERSON, 617(TLS):
  14MAR75-284
SHAW, D.L. GALLEGOS: DOÑA BÁRBARA.
  M. WILSON, 402(MLR):JUL74-681
SHAW, D.L. A LITERARY HISTORY OF
SPAIN: THE NINETEENTH CENTURY.*
  J.R. CORTINA, 399(MLJ):NOV73-376
  191(ELN):SEP73(SUPP)-173
SHAW, G.B. COLLECTED LETTERS, 1898-
1910.* (D.H. LAURENCE, ED)
  S.P. ALBERT, 572:JAN73-33
  R. EYRE, 214:VOL6#22-61
  F.P.W. MC DOWELL, 295:APR74-1039

SHAW, G.B. COLLECTED PLAYS WITH
THEIR PREFACES. (D.H. LAURENCE, ED)
J. SIMON, 441:2NOV75-1
SHAW, I. NIGHTWORK.
C. LEHMANN-HAUPT, 441:18SEP75-45
K. ROOSEVELT, 441:7SEP75-41
D. WILSON, 617(TLS):7NOV75-1325
442(NY):20OCT75-169
SHAW, J. THE SELF IN SOCIAL WORK.
P. WILLMOTT, 617(TLS):7FEB75-147
SHAW, M., ED. ACCORDING TO OUR
ANCESTORS.
L. CAMPBELL, 350:JUN74-394
SHAW, N. ALL GOD'S DANGERS.* (T.
ROSENGARTEN, ED)
W. NICHOLS, 31(ASCH):SPRING75-310
SHAW, S. THE CHRISTENING.
M. JOHNSON, 617(TLS):8AUG75-902
SHAW, S.J. BETWEEN OLD & NEW.*
E. BIRNBAUM, 318(JAOS):OCT-DEC73-
560
SHAW, T. IGBO-UKWU.
F. WILLETT, 69:JAN73-88
SHEA, W.R. GALILEO'S INTELLECTUAL
REVOLUTION.
R.E. BUTTS, 154:SEP73-531
M.S. MAHONEY, 319:JAN75-101
SHEAD, R. CONSTANT LAMBERT.*
C. PALMER, 410(M&L):APR74-241
SHEARER, J. MUSIC & DRAMA.
A.C. KEYS, 67:MAY74-96
SHEARMAN, J. RAPHAEL'S CARTOONS IN
THE COLLECTION OF HER MAJESTY THE
QUEEN & THE TAPESTRIES FOR THE SIS-
TINE CHAPEL. THE VATICAN STANZE.
C. GOULD, 39:JUN73-621
SHEATS, P.D. THE MAKING OF WORDS-
WORTH'S POETRY 1785-1798.*
J.A.W. HEFFERNAN, 591(SIR):SUMMER
74-255
S.M. SPERRY, 301(JEGP):JUL74-445
SHECHNER, M. JOYCE IN NIGHTTOWN.
C.G. ANDERSON, 329(JJQ):SPRING75-
335
SHECKLEY, R. OPTIONS.
G. JONAS, 441:24AUG75-30
SHEED, W. MUHAMMAD ALI.
A. BROYARD, 441:15SEP75-19
L. FINGER, 617(TLS):31OCT75-1284
W. HINCKLE, 441:21SEP75-2
G. WILLS, 453:30OCT75-3
SHEEHAN, B.W. SEEDS OF EXTINCTION.*
Y. KAWASHIMA, 639(VQR):WINTER74-
144
SHEEHY, G. HUSTLING.
S. TOTH, 109:SPRING/SUMMER74-127
SHEIKH, M.S. STUDIES IN MUSLIM
PHILOSOPHY.
R.E. ABU SHANAB, 319:JAN75-100
SHELDON, M. THE DEATH OF A LEADER.
R. SUTHERLAND, 102(CANL):AUTUMN73-
111
SHELDON, R. - SEE SHKLOVSKY, V.
SHELLABARGER, S. THE CHEVALIER
BAYARD.
R. O'GORMAN, 399(MLJ):DEC73-436
SHELLEY, P.B. THE COMPLETE POETICAL
WORKS OF PERCY BYSSHE SHELLEY.
(VOL 1) (N. ROGERS, ED)
P.H. BUTTER, 402(MLR):APR74-383
S.C., 191(ELN):SEP73(SUPP)-59
D.H. REIMAN, 301(JEGP):APR74-250
"SHELTER."
R. NORTH, 362:24APR75-542

SHENG, Y. SUN YAT-SEN UNIVERSITY IN
MOSCOW & THE CHINESE REVOLUTION.
J.P. HARRISON, 293(JAST):NOV72-147
SHENKER, I. WORDS & THEIR MASTERS.
C.T. WHALEY, 584(SWR):SUMMER74-327
SHEPARD, L. THE HISTORY OF STREET
LITERATURE.
O.W. FERGUSON, 579(SAQ):AUTUMN74-
573
SHEPARD, L. JOHN PITTS.*
A.W. WONDERLEY, 582(SFQ):JUN73-146
SHEPARD, L. - SEE DAVE, H.T.
SHEPARD, S. HAWK MOON.
J.D. BELLAMY, 473(PR):2/1974-314
SHEPARD, T. GOD'S PLOT. (M. MC GIF-
FERT, ED)
D.B. RUTMAN, 432(NEQ):JUN73-310
D.E. STANNARD, 165:WINTER75-338
SHEPHERD, G. THE NATURE OF ALLITER-
ATIVE POETRY IN LATE MEDIEVAL ENG-
LAND.
G.C. BRITTON, 447(N&Q):JAN73-29
SHEPHERD, J. THE FOREST KILLERS.
E. ABBEY, 441:20JUL75-6
SHEPHERD, W., COMP. SHEPHERD'S
GLOSSARY OF GRAPHIC SIGNS & SYM-
BOLS.
V.E. HANZELI, 399(MLJ):NOV73-372
SHEPPARD, F., ED. LONDON 1808-1870.*
A. WELSH, 155:MAY73-123
SHEPPARD, F.H.W., GENERAL ED. SURVEY
OF LONDON. (VOL 37)
S. CORBYN, 135:JUN73-151
SHERBURNE, J.C. JOHN RUSKIN, OR THE
AMBIGUITIES OF ABUNDANCE.
G.P. LANDOW, 637(VS):DEC73-228
SHERIDAN, J.E. CHINA IN DISINTE-
GRATION.
442(NY):17NOV75-195
SHERIDAN, R.B. THE DRAMATIC WORKS
OF RICHARD BRINSLEY SHERIDAN.*
(C. PRICE, ED)
P.W. DAY, 67:NOV74-225
SHERMAN, J. CHAIM THE SLAUGHTERER.
S. DRAGLAND, 198:WINTER75-115
F.W. WATT, 99:JUN75-40
SHERMAN, J.R. INVISIBLE POETS.
D. MAC LEOD, 617(TLS):13JUN75-675
SHERMAN, R.B. THE REPUBLICAN PARTY
& BLACK AMERICA, 1896-1933.
639(VQR):SPRING74-XLVIII
SHEROVER, C.M. HEIDEGGER, KANT &
TIME.*
H. HOPPE, 342:BAND64HEFT1-131
SHERRINGTON, R.J. THREE NOVELS BY
FLAUBERT.*
B.F. BART, 546(RR):NOV73-310
SHERRY, N. CONRAD'S WESTERN WORLD.*
R. LAWRENCE, 175:SPRING72-32
R.J. NELSON, 502(PRS):SUMMER73-179
295:FEB74-564
SHERWIN, J.J. IMPOSSIBLE BUILDINGS.*
M.G. PERLOFF, 659:WINTER75-84
SHERWIN, M.J. A WORLD DESTROYED.
V.K. MC ELHENY, 441:12NOV75-37
G. SMITH, 441:21DEC75-4
442(NY):8DEC75-199
SHERWIN, W.K., JR., ED & TRANS.
"DEEDS OF FAMOUS MEN (DE VIRIS IL-
LUSTRIBUS)."
R.T. BRUÈRE, 122:JAN74-73
G.V. SUMNER, 487:SUMMER73-209

338

SHERWOOD, J.M. GEORGES MANDEL &
THE THIRD REPUBLIC.*
J.M. TAYLOR, 447(N&Q):SEP73-353
SHERZER, J. - SEE SWADESH, M.
SHESGREEN, S. - SEE HOGARTH, W.
SHESTOV, L. DOSTOEVSKY, TOLSTOY &
NIETZSCHE.*
R.E. MATLAW, 574(SEEJ):SPRING72-
101
SHETTER, W.Z. THE PILLARS OF SOCI-
ETY.*
J. TROMP, 202(FMOD):JUN73-418
SHEWELL-COOPER, W.E. THE COMPOST
FLOWER GROWER.
617(TLS):22AUG75-954
SHEWELL-COOPER, W.E. COMPOST GAR-
DENING.
617(TLS):7FEB75-149
SHIBLES, W. DEATH.
C. RICKS, 617(TLS):18JUL75-790
SHIBLES, W.A. ANALYSIS OF METAPHOR
IN THE LIGHT OF W.M. URBAN'S THE-
ORIES.*
M. OSBORN, 480(P&R):SUMMER73-197
SHIBLES, W.A. METAPHOR.*
Z. FOLEJEWSKI, 574(SEEJ):SUMMER72-
250
E.B. GREENWOOD, 206:NOV73-607
H. JECHOVA', 549(RLC):APR-JUN73-
338
SHIBLES, W.A. MODELS OF ANCIENT
GREEK PHILOSOPHY.
J.M. COOPER, 124:NOV72-168
SHIELDS, C. INTERSECT.
D. BESSAI, 99:JUL75-36
SHIELS, T. ENTERTAINING WITH "ESP."
R. HAYNES, 617(TLS):31JAN75-113
SHIFFERT, E.M. & SAWA YUKI, EDS &
TRANS. ANTHOLOGY OF MODERN JAPAN-
ESE POETRY.
M. BROCK, 285(JAPQ):JAN-MAR74-101
SHIH, C-W. INJUSTICE TO TOU O (TOU
O YUAN).
D.R. JOHNSON, 352(LE&W):VOL16#4-
1248
SHILLER, R.E. NEW METHODS OF KNOW-
LEDGE & VALUE.
P. DUBOIS, 542:JUL-SEP73-373
SHILLONY, B-A. REVOLT IN JAPAN.*
639(VQR):SPRING74-LIV
SHILS, E. THE INTELLECTUALS & THE
POWERS & OTHER ESSAYS.
G. POGGI, 111:3MAY74-133
SHIMIZU, J. CONFLICT OF LOYALTIES.
R.D. LINDER, 551(RENQ):SUMMER73-
191
SHINAGEL, M., ED. A CONCORDANCE TO
THE POEMS OF JONATHAN SWIFT.*
C.J. HORNE, 402(MLR):APR74-376
SHINZŌ, K. & TANABE KEN'ICHI - SEE
UNDER KIUCHI SHINZŌ & TANABE KEN'-
ICHI
SHIPP, G.P. STUDIES IN THE LANGUAGE
OF HOMER. (2ND ED)
W.M. SEAMAN, 124:MAR74-299
SHIPPEY, T.A. OLD ENGLISH VERSE.*
R.B. BURLIN, 589:OCT74-758
F. DIEKSTRA, 433:JUL73-314
M.R. GODDEN, 301(JEGP):JAN74-108
M.E. GOLDSMITH, 382(MAE):1974/2-
147
S.B. GREENFIELD, 447(N&Q):JAN73-24
R.M. WILSON, 175:SPRING73-27

SHIPWAY, G. FREE LANCE.
M. LEVIN, 441:14SEP75-42
SHIRE, H.M. SONG, DANCE & POETRY OF
THE COURT OF SCOTLAND UNDER KING
JAMES VI.*
M-A. DE KISCH, 189(EA):JAN-MAR73-
59
W. MAYNARD, 179(ES):JUN73-278
SHIRLEY, F.A. - SEE WEBSTER, J.
SHIRLEY, J. & OTHERS. TROIS MASQUES
À LA COUR DE CHARLES IER D'ANGLE-
TERRE. (M. LEFKOWITZ, ED)
R. DONINGTON, 317:FALL73-495
SHIRLEY, R. THE KITTEN.
D.M. DAY, 157:SPRING73-84
SHIROKOGOROFF, S.M. ETHNOLOGICAL &
LINGUISTICAL ASPECTS OF THE URAL-
ALTAIC HYPOTHESIS.
R. ANTTILA, 215(GL):VOL13#1-37
SHIVELY, D.H., ED. TRADITION & MOD-
ERNIZATION IN JAPANESE CULTURE.*
W.B. HAUSER, 318(JAOS):OCT-DEC73-
630
SHIVERS, A.S. JESSAMYN WEST.*
L. BANKS, 649(WAL):SPRING&SUMMER
73-79
SHKLOVSKY, V. MAYAKOVSKY & HIS
CIRCLE. (L. FEILER, ED & TRANS)
T.J. BINYON, 617(TLS):16MAY75-540
R. SHELDON, 550(RUSR):OCT73-445
SHKLOVSKY, V. A SENTIMENTAL JOUR-
NEY.
R.K. WILSON, 574(SEEJ):FALL72-352
SHKLOVSKY, V. ZOO, OR LETTERS NOT
ABOUT LOVE.* (R. SHELDON, ED &
TRANS)
M. FRIEDBERG, 574(SEEJ):SUMMER72-
234
C.V. PONOMAREFF, 104:FALL73-431
SHOCKLEY, J.S. CHICANO REVOLT IN A
TEXAS TOWN.
W. GARD, 584(SWR):SUMMER74-V
SHOLL, B. CHANGING FACES.
H. VENDLER, 441:6APR75-4
SHONAGON, S. THE PILLOW BOOK OF SEI
SHONAGON. (I. MORRIS, ED & TRANS)
L.M. ZOLBROD, 352(LE&W):VOL16#3-
1080
SHORE, W. SOCIAL SECURITY.
H.D. SHAPIRO, 441:16NOV75-8
SHORES, D.L. A DESCRIPTIVE SYNTAX
OF THE PETERBOROUGH CHRONICLE FROM
1122 TO 1154.*
C. CLARK, 382(MAE):1974/1-47
SHORT, A. THE COMMUNIST INSURREC-
TION IN MALAYA 1948-60.
M. LIEFER, 617(TLS):5DEC75-1441
SHORT, C. THE OLD ONE & THE WIND.
M. CARY, 134(CP):FALL73-82
F. MORAMARCO, 651(WHR):WINTER74-90
K. SANDBERG, 109:SPRING/SUMMER74-
142
639(VQR):WINTER74-XI
SHORT, M. GUSTAV HOLST.
H. OTTAWAY, 415:DEC74-1047
SHORT, M. - SEE HOLST, G.
SHORTER, A. EAST AFRICAN SOCIETIES.
J-S. LA FONTAINE, 617(TLS):3JAN75-
8
SHORTER, E. THE MAKING OF MODERN
SOCIETY.
C. LASCH, 453:11DEC75-50

SHORTER, E. THE MAKING OF THE MOD-
ERN FAMILY.
  C. LASCH, 453:13NOV75-33
  C. LEHMANN-HAUPT, 441:25NOV75-41
  J.H. PLUMB, 441:21DEC75-3
SHOWALTER, E., JR. THE EVOLUTION OF
THE FRENCH NOVEL: 1641-1782.
  G. MAY, 131(CL):FALL73-369
SHRODER, M.Z., ED. LE DIX-NEUVIÈME
SIÈCLE.
  G.R. BESSER, 399(MLJ):NOV74-359
SHROEDER, P.W. AUSTRIA, GREAT BRIT-
AIN, & THE CRIMEAN WAR.
  B.D. GOOCH, 637(VS):DEC73-217
SHUCKBURGH, E.S. - SEE SOPHOCLES
SHUGARMAN, D., ED. THINKING ABOUT
CHANGE.
  I. DAVIES, 99:JAN75-40
SHUKLA, N.S. LE KARNĀNANDA DE
KRSNADĀSA.
  O. VON HINÜBER, 182:VOL26#13/14-
  470
SHULAR, A.C., T. YBARRA-FRAUSTO & J.
SOMMERS - SEE UNDER CASTAÑEDA SHU-
LAR, A., T. YBARRA-FRAUSTO & J. SOM-
MERS
SHULMAN, F.J. DOCTORAL DISSERTA-
TIONS ON SOUTH ASIA, 1966-1970.
  G.R. NUNN, 293(JAST):NOV72-126
SHULMAN, F.J., ED. JAPAN & KOREA.
  G.R. NUNN, 293(JAST):NOV72-126
  W.W. SMITH, JR., 318(JAOS):OCT-DEC
  73-631
SHULMAN, M. CORONER.
  S. SINCLAIR, 99:DEC75/JAN76-41
SHUMAKER, W. THE OCCULT SCIENCES IN
THE RENAISSANCE.*
  S.K. HENINGER, JR., 255(HAB):WIN-
  TER73-51
  M. MURRIN, 301(JEGP):JUL74-423
  D.W. PEARSON, 568(SCN):FALL74-52
  R.H. WEST, 219(GAR):SPRING73-137
SHUPTRINE, H. & J. DICKEY. JERICHO.*
  E.N. EVANS, 441:9FEB75-4
SHUTTLE, P. WAILING MONKEY EMBRAC-
ING A TREE.*
  J. MELLORS, 364:JUN/JUL74-135
SHUZO KUKI. IKI NO KŌZŌ.
  A. HOSOI & J. PIGEOT, 98:JAN73-40
SHVARTS, Y. THREE PLAYS. (A. PY-
MAN, ED)
  L.R. SIMARD, 574(SEEJ):FALL72-355
SIBLEY, F.N., ED. PERCEPTION.*
  J.M. HINTON, 483:JAN73-91
SIBLEY, G.M. THE LOST PLAYS &
MASQUES 1500-1642.
  C. LEECH, 551(RENQ):AUTUMN73-364
SIBLEY, M.M. GEORGE W. BRACKENRIDGE.
  W. GARD, 584(SWR):WINTER74-98
SICILIANO, E. MORAVIA.
  400(MLN):JAN73-169
SICILIANO, I. LES CHANSONS DE GESTE
ET L'ÉPOPÉE.
  F. KOENIG, 545(RPH):FEB74-424
SIDDHASENA DIVĀKARA. SIDDHASENA'S
NYĀYĀVATĀRA & OTHER WORKS. (A.N.
UPADHYE, ED)
  L. STERNBACH, 318(JAOS):JUL-SEP73-
  377
SIDDIQI, I.T. & Q.M.A. A FOURTEENTH
CENTURY ARAB ACCOUNT OF INDIA UNDER
SULTAN MUHAMMAD BIN TUGHLAQ.
  H.K. SHERWANI, 273(IC):JUL73-279

SIDDONS, A.R. JOHN CHANCELLOR MAKES
ME CRY.
  E. BOMBECK, 441:13APR75-18
SIDER, R.D. ANCIENT RHETORIC & THE
ART OF TERTULLIAN.*
  W.H.C. FREND, 123:MAR74-76
SIDERAS, A. AESCHYLUS HOMERICUS.
  J. PERADOTTO, 121(CJ):APR/MAY74-
  377
SIDEY, H. PORTRAIT OF A PRESIDENT.
  G. WILLS, 453:16OCT75-18
SIDNELL, M.J., G.P. MAYHEW & D.R.
CLARK - SEE YEATS, W.B.
SIDNEY, P. THE COUNTESS OF PEM-
BROKE'S ARCADIA. (J. ROBERTSON,
ED)
  R.P. CORBALLIS, 67:MAY74-80
SIDNEY, P. SIR PHILIP SIDNEY: SEL-
ECTED POEMS. (K. DUNCAN-JONES, ED)
  R.F. HILL, 402(MLR):OCT74-841
SIDŌ, M., B. ZALÁNYI & Z. SCHRÉTER.
NEUE PALÄONTOLOGISCHE ERGEBNISSE
AUS DEM OBERPALÄOZOIKUM DES BÜKKGE-
BIRGES.
  H. RIEBER, 182:VOL26#23/24-879
SIEBENMANN, G. DIE NEUERE LITERATUR
LATEINAMERIKAS UND IHRE REZEPTION
IM DEUTSCHEN SPRACHRAUM.
  H. ROGMANN, 72:BAND211HEFT1/3-238
SIEBENSCHUH, W.R. FORM & PURPOSE IN
BOSWELL'S BIOGRAPHICAL WORKS.
  J.T. BOULTON, 677:VOL4-303
  C.J. RAWSON, 175:SUMMER73-76
  J.C. RIELY, 481(PQ):JUL73-473
"AU SIÈCLE DES LUMIÈRES."
  M. RAEFF, 104:SPRING73-120
"LE SIÈCLE D'OR DE L'IMPRIMERIE
LYONNAISE."
  A. HOBSON, 617(TLS):19DEC75-1524
SIEGEL, B. ISAAC BASHEVIS SINGER.
  A. EASSON, 447(N&Q):SEP73-345
SIEGEL, J.E. VAL LEWTON.
  J.E. NOLAN, 200:MAY73-301
SIEGEL, M.B. AT THE VANISHING
POINT.*
  S.J. COHEN, 290(JAAC):SUMMER74-573
SIEGEL, R. THE BEASTS & THE EL-
DERS.*
  M. MADIGAN, 385(MQR):SPRING75-220
  A. OSTROFF, 651(WHR):SUMMER74-296
  639(VQR):SPRING74-LVII
SIEP, L. HEGELS FICHTEKRITIK UND
DIE WISSENSCHAFTSLEHRE VON 1804.
  U. WIEDNER, 53(AGP):BAND55HEFT3-
  349
SIETZ, R. THEODOR KIRCHNER.
  G. ABRAHAM, 410(M&L):APR74-239
SIEWERT, P. DER EID VON PLATAIAI.
  N. ROBERTSON, 487:WINTER73-413
SIFAKIS, G.M. PARABASIS & ANIMAL
CHORUSES.*
  D.H. GARRISON, 24:SUMMER74-180
  L.B. LAWLER, 121(CJ):APR/MAY74-376
  D.M. MAC DOWELL, 123:NOV74-198
  J. VAIO, 124:MAY73-472
ŠIGAREVSKAJA, N.A. OČERKI PO SIN-
TAKSISU SOVREMENNOJ FRANCUZSKOJ
RAZGOVORNOJ REČI.
  J. VEYRENC, 353:15OCT73-126
SIGELOVÁ, J. APPU-MÄRCHEN UND
HEDAMMU-MYTHUS.
  G. NEUMANN, 260(IF):BAND78-240
  G. WILHELM, 343:BAND17HEFT2-206

"SIGNATURE ANTHOLOGY."
  D. LODGE, 617(TLS):26DEC75-1533
SILBERSTANG, E. LOSERS, WEEPERS.
  N. CALLENDAR, 441:23MAR75-35
SILBERSTEIN, G.E. THE TROUBLED
ALLIANCE.
  H. HANAK, 575(SEER):JUL74-473
SILBURN, L., ED & TRANS. HYMNES DE
ABHINAVAGUPTA.
  W. HALBFASS, 318(JAOS):APR-JUN73-
  244
SĪLIS NA CEAPAICH [SĪLEAS MAC DON-
ALD]. BÀRDACHD SHĪLIS NA CEAPAICH
(POEMS & SONGS BY SĪLEAS MAC DON-
ALD). (C. Ō BAOILL, ED)
  W. GILLIES, 595(SCS):VOL18-143
SILKIN, J. OUT OF BATTLE.*
  B. BERGONZI, 541(RES):AUG73-373
  G. DONALDSON, 184(EIC):OCT73-419
  H. SERGEANT, 175:AUTUMN73-121
SILKIN, J. THE PRINCIPLE OF WATER.*
  R. GARFITT, 364:AUG/SEP74-110
SILL, G.G. A HANDBOOK OF SYMBOLS IN
CHRISTIAN ART.
  A. BROYARD, 441:4DEC75-39
SILL, U. NOMINA SACRA IM ALTKIRCH-
ENSLAVISCHEN BIS ZUM 11. JAHRHUN-
DERT.
  H. LEEMING, 575(SEER):OCT74-609
SILLITOE, A. STORM.
  D. ABSE, 617(TLS):28FEB75-214
SILVER, I. THE INTELLECTUAL EVOLU-
TION OF RONSARD.* (VOL 1)
  T.M. GREENE, 188(ECR):FALL73-260
SILVER, I. - SEE DE RONSARD, P.
SILVERA, A. - SEE HALÉVY, D.
SILVERBERG, J., ED. SOCIAL MOBILITY
IN THE CASTE SYSTEM IN INDIA.
  J.P. MENCHER, 293(JAST):MAY73-533
SILVERBERG, R. BORN WITH THE DEAD.
  S. CLARK, 617(TLS):8AUG75-903
  G. JONAS, 441:24AUG75-29
SILVERBERG, R. SUNDANCE & OTHER
SCIENCE FICTION STORIES.
  617(TLS):23MAY75-555
SILVERMAN, J. FOLK BLUES.
  H. OSTER, 650(WF):JAN73-60
SILVERMAN, J. - SEE HANDY, W.C.
SILVERSTEIN, M. - SEE WHITNEY, W.D.
SILVEY, R. WHO'S LISTENING?
  S. HOOD, 617(TLS):28FEB75-226
  H. TAYLOR, 362:6FEB75-187
ŠIMÁČOVÁ, J. & E. MACHÁČKOVÁ, EDS.
TEATRALIA ZÁMECKÉ KNIHOVNY Z KŘIMIC.
  H-J. KRÜGER, 182:VOL26#20-745
SIMAK, C.D. THE BEST OF CLIFFORD D.
SIMAK. (A. WELLS, ED) CEMETERY
WORLD.
  E. KORN, 617(TLS):8AUG75-903
SIMENON, G. BETTY.
  M. LEVIN, 441:16FEB75-12
  442(NY):3FEB75-94
SIMENON, G. THE HOUSE ON QUAI
NOTRE DAME.
  T. LASK, 441:21SEP75-38
SIMENON, G. MAIGRET & THE LONER.
  A. BROYARD, 441:11MAR75-39
  M. LASKI, 362:20MAR75-380
  442(NY):7APR75-139
SIMENON, G. MAIGRET & THE MAN ON
THE BENCH.
  A. BROYARD, 441:4AUG75-17

SIMEON, R. ENCIKLOPEDIJSKI RJEČNIK
LINGVISTIČKIH NAZIVA.
  O. AKHMANOVA, 353:1MAY73-101
SIMIC, C. RETURN TO A PLACE LIT BY
A GLASS OF MILK.
  J. ATLAS, 491:FEB75-295
  G. HITCHCOCK, 651(WHR):AUTUMN74-
  403
SIMKINS, P.D. & F.L. WERNSTEDT.
PHILIPPINE MIGRATION.
  D.E. VOTH, 293(JAST):FEB73-383
SIMMONDS, J.D. MASQUES OF GOD.*
  J. BENNETT, 541(RES):AUG73-332
  A.R. BOWERS, 502(PRS):WINTER73/74-
  366
  D.G. DONOVAN, 577(SHR):SUMMER73-
  341
  D.C. GUNBY, 67:MAY74-83
  H. SERGEANT, 175:SPRING73-28
  R.E. WIEHE, 179(ES):DEC73-593
  R. WILCHER, 677:VOL4-287
SIMMONDS, J.D., ED. MILTON STUDIES.
(VOL 1)
  J.S. DEES, 38:BAND91HEFT3-402
SIMMONDS, J.D., ED. MILTON STUDIES.*
(VOL 2)
  G. BULLOUGH, 175:SPRING72-24
  J.S. DEES, 38:BAND91HEFT3-402
  M-S. RØSTVIG, 179(ES):OCT73-512
SIMMONDS, J.D., ED. MILTON STUDIES.
(VOL 3)
  G. BULLOUGH, 175:SPRING72-24
  D.D.C. CHAMBERS, 541(RES):FEB73-83
  J.S. DEES, 38:BAND91HEFT3-402
  B. RUDDICK, 148:SPRING72-90
  H. SCHULTZ, 551(RENQ):WINTER73-539
SIMMONDS, J.D., ED. MILTON STUDIES.*
(VOL 4)
  G. BULLOUGH, 175:SUMMER73-74
SIMMONDS, J.D., ED. MILTON STUDIES.
(VOL 5)
  639(VQR):AUTUMN74-CXXVI
SIMMONS, I.G. THE ECOLOGY OF NAT-
URAL RESOURCES.
  K. MELLANBY, 617(TLS):17JAN75-55
SIMMONS, J. THE LONG SUMMER STILL
TO COME.
  H. MURPHY, 159(DM):SUMMER73-112
SIMMONS, J. WEST STRAND VISIONS.
  T. EAGLETON, 617(TLS):28FEB75-214
SIMMS, E. BIRDS OF TOWN & SUBURB.
  617(TLS):31OCT75-1313
SIMMS, W.G. STORIES & TALES. (J.C.
GUILDS, ED)
  M.J. SHILLINGSBURG, 578:SPRING75-
  133
SIMON, C. CONDUCTING BODIES.*
  E. KORN, 617(TLS):11JUL75-753
SIMON, C. LES CORPS CONDUCTEURS.*
  C. DU VERLIE, 207(FR):APR73-1072
SIMON, C. LEÇON DE CHOSES.
  J. STURROCK, 617(TLS):3OCT75-1151
SIMON, C. TRIPTYQUE.
  L.S. ROUDIEZ, 207(FR):MAY73-1251
SIMON, E. DAS ANTIKE THEATER.
  G.B. WAYWELL, 303:VOL93-268
SIMON, G.T. THE BIG BANDS.
  R. DAVIES, 617(TLS):6JUN75-629
SIMON, I. NEO-CLASSICAL CRITICISM
1660-1800.*
  T.A. BIRRELL, 179(ES):AUG73-390

SIMON, J.K., ED. MODERN FRENCH
CRITICISM.*
  G.H. BAUER, 207(FR):DEC72-424
  L.S. ROUDIEZ, 546(RR):NOV73-296
SIMON, J.Y. - SEE GRANT, J.D.
SIMON, L. A LA DÉCOUVERTE DE HAN
RYNER.
  F.B. CONEM, 535(RHL):JAN-FEB73-157
SIMON, M. LA CIVILISATION DE L'AN-
TIQUITÉ ET LE CHRISTIANISME.
  D. REUILLARD, 98:JUL73-675
SIMON, M.A. THE MATTER OF LIFE.
  E.M., 543:SEP72-173
  M. RUSE, 154:MAR73-157
SIMON, R.L. THE BIG FIX.
  J. HAMILTON-PATERSON, 617(TLS):
  10JAN75-29
SIMON, R.L. WILD TURKEY.
  N. CALLENDAR, 441:6JUL75-14
SIMON, U. STORY & FAITH.
  E.J. TINSLEY, 617(TLS):29AUG75-977
SIMÓN DÍAZ, J. LA BIBLIOGRAFÍA.*
  K. WHINNOM, 86(BHS):JUL73-278
DE SIMONE, C. DIE GRIECHISCHEN
ENTLEHNUNGEN IM ETRUSKISCHEN.
(VOL 2)
  R. PFISTER, 260(IF):BAND78-261
SIMONE, F., ED. CULTURE ET POLI-
TIQUE EN FRANCE À L'ÉPOQUE DE L'HUM-
ANISME ET DE LA RENAISSANCE.
  617(TLS):100CT75-1210
SIMONE, F., ED. DIZIONARIO CRITICO
DELLA LETTERATURA FRANCESE.*
  L. PERTILE, 402(MLR):JAN74-163
SIMONI, A.E.C., COMP. PUBLISH & BE
FREE.
  M.R.D. FOOT, 617(TLS):28NOV75-1408
SIMONS, G.L. THE SIMONS BOOK OF
SEXUAL RECORDS.
  617(TLS):10JAN75-34
SIMONS, M.A. AMITIÉ ET PASSION.
  P-P. CLÉMENT, 400(MLN):MAY73-888
SIMONSON, H.P. JONATHAN EDWARDS.
  W.J. SCHEICK, 165:SPRING75-95
SIMPKINS, C.O. COLTRANE.
  G. GIDDINS, 441:10AUG75-16
  M. WATKINS, 441:28JUN75-25
"SIMPOSIO 'VALDÉS-SALAS'."
  D.W. LOMAX, 86(BHS):APR73-169
SIMPSON, C.M. - SEE HAWTHORNE, N.
SIMPSON, E. THE MAZE.
  A. BROYARD, 441:27MAR75-29
  J.C. OATES, 441:6APR75-1
  442(NY):28APR75-137
SIMPSON, J., ED & TRANS. ICELANDIC
FOLKTALES & LEGENDS.*
  R.L. GREEN, 203:AUTUMN73-258
  J. HARRIS, 573(SSF):SUMMER73-295
SIMPSON, L. ADVENTURES OF THE LET-
TER I.*
  G. LINDOP, 148:WINTER72-379
SIMPSON, L. THREE ON THE TOWER.
  H. LEIBOWITZ, 441:5OCT75-1
  R.R. LINGEMAN, 441:15JUL75-37
  442(NY):26MAY75-120
SIMPSON, L.P. THE MAN OF LETTERS IN
NEW ENGLAND & THE SOUTH.*
  J.M. COX, 569(SR):WINTER74-163
  D. FLOWER, 432(NEQ):SEP74-478
  G.B. TENNYSON, 445(NCF):SEP73-247
SIMPSON, M. THE CHROME CONNECTION.
  M. LASKI, 362:5JUN75-748
SIMPSON, R., ED. THE SYMPHONY.
  E. HELM, 412:MAY73-176

SIMPSON, R.H. & J.F. LAZENBY. THE
CATALOGUE OF THE SHIPS IN HOMER'S
"ILIAD."
  J.K. ANDERSON, 121(CJ):DEC73/JAN
  74-180
SIMPSON, W.K. PAPYRUS REISNER III.
  L.H. LESKO, 318(JAOS):OCT-DEC73-
  587
SINCLAIR, A. DYLAN THOMAS.
  D. DAVIE, 441:9NOV75-7
SINCLAIR, D., ED. NINETEENTH CEN-
TURY NARRATIVE POEMS.
  R. DANIELLS, 102(CANL):SPRING73-
  108
SINCLAIR, J.M. A COURSE IN SPOKEN
ENGLISH: GRAMMAR.
  A.R. TELLIER, 189(EA):JUL-SEP73-
  347
SINCLAIR, K.V., ED. TRISTAN DE NAN-
TEUIL, CHANSON DE GESTE INÉDITE.*
  E. RUHE, 439(NM):1973/2-364
SINCLAIR, M. A LONG TIME SLEEPING.
  617(TLS):11JUL75-784
SINCLAIR, N. ACTING PECULIAR.
  D.M. DAY, 157:SPRING73-84
SINEL, A. THE CLASSROOM & THE
CHANCELLERY.*
  W.A. KOHLS, 104:WINTER74-601
SINFIELD, A. THE LANGUAGE OF TENNY-
SON'S "IN MEMORIAM."*
  C.P.R. TYZACK, 349:FALL73-297
SINGARIMBUN, M. KINSHIP, DESCENT &
ALLIANCE AMONG THE KARO BATAK.
  R.H. BARNES, 617(TLS):21NOV75-1394
SINGELENBERG, P. H.P. BERLAGE.
  H. SEARING, 576:OCT73-253
SINGER, I.B. A CROWN OF FEATHERS.*
  B. ALLEN, 249(HUDR):SPRING74-119
  W. PEDEN, 569(SR):FALL74-712
  639(VQR):WINTER74-X
SINGER, I.B. ENEMIES, A LOVE STORY.*
  C. LEVIANT, 390:MAR73-74
SINGER, I.B. PASSIONS.
  R. SALE, 441:2NOV75-7
SINGER, K. MIRROR, SWORD & JEWEL.*
  D. KEENE, 285(JAPQ):OCT-DEC73-461
SINGER, M. WHEN A GREAT TRADITION
MODERNIZES.
  R.D. LAMBERT, 293(JAST):MAY73-518
SINGERIE, A. HOW TO FIX IT.
  P. BRACKEN, 441:27APR75-30
SINGH, B. FOUNDATIONS OF INDIAN
PHILOSOPHY.
  L.S. ROUNER, 485(PE&W):JUL73-402
SINGH, G. EUGENIO MONTALE.*
  H. ENRICO, 401(MLQ):JUN74-209
SINGH, K. - SEE "HYMNS OF GURU
NANAK"
SINGH, S.U. SHELLEY & THE DRAMATIC
FORM.
  P.H. BUTTER, 677:VOL4-314
SINGLETON, C.S. - SEE BOCCACCIO, G.
SINGLETON, C.S. - SEE DANTE ALIGH-
IERI
SINISGALLI, L. MOSCHE IN BOTTIGLIA.
  K. BOSLEY, 617(TLS):31OCT75-1308
SINOS, S. DIE VORKLASSISCHEN HAUS-
FORMEN IN DER ÄGÄIS.
  J. BOARDMAN, 123:MAR74-123
  J.W. GRAHAM, 487:SUMMER73-202
SINSON, J.C. JOHN KEATS & THE
ANATOMY OF MELANCHOLY.
  S.M.S., 191(ELN):SEP73(SUPP)-52

SIODMAK, C. CITY IN THE SKY.
J. HAMILTON-PATERSON, 617(TLS):
8AUG75-903
SIPE, D.L. SHAKESPEARE'S METRICS.
H-J. DILLER, 38:BAND91HEFT4-528
"SIR GAWAIN & THE GREEN KNIGHT."*
(R.A. WALDRON, ED)
G. SCHELSTRAETE, 179(ES):FEB72-88
SIRCELLO, G. MIND & ART.
K.R.M., 543:JUN73-766
SIROVÁTKA, O., ED. TSCHECHISCHE
VOLKSMÄRCHEN.
M. BOŠKOVIĆ-STULLI, 196:BAND14
HEFT3-274
SISAM, C. & K., EDS. THE OXFORD
BOOK OF MEDIEVAL ENGLISH VERSE.*
K. REICHL, 38:BAND91HEFT4-521
A.V.C. SCHMIDT, 184(EIC):JAN72-92
SISLER, R. THE GIRLS.*
P. DREVNIG, 73:FALL73-43
SISSMAN, L.E. INNOCENT BYSTANDER.
D.C. ANDERSON, 441:21DEC75-22
SISSON, C.H. COLLECTED POEMS &
SELECTED TRANSLATIONS.
R. GARFITT, 364:OCT/NOV74-114
SISSON, C.H. ENGLISH POETRY 1900-
1950.
295:FEB74-503
SISSON, C.J. THE BOAR'S HEAD THE-
ATRE.* (S. WELLS, ED)
P. EDWARDS, 447(N&Q):APR73-146
R.A. FOAKES, 175:AUTUMN72-107
M.A. SHAABER, 551(RENQ):SPRING73-
85
SISSON, C.J. LOST PLAYS OF SHAKE-
SPEARE'S AGE.
C. LEECH, 551(RENQ):AUTUMN73-364
SISSON, R. THE CONGRESS PARTY IN
RAJASTHAN.
E.C. MOULTON, 318(JAOS):OCT-DEC73-
620
D.B. ROSENTHAL, 293(JAST):NOV72-
185
SISSON, R. & L.L. SHRADER. LEGIS-
LATIVE RECRUITMENT & POLITICAL
INTEGRATION.
C.P. BHAMBHRI, 293(JAST):MAY73-530
N.D. PALMER, 302:JAN73-192
SITTA, H. SEMANTEME UND RELATIONEN.
W. ABRAHAM, 361:DEC73-335
SITTER, J.E. THE POETRY OF POPE'S
"DUNCIAD."*
D. NOKES, 541(RES):AUG73-340
C.J. RAWSON, 175:SPRING73-29
C.J. RAWSON, 677:VOL4-300
SITTERDING, M. LE VALLON DES VAUX.
R. PITTIONI, 182:VOL26#20-754
SITWELL, O. QUEEN MARY & OTHERS.*
M. HOLROYD, 441:27APR75-26
SITWELL, S. FOR WANT OF THE GOLDEN
CITY.
D. SCHIER, 109:SPRING/SUMMER74-147
M.S. YOUNG, 39:SEP73-236
SITWELL, S. SPAIN.
T. LAMBERT, 617(TLS):30MAY75-606
SIVERTSEN, E. FONOLOGI.
G.F. MEIER, 682(ZPSK):BAND26HEFT
3/4-450
SIWEK, P. L'AUTHENTICITÉ DU TRAITÉ
"DE L'AME" D'ARISTOTE.
P. LOUIS, 555:VOL47FASC2-335
SJÖBERG, L. A READER'S GUIDE TO
GUNNAR EKELÖF'S "A MÖLNA ELEGY."
M. MATTSSON, 563(SS):FALL74-452

SJÖWALL, M. & P. WAHLÖÖ. COP KILLER.
P. ADAMS, 61:JUN75-95
N. CALLENDAR, 441:20JUL75-26
P.D. JAMES, 617(TLS):26SEP75-1079
SJÖWALL, M. & P. WAHLÖÖ. MURDER AT
THE SAVOY.
K. MC SWEENEY, 529(QQ):SPRING73-
152
SKAGGS, D.C. ROOTS OF MARYLAND DEM-
OCRACY, 1753-1776.
J. HAW, 656(WMQ):APR74-322
SKAGGS, M.M. THE FOLK OF SOUTHERN
FICTION.*
J.M. COX, 569(SR):WINTER74-163
B. HITCHCOCK, 577(SHR):FALL73-446
T.D. YOUNG, 579(SAQ):SUMMER74-413
SKARD, V. NORSK SPRÅKHISTORIE.
(VOL 2)
S.R. SMITH, 563(SS):SPRING74-179
SKEAT, W.O. GEORGE STEPHENSON.
J. LEE, 617(TLS):14MAR75-283
SKEI, A.B. - SEE HANDL, J.
SKELTON, R. J.M. SYNGE. J.M. SYNGE
& HIS WORLD.
R. HOGAN, 295:APR74-1031
SKELTON, R. TIMELIGHT.
D. ABSE, 617(TLS):28FEB75-214
R. MATHEWS, 99:APR/MAY75-64
SKELTON, R., ED & TRANS. TWO HUN-
DRED POEMS FROM THE GREEK ANTHOLOGY.
T.G. ROSENMEYER, 124:NOV72-169
SKELTON, R. THE WRITINGS OF J.M.
SYNGE.*
D. BALL, 447(N&Q):NOV73-440
R. HOGAN, 295:APR74-1031
SKELTON, R. - SEE YEATS, J.B.
SKELTON, R.A., COMP. COUNTY ATLASES
OF THE BRITISH ISLES, 1579-1850.*
(VOL 1)
R. HYDE, 325:OCT73-681
SKELTON, R.A. MAPS.*
R.E. EHRENBERG, 14:OCT73-558
J.B. POST, 503:AUTUMN73-148
SKENE, R. THE CUCHULAIN PLAYS OF
W.B. YEATS.
G. HOUGH, 617(TLS):14FEB75-160
SKIDELSKY, R. OSWALD MOSLEY.
J. GRIGG, 362:3APR75-450
A. HOWARD, 441:11MAY75-7
J. VINCENT, 617(TLS):4APR75-350
442(NY):18AUG75-84
SKILTON, D. ANTHONY TROLLOPE & HIS
CONTEMPORARIES.*
A.O.J. COCKSHUT, 541(RES):MAY73-
233
SKINNER, B.F. ABOUT BEHAVIORISM.*
R. CLAIBORNE, 473(PR):4/1974-613
N.S. SUTHERLAND, 617(TLS):28FEB75-
216
SKINNER, B.F. BEYOND FREEDOM & DIG-
NITY.*
A. HERON, 381:MAR73-101
SKINNER, C.M. MYTHS & LEGENDS OF
OUR OWN LAND.
L.C. KEATING, 582(SFQ):JUN73-148
SKJELVER, M.C. NINETEENTH CENTURY
HOMES OF MARSHALL, MICHIGAN.
M.B. LAPPING, 576:OCT73-262
SKLAR, K.K. CATHARINE BEECHER.*
676(YR):SPRING74-V
SKLAR, R. MOVIE-MADE AMERICA.
A. HACKER, 441:9NOV75-42

343

ŠKREB, Z., ED. UMJETNOST RIJEČI -
THE ART OF THE WORD.
  J. STRELKA, 131(CL):WINTER73-87
SKRINE, C.P. & P. NIGHTINGALE.
MACARTNEY AT KASHGAR.
  R. QUESTED, 302:JUL73-265
SKROTZKI, D. DIE GEBÄRDE DES ERRÖ-
TENS IN WERK HEINRICH VON KLEISTS.
  I.F., 191(ELN):SEP73(SUPP)-149
SKULTANS, V., ED. MADNESS & MORALS.
  P. LOMAS, 617(TLS):25JUL75-832
SKUTSCH, O. & OTHERS. ENNIUS.
  J-P. CÈBE, 555:VOL47FASC2-352
  J.K. NEWMAN, 124:FEB74-233
ŠKVORECKÝ, J. MISS SILVER'S PAST.
  T. LASK, 441:21SEP75-38
  G. WOODCOCK, 99:NOV75-35
  442(NY):15SEP75-130
SLADE, J.W. THOMAS PYNCHON.
  E. MENDELSON, 617(TLS):13JUN75-666
SLATE, S.J. AS LONG AS THE RIVERS
RUN.
  J.E. TALMADGE, 219(GAR):WINTER73-
  618
SLATER, M., ED. THE CATALOGUE OF
THE SUZANNET CHARLES DICKENS COL-
LECTION.
  P. COLLINS, 617(TLS):5DEC75-1464
SLATER, M., ED. DICKENS 1970.
  H. REINHOLD, 38:BAND91HEFT1-131
SLATER, P. A FIELD GUIDE TO AUS-
TRALIAN BIRDS: PASSERINES.
  617(TLS):8AUG75-906
SLATER, W.J., ED. LEXICON TO PIN-
DAR.*
  C. SEGAL, 121(CJ):OCT/NOV72-79
SLATTERY, M.F. HAZARD, FORM &
VALUE.*
  S.S. HAFEZI, 613:SPRING73-138
  K.R.M., 543:MAR73-546
SLAVÍKOVÁ, M. A STATISTICAL ANALY-
SIS OF SWAHILI MORPHOLOGY.
  S. BRAUNER, 682(ZPSK):BAND26HEFT
  3/4-393
SLAVITT, D.R. VITAL SIGNS.
  H. VENDLER, 441:7SEP75-6
SLEEMAN, W.H. SLEEMAN IN OUDH.*
(ED & ABRIDGED BY P.D. REEVES)
  R. CALLAHAN, 318(JAOS):APR-JUN73-
  249
  T.R. METCALF, 293(JAST):NOV72-179
SLENTE, F., ED. BIBLIOGRAFI OVER
STEEN EILER RASMUSSENS FORFATTER-
SKAB.
  E. ZIMMERMANN, 182:VOL26#11/12-385
SLESAR, H. THE THING AT THE DOOR.*
  T.J. BINYON, 617(TLS):26DEC75-1544
SLESSAREV, H. EDUARD MÖRIKE.*
  R.M. BROWNING, 222(GR):MAR73-153
SLIM, H.C. A GIFT OF MADRIGALS &
MOTETS.
  P.H.L., 414(MQ):JUL73-477
SLIVE, S. FRANS HALS. (VOLS 1&2)
  H. GERSON, 90:MAR73-170
SLIVE, S. FRANS HALS. (VOL 3)
  C. WHITE, 617(TLS):28NOV75-1413
SLOANE, E. THE LITTLE RED SCHOOL-
HOUSE.
  V.H. KELLEY, 50(ARQ):SPRING73-88
SLOBIN, D.I., ED. THE ONTOGENESIS
OF GRAMMAR.
  P. MENYUK, 269(IJAL):JAN73-55
SLOBIN, D.I. PSYCHOLINGUISTICS.*
  J. PRŮCHA, 353:1APR73-123

SŁONIMSKI, A. 138 WIERSZY.
  R.K. WILSON, 574(SEEJ):WINTER73-
  469
SLONIMSKY, N. MUSIC OF LATIN AMERI-
CA.
  L. SALTER, 415:JAN74-39
SLOTKIN, R. REGENERATION THROUGH
VIOLENCE.*
  I.H. BARTLETT, 432(NEQ):MAR74-145
  M.J. COLACURCIO, 165:WINTER75-333
  D. GRIMSTED, 656(WMQ):JAN74-143
  H.N. SMITH, 131(CL):WINTER74-74
SLUNG, M.B., ED. CRIME ON HER MIND.
  M.E. GALE, 441:1JUN75-5
SLUSSER, R.M. THE BERLIN CRISIS OF
1961.
  D.L. BARK, 550(RUSR):OCT73-454
SMABY, R.M. PARAPHRASE GRAMMARS.
  B. BRAINERD, 361:VOL31#1-67
SMALL, G.L. THE BLUE WHALE.
  J.Z. YOUNG, 453:17JUL75-3
SMALLEY, B. THE BECKET CONFLICT &
THE SCHOOLS.
  A. MOREY, 382(MAE):1974/3-310
SMALLEY, B. - SEE LEWES, G.H.
SMALLWOOD, J. I CHOSE CANADA.
  P.B. WAITE, 150(DR):WINTER73/74-
  765
  G. WOODCOCK, 102(CANL):WINTER74-95
SMART, A. THE ASSISI PROBLEM & THE
ART OF GIOTTO.*
  D. ROBINSON, 90:MAR73-183
  D. WILKINS, 551(RENQ):SPRING73-36
"CHRISTOPHER SMART." (M. WALSH, ED)
  J.D. JUMP, 148:SUMMER72-187
SMART, J.J.C. & B. WILLIAMS. UTILI-
TARIANISM - FOR & AGAINST.
  P. PETTIT, 111:26OCT73-26
  P. SINGER, 518:MAY74-22
SMART, N. THE CONCEPT OF WORSHIP.
  D. BASTOW, 518:JAN74-24
  G. SLATER, 479(PHQ):JUL73-283
SMART, N. THE PHILOSOPHY OF RELI-
GION.*
  K. BRITTON, 482(PHR):APR73-263
SMART, N. THE SCIENCE OF RELIGION &
THE SOCIOLOGY OF KNOWLEDGE.
  639(VQR):SUMMER74-CII
SMEED, J.W. FAUST IN LITERATURE.
  W. WITTE, 617(TLS):3OCT75-1149
SMELSER, R.M. THE SUDETEN PROBLEM
1933-1938.
  J.W. BRUEGEL, 617(TLS):3OCT75-1132
SMETS, G. AESTHETIC JUDGMENT &
AROUSAL.
  E.L. WALKER, 290(JAAC):WINTER74-
  231
SMIDT, K. MEMORIAL TRANSMISSION &
QUARTO COPY IN "RICHARD III."*
  J. GERRITSEN, 179(ES):JUN73-280
SMILEY, D.V. CANADA IN QUESTION.
  H.G. THORBURN, 529(QQ):SUMMER73-
  282
SMIT, J. - SEE POTGIETER, E.J. &
C.B. HUET
SMITH, A. POWERS OF MIND.
  E. FIRST, 441:2NOV75-2
  M. GARDNER, 453:11DEC75-46
  C. LEHMANN-HAUPT, 441:20OCT75-31
SMITH, A.C.H. ORGHAST AT PERSEPOL-
IS.*
  A. BRODY, 109:FALL/WINTER73/74-119
  D. WRIGHT, 157:SPRING73-81

SMITH, A.C.H. PAPER VOICES.
P. WHITEHEAD, 362:22MAY75-683
SMITH, A.H. COUNTY & COURT.
V. PEARL, 617(TLS):8AUG75-893
SMITH, A.H. THE SPREAD OF PRINTING:
SOUTH AFRICA.*
D.H. VARLEY, 354:MAR73-74
SMITH, A.J., ED. JOHN DONNE, ESSAYS
IN CELEBRATION.
G. BULLOUGH, 175:SUMMER73-74
J. GRUNDY, 677:VOL4-285
T.J. KELLY, 140(CR):#16-91
W. VON KOPPENFELS, 182:VOL26#1/2-
29
P. LEGOUIS, 189(EA):OCT-DEC73-470
A.F. MAROTTI, 141:SUMMER74-260
M.V. SMITH, 541(RES):NOV73-483
SMITH, A.J.M., ED. THE BOOK OF
CANADIAN PROSE. (VOLS 1&2)
A. APPENZELL, 102(CANL):AUTUMN74-
100
SMITH, B., ED. CONCERNING CONTEM-
PORARY ART.
R. SCRUTON, 617(TLS):25JUL75-847
SMITH, B. & W-G. WENG. CHINA.
639(VQR):WINTER74-XXX
SMITH, B.H., JR. TRADITIONAL IM-
AGERY OF CHARITY IN "PIERS PLOWMAN."
W. ERZGRÄBER, 38:BAND91HEFT3-394
SMITH, C. THE BEST OF CORDWAINER
SMITH. NORSTRILIA.
G. JONAS, 441:23MAR75-30
SMITH, C. - SEE "POEMA DE MIO CID"
SMITH, C., WITH M. BERMEJO MARCOS &
E. CHANG-RODRÍGUEZ. COLLINS SPAN-
ISH-ENGLISH ENGLISH-SPANISH DIC-
TIONARY.*
P. RUSSELL-GEBBETT, 86(BHS):JAN73-
71
B. STEEL, 238:MAY73-511
R.J. STEINER, 399(MLJ):MAR74-132
SMITH, C.B. TROY STATE UNIVERSITY
1937-1970.
H.E. STERKX, 9(ALAR):JUL73-229
SMITH, C.M. REVEREND RANDOLLPH &
THE WAGES OF SIN.
N. CALLENDAR, 441:16FEB75-16
SMITH, C.N. - SEE DE MONTCHRESTIEN,
A.
SMITH, C.R. & D.M. HUNSACKER. THE
BASES OF ARGUMENT.
N.C. COOK, 583:SPRING74-306
SMITH, C.W. COUNTRY MUSIC.
J. CHARYN, 441:7SEP75-41
442(NY):1SEP75-66
SMITH, C.W. THIN MEN OF HADDAM.*
W. GARD, 584(SWR):SPRING74-V
SMITH, D. THE FINAL FIRE.
M. LEVIN, 441:28DEC75-20
SMITH, D. THE FISHERMAN'S WHORE.
V. YOUNG, 249(HUDR):WINTER74/75-
597
SMITH, D. KONFRONTATION.
R.M. BROWNING, 399(MLJ):JAN-FEB74-
74
SMITH, D. THE KREMLIN PLOT.
N. CALLENDAR, 441:30MAR75-24
SMITH, D. SMITH'S MOSCOW.
S.F. STARR, 441:19JAN75-28
SMITH, D.C., JR. THE MAFIA MYSTIQUE.
C. LEHMANN-HAUPT, 441:13JAN75-27
T. PLATE, 441:23MAR75-4
SMITH, D.E. PRAIRIE LIBERALISM.
D. SMITH, 99:APR/MAY75-40

SMITH, D.I.B. EDITING SEVENTEENTH
CENTURY PROSE.
R.D. HUME, F. KEARNEY & G.B.
EVANS, 481(PQ):JUL73-330
SMITH, D.I.B. - SEE MARVELL, A.
SMITH, D.J. BULL ISLAND.
C.J. BANGS, 448:VOL13#2-102
SMITH, E. SOME VERSIONS OF THE FALL.
M. LEBOWITZ, 676(YR):WINTER74-308
639(VQR):WINTER74-XX
SMITH, E.A. WHIG PRINCIPLES & PARTY
POLITICS.
N. GASH, 617(TLS):21NOV75-1390
SMITH, E.C. NEW DICTIONARY OF AMER-
ICAN FAMILY NAMES.
K.B. HARDER, 424:DEC73-271
SMITH, E.E. & J.E. HALEY. LIFE ON
THE TEXAS RANGE.
W. GARD, 584(SWR):WINTER74-98
SMITH, F., ED. PSYCHOLINGUISTICS &
READING.
R.N. ST. CLAIR, 351(LL):DEC74-313
SMITH, F.G. D.H. LAWRENCE: "THE
RAINBOW."
E. DELAVENAY, 189(EA):JUL-SEP73-
323
SMITH, G. CANADA & THE CANADIAN
QUESTION.
W.P. WARD, 529(QQ):WINTER73-626
SMITH, H. SHAKESPEARE'S ROMANCES.*
L. DANSON, 191(ELN):JUN74-299
R.A. FOAKES, 175:SUMMER73-72
G. LAMBIN, 189(EA):JUL-SEP73-354
R. ORNSTEIN, 405(MP):MAY74-425
N. RABKIN, 401(MLQ):JUN74-187
SMITH, H.D., 2D. JAPAN'S FIRST STU-
DENT RADICALS.
K.B. PYLE, 293(JAST):AUG73-705
SMITH, H.E. & OTHERS. THAI RURAL
FAMILIES.
C.F. KEYES, 293(JAST):FEB73-376
SMITH, I.C. - SEE UNDER CRICHTON
SMITH, I.
SMITH, J. ENTERING ROOMS.*
A. CLUYSENAAR, 565:VOL14#4-75
SMITH, J. SHAKESPEARIAN & OTHER
ESSAYS.*
A. FAIRLIE, 208(FS):OCT74-490
SMITH, J.D., ED. THE PERSONAL DIS-
TRIBUTION OF INCOME & WEALTH.
A. HACKER, 453:1MAY75-9
SMITH, J.E. THE ANALOGY OF EXPERI-
ENCE.
G. WILLIAMS, 484(PPR):DEC73-293
SMITH, J.E. - SEE CLAY, L.D.
SMITH, J.H. CONSTANTINE THE GREAT.*
H.A. DRAKE, 121(CJ):FEB/MAR74-249
SMITH, J.H. - SEE FOXE, J.
SMITH, J.I., ED. SELECTED JUDICIARY
CASES 1624-1650. (VOL 3)
617(TLS):22AUG75-954
SMITH, J.L. MELODRAMA.
617(TLS):21FEB75-204
SMITH, J.M., JR. THE HISTORY OF THE
SARBADĀR DYNASTY, 1336-1381 A.D. &
ITS SOURCES.
R.W. BULLIET, 318(JAOS):OCT-DEC73-
559
SMITH, L. FANCY STRUT.
639(VQR):WINTER74-VIII
SMITH, M. THE DEATH OF THE DETEC-
TIVE.*
R. FOSTER, 617(TLS):15AUG75-913
N. HEPBURN, 362:2OCT75-453

SMITH, M. TIMES & LOCATIONS.
A. CLUYSENAAR, 565:VOL14#2-62
SMITH, M.A. FRANÇOIS MAURIAC.*
D.H. MORRIS 4TH, 577(SHR):WINTER
73-103
SMITH, M.A. PROSPER MÉRIMÉE.
A.S. ROSENTHAL, 399(MLJ):NOV74-358
SMITH, M.G. THE ECONOMY OF HAUSA
COMMUNITIES OF ZARIA.
A.H.M. KIRK-GREENE, 315(JAL):VOL11
PT3-92
SMITH, M.G. - SEE MC CULLERS, C.
SMITH, M.J., COMP. AN INVENTORY OF
THE PAPERS OF DENNIS J. ROBERTS IN
THE PHILLIPS MEMORIAL LIBRARY OF
PROVIDENCE COLLEGE.
K.J. PIKE, 14:JUL73-412
SMITH, M.J. WHEN I SAY NO, I FEEL
GUILTY.
L.C. LEWIN, 441:13APR75-6
SMITH, P. & C. DANIEL. THE CHICKEN
BOOK.
R. LASSON, 441:24AUG75-4
442(NY):1SEP75-67
SMITH, P.C.F. - SEE BOWEN, A.
SMITH, P.D., JR. A COMPARISON OF
THE COGNITIVE & AUDIOLINGUAL AP-
PROACHES TO FOREIGN LANGUAGE IN-
STRUCTION.
G.F. CARR, 353:1APR73-119
SMITH, P.D., JR. TOWARD A PRACTICAL
THEORY OF SECOND LANGUAGE INSTRUC-
TION.*
H.S. MADSEN, 399(MLJ):SEP-OCT73-
277
SMITH, P.M. CLÉMENT MAROT.*
E. BALMAS, 535(RHL):SEP-OCT73-883
D. STONE, JR., 546(RR):JAN74-57
SMITH, P.S. AIR FREIGHT.
617(TLS):21MAR75-320
SMITH, R. LORD NELSON TAVERN.
S. ESCHE, 606(TAMR):NOV74-85
A. SCOTT, 296:VOL4#1-197
SMITH, R. LYRIC & POLEMIC.
A.E. AUSTIN, 141:SPRING74-185
G. BUTLER, 180(ESA):MAR74-53
N. GORDIMER, 364:APR/MAY74-115
W.H. NEW, 102(CANL):WINTER74-87
F.T. PRINCE, 150(DR):AUTUMN73-581
J.N. WYSONG, 529(QQ):AUTUMN73-484
295:FEB74-555
SMITH, R.C. FREI JOSÉ DE SANTO
ANTÓNIO FERREIRA VILAÇA.
J. BURY, 90:DEC73-813
SMITH, R.M., ED. SOUTHEAST ASIA.
617(TLS):7FEB75-149
SMITH, S. COLLECTED POEMS.
J. BAYLEY, 362:25SEP75-409
SMITH, S. SCORPION & OTHER POEMS.*
D. GRANT, 148:SPRING72-92
SMITH, S. & P. RAZZELL. THE POOLS
WINNERS.
E.S. TURNER, 362:20MAR75-368
SMITH, T.L. BRAZILIAN SOCIETY.
A. HENNESSEY, 617(TLS):12DEC75-
1497
SMITH, T.L. THE DEVIL & WEBSTER
DANIELS.
N. CALLENDAR, 441:21DEC75-17
SMITH, V. VANCE & NETTIE PALMER.
C. HADGRAFT, 71(ALS):OCT75-217
SMITH, V. VALLE-INCLÁN: "TIRANO
BANDERAS."*
D. LING, 238:MAY73-528

SMITH, V.E. THE JONES MEN.*
R. DAVIES, 617(TLS):30MAY75-585
SMITH, V.L. ANTON CHEKHOV & THE
LADY WITH THE DOG.*
R.F. CHRISTIAN, 402(MLR):OCT74-952
SMITH, W. FLAGS.
G. WARD & R. STROZIER, 441:7DEC75-
94
SMITH, W.D. STRETCHING THEIR
BODIES.
617(TLS):7MAR75-261
SMITH, W.E. & A.M. MINAMATA.
R.R. LINGEMAN, 441:7JUL75-23
P. THEROUX, 441:8JUN75-2
SMITH, W.G., COMP. THE OXFORD DIC-
TIONARY OF ENGLISH PROVERBS. (3RD
ED REV BY F.P. WILSON)
H.M. HULME, 179(ES):FEB73-83
SMITH, W.H.B. SMALL ARMS OF THE
WORLD.
617(TLS):31JAN75-121
SMITH, W.J. THE STREAKS OF THE
TULIP.
L.T.L., 502(PRS):FALL73-280
SMITHERS, D.L. THE MUSIC & HISTORY
OF THE BAROQUE TRUMPET BEFORE
1721.*
M.H. FRANK, 568(SCN):WINTER74-86
E. HALFPENNY, 410(M&L):APR74-226
E.H. TARR, 415:SEP74-748
SMITS, K. DIE FRÜHMITTELHOCHDEUT-
SCHE WIENER GENESIS.*
J.S. GROSECLOSE, 406:SPRING74-100
H. RUPP, 182:VOL26#13/14-484
D.A. WELLS, 402(MLR):JUL74-693
SMUDA, M. BECKETTS PROSA ALS META-
SPRACHE.
H. OPPEL, 430(NS):SEP73-500
SMURL, J.F. RELIGIOUS ETHICS.
S.C. CRAWFORD, 485(PE&W):OCT73-549
SMUTS, J.C. WALT WHITMAN.* (A.L.
MC LEOD, ED)
A. LOZYNSKY, 646(WWR):SEP73-119
SMYTH, C.H. BRONZINO AS DRAUGHTSMAN.
F. GIBBONS, 551(RENQ):SUMMER73-197
C. GOULD, 39:OCT73-320
SMYTH, P. CONVERSIONS.
J. PARISI, 491:JUL75-219
SMYTH, W.R. THESAURUS CRITICUS AD
SEXTI PROPERTII TEXTUM.*
A.A. BARRETT, 122:JAN74-58
SMYTHE, D. GREEN DOORS.
J.M.P., 134(CP):FALL73-88
SMYTHE, H. HISTORICAL SKETCH OF
PARKER COUNTY & WEATHERFORD, TEXAS.
W. GARD, 584(SWR):WINTER74-98
"SNAP OUT OF IT."
D.M. DAY, 157:WINTER73-89
SNEED, J.D. THE LOGICAL STRUCTURE
OF MATHEMATICAL PHYSICS.
C.A. HOOKER, 486:MAR73-130
SNELGROVE, D., J. MAYNE & B. TAYLOR
- SEE HARDIE, M.
SNELL, B. SZENEN AUS GRIECHISCHEN
DRAMEN.*
F. JOUAN, 555:VOL47FASC2-329
SNELL, B., ED. TRAGICORUM GRAECORUM
FRAGMENTA. (VOL 1)
C.J. HERINGTON, 124:MAY73-463
SNODGRASS, A.M. THE DARK AGE OF
GREECE.
P. MAC KENDRICK, 124:MAR73-370
SNODGRASS, W.D. IN RADICAL PURSUIT.
M. WOOD, 453:17APR75-15

SNOW, C.P. IN THEIR WISDOM.*
P. VANSITTART, 364:FEB/MAR75-130
442(NY):13JAN75-90
SNOW, C.P. TROLLOPE.
A. BROYARD, 441:12DEC75-45
N. DENNIS, 453:11DEC75-34
C.H. SISSON, 617(TLS):5DEC75-1464
R. TOWERS, 441:16NOV75-5
SNOW, L.W. CHINA ON STAGE.
W.J. MESERVE, 397(MD):JUN73-104
SNUKAL, R. HIGH TALK.
A.N. JEFFARES, 569(SR):WINTER74-
108
639(VQR):WINTER74-XX
SNYDER, G. MANZANITA.
D.I. JANIK, 114(CHIR):VOL25#4-142
SNYDER, G. TURTLE ISLAND.
R. HOWARD, 491:SEP75-346
H. LEIBOWITZ, 441:23MAR75-2
SNYDER, W.U. THOMAS WOLFE.
B.B. HILLJE, 219(GAR):WINTER73-605
295:FEB74-826
SNYMAN, J.W. AN INTRODUCTION TO THE
!XŨ (!KUNG) LANGUAGE.
A.N. TUCKER, 69:APR73-168
SOARES, M. PORTUGAL'S STRUGGLE FOR
LIBERTY.
C.R. BOXER, 617(TLS):4JUL75-740
SOAVI, G. MEMORIE DI UN MILIAR-
DARIO.
617(TLS):31OCT75-1310
SOBEJANO, G. NOVELA ESPAÑOLA DE
NUESTRO TIEMPO (EN BUSCA DEL
PUEBLO PERDIDO).*
J. ALBERICH, 86(BHS):APR73-186
U.J. DE WINTER, 240(HR):AUTUMN73-
708
SOBEL, I.P. THE VIRUS KILLER.
M. LEVIN, 441:4MAY75-53
SOBEL, R. N.Y.S.E.
K. KOYEN, 441:7SEP75-38
SOBELL, M. ON DOING TIME.*
R.R. LINGEMAN, 441:24JUN75-37
SOBLE, R. SMART MONEY IN HARD TIMES.
B.G. MALKIEL, 441:26JAN75-19
SOBLE, R.L. & R.E. DALLOS. THE IM-
POSSIBLE DREAM.*
P. GROSE, 441:26FEB75-39
442(NY):17MAR75-126
SOBOUL, A. THE FRENCH REVOLUTION:
1787-1799.
R. DARNTON, 453:20CT75-17
C. LUCAS, 617(TLS):31JAN75-114
SOBRINO, J., J.B. SILMAN & F. VER-
GARA. REPASO DE ESPAÑOL.*
J.B. DALBOR, 399(MLJ):JAN-FEB74-79
"SOCIOLOGI E CENTRI DI POTERE IN
ITALIA."
E. NAMER, 542:JAN-MAR73-62
SÖDERBERGH, R. READING IN EARLY
CHILDHOOD.
J. PRŮCHA, 353:15SEP73-119
SÖDERHOLM, T. THE END-RHYMES OF
MARVELL, COWLEY, CRASHAW, LOVELACE
& VAUGHAN.*
P.M. WOLFE, 350:DEC74-742
SOECHTING, D. DIE PORTRÄTS DES SEP-
TIMIUS SEVERUS.
M.A.R. COLLEDGE, 313:VOL63-281
SOELLNER, R. SHAKESPEARE'S PATTERNS
OF SELF-KNOWLEDGE.
M. MC CANLES, 141:SPRING74-172
A. STEIN, 301(JEGP):JUL74-430

SOGRAFI, A.S. LE CONVENIENZE E LE
INCONVENIENZE TEATRALI. (G.F.
MALIPIERO, ED)
M.F., 228(GSLI):VOL150FASC470/471-
475
SOIRON, R. DER BEITRAG DER SCHWEI-
ZER AUSSENPOLITIK ZUM PROBLEM DER
FRIEDENSORGANISATION AM ENDE DES 1.
WELTKRIEGES.
A. WAHL, 182:VOL26#5/6-183
SOKOLOV, R. NATIVE INTELLIGENCE.
M. MEWSHAW, 441:11MAY75-45
SOKOLOVA, T. & K. ORLOVA. RUSSIAN
FURNITURE IN THE COLLECTION OF THE
HERMITAGE.
M. CHAMOT, 39:DEC73-514
DE SOLA PINTO, V. & F.W. ROBERT -
SEE LAWRENCE, D.H.
SOLBERG, R. INVENTIVE JEWELRY-
MAKING.
J-M.R., 139:APR73-13
SOLDEVILA, F., ED. JAUME I, BERNAT
DESCLOT, RAMON MUNTANER, PERE III:
LES QUATRE GRANS CRÒNIQUES. LIBRE
DELS FEYTS DEL REY EN JACME, EDI-
CIÓN FACSÍMIL DEL MANUSCRITO DE
POBLET (1343) CONSERVADO EN LA
BIBLIOTECA UNIVERSITARIA DE BARCE-
LONA.
R.I. BURNS, 589:APR74-382
SOLIN, H. BEITRÄGE ZUR KENNTNIS DER
GRIECHISCHEN PERSONENNAMEN IN ROM.*
(VOL 1)
H. PETERSEN, 122:OCT74-302
G. SERBAT, 555:VOL47FASC1-188
SOLL, I. AN INTRODUCTION TO HEGEL'S
METAPHYSICS.*
A. QUINTON, 453:29MAY75-34
SOLLERS, P. H.
R. BARTHES, 98:NOV73-965
SOLLERS, P. THE PARK.
A-H. GREET, 207(FR):MAY73-1252
SOLMSSEN, A.R.G. THE COMFORT LET-
TER.
M. LEVIN, 441:15JUN75-26
SOLNEY, P. THE HUNTER HOME.
D.M. DAY, 157:SPRING73-84
SOLOMON, R.C. THE EXISTENTIALISTS
& THEIR NINETEENTH-CENTURY BACK-
GROUNDS.
R. SCHACHT, 482(PHR):APR74-268
SOLOMON, R.C. FROM RATIONALISM TO
EXISTENTIALISM.
R.J. DEVETTERE, 258:JUN73-287
W.G., 543:DEC72-367
SOLOMON, R.C., ED. PHENOMENOLOGY &
EXISTENTIALISM.
R.J. DEVETTERE, 258:JUN73-287
SOLOMON, R.H. MAO'S REVOLUTION &
THE CHINESE POLITICAL CULTURE.
C-T. HSÜEH, 302:JUL73-264
T-A. METZGER, 293(JAST):NOV72-101
F.W. MOTE, 293(JAST):NOV72-107
SOLOTAROFF, R. DOWN MAILER'S WAY.
M. MASON, 617(TLS):8AUG75-891
R. MERRILL, 651(WHR):AUTUMN74-387
S. PINSKER, 659:SUMMER75-386
V. STRANDBERG, 27(AL):JAN75-600
SOLOUKHIN, V. SEARCHING FOR ICONS
IN RUSSIA.*
M. CHAMOT, 39:DEC73-514
SOLOVIEFF, G., ED. MADAME DE STAËL,
SES AMIS, SES CORRESPONDANTS.
S. COLSAËT, 535(RHL):JUL-AUG73-707

SOLOVIEV, V. STIKHOTVORENIYA I
SHUTOCHNYE P'ESY. (Z.G. MINTS, ED)
A. PYMAN, 617(TLS):25JUL75-857
SOLZHENITSYN, A. AUGUST 1914.*
(RUSSIAN TITLE: AVGUST CHETYRNADT-
SATOGO.)
R.P. BROWDER, 50(ARQ):SPRING73-90
SOLZHENITSYN, A. BODALSYA TELENOKS
DUBOM.
J.B. DUNLOP, 617(TLS):11APR75-386
SOLZHENITSYN, A. THE GULAG ARCHI-
PELAGO, 1918-1956.* (RUSSIAN TITLE:
ARKHIPELAG GULAG, 1918-1956.) (VOL
1)
K. FITZLYON, 364:APR/MAY74-110
M. MUDRICK, 249(HUDR):WINTER74/75-
589
A.E. SENN, 59(ASOC):FALL-WINTER74-
491
S. SPENDER, 473(PR):4/1974-553
SOLZHENITSYN, A. THE GULAG ARCHI-
PELAGO, 1918-1956. (RUSSIAN TITLE:
ARKHIPELAG GULAG, 1918-1956.) (VOL
2)
P. BLAKE, 441:26OCT75-1
K. FITZLYON, 364:DEC74/JAN75-112
L. SCHAPIRO, 453:13NOV75-10
P. WINDSOR, 362:4DEC75-750
SOLZHENITSYN, A. PRUSSKIE NOCHI.
L. KOEHLER, 104:WINTER74-581
SOLZHENITSYN, A. & OTHERS. FROM
UNDER THE RUBBLE. (M. SCAMMELL, ED)
N. BLIVEN, 442(NY):22SEP75-127
R.R. LINGEMAN, 441:25AUG75-25
B. SHRAGIN, 453:26JUN75-35
P. WINDSOR, 362:16OCT75-517
SOMERVILLE-LARGE, P. COUCH OF
EARTH.
617(TLS):9MAY75-501
SOMERVILLE-LARGE, P. IRISH ECCEN-
TRICS.
A. BOYLE, 362:13NOV75-657
C. DAVIDSON, 617(TLS):17OCT75-1237
S. HELGESEN, 441:16NOV75-62
SOMMER, R. DESIGN AWARENESS.
W.C. MILLER, 505:JUL73-128
SOMMERSTEIN, A.H. THE SOUND PATTERN
OF ANCIENT GREEK.
B. NEWTON, 487:AUTUMN73-292
SOMVILLE, L. DEVANCIERS DU SURRÉAL-
ISME.*
M. BERTRAND, 188(ECR):SUMMER73-166
M.A. CAWS, 546(RR):MAY74-234
S. FAUCHEREAU, 98:NOV73-997
SONDHI, M.L. NON APPEASEMENT.
L.J. KAVIC, 293(JAST):FEB73-357
SONG, B-S. AN ANNOTATED BIBLIOGRA-
PHY OF KOREAN MUSIC.
B.B. SMITH, 187:MAY75-318
"THE SONG OF ROLAND."* (R. HARRI-
SON, TRANS)
W.G. VAN EMDEN, 208(FS):JUL74-308
SONNTAG, J.M. NIFADES.
270:VOL23#2-42
SONSTROEM, D. ROSSETTI & THE FAIR
LADY.*
M. GREENE, 219(GAR):WINTER73-601
SONTHEIMER, K. & W. BLEEK. DIE DDR.
J. GOMEZ, 556(RLV):1973/5-477
SONTHEIMER, K. & W. BLEEK. THE GOV-
ERNMENT & POLITICS OF EAST GERMANY.
L. HOLMES, 617(TLS):24OCT75-1266

SOPEÑA IBÁÑEZ, F. ARTE Y SOCIEDAD
EN GALDÓS.*
E. RODGERS, 86(BHS):JAN73-96
SOPER, A. TEXTUAL EVIDENCE FOR THE
SECULAR ARTS OF CHINA IN THE PERIOD
FROM LIU SUNG THROUGH SUI.
C. HSI, 54:MAR73-137
SOPHOCLES. ANTIGONE.* (R.E. BRAUN,
TRANS)
G.E. DIMOCK, JR., 676(YR):SUMMER
74-573
SOPHOCLES. THE "ANTIGONE" OF SOPH-
OCLES. (R.C. JEBB, ED; ABRIDGED BY
E.S. SHUCKBURGH)
V.L. MAGBOO, 124:APR-MAY74-396
SOPHOCLES. SOFOCLE, "EDIPO RE."
(O. LONGO, ED)
E.W. WHITTLE, 123:NOV74-288
SORABJI, R. ARISTOTLE ON MEMORY.*
J.D.G. EVANS, 483:OCT73-404
W.A.F., 543:MAR73-546
W. LESZL, 548(RCSF):OCT-DEC73-476
R.K. SPRAGUE, 124:MAR74-313
SORDI, M., ED. CONTRIBUTI DELL'IS-
TITUTO DI STORIA ANTICA.
J-C. RICHARD, 555:VOL47FASC2-377
SORELL, W. - SEE WIGMAN, M.
SÖRENSEN, E. MODERN ENGLISH TEXTS
FOR COMPREHENSION & ANALYSIS.
K. OLTMANN, 430(NS):JUL73-381
SØRENSEN, K. ENGELSKE LÅN I DANSK.
R.W.Z., 179(ES):DEC73-619
SORLIN, P. LA SOCIÉTÉ FRANÇAISE
II/1914-1968.* [ENTRY IN PREV WAS
OF VOLS 1&2]
B.A. LENSKI, 207(FR):APR73-1090
SORRENTINO, G. SPLENDIDE-HÔTEL.
H. CARRUTH, 249(HUDR):AUTUMN74-475
"THE SORROW & THE PITY."
D. MAINFROY, 617(TLS):10JAN75-28
SORSBY, A., ED. TENEMENTS OF CLAY.
M. HURST, 617(TLS):2MAY75-489
SŌSEKI, N. GRASS ON THE WAYSIDE
(MICHIKUSA).
M. RYAN, 318(JAOS):JAN-MAR73-90
SŌSEKI, N. LIGHT & DARKNESS.
J. RUBIN, 318(JAOS):OCT-DEC73-627
SOTIROPOULOS, D. NOUN MORPHOLOGY OF
MODERN DEMOTIC GREEK.
B. NEWTON, 320(CJL):FALL74-188
SOTO, O.N., ED. ESPAÑA E HISPANO-
AMÉRICA.
D. CASTIEL, 238:MAY73-526
E.M. MALINAK, 399(MLJ):MAR74-135
SOTO, O.N. REPASO DE GRAMÁTICA.
I.E. STANISLAWCZYK, 238:MAR73-197
DE SOUSA-LEÃO, J. FRANS POST (1612-
80).
M. HUGGLER, 182:VOL26#11/12-423
SOUSTER, R. CHANGE-UP.
M. BAXTER, 99:DEC75/JAN76-48
G. MC WHIRTER, 198:SPRING75-132
L. SANDLER, 606(TAMR):MAR75-88
F.W. WATT, 99:JUN75-40
SOUSTER, R. SELECTED POEMS.
M. DOYLE, 102(CANL):WINTER74-123
SOUTH, A., COMP. RECORDS OF THE
HEADQUARTERS OF THE ARMY: RECORD
GROUP 108.
D.B. GRACY 2D, 14:APR73-249
"SOUTHEAST ASIA'S ECONOMY IN THE
1970'S."*
F.H. GOLAY, 293(JAST):AUG73-731

SOUTHERN, E. THE MUSIC OF BLACK
AMERICANS.*
 H. OSTER, 650(WF):JAN73-60
SOUTHERN, E., ED. READINGS IN BLACK
AMERICAN MUSIC.
 M. PETERSON, 470:JAN73-33
SOUTHERN, R. THE STAGING OF PLAYS
BEFORE SHAKESPEARE.
 J.C. TREWIN, 157:SUMMER73-74
"A SOUTHERN ALBUM."
 E. HOAGLAND, 441:7DEC75-4
SOUTHERNE, T. THE WIVES EXCUSE.
(R.R. THORNTON, ED)
 J. FREEHAFER, 566:AUTUMN73-39
SOUTHERTON, P. THE STORY OF A
PRISON.
 G. PLAYFAIR, 617(TLS):26SEP75-1105
SOUTHWORTH, H.R. LA DESTRUCTION DE
GUERNICA.
 H. THOMAS, 617(TLS):11APR75-392
SOVA, L.Z. ANALITIČESKAJA LINGVIS-
TIKA.
 J. KRISTOPHSON, 353:1AUG73-122
SOWELL, T. CLASSICAL ECONOMISTS RE-
CONSIDERED.
 L. ROBBINS, 617(TLS):1AUG75-870
SOWINSKI, B. DEUTSCHE STILISTIK.
 P. SCHÄUBLIN, 220(GL&L):APR74-252
SOYINKA, W. COLLECTED PLAYS 1.
 A. RENDLE, 157:WINTER73-87
SOYINKA, W. DEATH & THE KING'S
HORSEMAN.
 D.A.N. JONES, 617(TLS):17OCT75-
 1238
SOYINKA, W. THE JERO PLAYS.* SEAS-
ON OF ANOMY.
 J. MELLORS, 364:APR/MAY74-135
SOYINKA, W. A SHUTTLE IN THE CRYPT.
 A. CLUYSENAAR, 565:VOL14#1-70
SOZZI, G.P. JEHAN RICTUS.
 C. MIGNOT-OGLIASTRI, 535(RHL):
 JAN-FEB73-155
SPACKS, B. SOMETHING HUMAN.*
 M. MADIGAN, 385(MQR):SPRING75-220
SPACKS, P.M. AN ARGUMENT OF IMAGES.*
 A. WILLIAMS, 191(ELN):MAR74-222
SPACKS, P.M. THE FEMALE IMAGINATION.
 P. BEER, 441:11MAY75-42
SPACKS, P.M., ED. LATE AUGUSTAN
POETRY.
 566:AUTUMN73-35
SPAE, J.J. SHINTO MAN.
 A. BLOOM, 485(PE&W):OCT73-547
SPAETHLING, R. & E. WEBER, EDS.
LITERATUR I.
 J.E. CREAN, JR., 399(MLJ):SEP-OCT
 73-299
 D. SEVIN, 221(GQ):NOV73-657
SPALDING, R. THE IMPROBABLE PURI-
TAN.
 G. MACDONALD, 362:6MAR75-317
 B. WORDEN, 617(TLS):21FEB75-192
SPANGENBERG, K. BAUMHAUERS STROMER-
GESPRÄCHE IN ROTWELSCH.
 M. CALIEBE, 657(WW):MAR/APR73-139
SPARK, M. THE ABBESS OF CREWE.*
 J. UPDIKE, 442(NY):6JAN75-76
SPARK, M. THE HOTHOUSE BY THE EAST
RIVER.*
 M. PRICE, 676(YR):AUTUMN73-80
SPARK, M. NOT TO DISTURB.*
 J.C. FIELD, 556(RLV):1973/1-92

SPARKMAN, L., P.D. SMITH, JR. & D.E.
WOLFE. DIALOGUE AFRICAIN CONTEMPOR-
AIN. (LEVEL 1)
 J. DECOCK, 207(FR):MAY73-1267
SPARKS, E.H. THE MUSIC OF NOEL
BAULDEWEYN.*
 M. PICKER, 414(MQ):OCT73-643
SPARSHOTT, F.E. LOOKING FOR PHILOS-
OPHY.
 R.E. CARTER, 529(QQ):SUMMER73-308
 F.H. PAGE, 150(DR):AUTUMN73-568
SPEAIGHT, G., ED. BAWDY SONGS OF
THE EARLY MUSIC HALL.
 P. KEATING, 617(TLS):26DEC75-1534
SPEAIGHT, R. THE COMPANION GUIDE TO
BURGUNDY.
 S. PAKENHAM, 617(TLS):19DEC75-1504
SPEAIGHT, R. SHAKESPEARE ON THE
STAGE.*
 P. JAMES, 157:WINTER73-80
 639(VQR):AUTUMN74-CXXVI
SPEAIGHT, R. - SEE BRIDGES-ADAMS, W.
SPEAR, R.E. CARAVAGGIO & HIS FOL-
LOWERS.
 R. ENGGASS, 54:SEP73-460
SPEAR, R.E. RENAISSANCE & BAROQUE
PAINTINGS FROM THE SCIARRA & FIANO
COLLECTIONS.
 E. YOUNG, 39:SEP73-239
SPEARING, A.C. CRITICISM & MEDIEVAL
POETRY. (2ND ED)
 H. COOPER, 382(MAE):1974/2-213
SPEARING, A.C. THE GAWAIN-POET.*
 H. BOYD, 180(ESA):SEP73-107
 E. REISS, 191(ELN):MAR74-213
SPEARS, M.K. DIONYSUS & THE CITY.*
 P. ROBERTS, 541(RES):FEB73-108
 H. SERGEANT, 175:SUMMER72-75
SPECK, E.B., ED. MODY BOATRIGHT,
FOLKLORIST.
 J.W. BYRD, 584(SWR):WINTER74-89
SPECTOR, J.J. THE AESTHETICS OF
FREUD.
 A.W. BRINK, 529(QQ):WINTER73-620
SPECTOR, J.J. DELACROIX: THE DEATH
OF SARDANAPALUS.
 A. BROOKNER, 617(TLS):10JAN75-35
SPECTOR, M. METHODOLOGICAL FOUNDA-
TIONS OF RELATIVISTIC MECHANICS.
 P. KIRSCHENMANN, 486:SEP73-459
SPEER, A. INSIDE THE THIRD REICH.*
(GERMAN TITLE: ERINNERUNGEN.)
 D. VON KUENSSBERG-JEHLE, 221(GQ):
 MAR73-284
 B.M. LANE, 576:DEC73-341
SPEIRS, J. POETRY TOWARDS NOVEL.*
 I. SIMON, 556(RLV):1973/6-569
 G. THOMAS, 175:SPRING72-27
SPEIRS, L. TOLSTOY & CHEKHOV.*
 T.G. WINNER, 399(MLJ):DEC73-440
SPELL, J.R. BRIDGING THE GAP.
(L.M. SPELL, ED)
 E.J. MULLEN, 399(MLJ):MAR73-146
 D.L. SHAW, 86(BHS):JUL73-320
SPELLERBERG, G. VERHÄNGNIS UND
GESCHICHTE.*
 F. KIMMICH, 222(GR):MAY73-229
SPENCE, J.D. EMPEROR OF CHINA.*
 C.P. FITZGERALD, 617(TLS):30MAY75-
 592
SPENCER, C. NAHUM TATE.*
 R.D. HUME, 481(PQ):JUL73-584

SPURLING, H. IVY WHEN YOUNG.*
  G. CAVALIERO, 111:30MAY74-166
SQUAROTTI, G.B. - SEE UNDER BÀRBERI
  SQUAROTTI, G.
SQUEGLIA, M. ALL ABOUT REPAIRING
  SMALL APPLIANCES.
  P. BRACKEN, 441:27APR75-30
SQUIBB, G.D. FOUNDER'S KIN.
  J.A.W.B., 382(MAE):1974/3-320
SQUIRES, M. THE PASTORAL NOVEL.
  J.I.M. STEWART, 617(TLS):18APR75-
  415
SQUIRES, R. ALLEN TATE.*
  A. BROWN, 141:SPRING72-201
SQUIRES, R., ED. ALLEN TATE & HIS
  WORK.*
  W.G.R., 502(PRS):SUMMER73-186
SQUIRES, R. WAITING IN THE BONE.
  H. BAKER, 598(SOR):SUMMER75-644
"ŚRAUTAKOŚA." (SANSKRIT SECTION,
  VOL 2, PT 1) (C.G. KASHIKAR, ED)
  L. ROCHER, 318(JAOS):JUL-SEP73-376
SREEKRISHNA SARMA, E.R., COMP. IND-
  ISCHE HANDSCHRIFTEN. (PT 3)
  J. FILLIOZAT, 182:VOL26#13/14-449
SREEKRISHNA SARMA, E.R., ED. KAUṢĪ-
  TAKI-BRĀHMAṆA. (PT 1)
  J. FILLIOZAT, 182:VOL26#13/14-456
STAAL, J.F., ED. A READER ON THE
  SANSKRIT GRAMMARIANS.
  E.P. HAMP, 269(IJAL):JUL73-201
  T.S. PAIK, 350:SEP74-591
STABLER, A.P. THE LEGEND OF MAR-
  GUERITE DE ROBERVAL.
  S.E. MORISON, 432(NEQ):JUN73-305
STACCHINI, V.G. LA NARRATIVA DI
  VITALIANO BRANCATI.
  F. ALFONSI, 276:SPRING73-105
STACE, C. & D.V. JONES. STILUS
  ARTIFEX.
  P.L. SMITH, 124:MAY73-487
STACEY, C.P., ED. HISTORICAL DOCU-
  MENTS OF CANADA.* (VOL 5)
  G.F.G. STANLEY, 529(QQ):WINTER73-
  625
STACEY, M. & OTHERS. POWER, PERSIS-
  TENCE & CHANGE.
  P. WILLMOTT, 617(TLS):9MAY75-508
STACHIW, M. & J. SZTENDERA. WESTERN
  UKRAINE AT THE TURNING POINT OF
  EUROPE'S HISTORY, 1918-1923. (J.L.
  STACHIW, ED)
  O.W. GERUS, 104:SUMMER73-272
STACHOWIAK, H. RATIONALISMUS IM
  URSPRUNG.*
  J. BARNES, 393(MIND):APR73-292
STACK, E.M. LE PONT NEUF. (2ND ED)
  G.R. DANNER, 207(FR):OCT72-241
VON STACKELBERG, J. VON RABELAIS
  BIS VOLTAIRE.*
  E. KOPPEN, 52:BAND8HEFT3-335
  P.H. MEYER, 546(RR):JAN74-61
STACPOOLE, J. WILLIAM MASON - THE
  FIRST NEW ZEALAND ARCHITECT.
  P. HOWELL, 46:MAR73-212
STADE, G., ED. SIX MODERN BRITISH
  NOVELISTS.
  R.F. KENNEDY, 268:JUL75-180
STADLER, U. DER EINSAME ORT.*
  F.M. RENER, 221(GQ):NOV73-616
STADTER, P.A., ED. THE SPEECHES IN
  THUCYDIDES.
  639(VQR):AUTUMN74-CLIV

STADTFELD, C.K. FROM THE LAND &
  BACK.
  R. KIRK, 219(GAR):SPRING73-125
STÄDTKE, K., ED. DIE UNHEIMLICHE
  WAHRSAGUNG.
  J.D. SIMONS, 104:FALL73-424
STAEHLE, W.H. ORGANISATION UND
  FÜHRUNG SOZIO-TECHNISCHER SYSTEME.
  M.W. GILLO, 182:VOL26#5/6-147
MADAME DE STAËL. TEN YEARS OF
  EXILE. (D. BEIK, TRANS)
  R. MULHAUSER, 446:SPRING-SUMMER74-
  185
STAFF, E. THE HOSTAGE OF TOLEDO.
  D.M. DAY, 157:WINTER73-89
STAFFORD, W. SOMEDAY, MAYBE.*
  L. LIEBERMAN, 676(YR):SPRING74-453
  P. RAMSEY, 569(SR):SPRING74-400
  J.K. ROBINSON, 598(SOR):SUMMER75-
  668
  P. ZWEIG, 473(PR):4/1974-604
"STAFFORDSHIRE RECORD OFFICE CUMULA-
  TIVE HAND LIST." (PT 1)
  E. WELCH, 325:APR73-615
"STAGE DESIGN SINCE 1960."
  D. WRIGHT, 157:AUTUMN73-78
STAHL, W.H., WITH R. JOHNSON & E.L.
  BURGE. MARTIANUS CAPELLA & THE
  SEVEN LIBERAL ARTS.* (VOL 1)
  R. BERNABEI, 124:SEP72-46
  C. WITKE, 589:JAN74-155
STAHN, E. DAS AFRIKA DER VATERLÄN-
  DER.
  R. OLIVER, 617(TLS):17OCT75-1239
STALEY, A. THE PRE-RAPHAELITE LAND-
  SCAPE.*
  A.D. CULLER, 676(YR):WINTER74-287
  R. EDWARDS, 39:NOV73-403
STALEY, T.F. & B. BENSTOCK, EDS.
  APPROACHES TO "ULYSSES."
  295:FEB74-684
STALLEY, R.A. ARCHITECTURE & SCULP-
  TURE IN IRELAND 1150-1350.
  J. BECKWITH, 39:SEP73-238
STALLKNECHT, N.P. GEORGE SANTA-
  YANA.*
  R. ASSELINEAU, 189(EA):JAN-MAR73-
  117
STALLMACH, J. ATE.
  F.J. LE MOINE, 121(CJ):DEC73/JAN
  74-149
STALLMAN, R.W. STEPHEN CRANE.
  L. LINDER, 569(SR):SUMMER74-LXIV
  G.T. TANSELLE, 445(NCF):MAR74-486
STALLWORTHY, J. WILFRED OWEN.*
  C. BEDIENT, 441:14SEP75-27
  P. DICKINSON, 364:FEB/MAR75-120
  K. MILLER, 453:16OCT75-27
  D. THOMAS, 362:9JAN75-60
STALLYBRASS, M.O. - SEE FORSTER, E.M.
STAMBAUGH, J. NIETZSCHE'S THOUGHT
  OF ETERNAL RETURN.*
  W.J. GRIFFITH, 319:OCT75-536
  C. MURIN, 255(HAB):SPRING73-115
STAMBOLIAN, G. MARCEL PROUST & THE
  CREATIVE ENCOUNTER.*
  A. SONNENFELD, 401(MLQ):DEC74-432
STAMM, R. THE SHAPING POWERS AT
  WORK.*
  J.T. FAIN, 570(SQ):SUMMER73-348
STAMPFER, J. JOHN DONNE & THE META-
  PHYSICAL GESTURE.
  T.A. BIRRELL, 179(ES):FEB73-71

STANDEN, M. THE DREAMLAND TREE.
E. GLOVER, 565:VOL14#2-36
STANFORD, D., ED. PRE-RAPHAELITE
WRITING.
R. NYE, 364:APR/MAY74-142
STANFORD, W.B. & J.V. LUCE. THE
QUEST FOR ULYSSES.
G. GRIGSON, 362:6MAR75-316
STANKIEWICZ, E. - SEE BAUDOUIN DE
COURTENAY, J.
STANKIEWICZ, E. & D.S. WORTH. A
SELECTED BIBLIOGRAPHY OF SLAVIC
LINGUISTICS.* (VOL 2)
L.L. THOMAS, 574(SEEJ):SUMMER73-
251
STANKIEWICZ, W.J. WHAT IS BEHAVIOR-
ALISM?
A. SHALOM, 154:SEP73-547
STANLEY, A. PRE-RAPHAELITE LAND-
SCAPE.
M. ROSENTHAL, 135:DEC73-295
STANLEY, G.F.G. CANADA INVADED,
1775-1776.*
P.B. WAITE, 150(DR):WINTER73/74-
783
STANLEY, H. "CAN YOU HEAR ME,
MOTHER?"
P. KEATING, 617(TLS):26DEC75-1534
STANLEY, P.W. A NATION IN THE MAK-
ING.
R.E. WELCH, JR., 432(NEQ):DEC74-
633
STANLEY, R. KING GEORGE'S KEYS.
D. HUNT, 617(TLS):28MAR75-344
STANTON, P. PUGIN.
P.F. NORTON, 576:MAR73-75
M.D. ROSS, 54:MAR73-156
STANTON, W. THE GREAT UNITED STATES
EXPLORING EXPEDITION OF 1838-1842.
A. WHITMAN, 441:22NOV75-27
STANZEL, F. NARRATIVE SITUATIONS IN
THE NOVEL.*
P. STEVICK, 454:FALL73-71
STAPLETON, L. THE ELECTED CIRCLE.
W. BERTHOFF, 27(AL):NOV74-393
639(VQR):AUTUMN74-CXXII
STARCK, T. & J.C. WELLS, EDS. ALT-
HOCHDEUTSCHES GLOSSENWÖRTERBUCH.*
(2ND SER) (PT 1)
H. VON GADOW, 72:BAND211HEFT1/3-99
STARCK, T. & J.C. WELLS, EDS. ALT-
HOCHDEUTSCHES GLOSSENWÖRTERBUCH.
(2ND SER) (PT 2)
H. VON GADOW, 72:BAND211HEFT1/3-
104
STARK, F. LETTERS. (VOL 1) (L.
MOOREHEAD, ED)
E. MONROE, 617(TLS):7FEB75-132
STARKE, C.J. BLACK PORTRAITURE IN
AMERICAN FICTION.
J.F. YELLIN, 141:FALL72-399
STARKIE, E. FLAUBERT THE MASTER.*
J. CRUICKSHANK, 402(MLR):APR74-422
M. TILLETT, 208(FS):JAN74-96
STAROBINSKI, J. LES MOTS SOUS LES
MOTS.*
J-M. REY, 98:FEB73-137
STAROBINSKI, J. TROIS FUREURS.
G. STEINER, 617(TLS):24JAN75-75
STAROSTE, W. RAUM UND REALITÄT IN
DICHTERISCHER GESTALTUNG.* (G.
WUNBERG, ED)
D.G. LITTLE, 402(MLR):APR74-458
H. REISS, 133:1973/2-188

STARR, C.G. ATHENIAN COINAGE, 480-
449 B.C.*
W.G. MOON, 121(CJ):FEB/MAR74-276
S.I. OOST, 122:JAN73-76
STARR, K. AMERICANS & THE CALIFOR-
NIA DREAM, 1850-1915.*
K. JEFFREY, 109:FALL/WINTER73/74-
144
STARR, R. HOUSING & THE MONEY MAR-
KET.
A. TALBOT, 441:3AUG75-12
STARR, S.F. DECENTRALIZATION &
SELF-GOVERNMENT IN RUSSIA, 1830-
1870.
H.A. MC FARLIN, 104:WINTER73-551
W.M. PINTNER, 550(RUSR):APR73-200
STARR, S.F. - SEE VON HAXTHAUSEN, A.
STARR, S.Z. JENNISON'S JAYHAWKERS.
639(VQR):AUTUMN74-CXLIII
STATES, B.O. IRONY & DRAMA.*
H.B. NORLAND, 502(PRS):SPRING73-83
STATIUS. P. PAPINI STATI, "THEBAI-
DOS" LIBER X. (R.D. WILLIAMS, ED)
E. COURTNEY, 313:VOL63-308
STAUDER, J. THE MAJANGIR.
H. BLACKHURST, 69:JAN73-84
STAVELEY, E.S. GREEK & ROMAN VOTING
& ELECTIONS.
B.M. CAVEN, 313:VOL63-263
E.S. GRUEN, 24:WINTER74-417
J.A.O. LARSEN, 122:JUL73-225
R.J. ROWLAND, JR., 124:MAR73-368
STAVISKY, A.Y. SHAKESPEARE & THE
VICTORIANS.
A.M. EASTMAN, 570(SQ):SPRING73-228
STEAD, C. THE LITTLE HOTEL.*
P. ADAMS, 61:JUN75-95
H. CALISHER, 441:11MAY75-6
C. LEHMANN-HAUPT, 441:16JUN75-25
C. RICKS, 453:26JUN75-13
J. UPDIKE, 442(NY):18AUG75-79
STEADMAN, J.M. DISEMBODIED LAUGH-
TER.*
J.H. MARTIN, 131(CL):SUMMER73-273
D. MEHL, 182:VOL26#1/2-31
W.M. TEMPLE, 382(MAE):1974/3-293
R.M. WILSON, 175:AUTUMN73-112
STEADMAN, P. ENERGY, ENVIRONMENT &
BUILDING.
A.C. HARDY, 617(TLS):26SEP75-1109
STEANE, J.B. THE GRAND TRADITION.*
H. ROSENTHAL, 415:OCT74-846
STEANE, J.B. MARLOWE.
M.T. JONES-DAVIES, 189(EA):JUL-SEP
73-358
STEBBINS, T.E., JR. THE LIFE &
WORKS OF MARTIN JOHNSON HEADE.
J. RUSSELL, 441:7DEC75-24
STEEGMULLER, F. - SEE DUNCAN, I.
STEEGMULLER, F. - SEE FLAUBERT, G.
STEELE, E. HUGH WALPOLE.
B.E. TEETS, 177(ELT):VOL16#3-238
STEELE, E.D. IRISH LAND & BRITISH
POLITICS.
J. LEE, 617(TLS):9MAY75-505
STEELE, I.K. GUERILLAS & GRENA-
DIERS.
G.L. COOK, 255(HAB):WINTER73-71
STEELE, J. - SEE PHILIPS, P.
STEELE, R. THE PLAYS OF RICHARD
STEELE.* (S.S. KENNY, ED)
D.F. BOND, 405(MP):AUG73-93
J. DULCK, 189(EA):APR-JUN73-227
F. RAU, 224(GRM):BAND23HEFT3-376

STEELE, S.B. FORTY YEARS IN CANADA.
W.P. WARD, 529(QQ):WINTER73-626
STEELE, T.J. SANTOS & SAINTS.
W. GARD, 584(SWR):SUMMER74-V
STEELE, W.D. DIAMOND WEDDING.
M. BUCCO, 649(WAL):SPRING&SUMMER
73-77
STEENE, B. THE GREATEST FIRE.*
J. SEITZ, 563(SS):FALL74-447
STEFANOVA, L. THE MEXICAN VOLCANOES
ARE SMOKING.
270:VOL23#1-18
STEFFAN, T.G. - SEE LORD BYRON
STEFFENSEN, S., ED. NERTHUS III.
P.M. MITCHELL, 563(SS):WINTER74-75
G. MÜLLER, 597(SN):VOL45#2-431
STEGER, H., CHIEF ED. TEXTE GESPRO-
CHENER DEUTSCHER STANDARDSPRACHE 1.
R.R.K. HARTMANN, 353:1DEC73-103
B.J. KOEKKOEK, 221(GQ):MAR73-240
STEGER, H., ED. VORSCHLÄGE FÜR
EINE STRUKTURALE GRAMMATIK DES
DEUTSCHEN.
L. PAUL, 260(IF):BAND78-338
STEGMANN, T.D. CERVANTES' MUSTER-
ROMAN "PERSILES."
A.K. FORCIONE, 400(MLN):MAR73-434
STEGMÜLLER, W. PERSONELLE UND STAT-
ISTISCHE WAHRSCHEINLICHKEIT. (1ST
HALF)
L. KRÜGER, 311(JP):4SEP75-499
STEGMÜLLER, W. PROBLEME UND RESUL-
TATE DER WISSENSCHAFTSTHEORIE UND
ANALYTISCHEN PHILOSOPHIE. (VOL 1)
G. FREY, 536:JUN73-136
STEGMÜLLER, W. PROBLEME UND RESUL-
TATE DER WISSENSCHAFTSTHEORIE UND
ANALYTISCHEN PHILOSOPHIE.* (VOL 2)
B. KANITSCHEIDER, 536:JUN73-143
STEGNER, W. THE UNEASY CHAIR.*
H.M. JONES, 27(AL):JAN75-579
STEGNER, W. - SEE DE VOTO, B.
STEIN, C. L'ENFANT IMAGINAIRE.
N. ABRAHAM, 98:DEC71-1102
STEIN, G. THE GEOGRAPHICAL HISTORY
OF AMERICA OR THE RELATION OF HUMAN
NATURE TO THE HUMAN MIND.
N. SCHMITZ, 473(PR):2/1974-283
STEIN, G. PRIMÄRE UND SEKUNDÄRE AD-
JEKTIVE IM FRANZÖSISCHEN UND ENG-
LISCHEN.
D. GÖTZ, 38:BAND91HEFT3-382
STEIN, G.P. THE WAYS OF MEANING IN
THE ARTS.*
A. BERLEANT, 484(PPR):SEP73-114
STEIN, J.M. POEM & MUSIC IN THE
GERMAN LIED FROM GLUCK TO HUGO
WOLF.*
C.S. BROWN, 222(GR):MAY73-230
J.F. FETZER, 131(CL):FALL73-367
R. HOLLOWAY, 402(MLR):OCT74-923
R.M. LONGYEAR, 149:SEP74-255
J.M. ROSS, 89(BJA):SUMMER73-312
J.L.S., 191(ELN):SEP73(SUPP)-138
J. STRELKA, 133:1973/2-184
STEIN, L. - SEE SCHOENBERG, A.
STEIN, R.A. TIBETAN CIVILIZATION.*
M.S.Y. LOO, 293(JAST):NOV72-166
STEIN, S. THE CHILDKEEPER.
C. LEHMANN-HAUPT, 441:13NOV75-45
K. ROOSEVELT, 441:7SEP75-41
STEIN, S. LIVING ROOM.*
J. BARNES, 617(TLS):9MAY75-501
N. HEPBURN, 362:5JUN75-746

STEIN, W. CRITICISM AS DIALOGUE.*
V. BUCKLEY, 148:SPRING72-75
STEIN-WILKESHUIS, M.W. HET KIND IN
DE OUDIJSLANDSE SAMENLEVING.
T. HOMAN, 433:OCT73-401
STEINBACH, R. DIE DEUTSCHEN OSTER-
UND PASSIONSSPIELE.
W.F. MICHAEL, 222(GR):NOV73-315
STEINBECK, J. STEINBECK: A LIFE IN
LETTERS. (E. STEINBECK & R. WALL-
STEN, EDS)
S. MALOFF, 441:26OCT75-5
STEINBERG, A. SAM RAYBURN.
R. DUGGER, 441:6JUL75-2
R.R. LINGEMAN, 441:29JUL75-27
442(NY):8SEP75-126
STEINBERG, D.D. & L.A. JAKOBOVITS,
EDS. SEMANTICS.*
H.E. BREKLE, 343:BAND17HEFT1-76
R.D., 179(ES):APR73-200
R.D. EAGLESON, 67:NOV74-245
J.L., 543:SEP72-175
F.R. PALMER, 297(JL):SEP73-361
P.A.M. SEUREN, 433:APR73-198
STEINBERG, E.R. THE STREAM OF CON-
SCIOUSNESS & BEYOND IN "ULYSSES."*
G. ECKLEY, 659:AUTUMN75-504
STEINBERG, L. MICHELANGELO'S LAST
PAINTINGS.
J. RUSSELL, 441:23NOV75-7
STEINBERG, L. OTHER CRITERIA.*
C. BARRETT, 592:JUL-AUG73-49
A. DANTO, 290(JAAC):SUMMER74-568
STEINBERG, S. THE INSPECTOR.
C. BEDIENT, 473(PR):4/1974-643
STEINDL, E. - SEE LUCIAN
STEINECKE, H., ED. FAUST.
I.F., 191(ELN):SEP73(SUPP)-150
STEINECKE, H., ED. THEORIE UND
TECHNIK DES ROMANS IM 19. JAHRHUN-
DERT.*
E. MC INNES, 220(GL&L):JAN74-162
STEINECKE, H. - SEE HOFFMANN, E.T.A.
STEINER, B.E. SAMUEL SEABURY, 1729-
1796.*
H.R. CEDERBERG, 481(PQ):JUL73-404
C.K. SHIPTON, 432(NEQ):JUN73-298
STEINER, E. THE SLOVAK DILEMMA.
F.L. CARSTEN, 575(SEER):APR74-319
STEINER, G. AFTER BABEL.
N. BLIVEN, 442(NY):5MAY75-139
D.S. CARNE-ROSS, 453:30OCT75-38
D. DAVIE, 617(TLS):31JAN75-98
G.H. HARTMAN, 441:8JUN75-21
C. LEHMANN-HAUPT, 441:7MAY75-43
J. WEIGHTMAN, 362:30JAN75-154
STEINER, G. EXTRATERRITORIAL.*
295:FEB74-482
STEINER, G. IN BLUEBEARD'S CASTLE.*
H. PESCHMANN, 175:SPRING72-30
295:FEB74-482
STEINER, G. JAKOBINERSCHAUSPIEL
UND JAKOBINERTHEATER.
J. HERMAND, 406:WINTER74-438
STEINER, J. DIE BÜHNENANWEISUNG.*
C.L. HART-NIBBRIG, 657(WW):MAY/JUN
73-213
STEINER, M. MATHEMATICAL KNOWLEDGE.
J.E.J. ALTHAM, 617(TLS):19SEP75-
1043
STEINER, N.H. A CLOSER LOOK AT
ARIEL.*
H. WILLIAMS, 364:OCT/NOV74-64

STEINER, R. THE BANTAM NEW COLLEGE
FRENCH & ENGLISH DICTIONARY. THE
NEW COLLEGE FRENCH & ENGLISH DIC-
TIONARY.
   P.F. CHOLAKIAN, 399(MLJ):APR73-214
STEINER, R.J. TWO CENTURIES OF
SPANISH & ENGLISH BILINGUAL LEXI-
COGRAPHY: 1590-1880.
   H.H. CARTER, 240(HR):SUMMER73-592
   F.G. SALINERO, 399(MLJ):APR73-215
STEINGRUBER, J.D. ARCHITECTURAL
ALPHABET. (B.L. WOLPE, ED)
   R. MC LEAN, 135:FEB73-139
STEINHAUER, H., ED & TRANS. TEN
GERMAN NOVELLAS.
   W.L. HAHN, 221(GQ):MAR73-293
STEINHOFF, H-H. BIBLIOGRAPHIE ZU
GOTTFRIED VON STRASSBURG.*
   O. SAYCE, 402(MLR):JAN74-219
   A. SNOW, 221(GQ):MAR73-277
STEINITZ, R., WITH E. LANG. ADVERB-
IAL-SYNTAX.*
   D. CLÉMENT & S. KANNGIESSER,
   260(IF):BAND77HEFT2/3-369
STEINMETZ, H. - SEE GOTTSCHED, J.C.
VON STEINSDORFF, S., ED. DER BRIEF-
WECHSEL ZWISCHEN BETTINE BRENTANO
UND MAX PROKOP VON FREYBERG.
   E. STOPP, 402(MLR):OCT73-922
STEINWACHS, G. MYTHOLOGIE DES SUR-
REALISMUS ODER DIE RÜCKVERWANDLUNG
VON KULTUR IN NATUR.*
   R. KUHN, 207(FR):FEB73-629
STEINWEG, R. DAS LEHRSTÜCK.
   F.L. BORCHARDT, 221(GQ):NOV73-605
STEINWENTER, A. DIE STREITBEENDI-
GUNG DURCH URTEIL, SCHIEDSSPRUCH
UND VERGLEICH NACH GRIECHISCHEM
RECHTE.* (2ND ED)
   G. HEILBRUNN, 124:FEB73-310
   L. ROCHER, 318(JAOS):JUL-SEP73-376
STELL, W.J. SCENERY.
   J. VAN DER POLL, 583:FALL73-95
STELLMACH, B. FOUR AUSTRALIAN
PLAYS.
   A.A. PHILLIPS, 381:JUN73-189
STEMBER, S. THE BICENTENNIAL GUIDE
TO THE AMERICAN REVOLUTION.*
   G.F. SCHEER, 441:6APR75-2
STEMMLER, T. LITURGISCHE FEIERN UND
GEISTLICHE SPIELE.
   H-J. DILLER, 179(ES):OCT73-497
STEMMLER, T., ED. MEDIEVAL ENGLISH
LOVE-LYRICS.
   H.O., 430(NS):AUG73-449
STEMPEL, W-D., ED. BEITRÄGE ZUR
TEXTLINGUISTIK.
   W. THÜMMEL, 343:BAND16HEFT1-37
STEMPEL, W-D., ED. TEXTE DER RUS-
SISCHEN FORMALISTEN. (VOL 2)
   V. TERRAS, 550(RUSR):JAN73-92
STEMPOWSKI, J. [P. HOSTOWIEC] OD
BERDYCZOWA DO RZYMU.
   H. WEINTRAUB, 574(SEEJ):FALL72-359
STENDHAL. MEMOIRS OF AN EGOIST.
(D. ELLIS, TRANS)
   P.N. FURBANK, 362:5JUN75-741
   G. STRICKLAND, 617(TLS):4JUL75-741
STENHOUSE, D. THE EVOLUTION OF
INTELLIGENCE.
   A. HEIM, 617(TLS):24JAN75-88
STENHOUSE, T. LIVES ENSHRINED IN
LANGUAGE.
   K.B. HARDER, 424:JUN73-120

STENIUS, E. CRITICAL ESSAYS.
   R. BLANCHÉ, 542:JUL-SEP73-374
STENZEL, B., ED. CHANSONS DE
FRANCE.
   H. PULS, 430(NS):MAR73-177
STEPANOV, N. IVAN KRYLOV.
   P.R. HART, 574(SEEJ):SUMMER73-226
STEPHAN, J.J. THE KURIL ISLANDS.
   R. STORRY, 617(TLS):11APR75-405
STEPHAN, P. PAUL VERLAINE & THE
DECADENCE 1882-90.
   A.G. LEHMANN, 617(TLS):18APR75-436
STEPHAN, R. GOLDENES ZEITALTER UND
ARKADIEN.
   W. ENGLER, 52:BAND8HEFT3-338
   P. POLLARD, 208(FS):OCT74-473
   H. THOMA, 224(GRM):BAND23HEFT3-376
STEPHENS, A. RAINER MARIA RILKE'S
"GEDICHTE AN DIE NACHT."*
   U. FÜLLEBORN, 564:OCT73-267
   L.S. PICKLE, 399(MLJ):DEC73-433
   205(FMLS):APR73-216
STEPHENS, D.G., ED. WRITERS OF THE
PRAIRIES.
   H. KREISEL, 102(CANL):SUMMER74-88
STEPHENS, J. LETTERS OF JAMES
STEPHENS. (R.J. FINNERAN, ED)
   R. ELLMANN, 441:12OCT75-16
STEPHENS, M. EXILES ALL.
   A. CLUYSENAAR, 565:VOL14#4-75
STEPHENS, M. THE QUESTION OF FLAN-
NERY O'CONNOR.*
   D. EGGENSCHWILER, 301(JEGP):OCT74-
   569
   C. KATZ, 27(AL):MAY74-241
STEPHENSON, R. 5,000 MILES IN A
CATAMARAN.
   617(TLS):14FEB75-177
STERKX, H.E. PARTNERS IN REBELLION.
   L.N. ALLEN, 9(ALAR):JAN73-73
STERN, D. FINAL CUT.
   D. FREEMAN, 441:18MAY75-46
   442(NY):12MAY75-142
STERN, G. WAR, WEIMAR & LITERATURE.
   W.V. BLOMSTER, 399(MLJ):NOV73-380
   H.F. PFANNER, 221(GQ):MAY73-432
   U. WEISSTEIN, 400(MLN):APR73-648
   J.J. WHITE, 402(MLR):APR74-466
STERN, G., G. MERKEL & J. GLENN -
SEE "LESSING YEARBOOK"
STERN, H.R. & R. NOVAK. A HANDBOOK
OF ENGLISH-GERMAN IDIOMS & USEFUL
EXPRESSIONS.
   J.V. ROOD, 399(MLJ):NOV74-362
STERN, J.P. HITLER.
   G. BARRACLOUGH, 453:3APR75-11
   J. JOLL, 617(TLS):4JUL75-721
STERN, J.P. ON REALISM.
   F. JAMESON, 125:JUN74-346
   D. NEWTON-DE MOLINA, 402(MLR):
   JAN74-137
STERN, K. LOVE & SUCCESS & OTHER
ESSAYS.
   M.P. DUMONT, 441:13JUL75-10
STERN, M. THE SUN & THE CLOUDS.
   F. FREIDENREICH, 287:MAR73-32
STERN, M. - SEE ALCOTT, L.M.
STERN, R. THE BOOKS IN FRED HAMP-
TON'S APARTMENT.*
   W. PRITCHARD, 364:AUG/SEP74-147
STERN, R. OTHER MEN'S DAUGHTERS.*
   M. PRICE, 676(YR):SUMMER74-554

STERN, R.A.M. GEORGE HOWE.
  R. BANHAM, 617(TLS):19SEP75-1046
  P. GOLDBERGER, 441:6SEP75-17
STERN, R.M. POWER.
  M. LEVIN, 441:10AUG75-14
STERN, S. WITH THE WEATHERMEN.
  S. BROWNMILLER, 441:15JUN75-6
STERN, S.M. HISPANO-ARABIC STROPHIC
POETRY. (L.P. HARVEY, ED)
  J.F.P. HOPKINS, 617(TLS):22AUG75-
  948
STERNBACH, L. CĀṆAKYA-NĪTI-TEXT-
TRADITION (CĀṆAKYA-NĪTI-ŚĀKHĀ-SAṂ-
PRADĀYAḤ). (VOL 2, PTS 1-3)
  R.N. DANDEKAR, 318(JAOS):JAN-MAR73-
  110
  L. ROCHER, 318(JAOS):JUL-SEP73-373
STERNBERGER, D. HEINRICH HEINE UND
DIE ABSCHAFFUNG DER SÜNDE.*
  J.L.S., 191(ELN):SEP73(SUPP)-138
STERNLICHT, S. JOHN WEBSTER'S IM-
AGERY & THE WEBSTER CANON [TO-
GETHER WITH] DE SILVA, D. WIT &
THE MORAL SENSE IN "VOLPONE" & THE
MAJOR COMEDIES.*
  R. BERRY, 677:VOL4-283
STETTINIUS, E.R., JR. THE DIARIES
OF EDWARD R. STETTINIUS, JR., 1943-
1946. (T.M. CAMPBELL & G.C. HER-
RING, EDS)
  K.G.M. ROSS, 617(TLS):5DEC75-1441
STEVEN, S. OPERATION SPLINTER FAC-
TOR.
  W. SHAWCROSS, 453:23JAN75-41
STEVENS, C. THE GRAVY TRAIN HIT.
  N. CALLENDAR, 441:26JAN75-24
STEVENS, G. STANFIELD.
  A.P. PROSS, 150(DR):WINTER73/74-
  762
  G. WOODCOCK, 102(CANL):WINTER74-95
STEVENS, J. MEDIEVAL ROMANCE.
  R.M. WILSON, 175:AUTUMN73-112
STEVENS, J. - SEE TAYLOR, M.
STEVENS, J.R. - SEE KENNEDY, D.
STEVENS, M. V. SACKVILLE-WEST.*
  I. LINDBLAD, 597(SN):VOL45#1-184
STEVENS, P. BREAD CRUSTS & GLASS.*
  M. ANDRÉ, 529(QQ):AUTUMN73-471
STEVENS, P. A FEW MYTHS.
  R. GUSTAFSON, 102(CANL):WINTER73-
  105
STEVENS, P.B. GOD SAVE IRELAND!
  R. EDER, 441:13APR75-28
STEVENS, P.T. - SEE EURIPIDES
STEVENS, R. & R. WELFARE MEDICINE
IN AMERICA.
  H. SCHWARTZ, 441:26MAR75-35
STEVENS, S.K., D.H. KENT & A.L.
LEONARD - SEE BOUQUET, H.
STEVENSON, A. TRAVELLING BEHIND
GLASS.* CORRESPONDENCES.*
  R. GARFITT, 364(OCT/NOV74-116
STEVENSON, B. STEVENSON'S BOOK OF
QUOTATIONS.
  V. GLENDINNING, 617(TLS):30MAY75-
  604
STEVENSON, C.H. THE SPANISH LANGU-
AGE TODAY.*
  J. GONZÁLEZ MUELA, 240(HR):SUMMER
  73-593
  R.G. KEIGHTLEY, 297(JL):FEB73-204
STEVENSON, J. & R. QUINAULT, EDS.
POPULAR PROTEST & PUBLIC ORDER.
  G. RUDÉ, 617(TLS):26SEP75-1086

STEVENSON, L. THE PRE-RAPHAELITE
POETS.*
  J.R. REED, 301(JEGP):JAN74-133
  H.E. ROBERTS, 637(VS):SEP73-122
  D. SONSTROEM, 191(ELN):DEC73-148
STEVENSON, MRS. S. THE RITES OF
TWICE BORN.
  J.C. SIKORA, 293(JAST):MAY73-535
STEVENSON, W.H. - SEE BLAKE, W.
STEWART, A.T.Q. THE PAGODA WAR.
  B.D. GOOCH, 637(VS):DEC73-217
  O.B. POLLAK, 293(JAST):AUG73-740
STEWART, D.O. BY A STROKE OF LUCK.
  C. TOMKINS, 441:14DEC75-5
  617(TLS):19DEC75-1507
STEWART, D.O. MR. & MRS. HADDOCK
ABROAD.
  C. TOMKINS, 441:14DEC75-5
STEWART, G. DICKENS & THE TRIALS
OF IMAGINATION.
  P. COLLINS, 617(TLS):19SEP75-1066
STEWART, G. & G. RAWLYK. A PEOPLE
HIGHLY FAVOURED OF GOD.*
  S.W. JACKMAN, 432(NEQ):MAR73-131
STEWART, G.R. AMERICAN PLACE-NAMES.*
  W. ZELINSKY, 215(GL):VOL13#1-43
STEWART, H., ED & TRANS. A CHIME
OF WINDBELLS.
  S. MATSUI, 302:JAN73-173
STEWART, J. CURVING ROAD.
  J.D. O'HARA, 441:26OCT75-50
STEWART, J.I.M. THE GAUDY.*
  442(NY):28APR75-138
STEWART, J.I.M. YOUNG PATTULLO.
  L. PULVERTAFT, 617(TLS):6JUN75-617
STEWART, K. COOKING & EATING.
  S. CAMPBELL, 617(TLS):12DEC75-1491
STEWART, P.D. INNOCENT GENTILLET E
LA SUA POLEMICA ANTIMACHIAVELLICA.
  C.W., 275(IQ):SPRING74-105
STEWART, R. BETHUNE.*
  G. WOODCOCK, 102(CANL):WINTER74-95
STEWART, R. THE POLITICS OF PROTEC-
TION.
  J.M. PREST, 447(N&Q):AUG73-319
STEWART, S. BOOK COLLECTING.
  R.D. PRATT, 503:SPRING73-48
STEWART, Z. - SEE NOCK, A.D.
STICCA, S. THE LATIN PASSION PLAY.*
  P.J. ARCHAMBAULT, 593:FALL74-284
STICCA, S., ED. THE MEDIEVAL DRAMA.
  N. DENNY, 382(MAE):1974/1-84
STIEBER, Z. ZARYS GRAMATYKI PORÓW-
NAWCZEJ JĘZYKÓW SŁOWIAŃSKICH: FONO-
LOGIA.
  E. STANKIEWICZ, 279:VOL16-179
STIEHM, L., ED. ADALBERT STIFTER.
  L. BODI, 67:MAY74-120
STIER, H.E. DIE GESCHICHTLICHE
BEDEUTUNG DES HELLENENNAMENS.
  É. WILL, 555:VOL47FASC2-323
STIGLER, R. & OTHERS. THE OLD WORLD.
  N. HAMMOND, 617(TLS):15AUG75-918
STILLINGER, J. THE HOODWINKING OF
MADELINE & OTHER ESSAYS ON KEATS'S
POEMS.*
  A. RODWAY, 541(RES):NOV73-504
  G. THOMAS, 175:AUTUMN72-113
  H. VIEBROCK, 38:BAND91HEFT4-537
STILLINGER, J. THE TEXTS OF KEATS'S
POEMS.
  M. ALLOTT, 617(TLS):12DEC75-1498
STILLMAN, B. - SEE DOSTOEVSKY, A.

STILLMAN, P.G.G. ROMAN RULERS & REBELS.
  H. HAYDEN, 124:MAR73-366
STIMSON, G. & B. WEBB. GOING TO SEE THE DOCTOR.
  617(TLS):8AUG75-906
STIRLING, B. THE SHAKESPEARE SONNET ORDER.
  J. HASLER, 179(ES):FEB73-70
STIRLING, J. BUILDINGS & PROJECTS.
  M. GIROUARD, 617(TLS):29AUG75-964
STITES, F.N. PRIVATE INTEREST & PUBLIC GAIN.
  A.S. KONEFSKY, 432(NEQ):JUN73-327
STOBIE, M.R. FREDERICK PHILIP GROVE.
  S.E. MC MULLIN, 102(CANL):SPRING 74-107
  J.G. MOSS, 150(DR):SUMMER73-369
  D.O. SPETTIGUE, 529(QQ):AUTUMN73-465
STOCCHI, M.P. - SEE VERONESE, A.
STOCK, B. MYTH & SCIENCE IN THE TWELFTH CENTURY.
  K. FOSTER, 402(MLR):JUL74-605
  P.G. WALSH, 382(MAE):1974/2-163
STOCK, F. KOTZEBUE IM LITERARISCHEN LEBEN DER GOETHEZEIT.
  A. BEHRMANN, 52:BAND8HEFT3-342
STOCK, R.D. SAMUEL JOHNSON & NEO-CLASSICAL DRAMATIC THEORY.
  P.K. ALKON, 401(MLQ):JUN74-205
  L. DAMROSCH, JR., 301(JEGP):JUL74-442
  E. HNATKO, 141:SUMMER74-262
STOCKBRIDGE, G. HORDES OF THE RED BUTCHER.
  N. CALLENDAR, 441:23FEB75-40
STOCKHAUSEN, K. STOCKHAUSEN. (J. COTT, ED)
  P. GRIFFITHS, 415:SEP74-752
STOCKS, B. TROUBLE ON HELICON.
  D.M. DAY, 157:WINTER73-89
STOCKTON, D. CICERO.*
  A.W. LINTOTT, 123:MAR74-66
  S.E. SMETHURST, 124:SEP-OCT73-54
STOCKWELL, R.P. & R.K.S. MACAULAY, EDS. LINGUISTIC CHANGE & GENERATIVE THEORY.
  W.L. BALLARD, 35(AS):FALL-WINTER 71-254
  F.W. HOUSEHOLDER, 350:SEP74-555
STOCKWIN, J.A.A. JAPAN.
  E.J. HOBSBAWM, 453:17JUL75-27
  R. STORRY, 617(TLS):12SEP75-1027
STOEBKE, R. DIE VERHALTNISWÖRTER IN DEN OSTSEEFINNISCHEN SPRACHEN.
  G.F. MEIER, 682(ZPSK):BAND26HEFT 3/4-451
STOIAN, I. ÉTUDES HISTRIENNES.
  J. ANDRÉ, 555:VOL47FASC2-368
STOJANOVIĆ, S. BETWEEN IDEALS & REALITY.*
  F.B. SINGLETON, 575(SEER):JUL74-478
STOKER, B. THE ANNOTATED DRACULA. (L. WOLF, ED)
  P. ADAMS, 61:AUG75-88
  C. LEHMANN-HAUPT, 441:16JUL75-41
  G. WARD & R. STROZIER, 441:7DEC75-94
STOKER, B. THE BRAM STOKER BEDSIDE COMPANION.
  C. FRAYLING, 364:JUN/JUL74-103

STOKER, J.T. - SEE MOLIÈRE, J.B.P.
STOKES, A. THE IMAGE IN FORM.* (R. WOLLHEIM, ED)
  V.C. ALDRICH, 290(JAAC):FALL73-132
STOKES, H.S. THE LIFE & DEATH OF YUKIO MISHIMA.
  H. ISHIGURO, 453:11DEC75-48
  R. SCRUTON, 617(TLS):11APR75-388
STOKES, J. RESISTIBLE THEATRES.
  M.R. BOOTH, 637(VS):SEP73-110
  N. MARSHALL, 157:SPRING73-78
STOKES, M.C. ONE & MANY IN PRESOCRATIC PHILOSOPHY.*
  G.E.R. LLOYD, 303:VOL93-244
  R.K. SPRAGUE, 122:JUL74-237
STOKKE, O., ED. REPORTING AFRICA.
  R.G. WILLIS, 69:OCT73-360
STOLL, A. SCARRON ALS UBERSETZER QUEVEDOS.
  D. REICHARDT, 549(RLC):OCT-DEC73-634
STOLL, J.E. THE NOVELS OF D.H. LAWRENCE.
  N. ALFORD, 376:JAN73-159
  D.J. CAHILL, 219(GAR):WINTER73-588
  A.C. HEATH, 295:FEB74-698
STOLLER, R.J. THE TRANSSEXUAL EXPERIMENT.
  I. ROSEN, 617(TLS):18JUL75-796
STOLOFF, C. DYING TO SURVIVE.*
  J. SYLVESTER, 661:SUMMER73-109
STOLZ, F., A. DE BRUNNER & W. SCHMID. STORIA DELLA LINGUA LATINA.
  D.C. SWANSON, 121(CJ):OCT/NOV72-91
STONE, A. THE BANISHMENT.
  R. DRAKE, 396(MODA):SPRING74-221
STONE, D., JR. FRENCH HUMANIST TRAGEDY.
  A. LEVI, 617(TLS):10JAN75-27
STONE, D.D. NOVELISTS IN A CHANGING WORLD.*
  B.F. FISHER 4TH, 177(ELT):VOL16#3-234
  M. HARRIS, 72:BAND211HEFT1/3-128
  A.R. TINTNER, 594:FALL73-408
STONE, G. A LEGEND OF WOLF SONG.
  M. LEVIN, 441:18MAY75-50
STONE, G. THE SMALLEST SLAVONIC NATION.*
  L. NEWMAN, 574(SEEJ):FALL72-382
STONE, I. THE GREEK TREASURE.
  P. ANDREWS, 441:12OCT75-48
  H. MITGANG, 441:10OCT75-41
STONE, L., ED. THE UNIVERSITY IN SOCIETY.
  H. KEARNEY, 617(TLS):24OCT75-1267
  R. STORR, 99:DEC75/JAN76-62
  H. TREVOR-ROPER, 362:4DEC75-756
STONE, R. DOG SOLDIERS.*
  R. DAVIES, 617(TLS):30MAY75-585
  J. KLEIN, 31(ASCH):AUTUMN75-686
  D. MAY, 362:5JUN75-746
  R. SALE, 453:3APR75-9
STONE, R.H. REINHOLD NIEBUHR.
  W. GANGI, 613:SPRING73-150
STONE, R.K. MIDDLE ENGLISH PROSE STYLE.*
  S.S. HUSSEY, 447(N&Q):AUG73-302
STONES, E., WITH D. ANDERSON. EDUCATIONAL OBJECTIVES & THE TEACHING OF EDUCATIONAL PSYCHOLOGY.
  A-M. GOGUEL, 182:VOL26#3/4-80

STOPA, R. STRUCTURE OF BUSHMAN &
ITS TRACES IN INDO-EUROPEAN.
A.N. TUCKER, 69:JUL73-276
STOPPARD, T. ARTIST DESCENDING A
STAIRCASE [&] WHERE ARE THEY NOW.
A. RENDLE, 157:WINTER73-87
STORA, N. BURIAL CUSTOMS OF THE
SKOLT LAPPS.
R. VIRTANEN, 582(SFQ):MAR73-85
STORASKA, F. HOW TO SAY NO TO A
RAPIST - & SURVIVE.
A. BROYARD, 441:27FEB75-39
STOREY, A. BROTHERS KEEPERS.
N. HEPBURN, 362:6NOV75-622
J. MILLER, 617(TLS):31OCT75-1285
STOREY, C., ED. LA VIE DE SAINT
ALEXIS.
J.J. DUGGAN, 545(RPH):AUG73-134
STOREY, D. PASMORE.*
M. PRICE, 676(YR):SUMMER74-554
P.M. SPACKS, 249(HUDR):SUMMER74-
288
STOREY, E. A MAN IN WINTER.
A. CLUYSENAAR, 565:VOL14#2-62
STOREY, E. THE SOLITARY LANDSCAPE.
P. HORN, 617(TLS):19DEC75-1512
STORM, T. BRIEFE. (P. GOLDAMMER,
ED)
617(TLS):28FEB75-232
STORM, T. IMMENSEE. (J.M. RITCHIE,
ED)
E. MC INNES, 220(GL&L):JAN74-162
STORM, T. THEODOR STORM: SYLTER
NOVELLE/DER SCHIMMELREITER. (K.E.
LAAGE, ED)
E. MC INNES, 220(GL&L):JAN74-160
J.U. TERPSTRA, 433:JAN73-104
STORM, T. & P. HEYSE. THEODOR
STORM - PAUL HEYSE BRIEFWECHSEL.*
(VOLS 1&2) (C.A. BERND, ED)
L.W. KAHN, 222(GR):JAN73-58
J.U. TERPSTRA, 433:OCT73-418
STORM, T. & P. HEYSE. THEODOR
STORM - PAUL HEYSE BRIEFWECHSEL.
(VOL 3) (C.A. BERND, ED)
S.S. PRAWER, 617(TLS):11APR75-404
STORM, T. & E. SCHMIDT. THEODOR
STORM - ERICH SCHMIDT BRIEFWECHSEL.
(VOL 1) (K.E. LAAGE, ED)
C.A. BERND, 301(JEGP):JAN74-90
W.A. COUPE, 402(MLR):OCT74-931
A.F. GOESSL, 406:FALL74-310
STORZ, G. HEINRICH HEINES LYRISCHE
DICHTUNG.*
O.W. JOHNSTON, 221(GQ):NOV73-624
STOTT, W. DOCUMENTARY EXPRESSION &
THIRTIES AMERICA.*
J. RAEBURN, 651(WHR):SPRING74-188
A.E. STONE, 131(CL):FALL74-376
T. TANNER, 364:APR/MAY74-122
STOUT, N.R. THE ROYAL NAVY IN
AMERICA, 1760-1775.
I.D. GRUBER, 656(WMQ):JUL74-503
STOUT, R. A FAMILY AFFAIR.
N. CALLENDAR, 441:7SEP75-39
442(NY):13OCT75-179
STOVALL, F. THE FOREGROUND OF
"LEAVES OF GRASS."
J.J. RUBIN, 87(AL):NOV74-403
STOVE, D.C. PROBABILITY & HUME'S
INDUCTIVE SCEPTICISM.
I.M. FOWLIE, 518:MAY74-24
I. HINCKFUSS, 63:DEC74-269
[CONTINUED]

[CONTINUING]
D.W. LIVINGSTON, 319:JUL75-413
J. NOXON, 154:DEC73-735
STOW, J. A SURVEY OF LONDON.
W.G. ZEEVELD, 551(RENQ):SUMMER73-
217
STOY, R.H., ED. EVERYMAN'S ASTRON-
OMY.
617(TLS):14FEB75-177
STRABO. STRABON, "GEOGRAPHIE."
(VOL 7) (F. LASSERRE, ED & TRANS)
J.E. STAMBAUGH, 124:MAR73-357
STRACHEY, L. THE REALLY INTERESTING
QUESTION.
J. GLOVER, 565:VOL14#3-22
STRADA, V., ED. RUSSIA. (VOL 1)
I. DE MADARIAGA, 617(TLS):4JUL75-
716
STRAND, J. NOTES ON VALERIUS FLAC-
CUS' "ARGONAUTICA."*
J. ANDRÉ, 555:VOL47FASC1-164
STRAND, M. THE STORY OF OUR LIVES.*
F. MORAMARCO, 651(WHR):WINTER74-94
J.N. MORRIS, 249(HUDR):SPRING74-
117
P. RAMSEY, 569(SR):SPRING74-398
639(VQR):WINTER74-XIV
STRANG, B.M.H. A HISTORY OF ENG-
LISH.*
K.C. PHILLIPPS, 179(ES):APR72-184
STRANGE, A. ELECTRONIC MUSIC.*
P. GRIFFITHS, 415:DEC74-1048
H.S. HOWE, JR., 513:SPRING-SUMMER
73-249
STRASBURGER, H. HOMER UND DIE
GESCHICHTSSCHREIBUNG.
F.M. WASSERMANN, 124:MAY73-497
STRASSER, R. HERMAN GRIMM.
W.D. ROBSON-SCOTT, 402(MLR):OCT74-
932
STRATFORD, A.H. AIRPORTS & THE
ENVIRONMENT.
T.C. BARKER, 617(TLS):21MAR75-318
STRATFORD, J. THE ARTS COUNCIL COL-
LECTION OF MODERN LITERARY MANU-
SCRIPTS 1963-1972.*
A. BELL, 617(TLS):5SEP75-1002
STRATFORD, P., ED. STORIES FROM
QUÉBEC.
G. DAVIES, 198:SUMMER75-117
STRATFORD, P. - SEE GREENE, G.
STRATMAN, C.J. AMERICAN THEATRICAL
PERIODICALS, 1798-1967.
H. KOSOK, 447(N&Q):SEP73-353
STRATMAN, C.J., ED. BRITAIN'S
THEATRICAL PERIODICALS 1720-1967.
L-L. MARKER, 397(MD):JUN73-110
STRATMANN, G., ED. AUGUSTAN POETRY.
H.O., 430(NS):AUG73-450
I. SIMON, 556(RLV):1973/6-566
STRATMANN, R. DER EBENIST JEAN-
FRANÇOIS OEBEN.
P. THORNTON, 39:OCT73-314
STRAUMANN, H. WILLIAM FAULKNER.
G. VAN CROMPHOUT, 179(ES):APR72-
173
STRAUS, D. SHOWCASES.*
V. GLENDINNING, 617(TLS):9MAY75-
503
STRAUSS, C.N. EARTH BELOW, HEAVEN
ABOVE.
C. COPPOLA, 318(JAOS):JUL-SEP73-
394

STRAUSS, L.   XENOPHON'S SOCRATES.*
   T. IRWIN, 482(PHR):JUL74-409
   S. ROSEN, 124:MAY73-470
   C. SCHLAM, 399(MLJ):JAN-FEB74-62
STRAUSS, W.   THE COMPLETE ENGRAVINGS,
ETCHINGS & DRYPOINTS OF ALBRECHT
DÜRER.
   C. WHITE, 39:DEC73-518
STRAUSS, W.A.   DESCENT & RETURN.*
   G.L. BRUNS, 295:FEB74-407
   B. JUDEN, 208(FS):APR74-206
STRAUSS, W.L., ED.   THE COMPLETE
DRAWINGS OF ALBRECHT DÜRER.
   J. RUSSELL, 441:27JUL75-2
STRAVINSKY, T.   CATHERINE & IGOR
STRAVINSKY.*
   E.W. WHITE, 607:#104-41
STRAWSON, P.F.   INDIVIDUALS.
   J. CARGILE, 316:JUN73-320
STRAWSON, P.F.   LOGICO-LINGUISTIC
PAPERS.
   R. BLANCHÉ, 542:JUL-SEP73-375
   H. LAYCOCK, 529(QQ):SPRING73-131
STRAWSON, P.F.   SUBJECT & PREDICATE
IN LOGIC & GRAMMAR.
   P. GEACH, 617(TLS):28FEB75-215
STRAYER, J.R.   MEDIEVAL STATECRAFT
& THE PERSPECTIVES OF HISTORY.*
   W. ROTHWELL, 208(FS):JAN74-50
STRECH, H.   THEODOR FONTANE: DIE
SYNTHESE VON ALT UND NEU.*
   H. WETZEL, 564:MAR73-81
STREET, B.V.   THE SAVAGE IN LITERA-
TURE.
   P. KEATING, 617(TLS):8AUG75-899
STREET, J.   PLANTS FOR PERFORMANCE.
   C. SYKES, 617(TLS):7MAR75-258
STREETER, T.   THE ART OF THE JAPAN-
ESE KITE.
   C. HART, 617(TLS):7FEB75-136
STRELKA, J.   DIE GELENKTEN MUSEN.*
   L. HÖNNIGHAUSEN, 52:BAND8HEFT2-171
STRELKA, J.   VERGLEICHENDE LITERA-
TURKRITIK.*
   K. WEISSENBERGER, 133:1973/2-176
STRELKA, J.P., ED.   ANAGOGIC QUALI-
TIES OF LITERATURE.
   P. HERNADI, 221(GQ):NOV73-606
STRELKA, J.P., ED.   PATTERNS OF LIT-
ERARY STYLE.
   R.A. SAYCE, 307:#2-110
   H. WAGENER, 399(MLJ):MAR73-141
STREVENS, P.   SEAFARING.   (BK 1)
   J.R. EWER, 399(MLJ):SEP-OCT74-298
STRICK, P., ED.   ANTIGRAV.
   T.A. SHIPPEY, 617(TLS):23MAY75-554
STRIK-STRIKFELDT, W.   AGAINST STALIN
& HITLER.
   G.P. HOLMAN, JR., 396(MODA):SUMMER
   74-330
STRINDBERG, A.   GETTING MARRIED.
   (M. SANDBACH, ED & TRANS)
   J.W., 114(CHIR):VOL25#3-120
STRINDBERG, A.   PRE-INFERNO PLAYS.
A DREAM PLAY & FOUR CHAMBER PLAYS.
   (W. JOHNSON, TRANS OF BOTH)
   M. MATTSSON, 563(SS):FALL74-444
STRITTMATTER, E.   DIE BLAUE NACHTI-
GALL ODER DER ANFANG VON ETWAS.
   O. REINCKE, 654(WB):3/1973-143
STRITTMATTER, E.   DER WUNDERTÄTER.
   (VOL 2)
   F. WAGNER, 654(WB):10/1973-142

STROH, W.   DIE RÖMISCHE LIEBESELEGIE
ALS WERBENDE DICHTUNG.
   G.N. SANDY, 487:SPRING73-88
STROHSCHNEIDER-KOHRS, I.   LITERAR-
ISCHE STRUKTUR UND GESCHICHTLICHER
WANDEL.
   K. MÜLLER-VOLLMER, 133:1973/1-71
STRÖMBÄCK, D., ED.   LEADING FOLKLOR-
ISTS OF THE NORTH.*
   R.A. REUSS, 292(JAF):JUL-SEP73-298
STRONG, R.   SPLENDOR AT COURT.*
   A.B. KERNAN, 676(YR):SPRING74-434
STRONG, R.   VAN DYCK: CHARLES I ON
HORSEBACK.*
   M. TOYNBEE, 90:NOV73-753
STROUD, D.   GEORGE DANCE.*
   C. MUSGRAVE, 90:JAN73-48
STROUD, R.S.   DRAKON'S LAW ON HOMI-
CIDE.*
   A.L. BOEGEHOLD, 122:APR73-152
STROUT, C.   THE NEW HEAVENS & NEW
EARTH.
   639(VQR):SPRING74-XLVI
"STRUCTURES SOCIALES ET DÉMOCRATIE
ÉCONOMIQUE."
   D. VICTOROFF, 542:JAN-MAR73-100
STRUEVER, N.S.   THE LANGUAGE OF HIS-
TORY IN THE RENAISSANCE.*
   S. KINSNER, 125:JUN74-331
   D.J. WILCOX, 551(RENQ):SPRING73-43
STRUGATSKI, A. & B.   HARD TO BE A
GOD.
   E. MORGAN, 617(TLS):23MAY75-555
STRUNK, O.   ESSAYS ON MUSIC IN THE
WESTERN WORLD.
   C. ROSEN, 453:6FEB75-32
STRUVE, G.   RUSSIAN LITERATURE UNDER
LENIN & STALIN, 1917-1953.*
   T.J. BINYON, 402(MLR):JAN74-235
   R. EKMANIS, 125:OCT73-79
   295:FEB74-378
STRUVE, N., ED.   ANTHOLOGIE DE LA
POÉSIE RUSSE.
   R. BARTHÉLEMY-VOGELS, 556(RLV):
   1973/2-185
STRUVE, W.   ELITES AGAINST DEMOCRA-
CY.
   639(VQR):SPRING74-LI
STUART, C. - SEE LORD REITH
STUART, D.   THE OTHER HAND.
   J. PARISI, 491:JUL75-219
STUART, F.   REDEMPTION.   BLACK
LIST - SECTION H.
   V. GLENDINNING, 617(TLS):9MAY75-
   501
STUART, J.   IKONS.
   R. CORMACK, 617(TLS):26DEC75-1536
STUART, J.   LAND OF THE FOX.
   M. LEVIN, 441:23FEB75-38
STUART, R.C.   THE COLLECTIVE FARM IN
SOVIET AGRICULTURE.*
   J.R. MILLAR, 104:SUMMER73-278
STUBBERUD, T.   DET LITTERAERE UTT-
RYKK.
   M. PAHUUS, 290(JAAC):WINTER74-223
STUBBINGS, F.H.   PREHISTORIC GREECE.
   J. BOARDMAN, 123:NOV74-303
"STÜCKE GEGEN DEN FASCHISMUS."
   C.L. HART-NIBBRIG, 657(WW):MAY/JUN
   73-216
STUCKEY, W.J.   CAROLINE GORDON.
   J.E. BROWN, 577(SHR):FALL73-452

STUCKY-SCHÜRER, M. DIE PASSIONSTEP-
PICHE VON SAN MARCO IN VENEDIG.
  L. VON WILCKENS, 683:BAND36HEFT
  2/3-214
"STUDI CLASICE." (VOL 14)
  J. ANDRÉ, 555:VOL47FASC2-379
"STUDI DI GRAMMATICA ITALIANA."
  (VOL 1)
  D.D., 275(IQ):SUMMER73-117
"STUDIER I MODERN SPRÅKVETENSKAP."
  J.R. SIMON, 189(EA):APR-JUN73-219
"STUDIES IN CHILD PSYCHOANALYSIS:
PURE & APPLIED."
  M. JAMES, 617(TLS):18JUL75-806
STUEWER, R.H., ED. HISTORICAL &
PHILOSOPHICAL PERSPECTIVES OF
SCIENCE.*
  R.N. GIERE, 84:SEP73-282
  N. KOERTGE, 482(PHR):APR73-239
STUHLMANN, G. - SEE NIN, A.
STUIP, R.E.V. LA CHASTELAINE DE
VERGI.
  R.T. PICKENS, 207(FR):MAR73-819
STULTZ, N.M. AFRIKANER POLITICS IN
SOUTH AFRICA 1934-1948.
  J. LEWIN, 617(TLS):17OCT75-1243
"STURLUNGA SAGA."* (VOL 1) (J.H.
MC GREW, TRANS)
  O.J. ZITZELSBERGER, 222(GR):JAN73-
  82
STURM, H., ED. THE "LIBRO DE LOS
BUENOS PROVERBIOS."
  J. GULSOY, 545(RPH):FEB74-441
  H. SIEBER, 400(MLN):MAR73-405
  B.B. THOMPSON, 546(RR):MAR74-151
  F.M. WALTMAN, 238:SEP73-730
STURROCK, J. THE FRENCH NEW NOVEL.
  D. MC WILLIAMS, 295:FEB74-439
STURROCK, J. THE WILFUL LADY.
  T.J. BINYON, 617(TLS):26DEC75-1544
STURSBERG, P. DIEFENBAKER.
  J.L. GRANATSTEIN, 99:DEC75/JAN76-
  32
STYAN, J.L. CHEKHOV IN PERFORMANCE.*
  J. FLUDAS, 223:SEP73-333
  T.G. WINNER, 550(RUSR):JUL73-326
STYLOW, A.U. LIBERTAS UND LIBERALI-
TAS.
  R. SEAGER, 313:VOL63-256
  S.E. SMETHURST, 487:SUMMER73-210
STYRON, R. THIEVES' AFTERNOON.
  P. RAMSEY, 569(SR):SPRING74-404
SUARÈS, G. ANDRÉ MALRAUX.
  D.A.N. JONES, 362:13FEB75-221
  E. WEEKS, 61:FEB75-120
SUBRAHMANYAM, P.S. DRAVIDIAN VERB
MORPHOLOGY.
  H.F. SCHIFFMAN, 318(JAOS):JUL-SEP
  73-386
SUCH, P. RIVERRUN.*
  D. BARBOUR, 102(CANL):SUMMER74-82
  M. ENGEL, 606(TAMR):OCT74-84
  M.W. WRIGHT, 150(DR):WINTER73/74-
  775
SUCH, P. SOUNDPRINTS.
  102(CANL):SUMMER73-127
SUCKLING, J. THE WORKS OF SIR JOHN
SUCKLING: THE NON-DRAMATIC WORKS.*
  (T. CLAYTON, ED) THE WORKS OF SIR
JOHN SUCKLING: THE PLAYS.* (L.A.
BEAURLINE, ED)
  M. CRUM, 541(RES):NOV73-490
  R. ELLRODT, 189(EA):OCT-DEC73-479
  M.R. WOODHEAD, 447(N&Q):DEC73-474

SUCKSMITH, H.P. THE NARRATIVE ART
OF CHARLES DICKENS.
  L. LANE, JR., 594:SPRING73-125
  C.W. THOMSEN, 38:BAND91HEFT4-545
SUDERMANN, H. LITAUISCHE GESCHICH-
TEN. (B.J. KENWORTHY, ED)
  J. OSBORNE, 220(GL&L):APR74-272
SUFFIAN BIN HASHIM, T.S.M. AN IN-
TRODUCTION TO THE CONSTITUTION OF
MALAYSIA.
  W.R. ROFF, 293(JAST):MAY73-558
SUGAR, P.F. & D.W. TREADGOLD - SEE
ROTHSCHILD, J.
DE SUGNY, O., ED. COLLOQUE COMMÉM-
ORATIF DU QUATRIÈME CENTENAIRE DE
LA NAISSANCE D'HONORÉ D'URFÉ.
  R.G. MC GILLIVRAY, 546(RR):JAN74-
  59
SUHL, B. JEAN-PAUL SARTRE.*
  C. FRANÇOIS, 207(FR):MAR73-844
SUKENICK, R. 98.6.
  T. LE CLAIR, 441:18MAY75-6
SUKENICK, R. OUT.*
  L.S. BERGMANN, 114(CHIR):VOL25#3-9
  R. FEDERMAN, 473(PR):1/1974-137
ŠUKIN, A.N. RUSSKIJ JAZYK V DIALO-
GAX.
  J.R. HOLBROOK, 574(SEEJ):SUMMER73-
  247
SULEIMAN, E.N. POLITICS, POWER, &
BUREAUCRACY IN FRANCE.
  S. ENGLUND, 453:15MAY75-33
SULEIMAN, S. - SEE NIZAN, P.
SULLIVAN, M. THE ARTS OF CHINA.
  639(VQR):SPRING74-LX
SULLIVAN, M. THE MEETING OF EASTERN
& WESTERN ART.*
  R.H. LEARY, 60:SEP-OCT74-78
SULLIVAN, M. WATCH HOW YOU GO.
  F.W. DILLISTONE, 617(TLS):5DEC75-
  1465
SULLIVAN, M. - SEE CIBBER, C.
SULLIVAN, M.R. BROWNING'S VOICES
IN "THE RING & THE BOOK."*
  J.C. MAXWELL, 447(N&Q):JUL73-269
SULLIVAN, W. DEATH BY MELANCHOLY.*
  J.M. COX, 569(SR):WINTER74-163
  I. MALIN, 219(GAR):SPRING73-128
SULLOWAY, A.G. GERARD MANLEY HOP-
KINS & THE VICTORIAN TEMPER.*
  J. BUMP, 651(WHR):WINTER74-81
  J. FERNS, 529(QQ):SUMMER73-318
  J.H. FOX, 405(MP):MAY74-462
  W.S. JOHNSON, 191(ELN):MAR74-230
  J.D. JUMP, 541(RES):NOV73-512
  A. POLLARD, 148:SUMMER73-191
  M. SMITH, 577(SHR):FALL73-435
SULTANA, D. SAMUEL TAYLOR COLERIDGE
IN MALTA & ITALY.
  H.B. DE GROOT, 179(ES):APR73-182
SÜLTEMEYER, I. - SEE ROTH, J.
SUMAROKOV, A.P. SELECTED TRAGEDIES
OF A.P. SUMAROKOV.* (R. & R. FOR-
TUNE, TRANS)
  R. ŠILBAJORIS, 574(SEEJ):SPRING72-
  91
SÜMER, F., A.E. UYSAL & W.S. WALKER,
EDS & TRANS. THE BOOK OF DEDE
KORKUT.
  W.H. JANSEN, 292(JAF):OCT-DEC73-
  393
"SUMERIAN ART."
  J.V. CANBY, 318(JAOS):JUL-SEP73-
  402

SUMMERS, H. HOW THEY CHOSE THE
DEAD.
  W. PEDEN, 569(SR):FALL74-712
SUMMERS, J.H. THE HEIRS OF DONNE &
JONSON.*
  A. SACKTON, 141:WINTER72-89
SUMMERS, M. THE SKATING PARTY.
  M. BAXTER, 99:DEC75/JAN76-48
SUMMERS, N. A PROSPECT OF SOUTHWELL.
  617(TLS):7MAR75-261
SUMMERS, V., COMP. THE TEMPEST.
  M. LAURIE, 415:NOV74-948
SUMMERSON, J., ED. CONCERNING
ARCHITECTURE.*
  G.R. COLLINS, 54:SEP73-472
SUMMERSON, J. VICTORIAN ARCHITEC-
TURE.*
  P.F. NORTON, 576:MAR73-75
SUMPTION, J. PILGRIMAGE.
  G. CONSTABLE, 617(TLS):22AUG75-949
SUNDARAM, P.K. ADVAITA EPISTEMOLOGY
WITH SPECIAL REFERENCE TO IṢṬASID-
DHI.
  T.E. JACKSON, 485(PE&W):JUL73-406
SUNDBY, B. FRONT-SHIFTED "ING" &
"ED" GROUPS IN PRESENT-DAY ENG-
LISH.*
  R.W. ZANDVOORT, 179(ES):FEB72-85
SUPER, R.H. THE TIME-SPIRIT OF
MATTHEW ARNOLD.*
  J-C. RO JAHN, 38:BAND91HEFT2-262
SUPER, R.H. - SEE ARNOLD, M.
SUPERANSKAJA, A.V. UDARENIE V ZAIM-
STVOVANNYX SLOVAX V SOVREMENNOM
RUSSKOM JAZYKE.
  D.B. JOHNSON, 353:15FEB73-107
SUPPES, P. A PROBABILISTIC THEORY
OF CAUSALITY.*
  M. BUNGE, 84:DEC73-409
"A SUPPLEMENT TO THE OXFORD ENGLISH
DICTIONARY."* (VOL 1) (R.W. BURCH-
FIELD, ED)
  D.C. BAKER, 191(ELN):DEC73-156
  S. POTTER, 541(RES):NOV73-461
  T. PYLES, 35(AS):FALL-WINTER71-237
SUPRUN, A.E. LEKCII PO JAZYKOZNAN-
IJU.
  J. VEYRENC, 353:1NOV73-119
SURTEES, V. CHARLOTTE CANNING.
  J. GRIGG, 362:28AUG75-284
  E. STOKES, 617(TLS):29AUG75-967
SURTEES, V. THE PAINTINGS & DRAW-
INGS OF DANTE GABRIEL ROSSETTI
(1828-1882).*
  M. GREENE, 219(GAR):WINTER73-601
  B. NICOLSON, 90:FEB73-73
SURYANARAYANA SASTRI, S.S. - SEE
DHARMARĀJA ADHVARIN
SUSANN, J. ONCE IS NOT ENOUGH.
  A. ROBERTSON, 648:OCT73-63
"'SUSANNAH,' AN ALLITERATIVE POEM OF
THE FOURTEENTH CENTURY."* (A.
MISKIMIN, ED)
  F. DIEKSTRA, 433:JUL73-313
SUSSEX, R.T. HENRI BOSCO, POET-
NOVELIST.
  205(FMLS):JUL73-310
SUTCLIFFE, A. THE AUTUMN OF CENTRAL
PARIS.
  N. MILLER, 576:MAR73-67
SUTHERLAND, A. GYPSIES.
  P. ANDREWS, 441:9NOV75-29

SUTHERLAND, F. THE STYLE OF INNO-
CENCE.
  D. CAMERON, 102(CANL):AUTUMN74-104
  S.L. DRAGLAND, 529(QQ):WINTER73-
  653
SUTHERLAND, J. DANIEL DEFOE.*
  G. BULLOUGH, 175:SUMMER72-70
  M. SCHONHORN, 541(RES):FEB73-87
SUTHERLAND, J. ESSAYS, CONTROVER-
SIES & POEMS. (M. WADDINGTON, ED)
  P. MORLEY, 102(CANL):SPRING74-103
SUTHERLAND, J., ED. THE OXFORD BOOK
OF LITERARY ANECDOTES.
  C. LEHMANN-HAUPT, 441:22JUL75-29
  F. MUIR, 617(TLS):20JUN75-688
  A. QUINTON, 362:24JUL75-123
  442(NY):22SEP75-131
SUTHERLAND, M. THE FLEDGLING.
  S. MILLAR, 617(TLS):17JAN75-49
SUTSCHKOW, B. HISTORISCHE SCHICK-
SALE DES REALISMUS.
  H. KÄHLER, 654(WB):8/1973-176
SUTTON, D. - SEE FRY, R.
SUTTON, G.M. PORTRAITS OF MEXICAN
BIRDS.
  R. CARAS, 441:7DEC75-92
SUTTON, W. AMERICAN FREE VERSE.*
  V. STRANDBERG, 27(AL):NOV74-404
SUTTON, W.A. THE ROAD TO WINESBURG.*
  D.D. ANDERSON, 295:FEB74-530
SUZUKI, D.T. SENGAI, THE ZEN MASTER.
  M. MEDLEY, 39:JUL73-66
ŠVEDOVA, N.J., ED. GRAMMATIKA SOV-
REMENNOGO RUSSKOGO LITERATURNOGO
JAZYKA.
  A. ISAČENKO, 350:JUN74-383
SVENDSEN, C. NOTATER OM KAREN
BLIXEN.
  E. BREDSDORFF, 617(TLS):24OCT75-
  1269
SVIRIN, A.N. EARLY RUSSIAN JEWELRY
WORK, XI-XVII CENTURY.
  M. CHAMOT, 39:DEC73-514
SWADESH, F.L. LOS PRIMEROS POBLA-
DORES.
  W. GARD, 584(SWR):SUMMER74-V
SWADESH, M. THE ORIGIN & DIVERSIFI-
CATION OF LANGUAGE. (J. SHERZER,
ED)
  S.C. GUDSCHINSKY, 269(IJAL):JAN73-
  52
SWADOS, H. CELEBRATION.
  A. BROYARD, 441:5MAR75-39
  T. LE CLAIR, 441:9MAR75-4
  D. WAKEFIELD, 61:APR75-91
  442(NY):21APR75-144
SWAIN, J.O. JUAN MARÍN - CHILEAN.*
  B.A. SHAW, 399(MLJ):JAN-FEB73-74
SWAINSON, D., ED. OLIVER MOWAT'S
ONTARIO.
  G.N. EMERY, 529(QQ):WINTER73-628
SWALES, M. ARTHUR SCHNITZLER.*
  L. BODI, 67:MAY74-122
  205(FMLS):JUL73-310
SWALES, M. - SEE SCHNITZLER, A.
SWALLOW, C. THE SICK MAN OF EUROPE.
  M.S. ANDERSON, 575(SEER):JUL74-466
SWAN, A.J. RUSSIAN MUSIC & ITS
SOURCES IN CHANT & FOLK-SONG.*
  A.B. MC MILLIN, 575(SEER):OCT74-
  618
SWAN, B.F. THE SPREAD OF PRINTING:
THE CARIBBEAN AREA.*
  K.E. INGRAM, 354:MAR73-72

360

SWANN, D. SWANN'S WAY OUT.
D.A.N. JONES, 617(TLS):11APR75-389
SWANSTON, H.F.G. IDEAS OF ORDER.
617(TLS):22AUG75-954
SWARTHOUT, G. THE SHOOTIST.
P. CAMPBELL, 617(TLS):9MAY75-501
M. LASKI, 362:5JUN75-748
M. LEVIN, 441:2FEB75-12
SWARTZ, H.M. & M. - SEE DISRAELI, B.
SWARTZ, M.L. - SEE IBN AL-JAWZI
SWEARER, D.K., ED. SECRETS OF THE
LOTUS.
L.O. GOMEZ, 485(PE&W):JAN-APR73-
253
SWEDENBERG, H.T., JR., ED. ENGLAND
IN THE RESTORATION & EARLY EIGHT-
EENTH CENTURY.*
P. ROGERS, 541(RES):AUG73-338
SWEDENBERG, H.T., JR. - SEE DRYDEN,
J.
SWEENEY, A. MALAY SHADOW PUPPETS.
W.P. MALM, 293(JAST):AUG73-745
SWEENEY, J.J. AFRICAN SCULPTURE.
D.J. CROWLEY, 2:AUTUMN73-84
SWEENEY, L. INFINITY IN THE PRE-
SOCRATICS.
T.H., 543:MAR73-547
SWEET, H. A HANDBOOK OF PHONETICS.
I. LEHISTE, 269(IJAL):APR73-123
SWERLING, A. STRINDBERG'S IMPACT IN
FRANCE 1920-1960.*
B.L. KNAPP, 546(RR):MAY74-235
SWIFT, J. THE WRITINGS OF JONATHAN
SWIFT. (R.A. GREENBERG & W.B.
PIPER, EDS)
566:AUTUMN73-34
SWIGG, R. LAWRENCE, HARDY & AMERI-
CAN LITERATURE.*
R. BEARDS, 295:FEB74-450
E. DELAVENAY, 189(EA):JUL-SEP73-
322
T. ROGERS, 175:SPRING73-33
K. WIDMER, 594:WINTER73-547
SWINBURNE, A.C. A CHOICE OF SWIN-
BURNE'S VERSE. (R. NYE, ED)
K. MC SWEENEY, 529(QQ):AUTUMN73-
482
SWINBURNE, A.C. SWINBURNE AS CRIT-
IC.* (C.K. HYDER, ED)
K. MC SWEENEY, 529(QQ):AUTUMN73-
482
L. ORMOND, 677:VOL4-331
SWINBURNE, R. AN INTRODUCTION TO
CONFIRMATION THEORY.
R. BLANCHE, 542:OCT-DEC73-479
SWINDELL, L. SCREWBALL.
R. BRANTLEY, 441:30NOV75-55
SWINDLER, W.F. COURT & CONSTITUTION
IN THE TWENTIETH CENTURY.
639(VQR):SUMMER74-C
SWINGLEHURST, E. THE ROMANTIC JOUR-
NEY.
A. DROYARD, 441:19SEP75-41
SWINTON, G. SCULPTURE OF THE
ESKIMO.*
M. WILLIAMSON, 96:FEB/MAR73-86
G. WOODCOCK, 102(CANL):SPRING73-97
SYED, A.H. CHINA & PAKISTAN.
H. TINKER, 617(TLS):31OCT75-1288
SYFRET, R. - SEE MILTON, J.
SYKES, A. HAROLD PINTER.
S.H. GALE, 295:FEB74-746

SYKES, C. EVELYN WAUGH.
C. LEHMANN-HAUPT, 441:19NOV75-33
A. QUINTON, 362:9OCT75-483
P. STANSKY, 441:30NOV75-2
A. WILSON, 617(TLS):30CT75-1116
SYKES, S.W. & J.P. CLAYTON, EDS.
CHRIST, FAITH & HISTORY.
483:APR73-199
SYLVESTER, A.J. LIFE WITH LLOYD
GEORGE. (C. CROSS, ED)
A. BOYLE, 362:12JUN75-788
A. CRAIG, 99:DEC75/JAN76-61
J. GRIGG, 617(TLS):30MAY75-582
SYLVESTER, D. INTERVIEWS WITH FRAN-
CIS BACON.
W. FEAVER, 362:15MAY75-652
S. SPENDER, 617(TLS):21MAR75-290
SYLVESTER, R.S., ED. ST. THOMAS
MORE.*
H.W. DONNER, 597(SN):VOL45#2-448
W.L. GODSHALK, 551(RENQ):SUMMER73-
210
L. MILES, 677:VOL4-252
R.W.Z., 179(ES):FEB73-98
SYME, R. EMPERORS & BIOGRAPHY.*
A.J. GRAHAM, 313:VOL63-259
SYMEONOGLOU, S. KADMEIA I.
E. BIELEFELD, 182:VOL26#1/2-46
"LA SYMÉTRIE COMME PRINCIPE HEURIS-
TIQUE DANS LES DIFFÉRENTES SCI-
ENCES."
R. BLANCHE, 542:JUL-SEP73-375
SYMINGTON, R.T.K. BRECHT UND SHAKE-
SPEARE.*
C.L. HART-NIBBRIG, 657(WW):MAY/JUN
73-216
SYMMACHUS. SYMMAQUE, LETTRES. (VOL
1, BKS 1-11) (J.P. CALLU, ED &
TRANS)
M.P. CUNNINGHAM, 124:MAR74-294
SYMONDS, J. LETTERS FROM ENGLAND.
A. BARNES, 617(TLS):18JUL75-793
N. HEPBURN, 362:21AUG75-254
SYMONDS, J. PROPHECY & THE PARA-
SITES.
J. DECK, 441:16NOV75-78
SYMONS, J. THE PLAYERS & THE GAME.
K. MC SWEENEY, 529(QQ):SPRING73-
152
SYMONS, J. THE THIRTIES.
D.A.N. JONES, 617(TLS):31OCT75-
1300
SYMONS, J. A THREE PIPE PROBLEM.
N. CALLENDAR, 441:20JUL75-26
P. FRENCH, 617(TLS):21FEB75-184
M. LASKI, 362:20MAR75-380
442(NY):2JUN75-112
SYNAN, E.A. - SEE GODFREY OF SAINT
VICTOR
SYNGE, J.M. LETTERS TO MOLLY.* (A.
SADDLEMYER, ED)
R. HOGAN, 295:APR74-1031
N.H. MACKENZIE, 529(QQ):SPRING73-
127
SYRETT, H.C. - SEE HAMILTON, A.
SZABLOWSKI, J., ED. THE FLEMISH
TAPESTRIES AT WAWEL CASTLE IN CRA-
COW.
G.W. DIGBY, 39:OCT73-318
M.B. MC NAMEE, 377:NOV74-177
SZABO, A. ANFÄNGE DER GRIECHISCHEN
MATHEMATIK.
H. SINACEUR, 542:JUL-SEP73-375

SZABÓ, L. SELKUP TEXTS WITH PHON-
ETIC INTRODUCTION & VOCABULARY.
  G.F. MEIER, 682(ZPSK):BAND26HEFT
  1/2-208
SZABOLCSI, H. MAGYARORSZÁGI BÚTOR-
MÜVESZET A 18-19. SZÁZAD FORDULÓJÁN.
  P. THORNTON, 39:OCT73-314
SZAMUELY, T. THE RUSSIAN TRADITION.
  H. SHUKMAN, 617(TLS):8AUG75-900
SZANTO, G.H. NARRATIVE CONSCIOUS-
NESS.
  P. BROOKS, 207(FR):APR73-1031
  S. SEARS, 149:SEP74-270
  S. SPENCER, 659:SPRING75-249
  295:FEB74-496
SZARKOWSKI, J. LOOKING AT PHOTO-
GRAPHS.
  C.W. MILLARD, 249(HUDR):WINTER
  74/75-579
SZASZ, T. CEREMONIAL CHEMISTRY.
  G.M. CARSTAIRS, 617(TLS):25JUL75-
  831
SZASZ, T.S. THE AGE OF MADNESS.
  C.M. HOLLOWAY, 617(TLS):4JUL75-742
SZCZUCKI, L., ED. WOKÓŁ DZIEJÓW I
TRADYCJI ARIANIZMU.
  W. WEINTRAUB, 551(RENQ):WINTER73-
  476
VON SZELISKI, J. TRAGEDY & FEAR.*
  295:FEB74-509
SZEMERÉNYI, O. EINFÜHRUNG IN DIE
VERGLEICHENDE SPRACHWISSENSCHAFT.
  F.O. LINDEMAN, 260(IF):BAND78-201
  W. MEID, 343:BAND16HEFT1-41
  C.V.J. RUSS, 402(MLR):APR74-359
SZEMERÉNYI, O. RICHTUNGEN DER MOD-
ERNEN SPRACHWISSENSCHAFT. (VOL 1)
  R. GODEL, 343:BAND16HEFT1-87
SZEMLER, G.J. THE PRIESTS OF THE
ROMAN REPUBLIC.
  J.E.A. CRAKE, 487:AUTUMN73-312
  G.W. HOUSTON, 124:SEP-OCT73-51
  T.P. WISEMAN, 313:VOL63-266
SZINAI, M. & L. SZÜCS - SEE BETHLEN,
I.
SZLIFERSZTEJNOWA, S. KATEGORIA
STRONY (Z HISTORII MYŚLI LINGWIST-
YCZNEJ).
  K. HELTBERG, 353:1OCT73-124
SZÖVÉRFFY, J. WELTLICHE DICHTUNGEN
DES LATEINISCHEN MITTELALTERS.
  (VOL 1)
  H. HOMANN, 221(GQ):MAY73-450
SZULC, T. CZECHOSLOVAKIA SINCE
WORLD WAR II.
  M.P. MABEY, 104:SPRING74-165
SZULC, T. THE ENERGY CRISIS.
  G. BARRACLOUGH, 453:23JAN75-20

TAAFFE, J.G. ABRAHAM COWLEY.
  D.G. DONOVAN, 577(SHR):FALL73-440
TABER, G.M. PATTERNS & PROSPECTS OF
COMMON MARKET TRADE.
  D. ROBERTSON, 617(TLS):7FEB75-144
TABORI, P. CRIME & THE OCCULT.
  617(TLS):7MAR75-261
TACCOLA - SEE UNDER DI JACOPO, M.
TACITUS. THE ANNALS OF TACITUS.
  (BKS 1-6, VOL 1) (F.R.D. GOODYEAR,
  ED)
  T.D. BARNES, 124:MAR74-311
  G.B.A. FLETCHER, 313:VOL63-294

TACITUS. P. CORNELI TACITI "HISTOR-
IARUM." (BK 2) (I. SCHINZEL, ED)
  R.H. MARTIN, 123:NOV74-209
TACITUS. P. CORNELIUS TACITUS, "DIE
HISTORIEN." (VOL 3, BK 3) (H.
HEUBNER, ED)
  K. WELLESLEY, 313:VOL63-296
TADIÉ, J-Y. PROUST ET LE ROMAN.
  M. RAIMOND, 535(RHL):NOV-DEC73-
  1110
TAEGER, B. ZAHLENSYMBOLIK BEI
HRABAN, BEI HINCMAR - UND IM
"HELIAND"?
  P.W. TAX, 589:APR74-383
TAGLIAFERRI, A. STRUTTURE SOCIALI E
SISTEMI ECONOMICI PRECAPITALISTICI.
  H.C. KRUEGER, 589:OCT74-760
DE LA TAILLE, J. JACQUES DE LA
TAILLE'S "LA MANIÈRE."* (P. HAN,
ED)
  M. GLATIGNY, 535(RHL):NOV-DEC73-
  1054
"THE TAIN." (T. KINSELLA, TRANS)
  J.M. PURCELL, 134(CP):FALL73-86
TAKAHASHI, S. TRADITIONAL WOOD-
BLOCK PRINTS OF JAPAN.
  C. DRESSER, 592:MAR73-145
TAKEUTI, G. & W.M. ZARING. INTRO-
DUCTION TO AXIOMATIC SET THEORY.
  F.R. DRAKE, 316:SEP73-530
"TAL COMO ES."
  D.R. MC KAY, 399(MLJ):SEP-OCT74-
  294
TALADOIRE, B-A. TÉRENCE.
  J. PERRET, 555:VOL47FASC1-153
TALBERT, R.J.A. TIMOLEON & THE RE-
VIVAL OF GREEK SICILY 344-317 B.C.
  H.D. WESTLAKE, 617(TLS):7MAR75-254
TALBOTT, S. - SEE KHRUSHCHEV, N.S.
TALEV, I. SOME PROBLEMS OF THE
SECOND SOUTH SLAVIC INFLUENCE IN
RUSSIA.
  H.G. LUNT, 574(SEEJ):WINTER73-488
TALL, D. EIGHT COLORS WIDE.
  R. GARFITT, 364:FEB/MAR75-111
TALOUMIS, G. HOUSE PLANTS FOR FIVE
EXPOSURES.
  J. CANADAY, 441:13APR75-16
TAMAS, G., ED. AUFSÄTZE ÜBER LOGIK.
  R. BLANCHÉ, 542:JUL-SEP73-378
TANAKA, I. SHUBUN TO SESSHU.
  C. DRESSER, 592:MAR73-145
TANAKA, K. NIPPON KAIZO, RON.
  R.L. BROWN, 270:VOL23#4-91
TANAKA, S. THE TEA CEREMONY.*
  D. STORRY, 285(JAPQ):APR-JUN74-208
TÁNASE, E. & A-M. CHOIX DE POÉSIES
FRANÇAISES EN ORTHOGRAPHIE PHONÉT-
IQUE.
  G.F. MEIER, 682(ZPSK):BAND26HEFT
  3/4-453
TANDON, P. BEYOND PUNJAB: 1937-1960.
  N.G. BARRIER, 293(JAST):NOV72-200
TANGE, K. KATSURA.
  J. RAWSON, 463:AUTUMN73-316
  S. SITWELL, 39:AUG73-148
TANGE, K. NIPPON KENCHIKU.
  270:VOL23#2-41
TANNENBAUM, F. THE FUTURE OF DEMO-
CRACY IN LATIN AMERICA. (J. MAIER
& R.W. WEATHERHEAD, EDS)
  P. WINN, 441:9MAR75-6
TANNER, A.C. A MORMON MOTHER.
  D. BITTON, 651(WHR):AUTUMN74-398

TANNER, T. CITY OF WORDS.*
  T. COLSON, 268:JAN75-71
  J.L. GREEN, 295:FEB74-497
  M. PÜTZ, 430(NS):MAR73-171
TANOUS, P. & P. RUBINSTEIN. THE
PETRODOLLAR TAKEOVER.
  M. LEVIN, 441:27JUL75-11
TANSELLE, G.T. GUIDE TO THE STUDY
OF UNITED STATES IMPRINTS.*
  P. SNOW, 402(MLR):JAN74-161
  A. WILLIAM, 503:WINTER73-195
TANZER, M. THE ENERGY CRISIS.
  G. BARRACLOUGH, 453:7AUG75-23
T'AO CH'IEN. THE POETRY OF T'AO
CH'IEN. (J.R. HIGHTOWER, TRANS)
  L.M. FUSEK, 318(JAOS):JAN-MAR73-82
TAPIÉ, V-L. THE RISE & FALL OF THE
HABSBURG MONARCHY.
  A.J. BANNAN, 613:SPRING73-151
  T. SPIRA, 104:WINTER74-606
TARABOUKINE, N. LE DERNIER TABLEAU.
(A.B. NAKOV, ED)
  J. MILNER, 592:MAR73-143
TARASSUK, L. ANTIQUE EUROPEAN &
AMERICAN FIREARMS AT THE HERMITAGE
MUSEUM, LENINGRAD.
  J. HAYWARD, 90:MAR73-182
TARG, W. INDECENT PLEASURES.
  R. KLUGER, 441:9NOV75-16
TARGET, G.W. BERNADETTE.
  J. HORGAN, 362:8MAY75-620
TARGET, G.W. STRIKE THE STRIKERS.
  R. FOSTER, 617(TLS):31OCT75-1285
TARLING, N. BRITAIN, THE BROOKES &
BRUNEI.
  I.D. BLACK, 293(JAST):NOV72-214
  C. CRISSWELL, 302:JAN73-182
TARN, N. LYRICS FOR THE BRIDE OF
GOD.
  H. VENDLER, 441:7SEP75-6
TARNAWSKI, W. CONRAD.
  B. KOCÓWNA, 575(SEER):OCT74-630
TAROT, R. HUGO VON HOFMANNSTHAL.*
  R.C. NORTON, 221(GQ):JAN73-101
TARRANT, R., ED & TRANS. GREEK &
LATIN LYRIC POETRY IN TRANSLATION.
  D.A. CAMPBELL, 487:WINTER73-420
TART, C.T., ED. ALTERED STATES OF
CONSCIOUSNESS.
  J. BRUNO, 98:MAY73-418
TASCH, P.A. THE DRAMATIC COBBLER.*
  M.S. AUBURN, 405(MP):FEB74-337
TASHJIAN, D. SKYSCRAPER PRIMITIVES.
  J.R. MELLOW, 441:29JUN75-6
TASHJIAN, D. & A. MEMORIALS FOR
CHILDREN OF CHANGE.*
  M.G. WILLIAMS, 432(NEQ):DEC74-612
TASKER, J. - SEE LEAVIS, F.R.
DE TASSIS, J. & C. DE VILLAMEDIANA.
OBRAS. (J.M. ROZAS, ED)
  J.W. DÍAZ, 241:JAN73-82
TASZYCKI, W. ONOMASTYKA I HISTORIA
JĘZYKA POLSKIEGO.
  M.Z. BROOKS, 353:15FEB73-125
TATE, A. MEMOIRS & OPINIONS.
  G. CORE, 441:12OCT75-4
TATE, D.J.M. THE MAKING OF MODERN
SOUTH-EAST ASIA. (VOL 1)
  J.R.W. SMAIL, 293(JAST):AUG73-729
TATE, J. ABSENCES.
  N. LAVERS, 134(CP):SPRING73-88
TATE, R.B. - SEE DEL PULGAR, F.
TATE, R.B. & I.R. MACPHERSON - SEE
MANUEL, J.

TATEO, F. QUESTIONI DI POETICA
DANTESCA.
  M. MARTI, 228(GSLI):VOL150FASC470/
  471-411
  C.W., 275(IQ):FALL-WINTER73(VOL17
  #66)-61
TATEO, F. UMANESIMO ETICO DI GIO-
VANNI PONTANO.
  C.W., 275(IQ):SUMMER73-107
TATHAM, M.A.A. ENGLISH STRUCTURE
MANIPULATION DRILLS.
  K. OLTMANN, 430(NS):JUL73-386
TAUBE, M., COMP. TIBETISCHE HAND-
SCHRIFTEN UND BLOCKDRUCKE.
  J. FILLIOZAT, 182:VOL26#13/14-451
TAULI, V. INTRODUCTION TO A THEORY
OF LANGUAGE PLANNING.*
  G. MEINHOLD, 682(ZPSK):BAND26HEFT
  6-725
TAVE, S.M. SOME WORDS OF JANE AUS-
TEN.
  W.E. ANDERSON, 445(NCF):MAR74-492
  D. MANSELL, 301(JEGP):OCT74-556
  K.L. MOLER, 502(PRS):WINTER73/74-
  366
  M. TAYLOR, 268:JAN75-88
  639(VQR):SUMMER74-LXXIV
TAX, P. WORT, SINNBILD, ZAHL IM
TRISTANROMAN. (2ND ED)
  J.S. GROSECLOSE, 406:SPRING74-98
  W.A. TRINDADE, 382(MAE):1974/2-173
TAX, P.W. - SEE NOTKER DER DEUTSCHE
TAYLER, I. BLAKE'S ILLUSTRATIONS
TO THE POEMS OF GRAY.*
  I.H. CHAYES, 591(SIR):SPRING74-155
  D. HIRST, 541(RES):FEB73-95
  M.D. PALEY, 141:WINTER72-93
  G. THOMAS, 175:AUTUMN72-113
  A. WATSON, 54:SEP73-465
TAYLOR, A. ICE AGE.
  E. BALDERSTON, 581:MAR74-86
TAYLOR, A.J., ED. THE STANDARD OF
LIVING IN BRITAIN IN THE INDUSTRIAL
REVOLUTION.
  H. PERKIN, 617(TLS):4JUL75-737
TAYLOR, A.J.P. THE SECOND WORLD
WAR.
  H. THOMAS, 362:24APR75-537
TAYLOR, A.J.P. - SEE LLOYD GEORGE,
D. & F. STEVENSON
TAYLOR, B. CONSTABLE.*
  P. CONRAD, 617(TLS):15AUG75-911
TAYLOR, B. STUBBS.
  J. HAYES, 90:APR73-256
TAYLOR, C. THE CAMBRIDGESHIRE LAND-
SCAPE.*
  D. KNOWLES, 111:FEB74-81
TAYLOR, D.S., WITH B.B. HOOVER - SEE
CHATTERTON, T.
TAYLOR, E. MRS. PALFREY AT THE
CLAREMONT.
  J.C. FIELD, 556(RLV):1973/1-95
TAYLOR, E.R. WELCOME EUMENIDES.*
  R. MAZZOCCO, 453:3APR75-20
TAYLOR, G. PLACE OF THE DAWN.
  M. LEVIN, 441:26OCT75-55
TAYLOR, G.R. HOW TO AVOID THE FUT-
URE.
  A. CHALFONT, 617(TLS):19DEC75-1523
TAYLOR, I., P. WALTON & J. YOUNG,
EDS. CRITICAL CRIMINOLOGY.
  T. MORRIS, 617(TLS):22AUG75-940

TAYLOR, J. SUPERMINDS.
 J. BELOFF, 362:1MAY75-587
 J. COHEN, 617(TLS):25JUL75-846
 M. GARDNER, 453:30OCT75-14
TAYLOR, J.L. A PORTUGUESE-ENGLISH
DICTIONARY. (REV)
 C. STAVROU, 240(HR):AUTUMN73-712
TAYLOR, J.R. THE SECOND WAVE.*
 W. HABICHT, 72:BAND211HEFT1/3-168
TAYLOR, J.R. - SEE GREENE, G.
TAYLOR, M. THE SCOTS COLLEGE IN
SPAIN.
 D.R. WAGG, 86(BHS):JUL73-298
TAYLOR, M. MARY TAYLOR, FRIEND OF
CHARLOTTE BRONTË. (J. STEVENS, ED)
 E.A. KNIES, 445(NCF):DEC73-359
TAYLOR, M.A. BOTTOM, THOU ART
TRANSLATED.
 J.B. FORT, 189(EA):OCT-DEC73-467
 A. GERSTNER-HIRZEL, 182:VOL26#19-
 678
 W. HABICHT, 72:BAND211HEFT1/3-119
TAYLOR, R. FREEDOM, ANARCHY, & THE
LAW.
 R.E. SANTONI, 484(PPR):JUN74-616
TAYLOR, R. WITH HEART & MIND.
 C.F. POOLE, 150(DR):SUMMER73-381
TAYLOR, R.B. CHAVEZ & THE FARM
WORKERS.
 F. CARNEY, 453:13NOV75-39
 P. SHABECOFF, 441:11JUL75-33
TAYLOR, R.R. THE WORD IN STONE.
 S. BAYLEY, 617(TLS):12DEC75-1492
TAYLOR, S.W. & E. LUCIE-SMITH, EDS.
FRENCH POETRY TODAY.*
 M.A. CAWS, 207(FR):MAY73-1253
TAYLOR, W.D. AMÉLIE RIVES.
 639(VQR):WINTER74-XXVI
TEAL, J. & M. THE SARGASSO SEA.
 442(NY):18AUG75-84
"TEATRO LATINOAMERICANO DE AGITA-
CIÓN."
 G. WOODYARD, 238:DEC73-1125
TEDESCHI, T.R. - SEE UNDER RADINI
TEDESCHI, T.
TEDLOCK, D., ED & TRANS. FINDING
THE CENTER.
 L.J. EVERS, 502(PRS):SPRING73-79
 S. NEWMAN, 269(IJAL):OCT73-261
TEEPLE, G., ED. CAPITALISM & THE
NATIONAL QUESTION IN CANADA.*
 H.G. THORBURN, 529(QQ):AUTUMN73-
 455
TEETS, B.E. & H.E. GERBER, COMPS.
JOSEPH CONRAD.*
 D. LODGE, 354:JUN73-166
 G. MORGAN, 255(HAB):SUMMER73-229
 T.C. MOSER, 136:VOL5#1-56
 N. SHERRY, 637(VS):MAR74-336
 295:FEB74-564
TEEUW, A. MODERN INDONESIAN LITERA-
TURE.
 J.M. ECHOLS, 318(JAOS):JUL-SEP73-
 391
TEICH, M. & R. YOUNG, EDS. CHANGING
PERSPECTIVES IN THE HISTORY OF
SCIENCE.*
 E. MC MULLIN, 111:FEB74-76
TEICHMAN, J. THE MIND & THE SOUL.*
 R. MONTAGUE, 518:OCT74-30
TEILHARD DE CHARDIN, P. TOWARD THE
FUTURE.
 A. DYSON, 617(TLS):25APR75-464
TELLER, W. - SEE WHITMAN, W.

TELLEZ, A. SABATÉ. FACERÍAS.
 P. PRESTON, 617(TLS):24JAN75-74
TELLINI, G. LA TELA DI FUMO.
 M.C., 228(GSLI):VOL150FASC469-157
TEMKIN, O. GALENISM.*
 J. SCARBOROUGH, 319:OCT75-521
 J. STAROBINSKI, 453:26JUN75-15
TEMPERLEY, H. BRITISH ANTISLAVERY,
1833-1870.
 C.D. RICE, 637(VS):DEC73-233
TEMPIO, D. OPERE SCELTE. (C. MUSU-
MARRA, ED)
 E. BIGI, 228(GSLI):VOL150FASC469-
 149
TEMPLETON, C. THE KIDNAPPING OF
THE PRESIDENT.
 N. CALLENDAR, 441:20JUL75-26
TEMPORINI, H., ED. AUFSTIEG UND
NIEDERGANG DER RÖMISCHEN WELT.
(VOL 1)
 A.E. ASTIN, 313:VOL63-247
"TENDÊNCIAS DA LITERATURA CONTEM-
PORÂNEA."
 G.G. CURTIS, 238:MAR73-181
TENDRYAKOV, V. THREE, SEVEN, ACE.
 639(VQR):SUMMER74-LXXXII
TENNANT, E. THE LAST OF THE COUNTRY
HOUSE MURDERS.
 S. CLARK, 617(TLS):31JAN75-102
 S. MAITLAND, 362:13FEB75-222
TENNANT, P.E. THÉOPHILE GAUTIER.
 J. RICHARDSON, 617(TLS):28MAR75-
 342
TENNYSON, A. A VARIORUM EDITION OF
TENNYSON'S "IDYLLS OF THE KING."
(J. PFORDRESHER, ED)
 U.C. KNOEPFLMACHER, 637(VS):MAR74-
 344
TENNYSON, C. & H. DYSON. THE TENNY-
SONS.
 A. BELL, 617(TLS):14MAR75-274
TENNYSON, E. THE LETTERS OF EMILY
LADY TENNYSON. (J.O. HOGE, ED)
 A. BELL, 617(TLS):14MAR75-274
TENZIN GYATSO - SEE UNDER GYATSO, T.
TERKEL, S. WORKING.*
 R. COLES, 639(VQR):AUTUMN74-622
 T. COTTLE, 617(TLS):19DEC75-1523
 N. MILLS, 676(YR):SUMMER74-566
 R. WEAVER, 606(TAMR):MAR75-101
TERNES, A., ED. ANTS, INDIANS, &
LITTLE DINOSAURS.
 D.C. ANDERSON, 441:23NOV75-28
 A. BROYARD, 441:28AUG75-37
TERNI, E.A. - SEE UNDER ARAGONE
TERNI, E.
TERRILL, R. FACES OF CHINA.
 617(TLS):21MAR75-319
TERRILL, R. FLOWERS ON AN IRON
TREE.
 J.A. & J.L. COHEN, 441:5OCT75-5
TERRUWE, A.A. & C.W. BAARS. LOVING
& CURING THE NEUROTIC.
 D.W. CARROLL, 613:WINTER73-550
TERRY, A. A LITERARY HISTORY OF
SPAIN: CATALAN LITERATURE.
 J.M. SOBRÉ, 131(CL):FALL74-358
TERRY, A. ANTONIO MACHADA: "CAMPOS
DE CASTILLA."
 E. RODGERS, 402(MLR):JUL74-683
TERRY, M. COUPLINGS & GROUPINGS.
 S. TOTH, 109:SPRING/SUMMER74-127

TERTULLIAN. ADVERSUS MARCIONEM.
(E. EVANS, ED & TRANS)
R.D. SIDER, 124:MAY73-493
TERTULLIAN. TERTULLIANI "ADVERSUS
MARCIONEM." (C. MORESCHINI, ED)
J. ANDRÉ, 555:VOL47FASC1-170
E. EVANS, 123:MAR74-165
TERTULLIAN. TERTULLIEN, "LA TOIL-
ETTE DES FEMMES." (M. TURCAN, ED)
J. ANDRÉ, 555:VOL47FASC1-171
TERTZ, A. GOLOS IZ KHORA.
L.M. TIKOS, 268:JUL75-168
"LA TERZA ROMA."
S. KOSTOF, 576:OCT73-239
TESAURO, P. - SEE DE BERCEO, G.
TESDORPF, I-M. DIE AUSEINANDERSET-
ZUNG MATTHEW ARNOLDS MIT HEINRICH
HEINE.
C.R. OWEN, 400(MLN):APR73-632
J.L.S., 191(ELN):SEP73(SUPP)-138
TESSARI, R. LA COMMEDIA DELL'ARTE
NEL SEICENTO.
C.R., 275(IQ):FALL-WINTER73(VOL17
#66)-67
TETEL, M. MARGUERITE DE NAVARRE'S
"HEPTAMERON."*
B. BEAULIEU, 255:FALL73-320
TETEL, M. RABELAIS ET L'ITALIE.
P.E. BONDANELLA, 276:SPRING73-97
TEUNISSEN, J.J. & E.J. HINZ, EDS.
A KEY INTO THE LANGUAGE OF AMERICA.
R. VAN DER BEETS, 165:WINTER75-337
TEUTEBERG, N.J. & G. WIEGELMANN. DER
WANDEL DER NAHRUNGSGEWOHNHEITEN
UNTER DEM EINFLUSS DER INDUSTRIAL-
ISIERUNG.
E. ETTLINGER, 203:SPRING73-83
TEUTSCHMANN, J. PETAR HEKTOROVIĆ
(1487-1572) UND SEIN "RIBANJE I
RIBARSKO PRIGOVARANJE."
A. KADIĆ, 574(SEEJ):FALL72-378
THACKERAY, W.M. A SHABBY GENTEEL
STORY.
G.P. LANDOW, 454:SPRING74-269
THACKRAY, A. JOHN DALTON.
L.G. WILSON, 637(VS):SEP73-114
THADEN, E.C. RUSSIA SINCE 1801.*
M. KATZ, 104:SUMMER73-263
THAKER, J.P., ED. LAGHU-PRABANDHA-
SAÑGRAHA.
R. ROCHER, 318(JAOS):JUL-SEP73-382
VAN THAL, H., ED. THE PRIME MINIS-
TERS.* (VOL 1)
S. KOSS, 617(TLS):16MAY75-528
VAN THAL, H., ED. THE PRIME MINIS-
TERS. (VOL 2)
J. GRIGG, 362:22MAY75-684
S. KOSS, 617(TLS):16MAY75-528
VAN THAL, H. - SEE COLLINS, W.
THALE, M. - SEE PLACE, F.
THALMANN, M. THE LITERARY SIGN
LANGUAGE OF GERMAN ROMANTICISM.
L. DIECKMANN, 131(CL):WINTER74-94
K. KROEBER, 290(JAAC):FALL73-133
THALMANN, M. ROMANTIKER ALS POETO-
LOGEN.*
L.J. RIPPLEY, 400(MLN):APR73-626
THATCHER, D.S. NIETZSCHE IN ENG-
LAND, 1890-1914.*
G.B., 502(PRS):SPRING73-91
T. GIBBONS, 541(RES):AUG73-363
C. KOELB, 405(MP):AUG73-101

THAYNE, E.L. UNTIL ANOTHER DAY FOR
BUTTERFLIES.
F. MORAMARCO, 651(WHR):WINTER74-91
"THEATER IN DER ZEITENWENDE."
K. PFÜTZNER, 654(WB):5/1973-173
"LE THÉÂTRE, 1971." (PT 1)
B.L. KNAPP, 207(FR):OCT72-236
THEBERGE, J.D., ED. SOVIET SEAPOWER
IN THE CARIBBEAN.
R.W. HERRICK, 550(RUSR):APR73-217
THEMISTIUS. THEMISTII ORATIONES
QUAE SUPERSUNT. (VOL 2) (G. DOWNEY
& A.F. NORMAN, EDS)
P. CHANTRAINE, 555:VOL47FASC1-140
G. DAGRON, 303:VOL93-237
G.O. ROWE, 124:MAY73-467
THEOCRITUS. SELECT POEMS. (K.J.
DOVER, ED)
E.K. BORTHWICK, 303:VOL93-230
G. GIANGRANDE, 123:MAR74-29
THÉODORIDÈS, J. STENDHAL DU CÔTE DE
LA SCIENCE.
C.F. COATES, 207(FR):APR73-1015
J.S.P., 191(ELN):SEP73(SUPP)-101
THEODOULOU, C. GREECE & THE ENTENTE
AUGUST 1, 1914 - SEPTEMBER 25, 1916.
E.G. HELMREICH, 104:SPRING74-159
THEOPHRASTUS. THE CHARACTER SKET-
CHES.* (W. ANDERSON, ED & TRANS)
J.J. BUCHANAN, 124:NOV72-170
THEOPHRASTUS. DE IGNE.* (V. COU-
TANT, ED & TRANS)
J. OWENS, 124:MAY73-468
THÉRIAULT, Y. ASHINI. N'TSUK.
H. COWAN, 102(CANL):WINTER74-125
THÉRIAULT, Y. LE DERNIER HAVRE.
CUL DE SAC.
R. SUTHERLAND, 102(CANL):WINTER73-
114
THERNSTROM, S. THE OTHER BOSTON-
IANS.
R.M. JOHNSON, 432(NEQ):JUN74-333
THEROUX, J. SAINT JACK.*
639(VQR):WINTER74-VIII
THEROUX, P. THE BLACK HOUSE.*
D. DURRANT, 364:FEB/MAR75-135
R. SALE, 249(HUDR):WINTER74/75-628
THEROUX, P. THE GREAT RAILWAY
BAZAAR.
R. BLYTHE, 362:4DEC75-754
A. BROYARD, 441:20AUG75-37
R. TOWERS, 441:24AUG75-1
R.E.M. WHITAKER, 442(NY):29DEC75-
53
THEROUX, P. V.S. NAIPAUL.*
E. GLOVER, 565:VOL14#2-36
THEROUX, P. SINNING WITH ANNIE.*
M. MASON, 617(TLS):14MAR75-269
J. MELLORS, 362:22MAY75-685
THERRIEN, V. LA RÉVOLUTION DE
GASTON BACHELARD EN CRITIQUE LIT-
TÉRAIRE.*
C.A. HACKETT, 208(FS):APR74-233
THÉVENOT, E. LE BEAUNOIS GALLO-
ROMAIN.
E.M. WIGHTMAN, 313:VOL63-285
THIBAULT, P. SAVOIR ET POUVOIR.
L. PAQUET, 154:SEP73-552
E. WINANCE, 319:APR75-262
THIEL, E. & G. ROHR, EDS. LIBRETTI.
A.H. KING, 182:VOL26#9-300
VAN THIEL, H. DER ESELSROMAN.*
(VOL 1)
P.G. WALSH, 123:NOV74-215

VAN THIEL, H. DER ESELSROMAN.*
(VOL 2)
J. ANDRÉ, 555:VOL47FASC1-168
C. SCHLAM, 124:MAY73-481
P.G. WALSH, 123:NOV74-215
VAN THIEL, H. MITTELLATEINISCHE
TEXTE.
J.J. KEANEY, 124:MAR74-306
VAN THIEL, H. PETRON.*
R. BECK, 487:SPRING73-94
THIEME, P. KLEINE SCHRIFTEN.
J.W. DE JONG, 318(JAOS):JAN-MAR73-
109
THIHER, A. CÉLINE.*
C. KRANCE, 405(MP):MAY74-464
THIRION, A. RÉVOLUTIONNAIRES SANS
RÉVOLUTION.
M. BERTRAND, 188(ECR):SUMMER73-166
THIRSK, J. & J.P. COOPER, EDS.
SEVENTEENTH-CENTURY ECONOMIC DOCU-
MENTS.
J.S. KEPLER, 481(PQ):JUL73-373
THODY, P. ALDOUS HUXLEY.
P. VITOUX, 402(MLR):APR74-392
THODY, P. SARTRE.
F. BUSI, 207(FR):DEC72-425
H•F., 543:DEC72-368
THOMAS OF ERFURT. GRAMMATICA SPECU-
LATIVA. (G.L. BURSILL-HALL, ED &
TRANS)
M.W. BLOOMFIELD, 589:JAN74-102
W•F. BOLTON, 297(JL):SEP73-365
P•H. SALUS, 320(CJL):SPRING74-86
THOMAS, A. BLOWN FIGURES.
M. TAYLOR, 198:SUMMER75-113
THOMAS, A. HOPKINS THE JESUIT.*
G.A.M. JANSSENS, 179(ES):DEC72-569
THOMAS, A. MUNCHMEYER [&] PROSPERO
ON THE ISLAND.
H. ROSENGARTEN, 102(CANL):WINTER
73-111
THOMAS, A. SONGS MY MOTHER TAUGHT
ME.*
G. WOODCOCK, 102(CANL):SPRING74-96
THOMAS, A.G. GREAT BOOKS & BOOK
COLLECTORS.
A. HOBSON, 617(TLS):8AUG75-904
THOMAS, A.V. DICTIONNAIRE DES
DIFFICULTÉS DE LA LANGUE FRANÇAISE.
C. SANDERS, 208(FS):APR74-237
THOMAS, C. THE MANAWAKA WORLD OF
MARGARET LAURENCE.
M. ROSS, 99:OCT75-39
THOMAS, C. OUR NATURE - OUR VOICES.
M.J. EDWARDS, 102(CANL):AUTUMN74-
96
THOMAS, D. CARDIGAN.
P. ADAMS, 61:APR75-100
J. CLIVE, 231:DEC75-96
M. EDELMAN, 441:30MAR75-3
THOMAS, D. OEUVRES. (M. NATHAN &
D. ROCHE, EDS)
A•R. TELLIER, 189(EA):APR-JUN73-
238
THOMAS, D. THE POEMS. (D. JONES,
ED)
A•R. TELLIER, 189(EA):OCT-DEC73-
488
THOMAS, D. DYLAN THOMAS: EARLY
PROSE WRITINGS. (W. DAVIES, ED)
A. YOUNG, 148:SUMMER72-188
THOMAS, D.M. LOVE & OTHER DEATHS.
A. MACLEAN, 617(TLS):1AUG75-866

THOMAS, E. COLLECTED POEMS.
W.A. SUTTON, 598(SOR):SUMMER75-691
THOMAS, E. LOUISE MICHEL, OU LA
VELLÉDA DE L'ANARCHIE.
B. BRAUDE, 207(FR):OCT72-176
THOMAS, G. ISSELS.
H. MILLER, 362:31JUL75-154
617(TLS):31OCT75-1313
THOMAS, G. MASK OF ANUBIS.
G. TYLER, 157:AUTUMN73-75
THOMAS, H. DATELINE: WHITE HOUSE.
R. REEVES, 441:30NOV75-20
THOMAS, H. GOYA: THE THIRD OF MAY,
1808.*
T. CROMBIE, 39:MAR73-318
E. YOUNG, 90:NOV73-753
THOMAS, H. TRISTAN LE DÉPOSSÉDÉ.
A. FABRE-LUCE, 98:OCT73-959
THOMAS, J. THE NORTH BRITISH RAIL-
WAY. (VOL 2)
617(TLS):4APR75-380
THOMAS, J.C. CHASIN' THE TRANE.
G. GIDDINS, 441:10AUG75-16
M. WATKINS, 441:28JUN75-25
THOMAS, J. THE THEORY & PRACTICE
OF CREOLE GRAMMAR.*
J. NICHOLS, 545(RPH):MAY74-532
THOMAS, J.M.C. & OTHERS. CONTES,
PROVERBES, DEVINETTES OU ÉNIGMES,
CHANTS ET PRIÈRES NGBAKA-MA'BO
(RÉPUBLIQUE CENTRAFRICAINE).
J. KNAPPERT, 69:APR73-168
THOMAS, J.O. - SEE UNDER ORAM
THOMAS, J.
THOMAS, K. RELIGION & THE DECLINE
OF MAGIC.
R.H. ROBBINS, 551(RENQ):SPRING73-
70
W. STARK, 613:SPRING73-143
THOMAS, L. THE COMIC SPIRIT IN
NINETEENTH-CENTURY GERMANY.
C•P. MAGILL, 220(GL&L):APR74-268
THOMAS, L. STAND UP VIRGIN SOLDIERS.
J. MELLORS, 362:9OCT75-485
THOMAS, L.H. THE RENAISSANCE OF
CANADIAN HISTORY.
R. COOK, 99:APR/MAY75-13
THOMAS, L-V. ANTHROPOLOGIE DE LA
MORT.
C. RICKS, 617(TLS):18JUL75-790
THOMAS, M.H. - SEE SEWALL, S.
THOMAS, N. HANDLUNGSSTRUKTUR UND
DOMINANTE MOTIVIK IM DEUTSCHEN
PROSAROMAN DES 15. UND FRÜHEN 16.
JAHRHUNDERTS.
J. SCHMIDT, 680(ZDP):BAND92HEFT3-
463
THOMAS, P.D.G. BRITISH POLITICS &
THE STAMP ACT CRISIS.
J. BREWER, 617(TLS):4JUL75-725
THOMAS, R. THE MONEY HARVEST.
T.J. BINYON, 617(TLS):19DEC75-1508
N. CALLENDAR, 441:5OCT75-47
THOMAS, R.S. H'M.*
T. EAGLETON, 565:VOL14#1-65
THOMAS, T. & J. BERRY. THE BUSBY
BERKELEY BOOK.
J. SPRINGER, 200:OCT73-495
M. TORME, 441:19OCT75-6
THOMAS, W. BILINGUALE UDĀNAVARGA-
TEXTE DER SAMMLUNG HOERNLE.
M.J. DRESDEN, 318(JAOS):JUL-SEP73-
370

[CONTINUED]

THOMAS, W. BILINGUALE UDANAVARGA-
TEXTE DER SAMMLUNG HOERNLE. [CON-
TINUING]
  O. VON HINÜBER, 343:BAND16HEFT2-
  218
THOMASON, R.H. - SEE MONTAGUE, R.
THOMIS, M.I. THE TOWN LABOURER &
THE INDUSTRIAL REVOLUTION.
  H. PERKIN, 617(TLS):7MAR75-256
THOMKE, H. HYMNISCHE DICHTUNG DES
EXPRESSIONISMUS.
  G. BENDA, 406:SPRING74-81
  K. WEISSENBERGER, 301(JEGP):APR74-
  303
THOMPSON, A.A. THE SWISS LEGACY.
  N. CALLENDAR, 441:19JAN75-37
THOMPSON, C.W. VICTOR HUGO & THE
GRAPHIC ARTS (1820-1833).*
  P. BRADY, 546(RR):JAN73-77
THOMPSON, D. COPTIC TEXTILES IN THE
BROOKLYN MUSEUM.
  J. BECKWITH, 90:AUG73-547
THOMPSON, D. DANTE'S EPIC JOURNEYS.
  A.F. NAGEL, 401(MLQ):DEC74-418
THOMPSON, E.M. RUSSIAN FORMALISM &
ANGLO-AMERICAN NEW CRITICISM.*
  W.E. HARKINS, 574(SEEJ):FALL72-337
  L.G. LEIGHTON, 550(RUSR):JAN73-100
THOMPSON, E.P. WHIGS & HUNTERS.
  R. MITCHISON, 362:13NOV75-656
THOMPSON, G. LONDON STATUES.
  90:APR73-267
THOMPSON, G.R. POE'S FICTION.*
  R. ASSELINEAU, 189(EA):OCT-DEC73-
  496
  N. BAYM, 301(JEGP):JAN74-146
  H. KERR, 651(WHR):SPRING74-183
THOMPSON, H.A. & R.E. WYCHERLEY.
THE ATHENIAN AGORA.
  S.I. OOST, 122:JUL74-236
THOMPSON, J. AT THE EDGE OF THE
CHOPPING THERE ARE NO SECRETS.
  R. GIBBS, 198:WINTER75-134
THOMPSON, J. KIERKEGAARD.
  676(YR):AUTUMN73-VI
THOMPSON, K. ACROSS FROM THE FLORAL
PARK.*
  M. LEVIN, 441:5JAN75-21
THOMPSON, K., ED. STORIES FROM
ATLANTIC CANADA.
  P. MORLEY, 529(QQ):AUTUMN73-468
THOMPSON, K. THE TENANTS WERE COR-
RIE & TENNIE.*
  A. APPENZELL, 102(CANL):AUTUMN73-
  95
  R. MC CARTHY, 150(DR):SUMMER73-359
  A. MAC KINNON, 529(QQ):WINTER73-
  649
THOMPSON, K.F. MODESTY & CUNNING.*
  P.A. JORGENSEN, 405(MP):NOV73-197
THOMPSON, K.L. A DICTIONARY OF
TWENTIETH-CENTURY COMPOSERS 1911-
1971.*
  C. MAC DONALD, 607:JUN73-46
THOMPSON, L. ROBERT FROST: THE
YEARS OF TRIUMPH, 1915-1938.
  M. GAULL, 295:FEB74-612
THOMPSON, P. WILLIAM BUTTERFIELD.*
  P.F. NORTON, 576:MAR73-75
THOMPSON, P. THE CREATION FRAME.
  H. CARRUTH, 249(HUDR):SUMMER74-311
  P. RAMSEY, 569(SR):SPRING74-395
THOMPSON, P. THE EDWARDIANS.
  S. KOSS, 617(TLS):5DEC75-1435

THOMPSON, P. - SEE CONSTANT, B.
THOMPSON, R.F. AFRICAN ART IN
MOTION.
  W. BASCOM, 2:SUMMER74-85
  J. BLACKING, 617(TLS):5SEP75-989
THOMPSON, T.W. WORDSWORTH'S HAWKS-
HEAD.* (R. WOOF, ED)
  M.F. SCHULZ, 173(ECS):SPRING74-378
THOMPSON, W.I. PASSAGES ABOUT
EARTH.*
  W.A. SEDELOW, JR., 639(VQR):
  AUTUMN74-627
LORD THOMSON. AFTER I WAS 60.
  K. DAVEY, 99:DEC75/JAN76-40
  W. HARDCASTLE, 362:3JUL75-28
THOMSON, A.G. THE PAPER INDUSTRY IN
SCOTLAND, 1590-1861.
  617(TLS):25APR75-465
THOMSON, B. THE PREMATURE REVOLU-
TION.*
  T.J. BINYON, 402(MLR):JAN74-235
  L.J. SHEIN, 104:WINTER74-590
  295:FEB74-379
THOMSON, D. AN INTRODUCTION TO
GAELIC POETRY.*
  K. MILLER, 453:15MAY75-40
THOMSON, D. WOODBROOK.*
  R. FOSTER, 617(TLS):7FEB75-146
THOMSON, J. THE LONG REVENGE.
  N. CALLENDAR, 441:24AUG75-27
THOMSON, P. THE GROTESQUE.*
  H. PRIESSNITZ, 72:BAND211HEFT1/3-
  82
  N. SUCKLING, 208(FS):OCT74-488
THOMSON, P., ED. WYATT: THE CRITI-
CAL HERITAGE.
  A. LATHAM, 617(TLS):11APR75-391
THOMSON, P. - SEE ELWIN, M.
THOMSON, R.W., ED & TRANS. THE
TEACHING OF SAINT GREGORY.
  M.E. STONE, 318(JAOS):OCT-DEC73-
  591
THONSSEN, L., A.C. BAIRD & W.W.
BRADEN. SPEECH CRITICISM. (2ND
ED)
  H.H. MARTIN, 480(P&R):SPRING73-126
THORBURN, D. & G. HARTMAN, EDS.
ROMANTICISM.
  J. CULLER, 676(YR):SPRING74-439
  R.H. FOGLE, 569(SR):SPRING74-383
THORDARSON, B. TRUDEAU & FOREIGN
POLICY.
  102(CANL):SUMMER73-127
THOREAU, H.D. THE ILLUSTRATED WAL-
DEN.
  M.I. LOWANCE, JR., 432(NEQ):JUN74-
  330
THOREAU, H.D. MAINE WOODS. (J.J.
MOLDENHAUER, ED)
  D. LYTTLE, 255:FALL73-333
THOREAU, H.D. REFORM PAPERS. (W.
GLICK, ED)
  R.W. BRADFORD, 27(AL):JAN75-588
THOREAU, H.D. THOREAU'S VISION.
(C.R. ANDERSON, ED)
  A.C. KERN, 27(AL):NOV74-402
THORENSEN, F. ØRNEN PÅ HARM. JOM-
FRUEN PÅ HARM. BRØDRENE PÅ HARM.
LANGFERD MOT VEST.
  E. HASLUND, 270:VOL23#4-92
THORNBURY, W. THE LIFE OF J.M.W.
TURNER, R.A.
  G. REYNOLDS, 39:FEB73-196

THORNE, S.E. - SEE "BRACTON ON THE
LAWS & CUSTOMS OF ENGLAND"
THORNTON, A. PEOPLE & THEMES IN
HOMER'S "ODYSSEY."*
  H.W. CLARKE, 121(CJ):FEB/MAR74-253
THORNTON, R.C. THE BEAR & THE DRA-
GON.
  R.L. WALKER, 550(RUSR):APR73-189
THORNTON, R.R. - SEE SOUTHERNE, T.
THORPE, J. PRINCIPLES OF TEXTUAL
CRITICISM.*
  W.R. LE FANU, 541(RES):AUG73-382
  W. MILGATE, 191(ELN):MAR74-241
  G.R. PROUDFOOT, 354:MAR73-77
THORPE, J. WATCHING THE P'S & Q'S.
  E.L. STEEVES, 517(PBSA):APR-JUN74-
  189
THORPE, L. - SEE HELDRIS DE CORNU-
ÄLLE
THORPE, W.H. ANIMAL NATURE & HUMAN
NATURE.
  N. TINBERGEN, 617(TLS):28FEB75-216
THORSON, J.T. WANTED: A SINGLE
CANADA.
  J.M. BECK, 150(DR):AUTUMN73-583
  C.L. BROWN-JOHN, 628:SPRING74-93
  H.G. THORBURN, 529(QQ):WINTER73-
  623
THRAPP, D.J. VICTORIO & THE MIMBRES
APACHES.
  W. GARD, 584(SWR):SUMMER74-V
  639(VQR):SUMMER74-LXXXIX
THRELFALL, R. SERGEI RACHMANINOFF.
  G. NORRIS, 415:JAN74-42
THROMBLEY, W.G. & W.J. SIFFIN. THAI-
LAND POLITICS, ECONOMY, & SOCIO-
CULTURAL SETTING.
  J.K. MUSGRAVE, 293(JAST):FEB73-373
THUBRON, C. JOURNEY INTO CYPRUS.
  D. HUNT, 617(TLS):6JUN75-632
THUMMER, E. - SEE PINDAR
THURLEY, G. THE IRONIC HARVEST.
  D. DAVIE, 617(TLS):8AUG75-899
THURLOW, C.E. & OTHERS, COMPS. THE
JEFFERSON PAPERS OF THE UNIVERSITY
OF VIRGINIA.
  639(VQR):SUMMER74-XCIII
THURMAN, H. - SEE SCHREINER, O.
THUROT, F. TABLEAU DES PROGRÈS DE
LA SCIENCE GRAMMATICALE.* (A.
JOLY, ED)
  J. LAVÉDRINE, 189(EA):APR-JUN73-
  218
THWAITE, A. INSCRIPTIONS.*
  A. CLUYSENAAR, 565:VOL14#4-75
  H. SERGEANT, 175:AUTUMN73-121
THWAITE, A. NEW CONFESSIONS.*
  R. GARFITT, 364:AUG/SEP74-112
TIBBLE, A. LABYRINTH.
  A. CLUYSENAAR, 565:VOL14#2-62
TIBBLE, A. - SEE CLARE, J.
TIBBLE, J.W. & A. JOHN CLARE.
  J.E. RAPF, 591(SIR):WINTER74-79
  J. WAINWRIGHT, 565:VOL14#3-42
TIBENSKÝ, J. & OTHERS. SLOVENSKO:
DEJINY.
  W. BROWNE, 104:SUMMER73-276
TIBULLUS. ALBII TIBULLI ALIORUMQUE
CARMINUM LIBRI TRES. (3RD ED)
(F.W. LENZ & G.C. GALINSKY, EDS)
  G. LUCK, 24:FALL74-300

TICHER, K. IRISH SILVER IN THE
ROCOCO PERIOD.
  C. OMAN, 39:JUL73-72
  J. STUART, 135:AUG73-317
TIECK, L., F. SCHLEGEL & A.W.
SCHLEGEL. LUDWIG TIECK UND DIE
BRÜDER SCHLEGEL: BRIEFE. (E. LOH-
NER, ED)
  F. GRIES, 406:SPRING74-108
  W.J.L., 191(ELN):SEP73(SUPP)-159
  W. LILLYMAN, 221(GQ):MAY73-428
"LUDWIG TIECK."* (U. SCHWEIKERT,
ED)
  W. LILLYMAN, 221(GQ):MAY73-428
TIEMPO, E.K. A STREAM AT DALTON
PASS & OTHER STORIES.
  L. CASPER, 352(LE&W):VOL16#3-1099
TIEN, H-M. GOVERNMENT & POLITICS IN
KUOMINTANG CHINA, 1927-1937.
  R.A. KAPP, 293(JAST):MAY73-515
TIEPELMANN, K. VERMÖGENSPOLITIK UND
UNTERNEHMENSKONZENTRATION.
  K. MELLEROWICZ, 182:VOL26#17/18-
  595
TIERNEY, B. ORIGINS OF PAPAL INFAL-
LIBILITY, 1150-1350.
  G. POST, 589:OCT74-762
TIERNEY, F.M. - SEE PACEY, D.
TIERSKY, R. FRENCH COMMUNISM 1920-
1972.
  D. JOHNSON, 617(TLS):22AUG75-942
TIESLER, I. GÜNTER GRASS: "KATZ
UND MAUS."*
  K. HASSELBACH, 221(GQ):MAR73-263
TIETZ, M. SAINT FRANÇOIS DE SALES'
"TRAITÉ DE L'AMOUR DE DIEU" (1616)
UND SEINE SPANISCHEN VORLÄUFER CRIS-
TÓBAL DE FONSECA, DIEGO DE ESTELLA,
LUIS DE GRANADA, SANTA TERESA DE
JESÚS UND JUAN DE JESÚS MARÍA.
  P. SÉROUET, 182:VOL26#23/24-871
TIGER, V. WILLIAM GOLDING.
  G. CLIFFORD, 617(TLS):8AUG75-891
TIKKU, G.L. PERSIAN POETRY IN KASH-
MIR, 1339-1846.*
  M.A. JAZAYERY, 352(LE&W):VOL16#4-
  1254
TILANDER, G. - SEE PHÉBUS, G.
TILDON, E.T. THE ANGLO-SAXON AGONY.
  H.A. LARRABEE, 432(NEQ):DEC73-648
TILLETT, M. STENDHAL.*
  J. MITCHELL, 402(MLR):JAN74-181
TILLEY, P. FADE-OUT.
  M. LEVIN, 441:27JUL75-11
TILLICH, H. FROM TIME TO TIME.
  M. ELLMANN, 676(YR):SUMMER74-602
  P. HEBBLETHWAITE, 617(TLS):29AUG
  75-977
  D. TRILLING, 473(PR):1/1974-120
TILLIETTE, X. SCHELLING.
  M.H., 191(ELN):SEP73(SUPP)-155
  F. MARTI, 319:APR75-263
TILLOTSON, G. - SEE LEISHMAN, J.B.
TILLOTSON, G. & B. JENKINS - SEE
JOHNSON, S.
TIMBERLAKE, C.E., ED. ESSAYS ON
RUSSIAN LIBERALISM.*
  T. EMMONS, 104:WINTER73-552
  A.G. MAZOUR, 550(RUSR):APR73-218
"A TIME TO CHOOSE."
  G. BARRACLOUGH, 453:23JAN75-20
"THE TIMES ANTHOLOGY OF GHOST STOR-
IES."
  M. MASON, 617(TLS):28NOV75-1407

TIMM, E. DIE ÜBERLIEFERUNG DER
LIEDER OSWALDS VON WOLKENSTEIN.
 W. SALMEN, 182:VOL26#9-302
TIMOFIEWITSCH, W. CORPUS PALLADIAN-
UM. (VOL 3: LA CHIESA DEL REDEN-
TORE.)
 M.N. ROSENFELD, 576:DEC73-335
 F.J.B. WATSON, 39:MAY73-531
TIMPANARO, S. CLASSICISMO E ILLUM-
INISMO NELL' OTTOCENTO ITALIANO.
(2ND ED)
 L. TOSCHI, 275(IQ):SUMMER73-114
TIMPANARO, S. DIE ENTSTEHUNG DER
LACHMANNSCHEN METHODE.
 N.G. WILSON, 123:MAR74-144
TIMPE, D. ARMINIUS-STUDIEN.*
 E.M. WIGHTMAN, 124:SEP72-52
TINDALL, G. THE TRAVELLER & HIS
CHILD.
 S. CLAPP, 617(TLS):20JUN75-689
 J. MELLORS, 362:19JUN75-821
TINDALL, W.Y. THE JOYCE COUNTRY.
 J.S. ATHERTON, 617(TLS):12DEC75-
 1483
TINDALL, W.Y. - SEE ALAZRAKI, J.
TING-JUI, H. - SEE UNDER HO TING-JUI
TINGSTEN, H. VICTORIA & THE VIC-
TORIANS. (D. & E.L. GREY, EDS &
TRANS)
 R.C. TOBIAS, 637(VS):DEC73-213
TINKER, C. THE TRANSLATIONS OF BEO-
WULF.
 T. SHIPPEY, 617(TLS):29AUG75-974
TINKLER, J.D. VOCABULARY & SYNTAX
OF THE OLD ENGLISH VERSION IN THE
PARIS PSALTER.*
 K.R. GRINDA, 38:BAND91HEFT4-494
TINLAND, F., ED. HISTOIRE D'UNE
JEUNE FILLE SAUVAGE.*
 J.L. CARR, 402(MLR):OCT74-875
 L.C. ROSENFIELD, 207(FR):DEC72-404
 C. SCHUWER, 542:JAN-MAR73-69
TINLAND, F. L'HOMME SAUVAGE.
 C. SCHUWER, 542:JAN-MAR73-68
TIPTON, I.C. BERKELEY.*
 E. MATTHEWS, 518:MAY74-26
TIPTREE, J., JR. TEN THOUSAND
LIGHT-YEARS FROM HOME.
 J. HAMILTON-PATERSON, 617(TLS):
 8AUG75-903
TIPTREE, J., JR. WARM WORLDS &
OTHERWISE.
 G. JONAS, 441:23MAR75-31
TIRSO DE MOLINA. POESÍAS LÍRICAS.*
(E. JAREÑO, ED)
 R.M. PRICE, 86(BHS):JAN73-88
TIRYAKIAN, E.A., ED. ON THE MARGIN
OF THE VISIBLE.
 B. WILSON, 617(TLS):21FEB75-203
"TIRYNS: FORSCHUNGEN UND BERICHTE."
 J. BOARDMAN, 123:MAR74-158
TISCHLER, H. - SEE APEL, W.
TISCHLER, N.M. BLACK MASKS.*
 G. WÖLK, 447(N&Q):SEP73-357
TISON-BRAUN, M. NATHALIE SARRAUTE
OU LA RECHERCHE DE L'AUTHENTICITÉ.
 J. SCHWARCZ, 207(FR):OCT72-171
TITTA ROSA, G. VITA LETTERARIA DEL
NOVECENTO.
 G.P. PIERCE, 275(IQ):SPRING74-113
TIUSANEN, T. O'NEILL'S SCENIC IM-
AGES.*
 G. HOFFMANN, 38:BAND91HEFT2-265

TIXONOV, A.N. PROBLEMY SOSTAVLENIJA
GNEZDOVOGO SLOVOOBRAZOVATEL'NOGO
SLOVARJA SOVREMENNOGO RUSSKOGO JAZ-
YKA.
 D.S.W., 279:VOL16-197
TKACZYK, W. DER TAG IST GROSS.
 M. DAU, 654(WB):5/1973-155
TKADLECKOVÁ-VANTUCHOVÁ, J. ČESI A
SLOVÁCI V NÁRODNOOSLOBODZOVACOM
BOJI DO RAKÚSKOUHORSKÉHO VYROVNAN-
IA ROKU 1867.
 Y. JELINEK, 104:SPRING74-158
TOBEY, P. PIRATING PLANTS.
 J. CANADAY, 441:13APR75-16
TOBI, S. EUGÈNE IONESCO OU A LA
RECHERCHE DU PARADIS PERDU.
 D. KNOWLES, 208(FS):JUL74-354
TOBIAS, G.W.R. & B.H.C. TURVEY.
ENGLISH-KWANYAMA DICTIONARY.
 J. LUKAS, 182:VOL26#17/18-599
TOBIAS, H.J. THE JEWISH BUND IN
RUSSIA FROM ITS ORIGINS TO 1905.
 R.K. DEBO, 104:WINTER73-554
 H. SHUKMAN, 550(RUSR):APR73-201
TOBIAS, J.J. PRINCE OF FENCES.
 P. KEATING, 617(TLS):11APR75-394
TOBIN, J. THE NEW ECONOMICS ONE
DECADE OLDER.
 H.G. JOHNSON, 617(TLS):7FEB75-139
TOBIN, R.W. RACINE & SENECA.*
 M-R. CARRÉ, 399(MLJ):NOV73-362
 B. CHÉDOZEAU, 535(RHL):NOV-DEC73-
 1066
 R.C. KNIGHT, 402(MLR):JUL74-639
TOBIN, R.W. & J.D. ERICKSON, EDS.
PATHS TO FREEDOM.
 S. HAIG, 207(FR):MAR73-824
TOBIN, T. - SEE PITCAIRNE, A.
TODD, C. VOLTAIRE'S DISCIPLE.*
 R. SAISSELIN, 400(MLN):MAY73-878
TODD, G., ED. CURRENT ISSUES IN
TEACHING FRENCH.
 T.G. BROWN, 207(FR):APR73-1092
 W.R. HEROLD, 399(MLJ):APR73-225
TODD, J.M. REFORMATION.
 J.F. KELLY, 613:SPRING73-153
TODD, O. LES CANARDS DE CA MAO.
 D. LEITCH, 617(TLS):100CT75-1172
TODD, O. THE YEAR OF THE CRAB.
 N. HEPBURN, 362:5JUN75-746
TODD, W. HISTORY AS APPLIED SCIENCE.
 W.H. WALSH, 125:OCT73-84
TODD, W.B., ED. HUME & THE ENLIGHT-
ENMENT.
 J.M. CAMERON, 617(TLS):11JUL75-777
TODDS, W. PATRICK HADLEY.
 C. PALMER, 415:JUN74-478
TODOROV, T. THE FANTASTIC.
 J. CULLER, 676(YR):SPRING74-439
TODOROV, T. GRAMMAIRE DU DÉCAMÉRON.
 A.L. LEPSCHY, 353:1JAN73-98
TODOROV, T. INTRODUCTION À LA LIT-
TÉRATURE FANTASTIQUE.* (GERMAN
TITLE: EINFÜHRUNG IN DIE FANTAS-
TISCHE LITERATUR.)
 G. GENOT, 492:#9-93
TODRANI, J. CANO.
 S. MAX, 207(FR):FEB73-669
TOFFLER, A. THE ECO-SPASM REPORT.
 R.R. LINGEMAN, 441:31MAR75-29
 H. STEPHENSON, 617(TLS):8AUG75-894
TOFT, J. THE HOUSE OF THE AROUS-
ING.*
 364:OCT/NOV74-143

TOWN, H. ALBERT FRANCK, KEEPER OF
THE LANES.
N. STEED, 99:APR/MAY75-64
TOWNEND, P. ZOOM.
N. CALLENDAR, 441:29JUN75-30
TOWNS, E. HAVE THE PUBLIC SCHOOLS
"HAD IT"?
T.W. ROGERS, 396(MODA):FALL74-435
TOWNSEND, C.E. CONTINUING WITH
RUSSIAN.
R.L. BAKER, 574(SEEJ):SPRING72-113
TOWNSEND, P. THE LAST EMPEROR.
J. GRIGG, 362:6NOV75-621
TOWNSHEND, D.J. GLAND TIME.
P. CAMPBELL, 617(TLS):7FEB75-129
M. LEVIN, 441:2NOV75-55
TOYNBEE, A. SOME PROBLEMS OF GREEK
HISTORY.
J.A.S. EVANS, 122:APR73-132
TOYNBEE, A. A STUDY OF HISTORY.
(ABRIDGED)
R.N. STROMBERG, 125:OCT73-97
TOZZI, P. STORIA PADANA ANTICA.
R.M. OGILVIE, 123:NOV74-306
TRABANT, J. ZUR SEMIOLOGIE DES LIT-
ERARISCHEN KUNSTWERKS.
U.A. MUNNICH, 221(GQ):NOV73-633
TRABUT-CUSSAC, J-P. L'ADMINISTRA-
TION ANGLAISE EN GASCOGNE SOUS
HENRY III ET ÉDOUARD I DE 1254 Ã
1307.
E.A.R. BROWN, 589:OCT74-765
TRACHTENBERG, A. - SEE FRANK, W.
TRACHTENBERG, I. SO SLOW THE DAWN-
ING.*
M. SILVERSTEIN, 287:MAY73-42
TRACHTENBERG, M. THE CAMPANILE OF
FLORENCE CATHEDRAL, "GIOTTO'S
TOWER."*
F. BUCHER, 54:JUN73-290
TRACY, C. - SEE JOHNSON, S.
TRACY, H. IN A YEAR OF GRACE.
V. GLENDINNING, 617(TLS):22AUG75-
951
442(NY):23JUN75-108
TRACY, T.J. & S.J. PHYSIOLOGICAL
THEORY & THE DOCTRINE OF THE MEAN
IN PLATO & ARISTOTLE.*
D.Z. ANDRIOPOULOS, 121(CJ):APR/MAY
74-369
TRAEGER, J. DER REITENDE PAPST.
E. GARMS-CORNIDES, 54:SEP73-451
TRAHERNE, T. CHRISTIAN ETHICS.
(G.R. GUFFEY, ED)
R. ELLRODT, 189(EA):OCT-DEC73-477
TRAIN, J. DANCE OF THE MONEY BEES.
P. GROSE, 441:26FEB75-39
TRAPP, F.A. THE ATTAINMENT OF DELA-
CROIX.*
P. JOANNIDES, 90:AUG73-549
C.R. WALKER, 127:WINTER73/74-170
TRAUGOTT, E.C. A HISTORY OF ENGLISH
SYNTAX.
E.P. HAMP, 269(IJAL):APR73-130
S. STEELE, 35(AS):FALL-WINTER71-
270
"TRAVAUX LINGUISTIQUES DE PRAGUE."
(VOL 4)
G. SOHALIOH, 72:BAND211HEFT1/3-254
TRAVEN, B. THE KIDNAPPED SAINT.
(R.E. LUJAN, M.C. KLEIN & H.A.
KLEIN, EDS)
A. CHEUSE, 441:19OCT75-34

TRAVEN, B. MACARIO. (S.R. WILSON,
ED)
C.F. WHITMER, 238:MAR73-192
TRAVERS, P.L. ABOUT THE SLEEPING
BEAUTY.
J. COTT, 441:28SEP75-27
TRAVIS, G. THE COTTAGE.
E.M. EWING, 441:11MAY75-10
TRAVLOS, J. PICTORIAL DICTIONARY OF
ANCIENT ATHENS.
D.M. LEWIS, 123:MAR74-110
TRAYNOR, S. THE HARDENING GROUND.
J. MONTAGUE, 617(TLS):4JUL75-718
TREADGOLD, D.W. THE WEST IN RUSSIA
& CHINA.
D.C. PRICE, 104:WINTER74-598
TREASE, G. LAUGHTER AT THE DOOR.*
M. BISHOP, 617(TLS):3JAN75-18
TREASE, G. LONDON.
P. METCALF, 617(TLS):24OCT75-1272
TREE, R. WHEN THE MOON WAS HIGH.
A. FORBES, 617(TLS):18JUL75-792
TREGGIARI, S. ROMAN FREEDMEN DURING
THE LATE REPUBLIC.
J-C. DUMONT, 555:VOL47FASC1-181
TREIP, M. MILTON'S PUNCTUATION &
CHANGING ENGLISH USAGE 1582-1676.*
G. BULLOUGH, 175:SPRING72-24
R. LEJOSNE, 189(EA):JAN-MAR73-101
TREISTMAN, J.M. THE PREHISTORY OF
CHINA.*
S.M. BARD, 302:JAN73-162
TRELOAR, B. MOLIÈRE: LES PRÉCIEUSES
RIDICULES.
C.N. SMITH, 208(FS):JAN74-67
TREMAYNE, S. SELECTED & NEW POEMS.
H. SERGEANT, 175:AUTUMN73-121
TREMEL, F. WIRTSCHAFTS- UND SOZIAL-
GESCHICHTE ÖSTERREICHS.
K. SCHIB, 182:VOL26#3/4-125
TREML, V.G. & J.P. HARDT, EDS.
SOVIET ECONOMIC STATISTICS.
R.C. STUART, 104:SUMMER73-279
TRENCH, C.C. GEORGE II.
H.T.D., 566:SPRING74-97
TRENCKNER, V. A CRITICAL PĀLI DIC-
TIONARY. (VOL 2, FASC 6) (L. ALS-
DORF, ED)
L.A. SCHWARZSCHILD, 318(JAOS):
JUL-SEP73-376
TRENCKNER, V. A CRITICAL PĀLI DIC-
TIONARY. (VOL 2, FASC 7) (L. ALS-
DORF, ED)
C. CAILLAT, 260(IF):BAND78-247
TRENDALL, A.D. & T.B.L. WEBSTER.
ILLUSTRATIONS OF GREEK DRAMA.
R.M. COOK, 123:MAR74-107
E. KEULS, 124:APR73-430
B.A. SPARKES, 303:VOL93-269
TRENT, P. THE IMAGE MAKERS.
200:FEB73-113
"TRES OBRAS DE TEATRO."
G. WOODYARD, 238:MAR73-182
TRESCOTT, P.B. THAILAND'S MONETARY
EXPERIENCE.
P.F. BELL, 293(JAST):NOV72-220
"TRÉSOR DE LA LANGUE FRANÇAISE."*
(VOL 1) (P. IMBS, GENERAL ED)
V. VÄÄNÄNEN, 439(NM):1973/1-182
"TRÉSOR DE LA LANGUE FRANÇAISE."
(VOL 2) (P. IMBS, ED)
V. VÄÄNÄNEN, 439(NM):1973/3-543

"TRÉSOR DE LA LANGUE FRANÇAISE."
(VOL 3) (P. IMBS, ED)
  D. MC MILLAN, 617(TLS):30MAY75-589
TRETHOWAN, I. THE ABSOLUTE & THE
ATONEMENT.
  W.L.P., 543:DEC72-368
TREVOR, E. NIGHT STOP.
  N. CALLENDAR, 441:11MAY75-26
TREVOR, L. CODE 1013: ASSASSIN.
  N. CALLENDAR, 441:25MAY75-16
TREVOR, M. THE ARNOLDS.
  A.D. CULLER, 676(YR):WINTER74-287
  P.J. MC CARTHY, 637(VS):MAR74-339
TREVOR, W. ANGELS AT THE RITZ.
  V. CUNNINGHAM, 617(TLS):24OCT75-
1255
TREW, A. THE ZHUKOV BRIEFING.
  T.J. BINYON, 617(TLS):26DEC75-1544
"A TRIBUTE TO WYSTAN HUGH AUDEN."
  P. DAVISON, 354:DEC73-361
TRICAUD, F. - SEE HOBBES, T.
TRICKETT, R. BROWNING'S LYRICISM.*
  J.C. MAXWELL, 447(N&Q):JUL73-269
TRIEM, E. E.E. CUMMINGS.
  A. EASSON, 447(N&Q):SEP73-345
TRIFKOVIČ, M. LE MANCAGNE.
  J. KARLIK, 315(JAL):VOL11PT2-96
TRIGG, R. REASON & COMMITMENT.
  T. MAUTNER, 63:AUG74-185
  H.O. MOUNCE, 518:JAN74-26
TRILLING, L. THE MIDDLE OF THE
JOURNEY.
  J. BAYLEY, 617(TLS):11APR75-399
TRILLING, L. SINCERITY & AUTHENTI-
CITY.*
  A.R. CHISHOLM, 67:MAY74-104
  J.H. RALEIGH, 191(ELN):JUN74-320
  J. WAIN, 148:SUMMER73-173
TRIM, J. ENGLISH PRONUNCIATION
ILLUSTRATED. (NEW ED)
  617(TLS):26SEP75-1092
VON TRIMBERG, H. DER RENNER.* (G.
EHRISMANN, ED; REV BY G. SCHWEIKLE)
  O. SAYCE, 402(MLR):JAN74-221
TRINQUET, R. LA JEUNESSE DE MON-
TAIGNE.
  D.M. FRAME, 546(RR):MAR74-124
  M. GUTWIRTH, 207(FR):OCT72-147
TRIPATHI, R.K. PROBLEMS OF PHILOSO-
PHY & RELIGION.
  J.M. KOLLER, 485(PE&W):OCT73-545
TRIPP, C.A. THE HOMOSEXUAL MATRIX.
  P-L. ADAMS, 61:DEC75-118
  H. HENDIN, 441:26OCT75-35
  C. LEHMANN-HAUPT, 441:19DEC75-37
TRIPP, E. CROWELL'S HANDBOOK OF
CLASSICAL MYTHOLOGY.
  D.P. HARMON, 124:APR-MAY74-404
TRISTAN L'HERMITE, F. LETTRES MES-
LÉES. (C. GRISÉ, ED)
  C. ABRAHAM, 399(MLJ):SEP-OCT74-275
TROFIMENKOFF, S.M. ACTION FRANÇAISE.
  P. DIRKS, 99:JUL75-35
TROGU, G. VARIANTI-INVARIABILI.
  R. BLANCHÉ, 542:JUL-SEP73-378
TROTSKY, L. 1905.* (A. BOSTOCK,
TRANS)
  A.G. MAZOUR, 550(RUSR):JAN73-100
TROTTER, G.D. & K. WHINNOM, EDS.
LA COMEDIA THEBAIDA.
  B.M. DAMIANI, 400(MLN):MAR73-417
TROUILLARD, J. L'UN ET L'ÂME SELON
PROCLOS.
  É. DES PLACES, 555:VOL47FASC2-342

TROUPE, Q. & R. SCHULTE, EDS. GIANT
TALK.
  J. SLATER, 441:30NOV75-56
TROUSSON, R. ROUSSEAU ET SA FOR-
TUNE LITTÉRAIRE.*
  D.G. CREIGHTON, 207(FR):DEC72-406
  J-L. LECERCLE, 535(RHL):JAN-FEB73-
137
  J.S. SPINK, 208(FS):JUL74-327
  191(ELN):SEP73(SUPP)-72
TROUSSON, R. LE THÈME DE PROMÉTHÉE
DANS LA LITTÉRATURE EUROPÉENNE.
  G. BESSE, 542:JAN-MAR73-121
TROUSSON, R. - SEE FOUGEROT DE MON-
BRON, L-C.
TROUSSON, R. - SEE MERCIER, L-S.
TROYAT, H. DIVIDED SOUL.*
  B.M. COHEN, 584(SWR):SUMMER74-334
TROYAT, H. GOGOL.
  P. DEBRECZENY, 574(SEEJ):SUMMER72-
227
  A. DE JONGE, 617(TLS):7MAR75-251
TROYAT, H. LA PIERRE, LA FEUILLE ET
LES CISEAUX.
  C. FRANÇOIS, 207(FR):FEB73-670
TROYAT, H. & OTHERS. DOSTOÏEVSKI.
  H.H. KELLER, 574(SEEJ):WINTER72-
473
TRUBETZKOY, N.S. VORLESUNGEN ÜBER
DIE ALTRUSSISCHE LITERATUR.
  V. TERRAS, 574(SEEJ):FALL73-323
TRUCHET, J., ED. THÉÂTRE DU XVIIIE
SIÈCLE. (VOL 2)
  W.D. HOWARTH, 208(FS):OCT74-457
TRUDEAU, G. THE DOONESBURY CHRON-
ICLES.
  R.R. LINGEMAN, 441:7DEC75-7
TRUDEAU, P.E., ED. THE ASBESTOS
STRIKE.
  R. COOK, 99:FEB75-35
TRUDEL, M. THE BEGINNINGS OF NEW
FRANCE, 1524-1663.*
  M. WADE, 529(QQ):AUTUMN73-477
  102(CANL):SUMMER74-124
TRUEBLOOD, A.S. EXPERIENCE & ARTIS-
TIC EXPRESSION IN LOPE DE VEGA.
  A. PATERSON, 617(TLS):5SEP75-1004
TRUFFAUT, F. LES FILMS DE MA VIE.
  L. BRAUDY, 617(TLS):21NOV75-1374
TRUMAN, M. HARRY S. TRUMAN.
  J.A. NUECHTERLEIN, 529(QQ):AUTUMN
73-491
TRUNK, I. JUDENRAT.*
  A. DONAT, 390:JAN73-66
TRUSS, J. BIRD AT THE WINDOW.
  H. PORTER, 296:VOL4#3-180
TRUSSLER, S. JOHN ARDEN.
  A.C. EDWARDS, 397(MD):DEC73-394
TRUTMANN, A. STUDIEN ZUM ADJEKTIV
IM GOTISCHEN.
  E. SEEBOLD, 343:BAND16HEFT2-189
TRYON, T. A DISCOURSE OF THE
CAUSES, NATURES & CURE OF PHRENSIE,
MADNESS OR DISTRACTION (1689).
  566:SPRING74-99
TS'AO CHAO. CHINESE CONNOISSEUR-
SHIP, THE KO KU YAO LUN.* (P.
DAVID, ED & TRANS)
  W. WATSON, 90:MAR73-181
TSATSOS, J. THE SWORD'S FIERCE
EDGE.
  M. SAVVAS, 385(MQR):FALL75-477

TSCHIRCH, F. GESCHICHTE DER DEUT-
SCHEN SPRACHE.
  H.R. PLANT, 353:15FEB73-88
TSCHIRKY, R. HEIMITO VON DODERERS
"POSAUNEN VON JERICHO."
  M. SWALES, 402(MLR):APR74-471
  F. TROMMLER, 133:1973/3-284
TSCHIŽEWSKIJ, D., ED. DIE NESTOR-
CHRONIK.
  W.W. DERBYSHIRE, 574(SEEJ):SUMMER
  72-268
TSCHIŽEWSKIJ, D., ED. SLAVISCHE
BAROCKLITERATUR, I.
  A. HIPPISLEY, 574(SEEJ):SPRING72-
  89
TSE-TUNG, M. - SEE UNDER MAO TSE-
TUNG
TSIAPERA, M. A DESCRIPTIVE ANALYSIS
OF CYPRIOT MARONITE ARABIC.*
  P.A. SCHREIBER, 350:DEC74-748
TSIRKAS, S. DRIFTING CITIES.
  P. LEVI, 617(TLS):14NOV75-1356
TSO-LIANG, H. - SEE UNDER HSIAO TSO-
LIANG
TSUNG-SAN, M. - SEE UNDER MOU TSUNG-
SAN
TSUZAKI, S.M. ENGLISH INFLUENCES ON
MEXICAN SPANISH IN DETROIT.*
  W. WOLFRAM, 215(GL):VOL13#1-71
TSVETAYEVA, M. SELECTED POEMS.*
  S. KARLINSKY, 550(RUSR):JAN73-101
TUCHMAN, B.W. SAND AGAINST THE WIND.
  H. SCHMIDT, 302:JUL73-263
TUCHMAN, B.W. STILWELL & THE AMERI-
CAN EXPERIENCE IN CHINA, 1911-
1945.*
  E. FRIEDMAN, 318(JAOS):APR-JUN73-
  217
TUCHOLSKY, K. DEUTSCHLAND, DEUTSCH-
LAND ÜBER ALLES.
  R. GRIMM, 406:SUMMER74-184
TUCKER, N. THE COMPLETE PUBLISHED
POEMS OF NATHANIEL TUCKER TOGETHER
WITH "COLUMBINUS A MASK." (L.
LEARY, ED)
  J.A.L. LEMAY, 27(AL):MAY74-227
TUCKER, R.C. THE MARXIAN REVOLU-
TIONARY IDEA.
  A.W. WOOD, 543:SEP72-118
TUCKER, R.C. STALIN AS REVOLUTION-
ARY, 1879-1929.*
  P. DEMETZ, 676(YR):WINTER74-291
  A. GYORGY, 104:WINTER74-604
  D.E. POWELL, 639(VQR):SPRING74-314
TUCKER, S.I. ENTHUSIASM.*
  J.L. DELAPLAIN, 481(PQ):JUL73-406
  P.J. KORSHIN, 141:FALL73-368
  K.C. PHILLIPPS, 179(ES):DEC73-585
  C.J. RAWSON, 175:SUMMER73-75
  G. STORMS, 433:JUL73-312
TUCKER, W. ICE & IRON.
  T.A. SHIPPEY, 617(TLS):23MAY75-554
TUCKETT, A. THE BLACKSMITHS' HIS-
TORY.
  P. HOLLIS, 617(TLS):4JUL75-737
TUCKEY, J.S. - SEE TWAIN, M.
TUDOR, A. IMAGE & INFLUENCE.
  S. HARTOG, 617(TLS):28FEB75-227
TUFTE, V. THE POETRY OF MARRIAGE.
  A. AVNI, 131(CL):WINTER73-89
TUGGLE, W.O. SHEM, HAM & JAPHETH.*
(E. CURRENT-GARCIA, WITH D.B. HAT-
[CONTINUED]

[CONTINUING]
FIELD, EDS)
  L. LEARY, 577(SHR):FALL73-445
  H.S. MARKS, 9(ALAR):JUL73-233
TUGWELL, R.G. THE EMERGING CONSTI-
TUTION.
  H.J. ABRAHAM, 639(VQR):AUTUMN74-
  614
TULARD, J. LE MYTHE DE NAPOLÉON.*
  A. CAPRIO, 207(FR):OCT72-160
  M. DESCOTES, 535(RHL):SEP-OCT73-
  916
TULLY, A. THE BRAHMIN ARRANGEMENT.
  N. CALLENDAR, 441:12JAN75-22
TUMANJAN, H. DAS TAUBENKLOSTER.
  A. LATCHINIAN, 654(WB):2/1973-167
TUMBUSCH, T. COMPLETE PRODUCTION
GUIDE TO MODERN MUSICAL THEATRE.
  J. VAN DER POLL, 583:FALL73-95
TUMINS, V.A. TSAR IVAN IV'S REPLY
TO JAN ROKYTA.*
  A.M. KLEIMOLA, 574(SEEJ):FALL72-
  386
TUMMERS, N.H.M. J.L. MATHIEU LAU-
WERIKS.
  H. SEARING, 576:OCT73-253
TUNICKIJ, N.L. MONUMENTA AD SS
CYRILLI ET METHODII SUCCESSORUM
VITAS RESQUE GESTAS PERTINENTIA.
  F.C.M. KITCH, 575(SEER):OCT74-635
TUOMELA, R. THEORETICAL CONCEPTS.
  H.E. KYBURG, JR., 311(JP):4SEP75-
  491
TUPLIN, W.A. GREAT WESTERN POWER.
  617(TLS):4JUL75-737
TURCAN, M. - SEE TERTULLIAN
TURGENEV, I.S. THE PORTRAIT GAME.
(M. MAINWARING, ED)
  639(VQR):SPRING74-LX
TURGENEV, I.S. RUDIN.
  A. KELLY, 617(TLS):6JUN75-629
TURK, L.H. & E.M. ALLEN. EL ESPAÑOL
AL DÍA. (4TH ED)
  R.W. HATTON, 238:DEC73-1137
TURNBULL, C.M. THE MOUNTAIN PEOPLE.*
  T.O. BEIDELMAN, 69:APR73-170
TURNELL, M. JEAN RACINE - DRAMA-
TIST.*
  R.C. KNIGHT, 208(FS):OCT74-453
  C. ROSENBERG, 50(ARQ):SPRING73-81
  I. WARDLE, 214:VOL6#22-65
TURNER, D.G. UNAMUNO'S WEBS OF
FATALITY.
  J. BUTT, 617(TLS):23MAY75-570
TURNER, E.G. GREEK MANUSCRIPTS OF
THE ANCIENT WORLD.*
  S.G. DAITZ, 124:OCT72-113
  N.G. WILSON, 123:MAR74-91
TURNER, E.S. AMAZING GRACE.
  G. ANNAN, 617(TLS):3OCT75-1117
  R. SCOTT, 362:18SEP75-384
TURNER, F. SHAKESPEARE & THE NATURE
OF TIME.*
  P. EDWARDS, 677:VOL4-269
TURNER, F.M. BETWEEN SCIENCE &
RELIGION.*
  A.R. LOUCH, 319:APR75-273
  639(VQR):SUMMER74-CII
TURNER, F.W., 3D, ED. THE PORTABLE
NORTH AMERICAN INDIAN READER.
  639(VQR):AUTUMN74-CLVIII
TURNER, H.L. TOWN DEFENCES IN ENG-
LAND & WALES.
  C. TADGELL, 46:JAN73-80

TURNER, I. PETER LALOR.
H.W. RHODES, 67:NOV74-233
TURNER, J. COGNITIVE DEVELOPMENT.
I. HUNTER, 617(TLS):6JUN75-629
TURNER, M.R. & A. MIALL, EDS. JUST
A SONG AT TWILIGHT.
P. KEATING, 617(TLS):26DEC75-1534
TURNER, P. - SEE BROWNING, R.
TURNER, P. & R. WOOD. P.H. EMERSON.*
H. KRAMER, 441:7DEC75-84
TURNER, R.F. VIETNAMESE COMMUNISM.
D. DUNCANSON, 617(TLS):19SEP75-
1042
TURNER, V. DRAMA, FIELDS, & META-
PHORS.*
W.S. DILLON, 31(ASCH):SUMMER75-515
TURNEY, C. BYRON'S DAUGHTER.*
E.E.B., 191(ELN):SEP73(SUPP)-39
TURTON, G. THE SYRIAN PRINCESSES.
P. GREEN, 617(TLS):17JAN75-64
TUSCANO, P. POETICA E POESIA DI
TOMMASO CAMPANELLA.
A.N. MANCINI, 400(MLN):JAN73-125
TUSCHLING, B. METAPHYSISCHE UND
TRANSZENDENTALE DYNAMIK IN KANTS
"OPUS POSTUMUM."
W. VON LEYDEN, 393(MIND):APR73-293
TUSELL, J. HISTORIA DE LA DEMOCRA-
CIA CRISTIANA EN ESPAÑA.
R. CARR, 617(TLS):11APR75-393
TUSHNET, L. THE PAVEMENT OF HELL.
617(TLS):10OCT75-1178
TUSIANI, J., ED & TRANS. ITALIAN
POETS OF THE RENAISSANCE.*
T.G. BERGIN, 551(RENQ):AUTUMN73-
345
F. CERRETA, 276:AUTUMN73-449
TUTE, W. NEXT SATURDAY IN MILAN.
617(TLS):2MAY75-492
TUTTLETON, J.W. THE NOVEL OF MAN-
NERS IN AMERICA.*
D. MARDER, 454:FALL73-81
J.L. MARSH, 219(GAR):FALL73-451
C.C. WALCUTT, 445(NCF):SEP73-236
295:FEB74-498
TUVILL, D. ESSAYS POLITIC & MORAL
& ESSAYS MORAL & THEOLOGICAL.*
(J.L. LIEVSAY, ED)
F. LAGARDE, 189(EA):JAN-MAR73-94
TWADDLE, M., ED. EXPULSION OF A
MINORITY.
Y. GAI, 617(TLS):4JUL75-738
TWERSKY, I. & G.H. WILLIAMS - SEE
WOLFSON, H.A.
TWAIN, M. THE GREAT LANDSLIDE CASE.
(F. ANDERSON & E.M. BRANCH, EDS)
H. PARKER, 445(NCF):SEP73-228
TWAIN, M. MARK TWAIN'S FABLES OF
MAN.* (J.S. TUCKEY, ED)
H. PARKER, 445(NCF):SEP73-225
TWAIN, M. MARK TWAIN'S HANNIBAL,
HUCK & TOM. (W. BLAIR, ED) MARK
TWAIN'S MYSTERIOUS STRANGER MANU-
SCRIPTS. (W. GIBSON, ED) MARK
TWAIN'S CORRESPONDENCE WITH HENRY
HUDDLESTON ROGERS, 1893-1909. (L.
LEARY, ED)
O. ÖVERLAND, 179(ES):AUG72-372
TWAIN, M. THE WORKS OF MARK TWAIN.*
(VOL 2: ROUGHING IT.) (F.R. ROGERS
& P. BAENDER, EDS)
H. PARKER, 445(NCF):SEP73-225

TWIGGS, R.D. PAN-AFRICAN LANGUAGE
IN THE WESTERN HEMISPHERE.
R.E. WOOD, 399(MLJ):SEP-OCT74-300
TWIGGY. AN AUTOBIOGRAPHY.
A. FORBES, 617(TLS):19DEC75-1510
TWITCHETT, D.C. FINANCIAL ADMINIS-
TRATION UNDER THE T'ANG DYNASTY.
(2ND ED)
J.T.C. LIU, 318(JAOS):APR-JUN73-
215
TWOMBLY, R.C. FRANK LLOYD WRIGHT.
L.K. EATON, 505:AUG73-94
D. HOFFMANN, 44:APR73-14
TWYCROSS, M. THE MEDIEVAL ANADYO-
MENE.*
J.M. STEADMAN, 382(MAE):1974/1-83
TYABJI, B. "THE SELF IN SECULARISM."
M.F. RAHMAN, 273(IC):APR73-186
TYLER, A. CELESTIAL NAVIGATION.*
S. CLAPP, 617(TLS):23MAY75-577
J.L. HALIO, 598(SOR):AUTUMN75-942
TYLER, J.A., ED. A CONCORDANCE TO
THE FABLES & TALES OF JEAN DE LA
FONTAINE.
F.R.P. AKEHURST, 113:FALL73-170
TYLER, R. THE COWBOY.
G. WARD & R. STROZIER, 441:7DEC75-
94
TYLER, R. THE PROSE OF ROYALL
TYLER.* (M.B. PÉLADEAU, ED)
F. MURPHY, 432(NEQ):MAR73-143
TYMIENIECKA, A-T., ED. ANALECTA
HUSSERLIANA. (VOL 2)
E. WINANCE, 319:APR75-277
TYNAN, K. THE SUMMER AEROPLANE.
M. JOHNSON, 617(TLS):25APR75-445
"TYPOLOGIE DES SOURCES DU MOYEN ÂGE
OCCIDENTAL." (FASC 1-5)
G. CONSTABLE, 589:APR74-386
TYRMAND, L., ED. EXPLORATIONS IN
FREEDOM.
X. GASIOROWSKA, 574(SEEJ):SPRING72-
112
TYROWICZ, M. PRAWDA I MIT W BIO-
GRAFII JULIANA MACIEJA GOSLARA
1820-1852.
P. BROCK, 497(POLR):VOL18#4-108
TYRRELL, B. BERNARD LONERGAN'S
PHILOSOPHY OF GOD.
A. KENNY, 617(TLS):7FEB75-145
TYRRELL, G. LETTRES DE GEORGES
TYRRELL À HENRI BREMOND. (A.
LOUIS-DAVID, ED & TRANS)
L.F. BARMANN, 613:SPRING73-155
TYSDAHL, B.J. JOYCE & IBSEN.
P. SWINDEN, 148:SPRING72-91
TYSON, A., ED. BEETHOVEN STUDIES.
(VOL 1)
W. DRABKIN, 415:AUG74-658
D. MATTHEWS, 617(TLS):20JUN75-702
TYUTCHEV, F.I. POEMS & POLITICAL
LETTERS. (J. ZELDIN, ED & TRANS)
T.J. BINYON, 617(TLS):10JAN75-38
TZARA, T. LE COEUR À GAZ.
S. FAUCHEREAU, 98:NOV73-997
TZARA, T. LAMPISTERIES, SEPT MANI-
FESTES DADA.
S. FAUCHEREAU, 98:APR73-375
TZERMIAS, P. NEUGRIECHISCHE GRAM-
MATIK.
E. TRAPP, 260(IF):BAND77HEFT2/3-
312

TZONIS, A. TOWARDS A NON-OPPRESSIVE
ENVIRONMENT.
F. CHOAY, 98:APR73-293

UBEIKAITĖ, A., ED. LIETUVOS TSR
MOKSLŲ AKADEMIJOS LEIDINIŲ BIBLIO-
GRAFIJA 1969.
W.R. SCHMALSTIEG, 574(SEEJ):SUMMER
72-273
UCHASTKINA, Z.V. RAZVITIE BUMAZH-
NOGO PROIZVODSTVA V ROSSII.
354:MAR73-86
UČIDA, N. DER BENGALI-DIALEKT VON
CHITTAGONG.*
V. MILTNER, 353:1JUL73-93
UDALL, S., C. CONCONI & D. OSTER-
HOUT. THE ENERGY BALLOON.
P. ADAMS, 61:JAN75-90
UEDING, G. SCHILLERS RHETORIK.*
K.L. BERGHAHN, 406:WINTER74-401
UEHLING, T.E., JR. THE NOTION OF
FORM IN KANT'S CRITIQUE OF AESTHET-
IC JUDGMENT.*
R.K., 543:DEC72-369
P. LEECH, 290(JAAC):FALL73-122
"JERRY N. UELSMANN: SILVER MEDITA-
TIONS."
H. KRAMER, 441:7DEC75-86
UIBOPUU, V. SIMILARKOMPARATIVE KON-
STRUKTIONEN IM FINNISCHEN UND EST-
NISCHEN, INSBESONDERE IN DER MOD-
ERNEN SCHRIFTSPRACHE.*
G. MUST, 343:BAND16HEFT1-112
UKENA, P. - SEE VON HUTTEN, U.
UKENA, P. - SEE SEITZ, A.
ULAM, A. THE FALL OF THE AMERICAN
UNIVERSITY.*
R. BUFFINGTON, 569(SR):WINTER74-
147
ULAM, A.B. STALIN.*
A. GYORGY, 104:WINTER74-604
D.E. POWELL, 639(VQR):SPRING74-314
ULBERT, G. DAS RÖMISCHE DONAU-KAS-
TELL RISSTISSEN. (PT 1)
G. WEBSTER, 313:VOL63-314
ULČ, O. POLITICS IN CZECHOSLOVAKIA.
V. KUSIN, 617(TLS):22AUG75-953
ULLMAN, B.L. & P.A. STADTER. THE
PUBLIC LIBRARY OF RENAISSANCE
FLORENCE.*
M.T. GRENDLER, 124:FEB74-228
D.M. ROBATHAN, 24:FALL74-320
ULLMAN, P.L. MARIANO DE LARRA &
SPANISH POLITICAL RHETORIC.*
J. HERRERO, 400(MLN):MAR73-475
J.K. LESLIE, 405(MP):NOV73-226
L. LORENZO-RIVERO, 399(MLJ):JAN-
FEB73-68
ULLMANN, L. - SEE LABAN, R.
ULLMANN, S. SPRACHE UND STIL.
G. FRITZ, 343:BAND17HEFT2-199
ULLMANN, W. LAW & POLITICS IN THE
MIDDLE AGES.
G. LEFF, 617(TLS):8AUG75-901
ULMAN, C.H. SATIRE & THE CORRESPON-
DENCE OF SWIFT.
566:AUTUMN73-34
ULMER, B. MARTIN OPITZ.
H. WAGENER, 399(MLJ):NOV73-378

ULRICH, W. SEMANTISCHE UNTERSUCHUN-
GEN ZUM WORTSCHATZ DES KIRCHEN-
LIEDES IM 16. JAHRHUNDERT.
M. KAEMPFERT, 680(ZDP):BAND92HEFT
2-278
C.V.D. KETTERIJ, 433:OCT73-412
ULRICH, W. WÖRTERBUCH: LINGUIS-
TISCHE GRUNDBEGRIFFE.
M. HELLINGER, 430(NS):MAY73-287
UMBRAL, F. DIARIO DE UN SNOB. RE-
TRATO DE UN JOVEN MALVADO.
G. BROWN, 617(TLS):23MAY75-576
DE UNAMUNO, M. THE AGONY OF CHRIS-
TIANITY & ESSAYS ON FAITH.
639(VQR):AUTUMN74-CLII
DE UNAMUNO, M. NIEBLA. (M.J. VAL-
DÉS, ED)
J.W. DÍAZ, 238:SEP73-753
DE UNAMUNO, M. THE TRAGIC SENSE OF
LIFE IN MEN & NATIONS.
H. REGNERY, 396(MODA):WINTER74-98
UNBEGAUN, B.O. RUSSIAN SURNAMES.*
M. BENSON, 574(SEEJ):FALL73-358
E.C. SMITH, 424:JUN73-114
D.S. WORTH, 550(RUSR):OCT73-444
UNBEGAUN, B.O., WITH D.P. COSTELLO
& W.F. RYAN - SEE WHEELER, M.
UNDERWOOD, M. THE JUROR.
N. CALLENDAR, 441:11MAY75-26
617(TLS):4APR75-353
UNGER, H. GEISTLICHER HERZEN BAVN-
GART.
B.D. HAAGE, 433:OCT73-415
UNGER, P. IGNORANCE.
A.J. AYER, 617(TLS):5SEP75-992
UNGERN-STERNBERG VON PÜRKEL, J. UN-
TERSUCHUNGEN ZUM SPÄTREPUBLIKANIS-
CHEN NOTSTANDRECHT.
U. HALL, 313:VOL63-253
UNSELD, S. BEGEGNUNGEN MIT HERMANN
HESSE.
T. ZIOLKOWSKI, 617(TLS):26SEP75-
1108
UNSELD, S., ED. PETER SUHRKAMP.
E. ROLL, 617(TLS):30CT75-1134
UNVERHAU, D. APPROBATIO - REPROBA-
TIO.
R. FOLZ, 182:VOL26#19-695
UNWIN, P. THE PUBLISHING UNWINS.
295:FEB74-379
UPADHYAYA, K.N. EARLY BUDDHISM &
THE BHAGAVADGITA.
B.G. GOKHALE, 318(JAOS):APR-JUN73-
245
UPADHYE, A.N. - SEE SIDDHASENA DIVĀ-
KARA
UPDIKE, J. BECH VOYAGE.
N. KATTAN, 98:FEB73-191
UPDIKE, J. A MONTH OF SUNDAYS.
A. BROYARD, 441:19FEB75-35
R. DINNAGE, 617(TLS):4JUL75-713
T.R. EDWARDS, 453:3APR75-18
N. HEPBURN, 362:3JUL75-30
G. STADE, 441:23FEB75-4
G. STEINER, 442(NY):10MAR75-116
E. WEEKS, 61:MAR75-141
UPDIKE, J. PICKED-UP PIECES.
A. BROYARD, 441:2DEC75-37
L. GRAVER, 441:30NOV75-39
UPTON, A.F. FINLAND 1939-1940.
D. KIRBY, 617(TLS):7MAR75-244
URANG, G. SHADOWS OF HEAVEN.
R. DETWEILER, 295:FEB74-405

URBAN, R. HISTORISCHE UNTERSUCHUN-
GEN ZUM DOMITIANBILD DES TACITUS.*
T.F. BAXTER, 487:SUMMER73-207
R.H. MARTIN, 123:MAR74-154
URBAN, Z. POZAPOMENUTÁ TVÁŘ BOŽENY
NĚMCOVÉ.*
M.N. BANERJEE, 574(SEEJ):SUMMER72-
247
URE, P. ELIZABETHAN & JACOBEAN
DRAMA. (J.C. MAXWELL, ED)
D. DONOGHUE, 617(TLS):17JAN75-51
URE, P. YEATS & ANGLO-IRISH LITERA-
TURE. (C.J. RAWSON, ED)
D. DONOGHUE, 617(TLS):17JAN75-51
F.S.L. LYONS, 617(TLS):10OCT75-
1187
URE, P. - SEE FORD, J.
URONDO, F. TEATRO.
P.J. SCHOENBACH, 238:MAY73-507
URQUHART, B. HAMMARSKJOLD.
M. MANDELBAUM, 676(YR):AUTUMN73-
151
URQUHART, T. THE ADMIRABLE URQU-
HART. (R. BOSTON, ED)
R. MITCHISON, 362:26JUN75-853
E. MORGAN, 617(TLS):24OCT75-1254
URRY, J. REFERENCE GROUPS & THE
THEORY OF REVOLUTION.
J. DUNN, 111:3MAY74-136
URSU, H.I. MOLDOVA ÎN CONTEXTUL
POLITIC EUROPEAN (1517-1527).
D.J. DELETANT, 575(SEER):JUL74-472
DE USANDIZAGA Y MENDOZA, P.M. EL
CHINGOLÉS.
J.R. REYNA, 292(JAF):JUL-SEP73-309
USBORNE, R. CLUBLAND HEROES.
LORD LAMBTON, 617(TLS):14MAR75-268
USIGLI, R. CORONA DE FUEGO. (R.E.
BALLINGER, ED)
G.J. EDBERG, 238:SEP73-748
W.P. SCOTT, 399(MLJ):DEC73-441
USINGER, F. - SEE GUNDOLF, F.
USPENSKIJ, B.A. POĖTIKA KOMPOZICII.
L.A. FOSTER, 574(SEEJ):FALL72-339
USPENSKY, B. A POETICS OF COMPOSI-
TION.
639(VQR):SUMMER74-LXXX
USSERY, H.E. CHAUCER'S PHYSICIAN.*
R.T. DAVIES, 447(N&Q):JAN73-30
J.E. GRENNEN, 589:JAN74-158
J. MANN, 382(MAE):1974/2-195
C.H. TALBOT, 541(RES):MAY73-201
UTLEY, F.L., L.Z. BLUM & A.F. KIN-
NEY, EDS. BEAR, MAN & GOD.
R. ASSELINEAU, 189(EA):OCT-DEC73-
493
UTLEY, T.E. LESSONS OF ULSTER.
D. ANDERSON, 362:18DEC75-837

VÄÄNÄNEN, V. ÉTUDE SUR LA TEXTE ET
LA LANGUE DES TABLETTES ALBERTINI.
M. GONZÁLEZ-HABA, 343:BAND16HEFT1-
92
VÄÄNÄNEN, V. INTRODUCTION AU LATIN
VULGAIRE.* (2ND ED)
B. LÖFSTEDT, 260(IF):BAND77HEFT
2/3-319
VÄÄNÄNEN, V. - SEE CASTRÉN, P. & H.
LILIUS
VACCARO, A.M. MOSTRA DEI MATERIALI
DELLA TUSCIA LONGOBARDA NELLE RAC-
[CONTINUED]

[CONTINUING]
COLTE PUBBLICHE TOSCANE.
E.M. BOGGESS, 124:DEC73-JAN74-178
VACHEK, J. DYNAMIKA FONOLOGICKÉHO
SYSTÉMU SOUČASNÉ SPISOVNÉ ČEŠTINY.
G.F. MEIER, 682(ZPSK):BAND26HEFT
3/4-453
VĀCISSARATHERA. THE CHRONICLE OF
THE THŪPA & THE THŪPAVAMSA. (N.A.
JAYAWICKRAMA, ED & TRANS)
O. VON HINÜBER, 318(JAOS):JUL-SEP
73-385
VACULÍK, L. THE GUINEA PIGS.*
(GERMAN TITLE: DER MEERSCHWEIN-
CHEN.)
E. OSERS, 364:FEB/MAR75-137
VAGO, B. THE SHADOW OF THE SWAS-
TIKA.
F.L. CARSTEN, 617(TLS):7MAR75-244
VAID, K.N. THE OVERSEAS INDIAN COM-
MUNITY IN HONG KONG.
O. UL HAQ, 302:JUL73-269
VAIL, V.H. & K. SPARKS. MODERN GER-
MAN.*
J.J. MULLIGAN, 221(GQ):JAN73-145
VAIL, V.H., K. SPARKS & T. HUBER.
THOMAS MANNS TONIO KRÖGER ALS WEG
ZUR LITERATUR.
E. FREDERIKSEN, 399(MLJ):NOV74-365
VALAORITIS, N. DIPLOMATIC RELATIONS.
S. TORREGIAN, 114(CHIR):VOL25#3-
166
VALDÉS, H. DIARY OF A CHILEAN CON-
CENTRATION CAMP.
A. ANGELL, 617(TLS):19SEP75-1042
VALDÉS, M.J. - SEE DE UNAMUNO, M.
VALDESPINO, A. JORGE MAÑACH Y SU
GENERACIÓN EN LAS LETRAS CUBANAS.
A.B. HENKIN, 238:DEC73-1124
VALDEZ, L. & S. STEINER, EDS. AZT-
LÁN.
J. HANCOCK, 399(MLJ):APR73-228
VALDMAN, A. BASIC COURSE IN HAITIAN
CREOLE.
G.F. MEIER, 682(ZPSK):BAND26HEFT
3/4-456
J. NICHOLS, 545(RPH):NOV73-218
VALDMAN, A., S. BELASCO & F. STEIN-
ER. SON ET SENS.
N.A. POULIN, 207(FR):FEB73-687
VALE, M.G.A. CHARLES VII.
442(NY):12MAY75-143
VALENCY, M. THE CART & THE TRUM-
PET.*
E. REUBEN, 637(VS):MAR74-340
K.T. VON ROSADOR, 72:BAND211HEFT
1/3-152
H.F. SALERNO, 191(ELN):JUN74-313
639(VQR):WINTER74-XVII
VALENTE, J.A. EL FIN DE LA EDAD DE
PLATA.
J.M. COHEN, 617(TLS):23MAY75-576
VALENTE, J.A. - SEE DE MOLINOS, M.
VALENTIN, P. & G. ZINK, EDS. MÉLAN-
GES POUR JEAN FOURQUET.*
R.G. FINCH, 220(GL&L):OCT73-70
E. SEEBOLD, 260(IF):BAND77HEFT2/3-
367
VALENTINER, T. - SEE KANT, I.
VALENTINI, A. LETTURE DI MONTRALE.
I.P., 275(IQ):SUMMER73-115

VALERA, J. MORSAMOR. (J.B. AVALLE-
ARCE, ED)
  M. BERMEJO-MARCOS, 86(BHS):APR73-
  182
VALÉRY, P. CAHIERS I. (J. ROBIN-
SON, ED)
  C.M. CROW, 208(FS):JAN74-104
VALÉRY, P. LEONARDO, POE & MALLAR-
MÉ. (J. MATHEWS, ED)
  J.D. ERICKSON, 188(ECR):FALL73-252
VALÉRY, P. SELECTED WRITINGS OF
PAUL VALÉRY.
  J.T. JOHNSON, JR., 399(MLJ):MAR74-
  143
VALETTE, R.M. DIRECTIONS IN FOREIGN
LANGUAGE TESTING.
  P. SIEGEL, 207(FR):MAY73-1258
VALETTE, R.M. & R.S. DISICK. MOD-
ERN LANGUAGE PERFORMANCE OBJEC-
TIVES & INDIVIDUALIZATION.
  P.E. ARSENAULT, 399(MLJ):DEC73-441
  F.M. GRITTNER, 207(FR):MAY73-1262
  J.L. WALKER, 238:SEP73-747
VALGARDSON, W.D. BLOODFLOWERS.*
  E. DURIE, 606(TAMR):1STQTR74-90
VALGEMAE, M. ACCELERATED GRIMACE.*
  295:FEB74-409
VALI, F.A. THE TURKISH STRAITS &
NATO.*
  R.W. HERRICK, 550(RUSR):JAN73-102
VÄLIKANGAS, O. LES TERMES D'APPEL-
LATION ET D'INTERPELLATION DANS
"LA COMÉDIE HUMAINE" D'HONORÉ DE
BALZAC.
  M.G. WORTHINGTON, 545(RPH):NOV73-
  228
DE VALINCOUR, J-B-H.D.T. LETTRES À
MADAME LA MARQUISE...SUR LE SUJET
DE LA PRINCESSE DE CLÈVES.
  S.W. TIEFENBRUN, 207(FR):MAY73-
  1222
DE VALK, A. MORALITY & LAW IN CAN-
ADIAN POLITICS.
  I. GENTLES, 99:APR/MAY75-22
VAN DER VALK, M. - SEE EUSTATHIUS
VALLA, L. COLLATIO NOVI TESTAMENTI.
(A. PEROSA, ED)
  M. DE PANIZZA LORCH, 551(RENQ):
  SPRING73-44
VALLA, L. DE VERO FALSOQUE BONO.*
(M. DE PANIZZA LORCH, ED)
  A. SOONS, 551(RENQ):SUMMER73-182
VALLANCE, E., ED. THE STATE, SOCI-
ETY & SELF-DESTRUCTION.
  Z. BANKOWSKI, 617(TLS):26SEP75-
  1089
VALLAS, L. CLAUDE DEBUSSY.
  R. NICHOLS, 415:APR74-307
VALLEJO, A.B. - SEE UNDER BUERO
VALLEJO, A.
VALLÈS, J. LE BACHELIER. (W.D.
REDFERN, ED)
  205(FMLS):APR73-216
VALLÈS, J. OEUVRES. (VOL 1) (R.
BELLET, ED)
  W.D. REDFERN, 617(TLS):3OCT75-1147
VALLI, D. ROMAGNOSI E MANZONI TRA
REALTÀ E STORIA.
  W.T.S., 191(ELN):SEP73(SUPP)-171
VALLONE, A. DANTE.
  J. CHIERICI, 276:WINTER73-589
  M. MARTI, 228(GSLI):VOL150FASC470/
  471-411

VALLONE, A. LETTURA INTERNA DELLE
RIME DI DANTE.
  G. CAMBON, 275(IQ):SUMMER73-96
VALLOTTON, M. & C. GEORG. FELIX
VALLOTTON.
  S. WHITFIELD, 90:JUN73-403
VALPREDA, P. THE VALPREDA PAPERS.
  G. POGGI, 617(TLS):31OCT75-1294
VALVERDE, J.M. AZORÍN.
  L. LIVINGSTONE, 400(MLN):MAR73-485
VAN BRUNT, H.L. INDIAN TERRITORY.
  R. LATTIMORE, 249(HUDR):AUTUMN74-
  470
VAN CLEVE, T.C. THE EMPEROR FRED-
ERICK II OF HOHENSTAUFEN: "IMMUTA-
TOR MUNDI."
  J.M. POWELL, 589:JAN74-159
VAN DER BEETS, R., ED. HELD CAPTIVE
BY INDIANS.
  J. AXTELL, 656(WMQ):OCT74-688
  R.N. ELLIS, 651(WHR):SPRING74-192
  F.W. TURNER 3D, 165:WINTER75-345
  639(VQR):WINTER74-XXIV
VAN DER POEL, C.J. THE SEARCH FOR
HUMAN VALUES.
  W.E.M., 543:SEP72-177
VAN DER TUUK, H.N. A GRAMMAR OF
TOBA BATAK.
  J.M. ECHOLS, 318(JAOS):APR-JUN73-
  251
VAN DE WAAL, H. ABRIDGED EDITION OF
THE ICONCLASS SYSTEM.
  D. CARTER, 54:DEC73-653
VAN DOREN, M. GOOD MORNING.*
  J.N. MORRIS, 249(HUDR):SPRING74-
  109
  A. OSTROFF, 651(WHR):SUMMER74-299
VAN DUSSELDORP, D.B.W.M. PLANNING
OF SERVICE CENTRES IN RURAL AREAS
OF DEVELOPING COUNTRIES.
  S.F. RICHARDS, 302:JAN73-188
VAN DUYN, M. MERCIFUL DISGUISES.*
  H. CARRUTH, 249(HUDR):SUMMER74-311
  S. YENSER, 491:JUN75-167
  H. ZINNES, 109:SPRING/SUMMER74-122
  639(VQR):WINTER74-XI
VAN DYKEN, S. SAMUEL WILLARD, 1640-
1707.*
  D.B. RUTMAN, 432(NEQ):MAR73-149
VAN GREENAWAY, P. TAKE THE WAR TO
WASHINGTON.
  N. CALLENDAR, 441:21SEP75-42
VAN HOLTHOON, F.L. THE ROAD TO
UTOPIA.
  G. BRYKMAN, 542:JAN-MAR73-62
  A. HOLLOWAY, 479(PHQ):APR73-165
VANN, J.D. GRAHAM GREENE.
  R.M. DAVIS, 594:WINTER73-530
VAN NESS, P. REVOLUTION & CHINESE
FOREIGN POLICY.
  E. WICKBERG, 318(JAOS):JAN-MAR73-
  87
VAN NIEL, R. A SURVEY OF HISTORICAL
SOURCE MATERIALS IN JAVA & MANILA.*
  M.C. RICKLEFS, 318(JAOS):APR-JUN73-
  233
VANNIER, B. L'INSCRIPTION DU CORPS.
  R. VIRTANEN, 446:SPRING-SUMMER74-
  190
VAN RYSSELBERGHE, M. LES CAHIERS DE
LA PETITE DAME.
  P. FAWCETT, 617(TLS):4JUL75-741

VAN SCHREEVEN, W.J., COMP. REVOLU-
TIONARY VIRGINIA. (VOL 1)
639(VQR):SPRING74-XLII
VANSINA, J. LA LEGENDE DU PASSE.
L. HARRIES, 292(JAF):OCT-DEC73-401
VANSITTART, P. DICTATORS.
J. SYMONS, 364:OCT/NOV74-141
VAN SYOC, W.B. & F.S. LET'S LEARN
ENGLISH, ADVANCED COURSE. (BKS 5&6)
E.M. ANTHONY, 399(MLJ):JAN-FEB73-
76
VAN VOGT, A.E. THE MAN WITH A
THOUSAND NAMES.
E. KORN, 617(TLS):8AUG75-903
VAN WALLEGHEN, M. THE WICHITA
POEMS.
J.N. MORRIS, 249(HUDR):SPRING74-
114
VAN ZILE, J. DANCE IN INDIA.
S. YOUNGERMAN, 187:SEP75-493
VÁRADY, L. DAS LETZTE JAHRHUNDERT
PANNONIENS (376-476).*
J.J. WILKES, 313:VOL63-260
VARÂHAMIHIRA. THE PAÑCASIDDHÂNTIKÂ
OF VARÂHAMIHIRA. (O. NEUGEBAUER &
D. PINGREE, EDS)
K.S. SHUKLA, 318(JAOS):JUL-SEP73-
386
VARANINI, G., ED. LAUDE DUGENTESCHE.
D.D., 275(IQ):FALL-WINTER73(VOL17
#66)-59
VARANINI, G. & G.P. MARCHI. PAGINE
INTRODUTTIVE ALLO STUDIO DELLA LET-
TERATURA ITALIANA. (2ND ED)
B.L., 275(IQ):SPRING74-115
VARANNAI, A. ANGLIAI VISSZHANG.
N. MASTERMAN, 617(TLS):11APR75-406
VARDUL', I.F., ED. JAZYKOVYE UNI-
VERSALII I LINGVISTIČESKAJA TIPO-
LOGIJA.
B. PANZER, 353:15OCT73-92
VARENNE, J., ED & TRANS. DEVI UPAN-
IŞAD.
L. ROCHER, 318(JAOS):JUL-SEP73-375
VARENNE, J. GRAMMAIRE DU SANSKRIT.
F. BADER, 555:VOL47FASC2-315
L. DEROY, 556(RLV):1973/2-189
H. QUELLET, 343:BAND16HEFT2-157
VARENNE, J., ED & TRANS. UPANISHADS
DU YOGA.
W. HALBFASS, 318(JAOS):JUL-SEP73-
384
VARÈSE, L. VARÈSE. (VOL 1)
M. PETERSON, 470:MAR74-30
VAREY, J.E. PÉREZ GALDÓS: "DOÑA
PERFECTA."*
E. RODGERS, 86(BHS):JUL73-303
P.L. ULLMAN, 238:MAY73-529
VAREY, J.E., ED. GALDÓS STUDIES.
J. HERRERO, 86(BHS):JAN73-92
T.A. SACKETT, 546(RR):NOV73-321
VAREY, J.E. LOS TÍTERES Y OTROS
DIVERTIMIENTOS POPULARES DE MAD-
RID: 1758-1840.
H.F. GRANT, 402(MLR):OCT74-903
VAREY, J.E., N.D. SHERGOLD & J.
SAGE - SEE VÉLEZ DE GUEVARA, J.
VARGAS LLOSA, M. CONVERSATION IN
THE CATHEDRAL.
S.J. LEVINE, 441:23MAR75-1
M. WOOD, 453:20MAR75-27
VARGAS LLOSA, M. PANTALEÓN Y LAS
VISITADORAS.
N. MADRID-MALO, 263:JUL-SEP74-312

VARGISH, T. NEWMAN.*
J. ARTZ, 38:BAND91HEFT4-540
VARGO, E.P. RAINSTORMS & FIRE.
R. HAUGH, 385(MQR):FALL75-473
S.D. WARNER, 27(AL):JAN75-601
VARLEY, H.P. JAPANESE CULTURE.
E.P. TSURMI, 529(QQ):WINTER73-637
VARMA, G.S. VAAGRI BOLI, AN INDO-
ARYAN LANGUAGE.
K. DE VREESE, 318(JAOS):JAN-MAR73-
115
VARMA, S.P. STRUGGLE FOR THE HIMA-
LAYAS. (2ND ED)
R.L. DIAL, 293(JAST):FEB73-361
"VARNEY THE VAMPIRE."
C. FRAYLING, 364:JUN/JUL74-102
VARRO. VARRON, "SATIRES MÉNIPPÉES."
(VOL 1) (J-P. CÈBE, ED & TRANS)
R. ASTBURY, 313:VOL63-304
VARVARO, A. BÉROUL'S "ROMANCE OF
TRISTAN."*
G.J. HALLIGAN, 67:MAY74-113
"VASARELY."
J.R. MELLOW, 441:7DEC75-2
DE VASCONCELLOS, J.L. ESQUISSE
D'UNE DIALECTOLOGIE PORTUGAISE.
(2ND ED)
A.J. NARO, 240(HR):SUMMER73-594
DE VASCONCELOS, J.M. - SEE UNDER
MAURO DE VASCONCELOS, J.
VASIL, R.K. POLITICS IN A PLURAL
SOCIETY.
R.O. TILMAN, 293(JAST):NOV72-212
VASSALL, J. VASSALL.
J. GRIGG, 362:23JAN75-124
DEL VASTO, L. RETURN TO THE SOURCE.
A. BHARATI, 293(JAST):NOV72-195
VATIN, C. RECHERCHES SUR LE MARIAGE
ET LA CONDITION DE LA FEMME MARIÉE
À L'ÉPOQUE HELLÉNISTIQUE.
S.C. HUMPHREYS, 303:VOL93-258
VATSYAYAN, S.H. [AGYEYA] FIRST PER-
SON, SECOND PERSON.
C. COPPOLA, 318(JAOS):APR-JUN73-
247
VATUK, S. KINSHIP & URBANIZATION.
A.D. ROSS, 293(JAST):AUG73-728
DE VAUCELLES, L. "LE NOUVELLISTE DE
LYON" ET LA DÉFENSE RELIGIEUSE
(1879-1889).
L. LE GUILLOU, 535(RHL):NOV-DEC73-
1097
VAUDEVILLE, C. L'INVOCATION.
R.S. MC GREGOR, 318(JAOS):OCT-DEC
73-619
DE VAUGELAS, C.F. REMARQUES SUR LA
LANGUE FRANÇAISE. (R. LAGANE, ED)
209(FM):APR73-194
VAUGHAN, A. AMERICAN GENESIS.
J.H. ELLIOTT, 453:15MAY75-3
VAUGHAN, A.T. & G.A. BILLIAS, EDS.
PERSPECTIVES ON EARLY AMERICAN
HISTORY.
M. ZUCKERMAN, 656(WMQ):OCT74-680
VAUGHAN, J.D. THE MANNERS & CUSTOMS
OF THE CHINESE OF THE STRAITS SET-
TLEMENTS.
H.K. KAUFMAN, 293(JAST):NOV72-215
VAUGHAN, M. CHALKY.
M. LEVIN, 441:22JUN75-14
VAUGHAN, M. & M.S. ARCHER. SOCIAL
CONFLICT & EDUCATIONAL CHANGE IN
ENGLAND & FRANCE 1789-1848.
D.F. BRADSHAW, 208(FS):OCT74-491

VAUGHAN, R. THE GRAND GESTURE.
  C. LEHMANN-HAUPT, 441:16SEP75-45
VAUGHAN, R. VALOIS BURGUNDY.
  M. VALE, 617(TLS):5SEP75-1005
DE VAUX DE FOLETIER, F. MILLE ANS
  D'HISTOIRE DES TSIGANES.
  J. MOREL, 535(RHL):JAN-FEB73-163
VAWTER, B. THIS MAN JESUS.
  G. STANTON, 617(TLS):18JUL75-812
VÁZQUEZ, A.S. - SEE UNDER SÁNCHEZ
  VÁZQUEZ, A.
VÁZQUEZ, J.A. - SEE UNDER AMOR Y
  VÁZQUEZ, J.
VÁZQUEZ CUESTA, P. & M. MENDES DA
  LUZ. GRAMÁTICA PORTUGUESA.* (3RD
  ED)
  N.J. LAMB, 86(BHS):APR73-189
VEATCH, H.B. FOR AN ONTOLOGY OF
  MORALS.*
  J.J. KUPPERMAN, 482(PHR):APR73-244
  M.H.R., 543:JUN73-770
  M.H. ROBINS, 258:MAR73-135
VEBLEN, T. ESSAYS REVIEWS & RE-
  PORTS. (J. DORFMAN, ED)
  D. MAC RAE, 617(TLS):25JUL75-824
VEBR, L., ED. KNIHTISK A UNIVERSITA
  KARLOVA.
  J.S.G. SIMMONS, 78(BC):AUTUMN73-
  390
VÉDRINE, H. LES PHILOSOPHIES DE LA
  RENAISSANCE.
  H.F., 543:DEC72-370
DE LA VEGA, G.L.L. - SEE UNDER LOBO
  LASSO DE LA VEGA, G.
DE VEGA, L. EL ARTE NUEVO DE HACER
  COMEDIAS EN ESTE TIEMPO. (J. DE
  JOSÉ PRADES, ED)
  J. ARCE, 202(FMOD):JUN73-397
DE VEGA, L. A CRITICAL EDITION OF
  LOPE DE VEGA'S "LAS ALMENAS DE
  TORO." (T.E. CASE, ED)
  J.A. CASTAÑEDA, 238:SEP73-733
  C. IRANZO DE EBERSOLE, 241:SEP73-
  90
DE VEGA, L. LA FIANZA SATISFECHA.*
  (W.M. WHITBY & R.R. ANDERSON, EDS)
  A.A. HEATHCOTE, 86(BHS):JUL73-296
  W.C. MC CRARY, 551(RENQ):SPRING73-
  59
DE VEGA, L. LO QUE PASA EN UNA
  TARDE. (R.A. PICERNO, ED)
  L.C. PÉREZ, 238:SEP73-732
DE VEGA, L. EL PEREGRINO EN SU PAT-
  RIA. (M.A. PEYTON, ED)
  V. DIXON, 86(BHS):OCT73-397
  F.C. HAYES, 399(MLJ):DEC73-429
  R.H. KOSSOFF, 405(MP):FEB74-331
  V.G. WILLIAMSEN, 238:MAR73-174
DE VEGA, L. PERIBÁÑEZ Y EL COMENDA-
  DOR DE OCAÑA. (W.S. MITCHELL, ED)
  EL ACERO DE MADRID. (A. BERGOUNI-
  OUX, J. LEMARTINEL & G. ZONANA,
  EDS)
  P.N. DUNN, 86(BHS):APR73-176
DE VEGA, L. VIDA Y MUERTE DE SANTA
  TERESA DE JESÚS. (E. ARAGONE TER-
  NI, ED)
  J.G. FUCILLA, 240(HR):AUTUMN73-700
DE VEGA, L. & C. DE MONROY. FUENTE
  OVEJUNA, DOS COMEDIAS. (F. LÓPEZ
  ESTRADA, ED)
  A. SOONS, 240(HR):WINTER73-102
VEIT, W., ED. CAPTAIN JAMES COOK.
  A.O.A., 149:DEC74-360

VEITH, W.H. INTERSYSTEMARE PHONOLO-
  GIE.
  H. PENZL, 343:BAND17HEFT2-188
VAN DER VEKENE, E. BEMERKENSWERTE
  EINBÄNDE IN DER NATIONALBIBLIOTHEK
  ZU LUXEMBOURG.
  A. HOBSON, 617(TLS):19DEC75-1524
  O. MAZAL, 182:VOL26#11/12-387
VELASCO, G.R. LABOR LEGISLATION
  FROM AN ECONOMIC POINT OF VIEW.
  W.H. HUTT, 396(MODA):FALL74-429
VÉLEZ DE GUEVARA, J. LOS CELOS
  HACEN ESTRELLAS.* (J.E. VAREY,
  N.D. SHERGOLD & J. SAGE, EDS)
  C. IRANZO DE EBERSOLE, 241:JAN73-
  83
  W.F. KING, 405(MP):NOV73-210
  M. WILSON, 86(BHS):APR73-178
VELLACOTT, P. IRONIC DRAMA.
  O. TAPLIN, 617(TLS):15AUG75-919
VELLACOTT, P. SOPHOCLES & OEDIPUS.
  C.J. HERINGTON, 124:SEP72-47
  E.W. WHITTLE, 123:NOV74-196
VELTSOS, G.S. SEMEIOLOGIA TON POLI-
  TIKON THESMON.
  M. DRAGOUMIS, 617(TLS):14NOV75-
  1363
"IVAN VELYČKOVSKYJ: TWORY."
  D. TSCHIŽEWSKIJ, 72:BAND211HEFT
  1/3-248
VELZ, J.W. SHAKESPEARE & THE CLASSI-
  CAL TRADITION.
  D. GREENWOOD, 570(SQ):WINTER73-94
VENDITTI, A. CORPUS PALLADIANUM.
  (VOL 4: LA LOGGIA DEL CAPITANIATO
  DI VICENZA.)
  C.K. LEWIS, 127:WINTER73/74-176
  M.N. ROSENFELD, 576:DEC73-335
  F.J.B. WATSON, 39:MAY73-531
VENDLER, H. THE POETRY OF GEORGE
  HERBERT.
  F. KERMODE, 441:6JUL75-13
  I.A. RICHARDS, 617(TLS):28NOV75-
  1417
VENDLER, Z. RES COGITANS.
  C.F.B., 543:JUN73-770
VENEZKY, R.L. THE STRUCTURE OF ENG-
  LISH ORTHOGRAPHY.*
  A. BRISAU, 179(ES):JUN72-275
VENGEROV, S.A., ED. RUSSKAYA LITER-
  ATURA XX VEKA.
  J.D. ELLSWORTH, 575(SEER):JAN74-
  153
VENTURI, R., D.S. BROWN & S. IZEN-
  OUR. LEARNING FROM LAS VEGAS.*
  M.C. BEARDSLEY, 290(JAAC):WINTER
  74-245
  G. WOLF, 576:OCT73-258
VERBRAEKEN, R. JACQUES-LOUIS DAVID
  JUGÉ PAR SES CONTEMPORAINS ET PAR
  LA POSTERITÉ.
  F.J.B. WATSON, 39:DEC73-512
VERCIER, B. LES CRITIQUES DE NOTRE
  TEMPS ET SAINT-EXUPÉRY.
  H. GODIN, 208(FS):JUL74-348
VERCORS. COMME UN FRÈRE.
  J. KOLBERT, 399(MLJ):APR74-207
VERDI, G. LETTERS OF GIUSEPPE
  VERDI. (C. OSBORNE, ED & TRANS)
  R. CRAFT, 453:20MAR75-3
  P. GOSSETT, 414(MQ):OCT73-633
VERDI, G. SEVEN VERDI LIBRETTOS.
  (W. WEAVER, TRANS)
  R. CRAFT, 453:20MAR75-3

VERDIER, C. LES ÉOLISMES NON-
ÉPIQUES DE LA LANGUE DE PINDARE.
  B. FORSSMAN, 343:BAND17HEFT2-164
VERDIER, P., P. BRIEGER & M.F. MONT-
PETIT. ART & THE COURTS.
  G. ZARNECKI, 39:JUN73-623
VERDÍN DÍAZ, G. INTRODUCCIÓN AL
ESTILO INDIRECTO LIBRE EN ESPAÑOL.
  B.R. LAVANDERA, 545(RPH):AUG73-101
VERGA, G. LETTERE D'AMORE. (G.
RAYA, ED)
  C.R., 275(IQ):FALL-WINTER73(VOL17
  #66)-69
  E. SACCONE, 400(MLN):JAN73-142
VERGA, L. IL PENSIERO FILOSOFICO E
SCIENTIFICO DI ANTOINE ARNAULD.
(VOL 1)
  M.A. FINOCCHIARO, 319:OCT75-529
VERGIL. THE "AENEID" OF VIRGIL.
(A. MANDELBAUM, TRANS)
  W.S. ANDERSON, 124:MAR73-354
  G.S. FRASER, 473(PR):2/1974-289
VERGIL. LANDLEBEN. (J. & M. GÖTTE,
EDS)
  B.F. DICK, 124:NOV72-174
VERGIL. P. VERGILI MARONIS "AENEI-
DOS" LIBER I.* (R.G. AUSTIN, ED)
  E.W. LEACH, 124:SEP72-42
  G. LUCK, 24:SUMMER74-176
  W.S. MAGUINNESS, 123:NOV74-207
VERGO, P. ART IN VIENNA, 1898-1918.
  C.E. SCHORSKE, 453:11DEC75-39
VERGOPOULOS, K. TO AGROTIKON ZU-
TIMA STIN ELLADA.
  P.J. VATIKIOTIS, 617(TLS):14NOV75-
  1366
VERHEUL, K. THE THEME OF TIME IN
THE POETRY OF ANNA AXMATOVA.*
  R.D.B. THOMSON, 574(SEEJ):FALL72-
  350
VERHEUS, S.L. ZEUGNIS UND GERICHT.
  B.P. COPENHAVER, 551(RENQ):AUTUMN
  73-325
VERHEYEN, E. THE PAINTINGS IN THE
"STUDIOLO" OF ISABELLA D'ESTE AT
MANTUA.
  C.H. CLOUGH, 39:MAY73-533
  C. GOULD, 54:JUN73-300
VERHOEVEN, C. THE PHILOSOPHY OF
WONDER.
  H.F., 543:DEC72-371
VERKUYL, H.J. ON THE COMPOSITIONAL
NATURE OF THE ASPECTS.
  J.W. DE VRIES, 204(FDL):DEC73-307
VERKUYL, P.E.L. BATTISTA GUARINI'S
"IL PASTOR FIDO" IN DE NEDERLANDSE
DRAMATISCHE LITERATUUR.*
  E.B., 228(GSLI):VOL150FASC469-153
VERLAINE, P. OEUVRES EN PROSE COM-
PLÈTES. (J. BOREL, ED)
  R.T. DENOMMÉ, 446:SPRING-SUMMER74-
  197
VERMASEREN, M.J. MITHRIACA. (VOL 1)
  M.W. FREDERIKSEN, 313:VOL63-274
  R.E. WITT, 123:MAR74-157
VERNADSKY, G. & OTHERS, EDS. A
SOURCE BOOK FOR RUSSIAN HISTORY
FROM EARLY TIMES TO 1917. (VOLS
1&3)
  H.G. LUNT, 574(SEEJ):FALL73-361
  J.L. WIECZYNSKI, 104:WINTER73-537
VERNADSKY, G. & OTHERS, EDS. A
SOURCE BOOK FOR RUSSIAN HISTORY
  [CONTINUED]

[CONTINUING]
FROM EARLY TIMES TO 1917. (VOL 2)
  H.G. LUNT, 574(SEEJ):FALL73-361
  N.E. SAUL, 481(PQ):JUL73-375
  J.L. WIECZYNSKI, 104:WINTER73-537
VERNADSKY, G. & R.T. FISHER, JR. -
SEE PUSHKAREV, S.G.
VERNANT, J-P., ED. DIVINATION ET
RATIONALITÉ.
  M. FREEDMAN, 617(TLS):14FEB75-171
VERNANT, J-P. & P. VIDAL-NAQUET.
MYTHE ET TRAGÉDIE EN GRÈCE ANCIENNE.
  J.A. HALDANE, 303:VOL93-241
  N. LORAUX, 98:OCT73-908
VERNIER, J-P. H.G. WELLS ET SON
TEMPS.
  F. SCARFE, 189(EA):JUL-SEP73-309
VERNIER, R. LETTRES DE L'INTÉRIEUR.
  R.R. HUBERT, 207(FR):MAR73-869
VERNOIS, P. LA DYNAMIQUE THÉÂTRALE
D'EUGÈNE IONESCO.
  A. DEMAITRE, 207(FR):MAY73-1236
VERNON, J. THE GARDEN & THE MAP.*
  D. ROBY, 651(WHR):SPRING74-190
VERNON, R., ED. BIG BUSINESS & THE
STATE.
  N. FAITH, 617(TLS):2MAY75-486
VERONESE, A. (AGLAIA ANASSILLIDE)
NOTIZIE DELLA SUA VITA SCRITTE DA
LEI MEDESIMA. (M.P. STOCCHI, ED)
  M. FUBINI, 228(GSLI):VOL150FASC472-
  626
VEROSTA, S. THEORIE UND REALITÄT
VON BÜNDNISSEN.
  F.R. BRIDGE, 575(SEER):JUL74-468
"VERS L'UTOPIE DU LIVRE."
  R. FEDERMAN, 207(FR):FEB73-671
VERSNEL, H.S. TRIUMPHUS.*
  J.E. PHILLIPS, 124:FEB74-232
VÉRTES, E. DIE OSTJAKISCHEN PRONOM-
INA.
  G.F. MEIER, 682(ZPSK):BAND26HEFT
  1/2-213
  E. SCHIEFER, 343:BAND16HEFT1-109
VERVLIET, H.D.L., ED. THE BOOK
THROUGH FIVE THOUSAND YEARS.
  D. COOMBS, 135:AUG73-316
  R.D. PRATT, 503:AUTUMN73-148
VERWEY, H.D. - SEE UNDER DE LA FON-
TAINE VERWEY, H.
VERWEYEN, T. DER "ARME HEINRICH"
HARTMANNS VON AUE.
  R.C.J. ENDRES, 221(GQ):SEP73-151
VERZERA, A. LA POESIA DI TOMMASO
CAMPANELLA.
  A.N. MANCINI, 400(MLN):JAN73-125
VESCOVINI, G.F. - SEE CUSANO, N.
VESEY, G., ED. PHILOSOPHY & THE
ARTS.
  W. CHARLTON, 518:JAN74-30
VESEY, G.N.A., ED. REASON & REALITY.
  A. FLEW, 479(PHQ):OCT73-358
  R. HARRISON, 483:JUL73-303
VESTAL, S. HAPPY HUNTING GROUNDS.
  M. LEVIN, 441:14DEC75-32
VIANSINO, G. INTRODUZIONE ALLO
STUDIO CRITICO DELLA LETTERATURA
LATINA.*
  E.T. SILK, 24:SUMMER74-165
VIAZZI, G. STUDI E DOCUMENTI PER IL
LUCINI.
  400(MLN):JAN73-170
VIAZZI, G. - SEE LUCINI, G.P.

VIAZZI, G. & V. SCHEIWILLER, EDS.
POETI SIMBOLISTI E LIBERTY IN
ITALIA. (VOL 2)
A.D.B., 228(GSLI):VOL150FASC469-
156
VICENTE, G. FARCES & FESTIVAL
PLAYS. (T.R. HART, ED)
J. BROTHERTON, 67:MAY74-132
T.F. EARLE, 402(MLR):OCT74-900
R.M. WALKER, 131(CL):SUMMER74-282
VICHIN PANUPONG. INTER-SENTENCE
RELATIONS IN MODERN CONVERSATIONAL
THAI.
R.B. NOSS, 302:JAN73-179
VICI, A.B. - SEE UNDER BUSIRI VICI,
A.
VICINUS, M. THE INDUSTRIAL MUSE.
R. FULLER, 362:27MAR75-420
P. KEATING, 617(TLS):31JAN75-104
VICKERS, B. FRANCIS BACON & RENAIS-
SANCE PROSE.
M. CRANE, 570(SQ):WINTER73-94
VICKERS, B., ED. SHAKESPEARE: THE
CRITICAL HERITAGE.* (VOL 1)
C.T.P., 566:SPRING74-101
VICKERS, B. TOWARDS GREEK TRAGEDY.*
D. GRENE, 31(ASCH):SUMMER75-509
VICKERS, B., ED. THE WORLD OF JONA-
THAN SWIFT.
P. DANCHIN, 179(ES):APR72-166
VICKERY, J.B. ROBERT GRAVES & THE
WHITE GODDESS.*
L. FEDER, 295:FEB74-623
VICKERY, J.B. THE LITERARY IMPACT
OF "THE GOLDEN BOUGH."*
M. LEBOWITZ, 676(YR):WINTER74-308
R. TELEKY, 627(UTQ):FALL73-91
G.B. TENNYSON, 445(NCF):DEC73-367
QUEEN VICTORIA. ADVICE TO A GRAND-
DAUGHTER. (R. HOUGH, ED)
G. BATTISCOMBE, 617(TLS):26DEC75-
1532
K. EVANS & LORD MOUNTBATTEN, 362:
20NOV75-686
QUEEN VICTORIA. YOUR DEAR LETTER.
(R. FULFORD, ED)
R.C. TOBIAS, 637(VS):DEC73-210
"VICTORIA & ALBERT MUSEUM YEARBOOK."
(NO. 3)
B.D.H. MILLER, 463:WINTER73-438
"A VICTORIAN ALBUM."
H. KRAMER, 441:7DEC75-84
"VICTORIAN CHURCH ART."
P.F. NORTON, 576:MAR73-75
VIDAL, A.B. - SEE UNDER BARRERA
VIDAL, A.
VIDAL, G. BURR.*
639(VQR):SPRING74-LV
VIDAL, G. COLLECTED ESSAYS 1952-
1972.
P. BAILEY, 364:DEC74/JAN75-133
R. PADEL, 617(TLS):21FEB75-188
VIDAL, G. MYRON.*
E. TENNANT, 362:10APR75-486
F. WYNDHAM, 617(TLS):11APR75-389
VIDAL, H. JOSÉ DONOSO.
J. DURÁN CERDA, 263:JUL-SEP74-287
VIDAL, R. ABRIL ISSIA. (W.H.W.
FIELD, ED)
T. NEWCOMBE, 402(MLR):OCT74-862
VIDAL, R. THE "RAZOS DE TROBAR" OF
RAIMON VIDAL & ASSOCIATED TEXTS.*
(J.H. MARSHALL, ED)
T.R. HART, 400(MLN):MAR73-398
[CONTINUED]

[CONTINUING]
P. SKÅRUP, 589:APR74-361
L.T. TOPSFIELD, 382(MAE):1974/2-
166
VIDAL-NAQUET, P. OEDIPE À ATHÈNES.
N. LORAUX, 98:OCT73-908
VIDMAN, L. ISIS UND SARAPIS BEI DEN
GRIECHEN UND RÖMERN.*
E. WILL, 555:VOL47FASC1-143
VIEBROCK, H. - SEE LOWE, R. & J.
BRIGHT
VIELWAHR, A. LA VIE ET L'OEUVRE DE
SÉNAC DE MEILHAN.
P.H. MEYER, 546(RR):MAR74-138
V. MYLNE, 535(RHL):SEP-OCT73-901
VIER, J. GIDE.
D. MOUTOTE, 535(RHL):JAN-FEB73-158
VIER, J. HISTOIRE DE LA LITTÉRATURE
FRANÇAISE: XVIIIE SIÈCLE.* (VOLS
1&2)
R. TROUSSON, 549(RLC):APR-JUN73-
351
VIETH, D.M. - SEE DRYDEN, J.
VIETTA, S. SPRACHE UND SPRACHRE-
FLEXION IN DER MODERNEN LYRIK.
K. WEISSENBERGER, 221(GQ):SEP73-
138
VIGAR, P. THE NOVELS OF THOMAS
HARDY.
J.I.M. STEWART, 617(TLS):18APR75-
415
DE VIGNEULLES, P. LES CENT NOU-
VELLES. (C.H. LIVINGSTON, WITH
F.R. LIVINGSTON & R.H. IVY, JR.,
EDS)
B.C. BOWEN, 551(RENQ):WINTER73-512
DE VIGNY, A. LES CONSULTATIONS DU
DOCTEUR NOIR. (F. GERMAIN, ED)
D.G. CHARLTON, 208(FS):JUL74-338
VIIRLAID, A. GRAVES WITHOUT CROSSES.
M. WOLFE, 102(CANL):WINTER74-99
VILJAMAA, T. STUDIES IN GREEK ENCO-
MIASTIC POETRY OF THE EARLY BYZAN-
TINE PERIOD.
C.A. TRYPANIS, 122:APR74-131
VILLA, E. - SEE ZENA, R.
VILLARET, B. DEUX SOLEILS POUR
ARTUBY.
H. MICHOT-DIETRICH, 207(FR):APR73-
1074
VILLAVERDE, C. CECILIA VALDÉS O LA
LOMA DEL ÁNGEL. (O. BLONDET & A.
TUDISCO, EDS)
E. GUILLERMO, 263:APR-JUN74-182
VILLEGAS, J. LA ESTRUCTURA MÍTICA
DEL HÉROE.
R.A. CARDWELL, 402(MLR):JUL74-687
VILLEGAS, J. LA INTERPRETACIÓN DE
LA OBRA DRAMÁTICA.
A.A. BORRÁS, 238:SEP73-736
DE VILLIERS, G. CHECKPOINT CHARLIE.
N. CALLENDAR, 441:29JUN75-30
VIÑAS, A. LA ALEMANIA NAZI Y EL
18 DE JULIO.
P. PRESTON, 617(TLS):23MAY75-557
VINAVER, E. THE RISE OF ROMANCE.*
G.C. BRITTON, 447(N&Q):JAN73-28
A. CRÉPIN, 189(EA):JUL-SEP73-351
B.N. SARGENT, 405(MP):MAY74-405
E. VANCE, 546(RR):JAN74-52
R.M. WILSON, 175:SPRING72-23
VINAVER, E. - SEE MALORY, T.

VINAY, G. L'AMERICA MUSICALE DI
CHARLES IVES.
  P. DICKINSON, 415:NOV74-947
VINCENT, W.A.L. THE GRAMMAR SCHOOLS.
  P.A. SLACK, 447(N&Q):AUG73-316
DA VINCI, L. - SEE UNDER LEONARDO DA
VINCI
VINÇON, H. TOPOGRAPHIE.*
  D. BERGER, 221(GQ):MAR73-260
VINER, J. THE ROLE OF PROVIDENCE
IN THE SOCIAL ORDER.
  C.N. STOCKTON, 481(PQ):JUL73-407
VINOGRADOV, V.V. THE HISTORY OF THE
RUSSIAN LITERARY LANGUAGE FROM THE
SEVENTEENTH CENTURY TO THE NINE-
TEENTH.
  C.N. LEE, 574(SEEJ):SPRING72-123
VINOKUR, G.O. THE RUSSIAN LANGU-
AGE.* (J. FORSYTH, ED)
  S.P. HILL, 574(SEEJ):SPRING72-120
VINTON, J., ED. DICTIONARY OF CON-
TEMPORARY MUSIC.*
  639(VQR):SUMMER74-CVII
VIPOND, D. NIGHT OF THE SHOOTING
STAR.
  N. CALLENDAR, 441:26OCT75-54
VIRGIL - SEE UNDER VERGIL
VIRIEUX, D. - SEE MADAME DE DURAS
"THE VISCONTI HOURS."* (M. MEISS &
E.W. KIRSCH, EDS)
  T. LASK, 55:NOV72-16
VISCOTT, D. HOW TO LIVE WITH AN-
OTHER PERSON.
  L.C. LEWIN, 441:13APR75-6
VISHNYAKOVA-AKIMOVA, V.V. TWO YEARS
IN REVOLUTIONARY CHINA, 1925-1927.*
  E.P. TRANI, 550(RUSR):JAN73-102
"A VISION OF CANADA: THE MC MICHAEL
CANADIAN COLLECTION."
  K. MC SWEENEY, 529(QQ):AUTUMN73-
  500
VISSER, F.T. AN HISTORICAL SYNTAX
OF THE ENGLISH LANGUAGE. (PT 3,
1ST HALF)
  B. CARSTENSEN, 430(NS):JAN73-44
  H.W. VIETHEN, 38:BAND91HEFT3-371
VITA, L. STORIA DELLA POESIA DEL
DOPOGUERRA.
  J.V. GRECO, 399(MLJ):NOV73-367
VITALIS, O. - SEE UNDER ORDERIC VI-
TALIS
VITESTAM, G., ED. KANZ AL-MULŪK FĪ
KAIFIYYAT AS-SULŪK.
  J.M. KELLY, 318(JAOS):JAN-MAR73-97
VITRIA, M.P., ED. POESÍAS PATRIÓT-
ICAS MEXICANAS.
  P. JOHNSON, 399(MLJ):SEP-OCT73-302
VITTORINI, D., ED. ITALIAN SHORT
STORIES 2.
  G. LAZZARINO, 399(MLJ):DEC73-445
VITTORINI, E. WOMEN OF MESSINA.*
  N. HEPBURN, 362:21AUG75-254
  I. QUIGLY, 617(TLS):18JUL75-793
  P.M. SPACKS, 249(HUDR):SUMMER74-
  283
VITZ, E.B. THE CROSSROAD OF INTEN-
TIONS.
  E. MOLES, 617(TLS):12SEP75-1032
VIVANTE, P. THE HOMERIC IMAGINA-
TION.*
  C.R. BEYE, 24:WINTER74-394
VLACK, D. ART DECO ARCHITECTURE IN
NEW YORK.
  P. GOLDBERGER, 441:2MAR75-6

VLADIMIROV, L. THE RUSSIAN SPACE
BLUFF.
  G.P. HOLMAN, JR., 396(MODA):SUMMER
  74-328
VLASTO, A.P. THE ENTRY OF THE SLAVS
INTO CHRISTENDOM.*
  H.G. LUNT, 574(SEEJ):SUMMER72-269
VOCOLO, J.M. & E.H. MIYARES, JR.
BOSQUEJOS DE MÉXICO Y CENTROAMÉR-
ICA.
  M.W. COATES, 238:MAY73-529
  R. LARSON, 399(MLJ):JAN-FEB74-79
VOEGELIN, E. ORDER & HISTORY. (VOL
4) FROM ENLIGHTENMENT TO REVOLU-
TION.
  G. SEBBA, 598(SOR):AUTUMN75-918
VOELKE, A-J. L'IDÉE DE VOLONTÉ DANS
LE STOÏCISME.
  J.B. GOULD, 319:JUL75-404
VOGEL, E.F. JAPAN'S NEW MIDDLE
CLASS.
  L. HOLLERMAN, 285(JAPQ):APR-JUN73-
  227
VOGEL, I. DIE AFFEKTIVE INTENSIV-
IERUNG DER ADJEKTIVA MIT HILFE DES
VERGLEICHS IM ALTFRANZÖSISCHEN.
  M. SANDMANN, 545(RPH):MAY74-534
VOGEL, J.F. DANTE GABRIEL ROSSET-
TI'S VERSECRAFT.*
  M. GREENE, 219(GAR):WINTER73-601
VOGEL, L. THE COLUMN OF ANTONINUS
PIUS.
  D.K. HAGEL, 255:FALL73-302
VOGEL, L.E. ALEKSANDR BLOK: THE
JOURNEY TO ITALY.*
  I. MASING-DELIC, 574(SEEJ):SUMMER
  73-232
VOGEL, R., ED. THE GERMAN PATH TO
ISRAEL.
  R.M. DE VORE, 497(POLR):VOL18#4-
  103
VOGELGESANG, S. THE LONG DARK NIGHT
OF THE SOUL.*
  P. STEINFELS, 231:JAN75-80
VON DER VOGELWEIDE, W. - SEE UNDER
WALTHER VON DER VOGELWEIDE
VOGT, H. GRAMMAIRE DE LA LANGUE
GÉORGIENNE.
  D.M. LANG, 297(JL):FEB73-187
VOGT, H., WITH OTHERS. NEUE MUSIK
SEIT 1945.*
  F. STERNFELD, 410(M&L):JUL74-329
VOGT, J. ANCIENT SLAVERY & THE
IDEAL OF MAN.
  M.I. FINLEY, 617(TLS):14NOV75-1348
VOGT, J., ED. BIBLIOGRAPHIE ZUR
ANTIKEN SKLAVEREI.
  J.H.W.G. LIEBESCHUETZ, 313:VOL63-
  311
  G.E.M. DE STE. CROIX, 123:NOV74-
  304
VOGT, J., ED. DER KRIMINALROMAN.
  D.L. ASHLIMAN, 131(CL):SPRING73-
  187
VOGT, J. SKLAVEREI UND HUMANITÄT.
(2ND ED)
  F. LASSERRE, 182:VOL26#5/6-172
"VOGUE POSTER BOOK."
  J-C. SUARES, 441:5OCT75-22
VOIGT, K. ITALIENISCHE BERICHTE AUS
DEM SPÄTMITTELALTERLICHEN DEUTSCH-
LAND.
  F.R. HAUSMANN, 72:BAND211HEFT1/3-
  86

VOIGT, W., ED. XVII. DEUTSCHER
ORIENTALISTENTAG VOM 21. BIS 27.
JULI 1968 IN WÜRZBURG: VORTRÄGE.
J.L. MALONE, 353:15MAR73-87
VOITL, H., ED. DER SPRACHPRAKTISCHE
TEIL DES STUDIUMS DER ANGLISTIK.
G. FEUERSTEIN, 430(NS):APR73-238
VÖLKER, G., ED. VOM ANTICHRIST.
W.F. SCHERER, 406:SUMMER74-209
VÖLKER, W. MÄRCHENHAFTE ELEMENTE
BEI CHRÉTIEN DE TROYES.
E. KENNEDY, 208(FS):OCT74-437
DE VOLTAIRE, F.M.A. THE COMPLETE
WORKS OF VOLTAIRE. (VOLS 99-105)
(T. BESTERMAN, ED)
C. TODD, 402(MLR):APR74-407
DE VOLTAIRE, F.M.A. HISTOIRE DE LA
GUERRE DE 1741.* (J. MAURENS, ED)
M. LAURENT-HUBERT, 535(RHL):JUL-
AUG73-702
DE VOLTAIRE, F.M.A. ZADIG & OTHER
STORIES. (H.T. MASON, ED)
W.H. BARBER, 208(FS):JAN74-79
VONDRA, J. PAUL ZWILLING.
P. CAMPBELL, 617(TLS):22AUG75-951
VONNEGUT, K., JR. BREAKFAST OF
CHAMPIONS.*
P. STEVICK, 473(PR):2/1974-302
VONNEGUT, K., JR. HAPPY BIRTHDAY,
WANDA JUNE.
A. RENDLE, 157:AUTUMN73-81
VONNEGUT, K., JR. WAMPETERS FOMA &
GRANFALLOONS.*
A. DUCHÊNE, 617(TLS):11APR75-387
VONNEGUT, M. THE EDEN EXPRESS.
A.C.J. BERGMAN, 441:26OCT75-7
R. TODD, 61:OCT75-105.
VOORHOEVE, P., COMP. SÜDSUMATRAN-
ISCHE HANDSCHRIFTEN.
J. FILLIOZAT, 182:VOL26#13/14-452
"VOPOROSY STILISTIKI."
D. TSCHIŽEWSKIJ, 72:BAND211HEFT
1/3-253
VORDTRIEDE, W. - SEE VON BACHERACH,
T. & K. GUTZKOW
VORDTRIEDE, W. - SEE YEATS, W.B.
VORPAHL, B.M. MY DEAR WISTER.
R.A. RORIPAUGH, 649(WAL):SPRING&
SUMMER73-77
VOSSKAMP, W. ROMANTHEORIE IN
DEUTSCHLAND.
T.P. SAINE, 301(JEGP):OCT74-583
"VOX CONCISE SPANISH & ENGLISH DIC-
TIONARY." "VOX NEW COMPACT SPANISH
& ENGLISH DICTIONARY."
R.J. PENNY, 402(MLR):OCT74-896
"VOX SHORTER SPANISH & ENGLISH DIC-
TIONARY."
R.J. PENNY, 402(MLR):OCT74-896
J. STEVENSON, 67:MAY74-135
VRANICH, S.B. - SEE DE ARGUIJO, J.
VREULS, D. ARE WE THERE YET?
A. BROYARD, 441:2MAY75-39
T. LE CLAIR, 441:25MAY75-18
DE VRIEND, H.J., ED. THE OLD ENG-
LISH "MEDICINA DE QUADRUPEDIBUS."
A. CRÉPIN, 189(EA):JUL-SEP73-348
A. HUDSON, 541(RES):MAY73-250
VROOMAN, J.R. VOLTAIRE'S THEATRE.*
V. BOWEN, 546(RR):MAR74-130
J. UNDANK, 400(MLN):MAY73-873
VUCINICH, W.S., ED. RUSSIA & ASIA.
R.E. KANET, 104:WINTER74-600
G. TOKMAKOFF, 550(RUSR):OCT73-443

VUILLEMIN, J. LE DIEU D'ANSELME ET
LES APPARENCES DE LA RAISON.*
B.M.B., 543:DEC72-372
VUILLEMIN, J. LA LOGIQUE ET LE
MONDE SENSIBLE.
H. BARREAU, 542:JUL-SEP73-379
E. VON SAVIGNY, 53(AGP):BAND55
HEFT3-338
VUKANOVICH, E.I. ZVUKOVAIA FAKTURA
STIKHOTVORENII SBORNIKA B.L. PAS-
TERNAKA "SESTRA MOIA ZHIZN."*
R.D.B. THOMSON, 104:FALL73-420
VYGOTSKY, L.S. THE PSYCHOLOGY OF
ART.*
M. RADER, 399(MLJ):SEP-OCT73-291
VYVYAN, J. SHAKESPEARE & PLATONIC
BEAUTY.
V.K. WHITAKER, 570(SQ):SUMMER73-
349

WAAGE, F.O., JR. - SEE ROWLANDS, S.
WACHER, J. THE TOWNS OF ROMAN
BRITAIN.
B. CUNLIFFE, 617(TLS):12SEP75-1016
WACHINGER, B. SÄNGERKRIEG.
F.H. BÄUML, 301(JEGP):OCT74-579
WÄCHTERSHÄUSER, W. DAS VERBRECHEN
DES KINDESMORDES IM ZIETALTER DER
AUFKLÄRUNG.
G. MAY, 182:VOL26#13/14-474
WÄCHTLER, K. DAS STUDIUM DER ENG-
LISCHEN SPRACHE.
B. CARSTENSEN, 430(NS):JAN73-48
WÄCHTLER, K. - SEE GLEASON, H.A., JR.
WACKENRODER, W.H. WILHELM HEINRICH
WACKENRODER'S "CONFESSIONS" & "FAN-
TASIES."* (M.H. SCHUBERT, ED &
TRANS)
J.D. ZIPES, 399(MLJ):DEC73-435
WACKERNAGEL-JOLLES, B. UNTERSUCH-
UNGEN ZUR GESPROCHENEN SPRACHE.
K-H. BAUSCH, 657(WW):MAR/APR73-136
WADDELL, J.R.E. AN INTRODUCTION TO
SOUTHEAST ASIAN POLITICS.
D.A. WILSON, 293(JAST):AUG73-731
WADDINGTON, M. DRIVING HOME.*
C. LEVENSON, 529(QQ):AUTUMN73-469
T. WAYMAN, 102(CANL):SPRING73-85
WADDINGTON, M. - SEE SUTHERLAND, J.
WADE, I.O. THE INTELLECTUAL ORIGINS
OF THE FRENCH ENLIGHTENMENT.*
J. LOUGH, 402(MLR):JUL74-642
P.H. MEYER, 207(FR):MAR73-829
R. SHACKLETON, 131(CL):FALL74-361
WADE, J. THE TRADE OF THE TRICKS.
R. HAYNES, 617(TLS):31JAN75-113
WADEY, M.T. SLEIGHT OF HEART.
S. CLAPP, 617(TLS):30MAY75-584
WADSWORTH, J.B., ED. THE COMEDY OF
EROS.* (N.A. SHAPIRO, TRANS)
B.L.O. RICHTER, 207(FR):OCT72-195
DE WAELHENS, A. LA PSYCHOSE.
W.V.E., 543:SEP72-157
J.N. KAUFMANN, 154:MAR73-189
WAGAR, W. GOOD TIDINGS.
H.W.S., 319:OCT75-549
WAGAR, W.W., ED. HISTORY OF THE
IDEA OF MANKIND.
H.D. LONG, 485(PE&W):JAN-APR73-266

WAGENFELD, M. AUSGLEICHSANSPRÜCHE
UNTER SOLIDARISCH HAFTENDEN DELIKTS-
SCHULDNERN IM ENGLISCHEN UND DEUT-
SCHEN RECHT.
  W.G. BECKER, 182:VOL26#19-655
WAGENKNECHT, C. WECKHERLIN UND
OPITZ.*
  P.N. SKRINE, 402(MLR):JAN74-225
WAGENKNECHT, D. BLAKE'S NIGHT.*
  D.R. FAULKNER, 676(YR):SUMMER74-
  590
  S.R. HOOVER, 401(MLQ):DEC74-430
  D.K. MOORE, 301(JEGP):JUL74-444
  T. WEISKEL, 591(SIR):SPRING74-172
  639(VQR):SUMMER74-LXXVI
WAGENKNECHT, E. RALPH WALDO EMER-
SON.
  639(VQR):AUTUMN74-CXXXIV
WAGER, W. TELEFON.
  N. CALLENDAR, 441:13APR75-30
WAGER, W. - SEE WÖRNER, K.H.
WAGLEY, C. AN INTRODUCTION TO BRA-
ZIL. (REV)
  J.C. KINNEAR, 86(BHS):APR73-198
WAGMAN, F. MAGIC MAN, MAGIC MAN.
  M. LEVIN, 441:2FEB75-10
WAGNER, A. DIE WACHSTUMSZYKLEN IN
DER BUNDESREPUBLIK DEUTSCHLAND.
  A. OCKER, 182:VOL26#5/6-150
WAGNER, E. DER LANDKREIS ALTENA
(REGIERUNGSBEZIRK ARNSBERG).
  P. VOSSELER, 182:VOL26#21/22-828
WAGNER, E. MUNDARTGEOGRAPHIE DES
SÜDLICHEN BAYREUTHER RAUMES UND
SEINER NEBENLANDSCHAFTEN.
  G. BELLMANN, 680(ZDP):BAND92HEFT1-
  142
WAGNER, H. CRÉBILLON FILS.
  W. SCHULZE, 72:BAND211HEFT1/3-228
WAGNER, H. JAN VAN DER HEYDEN 1637-
1712.
  E.H. BEGEMANN, 90:JUN73-401
WAGNER, H. STUDIES IN THE ORIGINS
OF THE CELTS & OF EARLY CELTIC CIV-
ILISATION.
  H. BIRKHAN, 343:BAND16HEFT2-201
WAGNER, L.W. PHYLLIS MC GINLEY.
  295:FEB74-714
WAGNER, R. EIN NÜCZ UND SCHONE LER
VON DER AYGEN ERKANTNUSS.*
  D. BLAMIRES, 382(MAE):1974/3-307
WAGNER, R. RICHARD WAGNER: STORIES
& ESSAYS. (C. OSBORNE, ED)
  R. ANDERSON, 415:AUG74-659
WAGNER, R. WAGNER WRITES FROM
PARIS.* (R. JACOBS & G. SKELTON,
EDS & TRANS)
  R. ANDERSON, 415:AUG74-659
  J. DEATHRIDGE, 410(M&L):JAN74-97
WAGONER, D. RIVERBED.*
  P. GOW, 448:VOL13#2-103
  A. HELMS, 473(PR):1/1974-151
  R.J. SMITH, 598(SOR):SPRING75-464
WAGONER, D. THE ROAD TO MANY A WON-
DER.*
  R. SALE, 249(HUDR):WINTER74/75-624
WAGONER, D. SLEEPING IN THE WOODS.
  R. HOWARD, 491:SEP75-346
WAGONER, D. TRACKER.
  M. LEVIN, 441:12OCT75-49
WAIN, J. FENG.
  R. PADEL, 617(TLS):26SEP75-1080

WAIN, J., ED. INTERPRETATIONS.
(NEW ED)
  B. BERGONZI, 148:SPRING73-59
WAIN, J. SAMUEL JOHNSON.*
  A. BROYARD, 441:13FEB75-31
  I. EHRENPREIS, 453:20FEB75-3
  J. RICHARDSON, 231:JUL75-87
  C. RICKS, 441:16MAR75-6
  G. STEINER, 442(NY):28APR75-135
WAINWRIGHT, E. LYING IN WAIT.
  S. CURTIS, 148:SPRING72-85
WAINWRIGHT, J. THE HARD HIT.
  N. CALLENDAR, 441:18MAY75-47
WAINWRIGHT, J. SQUARE DANCE.
  N. CALLENDAR, 441:6JUL75-14
WAISMANN, F. HOW I SEE PHILOSOPHY.
(R. HARRÉ, ED)
  A. CHURCH, 316:DEC73-663
WAIT, R.J.C. THE BACKGROUND OF
SHAKESPEARE'S SONNETS.*
  A.R. YOUNG, 255(HAB):SPRING73-138
WAITES, N., ED. TROUBLED NEIGHBOURS.
  M. ANDERSON, 208(FS):JUL74-364
WAITH, E.M. IDEAS OF GREATNESS.*
  G.R. HIBBARD, 677:VOL4-264
  P. LEGOUIS, 189(EA):OCT-DEC73-473
  E. MACKENZIE, 541(RES):FEB73-85
  M.E. PRIOR, 405(MP):NOV73-199
  S.G. PUTT, 175:SPRING72-26
WAKE, J. & D.C. WEBSTER - SEE EATON,
D.
WAKELIN, M.F. ENGLISH DIALECTS.
  H. HARGREAVES, 541(RES):NOV73-464
  J.D.A. WIDDOWSON, 203:AUTUMN73-256
WAKELYN, J.L. THE POLITICS OF A
LITERARY MAN.*
  M.J. SHILLINGSBURG, 578:SPRING75-
  133
WAKOSKI, D. DANCING ON THE GRAVE OF
A SON OF A BITCH.
  H. CARRUTH, 249(HUDR):SUMMER74-311
WAKOSKI, D. THE MOTORCYCLE BETRAYAL
POEMS.*
  P. CALLAHAN, 134(CP):SPRING73-81
  D. HULBERT, 502(PRS):SPRING73-81
WAKOSKI, D. SMUDGING.* GREED,
PARTS 8, 9, 11.*
  M.G. PERLOFF, 659:WINTER75-84
WAKOSKI, D. TRILOGY.
  G. HITCHCOCK, 651(WHR):AUTUMN74-
  406
WAKOSKI, D. VIRTUOSO LITERATURE FOR
TWO & FOUR HANDS.
  H. VENDLER, 441:6APR75-4
WALCOTT, D. ANOTHER LIFE.*
  L. LIEBERMAN, 676(YR):AUTUMN73-113
  639(VQR):WINTER74-XIV
WALD, M. & M. WERNER, EDS. THREE
MAJOR SCREENPLAYS.
  R. CAMPION, 200:FEB73-116
WALDAU, R.S. VINTAGE YEARS OF THE
THEATRE GUILD, 1928-1939.
  R.R. FINDLAY, 397(MD):SEP73-207
  295:FEB74-380
WALDHORN, A. A READER'S GUIDE TO
ERNEST HEMINGWAY.*
  K. MC SWEENEY, 529(QQ):AUTUMN73-
  498
WALDRON, R.A. - SEE "SIR GAWAIN &
THE GREEN KNIGHT"
WALDROP, R. AGAINST LANGUAGE? THE
AGGRESSIVE WAYS OF THE CASUAL
STRANGER.
  J. GUGLIELMI, 98:FEB73-189

WALDSCHMIDT, E., ED. SANSKRITHAND-
SCHRIFTEN AUS DEN TURFANFUNDEN.
(PTS 2&3)
  J. FILLIOZAT, 182:VOL26#13/14-450
WALDWEI-WIEGELMANN, H., ED. NEUERE
DDR-LITERATUR.
  R.F. AMBACHER, 399(MLJ):NOV74-361
WALETT, F.G. - SEE PARKMAN, E.
WALEY, P. - SEE DE FLORES, J.
WALKER, A., ED. THE CHOPIN COMPAN-
ION.
  M. PETERSON, 470:MAY73-15
WALKER, A. HOLLYWOOD U.K.
  M. SCHUMACH, 441:12APR75-25
WALKER, B.G. SAMPLER KNITTING.
  M.W. PHILLIPS, 139:DEC73-59
WALKER, D.L. & J.E. SISSON 3D, EDS.
THE FICTION OF JACK LONDON.
  E. LABOR, 573(SSF):FALL73-431
WALKER, F. IRREVERENT PILGRIMS.
  H. BEAVER, 617(TLS):4JUL75-733
WALKER, J. GLOSSARY OF ART, ARCHI-
TECTURE & DESIGN SINCE 1945.
  C. PHILLPOT, 592:NOV73-208
WALKER, J. SELF-PORTRAIT WITH
DONORS.
  R. WOLLHEIM, 453:1MAY75-29
WALKER, J. TO WILL ONE THING.
  G.J. STACK, 484(PPR):JUN74-607
WALKER, R.L., ED. PROSPECTS IN THE
PACIFIC.
  E. FRIEDMAN, 293(JAST):MAY73-507
WALKER, R.M., ED. ESTORIA DE SANTA
MARÍA EGIÇIACA.
  B. DUTTON, 400(MLN):MAR73-403
  205(FMLS):APR73-212
WALKER, S. SPORTING ART.
  B. HARRISON, 637(VS):SEP73-123
WALKUP, E. & O. OTIS. THE RACE.
  A. ROSS, 364/AUG/SEP74-114
WALL, C.E. CUMULATIVE AUTHOR INDEX
FOR POOLE'S INDEX TO PERIODICAL
LITERATURE 1802-1906.
  R.D. ALTICK, 445(NCF):SEP73-241
WALL, R. INTRODUCTION TO MATHEMAT-
ICAL LINGUISTICS.
  G.B. PECK, 399(MLJ):MAR74-151
WALLACE, E. THE AFRICAN MILLION-
AIRE.
  A. RENDLE, 157:SPRING73-82
WALLACE, G., JR., WITH J. GREGORY.
THE WALLACES OF ALABAMA.
  M. FRADY, 453:30OCT75-16
WALLACE, I. PROMISE ME YOU'LL SING
MUD!
  E.S. TURNER, 617(TLS):19DEC75-1506
WALLACE, K.R. UNDERSTANDING DIS-
COURSE.
  R.P. HART, 480(P&R):WINTER73-67
WALLACE, W.A. CAUSALITY & SCIENTIF-
IC EXPLANATION.* (VOL 1) [ENTRY IN
PREV WAS OF VOLS 1&2]
  M. MC VAUGH, 385(MQR):WINTER75-116
  E.H. MADDEN, 543:JUN73-723
  L.C. RICE, 486:JUN73-321
  A.B.W., 543:MAR73-549
WALLACE-CRABBE, C. MELBOURNE OR THE
BUSH.
  B. BENNETT, 71(ALS):OCT75-222
WALLDORF, H. CLEMENS BRENTANO.
  J.F.F., 191(ELN):SEP73(SUPP)-119
WALLECHINSKY, D. & I. WALLACE. THE
PEOPLE'S ALMANAC.
  W. ZINSSER, 441:14DEC75-4

WALLER, I. DESIGNING WITH THREAD.
  M.W. PHILLIPS, 139:DEC73-59
WALLERSTEIN, I. THE MODERN WORLD-
SYSTEM.*
  K. THOMAS, 453:17APR75-26
WALLICH-CLIFFORD, A. NO FIXED ABODE.
  P. WILLMOTT, 617(TLS):2MAY75-488
WALLICZEK, W. RUDOLF VON EMS, "DER
GUOTE GÊRHART."
  H. ADOLF, 182:VOL26#23/24-860
WALLING, W.A. MARY SHELLEY.
  S.C., 191(ELN):SEP73(SUPP)-56
WALLIS, J. GRAMMAR OF THE ENGLISH
LANGUAGE & A TREATISE ON SPEECH.*
(J.A. KEMP, ED & TRANS)
  W.F. BOLTON, 297(JL):SEP73-365
  J.K. CHAMBERS, 320(CJL):SPRING74-
  83
  M. 'ESPINASSE, 541(RES):AUG73-334
WALLIS, R., ED. SECTARIANISM.
  B. WILSON, 617(TLS):26SEP75-1107
WALLIS, R.T. NEOPLATONISM.
  A.H. ARMSTRONG, 123:NOV74-227
  E.L. MINAR, JR., 124:FEB74-246
  J.M. RIST, 303:VOL93-249
WALLOT, J-P. UN QUÉBEC QUI BOUGEAIT.
  J.E. IGARTUA, 99:MAR75-35
WALLWORK, E. DURKHEIM.
  D. LA CAPRA, 482(PHR):OCT74-533
WALLWORK, K.L. DERELICT LAND.
  K. WARREN, 617(TLS):7FEB75-143
WALPOLE, H. SELECTED LETTERS OF
HORACE WALPOLE.* (W.S. LEWIS, ED)
  S. PICKERING, JR., 569(SR):SUMMER
  74-LII
WALPOLE, H. HORACE WALPOLE'S COR-
RESPONDENCE. (VOLS 37-39) (W.S.
LEWIS & OTHERS, EDS)
  J. SUTHERLAND, 617(TLS):25APR75-
  447
WALSER, M. DIE GALLISTL'SCHE KRANK-
HEIT.
  U. REINHOLD, 654(WB):1/1973-166
WALSH, A.E. & J. PAXTON. COMPETI-
TION POLICY.
  B. HINDLEY, 617(TLS):10OCT75-1215
WALSH, C. THE END OF NATURE.
  B. HOWARD, 491:APR75-44
WALSH, D.D. - SEE NERUDA, P.
WALSH, D.D. & H.G. STURM. REPASO.*
(REV)
  S.H. TILLES, 399(MLJ):MAR73-142
WALSH, G. GENTLEMAN JIMMY WALKER.*
  R.F. SHEPARD, 441:16FEB75-20
WALSH, J.E. THE HIDDEN LIFE OF
EMILY DICKINSON.*
  D.E. STANFORD, 295:FEB74-576
WALSH, M. - SEE "CHRISTOPHER SMART"
WALSH, M.M.B. DOLLY PURDO.
  M. LEVIN, 441:17AUG75-25
WALSH, P.G. THE ROMAN NOVEL.*
  G. SCHMELING, 121(CJ):DEC73/JAN74-
  182
WALSH, W. COMMONWEALTH LITERATURE.
  R. MANE, 189(EA):OCT-DEC73-492
  W.H. NEW, 102(CANL):WINTER74-87
  H. SERGEANT, 175:AUTUMN73-121
  D. SPETTIGUE, 255:FALL73-342
WALSH, W. D.J. ENRIGHT.
  J. BAYLEY, 362:20NOV75-681
WALTER, E. DEAD WOMAN.
  617(TLS):26DEC75-1533

WALTER, G. LA CONJURATION DU NEUF
THERMIDOR.
  C. LUCAS, 617(TLS):31JAN75-114
WALTER, H. - SEE BUSCHOR, E.
WALTER, O. DIE ERSTEN UNRUHEN.
  M. KANE, 270:VOL23#2-45
WALTERS, A.A. NOISE & PRICES.
  D. PEARCE, 617(TLS):23MAY75-563
WALTERS, D. FLANNERY O'CONNOR.
  N.Y. HOFFMAN, 573(SSF):SUMMER73-
  294
WALTERS, G.B., JR. THE SIGNIFICANCE
OF DIDEROT'S "ESSAI SUR LE MÉRITE
ET LA VERTU."
  J.R. LOY, 546(RR):MAY74-231
WALTHER, J.A. NEW TESTAMENT GREEK
WORKBOOK.
  W.L. WATSON, 399(MLJ):APR73-219
WALTHER, M. METAPHYSIK ALS ANTI-
THEOLOGIE.
  H.W. BRANN, 258:MAR73-150
WALTHER, M.S. LA PRÉSENCE DE STEN-
DHAL AUX ETATS-UNIS 1818-1920.
  M. TURNELL, 617(TLS):13JUN75-673
WALTHER VON DER VOGELWEIDE. DIE
LIEDER.* (F. MAURER, ED)
  H. TIEFENBACH, 182:VOL26#15/16-542
WALTON, C. DE LA RECHERCHE DU
BIEN.*
  R.A. WATSON, 481(PQ):JUL73-551
WALTON, D. WAITING IN LINE.
  J. DECK, 441:16NOV75-78
WALTON, G. EDITH WHARTON.
  B.H. GELFANT, 295:FEB74-819
WALTON, H., JR. BLACK POLITICAL
PARTIES.
  E.W. HEDLIN, 579(SAQ):SPRING74-276
WALTON, J.K. THE QUARTO COPY FOR
THE FIRST FOLIO OF SHAKESPEARE.*
  R.A. FOAKES, 175:SUMMER72-67
  D. HAMER, 541(RES):FEB73-70
  R.K. TURNER, JR., 405(MP):NOV73-
  191
WALTON, P.H. THE DRAWINGS OF JOHN
RUSKIN.*
  J.B. GORDON, 141:WINTER74-77
  J. HAYMAN, 376:JUL73-137
  G.P. LANDOW, 301(JEGP):APR74-262
WALTON, R.G. WOMEN IN SOCIAL WORK.
  P. WILMOTT, 617(TLS):22AUG75-940
WALVIN, J. THE PEOPLE'S GAME.
  R. DAVIES, 617(TLS):31JAN75-105
WALZ, W.R. DER SCHUTZINHALT DES
PATENTRECHTS IM RECHT DER WETTBE-
WERBSBESCHRÄNKUNGEN.
  H. RASCH, 182:VOL26#5/6-145
WALZER, M., ED. REGICIDE & REVOLU-
TION.*
  639(VQR):SUMMER74-XCVII
WALZER, P-O. - SEE COMTE DE LAUTRÉA-
MONT & G. NOUVEAU
WAMBAUGH, J. THE CHOIRBOYS.
  P-L. ADAMS, 61:NOV75-124
  J. LEONARD, 441:2NOV75-6
WANDRUSZKA, M. INTERLINGUISTIK.
  W. MAŃCZAK, 353:1AUG73-114
  E.W., 75:4/1973-192
WANDRUSZKA, M. SPRACHEN - VERGLEICH-
BAR UND UNVERGLEICHLICH.
  R.R.K. HARTMANN, 353:1DEC73-99
WANDYCZ, P.S. THE LANDS OF PARTI-
TIONED POLAND 1795-1918.
  H. SETON-WATSON, 617(TLS):5DEC75-
  1440

WANG CHIH-YÜAN. BERICHT ÜBER DIE
VERTEIDIGUNG DER STADT TE-AN WÄH-
REND DER PERIODE K'AI-HSI 1205-1208.
  C.A. PETERSON, 318(JAOS):APR-JUN73-
  216
WANG, H. FROM MATHEMATICS TO PHIL-
OSOPHY.*
  S. READ, 518:OCT74-12
WANG, J.C-Y. CHIN SHENG-T'AN.
  C. WIVELL, 293(JAST):MAY73-511
WANG, W.S-Y. & A. LYOVIN, COMPS.
CLIBOC: CHINESE LINGUISTICS BIBLIO-
GRAPHY ON COMPUTER.*
  P.L-M. SERRUYS, 318(JAOS):APR-JUN
  73-214
WANG WEI. HIDING THE UNIVERSE.
(YIP WAI-LIM, TRANS)
  H.K. JOSEPHS, 244(HJAS):VOL33-270
WÄNGLER, H-H., R.L. KYES & G.A.C.
SCHERER. CONTEMPORARY GERMAN. (2ND
ED)
  E.E. THEOBALD, 221(GQ):MAY73-487
WAPNEWSKI, P. DIE LYRIK WOLFRAMS
VON ESCHENBACH.
  S.M. JOHNSON, 301(JEGP):JAN74-75
  P. SALMON, 182:VOL26#7/8-215
WARBURTON, I.P. ON THE VERB IN
MODERN GREEK.*
  D.Q. ADAMS, 361:SEP73-143
  B. NEWTON, 297(JL):SEP73-331
WARCH, R. SCHOOL OF THE PROPHETS.
  N.S. FIERING, 656(WMQ):APR74-314
  J.M. HOFFMAN, 432(NEQ):JUN74-311
  639(VQR):SPRING74-XLII
WARD, A. BOOK PRODUCTION, FICTION &
THE GERMAN READING PUBLIC, 1740-
1800.
  W.H. BRUFORD, 617(TLS):28FEB75-231
WARD, A.C. LONGMAN COMPANION TO
TWENTIETH CENTURY LITERATURE.
  295:FEB74-359
WARD, A.G. & OTHERS. THE QUEST FOR
THESEUS.*
  P. LEVI, 447(N&Q):AUG73-320
WARD, B. & R. DUBOS. ONLY ONE
EARTH.* (SPANISH TITLE: UNA SOLA
TIERRA. FRENCH TITLE: NOUS N'AVONS
QU'UNE TERRE.)
  R.F. SHAW, 529(QQ):SUMMER73-285
WARD, C. & A. FYSON. STREETWORK.
  617(TLS):7NOV75-1342
WARD, D. THE DIVINE TWINS.
  H. BIEZAIS, 260(IF):BAND77HEFT2/3-
  275
WARD, D. T.S. ELIOT BETWEEN TWO
WORLDS.
  P. GRAY, 111:23NOV73-55
  L. UNGER, 27(AL):JAN75-595
WARD, D. JONATHAN SWIFT.
  C.T.P., 566:SPRING74-93
WARD, H.M. STATISM IN PLYMOUTH
COLONY.
  J.D. KRUGLER, 656(WMQ):JUL74-521
WARD, J.A. THE MAN HAUPT.
  639(VQR):SUMMER74-LXXXIX
WARD, J.H. A BIBLIOGRAPHY OF PHIL-
IPPINE LINGUISTICS & MINOR LANGU-
AGES.
  A.M. STEVENS, 293(JAST):MAY73-570
WARD, K. THE DEVELOPMENT OF KANT'S
VIEW OF ETHICS.
  A.C. EWING, 483:JAN73-96
  W.A.S., 543:JUN73-772
  W.H. WERKMEISTER, 319:JAN75-113

WARD, M. THE TRAGICOMEDY OF PEN
BROWNING.
T.J. COLLINS, 637(VS):DEC73-234
J.W. GILSDORF, 502(PRS):WINTER73/
74-367
M. HANCHER, 402(MLR):APR74-389
WARD, N. THE SIMPLE COBLER OF AGGA-
WAM IN AMERICA. (P.M. ZALL, ED)
H.T. MESEROLE, 405(MP):AUG73-84
WARD, R.E. - SEE FAULKNER, G.
WARD, W.S. BRITISH PERIODICALS &
NEWSPAPERS, 1789-1832.
R.M. WILES, 481(PQ):JUL73-332
WARDER, A.K. INDIAN BUDDHISM.*
P. BJAALAND & A.E. LEDERMAN,
485(PE&W):OCT73-537
WARDHAUGH, R. TOPICS IN APPLIED
LINGUISTICS.
T.G. BROWN, 399(MLJ):NOV74-375
WARDLE, D. ENGLISH POPULAR EDUCA-
TION 1780-1970.
P.A. SLACK, 447(N&Q):AUG73-316
WARDLE, D.B. DOCUMENT REPAIR.*
A.D. BAYNES-COPE, 325(OCT73-677
WARDLE, R.M. HAZLITT.*
S.M. TAVE, 405(MP):FEB74-341
WARDMAN, A. PLUTARCH'S LIVES.*
639(VQR):AUTUMN74-CLIV
WARDROPPER, B.W., ED. SPANISH POET-
RY OF THE GOLDEN AGE.*
T.R. HART, 399(MLJ):MAR73-152
WARDROPPER, B.W., ED. TEATRO ESPAÑOL
DEL SIGLO DE ORO.
F.M. CLARK, 241:JAN73-80
R.L. FIORE, 238:MAY73-535
W.T. MC CREADY, 240(HR):SPRING73-
438
N. MAC KINNON, 238:MAY73-534
F.G. VINSON, 399(MLJ):JAN-FEB73-67
WARHOL, A. THE PHILOSOPHY OF ANDY
WARHOL.
B. GOLDSMITH, 441:14SEP75-4
442(NY):27OCT75-167
WARINGHIEN, G., CHIEF ED. PLENA
ILUSTRITA VORTARO DE ESPERANTO.
D. BLANKE, 682(ZPSK):BAND26HEFT1/2-
144
WARK, R.R. DRAWINGS BY THOMAS ROW-
LANDSON IN THE HUNTINGTON COLLEC-
TION.
P. CONRAD, 617(TLS):12SEP75-1026
WARKENTIN, G. - SEE REANEY, J.
WARMINGTON, B.H. NERO.
B. BALDWIN, 121(CJ):DEC73/JAN74-
153
WARNANT, L. DICTIONNAIRE DE LA
PRONONCIATION FRANÇAISE. (3RD ED)
N.L. CORBETT, 545(RPH):FEB74-392
WARNER, F. MAQUETTES [&] LYING
FIGURES.
H. COOKE, 159(DM):WINTER/SPRING73-
131
WARNER, K.Q. VOIX FRANÇAISES DU
MONDE NOIR.
N.D. SAVAGE, 207(FR):FEB73-680
WARNER, O. NELSON.
C.L. MEE, JR., 441:7DEC75-42
WARNER, P. THE CRIMEAN WAR.
B.D. GOOCH, 637(VS):DEC73-217
WARNER, R. DUTCH & FLEMISH FLOWER &
FRUIT PAINTERS OF THE XVIITH &
XVIIITH CENTURIES.
C. BROWN, 617(TLS):12DEC75-1492

WARNER, S.T. THE INNOCENT & THE
GUILTY.
J.L. ABBOTT, 573(SSF):WINTER73-111
WARNERS, J.D.P. & L.P. RANK. BAC-
CHUS.* (VOL 2)
F.L. UTLEY, 545(RPH):FEB74-439
WARNKE, F.J. VERSIONS OF BAROQUE.*
A.R. CIRILLO, 405(MP):MAY74-430
T.M. GREENE, 131(CL):SPRING73-167
M. MARGITIC, 141:WINTER73-77
A. SCAGLIONE, 149:SEP74-257
J. VOISINE, 549(RLC):APR-JUN73-342
WARNOCK, G.J. THE OBJECT OF MORAL-
ITY.*
K. BAIER, 482(PHR):APR73-269
WARNOCK, M., ED. SARTRE.
T.R.F., 543:SEP72-177
WARRACK, J. TCHAIKOVSKY.
A. FITZLYON, 364:APR/MAY74-128
WARREN, M. CROWDED CANVAS.
F.R. BARRY, 617(TLS):28MAR75-345
WARREN, P. MINOAN STONE VASES.*
E. VERMEULE, 121(CJ):DEC73/JAN74-
177
WARREN, R., JR., COMP. CHARLES E.
IVES: DISCOGRAPHY.
P. DICKINSON, 415:NOV74-947
412:MAY73-175
WARREN, R.P. DEMOCRACY & POETRY.
C. BEDIENT, 441:3AUG75-17
A. BROYARD, 441:23JUN75-25
WARREN, R.P. OR ELSE.*
C. RICKS, 441:23FEB75-6
WARREN, W.L. HENRY II.
C.W. HOLLISTER & T.K. KEEFE, 377:
JUL74-119
VON WARTBURG, W. EINFÜHRUNG IN
PROBLEMATIK UND METHODIK DER
SPRACHWISSENSCHAFT. (3RD ED)
R. BAEHR, 430(NS):APR73-237
W. ROTHE, 260(IF):BAND78-204
K. STRUNK, 343:BAND17HEFT1-101
WARTELLE, A. HISTOIRE DU TEXTE
D'ESCHYLE DANS L'ANTIQUITÉ.
C.J. HERINGTON, 24:FALL74-286
W.C. SCOTT, 124:FEB74-241
N.G. WILSON, 123:NOV74-286
WASHBURN, W.E. THE INDIAN IN AMER-
ICA.
A. WHITMAN, 441:8MAR75-23
WASHINGTON, B.T. THE BOOKER T.
WASHINGTON PAPERS. (VOLS 1&2)
(L.R. HARLAN & OTHERS, EDS)
N.C. BURCKEL, 14:APR73-241
W.S. HOOLE, 9(ALAR):APR73-146
WASIOLEK, E. - SEE DOSTOEVSKY, F.M.
WASON, B. THE LANGUAGE OF COOKERY.
M.F.K. FISHER, 442(NY):10NOV75-183
WASSERMAN, E.R. SHELLEY.*
S. CURRAN, 141:SUMMER72-295
G. THOMAS, 175:SPRING72-27
M. WILSON, 191(ELN):SEP73-64
WASSERMAN, J. LEONARDO DA VINCI.
J. RUSSELL, 441:7DEC75-3
WASSERMAN, P. & E. HERMAN, EDS.
MUSEUM MEDIA.
J. POVEY, 2:SUMMER74-89
WASSERSTROM, W. THE LEGACY OF VAN
WYCK BROOKS.*
295:FEB74-551
WASSON, R.G. SOMA.*
T. HARRISSON, 463:SPRING73-85

WASWO, R. THE FATAL MIRROR.*
  J. REES, 541(RES):NOV73-470
  G. STITT, 255:FALL73-327
WATERHOUSE, K. BILLY LIAR ON THE
MOON.
  N. HEPBURN, 362:6NOV75-622
  D.A.N. JONES, 617(TLS):24OCT75-
  1255
WATERMAN, C.F. FISHING IN AMERICA.
  R. SMITH, 441:7DEC75-30
WATERMAN, J.T. PERSPECTIVES IN LIN-
GUISTICS.* (2ND ED)
  J. FELLMAN, 361:SEP73-140
WATERS, H.A. PAUL CLAUDEL.
  D.H. MORRIS 4TH, 577(SHR):WINTER
  73-103
WATERS, I. FOLKLORE & DIALECT OF
THE LOWER WYE VALLEY.
  J. SIMPSON, 203:WINTER73-344
WATERS, M.L. & E.A. LITTLE, EDS.
FENÊTRES SUR LA VIE.
  A. CAPRIO, 207(FR):FEB73-681
WATERSTON, E. SURVEY.*
  M.J. EDWARDS, 102(CANL):AUTUMN74-
  96
WATKIN, D. THE LIFE & WORK OF C.R.
COCKERELL.
  J.M. CROOK, 617(TLS):1AUG75-868
WATKIN, D.J., ED. SALE CATALOGUES
OF LIBRARIES OF EMINENT PERSONS.
(VOL 4: ARCHITECTS.)
  J. LEES-MILNE, 39:JUL73-69
WATKINS, F.C. THE FLESH & THE WORD.*
  O. CARGILL, 295:FEB74-452
WATKINS, F.C. & C.H. YESTERDAY IN
THE HILLS.
  569(SR):WINTER74-XIV
WATKINS, G. GESUALDO.*
  D. ARNOLD, 415:MAR74-219
  639(VQR):AUTUMN74-CXXX
WATKINS, O.C. THE PURITAN EXPERI-
ENCE.*
  D.B. SHEA, JR., 481(PQ):JUL73-455
WATMOUGH, D. "ASHES FOR EASTER" &
OTHER MONODRAMAS.
  A. PARKIN, 102(CANL):WINTER74-108
WATSON, A. THE LAW OF SUCCESSION IN
THE LATER ROMAN REPUBLIC.
  J. CROOK, 123:NOV74-240
WATSON, A. ROMAN PRIVATE LAW AROUND
200 B.C.
  J. CROOK, 123:NOV74-239
WATSON, A. & P.E.S. WHALLEY. THE
DICTIONARY OF BUTTERFLIES & MOTHS
IN COLOR.
  H.E. EVANS, 441:7DEC75-92
WATSON, B. CHINESE LYRICISM.*
  Y.C. LIU, 293(JAST):NOV72-136
WATSON, B. - SEE "CHINESE RHYME-
PROSE"
WATSON, C. THE NAKED NUNS.
  617(TLS):20JUN75-692
WATSON, C. SIX NUNS & A SHOTGUN.
  P. ADAMS, 61:FEB75-122
  N. CALLENDAR, 441:16MAR75-32
WATSON, G. THE LITERARY CRITICS.
(2ND ED)
  566:SPRING74-101
WATSON, G., ED. LITERARY ENGLISH
SINCE SHAKESPEARE.
  E.B. GREENWOOD, 206:NOV73-607
WATSON, G. THE LITERARY THESIS.*
  C. RAINE, 447(N&Q):JUL73-280

WATSON, G., ED. THE NEW CAMBRIDGE
BIBLIOGRAPHY OF ENGLISH LITERA-
TURE.* (VOL 2)
  E. ROTHSTEIN, 405(MP):NOV73-176
WATSON, G.H. COLOMBIA, ECUADOR &
VENEZUELA.
  M.D. DEAS, 86(BHS):OCT73-421
WATSON, G.R. THE ROMAN SOLDIER.
  T.B. JONES, 121(CJ):OCT/NOV72-80
WATSON, H. CLAUDEL'S IMMORTAL HER-
OES.*
  E.T. DUBOIS, 402(MLR):APR74-423
  W.H. MATHESON, 399(MLJ):JAN-FEB73-
  50
  H.A. WATERS, 207(FR):FEB73-625
WATSON, I. THE EMBEDDING.
  G. JONAS, 441:20JUL75-12
WATSON, I. THE JONAH KIT.
  E. KORN, 617(TLS):23MAY75-554
WATSON, R. CHRISTMAS IN LAS VEGAS.*
  K.S. BYER, 219(GAR):SPRING73-110
WATSON, W. ANCIENT CHINA.
  N. HAMMOND, 617(TLS):28MAR75-335
WATT, D. FROM HERESY TOWARD TRUTH.
  R.E. MILLER, 432(NEQ):JUN73-325
WATT, J.R. THE DISTRICT MAGISTRATE
IN LATE IMPERIAL CHINA.
  S.M. JONES, 293(JAST):FEB73-317
WATT, W.M. THE FORMATIVE PERIOD OF
ISLAMIC THOUGHT.
  R.E. ABU SHANAB, 319:APR75-250
  R. PARET, 182:VOL26#17/18-580
WATT, W.M. - SEE "BELL'S INTRODUC-
TION TO THE QUR'ÂN"
WATTENBERG, B.J. THE REAL AMERICA.*
  S.S. WOLIN, 453:6FEB75-15
WATTERS, R.E. A CHECKLIST OF CAN-
ADIAN LITERATURE & BACKGROUND MAT-
ERIALS, 1628-1960. (2ND ED)
  P.C. NOEL-BENTLEY, 255:FALL73-340
  G.W., 102(CANL):SUMMER73-127
WATTS, D.A. - SEE ROTROU, J.
WATTS, D.G. THE LEARNING OF HISTORY.
  J. HERBST, 125:OCT73-96
WATTS, E.S. ERNEST HEMINGWAY & THE
ARTS.*
  S.N. GREBSTEIN, 295:FEB74-636
WATTS, I. DIVINE SONGS ATTEMPTED IN
EASY LANGUAGE FOR THE USE OF CHILD-
REN.
  M.E. BROWN, 447(N&Q):JUN73-224
WATTS, J. & P. WHITE. THE BAYONET
BOOK.
  617(TLS):17OCT75-1234
WATZLAWICK, P., J. WEAKLAND & R.
FISCH. CHANGE.
  E. FIRST, 453:20FEB75-8
WAUGH, E. ROSSETTI.
  D.A.N. JONES, 362:20NOV75-683
WAUGH, H. MIRROR MIRROR.*
  G. DAVENPORT, 441:8JUN75-6
WAYMAN, T. FOR & AGAINST THE MOON.
  S. SOLECKI, 99:JAN75-46
WAYMAN, T. WAITING FOR WAYMAN.
  G. BOWERING, 102(CANL):SPRING74-
  112
  A. SAFARIK, 606(TAMR):1STQTR74-86
  P. STEVENS, 529(QQ):WINTER73-656
WAYMENT, H.G. THE WINDOWS OF KING'S
COLLEGE CHAPEL, CAMBRIDGE.*
  R. BECKSMANN, 683:BAND36HEFT2/3-
  180
  W. COLE, 39:DEC73-520
  Y. VANDEN BEMDEN, 54:DEC73-635

WEALES, G. CLIFFORD ODETS, PLAY-
WRIGHT.*
  R. HOGAN, 295:FEB74-735
WEARING, J.P. - SEE PINERO, A.
WEATHERBY, H.L. CARDINAL NEWMAN IN
HIS AGE.*
  J.M. CAMERON, 191(ELN):MAR74-227
  N. KING, 141:SPRING74-176
  P.G. STANWOOD, 568(SCN):SPRING-
  SUMMER74-21
  T. VARGISH, 637(VS):SEP73-124
WEATHERFORD, R.M., ED. STEPHEN
CRANE: THE CRITICAL HERITAGE.
  L. LINDER, 569(SR):SUMMER74-LXIV
  G. MONTEIRO, 517(PBSA):OCT-DEC74-
  455
  T. WORTHAM, 445(NCF):MAR74-497
WEATHERS, W. THE LONESOME GAME.
  J. ZUCKERMAN, 573(SSF):SPRING73-
  222
WEAVER, G. THE ENTOMBED MAN OF
THULE.
  J.D. BELLAMY, 473(PR):2/1974-314
  J. SCHWARTZ, 573(SSF):SPRING73-216
WEAVER, G. GIVE HIM A STONE.
  M. LEVIN, 441:20JUL75-23
WEAVER, G. SUCH WALTZING WAS NOT
EASY.
  J.D. O'HARA, 441:26OCT75-50
WEAVER, H. & P.H. BERGERON - SEE
POLK, J.K.
WEAVER, M. WILLIAM CARLOS WILLIAMS.*
  S. FERGUSON, 219(GAR):SUMMER73-291
  J. MAZZARO, 141:SUMMER72-302
  M. NEUSSENDORFER, 613:SPRING73-130
WEAVER, P.R.C. FAMILIA CAESARIS.
  S. TREGGIARI, 124:FEB74-234
WEAVER, R. & W. TOYE, EDS. THE OX-
FORD ANTHOLOGY OF CANADIAN LITERA-
TURE.
  P. BARCLAY, 102(CANL):AUTUMN74-98
WEBB, C. THE ABOLITIONIST OF CLARK
GABLE PLACE.
  J. YOHALEM, 441:18MAY75-41
WEBB, C. ORPHANS & OTHER CHILDREN.*
  D. LODGE, 617(TLS):4APR75-353
  J. MELLORS, 362:22MAY75-685
WEBB, E. THE PLAYS OF SAMUEL BECK-
ETT.
  R.F. SMITH, 376:JUL73-140
WEBB, J.F. CARNAVARON'S CASTLE.
  E.M. EWING, 441:11MAY75-10
WEBBER, J. THE ELOQUENT "I."*
  I. SIMON, 179(ES):FEB72-70
WEBER, E., ED. L'INTERPRÉTATION DE
LA MUSIQUE FRANÇAISE AUX XVIIE ET
XVIIIE SIÈCLES.
  L. SALTER, 617(TLS):7MAR75-259
WEBER, E. - SEE VON HOFMANNSTHAL, H.
& R. BEER-HOFMANN
WEBER, E-H. LA CONTROVERSE DE 1270
À L'UNIVERSITÉ DE PARIS ET SON
RETENTISSEMENT SUR LA PENSÉE DE S.
THOMAS D'AQUIN.
  W.H. PRINCIPE, 589:JAN74-163
WEBER, F.J. - SEE PLATO
WEBER, G.W. "WYRD."*
  M.M. GATCH, 589:OCT74-771
WEBER, H. DAS ERWEITERTE ADJEKTIV-
UND PARTIZIPIALATTRIBUT IM DEUT-
SCHEN.*
  O. LUDWIG, 343:BAND16HEFT2-218

WEBER, H. HUGO VON HOFMANNSTHAL:
BIBLIOGRAPHIE DER WERKE.*
  M.E. GILBERT, 402(MLR):OCT74-939
  K.W. JONAS, 400(MLN):APR73-639
WEBER, H-D. FRIEDRICH SCHLEGELS
"TRANSZENDENTALPOESIE."
  L.R. FURST, 220(GL&L):APR74-266
WEBER, H-D. ÜBER EINE THEORIE DER
LITERATURKRITIK.*
  D. HARTH, 224(GRM):BAND23HEFT4-486
  R.M., 191(ELN):SEP73(SUPP)-111
WEBER, J-P. DOMAINES THÉMATIQUES.
GENÈSE DE L'OEUVRE POÉTIQUE.
  M. CHASTAING, 542:APR-JUN73-215
WEBER, M. 48 SMALL POEMS.*
  J.H., 502(PRS):FALL73-279
WEBER, M. LE JUDAÏSME ANTIQUE.
  R. GOETSCHEL, 542:JAN-MAR73-106
WEBER, N. THE LIFE SWAP.*
  J. SYMONS, 617(TLS):4JUL75-712
WEBER, R.W. DIE AUSSAGE DER FORM.
  G. VAN CROMPHOUT, 179(ES):JUN73-
  302
WEBER-KELLERMANN, I. DEUTSCHE
VOLKSKUNDE ZWISCHEN GERMANISTIK
UND SOZIALWISSENSCHAFTEN.
  W.F.H. NICOLAISEN, 292(JAF):
  JUL-SEP73-295
WEBSTER, B.S. YEATS.
  G. HOUGH, 617(TLS):14FEB75-160
  A.N. JEFFARES, 569(SR):WINTER74-
  108
WEBSTER, G. THE CORNOVII.
  S. FRERE, 617(TLS):12SEP75-1017
WEBSTER, J. THE DEVIL'S LAW-CASE.
(F.A. SHIRLEY, ED)
  F. LAGARDE, 189(EA):JAN-MAR73-93
WEBSTER, J. THE WHITE DEVIL. (J.
FEATHER, ED)
  J.J. YOCH, JR., 568(SCN):SPRING-
  SUMMER74-14
WEBSTER, R. NEW DIALOGUE WITH
ANGLO-AMERICAN PHILOSOPHY.
  C.F.B., 543:JUN73-773
WEBSTER, T.B.L. THE GREEK CHORUS.
  T.V. BUTTREY, 122:APR74-147
WEBSTER, T.B.L. AN INTRODUCTION TO
MENANDER.
  P. LEVI, 617(TLS):11JUL75-757
WEBSTER, T.B.L. STUDIES IN LATER
GREEK COMEDY. (2ND ED)
  W.T. MAC CARY, 122:APR74-136
WECHSBERG, J. VERDI.
  R. CRAFT, 453:20MAR75-3
WECHSBERG, J. THE WALTZ EMPERORS.
  639(VQR):SUMMER74-XC
WECHSLER, H.J. MIRROR TO THE SON OF
HEAVEN.
  C.P. FITZGERALD, 617(TLS):19DEC75-
  1522
WEDDLE, R.S. WILDERNESS MANHUNT.
  J. FENNELL, 263:OCT-DEC74-463
WEEKES, B. & OTHERS. INDUSTRIAL
RELATIONS & THE LIMITS OF LAW.
  R.J. BEISHON, 617(TLS):7NOV75-1341
WEEKS, D. CORVO.
  295:FEB74-568
WEEKS, K.R. THE CLASSICAL CHRIS-
TIAN TOWNSITE AT ARMINNA WEST.
  J.D. SEGER, 318(JAOS):JAN-MAR73-74
WEES, W.C. VORTICISM & THE ENGLISH
AVANT-GARDE.*
  E. GREENE, 255(HAB):SUMMER73-235
  295:FEB74-409

WEHDEKING, V.C. DER NULLPUNKT.*
R.F. ABT, 221(GQ):JAN73-89
WEHLE, W. FRANZÖSISCHER ROMAN DER
GEGENWART.
V.A. LA CHARITÉ, 546(RR):MAR74-146
Z. TAKACS, 182:VOL26#1/2-37
WEI, T.S. MU T'IEN-TZU CHÜAN CHIN-
K'AO.
L.Y. CHIU, 302:JAN73-167
WEI, W. - SEE UNDER WANG WEI
WEIBEL, V. NAMENKUNDE DES LANDES
SCHWYZ.
E.H. YARRILL, 182:VOL26#11/12-408
WEIDHORN, M. DREAMS IN SEVENTEENTH-
CENTURY ENGLISH LITERATURE.*
J.R. MULDER, 551(RENQ):WINTER73-
540
WEIDHORN, M. RICHARD LOVELACE.
D.G. DONOVAN, 577(SHR):FALL73-440
WEIGAND, H. STUDIEN ZUR MINNE UND
EHE IN WOLFRAMS "PARZIVAL" UND
HARTMANNS "ARTUS"EPIK.
J.F. POAG, 301(JEGP):APR74-282
WEIHER, E. DER NEGATIVE VERGLEICH
IN DER RUSSISCHEN VOLKSPOESIE.
F.J. OINAS, 574(SEEJ):SPRING73-88
WEIL, J.L. MY MUSIC BENT.
W.G. REGIER, 502(PRS):FALL73-274
WEIL, M.S. THE HISTORY & DECORATION
OF THE PONTE S ANGELO.
S. PEPPER, 617(TLS):4APR75-378
WEILER, G. MAUTHNER'S CRITIQUE OF
LANGUAGE.*
R.H. STOOTHOFF, 479(PHQ):JAN73-81
WEILER, P. IN THE LAST RESORT.
S. GRANT & H. RYAN, 99:APR/MAY75-
18
WEILL, G. A WOMAN'S EYES.
N. CALLENDAR, 441:4MAY75-54
WEIMANN, R. LITERATURGESCHICHTE
UND MYTHOLOGIE.*
C. TRILSE, 654(WB):9/1973-180
WEIMANN, R., ED. TRADITION IN DER
LITERATURGESCHICHTE.
W. GIRNUS, 654(WB):10/1973-174
WEIN, H. KENTAURISCHE PHILOSOPHIE.
G.J. STACK, 321:SUMMER73-156
WEINBERG, B., ED. TRATTATI DI POET-
ICA E RETORICA DEL CINQUECENTO.
(VOL 2)
B. CORRIGAN, 551(RENQ):SUMMER73-
186
WEINBERG, D.H. LES JUIFS À PARIS DE
1933 À 1939.
R. COBB, 617(TLS):10OCT75-1176
WEINBERG, E.A. THE DEVELOPMENT OF
SOCIOLOGY IN THE SOVIET UNION.
617(TLS):14FEB75-162
WEINBERG, G.L. GERMANY & THE SOVIET
UNION, 1939-1941.
R.G. WESSON, 550(RUSR):APR73-218
WEINBERG, J.R. DER WIRKLICHKEITS-
KONTAKT UND SEINE PHILOSOPHISCHEN
DEUTUNGEN.
A.G., 543:JUN73-774
WEINBERG, K. ON GIDE'S "PROMÉTHÉE."*
E.R.J. HANCHETT, 188(ECR):FALL73-
266
L.D. JOINER, 399(MLJ):DEC74-423
WEINBROT, H.D., ED. NEW ASPECTS OF
LEXICOGRAPHY.*
W.H. BROWN, JR., 173(ECS):SUMMER
74-494
A. BRUTEN, 447(N&Q):AUG73-298

WEINER, J. MANTILLAS IN MUSCOVY.*
L.B. TURKEVICH, 240(HR):SUMMER73-
570
V. VON WIREN, 574(SEEJ):SPRING72-
92
WEINER, J. & K. MIRKES. WATERMARK-
ING.
G.M. CUNHA, 14:APR73-253
WEINGAERTNER, D.G. DIE AEGYPTENREISE
DES GERMANICUS.
D. FISHWICK, 313:VOL63-255
WEINGARTNER, J.J. HITLER'S GUARD.
H. FRAENKEL, 617(TLS):11APR75-408
WEINGARTNER, R.A. THE UNITY OF THE
PLATONIC DIALOGUE.
K.W. HARRINGTON, 484(PPR):SEP73-
132
J. KING & J.W. DYE, 319:APR75-247
WEINREICH, M. HISTORY OF THE YID-
DISH LANGUAGE.
W. GLICKSMAN, 399(MLJ):DEC74-431
WEINREICH, O. DIE SUFFIXABLÖSUNG
BEI DEN NOMINA AGENTIS WÄHREND DER
ALTHOCHDEUTSCHEN PERIODE.*
G. CUBBIN, 220(GL&L):APR74-252
B. MURDOCH, 402(MLR):JAN74-214
WEINREICH, U. ERKUNDUNGEN ZUR
THEORIE DER SEMANTIK.*
H.E. BREKLE, 260(IF):BAND78-213
H.J. VERKUYL, 433:OCT73-409
WEINRYB, B.D. THE JEWS OF POLAND.
M.A. COHEN, 497(POLR):VOL18#4-100
WEINSTEIN, F. & G.M. PLATT. THE
WISH TO BE FREE.
C. LASCH, 453:13NOV75-33
C. LASCH, 453:27NOV75-37
WEINSTEIN, L. HIPPOLYTE TAINE.*
T.H. GOETZ, 399(MLJ):SEP-OCT73-283
WEINSTEIN, M.E. JAPAN'S POSTWAR
DEFENSE POLICY, 1947-1968.
G.K. GOODMAN, 318(JAOS):OCT-DEC73-
631
WEINSTEIN, P.M. HENRY JAMES & THE
REQUIREMENTS OF THE IMAGINATION.*
E. RECCHIA, 141:WINTER73-83
J.P. TOMPKINS, 295:FEB74-662
WEINSTOCK, J.M., ED. SAGA OG SPRÅK.
H. BENEDIKTSSON, 563(SS):SPRING74-
169
WEINSTOCK, S. DIVUS JULIUS.
J-C. DUMONT, 555:VOL47FASC1-185
A. MICHELS, 124:MAR73-363
C.B. PASCAL, 122:APR73-130
G.V. SUMNER, 24:FALL74-304
WEINTRAUB, S. BEARDSLEY.
T. GIBBONS, 89(BJA):SUMMER73-305
WEINTRAUB, S. JOURNEY TO HEART-
BREAK.* (BRITISH TITLE: BERNARD
SHAW 1914-1918.)
J-C. AMALRIC, 189(EA):OCT-DEC73-
487
T-F. EVANS, 571:SUMMER73-263
A.P. HINCHLIFFE, 148:WINTER73-381
WEINTRAUB, S., ED. "SAINT JOAN:"
FIFTY YEARS AFTER.
K. REARDON, 579(SAQ):AUTUMN74-571
639(VQR):WINTER74-XVII
WEIR, A. A CENTURY OF QUATRAINS.
F. HARVEY, 159(DM):WINTER/SPRING
73-115
WEIR, M. STEPPING INTO THE SPOT-
LIGHT.
E.S. TURNER, 617(TLS):19DEC75-1506

WEISBACH, R. MENSCHENBILD, DICHTER
UND GEDICHT.
  K-D. HÄHNEL, 654(WB):8/1973-187
WEISBACH, R. WIR UND DER EXPRES-
SIONISMUS.
  U. REINHOLD, 654(WB):10/1973-182
WEISBAND, E. & T.M. FRANCK. RESIG-
NATION IN PROTEST.
  F. FERRETTI, 441:31MAY75-25
  R. MANNING, 61:OCT75-106
  R. REEVES, 441:4MAY75-2
  442(NY):23JUN75-108
WEISE, C. SÄMTLICHE WERKE. (VOLS
1&3) (J.D. LINDBERG, ED)
  J.N. HARDIN, 221(GQ):SEP73-175
WEISE, C. SÄMTLICHE WERKE. (VOLS
4&5) (J.D. LINDBERG, ED)
  R.R. HEITNER, 301(JEGP):JAN74-83
WEISE, E. DIE AMTSGEWALT VON PAPST
UND KAISER UND DIE OSTMISSION BE-
SONDERS IN DER 1. HÄLFTE DES 13.
JAHRHUNDERTS.
  P. HERDE, 589:JAN74-167
WEISE, E.A., ED. DIE STAATSCHRIFTEN
DES DEUTSCHEN ORDENS IN PREUSSEN
IM 15 JAHRHUNDERT. (VOL 1)
  C.A.F. MEEKINGS, 325:APR73-617
WEISGERBER, J. FAULKNER ET DOSTOI-
ÈVSKI.
  G. VAN CROMPHOUT, 179(ES):AUG72-
  374
WEISHEIPL, J.A. FRIAR THOMAS
D'AQUINO.*
  O. LEWRY, 617(TLS):24OCT75-1273
WEISS, A. LE DESTIN DES GRANDES
OEUVRES DRAMATIQUES.
  F. HEIDSIECK, 542:APR-JUN73-216
WEISS, D.A. INTRODUCTION TO FUNC-
TIONAL VOICE THERAPY.
  W. GOLDHAN, 682(ZPSK):BAND26HEFT
  6-712
WEISS, E. DEUTSCH.
  K.W. MOERSCHNER, 399(MLJ):DEC74-
  428
WEISS, K. & E. GOODGOLD. TO BE CON-
TINUED.
  R. CAMPION, 200:FEB73-113
WEISS, R.S. MARITAL SEPARATION.
  M. HUNT, 441:30NOV75-4
WEISS, T. THE BREATH OF CLOWNS &
KINGS.*
  R.E. BURKHART, 179(ES):DEC73-590
WEISS, T. THE WORLD BEFORE US.*
  W.G.R., 502(PRS):SPRING73-93
WEISSBORT, D. IN AN EMERGENCY.
  A. CLUYSENAAR, 565:VOL14#2-62
WEISSMAN, F. - SEE LARBAUD, V.
WEISSTEIN, U. COMPARATIVE LITERA-
TURE & LITERARY THEORY. (GERMAN
TITLE: EINFÜHRUNG IN DIE VERGLEICH-
ENDE LITERATURWISSENSCHAFT.)
  S.L. FLAXMAN, 131(CL):WINTER73-91
  A.F. NAGEL, 113:SPRING74-90
  J. VOISINE, 549(RLC):JUL-SEP73-465
WEITZ, S., ED. NONVERBAL COMMUNICA-
TION.
  C.M. HOLLOWAY, 617(TLS):14NOV75-
  1354
WEITZMAN, A.J. SEE MAÑANA, G.P.
WEITZMANN, K. ILLUSTRATED MANU-
SCRIPTS AT ST. CATHERINE'S MONAS-
TERY ON MOUNT SINAI.
  J.N. BIRDSALL, 354:DEC73-344

WELCH, C. & L. EMERGENCE.
  J. BAILIFF, 399(MLJ):DEC74-420
WELCH, D.A. A BIBLIOGRAPHY OF AMER-
ICAN CHILDREN'S BOOKS PRINTED PRIOR
TO 1821.
  J. ALDEN, 432(NEQ):SEP73-491
WELCH, J. WINTER IN THE BLOOD.*
  E. WEEKS, 61:JAN75-88
WELCH, S.C. A KING'S BOOK OF KINGS.
  M. LEVEY, 39:AUG73-151
WELCOME, J. THE SPORTING EMPRESS.
  H. D'AVIGDOR-GOLDSMID, 617(TLS):
  16MAY75-544
WELDER-STEINBERG, A. GESCHICHTE DER
JUDEN IN DER SCHWEIZ VOM 16. JAHR-
HUNDERT BIS NACH DER EMANZIPATION.
(F. GUGGENHEIM-GRÜNBERG, ED)
  R. HAUSWIRTH, 182:VOL26#10-376
WELDON, F. FEMALE FRIENDS.*
  N. HEPBURN, 362:27FEB75-285
  D.A.N. JONES, 617(TLS):28FEB75-213
  L.E. SISSMAN, 442(NY):3MAR75-96
WELLEK, R. DISCRIMINATIONS.*
  R.A. SAYCE, 447(N&Q):AUG73-314
WELLEK, R. - SEE MASARYK, T.G.
WELLENREUTHER, H. GLAUBE UND POLI-
TIK IN PENNSYLVANIA 1681-1776.
  D. ROTHERMUND, 656(WMQ):JAN74-154
WELLES, C. THE LAST DAYS OF THE
CLUB.
  C. LEHMANN-HAUPT, 441:11NOV75-35
  442(NY):29DEC75-56
WELLESZ, E. & F. STERNFELD, EDS.
THE NEW OXFORD HISTORY OF MUSIC.*
(VOL 7)
  A. HUTCHINGS, 410(M&L):OCT74-465
WELLMAN, C. CHALLENGE & RESPONSE.*
  M. SINGER, 482(PHR):APR74-254
WELLS, A. - SEE HERBERT, F.
WELLS, A. - SEE SIMAK, C.D.
WELLS, C.M. THE GERMAN POLICY OF
AUGUSTUS.*
  J-C. RICHARD, 555:VOL47FASC1-185
WELLS, G.A. DID JESUS EXIST?
  G. STANTON, 617(TLS):29AUG75-977
WELLS, H.W. TRADITIONAL CHINESE
HUMOR.*
  D.R. KNECHTGES, 318(JAOS):OCT-DEC
  73-633
  Y.W. MA, 399(MLJ):SEP-OCT73-305
WELLS, J.A. THE PEABODY STORY.
  B.F. TOLLES, JR., 432(NEQ):JUN74-
  322
WELLS, S. LITERATURE & DRAMA.
  R. AHRENS, 72:BAND21HEFT1/3-116
  R. WARREN, 447(N&Q):APR73-149
WELLS, S., ED. SHAKESPEARE.
  S. BARNET, 402(MLR):OCT74-843
WELLS, S. - SEE SISSON, C.J.
WELLS, W. TYCOONS & LOCUSTS.
  J.F. LIGHT, 27(AL):MAY74-238
WELLWARTH, G.E., ED. THE NEW WAVE
SPANISH DRAMA.
  J.W. DÍAZ, 241:MAY73-72
WELLWARTH, G.E. SPANISH UNDERGROUND
DRAMA.
  R.C. COX, JR., 160:WINTER72/73-134
WELSCH, R. SHINGLING THE FOG &
OTHER PLAINS LIES.
  R.S. TALLMAN, 292(JAF):OCT-DEC73-
  404

391

WELSH, A.   THE CITY OF DICKENS.*
   T.J. CRIBB, 541(RES):MAY73-230
   S. GILL, 447(N&Q):JUL73-277
   L. LANE, JR., 594:SPRING73-125
   A. MAACK, 430(NS):JAN73-52
WELTY, E.   ONE TIME, ONE PLACE.*
   C. RICH, 577(SHR):SUMMER73-346
WELZ, D.   SELBSTSYMBOLIK DES ALTEN
GOETHE.
   C.P. MAGILL, 220(GL&L):APR74-265
WENK, K., COMP.   THAI-HANDSCHRIFTEN.
   (PT 2)
   J. FILLIOZAT, 182:VOL26#13/14-449
WENTE, M. - SEE DIEFENBAKER, J.G.
WENZEL, G.   THOMAS MANN UND DIE
TRADITION.
   G. WENZEL, 654(WB):7/1973-187
WERBA, H.   INTERMEDIATE GERMAN.
   S. BAUSCHINGER, 399(MLJ):APR73-222
   M.E. GOTTSCHALK, 221(GQ):SEP73-184
WERBOW, S.S., ED.   FORMAL ASPECTS OF
MEDIEVAL GERMAN POETRY.*
   J.F. POAG, 221(GQ):MAY73-460
VAN DER WERF, H.   THE CHANSONS OF
THE TROUBADOURS & TROUVÈRES.*
   M.G. PIFER, 399(MLJ):SEP-OCT74-273
   R. STEINER, 317:FALL73-488
   H. TISCHLER, 589:OCT74-767
WERKMÜLLER, D.   ÜBER AUFKOMMEN UND
VERBREITUNG DER WEISTÜMER.
   E.A. PHILIPPSON, 301(JEGP):JUL74-
   388
WERNER, A.   INNESS LANDSCAPES.
   J.C. SLOANE, 579(SAQ):AUTUMN74-571
WERNER, J. - SEE BOSWELL, J.
WERNER, O.   EINFÜHRUNG IN DIE STRUK-
TURELLE BESCHREIBUNG DES DEUTSCH-
EN.*   (PT 1)
   U. SCHEUERMANN, 260(IF):BAND77HEFT
   2/3-348
WERNER, O.   PHONEMIK DES DEUTSCHEN.
   D.A. BECKER, 406:SPRING74-77
WERNER, O. & B. NAUMANN, EDS.   FOR-
MEN MITTELALTERLICHER LITERATUR.
   R. HARVEY, 220(GL&L):OCT73-71
WERNER, R.   SKEPTIZISMUS, ÄSTHETIZ-
ISMUS, AKTIVISMUS.
   R.N. LINN, 406:FALL74-314
WERNER, S.   DIDEROT'S GREAT SCROLL.
   H.T. MASON, 617(TLS):12SEP75-1032
WERTENBAKER, L.   PERILOUS VOYAGE.
   M. LEVIN, 441:17AUG75-24
WERTHEIM, W.F.   BUITEN DE GRENZEN.
   W.H. FREDERICK, 293(JAST):AUG73-
   737
WERTHEIMER, R.   THE SIGNIFICANCE OF
SENSE.*
   J.H. BENSON, 483:OCT73-401
   R.S. DOWNIE, 479(PHQ):APR73-185
   G. HARMAN, 482(PHR):APR73-235
WESENCRAFT, C.F. WITH PIKE & MUSKET.
   B. HILL, 617(TLS):26DEC75-1543
WESKER, A.   LOVE LETTERS ON BLUE
PAPER.*
   A. KAZIN, 441:3AUG75-6
   442(NY):9JUN75-126
WESLING, D.   WORDSWORTH & THE ADE-
QUACY OF LANDSCAPE.
   M. JACOBUS, 447(N&Q):FEB73-68
WESSELY, O.   MUSIK.
   E. SAMS, 415:JAN74-39
   J.A. WESTRUP, 410(M&L):JAN74-89

WESSÉN, E.   SCHWEDISCHE SPRACHGE-
SCHICHTE.*   (VOLS 1-3)
   J. WEINSTOCK, 563(SS):SUMMER74-285
WESSON, R.G.   THE SOVIET RUSSIAN
STATE.*
   J.A. ARMSTRONG, 550(RUSR):JAN73-81
WEST, A.   MORTAL WOUNDS.
   S. RUDIKOFF, 249(HUDR):SUMMER74-
   273
   639(VQR):SUMMER74-XC
WEST, E.G.   EDUCATION & THE INDUS-
TRIAL REVOLUTION.
   H. SILVER, 617(TLS):7NOV75-1340
WEST, J.   THE MASSACRE AT FALL
CREEK.
   E. FISHER, 441:27APR75-32
   E. WEEKS, 61:MAY75-100
   442(NY):5MAY75-143
WEST, J.B. & M.L. KOTZ.   UPSTAIRS AT
THE WHITE HOUSE.
   E.S. TURNER, 617(TLS):14FEB75-155
WEST, M.   HARLEQUIN.*
   A. BENTLEY, 268:JAN75-87
WEST, M.L.   EARLY GREEK PHILOSOPHY &
THE ORIENT.
   E.D. HARTER, 485(PE&W):JAN-APR73-
   256
   G.S. KIRK, 123:MAR74-82
WEST, M.L., ED.   IAMBI ET ELEGI
GRAECI ANTE ALEXANDRUM CANTATI.
   (VOL 1)
   D.E. GERBER, 124:APR-MAY74-393
WEST, M.L., ED.   IAMBI ET ELEGI
GRAECI ANTE ALEXANDRUM CANTATI.
   (VOL 2)
   D. CLAY, 24:WINTER74-397
   D. YOUNG, 303:VOL93-221
WEST, M.L.   TEXTUAL CRITICISM & EDI-
TORIAL TECHNIQUE.
   R.J. TARRANT, 487:AUTUMN73-395
"MAE WEST ON SEX, HEALTH & ESP."
   M. DAVSON, 362:5JUN75-740
WEST, R.   VICTORY IN VIETNAM.
   J. BIERMAN, 362:6MAR75-317
   H. TOYE, 617(TLS):18APR75-424
"WEST COAST THEATRICAL DIRECTORY
1972."
   200:FEB73-112
WESTERINCK, L.G. - SEE ARETHAS
WESTERLUND, G. & E. HUGHES.   MUSIC
OF CLAUDIO MONTEVERDI.
   T. WALKER, 415:JUL74-571
VON WESTERNHAGEN, C.   DIE ENTSTEHUNG
DES "RING."
   G. ABRAHAM, 410(M&L):OCT74-474
WESTHEIMER, D.   THE AVILA GOLD.
   T.J. BINYON, 617(TLS):19DEC75-1508
   N. CALLENDAR, 441:12JAN75-18
WESTLAKE, D.E.   BROTHERS KEEPERS.
   M. LEVIN, 441:5OCT75-48
WESTLAKE, D.E.   HELP, I AM BEING
HELD PRISONER.*
   M. LASKI, 362:20NOV75-684
WESTLAKE, D.E.   TWO MUCH.
   N. CALLENDAR, 441:18MAY75-47
WESTLAKE, H.D.   INDIVIDUALS IN THU-
CYDIDES.
   G. DONINI, 122:APR74-133
WESTLAND, P.   A TASTE OF THE COUN-
TRY.
   617(TLS):22AUG75-954
WESTON, C.   SUSANNAH SCREAMING.
   N. CALLENDAR, 441:16NOV75-74

WESTON, M. MORALITY & THE SELF.
M. WARNOCK, 617(TLS):22AUG75-938
WESTRICH, S.A. THE ORMÉE OF BOR-
DEAUX.
D. HIGGS, 529(QQ):WINTER73-634
VAN DE WETERING, J. A GLIMPSE OF
NOTHINGNESS.
P. KAGAN, 441:29JUN75-21
WETHEY, H.E. TITIAN. (VOL 2)
J. MAXON, 90:APR73-254
D. ROSAND, 551(RENQ):WINTER73-497
WETHEY, H.E. TITIAN. (VOL 3)
J. POPE-HENNESSY, 617(TLS):15AUG
75-910
WETTSTEIN, J. LA FRESQUE ROMANE.
C. NORDENFALK, 54:SEP73-441
WETZEL, J.H. CARL SPITTELER.
V. LO CICERO, 301(JEGP):JUL74-414
WEVERS, J.W. & D.B. REDFORD, EDS.
STUDIES ON THE ANCIENT PALESTINIAN
WORLD.
A.R. MILLARD, 318(JAOS):JUL-SEP73-
398
WEYERGRAF, B. DER SKEPTISCHE BÜR-
GER.
A. PHELAN, 402(MLR):OCT74-919
WEYMOUTH, L., ED. THOMAS JEFFERSON.*
P.F. BOLLER, JR., 584(SWR):SUMMER
74-321
WEZEL, J.C. HERRMANN UND ULRIKE.
W. VOSSKAMP, 680(ZDP):BAND92HEFT4-
590
WHALLON, W. FORMULA, CHARACTER, &
CONTEXT.*
H.L. ROGERS, 179(ES):OCT72-455
WHARTON, E. THE GHOST STORIES OF
EDITH WHARTON.
R.W.B. LEWIS, 617(TLS):13JUN75-644
J. MELLORS, 362:18SEP75-386
WHEATLEY, J. LANGUAGE & RULES.*
R.J. MATTHEWS, 353:1APR73-107
WHEATLEY, J.H. PATTERNS IN THACKER-
AY'S FICTION.*
G. KRIEGER, 430(NS):MAY73-290
WHEATLEY, P. THE PIVOT OF THE FOUR
QUARTERS.*
D.N. KEIGHTLEY, 318(JAOS):OCT-DEC
73-527
WHEELER, G. EASY COME.
N. CALLENDAR, 441:19JAN75-36
WHEELER, L. "PARADISE LOST" & THE
MODERN READER.
A.M. MC LEAN, 568(SCN):WINTER74-71
WHEELER, M. THE OXFORD RUSSIAN-
ENGLISH DICTIONARY.* (B.O. UNBE-
GAUN, WITH D.P. COSTELLO & W.F.
RYAN, EDS)
W.W. DERBYSHIRE, 399(MLJ):NOV74-
368
J.L. LISTON, 574(SEEJ):WINTER72-
498
WHEELER, R. VOICES OF 1776.*
W.R. HIGGINS, 579(SAQ):SPRING74-
281
WHEELER, R.S. THE CHILDREN OF DARK-
NESS.
T.W. ROGERS, 396(MODA):FALL74-436
WHEELER, R.S. THE POLITICS OF PAK-
ISTAN.
A. AHMAD, 318(JAOS):JAN-MAR73-98
WHEELER-BENNETT, J. KNAVES, FOOLS &
HEROES.*
442(NY):26MAY75-119

WHEELWRIGHT, J. COLLECTED POEMS OF
JOHN WHEELWRIGHT.* (A.H. ROSEN-
FELD, ED)
L. LEARY, 432(NEQ):MAR74-153
WHELDALL, K. SOCIAL BEHAVIOUR.
I. HUNTER, 617(TLS):6JUN75-629
WHEWAY, J. THE GREEN TABLE OF
INFINITY.
E. GLOVER, 565:VOL14#4-69
WHINNEY, M. CHRISTOPHER WREN.*
H.M. AUSTIN, 481(PQ):JUL73-422
WHISTLER, L. THE IMAGE ON THE
GLASS. THE INITIALS IN THE HEART.
V. GLENDINNING, 617(TLS):12DEC75-
1478
WHITAKER, M-J. LA STRUCTURE DU
MONDE IMAGINAIRE DE RIMBAUD.
R. CHAMBERS, 67:MAY74-111
WHITAKER, W.B. VICTORIAN & EDWARD-
IAN SHOP WORKERS.
J.A. BANKS, 637(VS):JUN74-439
WHITBOURN, C.J., ED. KNAVES &
SWINDLERS.
R. MOORE, 268:JUL75-186
WHITBREAD, L.G. - SEE FULGENTIUS
WHITBY, W.M. & R.R. ANDERSON - SEE
DE VEGA, L.
WHITCOMBE, E. AGRARIAN CONDITIONS
IN NORTHERN INDIA. (VOL 1)
T.R. METCALF, 293(JAST):FEB73-344
WHITE, B.L. THE FIRST THREE YEARS
OF LIFE.
J. CHURCH, 441:28DEC75-4
WHITE, B.R. THE ENGLISH SEPARATIST
TRADITION.
L.D. GELLER, 432(NEQ):JUN73-302
WHITE, C. REMBRANDT AS AN ETCHER.
L.J. SLATKES, 56:AUTUMN73-250
WHITE, C. & K.G. BOON. REMBRANDT'S
ETCHINGS.*
L.J. SLATKES, 56:AUTUMN73-250
WHITE, D.H. POPE & THE CONTEXT OF
CONTROVERSY.*
P. ROBERTS, 447(N&Q):NOV73-430
WHITE, E.W. ANNE BRADSTREET.*
C.J. GEFVERT, 141:SPRING73-184
WHITE, H.B. COPP'D HILLS TOWARDS
HEAVEN.*
J.W. VELZ, 570(SQ):AUTUMN73-482
WHITE, J., ED. THE HIGHEST STATE OF
CONSCIOUSNESS.
J. BRUNO, 98:MAY73-418
WHITE, J.J. MYTHOLOGY IN THE MODERN
NOVEL.
D. DODDS, 399(MLJ):JAN-FEB73-58
P. MERIVALE, 295:FEB74-390
P. STEVICK, 454:FALL73-71
C. TATHAM, 125:JUN74-375
WHITE, J.M. SEND FOR MR. ROBINSON!
N. CALLENDAR, 441:27JUL75-17
WHITE, J.M.B. - SEE UNDER BLANCO
WHITE, J.M.
WHITE, L. THE MEXICO RUN.
N. CALLENDAR, 441:23FEB75-40
WHITE, L. A RICH & DANGEROUS GAME.
N. CALLENDAR, 441:9FEB75-16
WHITE, L.J. INDUSTRIAL CONCENTRA-
TION & ECONOMIC POWER IN PAKISTAN.
639(VQR):AUTUMN74-CLI
WHITE, M. DOCUMENTS IN THE HISTORY
OF AMERICAN PHILOSOPHY.*
483:APR73-199

WHITE, M. PRAGMATISM & THE AMERICAN
MIND.
 G. ISEMINGER, 109:SPRING/SUMMER74-
 144
WHITE, M. SCIENCE & SENTIMENT IN
AMERICA.*
 T.A. GOUDGE, 488:SEP73-270
 M. MANDELBAUM, 482(PHR):OCT73-517
 483:APR73-199
WHITE, P. THE COCKATOOS.*
 A. BROYARD, 441:14JAN75-37
 J. MELLORS, 362:9JAN75-61
 E. WELTY, 441:19JAN75-4
WHITE, P. THE EYE OF THE STORM.*
 P.R. BEATSON, 581:SEP74-219
 D. GREEN, 381:DEC73-395
 P.M. SPACKS, 249(HUDR):SUMMER74-
 283
WHITE, R.J. THOMAS HARDY & HISTORY.
 J.I.M. STEWART, 617(TLS):18APR75-
 415
WHITE, R.J. - SEE COLERIDGE, S.T.
WHITE, R.L. - SEE ANDERSON, S. & G.
STEIN
WHITE, T.D. THE ANGLO-IRISH.
 J. RYAN, 159(DM):AUTUMN72-122
WHITE, T.D. THE DISTANCE & THE
DARK.*
 H. MURPHY, 159(DM):SUMMER73-113
WHITE, T.H. BREACH OF FAITH.
 A. BROYARD, 441:12MAY75-31
 A. LEWIS, 442(NY):11AUG75-81
 W. SHAWCROSS, 453:17JUL75-6
 R. TODD, 61:JUL75-73
 S.R. WEISMAN, 441:11MAY75-1
WHITEHEAD, A.N. SCIENCE & THE MOD-
ERN WORLD.
 J. NORTH, 617(TLS):21FEB75-186
WHITEHEAD, G.E. WARM GREENHOUSE
PLANTS.
 617(TLS):21NOV75-1397
WHITEHEAD, J.S. THE SEPARATION OF
COLLEGE & STATE.
 W.G. MC LOUGHLIN, 639(VQR):WINTER
 74-117
WHITEHOUSE, D. & R. ARCHAEOLOGICAL
ATLAS OF THE WORLD.
 N. HAMMOND, 617(TLS):30CT75-1158
WHITELEY, C.H. MIND IN ACTION.
 N.F. BUNNIN, 518:MAY74-28
WHITELEY, W.H., ED. LANGUAGE USE &
SOCIAL CHANGE.
 M. HOUIS, 315(JAL):VOL11PT2-93
 R.B. LE PAGE, 297(JL):FEB73-140
WHITMAN, C.H. EURIPIDES & THE FULL
CIRCLE OF MYTH.
 O. TAPLIN, 617(TLS):15AUG75-919
WHITMAN, R. THE PASSION OF LIZZIE
BORDEN.
 J.T. MC DONNELL, 109:FALL/WINTER
 73/74-107
WHITMAN, W. LEAVES OF GRASS. (S.
BRADLEY & H.W. BLODGETT, EDS)
 S.A. BLACK, 141:SPRING74-186
WHITMAN, W. WALT WHITMAN'S CAMDEN
CONVERSATIONS.* (W. TELLER, ED)
 E.F. CARLISLE, 27(AL):MAR74-113
 639(VQR):WINTER74-XXVIII
WHITNEY, M.S. CRITICAL REACTIONS &
THE CHRISTIAN ELEMENT IN THE POET-
RY OF PIERRE DE RONSARD.*
 N. ARONSON, 399(MLJ):DEC73-427
 J. PINEAUX, 535(RHL):JAN-FEB73-121

WHITNEY, P.A. SPINDRIFT.
 M. LEVIN, 441:18MAY75-50
WHITNEY, P.A. SKYE CAMERON. SNOW-
FIRE.
 E.M. EWING, 441:11MAY75-10
WHITNEY, W.D. WHITNEY ON LANGUAGE.*
(M. SILVERSTEIN, ED)
 K. CONNORS, 545(RPH):AUG73-69
 R.A. HALL, JR., 399(MLJ):APR73-220
 E.F.K. KOERNER, 318(JAOS):OCT-DEC
 73-617
WHITTEMORE, E. QUIN'S SHANGHAI
CIRCUS.*
 617(TLS):11APR75-388
WHITTEMORE, R. THE MOTHER'S BREAST
& THE FATHER'S HOUSE.
 J. PARISI, 491:JUL75-219
WHITTEMORE, R. WILLIAM CARLOS
WILLIAMS.
 P. DAVISON, 61:NOV75-120
 C. LEHMANN-HAUPT, 441:23DEC75-23
 H. LEIBOWITZ, 441:50CT75-1
 H. VENDLER, 453:13NOV75-17
WHITTINGTON-EGAN, R. THE RIDDLE OF
BIRDHURST RISE.
 R. DAVIES, 617(TLS):26SEP75-1097
WHITTLE, A.R. TRUMBULL STICKNEY.
 J.W. CROWLEY, 27(AL):JAN75-591
WHITTLESEY, E.S. SYMBOLS & LEGENDS
IN WESTERN ART.
 E. FINKENSTAEDT, 124:MAY73-485
WHITTON, T. & W. INSIDE SYDNEY'S
BOOKSHOPS.
 G.A.W., 581:MAR74-102
"WHOLE EARTH EPILOG."
 R. NORTH, 362:24APR75-542
WHORTON, J. BEFORE SILENT SPRING.
 K. MELLANBY, 617(TLS):18APR75-419
WHYTE, A. NEW CINEMA IN EASTERN
EUROPE.
 S.P. HILL, 574(SEEJ):WINTER72-512
WHYTE, R.O. RURAL NUTRITION IN
CHINA.
 G.M. KNEEBONE, 302:JUL73-262
WIBBERLY, L. 1776 - & ALL THAT.
 M. KITMAN, 441:28DEC75-8
WICK, C. THE FACELESS MAN.
 N. CALLENDAR, 441:15JUN75-25
WICKER, B. THE STORY-SHAPED WORLD.
 G. JOSIPOVICI, 617(TLS):30CT75-
 1118
WICKER, T. A TIME TO DIE.
 P. ADAMS, 61:MAY75-103
 C. LEHMANN-HAUPT, 441:6MAR75-41
 K. VONNEGUT, JR., 441:9MAR75-2
 G. WILLS, 453:3APR75-3
 442(NY):21APR75-144
WICKHAM, G. EARLY ENGLISH STAGES
1300 TO 1660.* (VOL 2, PT 2)
 P. EDWARDS, 447(N&Q):APR73-146
 W.C. MC AVOY, 377:JUL74-122
WICKHAM, G. THE MEDIEVAL THEATRE.
 A.C. CAWLEY, 617(TLS):7MAR75-247
WIDEMAN, J.E. THE LYNCHERS.*
 J.M. FLORA, 385(MQR):WINTER75-101
"WIDENER LIBRARY SHELFLIST, 40: FIN-
NISH & BALTIC HISTORY & LITERA-
TURES."*
 F.J. OINAS, 574(SEEJ):WINTER72-493
"WIDENER LIBRARY SHELFLIST, 47 & 48:
FRENCH LITERATURE."
 D.L. RUBIN, 399(MLJ):DEC74-421

WIDMANN, H., ED. DER GEGENWAERTIGE
STAND DER GUTENBERG-FORSCHUNG.
 H. LEHMANN-HAUPT, 517(PBSA):APR-
 JUN74-197
WIDMANN, H. TÜBINGEN ALS VERLAGS-
STADT.
 J.L. FLOOD, 354:SEP73-257
WIDMANN, H. - SEE "GUTENBERG JAHR-
BUCH"
WIEBE, R. STORIES FROM WESTERN
CANADA.*
 D. BAILEY, 529(QQ):SPRING73-99
WIEBE, R. THE TEMPTATIONS OF BIG
BEAR.
 D. BARBOUR, 102(CANL):SUMMER74-82
 D.W. DOERKSEN, 198:SPRING75-128
WIEBE, R. WHERE IS THE VOICE COMING
FROM?
 S. ESCHE, 606(TAMR):NOV74-85
WIEBE, R.H. THE SEGMENTED SOCIETY.
 J.R. POLE, 617(TLS):13JUN75-677
WIECZYNSKI, J.L. - SEE PLATONOV,
S.F.
WIELAND, C.M. - SEE LUCIAN
WIELING, H.J. TESTAMENTAUSLEGUNG
IM RÖMISCHEN RECHT.
 A.A. SCHILLER, 124:FEB74-231
WIEMAN, H.N. RELIGIOUS EXPERIENCE
& SCIENTIFIC METHOD.
 J.M.V., 543:SEP72-178
WIENANDT, E., ED. OPINIONS ON
CHURCH MUSIC.
 A. BOND, 415:NOV74-950
WIENER, M.J. BETWEEN TWO WORLDS.
 M. ROSE, 637(VS):MAR74-319
WIENERS, J. SELECTED POEMS.
 M.G. PERLOFF, 659:WINTER75-84
WIENOLD, G. FORMULIERUNGSTHEORIE -
POETIK - STRUKTURELLE LITERATURGE-
SCHICHTE AM BEISPIEL DER ALTENG-
LISCHEN DICHTUNG.*
 U. FRIES, 72:BAND211HEFT3/6-421
WIENOLD, G. GENUS UND SEMANTIK.
 G.F. MEIER, 682(ZPSK):BAND26HEFT
 1/2-210
WIENOLD, G. SEMIOTIK DER LITERATUR.
 A.P. FOULKES, 131(CL):SPRING74-177
 E.E. GEORGE, 301(JEGP):APR74-305
 J. THOMAS, 209(FM):JUL73-308
WIERENGA, L. "LA TROADE" DE ROBERT
GARNIER.*
 J. PINEAUX, 535(RHL):JAN-FEB73-121
 R.W. TOBIN, 546(RR):JAN74-60
WIERUSZOWSKI, H. POLITICS & CULTURE
IN MEDIEVAL SPAIN & ITALY.
 C.T. DAVIS, 589:JAN74-169
VON WIESE, B., ED. DEUTSCHE DICHTER
DER ROMANTIK.*
 D. BRÜGGEMANN, 182:VOL26#11/12-416
 R.M., 191(ELN):SEP73(SUPP)-111
 M. THALMANN, 680(ZDP):BAND92HEFT2-
 285
VON WIESE, B., ED. DEUTSCHE DRAMA-
TURGIE VOM NATURALISMUS BIS ZUR
GEGENWART.
 C.L. HART-NIBBRIG, 657(WW):MAY/JUN
 73-212
VON WIESE, B., ED. SCHLEGEL UND
DIE ROMANTIK.
 R.S. STRUC, 221(GQ):MAR73-273
WIESEL, E. CÉLÉBRATION HASSIDIQUE
(PORTRAITS ET LÉGENDES).
 J. KOLBERT, 207(FR):FEB73-673

WIESEL, E. NIGHT, DAWN, THE ACCI-
DENT.*
 J.K. CRANE, 573(SSF):FALL73-428
WIESEL, E. SOULS ON FIRE.*
 A.L. BERGER, 390:FEB73-77
WIESENGRUNG-ADORNO, T. - SEE UNDER
ADORNO, T.W.
WIESER, M. LA FORTUNE D'UHLAND EN
FRANCE.
 L.R. FURST, 131(CL):FALL73-363
 G.J. SAYN, 546(RR):MAR74-140
 M-O. SWEETSER, 149:DEC74-355
WIESINGER, P. PHONETISCH-PHONOLO-
GISCHE UNTERSUCHUNGEN ZUR VOKALENT-
WICKLUNG IN DEN DEUTSCHEN DIALEK-
TEN.*
 B.A. LEWIS, 399(MLJ):MAR73-138
 W. THÜMMEL, 260(IF):BAND78-334
WIESNER, H., I. ZIVSA & C. STOLL.
BIBLIOGRAPHIE DER PERSONALBIBLIO-
GRAPHIEN ZUR DEUTSCHEN GEGENWARTS-
LITERATUR.
 E. BOA, 402(MLR):APR74-470
WIESNER, W.T. - SEE ST. AMBROSE
WIESSNER, E. DER WORTSCHATZ VON
HEINRICH WITTENWILERS "RING."
 D. BLAMIRES, 402(MLR):APR74-452
WIGGAN, R. SO YOU WANT TO BE AN
AIR HOSTESS.
 617(TLS):18JUL75-802
WIGGINS, M. BABE.
 M. LEVIN, 441:11MAY75-22
WIGGINTON, B.E., ED. THE FOXFIRE
BOOK.*
 A.E. FIFE, 292(JAF):APR-JUN73-196
WIGHT, J.A. BRICK BUILDING IN ENG-
LAND TO 1550.
 A. CLIFTON-TAYLOR, 135:FEB73-139
WIGHTMAN, E.M. ROMAN TRIER & THE
TREVERI.
 R.L. HOHLFELDER, 121(CJ):FEB/MAR74-
 254
WIGHTMAN, M. THE FACES OF GERMANY.
 C. BAIER, 220(GL&L):APR74-251
WIGMAN, M. THE MARY WIGMAN BOOK.
 (W. SORELL, ED & TRANS)
 A. KISSELGOFF, 441:19JUL75-21
WILBER, D.N. PERSEPOLIS.*
 R.W. CARRUBBA, 124:OCT72-121
WILBERT, J. ZUR KENNTNIS DER YABA-
RANA.
 M. CENTLIVRES, 343:BAND16HEFT2-228
WILCOX, A.M.C. - SEE MAURIAC, F.
WILCZYNSKI, J. TECHNOLOGY IN COME-
CON.
 R.W. DAVIES, 617(TLS):14FEB75-175
WILD, P. COCHISE.
 J.R. CARPENTER, 491:DEC74-166
 L.S. FALLIS, 50(ARQ):WINTER73-377
 P. RAMSEY, 569(SR):SPRING74-394
 639(VQR):SUMMER74-LXXXIV
WILD, P. NEW & SELECTED POEMS.
 P. NELSON, 109:SPRING/SUMMER74-131
WILDE, A. CHRISTOPHER ISHERWOOD.
 A.A. DE VITIS, 295:FEB74-656
WILDE, J. VENETIAN ART FROM BELLINI
TO TITIAN.
 C. GOULD, 617(TLS):10OCT75-1196
WILDENHAIN, M. THE INVISIBLE CORE.
 R.H. PROTHRO, JR., 139:DEC73-15
WILDENSTEIN, D. CLAUDE MONET. (VOL
1)
 R. PICKVANCE, 617(TLS):26DEC75-
 1536

WILDENSTEIN, D. & G. LOUIS DAVID.
F.J.B. WATSON, 39:DEC73-512
WILDER, F.L. ENGLISH SPORTING
PRINTS.
G. REYNOLDS, 617(TLS):14FEB75-174
WILDER, T. THEOPHILUS NORTH.*
639(VQR):SPRING74-LV
WILDERS, J. & H. DE QUEHEN - SEE
BUTLER, S.
WILDHAGEN, K. & W. HÉRAUCOURT. ENG-
LISCH-DEUTSCHES DEUTSCH-ENGLISCHES
WÖRTERBUCH.* (VOL 2: DEUTSCH-ENG-
LISCH.) (2ND ED)
D. DUCKWORTH, 72:BAND211HEFT3/6-
415
WILDING, M. MILTON'S "PARADISE
LOST."*
A.J. SMITH, 541(RES):FEB73-76
WILDMAN, E. MONTEZUMA'S BALL.
S.I. BELLMAN, 573(SSF):SPRING73-
220
WILDMAN, E. NUCLEAR LOVE.*
A. ARIAS-MISSON, 114(CHIR):VOL25
#1-170
VON WILDONIE, H. - SEE UNDER HERRAND
VON WILDONIE
WILES, J. DELHI IS FAR AWAY.
S. BRATA, 617(TLS):7FEB75-146
WILGUS, D.K., WITH C. SOMMER, EDS.
FOLKLORE INTERNATIONAL.
R. GRAMBO, 196:BAND14HEFT3-272
WILHELM, B. LETTRES DU CANADA.
A. CAPRIO, 207(FR):MAR73-870
WILHELM, J. NOUVEAU ROMAN UND
ANTI-THÉÂTRE.
K. BAHNERS, 430(NS):SEP73-506
WILHELM, J.J. MEDIAEVAL SONG.
B. RAW, 447(N&Q):NOV73-437
WILHELM, P. TRAVELS IN NORTH AMER-
ICA, 1822-1824.
W. GARD, 584(SWR):SUMMER74-V
WILKES, G.A. - SEE GREVILLE, F.
WILKES, J.J. DALMATIA.
S. SKEFICH, 121(CJ):FEB/MAR74-260
WILKES, P. TRYING OUT THE DREAM.
C. LEHMANN-HAUPT, 441:4MAR75-37
WILKINS, B.T. HEGEL'S PHILOSOPHY OF
HISTORY.*
A. QUINTON, 453:12JUN75-39
WILKINS, D.A. LINGUISTICS IN LAN-
GUAGE TEACHING.*
A. ANDREYEWSKY, 574(SEEJ):FALL73-
353
R. FILIPOVIĆ, 399(MLJ):JAN-FEB74-
60
R. ST. CLAIR, 351(LL):JUN74-163
WILKINS, E.H. A HISTORY OF ITALIAN
LITERATURE. (REV BY T.G. BERGIN)
J.H. WHITFIELD, 617(TLS):31OCT75-
1310
WILKINS, K.S. A STUDY OF THE WORKS
OF CLAUDE BUFFIER.
J.N. PAPPAS, 546(RR):JAN73-73
WILKINS, M. THE MATURING OF MULTI-
NATIONAL ENTERPRISE.
R.L. HEILBRONER, 453:20MAR75-6
WILKINS, N., ED. TWO MIRACLES.
D. EVANS, 447(N&Q):AUG73-302
WILKINS, N. - SEE DE MACHAUT, G.
WILKINS, R.H. THE HIDDEN ALCOHOLIC
IN GENERAL PRACTICE.
617(TLS):4APR75-380

WILKINSON, F. ANTIQUE GUNS & GUN
COLLECTING.
617(TLS):26DEC75-1543
WILKINSON, R. THE BROKEN REBEL.
W.P. IRVINE, 529(QQ):WINTER73-661
WILKINSON, W.R.T. INDIAN COLONIAL
SILVER.
J. BANISTER, 135:JUL73-228
WILKINSON-LATHAM, J. BRITISH CUT &
THRUST WEAPONS.
N. HALL, 135:MAR73-216
WILKS, I. ASANTE IN THE NINETEENTH
CENTURY.
L. MAIR, 617(TLS):4JUL75-739
R. RATHBONE, 362:19JUN75-820
WILKS, Y.A. GRAMMAR, MEANING & THE
MACHINE ANALYSIS OF LANGUAGE.
C.J.E. BALL, 447(N&Q):FEB73-59
WILKINSON, G., ED. TURNER'S EARLY
SKETCHBOOKS.*
G. REYNOLDS, 39:FEB73-196
WILLARD, N. CHILDHOOD OF THE MAGI-
CIAN.
J.M. FLORA, 385(MQR):WINTER75-101
WILLE, K. DIE SIGNATUR DER MELAN-
CHOLIE IM WERK CLEMENS BRENTANOS.*
J.F. FETZER, 221(GQ):JAN73-109
WILLE, L. FOREVER OPEN, CLEAR &
FREE.
D.J. SHANNON, 44:JAN-FEB73-12
WILLEFORD, W. THE FOOL & HIS SCEP-
TER.
W. KAISER, 570(SQ):SPRING73-228
WILLENS, L. VOLTAIRE'S COMIC THE-
ATRE.
H.T. MASON, 617(TLS):12SEP75-1032
WILLER, J. PARAMIND.*
A. APPENZELL, 102(CANL):AUTUMN73-
95
WILLETT, J. EXPRESSIONISM.*
B. ASHMORE, 214:VOL6#21-120
WILLETT, R. MODERN GAME SHOOTING.
C. WORDSWORTH, 617(TLS):19DEC75-
1504
WILLEY, B. SAMUEL TAYLOR COLERIDGE.
W.J.B. OWEN, 541(RES):MAY73-222
WILLEY, F. THE HONOURABLE MEMBER.
617(TLS):17JAN75-65
WILLIAM OF OCKHAM - SEE UNDER OCKHAM
WILLIAM OF ST. THIERRY. ON CONTEM-
PLATING GOD. (SISTER PENELOPE,
TRANS) THE GOLDEN EPISTLE. (T.
BERKELEY, TRANS)
T.M. TOMASIC, 613:AUTUMN73-425
WILLIAMS, A. GENTLEMAN TRAITOR.
T. BUCKLEY, 441:21DEC75-18
617(TLS):31JAN75-101
WILLIAMS, A.M., ED. CONVERSATIONS
AT LITTLE GIDDING.*
F.L. HUNTLEY, 191(ELN):SEP73-59
WILLIAMS, B. MORALITY.
O. NELL, 311(JP):19JUN75-334
D.A. ROHATYN, 258:DEC73-590
WILLIAMS, C.J. MADAME VESTRIS.
J. HAMILTON, 157:AUTUMN73-73
WILLIAMS, F.B., JR. - SEE ROGERS, T.
WILLIAMS, G. EASTERN TURKEY.
R.R. FEDDEN, 46:MAY73-344
WILLIAMS, G. TWO SKETCHES OF WOMAN-
HOOD.
R. BUCKLER, 362:1MAY75-590
WILLIAMS, G.G. GUIDE TO LITERARY
LONDON.
C.T.P., 566:AUTUMN73-41

WILLIAMS, G.W. - SEE CRASHAW, R.
WILLIAMS, H. SOME SWEET DAY.
  R. GARFITT, 617(TLS):29AUG75-960
WILLIAMS, H.A. POVERTY, CHASTITY &
OBEDIENCE.
  P. HEBBLETHWAITE, 617(TLS):2MAY75-
  474
WILLIAMS, I., ED. ARMES PRYDEIN.
  B.L. JONES, 382(MAE):1974/2-181
WILLIAMS, I., ED. MEREDITH: THE
CRITICAL HERITAGE.*
  M. HARRIS, 72:BAND211HEFT1/3-128
WILLIAMS, J. AN EAR IN BARTRAM'S
TREE.
  A. HELMS, 473(PR):1/1974-151
WILLIAMS, J. & OTHERS. THE WORLD OF
TITIAN.
  E. YOUNG, 39:JUL73-66
WILLIAMS, J.A. THE MAN WHO CRIED I
AM.
  W.M. BURKE, 145(CRIT):VOL15#3-5
WILLIAMS, J.A., ED. THEMES OF IS-
LAMIC CIVILIZATION.
  J.A. BELLAMY, 318(JAOS):JUL-SEP73-
  368
WILLIAMS, J.E.H. - SEE UNDER HALL
WILLIAMS, J.E.
WILLIAMS, K., ED. SWIFT: THE CRITI-
CAL HERITAGE.
  P. ROBERTS, 447(N&Q):NOV73-430
WILLIAMS, L.A. ROAD TRANSPORT IN
CUMBRIA IN THE NINETEENTH CENTURY.
  J. BUTT, 617(TLS):30OCT75-1160
WILLIAMS, M. HALFWAY FROM HOXIE.
  639(VQR):WINTER74-XI
WILLIAMS, M. THOMAS HARDY & RURAL
ENGLAND.*
  D. KRAMER, 445(NCF):DEC73-347
  B. LUPINI, 175:SUMMER73-68
  H. OREL, 191(ELN):SEP73-72
  F.B. PINION, 541(RES):MAY73-235
  R.C. SCHWEIK, 177(ELT):VOL16#2-135
  A. SHELSTON, 148:SPRING73-93
WILLIAMS, M. THE POETRY OF JOHN
CROWE RANSOM.*
  R. BUFFINGTON, 577(SHR):FALL73-
  450
  W.G.R., 502(PRS):FALL73-281
  T.D. YOUNG, 219(GAR):SUMMER73-275
WILLIAMS, M. - SEE PARRA, N.
WILLIAMS, R. THE COUNTRY & THE
CITY.*
  M. BYRD, 473(PR):1/1974-132
  W.J. KEITH, 627(UTQ):WINTER74-169
  L. MARX, 569(SR):SPRING74-351
  C.T.P., 568:AUTUMN73-36
  G.B. TENNYSON, 445(NCF):DEC73-367
  E.P. THOMPSON, 453:6FEB75-34
  A. TRACHTENBERG, 676(YR):SUMMER74-
  610
  568(SCN):FALL74-62
WILLIAMS, R., ED. GEORGE ORWELL.*
  M. CRANSTON, 617(TLS):11APR75-387
WILLIAMS, R. TELEVISION.
  J. LEONARD, 441:30NOV75-6
WILLIAMS, R.C. CULTURE IN EXILE.*
  P. SCHEIBERT, 104:SUMMER73-263
  R. SHELDON, 550(RUSR):JAN73-90
WILLIAMS, R.D. - SEE STATIUS
WILLIAMS, R.L. THE MORTAL NAPOLÉON
III.*
  R. MERKER, 207(FR):OCT72-193

WILLIAMS, S.A. GIVE BIRTH TO
BRIGHTNESS.*
  295:FEB74-440
WILLIAMS, T. EIGHT MORTAL LADIES
POSSESSED.*
  J.H. ADLER, 578:FALL75-165
  G. ANNAN, 617(TLS):1AUG75-865
  W. PEDEN, 569(SR):FALL74-712
WILLIAMS, T. THE HAIR OF HAROLD
ROUX.*
  R. BUCKLER, 362:11SEP75-349
  M. IRWIN, 617(TLS):13JUN75-643
WILLIAMS, T. MEMOIRS.
  C. LEHMANN-HAUPT, 441:7NOV75-41
  J. RICHARDSON, 441:2NOV75-42
WILLIAMS, T. MOISE & THE WORLD OF
REASON.
  C. LEHMANN-HAUPT, 441:15MAY75-47
  K. ROOSEVELT, 441:13JUL75-26
  442(NY):26MAY75-118
WILLIAMS, T. OUT CRY.
  639(VQR):WINTER74-XVI
WILLIAMS, T.A. MALLARMÉ & THE LAN-
GUAGE OF MYSTICISM.*
  R.G. COHN, 535(RHL):SEP-OCT73-920
WILLIAMS, T.B. AIRSHIP PILOT NO. 28.
  617(TLS):10JAN75-41
WILLIAMS, W.C. THE EMBODIMENT OF
KNOWLEDGE. (R. LOEWINSOHN, ED)
  H. VENDLER, 453:13NOV75-17
WILLIAMSON, A. THOMAS PAINE.*
  C.B. CONE, 656(WMQ):OCT74-698
  E. FONER, 453:15MAY75-42
WILLIAMSON, A. PITY THE MONSTERS.
  G. PEARSON, 617(TLS):4JUL75-719
  B. WALLENSTEIN, 659:SUMMER75-397
WILLIAMSON, A. WILKES.
  G. CURTIS, 617(TLS):24JAN75-72
WILLIAMSON, D. THE REMOVALIST.*
  A.A. PHILLIPS, 381:JUN73-189
WILLIAMSON, H.D. THE YEAR OF THE
KOALA.
  H. BORLAND, 441:23NOV75-44
WILLIAMSON, J.G. LATE NINETEENTH-
CENTURY AMERICAN DEVELOPMENT.
  D. MC CLOSKEY, 617(TLS):12DEC75-
  1480
WILLIAMSON, J.V. & V.M. BURKE, EDS.
A VARIOUS LANGUAGE.*
  J. APPLEBY, 35(AS):SPRING-SUMMER
  71-158
  C.W. MC CORD, 583:WINTER73-197
WILLIAMSON, K., ED. IGBO-ENGLISH
DICTIONARY, BASED ON THE ONITSHA
DIALECT.
  F.D.D. WINSTON, 315(JAL):VOL11PT3-
  97
WILLINGHAM, C. THE BIG NICKEL.
  S. MALOFF, 441:23MAR75-10
WILLIS, A.J., COMP. PORTSMOUTH
RECORD SERIES: BOROUGH SESSIONS
PAPERS 1653-1688.* (M.J. HOAD, ED)
  B.R. MASTERS, 325:OCT73-672
WILLIS, J. LATIN TEXTUAL CRITICISM.
  C.E. FINCH, 377:JUL74-115
  A.F. STOCKER, 124:SEP-OCT73-40
  R.J. TARRANT, 487:AUTUMN73-295
WILLIS, J. DE MARTIANO CAPELLA
EMENDANDO.*
  F.R.D. GOODYEAR, 123:NOV74-299
WILLIS, P., ED. FUROR HORTENSIS.
  C. SYKES, 617(TLS):20JUN75-703

WILLIS, R.C. AN ESSENTIAL COURSE IN
MODERN PORTUGUESE. (REV)
A. HOWER, 399(MLJ):APR73-231
WILLIS, R.S. - SEE RUIZ, J.
WILLIS, T. THE LEFT-HANDED SLEEPER.
617(TLS):10OCT75-1174
WILLIS, T. WESTMINSTER ONE.
N. CALLENDAR, 441:20JUL75-26
WILLISON, I.R., ED. THE NEW CAM-
BRIDGE BIBLIOGRAPHY OF ENGLISH
LITERATURE. (VOL 4)
J.S. RYAN, 67:MAY74-102
WILLMOTT, W.E., ED. ECONOMIC OR-
GANIZATION IN CHINESE SOCIETY.
F.C. HUNG, 293(JAST):NOV72-153
WILLWERTH, J. JONES.
A. GOTTLIEB, 441:16FEB75-5
442(NY):17MAR75-127
WILLY, M. THE METAPHYSICAL POETS.
T.A. BIRRELL, 179(ES):AUG73-390
WILMERDING, J. WINSLOW HOMER.
T. CRAIG, 592:JUL-AUG73-55
D. FLOWER, 432(NEQ):MAR73-135
B.D. MANGRUM, 255(HAB):SUMMER73-
197
WILMORE, S.B. SWANS OF THE WORLD.
617(TLS):14FEB75-177
WILSON, A. AS IF BY MAGIC.*
B. HARDY, 155:SEP73-182
J.M. FLORA, 385(MQR):WINTER75-101
M. PRICE, 676(YR):SUMMER74-554
639(VQR):SUMMER74-LXXXII
WILSON, A. THE WORLD OF CHARLES
DICKENS.*
L. LANE, JR., 594:SPRING73-125
WILSON, A.E. - SEE NAVAGERO, A.
WILSON, A.H. LORD, IT'S ME AGAIN.
H. VENDLER, 441:7SEP75-6
WILSON, A.J. ELECTORAL POLITICS IN
AN EMERGENT STATE.
W.H. MORRIS-JONES, 617(TLS):19DEC
75-1526
WILSON, A.M. DIDEROT.*
O. FELLOWS, 546(RR):NOV74-310
R.L. FRAUTSCHI, 207(FR):MAY73-1223
A. KNODEL, 173(ECS):FALL73-93
G. MAY, 399(MLJ):SEP-OCT73-285
J.S. SPINK, 208(FS):OCT74-460
R.E. TAYLOR, 481(PQ):JUL73-489
A. VARTANIAN, 322(JHI):APR-JUN73-
303
WILSON, B. MAGIC & THE MILLENNIUM.
R. JOBLING, 111:FEB74-79
WILSON, D. ATOMS OF TIME PAST.
J. COLES, 617(TLS):24OCT75-1272
WILSON, D. PRESUPPOSITIONS & NON-
TRUTH-CONDITIONAL SEMANTICS.
R. HARNISH, 617(TLS):19SEP75-1067
WILSON, D.B. - SEE GARNIER, R.
WILSON, E. AMERICAN PAINTER IN
PARIS.
A.D. BREESKIN, 127:SPRING74-280
WILSON, E. THE DEVILS & CANON BAR-
HAM.
K. MC SWEENEY, 529(QQ):WINTER73-
670
WILSON, E. NEEDLEPLAY.
B. GUTCHEON, 441:7DEC75-74
WILSON, E. THE TWENTIES. (L. EDEL,
ED)
L.M. DABNEY, 231:JUN75-88
I. EHRENPREIS, 453:12JUN75-3
J. EPSTEIN, 441:15JUN75-1
[CONTINUED]

[CONTINUING]
C. LEHMANN-HAUPT, 441:29MAY75-39
K.S. LYNN, 31(ASCH):AUTUMN75-677
442(NY):9JUN75-126
WILSON, E. UPSTATE.*
295:FEB74-380
WILSON, E. A WINDOW ON RUSSIA.*
R. GREGG, 550(RUSR):APR73-219
WILSON, E.C. SHAKESPEARE, SANTAYANA,
& THE COMIC.
S.J. GREENBLATT, 676(YR):SPRING74-
447
WILSON, E.M. & D. MOIR. A LITERARY
HISTORY OF SPAIN: THE GOLDEN AGE;
DRAMA 1492-1700.
C.V. AUBRUN, 86(BHS):APR73-171
J.R. CORTINA, 399(MLJ):JAN-FEB74-
80
400(MLN):MAR73-507
WILSON, E.O. SOCIOBIOLOGY.
J. PFEIFFER, 441:27JUL75-15
L. THOMAS, 231:NOV75-96
C.H. WADDINGTON, 453:7AUG75-30
WILSON, E.T. RUSSIA & BLACK AFRICA
BEFORE WORLD WAR II.
M. HOLDSWORTH, 617(TLS):25APR75-
463
WILSON, F.P. - SEE SMITH, W.G.
WILSON, G.B. THREE HUNDRED YEARS OF
AMERICAN DRAMA & THEATRE.
B. WHITAKER, 583:WINTER73-203
WILSON, H.B. DEMOCRACY & THE WORK-
PLACE.
W. JOHNSON, 99:APR/MAY75-52
WILSON, H.S. MC CLURE'S MAGAZINE &
THE MUCKRAKERS.
T.H. TOWERS, 295:FEB74-380
WILSON, J. CB: A LIFE OF SIR HENRY
CAMPBELL-BANNERMAN.
H.R. WINKLER, 637(VS):JUN74-450
WILSON, J. WEAVING IS CREATIVE.
M.W. PHILLIPS, 139:JUN73-57
WILSON, J. HERBERT HOOVER.
R. RADOSH, 441:17AUG75-19
WILSON, J.M. ISAAC ROSENBERG.
K. MILLER, 453:16OCT75-27
W.W. ROBSON, 617(TLS):29AUG75-958
D. THOMAS, 362:4SEP75-318
WILSON, J.Q. THINKING ABOUT CRIME.
N. BLIVEN, 442(NY):22DEC75-93
S. RAAB, 441:16AUG75-17
M.E. WOLFGANG, 441:20JUL75-19
WILSON, J.R.S. EMOTION & OBJECT.*
J.C.B. GOSLING, 479(PHQ):JUL73-270
P. JONES, 483:JUL73-305
H. MORICK, 154:JUN73-338
I. THALBERG, 482(PHR):APR74-278
WILSON, K. MIDWATCH.*
M. PERLBERG, 491:JUN75-172
WILSON, M. THE LIFE OF WILLIAM
BLAKE.* (NEW ED) (G. KEYNES, ED)
J.B. BEER, 447(N&Q):AUG73-305
M.F. SCHULZ, 173(ECS):FALL73-120
WILSON, M. RELIGION & THE TRANSFOR-
MATION OF SOCIETY.
R.G. WILLIS, 69:JAN73-82
WILSON, M.R. COPTIC FUTURE TENSES.*
J. ZANDEE, 353:JUL73-123
WILSON, N.G., ED. AN ANTHOLOGY OF
BYZANTINE PROSE.*
A.R. LITTLEWOOD, 487:SPRING73-96
D.M. NICOL, 123:MAR74-137

WILSON, R.J.A. A GUIDE TO THE ROMAN
REMAINS IN BRITAIN.
617(TLS):30MAY75-607
WILSON, R.K. THE LITERARY TRAVEL-
OGUE.
G.S. SMITH, 402(MLR):OCT74-949
WILSON, R.R. INTERNATIONAL LAW &
CONTEMPORARY COMMONWEALTH ISSUES.*
A.H. JEEVES, 529(QQ):SPRING73-118
WILSON, S. I COULD BE HAPPY.
E.S. TURNER, 617(TLS):9MAY75-503
WILSON, S. IVOR.
G. ANNAN, 617(TLS):19DEC75-1506
WILSON, S., JR. & B. LEMANN. NEW
ORLEANS ARCHITECTURE. (VOL 2)
J. HNEDAK, 576:OCT73-261
WILSON, S.R. - SEE TRAVEN, B.
WILSON, V. & B. WATTENMAKER. ENTEN-
DER, LEER Y ESCRIBIR.
D.A. KLEIN, 238:DEC73-1138
WILSON, W.R., ED & TRANS. HŌGEN
MONOGATARI, TALE OF THE DISORDER
IN HOGEN.*
H. MC CULLOUGH, 318(JAOS):APR-JUN
73-223
WILTSE, C.M., ED. THE MICROFILM
EDITION OF THE PAPERS OF DANIEL
WEBSTER.
D.A. YANCHISIN, 14:OCT73-566
WIMMEL, W., ED. FORSCHUNGEN ZUR
RÖMISCHEN LITERATUR.
M.P. CUNNINGHAM, 122:APR73-134
WIMPFELING, J. & B. RHENANUS. DAS
LEBEN DES JOHANNES GEILER VON KAY-
SERSBERG. (O. HERDING, ED)
V.A. TUMINS, 551(RENQ):SUMMER73-
206
WIMSATT, J. CHAUCER & THE FRENCH
LOVE POETS.
J.R. COLLINS, 382(MAE):1974/1-80
WIMSATT, W.K., ED. LITERARY CRITI-
CISM.
F. KERMODE, 617(TLS):11JUL75-751
WIMSATT, W.K., ED. VERSIFICATION.
J. BAILEY, 574(SEEJ):WINTER73-471
H. GROSS, 131(CL):FALL74-369
WIN, U.K. - SEE UNDER KYAW WIN, U
WINCH, P. ETHICS & ACTION.
483:APR73-198
WINCHELL, W. WINCHELL EXCLUSIVE.
W. MARKFIELD, 441:9NOV75-5
WINCHESTER, S. IN HOLY TERROR.
J. HORGAN, 362:16JAN75-88
G. Ó TUATHAIGH, 617(TLS):18APR75-
424
WINCKELMANN, J.J. WRITINGS ON ART.*
(D. IRWIN, ED)
P. CONNISBEE, 592:MAR73-146
D. DIANG, 124:FEB74-230
R. WOODFIELD, 89(BJA):WINTER73-86
WIND, E., WITH G.L. HARRISS - SEE
MC FARLANE, K.B.
WIND, H.W. THE STORY OF AMERICAN
GOLF. (REV)
R. SMITH, 441:7DEC75-30
WINDFUHR, M. DIE UNZULANGLICHE
GESELLSCHAFT.
J.L.S., 191(ELN):SEP73(SUPP)-139
LORD WINDLESHAM. POLITICS IN PRAC-
TICE.
B. TREND, 617(TLS):20JUN75-686
WINDRICH, E. THE RHODESIAN PROBLEM.
R. HODDER-WILLIAMS, 617(TLS):
17OCT75-1241

WINFREY, C. STARTS & FINISHES.
P.S. PRESCOTT, 441:14SEP75-20
WING, D., COMP. SHORT-TITLE CATA-
LOGUE OF BOOKS PRINTED IN ENGLAND,
SCOTLAND, IRELAND, WALES, & BRITISH
AMERICA & OF ENGLISH BOOKS PRINTED
IN OTHER COUNTRIES, 1641-1700.
(VOL 1)
A. BRAUER, 182:VOL26#15/16-519
WINGATE, J. BELOW THE HORIZON.*
M. LEVIN, 441:6APR75-14
WINGE, M. OMKRING HAABLØSE SLAEG-
TER.
C.S. GRAY, 563(SS):WINTER74-76
WINIKER, R. MADAME DE CHARRIÈRE.
A. FAIRLIE, 208(FS):APR74-201
L. VERSINI, 535(RHL):NOV-DEC73-
1087
WINKELMAN, J. THE POETIC STYLE OF
ERICH KÄSTNER.
L. DHORITY, 599:SPRING73-231
WINNER, T.G. THE ORAL ART & LITERA-
TURE OF THE KAZAKHS OF RUSSIAN CEN-
TRAL ASIA.
E. FRANKLE, 182:VOL26#3/4-98
WINNIFRITH, T. THE BRONTËS & THEIR
BACKGROUND.
J. MILLGATE, 637(VS):MAR74-343
N. SHERRY, 402(MLR):JUL74-626
G. THOMAS, 175:SUMMER73-80
WINOCK, M. HISTOIRE POLITIQUE DE
LA REVUE "ESPRIT" 1930-1950.
M. STANTON, 617(TLS):10OCT75-1203
WINOCK, M. & J-P. AZÉMA. LES COM-
MUNARDS.
G. CRICHFIELD, 207(FR):FEB73-647
WINSLOW, O.E. A DESTROYING ANGEL.
J.M. QUEN, 432(NEQ):SEP74-488
639(VQR):SUMMER74-CVI
WINTER, C. GOTTFRIED KELLER.
H. LAUFHÜTTE, 680(ZDP):BAND92HEFT
2-301
WINTER, D.G. - SEE RANK, O.
WINTER, E. BAROCK, ABSOLUTISMUS UND
AUFKLÄRUNG IN DER DONAUMONARCHIE.
E. WANGERMANN, 575(SEER):JAN74-141
WINTER, F.E. GREEK FORTIFICATIONS.*
J.K. ANDERSON, 121(CJ):FEB/MAR74-
274
WINTER, J.M., ED. WAR & ECONOMIC
DEVELOPMENT.
A.S. MILWARD, 617(TLS):15AUG75-923
WINTER, M.H. THE PRE-ROMANTIC
BALLET.
R. FISKE, 617(TLS):28FEB75-228
WINTERBOTTOM, M. PROBLEMS IN QUIN-
TILIAN.*
P.K. MARSHALL, 24:SPRING74-80
WINTERBOTTOM, M., ED. THREE LIVES
OF ENGLISH SAINTS.
J.W. BINNS, 402(MLR):JUL74-614
H. GNEUSS, 447(N&Q):DEC73-479
M. GÖRLACH, 72:BAND21HEFT3/6-426
WINTERBOTTOM, M. - SEE QUINTILIAN
WINTERS, Y. UNCOLLECTED ESSAYS &
REVIEWS.* (F. MURPHY, ED)
P. BAILEY, 364:DEC74/JAN75-133
H. KAYE, 598(SOR):SUMMER75-652
639(VQR):SUMMER74-LXXII
WINWARD, W. FIVES WILD.
617(TLS):10OCT75-1174
WIPLINGER, F. PHYSIS UND LOGOS.
F. LASSERRE, 182:VOL26#15/16-558

WIRKUS, T.E. & H.P. ERICKSON. COM-
MUNICATION & THE TECHNICAL MAN.
J.C. MELE, 583:FALL73-98
WIRSING, A. DAS EHELICHE GÜTERRECHT
DER DDR, TEIL EINER SOZIALISTISCHEN
GESETZGEBUNG.
S. MAMPEL, 182:VOL26#11/12-403
"WIRTSCHAFT UND ÖFFENTLICHE MEINUNG."
M. ROCK, 182:VOL26#19-661
WIRTZ, U. DIE SPRACHSTRUKTUR GOTT-
FRIED BENNS.
O.H. OLZIEN, 224(GRM):BAND23HEFT4-
494
WISBEY, R.A. A COMPLETE CONCORDANCE
TO THE "ROLANDSLIED" (HEIDELBERG
MANUSCRIPT).
W. LENDERS, 680(ZDP):BAND92HEFT1-
119
WISBEY, R.A. A COMPLETE CONCORDANCE
TO THE VORAU & STRASSBURG "ALEXAN-
DER." A COMPLETE WORD-INDEX TO THE
"SPECULUM ECCLESIAE" (EARLY MIDDLE
HIGH GERMAN & LATIN).
W. LENDERS, 680(ZDP):BAND92HEFT1-
118
WISBEY, R.A., ED. THE COMPUTER IN
LITERARY & LINGUISTIC RESEARCH.*
J.M. SINCLAIR, 354:JUN73-170
"WISDEN: CRICKETERS' ALMANACK 1975."
617(TLS):30MAY75-607
WISE, G. AMERICAN HISTORICAL EX-
PLANATIONS.
D. LEVIN, 125:JUN74-341
WISE, J.N. SIR THOMAS BROWNE'S
"RELIGIO MEDICI" & TWO SEVENTEENTH-
CENTURY CRITICS.
F.L. HUNTLEY, 551(RENQ):WINTER73-
546
WISEMAN, A. CRACKPOT.
M. ENGEL, 606(TAMR):MAR75-91
WISEMAN, T.P. CINNA THE POET.
P. GREEN, 617(TLS):2MAY75-478
WISEMAN, T.P. NEW MEN IN THE ROMAN
SENATE.
E.S. GRUEN, 121(CJ):FEB/MAR74-251
A.W. LINTOTT, 123:NOV74-261
M.G. MORGAN, 313:VOL63-252
S.I. OOST, 122:JAN73-75
A.M. WARD, 124:SEP72-51
WISHARD, A. & E. DILLER, EDS. SPIEL
UND SPRACHE.
A. BONAWITZ, 399(MLJ):APR73-223
WISSE, R.R. THE SCHLEMIEL AS MODERN
HERO.*
A. AVNI, 131(CL):FALL73-361
M.J. FRIEDMAN, 295:FEB74-436
A. GUTTMANN, 141:FALL72-396
WITKE, C. LATIN SATIRE.*
R. SELDEN, 313:VOL63-299
B. WALKER, 122:APR73-146
WITKE, C. NUMEN LITTERARUM.*
M.P. CUNNINGHAM, 122:OCT74-296
P.G. WALSH, 123:NOV74-221
WITKIEWICZ, S.I. DRAMATY. (2ND ED
REV BY K. PUZYNA)
D. GEROULD, 497(POLR):VOL18#1/2-
152
WITKIEWICZ, S.I. 622 UPADKI BUNGA
CZYLI DEMONICZNA KOBIETA. (A.
MICIŃSKA, ED)
D. GEROULD, 497(POLR):VOL18#1/2-
139

WITKIEWICZ, S.I. W MAŁYM DWORKU.
D. GEROULD, 497(POLR):VOL18#1/2-
154
WITONSKI, P. WHAT WENT WRONG WITH
AMERICAN EDUCATION & HOW TO MAKE IT
RIGHT.
R. BUFFINGTON, 569(SR):WINTER74-
147
WITONSKI, P., ED. THE WISDOM OF
CONSERVATISM.
H.B. GOW, 396(MODA):SUMMER74-318
WITT, R.E. ISIS IN THE GRAECO-
ROMAN WORLD.*
R.J. LENARDON, 124:OCT72-115
O. MURRAY, 123:NOV74-235
C.B. PASCAL, 122:APR73-148
WITTE, B. DIE WISSENSCHAFT VOM
GUTEN UND BOSEN.*
R. HOGAN, 319:OCT75-520
WITTE, E., ED. DAS INFORMATIONSVER-
HALTEN IN ENTSCHEIDUNGSPROZESSEN.
A. HÜFNER, 182:VOL26#15/16-535
WITTGENSTEIN, L. LETTERS TO C.K.
OGDEN. (G.H. VON WRIGHT, ED)
J. BURNHEIM, 63:AUG74-181
483:OCT73-408
WITTGENSTEIN, L. ON CERTAINTY.*
(G.E.M. ANSCOMBE & G.H. VON WRIGHT,
EDS)
J. BOGEN, 482(PHR):JUL74-364
WITTGENSTEIN, L. PHILOSOPHICAL RE-
MARKS. (R. HARGREAVES & R. WHITE,
TRANS)
D. PEARS, 617(TLS):12SEP75-1015
WITTGENSTEIN, L. PROTOTRACTATUS.*
(B.F. MC GUINNESS, T. NYBERG & G.H.
VON WRIGHT, EDS)
R.W. NEWELL, 483:JAN73-97
R. RHEES, 482(PHR):OCT73-530
WITTIG, M. THE LESBIAN BODY.
V. CUNNINGHAM, 617(TLS):15AUG75-
913
W. FEAVER, 362:14AUG75-221
J. STURROCK, 441:23NOV75-18
WITTKOWER, R. GOTHIC VS. CLASSIC.*
PALLADIO & PALLADIANISM.* (BRITISH
TITLE: PALLADIO & ENGLISH PALLADI-
ANISM.)
A. BLUNT, 453:3APR75-34
WITTKOWER, R. STUDIES IN THE ITAL-
IAN BAROQUE.
J. RYKWERT, 617(TLS):7NOV75-1323
WITTKOWER, R. & I.B. JAFFE, EDS.
BAROQUE ART.*
C.J. MC NASPY, 613:SUMMER73-305
WITTMAN, G. A MATTER OF INTELLI-
GENCE.
N. CALLENDAR, 441:30NOV75-63
WITTMANN, R. DIE FRÜHEN BUCHHÄND-
LERZEITSCHRIFTEN ALS SPIEGEL DES
LITERARISCHEN LEBENS.
R. SCHOLL, 301(JEGP):JUL74-395
WITTREICH, J.A., JR., ED. CALM OF
MIND.
D.T. MACE, 541(RES):MAY73-210
WITTREICH, J.A., JR. THE ROMANTICS
ON MILTON.
K. MUIR, 447(N&Q):FEB73-77
J.R. MULDER, 568(SCN):SPRING-SUM-
MER74-4
WITTSCHIER, H.W. DIE LYRIK DER
PLÉIADE.
G. CASTOR, 402(MLR):APR74-401

WLASSICS, T. INTERPRETAZIONI DI
PROSODIA DANTESCA.
  D.H. HIGGINS, 402(MLR):APR74-427
WODEHOUSE, P.G. THE CAT-NAPPERS.
  R.M. STROZIER, 441:27APR75-23
  E. WEEKS, 61:MAY75-100
WODTKE, F.W. - SEE BENN, G.
WOEHRLIN, W.F. CHERNYSHEVSKII.*
  V. TERRAS, 574(SEEJ):SPRING72-97
WOHLFARTH, H. JOHANN CHRISTOPH
FRIEDRICH BACH.
  E. HELM, 317(FALL73-496
WOIWODE, L. BEYOND THE BEDROOM WALL.
  J. GARDNER, 441:28SEP75-1
  A. HELLER, 61:OCT75-108
  C. LEHMANN-HAUPT, 441:14OCT75-41
  R. SALE, 453:13NOV75-31
  442(NY):29DEC75-55
WOJCIECHOWSKI, M. DIE POLNISCH-
DEUTSCHEN BEZIEHUNGEN, 1933-1938.
  F.L. CARSTEN, 575(SEER):JAN74-155
WOJNAR, I. ESTHÉTIQUE ET PÉDAGOGIE.
  C. SCHUWER, 542:APR-JUN73-217
WOJTYSKA, H.D. CARDINAL HOSIUS,
LEGATE TO THE COUNCIL OF TRENT.
  S.A. MATCZAK, 497(POLR):VOL18#3-93
WOLANDT, G. IDEALISMUS UND FAKTIZI-
TÄT.
  E. SCHAPER, 89(BJA):WINTER73-92
WOLBERGS, T. GRIECHISCHE RELIGIÖSE
GEDICHTE DER ERSTEN NACHCHRISTLICH-
EN JAHRHUNDERTE. (VOL 1)
  C.W. MACLEOD, 123:MAR74-131
WOLF, C. UNTER DEN LINDEN.
  R. LAST, 617(TLS):10OCT75-1208
WOLF, E., 2D. THE LIBRARY OF JAMES
LOGAN OF PHILADELPHIA, 1674-1751.
  C. EVANS, 617(TLS):5SEP75-1002
WOLF, H. DIE SPRACHE DES JOHANNES
MATHESIUS.
  J. ERBEN, 680(ZDP):BAND92HEFT3-474
WOLF, J.U. BEGINNING CEBUANO. (PT
1)
  G.F. MEIER, 682(ZPSK):BAND26HEFT
  1/2-215
WOLF, L. A DREAM OF DRACULA.
  R. MAC GILLIVRAY, 529(QQ):AUTUMN
  73-483
WOLF, L. - SEE STOKER, B.
WOLFE, D.L. CURSO INTERMEDIO DE
ESPAÑOL.
  R.K. CRISPIN, 399(MLJ):DEC73-431
  F.E. PORRATA, 238:MAR73-191
WOLFE, D.M. MILTON & HIS ENGLAND.*
  R. LEJOSNE, 189(EA):JAN-MAR73-100
WOLFE, D.M. - SEE MILTON, J.
WOLFE, G. PEACE.
  M. LEVIN, 441:13JUL75-34
WOLFE, L. PLAYING AROUND.
  R.W. LAMB, 441:22JUN75-6
  C. LEHMANN-HAUPT, 441:20JUN75-39
WOLFE, M. THE TWO-STAR PIGEON.
  N. CALLENDAR, 441:16FEB75-16
WOLFE, P. GRAHAM GREENE.
  R.M. DAVIS, 594:WINTER73-530
  H.D. SPEAR, 295:FEB74-625
WOLFE, P. MARY RENAULT.
  E.C. BOGLE, 577(SHR):WINTER73-100
WOLFE, T. THE PAINTED WORD.
  C. LEHMANN-HAUPT, 441:27MAY75-33
  B. ROSE, 453:26JUN75-26
  J. RUSSELL, 441:15JUN75-4

WOLFE, T. & E.W. JOHNSON, EDS. THE
NEW JOURNALISM.
  S. DONALDSON, 569(SR):SUMMER74-527
  S. MINOGUE, 362:1MAY75-589
  A. TRACHTENBERG, 473(PR):2/1974-
  296
WOLFE, W. FROM RADICALISM TO SOCIAL-
ISM.
  S. KOSS, 617(TLS):21NOV75-1390
WÖLFEL, K., ED. JAHRBUCH DER JEAN-
PAUL-GESELLSCHAFT. (1970)
  W.R. MAURER, 221(GQ):NOV73-645
WOLFER, V.E. REBECCA WEST.
  H. WEBER, 182:VOL26#15/16-554
WOLFF, E. CHOU TSO-JEN.*
  C.L. ALBER, 352(LE&W):VOL16#3-1051
  D.E. POLLARD, 302:JAN73-163
  W.L.Y. YANG, 293(JAST):NOV72-149
WOLFF, G. THE SIGHTSEER.*
  639(VQR):SUMMER74-LXXXII
WOLFF, H.J. "NORMENKONTROLLE" UND
GESETZESBEGRIFF IN DER ATTISCHEN
DEMOKRATIE.*
  R.A. DE LAIX, 124:FEB74-236
WOLFF, J.U. BEGINNING CEBUANA.
(PT 2)
  G.F. MEIER, 682(ZPSK):BAND26HEFT
  3/4-428
WOLFF, J.U. BEGINNING INDONESIAN.
  M. SOEMARMO, 293(JAST):MAY73-565
WOLFF, K. THE TEACHING OF ARTUR
SCHNABEL.
  A. BUSH, 607:SEP73-43
WOLFF, L. - SEE HARTMANN VON AUE
WOLFF, R.J. ON ART & LEARNING.
  C. HESS, 186(ETC.):MAR73-104
WOLFF, R.L. STRANGE STORIES & OTHER
EXPLORATIONS IN VICTORIAN FICTION.*
  V. GLENDINNING, 617(TLS):4APR75-
  352
  W.V. HARRIS, 573(SSF):WINTER73-108
  G.B. TENNYSON, 445(NCF):DEC73-367
WOLFF, R.P. IN DEFENSE OF ANARCHISM.
  M.S. PRITCHARD, 321:WINTER73-296
  M.B.E. SMITH, 321:WINTER73-290
WOLFF, T. UGLY RUMOURS.
  V. CUNNINGHAM, 617(TLS):14MAR75-
  269
WOLFF, T. - SEE PUSHKIN, A.
WOLFFE, B.P. THE ROYAL DEMESNE IN
ENGLISH HISTORY.
  M. HASTINGS, 589:JAN74-171
WOLFGANG, M.E., R.M. FIGLIO & T.
SELLIN. DELINQUENCY IN A BIRTH
COHORT.
  I. GLASSER, 231:FEB75-118
WOLFRAM, H., ED. INTITULATIO.
(VOL 2)
  R. FOLZ, 182:VOL26#21/22-823
WOLFRAM, R. PRINZIPIEN UND PROBLEME
DER BRAUCHTUMSFORSCHUNG.
  B. GUNDA, 203:SUMMER73-168
WOLFRAM, W.A. A SOCIOLINGUISTIC
DESCRIPTION OF DETROIT NEGRO SPEECH.
  R.B. LE PAGE, 353:15DEC73-119
"KARL WOLFSKEHL 1869-1969."
  A. STRAUSS, 220(GL&L):JAN74-164
WOLFSON, H.A. STUDIES IN THE HIS-
TORY OF PHILOSOPHY & RELIGION.
(VOL 1) (I. TWERSKY & G.H. WILLIAMS,
EDS)
  D.S. ROBINSON, 484(PPR):JUN74-601

WOLFSON, L. LE SCHIZO ET LES LAN-
GUES.
P. AUSTER, 453:6FEB75-30
WOLGAST, E. DIE WITTENBERGER
LUTHER-AUSGABE.*
L.W. SPITZ, 551(RENQ):WINTER73-473
WOLITZ, S. THE PROUSTIAN COMMUNITY.
F. BUSI, 207(FR):MAR73-841
VON WOLKENSTEIN, O. ABBILDUNGEN ZUR
ÜBERLIEFERUNG I. (H. MOSER & U.
MÜLLER, EDS)
G.F. JONES, 406:FALL74-294
WOLKERS, J. TURKISH DELIGHT.*
A. ROSS, 364:DEC74/JAN75-140
WOLLHEIM, D.A., ED. THE 1975 ANNUAL
WORLD'S BEST SF.
G. JONAS, 441:29JUN75-25
WOLLHEIM, D.A., ED. THE WORLD'S
BEST SF SHORT STORIES NO. 1.
J. HAMILTON-PATERSON, 617(TLS):
5DEC75-1438
WOLLHEIM, R., ED. FREUD.*
W. GASS, 453:17APR75-3
W. GASS, 453:1MAY75-24
WOLLHEIM, R. ON ART & THE MIND.*
C. BARRETT, 617(TLS):7FEB75-137
WOLLHEIM, R. - SEE STOKES, A.
WÖLLNER, G. E.T.A. HOFFMANN UND
FRANZ KAFKA.
S.P.S., 191(ELN):SEP73(SUPP)-145
WOLLSTONECRAFT, M. MARIA, OR THE
WRONGS OF A WOMAN.
N. BLIVEN, 442(NY):26MAY75-117
WOLPE, B.L. - SEE STEINGRUBER, J.D.
WOLTERS, O.W. THE FALL OF SRIVIJAYA
IN MALAY HISTORY.
A. TEEUW, 293(JAST):NOV72-206
WOLTERS, R. THE NEW NEGRO ON CAMPUS.
G. SHEPPERSON, 617(TLS):13JUN75-
656
WOLTERSTORFF, N. ON UNIVERSALS.*
M. STRATTON, 484(PPR):JUN74-610
WOOD, C. THE DICTIONARY OF VICTOR-
IAN PAINTERS.*
G. REYNOLDS, 39:FEB73-196
WOOD, D. THE PLOTTERS OF CABBAGE
PATCH CORNER.
A. RENDLE, 157:SUMMER73-79
WOOD, J. NORTH KILL.
M. LASKI, 362:20MAR75-380
WOOD, M. AMERICA IN THE MOVIES.
D. BROMWICH, 441:3AUG75-4
R. EDER, 441:20SEP75-27
WOOD, M. EDWARD.
D.M. DAY, 157:AUTUMN73-86
WOOD, M. STENDHAL.
M. GUTWIRTH, 399(MLJ):JAN-FEB73-51
K.G. MC WATTERS, 402(MLR):APR74-
418
M. TILLETT, 208(FS):APR74-208
WOOD, M. TOP TABLE.
D.M. DAY, 157:WINTER73-89
WOOD, O.P. & G. PITCHER, EDS. RYLE.*
P. DUBOIS, 542:APR-JUN73-230
WOOD, P.H. BLACK MAJORITY.*
639(VQR):AUTUMN74-CXLII
WOOD, R.E., ED. THE FUTURE OF META-
PHYSICS.*
W. GERBER, 322(JHI):OCT-DEC73-669
WOOD, T.E.B. THE WORD "SUBLIME" &
ITS CONTEXT, 1650-1760.
J.A. ARIETI, 568(SCN):WINTER74-74
G.R. SMITH, 566:SPRING74-96

WOOD, W. BILLYBOY.
M. LEVIN, 441:10AUG75-14
WOODARD, W.P. THE ALLIED OCCUPATION
OF JAPAN 1945-1952 & JAPANESE RE-
LIGIONS.
J.A. DATOR, 293(JAST):NOV72-159
K.B. PYLE, 318(JAOS):JUL-SEP73-414
WOODCOCK, G. DAWN & THE DARKEST
HOUR.*
P. GROSSKURTH, 102(CANL):SPRING73-
117
J. MECKIER, 295:FEB74-652
T. ROGERS, 175:SPRING73-33
WOODCOCK, G. GABRIEL DUMONT.
M. LAURENCE, 99:DEC75/JAN76-28
WOODCOCK, G. INTO TIBET.*
T.V. WYLIE, 318(JAOS):APR-JUN73-
227
WOODCOCK, G. HERBERT READ.
J. GLOVER, 565:VOL14#3-22
WOODCOCK, G. THE REJECTION OF POLI-
TICS & OTHER ESSAYS.
C.L. BROWN-JOHN, 628:SPRING74-93
G. GEDDES, 376:APR73-233
R. ROBERTSON, 529(QQ):SUMMER73-288
R. SMITH, 150(DR):AUTUMN73-577
WOODCOCK, G. WHO KILLED THE BRITISH
EMPIRE?*
442(NY):6JAN75-82
WOODESON, J. MARK GERTLER.*
P. SKIPWITH, 135:FEB73-139
WOODFORD, P.E., R.G. MARSHALL & C.J.
SCHMITT. ESPAÑOL. (3RD ED)
J. CARFORA, 238:DEC73-1134
WOODHAM-SMITH, C. QUEEN VICTORIA.*
(VOL 1)
E. LONGFORD, 637(VS):SEP73-103
WOODHEAD, A.G., ED. SUPPLEMENTUM
EPIGRAPHICUM GRAECUM. (VOL 25)
M.P. SPEIDEL, 124:MAR74-301
WOODHEAD, A.G. THUCYDIDES ON THE
NATURE OF POWER.*
R.J. LENARDON, 121(CJ):DEC73/JAN
74-189
WOODHOUSE, A.S.P. THE HEAVENLY
MUSE. (H. MAC CALLUM, ED)
R. DANIELLS, 150(DR):SUMMER73-356
G.D. HAMILTON, 125:JUN74-392
J.S. LAWRY, 255:FALL73-329
M. MAC LURE, 627(UTQ):FALL73-87
K. MC SWEENEY, 529(QQ):SUMMER73-
322
B. RAJAN, 102(CANL):SUMMER74-84
J.A. WITTREICH, JR., 568(SCN):WIN-
TER74-69
WOODHOUSE, A.S.P. & D. BUSH, EDS.
A VARIORUM COMMENTARY ON THE POEMS
OF JOHN MILTON.* (VOL 2, PT 1)
W. BLISSETT, 627(UTQ):FALL73-90
G. BULLOUGH, 175:SUMMER73-74
K.W. GRANSDEN, 184(EIC):JUL73-302
W.B. HUNTER, JR., 405(MP):MAY74-
435
R. NASH, 141:SUMMER73-284
G.F. SENSABAUGH, 551(RENQ):SPRING
73-92
WOODHOUSE, A.S.P. & D. BUSH, EDS.
A VARIORUM COMMENTARY ON THE POEMS
OF JOHN MILTON.* (VOL 2, PT 2)
W. BLISSETT, 627(UTQ):FALL73-90
G. BULLOUGH, 175:SUMMER73-74
K.W. GRANSDEN, 184(EIC):JUL73-302
W.B. HUNTER, JR., 405(MP):MAY74-
435   [CONTINUED]

WOODHOUSE, A.S.P. & D. BUSH, EDS.
A VARIORUM COMMENTARY ON THE POEMS
OF JOHN MILTON.* (VOL 2, PT 2)
[CONTINUING]
  R. NASH, 141:SUMMER73-284
  T.J. O'KEEFFE, 568(SCN):WINTER74-
  71
  G.F. SENSABAUGH, 551(RENQ):SPRING
  73-92
WOODHOUSE, A.S.P. & D. BUSH, EDS.
A VARIORUM COMMENTARY ON THE POEMS
OF JOHN MILTON. (VOL 2, PT 3)
  W. BLISSETT, 627(UTQ):FALL73-90
  G. BULLOUGH, 175:SUMMER73-74
  K.W. GRANSDEN, 184(EIC):JUL73-302
  G.F. SENSABAUGH, 551(RENQ):SPRING
  73-92
WOODHOUSE, C.P. THE VICTORIANA COL-
LECTOR'S HANDBOOK.
  G. WILLS, 39:AUG73-152
WOODHOUSE, J.R. - SEE BORGHINI, V.
WOODMAN, D. HIMALAYAN FRONTIERS.
  M.W. FISHER, 293(JAST):FEB73-334
WOODMAN, R.G. JAMES REANEY.
  C. THOMAS, 102(CANL):SPRING73-103
WOODMAN, T. & D. WEST, EDS. QUALITY
& PLEASURE IN LATIN POETRY.
  C. MACLEOD, 617(TLS):2MAY75-478
WOODRESS, J. WILLA CATHER.*
  J.H. RANDALL 3D, 295:FEB74-558
WOODRESS, J., WITH T. LUDINGTON & J.
ARPAD, EDS. ESSAYS MOSTLY ON PERI-
ODICAL PUBLISHING IN AMERICA.*
  G.B. TENNYSON, 445(NCF):SEP73-247
WOODRUFF, W. AMERICA'S IMPACT ON
THE WORLD.
  W. MC NEILL, 617(TLS):29AUG75-970
WOODS, L. & OTHERS, WITH B. SLOTE.
WILLA CATHER.
  639(VQR):SUMMER74-LXXXVIII
WOODS, M. EARLY MORNING MATINS.
  F. HARVEY, 159(DM):WINTER/SPRING
  73-115
WOODS, R.G. & R.S. BARROW. AN IN-
TRODUCTION TO PHILOSOPHY OF EDUCA-
TION.
  617(TLS):14MAR75-271
WOODS, S. DONE TO DEATH. A SHOW OF
VIOLENCE.
  N. CALLENDAR, 441:9NOV75-55
WOODSWORTH, A. THE "ALTERNATIVE"
PRESS IN CANADA.
  G.W., 102(CANL):WINTER73-128
WOODSWORTH, J.S. MY NEIGHBOR.
STRANGERS WITHIN OUR GATES, OR
COMING CANADIANS.
  W.P. WARD, 529(QQ):SPRING73-114
WOOF, R. - SEE THOMPSON, T.W.
WOOLF, C. A BIBLIOGRAPHY OF FRED-
ERICK ROLFE, BARON CORVO. (2ND ED)
  B.C. BLOOMFIELD, 354:JUN73-167
  D. WEEKS, 503:AUTUMN72-159
WOOLF, R. THE ENGLISH MYSTERY
PLAYS.*
  A.C. CAWLEY, 402(MLR):JUL74-614
  N. DENNY, 382(MAE):1974/1-84
  S.J. KAHRL, 191(ELN):MAR74-210
  A. NELSON, 405(MP):MAY74-409
  B. RAW, 447(N&Q):SEP73-344
  R.M. WILSON, 175:SPRING73-27
WOOLF, R. THE ENGLISH RELIGIOUS
LYRIC IN THE MIDDLE AGES.
  R.W.V. ELLIOTT, 179(ES):AUG72-352

WOOLF, V. THE LETTERS OF VIRGINIA
WOOLF. (VOL 1) (BRITISH TITLE: THE
FLIGHT OF THE MIND.) (N. NICOLSON &
J. TRAUTMANN, EDS)
  A. BELL, 617(TLS):19SEP75-1038
  M. DRABBLE, 362:18SEP75-382
  R. EDER, 441:6DEC75-27
  E. MOERS, 441:23NOV75-2
WOOLF, V. LA MORT DE LA PHALÈNE.
(H. BOKANOWSKI, TRANS)
  J. GUIGUET, 189(EA):JUL-SEP73-338
WOOLFOLK, W. THE PRESIDENT'S DOC-
TOR.
  N. CALLENDAR, 441:18MAY75-47
WOOLFOLK, W. & J. THE GREAT AMERI-
CAN BIRTH RITE.
  J. WILSON, 441:22JUN75-7
WOOLHAM, F. AVIARY BIRDS IN COLOUR.
  617(TLS):17JAN75-65
WOOLHOUSE, R.S. LOCKE'S PHILOSOPHY
OF SCIENCE & KNOWLEDGE.*
  D.R.P., 543:DEC72-373
  R. RUBIN, 482(PHR):OCT73-531
  J.W. YOLTON, 319:OCT75-505
WOOLLEY, A.R. CLARENDON GUIDE TO
OXFORD. (3RD ED)
  617(TLS):14MAR75-276
WOOLLEY, P. CREATIVE SURVIVAL FOR
SINGLE MOTHERS.
  A. NELSON, 441:6JUL75-4
WOOTTON, B. INCOMES POLICY.
  D. LAIDLER, 617(TLS):18APR75-433
WORBOYS, A. THE LION OF DELOS.
  N. CALLENDAR, 441:12JAN75-22
WORCESTER, D.E. BRAZIL.
  639(VQR):AUTUMN74-CXLVII
WORDSWORTH, J. WILLIAM WORDSWORTH,
1770-1969.
  F. MC COMBIE, 447(N&Q):MAR73-119
WORDSWORTH, W. THE PROSE WORKS OF
WILLIAM WORDSWORTH. (W.J.B. OWEN
& J.W. SMYSER, EDS)
  A. GOMME, 617(TLS):17JAN75-61
  J.C. MAXWELL, 402(MLR):OCT74-846
WORDSWORTH, W. & D. THE LETTERS OF
WILLIAM & DOROTHY WORDSWORTH. (VOL
2, PT 1) (E. DE SELINCOURT, ED; 2ND
ED REV BY M. MOORMAN)
  H. SCHNYDER, 179(ES):DEC72-568
WORDSWORTH, W. & D. THE LETTERS OF
WILLIAM & DOROTHY WORDSWORTH. (VOL
3, PT 2) (2ND ED) (E. DE SELIN-
COURT, ED; REV BY M. MOORMAN & A.G.
HILL)
  J.C. MAXWELL, 447(N&Q):FEB73-72
  H. SCHNYDER, 179(ES):DEC72-568
"WORKPAPERS IN TEACHING ENGLISH AS A
SECOND LANGUAGE." (VOL 6)
  W.R. SLAGER, 399(MLJ):MAR74-138
"WORLD ARMAMENTS & DISARMAMENT:
SIPRI YEARBOOK, 1975."
  E. ROTHSCHILD, 453:20CT75-7
"WORLD BANK ANNUAL REPORT 1974."
  G. BARRACLOUGH, 453:23JAN75-20
"WORLD GUIDE TO TECHNICAL INFORMA-
TION & DOCUMENTATION SERVICES."
  J.R. GOODSTEIN, 14:JUL73-419
"WORLD HUNGER: CAUSES & REMEDIES."
  G. BARRACLOUGH, 453:23JAN75-20
WÖRNER, K.H. HISTORY OF MUSIC.
(5TH ED) (W. WAGER, ED & TRANS)
  P. DENNISON, 410(M&L):JUL74-352

WOROSZYLSKI, W. THE LIFE OF MAYA-
KOVSKY.
P. ROUVE, 214:VOL6#21-114
WORSLEY, G. THEY CALL ME GUMP.
M. RICHLER, 441:5JAN75-6
"WÖRTERBUCH DER DEUTSCHEN AUS-
SPRACHE." (2ND ED)
M.H. FOLSOM, 353:15APR73-126
WORTH, D.S. DICTIONARY OF WESTERN
KAMCHADAL.
B. COLLINDER, 343:BAND16HEFT1-105
A.P. VOLODIN, 215(GL):VOL13#2-113
WORTH, G.J. WILLIAM HARRISON AINS-
WORTH.
155:SEP73-192
WORTH, K., ED. BECKETT THE SHAPE
CHANGER.
J. MOYNAHAN, 617(TLS):17OCT75-1226
WORTLEY, W.V. TALLEMANT DES RÉAUX.
H. DE LEY, 400(MLN):MAY73-851
WRAY, E., C. ROSENFIELD & D. BAILEY.
TEN LIVES OF THE BUDDHA.*
H.D. GINSBURG, 293(JAST):MAY73-559
WREDE, H. DIE SPÄTANTIKE HERMEN-
GALERIE VON WELSCHBILLIG.
J.P. WILD, 313:VOL63-287
WREN, M.K. A MULTITUDE OF SINS.
N. CALLENDAR, 441:3AUG75-24
WRIGHT, A. BLAKE'S "JOB."*
I.H. CHAYES, 591(SIR):SPRING74-155
S. CURRAN, 405(MP):MAY74-450
M. EAVES, 173(ECS):WINTER73/74-226
J.E. GRANT, 481(PQ):JUL73-467
J. KING, 255(HAB):SPRING73-122
G. THOMAS, 175:AUTUMN73-118
WRIGHT, A. FIRST PERSONS.
639(VQR):SPRING74-LV
WRIGHT, A. THE SHRINKING MAP.
A. CLUYSENAAR, 565:VOL14#1-70
WRIGHT, A.L. & J.H. MC GILLIVRAY.
LET'S LEARN ENGLISH, BEGINNING
COURSE. (BKS 1&2) (4TH ED)
E.M. ANTHONY, 399(MLJ):JAN-FEB73-
76
WRIGHT, B. - SEE FROMENTIN, E. & E.
BELTREMIEUX
WRIGHT, B. & P. MOISY. GUSTAVE
MOREAU ET EUGÈNE FROMENTIN.
H. LANDOLT, 182:VOL26#7/8-229
T. MELLORS, 208(FS):JUL74-343
WRIGHT, C. BLOODLINES.
H. VENDLER, 441:7SEP75-6
WRIGHT, C. HARD FREIGHT.*
G. BURNS, 584(SWR):WINTER74-103
J.R. CARPENTER, 491:DEC74-166
J.N. MORRIS, 249(HUDR):SPRING74-
106
P. RAMSEY, 569(SR):SPRING74-399
WRIGHT, C.E. FONTES HARLEIANI.
A.N.L. MUNBY, 78(BC):SPRING73-103
A.G. WATSON, 325:APR73-603
WRIGHT, E.O., ED. THE POLITICS OF
PUNISHMENT.
J. ULLAND, 109:FALL/WINTER73/74-
102
WRIGHT, F.L. AN ORGANIC ARCHITEC-
TURE. GENIUS & THE MOBOCRACY.*
(NEW ED) THE INDUSTRIAL REVOLU-
TION RUNS AWAY.
R.G. WILSON, 576:OCT73-262
WRIGHT, G. JOG RUMMAGE.
P. ADAMS, 61:MAR75-146

VON WRIGHT, G.H. CAUSALITY & DETER-
MINISM.
L.J. COHEN, 617(TLS):15AUG75-914
VON WRIGHT, G.H. EXPLANATION & UN-
DERSTANDING.*
J. KIM, 482(PHR):JUL73-380
S. TOULMIN, 479(PHQ):APR73-176
J.W. YOLTON, 488:MAR73-81
VON WRIGHT, G.H., ED. PROBLEMS IN
THE THEORY OF KNOWLEDGE.
B.G.H., 543:JUN73-771
VON WRIGHT, G.H. - SEE WITTGENSTEIN,
L.
WRIGHT, J. COLLECTED POEMS.*
J. SEAY, 219(GAR):SPRING73-71
WRIGHT, J. TWO CITIZENS.*
E. ENGELBERG, 598(SOR):SPRING75-
440
L. LIEBERMAN, 676(YR):SPRING74-453
P. NELSON, 109:SPRING/SUMMER74-131
M.G. PERLOFF, 659:WINTER75-84
P. RAMSEY, 569(SR):SPRING74-394
H. TAYLOR, 385(MQR):WINTER75-92
WRIGHT, K. TREBLE POETS I.
R. GARFITT, 364:FEB/MAR75-111
WRIGHT, L., H. MORRISON & K.F. WONG.
VANISHING WORLD.
T.T., 293(JAST):NOV72-227
WRIGHT, L.M., JR. FISHING THE DRY
FLY AS A LIVING INSECT.
H. HENKIN, 441:29JUN75-17
WRIGHT, L.R. THE ORIGINS OF BRITISH
BORNEO.*
K.G. TREGONNING, 318(JAOS):JUL-SEP
73-406
WRIGHT, M., WITH D. BROWN, EDS. THE
COMPLETE INDOOR GARDENER.
J. CANADAY, 441:13APR75-7
WRIGHT, N. - SEE GREENOUGH, H.
WRIGHT, S. - SEE IRVING, W.
WRIGHT, R.B. IN THE MIDDLE OF A
LIFE.*
P. MOORE, 606(TAMR):OCT74-85
WRIGHT, T. THE LIFE OF WILLIAM
BLAKE.
M.F. SCHULZ, 173(ECS):FALL73-120
WRIGHT, W.F. ARNOLD BENNETT, ROMAN-
TIC REALIST.
J. HEPBURN, 405(MP):NOV73-233
WRIGHT, W.R. BRITISH-OWNED RAILWAYS
IN ARGENTINA.
617(TLS):8AUG75-906
WU HAN. HAI JUI DISMISSED FROM
OFFICE.
J.R. PUSEY, 293(JAST):NOV72-226
WU, R-I. THE STRATEGY OF ECONOMIC
DEVELOPMENT.
S.P.S. HO, 293(JAST):MAY73-517
WULBERN, J.H. BRECHT & IONESCO.*
C. PHILLABAUM, 295:FEB74-454
K.S. WHITE, 188(ECR):SUMMER73-179
"WULFSTAN'S CANONS OF EDGAR." (R.
FOWLER, ED)
A. CAMPBELL, 447(N&Q):MAR73-103
D.B. LOOMIS, 382(MAE):1974/2-151
WUNBERG, G., ED. HOFMANNSTHAL IM
URTEIL SEINER KRITIKER.
T.P. BALDWIN, 406:SUMMER74-182
M.E. GILBERT, 402(MLR):OCT74-938
WUNBERG, G. - SEE STAROSTE, W.
WUNDERLI, P. DIE OKZITANISCHEN
BIBELÜBERSETZUNGEN DES MITTELALTERS
- GELÖSTE UND UNGELÖSTE FRAGEN.
J.R. SMEETS, 433:OCT73-405

WUNDERLICH, D. TEMPUS UND ZEITREF-
ERENZ IM DEUTSCHEN.*
H.J. VERKUYL, 361:VOL31#2/3-271
WUNDERLICH, H.G. THE SECRET OF
CRETE.
P. ADAMS, 61:JAN75-91
G. BIBBY, 441:2MAR75-10
WURFEL, D., ED. MEIJI JAPAN'S
CENTENNIAL.*
C. TOTMAN, 318(JAOS):APR-JUN73-224
WURLITZER, R. QUAKE.*
E. BUTSCHER, 109:FALL/WINTER73/74-
131
WURM, M. APOKERYXIS, ABDICATIO UND
EXHEREDATIO.
E.R. MIX, 124:MAY73-499
WYATT, D.K. THE POLITICS OF REFORM
IN THAILAND.
W.F. VELLA, 293(JAST):AUG73-744
WYATT, T. COLLECTED POEMS OF SIR
THOMAS WYATT. (K. MUIR & P. THOM-
SON, EDS)
J. DAALDER, 184(EIC):OCT73-399
WYATT, W.F., JR. THE GREEK PROTHET-
IC VOWEL.*
J.W. POULTNEY, 24:WINTER74-406
O. SZEMERÉNYI, 487:SUMMER73-180
WYLDER, E. THE LAST FACE.*
G. THOMAS, 175:AUTUMN73-118
WYLLIE, J. SKULL STILL BONE.
N. CALLENDAR, 441:8JUN75-16
WYNAND, D. SNOWSCAPES.
P. THOMAS, 198:FALL75-129
WYNDHAM, F. OUT OF THE WAR.
V. GLENDINNING, 617(TLS):31JAN75-
101
J. MELLORS, 362:20FEB75-253
WYNDHAM, F. & D. KING, EDS. TROT-
SKY.*
B.D. WOLFE, 550(RUSR):JUL73-315
WYNDHAM, J. THE MAN FROM BEYOND &
OTHER STORIES.
J. HAMILTON-PATERSON, 617(TLS):
23MAY75-555
WYNNE-TYSON, J. FOOD FOR A FUTURE.
L. BURKHOLDER, 617(TLS):29AUG75-
973
WYSLING, H., ED. THOMAS MANN.
(VOL 1)
T.J.R., 617(TLS):10OCT75-1207
WYSLING, H. ZUR SITUATION DES
SCHRIFTSTELLERS IN DER GEGENWART.
S. ELKHADEM, 268:JUL75-182
WYTRZENS, G. BIBLIOGRAPHISCHE EIN-
FÜHRUNG IN DAS STUDIUM DER SLAVIS-
CHEN LITERATUREN.*
N.W. INGHAM, 574(SEEJ):FALL73-322

PROFESSOR X. THIS BEATS WORKING FOR
A LIVING.
J.M. LALLEY, 396(MODA):SPRING74-
197
XENOPHON. XÉNOPHON, "CYROPÉDIE I."
(BKS 1&2) (M. BIZOS, ED & TRANS)
P. CHANTRAINE, 555:VOL47FASC1-134
XETSO, G. EVGENIJ BARATYNSKIJ.
M. DALTON, 574(SEEJ):WINTER73-455
XIRAU, R. GENIO Y FIGURA DE SOR
JUANA INÉS DE LA CRUZ.
G. SABÁT DE RIVERS, 400(MLN):MAR
73-458

XUEREB, P. MELITENSIA.
H. ALKER, 182:VOL26#23/24-840

YAGER, J.A. & E.B. STEINBERG. ENER-
GY & US FOREIGN POLICY.
G. BARRACLOUGH, 453:7AUG75-23
YAKIR, P. A CHILDHOOD IN PRISON.*
(R. CONQUEST, ED)
D.V. POSPIELOVSKY, 550(RUSR):OCT
73-441
YAMAGUCHI, H. ESSAYS TOWARDS ENG-
LISH SEMANTICS.* (2ND ED)
S. ULLMANN, 361:VOL31#1-71
YAMAMURA, K. A STUDY OF SAMURAI
INCOME & ENTREPRENEURSHIP.
R. STORRY, 617(TLS):21MAR75-319
YANAGI, S. THE UNKNOWN CRAFTSMAN.
J. LARSON, 139:JUN73-9
YANEY, G.L. THE SYSTEMATIZATION OF
RUSSIAN GOVERNMENT.*
J. KEEP, 104:WINTER74-569
YARDENI, M. LA CONSCIENCE NATIONALE
EN FRANCE PENDANT LES GUERRES DE
RELIGION (1559-1598).*
T.C. CAVE, 208(FS):JAN74-62
YARLOTT, G. COLERIDGE & THE ABYS-
SINIAN MAID.
R. GERBER, 38:BAND91HEFT3-410
YARMOLINSKY, A. DOSTOEVSKY.*
L. GLEIMAN, 613:SPRING73-131
YARMOLINSKY, A. - SEE CHEKHOV, A.
YARROW, P.J. - SEE CORNEILLE, T. &
D. DE VISÉ
YASUDA, K. - SEE "LAND OF THE REED
PLAINS"
YATES, B. DEAD IN THE WATER.
N. CALLENDAR, 441:16NOV75-74
YATES, F.A. ASTRAEA.
J.H. ELLIOTT, 453:20FEB75-32
P.N. FURBANK, 362:10APR75-481
YATES, F.A. THE ROSICRUCIAN EN-
LIGHTENMENT.
P.F. CORBIN, 402(MLR):JAN74-149
YATES, F.A. SHAKESPEARE'S LAST
PLAYS.
C.L. BARBER, 453:16OCT75-33
P.N. FURBANK, 362:10APR75-481
YATES, J.M. THE ABSTRACT BEAST.*
G. AMABILE, 150(DR):SPRING73-167
D. DUFFY, 102(CANL):SPRING73-125
YATES, J.M. BREATH OF THE SNOW
LEOPARD.
M.T. LANE, 198:SUMMER75-121
YATES, J.M., ED. VOLVOX.*
B. OPALA, 102(CANL):WINTER74-92
D. WYNAND, 376:JAN73-163
YATES, R. DISTURBING THE PEACE.
A. BROYARD, 441:9SEP75-43
G. LYONS, 441:5OCT75-6
R. TODD, 61:OCT75-104
YATES, W.E. GRILLPARZER.*
A. BURKHARD, 400(MLN):APR73-630
W.A. LITTLE, 221(GQ):SEP73-146
205(FMLS):OCT73-408
YATES, W.E. NESTROY.*
K. SEGAR, 617(TLS):30CT75-1148
"YEARBOOK OF ITALIAN STUDIES."
E. SACCONE, 400(MLN):JAN73-172
"THE YEARBOOK OF THE FOLKLORE AR-
CHIVES IN HAIFA." (VOLS 1-6) (D.
NOY & Z. KAGAN, EDS)
E. SCHOENFELD, 196:BAND14HEFT3-263

"THE YEAR'S WORK IN ENGLISH STUD-
IES." (VOLS 47-51)
 B. FABIAN, 72:BAND211HEFT1/3-106
"THE YEAR'S WORK IN MODERN LANGUAGE
STUDIES." (VOL 34, 1972) (G.
PRICE, ED)
 S. ULLMANN, 208(FS):JUL74-373
YEATS, J.B. THE COLLECTED PLAYS OF
JACK B. YEATS.* (R. SKELTON, ED)
 R. HOGAN, 295:APR74-1031
YEATS, W.B. DRUID CRAFT, THE WRIT-
ING OF "THE SHADOWY WATERS."*
(M.J. SIDNELL, G.P. MAYHEW & D.R.
CLARK, EDS)
 D.R.C. MARSH, 67:MAY74-95
YEATS, W.B., ED. FAIRY & FOLK TALES
OF IRELAND.
 A.N. JEFFARES, 569(SR):WINTER74-
 108
YEATS, W.B. MEMOIRS. (D. DONOGHUE,
ED)
 G.M. HARPER, 598(SOR):SPRING75-452
 A.N. JEFFARES, 569(SR):WINTER74-
 108
 K. MC SWEENEY, 529(QQ):AUTUMN73-
 497
 G. MONSMAN, 579(SAQ):SUMMER74-407
 H. PESCHMANN, 175:SUMMER73-83
YEATS, W.B. WERKE I. (W. VORD-
TRIEDE, ED; S. ANDRES & OTHERS,
TRANS)
 J. UTZ, 72:BAND211HEFT1/3-142
YEHOSHUA, B-Z. TZ'VA'AT AV.
 E. SCHOENFELD, 196:BAND14HEFT1/2-
 168
YELLIN, J.F. THE INTRICATE KNOT.
 H.A. BAKER, JR., 27(AL):JAN75-587
YEN CHIH-T'UI. FAMILY INSTRUCTIONS
FOR THE YEN CLAN. (TENG SSU-YÜ,
TRANS)
 A.E. DIEN, 318(JAOS):JAN-MAR73-83
YETMAN, N.R., ED. LIFE UNDER THE
"PECULIAR INSTITUTION."
 A.W. WONDERLY, 582(SFQ):DEC73-411
YEVTUSHENKO, Y. STOLEN APPLES.*
 G.S. FRASER, 473(PR):2/1974-289
 D. PHILLIPS, 50(ARQ):SPRING73-86
 J.A. TAUBMAN, 574(SEEJ):WINTER72-
 488
YIN, J. SINO-SOVIET DIALOGUE ON THE
PROBLEM OF WAR.
 R.L. WALKER, 550(RUSR):APR73-189
YNDURÁIN, D. ANÁLISIS FORMAL DE LA
POESÍA DE ESPRONCEDA.
 191(ELN):SEP73(SUPP)-177
YNDURÁIN, F. RELECCIÓN DE CLÁSICOS.
 M. DURÁN, 240(HR):WINTER73-101
YOGASWAMI. SONGS & SAYINGS OF YOGA-
SWAMI.
 A. PIATIGORSKY, 617(TLS):3JAN75-20
YORK, A. THE FASCINATOR.
 N. CALLENDAR, 441:2NOV75-51
YORK, T. WE, THE WILDERNESS.
 A. APPENZELL, 102(CANL):AUTUMN73-
 95
YOSHIDA, M. IN SEARCH OF PERSIAN
POTTERY.
 M. LEVEY, 39:AUG73-151
YOUNG, A. COMPLETE POEMS.* (L.
CLARK, ED)
 L. NORRIS, 364:JUN/JUL74-132
YOUNG, A. WHO IS ANGELINA?
 C. LEHMANN-HAUPT, 441:23JAN75-37
 M. LEVIN, 441:9FEB75-10

YOUNG, A. - SEE RICKWORD, E.
YOUNG, D. BOXCARS.*
 J.N. MORRIS, 249(HUDR):SPRING74-
 111
YOUNG, D. THE HEART'S FOREST.*
 R. BERRY, 677:VOL4-272
 D. CRAWLEY, 529(QQ):WINTER73-639
 L. DANSON, 191(ELN):JUN74-299
 M. GRIVELET, 189(EA):OCT-DEC73-465
 C. HOY, 569(SR):SPRING74-363
 A.C. KIRSCH, 405(MP):MAY74-424
 N. RABKIN, 401(MLQ):JUN74-187
 A.R. YOUNG, 150(DR):SUMMER73-363
YOUNG, D.C. PINDAR, "ISTHMIAN 7."
 M.M. WILLCOCK, 123:MAR74-14
YOUNG, E. THE CORRESPONDENCE OF
EDWARD YOUNG 1683-1765.* (H. PET-
TIT, ED)
 A. PARREAUX, 189(EA):JAN-MAR73-105
 C.J. RAWSON, 677:VOL4-299
YOUNG, F. & P. PETZOLD. THE WORK
OF THE MOTION PICTURE CAMERAMAN.
 R. PICKARD, 200:JUN-JUL73-371
YOUNG, M. & P. WILLMOTT. THE
SYMMETRICAL FAMILY.*
 E.R. LEACH, 111:3MAY74-135
YOUNG, M.T. SAINT-EXUPÉRY: "VOL DE
NUIT."*
 H. GODIN, 208(FS):JAN74-110
YOUNG, P. THREE BAGS FULL.
 I. MALIN, 594:SPRING73-148
 295:FEB74-499
YOUNG, P. - SEE HEMINGWAY, E.
YOUNG, P.D. TWO OF THE MISSING.
 J.S. KUNEN, 441:9MAR75-10
YOUNG, P.M. SIR ARTHUR SULLIVAN.
 M. PETERSON, 470:NOV72-46
YOUNG, R. FREEDOM, RESPONSIBILITY
& GOD.
 A.K., 617(TLS):5DEC75-1466
YOUNG, R.E., A.L. BECKER & K.L.
PIKE. RHETORIC.
 R.J. REDDICK, 113:SPRING73-61
YOUNG, V. ON FILM.*
 R. CAMPION, 200:APR73-234
 295:FEB74-524
YOUNG, W.C., ED. DOCUMENTS OF AMER-
ICAN THEATER HISTORY.* (VOLS 1&2)
 L.S. THOMPSON, 263:JUL-SEP74-314
YOUNG, W.D. DEMOCRACY & DISCONTENT.
 G.L. COOK, 255(HAB):WINTER73-71
YOUNGER, P. INTRODUCTION TO INDIAN
RELIGIOUS THOUGHT.
 R.F. OLSON, 485(PE&W):OCT73-550
YOUNT, J. THE TRAPPER'S LAST SHOT.*
 B. ALLEN, 249(HUDR):SPRING74-119
 J. HAMILTON-PATERSON, 617(TLS):
 3JAN75-5
YOURCENAR, M. THÉÂTRE II.
 L. RIÈSE, 207(FR):MAY73-1256
YOURGRAU, W. & A. VAN DER MERWE,
EDS. PERSPECTIVES IN QUANTUM
THEORY.
 M.N. AUDI, 486:JUN73-323
 M.R. GARDNER, 84:MAR73-72
YOYO, É. SAINT-JOHN PERSE ET LE
CONTEUR.
 R. LITTLE, 208(FS):JUL74-346
 C.N. RIGOLOT, 400(MLN):MAY73-924
YU, B. AKUTAGAWA.
 YOSHIO IWAMOTO, 293(JAST):AUG73-
 706

YU, B.   NATSUME SŌSEKI.
R.N. MC KINNON, 293(JAST):NOV72-
157
YU, L. - SEE UNDER LU YU
YU, P-K., COMP.   CHINESE HISTORY:
INDEX TO LEARNED ARTICLES.   (VOL 2)
T-H. TSIEN, 244(HJAS):VOL33-291
YU-NING, L. - SEE UNDER LI YU-NING
YUILL, P.B.   THE BORNLESS KEEPER.
N. CALLENDAR, 441:6JUL75-14
YURICK, S.   AN ISLAND DEATH.
D. GRUMBACH, 441:20APR75-5
YURIEFF, Z.   JOSEPH WITTLIN.
E. VARDAMAN, 574(SEEJ):FALL73-350
YURKIEVICH, S.   FUNDADORES DE LA
NUEVA POESÍA LATINOAMERICANA.
M-L. GAZARIAN, 238:DEC73-1129
J. HIGGINS, 86(BHS):OCT73-420

ZACHWATOWICZ, J.   POLISH ARCHITEC-
TURE.
T. MULLALY, 135:DEC73-295
ZAEHNER, R.C.   DRUGS, MYSTICISM &
MAKE-BELIEVE.
K. MC SWEENEY, 529(QQ):SPRING73-
149
ZAEHNER, R.C. EVOLUTION & RELIGION.*
B. BRUTEAU, 258:MAR73-147
ZAHN, H.E.   EURO-WIRTSCHAFTSWÖRTER-
BUCH IN DREI SPRACHEN - DEUTSCH-
ENGLISCH-FRANZÖSISCH.
H. SCHWARZ, 75:2/1973-99
ZAIMOV, K.   ÜBER DIE PATHOPHYSIOLO-
GIE DER AGNOSIEN, APHASIEN, APRAX-
IEN UND DER ZERFAHRENHEIT DES DEN-
KENS BEI DER SCHIZOPHRENIE.
G.F. MEIER, 682(ZPSK):BAND26HEFT
3/4-460
ZAIONCHKOVSKII, P.A., ED.   SPRAVOCH-
NIKI PO ISTORII DOREVOLIUTSIONNOI
ROSSII.*
C.A. RUUD, 104:WINTER74-597
ZAITZEVSKY, C.   THE ARCHITECTURE OF
WILLIAM RALPH EMERSON 1833-1917.
E. PEARSON, 576:OCT73-250
ZALDIVAR, G.   EL VISITANTE.
G. SABÁT DE RIVERS, 400(MLN):MAR
73-505
ZALL, P.M. - SEE WARD, N.
ZAMPETTI, P.   GIOVANNI BOCCATI.
L. VERTOVA, 90:SEP73-609
ZAMPETTI, P.   PAINTINGS FROM THE
MARCHES: GENTILE TO RAPHAEL.*
L. VERTOVA, 90:SEP73-608
ZAMYATIN, Y.   THE DRAGON & OTHER
STORIES.   (M. GINSBERG, ED & TRANS)
E. MORGAN, 617(TLS):18APR75-422
ZAMYATIN, Y.   WE.
A.M. SHANE, 574(SEEJ):WINTER72-482
ZANDVOORT, R.W.   COLLECTED PAPERS
II.*
A-M. VANDENBERGEN, 179(ES):AUG72-
375
ZANETTI, D.E.   LA DEMOGRAFIA DEL
PATRIZIATO MILANESE NEI SECOLI
XVII, XVIII, XIX.
C-M. CIPOLLA, 617(TLS):31OCT75-
1295
ZANZOTTO, A.   PASQUE.
F. FORTINI, 617(TLS):31OCT75-1308

ZARETSKY, I.I. & M.P. LEONE, EDS.
RELIGIOUS MOVEMENTS IN CONTEMPOR-
ARY AMERICA.*
M. FELLMAN, 99:DEC75/JAN76-63
D. MARTIN, 617(TLS):13JUN75-676
442(NY):14APR75-127
ZASLAWSKY, F. - SEE LUKASIEWICZ, J.
ZASLOFF, J.J. & A.E. GOODMAN.   INDO-
CHINA IN CONFLICT.
J. RACE, 293(JAST):NOV72-219
ZATURENSKA, M.   THE HIDDEN WATERFALL.
R.B. SHAW, 491:MAY75-100
ZAVALA, I.M.   IDEOLOGÍA Y POLÍTICA
EN LA NOVELA ESPAÑOLA DEL SIGLO
XIX.*
D.T. GIES, 238:DEC73-1119
191(ELN):SEP73(SUPP)-174
ZAVALA, I.M.   MASONES, COMUNEROS Y
CARBONARIOS.*
J. HERRERO, 400(MLN):MAR73-473
ZEGGER, R.E.   JOHN CAM HOBHOUSE.
J.M. PREST, 637(VS):JUN74-449
"DAS ZEITBUDGET DER BEVÖLKERUNG."
S. TÜMMLER, 654(WB):5/1973-183
ZEITLER, R.   DIE KUNST DES 19. JAHR-
HUNDERTS.
R-M. BISANZ, 127:WINTER73/74-168
ZELAZNY, R.   SIGN OF THE UNICORN.
M. WOOD, 453:2OCT75-3
ZELDIN, J. - SEE TYUTCHEV, F.I.
ZELDIN, T.   FRANCE 1848-1945.*
(VOL 1)
H. BROGAN, 111:30MAY74-165
639(VQR):SPRING74-LI
ZELL, C-A.   UNTERSUCHUNGEN ZUM PROB-
LEM DER GEISTLICHEN BAROCKLYRIK MIT
BESONDERER BERÜCKSICHTIGUNG DER
DICHTUNG JOHANN HEERMANNS (1585-
1647).
R.T. LLEWELLYN, 402(MLR):APR74-455
ZELLER, B.   PORTRAIT OF HESSE.
K.J. FICKERT, 295:FEB74-642
ZELLER, E.   GRUNDRISS DER GESCHICHTE
DER GRIESCHISCHEN PHILOSOPHIE.
R. CADENBACH, 53(AGP):BAND55HEFT3-
348
ZELLER, H. & A. ZÄCH - SEE MEYER,
C.F.
ZEMAN, H.   DIE DEUTSCHE ANAKREON-
TISCHE DICHTUNG.*
A. MENHENNET, 402(MLR):OCT74-917
ZEMAN, J.J.   MODAL LOGIC.*
R. BLANCHÉ, 542:OCT-DEC73-479
ZEMCOVSKIJ, I.I., COMP.   POZZIJA
KREST'JANSKIX PRAZDNIKOV.
F.J. OINAS, 574(SEEJ):SUMMER72-226
ZEMP, H.   MUSIQUE DAN.
A.M. JONES, 69:APR73-176
ZENA, R.   ROMANZI E RACCONTI.   (E.
VILLA, ED)
A.D.B., 228(GSLI):VOL150FASC469-
154
ZENK, G.   KONZENTRATIONSPOLITIK IN
DÄNEMARK, NORWEGEN UND FINNLAND.
F.F. GUNDERSEN, 182:VOL26#17/18-
588
ZEN'KOVSKIJ, S.   RUSSKOE STAROOBR-
JADČESTVO.*
H.A. STAMMLER, 574(SEEJ):SUMMER73-
224
ZENKOVSKY, S.A. - SEE ČIŽEVSKIJ, D.